The Norton Reader

The Norton Reader

An Anthology of Expository Prose

Arthur M. Eastman, *General Editor*
UNIVERSITY OF MICHIGAN

Caesar Blake
UNIVERSITY OF MICHIGAN

Hubert M. English, Jr.
UNIVERSITY OF MICHIGAN

Alan B. Howes
UNIVERSITY OF MICHIGAN

Robert T. Lenaghan
UNIVERSITY OF MICHIGAN

Leo F. McNamara
UNIVERSITY OF MICHIGAN

James Rosier
UNIVERSITY OF PENNSYLVANIA

W · W · NORTON & COMPANY · INC · *New York*

Copyright © 1965 by W. W. Norton & Company, Inc.

Published simultaneously in the Dominion of Canada by
George J. MacLeod Limited, Toronto

Since this page cannot legibly accommodate
all the copyright notices, the pages following
constitute an extension of the copyright page.

Library of Congress Catalog Card No. 65-12518

Book design by John Woodlock

PRINTED IN THE UNITED STATES OF AMERICA FOR THE PUBLISHERS BY W.P.C.

1 2 3 4 5 6 7 8 9

ACKNOWLEDGMENTS

James Agee: from *Let Us Now Praise Famous Men*. Copyright 1939 by Houghton Mifflin Company. Reprinted by permission of the publisher.

Hannah Arendt: from *Eichmann in Jerusalem*. Copyright © 1963 by Hannah Arendt. Reprinted by permission of The Viking Press, Inc.

W. H. Auden: from *The Dyer's Hand*. Copyright © 1962 by W. H. Auden. Reprinted by permission of Random House, Inc.

James Baldwin: from *Notes of a Native Son*. Copyright © 1955 by James Baldwin. Reprinted by permission of the Beacon Press.

Margaret Banning: from *Letters to Susan*. Copyright 1934 by Margaret Culkin Banning. Reprinted by permission of Brandt & Brandt.

George W. Beadle: from *Phoenix*, Vol. II, No. 1, September 1963. Reprinted by permission of the author and the Michigan Memorial–Phoenix Project.

Carl Becker: from *Modern Democracy*. Copyright 1941 by Yale University Press. Reprinted by permission of the Press.

Max Beerbohm: from *And Even Now*. Copyright 1921 by E. P. Dutton & Company, Inc.; renewal 1949 by Max Beerbohm. Published in Canada by William Heinemann Ltd. Publishers. Reprinted by permission of the publishers.

Henri Bergson: from "Laughter," which is contained in the book, *Comedy*, by Wylie Sypher. Copyright © 1956 by Wylie Sypher. Reprinted by permission of Doubleday & Company, Inc.

Bruno Bettelheim: from *The Informed Heart*. Copyright © 1960 by The Free Press, A Corporation. Reprinted by permission of the publisher.

Wayne C. Booth: from an address to the Illinois Council of College Teachers in 1963. Reprinted by permission of the author.

Jacob Bronowski: from *Science and Human Values*. Copyright © 1956 by J. Bronowski. Reprinted by permission of Julian Messner, Inc.

Van Wyck Brooks: from *The Ordeal of Mark Twain*. Copyright 1920 by E. P. Dutton, Inc., renewal 1948 by Van Wyck Brooks. Reprinted by permission of the publishers.

Martin Buber: from *Pointing the Way*. Copyright © 1957 by Martin Buber. Reprinted by permission of Harper & Row, Publishers, Inc.

J. B. Bury: from *Selected Essays of J. B. Bury*, 1930. Reprinted by permission of the Trustees of the Will of the late Mrs. Jane Bury Bagnall.

Edward Hallett Carr: from *What Is History?* Copyright © 1961 by Edward Hallett Carr. Reprinted by permission of Alfred A. Knopf, Inc., and The Macmillan Company Ltd. of Canada.

W. J. Cash: from *The Mind of the South*. Copyright 1941 by Alfred A. Knopf, Inc. Reprinted by permission of the publisher.

Kenneth Clark: from *Encounter*, January 1963. Reprinted by permission of the author and *Encounter*.

Robert Coles: from *The Atlantic Monthly*, July 1961. Reprinted by permission of the author.

Geoffrey Crowther: pp. 225ff. from *The Atlantic Monthly*, April 1960. Reprinted by permission of the author. Pp. 235ff. from *Michigan Alumnus Quarterly Review*, Summer 1960. Reprinted by permission of the Review.

Edward S. Deevey, Jr.: from *Scientific American*, October 1958, Vol. 199, No. 4. Copyright © 1958 by Scientific American, Inc. All rights reserved. Reprinted by permission of Scientific American, Inc.

John Dos Passos: from *U.S.A.* Copyright 1930, 1932, 1934, 1935, 1936, 1937 by John Dos Passos; published by Houghton Mifflin Company. Reprinted by permission of the author.

William O. Douglas: "The Six Poorest of Us" from *Strange Lands and Friendly People*. Copyright 1951 by William O. Douglas. Reprinted with the permission of Harper & Row, Publishers, Inc.

A. S. Eddington: from *The Nature of the Physical World*. Copyright 1928 by Cambridge University Press. Reprinted by permission of the publisher.

Ralph Waldo Emerson: from *The Heart of Emerson's Journals*, ed. by Bliss Perry. Copyright 1926 by Houghton Mifflin Company. Reprinted by permission of the publisher.

Desiderius Erasmus: from *The Education of a Christian Prince*, 1936, tr. by Lester K. Born. Reprinted by permission of Columbia University Press.

Thomas F. Farrell: from *Atomic Energy for Military Purposes* by H. D. Smyth. Copyright 1945 by Princeton University Press. Reprinted by permission of the publisher.

Donald Fleming: from *Victorian Studies* IV, March 1961. Reprinted by permission of the author and *Victorian Studies*.

E. M. Forster: from *Two Cheers for Democracy*. Copyright 1939 by E. M. Forster. Reprinted by permission of Harcourt, Brace & World, Inc., and Edward Arnold, Ltd.

Anatole France: from *On Life and Letters*. Copyright 1924 by Dodd, Mead & Company. Reprinted by permission of the publisher.

W. Nelson Francis: from *Quarterly Journal of Speech*, October 1954. Reprinted by permission of the Speech Association of America.

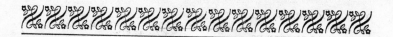

Contents

ON CIVILIZATION
Manners and Marriage · Discrimination · Poverty ·
The Machine

ON LITERATURE AND THE ARTS
Standards · Humor · Poetry

ON ETHICS
Moral Traits · Advice · Judgment

ON GOVERNMENT
Prince or President · Conflict · Democracy · Law

ON HISTORY
Men · Events · Philosophies

ON SCIENCE
Aims · Perspectives · Applications

ON RELIGION

Preface

A good anthology, like a good banquet, offers food for every taste, and all of it of high quality. The quality of the offerings in *The Norton Reader* the individual must determine for himself, but the editors have tried to insure quality by screening their selections again and again and by calling on a good many readers across the country to screen yet further. Undoubtedly some pieces here are better than others; undoubtedly some fall short of the highest mark; but the editors rest confident that *The Norton Reader* offers very little that is not very good.

Where there is such a range of material, and so much of it, the mind naturally needs some kind of guideline or organization to help it know where it is and in relation to what. The organization of *The Norton Reader* is alternately thematic and formal. It begins with a series of essays focusing on personal experience, then turns briefly to an examination of journals, a form of writing which, as the headnote suggests, significantly relates to the essay. And so throughout: selections grouped under a common thematic heading, then selections illustrating an important prose form. The eleven thematic sections follow a simple and natural arrangement, though the reader may wish to make a different one for himself. They begin with personal experience, turn to the equipment and training with which a person confronts and masters experience—his language, his education, his mind; then look broadly outward at certain insistent concerns of our civilization—manners and marriage, discrimination, poverty, the machine; and develop, finally, along the great traditional lines of a liberating education—art, morality, politics, history, science, religion.

Since readers are for writers, the editors have tried to help those who wish help. Headnotes to the five sections on Prose Forms indicate ways in which these relate to the writing of essays. Approximately one-half of the selections are followed by questions on form and content designed to help the student help himself. And at the book's back there is the Compendious Rhetoric, a comprehensive survey of the main headings of the art of writing, with references to especially relevant material in the body of the book. Further help we fear would be intrusive. Teachers, at least, tend to like to go by their own paces along roads of their own choosing. To students, though, we offer this counsel for occasions when they have essays to write but find nothing to say. Turn to the Prose Forms. Select one piece—

journal entry, letter, apothegm, character, parable. What does it say? You could write about that. How does it say it? You could write about that. Could you do something like it? Do it. Write your own. You will find yourself writing—and learning to write better in the process.

The relation of journal and letter, apothegm, character, and parable to a book subtitled *An Anthology of Expository Prose* needs, perhaps, a word of explanation. In our selections we have tried to indicate the range and the definition of the expository, and while it is common to divide the methods of discourse into four separated categories—description, narration, exposition, and argumentation— it is clear that each method can call on the others for its own purposes: narration may set forth or expose; exposition may present its case by argument. What we have called Prose Forms lie at the boundaries between exposition and other kinds of discourse or literature. The journal or diary is expository but it is also narrative. The letter sets forth, like an essay, but partakes of oratory, of monologue, and, if it is good, of dialogue. The character manifestly defines moral nature, but it belongs to the novel and the drama as much as to the essay. The apothegm cleanly makes its statement, but in its economy, its imagery, its cadence, and its twist it belongs to poetry: it is first cousin to the couplets of Pope, close kin to the striking lines of Donne and the metaphysicals. And the parable no less than the outright essay makes its point, but its form is narrative and its matter fictive, not factual.

The Prose Forms, then, define the boundaries of expository prose. They do something more. They offer, in their purity, what might be called the elements or archetypes of exposition. The journal entry as testimony, the apothegm as authority, the parable as illustration— these are the materials out of which good essays are made. To focus on them, if only briefly, is to discover some of the principal sources of expository power.

We have tried to achieve a reader in which students as well as teachers will proceed on their own initiative simply because there is so much and such varied delight. The material in the Prose Forms sections particularly offers itself for quick delectation, as in Bierce's definitions (under Apothegms) or Thurber's fables. And each of the major sections contains essays surprising, exciting, mentally explosive. The section On Mind includes, for example, Bronowski's compelling identification of the creative process in science and the creative process in art as one and the same; Milgram's fascinating and (to some) appalling account of "A Behavioral Study of Obedience," wherein subjects were commanded to inflict increasing pain on their visibly suffering fellows—and did; and March's mordant fable on the malice of displaced love, "The Dog and Her Rival."

The editors assume that the very variety of the book in tone, style, length, and seriousness will contribute to enjoyment. We would hope, too, that readers find pleasure as they discover and continue to discover patterns of connection between one part of the book and another. Not all the letters are in Prose Forms: Letters, nor is all the moral advice to be found in On Ethics. Bettelheim's "A Victim," an account of his imprisonment in a Nazi concentration camp, appears in Personal Report, but it links with Sartre's "Portrait of an Antisemite" in On Civilization and with Arendt's "Denmark and the Jews" in On History. Liebling's "Poet and Pedagogue," an analytic history of a prize fight between Cassius Clay and Sonny Banks, appears in Personal Experience but links, as a chronicle of a conflict, with the pieces in On History; Thoreau's "Battle of the Ants," which is in On History, links with Goetsch's "Warfare and Hunting," which is all about ants and appears, appropriately enough, in On Science. Of such links there are literally hundreds, the discovery of which offers new perspectives on subject and style.

Such delights we may hope that teachers and students will find on their own, but the editors would call attention to three in especial: the Album of Styles in On Language, which contains superb and representative short passages from the great prose expositors of England's past centuries; the final pieces in On Government—dissenting judicial opinions that combine argument, human interest, and high literacy; and, in On Religion, the extraordinarily similar and yet extraordinarily different specimens of pulpit oratory by Hopkins, Donne, Edwards, and Joyce.

At the end of the long task of making this book, it is a pleasure for the editors to acknowledge the generous and stimulating help they have received from colleagues: Professors Robert D. Bamberg of the University of Pennsylvania, James H. Broderick of Bryn Mawr College, Frederick Candelaria of the University of Oregon, Don L. Cook of the University of Indiana, John P. Cutts of Wayne State University, John Doebler of Dickinson University, J. R. Gaskin of the University of North Carolina, Fabian Gudas of Louisiana State University, Eugene Hardy of the University of Nebraska, W. Donald Head of San Jose State College, Harold D. Kelling of the University of Colorado, Cecil M. McCulley of the College of William and Mary, Joseph P. Roppolo of Tulane University, Fred A. Tarpley of East Texas University, and Harris W. Wilson of the University of Illinois. Professor David J. DeLaura of the University of Texas, Scott Elledge of Cornell University, Donald J. Gray of the University of Indiana, and Hulon Willis of Bakersfield College offered counsel of especial abundance from early on until the very end. To the wise editorial eye and steady if critical encouragement of John G. Benedict of W. W. Norton & Company, Inc., we happily acknowledge that we owe most of all.

Arthur M. Eastman

The Norton Reader

Personal Report

DYLAN THOMAS
Memories of Christmas

One Christmas was so much like another, in those years, around the sea-town corner now, and out of all sound except the distant speaking of the voices I sometimes hear a moment before sleep, that I can never remember whether it snowed for six days and six nights when I was twelve or whether it snowed for twelve days and twelve nights when I was six; or whether the ice broke and the skating grocer vanished like a snowman through a white trap-door on that same Christmas Day that the mince-pies finished Uncle Arnold and we tobogganed down the seaward hill, all the afternoon, on the best tea-tray, and Mrs. Griffiths complained, and we threw a snowball at her niece, and my hands burned so, with the heat and the cold, when I held them in front of the fire, that I cried for twenty minutes and then had some jelly.

All the Christmases roll down the hill towards the Welsh-speaking sea, like a snowball growing whiter and bigger and rounder, like a cold and headlong moon bundling down the sky that was our street; and they stop at the rim of the ice-edged, fish-freezing waves, and I plunge my hands in the snow and bring out whatever I can find; holly or robins or pudding, squabbles and carols and oranges and tin whistles, and the fire in the front room, and bang go the crackers, and holy, holy, holy, ring the bells, and the glass bells shaking on the tree, and Mother Goose, and Struwelpeter[1] —oh! the baby-burning flames and the clacking scissorman!—Billy Bunter[2] and Black Beauty, Little Women and boys who have three helpings, Alice and Mrs. Potter's badgers,[3] penknives, teddy-bears

---

1. The title character of *Struwelpeter (Slovenly Peter), or Merry Tales and Funny Pictures*, a children's book originally in German, by Dr. Heinrich Hoffmann, containing gaily grim admonitory narratives in verse about little Pauline, for example, who played with matches and got burned up; or the little boy who sucked his thumbs until the tall scissorman cut them off.

2. The humorous fat boy in Frank Richards' tales of English school life.

3. Beatrix Potter, creator of *Peter Rabbit* and other animal tales for children, among them *The Tale of Mr. Tod*, a badger.

1

—named after a Mr. Theodore Bear, their inventor, or father, who died recently in the United States—mouth-organs, tin-soldiers, and blancmange, and Auntie Bessie playing "Pop Goes the Weasel" and "Nuts in May" and "Oranges and Lemons" on the untuned piano in the parlor all through the thimble-hiding musical-chairing blind-man's-buffing party at the end of the never-to-be-forgotten day at the end of the unremembered year.

In goes my hand into that wool-white bell-tongued ball of holi-days resting at the margin of the carol-singing sea, and out come Mrs. Prothero and the firemen.

It was on the afternoon of the day of Christmas Eve, and I was in Mrs. Prothero's garden, waiting for cats, with her son Jim. It was snowing. It was always snowing at Christmas; December, in my memory, is white as Lapland, though there were no reindeers. But there were cats. Patient, cold, and callous, our hands wrapped in socks, we waited to snowball the cats. Sleek and long as jaguars and terrible-whiskered, spitting and snarling they would slink and sidle over the white back-garden walls, and the lynx-eyed hunters, Jim and I, fur-capped and moccasined trappers from Hudson's Bay off Eversley Road, would hurl our deadly snowballs at the green of their eyes. The wise cats never appeared. We were so still, Eskimo-footed arctic marksmen in the muffling silence of the eternal snows—eternal, ever since Wednesday—that we never heard Mrs. Prothero's first cry from her igloo at the bottom of the garden. Or, if we heard it at all, it was, to us, like the far-off challenge of our enemy and prey, the neighbor's Polar Cat. But soon the voice grew louder. "Fire!" cried Mrs. Prothero, and she beat the dinner-gong. And we ran down the garden, with the snow-balls in our arms, towards the house, and smoke, indeed, was pour-ing out of the dining-room, and the gong was bombilating, and Mrs. Prothero was announcing ruin like a town-crier in Pompeii. This was better than all the cats in Wales standing on the wall in a row. We bounded into the house, laden with snowballs, and stopped at the open door of the smoke-filled room. Something was burning all right; perhaps it was Mr. Prothero, who always slept there after midday dinner with a newspaper over his face; but he was standing in the middle of the room, saying "A fine Christmas!" and smacking at the smoke with a slipper.

"Call the fire-brigade," cried Mrs. Prothero as she beat the gong.

"They won't be there," said Mr. Prothero, "it's Christmas."

There was no fire to be seen, only clouds of smoke and Mr. Prothero standing in the middle of them, waving his slipper as though he were conducting.

"Do something," he said.

And we threw all our snowballs into the smoke—I think we

missed Mr. Prothero—and ran out of the house to the telephone-box.
"Let's call the police as well," Jim said.
"And the ambulance."
"And Ernie Jenkins, he likes fires."

But we only called the fire-brigade, and soon the fire-engine
came and three tall men in helmets brought a hose into the house
and Mr. Prothero got out just in time before they turned it on.
Nobody could have had a noisier Christmas Eve. And when the
firemen turned off the hose and were standing in the wet and
smoky room, Jim's aunt, Miss Prothero, came downstairs and
peered in at them. Jim and I waited, very quietly, to hear what
she would say to them. She said the right thing, always. She
looked at the three tall firemen in their shining helmets, standing
among the smoke and cinders and dissolving snowballs, and she
said: "Would you like something to read?"

Now out of that bright white snowball of Christmas gone
comes the stocking, the stocking of stockings, that hung at the foot
of the bed with the arm of a golliwog dangling over the top and
small bells ringing in the toes. There was a company, gallant and
scarlet but never nice to taste though I always tried when very
young, of belted and busbied and musketed lead soldiers so soon
to lose their heads and legs in the wars on the kitchen table after
the tea-things, the mince-pies, and the cakes that I helped to make
by stoning the raisins and eating them, had been cleared away;
and a bag of moist and many-colored jelly-babies and a folded
flag and a false nose and a tram-conductor's cap and a machine
that punched tickets and rang a bell; never a catapult; once, by a
mistake that no one could explain, a little hatchet; and a rubber-
buffalo, or it may have been a horse, with a yellow head and
haphazard legs; and a celluloid duck that made, when you pressed
it, a most unducklike noise, a mewing moo that an ambitious cat
might make who wishes to be a cow; and a painting-book in which
I could make the grass, the trees, the sea, and the animals any color
I pleased: and still the dazzling sky-blue sheep are grazing in the
red field under a flight of rainbow-beaked and pea-green birds.

Christmas morning was always over before you could say Jack
Frost. And look! suddenly the pudding was burning! Bang the
gong and call the fire-brigade and the book-loving firemen! Someone found the silver three-penny-bit with a currant on it; and the
someone was always Uncle Arnold. The motto in my cracker read:

> Let's all have fun this Christmas Day,
> Let's play and sing and shout hooray!

and the grown-ups turned their eyes towards the ceiling, and
Auntie Bessie, who had already been frightened, twice, by a clock-

work mouse, whimpered at the sideboard and had some elderberry wine. And someone put a glass bowl full of nuts on the littered table, and my uncle said, as he said once every year: "I've got a shoe-nut here. Fetch me a shoehorn to open it, boy."

And dinner was ended.

And I remember that on the afternoon of Christmas Day, when the others sat around the fire and told each other that this was nothing, no, nothing, to the great snowbound and turkey-proud yule-log-crackling holly-berry-bedizined and kissing-under-the-mistletoe Christmas when *they* were children, I would go out, school-capped and gloved and mufflered, with my bright new boots squeaking, into the white world on to the seaward hill, to call on Jim and Dan and Jack and to walk with them through the silent snowscape of our town.

We went padding through the streets, leaving huge deep footprints in the snow, on the hidden pavements.

"I bet people'll think there's been hippoes."

"What would you do if you saw a hippo coming down Terrace Road?"

"I'd go like this, bang! I'd throw him over the railings and roll him down the hill and then I'd tickle him under the ear and he'd wag his tail . . . ."

"What would you do if you saw *two* hippoes . . . ?"

Iron-flanked and bellowing he-hippoes clanked and blundered and battered through the scudding snow towards us as we passed by Mr. Daniel's house.

"Let's post Mr. Daniel a snowball through his letter box."

"Let's write things in the snow."

"Let's write 'Mr. Daniel looks like a spaniel' all over his lawn."

"Look," Jack said, "I'm eating snow-pie."

"What's it taste like?"

"Like snow-pie," Jack said.

Or we walked on the white shore.

"Can the fishes see it's snowing?"

"They think it's the sky falling down."

The silent one-clouded heavens drifted on to the sea.

"All the old dogs have gone."

Dogs of a hundred mingled makes yapped in the summer at the sea-rim and yelped at the trespassing mountains of the waves.

"I bet St. Bernards would like it now."

And we were snowblind travelers lost on the north hills, and the great dewlapped dogs, with brandy-flasks round their necks, ambled and shambled up to us, baying "Excelsior."

We returned home through the desolate poor sea-facing streets where only a few children fumbled with bare red fingers in the thick wheel-rutted snow and catcalled after us, their voices fading away, as we trudged uphill, into the cries of the dock-birds and the hooters of ships out in the white and whirling bay.

Bring out the tall tales now that we told by the fire as we roasted chestnuts and the gaslight bubbled low. Ghosts with their heads under their arms trailed their chains and said "whooo" like owls in the long nights when I dared not look over my shoulder; wild beasts lurked in the cubby-hole under the stairs where the gas-meter ticked. "Once upon a time," Jim said, "there were three boys, just like us, who got lost in the dark in the snow, near Bethesda Chapel, and this is what happened to them . . ." It was the most dreadful happening I had ever heard.

And I remember that we went singing carols once, a night or two before Christmas Eve, when there wasn't the shaving of a moon to light the secret, white-flying streets. At the end of a long road was a drive that led to a large house, and we stumbled up the darkness of the drive that night, each one of us afraid, each one holding a stone in his hand in case, and all of us too brave to say a word. The wind made through the drive-trees noises as of old and unpleasant and maybe web-footed men wheezing in caves. We reached the black bulk of the house.

"What shall we give them?" Dan whispered.

" 'Hark the Herald'? 'Christmas comes but Once a Year'?"

"No," Jack said: "We'll sing 'Good King Wenceslas.' I'll count three."

One, two, three, and we began to sing, our voices high and seemingly distant in the snow-felted darkness round the house that was occupied by nobody we knew. We stood close together, near the dark door.

> Good King Wenceslas looked out
> On the Feast of Stephen.

And then a small, dry voice, like the voice of someone who has not spoken for a long time, suddenly joined our singing: a small, dry voice from the other side of the door: a small, dry voice through the keyhole. And when we stopped running we were outside *our* house; the front room was lovely and bright; the gramophone was playing; we saw the red and white balloons hanging from the gas-bracket; uncles and aunts sat by the fire; I thought I smelt our supper being fried in the kitchen. Everything was good again, and Christmas shone through all the familiar town.

"Perhaps it was a ghost," Jim said.

"Perhaps it was trolls," Dan said, who was always reading.

"Let's go in and see if there's any jelly left," Jack said. And we did that.

WALLACE STEGNER
The Town Dump

The town dump of Whitemud, Saskatchewan, could only have been a few years old when I knew it, for the village was born in 1913 and I left there in 1919. But I remember the dump better than I remember most things in that town, better than I remember most of the people. I spent more time with it, for one thing; it has more poetry and excitement in it than people did.

It lay in the southeast corner of town, in a section that was always full of adventure for me. Just there the Whitemud River left the hills, bent a little south, and started its long traverse across the prairie and international boundary to join the Milk. For all I knew, it might have been on its way to join the Alph: simply, before my eyes, it disappeared into strangeness and wonder.

Also, where it passed below the dumpground, it ran through willowed bottoms that were a favorite campsite for passing team-sters, gypsies, sometimes Indians. The very straw scattered around those camps, the ashes of those strangers' campfires, the manure of their teams and saddle horses, were hot with adventurous possibilities.

It was as an extension, a living suburb, as it were, of the dumpground that we most valued those camps. We scoured them for artifacts of their migrant tenants as if they had been archaeological sites full of the secrets of ancient civilizations. I remember toting around for weeks the broken cheek strap of a bridle. Somehow or other its buckle looked as if it had been fashioned in a far place, a place where they were accustomed to flatten the tongues of buckles for reasons that could only be exciting, and where they made a habit of plating the metal with some valuable alloy, probably silver. In places where the silver was worn away the buckle underneath shone dull yellow: probably gold.

It seemed that excitement liked that end of town better than our end. Once old Mrs. Gustafson, deeply religious and a little raddled in the head, went over there with a buckboard full of trash, and as she was driving home along the river she looked and saw a spent catfish, washed in from Cypress Lake or some other part of the watershed, floating on the yellow water. He was two feet long, his whiskers hung down, his fins and tail were limp. He was a kind of fish that no one had seen in the Whitemud in the three or four years of the town's life, and a kind that none of us children had ever seen anywhere. Mrs. Gustafson had never seen one like him either; she perceived at once that he was the devil, and she whipped up the team and reported him at Hoffman's elevator.

We could hear her screeching as we legged it for the river to see for ourselves. Sure enough, there he was. He looked very tired, and he made no great effort to get away as we pushed out a half-sunken rowboat from below the flume, submerged it under him, and brought him ashore. When he died three days later we experimentally fed him to two half-wild cats, but they seemed to suffer no ill effects.

At that same end of town the irrigation flume crossed the river. It always seemed to me giddily high when I hung my chin over its plank edge and looked down, but it probably walked no more than twenty feet above the water on its spidery legs. Ordinarily in summer it carried about six or eight inches of smooth water, and under the glassy hurrying of the little boxed stream the planks were coated with deep sun-warmed moss as slick as frogs' eggs. A boy could sit in the flume with the water walling up against his back, and grab a cross brace above him, and pull, shooting himself sledlike ahead until he could reach the next brace for another pull and another slide, and so on across the river in four scoots.

After ten minutes in the flume he would come out wearing a dozen or more limber black leeches, and could sit in the green shade where darning needles flashed blue, and dragonflies hummed and darted and stopped, and skaters dimpled slack and eddy with their delicate transitory footprints, and there stretch the leeches out one by one while their sucking ends clung and clung, until at last, stretched far out, they let go with a tiny wet *puk* and snapped together like rubber bands. The smell of the river and the flume and the clay cutbanks and the bars of that part of the river was the smell of wolf willow.

But nothing in that end of town was as good as the dumpground that scattered along a little runoff coulee dipping down toward the river from the south bench. Through a historical process that went back, probably, to the roots of community sanitation and distaste for eyesores, but that in law dated from the Unincorporated Towns Ordinance of the territorial government, passed in 1888, the dump was one of the very first community enterprises, almost our town's first institution.

More than that, it contained relics of every individual who had ever lived there, and of every phase of the town's history.

The bedsprings on which the town's first child was begotten might be there; the skeleton of a boy's pet colt; two or three volumes of Shakespeare bought in haste and error from a peddler, later loaned in carelessness, soaked with water and chemicals in a house fire, and finally thrown out to flap their stained eloquence in the prairie wind.

Broken dishes, rusty tinware, spoons that had been used to mix paint; once a box of percussion caps, sign and symbol of the carelessness that most of those people felt about all matters of personal or public safety. We put them on the railroad tracks and were anonymously denounced in the *Enterprise*. There were also old iron, old brass, for which we hunted assiduously, by night conning junkmen's catalogues and the pages of the *Enterprise* to find how much wartime value there might be in the geared insides of clocks or in a pound of tea lead carefully wrapped in a ball whose weight astonished and delighted us. Sometimes the unimaginable outside world reached in and laid a finger on us. I recall that, aged no more than seven, I wrote a St. Louis junk house asking if they preferred their tea lead and tinfoil wrapped in balls, or whether they would rather have it pressed flat in sheets, and I got back a typewritten letter in a window envelope instructing me that they would be happy to have it in any way that was convenient for me. They added that they valued my business and were mine very truly. Dazed, I carried that windowed grandeur around in my pocket until I wore it out, and for months I saved the letter as a souvenir of the wondering time when something strange and distinguished had singled me out.

We hunted old bottles in the dump, bottles caked with dirt and filth, half buried, full of cobwebs, and we washed them out at the horse trough by the elevator, putting in a handful of shot along with the water to knock the dirt loose; and when we had shaken them until our arms were tired, we hauled them off in somebody's coaster wagon and turned them in at Bill Anderson's pool hall, where the smell of lemon pop was so sweet on the dark pool-hall air that I am sometimes awakened by it in the night, even yet.

Smashed wheels of wagons and buggies, tangles of rusty barbed wire, the collapsed perambulator that the French wife of one of the town's doctors had once pushed proudly up the planked sidewalks and along the ditchbank paths. A welter of foul-smelling feathers and coyote-scattered carrion which was all that remained of somebody's dream of a chicken ranch. The chickens had all got some mysterious pip at the same time, and died as one, and the dream lay out there with the rest of the town's history to rustle to the empty sky on the border of the hills.

There was melted glass in curious forms, and the half-melted office safe left from the burning of Bill Day's Hotel. On very lucky days we might find a piece of the lead casing that had enclosed the wires of the town's first telephone system. The casing was just the right size for rings, and so soft that it could be whittled with a jackknife. It was a material that might have made artists of us. If we had been Indians of fifty years before, that bright soft metal would have enlisted our maximum patience and craft and come out as ring and metal and amulet inscribed with the symbols of our observed world. Perhaps there were too many ready-made alternatives in the local drug, hardware, and general stores; perhaps our feeble artistic response was a measure of the insufficiency of the challenge we felt. In any case I do not remember that we did any more with the metal than to shape it into crude seal rings with our initials or pierced hearts carved in them; and these, though they served a purpose in juvenile courtship, stopped something short of art.

The dump held very little wood, for in that country anything burnable got burned. But it had plenty of old iron, furniture, papers, mattresses that were the delight of field mice, and jugs and demijohns that were sometimes their bane, for they crawled into the necks and drowned in the rain water or redeye that was inside.

If the history of our town was not exactly written, it was at least hinted, in the dump. I think I had a pretty sound notion even at eight or nine of how significant was that first institution of our forming Canadian civilization. For rummaging through its foul purlieus I had several times been surprised and shocked to find relics of my own life tossed out there to rot or blow away.

The volumes of Shakespeare belonged to a set that my father had bought before I was born. It had been carried through successive moves from town to town in the Dakotas, and from Dakota to Seattle, and from Seattle to Bellingham, and Bellingham to Redmond, and from Redmond back to Iowa, and from there to Saskatchewan. Then, stained in a stranger's house fire, these volumes had suffered from a house-cleaning impulse and been thrown away for me to stumble upon in the dump. One of the Cratchet girls had borrowed them, a hatchet-faced, thin, eager, transplanted Cockney girl with a frenzy, almost a hysteria, for reading. And yet somehow, through her hands, they found the dump, to become a symbol of how much was lost, how much thrown aside, how much carelessly or of necessity given up, in the making of a new country. We had so few books that I was familiar with them all, had handled them, looked at their pictures, perhaps even read them. They were the lares and penates, part of the skimpy impedimenta of household gods we had brought with us into Latium.[1] Finding those three thrown away was a little like finding my own name on a gravestone.

And yet not the blow that something else was, something that

---

1. In Roman families the lares and penates were the ancestral, household gods; they came to embody the con-tinuity of the family. Cf. Virgil, *Aeneid* I. 1-7.

impressed me even more with the dump's close reflection of the town's intimate life. The colt whose picked skeleton lay out there was mine. He had been incurably crippled when dogs chased our mare, Daisy, the morning after she foaled. I had labored for months to make him well; had fed him by hand, curried him, exercised him, adjusted the iron braces that I had talked my father into having made. And I had not known that he would have to be destroyed. One weekend I turned him over to the foreman of one of the ranches, presumably so that he could be cared for. A few days later I found his skinned body, with the braces still on his crippled front legs, lying on the dump.

Not even that, I think, cured me of going there, though our parents all forbade us on pain of cholera or worse to do so. The place fascinated us, as it should have. For this was the kitchen midden of all the civilization we knew; it gave us the most tantalizing glimpses into our lives as well as into those of the neighbors. It gave us an aesthetic distance from which to know ourselves.

The dump was our poetry and our history. We took it home with us by the wagonload, bringing back into town the things the town had used and thrown away. Some little part of what we gathered, mainly bottles, we managed to bring back to usefulness, but most of our gleanings we left lying around barn or attic or cellar until in some renewed fury of spring cleanup our families carted them off to the dump again, to be rescued and briefly treasured by some other boy with schemes for making them useful. Occasionally something we really valued with a passion was snatched from us in horror and returned at once. That happened to the mounted head of a white mountain goat, somebody's trophy from old times and the far Rocky Mountains, that I brought home one day in transports of delight. My mother took one look and discovered that his beard was full of moths.

I remember that goat; I regret him yet. Poetry is seldom useful, but always memorable. I think I learned more from the town dump than I learned from school: more about people, more about how life is lived, not elsewhere but here, not in other times but now. If I were a sociologist anxious to study in detail the life of any community, I would go very early to its refuse piles. For a community may be as well judged by what it throws away —what it has to throw away and what it chooses to—as by any other evidence. For whole civilizations we have sometimes no more of the poetry and little more of the history than this.

QUESTIONS FOR STUDY, DISCUSSION, AND WRITING

1. *Stegner begins his reminiscence of the town dump by saying that it had "poetry and excitement" in it. In what ways does he seek to convey those qualities to the reader?*

2. Is Stegner's description of the dump and its surroundings vivid to you? Where does his writing directly appeal to the senses, and which senses are called into play?

3. In his second paragraph Stegner speaks of the Alph, the "sacred river" of Coleridge's poem "Kubla Khan." Why? How does allusion to that poem help him convey the strangeness and wonder he then felt?

4. In paragraphs 5-8 Stegner departs, as he had departed to a lesser degree in the two preceding paragraphs, from his description of the dump. Explain how that departure is justified and whether the writing there is appropriate to the essay as a whole.

5. Why does Stegner say (p. 9) that finding the three volumes of Shakespeare in the dump was "a little like finding my own name on a gravestone"? What is the purpose and effect of his allusion to Virgil's Aeneid in the sentence just before that?

6. Through what particular details does Stegner portray the dump as a record of his childhood? How is it shown to be also a record of the brief history of the town? In what respects does it reflect and suggest more widely yet, European and American history and culture and, ultimately, the ancient past, the foundations of civilization? Explain how and to what effect Stegner's focus on the dump enables these considerations to widen in scope but remain associated.

ALLAN SEAGER

The Joys of Sport at Oxford

During my first week at Oxford I decided not to go out for any sports in the fall, or Michaelmas, term. My college offered Rugby, soccer, field hockey and something referred to as "the boats." I had never done any of these. They were all outdoor sports, and outdoors was where it was raining. For a fee I could also have joined a team of chaps who trotted informally through the dripping countryside in mild competition with a group from another college. Or I could have subscribed to a beagling club and worn a green coat, stout laced boots and a hemispheric little green velvet cap and legged it over the fields behind the dogs in search of hares and perhaps gotten a furry paw glued to a wooden shield as a trophy to hang in my room. The rain discouraged me, however. I got soggy enough walking to lectures. The fall term seemed a good time to lie up in front of a fire and get a good start on my reading.

I did this. I read heavily, but after three weeks I noticed a nervousness coming over me. And after the fourth week I knew what it was. I had been getting up every half hour to look out of the window. Now, there was nothing to look at out of my window but the college coal pile and beyond it a 15-foot wall topped with broken glass to keep students from climbing in after midnight. I was looking for a girl. I had got used to having dates at home but, after a day or two of scrutiny, I could tell that I was not likely to see one poised like a mountain goat on top of the coal.

I had won a Rhodes scholarship because I was the only man at the state examination who had worn a stiff collar—an Arrow, I believe. I did not wear it to Oxford. Instead I bought shirts with what we used to call bootlegger (tab) collars, a tweed jacket and gray flannel "bags." Not knowing that Americans move differently from the English—looser, somehow—and that you can identify one as far as you can see him, I believed my attire made me indistinguishable from an Old Etonian, and I had peeped at the English girls in the lecture halls, thinking that I had at least an even start with the Englishmen. I was appalled at what I saw.

There are four women's colleges at Oxford. Most of their undergraduates were going to be schoolmistresses and looked it. They wore rugged tweeds full of sticks of heather and twigs of gorse than stank in the wet weather, and they had big, frightening muscles in their legs from bike riding. A beautiful American girl would, I thought, be glad to make the acquaintance of a compatriot because of her loneliness.

I spotted an American girl in one of my lectures and she was beautiful. By asking around among other Americans I learned her name, which I have forgotten, and her address. I called. A maid let me in and went to fetch her. When she came in I said, "I wonder if you would care to drink some sherry with me this afternoon and bring a friend." I didn't want her friend, but the university had ruled that young women could visit young men's rooms only in pairs.

"I don't think so," she said coldly.

"Tea, perhaps?"

"No."

"Ah, milk?"

She walked out.

I didn't know then, as I came to later, that American girls in Oxford don't want to meet Americans; they want to meet Englishmen.

After this rebuff I might have lingered before my fire until spring in a dangerous inertia, dangerous because the elements of English diet are extremely reluctant to move without help after you have ingested them. But I was asked to go on the river. I was flattered to be asked, and I went.

The river is the Thames, but it is mysteriously called the Isis where it flows through Oxford, and the way to it is past the walled garden where Lewis Carroll, himself an admirer of girls—but girls rather younger than those who interested me—wrote *Alice in Wonderland* while he was a don at Christ Church. Then you go down a long alley under tremendous elms and you come to the college barges. They are houseboats, really, and they never go anyplace. They are moored tight to the bank and are used as dressing rooms. They are painted white, highly ornamented with colored moldings, and they made a pretty sight lined up along the riverbank.

The only rowing I had done was to pull a flat-bottomed rowboat over the weed beds of small lakes after bass. I was not the only novice, however, and we all had to put up with two or three days of "we call this an oar" kind of instruction before they let us sit down and try to put our backs into it. The president of the Boat Club, Tom Smith, was the coach. There was no professional coaching in any sport—there still isn't—except that the varsity cricketers and swimmers had professionals come to look at them occasionally during the season. Tom Smith told me I might make a No. 6, and he gave me politely to know that Six was supposed to move a lot of water. At 12 stone 9 (180 and one-half pounds) I was the biggest man in the boat and, as I found out later, in the college. The English had been children during World War I. They had grown up on rationed food, and I think this is why they were not very big.

At my college we were lucky. We began the season in a proper shell no thicker than a cigar box. I saw an unfortunate youth step right through it into the river because he had not set his foot exactly on the keel when he climbed in. We also had movable seats on little wheels and swivel rowlocks (pronounced "rollocks"). I kept hearing a saying: "English rowing is 10 years behind the times; Cambridge rowing is 20 years behind the times. Oxford rowing is 40 years behind the times."

The varsity boat and those of some of the colleges began training exactly as their forefathers had done when Victoria was a young queen. In the first weeks of the season the varsity eight swung grandly down the river in a craft that resembled the war canoe of some obscure tribe. It was heavy enough for the open sea. It had board seats and the rowlocks were merely two straight pegs you laid the oars between. A month's workouts in this scow certainly preserved tradition, but it also gave a man a set of boils as big as walnuts. A varsity oarsman spent more time on his feet than a cop, and when he sat down he bellowed. With such a fine start, the boils lasted all season even after the varsity shifted to the shell they would use against Cambridge. At my college, Oriel, we avoided all this pain. Daringly unorthodox, we rowed the Jesus style.

This was not blasphemy and we did not kneel in prayer before taking to the water. The Jesus style was developed at Jesus College, Cambridge by a man named Steve Fairbairn. Succinctly put, it was "blade form." This meant that if your oar blade was right, nothing else mattered. Opposed to this was the practice of the varsity, all the other colleges and, I believe, American crews, called body form, which meant that if your body was correctly poised, the blade had to be right.

A body-form crew was coached right down to its fingernails. You were supposed to keep a straight back, to stare perpetually at the fifth or sixth cervical vertebra of the man in front of you and never move your head. A body form crew is impressive to watch. The muscular decorum makes its members look virtuous and clean-limbed. Perhaps this is its own reward, for a blade-form crew, rowing with backs bending comfortably and gandering around at the blades, may look raffish and sloppy but probably is going as fast as the body-form boys.

We trained all the fall into December. It was mostly just rowing. The Thames is a canal with locks all the way to London and, if we were taking a long paddle, say, eight or 10 miles, we had to pass Iffley lock when we went one way and Osney lock when we went the other. I can remember sitting in Osney lock one dark afternoon, waiting for it to fill, with ice forming on the oars and flakes of snow as big as goose feathers wetting the back of my skimpy little Jaegar shirt, and it was no consolation to remember that the Miller's Wife in *The Canterbury Tales* had probably lived within a furlong.

On short days when we stayed within Iffley lock we were coached by Tom Smith riding a bicycle beside us on the towpath. I doubt if we rowed as much as Washington or Yale. There was no other training. Beer was believed strengthening; gin would keep coxswains small. No one spoke of cigarettes at all. As green as I was, I didn't know whether I was in shape or not, but it didn't make much difference, because term ended about the middle of December and I took off for six weeks in Paris.

The Bump Races come in two sets, late in January and early in May. They are rowed for six days, Thursday through Saturday and Monday through Wednesday. The colloquial name for the January races is Toggers; the formal one, Torpids; but no one could tell me why. The May races are called Eights, and they are quite social. If you have a girl, you bring her, give her luncheons of hock and lobster mayonnaise and she sits on the top of your barge to watch you sweat. Toggers are grimmer because January is grimmer.

Bump races are examples of much made of little. The Thames is a small river at Oxford; in fact, I think Ralph Boston could jump over it at a place called the Gut if he took a good run. There were about 25 rowing colleges at Oxford, and each college put two boats in the river, the larger colleges, like Balliol, three, sometimes four, so there were perhaps 60 in all. I doubt if you could row 60 eight-oared shells abreast at Poughkeepsie, and you certainly can't on the Isis, so they start one behind another and chase the one in front.

Small stakes are driven into the bank 60 feet apart. To each stake a rope 60 feet long is fixed. The cox holds the other end and lets the boat drift until it is taut. Each boat has a starter. Five minutes before time all the starters gather at a little brass cannon in a hayfield to synchronize their stopwatches with a chronometer. Then they come back and stand on the bank beside their boats saying, "Two minutes gone. Three minutes gone," to the yawning oarsmen in the river below. In the last minute they count off the quarters, and finally, "10, 9, 8, 7, 6, 5, 4, come forward, are you ready?" and "Bang!" goes the little brass cannon. The college bargeman gives you a hell of a shove with a boathook and away you go, the cox howling the beat at about 50 strokes a minute. It is very common to black out completely during the first 30 seconds. As soon as you are under way, the stroke drops to about 40, but not much less, because the course from Iffley lock to the top of the barges is only about a mile and a half.

Most of the members of your college are scrambling along the towpath beside you, yelling and shooting off guns. You can't tell whether the boat behind you is gaining, because you are watching Stroke's oar or your own, but if the cox's voice rises to a scream and he starts counting to raise the beat you know you are overtaking the boat ahead. When your bow overlaps his stern, the cox turns the rudder sharply. Bow touches stern. This is the bump.

When you make a bump, the next day your boat starts in the place of the bumped boat. You go up or down each day according to your prowess. The final aim, which may take several years to achieve, is to become Head of the River, the first boat in line.

I came back from Paris not in the best of shape. A wisdom tooth had started acting up. It ached and swelled monotonously. I made my apologies to Tom Smith, and he found another Six. For a week I tried to ignore it, hoping the swelling would go away. It didn't and I asked the dean to recommend a dentist. I found this man in what I took to be a large bedroom with the bed moved out. The walls were covered with flowered wallpaper, and a chromo of Watts's *Hope*[1] hung on the wall. He sat me down in a chair with four legs. He took a look and, as God is my judge, he prescribed an infusion of camomile and poppyhead—not opium, poppyhead—with which to bathe the afflicted parts. I was not sleeping much and I was smoking about 50 Players a day, but I bathed away conscientiously. It didn't do any good. The swelling went gruesomely on. When I looked as if I were trying to conceal a scarlet pippin in my cheek I went back to the dentist and said, "Lance this, will you?" He bumbled and said at last, "I can't. I'm not a dental surgeon." So he took me to a real surgeon, who had his learning son in the office, and

---

1. An allegorical painting of a female figure seated on the globe, peeping from beneath a blindfold. She bends over a lyre on which only one string remains; the sky is dark except for one star.

there before a blazing coal fire the three together gave me gas and lanced it. Afterward I didn't feel good, but at least I didn't feel like a bomb about to go off.

That night I was sitting in front of my fire, reading and bathing my wound with a little neat whisky when Tom Smith knocked at my door. He said that his No. 6 had just come down with a bad case of flu. Toggers started the next day. Would I care to fill in? It was so casual and the honor of the U.S.A. depended so heavily on it that I said I would be delighted—which was a lie.

On the first day of Toggers I was personally lucky. I had to row only the first six strokes. When the little brass cannon went off, we laid into the first strokes hard. The cox had just shouted, "Six!" when No. 7 in front of me caught a crab. If you are quick you can sometimes lie flat and let the oar pass over your head. Seven was not quick. He was probably blacked out, and the butt of the oar caught him in the belly and jackknifed him out of the boat. Falling, he broke his oar smack off at the rowlock. The boat staggered. There were cries of "Man overboard!" and Dawson-Grove, the cox, was yelling oaths like a banshee. I don't believe it is possible to overturn an eight-oared boat, but we nearly made it. In the confusion, Exeter came tearing into us from behind and sheared off all the oars on the bow side. It was a mess. No. 7 avoided having Exeter's keel bash his head in by cannily staying under water until after the collision; then he swam soggily ashore. Our race was over for that day and I was barely winded.

The next day, with new oars, we caught St. John's on the Green Bank and made a bump. In fact, we made five bumps in all during Toggers. If a boat makes five bumps in Toggers or four in Eights the college is required by custom to stand its members a Bump supper. It is a big jollification in honor of the Boat Club. The manciple (head chef) outdoes himself and provides a really good meal, with fresh soup (I think) and champagne at will. Alumni gather and there are sherry parties. Since many Oriel undergraduates study theology, many of its graduates are parsons, but Church of England clergy are not stuffy. They go to sherry parties, and they don't stand around with a glass in their hands for the look of things, either.

At our Bump supper the hall was in an uproar because of the sherry parties beforehand. Cheers were started but forgotten. Boating songs were begun, broken off and begun again. A stately portrait of Matthew Arnold, once an Oriel don, hung on the wall. A swaying youth, his boiled shirt coming out in welts from spilled champagne, pegged an orange from the centerpiece clean through Matthew's jaw just at the muttonchop. A bonfire sprang up in the front quad, fed by side tables, chairs and Van Gogh reproductions. The son of a Scottish laird broke into the provost's lodgings, stole all the shoes belonging to that good old man (now knighted for his translations of Aristotle) and hurled them all into the flames.

High above the quad in a third-floor bedroom a man named Antony Henley crouched, waiting for the supper to finish. Tony had collected half the chamber pots in the college. (They used them then, and it is no more than even money they use them now.) In a room directly opposite, another man had collected the other half. A rope hung in a curve from one window to the other. At last the dons appeared under the porch of the hall, chatting only less than boisterously from the champagne. They were in full fig—dinner jackets, long M.A. gowns and mortarboards. They walked down the steps in the wavering light of the bonfire. At that moment a shower of broken crockery fell on their heads. Tony and his friend were sticking the rope ends through the pot handles and letting them slide down the rope two at a time. When they met they broke and fell on the dean, the provost, the bursar, the Goldsmith's reader, a bishop or two and other dignitaries. Big joke. The party went on all night, consuming untold bottles of Pommery and Piper-Heidsieck and much of the movable furniture of the college. At one point, I was told, seven drunken archdeacons danced around the bonfire, a spectacle very likely unmatched since the martyrdom of Ridley and Latimer, who were burned years earlier in Broad Street and from the top of whose Gothic monument the Oxford Alpine Club hangs a chamber pot each year.

The next morning the groans of hangover were decently stifled by the mists in the quad. The scouts were out with rakes and shovels, cleaning away the empties, the shards of crockery and the ashes of the bonfire strewn with the nails and eyelets of the provost's shoes. Antony Henley was haled before the dean, presented with a bill for upward of 150 chamber pots and laughingly fined £10. Toggers were over. I have never rowed since nor drunk so much champagne.

I was not, so to speak, an oarsman by trade, I was a swimmer. The rowing I had done, while exhausting and in some ways amusing, merely passed the time until the swimming season opened in the third, or Hilary, term. The trouble was I couldn't find anyplace to "go out" for swimming. There was no varsity pool, I discovered. But I heard somewhere that the swimmers used the Merton Street Baths.

The Baths were in a grubby brick building, built long before with what seemed an ecclesiastical intent, for they had long Gothic windows in front. The pool itself, gently steaming in the cold of the building, was a gloomy tank, trapezoidal in shape, and I learned later that it was 25 yards long on one side and exactly 22 and one-half yards long on the other—which made for some tricky finishes in a race. The bathing master said there hadn't been any gentlemen from the varsity near the place in months. He suggested that I see Mr. Pace in Merton College, the club president.

After I had knocked, Pace opened his door six inches, no more.
"Yes?" he said.

"Mr. Pace?"

"Yes," he said.

"My name is Seager."

"Yes?" he said.

"I wanted to ask you about the swimming."

"Oh. Ah," he said. Then he opened the door. "Do come in."

I went in.

"Seager? Oh, yes. Someone mentioned your name. From the
States, aren't you? Mitchigan? A good club, I believe."

"We were national champions last year."

"Really? Just what did you want to know?"

"When do you start training?"

"Oh, I'll let you know. I'll send you a note round the week before
we begin. Will that do?"

It was the Oxford manner again. He was effortlessly making my
enthusiasm seem not only comic but childishly comic. However, it
is just as well to be candid. I was after their records, and I didn't
know then that he was Oxford's best sprinter. "I'd like to start now,"
I said, "I'm not in very good shape."

"I daresay you could use the Baths. Cost you a bob a time until
we start meeting."

He waved his hand nonchalantly.

"Cheers," he said, and I left.

It was only later that I learned I had committed a faux pas. I
was always finding out things later. You did not "go out" for the
varsity. College sports, O.K.—you could turn up whenever you liked.
But the varsity was strictly invitational, so much so that in my day
the Varsity Boat Club had never used an American oar. There was
a faint general resentment of Americans and Colonials taking over
Oxford sports. However, I paid my shilling and trundled a slow half
mile every day up and down the bath. It was like swimming in
church.

In a couple of weeks Pace sent his note round and the season
opened. I was astounded. It was not so much that they swam badly
—I had more or less expected that from their record times—it was
that they worked so little. In fact, they didn't *work* at all. They
swam until they felt tired and quit for the day, refreshed. Where
was the old pepper, the old fight? Slowly I began to comprehend
the English attitude toward sports, which, unless Dr. Bannister
changed it drastically with his great meticulous mile, is this: sports
are for fun. If you are good at one or two of them, it is somewhat
in the nature of a divine gift. Since the gift is perpetual, it is there
every day and you can pull out a performance very near your best
any time. With a little practice to loosen the muscles and clear the

pipes, you are ready for the severest tests.

I was drinking beer one night in Balliol College with several men, one of them an Olympic runner, a 1,500-meter man. It is rare that a subject so trivial as sports would come up in Balliol, the intellectual center of England, but it came up and eventually came down to the question of how fast could this Olympic man run 1,500 meters at the moment? We all piled into a couple of taxis and drove out to the Oxford Sports Ground, where there was a cinder track. The runner, full of confidence and beer, supplied a stopwatch and a flashlight, and there in his street clothes, in the rain, in the dead of night, this man took off and ran 1,500 meters in just over four minutes. This proved to me that the English were right, but it did not prove to me that I was wrong. I knew I could not swim 100 yards in less than a minute, untrained.

But I stayed untrained. It seemed to be overly zealous to go on chugging up and down after all the other members of the club had showered, dressed and come to stand at the edge of the bath to watch me as if I were a marine curiosity, like a dugong. I tried it a couple of times and quit. I swam as little as they did, no more. Then there was the problem of entertainment after the matches— they didn't call them meets. There was little university swimming in England, so our competition was usually a town club whose members might be aquatic plumbers and carpenters—not gentlemen, you see. With a splendid condescension, we set out a table loaded with whisky, beer and wine after each match, and we had to drink to make our guests feel at home so that caste differences would be concealed and we could pretend to be all jolly good sportsmen together. After a match, say, in London with the Paddington police, the coppers would set out a table of whisky, beer and wine, and we had to drink to show our appreciation of their hospitality. This drinking was not a detestable chore, but it meant that, with two matches a week, we were getting mildly stoned twice a week just in the way of business. This was not how I had been taught to train, and it came over me suddenly how far morality had invaded sports in the U.S.

I won all my races except one, but the times were shamefully slow and I was chased right down to the wire in all of them. In May, John Pace had the whole club to tea in his rooms. There was an hour of conversation interspersed with tomato and cucumber sandwiches. Then Pace stood up by the chimney piece. "Now, chaps," he began facetiously (I never heard anyone use "chaps" except facetiously). "You know we swim the Tabs two weeks from now." "Tabs" meant Cambridge, from the latin *Cantabrigia*. "Please smoke only after meals and cut down your beer to a pint a day. And do try to swim every day between now and then."

People clapped and cried, "Hear! Hear!" as if Pace had been in the House of Commons. I gathered we were in hard training from then on. I had not gone under 61 seconds for 100 yards yet, and I had heard that Cambridge had a fancy Dan named Hill who had done 58. I was scared.

Someone said, "This rationing of beer, John. What if we're sconced?"

"Behave yourselves and you won't be," Pace said.

In Oxford dining halls a sconce is a penalty exacted in the spring of the year for some breach of taste or decorum. It is a welcome penalty, eagerly exacted. If you showed up late for dinner or wearing something odd like a turtleneck sweater or if you said something that could be remotely construed as offensive, you were sconced. Once I said something slightly off color.

"We'll have a sconce on you for that," the man next to me said. He wrote my offense in Latin on the back of a menu, "*Seager dixit obscenissime*"[2] and had a waiter take it up to high table to be approved by the dean. It was a formality. The dean always approved sconces. "What will you take it in?" I was asked. In theory you had to drink a silver quart pot of some liquid, bottoms up. In practice you had no choice; custom said old beer. Once I saw a man take it in fresh cow's milk and he never lived it down. It is the sort of thing planters discuss in Kenya and Borneo 20 years later.

The strength of English beer is indicated by the number of Xs on the barrel. Ale is the weakest, one X. Bitter beer is two Xs. Old beer is five Xs, about as strong as sherry. It is never iced, but in college it comes from the cellars and it might as well be. It looks almost coal-black and it is as thick as stout. It is hard but not impossible to drink it all down at one go. If you do, the man who sconced you has to pay for it. If you fail, it is passed around the table like a loving cup. But the minute you set the pot down empty, you're drunk.

The Cambridge match was held at the Bath Club, then on Dover Street, London. It was a posh club. (I like the origin of posh. When people used to tour the Orient from England the most expensive cabins on the P&O boats, those that made the most of the prevailing winds and the least of the sun, were on the port side going and the starboard side returning, so the luggage for those cabins was marked P.O.S.H., that is "port out, starboard home.") We took an afternoon train down to London already dressed in white ties, black trousers and our blazers, and with an affectation of gaiety we sauntered up Piccadilly in the early evening and into the Bath Club. I knew I had to fear this Cambridge speedster, Hill, who had done 58 seconds, because I had done only 61 that season. (I had done 61 when I was a long, wheyfaced boy of 15 in high school in Tennessee.) My fear was degrading. That's why I was mad: it was a real

---

2. "Seager spoke most obscenely."

fear. And I felt that my teammates had begun to wonder when I was going to demonstrate that I didn't fit one of the stock British images of the American, lots of noise and no performance.

I figured I could take Hill in the 50 if I scrambled, but in the 100 I knew I would have to swim and I figured I could swim about 75 yards before I blew up. Since the English started slow and finished fast, I figured I would start fast, get a big lead, frighten him and finish on whatever I had left.

The Bath Club looked like a court levee, the ladies in those English evening gowns, the men in white ties and tail coats, and the Old Blues[3] wore their blazers. Diamonds glittered. I detected dowagers with lorgnons, a colorful throng, posh. The club pool was 25 yards long on both sides, but it was dark at one end. Since you can bump your head into a goose egg or even oblivion if you slam into a turn you can't see, I wet a towel and hung it over the far end in my lane to make a white spot. As I walked back I heard resentful murmurs from the spectators. "He's an Ameddican," as if what I had done were cunning and illicit.

The 50-yard race went as I had expected. I scrambled. I won in a record time of 25 seconds. I went back to the dressing room to worry about the 100. Hill was a little fleshy fellow whose fat might hide more stamina than I had.

I swam the first two lengths of the 100 in 25 seconds, and after the third length I looked back at Hill. He was 30 feet behind, but I was not encouraged because I could tell I was going to blow up. I blew and finished the last 25 yards with a frantic overhand, dazzled by fatigue, my head out all the way so I could breathe. But I won by a yard, and they said it was a new record, 57 seconds. My teammates shouted and pounded me on the back as if I had done well. My shabby little victories gave Oxford the match.

The adulation of the English for sports figures is greater than that in this country, possibly because a sound sports record keeps a chap from being too "clever"—which is repugnant (Churchill was too clever by half, right up until the blitz). Let a man die who has not specially distinguished himself as an admiral, a cabinet member or a press lord, and if he has been a Blue, Oxon or Cantab, the obituary will very likely be headed OLD BLUE'S DEMISE. That is what is important. A few months after my victories I was having tea with some people at a public tearoom in Oxford.

A man came up to the table, a student, and said to me, "Is this Mr. Seager, the famous swimmer?"

I looked him straight in the eye for maybe three seconds. He seemed to be perfectly serious. "I'm Seager," I answered finally.

"May I shake your hand?" he said.

I shook hands and he went away pleased, apparently. Nobody at

3. Former varsity athletes from Oxford and Cambridge.

my table seemed to think that any of this was strange, and I let my self-esteem expand a little.

I didn't get punctured for two years. I was back in Ann Arbor then and happened to run into Matt Mann, my former coach.

"Say, I hear you got a couple of English records," he said. Matt was born in Yorkshire, and he had held English records himself.

"Yes," I said. I couldn't look at him.

"What were your times?"

"Twenty-five. Fifty-seven," I mumbled. I had been a bad boy.

"Fifty-seven! Were you dragging something?" he said jovially.

Surprising myself, I said defiantly, "Matt, it was fun."

And it had been, all of it, the massive courtesy of the swimming policemen, the singing in the pub afterward, the soiree at the Bath Club—not real glory, which means work, but a hell of a lot of fun.

QUESTIONS FOR STUDY, DISCUSSION, AND WRITING

1. At some points Seager describes the Oxford manner and pictures himself as an outsider. Give some examples. Are there instances where Seager presents himself in the Oxford manner?
2. What characteristics of the English view of sports does Seager stress. How are these characteristics reflected in other areas of Oxford life?
3. Seager's narrative permits him to use a wide range of language, including British and American diction, and of usage, reaching from the relatively formal to slang. What kinds of effects does Seager achieve with this variety of language?
4. When Seager draped a wet towel at the end of his lane, was that gamesmanship (see Potter, pp. 636–644)? Did he display Rhodesmanship in the state examination?
5. What is Seager's attitude toward the experiences he recounts? How is that attitude expressed in his tone? Does it vary?
6. Consider a nation or smaller social group with which you are familiar. What does its attitude toward sports reveal about the nation or group? Write an essay showing the evidence for your view.

A. J. LIEBLING
Poet and Pedagogue

When Floyd Patterson regained the world heavyweight championship by knocking out Ingemar Johansson in June, 1960, he so excited a teenager named Cassius Marcellus Clay, in Louisville, Kentucky, that Clay, who was a good amateur light heavyweight, made up a ballad in honor of the victory. (The tradition of pugilistic poetry is old; according to Pierce Egan, the Polybius of the London Prize Ring, Bob Gregson, the Lancashire Giant, used "to recount the deeds of his Brethren of the Fist in heroic verse, like the Bards of Old." A sample Gregson couplet was "The British lads that's here/Quite strangers are to fear." He was not a very good fighter, either.) At the time, Clay was too busy training for the Olympic boxing tournament in Rome that summer to set his ode down on paper, but he memorized it, as Homer and Gregson must have done with their things, and then polished it up in his head. "It took me about three days to think it up," Clay told me a week or so ago, while he was training in the Department of Parks gymnasium, on West Twenty-eighth Street, for his New York debut as a professional, against a heavyweight from Detroit named Sonny Banks. In between his composition of the poem and his appearance on Twenty-eighth Street, Clay had been to Rome and cleaned up his Olympic opposition with aplomb, which is his strongest characteristic. The other finalist had been a Pole with a name that it takes two rounds to pronounce, but Cassius had not tried. A book that I own called *Olympic Games: 1960*, translated from the German, says "Clay fixes the Pole's punch-hand with an almost hypnotic stare and by nimble dodging renders his attacks quite harmless." He thus risked being disqualified for holding and hitting, but he got away with it. He had then turned professional under social and financial auspices sufficient to launch a bank, and had won ten tryout bouts on the road. Now he told me that Banks, whom he had never seen, would be no problem.

I had watched Clay's performance in Rome and had considered it attractive but not probative. Amateur boxing compares with professional boxing as college theatricals compare with stealing scenes from Margaret Rutherford. Clay had a skittering style, like a pebble scaled over water. He was good to watch, but he seemed to make only glancing contact. It is true that the Pole finished the three-round bout helpless and out on his feet, but I thought he had just run out of puff chasing Clay, who had then cut him to pieces. ("Pietrzykowski is done for," the Olympic book says. "He gazes helplessly into his corner of the ring; his legs grow heavier and he cannot escape his rival.") A boxer who uses his legs as much as Clay used his in Rome risks deceleration in a longer bout. I had been more impressed by Patterson when he was an Olympian, in 1952; he had knocked out his man in a round.

At the gym that day, Cassius was on a mat doing situps when Mr. Angelo Dundee, his trainer, brought up the subject of the ballad. "He is smart," Dundee said. "He made up a poem." Clay had his hands locked behind his neck, elbows straight out, as he bobbed up and down. He is a golden-brown young man, big-chested and long-legged, whose limbs have the smooth, rounded look that Joe Louis's used to have, and that frequently denotes fast muscles. He is twenty years old and six feet two inches tall, and he weighs a hundred and ninety-five pounds.

"I'll say it for you," the poet announced, without waiting to be wheedled or breaking cadence. He began on a rise: "You may talk about Sweden [down and up again], You may talk about Rome [down and up again], But Rockville Centre is Floyd Patterson's home [down]."

He is probably the only poet in America who can recite this way. I would like to see T. S. Eliot try.

Clay went on, continuing his ventriflexions: "A lot of people said that Floyd couldn't fight, But you should have seen him on that comeback night."

There were some lines that I fumbled; the tempo of situps and poetry grew concurrently faster as the bardic fury took hold. But I caught the climax as the poet's voice rose: "He cut up his eyes and mussed up his face, And that last left hook knocked his head out of place!"

Cassius smiled and said no more for several situps, as if waiting for Johansson to be carried to his corner. He resumed when the Swede's seconds had had time to slosh water in his pants and bring him around. The fight was done; the press took over: "A reporter asked: 'Ingo, will a rematch be put on?' Johansson said: 'Don't know. It might be postponed.'"

The poet did a few more silent strophes, and then said:

"If he would have stayed in Sweden, He wouldn't have took that beatin'."

Here, overcome by admiration, he lay back and laughed. After a minute or two, he said, "That rhymes. I like it."

There are trainers I know who, if they had a fighter who was a poet, would give up on him, no matter how good he looked, but Mr. Dundee is of the permissive school. Dundee has been a leading Italian name in the prize-fighting business in this country ever since about 1910, when a manager named Scotty Monteith had a boy named Giuseppe Carrora whom he rechristened Johnny Dundee. Johnny became the hottest lightweight around; in 1923, in the twilight of his career, he boiled down and won the featherweight championship of the world. Clay's trainer is a brother of Chris Dundee, a promoter in Miami Beach, but they are not related to Johnny, who is still around, or to Joe and Vince Dundee, brothers out of Baltimore, who were welterweight and middleweight champions, respectively, in the late twenties and early thirties, and who are not related to Johnny, either.

"He is very talented," Dundee said while Clay was dressing. It was bitter cold outside, but he did not make Clay take a cold shower before putting his clothes on. "He likes his shower better at the hotel," he told me. It smacked of progressive education. Elaborating on Clay's talent, Dundee said, "He will jab you five or six times going away. Busy hands. And he has a left uppercut." He added that Clay, as a business enterprise, was owned and operated by a syndicate of ten leading citizens of Louisville, mostly distillers. They had given the boy a bonus of ten thousand dollars for signing up, and paid him a monthly allowance and his training expenses whether he fought or not—a research fellowship. In return, they took half his earnings when he had any. These had been inconsiderable until his most recent fight, when he made eight thousand dollars. His manager of record (since somebody has to sign contracts) was a member of this junta—Mr. William Faversham, a son of the old matinee idol. Dundee, a tutor in attendance, was a salaried employee. "The idea was he shouldn't be rushed," Dundee said. "Before they hired me, we had a conference about his future like he was a serious subject."

It sounded like flying in the face of the old rule that hungry fighters make the best fighters. I know an old-style manager named Al Weill, who at the beginning of the week used to give each of his fighters a five-dollar meal ticket that was good for five dollars and fifty cents in trade at a coffeepot on Columbus Avenue. A guy had to win a fight to get a second ticket before the following Monday. "It's good for them," Weill used to say. "Keeps their mind on their work."

That day in the gym, Clay's boxing had consisted of three rounds with an amateur light heavyweight, who had been unable to keep away from the busy hands. When the sparring partner covered his head with his arms, the poet didn't bother to punch to the body. "I'm a head-hunter," he said to a watcher who called his attention to this omission. "Keep punching at a man's head, and it mixes his mind." After that, he had skipped rope without a rope. His flippancy would have horrified Colonel John R. Stingo, an ancient connoisseur, who says, "Body-punching is capital investment," or the late Sam Langford, who, when asked why he punched so much for the body, said, "The head got eyes."

Now Cassius reappeared, a glass of fashion in a snuff-colored suit and one of those lace-front shirts, which I had never before known anybody with nerve enough to wear, although I had seen them in shirt-shop windows on Broadway. His tie was like two shoestring ends laid across each other, and his smile was white and optimistic. He did not appear to know how badly he was being brought up.

Just when the sweet science appears to lie like a painted ship upon a painted ocean, a new Hero, as Pierce Egan would term him, comes along like a Moran tug to pull it out of the doldrums. It was because Clay had some of the Heroic aura about him that I went uptown the next day to see Banks, the *morceau*[1] chosen for the

1. Short musical piece.

prodigy to perform in his big-time debut. The exhibition piece is usually a fighter who was once almost illustrious and is now beyond ambition, but Banks was only twenty-one. He had knocked out nine men in twelve professional fights, had won another fight on a decision, and had lost two, being knocked out once. But he had come back against the man who stopped him and had knocked him out in two rounds. That showed determination as well as punching power. I had already met Banks, briefly, at a press conference that the Madison Square Garden Corporation gave for the two incipient Heroes, and he seemed the antithesis of the Kentucky bard—a grave, quiet young Deep Southerner. He was as introverted as Clay was extro. Banks, a lighter shade than Clay, had migrated to the automobile factories from Tupelo, Mississippi, and boxed as a professional from the start, to earn money. He said at the press conference that he felt he had "done excellently" in the ring, and that the man who had knocked him out, and whom he had subsequently knocked out, was "an excellent boxer." He had a long, rather pointed head, a long chin, and the kind of inverted-triangle torso that pro-proletarian artists like to put on their steelworkers. His shoulders were so wide that his neat ready-made suit floated around his waist, and he had long, thick arms.

Banks was scheduled to train at two o'clock in the afternoon at Harry Wiley's Gymnasium, at 137th Street and Broadway. I felt back at home in the fight world as soon as I climbed up from the subway and saw the place—a line of plate-glass windows above a Latin-American bar, grill, and barbecue. The windows were flecked with legends giving the hours when the gym was open (it wasn't), the names of fighters training there (they weren't and half of them had been retired for years), and plugs for physical fitness and boxing instruction. The door of the gym—"Harry Wiley's Clean Gym," the sign on it said—was locked, so I went into the Latin-American place and had a beer while I waited. I had had only half the bottle when a taxi drew up at the curb outside the window and five colored men—one little and four big—got out, carrying bags of gear. They had the key for the gym. I finished my beer and followed them.

By the time I got up the stairs, the three fellows who were going to spar were already in the locker room changing their clothes, and the only ones in sight were a big, solid man in a red jersey, who was laying out the gloves and bandages on a rubbing table, and a wispy little chap in an olive-green sweater, who was smoking a long rattail cigar. His thin black hair was carefully marcelled along the top of his narrow skull, a long gold watch chain danged from his fob pocket, and he exuded an air of elegance, precision, and authority, like a withered but still peppery mahout in charge of a string of not quite bright elephants. Both men appeared occupied with their thoughts, so I made a tour of the room before intruding, reading a series of didactic signs that the proprietor had put up among the photographs of prize fighters and pin-up girls. "Road Work Builds Your Legs," one sign said, and another, "Train Every Day—Great Fighters Are Made That Way." A third admonished, "The Gentleman Boxer Has the Most Friends." "Ladies Are Fine—At the Right Time," another said. When I had absorbed them all, I got around to the big man. "Clay looks mighty fast," I said to him by way of an opening.

He said, "He may not be if a big fellow go after him. That amateur stuff don't mean too much." He himself was Johnny Summerlin, he told me, and he had fought a lot of good heavyweights in his day. "Our boy don't move so fast, but he got fast hands," he said. "He don't discourage easy, either. If we win this one, we'll be all set." I could see that they would be, because Clay has been getting a lot of publicity, and a boxer's fame, like a knight's armor, becomes the property of the fellow who licks him.

Banks now came out in ring togs, and, after greeting me, held out his hands to Summerlin to be bandaged. He looked even more formidable without his street clothes. The two other fighters, who wore their names on their dressing robes, were Cody Jones, a heavyweight as big as Banks, and Sammy Poe, nearly as big. Poe, although a Negro, had a shamrock on the back of his robe—a sign that he was a wag. They were both Banks stablemates from Detroit, Summerlin said, and they had come along to spar with him. Jones had had ten fights and had won eight, six of them by knockouts. This was rougher opposition than any amateur light heavyweight. Banks, when he sparred with Jones, did not scuffle around but practiced purposefully a pattern of coming in low, feinting with head and body to draw a lead, and then hammering in hooks to body and head, following the combination with a right cross. His footwork was neat and geometrical but not flashy —he slid his soles along the mat, always set to hit hard. Jones, using his right hand often, provided rough competition but no substitute for Clay's blinding speed. Poe, the clown, followed Jones. He grunted and howled "Whoo-huh-huh!" every time he threw a punch, and Banks howled back; it sounded like feeding time at a zoo. This was a lively workout.

After the sparring, the little man, discarding his cigar, got into the ring alone with Banks. He wore huge sixteen- or eighteen-ounce sparring gloves, which he held, palm open, toward the giant, leading him in what looked like a fan dance. The little man, covering his meagre chest with one glove, would hold up the other, and Banks would hit it. The punch coming into the glove sounded like a fast ball striking a catcher's mitt. By his motions the trainer indicated a scenario, and Banks, from his crouch, dropped Clay ten or fifteen times this way, theoretically. Then the slender man called a halt and sent Banks to punch the bag. "Remember," he said, "you got to keep on top of him—keep the pressure on."

As the little man climbed out of the ring, I walked around to him and introduced myself. He said that his name was Theodore McWhorter, and that Banks was his baby, his creation—he had taught him everything. For twenty years, McWhorter said, he had run a gymnasium for boxers in Detroit—the Big D. (I supposed it must be pretty much like Wiley's, where we were talking.) He had trained hundreds of neighborhood boys to fight, and had had some good fighters in his time, like Johnny Summerlin, but never a champion. Something always went wrong.

There are fellows like this in almost every big town. Cus D'Amato, who brought Patterson through the amateurs and still has him, used to be one of them, with a one-room gym on Fourteenth Street, but he is among the few who ever hit the mother lode. I could see that McWhorter was a good teacher—such men often are. They are never former champions or notable boxers. The old star is impatient with beginners. He secretly hopes that they won't be as good as he was, and this is a self-defeating quirk in an instructor. The man with the little gym wants to prove himself vicariously. Every promising pupil, consequently, is himself, and he gets knocked out with every one of them, even if he lives to be eighty. McWhorter, typically, said he had been an amateur bantamweight in the thirties but had never turned pro, because times were so hard then that you could pick up more money boxing amateur. Instead of medals, you would get certificates redeemable for cash—two, three, five dollars, sometimes even ten. Once you were a pro, you might not get two fights a year. Whatever his real reason, he had not gone on.

"My boy never got nothing easy," he said. "He don't expect it. Nobody give him nothing. And a boy like that, when he got a chance to be something, he's dangerous."

"You think he's really got a chance?" I asked.

"If we didn't think so, we wouldn't have took the match," Mr. McWhorter said. "You can trap a man," he added mysteriously. "Flashy boxing is like running. You got a long lead, you can run freely. The other kid's way behind, you can sit down and play, get up fresh, and run away from him again. But you got a man running after you with a knife or a gun, pressing it in your back, you feel the pressure. You can't run so free. I'm fighting Clay my way." The substitution of the first for the third person in conversation is managerial usage. I knew that McWhorter would resubstitute

Banks for himself in the actual fight.

We walked over to the heavy bag, where Banks was working. There was one other downtown spectator in the gym, and he came over and joined us. He was one of those anonymous experts, looking like all his kind, whom I have been seeing around gyms and fight camps for thirty years. "You can tell a Detroit fighter every time," he said. "They're well trained. They got the fundamentals. They can hit. Like from Philadelphia the fighters got feneese."

Mr. McWhorter acknowledged the compliment. "We have some fine trainers in Detroit," he said.

Banks, no longer gentle, crouched and swayed before the bag, crashing his left hand into it until the thing jigged and clanked its chains.

"Hit him in the belly like that and you got him," the expert said. "He can't take it there."

Banks stopped punching the bag and said, "Thank you, thank you," just as if the expert had said something novel.

"He's a good boy," McWhorter said as the man walked away. "A polite boy."

When I left to go downtown, I felt like the possessor of a possibly valuable secret. I toyed with the notion of warning the butterfly Cassius, my fellow-litterateur, of his peril, but decided that I must remain neutral and silent. In a dream the night before the fight, I heard Mr. McWhorter saying ominously, "You can trap a man." He had grown as big as Summerlin, and his cigar had turned into an elephant goad.

The temperature outside the Garden was around fifteen degrees on the night of the fight, and the crowd that had assembled to see Clay's debut was so thin that it could more properly be denominated a quorum. Only fans who like sociability ordinarily turn up for a fight that they can watch for nothing on television, and that night the cold had kept even the most gregarious at home. (The boxers, however, were sure of four thousand dollars apiece from television.) Only the sportswriters, the gamblers, and the fight mob were there—nonpayers all—and the Garden management, solicitous about how the ringside would look to the television audience, had to coax relative strangers into the working press section. This shortage of spectators was too bad, because there was at least one red-hot preliminary, which merited a better audience. It was a six-rounder between a lad infelicitously named Ducky Dietz—a hooker and body puncher—and a light heavy from western Pennsylvania named Tommy Gerarde, who preferred a longer range but punched more sharply. Dietz, who shouldn't have, got the decision, and the row that followed warmed our little social group and set the right mood for the main event.

The poet came into the ring first, escorted by Dundee; Nick Florio, the brother of Patterson's trainer, Dan Florio; and a fellow named Gil Clancy, a physical-education supervisor for the Department of Parks, who himself manages a good welterweight named Emile Griffith. (Griffith, unlike Clay, is a worrier. "He is always afraid of being devalued," Clancy says.) As a corner, it was the equivalent of being represented by Sullivan & Cromwell.[2] Clay, who I imagine regretted parting with his lace shirt, had replaced it with a white robe that had a close-fitting red collar and red cuffs. He wore white buckskin bootees that came high on his calves, and taking hold of the ropes in his corner, he stretched and bounced like a ballet dancer at the bar. In doing so, he turned his back to the other, or hungry, corner before Banks and his faction arrived.

Banks looked determined but slightly uncertain. Maybe he was trying to remember all the things McWhorter had told him to do. He was accompanied by McWhorter, Summerlin, and Harry Wiley, a plump, courtly colored man, who runs the clean gym. McWhorter's parchment brow was wrinkled with concentration, and his mouth was set. He looked like a producer who thinks he may have a hit and doesn't want to jinx it. Summerlin was stolid; he may have been remembering the nights when he had not quite made it. Wiley was comforting and solicitous. The weights were announced: Clay, 194½; Banks, 191¼. It was a difference too slight to count between heavyweights. Banks, wide-shouldered, narrow-waisted, looked as if he would be the better man at slinging a sledge or lifting weights; Clay, more cylindrically formed—arms, legs, and torso—moved more smoothly.

When the bell rang, Banks dropped into the crouch I had seen him rehearse, and began the stalk after Clay that was to put the pressure on him. I felt a species of complicity. The poet, still wrapped in certitude, jabbed, moved, teased, looking the *Konzerstuck*[3] over before he banged the ivories. By nimble dodging, as in Rome, he rendered the hungry fighter's attack quite harmless, but this time without keeping his hypnotic stare fixed steadily enough on the punch-hand. They circled around for a minute or so, and then Clay was hit, but not hard, by the left hand. He moved to his own left, across Bank's field of vision, and Banks, turning with him, hit him again, but this time full, with the rising left hook he had worked on so faithfully. The poet went down, and the three men crouching below Banks's corner must have felt, as they listened to the count, like a Reno tourist who hears the silver-dollar jackpot come rolling down. It had been a solid shot—no fluke—and where one shot succeeds, there is no reason to think that another won't. The poet rose at the count of

2. A prominent New York law firm.   3. A freer form of the concerto.

two, but the referee, Ruby Goldstein, as the rules in New York require, stepped between the boxers until the count reached eight, when he let them resume. Now that Banks knew he could hit Clay, he was full of confidence, and the gamblers, who had made Clay a 5-1 favorite, must have had a bad moment. None of them had seen Clay fight, and no doubt they wished they hadn't been so credulous. Clay, I knew, had not been knocked down since his amateur days, but he was cool. He neither rushed after Banks, like an angry kid, nor backed away from him. Standing straight up, he boxed and moved—cuff, slap, jab, and stick, the busy hands stinging like bees. As for Banks, success made him forget his whole plan. Instead of keeping the pressure on—he forgot his right hand and began winging left hooks without trying to set Clay up for them. At the end of the round, the poet was in good shape again, and Banks, the more winded of the two, was spitting a handsome quantity of blood from the jabs that Clay had landed going away. Nothing tires a man more than swinging uselessly. Nevertheless, the knockdown had given Banks the round. The hungry fighter who had listened to his pedagogue was in front, and if he listened again, he might very well stay there.

It didn't happen. In the second round, talent asserted itself. Honest effort and sterling character backed by solid instruction will carry a man a good way, but unlearned natural ability has a lot to be said for it. Young Cassius, who will never have to be lean, jabbed the good boy until he had spread his already wide nose over his face. Banks, I could see, was already having difficulty breathing, and the intellectual pace was just too fast. He kept throwing that left hook whenever he could get set, but he was like a man trying to fight off wasps with a shovel. One disadvantage of having had a respected teacher is that whenever the pupil gets in a jam he tries to remember what the professor told him, and there just isn't time. Like the Pole's in the Olympics, Bank's legs grew heavier, and he could not escape his rival. He did not, however, gaze helplessly into his corner of the ring; he kept on trying. Now Cassius, having mixed the mind, began to dig in. He would come in with a flurry of busy hands, jabbing and slapping his man off balance, and then, in close, drive a short, hard right to the head or a looping left to the slim waist. Two-thirds of the way through the round, he staggered Banks, who dropped forward to his glove tips, though his knees did not touch canvas. A moment later, Clay knocked him down fairly with a right hand, but McWhorter's pupil was not done.

The third round was even less competitive; it was now evident that Banks could not win, but he was still trying. He landed the last, and just about the hardest, punch of the round—a good left hook to the side of the poet's face. Clay looked surprised.

Between the third and fourth rounds, the Boxing Commission physician, Dr. Schiff, trotted up the steps and looked into Banks' eyes. The Detroit lad came out gamely for the round, but the one-minute rest had not refreshed him. After the first flurry of punches, he staggered, helpless, and Goldstein stopped the match. An old fighter, brilliant but cursed with a weak jaw, Goldstein could sympathize.

When it was over, I felt that my first social duty was to the stricken. Clay, I estimated, was the kind of Hero likely to be around for a long while, and if he felt depressed by the knock-down, he had the contents of ten distilleries to draw upon for stimulation. I therefore headed for the loser's dressing room to condole with Mr. McWhorter, who had experienced another almost. When I arrived, Banks, sitting up on the edge of a rubbing table, was shaking his head, angry at himself, like a kid outfielder who has let the deciding run drop through his fingers. Summerlin was telling him what he had done wrong: "You can't hit any-body throwing just one punch all the time. You had him, but you lost him. You forgot to keep crowding." Then the unquench-able pedagogue said, "You're a better fighter than he is, but you lost your head. If you can only get him again. . . ." But poor Banks looked only half convinced. What he felt, I imagine, was that he had had Clay, and that it might be a long time before he caught him again. If he had followed through, he would have been in line for dazzling matches—the kind that bring you five figures even if you lose. I asked him what punch had started him on the downgrade, but he just shook his head. Wiley, the gym proprietor, said there hadn't been any one turning point. "Things just went sour gradually all at once," he declared. "You got to respect a boxer. He'll pick you and peck you, peck you and pick you, until you don't know where you are."

ROBERT COLES
A Young Psychiatrist Looks at His Profession

Recently, in the emergency ward of the Children's Hospital in Boston, an eight-year-old girl walked in and asked to talk to a psy-chiatrist about her "worries." I was called to the ward, and when we ended our conversation I was awake with sorrow and hope for this young girl, but also astonished at her coming. As a child psychiatrist, I was certainly accustomed to the troubled mother who brings her child to a hospital for any one of a wide variety of emotional prob-lems. It was the child's initiative in coming which surprised me. I recalled a story my wife had told me. She was teaching a ninth-grade

English class, and they were starting to read the Sophoclean tragedy of *Oedipus*. A worldly thirteen-year-old asked the first question: "What is an Oedipus complex?" Somehow, in our time, psychiatrists have become the heirs of those who hear the worried and see the curious. I wondered, then, what other children in other times did with their troubles and how they talked of the Greeks. I wondered, too, about my own profession, its position and its problems, and about the answers we might have for ourselves as psychiatrists.

We appear in cartoons, on television serials, and in the movies. We are "applied" by Madison Avenue, and we "influence" writers. Acting techniques, even schools of painting are supposed to be derived from our insights, and Freud has become what Auden calls "a whole climate of opinion." Since children respond so fully to what is most at hand in the adult world, there should have been no reason for my surprise in that emergency ward. But this quick acceptance of us by children and adults alike is ironic, tells us something about this world, and is dangerous.

The irony is that we no longer resemble the small band of outcasts upon whom epithets were hurled for years. One forgets today just how rebellious Freud and his contemporaries were. They studied archaeology and mythology, were versed in the ancient languages, wrote well, and were a bit fiery, a bit eccentric, a bit troublesome, even for one another. Opinionated, determined, oblivious of easy welcome, they were fighters for their beliefs, and their ideas fought much of what the world then thought.

This is a different world. People today are frightened by the memory of concentration camps, by the possibility of atomic war, by the breakdown of old empires and old ways of living and believing. Each person shares the hopes and terrors peculiar to this age, not an age of reason or of enlightenment, but an age of fear and trembling. Every year brings problems undreamed of only a decade ago in New York or Vienna. Cultures change radically, values are different, even diseases change. For instance, cases of hysteria, so beautifully described by Freud, are rarely found today. A kind of innocence is lost; people now are less suggestible, less naïve, more devious. They look for help from many sources, and chief among them, psychiatrists. Erich Fromm, in honor of Paul Tillich's seventy-fifth birthday, remarked: "Modern man is lonely, frightened, and hardly capable of love. He wants to be close to his neighbor, and yet he is too unrelated and distant to be able to be close. . . . In search for closeness he craves knowledge; and in search for knowledge he finds psychology. Psychology becomes a substitute for love, for intimacy. . . ."

Now Freud and his knights are dead. Their long fight has won acclaim and increasing protection from a once reluctant society, and perhaps we should expect this ebb tide. Our very acclaim makes us more rigid and querulous. We are rent by rivalries, and early angers or stubborn idiosyncrasies have hardened into a variety of schools with conflicting ideas. We use proper names of early psychiatrists—Jung, Rank, Horney—to describe the slightest differences of emphasis or theory. The public is interested, but understandably confused. If it is any comfort to the public, so are psychiatrists, at times. Most of us can recall our moments of arrogance, only thinly disguised by words which daily become more like shibboleths, sound hollow, and are almost cant.

Ideas need the backing of institutions and firm social approval if they are to result in practical application. Yet I see pharisaic temples being built everywhere in psychiatry; pick up our journals and you will see meetings listed almost every week of the year and pages filled with abstracts of papers presented at them. These demand precious time in attendance and reading, and such time is squandered all too readily these days. Who of us, even scanting sleep, can keep up with this monthly tidal wave of minute or repetitive studies? And who among us doesn't smile or shrug, as he skims the pages, and suddenly leap with hunger at the lonely monograph that really says something? As psychiatrists we need to be in touch not only with our patients but with the entire range of human activity. We need time to see a play or read a poem, yet daily we sit tied to our chairs, listening and talking for hours on end. While this is surely a problem for all professions, it is particularly deadening for one which deals so intimately with people and which requires that its members themselves be alive and alert.

It seems to me that psychiatric institutions and societies too soon become bureaucracies, emphasizing form, detail, and compliance. They also breed the idea that legislation or grants of money for expansion of laboratories and buildings will provide answers where true knowledge is lacking. Whereas we desperately need more money for facilities and training for treatment programs, there can be a vicious circle of more dollars for more specialized projects producing more articles about less and less, and it may be that some projects are contrived to attract money and expand institutions rather than to form any spontaneous intellectual drive. We argue longer and harder about incidentals, such as whether our patients should sit up or lie down; whether we should accept or reject their gifts or answer their letters; how our offices should be decorated; or how we should talk to patients when they arrive or leave. We debate for hours about the difference between psychoanalysis and psychotherapy; about the advantages of seeing a person twice a week or three times a week; about whether we should give medications to people, and if so, in what way. For the plain fact is that, as we draw near the bureaucratic and the institutionalized, we draw near quibbling. Maybe it is too late, and much of this cannot be stopped. But it may be pleasantly nostalgic, if not instructive, to recall Darwin sailing on the *Beagle*, or Freud writing spirited letters of discovery to a close friend, or Sir Alexander Fleming stumbling upon a mold of penicillin in his laboratory—all in so simple and creative a fashion, and all with so little red tape and money.

If some of psychiatry's problems come from its position in the kind of society we have, other troubles are rooted in the very nature of our job. We labor with people who have troubled thoughts and feelings, who go awry in bed or in the office or with friends. Though we talk a great deal about our scientific interests, man's thoughts and feelings cannot be as easily understood or manipulated as atoms. The brain is where we think and receive impressions of the world, and it is in some ultimate sense an aggregate of atoms and molecules. In time we will know more about how to control and transform all cellular life, and at some point the cells of the brain will be known in all their intricate functions. What we now call "ego" or "unconscious" will be understood in terms of cellular action or biochemical and biophysical activity. The logic of the nature of all matter predicts that someday we will be able to arrange and rearrange ideas and feelings. Among the greatest mysteries before us are the unmarked pathways running from the peripheral nervous system to the thinking areas in the brain. The future is even now heralded by machines which think and by drugs which stimulate emotional states or affect specific moods, like depressions. Until these roads are thoroughly surveyed and the brain is completely understood, psychiatry will be as pragmatic or empirical as medicine.

Social scientists have taught us a great deal about how men think and how they get along with one another and develop from infancy to full age. We have learned ways of reaching people with certain problems and can offer much help to some of them. Often we can understand illnesses that we cannot so readily treat. With medicines, we can soften the lacerations of nervousness and fear, producing no solutions, but affording some peace and allowing the mind to seek further aid. Some hospitals now offer carefully planned communities where new friendships can arise, refuges where the unhappy receive individual medical and psychiatric attention. Clinics, though harried by small staffs and increasing requests, offer daily help for a variety of mental illnesses. Children come to centers devoted to the study and treatment of early emotional difficulties. If the etiologies are still elusive, the results of treatment are often considerable. Failures are glaring, but the thousands of desperate people who are helped are sometimes overlooked because of their very recovery. Indeed, it is possible that our present problems may give way to worse ones as we get to know more. The enormous difficulties of finding out about the neurophysiology of emotional life may ultimately yield to the Orwellian dilemma of a society in which physicists of the mind can change thoughts and control feelings at their will.

However, right now I think our most pressing concern is less the matter of our work than the manner of ourselves. For the individual psychiatrist, the instiutional rigidities affect his thoughts and attitudes, taint his words and feelings, and thereby his ability to treat patients. We become victims of what we most dread; our sensibilities die, and we no longer care or notice. We dread death of the heart— any heart under any moon. Yet I see Organization Men in psychiatry, with all the problems of deathlike conformity. Independent thinking by the adventurous has declined; psychiatric training has become more formal, more preoccupied with certificates and diplomas, more hierarchical. Some of the finest people in early dynamic psychiatry were artists, like Eric Erikson, schoolteachers, like August Aichhorn, or those, like Anna Freud, who had no formal training or occupation but motivations as personal as those of a brilliant and loyal daughter. Today we are obsessed with accreditation, recognition, levels of training, with status as scientists. These are the preoccupations of young psychiatrists. There are more lectures, more supervision, more examinations for specialty status, and thus the profession soon attracts people who take to these practices. Once there were the curious and bold; now there are the carefully well-adjusted and certified.

When the heart dies, we slip into wordy and doctrinaire caricatures of life. Our journals, our habits of talk become cluttered with jargon or the trivial. There are negative cathects, libido quanta, "presymbiotic, normal-autistic phases of mother-infant unity," and "a hierarchically stratified, firmly cathected organization of self-representations." Such dross is excused as a short cut to understanding a complicated message by those versed in the trade; its practitioners call on the authority of symbolic communication in the sciences. But the real test is whether we best understand by this strange proliferation of language the worries, fears, or loves in individual people. As the words grow longer and the concepts more intricate and tedious, human sorrows and temptations disappear, loves move away, envies and jealousies, revenge and terror dissolve. Gone are strong, sensible words with good meaning and the flavor of the real. Freud called Dostoevsky the greatest psychologist of all time, and long ago Euripedes described in *Medea* the hurt of the mentally ill. Perhaps we cannot expect to describe our patients with the touching accuracy and poetry used for Lady Macbeth or Hamlet or King Lear, but surely there are sparks to be kindled, cries to be heard, from people who are individuals.

If we become cold, and our language frosty, then our estrangement is complete. Living in an unreliable world, often lonely, and for this reason, attracted to psychiatry as a job with human contacts, we embrace icy reasoning and abstractions, a desperate shadow of the real friendships which we once desired. Estrangement may, indeed, thread through the entire fabric of our professional lives in America.

Cartoons show us pre-empted by the wealthy. A recent study from Yale by Doctor Redlich shows how few people are reached by psychiatrists, how much a part of the class and caste system in America we are. Separated from us are all the troubled people in villages and farms from Winesburg to Yoknapatawpha. Away from us are the wretched drunks and the youthful gangs in the wilderness of our cities. Removed from us are most of the poor, the criminal, the drug addicts. Though there are some low-cost clinics, their waiting lists are long, and we are all too easily and too often available to the select few of certain streets and certain neighborhoods.

Whereas in Europe the theologian or artist shares intimately with psychiatrists, we stand apart from them, afraid to recognize our common heritage. European psychiatry mingles with philosophers; produces Karl Jaspers, a psychiatrist who is a theologian, or Sartre, a novelist and philosopher who writes freely and profoundly about psychiatry. After four years of psychiatric training in a not uncultured city, I begin to wonder whether young psychiatrists in America are becoming isolated by an arbitrary definition of what is, in fact, our work. Our work is the human condition, and we might do well to talk with Reinhold Niebuhr about the "nature and destiny of man," or with J. D. Salinger about our Holden Caulfields. Perhaps we are too frightened and too insecure to recognize our very brothers. This is a symptom of the estranged.

In some way our hearts must live. If we truly live, we will talk clearly and avoid the solitary trek. In some way we must manage to blend poetic insight with a craft and unite intimately the rational and the intuitive, the aloof stance of the scholar with the passion and affection of the friend who cares and is moved. It seems to me that this is the oldest summons in the history of Western civilization. We can answer this request only with some capacity for risk, dare, and whim. Thwarting us at every turn of life is the ageless fear of uncertainty; it is hard to risk the unknown. If we see a patient who puzzles us, we can avoid the mystery and challenge of the unique through readily available diagnostic categories. There is no end to classifications and terminologies, but the real end for us may be the soul of man, lost in these words: "Name it and it's so, or call it and it's real." This is the language of children faced with a confusion of the real and unreal, and it is ironic, if human, to see so much of this same habit still among psychiatrists.

Perhaps, if we dared to be free, more would be revealed than we care to admit. I sometimes wonder why we do not have a journal in our profession which publishes anonymous contributions. We might then hear and feel more of the real give-and-take in all those closed offices, get a fuller flavor of the encounter between the two people, patient and psychiatrist, who are in and of themselves what we call psychotherapy. The answer to the skeptic who questions the worth of psychotherapy is neither the withdrawn posture of the adherent of a closed system who dismisses all inquiry as suspect nor an eruption of pseudoscientific verbal pyrotechnics. Problems will not be solved by professional arrogance or more guilds and rituals. For it is more by being than by doing that the meaningful and deeply felt communion between us and our patients will emerge. This demands as much honesty and freedom from us as it does from our patients, and as much trust on our part as we would someday hope to receive from them.

If the patient brings problems that may be understood as similar to those in many others, that may be conceptualized and abstracted, he is still in the midst of a life which is in some ways different from all others. We bring only ourselves; and so each meeting in our long working day is different, and our methods of treatment will differ in many subtle ways from those of all of our colleagues. When so much of the world faces the anthill of totalitarian living, it is important for us to affirm proudly the preciously individual in each human being and in ourselves as doctors. When we see patients, the knowledge and wisdom of many intellectual ancestors are in our brains, and hopefully, some life and affection in our hearts. The heart must carry the reasoning across those inches or feet of office room. The psychiatrist, too, has his life and loves, his sorrows and angers. We know that we receive from our patients much of the irrational, misplaced, distorted thoughts and feelings once directed at parents, teachers, brothers, and sisters. We also know that our patients attempt to elicit from us many of the attitudes and responses of these earlier figures. But we must strive for some neutrality, particularly in the beginning of treatment, so that our patients may be offered, through us and their already charged feelings toward us, some idea of past passions presently lived. Yet, so often this neutrality becomes our signal for complete anonymity. We try to hide behind our couches, hide ourselves from our patients. In so doing we prolong the very isolation often responsible for our patients' troubles, and if we persist, they will derive from the experience many interpretations, but little warmth and trust.

I think that our own lives and problems are part of the therapeutic process. Our feelings, our own disorders and early sorrows are for us in some fashion what the surgeon's skilled hands are for his work. His hands are the trained instruments of knowledge, lectures, traditions. Yet they are, even in surgery, responsive to the artistry, the creative and sensitive intuition of the surgeon as a man. The psychiatrist's hands are himself, his life. We are educated and prepared, able to see and interpret. But we see, talk, and listen through our minds, our memories, our persons. It is through our emotions that the hands of our healing flex and function, reach out, and finally touch.

We cannot solve many problems, and there are the world and the stars to dwarf us and give us some humor about ourselves. But we can hope that, with some of the feeling of what Martin Buber calls "I-Thou"[1] quietly and lovingly nurtured in some of our patients, there may be more friendliness about us. This would be no small happening, and it is for this that we must work. Alert against dryness and the stale, smiling with others and occasionally at ourselves, we can read and study; but maybe wince, shout, cry, and love, too. Really, there is much less to say than to affirm by living. I would hope that we would dare to accept ourselves fully and offer ourselves freely to a quizzical and apprehensive time and to uneasy and restless people.

1. The relationship between man and man and man and man and God, as distinct from   "I-it," the relationship between man and thing.

SAMUEL L. CLEMENS
Overland Stagecoaching[1]

As the sun went down and the evening chill came on, we made preparation for bed. We stirred up the hard leather letter-sacks, and the knotty canvas bags of printed matter (knotty and uneven because of projecting ends and corners of magazines, boxes and books). We stirred them up and redisposed them in such a way as to make our bed as level as possible. And we *did* improve it, too, though after all our work it had an upheaved and billowy look about it, like a little piece of a stormy sea. Next we hunted up our boots from odd nooks among the mail-bags where they had settled, and put them on. Then we got down our coats, vests, pantaloons and heavy woolen shirts, from the arm-loops where they had been swinging all day, and clothed ourselves in them—for, there being no ladies either at the stations or in the coach, and the weather being hot, we had looked to our comfort by stripping to our underclothing, at nine o'clock in the morning. All things being now ready, we stowed the uneasy Dictionary where it would lie as quiet as possible, and placed the water-canteens and pistols where we could find them in the dark. Then we smoked a final pipe, and swapped a final yarn; after which, we put the pipes, tobacco and bag of coin in snug holes and caves among the mail-bags, and then fastened down the coach curtains all around, and made the place as "dark as the inside of a cow," as the conductor phrased it in his picturesque way. It was certainly as dark as any place could be—nothing was even dimly visible in it. And finally, we rolled ourselves up like silk-worms, each person in his own blanket, and sank peacefully to sleep.

Whenever the stage stopped to change horses, we would wake

1. From Chapter IV of *Roughing It*. Twain's synoptic headings run as follows: "Making Our Bed—Assaults by the Unabridged—At a Station—Our Driver a Great and Shining Dignitary—Strange Place for a Front Yard—Accommodations—Double Portraits—An Heir-loom—Our Worthy Landlord—'Fixings and Things'—An Exile—Slumgullion—A Well Furnished Table—The Landlord Astonished—Table Etiquette—Wild Mexican Mules—Stage-Coaching and Railroading."

up, and try to recollect where we were—and succeed—and in a minute or two the stage would be off again, and we likewise. We began to get into country, now, threaded here and there with with little streams. These had high, steep banks on each side, and every time we flew down one bank and scrambled up the other, our party inside got mixed somewhat. First we would all be down in a pile at the forward end of the stage, nearly in a sitting posture, and in a second we would shoot to the other end, and stand on our heads. And we would sprawl and kick, too, and ward off ends and corners of mail-bags that came lumbering over us and about us; and as the dust rose from the tumult, we would all sneeze in chorus, and the majority of us would grumble, and probably say some hasty thing, like: "Take your elbow out of my ribs! Can't you quit crowding?"

Every time we avalanched from one end of the stage to the other, the Unabridged Dictionary would come too; and every time it came it damaged somebody. One trip it "barked" the Secretary's elbow; the next trip it hurt me in the stomach, and the third it tilted Bemis's nose up till he could look down his nostrils—he said. The pistols and coin soon settled to the bottom, but the pipes, pipe-stems, tobacco and canteens clattered and floundered after the Dictionary every time it made an assault on us, and aided and abetted the book by spilling tobacco in our eyes, and water down our backs.

Still, all things considered, it was a very comfortable night. It wore gradually away, and when at last a cold gray light was visible through the puckers and chinks in the curtains, we yawned and stretched with satisfaction, shed our cocoons, and felt that we had slept as much as was necessary. By and by, as the sun rose up and warmed the world, we pulled off our clothes and got ready for breakfast. We were just pleasantly in time, for five minutes afterward the driver sent the weird music of his bugle winding over the grassy solitudes, and presently we detected a low hut or two in the distance. Then the rattling of the coach, the clatter of our six horses' hoofs, and the driver's crisp commands, awoke to a louder and stronger emphasis, and we went sweeping down on the station at our smartest speed. It was fascinating—that old overland stagecoaching.

We jumped out in undress uniform. The driver tossed his gathered reins out on the ground, gaped and stretched complacently, drew off his heavy buckskin gloves with great deliberation and insufferable dignity—taking not the slightest notice of a dozen solicitious inquiries after his health, and humbly facetious and flattering accostings, and obsequious tenders of service, from five or six hairy and half-civilized station-keepers and hostlers who were nimbly unhitching our steeds and bringing the fresh team out of the stables—for in the eyes of the stage-driver of that day, station-keepers and hostlers were a sort of good enough low creatures, useful in their place, and helping to make up a world, but not the kind of beings which a person of distinction could afford to concern himself with; while, on the contrary, in the eyes of the station-keeper and the hostler, the stage-driver was a hero—a great and shining dignitary, the world's favorite son, the envy of the people, the observed of the nations. When they spoke to him they received his insolent silence meekly, and as being the natural and proper conduct of so great a man; when he opened his lips they all hung on his words with admiration (he never honored a particular individual with a remark, but addressed it with a broad generality to the horses, the stables, the surrounding country *and* the human underlings); when he discharged a facetious insulting personality at a hostler, that hostler was happy for the day; when he uttered his one jest —old as the hills, coarse, profane, witless, and inflicted on the same audience, in the same language, every time his coach drove up there—the varlets roared, and slapped their thighs, and swore it was the best thing they'd ever heard in all their lives. And how they would fly around when he wanted a basin of water, a gourd of the same, or a light for his pipe—but they would instantly insult a passenger if he so far forgot himself as to crave a favor at their hands. They could do that sort of insolence as well as the driver they copied it from—for, let it be borne in mind, the overland driver had but little less contempt for his passengers than he had for his hostlers.

The hostlers and station-keepers treated the really powerful *conductor* of the coach merely with the best of what was their idea of civility, but the *driver* was the only being they bowed down to and worshipped. How admiringly they would gaze up at him in his high seat as he gloved himself with lingering deliberation, while some happy hostler held the bunch of reins aloft, and waited patiently for him to take it! And how they would bombard him with glorifying ejaculations as he cracked his long whip and went careering away.

The station buildings were long, low huts, made of sun-dried, mud-colored bricks, laid up without mortar (*adobes*, the Spaniards call these bricks, and Americans shorten it to *'dobies*). The roofs, which had no slant to them worth speaking of, were thatched and then sodded or covered with a thick layer of earth, and from this sprung a pretty rank growth of weeds and grass. It was the first time we had ever seen a man's front yard on top of his house. The buildings consisted of barns, stable-room for twelve or fifteen horses, and a hut for an eating-room for passengers. This latter had bunks in it for the station-keeper and a hostler or two. You could rest your elbow on its eaves, and you had to bend in order to get in at the door. In place of a window there was a square hole about large enough for a man to crawl through, but this had no glass in it. There was no flooring, but the ground was packed hard. There was no stove, but the fireplace served all needful purposes. There were no shelves, no cupboards, no closets. In a corner stood an open sack of flour, and nestling against its base were a couple of black and venerable tin coffee-pots, a tin tea-pot, a litle bag of salt, and a side of bacon.

By the door of the station-keeper's den, outside, was a tin wash-basin, on the ground. Near it was a pail of water and a piece of yellow bar soap, and from the eaves hung a hoary blue woolen shirt, significantly—but this latter was the station-keeper's private towel, and only two persons in all the party might venture to use it—the stage-driver and the conductor. The latter would not, from a sense of decency; the former would not because he did not choose to encourage the advances of a station-keeper. We had towels—in the valise; they might as well have been in Sodom and Gomorrah. We (and the conductor) used our handkerchiefs, and the driver his pantaloons and sleeves. By the door, inside, was fastened a small old-fashioned looking-glass frame, with two little fragments of the original mirror lodged down in one corner of it. This arrangement afforded a pleasant double-barreled portrait of you when you looked into it, with one half of your head set up a couple of inches above the other half. From the glass frame hung the half of a comb by a string—but if I had to describe that patriarch or die, I believe I would order some sample coffins. It had come down from Esau and Samson, and had been accumulating hair ever since—along with certain impurities. In one corner of the room stood three or four rifles and muskets, together with horns and pouches of ammunition. The station-men wore pantaloons of coarse, country-woven stuff, and into the seat and the inside of the legs were sewed ample additions of buckskin, to do duty in place of leggings, when the man rode horseback—so the pants were half dull blue and half yellow, and unspeakably picturesque. The pants were stuffed into the tops of high boots, the heels whereof were armed with great Spanish spurs, whose little iron clogs and chains jingled with every step. The man wore a huge beard and mustachios, an old slouch hat, a blue woolen shirt, no suspenders, no vest, no coat—in a leathern sheath in his belt, a great long "navy" revolver (slung on right side, hammer to the front), and projecting from his boot a horn-handled bowie-knife. The furniture of the hut was neither gorgeous nor much in the way. The rocking-chairs and sofas were not present, and never had been, but they were represented by two three-legged stools, a pine-board bench four feet long, and two empty candle-boxes. The table was a greasy board on stilts, and the table-cloth and napkins had not come—and they were not looking for them, either. A battered tin platter, a knife and fork, and a tin pint cup, were at each man's place, and the driver had a queensware[2] saucer that had seen better days. Of course this duke sat at the head of the table. There was one isolated piece of table furniture that bore about it a touching air of grandeur in misfortune. This was the caster.[3] It was German silver, and crippled and rusty, but it was so preposterously out of place there that it was suggestive of a tattered exiled king among barbarians, and the majesty of its native position compelled respect even in its degradation. There was only one cruet left, and that was a stopperless, fly-specked, broken-necked thing, with two inches of vinegar in it, and a dozen preserved flies with their heels up and looking sorry they had invested there.

The station-keeper up-ended a disk of last week's bread, of the shape and size of an old-time cheese, and carved some slabs from it which were as good as Nicholson pavement, and tenderer.

He sliced off a piece of bacon for each man, but only the experienced old hands made out to eat it, for it was condemned army bacon which the United States would not feed to its soldiers in the forts, and the stage company had bought it cheap for the sustenance of their passengers and employes. We may have found this condemned army bacon further out on the plains than the section I am locating it in, but we *found* it—there is no gainsaying that.

Then he poured for us a beverage which he called "*Slumgullion,*" and it is hard to think he was not inspired when he named it. It really pretended to be tea, but there was too much dish-rag, and sand, and old bacon-rind in it to deceive the intelligent traveler. He had no sugar and no milk—not even a spoon to stir the ingredients with.

We could not eat the bread or the meat, nor drink the "slumgullion." And when I looked at that melancholy vinegar cruet, I thought of the anecdote (a very, very old one, even at that day) of the traveler who sat down to a table which had nothing on it but a mackerel and a pot of mustard. He asked the landlord if this was all. The landlord said:

"*All!* Why, thunder and lightning, I should think there was mackerel enough there for six."

"But I don't like mackerel."

"Oh—then help yourself to the mustard."

2. Cream-colored, glazed English earthenware.
3. Lazy Susan.

In other days I had considered it a good, a very good, anecdote, but there was a dismal plausibility about it, here, that took all the humor out of it.

Our breakfast was before us, but our teeth were idle.

I tasted and smelt, and said I would take coffee, I believed. The station-boss stopped dead still, and glared at me speechless. At last, when he came to, he turned away and said, as one who communes with himself upon a matter too vast to grasp:

"*Coffee!* Well, if that don't go clean ahead of me, I'm d——d!"

We could not eat, and there was no conversation among the hostlers and herdsmen—we all sat at the same board. At least there was no conversation further than a single hurried request, now and then, from one employe to another. It was always in the same form, and always gruffly friendly. Its western freshness and novelty startled me, at first, and interested me, but it presently grew monotonous, and lost its charm. It was:

"Pass the bread, you son of a skunk!" No, I forget—skunk was not the word; it seems to me it was still stronger than that; I know it was, in fact, but it is gone from my memory, apparently. However, it is no matter—probably it was too strong for print, anyway. It is the landmark in my memory which tells me where I first encountered the vigorous new vernacular of the occidental plains and mountains.

We gave up the breakfast, and paid our dollar apiece and went back to our mail-bag bed in the coach, and found comfort in our pipes. Right here we suffered the first diminution of our princely state. We left our six fine horses and took six mules in their place. But they were wild Mexican fellows, and a man had to stand at the head of each of them and hold him fast while the driver gloved and got himself ready. And when at last he grasped the reins and gave the word, the men sprung suddenly away from the mules' heads and the coach shot from the station as if it had issued from a cannon. How the frantic animals did scamper! It was a fierce and furious gallop—and the gait never altered for a moment till we reeled off ten or twelve miles and swept up to the next collection of little station-huts and stables.

So we flew along all day. At 2 P.M. the belt of timber that fringes the North Platte and marks its windings through the vast level floor of the Plains came in sight. At 4 P.M. we crossed a branch of the river, and at 5 P.M. we crossed the Platte itself, and landed at Fort Kearney, *fifty-six hours out from St. Joe*—THREE HUNDRED MILES!

QUESTIONS FOR STUDY, DISCUSSION, AND WRITING

1. Why does Twain make so much of the driver's gloves?
2. Today a bus driver is not a hero for most people. Why is Twain's driver a hero? Why aren't the passengers heroes?

3. Can you think of comparable examples of hero worship? What qualities are worshipped? What does the hero worship reveal about some fact or aspect of language? Explain.

4. Twain mentions many rather unpleasant details—the dirty comb, the "greasy board," the inedible food, etc. What modifies the unpleasantness of the impression?

5. What are the humorous devices Twain uses in such sentences as:

    a. "And we would sprawl and kick, too, and ward off ends and corners of mail-bags that came lumbering over us and about us; and as the dust rose from the tumult, we would all sneeze in chorus, and the majority of us would grumble, and probably say some hasty thing, like: 'Take your elbow out of my ribs! Can't you quit crowding?' "

    b. "One trip it [the unabridged dictionary] 'barked' the Secretary's elbow; the next trip it hurt me in the stomach, and the third it tilted Bemis's nose up till he could look down his nostrils—he said."

    c. "From the glass frame hung the half of a comb by a string—but if I had to describe that patriarch or die, I believe I would order some sample coffins."

    d. "The furniture of the hut was neither gorgeous nor much in the way. . . . The table was a greasy board on stilts, and the table-cloth and napkins had not come—and they were not looking for them, either."

    e. "There was only one cruet left, and that was a stopperless, fly-specked, broken-necked thing, with two inches of vinegar in it, and a dozen preserved flies with their heels up and looking sorry they had invested there."

    f. "The station-keeper up-ended a disk of last week's bread, of the shape and size of an old-time cheese, and carved some slabs from it which were as good as Nicholson pavement, and tenderer."

6. Twain once wrote: "The humorous story is told gravely: the teller does his best to conceal the fact that he even dimly suspects that there is anything funny about it. . . ." How accurately does this describe "Overland Stagecoaching"?

WALT WHITMAN
From Sumter to Bull Run[1]

Opening of the Secession War

News of the attack on Fort Sumter and *the flag* at Charleston harbor, S.C., was received in New York city late at night (13th April, 1861,) and was immediately sent out in extras of the newspapers. I had been to the opera in Fourteenth street that night, and after the performance was walking down Broadway toward twelve o'clock, on my way to Brooklyn, when I heard in

1. From *Specimen Days*.

the distance the loud cries of the newsboys, who came presently tearing and yelling up the street, rushing from side to side even more furiously than usual. I bought an extra and cross'd to the Metropolitan hotel (Niblo's) where the great lamps were still brightly blazing, and with a crowd of others, who gather'd impromptu, read the news, which was evidently authentic. For the benefit of some who had no papers, one of us read the telegram aloud, while all listen'd silently and attentively. No remark was made by any of the crowd, which had increas'd to thirty or forty, but all stood a minute or two, I remember, before they dispers'd. I can almost see them there now, under the lamps at midnight again.

National Uprising and Volunteering

I have said somewhere that the three Presidentiads[2] preceding 1861 show'd how the weakness and wickedness of rulers are just as eligible here in America under republican, as in Europe under dynastic influences. But what can I say of that prompt and splendid wrestling with secession slavery, the arch-enemy personified, the instant he unmistakably show'd his face? The volcanic upheaval of the nation, after that firing on the flag at Charleston, proved for certain something which had been previously in great doubt, and at once substantially settled the question of disunion. In my judgment it will remain as the grandest and most encouraging spectacle yet vouchsafed in any age, old or new, to political progress and democracy. It was not for what came to the surface merely—though that was important—but what it indicated below, which was of eternal importance. Down in the abysms of New World humanity there had form'd and harden'd a primal hard-pan of national Union will, determin'd and in the majority, refusing to be tamper'd with or argued against, confronting all emergencies, and capable at any time of bursting all surface bonds, and breaking out like an earthquake. It is, indeed, the best lesson of the century, or of America, and it is a mighty privilege to have been part of it. (Two great spectacles, immortal proofs of democracy, unequal'd in all the history of the past, are furnish'd by the Secession War—one at the beginning, the other at its close. Those are, the general, voluntary, arm'd upheaval, and the peaceful and harmonious disbanding of the armies in the summer of 1865.)

Contemptuous Feeling

Even after the bombardment of Sumter, however, the gravity of the revolt, and the power and will of the slave states for a strong and continued military resistance to national authority, were not at all realized at the North, except by a few. Nine-tenths of the people of the free states look'd upon the rebellion, as started in South

2. Presidency, term of Presidential office.

Carolina, from a feeling one-half of contempt, and the other half composed of anger and incredulity. It was not thought it would be join'd in by Virginia, North Carolina, or Georgia. A great and cautious national official predicted that it would blow over "in sixty days," and folks generally believ'd the prediction. I remember talking about it on a Fulton ferryboat with the Brooklyn mayor, who said he only "hoped the Southern fire-eaters would commit some overt act of resistance, as they would then be at once so effectually squelch'd, we would never hear of secession again—but he was afraid they never would have the pluck to really do anything." I remember, too, that a couple of companies of the Thirteenth Brooklyn, who rendezvou'd at the city armory, and started thence as thirty days' men, were all provided with pieces of rope, conspicuously tied to their musket barrels, with which to bring back each man a prisoner from the audacious South, to be led in a noose, on our men's early and triumphant return!

Battle of Bull Run, July, 1861

All this sort of feeling was destined to be arrested and reversed by a terrible shock—the battle of first Bull Run—certainly, as we now know it, one of the most singular fights on record. (All battles, and their results, are far more matters of accident than is generally thought; but this was throughout a casualty, a chance. Each side supposed it had won, till the last moment. One had, in point of fact, just the same right to be routed as the other. By a fiction, or series of fictions, the national forces at the last moment exploded in a panic and fled from the field.) The defeated troops commenced pouring into Washington over the Long Bridge at daylight on Monday, 22nd—day drizzling all through with rain. The Saturday and Sunday of the battle (20th, 21st,) had been parch'd and hot to an extreme—the dust, the grime and smoke, in layers, sweated in, follow'd by other layers again sweated in, absorbed by those excited souls—their clothes all saturated with the claypowder filling the air—stirr'd up everywhere on the dry roads and trodden fields by the regiments, swarming wagons, artillery, etc.—all the men with this coating of murk and sweat and rain, now recoiling back, pouring over the Long Bridge—a horrible march of twenty miles, returning to Washington baffled, humiliated, panic-struck. Where are the vaunts, and the proud boasts with which you went forth? Where are your banners, and your bands of music, and your ropes to bring back your prisoners? Well, there isn't a band playing—and there isn't a flag but clings ashamed and lank to its staff.

The sun rises, but shines not. The men appear, at first sparsely and shamefaced enough, then thicker, in the streets of Washington—appear in Pennsylvania avenue, and on the steps and basement entrances. They come along in disorderly mobs, some in squads, stragglers, companies. Occasionally, a rare regiment, in perfect order, with its officers (some gaps, dead, the true braves,) marching in silence, with lowering faces, stern, weary to sinking, all black and dirty, but every man with his musket, and stepping alive; but these are the exceptions. Sidewalks of Pennsylvania avenue, Fourteenth street, etc., crowded, jamm'd with citizens, darkies, clerks, everybody, lookers-on; women in the windows, curious expressions from faces, as those swarms of dirt-covered return'd soldiers there (will they never end?) move by; but nothing said, no comments; (half our lookers-on secesh[3] of the most venomous kind—they say nothing; but the devil snickers in their faces). During the forenoon Washington gets all over motley with these defeated soldiers—queer-looking objects, strange eyes and faces, drench'd (the steady rain drizzles on all day) and fearfully worn, hungry, haggard, blister'd in the feet. Good people (but not overmany of them either,) hurry up something for their grub. They set tables on the sidewalks—wagonloads of bread are purchas'd, swiftly cut in stout chunks. Here are two aged ladies, beautiful, the first in the city for culture and charm, they stand with store of eating and drink at an improvis'd table of rough plank, and give food, and have the store replenish'd from their house every half-hour all that day; and there in the rain they stand, active, silent, white-hair'd, and give food, though the tears stream down their cheeks, almost without intermission, the whole time. Amid the deep excitement, crowds and motion, and desperate eagerness, it seems strange to see many, very many, of the soldiers sleeping—in the midst of all, sleeping sound. They drop down anywhere, on the steps of houses, up close by the basements or fences, on the sidewalk, aside on some vacant lot, and deeply sleep. A poor seventeen- or eighteen-year-old boy lies there, on the stoop of a grand house; he sleeps so calmly, so profoundly. Some clutch their muskets firmly even in sleep. Some in squads; comrades, brothers, close together—and on them, as they lie, sulkily drips the rain.

As afternoon pass'd, and evening came, the streets, the barrooms, knots everywhere, listeners, questioners, terrible yarns, bugaboo, mask'd batteries, our regiment all cut up, etc.—stories and story tellers, windy, bragging, vain centers of street crowds. Resolution, manliness, seem to have abandon'd Washington. The principal hotel, Willard's, is full of shoulder straps—thick, crush'd, creeping with shoulder straps. (I see them, and must have a word with them. There you are, shoulder straps—but where are your companies? where are your men? Incompetents! never tell me of chances of battle, of getting stray'd, and the like. I think this is your work, this retreat, after all. Sneak, blow, put on airs there

---

3. Secessionist.

in Willard's sumptuous parlors and barrooms, or anywhere—no explanation shall save you. Bull Run is your work; had you been half or one-tenth worthy your men, this would never have happen'd.

Meantime, in Washington, among the great persons and their entourage, a mixture of awful consternation, uncertainty, rage, shame, helplessness, and stupefying disappointment. The worst is not only imminent, but already here. In a few hours—perhaps before the next meal—the secesh generals, with their victorious hordes, will be upon us. The dream of humanity, the vaunted Union we thought so strong, so impregnable—lo! it seems already smash'd like a china plate. One bitter, bitter hour—perhaps proud America will never again know such an hour. She must pack and fly—no time to spare. Those white palaces—the dome-crown'd capitol there on the hill, so stately over the trees—shall they be left—or destroy'd first? For it is certain that the talk among certain of the magnates and officers and clerks and officials everywhere, for twenty-four hours in and around Washington after Bull Run, was loud and undisguised for yielding out and out, and substituting the southern rule, and Lincoln promptly abdicating and departing. If the secesh officers and forces had immediately follow'd, and by a bold Napoleonic movement had enter'd Washington the first day, (or even the second,) they could have had things their own way, and a powerful faction north to back them. One of our returning colonels express'd in public that night, amid a swarm of officers and gentlemen in a crowded room, the opinion that it was useless to fight, that the southerners had made their title clear, and that the best course for the national government to pursue was to desist from any further attempt at stopping them, and admit them again to the lead, on the best terms they were willing to grant. Not a voice was rais'd against this judgment amid that large crowd of officers and gentlemen. (The fact is, the hour was one of the three or four of those crises we had then and afterward, during the fluctuations of four years, when human eyes appear'd at least just as likely to see the last breath of the Union as to see it continue.)

The Stupor Passes—Something Else Begins

But the hour, the day, the night pass'd, and whatever returns, an hour, a day, a night like that can never again return. The President, recovering himself, begins that very night—sternly, rapidly sets about the task of reorganizing his forces, and placing himself in positions for future and surer work. If there were nothing else of Abraham Lincoln for history to stamp him with, it is enough to send him with his wreath to the memory of all future time, that he endured that hour, that day, bitterer than gall—indeed a crucifixion day—that it did not conquer him—that he unflinchingly stemm'd it, and resolv'd to lift himself and the Union out of it.

Then the great New York papers at once appear'd, (commencing that evening, and following it up the next morning, and incessantly through many days afterwards,) with leaders that rang out over the land with the loudest, most reverberating ring of clearest bugles, full of encouragement, hope, inspiration, unfaltering defiance. Those magnificent editorials! They never flagg'd for a fortnight. *The Herald* commenced them—I remember the articles well. *The Tribune* was equally cogent and inspiriting—and *The Times, Evening Post,* and other principal papers, were not a whit behind. They came in good time, for they were needed. For in the humiliation of Bull Run, the popular feeling north, from its extreme of superciliousness, recoil'd to the depth of gloom and apprehension.

BRUNO BETTELHEIM
A Victim[1]

Many students of discrimination are aware that the victim often reacts in ways as undesirable as the action of the aggressor. Less attention is paid to this because it is easier to excuse a defendant than an offender, and because they assume that once the aggression stops the victim's reactions will stop too. But I doubt if this is of real service to the persecuted. His main interest is that the persecution cease. But that is less apt to happen if he lacks a real understanding of the phenomenon of persecution, in which victim and persecutor are inseparably interlocked.

Let me illustrate with the following example: in the winter of 1938 a Polish Jew murdered the German attaché in Paris, vom Rath. The Gestapo used the event to step up anti-Semitic actions, and in the camp new hardships were inflicted on Jewish prisoners. One of these was an order barring them from the medical clinic unless the need for treatment had originated in work accident.

Nearly all prisoners suffered from frostbite which often led to gangrene and then amputation. Whether or not a Jewish prisoner was admitted to the clinic to prevent such a fate depended on the whim of an SS private. On reaching the clinic entrance, the prisoner explained the nature of his ailment to the SS man, who then decided if he should get treatment or not.

I too suffered from frostbite. At first I was discouraged from

1. From "Behavior in Extreme Situations: Defenses," Chapter 5 of *The Informed Heart,* 1960.

trying to get medical care by the fate of Jewish prisoners whose attempts had ended up in no treatment, only abuse. Finally things got worse and I was afraid that waiting longer would mean amputation. So I decided to make the effort.

When I got to the clinic, there were many prisoners lined up as usual, a score of them Jews suffering from severe frostbite. The main topic of discussion was one's chances of being admitted to the clinic. Most Jews had planned their procedure in detail. Some thought it best to stress their service in the German army during World War I: wounds received or decorations won. Others planned to stress the severity of their frostbite. A few decided it was best to tell some "tall story," such as that an SS officer had ordered them to report at the clinic.

Most of them seemed convinced that the SS man on duty would not see through their schemes. Eventually they asked me about my plans. Having no definite ones, I said I would go by the way the SS man dealt with other Jewish prisoners who had frostbite like me, and proceed accordingly. I doubted how wise it was to follow a preconceived plan, because it was hard to anticipate the reactions of a person you didn't know.

The prisoners reacted as they had at other times when I had voiced similar ideas on how to deal with the SS. They insisted that one SS man was like another, all equally vicious and stupid. As usual, any frustration was immediately discharged against the person who caused it, or was nearest at hand. So in abusive terms they accused me of not wanting to share my plan with them, or of intending to use one of theirs; it angered them that I was ready to meet the enemy unprepared.

No Jewish prisoner ahead of me in the line was admitted to the clinic. The more a prisoner pleaded, the more annoyed and violent the SS became. Expressions of pain amused him; stories of previous services rendered to Germany outraged him. He proudly remarked that *he* could not be taken in by Jews, that fortunately the time had passed when Jews could reach their goal by lamentations.

When my turn came he asked me in a screeching voice if I knew that work accidents were the only reason for admitting Jews to the clinic, and if I came because of such an accident. I replied that I knew the rules, but that I couldn't work unless my hands were freed of the dead flesh. Since prisoners were not allowed to have knives, I asked to have the dead flesh cut away. I tried to be matter-of-fact, avoiding pleading, deference, or arrogance. He replied: "If that's all you want, I'll tear the flesh off myself." And he started to pull at the festering skin. Because it did not come off as easily as he may have expected, or for some other reason, he waved me into the clinic.

Inside, he gave me a malevolent look and pushed me into the treatment room. There he told the prisoner orderly to attend to the wound. While this was being done, the guard watched me closely for signs of pain but I was able to suppress them. As soon as the cutting was over, I started to leave. He showed surprise and asked why I didn't wait for further treatment. I said I had gotten the service I asked for, at which he told the orderly to make an exception and treat my hand. After I had left the room, he called me back and gave me a card entitling me to further treatment, and admittance to the clinic without inspection at the entrance.

* * *

Because my behavior did not correspond to what he expected of Jewish prisoners on the basis of his projection, he could not use his prepared defenses against being touched by the prisoner's plight. Since I did not act as the dangerous Jew was expected to, I did not activate the anxieties that went with his stereotype. Still he did not altogether trust me, so he continued to watch while I received treatment.

Throughout these dealings, the SS felt uneasy with me, though he did not unload on me the annoyance his uneasiness aroused. Perhaps he watched me closely because he expected that sooner or later I would slip up and behave the way his projected image of the Jew was expected to act. This would have meant that his delusional creation had become real.

THOMAS F. FARRELL
The New Mexico Test, July 16, 1945[1]

The scene inside the shelter was dramatic beyond words. In and around the shelter were some twenty-odd people concerned with last-minute arrangements. Included were Dr. Oppenheimer, the Director who had borne the great scientific burden of developing the weapon from the raw materials made in Tennessee and Washington, and a dozen of his key assistants, Dr. Kistiakowsky, Dr. Bainbridge, who supervised all the detailed arrangements for the test; the weather expert, and several others. Besides those, there were a handful of soldiers, two or three Army officers and one Naval officer. The shelter was filled with a great variety of instruments and radios.

For some hectic two hours preceding the blast, General Groves stayed with the Director. Twenty minutes before the zero hour,

1. From the War Department release on the New Mexico Test, July 16, 1945, Appendix 6 in Henry DeWolf Smyth, *Atomic Energy for Military Purposes,* 2d ed., 1945. Farrell was an Army major general at the time of this writing.

General Groves left for his station at the base camp, first because it provided a better observation point and second, because of our rule that he and I must not be together in situations where there is an element of danger which existed at both points.

Just after General Groves left, announcements began to be broadcast of the interval remaining before the blast to the other groups participating in and observing the test. As the time interval grew smaller and changed from minutes to seconds, the tension increased by leaps and bounds. Everyone in that room knew the awful potentialities of the thing that they thought was about to happen. The scientists felt that their figuring must be right and that the bomb had to go off but there was in everyone's mind a strong measure of doubt.

We were reaching into the unknown and we did not know what might come of it. It can safely be said that most of those present were praying—and praying harder than they had ever prayed before. If the shot were successful, it was a justification of the several years of intensive effort of tens of thousands of people—statesmen, scientists, engineers, manufacturers, soldiers, and many others in every walk of life.

In that brief instant in the remote New Mexico desert, the tremendous effort of the brains and brawn of all these people came suddenly and startlingly to the fullest fruition. Dr. Oppenheimer, on whom had rested a very heavy burden, grew tenser as the last seconds ticked off. He scarcely breathed. He held on to a post to steady himself. For the last few seconds, he stared directly ahead and then when the announcer shouted "Now!" and there came this tremendous burst of light followed shortly thereafter by the deep growling roar of the explosion, his face relaxed into an expression of tremendous relief. Several of the observers standing back of the shelter to watch the lighting effects were knocked flat by the blast.

The tension in the room let up and all started congratulating each other. Everyone sensed "This is it!" No matter what might happen now all knew that the impossible scientific job had been done. Atomic fission would no longer be hidden in the cloisters of the theoretical physicists' dreams. It was almost full grown at birth. It was a great new force to be used for good or for evil. There was a feeling in that shelter that those concerned with its nativity should dedicate their lives to the mission that it would always be used for good and never for evil.

Dr. Kistiakowsky threw his arms around Dr. Oppenheimer and embraced him with shouts of glee. Others were equally enthusiastic. All the pent-up emotions were released in those few minutes and all seemed to sense immediately that the explosion had far exceeded the most optimistic expectations and wildest hopes of the scientists.

All seemed to feel that they had been present at the birth of a new age—The Age of Atomic Energy—and felt their profound responsibility to help in guiding into right channels the tremendous forces which had been unlocked for the first time in history.

As to the present war, there was a feeling that no matter what else might happen, we now had the means to insure its speedy conclusion and save thousands of American lives. As to the future, there had been brought into being something big and something new that would prove to be immeasurably more important than the discovery of electricity or any of the other great discoveries which have so affected our existence.

The effects could well be called unprecedented, magnificent, beautiful, stupendous and terrifying. No man-made phenomenon of such tremendous power had ever occurred before. The lighting effects beggared description. The whole country was lighted by a searing light with the intensity many times that of the midday sun. It was golden, purple, violet, gray and blue. It lighted every peak, crevasse and ridge of the nearby mountain range with a clarity and beauty that cannot be described but must be seen to be imagined. It was that beauty the great poets dream about but describe most poorly and inadequately. Thirty seconds after, the explosion came first, the air blast pressing hard against the people and things, to be followed almost immediately by the strong, sustained, awesome roar which warned of doomsday and made us feel that we puny things were blasphemous to dare tamper with the forces heretofore reserved to the Almighty. Words are inadequate tools for the job of acquainting those not present with the physical, mental and psychological effects. It had to be witnessed to be realized.

MAX BEERBOHM

A Relic

Yesterday I found in a cupboard an old, small, battered portmanteau which, by the initials on it, I recognized as my own property. The lock appeared to have been forced. I dimly remembered having forced it myself, with a poker, in my hot youth, after some journey in which I had lost the key; and this act of violence was probably the reason why the trunk had so long ago ceased to travel. I unstrapped it, not without dust; it exhaled the faint scent of its long closure; it contained a tweed suit of Late Victorian pattern, some bills, some letters, a collar stud, and—something which, after I had wondered for a moment or two what on earth it was, caused me suddenly to murmur, "Down below, the sea rustled to and fro over the shingle."

Strange that these words had, year after long year, been existing in some obscure cell at the back of my brain—forgotten but all the while existing like the trunk in that cupboard. What released them, what threw open the cell door, was nothing but the fragment of a fan; just the butt-end of an inexpensive fan. The sticks are of white bone, clipped together with a semicircular ring that is not silver. They are neatly oval at the base, but variously jagged at the other end. The longest of them measures perhaps two inches. Ring and all, they have no market value; for a farthing is the least coin in our currency. And yet, though I had so long forgotten them, for me they are not worthless. They touch a chord. . . . Lest this confession raise false hope in the reader, I add that I did not know their owner.

I did once see her, and in Normandy, and by moonlight, and her name was Angélique. She was graceful, she was even beautiful. I was but nineteen years old. Yet even so I cannot say that she impressed me favorably. I was seated at a table of a café on the terrace of a casino. I sat facing the sea, with my back to the casino. I sat listening to the quiet sea, which I had crossed that morning. The hour was late, there were few people about. I heard the swing-door behind me flap open, and was aware of a sharp snapping and crackling sound as a lady in white passed quickly by me. I stared at her erect thin back and her agitated elbows. A short fat man passed in pursuit of her—an elderly man in a black alpaca jacket that billowed. I saw that she had left a trail of little white things on the asphalt. I watched the efforts of the agonized short fat man to overtake her as she swept wraithlike away to the distant end of the terrace. What was the matter? What had made her so spectacularly angry with him? The three or four waiters of the café were exchanging cynical smiles and shrugs, as waiters will. I tried to feel cynical, but was thrilled with excitement, with wonder and curiosity. The woman out yonder had doubled on her tracks. She had not slackened her furious speed, but the man waddlingly contrived to keep pace with her now. With every moment they became more distinct, and the prospect that they would presently pass by me, back into the casino, gave me that physical tension which one feels on a wayside platform at the imminent passing of an express. In the rushingly enlarged vision I had of them, the wrath on the woman's face was even more saliently the main thing than I had supposed it would be. That very hard Parisian face must have been as white as the powder that coated it. "Écoute, Angélique," gasped the perspiring bourgeois, "—écoute, je te supplie—."[1] The swing-door received them and was left swinging to and fro. I wanted to follow, but had not paid for my bock. I beckoned my

1. "Listen, Angélique . . . listen, I beg you—."

waiter. On his way to me he stooped down and picked up something which, with a smile and a shrug, he laid on my table: "*Il semble que Mademoiselle ne s'en servira plus.*"[2] This is the thing I now write of, and at sight of it I understood why there had been that snapping and crackling, and what the white fragments on the ground were.

I hurried through the rooms, hoping to see a continuation of that drama—a scene of appeasement, perhaps, or of fury still implacable. But the two oddly-assorted players were not performing there. My waiter had told me he had not seen either of them before. I suppose they had arrived that day. But I was not destined to see either of them again. They went away, I suppose, next morning; jointly or singly; singly, I imagine.

They made, however, a prolonged stay in my young memory, and would have done so even had I not had that tangible memento of them. Who were they, those two of whom that one strange glimpse had befallen me? What, I wondered, was the previous history of each? What, in particular, had all that tragic pother been about? Mlle. Angélique I guessed to be thirty years old, her friend perhaps fifty-five. Each of their faces was as clear to me as in the moment of actual vision—the man's fat shiny bewildered face; the taut white face of the woman, the hard red line of her mouth, the eyes that were not flashing, but positively dull, with rage. I presumed that the fan had been a present from him, and a recent present—bought perhaps that very day, after their arrival in the town. But what, *what* had he done that she should break it between her hands, scattering the splinters as who should sow dragon's teeth? I could not believe he had done anything much amiss. I imagined her grievance a trivial one. But this did not make the case less engrossing. Again and again I would take the fan-stump from my pocket, examining it on the palm of my hand, or between finger and thumb, hoping to read the mystery it had been mixed up in, so that I might reveal that mystery to the world. To the world, yes; nothing less than that. I was determined to make a story of what I had seen—a *conte* in the manner of great Guy de Maupassant. Now and again, in the course of the past year or so, it had occurred to me that I might be a writer. But I had not felt the impulse to sit down and write something. I did feel that impulse now. It would indeed have been an irresistible impulse if I had known just what to write.

I felt I might know at any moment, and had but to give my mind to it. Maupassant was an impeccable artist, but I think the secret of the hold he had on the young men of my day was not so much that we discerned his cunning as that we delighted in the simplicity which his cunning achieved. I had read a great number of his short stories, but none that had made me feel as though I, if I were a writ-

---

2. "It seems that Mademoiselle will not be using this any more."

er, mightn't have written it myself. Maupassant had an European reputation. It was pleasing, it was soothing and gratifying, to feel that one could at any time win an equal fame if one chose to set pen to paper. And now, suddenly, the spring had been touched in me, the time was come. I was grateful for the fluke by which I had witnessed on the terrace that evocative scene. I looked forward to reading the MS. of *The Fan*—tomorrow, at latest. I was not wildly ambitious. I was not inordinately vain. I knew I couldn't ever, with the best will in the world, write like Mr. George Meredith. Those wondrous works of his, seething with wit, with poetry and philosophy and what not, never had beguiled me with the sense that I might do something similar. I had full consciousness of not being a philospher, of not being a poet, and of not being a wit. Well, Maupassant was none of these things. He was just an observer like me. Of course he was a good deal older than I, and had observed a good deal more. But it seemed to me that he was not my superior in knowledge of life. I knew all about life through *him*.

Dimly, the initial paragraph of my tale floated in my mind. I—not exactly I myself, but rather that impersonal *je* familiar to me through Maupassant—was to be sitting at that table, with a bock before me, just as I *had* sat. Four or five short sentences would give the whole scene. One of these I had quite definitely composed. You have already heard it. "Down below, the sea rustled to and fro over the shingle."

These words, which pleased me much, were to do double duty. They were to recur. They were to be, by a fine stroke, the very last words of my tale, their tranquillity striking a sharp ironic contrast with the stress of what had just been narrated. I had, you see, advanced further in the form of my tale than in the substance. But even the form was as yet vague. What, exactly, was to happen after Mlle. Angélique and M. Joumand (as I provisionally called him) had rushed back past me into the casino? It was clear that I must hear the whole inner history from the lips of one or the other of them. Which? Should M. Joumand stagger out on to the terrace, sit down heavily at the table next to mine, bury his head in his hands, and presently, in broken words, blurt out to me all that might be of interest? . . .

"'And I tell you I gave up everything for her—everything.' He stared at me with his old hopeless eyes. 'She is more than the fiend I have described to you. Yet I swear to you, monsieur, that if I had anything left to give, it should be hers.'

"Down below, the sea rustled to and fro over the shingle."

Or should the lady herself be my informant? For a while, I rather leaned to this alternative. It was more exciting, it seemed to make the writer more signally a man of the world. On the other hand, it was less simple to manage. Wronged persons might be ever so communicative, but I surmised that persons in the wrong were reticent.

Mlle. Angélique, therefore, would have to be modified by me in appearance and behavior, toned down, touched up; and poor M. Joumand must look like a man of whom one could believe anything. . . .

"She ceased speaking. She gazed down at the fragments of her fan, and then, as though finding in them an image of her own life, whispered, 'To think what I once was, monsieur—what, but for him, I might be, even now!' She buried her face in her hands, then stared out into the night. Suddenly she uttered a short, harsh laugh.

"Down below, the sea rustled to and fro over the shingle."

I decided that I must choose the first of these two ways. It was the less chivalrous as well as the less lurid way, but clearly it was the more artistic as well as the easier. The *chose vue*, the *tranche de la vie*[3]—this was the thing to aim at. Honesty was the best policy. I must be nothing if not merciless. Maupassant was nothing if not merciless. He would not have spared Mlle. Angélique. Besides, why should I libel M. Joumand? Poor—no, not *poor* M. Joumand! I warned myself against pitying him. One touch of "sentimentality," and I should be lost. M. Joumand was ridiculous. I must keep him so. But—what was his position in life? Was he a lawyer perhaps—or the proprietor of a shop in the Rue de Rivoli? I toyed with the possibility that he kept a fan shop—that the business had once been a prosperous one, but had gone down, down, because of his infatuation for this woman to whom he was always giving fans—which she always smashed. . . .

" 'Ah monsieur, cruel and ungrateful to me though she is, I swear to you that if I had anything left to give, it should be hers; but,' he stared at me with his old hopeless eyes, 'the fan she broke tonight was the last—the last, monsieur—of my stock.' Down below,"—but I pulled myself together, and asked pardon of my Muse.

It may be that I had offended her by my fooling. Or it may be that she had a sisterly desire to shield Mlle. Angélique from my mordant art. Or it may be that she was bent on saving M. de Maupassant from a dangerous rivalry. Anyway, she withheld from me the inspiration I had so confidently solicited. I *could not* think what had led up to that scene on the terrace. I tried hard and soberly. I turned the *chose vue* over and over in my mind, day by day, and the fan-stump over and over in my hand. But the *chose à figurer*[4]—what, oh what, was that? Nightly I revisited the café, and sat there with an open mind—a mind wide-open to catch the idea that should drop into it like a ripe golden plum. The plum did not ripen. The mind remained wide-open for a week or more, but nothing except that phrase about the sea rustled to and fro in it.

A full quarter of a century has gone by. M. Joumand's death, so far too fat was he all those years ago, may be presumed. A temper so violent as Mlle. Angélique's must surely have brought its owner to the

3. The "thing seen," the "slice of life."
4. The "thing to imagine."

grave, long since. But here, all unchanged, the stump of her fan is; and once more I turn it over and over in my hand, not learning its secret—no, nor even trying to, now. The chord this relic strikes in me is not one of curiosity as to that old quarrel, but (if you will forgive me) one of tenderness for my first effort to write, and for my first hopes of excellence.

QUESTIONS FOR STUDY, DISCUSSION, AND WRITING

1. Each time Beerbohm speaks of the man, he changes or adds something. First he is "a short fat man," then he is "the agonized short fat man"; later he is "the perspiring bourgeois." Is this simply variety for variety's sake? Is it elegant variation—a demonstration of literary cleverness? If not, what is it?
2. Beerbohm chose to have the man rather than the woman tell him the story, he says, because "it was . . . more artistic as well as . . . easier." What precisely did he mean by "artistic"? What has honesty to do with it? Mercilessness? The "chose vue," the "tranche de la vie"?
3. Beerbohm seems to feel that his last version of the tale was more absurd, more offensive to his Muse than the earlier versions. Why?
4. The sentence which Beerbohm originally intended to use as a refrain in his tale of Mlle. Angélique and M. Joumand he uses as a refrain in this essay. Is the effect the same, different, or what? Explain.
5. Beerbohm might have ended his essay on a note of amusement at his youthful folly, at the absurd naiveté of hoping to achieve excellence cheaply and without effort. Would such an ending have been more in keeping with the essay's tone and values than the one he chose? More surprising? More satisfactory? Why or why not?
6. Young men, says Beerbohm, delighted in the simplicity which Maupassant's cunning achieved. Explain the paradox. In what senses might it be applied to Beerbohm's own writing?

CHARLES W. MORTON
The Boston *Evening Transcript:*
A Light Jab at the Past

When I went to work for the Boston *Evening Transcript* as a news reporter at the beginning of 1930, it seemed to me a wonderfully good break. I was thirty years old, and it had taken me almost eight years to disentangle myself from the hardware business. Yet, with barely a year of newspapering behind me, I was on the staff of this celebrated sheet. True, its circulation was somewhere around 38,000, but many of us, in office conjectures, felt that this figure could be boosted to 40,000—perhaps even 45,000—if we all pitched in on the news side. The fact that our circulation was slightly junior to that of evening papers in Passaic, New Jersey, Canton, Ohio, and Elmira, New York, impressed none of us. All we knew about circulation was that the *Transcript*, in some mysterious way, could get along without it.

The Depression was just at its onset. I doubt that any of us understood at the time why the stock market crash of a few months earlier did in fact mean the inevitable end of the paper. Our general reaction was that things were tough for the moment, so tough that they could only change for the better. Yet the real situation was that the *Transcript* had depended almost exclusively on financial advertising announcing new issues of all sorts of securities. On this category of display space, the *Transcript's* rate was approximately the same as that of the New York *Daily News*, which had a circulation more than twenty-five times as large as ours. The paper might have lived comfortably on this income had it continued, with relatively high revenues and the low production costs of a small circulation. But when financial advertising stopped, as it did, the paper had to begin suddenly to live on its fat.

At the beginning of 1930, in spite of the portents, the *Transcript's* news staff was far from pessimistic. There was a vague legend in the city room that whenever circulation shot up again to the 45,000 mark, the department stores would suddenly reinstate their advertising in the *Transcript*. The legend had a strange quality of reality for us; it was almost as if a committee representing the department stores would meet on a certain day, summon our advertising manager, and bestow on him a packet of lavish contracts. Meanwhile, as we were given to imagining, the committee was watching closely our circulation figures, awaiting only the reassurance of that additional five or seven thousand readers. At the time of my arrival, the paper was losing not more than $500 a day. My own part in this deficit was a wage of $55 a week and an expense account that ranged between $3 and $4 a month. The department store situation, we felt, was temporary, even though it had obtained for decades. It was bound to improve and eventually to bring a general lift in city room salaries. This would be especially true in the case of later arrivals, such as myself, who naturally received less pay than the veterans. It was one of the very first inequalities which would be ironed out just as soon as the deparment stores saw the light.

Working conditions at the *Transcript* were generally regarded by Boston newspapermen as ideal. The first of its three editions on weekdays closed at 10:30 A.M., and the local staff did not have to report for work until 8:15 A.M. Unlike morning-paper people, we were able to sleep nights. We had Sundays off, closed at 1:15 P.M. on Saturdays. We were allowed as much as fifteen or twenty minutes for lunch. If a man appeared five minutes late of a morning, in some instances he was not even admonished.

Practically everything in the *Transcript* was in a department. We had one called "Patriotic and Historical"; another was "The Churchman Afield"; and we had a big one entitled "Genealogical." Even our sports page was subdivided, with specialists who covered nothing but golf, or yachting, or horses and dogs.

So great was the degree of specialization that almost anything remotely relating to a department was handed over to its proprietor for expert treatment. Every year, for instance, a considerable number of Bostonians would be announced as ticket holders in the Irish Sweepstakes, and the news staff was sent out among them to find out what the winners would do with the money. These stories at times were odd and amusing, and the Boston Irish must have bought enough sweepstakes tickets over the years to build hospitals for most of the Western world. But no matter how numerous or queer the stories, the disposition of them was always assigned to the horse-and-dog editor, on the theory that these winnings were resulting from a horse race, the Grand National or the Derby. Ordinary news judgments confronted by such a circumstance, so the reasoning went, would be incompetent.

I have forgotten some of the nomenclature, but there were also departments dealing with schools and colleges, women's clubs, banks and real estate, necrology, and so on. By and large, the proprietor of one of these departments did nothing else. He was a specialist, an expert—indeed, he was known as an "editor," and in dealings with the outside world casually refer to himself as "one of the editors of the Boston *Evening Transcript*." In this sense, the paper must have had twenty or thirty editors. Their day was more leisurely than that of the news staff; they seemed to have to do a great deal of reading in the office, thumbing through the trade journals of their specialty, boning up on the latest caper among Sealyham breeders or road builders. Occasionally one would seize shears and a pot and paste up, verbatim, a long release from a press agent or advertising agency, and this would appear intact a few days later in the larger Wednesday or Saturday edition. Probably no other paper ever brought such joy and astonishment to publicists, and one can only imagine their reactions at finding the whole handout in a Saturday *Transcript* without even its lead rewritten, let alone abridged.

These "editors" were obliged to spend considerable time away from the office, at meetings and conventions. They traveled widely, but the technique was usually the same, and the signed story, arriving in great lumps of Western Union copy, usually bore a strange similarity to the mimeographed material which had already reached the office as third-class mail, advance copy.

I had been on the *Transcript* staff for about two weeks when I finally asked one of the other news reporters about one of the hard-reading editors.

"What does that fellow do?" I inquired.

The answer was brief but definitive: "If it isn't banks, he doesn't do it."

With so many desks occupied by editors, the *Transcript* maintained no rewrite staff as such. There would not have been room for one, and I dare say it would have seemed a needless expense. The news staff, consequently, did its own legwork and its own writing. If the story were in town and the hour suitable, the staff man rushed back to the office and wrote his story. He had to write his own heads, incidentally, and usually had to decide how big a head the story deserved. He then read copy on himself and as often as not popped the story, without further reading by anyone, into a tube to the composing room. It was up to the make-up man upstairs, then, to shuffle things around and locate them as he saw fit. If the reporter was particularly attracted by his story, he would mark it "Page One." If he had doubts about its future, he would even add "Must." In this way, the city editor undoubtedly found a lot of news in the paper each evening which he had never seen before. We were not altogether sure who the managing editor was at any given moment, but the same would have been true in his case. I don't intend to imply that we had any great turnover in managing editors but rather that the title and function were, for some years at any rate, a matter of conjecture.

Again for reasons obscure to me, this somewhat informal system seemed to work out happily enough. In the early part of the day, a certain amount of copy was read and pondered, but along toward closing time, the common practice was to railroad as much of it as seemed necessary. This gave the city editor an abundance of free time, so that he was able to keep a vigilant eye on how long the news staff took for lunch.

Apart from the assortment of editors, the *Transcript's* news staff included the normal list of beatmen—city hall, waterfront, police headquarters, and such—a wholly unpredictable string of suburban correspondents, many of whom were unheard from for months on end, and a hard core of a half-dozen or so writing reporters. We were all virtuosos, possessed, in the face of constantly diminishing evidence to support it, by the belief that all Boston, and much of the outside world, depended breathlessly each day on what we were about to write. Whereas this may have been true of press agents and public relations artificers, who would have been foolish indeed to omit clipping the first edition, in which so much of their "advance" copy was served forth intact, I doubt that other parts of the paper produced quite the impact on the reader that the writing of them did on us.

The average age of our circulation must have been the highest in the land, but we plugged along at the run of the news without realizing that the department of "Recent Deaths" was probably the hottest piece of reading matter in the paper for most of the customers. When the *Transcript* finally suspended publication in 1941, I overheard a dialogue between two elderly Bostonians which afforded a fair hindsight, it seems to me, on how we had been doing. The *Christian Science Monitor*, a paper celebrated for its reluctance to mention death from any cause whatever, was falling heir, temporarily, to some of the *Transcript's* circulation, and the two Bostonians were comparing notes.

The conversation, as they reached for their evening papers, went:

"Too bad about the *Transcript*."

"Great paper."

"What are you reading now?"

"*Globe*."

"I'm trying the *Monitor*."

"Well, I tried the *Monitor* a while ago, but I didn't like it. Couldn't tell who's dead or anything."

I must pull up for a moment at this point to explain that the *Transcript's* interest in necrology as something calling for the maximum journalistic effort was matched only by the attention it paid to football and the stock market. Nothing threw the city room into so much high-speed sleuthing and telephoning as a first-rank bereavement. A system of research into maiden names, grandparents, undergraduate clubs at Harvard, Junior League, Sewing Circle, and funeral arrangements was immediately set in motion. Anyone passing our two telephone booths could tell by the unctuous tones of the reporter inside that he was talking to the newly bereft relative of an influential corpse. A bedside manner beyond reproach, it became a stunt of the first order, part of the office repertory of conversational histrionics; the man who could get the most spuriously funereal or excessively sympathetic note into the clichés of the occasion rightly counted himself an artist, esteemed by all.

Great lumps of trivial detail which no other paper would have dreamed of publishing thus fortified the *Transcript's* obits. We were especially interested in the deaths of Harvard graduates and anyone with early New England ancestry, and this latter category would embrace at full length even those families which were no longer rich. When a really big death came along, someone who met all the tests—old family, Harvard, still rich—the response would be about the same as to a general conflagration. Other prominent citizens would be telephoned and induced to say for publication that they deeply regretted the death; our obituary editor would turn to; the male society editor of the *Transcript* would put in one of his rare appearances in the city room to see that no reference work lay unconsulted; other news projects were sidetracked as the pursuit of funeral arrangements was loosed. After a fury of telephoning, typing, pasting, and scanning, the obit would be sent along, the most lavish journalistic compliment the deceased had ever received. The extent of the obit was bound to surprise even the most infatuate relatives and friends of its subject.

If the *Transcript* went to town on a death, it outdid itself on a funeral. Whereas the death might have turned up first in the morning papers, most funerals were held during the *Transcript's* working hours. Here was another chance to demonstrate the solid virtues of an evening sheet, to teach the A.M.'s a lesson in how to clean up on a big story and leave nothing for the next day. It was not uncommon for us to send more staff to a funeral than to a murder trial, even though church services and burial seemed to have been worked out, as a general thing, on a fairly stable basis—that is, without disorders, arrests, or whatever it was that we expected to have happen at the obsequies which called for the vigilance of a smart news staff. It was no particular trick to get the names of the clergy, pallbearers, and the musical program over the phone, but we covered the funerals just the same to make sure that no slip-ups occurred. We spent most of our time outside, leaning up against churches, although in a fit of tenacity I once elbowed my way into a sort of minstrels' gallery at the funeral of a prominent banker and market rigger and sat in the middle of a bosomy quartet of female vocalists. A variation of this kind was well regarded by the rest of the city staff, in that it was hard to do and had, at the same time, a certain useless quality which appealed to all of us.

I believe it would be fair to take our obits as representing the ideal *Transcript* story. The obit was already too long, for the executives held that the longer the story, the harder the reporter had worked, an end in itself. A short story could not be so desirable as a long one, since it meant that the reporter had been frittering away his time in lunchrooms or worse—a correct estimate, I must add, since we did go to almost any lengths to get out of the office for a few hours.

The obit had a great deal less standing with other papers in Boston. This enabled the *Transcript* to harvest richly in the field of obituaries and to feel at ease in an appreciation of news values which other editors did not have enough sense to comprehend. The obit was authoritative, exhaustive, and uninteresting. It required more work than it was worth, and it was a story which other papers usually managed to do without. It was, in sum, what we used to call a "technical scoop."

It sounds absurd to say that the *Transcript* had a commercial interest in funerals, that what we published under "Recent Deaths" was by way of being a "reader," like one of the pasted-up stories describing plans for the regional convention of Frigidaire salesmen. I am sure that none of our executives, consciously, expected the legatees of a *Transcript* death to start an advertising campaign in the paper as a result of the handsome obit. But I could not escape the notion, watching so many pallbearers shouldering their burdens, that an excellent reason must underlie our interest. Wiser heads than mine had figured it out, and I was willing to give it a whirl. Although it was hard for me to see what use the beneficiaries of a Boston trust might want to make of our advertising columns, the answer might lie somewhere in the overlapping and mysterious intricacies of high finance. Perhaps the deceased himself had been the stumbling block, cherishing an old prejudice against the *Transcript* and preventing his associates from giving us a little business. Perhaps even now they were re-examining, in the light of our unique performance, their earlier judgments of newspaper media and rates. With the old man out of the way, a fresh approach was possible. New ties could be cemented in sorrow or in relief or whatever, and things would pick up again for the *Transcript*.

As I say, no one formally enunciated any such motives. I doubt if I could have discerned them at the time, yet they are perfectly plain to me today, and they offer almost the only explanation of why so many dissimilar people worked so hard for so little at projects so completely wide of the mark. Only good could follow such drudgery, we felt. But like the department stores, the heirs and successors never did get around to laying it on the line. A friend or flunky of the deceased with some literary flair or reputation would favor us with a memoir for the editorial page a week or two later, but that was about all. We even made a final stab at the proceedings in probate court, reporting faithfully the public bequests—the sums to be shared equally by the Animal Rescue League, the New England Home for Little Wanderers, the Boston Seaman's Friend Society, the Boston Society for the Care of Girls, the New England Anti-Vivisection Society, Trinity Church, and such—and the story always ended: "The residuary estate is to be held in trust for the widow during her lifetime . . . ." It was not that we actually expected to be mentioned in the will, yet my own vague impression was that the testator would have put the *Transcript* down on his list if he had only realized our great need.

A horde of charitable organizations preyed upon the *Transcript* in its latter years. No scheming merchant, if we had been blessed with the advertising of local retailers, would have coerced the paper into so many puffs, endorsements, and general publicity as these welfare organizations unblushingly exacted from the *Transcript*. True, they did carry paid announcements in the paper each week, but, I suspect, at nominal rates, and for every line of what they were buying, they obtained without charge truly fantastic hospitality for

1. Massachusetts Society for the Prevention of Cruelty to Animals.

their press releases. Like the fifty-fifty hash of rabbit and horse, one rabbit for one horse, the deal amounted to a half column of free space for every line of advertising. It became another of the despairing stunts with which the city staff idled away its time to see who could get into the paper verbatim the longest and worst press releases from this swarm of vultures.

Here again was a curious motivation. One would not expect a staff genuinely striving for the paper's success to cripple its pages with such pitiful rubbish. In this case, the whole thing was a queer, reverse English attempt to rid ourselves of the city editor.

As I have said, the news staff was an oddly assorted group, but it had a common characteristic, the blend of ignorance, egotism, and enthusiasm with which each of us viewed the *Transcript* and our own part in it. We were going to save the paper in spite of itself, and most of our momentum was spent on that hapless functionary, the city editor, who was in fact the only executive with whom we had to deal. So firmly was the discipline of our relationship fixed that none of us ever gave him a flat refusal or denounced him to his face, and it seems unlikely that he would have known what we were talking about had we tried to straighten him out. He was only the inheritor of the attitudes which he applied to us, but we detested him and, again in our innocence, were sure that, given his head, he would commit some supreme folly which would eliminate him. Thus, when it came to letting a handout from the Anti-Vivisection Society drivel move along without the touch of a pencil, we counted it a bitter medicine for the paper but one which might at least cure the *Transcript* of its city editor. Someone was bound to see the stuff and complain.

I recall putting up a whole treatise, unabridged, from the M.S.P.C.A.[1] on how to boil a live lobster without causing it pain, although the biological authority for the recipe was really no more than the fiat of the Society's publicity man. If anyone really cares, the method, as I remember it, was to start the lobster off in lukewarm water and bring it slowly to the boil. This is not only at direct variance with the approved water's-edge theory of beginning with boiling water, but if you stop to think of it, it sounds like a prolongation and refinement of whatever discomfort the lobster experiences. The press release explained that the lukewarm water made the lobster groggy and that it yielded up the spirit hardly aware that anything unusual was going on. I have mentioned this press release at times in trying to explain the *Transcript*, but it was always taken to be mere facetiousness on my part. All I can say is that I am willing to bet anyone that a deadpan telephone inquiry or visit to the M.S.P.C.A. will bring, even today, an official written instruction on how to boil a live lobster without

1. Massachusetts Society for the Prevention of Cruelty to Animals.

hurting it enough to give the Society grounds for action. (I have never seen any similar release from the Society with respect to oysters.)

I worked for the *Transcript* almost seven years. In five of them we were each presented with a turkey on Thanksgiving, or rather with a turkey order on some market. In the sixth there was no turkey order. We took three pay cuts—a 10, a 20, and a 40 per cent reduction; it may have been two twenties instead of the forty. At any rate, I left the paper in the summer of 1936 on a Saturday afternoon. With one stratagem or another, my wage had curved up slightly from its low. After running my legs off for six and a half years, I was getting only $10 a week less than when I had started.

E. B. WHITE
Once More to the Lake

One summer, along about 1904, my father rented a camp on a lake in Maine and took us all there for the month of August. We all got ringworm from some kittens and had to rub Pond's Extract on our arms and legs night and morning, and my father rolled over in a canoe with all his clothes on; but outside of that the vacation was a success and from then on none of us ever thought there was any place in the world like that lake in Maine. We returned summer after summer—always on August 1st for one month. I have since become a salt-water man, but sometimes in summer there are days when the restlessness of the tides and the fearful cold of the sea water and the incessant wind which blows across the afternoon and into the evening make me wish for the placidity of a lake in the woods. A few weeks ago this feeling got so strong I bought myself a couple of bass hooks and a spinner and returned to the lake where we used to go, for a week's fishing and to revisit old haunts.

I took along my son, who had never had any fresh water up his nose and who had seen lily pads only from train windows. On the journey over to the lake I began to wonder what it would be like. I wondered how time would have marred this unique, this holy spot— the coves and streams, the hills that the sun set behind, the camps and the paths behind the camps. I was sure the tarred road would have found it out and I wondered in what other ways it would be desolated. It is strange how much you can remember about places like that once you allow your mind to return into the grooves which lead back. You remember one thing, and that suddenly reminds you of another thing. I guess I remembered clearest of all the early mornings, when the lake was cool and motionless, remembered how the bedroom smelled of the lumber it was made of and of the wet woods whose scent entered through the screen. The partitions in the camp were thin and did not extend clear to the top of the rooms, and as I was always the first up I would dress softly so as not to wake the others, and sneak out into the sweet outdoors and start out in the canoe, keeping close along the shore in the long shadows of the pines. I remembered being very careful never to rub my paddle against the gunwale for fear of disturbing the stillness of the cathedral.

The lake had never been what you would call a wild lake. There were cottages sprinkled around the shores, and it was in farming country although the shores of the lake were quite heavily wooded. Some of the cottages were owned by nearby farmers, and you would live at the shore and eat your meals at the farmhouse. That's what our family did. But although it wasn't wild, it was a fairly large and undisturbed lake and there were places in it which, to a child at least, seemed infinitely remote and primeval.

I was right about the tar: it led to within half a mile of the shore. But when I got back there, with my boy, and we settled into a camp near a farmhouse and into the kind of summertime I had known, I could tell that it was going to be pretty much the same as it had been before—I knew it, lying in bed the first morning, smelling the bedroom, and hearing the boy sneak quietly out and go off along the shore in a boat. I began to sustain the illusion that he was I, and therefore, by simple transposition, that I was my father. This sensation persisted, kept cropping up all the time we were there. It was not an entirely new feeling, but in this setting it grew much stronger. I seemed to be living a dual existence. I would be in the middle of some simple act, I would be picking up a bait box or laying down a table fork, or I would be saying something, and suddenly it would be not I but my father who was saying the words or making the gesture. It gave me a creepy sensation.

We went fishing the first morning. I felt the same damp moss covering the worms in the bait can, and saw the dragonfly alight on the tip of my rod as it hovered a few inches from the surface of the water. It was the arrival of this fly that convinced me beyond any doubt that everything was as it always had been, that the years were a mirage and there had been no years. The small waves were the same, chucking the rowboat under the chin as we fished at anchor, and the boat was the same boat, the same color green and the ribs broken in the same places, and under the floor-boards the same fresh-water leavings and débris—the dead helgramite,[1] the wisps of moss, the rusty discarded fishook, the dried blood from yesterday's catch. We stared silently at the tips of our rods, at the dragonflies that came and went. I lowered the tip of mine into the water, tentatively, pensively dislodging the fly, which darted two feet away, poised, darted two feet back, and came to rest again a little farther

1. The nymph of the May-fly, used as bait.

up the rod. There had been no years between the ducking of this dragonfly and the other one—the one that was part of memory. I looked at the boy, who was silently watching his fly, and it was my hands that held his rod, my eyes watching. I felt dizzy and didn't know which rod I was at the end of.

We caught two bass, hauling them in briskly as though they were mackerel, pulling them over the side of the boat in a businesslike manner without any landing net, and stunning them with a blow on the back of the head. When we got back for a swim before lunch, the lake was exactly where we had left it, the same number of inches from the dock, and there was only the merest suggestion of a breeze. This seemed an utterly enchanted sea, this lake you could leave to its own devices for a few hours and come back to, and find that it had not stirred, this constant and trustworthy body of water. In the shallows, the dark, water-soaked sticks and twigs, smooth and old, were undulating in clusters on the bottom against the clean ribbed sand, and the track of the mussel was plain. A school of minnows swam by, each minnow with its small individual shadow, doubling the attendance, so clear and sharp in the sunlight. Some of the other campers were in swimming, along the shore, one of them with a cake of soap, and the water felt thin and clear and unsubstantial. Over the years there had been this person with the cake of soap, this cultist, and here he was. There had been no years.

Up to the farmhouse to dinner through the teeming, dusty field, the road under our sneakers was only a two-track road. The middle track was missing, the one with the marks of the hooves and the splotches of dried, flaky manure. There had always been three tracks to choose from in choosing which track to walk in; now the choice was narrowed down to two. For a moment I missed terribly the middle alternative. But the way led past the tennis court, and something about the way it lay there in the sun reassured me; the tape had loosened along the backline, the alleys were green with plantains and other weeds, and the net (installed in June and removed in September) sagged in the dry noon, and the whole place steamed with midday heat and hunger and emptiness. There was a choice of pie for dessert, and one was blueberry and one was apple, and the waitresses were the same country girls, there having been no passage of time, only the illusion of it as in a dropped curtain—the waitresses were still fifteen; their hair had been washed, that was the only difference—they had been to the movies and seen the pretty girls with the clean hair.

Summertime, oh summertime, pattern of life indelible, the fade-proof lake, the woods unshatterable, the pasture with the sweetfern and the juniper forever and ever, summer without end; this was the background, and the life along the shore was the design, the cottagers with their innocent and tranquil design, their tiny docks with the flagpole and the American flag floating against the white clouds in the blue sky, the little paths over the roots of the trees leading from camp to camp and the paths leading back to the outhouses and the can of lime for sprinkling, and at the souvenir counters at the store the miniature birch-bark canoes and the post cards that showed things looking a little better than they looked. This was the American family at play, escaping the city heat, wondering whether the newcomers in the camp at the head of the cove were "common" or "nice," wondering whether it was true that the people who drove up for Sunday dinner at the farmhouse were turned away because there wasn't enough chicken.

It seemed to me, as I kept remembering all this, that those times and those summers had been infinitely precious and worth saving. There had been jollity and peace and goodness. The arriving (at the beginning of August) had been so big a business in itself, at the railway station the farm wagon drawn up, the first smell of the pine-laden air, the first glimpse of the smiling farmer, and the great importance of the trunks and your father's enormous authority in such matters, and the feel of the wagon under you for the long ten-mile haul, and at the top of the last long hill catching the first view of the lake after eleven months of not seeing this cherished body of water. The shouts and cries of the other campers when they saw you, and the trunks to be unpacked, to give up their rich burden. (Arriving was less exciting nowadays, when you sneaked up in your car and parked it under a tree near the camp and took out the bags and in five minutes it was all over, no fuss, no loud wonderful fuss about trunks.)

Peace and goodness and jollity. The only thing that was wrong now, really, was the sound of the place, an unfamiliar nervous sound of the outboard motors. This was the note that jarred, the one thing that would sometimes break the illusion and set the years moving. In those other summertimes all motors were inboard; and when they were at a little distance, the noise they made was a sedative, an ingredient of summer sleep. They were one-cylinder and two-cylinder engines, and some were make-and-break and some were jump-spark,[2] but they all made a sleepy sound across the lake. The one-lungers throbbed and fluttered, and the twin-cylinder ones purred and purred, and that was a quiet sound too. But now the campers all had outboards. In the daytime, in the hot mornings, these motors made a petulant, irritable sound; at night, in the still evening when the afterglow lit the water, they whined about one's ears like mosquitoes. My boy loved our rented outboard, and his great desire was to achieve singlehanded mastery over it, and authority, and he soon learned the trick of choking it a little (but not too much), and the adjustment of the needle valve. Watching him

2. Methods of ignition timing.

I would remember the things you could do with the old one-cylinder engine with the heavy flywheel, how you could have it eating out of your hand if you got really close to it spiritually. Motor boats in those days didn't have clutches, and you would make a landing by shutting off the motor at the proper time and coasting in with a dead rudder. But there was a way of reversing them, if you learned the trick, by cutting the switch and putting it on again exactly on the final dying revolution of the flywheel, so that it would kick back against compression and begin reversing. Approaching a dock in a strong following breeze, it was difficult to slow up sufficiently by the ordinary coasting method, and if a boy felt he had complete mastery over his motor, he was tempted to keep it running beyond its time and then reverse it a few feet from the dock. It took a cool nerve, because if you threw the switch a twentieth of a second too soon you would catch the flywheel when it still had speed enough to go up past center, and the boat would leap ahead, charging bull-fashion at the dock.

We had a good week at the camp. The bass were biting well and the sun shone endlessly, day after day. We would be tired at night and lie down in the accumulated heat of the little bedrooms after the long hot day and the breeze would stir almost imperceptibly outside and the smell of the swamp drift in through the rusty screens. Sleep would come easily and in the morning the red squirrel would be on the roof, tapping out his gay routine. I kept remembering everything, lying in bed in the mornings—the small steamboat that had a long rounded stern like the lip of a Ubangi, and how quietly she ran on the moonlight sails, when the older boys played their mandolins and the girls sang and we ate doughnuts dipped in sugar, and how sweet the music was on the water in the shining night, and what it had felt like to think about girls then. After breakfast we would go up to the store and the things were in the same place—the minnows in a bottle, the plugs and spinners disarranged and pawed over by the youngsters from the boys' camp, the fig newtons and the Beeman's gum. Outside, the road was tarred and cars stood in front of the store. Inside, all was just as it had always been, except there was more Coca-Cola and not so much Moxie and root beer and birch beer and sarsaparilla. We would walk out with a bottle of pop apiece and sometimes the pop would backfire up our noses and hurt. We explored the streams, quietly, where the turtles slid off the sunny logs and dug their way into the soft bottom; and we lay on the town wharf and fed worms to the tame bass. Everywhere we went I had trouble making out which was I, the one walking at my side, the one walking in my pants.

One afternoon while we were there at that lake a thunderstorm came up. It was like the revival of an old melodrama that I had seen long ago with childish awe. The second-act climax of the drama of the electrical disturbance over a lake in America had not changed in any important respect. This was the big scene, still the big scene. The whole thing was so familiar, the first feeling of oppression and heat and a general air around camp of not wanting to go very far away. In midafternoon (it was all the same) a curious darkening of the sky, and a lull in everything that had made life tick; and then the way the boats suddenly swung the other way at their moorings with the coming of a breeze out of the new quarter, and the premonitory rumble. Then the kettle drum, then the snare, then the bass drum and cymbals, then crackling light against the dark, and the gods grinning and licking their chops in the hills. Afterward the calm, the rain steadily rustling in the calm lake, the return of light and hope and spirits, and the campers running out in joy and relief to go swimming in the rain, their bright cries perpetuating the deathless joke about how they were getting simply drenched, and the children screaming with delight at the new sensation of bathing in the rain, and the joke about getting drenched linking the generations in a strong indestructible chain. And the comedian who waded in carrying an umbrella.

When the others went swimming my son said he was going in too. He pulled his dripping trunks from the line where they had hung all through the shower, and wrung them out. Languidly, and with no thought of going in, I watched him, his hard little body, skinny and bare, saw him wince slightly as he pulled up around his vitals the small, soggy, icy garment. As he buckled the swollen belt suddenly my groin felt the chill of death.

QUESTIONS FOR STUDY, DISCUSSION, AND WRITING

1. White had not been back to the lake for many years. What bearing has this fact on the experience which the essay describes?
2. What has guided White in his selection of the details he gives about the trip? Why, for example, does he talk about the road, the dragonfly, the bather with the cake of soap?
3. How do the differences between boats of the past and boats of today relate to or support the point of the essay?
4. What is the meaning of White's last sentence? What relation has it to the sentence just preceding? How has White prepared us for this ending?
5. How would the narrative differ if it were told by the boy? What details of the scene might the boy emphasize? Why? Show what point the boy's selection of details might make.

Prose Forms: Journals

[Occasionally a man catches himself having said something aloud, obviously with no concern to be heard, even by himself. And all of us have overheard, perhaps while walking, a solitary person muttering or laughing softly or exclaiming abruptly. For oneself or another, something floats up from the world within, forces itself to be expressed, takes no real account of the time or the place, and certainly intends no conscious communication.

With more self-consciousness, and yet without a specific audience, a man sometimes speaks out at something that has momentarily filled his attention from the world without. A sharp play at the ball game, the twist of a political speech, an old photograph—something from the outer world impresses the mind, stimulates it, focuses certain of its memories and values, interests and needs. Thus stimulated, the man may wish to share his experience with another, to inform or amuse him, to rouse him to action or persuade him to a certain belief. Often, though, the man experiencing may want most to talk to himself, to give a public shape in words to his thoughts and feelings but for the sake of a kind of private dialogue with himself. Communication to another may be an ultimate desire, but the immediate motive is to articulate the experience for himself.

To articulate, to shape the experience in language for his own sake, one may keep a journal. Literally a day-book, the journal enables one to write down something about the experiences of a day which for a great variety of reasons may have been especially memorable or impressive. The journal entry may be merely a few words to call to mind a thing done, a person seen, a menu enjoyed at a dinner party. It may be concerned at length with a political crisis in the community, or a personal crisis in the home. It may even be as noble as it was with some pious men in the past who used the journal to keep a record of their consciences, a periodic reckoning of their moral and spiritual accounts. In its most public aspect, the idea of a journal calls to mind the newspaper or the record of proceedings like the Congressional Record. In its most closely private form, the journal becomes the diary.

For the person keeping a journal, whatever he experiences and wants to hold he can write down. But to get it down on paper begins another adventure. For he has to focus on what he has experienced, and to be able to say what, in fact, the experience is. What of it is new? What of it is remarkable because of associations in the memory it stirs up? Is this like anything I—or others—have experienced before? Is it a good or a bad thing to have happened? And why, specifically? The questions multiply themselves quickly, and as the journalist seeks to answer the appropriate ones, he begins to know what it is he contemplates. As he tries next to find the words that best represent his discovery, the experience becomes even more clear in its shape and meaning. We can imagine Emerson going to the ballet, being absorbed in the spectacle, thinking casually of this or that association the dancer and the movements suggest. When he writes about the experience in his journal, a good many questions, judgments, and speculations get tied up with the spectacle, and it is this complex of event and his total relation to it that becomes the experience he records. The simple facts of time, place, people, and actions drop down into a man's consciousness and set in motion ideas and feelings which give those facts their real meaning to that man.

Once this consciousness of events is formulated in words, the journal-keeper has it, not only in the sense of understanding what he has seen or felt or thought, but also in the sense of having it there before him to contemplate long after the event itself. When we read a carefully kept journal covering a long period and varied experiences, we have the pleasure of a small world re-created for us in the consciousness of one who experienced it. Even more, we feel the continuity, the wholeness, of the person himself. Something of the same feeling is there for the person who kept the journal: a whole world of events preserved in the form of their experienced reality, and with it the persistent self in the midst of that world. That world and that self are always accessible on the page, and ultimately, therefore, usably real.

Beyond the value of the journal as record, there is the instructive value of the habit of mind and hand journal keeping can assure. One begins to attend more carefully to what happens to him and around him. To have discovered, like Katherine Mansfield, that so apparently simple a thing as a pigeon sitting proudly on a tree can bring to mind the profoundest questions about the relation of God to His creatures, is to be thereafter a little more sensitive to all kinds of "simple" experience. Fact begins to be related to fact more readily, apparently dissimilar experiences may not be entirely different, the more and the less important begin to be discriminated. One begins to see what he is looking at, if he becomes accustomed to the characteristic method and form of the journal entry. All the while, one is learning the resources of language as a means of representing what he sees, and gaining skill and certainty in doing justice to experience and to his own consciousness when he writes.

The journal represents a discipline. It brings together an individual and a complex environment in a relation that teaches the individual something of himself, something of his world, and something of the meaning of their relation. There is scarcely a moment in a person's life when he is not poised for the lesson. When it comes with the promise of special force, there is the almost irresistible temptation to catch the impulse, give it form, make it permanent, assert its meaning. And so one commits himself to language. To have given up one's experience to words is to have begun marking out the limits and potential of its meaning. In the journal that meaning is developed and clarified to oneself primarily. When the whole intention of the development and the clarification is the consideration of another reader, the method of the journal redirects itself to become that of the essay.]

RALPH WALDO EMERSON: Journal

I like to have a man's knowledge comprehend more than one class of topics, one row of shelves. I like a man who likes to see a fine barn as well as a good tragedy.   [1828]

When a man has got to a certain point in his career of truth he becomes conscious forevermore that he must take himself for better, for worse, as his portion; that what he can get out of his plot of ground by the sweat of his brow is his meat, and though the wide universe is full of good, not a particle can he add to himself but through his toil bestowed on this spot. It looks to him indeed a little spot, a poor barren possession, filled with thorns, and a lurking place for adders and apes and wolves. But cultivation will work wonders. It will enlarge to his eye as it is explored. That little nook will swell to a world of light and power and love.   [1830]

The Religion that is afraid of science dishonors God and commits suicide.   [1831]

The things taught in colleges and schools are not an education, but the means of education.   [1831]

Don't tell me to get ready to die. I know not what shall be. The only preparation I can make is by fulfilling my present duties. This is the everlasting life.   [1832]

My aunt [Mary Moody Emerson] had an eye that went through and through you like a needle. "She was endowed," she said, "with the fatal gift of penetration." She disgusted everybody because she knew them too well.   [1832]

I am sure of this, that by going much alone a man will get more of a noble courage in thought and word than from all the wisdom that is in books.   [1833]

It is very easy in the world to live by the opinion of the world. It is very easy in solitude to be self-centered. But the finished man is he who in the midst of the crowd keeps with perfect sweetness the independence of solitude.   [1833]

I fretted the other night at the hotel at the stranger who broke into my chamber after midnight, claiming to share it. But after his lamp had smoked the chamber full and I had turned round to the wall in despair, the man blew out his lamp, knelt down at his bedside, and made in low whisper a long earnest prayer. Then was the relation entirely changed between us. I fretted no more, but respected and liked him.   [1835]

I believe I shall some time cease to be an individual, that the eternal tendency of the soul is to become Universal, to animate the last extremities of organization.   [1837]

It is very hard to be simple enough to be good.   [1837]

A man must have aunts and cousins, must buy carrots and turnips, must have barn and woodshed, must go to market and to the black-smith's shop, must saunter and sleep and be inferior and silly.   [1838]

How sad a spectacle, so frequent nowadays, to see a young man after ten years of college education come out, ready for his voyage of life—and to see that the entire ship is made of rotten timber, of rotten, honeycombed, traditional timber without so much as an inch of new plank in the hull.   [1839]

A sleeping child gives me the impression of a traveler in a very far country.   [1840]

In reading these letters of M.M.E. I acknowledge (with surprise that I could ever forget it) the debt of myself and my brothers to that old religion which, in those years, still dwelt like a Sabbath peace in the country population of New England, which taught privation, self-denial, and sorrow. A man was born, not for prosperity, but to suffer for the benefit of others, like the noble rock-maple tree which all around the villages bleeds for the service of man. Not praise, not men's acceptance of our doing, but the Spirit's holy errand through us, absorbed the thought. How dignified is this! how all that is called talents and worth in Paris and in Washington dwindles before it!   [1841]

All writing is by the grace of God. People do not deserve to have good writing, they are so pleased with bad. In these sentences that you show me, I can find no beauty, for I see death in every clause and every word. There is a fossil or a mummy character which pervades this book. The best sepulchers, the vastest catacombs, Thebes and Cairo, Pyramids, are sepulchers to me. I like gardens and nurseries. Give me initiative, spermatic, prophesying, man-making words.   [1841]

My garden is an honest place. Every tree and every vine are incapable of concealment, and tell after two or three months exactly what sort of treatment they have had. The sower may mistake and sow his peas crookedly: the peas make no mistake, but come up and show his line.   [1843]

When summer opens, I see how fast it matures, and fear it will be short; but after the heats of July and August, I am reconciled, like one who has had his swing, to the cool of autumn. So will it be with the coming of death. [1846]

In England every man you meet is some man's son; in America, he may be some man's father. [1848]

Every poem must be made up of lines that are poems. [1848]

Love is necessary to the righting the estate of woman in this world. Otherwise nature itself seems to be in conspiracy against her dignity and welfare; for the cultivated, high-thoughted, beauty-loving, saintly woman finds herself unconsciously desired for her sex, and even enhancing the appetite of her savage pursuers by these fine ornaments she has piously laid on herself. She finds with indignation that she is herself a snare, and was made such. I do not wonder at her occasional protest, violent protest against nature, in fleeing to nunneries, and taking black veils. Love rights all this deep wrong. [1848]

Natural Aristocracy. It is a vulgar error to suppose that a gentle-man must be ready to fight. The utmost that can be demanded of the gentleman is that he be incapable of a lie. There is a man who has good sense, is well informed, well-read, obliging, cultivated, capable, and has an absolute devotion to truth. He always means what he says, and says what he means, however courteously. You may spit upon him—nothing could induce him to spit upon you—no praises, and no possessions, no compulsion of public opinion. You may kick him—he will think it the kick of a brute—but he is not a brute, and will not kick you in return. But neither your knife and pistol, nor your gifts and courting will ever make the smallest impression on his vote or word; for he is the truth's man, and will speak and act the truth until he dies. [1849]

Love is temporary and ends with marriage. Marriage is the per-fection which love aimed at, ignorant of what it sought. Marriage is a good known only to the parties—a relation of perfect under-standing, aid, contentment, possession of themselves and of the world—which dwarfs love to green fruit. [1850]

I found when I had finished my new lecture that it was a very good house, only the architect had unfortunately omitted the stairs. [1851]

This filthy enactment [The Fugitive Slave Law] was made in the nineteenth century, by people who could read and write. I will not obey it, by God. [1851]

The head of Washington hangs in my dining-room for a few days past, and I cannot keep my eyes off of it. It has a certain Appalachian strength, as if it were truly the first-fruits of America,

and expressed the Country. The heavy, leaden eyes turn on you,
as the eyes of an ox in a pasture. And the mouth has gravity
and depth of quiet, as if this MAN had absorbed all the serenity
of America, and left none for his restless, rickety, hysterical
countrymen. [1852]

Henry [Thoreau] is military. He seemed stubborn and implacable;
always manly and wise, but rarely sweet. One would say that, as
Webster could never speak without an antagonist, so Henry does not
feel himself except in opposition. He wants a fallacy to expose,
a blunder to pillory, requires a little sense of victory, a roll of
the drums, to call his powers into full exercise. [1853]

Shall we judge the country by the majority or by the minority?
Certainly, by the minority. The mass are animal, in state of pupilage,
and nearer the chimpanzee. [1854]

All the thoughts of a turtle are turtle. [1854]

Resources or feats. I like people who can do things. When
Edward and I struggled in vain to drag our big calf into the barn,
the Irish girl put her finger into the calf's mouth, and led her in
directly. [1862]

George Francis Train said in a public speech in New York,
"Slavery is a divine institution." "So is hell," exclaimed an old
man in the crowd. [1862]

You complain that the Negroes are a base class. Who makes
and keeps the Jew or the Negro base, who but you, who exclude
them from the rights which others enjoy? [1867]

KATHERINE MANSFIELD: Journal[1]

March 21. Traveled with two brown women. One had a basket
of chickweed on her arm, the other a basket of daffodils. They
both carried babies bound, somehow, to them with a torn shawl.
Neat spare women with combed and braided hair. They slung talk
at each other across the bus. Then one woman took a piece of bread
from her sagging pocket and gave it to the baby, the other opened
her bodice and put the child to her breast. They sat and rocked
their knees and darted their quick eyes over the bus load. Busy and
indifferent they looked. [1914]

April 5. No bird sits a tree more proudly than a pigeon. It looks
as though placed there by the Lord. The sky was silky blue and
white, and the sun shone through the little leaves. But the children,

1. The triple dots in these entries are Mansfield's; they do not indicate deletions.

pinched and crooked, made me feel a bit out of love with God. [1914]

January 20. A stormy day. We walked back this morning. It has rained and snowed and hailed and the wind blows. The dog at the mill howls. A man far away is playing the bugle. I have read and sewed to-day, but not written a word. I want to to-night. It is so funny to sit quietly, while my heart is never for a moment still. I am dreadfully tired in head and body. This sad place is killing me. I live upon old made-up dreams; but they do not deceive either of us. [1914]

Wednesday [*December*]. To-day I am hardening my heart. I am walking all round my heart and building up the defenses. I do not mean to leave a loophole even for a tuft of violets to grow in. Give me a hard heart, O Lord! Lord, harden thou my heart! [1915]

I'm so hungry, simply empty, and seeing in my mind's eye just now a sirloin of beef, well browned with plenty of gravy and horse-radish sauce and baked potatoes, I nearly sobbed. There's nothing here to eat except omelettes and oranges and onions. It's a cold, sunny, windy day—the kind of day when you want a tremendous feed for lunch and an armchair in front of the fire to boa-constrict in afterwards. I feel sentimental about England now—English food, *decent* English *waste!* How much better than these thrifty French, whose flower gardens are nothing but potential salad bowls. There's not a leaf in France that you can't *faire une infusion avec,* not a blade that isn't *bon pour la cuisine.*[1] By God, I'd like to buy a pound of the best butter, put it on the window sill and watch it melt to spite 'em. They are a stingy, uncomfortable crew for all their lively scrapings. . . . For instance, their houses—what appalling furniture—and never one comfortable chair. If you want to talk the only possible thing to do is to go to bed. It's a case of either standing on your feet or lying in comfort under a puffed-up eiderdown. I quite understand the reason for what is called French moral laxity. You're simply forced into bed—no matter with whom. There's no other place for you. Supposing a *young* man comes to see about the electric light and will go on talking and pointing to the ceiling—or a friend drops in to tea and asks you if you believe in Absolute Evil. How can you give your mind to these things when you're sitting on four knobs and a square inch of cane? How much better to lie snug and *give yourself up to it.* [1916]

If only one could tell true love from false love as one can tell mushrooms from toadstools. With mushrooms it is so simple—you salt them well, put them aside and have patience. But with

1. "make tea with" . . . "good for eating."

love, you have no sooner lighted on anything that bears even the remotest resemblance to it than you are perfectly certain it is not only a genuine specimen, but perhaps *the* only genuine mushroom ungathered. It takes a dreadful number of toadstools to make you realize that life is not one long mushroom.   [1917]

The man in the room next to mine has the same complaint as I. When I wake in the night I hear him turning. And then he coughs. And I cough. And after a silence I cough. And he coughs again. This goes on for a long time. Until I feel we are like two roosters calling to each other at false dawn. From far-away hidden farms.   [1918]

She is little and grey, with a black velvet band round her hair, false teeth, and skinny little hands coming out of frills like the frills on cutlets.

As I passed her room one morning I saw her "worked" brush-and-comb bag and her Common Prayerbook.

Also, when she goes to the "Ladies," for some obscure reason she wears a little shawl. . . .

At the dining table, smiling brightly: "This is the first time I have ever traveled alone, or stayed by myself in a Strange Hotel. But my husband does not mind. As it is so Very Quiet. Of course, if it were a Gay Place—" And she draws in her chin, and the bead chain rises and falls on her vanished bosom.   [1918]

May 31. Work. Shall I be able to express one day my love of work—my desire to be a better writer—my longing to take greater pains. And the passion I feel. It takes the place of religion—it *is* my religion—of people—I create my people: of "life"—it *is* Life. The temptation is to kneel before it, to adore, to prostrate myself, to stay too long in a state of ecstasy before the idea of it. I must be more busy about my master's business.   [1919]

December 15. When I had gone to bed I realized what it was that had caused me to "give way." It was the effort of being up, with a heart that won't work. Not my lungs at all. My despair simply disappeared—yes, simply. The weather was lovely. Every morning the sun came in and drew more squares of golden light on the wall, I looked round my bed on to a sky like silk. The day opened slowly, slowly like a flower, and it held the sun long, long before it slowly, slowly folded. Then my homesickness went. I not only didn't want to be in England, I began to love Italy, and the thought of it—the sun—even when it was too hot—always the sun —and a kind of *wholeness* which was good to bask in.

All these two years I have been obsessed by the fear of death. This grew and grew and grew gigantic, and this it was that made me cling so, I think. Ten days ago it went, I care no more. It leaves me perfectly cold. . . . Life either stays or goes.

I must put down here a dream. The first night I was in bed here, *i.e.* after my first day in bed, I went to sleep. And suddenly I felt my whole body *breaking up*. It broke up with a violent shock—an earthquake—and it broke like glass. A long terrible shiver, you understand—the spinal cord and the bones and every bit and particle quaking. It sounded in my ears a low, confused din, and there was a sense of floating greenish brilliance, like broken glass. When I woke I thought that there had been a violent earthquake. But all was still. It slowly dawned upon me—the conviction that in that dream I died. I shall go on living now—it may be for months, or for weeks or days or hours. Time is not. In that dream I died. The *spirit* that is the enemy of death and quakes so and is so tenacious was shaken out of me. I am (December 15, 1919) a dead woman, and *I don't care*. It might comfort others to know that one gives up caring; but they'd not believe any more than I did until it happened. And, oh, how strong was its hold upon me! How I *adored* life and *dreaded* death!

I'd like to write my books and spend some happy time with J. (not very much faith withal) and see L. in a sunny place and pick violets—all kinds of flowers. I'd like to do heaps of things, really. But I don't mind if I do not do them. . . . Honesty (why?) is the only thing one seems to prize beyond life, love, death, everything. It alone remaineth. O you who come after me, will you believe it? At the end *truth* is the only thing *worth having*: it's more thrilling than love, more joyful and more passionate. It simply *cannot* fail. All else fails. I, at any rate, give the remainder of my life to it and it alone.   [1919]

What I feel is: She is never for one fraction of a second unconscious. If I sigh, I know that her head lifts. I know that those grave large eyes solemnly fix on me: Why did she sigh? If I turn she suggests a cushion or another rug. If I turn again, then it is my back. Might she try to rub it for me? There is no escape. All night: a faint rustle, the smallest cough, and her soft voice asks: "Did you speak? Can I do anything?" If I do absolutely nothing then she discovers my fatigue under my eyes. There is something profound and terrible in this eternal desire to establish contact.   [1920]

August. A sudden idea of the relationship between "lovers."
We are neither male nor female. We are a compound of both. I choose the male who will develop and expand the male in me; he chooses me to expand the female in him. Being made "whole," Yes, but that's a process. By love serve ye one another. . . . And why I choose *one* man for this rather than many

is for safety. We bind ourselves within a ring and that ring is as it were a wall against the outside world. It is our refuge, our shelter. Here the tricks of life will not be played. Here is *safety* for us to *grow*.

Why, I talk like a child!]1921[

Tidied all my papers. Tore up and ruthlessly destroyed much. This is always a great satisfaction. Whenever I prepare for a journey I prepare as though for death. Should I never return, all is in order. This is what life has taught me. [1922]

My first conversation with O. took place on August 30, 1922. On that occasion I began by telling him how dissatisfied I was with the idea that Life must be a lesser thing than we were capable of imagining it to be. I had the feeling that the same thing happened to nearly everybody whom I knew and whom I did not know. No sooner was their youth, with the little force and impetus characteristic of youth, done, than they stopped growing. At the very moment that one felt that now was the time to gather oneself together, to use one's whole strength, to take control, to be an adult, in fact, they seemed content to swap the darling wish of their hearts for innumerable little wishes. Or the image that suggested itself to me was that of a river flowing away in countless little trickles over a dark swamp.

They deceived themselves, of course. They called this trickling away—greater tolerance—wider interests—a sense of proportion—so that work did not rule out the possibility of "life." Or they called it an escape from all this mind-probing and self-consciousness—a simpler and therefore a better way of life. But sooner or later, in literature at any rate, there sounded an undertone of deep regret. There was an uneasiness, a sense of frustration. One heard, one thought one heard, the cry that began to echo in one's own being: "I have missed it. I have given up. This is not what I want. If this is all, then Life is not worth living."

But I *know* it is not all. How does one know that? Let me take the case of K.M. She has led, ever since she can remember, a very typically false life. Yet, through it all, there have been moments, instants, gleams, when she has felt the possibility of something quite other. [1922]

HENRY DAVID THOREAU: Journal

As the least drop of wine tinges the whole goblet, so the least particle of truth colors our whole life. It is never isolated, or simply added as treasure to our stock. When any real progress is made, we unlearn and learn anew what we thought we knew before. [1837]

The words of some men are thrown forcibly against you and adhere like burs. [1839]

Not by constraint or severity shall you have access to true wisdom, but by abandonment, and childlike mirthfulness. If you would know aught, be gay before it. [1840]

It is the man determines what is said, not the words. If a mean person uses a wise maxim, I bethink me how it can be interpreted so as to commend itself to his meanness; but if a wise man makes a commonplace remark, I consider what wider construction it will admit. [1840]

Nothing goes by luck in composition. It allows of no tricks. The best you can write will be the best you are. Every sentence is the result of a long probation. The author's character is read from title-page to end. Of this he never corrects the proofs. We read it as the essential character of a handwriting without regard to the flourishes. And so of the rest of our actions; it runs as straight as a ruled line through them all, no matter how many curvets about it. Our whole life is taxed for the least thing well done; it is its net result. How we eat, drink, sleep, and use our desultory hours, now in these indifferent days, with no eye to observe and no occasion [to] excite us, determines our authority and capacity for the time to come. [1841]

What does education often do? It makes a straight-cut ditch of a free, meandering book. [1850]

All perception of truth is the detection of an analogy; we reason from our hands to our head. [1851]

To set down such choice experiences that my own writings may inspire me and at last I may make wholes of parts. Certainly it is a distinct profession to rescue from oblivion and to fix the sentiments and thoughts which visit all men more or less generally, that the contemplation of the unfinished picture may suggest its harmonious completion. Associate reverently and as much as you can with your loftiest thoughts. Each thought that is welcomed and recorded is a nest egg, by the side of which more will be laid. Thoughts accidentally thrown together become a frame in which more may be developed and exhibited. Perhaps this is the main value of a habit of writing, of keeping a journal—that so we remember our best hours and stimulate ourselves. My thoughts are my company. They have a certain individuality and separate existence, aye, personality. Having by chance recorded a few disconnected thoughts and then brought them into juxtaposition, they suggest a whole new field in which it was possible to labor and to think. Thought begat thought. [1852]

What men call social virtues, good fellowship, is commonly but the virtue of pigs in a litter, which lie close together to keep each other warm. It brings men together in crowds and mobs in barrooms and elsewhere, but it does not deserve the name of virtue. [1852]

It is pardonable when we spurn the proprieties, even the sanctities, making them stepping-stones to something higher. [1858]

There is always some accident in the best things, whether thoughts or expressions or deeds. The memorable thought, the happy expression, the admirable deed are only partly ours. The thought came to us because we were in a fit mood; also we were unconscious and did not know that we had said or done a good thing. We must walk consciously only part way toward our goal, and then leap in the dark to our success. What we do best or most perfectly is what we have most thoroughly learned by the longest practice, and at length it falls from us without our notice, as a leaf from a tree. It is the *last* time we shall do it—our unconscious leavings. [1859]

The expression "a *liberal* education" originally meant one worthy of freemen. Such is education simply in a true and broad sense. But education ordinarily so called—the learning of trades and professions which is designed to enable men to earn their living, or to fit them for a particular station in life—is *servile*. [1859]

On Language
Words · Grammar · Style

WILLIAM MARCH
The Unspeakable Words

There were words in the Brett language considered so corrupting in their effect on others that if anyone wrote them or was heard to speak them aloud, he was fined and thrown into prison. The King of the Bretts was of the opinion that the words were of no importance one way or the other, and besides, everybody in the country knew them anyway; but his advisers disagreed, and at last, to determine who was right, a committee was appointed to examine the people separately.

At length everyone in the kingdom had been examined, and found to know the words quite well, without the slightest damage to themselves. There was then left only one little girl, a five-year-old who lived in the mountains with her deaf and dumb parents. The committee hoped that this little girl, at least, had never heard the corrupting words, and on the morning they visited her, they said solemnly: "Do you know the meaning of *poost, gist, duss, feng?*"

The little girl admitted that she did not, and then, smiling happily, she said, "Oh, you must mean *feek, kusk, dalu,* and *liben!*"

Those who don't know the words must make them up for themselves.

GERTRUDE STEIN
Poetry and Grammar[1]

Words have to do everything in poetry and prose and some writers write more in articles and prepositions and some say you should write in nouns, and of course one has to think of everything.

1. Excerpted from the essay with this title in *Lectures in America,* 1935.

A noun is a name of anything, why after a thing is named write about it. A name is adequate or it is not. If it is adequate then why go on calling it, if it is not then calling it by its name does no good.

People if you like to believe it can be made by their names. Call anybody Paul and they get to be a Paul call anybody Alice and they get to be an Alice perhaps yes perhaps no, there is something in that, but generally speaking, things once they are named the name does not go on doing anything to them and so why write in nouns. Nouns are the name of anything and just naming names is alright when you want to call a roll but is it any good for anything else. To be sure in many places in Europe as in America they do like to call rolls.

As I say a noun is a name of a thing, and therefore slowly if you feel what is inside that thing you do not call it by the name by which it is known. Everybody knows that by the way they do when they are in love and a writer should always have that intensity of emotion about whatever is the object about which he writes. And therefore and I say it again more and more one does not use nouns.

Now what other things are there beside nouns, there are a lot of other things beside nouns.

When you are at school and learn grammar grammar is very exciting. I really do not know that anything has ever been more exciting than diagraming sentences. I suppose other things may be more exciting to others when they are at school but to me undoubtedly when I was at school the really completely exciting thing was diagraming sentences and that has been to me ever since the one thing that has been completely exciting and completely completing. I like the feeling the everlasting feeling of sentences as they diagram themselves.

In that way one is completely possessing something and incidentally one's self. Now in that diagraming of the sentences of course there are articles and prepositions and as I say there are nouns but nouns as I say even by definition are completely not interesting, the same thing is true of adjectives. Adjectives are not really and truly interesting. In a way anybody can know always has known that, because after all adjectives effect nouns and as nouns are not really interesting the thing that effects a not too interesting thing is of necessity not interesting. In a way as I say anybody knows that because of course the first thing that anybody takes out of anybody's writing are the adjectives. You see of yourself how true it is that which I have just said.

Beside the nouns and the adjectives there are verbs and adverbs. Verbs and adverbs are more interesting. In the first place they have one very nice quality and that is that they can be so mistaken. It is wonderful the number of mistakes a verb can make and that is equally true of its adverb. Nouns and adjectives never can make mistakes can never be mistaken but verbs can be so endlessly, both as to what they do and how they agree or disagree with whatever they do. The same is true of adverbs.

In that way any one can see that verbs and adverbs are more interesting than nouns and adjectives.

Beside being able to be mistaken and to make mistakes verbs can change to look like themselves or to look like something else, they are, so to speak on the move and adverbs move with them and each of them find themselves not at all annoying but very often very much mistaken. That is the reason any one can like what verbs can do. Then comes the thing that can of all things be most mistaken and they are prepositions. Prepositions can live one long life being really being nothing but absolutely nothing but mistaken and that makes them irritating if you feel that way about mistakes but certainly something that you can be continuously using and everlastingly enjoying. I like prepositions the best of all, and pretty soon we will go more completely into that.

Then there are articles. Articles are interesting just as nouns and adjectives are not. And why are they interesting just as nouns and adjectives are not. They are interesting because they do what a noun might do if a noun was not so unfortunately so completely unfortunately the name of something. Articles please, a and an and the please as the name that follows cannot please. They the names that is the nouns cannot please, because after all you know well after all that is what Shakespeare meant when he talked about a rose by any other name.

I hope now no one can have any illusion about a noun or about the adjective that goes with the noun.

But an article an article remains as a delicate and a varied something and any one who wants to write with articles and knows how to use them will always have the pleasure that using something that is varied and alive can give. That is what articles are.

Beside that there are conjunctions, and a conjunction is not varied but it has a force that need not make any one feel that they are dull. Conjunctions have made themselves live by their work. They work and as they work they live and even when they do not work and in these days they do not always live by work still nevertheless they do live.

So you see why I like to write with prepositions and conjunctions and articles and verbs and adverbs but not with nouns and adjectives. If you read my writing you will you do see what I mean.

Of course then there are pronouns. Pronouns are not as bad as nouns because in the first place practically they cannot have adjectives go with them. That already makes them better than nouns.

Then beside not being able to have adjectives go with them, they of course are not really the name of anything. They represent some one but they are not its or his name. In not being his or its or her name they already have a greater possibility of being something than if they were as a noun is the name of anything. Now actual given names of people are more lively than nouns which are the name of anything and I suppose that this is because after all the name is only given to that person when they are born, there is at least the element of choice even the element of change and anybody can be pretty well able to do what they like, they may be born Walter and become Hub, in such a way they are not like a noun. A noun has been the name of something for such a very long time.

That is the reason that slang exists it is to change the nouns which have been names for so long. I say again. Verbs and adverbs and articles and conjunctions and prepositions are lively because they all do something and as long as anything does something it keeps alive.

QUESTIONS FOR STUDY, DISCUSSION, AND WRITING

1. What is there about nouns and adjectives that makes them uninteresting to Miss Stein?
2. What does Miss Stein mean when she says that verbs and adverbs are more interesting because "they can be so mistaken"? She says that nouns cannot be mistaken; is she right?
3. How does her love of verbs help to explain her feeling that there has never been anything "more exciting than diagraming sentences"?
4. How does Miss Stein's own style differ from more conventional prose styles? Does she write more in verbs, adverbs, and prepositions than in nouns and adjectives? What might her essay lose in effectiveness if it were written in a more conventional style?
5. Miss Stein says that "if you feel what is inside" a thing, "you do not call it by the name by which it is known." She says this can be shown by the way we act when we are in love and that "a writer should always have that intensity of emotion" about his subject. Other writers might say that you do not have to have strong convictions about a subject to write interestingly about it. Is the disagreement between these two views complete or only partial? Is one right and the other wrong? What are the assumptions about the nature and purpose of writing from which they start?

HERBERT SPENCER
Force in Words[1]

The Principle of Economy

Commenting on the seeming incongruity between his father's argumentative powers and his ignorance of formal logic, Tristram Shandy says: "It was a matter of just wonder with my worthy tutor, and two or three fellows of that learned society, that a man who knew not so much as the names of his tools, should be able to work after that fashion with them." Sterne's intended implication that a knowledge of the principles of reasoning neither makes, nor is essential to, a good reasoner, is doubtless true. Thus, too, is it with grammar. As Dr. Latham, condemning the usual school-drill in Lindley Murray,[2] rightly remarks: "Gross vulgarity is a fault to be prevented; but the proper prevention is to be got from habit—not rules." Similarly, there can be little question that good composition is far less dependent upon acquaintance with its laws, than upon practice and natural aptitude. A clear head, a quick imagination, and a sensitive ear, will go far towards making all rhetorical precepts needless. He who daily hears and reads well-framed sentences, will naturally more or less tend to use similar ones. And where there exists any mental idiosyncrasy—where there is a deficient verbal memory, or an inadequate sense of logical dependence, or but little perception of order, or a lack of constructive ingenuity; no amount of instruction will remedy the defect. Nevertheless, *some* practical result may be expected from a familiarity with the principles of style. The endeavor to conform to laws may tell, though slowly. And if in no other way, yet, as facilitating revision, a knowledge of the thing to be achieved—a clear idea of what constitutes a beauty, and what a blemish—cannot fail to be of service.

No general theory of expression seems yet to have been enunciated. The maxims contained in works on composition and rhetoric, are presented in an unorganized form. Standing as isolated dogmas —as empirical generalizations, they are neither so clearly apprehended, nor so much respected, as they would be were they deduced from some simple first principle. We are told that "brevity is the soul of wit." We hear styles condemned as verbose or involved. Blair says that every needless part of a sentence "interrupts the

---

1. From "Causes of Force in Language Which Depend Upon Economy of the Mental Energies," Part I of *The Philosophy of Style*, 1852.

2. Any of several school texts by the American-English grammarian Lindley Murray (1745-1826). His *English Grammar* (1795), *Reader* (1799), and *Spelling Book* (1804) were standard in virtually all schools. Other men mentioned in the course of this selection were eminent nineteenth-century (Latham) or eighteenth-century (Blair, Kames, Campbell) authorities on language.

description and clogs the image;" and again, that "long sentences fatigue the reader's attention." It is remarked by Lord Kames, that "to give the utmost force to a period, it ought, if possible, to be closed with that word which makes the greatest figure." That parentheses should be avoided and that Saxon words should be used in preference to those of Latin origin, are established precepts. But, however influential the truths thus dogmatically embodied, they would be much more influential if reduced to something like scientific ordination. In this, as in other cases, conviction will be greatly strengthened when we understand the *why*. And we may be sure that a comprehension of the general principle from which the rules of composition result, will not only bring them home to us with greater force, but will discover to us other rules of like origin.

On seeking for some clue to the law underlying these current maxims, we may see shadowed forth in many of them, the importance of economizing the reader's or hearer's attention. To so present ideas that they may be apprehended with the least possible mental effort, is the desideratum towards which most of the rules above quoted point. When we condemn writing that is wordy, or confused, or intricate—when we praise this style as easy, and blame that as fatiguing, we consciously or unconsciously assume this desideratum as our standard of judgment. Regarding language as an apparatus of symbols for the conveyance of thought, we may say that, as in a mechanical apparatus, the more simple and the better arranged its parts, the greater will be the effect produced. In either case, whatever force is absorbed by the machine is deducted from the result. A reader or listener has at each moment but a limited amount of mental power available. To recognize and interpret the symbols presented to him, requires part of this power; to arrange and combine the images suggested requires a further part; and only that part which remains can be used for realizing the thought conveyed. Hence, the more time and attention it takes to receive and understand each sentence, the less time and attention can be given to the contained idea; and the less vividly will that idea be conceived.

How truly language must be regarded as a hindrance to thought, though the necessary instrument of it, we shall clearly perceive on remembering the comparative force with which simple ideas are communicated by signs. To say, "Leave the room," is less expressive than to point to the door. Placing a finger on the lips is more forcible than whispering, "Do not speak." A beck of the hand is better than, "Come here." No phrase can convey the idea of surprise so vividly as opening the eyes and raising the eyebrows. A shrug of the shoulders would lose much by translation into words. Again, it may be remarked that when oral language is employed, the strongest effects are produced by interjections, which condense entire sentences into syllables. And in other cases, where custom allows us to express thoughts by single words, as in *Beware*, *Heigho*, *Fudge*, much force would be lost by expanding them into specific propositions. Hence, carrying out the metaphor that language is the vehicle of thought, there seems reason to think that in all cases the friction and inertia of the vehicle deduct from its efficiency; and that in composition, the chief, if not the sole thing to be done, is, to reduce this fiction and inertia to the smallest possible amount. Let us then inquire whether economy of the recipient's attention is not the secret of effect, alike in the right choice and collocation of words, in the best arrangement of clauses in a sentence, in the proper order of its principal and subordinate propositions, in the judicious use of simile, metaphor, and other figures of speech, and even in the rhythmical sequence of syllables.

Economy in the Use of Words

The greater forcibleness of Saxon English, or rather non-Latin English, first claims our attention. The several special reasons assignable for this may all be reduced to the general reason—economy. The most important of them is early association. A child's vocabulary is almost wholly Saxon. He says, *I have*, not *I possess*—*I wish*, not *I desire*, he does not reflect, he *thinks*; he does not beg for *amusement*, but for *play*; he calls things *nice* or *nasty*, not *pleasant* or *disagreeable*. The synonyms which he learns in after years, never become so closely, so organically connected with the ideas signified, as do these original words used in childhood; and hence the association remains less strong. But in what does a strong association between a word and an idea differ from a weak one? Simply in the greater ease and rapidity of the suggestive action. It can be in nothing else. Both of two words, if they be strictly synonymous, eventually call up the same image. The expression—It is *acid*, must in the the end give rise to the same thought as—It is *sour*; but because the term *acid* was learnt later in life, and has not been so often followed by the thought symbolized, it does not so readily arouse that thought as the term *sour*. If we remember how slowly and with what labor the appropriate ideas follow unfamiliar words in another language, and how increasing familiarity with such words brings greater rapidity and ease of comprehension; and if we consider that the same process must have gone on with the words of our mother tongue from childhood upwards, we shall clearly see that the earliest learnt and oftenest used words, will, other things equal, call up images with less loss of time and energy than their later learnt synonyms.

The further superiority possessed by Saxon English in its comparative brevity, obviously comes under the same generalization. If it be an advantage to express an idea in the smallest number of words, then will it be an advantage to express it in the smallest number of syllables. If circuitous phrases and needless expletives distract the attention and diminish the strength of the impression produced, then do surplus articulations do so. A certain effort, though commonly an inappreciable one, must be required to recognize every vowel and consonant. If, as all know, it is tiresome to listen to an indistinct speaker, or read a badly-written manuscript; and if, as we cannot doubt, the fatigue is a cumulative result of the attention needed to catch successive syllables; it follows that attention is in such cases absorbed by each syllable. And if this be true when the syllables are difficult of recognition, it will also be true, though in a less degree, when the recognition of them is easy. Hence, the shortness of Saxon words becomes a reason for their greater force. One qualification, however, must not be overlooked. A word which in itself embodies the most important part of the idea to be conveyed, especially when that idea is an emotional one, may often with advantage be a polysyllabic word. Thus it seems more forcible to say, "It is *magnificent*," than "It is *grand*." The word *vast* is not so powerful a one as *stupendous*. Calling a thing *nasty* is not so effective as calling it *disgusting*.

There seem to be several causes for this exceptional superiority of certain long words. We may ascribe it partly to the fact that a voluminous, mouth-filling epithet is, by its very size, suggestive of largeness or strength; witness the immense pomposity of sesquipedalian verbiage: and when great power or intensity has to be suggested, this association of ideas aids the effect. A further cause may be that a word of several syllables admits of more emphatic articulation; and as emphatic articulation is a sign of emotion, the unusual impressiveness of the thing named is implied by it. Yet another cause is that a long word (of which the latter syllables are generally inferred as soon as the first are spoken) allows the hearer's consciousness a longer time to dwell upon the quality predicated; and where, as in the above cases, it is to this predicated quality that the entire attention is called, an advantage results from keeping it before the mind for an appreciable time. The reasons which we have given for preferring short words evidently do not hold here. So that to make our generalization quite correct we must say, that while in certain sentences expressing strong feeling, the word which more especially implies that feeling may often with advantage be a many-syllabled or Latin one; in the immense majority of cases, each word serving but as a step to the idea embodied by the whole sentence, should, if possible, be a one-syllabled or Saxon one.

Once more, that frequent cause of strength in Saxon and other primitive words—their imitative character, may be similarly resolved into the more general cause. Both those directly imitative, as *splash, bang, whiz, roar*, etc., and those analogically imitative, as *rough, smooth, keen, blunt, thin, hard, crag*, etc., have a greater or less likeness to the things symbolized; and by making on the senses impressions allied to the ideas to be called up, they save part of the effort needed to call up such ideas, and leave more attention for the ideas themselves.

The economy of the recipient's mental energy, into which are thus resolvable the several causes of the strength of Saxon English, may equally be traced in the superiority of specific over generic words. That concrete terms produce more vivid impressions than abstract ones, and should, when possible, be used instead, is a thorough maxim of composition. As Dr. Campbell says, "The more general the terms are, the picture is the fainter; the more special they are, 'tis the brighter." We should avoid such a sentence as: "In proportion as the manners, customs, and amusements of a nation are cruel and barbarous, the regulations of their penal code will be severe." And in place of it we should write: "In proportion as men delight in battles, bull-fights, and combats of gladiators, will they punish by hanging, burning, and the rack."

This superiority of specific expressions is clearly due to a saving of the effort required to translate words into thoughts. As we do not think in generals but in particulars—as, whenever any class of things is referred to, we represent it to ourselves by calling to mind individual members of it; it follows that when an abstract word is used, the hearer or reader has to choose from his stock of images, one or more, by which he may figure to himself the genus mentioned. In doing this, some delay must arise—some force be expended; and if, by employing a specific term, an appropriate image can be at once suggested, an economy is achieved, and a more vivid impression produced.

RALPH WALDO EMERSON
The Language of the Street

The language of the street is always strong. What can describe the folly and emptiness of scolding like the word *jawing?* I feel too the force of the double negative, though clean contrary to our grammar rules. And I confess to some pleasure from the stinging rhetoric of a rattling oath in the mouths of truckmen and teamsters. How laconic and brisk it is by the side of a page of the *North American Review*. Cut these words and they would bleed; they are vascular and alive; they walk and run. Moreover they who speak them have this elegancy, that they do not trip in their speech. It is a shower of bullets, whilst Cambridge men and Yale men correct themselves and begin again at every half sentence.

GEORGE ORWELL
The Principles of Newspeak[1]

Newspeak was the official language of Oceania and had been devised to meet the ideological needs of Ingsoc, or English Socialism. In the year 1984 there was not as yet anyone who used Newspeak as his sole means of communication, either in speech or writing. The leading articles in the *Times* were written in it, but this was a tour de force which could only be carried out by a specialist. It was expected that Newspeak would have finally superseded Oldspeak (or Standard English, as we should call it) by about the year 2050. Meanwhile it gained ground steadily, all Party members tending to use Newspeak words and grammatical constructions more and more in their everyday speech. The version in use in 1984, and embodied in the Ninth and Tenth Edition of the Newspeak dictionary, was a provisional one, and contained many superfluous words and archaic formations which were due to be suppressed later. It is with the final, perfected version, as embodied in the Eleventh Edition of the dictionary, that we are concerned here.

The purpose of Newspeak was not only to provide a medium of expression for the world-view and mental habits proper to the devotees of Ingsoc, but to make all other modes of thought impossible. It was intended that when Newspeak had been adopted once and for all and Oldspeak forgotten, a heretical thought—that is, a thought diverging from the principles of Ingsoc—should be literally unthinkable, at least so far as thought is dependent on words. Its vocabulary was so constructed as to give exact and often very subtle expression to every meaning that a Party member could properly wish to express, while excluding all other meanings and also the possibility of arriving at them by indirect methods. This was done partly by the invention of new words, but chiefly by eliminating undesirable words and by stripping such words as remained of unorthodox meanings, and so far as possible of all secondary meanings whatever. To give a single example. The word *free* still existed in Newspeak, but it could only be used in such statements as "This dog is free from lice" or "This field is free from weeds." It could not be used in its old sense of "politically free" or "intellectually free," since political and intellectual freedom no longer existed even as concepts, and were therefore of necessity nameless. Quite apart from the suppression of definitely heretical words, reduction of vocabulary was regarded as an end in itself, and no word that could be dispensed with was allowed to survive. New-

1. Appendix to *1984*, Orwell's novel about the efforts of his hero, Winston Smith, to preserve his own identity in a totalitarian society of the future ruled by the dictator Big Brother.

speak was designed not to extend but to *diminish* the range of thought, and this purpose was indirectly assisted by cutting the choice of words down to a minimum.

Newspeak was founded on the English language as we now know it, though many Newspeak sentences, even when not containing newly created words, would be barely intelligible to an English-speaker of our own day. Newspeak words were divided into three distinct classes, known as the A vocabulary, the B vocabulary (also called compound words), and the C vocabulary. It will be simpler to discuss each class separately, but the grammatical peculiarities of the language can be dealt with in the section devoted to the A vocabulary, since the same rules held good for all three categories.

The A vocabulary. The A vocabulary consisted of words needed for the business of everyday life—for such things as eating, drinking, working, putting on one's clothes, going up and down stairs, riding in vehicles, gardening, cooking, and the like. It was composed almost entirely of words that we already possess—words like *hit*, *run*, *dog*, *tree*, *sugar*, *house*, *field*—but in comparison with the present-day English vocabulary, their number was extremely small, while their meanings were far more rigidly defined. All ambiguities and shades of meaning had been purged out of them. So far as it could be achieved, a Newspeak word of this class was simply a staccato sound expressing *one* clearly understood concept. It would have been quite impossible to use the A vocabulary for literary purposes or for political or philosophical discussion. It was intended only to express simple, purposive thoughts, usually involving concrete objects or physical actions.

The grammar of Newspeak had two outstanding peculiarities. The first of these was an almost complete interchangeability between different parts of speech. Any word in the language (in principle this applied even to very abstract words such as *if* or *when*) could be used either as verb, noun, adjective, or adverb. Between the verb and the noun form, when they were of the same root, there was never any variation, this rule of itself involving the destruction of many archaic forms. The word *thought*, for example, did not exist in Newspeak. Its place was taken by *think*, which did duty for both noun and verb. No etymological principle was involved here; in some cases it was the original noun that was chosen for retention, in other cases the verb. Even where a noun and verb of kindred meaning were not etymologically connected, one or other of them was frequently suppressed. There was, for example, no such word as *cut*, its meaning being sufficiently covered by the noun-verb *knife*. Adjectives were formed by adding the suffix *-ful* to the noun-verb, and adverbs by adding *-wise*. Thus, for example, *speedful* meant "rapid" and *speedwise* meant "quickly." Certain of our present-day adjectives, such as *good, strong, big, black, soft,* were retained, but their total number was very small. There was little need for them, since almost any adjectival meaning could be arrived at by adding *-ful* to a noun-verb. None of the now-existing adverbs was retained, except for a very few already ending in *-wise;* the *-wise* termination was invariable. The word *well,* for example, was replaced by *goodwise.*

In addition, any word—this again applied in principle to every word in the language—could be negatived by adding the affix *un-,* or could be strengthened by the affix *plus-,* or, for still greater emphasis *doubleplus-.* Thus, for example, *uncold* meant "warm," while *pluscold* and *doublepluscold* meant, respectively, "very cold" and "superlatively cold." It was also possible, as in present-day English, to modify the meaning of almost any word by prepositional affixes such as *ante-, post-, up-, down-,* etc. By such methods it was found possible to bring about an enormous diminution of vocabulary. Given, for instance, the word *good,* there was no need for such a word as *bad,* since the required meaning was equally well—indeed, better—expressed by *ungood.* All that was necessary, in any case where two words formed a natural pair of opposites, was to decide which of them to suppress. *Dark,* for example, could be replaced by *unlight,* or *light* by *undark,* according to preference.

The second distinguishing mark of Newspeak grammar was its regularity. Subject to a few exceptions which are mentioned below, all inflections followed the same rules. Thus, in all verbs the preterit and the past participle were the same and ended in *-ed.* The preterit of *steal* was *stealed,* the preterit of *think* was *thinked,* and so on throughout the language, all such forms as *swam, gave, brought, spoke, taken,* etc., being abolished. All plurals were made by adding *-s* or *-es* as the case might be. The plurals of *man, ox, life* were *mans, oxes, lifes.* Comparison of adjectives was invariably made by adding *-er, -est* (*good, gooder, goodest*), irregular forms and the *more, most* formation being suppressed.

The only classes of words that were still allowed to inflect irregularly were the pronouns, the relatives, the demonstrative adjectives, and the auxiliary verbs. All of these followed their ancient usage, except that *whom* had been scrapped as unnecessary, and the *shall, should* tenses had been dropped, all their uses being covered by *will* and *would.* There were also certain irregularities in word formation arising out of the need for rapid and easy speech. A word which was difficult to utter, or was liable to be incorrectly heard, was held to be ipso facto a bad word; occasionally therefore, for the sake of euphony, extra letters were inserted into a word or an archaic formation was retained. But this need made itself felt chiefly in connection with the B vocabulary. *Why* so great an importance was attached to ease of pronunciation will be made clear later in this essay.

The B vocabulary. The B vocabulary consisted of words which had been deliberately constructed for political purposes: words, that is to say, which not only had in every case a political implication, but were intended to impose a desirable mental attitude upon the person using them. Without a full understanding of the principles of Ingsoc it was difficult to use these words correctly. In some cases they could be translated into Oldspeak, or even into words taken from the A vocabulary, but this usually demanded a long paraphrase and always involved the loss of certain overtones. The B words were a sort of verbal shorthand, often packing whole ranges of ideas into a few syllables, and at the same time more accurate and forcible than ordinary language.

The B words were in all cases compound words.[2] They consisted of two or more words, or portions of words, welded together in an easily pronounceable form. The resulting amalgam was always a noun-verb, and inflected according to the ordinary rules. To take a single example: the word *goodthink*, meaning, very roughly, "orthodoxy," or, if one chose to regard it as a verb, "to think in an orthodox manner." This inflected as follows: noun-verb, *goodthink*; past tense and past participle, *goodthinked*; present participle, *goodthinking*; adjective, *goodthinkful*; adverb, *goodthinkwise*; verbal noun, *goodthinker*.

The B words were not constructed on any etymological plan. The words of which they were made up could be any parts of speech, and could be placed in any order and mutilated in any way which made them easy to pronounce while indicating their derivation. In the word *crimethink* (thought-crime), for instance, the *think* came second, whereas in *thinkpol* (Thought Police) it came first, and in the latter word *police* had lost its second syllable. Because of the greater difficulty in securing euphony, irregular formations were commoner in the B vocabulary than in the A vocabulary. For example, the adjectival forms of *Minitrue*, *Minipax*, and *Miniluv* were, respectively, *Minitruthful*, *Minipeaceful*, and *Minilovely*, simply because *-trueful*, *-paxful*, and *-loveful* were slightly awkward to pronounce. In principle, however, all B words could inflect, and all inflected in exactly the same way.

Some of the B words had highly subtilized meanings, barely intelligible to anyone who had not mastered the language as a whole. Consider, for example, such a typical sentence from a *Times* leading article as *Oldthinkers unbellyfeel Ingsoc.* The shortest ren-

---

2. Compound words, such as *speak-write*, were of course to be found in the A vocabulary, but these were merely con- venient abbreviations and had no special ideological color [Orwell's note].

dering that one could make of this in Oldspeak would be: "Those whose ideas were formed before the Revolution cannot have a full emotional understanding of the principles of English Socialism." But this is not an adequate translation. To begin with, in order to grasp the full meaning of the Newspeak sentence quoted above, one would have to have a clear idea of what is meant by Ingsoc. And, in addition, only a person thoroughly grounded in Ingsoc could appreciate the full force of the word *bellyfeel,* which implied a blind, enthusiastic acceptance difficult to imagine today; or of the word *oldthink;* which was inextricably mixed up with the idea of wickedness and decadence. But the special function of certain Newspeak words of which *oldthink* was one, was not so much to *express* meanings as to destroy them. These words, necessarily few in number, had had their meanings extended until they contained within themselves whole batteries of words which, as they were sufficiently covered by a single comprehensive term, could now be scrapped and forgotten. The greatest difficulty facing the compilers of the Newspeak dictionary was not to invent new words, but, having invented them, to make sure what they meant; to make sure, that is to say, what ranges of words they canceled by their existence.

As we have already seen in the case of the word *free,* words which had once borne a heretical meaning were sometimes retained for the sake of convenience, but only with the undesirable meanings purged out of them. Countless other words such as *honor, justice, morality, internationalism, democracy, science,* and *religion* had simply ceased to exist. A few blanket words covered them, and, in covering them, abolished them. All words grouping themselves round the concepts of liberty and equality, for instance, were contained in the single word *crimethink,* while all words grouping themselves round the concepts of objectivity and rationalism were contained in the single word *oldthink.* Greater precision would have been dangerous. What was required in a Party member was an outlook similar to that of the ancient Hebrew who knew, without knowing much else, that all nations other than his own worshipped "false gods." He did not need to know that these gods were called Baal, Osiris, Moloch, Ashtaroth, and the like; probably the less he knew about them the better for his orthodoxy. He knew Jehovah and the commandments of Jehovah; he knew, therefore, that all gods with other names or other attributes were false gods. In somewhat the same way, the Party member knew what constituted right conduct, and in exceedingly vague, generalized terms he knew what kinds of departure from it were possible. His sexual life, for example, was entirely regulated by the two Newspeak words *sexcrime* (sexual immorality) and *goodsex* (chastity). *Sexcrime* covered all sexual misdeeds whatever. It covered fornication, adultery, homosexuality, and other perversions, and, in addition, normal intercourse practiced for its own sake. There was no need to enumerate them separately, since they were all equally culpable, and in principle, all punishable by death. In the C vocabulary, which consisted of scientific and technical words, it might be necessary to give specialized names to certain sexual aberrations, but the ordinary citizen had no need of them. He knew what was meant by *goodsex*—that is to say, normal intercourse between man and wife, for the sole purpose of begetting children, and without physical pleasure on the part of the woman; all else was *sexcrime*. In Newspeak it was seldom possible to follow a heretical thought further than the perception that it was heretical; beyond that point the necessary words were nonexistent.

No word in the B vocabulary was ideologically neutral. A great many were euphemisms. Such words, for example, as *joycamp* (forced-labor camp) or *Minipax* (Ministry of Peace, i.e., Ministry of War) meant almost the exact opposite of what they appeared to mean. Some words, on the other hand, displayed a frank and contemptuous understanding of the real nature of Oceanic society. An example was *prolefeed*, meaning the rubbishy entertainment and spurious news which the Party handed out to the masses. Other words, again, were ambivalent, having the connotation "good" when applied to the Party and "bad" when applied to its enemies. But in addition there were great numbers of words which at first sight appeared to be mere abbreviations and which derived their ideological color not from their meaning but from their structure.

So far as it could be contrived, everything that had or might have political significance of any kind was fitted into the B vocabulary. The name of every organization, or body of people, or doctrine, or country, or institution, or public building, was invariably cut down into the familiar shape; that is, a single easily pronounced word with the smallest number of syllables that would preserve the original derivation. In the Ministry of Truth, for example, the Records Department, in which Winston Smith worked, was called *Recdep*, the Fiction Department was called *Ficdep*, the Teleprograms Department was called *Teledep*, and so on. This was not done solely with the object of saving time. Even in the early decades of the twentieth century, telescoped words and phrases had been one of the characteristic features of political language; and it had been noticed that the tendency to use abbreviations of this kind was most marked in totalitarian countries and totalitarian organizations. Examples were such words as *Nazi*, *Gestapo*, *Comintern*, *Inprecorr*, *Agitprop*. In the beginning the practice had been adopted as it were instinctively, but in Newspeak it was used with a conscious purpose. It was perceived that in thus abbreviating a name one narrowed and subtly altered its meaning, by cutting out most of the associations that would otherwise cling to it. The words *Communist*

International, for instance, call up a composite picture of universal human brotherhood, red flags, barricades, Karl Marx, and the Paris Commune. The word *Comintern,* on the other hand, suggests merely a tightly knit organization and a well-defined body of doctrine. It refers to something almost as easily recognized, and as limited in purpose, as a chair or a table. *Comintern* is a word that can be uttered almost without taking thought, whereas *Communist International* is a phrase over which one is obliged to linger at least momentarily. In the same way, the associations called up by a word like *Minitrue* are fewer and more controllable than those called up by *Ministry of Truth.* This accounted not only for the habit of abbreviating whenever possible, but also for the almost exaggerated care that was taken to make every word easily pronounceable.

In Newspeak, euphony outweighed every consideration other than exactitude of meaning. Regularity of grammar was always sacrificed to it when it seemed necessary. And rightly so, since what was required, above all for political purposes, were short clipped words of unmistakable meaning which could be uttered rapidly and which roused the minimum of echoes in the speaker's mind. The words of the B vocabulary even gained in force from the fact that nearly all of them were very much alike. Almost invariably these words—*goodthink, Minipax, prolefeed, sexcrime, joycamp, Ingsoc, bellyfeel, thinkpol,* and countless others—were words of two or three syllables, with the stress distributed equally between the first syllable and the last. The use of them encouraged a gabbling style of speech, at once staccato and monotonous. And this was exactly what was aimed at. The intention was to make speech, and especially speech on any subject not ideologically neutral, as nearly as possible independent of consciousness. For the purposes of everyday life it was no doubt necessary, or sometimes necessary, to reflect before speaking, but a Party member called upon to make a political or ethical judgment should be able to spray forth the correct opinions as automatically as a machine gun spraying forth bullets. His training fitted him to do this, the language gave him an almost foolproof instrument, and the texture of the words, with their harsh sound and a certain willful ugliness which was in accord with the spirit of Ingsoc, assisted the process still further.

So did the fact of having very few words to choose from. Relative to our own, the Newspeak vocabulary was tiny, and new ways of reducing it were constantly being devised. Newspeak, indeed, differed from almost all other languages in that its vocabulary grew smaller instead of larger every year. Each reduction was a gain, since the smaller the area of choice, the smaller the temptation to take thought. Ultimately it was hoped to make articulate speech issue from the larynx without involving the higher brain centers at all. This aim was frankly admitted in the Newspeak word *duckspeak,* meaning "to quack like a duck." Like various other words in the B vocabulary, *duckspeak* was ambivalent in meaning. Provided that the opinions which were quacked out were orthodox ones, it implied nothing but praise, and when the *Times* referred to one of the orators of the Party as a *doubleplusgood duckspeaker* it was paying a warm and valued compliment.

The C vocabulary. The C vocabulary was supplementary to the others and consisted entirely of scientific and technical terms. These resembled the scientific terms in use today, and were constructed from the same roots, but the usual care was taken to define them rigidly and strip them of undesirable meanings. They followed the same grammatical rules as the words in the other two vocabularies. Very few of the C words had any currency either in everyday speech or in political speech. Any scientific worker or technician could find all the words he needed in the list devoted to his own specialty, but he seldom had more than a smattering of the words occurring in the other lists. Only a very few words were common to all lists, and there was no vocabulary expressing the function of Science as a habit of mind, or a method of thought, irrespective of its particular branches. There was, indeed, no word for "Science," any meaning that it could possibly bear being already sufficiently covered by the word *Ingsoc.*

From the foregoing account it will be seen that in Newspeak the expression of unorthodox opinions, above a very low level, was well-nigh impossible. It was of course possible to utter heresies of a very crude kind, a species of blasphemy. It would have been possible, for example, to say *Big Brother is ungood.* But this statement, which to an orthodox ear merely conveyed a self-evident absurdity, could not have been sustained by reasoned argument, because the necessary words were not available. Ideas inimical to Ingsoc could only be entertained in a vague wordless form, and could only be named in very broad terms which lumped together and condemned whole groups of heresies without defining them in doing so. One could, in fact, only use Newspeak for unorthodox purposes by illegitimately translating some of the words back into Oldspeak. For example, *All mans are equal* was a possible Newspeak sentence, but only in the same sense in which *All men are redhaired* is a possible Oldspeak sentence. It did not contain a grammatical error, but it expressed a palpable untruth, i.e., that all men are of equal size, weight, or strength. The concept of political equality no longer existed, and this secondary meaning had accordingly been purged out of the word *equal.* In 1984, when Oldspeak was still the normal means of communication, the danger theoretically existed that in using Newspeak words one might remember their original meanings. In practice it was not difficult for any person well grounded in *doublethink* to avoid doing this, but within a couple of generations even the possibility of such a lapse would have vanished. A person growing up with Newspeak as his sole language would no more know that *equal* had once had the secondary meaning of "politically equal," or that *free* had once meant "intellectually free," than, for instance, a person who had never heard of chess would be aware of the secondary meanings attaching to *queen* and *rook*. There would be many crimes and errors which it would be beyond his power to commit, simply because they were nameless and therefore unimaginable. And it was to be foreseen that with the passage of time the distinguishing characteristics of Newspeak would become more and more pronounced—its words growing fewer and fewer, their meanings more and more rigid, and the chance of putting them to improper uses always diminishing.

When Oldspeak had been once and for all superseded, the last link with the past would have been severed. History had already been rewritten, but fragments of the literature of the past survived here and there, imperfectly censored, and so long as one retained one's knowledge of Oldspeak it was possible to read them. In the future such fragments, even if they chanced to survive, would be unintelligible and untranslatable. It was impossible to translate any passage of Oldspeak into Newspeak unless it either referred to some technical process or some very simple everyday action, or was already orthodox (*goodthinkful* would be the Newspeak expression) in tendency. In practice this meant that no book written before approximately 1960 could be translated as a whole. Prerevolutionary literature could only be subjected to ideological translation—that is, alteration in sense as well as language. Take for example the well-known passage from the Declaration of Independence:

> We hold these truths to be self-evident, that all men are created equal, that they are endowed by their Creator with certain inalienable rights, that among these are life, liberty and the pursuit of happiness. That to secure these rights, Governments are instituted among men, deriving their powers from the consent of the governed. That whenever any form of Government becomes destructive of those ends, it is the right of the People to alter or abolish it, and to institute new Government...

It would have been quite impossible to render this into Newspeak while keeping to the sense of the original. The nearest one could come to doing so would be to swallow the whole passage up in the single word *crimethink*. A full translation could only be an ideological translation, whereby Jefferson's words would be changed into a panegyric on absolute government.

A good deal of the literature of the past was, indeed, already being transformed in this way. Considerations of prestige made it desirable to preserve the memory of certain historical figures, while at the same time bringing their achievements into line with the philosophy of Ingsoc. Various writers, such as Shakespeare, Milton, Swift, Byron,

Dickens and some others were therefore in process of translation; when the task had been completed, their original writings, with all else that survived of the literature of the past, would be destroyed. These translations were a slow and difficult business, and it was not expected that they would be finished before the first or second decade of the twenty-first century. There were also large quantities of merely utilitarian literature—indispensable technical manuals and the like—that had to be treated in the same way. It was chiefly in order to allow time for the preliminary work of translation that the final adoption of Newspeak had been fixed for so late a date as 2050.

QUESTIONS FOR STUDY, DISCUSSION, AND WRITING

1. What is the purpose of Newspeak? What assumptions about the nature and uses of language make it possible to try to accomplish that purpose?
2. Why are three vocabularies necessary in Newspeak? How do they differ and what do they have in common? Are there comparable divisions into "vocabularies" in present-day English?
3. In the A vocabulary what, if anything, is lost by such substitutions as "ungood" for "bad," "unlight" for "dark," etc.? Why are the forms for verb inflections and for comparison of adjectives all made consistent?
4. In the B vocabulary why are all the words compound words? Why are words telescoped as much as possible? How do the purposes represented by these two facts about the B vocabulary differ from the purposes of language as we know it?
5. Why is there no word for science in the C vocabulary, although it is described as consisting "entirely of scientific and technical terms"?
6. Find a brief passage (from the Album of Styles, pp. 141–153, or the section On Ethics) and translate it into Newspeak.
7. How would Francis (essay following) analyze Newspeak? How would he apply the classifications of form, function, and meaning? Would he make any judgments about Newspeak as a language?

W. NELSON FRANCIS
Revolution in Grammar[1]

A long overdue revolution is at present taking place in the study of English grammar—a revolution as sweeping in its consequences as the Darwinian revolution in biology. It is the result of the application to English of methods of descriptive analysis originally de-

1. Mr. Francis writes "I'd appreciate a brief note saying that 'Revolution in Grammar' was written in 1954 and that a great deal has happened in the linguistic field since."

veloped for use with languages of primitive people. To anyone at all interested in language, it is challenging; to those concerned with the teaching of English (including parents), it presents the necessity of radically revising both the substance and the methods of their teaching.

A curious paradox exists in regard to grammar. On the one hand it is felt to be the dullest and driest of academic subjects, fit only for those in whose veins the red blood of life has long since turned to ink. On the other, it is a subject upon which people who would scorn to be professional grammarians hold very dogmatic opinions, which they will defend with considerable emotion. Much of this prejudice stems from the usual sources of prejudice—ignorance and confusion. Even highly educated people seldom have a clear idea of what grammarians do, and there is an unfortunate confusion about the meaning of the term "grammar" itself.

Hence it would be well to begin with definitions. What do people mean when they use the word "grammar"? Actually the word is used to refer to three different things, and much of the emotional thinking about matters grammatical arises from confusion among these different meanings.

The first thing we mean by "grammar" is "the set of formal patterns in which the words of a language are arranged in order to convey larger meanings." It is not necessary that we be able to discuss these patterns self-consciously in order to be able to use them. In fact, all speakers of a language above the age of five or six know how to use its complex forms of organization with considerable skill; in this sense of the word—call it "Grammar 1"—they are thoroughly familiar with its grammar.

The second meaning of "grammar"—call it "Grammar 2"—is "the branch of linguistic science which is concerned with the description, analysis, and formulization of formal language patterns." Just as gravity was in full operation before Newton's apple fell, so grammar in the first sense was in full operation before anyone formulated the first rule that began the history of grammar as a study.

The third sense in which people use the word "grammar" is "linguistic etiquette." This we may call "Grammar 3." The word in this sense is often coupled with a derogatory adjective: we say that the expression "he ain't here" is "bad grammar." What we mean is that such an expression is bad linguistic manners in certain circles. From the point of view of "Grammar 1" it is faultless; it conforms just as completely to the structural patterns of English as does "he isn't here." The trouble with it is like the trouble with Prince Hal in Shakespeare's play[2]—it is "bad," not in itself, but in the company it keeps.

As has already been suggested, much confusion arises from mixing

2. *Henry IV, Part 1.*

these meanings. One hears a good deal of criticism of teachers of English couched in such terms as "they don't teach grammar any more." Criticism of this sort is based on the wholly unproved assumption that teaching Grammar 2 will increase the student's proficiency in Grammar 1 or improve his manners in Grammar 3. Actually, the form of Grammar 2 which is usually taught is a very inaccurate and misleading analysis of the facts of Grammar 1; and it therefore is of highly questionable value in improving a person's ability to handle the structural patterns of his language. It is hardly reasonable to expect that teaching a person some inaccurate grammatical analysis will either improve the effectiveness of his assertions or teach him what expressions are acceptable to use in a given social context.

These, then, are the three meanings of "grammar": Grammar 1, a form of behavior; Grammar 2, a field of study, a science; and Grammar 3, a branch of etiquette.

Grammarians have arrived at some basic principles of their science, three of which are fundamental to this discussion. The first is that a language constitutes a set of behavior patterns common to the members of a given community. It is a part of what the anthropologists call the culture of the community. Actually it has complex and intimate relationships with other phases of culture such as myth and ritual. But for purposes of study it may be dealt with as a separate set of phenomena that can be objectively described and analyzed like any other universe of facts. Specifically, its phenomena can be observed, recorded, classified, and compared; and general laws of their behavior can be made by the same inductive process that is used to produce the "laws" of physics, chemistry, and the other sciences.

A second important principle of linguistic science is that each language or dialect has its own unique system of behavior patterns. Parts of this system may show similarities to parts of the systems of other languages, particularly if those languages are genetically related. But different languages solve the problems of expression and communication in different ways, just as the problems of movement through water are solved in different ways by lobsters, fish, seals, and penguins. A couple of corollaries of this principle are important. The first is that there is no such thing as "universal grammar," or at least if there is, it is so general and abstract as to be of little use. The second corollary is that the grammar of each language must be made up on the basis of a study of that particular language——a study that is free from preconceived notions of what a language should contain and how it should operate. The marine biologist does not criticize the octopus for using jet-propulsion to get him through the water instead of the methods of a self-respecting fish. Neither does the linguistic scientist express alarm or distress when he finds a language that seems to get along quite well without any words that correspond to what in English we call verbs.

A third principle on which linguistic science is based is that the analysis and description of a given language must conform to the requirements laid down for any satisfactory scientific theory. These are (1) simplicity, (2) consistency, (3) completeness, and (4) usefulness for predicting the behavior of phenomena not brought under immediate observation when the theory was formed. Linguistic scientists who have recently turned their attention to English have found that, judged by these criteria, the traditional grammar of English is unsatisfactory. It falls down badly on the first two requirements, being unduly complex and glaringly inconsistent within itself. It can be made to work, just as the Ptolemaic earth-centered astronomy can be, but at the cost of great elaboration and complication. The new grammar, like the Copernican sun-centered astronomy, solves the same problems with greater elegance, which is the scientist's word for the simplicity, compactness, and tidiness that characterize a satisfactory theory.

A brief look at the history of the traditional grammar of English will make apparent the reasons for its inadequacy. The study of English grammar is actually an outgrowth of the linguistic interest of the Renaissance. It was during the later Middle Ages and early Renaissance that the various vernacular languages of Europe came into their own. They began to be used for many kinds of writing which had previously always been done in Latin. As the vernaculars, in the hands of great writers like Dante and Chaucer, came of age as members of the linguistic family, a concomitant interest in their grammars arose. The earliest important English grammar was written by Shakespeare's contemporary, Ben Jonson.

It is important to observe that not only Ben Jonson himself but also those who followed him in the study of English grammar were men deeply learned in Latin and sometimes in Greek. For all their interest in English, they were conditioned from earliest school days to conceive of the classical languages as superior to the vernaculars. We still sometimes call the elementary school the "grammar school"; historically the term means the school where Latin grammar was taught. By the time the Renaissance or eighteenth-century scholar took his university degree, he was accustomed to use Latin as the normal means of communication with his fellow scholars. Dr. Samuel Johnson, for instance, who had only three years at the university and did not take a degree, wrote poetry in both Latin and Greek. Hence it was natural for these men to take Latin grammar as the norm, and to analyze English in terms of Latin. The grammarians of the seventeenth and eighteenth centuries who formulated the traditional grammar of English looked for the devices and distinctions of Latin grammar in English, and where they did not actually find them they imagined or created them. Of course, since English is a member of the Indo-European family of languages, to which Latin and Greek also belong, it did have many grammatical elements in common with them. But many of these had been obscured or wholly lost as a result of the extensive changes that had taken place in English—changes that the early grammarians inevitably conceived of as degeneration. They felt that it was their function to resist further change, if not to repair the damage already done. So preoccupied were they with the grammar of Latin as the ideal that they overlooked in large part the exceedingly complex and delicate system that English had substituted for the Indo-European grammar it had abandoned. Instead they stretched unhappy English on the Procrustean bed of Latin. It is no wonder that we commonly hear people say, "I didn't really understand grammar until I began to study Latin." This is eloquent testimony to the fact that the grammar "rules" of our present-day textbooks are largely an inheritance from the Latin-based grammar of the eighteenth century.

Meanwhile the extension of linguistic study beyond the Indo-European and Semitic families began to reveal that there are many different ways in which linguistic phenomena are organized—in other words, many different kinds of grammar. The tone-languages of the Orient and of North America, and the complex agglutinative languages of Africa, among others, forced grammarians to abandon the idea of a universal or ideal grammar and to direct their attention more closely to the individual systems employed by the multifarious languages of mankind. With the growth and refinement of the scientific method and its application to the field of anthropology, language came under more rigorous scientific scrutiny. As with anthropology in general, linguistic science at first concerned itself with the primitive. Finally, again following the lead of anthropology, linguistics began to apply its techniques to the old familiar tongues, among them English. Accelerated by the practical need during World War II of teaching languages, including English, to large numbers in a short time, research into the nature of English grammar has moved rapidly in the last fifteen years. The definitive grammar of English is yet to be written, but the results so far achieved are spectacular. It is now as unrealistic to teach "traditional" grammar of English as it is to teach "traditional" (i.e. pre-Darwinian) biology or "traditional" (i.e. four-element) chemistry. Yet nearly all certified teachers of English on all levels are doing so. Here is a cultural lag of major proportions.

Before we can proceed to a sketch of what the new grammar of English looks like, we must take account of a few more of the premises of linguistic science. They must be understood and accepted by anyone who wishes to understand the new grammar.

First, the spoken language is primary, at least for the original study of a language. In many of the primitive languages,[3] of course, where writing is unknown, the spoken language is the *only* form. This is in many ways an advantage to the linguist, because the written language may use conventions that obscure its basic structure. The reason for the primary importance of the spoken language is that language originates as speech, and most of the changes and innovations that occur in the history of a given language begin in the spoken tongue.

Secondly, we must take account of the concept of dialect. I suppose most laymen would define a dialect as "a corrupt form of a language spoken in a given region by people who don't know any better." This introduces moral judgments which are repulsive to the linguistic scholar. Let us approach the definition of a dialect from the more objective end, through the notion of a speech community. A speech community is merely a group of people who are in pretty constant intercommunication. There are various types of speech communities: local ones, like "the people who live in Tidewater Virginia"; class ones, like "the white-collar class"; occupational ones, like "doctors, nurses, and other people who work in hospitals"; social ones, like "clubwomen." In a sense, each of these has its own dialect. Each family may be said to have its own dialect; in fact, in so far as each of us has his own vocabulary and particular quirks of speech, each individual has his own dialect. Also, of course, in so far as he is a member of many speech communities, each individual is more or less master of many dialects and shifts easily and almost unconsciously from one to another as he shifts from one social environment to another.

In the light of this concept of dialects, a language can be defined as a group of dialects which have enough of their sound-system, vocabulary and grammar (Grammar 1, that is) in common to permit their speakers to be mutually intelligible in the ordinary affairs of life. It usually happens that one of the many dialects that make up a language comes to have more prestige than the others; in modern times it has usually been the dialect of the middle-class residents of the capital, like Parisian French and London English, which is so distinguished. This comes to be thought of as the standard dialect; in fact, its speakers become snobbish and succeed in establishing the belief that it is not a dialect at all, but the only proper form of the language. This causes the speakers of other dialects to become self-conscious and ashamed of their speech, or else aggressive and jingoistic about it—either of which is an acknowledgment of their feelings of inferiority. Thus one of the duties of the educational system

---

3. "Primitive languages" here is really an abbreviated statement for "languages used by peoples of relatively primitive culture"; it is not to be taken as implying anything simple or rudimentary about the languages themselves. Many languages included under the term, such as native languages of Africa and Mexico, exhibit grammatical complexities unknown to more "civilized" languages [Francis' note].

comes to be that of teaching the standard dialect to all so as to relieve them of feelings of inferiority, and thus relieve society of linguistic neurotics. This is where Grammar 3, linguistic etiquette, comes into the picture.

A third premise arising from the two just discussed is that the difference between the way educated people talk and the way they write is a dialectal difference. The spread between these two dialects may be very narrow, as in present-day America, or very wide, as in Norway, where people often speak local Norwegian dialects but write in the Dano-Norwegian *Riksmaal*. The extreme is the use of writers of an entirely different language, or at least an ancient and no longer spoken form of the language—like Sanskrit in northern India or Latin in western Europe during the Middle Ages. A corollary of this premise is that anyone setting out to write a grammar must know and make clear whether he is dealing with the spoken or the written dialect. Virtually all current English grammars deal with the written language only; evidence for this is that their rules for the plurals of nouns, for instance, are really spelling rules, which say nothing about pronunciation.

This is not the place to go into any sort of detail about the methods of analysis the linguistic scientist uses. Suffice it to say that he begins by breaking up the flow of speech into minimum sound-units, or phones, which he then groups into families called phonemes, the minimum significant sound-units. Most languages have from twenty to sixty of these. American English has forty-one: nine vowels, twenty-four consonants, four degrees of stress, and four levels of pitch. These phonemes group themselves into minimum meaningful units, called morphemes. These fall into two groups: free morphemes, those that can enter freely into many combinations with other free morphemes to make phrases and sentences; and bound morphemes, which are always found tied in a close and often indissoluble relationship with other bound or free morphemes. An example of a free morpheme is "dog"; an example of a bound morpheme is "un-" or "ex-." The linguist usually avoids talking about "words" because the term is very inexact. Is "instead of," for instance, to be considered one, two, or three words? This is purely a matter of opinion; but it is a matter of fact that it is made up of three morphemes.

In any case, our analysis has now brought the linguist to the point where he has some notion of the word-stock (he would call it the "lexicon") of his language. He must then go into the question of how the morphemes are grouped into meaningful utterances, which is the field of grammar proper. At this point in the analysis of English, as of many other languages, it becomes apparent that there are three bases upon which classification and analysis may be built: form, function, and meaning. For illustration let us take the word "boys" in the utterance "the boys are here." From the point of view of form, "boys" is a noun with the plural ending "s" (pronounced like "z"), preceded by the noun-determiner "the," and tied by concord to the verb "are," which it precedes. From the point of view of function, "boys" is the subject of the verb "are" and of the sentence. From the point of view of meaning, "boys" points out or names more than one of the male young of the human species, about whom an assertion is being made.

Of these three bases of classification, the one most amenable to objective description and analysis of a rigorously scientific sort is form. In fact, many conclusions about form can be drawn by a person unable to understand or speak the language. Next comes function. But except as it is revealed by form, function is dependent on knowing the meaning. In a telegraphic sentence like "ship sails today"[4] no one can say whether "ship" is the subject of "sails" or an imperative verb with "sails" as its object until he knows what the sentence means. Most shaky of all bases for grammatical analysis is meaning. Attempts have been made to reduce the phenomena of meaning to objective description, but so far they have not succeeded very well. Meaning is such a subjective quality that it is usually omitted entirely from scientific description. The botanist can describe the forms of plants and the functions of their various parts, but he refuses to concern himself with their meaning. It is left to the poet to find symbolic meaning in roses, violets, and lilies.

At this point it is interesting to note that the traditional grammar of English bases some of its key concepts and definitions on this very subjective and shaky foundation of meaning. A recent English grammar defines a sentence as "a group of words which expresses a complete thought through the use of a verb, called its predicate, and a subject, consisting of a noun or pronoun about which the verb has something to say."[5] But what is a complete thought? Actually we do not identify sentences this way at all. If someone says, "I don't know what to do," dropping his voice at the end, and pauses, the hearer will know that it is quite safe for him to make a comment without running the risk of interrupting an unfinished sentence. But if the speaker says the same words and maintains a level pitch at the end, the polite listener will wait for him to finish his sentence. The words are the same, the meaning is the same; the only difference is a slight one in the pitch of the final syllable—a purely formal distinction, which signals that the first utterance is complete, a sentence, while the second is incomplete. In writing we would translate these signals into punctuation: a period or exclamation point at the end of the first, a

4. This example is taken from C. C. Fries, *The Structure of English* (New York, 1952), p. 62. This important book will be discussed below [Francis' note].

5. Ralph B. Allen, *English Grammar* (New York, 1950), p. 187 [Francis' note].

comma or dash at the end of the second. It is the form of the utterance, not the completeness of the thought, that tells us whether it is a whole sentence or only part of one.

Another favorite definition of the traditional grammar, also based on meaning, is that of "noun" as "the name of a person, place, or thing"; or, as the grammar just quoted has it, "the name of anybody or anything, with or without life, and with or without substance or form."[6] Yet we identify nouns, not by asking if they name something, but by their positions in expressions and by the formal marks they carry. In the sentence, "The slithy toves did gyre and gimble in the wabe," any speaker of English knows that "toves" and "wabe" are nouns, though he cannot tell what they name, if indeed they name anything. How does he know? Actually because they have certain formal marks, like their position in relation to "the" as well as the whole arrangement of the sentence. We know from our practical knowledge of English grammar (Grammar 1), which we have had since before we went to school, that if we were to put meaningful words into this sentence, we would have to put nouns in place of "toves" and "wabe," giving something like "The slithy snakes did gyre and gimble in the wood." The pattern of the sentence simply will not allow us to say "The slithy arounds did gyre and gimble in the wooden."

One trouble with the traditional grammar, then, is that it relies heavily on the most subjective element in language, meaning. Another is that it shifts the ground of its classification and produces the elementary logical error of cross-division. A zoologist who divided animals into invertebrates, mammals, and beasts of burden would not get very far before running into trouble. Yet the traditional grammar is guilty of the same error when it defines three parts of speech on the basis of meaning (noun, verb, and interjection), four more on the basis of function (adjective, adverb, pronoun, conjunction), and one partly on function and partly on form (preposition). The result is that in such an expression as "a dog's life" there can be endless futile argument about whether "dog's" is a noun or an adjective. It is, of course, a noun from the point of view of form and an adjective from the point of view of function, and hence falls into both classes, just as a horse is both a mammal and a beast of burden. No wonder students are bewildered in their attempts to master the traditional grammar. Their natural clearness of mind tells them that it is a crazy patchwork violating the elementary principles of logical thought.

If the traditional grammar is so bad, what does the new grammar offer in its place?

It offers a description, analysis, and set of definitions and formulas —rules, if you will—based firmly and consistently on the easiest, or at least the most objective, aspect of language, form. Experts can

6. *Ibid.*, p. 1 [Francis' note].

quibble over whether "dog's" in "a dog's life" is a noun or an adjective, but anyone can see that it is spelled with "'s" and hear that it ends with a "z" sound; likewise anyone can tell that it comes in the middle between "a" and "life." Furthermore he can tell that something important has happened if the expression is changed to "the dog's alive," "the live dogs," or "the dogs lived," even if he doesn't know what the words mean and has never heard of such functions as modifier, subject, or attributive genitive. He cannot, of course, get very far into his analysis without either a knowledge of the language or access to someone with such knowledge. He will also need a minimum technical vocabulary describing grammatical functions. Just so the anatomist is better off for knowing physiology. But the grammarian, like the anatomist, must beware of allowing his preconceived notions to lead him into the error of interpreting before he describes —an error which often results in his finding only what he is looking for.

When the grammarian looks at English objectively, he finds that it conveys its meanings by two broad devices: the denotations and connotations of words separately considered, which the linguist calls "lexical meaning," and the significance of word-forms, word-groups, and arrangements apart from the lexical meanings of the words, which the linguist calls "structural meaning." The first of these is the domain of the lexicographer and the semanticist, and hence is not our present concern. The second, the structural meaning, is the business of the structural linguist, or grammarian. The importance of this second kind of meaning must be emphasized because it is often overlooked. The man in the street tends to think of the meaning of a sentence as being the aggregate of the dictionary meanings of the words that make it up; hence the widespread fallacy of literal translation—the feeling that if you take a French sentence and a French-English dictionary and write down the English equivalent of each French word you will come out with an intelligible English sentence. How ludicrous the results can be, anyone knows who is familiar with Mark Twain's retranslation from the French of his jumping frog story. One sentence reads, "Eh bien! I no saw not that that frog has nothing of better than each frog." Upon which Mark's comment is, 'if that isn't grammar gone to seed, then I count myself no judge."[7]

The second point brought out by a formal analysis of English is that it uses four principal devices of form to signal structural meanings:

1. Word order—the sequence in which words and word-groups are arranged.

7. Mark Twain, "The Jumping Frog; the Original Story in English; the Re-translation Clawed Back from the French, into a Civilized Language Once More, by Patient and Unremunerated Toil," *1601 . . . and Sketches Old and New (n.p., 1933), p. 50 [Francis' note].

2. Function-words—words devoid of lexical meaning which indicate relationships among the meaningful words with which they appear.

3. Inflections—alterations in the forms of words themselves to signal changes in meaning and relationship.

4. Formal contrasts—contrasts in the forms of words signaling greater differences in function and meaning. These could also be considered inflections, but it is more convenient for both the lexicographer and the grammarian to consider them separately.

Usually several of these are present in any utterance, but they can be separately illustrated by means of contrasting expressions involving minimum variation—the kind of controlled experiment used in the scientific laboratory.

To illustrate the structural meaning of word order, let us compare the two sentences "man bites dog" and "dog bites man." The words are identical in lexical meaning and in form; the only difference is in sequence. It is interesting to note that Latin expresses the difference between these two by changes in the form of the words, without necessarily altering the order: "homo canem mordet" or "hominem canis mordet." Latin grammar is worse than useless in understanding this point of English grammar.

Next, compare the sentences "the dog is the friend of man" and "any dog is a friend of that man." Here the words having lexical meaning are "dog," "is," "friend," and "man," which appear in the same form and the same order in both sentences. The formal differences between them are in the substitution of "any" and "a" for "the," and in the insertion of "that." These little words are function-words; they make quite a difference in the meanings of the two sentences, though it is virtually impossible to say what they mean in isolation.

Third, compare the sentences "the dog loves the man" and "the dogs loved the men." Here the words are the same, in the same order, with the same function-words in the same positions. But the forms of the three words having lexical meanings have been changed: "dog" to "dogs," "loves" to "loved," and "man" to "men." These changes are inflections. English has very few of them as compared with Greek, Latin, Russian, or even German. But it still uses them; about one word in four in an ordinary English sentence is inflected.

Fourth, consider the difference between "the dog's friend arrived" and "the dog's friendly arrival." Here the difference lies in the change of "friend" to "friendly," a formal alteration signaling a change of function from subject to modifier, and the change of "arrived" to "arrival," signaling a change of function from predicate to head-word in a noun-modifier group. These changes are of the same formal nature as inflections, but because they produce words of different lexical meaning, classifiable as different parts of speech, it is better to call them formal contrasts than inflections. In other words, it is logically quite defensible to consider "love," "loving," and "loved" as the same word in differing aspects and to consider "friend," "friendly," "friendliness," "friendship," and "befriend" as different words related by formal and semantic similarities. But this is only a matter of convenience of analysis, which permits a more accurate description of English structure. In another language we might find that this kind of distinction is unnecessary but that some other distinction, unnecessary in English, is required. The categories of grammatical description are not sacrosanct; they are as much a part of man's organization of his observations as they are of the nature of things.

If we are considering the spoken variety of English, we must add a fifth device for indicating structural meaning—the various musical and rhythmic patterns which the linguist classifies under juncture, stress, and intonation. Consider the following pair of sentences:

> Alfred, the alligator is sick.
> Alfred the alligator is sick.

These are identical in the four respects discussed above—word order, function-words, inflections, and word-form. Yet they have markedly different meanings, as would be revealed by the intonation if they were spoken aloud. These differences in intonation are to a certain extent indicated in the written language by punctuation —that is, in fact, the primary function of punctuation.

The examples so far given were chosen to illustrate in isolation the various kinds of structural devices in English grammar. Much more commonly the structural meaning of a given sentence is indicated by a combination of two or more of these devices: a sort of margin of safety which permits some of the devices to be missed or done away with without obscuring the structural meaning of the sentence, as indeed anyone knows who has ever written a telegram or a newspaper headline. On the other hand, sentences which do not have enough of these formal devices are inevitably ambiguous. Take the example already given, Fries's "ship sails today." This is ambiguous because there is nothing to indicate which of the first two words is performing a noun function and which a verb function. If we mark the noun by putting the noun-determining function-word "the" in front of it, the ambiguity disappears; we have either "the ship sails today" or "ship the sails today." The ambiguity could just as well be resolved by using other devices: consider "ship sailed today," "ship to sail today," "ship sail today," "shipping sails today," "shipment of sails today," and so on. It is simply a question of having enough formal devices in the sentence to indicate its structural meaning clearly.

How powerful the structural meanings of English are is illustrated by so-called "nonsense." In English, nonsense as a literary form often consists of utterances that have a clear structural meaning but use words that either have no lexical meanings, or whose lexical meanings are inconsistent one with another. This will become apparent if we subject a rather famous bit of English nonsense to formal grammatical analysis:

> All mimsy were the borogoves
> And the mome raths outgrabe.

This passage consists of ten words, five of them words that should have lexical meanings but don't, one standard verb, and four function-words. In so far as it is possible to indicate its abstract structure, it would be this:

> All ...y were the ..... s
> And the .... s ....

Although this is a relatively simple formal organization, it signals some rather complicated meanings. The first thing we observe is that the first line presents a conflict: word order seems to signal one thing, and inflections and function-words something else. Specifically, "mimsy" is in the position normally occupied by the subject, but we know that it is not the subject and that "borogoves" is. We know this because there is an inflectional tie between the form "were" and the "s" ending of "borogoves," because there is the noun-determiner "the" before it, and because the alternative candidate for subject "mimsy," lacks both of these. It is true that "mimsy" does have the function-word "all" before it, which may indicate a noun; but when it does, the noun is either plural (in which case "mimsy" would most likely end in "s"), or else the noun is what grammarians call a mass-word (like "sugar," "coal," "snow"), in which case the verb would have to be "was," not "were." All these formal considerations are sufficient to counteract the effect of word order and show that the sentence is of the type that may be represented thus:

> All gloomy were the Democrats.

Actually there is one other possibility. If "mimsy" belongs to the small group of nouns which don't use "s" to make the plural, and if "borogoves" has been so implied (but not specifically mentioned) in the context as to justify its appearing with the determiner "the," the sentence would then belong to the following type:

> (In the campaign for funds) all alumni were the canvassers.
> (In the drought last summer) all cattle were the sufferers.

But the odds are so much against this that most of us would be prepared to fight for our belief that "borogoves" are things that can be named, and that at the time referred to they were in a complete state of "mimsyness."

Moving on to the second line, "And the mome raths outgrabe," the first thing we note is that the "And" signals another parallel assertion to follow. We are thus prepared to recognize from the noun-determiner "the," the plural inflection "s," and the particular positions of "mome" and "outgrabe," as well as the continuing influence of the "were" of the preceding line, that we are dealing with a sentence of this pattern:

> And the lone rats agreed.

The influence of the "were" is particularly important here; it guides us in selecting among several interpretations of the sentence. Specifically, it requires us to identify "outgrabe" as a verb in the past tense, and thus a "strong" or "irregular" verb, since it lacks the characteristic past-tense ending "d" or "ed." We do this in spite of the fact that there is another strong candidate for the position of verb: that is, "raths," which bears a regular verb inflection and could be tied with "mome" as its subject in the normal noun-verb relationship. In such a case we should have to recognize "outgrabe" as either an adverb of the kind not marked by the form-contrast "ly," an adjective, or the past participle of a strong verb. The sentence would then belong to one of the following types:

> And the moon shines above.
> And the man stays aloof.
> And the fool seems outdone.

But we reject all of these—probably they don't even occur to us—because they all have verbs in the present tense, whereas the "were" of the first line combines with the "And" at the beginning of the second to set the whole in the past.

We might recognize one further possibility for the structural meaning of this second line, particularly in the verse context, since we are used to certain patterns in verse that do not often appear in speech of prose. The "were" of the first line could be understood as doing double duty, its ghost or echo appearing between "raths" and "outgrabe." Then we would have something like this:

> All gloomy were the Democrats
> And the home folks outraged.

But again the odds are pretty heavy against this. I for one am so sure that "outgrabe" is the past tense of a strong verb that I can give its present. In my dialect, at least, it is "outgribe."

The reader may not realize it, but in the last four paragraphs I have been discussing grammar from a purely formal point of view. I have not once called a word a noun because it names something (that is, I have not once resorted to meaning), nor have I called any word an adjective because it modifies a noun (that is, resorted to function). Instead I have been working in the opposite direction, from form toward function and meaning. I have used only criteria which are objectively observable, and I have assumed only a working knowledge of certain structural patterns and devices known to all speakers of English over the age of six. I did use some technical terms like "noun," "verb," and "tense," but only to save time; I could have got along without them.

If one clears his mind of the inconsistencies of the traditional grammar (not so easy a process as it might be), he can proceed with a similarly rigorous formal analysis of a sufficient number of representative utterances in English and come out with a descriptive grammar. This is just what Professor Fries did in gathering and studying the material for the analysis he presents in the remarkable book to which I have already referred, *The Structure of English*. What he actually did was to put a tape recorder into action and record about fifty hours of telephone conversation among the good citizens of Ann Arbor, Michigan. When this material was transcribed, it constituted about a quarter of a million words of perfectly natural speech by educated middle-class Americans. The details of his conclusions cannot be presented here, but they are sufficiently different from the usual grammar to be revolutionary. For instance, he recognizes only four parts of speech among the words with lexical meaning, roughly corresponding to what the traditional grammar calls substantives, verbs, adjectives and adverbs, though to avoid preconceived notions from the traditional grammar Fries calls them Class 1, Class 2, Class 3, and Class 4 words. To these he adds a relatively small group of function-words, 154 in his materials, which he divides into fifteen groups. These must be memorized by anyone learning the language; they are not subject to the same kind of general rules that govern the four parts of speech. Undoubtedly his conclusions will be developed and modified by himself and by other linguistic scholars, but for the present his book remains the most complete treatment extant of English grammar from the point of view of linguistic science.

Two vital questions are raised by this revolution in grammar. The first is, "What is the value of this new system?" In the minds of many who ask it, the implication of this question is, "We have been getting along all these years with traditional grammar, so it can't be so very bad. Why should we go through the painful process of unlearning and relearning grammar just because linguistic scientists have concocted some new theories?"

The first answer to this question is the bravest and most honest. It is that the superseding of vague and sloppy thinking by clear and precise thinking is an exciting experience in and for itself. To acquire insight into the workings of a language, and to recognize the infinitely delicate system of relationship, balance, and interplay that constitutes its grammar, is to become closely acquainted with one of man's most miraculous creations, not unworthy to be set beside the equally beautiful organization of the physical universe. And to find that its most complex effects are produced by the multi-layered organization of relatively simple materials is to bring our thinking about language into accord with modern thought in other fields, which is more and more coming to emphasize the importance of organization —the fact that an organized whole is truly greater than the sum of all its parts.

There are other answers, more practical if less philosophically valid. It is too early to tell, but it seems probable that a realisitic, scientific grammar should vastly facilitate the teaching of English, especially as a foreign language. Already results are showing here; it has been found that if intonation contours and other structural patterns are taught quite early, the student has a confidence that allows him to attempt to speak the language much sooner than he otherwise would.

The new grammar can also be of use in improving the native speaker's proficiency in handling the structural devices of his own language. In other words, Grammar 2, if it is accurate and consistent, can be of use in improving skill in Grammar 1. An illustration is that famous bugaboo, the dangling participle. Consider a specific instance of it, which once appeared on a college freshman's theme, to the mingled delight and despair of the instructor:

> Having eaten our lunch, the steamboat departed.

What is the trouble with this sentence? Clearly there must be something wrong with it, because it makes people laugh, although it was not the intent of the writer to make them laugh. In other words, it produces a completely wrong response, resulting in total breakdown of communication. It is, in fact, "bad grammar" in a much more serious way than are mere dialectal divergences like "he ain't here" or "he never seen none," which produce social reactions but communicate effectively. In the light of the new grammar, the trouble with our dangling participle is that the form, instead of leading to the meaning, is in conflict with it. Into the position which, in this pattern, is reserved for the word naming the eater of the lunch, the writer has inserted the word "steamboat." The resulting tug-of-war between form and meaning is only momentary; meaning quickly wins out, simply because our common sense tells us that steamboats don't eat lunches. But if the pull of the lexical meaning is not given a good deal of help from common sense, the form will conquer the meaning, or the two will remain in ambiguous equilibrium—as, for instance, in "Having eaten our lunch, the passengers boarded the steamboat." Writers will find it easier to avoid such troubles if they know about the forms of English and are taught to use the form to convey the meaning, instead of setting up tensions between form and meaning. This, of course, is what English teachers are already trying to do. The new grammar should be a better weapon in their arsenal than the traditional grammar since it is based on a clear understanding of the realities.

The second and more difficult question is, "How can the change from one grammar to the other be effected?" Here we face obstacles of a formidable nature. When we remember the controversies attending on revolutionary changes in biology and astronomy, we realize what a tenacious hold the race can maintain on anything it has once learned, and the resistance it can offer to new ideas. And remember that neither astronomy nor biology was taught in elementary schools. They were, in fact, rather specialized subjects in advanced education. How then change grammar, which is taught to everybody, from the fifth grade up through college? The vested interest represented by thousands upon thousands of English and Speech teachers who have learned the traditional grammar and taught it for many years is a conservative force comparable to those which keep us still using the chaotic system of English spelling and the unwieldy measuring system of inches and feet, pounds and ounces, quarts, bushels, and acres. Moreover, this army is constantly receiving new recruits. It is possible in my state to become certified to teach English in high school if one has had eighteen credit hours of college English—let us say two semesters of freshman composition (almost all of which is taught by people unfamiliar with the new grammar), two semesters of a survey course in English literature, one semester of Shakespeare, and one semester of the contemporary novel. And since hard-pressed school administrators feel that anyone who can speak English can in a pinch teach it, the result is that many people are called upon to teach grammar whose knowledge of the subject is totally inadequate.

There is, in other words, a battle ahead of the new grammar. It will have to fight not only the apathy of the general public but the ignorance and inertia of those who count themselves competent in the field of grammar. The battle is already on, in fact. Those who try to get the concepts of the new grammar introduced into the curriculum are tagged as "liberal" grammarians—the implication being, I suppose, that one has a free choice between "liberal" and "conservative" grammar, and that the liberals are a bit dangerous, perhaps even a touch subversive. They are accused of undermining standards, of holding that "any way of saying something is just as good as any other," of not teaching the fundamentals of good English. I trust that the readers of this article will see how unfounded these charges are. But the smear campaign is on. So far as I know, neither religion nor patriotism has yet been brought into it. When they are, Professor Fries will have to say to Socrates, Galileo, Darwin, Freud, and the other members of the honorable fraternity of the misunderstood, "Move over, gentlemen, and make room for me."

SAMUEL L. CLEMENS
Jim Baker on Bluejays[1]

Animals talk to each other, of course. There can be no question about that, but I suppose there are very few people who can understand them. I never knew but one man who could. I knew he could, however, because he told me so himself. He was a middle-aged, simple-hearted miner who had lived in a lonely corner of California among the woods and mountains a good many years, and had studied the ways of his only neighbors, the beasts and the birds, until he believed he could accurately translate any remark which they made. This was Jim Baker. According to Jim Baker, some animals have only a limited education and use only very simple words, and scarcely ever a comparison or a flowery figure; whereas certain other animals have a large vocabulary, a fine command of language and a ready and fluent delivery; consequently these latter talk a great deal; they like it, they are conscious of their talent, and they enjoy "showing off." Baker said that after long and careful observation, he had come to the conclusion that the bluejays were the best talkers he had found among the birds and beasts. Said he: "There's more *to* a bluejay than any other creature. He has got more moods, and more different kinds of feelings than other creatures; and, mind you, whatever a bluejay feels, he can put into language. And no mere commonplace language, either, but rattling, out-and-out booktalk—and bristling with metaphor too—just bristling! And as for command of language—why *you* never see a bluejay get stuck for a word. No man ever did. They just boil out of him! And another thing: I've noticed a good deal and there's no bird, or cow, or anything that uses as good grammar as a bluejay. You may say a cat uses good grammar. Well, a cat does—but you let a cat get excited once; you let a cat get to pulling fur with another cat on a shed, nights, and you'll hear grammar that will give you the lockjaw. Ignorant people think it's the *noise* which fighting cats make that is so aggravating but it ain't so; it's the sickening grammar they use. Now I've never heard a jay use bad grammar but very seldom, and when they do, they are as ashamed as a human, they shut right down and leave.

"You may call a jay a bird. Well, so he is, in a measure—because he's got feathers on him, and don't belong to no church, perhaps,

1. From *A Tramp Abroad* (1879), Volume I, Chapter 2.

but otherwise he is just as much a human as you be. And I'll tell
you for why. A jay's gifts and instincts and feelings and interests
cover the whole ground. A jay hasn't got any more principle than a
Congressman. A jay will lie, a jay will steal, a jay will deceive, a jay
will betray; and four times out of five, a jay will go back on his
solemnest promise. The sacredness of an obligation is a thing which
you can't cram into no bluejay's head. Now on top of all this there's
another thing, a jay can outswear any gentleman in the mines. You
think a cat can swear. Well, a cat can, but you give a bluejay a subject that calls for his reserve-powers and where is your cat? Don't
talk to *me*—I know too much about this thing. And there's yet
another thing, in the one little particular of scolding—just good,
clean, out-and-out scolding—a bluejay can lay over anything, human
or divine. Yes, sir, a jay is everything that a man is. A jay can cry, a
jay can laugh, a jay can feel shame, a jay can reason and plan and
discuss, a jay likes gossip and scandal, a jay has got a sense of humor,
a jay knows when he is an ass just as well as you do—maybe better.
If a jay ain't human, he better take in his sign, that's all."

QUESTIONS FOR STUDY, DISCUSSION, AND WRITING

1. On page 107 Francis says that the difference between the "old"
   grammar and the "new" is like the difference between Ptolemaic
   and Copernican astronomy. Earlier he has compared the revolution in grammar to the Darwinian revolution in biology. What do
   these analogies contribute to his main idea? What other analogies
   of this kind do you find elsewhere in the essay? What do you make
   of the fact that Francis uses so many analogies from natural and
   physical science?
2. How are form, function, and meaning important to each of the
   three grammars?
3. On page 111 Francis implies a comparison between the botanist
   and the ideal student of language when he says, "The botanist can
   describe the forms of plants and the functions of their various
   parts, but he refuses to concern himself with their meaning. It is
   left to the poet to find symbolic meaning in roses, violets, and
   lilies." What is the point of this comment? How exact is the
   comparison he suggests?
4. Read the passage from a story by Clemens.
   a. Which things would you not say in your dialect? If you
      rewrote the passage as you would speak it, what kinds of
      changes would you make?
   b. Which of Francis' three grammars does the speaker's implied
      definition most closely resemble?
   c. Comment on the passage, or portions of it, from the point of
      view of each of Francis' three grammars.
5. Compare Francis' view of grammar with that implied by Miss
   Stein (p. 86–89). What part of Francis' discussion would Miss
   Stein be most interested in? Explain.

6. Francis says that the linguist uses speech rather than writing as the basis for his analysis. Record some of your conversation on a particular subject (either with a tape recorder or in a notebook). Then write a short essay on the same subject, treating it as a "composition assignment." What differences can you discover between speech and writing? Which characteristics of speech can profitably be transferred to writing? Are there any which can not?
7. Francis suggests some ways in which tone of voice, intonation, pauses, and so forth can be approximated in writing. See how accurately you can record a conversation in written form. What devices can you use to achieve some of the effects of speech?
8. Analyze the following nonsense passage, using Francis' analysis of "Jabberwocky" as a model: "I lon the isc blely at frush, gribbling in the mornsy drib. I dobbed my tib, and he, unabit to humses, lagged it bobbily. I grid him in with musy nattle lud and balgered him for monry."

WAYNE C. BOOTH

Boring from Within: The Art of the Freshman Essay[1]

Last week I had for about the hundredth time an experience that always disturbs me. Riding on a train, I found myself talking with my seat-mate, who asked me what I did for a living. "I teach English." Do you have any trouble predicting his response? His face fell, and he groaned, "Oh, dear, I'll have to watch my language." In my experience there are only two other possible reactions. The first is even less inspiriting: "I hated English in school; it was my worst subject." The second, so rare as to make an honest English teacher almost burst into tears of gratitude when it occurs, is an animated conversation about literature, or ideas, or the American language— the kind of conversation that shows a continuing respect for "English" as something more than being sure about who and whom, lie and lay.

Unless the people you meet are a good deal more tactful or better liars than the ones I meet, you've had the two less favorable experiences many times. And it takes no master analyst to figure out why so many of our fellow citizens think of us as unfriendly policemen: it is because too many of us have seen ourselves as unfriendly policemen. I know of a high school English class in Indiana in which the students are explicitly told that their paper grades will not be affected by anything they say; required to write a paper a week, they are graded simply on the number of spelling and grammatical errors. What is more, they are given a standard form for their papers: each

1. Adapted by Mr. Booth from a speech delivered in May 1963 to the Illinois Council of College Teachers of English.

paper is to have three paragraphs, a beginning, a middle, and an end —or is it an introduction, a body, and a conclusion? The theory seems to be that if the student is not troubled about having to say anything, or about discovering a good way of saying it, he can then concentrate on the truly important matter of avoiding mistakes.

What's wrong with such assignments? What's wrong with getting the problem of correctness focused sharply enough so that we can really work on it? After all, we do have the job of teaching correct English, don't we? We can't possibly teach our hordes of students to be colorful writers, but by golly, we can beat the bad grammar out of them. Leaving aside the obvious fact that we *can't* beat the bad grammar out of them, not by direct assault, let's think a bit about what that kind of assignment does to the poor teacher who gives it. Those papers must be read, by someone, and unless the teacher has more trained assistance than you and I have, *she's* the victim. She can't help being bored silly by her own paper-reading, and we all know what an evening of being bored by a class's papers does to our attitude toward that class the next day. The old formula of John Dewey was that any teaching that bores the student is likely to fail. The formula was subject to abuse, quite obviously, since interest in itself is only one of many tests of adequate teaching. A safer formula, though perhaps also subject to abuse, might be: Any teaching that bores the teacher is sure to fail. And I am haunted by the picture of that poor woman in Indiana, week after week reading batches of papers written by students who have been told that nothing they say can possibly affect her opinion of those papers. Could any hell imagined by Dante or Jean-Paul Sartre match this self-inflicted futility?

I call it self-inflicted, as if it were a simple matter to avoid receiving papers that bore us. But unfortunately it is not. It may be a simple matter to avoid the *total* meaninglessness that the students must give that Indiana teacher, but we all know that it is no easy matter to produce interesting papers; our pet cures for boredom never work as well as they ought to. Every beginning teacher learns quickly and painfully that nothing works with all students, and that on bad days even the most promising ideas work with nobody.

As I try to sort out the various possible cures for those batches of boredom—in ink, double-spaced, on one side of the sheet, only, please —I find them falling into three groups: efforts to give the students a sharper sense of writing to an audience, efforts to give them some substance to express, and efforts to improve their habits of observation and of approach to their task—what might be called improving their mental personalities.

This classification, both obvious and unoriginal, is a useful one not only because it covers—at least I hope it does—all of our efforts to improve what our students can do but also because it reminds us that no one of the three is likely to work unless it is related to each of the others. In fact each of the three types of cure—"develop an awareness of audience," "give them something to say," and "enliven their writing personalities"—threatens us with characteristic dangers and distortions; all three together are indispensable to any lasting cure.

Perhaps the most obvious omission in that Indiana teacher's assignments is all sense of an audience to be persuaded, of a serious rhetorical purpose to be achieved. One tempting cure for this omission is to teach them to put a controversial edge on what they say. So we ask them to write a three-page paper arguing that China should be allowed into the UN or that women are superior to men or that American colleges are failing in their historic task. Then we are surprised when the papers turn out to be as boring as ever. The papers on Red China are full of abstract pomposities that the students themselves obviously do not understand or care about, since they have gleaned them in a desperate dash through the most readily available courses listed in the *Readers' Guide*. Except for the rare student who has some political background and awareness, and who thus might have written on the subject anyway, they manage to convey little more than their resentment at the assignment and their boredom in carrying it out. One of the worst batches of papers I ever read came out of a good idea we had at Earlham College for getting the whole student body involved in controversial discussion about world affairs. We required them to read Barbara Ward's *Five Ideas that Changed the World*; we even had Lady Barbara come to the campus and talk to everyone about her concern for the backward nations. The papers, to our surprise, were a discouraging business. We found ourselves in desperation collecting the boners that are always a sure sign, when present in great numbers, that students are thoroughly disengaged. "I think altruism is all right, so long as we practice it in our own interest." "I would be willing to die for anything fatal." "It sure is a doggie dog world."

It is obvious what had gone wrong: though we had ostensibly given the student a writing purpose, it had not become *his* purpose, and he was really no better off, perhaps worse, than if we had him writing about, say, piccolos or pizza. We might be tempted in revulsion from such overly ambitious failures to search for controversy in the students' own mundane lives. This may be a good move, but we should not be surprised when the papers on "Let's clean up the campus" or "Why must we have traffic fatalities?" turn out to be just as empty as the papers on the UN or the Congo. They may have more exclamation points and underlined adjectives, but they will not interest any teacher who would like to read papers for his own pleasure or edification. "People often fail to realize that nearly 40,000 people are killed on our highways each year. Must this carnage continue?" Well, I suppose it must, until people who write about it learn to see it with their own eyes, and hearts, instead of through a haze of cliché. The truth is that to make students assume a controversial pose before they have any genuine substance to be controversial about is to encourage dishonesty and slovenliness, and to ensure our own boredom. It may very well lead them into the kind of commercial concern for the audience which makes almost every *Reader's Digest* article intelligible to everyone over the chronological age of ten and boring to everyone over the mental age of fifteen. *Newsweek* magazine recently had a readability survey conducted on itself. It was found to be readable by the average twelfth grader, unlike *Time*, which is readable by the average eleventh grader. The editors were advised, and I understand are taking the advice, that by improving their "readability" by one year they could improve their circulation by several hundred thousand. Whether they will thereby lop off a few thousand adult readers in the process was not reported.

The only protection from this destructive type of concern for the audience is the control of substance, of having something solid to say. Our students bore us, even when they take a seemingly lively controversial tone, because they have nothing to say, to us or to anybody else. If and when they discover something to say, they will no longer bore us, and our comments will no longer bore them. Having something to say, they will be interested in learning how to say it better. Having something to say, they can be taught how to give a properly controversial edge to what will by its nature be controversial—nothing, after all, is worth saying that everybody agrees on already.

When we think of providing substance, we are perhaps tempted first to find some way of filling students' minds with a goodly store of general ideas, available on demand. This temptation is not necessarily a bad one. After all, if we think of the adult writers who interest us, most of them have such a store; they have read and thought about man's major problems, and they have opinions and arguments ready to hand about how men ought to live, how society ought to be run, how literature ought to be written. Edmund Wilson, for example, one of the most consistently interesting men alive, seems to have an inexhaustible flow of reasoned opinions on any subject that comes before him. Obviously our students are not going to interest us until they too have some ideas.

But it is not easy to impart ideas. It is not even easy to impart opinions, though a popular teacher can usually manage to get students to parrot his views. But ideas—that is, opinions backed with genuine reasoning—are extremely difficult to develop. If they were not, we wouldn't have a problem in the first place; we could simply send our students off with an assignment to prove their conviction that God does or does not exist or that the American high school system is the best on God's earth, and the interesting arguments would flow.

There is, in fact, no short cut to the development of reasoned ideas. Years and years of daily contact with the world of ideas are required before the child can be expected to begin formulating his own ideas and his own reasons. And for the most part the capacity to handle abstract ideas comes fairly late. I recently saw a paper of a bright high school sophomore, from a good private school, relating the economic growth of China and India to their political development and relative supply of natural resources. It was a terrible paper; the student's hatred of the subject, his sense of frustration in trying to invent generalizations about processes that were still too big for him, showed in every line. The child's parent told me that when the paper was returned by the geography teacher, he had pencilled on the top of one page, "Why do you mix so many bad ideas with your good ones?" The son was almost in tears, his father told me, with anger and helplessness. "He talks as if I'd put bad ideas in on purpose. *I* don't know a bad idea from a good one on this subject."

Yet with all this said, I am still convinced that general ideas are not only a resource but also a duty that cannot be dodged just because it is a dangerous one. There is nothing we touch, as English teachers, that is immune to being tainted by our touch; all the difference lies in how we go about it.

Ideas are a resource because adolescents are surprisingly responsive to any real encouragement to think for themselves, *if* methods of forced feeding are avoided. The seventeen-year-old who has been given nothing but commonplaces and clichés all his life and who finally discovers a teacher with ideas of his own may have his life changed, and, as I shall say in my final point, when his life is changed his writing is changed. Perhaps some of you can remember, as I can, a first experience with a teacher who could think for himself. I can remember going home from a conversation with my high school chemistry teacher and audibly vowing to myself: "Someday I'm going to be able to think for myself like that." There was nothing especially unconventional about Luther Gidding's ideas—at least I can remember few of them now. But what I cannot forget is the way he had with an idea, the genuine curiosity with which he approached it, the pause while he gave his little thoughtful cough, and then the bulldog tenacity with which he would argue it through. And I am convinced that though he never required me to write a line, he did more to improve my writing during the high school years than all of my English teachers put together. The diary I kept to record my sessions with him, never read by anyone, was the best possible writing practice.

If ideas, in this sense of speculation backed up with an attempt to think about things rigorously and constructively, are a great and often neglected resource, they are also our civic responsibility—a far more serious responsibility than our duty to teach spelling and grammar. It is a commonplace to say that democracy depends for its survival on an informed citizenry, but we all know that mere information is not what we are talking about when we say such things. What we mean is that democracy depends on a citizenry that can reason for themselves, on men who know whether a case has been proved, or at least made probable. Democracy depends, if you will forgive some truisms for a moment, on free choices, and choices cannot be in any sense free if they are made blind: free choice is, in fact, choice that is based on knowledge—not just opinions, but knowledge in the sense of reasoned opinion. And if that half of our population who do not go beyond high school do not learn from us how to put two and two together and how to test the efforts of others to do so, and if the colleges continue to fail with most of the other half, we are doomed to become even more sheeplike, as a nation, than we are already.

Papers about ideas written by sheep are boring; papers written by thinking boys and girls are interesting. The problem is always to find ideas at a level that will allow the student to *reason*, that is, to provide support for his ideas, rather than merely assert them in half-baked form. And this means something that is all too often forgotten by the most ambitious teachers—namely, that whatever ideas the student writes about must somehow be connected with his own experience. Teaching machines will never be able to teach the kind of writing we all want precisely, because no machine can ever know which general ideas relate, for a given student, to some meaningful experience. In the same class we'll have one student for whom philosophical and religious ideas are meaningful, another who can talk with confidence about entropy and the second law of thermodynamics, a third who can write about social justice, and a fourth who can discuss the phony world of Holden Caulfield. Each of them can do a good job on his own subject, because he has as part of his equipment a growing awareness of how conclusions in that subject are related to the steps of argument that support conclusions. Ideally, each of these students ought to have the personal attention of a tutor for an hour or so each week, someone who can help him sharpen those connections, and not force him to write on topics not yet appropriate to his interests or experience. But when these four are in a class of thirty or forty others, taught by a teacher who has three or four other similar sections, we all know what happens: the teacher is forced by his circumstances to provide some sort of mold into which all of the students can be poured. Although he is still better able to adapt to individual differences than a machine, he is unfortunately subject to boredom and fatigue, as a machine would not be. Instead of being the philosopher, scientist, political analyst, and literary critic that these four students require him to be, teaching them and learning from them at the same time, the teacher is almost inevitably tempted to force them all to write about the ideas he himself knows best. The result is that at least three of the four must write out of ignorance.

Now clearly the best way out of this impasse would be for legislatures and school boards and college presidents to recognize the teaching of English for what it is: the most demanding of all teaching jobs, justifying the smallest sections and the lightest course loads. No composition teacher can possibly concentrate on finding special interests, making imaginative assignments, and testing the effectiveness and cogency of papers if he has more than seventy-five students at a time; the really desirable limit would be about forty-five—three sections of fifteen students each. Nobody would ever expect a piano teacher, who has no themes to read, to handle the great masses of pupils that we handle. Everyone recognizes that for all other technical skills individual attention is required. Yet for this, the most delicate of all skills, the one requiring the most subtle interrelationships of training, character, and experience, we fling students and teachers into hopelessly impersonal patterns.

But if I'm not careful I'll find myself saying that our pupils bore us because the superintendents and college presidents hire us to be bored. Administrative neglect and misallocation of educational funds are basic to our problem, and we should let the citizenry know of the scandal on every occasion. But meanwhile, back at the ranch, we are faced with the situation as it now is: we must find some way to train a people to write responsibly even though the people, as represented, don't want this service sufficiently to pay for it.

The tone of political exhortation into which I have now fallen leads me to one natural large source of ideas as we try to encourage writing that is not just lively and controversial but informed and genuinely persuasive. For many students there is obviously more potential interest in social problems and forces, political controversy, and the processes of everyday living around them than in more general ideas. The four students I described a moment ago, students who can say something about philosophy, science, general political theory, or literary criticism, are rare. But most students, including these four, can in theory at least be interested in meaningful argument about social problems in which they are personally involved.

As a profession we have tried, over the past several decades, a variety of approaches attempting to capitalize on such interests. Papers on corruption in TV, arguments about race relations, analyses of distortions in advertising, descriptions of mass communication—these have been combined in various quantities with traditional subjects like grammar, rhetoric, and literature. The "communications" movement, which looked so powerful only a few years ago and which now seems almost dead, had at its heart a perfectly respectable notion, a notion not much different from the one I'm working with today: get them to write about something they know about, and make sure that they see their writing as an act of communication, not as a meaningless exercise. And what better material than other acts of communication.

The dangers of such an approach are by now sufficiently understood. As subject matter for the English course, current "communications media" can at best provide only a supplement to literature and analysis of ideas. But they can be a valuable supplement. Analysis in class of the appeals buried in a *New Yorker* or *Life* advertisement followed by a writing assignment requiring similar analyses can be a far more interesting introduction to the intricacies of style than assignments out of a language text on levels of usage or emotion-charged adjectives. Analysis of a *Time* magazine account, purporting to be objective news but in actual fact a highly emotional editorial, can be not only a valuable experience in itself, but it can lead to papers in which the students do say something to us. Stylistic analysis of the treatment of the same news events by two newspapers or weeklies of different editorial policy can lead to an intellectual awakening of great importance, and thus to papers that will not, cannot, bore the teacher. But this will happen only if the students' critical powers are genuinely developed. It wil not do simply to teach the instructor's own prejudices.

There was a time in decades not long past when many of the most lively English teachers thought of their job as primarily to serve as handmaids to liberalism. I had one teacher in college who confessed to me that his overriding purpose was to get students to read and believe *The Nation* rather than the editorials of their daily paper. I suppose that his approach was not entirely valueless. It seems preferable to the effort to be noncontroversial that marks too many English teachers in the '60's, and at least it stirred some of us out of our dogmatic slumbers. But unfortunately it did nothing whatever about teaching us to think critically. Though we graduated from his course at least aware—as many college graduates do not seem to be today—that you can't believe anything you read in the daily press until you have analyzed it and related it to your past experience and to other accounts, it failed to teach us that you can't believe what you read in *The Nation* either. It left the job undone of training our ability to think, because it concentrated too heavily on our opinions. The result was, as I remember, that my own papers in that course were generally regurgitated liberalism. I was excited by them, and that was something. But I can't believe that the instructor found reading them anything other than a chore. There was nothing in them that came from my own experience, my own notions of what would constitute evidence for my conclusions. There I was, in Utah in the depths of the depression, writing about the Okies when I could have been writing about the impoverished farmers all around me. I wrote about race relations in the south without ever having talked with a Negro in my life and without recognizing that the bootblack I occasionally saw in Salt Lake City in the Hotel Utah was in any way related to the problem of race relations.

The third element that accounts for our boring papers is the lack of character and personality in the writer. My life, my observations, my insights were not included in those papers on the Okies and race relations and the New Deal. Every opinion was derivative, every observation second-hand. I had no real opinions of my own, and my eyes were not open wide enough for me to make first-hand observations on the world around me. What I wrote was therefore characterless, without true personality, though often full of personal pronouns. My opinions had been changed, my *self* had not. The style was the boy, the opinionated, immature, uninformed boy; whether my teacher knew it or not—and apparently he did not—his real job was to make a man of me if he wanted me to write like a man.

Putting the difficulty in this way naturally leads me to what perhaps many of you have been impatient about from the beginning. Are not the narrative arts, both as encountered in great literature and as practiced by the students themselves, the best road to the infusion of individuality that no good writing can lack? Would not a real look at the life of that bootblack, and an attempt to deal with him in narrative, have led to a more interesting paper than all of my generalized attacks on the prejudiced southerners?

I think it would, but once again I am almost more conscious of the dangers of the cure than of the advantages. As soon as we make our general rule something like, "Have the students write a personal narrative on what they know about, what they can see and feel at first hand," we have opened the floodgates for those dreadful assignments that we all find ourselves using, even though we know better: "My Summer Vacation," "Catching My First Fish," and "Our Trip to the Seattle World's Fair." Here are personal experiences that call for personal observation and narration. What's wrong with them?

Quite simply, they invite triviality, superficiality, puerility. Our students have been writing essays on such non-subjects all their lives, and until they have developed some sort of critical vision, some way of looking at the world they passed through on their vacations or fishing trips, they are going to feed us the same old bromides that have always won their passing grades. "My Summer Vacation" is an invitation to a grocery list of items, because it implies no audience, no point to be made, no point of view, no character in the speaker. A bright student will make something of such an invitation, by dramatizing the comic family quarrel that developed two days out, or by comparing his view of the American motel system with Nabokov's in *Lolita*, or by remembering the types of people seen in the campgrounds. If he had his own eyes and ears open he might have seen, in a men's room in Grand Canyon last summer, a camper with a very thick French accent trying to convert a Brooklyn Jew into believing the story of the Mormon gold plates. Or he could have heard, at Mesa Verde, a young park ranger, left behind toward the end of the season by all of the experienced rangers, struggling ungrammatically through a set speech on the geology of the area and finally breaking down in embarrassment over his lack of education. Such an episode, really *seen*, could be used narratively to say something to other high school students about what education really is.

But mere narration can be in itself just as dull as the most abstract theorizing about the nature of the universe or the most derivative opinion-mongering about politics. Even relatively skilful narration, used too obviously as a gimmick to catch interest, with no real relation to the subject, can be as dull as the most abstract pomposities. We all know the student papers that begin like *Reader's Digest* articles, with stereotyped narration that makes one doubt the event itself: "On a dark night last January, two teen agers were seen etc., etc." One can open any issue of *Time* and find this so-called narrative interest plastered throughout. From the March 29 issue I find, among many others, the following bits of fantasy: #1: "A Bolivian father sadly surveyed his nation's seven universities, then made up his mind. 'I don't want my son mixed up in politics.' . . . So saying, he sent his son off to West Germany to college." So writing, the author sends me into hysterical laughter: the quote is phony, made up for the occasion to disguise the generality of the news item. #2: "Around 12:30 P.M. every Monday and Friday, an aging Cubana Airlines turbo-prop Britannia whistles to a halt at Mexico City's International Airport. Squads of police stand by. All passengers . . . without diplomatic or Mexican passports are photographed and questioned. . . . They always dodge questions. 'Why are you here? Where are you going?' ask the Mexicans. 'None of your business,' answer the secretive travelers." "Why should I go on reading?" ask I. #3: "At 6:30 one morning early this month, a phone shrilled in the small office off the bedroom of Egypt's President. . . . Nasser. [All early morning phones "shrill" for *Time*.] Already awake, he lifted the receiver to hear exciting news: a military coup had just been launched against the anti-Nasser government of Syria. The phone rang again. It was the Minister of Culture. . . . How should Radio Cairo handle the Syrian crisis? 'Support the rebels,' snapped Nasser." Oh lucky reporter, I sigh, to have such an efficient wiretapping service. #4: "In South Korea last week, a farmer named Song Kyu Il traveled all the way from the southern provinces to parade before Seoul's Duk Soo Palace with a placard scrawled in his own blood. . . . Farmer Song was thrown in jail, along with some 200 other demonstrators." That's the last we hear of Song, who is invented as an individual for this opening and then dropped. #5: "Defense Secretary Robert McNamara last spring stood beside President Kennedy on the tenth-deck bridge of the nuclear-powered carrier *Enterprise*. For as far as the eye could see, other U. S. ships deployed over the Atlantic seascape." Well, maybe. But for as far as the eye can see, the narrative clichés are piled, rank on rank. At 12:00 midnight last Thursday a gaunt, harried English professor could be seen hunched over his typewriter, a pile of *Time* magazines beside him on the floor. "What," he murmured to himself, sadly, "Whatever can we do about this trashy imitation of narration?"

Fortunately there is something we can do, and it is directly within our province. We can subject our students to models of genuine narration, with the sharp observation and penetrating critical judgment that underlies all good story telling, whether reportorial or fictional.

It is a truth universally acknowledged, that a single man in possession of a good fortune must be in want of a wife.

However little known the feelings or views of such a man may be on his first entering a neighborhood, this truth is so well fixed in the minds of the surrounding families, that he is considered as the rightful property of someone or other of their daughters.

"My dear Mr. Bennet," said his lady to him one day, "have you heard that Netherfield Park is let at last?"

And already we have a strong personal tone established, a tone of mocking irony which leaves Jane Austen's Mrs. Bennet revealed before us as the grasping, silly gossip she is. Or try this one:

I am an American, Chicago-born—Chicago, that somber city—and go at things as I have taught myself, free-style, and will make the record in my own way: first to knock, first admitted; sometimes an innocent knock, sometimes a not so innocent. But a man's character is his fate, says Heraclitus, and in the end there isn't any way to disguise the nature of the knocks by acoustical work on the door or gloving the knuckles.

Everybody knows there is no fineness or accuracy of suppression; if you hold down one thing you hold down the adjoining.

My own parents were not much to me, though I cared for my mother. She was simple-minded, and what I learned from her was not what she taught....

Do you catch the accent of Saul Bellow here, beneath the accent of his Augie March? You do, of course, but the students, many of them, do not. How do you know, they will ask, that Jane Austen is being ironic? How do you know, they ask again, that Augie is being characterized by his author through what he says? In teaching them how we know, in exposing them to the great narrative voices, ancient and modern, and in teaching them to hear these voices accurately, we are, of course, trying to change their lives, to make them new, to raise their perceptions to a new level altogether. Nobody can really catch these accents who has not grown up sufficiently to see through cheap substitutes. Or, to put it another way, a steady exposure to such voices is the very thing that will produce the maturity that alone can make our students ashamed of beclouded, commercial, borrowed spectacles for viewing the world.

It is true that exposure to good fiction will not in itself transform our students into good writers. Even the best-read student still needs endless hours and years of practice, with rigorous criticism. Fiction will not do the job of discipline in reasoned argument and of practice in developing habits of addressing a living audience. But in the great fiction they will learn what it means to look at something with full attention, what it means to see beneath the surface of society's platitudes. If we then give them practice in writing about things close to the home base of their own honest observations, constantly stretching their powers of generalization and argument but never allowing them to drift into pompous inanities or empty controversiality, we may have that rare but wonderful pleasure of witnessing the miracle: a man and a style where before there was only a bag of wind or a bundle of received opinions. Even when, as with most of our students, no miracles occur, we can hope for papers that we can enjoy reading. And as a final bonus, we might hope that when our students encounter someone on a train who says that he teaches English, their automatic response may be something other than looks of pity or cries of mock alarm.

QUESTIONS FOR STUDY, DISCUSSION, AND WRITING

1. Booth is writing for an audience of English teachers. In what ways might the essay differ if he were writing for an audience of students?
2. On page 129 Booth says he has "now fallen" into a "tone of political exhortation." (Tone may be defined as the reflection in language of the attitude a writer takes toward his subject or his audience or both.) What other "tones" are there in the essay? Why does Booth find it necessary to vary the tone?
3. What steps are necessary before an "opinion" can become a "reasoned opinion"? Select some subject on which you have a strong opinion and decide whether it is a reasoned opinion.
4. Booth characterizes the writing in the Reader's Digest and Time (pp. 132–133). What does he feel the two magazines have in common? Analyze an article from either one of these magazines to see how accurate you believe Booth's characterization to be.

W. SOMERSET MAUGHAM
Lucidity, Simplicity, Euphony[1]

I have never had much patience with the writers who claim from the reader an effort to understand their meaning. You have only to go to the great philosophers to see that it is possible to express with lucidity the most subtle reflections. You may find it difficult to understand the thought of Hume, and if you have no philosophical

1. Chapters 11, 12, and 13 of *The Summing Up*, 1938.

training its implications will doubtless escape you; but no one with any education at all can fail to understand exactly what the meaning of each sentence is. Few people have written English with more grace than Berkeley. There are two sorts of obscurity that you find in writers. One is due to negligence and the other to willfulness. People often write obscurely because they have never taken the trouble to learn to write clearly. This sort of obscurity you find too often in modern philosophers, in men of science, and even in literary critics. Here it is indeed strange. You would have thought that men who passed their lives in the study of the great masters of literature would be sufficiently sensitive to the beauty of language to write if not beautifully at least with perspicuity. Yet you will find in their works sentence after sentence that you must read twice to discover the sense. Often you can only guess at it, for the writers have evidently not said what they intended.

Another cause of obscurity is that the writer is himself not quite sure of his meaning. He has a vague impression of what he wants to say, but has not, either from lack of mental power or from laziness, exactly formulated it in his mind and it is natural enough that he should not find a precise expression for a confused idea. This is due largely to the fact that many writers think, not before, but as they write. The pen originates the thought. The disadvantage of this, and indeed it is a danger against which the author must be always on his guard, is that there is a sort of magic in the written word. The idea acquires substance by taking on a visible nature, and then stands in the way of its own clarification. But this sort of obscurity merges very easily into the willful. Some writers who do not think clearly are inclined to suppose that their thoughts have a significance greater than at first sight appears. It is flattering to believe that they are too profound to be expressed so clearly that all who run may read, and very naturally it does not occur to such writers that the fault is with their own minds which have not the faculty of precise reflection. Here again the magic of the written word obtains. It is very easy to persuade oneself that a phrase that one does not quite understand may mean a great deal more than one realizes. From this there is only a little way to go to fall into the habit of setting down one's impressions in all their original vagueness. Fools can always be found to discover a hidden sense in them. There is another form of willful obscurity that masquerades as aristocratic exclusiveness. The author wraps his meaning in mystery so that the vulgar shall not participate in it. His soul is a secret garden into which the elect may penetrate only after overcoming a number of perilous obstacles. But this kind of obscurity is not only pretentious; it is short-sighted. For time plays it an odd trick. If the sense is meagre time reduces it to a meaningless verbiage that no one thinks of reading. This is the fate that has befallen the lucubrations of those French writers who were seduced by the example of Guillaume Apollinaire. But occasionally it throws a sharp cold light on what had seemed profound and thus discloses the fact that these contortions of language disguised very commonplace notions. There are few of Mallarmé's poems now that are not clear; one cannot fail to notice that his thought singularly lacked originality. Some of his phrases were beautiful; the materials of his verse were the poetic platitudes of his day.

Simplicity is not such an obvious merit as lucidity. I have aimed at it because I have no gift for richness. Within limits I admire richness in others, though I find it difficult to digest in quantity. I can read one page of Ruskin with delight, but twenty only with weariness. The rolling period, the stately epithet, the noun rich in poetic associations, the subordinate clauses that give the sentence weight and magnificence, the grandeur like that of wave following wave in the open sea; there is no doubt that in all this there is something inspiring. Words thus strung together fall on the ear like music. The appeal is sensuous rather than intellectual, and the beauty of the sound leads you easily to conclude that you need not bother about the meaning. But words are tyrannical things, they exist for their meanings, and if you will not pay attention to these, you cannot pay attention at all. Your mind wanders. This kind of writing demands a subject that will suit it. It is surely out of place to write in the grand style of inconsiderable things. No one wrote in this manner with greater success than Sir Thomas Browne, but even he did not always escape this pitfall. In the last chapter of *Hydriotaphia* the matter, which is the destiny of man, wonderfully fits the baroque splendor of the language, and here the Norwich doctor produced a piece of prose that has never been surpassed in our literature; but when he describes the finding of his urns in the same splendid manner the effect (at least to my taste) is less happy. When a modern writer is grandiloquent to tell you whether or no a little trollop shall hop into bed with a commonplace young man you are right to be disgusted.

But if richness needs gifts with which everyone is not endowed, simplicity by no means comes by nature. To achieve it needs rigid discipline. So far as I know ours is the only language in which it has been found necessary to give a name to the piece of prose which is described as the purple patch; it would not have been necessary to do so unless it were characteristic. English prose is elaborate rather than simple. It was not always so. Nothing could be more racy, straightforward and alive than the prose of Shakespeare; but it must be remembered that this was dialogue written to be spoken. We do not know how he would have written if like Corneille he had composed prefaces to his plays. It may be that they would have been as euphuistic as the letters of Queen Elizabeth. But earlier prose, the prose of Sir Thomas More, for instance, is neither ponderous, flowery nor oratorical. It smacks of the English soil. To my mind King James's Bible has been a very harmful influence on English prose. I am not so stupid as to deny its great beauty. It is majestical. But the Bible is an oriental book. Its alien imagery has nothing to do with us. Those hyperboles, those luscious metaphors, are foreign to our genius. I cannot but think that not the least of the misfortunes that the Secession from Rome brought upon the spiritual life of our country is that this work for so long a period became the daily, and with many the only, reading of our people. Those rhythms, that powerful vocabulary, that grandiloquence, became part and parcel of the national sensibility. The plain, honest English speech was overwhelmed with ornament. Blunt Englishmen twisted their tongues to speak like Hebrew prophets. There was evidently something in the English temper to which this was congenial, perhaps a native lack of precision in thought, perhaps a naïve delight in fine words for their own sake, an innate eccentricity and love of embroidery, I do not know; but the fact remains that ever since, English prose has had to struggle against the tendency to luxuriance. When from time to time the spirit of the language has reasserted itself, as it did with Dryden and the writers of Queen Anne, it was only to be submerged once more by the pomposities of Gibbon and Dr. Johnson. When English prose recovered simplicity with Hazlitt, the Shelley of the letters and Charles Lamb at his best, it lost it again with De Quincey, Carlyle, Meredith and Walter Pater. It is obvious that the grand style is more striking than the plain. Indeed many people think that a style that does not attract notice is not style. They will admire Walter Pater's, but will read an essay by Matthew Arnold without giving a moment's attention to the elegance, distinction and sobriety with which he set down what he had to say.

The dictum that the style is the man is well known. It is one of those aphorisms that say too much to mean a great deal. Where is the man in Goethe, in his birdlike lyrics or in his clumsy prose? And Hazlitt? But I suppose that if a man has a confused mind he will write in a confused way, if his temper is capricious his prose will be fantastical, and if he has a quick, darting intelligence that is reminded by the matter in hand of a hundred things, he will, unless he has great self-control, load his pages with metaphor and simile. There is a great difference between the magniloquence of the Jacobean writters, who were intoxicated with the new wealth that had lately been brought into the language, and the turgidity of Gibbon and Dr. Johnson, who were the victims of bad theories. I can read every word that Dr. Johnson wrote with delight, for he had good sense, charm and wit. No one could have written better if he had not willfully set himself to write in the grand style. He knew good English when he saw it. No critic has praised Dryden's prose more aptly. He said of him that he appeared to have no art other than that of expressing with clearness what he thought with vigor. And one of his Lives he finished with the words: "Whoever wishes to attain an English style, familiar but not coarse, and elegant but not ostentatious, must give his days and nights to the volumes of Addison." But when he himself sat down to write it was with a very different aim. He mistook the orotund for the dignified. He had not the good breeding to see that simplicity and naturalness are the truest marks of distinction.

For to write good prose is an affair of good manners. It is, unlike verse, a civil art. Poetry is baroque. Baroque is tragic, massive and mystical. It is elemental. It demands depth and insight. I cannot but feel that the prose writers of the baroque period, the authors of King James's Bible, Sir Thomas Browne, Glanville, were poets who had lost their way. Prose is a rococo art. It needs taste rather than power, decorum rather than inspiration and vigor rather than grandeur. Form for the poet is the bit and the bridle without which (unless you are an acrobat) you cannot ride your horse; but for the writer of prose it is the chassis without which your car does not exist. It is not an accident that the best prose was written when rococo with its elegance and moderation, at its birth attained its greatest excellence. For rococo was evolved when baroque had become declamatory and the world, tired of the stupendous, asked for restraint. It was the natural expression of persons who valued a civilized life. Humor, tolerance and horse sense made the great tragic issues that had preoccupied the first half of the seventeenth century seem excessive. The world was a more comfortable place to live in and perhaps for the first time in centuries the cultivated classes could sit back and enjoy their leisure. It has been said that good prose should resemble the conversation of a well-bred man. Conversation is only possible when men's minds are free from pressing anxieties. Their lives must be reasonably secure and they must have no grave concern about their souls. They must attach importance to the refinements of civilization. They must value courtesy, they must pay attention to their persons (and have we not also been told that good prose should be like the clothes of a well-dressed man, appropriate but unobtrusive?), they must fear to bore, they must be neither flippant nor solemn, but always apt; and they must look upon "enthusiasm" with a critical glance. This is a soil very suitable for prose. It is not to be wondered at that it gave a fitting opportunity for the appearance of the best writer of prose that our modern world has seen, Voltaire. The writers of English, perhaps owing to the poetic nature of the language, have seldom reached the excellence that seems to have come so naturally to him. It is in so far as they have approached the ease, sobriety and precision of the great French masters that they are admirable.

Whether you ascribe importance to euphony, the last of the three characteristics that I mentioned, must depend on the sensitiveness of your ear. A great many readers, and many admirable writers, are devoid of this quality. Poets as we know have always made a great use of alliteration. They are persuaded that the repetition of a sound gives an effect of beauty. I do not think it does so in prose. It seems to me that in prose alliteration should be used only for a special reason; when used by accident it falls on the ear very disagreeably. But its accidental use is so common that one can only suppose that the sound of it is not universally offensive. Many writers without distress will put two rhyming words together, join a monstrous long adjective to a monstrous long noun, or between the end of one word and the beginning of another have a conjunction of consonants that almost breaks your jaw. These are trivial and obvious instances. I mention them only to prove that if careful writers can do such things it is only because they have no ear. Words have weight, sound and appearance; it is only by considering these that you can write a sentence that is good to look at and good to listen to.

I have read many books on English prose, but have found it hard to profit by them; for the most part they are vague, unduly theoretical, and often scolding. But you cannot say this of Fowler's *Dictionary of Modern English Usage*. It is a valuable work. I do not think anyone writes so well that he cannot learn much from it. It is lively reading. Fowler liked simplicity, straightforwardness and common sense. He had no patience with pretentiousness. He had a sound feeling that idiom was the backbone of a language and he was all for the racy phrase. He was no slavish admirer of logic and was willing enough to give usage right of way through the exact demesnes of grammar. English grammar is very difficult and few writers have avoided making mistakes in it. So heedful a writer as Henry James, for instance, on occasion wrote so ungrammatically that a schoolmaster, finding such errors in a schoolboy's essay, would be justly indignant. It is necessary to know grammar, and it is better to write grammatically than not, but it is well to remember that grammar is common speech formulated. Usage is the only test. I would prefer a phrase that was easy and unaffected to a phrase that was grammatical. One of the differences between French and English is that in French you can be grammatical with complete naturalness, but in English not invariably. It is a difficulty in writing English that the sound of the living voice dominates the look of the printed word. I have given the matter of style a great deal of thought and have taken great pains. I have written few pages that I feel I could not improve and far too many that I have left with dissatisfaction because, try as I would, I could do no better. I cannot say of myself what Johnson said of Pope: "He never passed a fault unamended by indifference, nor quitted it by despair." I do not write as I want to; I write as I can.

But Fowler had no ear. He did not see that simplicity may sometimes make concessions to euphony. I do not think a far-fetched, an archaic or even an affected word is out of place when it sounds better than the blunt, obvious one or when it gives a sentence a better balance. But, I hasten to add, though I think you may without misgiving make this concession to pleasant sound, I think you should make none to what may obscure your meaning. Anything is better than not to write clearly. There is nothing to be said against lucidity, and against simplicity only the possibility of dryness. This is a risk that is well worth taking when you reflect how much better it is to be bald than to wear a curly wig. But there is in euphony a danger that must be considered. It is very likely to be monotonous. When George Moore began to write, his style was poor; it gave you the impression that he wrote on wrapping paper with a blunt pencil. But he developed gradually a very musical English. He learnt to write sentences that fall away on the ear with a misty languor and it delighted him so much that he could never have enough of it. He did not escape monotony. It is like the sound of water lapping a shingly beach, so soothing that you presently cease to be sensible of it. It is so mellifluous that you hanker for some harshness, for an abrupt dissonance, that will interrupt the silky concord. I do not know how one can guard against this. I suppose the best chance is to have a more lively faculty of boredom than one's readers so that one is wearied before they are. One must always be on the watch for mannerisms and when certain cadences come too easily to the pen ask oneself whether they have not become mechanical. It is very hard to discover the exact point where the idiom one has formed to express oneself has lost its tang. As Dr. Johnson said: "He that has once studiously formed a style, rarely writes afterwards with complete ease." Admirably as I think Matthew Arnold's style was suited to his particular purposes, I must admit that his mannerisms are often irritating. His style was an instrument that he had forged once for all; it was not like the human hand capable of performing a variety of actions.

If you could write lucidly, simply, euphoniously and yet with liveliness you would write perfectly: you would write like Voltaire. And yet we know how fatal the pursuit of liveliness may be: it may result in the tiresome acrobatics of Meredith. Macaulay and Carlyle were in their different ways arresting; but at the heavy cost of naturalness. Their flashy effects distract the mind. They destroy their persuasiveness; you would not believe a man was very intent on ploughing a furrow if he carried a hoop with him and jumped through it at every other step. A good style should show no sign of effort. What is written should seem a happy accident. I think no one in France now writes more admirably than Collette, and such is the ease of her expression that you cannot bring yourself to believe that she takes any trouble over it. I am told that there are pianists who have a natural technique so that they can play in a manner that most executants can achieve only as the result of unremitting toil, and I am willing to believe that there are writers who are equally fortunate. Among them I was much inclined to place Colette. I asked her. I was exceedingly surprised to hear that she wrote everything over and over again. She told me that she would often spend a whole morning working upon a single page. But it does not matter how one gets the effect of ease. For my part, if I get it at all, it is only by strenuous effort. Nature seldom provides me with the word, the turn of phrase, that is appropriate without being far-fetched or commonplace.

QUESTIONS FOR STUDY, DISCUSSION, AND WRITING

Maugham draws attention to the two conflicting yet complementary approaches to style that have been traditional in literary criticism. One approach maintains that style is primarily a combination of qualities and devices that can be learned and produced; the other, that "style is the man," the reflection in language of a personality with all its attitudes and idiosyncracies. Using passages from the following Album, explore the two approaches. In any given passage what appears as impersonal technique or device, what as reflecting the special temperament or character of the author?

AN ALBUM OF STYLES

I

Men fear death as children fear to go in the dark; and as that natural fear in children is increased with tales, so is the other. Certainly, the contemplation of death as the wages of sin, and passage to another world, is holy and religious; but the fear of it, as a tribute due unto nature, is weak. Yet in religious meditations there is sometimes mixture of vanity and of superstition. You shall read in some of the friars' books of mortification that a man should think with himself what the pain is if he have but his finger's end pressed or tortured; and thereby imagine what the pains of death are, when the whole body is corrupted and dissolved; when many times death passeth with less pain than the torture of a limb; for the most vital parts are not the quickest of sense. And by him that spake only as a philosopher, and natural man, it was well said, *Pompa mortis magis terret, quam mors ipsa.*[1] Groans and convulsions, and a discolored face, and friends weeping, and blacks and obsequies, and the like, show death terrible. It is worthy the observing that there is no passion in the mind of man so weak, but it mates and masters the fear of death; and therefore death is no such terrible enemy when a man hath so many attendants about him that can win the combat of him. Revenge triumphs over death; love slights it; honor aspireth to it; grief flieth to it; fear preoccupateth it; nay, we read, after Otho the emperor had slain himself, pity, which is the tenderest of affections, provoked many to die out of mere compassion to their sovereign, and as the truest sort of followers. Nay, Seneca adds, niceness and satiety: *Cogita quamdiu eadem feceris; mori velle, non tantum fortis, aut miser, sed etiam fastidiosus potest.*[2] A man would die, though he were neither valiant nor miserable, only upon a weariness to do the same thing so oft over and over. It is no less worthy to observe, how little alteration in good spirits the approaches of death make: for they appear to be the same men till the last instant. Augustus Caesar died in a compliment, *Livia, conjugii nostri memor, vive et vale.*[3] Tiberius in dissimulation, as Tacitus saith of him, *Jam Tiberium vires et corpus, non dissimulatio, deserebant,*[4] Vespasion in a jest, sitting upon the stool, *Ut puto Deus fio.*[5] Galba with a sentence, *Feri, si ex re sit populi Romani,*[6] holding forth his neck; Septimus Severus in dispatch, *Adeste, se quid mihi restat agendum,*[7] and the like. Certainly the Stoics bestowed too much cost upon death, and by their great preparations made it appear more fearful. Better, saith he, *qui finem vitae extremum inter munera ponit naturae.*[8] It is as natural to die as to be born; and to a little infant, perhaps, the one is as painful as the other. He that dies in an earnest pursuit, is like one that is wounded in hot blood; who for the time scarce feels the hurt; and therefore a mind fixed and bent upon somewhat that is good, doth avert the dolors of death. But, above all, believe it, the sweetest canticle is *Nunc dimittis,*[9] when a man hath obtained worthy ends and expectations. Death hath this also, that it openeth the gate to good fame, and extinguisheth envy; *Extinctus amabitur idem.*[10]

—Francis Bacon, "Of Death"

1. "The retinue of death terrifies more than death itself."

2. "Consider how long you have been doing the same things: a man may be willing to die not only because he is brave, or wretched, but because he is sick of living."

3. "Farewell, Livia; live on remembering our marriage."

4. "Strength and spirit were deserting Tiberius then, but not his duplicity."

5. A pun is involved: "As I (cleanse myself; think), I am becoming a god."

6. "Strike, if it be for the good of the Roman people."

7. "Approach, if there is anything left for me to do."

8. "Who considers the end of life among the gifts of nature."

9. "Now dismiss [Thy servant, O Lord]": the words spoken by the Prophet Simeon (Luke ii, 29-32).

10. "The same man [who was envied in life] will be loved in death."

II

And therefore, restless inquietude for the diuturnity of our memories unto present considerations seems a vanity almost out of date, and superannuated piece of folly. We cannot hope to live so long in our names, as some have done in their persons. One face of Janus holds no proportion unto the other. 'Tis too late to be ambitious. The great mutations of the world are acted, or time may be too short for our designs. To extend our memories by monuments, whose death we daily pray for, and whose duration we cannot hope, without injury to our expectations in the advent of the last day, were a contradiction to our beliefs. We whose generations are ordained in this setting part of time, are providentially taken off from such imaginations; and, being necessitated to eye the remaining particle of futurity, are naturally constituted unto thoughts of the next world, and cannot excusably decline the consideration of that duration, which maketh pyramids pillars of snow, and all that's past a moment.

—Thomas Browne, *Hydriotaphia,* or *Urn Burial*

III

Whether others have this wonderful faculty of abstracting their ideas, they best can tell. For myself, I find indeed I have a faculty of imagining, or representing to myself, the ideas of those particular things I have perceived, and of variously compounding and dividing them. I can imagine a man with two heads, or the upper parts of a man joined to the body of a horse. I can consider the hand, the eye, the nose, each by itself abstracted or separated from the rest of the body. But then whatever hand or eye I imagine, it must have some particular shape and color. Likewise the idea of a man that I frame to myself, must be either of a white, or a black, or a tawny, a straight, or a crooked, a tall, or a low, or a middle-sized man. I cannot by any effort of thought conceive the abstract idea above described. And it is equally impossible for me to form the abstract idea of motion distinct from the body moving, and which is neither swift nor slow, curvilinear nor rectilinear; and the like may be said of all other abstract general ideas whatsoever. To be plain, I own myself able to abstract in one sense, as when I consider some particular parts or qualities separated from others, with which though they are united in some object, yet it is possible they may really exist without them. But I deny that I can abstract one from another, or conceive separately, those qualities which it is impossible should exist so separated; or that I can frame a general notion by abstracting from particulars in the manner aforesaid—which two last are the proper acceptations of *abstraction*. And there is ground to think most men will acknowledge themselves to be in my case. The generality of men which are simple and illiterate never pretend to abstract notions. It is said they are difficult, and not to be attained without pains and study. We may therefore reasonably conclude that, if such there be, they are confined only to the learned.

—George Berkeley, *The Principles of Human Knowledge*

IV

Of the wall [of China] it is very easy to assign the motives. It secured a wealthy and timorous nation from the incursions of Barbarians, whose unskillfulness in arts made it easier for them to supply their wants by rapine than by industry, and who from time to time poured in upon the habitations of peaceful commerce, as vultures descend upon domestic fowl. Their celerity and fierceness made the wall necessary, and their ignorance made it efficacious.

But for the pyramids no reason has ever been given adequate to the cost and labor of the work. The narrowness of the chambers proves that it could afford no retreat from enemies, and treasures might have been reposited at far less expense with equal security. It seems to have been erected only in compliance with that hunger of imagination which preys incessantly upon life, and must be always appeased by some employment. Those who have already all that they can enjoy, must enlarge their desires. He that has built for use, till use is supplied must begin to build for vanity, and extend his plan to the utmost power of human performance, that he may not be soon reduced to form another wish.

I consider this mighty structure as a monument of the insufficiency of human enjoyments. A king, whose power is unlimited, and whose treasures surmount all real and imaginary wants, is compelled to solace, by the erection of a pyramid, the satiety of dominion and tastelessness of pleasures, and to amuse the tediousness of declining life, by seeing thousands laboring without end, and one stone, for no purpose, laid upon another. Whoever thou art, that, not content with a moderate condition, imaginest happiness in royal magnificence, and dreamest that command or riches can feed the appetite of novelty with perpetual gratifications, survey the pyramids, and confess thy folly!

—Samuel Johnson, *Rasselas*

V

Moral philosophy, or the science of human nature, may be treated after two different manners; each of which has its peculiar merit, and may contribute to the entertainment, instruction, and reformation of mankind. The one considers man chiefly as born for action; and as influenced in his measures by taste and sentiment; pursuing one object, and avoiding another, according to the value which these objects seem to possess, and according to the light in which they present themselves. As virtue, of all objects, is allowed to be the most valuable, this species of philosophers paint her in the most amiable colors; borrowing all helps from poetry and eloquence, and treating their subject in an easy and obvious manner, and such as is best fitted to please the imagination, and engage the affections. They select the most striking observations and instances from common life; place opposite characters in a proper contrast; and alluring us into the paths of virtue by the views of glory and most illustrious examples. They make us *feel* the difference between vice and virtue; they excite and regulate our sentiments; and so they can but bend our hearts to the love of probity and true honor, they think, that they have fully attained the end of all their labors.

The other species of philosophers consider man in the light of a reasonable rather than an active being, and endeavor to form his understanding more than cultivate his manners. They regard human nature as a subject of speculation; and with a narrow scrutiny examine it, in order to find those principles, which regulate our understanding, excite our sentiments, and make us to approve or blame any particular object, action, or behavior. They think it a reproach to all literature, that philosophy should not yet have fixed, beyond controversy, the foundation of morals, reasoning, and criticism; and should forever talk of truth and falsehood, vice and virtue, beauty and deformity, without being able to determine the source of these distinctions. While they attempt this arduous task, they are deterred by no difficulties; but proceeding from particular instances to general principles they still push on their inquiries of principles more general, and rest not satisfied till they arrive at those original principles, by which, in every science, all human curiosity must be bounded. Though their speculations seem abstract, and even unintelligible to common readers, they aim at the approbation of the learned and the wise; and think themselves sufficiently compensated for the labor of their whole lives, if they can discover some hidden truths, which may contribute to the instruction of posterity.

—David Hume, *An Enquiry Concerning Human Understanding*

VI

Every day for at least ten years together did my father resolve to have it mended—'tis not mended yet: no family but ours would have borne with it an hour—and what is most astonishing, there was not a subject in the world upon which my father was so eloquent, as upon that of door-hinges. And yet at the same time, he was certainly one of the greatest bubbles to them, I think, that history can produce: his rhetoric and conduct were at perpetual handy-cuffs. Never did the parlor-door open—but his philosophy or his principles fell a victim to it; three drops of oyl with a feather, and a smart stroke of a hammer, had saved his honor for ever. Inconsistent soul that man is—languishing under wounds, which he has the power to heal —his whole life a contradiction to his knowledge—his reason, that

precious gift of God to him—(instead of pouring in oyl) serving but
to sharpen his sensibilities, to multiply his pains and render him
more melancholy and uneasy under them—poor unhappy creature,
that he should do so! Are not the necessary causes of misery in this
life enow, but he must add voluntary ones to his stock of sorrow,
struggle against evils which cannot be avoided, and submit to others,
which a tenth part of the trouble they create him, would remove
from his heart forever?

By all that is good and virtuous! if there are three drops of oyl to
be got, and a hammer to be found within ten miles of Shandy-Hall,
the parlor-door hinge shall be mended this reign.

—Laurence Sterne, *Tristram Shandy*

VII

The division of Europe into a number of independent states, connected, however, with each other, by the general resemblance of
religion, language, and manners, is productive of the most beneficial
consequences to the liberty of mankind. A modern tyrant, who should
find no resistance either in his own breast, or in his people, would
soon experience a gentle restraint from the example of his equals,
the dread of present censure, the advice of his allies, and the apprehension of his enemies. The object of his displeasure, escaping from
the narrow limits of his dominions, would easily obtain, in a happier
climate, a secure refuge, a new fortune adequate to his merit, the
freedom of complaint, and perhaps the means of revenge. But the
empire of the Romans filled the world, and when that empire fell
into the hands of a single person, the world became a safe and dreary
prison for his enemies. The slave of Imperial despotism, whether he
was condemned to drag his gilded chain in Rome and the senate,
or to wear out a life of exile on the barren rock of Seriphus, or
the frozen banks of the Danube, expected his fate in silent despair.
To resist was fatal, and it was impossible to fly. On every side he
was encompassed with a vast extent of sea and land, which he could
never hope to traverse without being discovered, seized, and restored
to his irritated master. Beyond the frontiers, his anxious view could
discover nothing, except the ocean, inhospitable deserts, hostile tribes
of barbarians, of fierce manners and unknown language, or dependent
kings, who would gladly purchase the emperor's protection by the
sacrifice of an obnoxious fugitive. "Wherever you are," said Cicero
to the exiled Marcellus, "remember that you are equally within the
power of the conqueror."

—Edward Gibbon, *The Decline and Fall of the Roman Empire*

VIII

The human species, according to the best theory I can form of it,
is composed of two distinct races, *the men who borrow*, and *the men*

who lend. To these two original diversities may be reduced all those impertinent classifications of Gothic and Celtic tribes, white men, black men, red men. All the dwellers upon earth, "Parthians, and Medes, and Elamites," flock hither, and do naturally fall in with one or other of these primary distinctions. The infinite superiority of the former, which I choose to designate as the *great race*, is discernible in their figure, port, and a certain instinctive sovereignty. The latter are born degraded. "He shall serve his brethren." There is something in the air of one of this cast, lean and suspicious; contrasting with the open, trusting, generous manners of the other.

Observe who have been the greatest borrowers of all ages—Alcibiades—Falstaff—Sir Richard Steele—our late incomparable Brinsley—what a family likeness in all four!

What a careless, even deportment hath your borrower! what rosy gills! what a beautiful reliance on Providence doth he manifest—taking no more thought than lilies! What contempt for money—accounting it (yours and mine especially) no better than dross. What a liberal confounding of those pedantic distinctions of *meum* and *tuum!* or rather, what a noble simplification of language (beyond Tooke), resolving these supposed opposites into one clear, intelligible pronoun adjective! What near approaches doth he make to the primitive *community*—to the extent of one half of the principle at least!

—Charles Lamb, "The Two Races of Men"

IX

There is hardly anything that shows the shortsightedness or capriciousness of the imagination more than traveling does. With change of place we change our ideas; nay, our opinions and feelings. We can by an effort indeed transport ourselves to old and long-forgotten scenes, and then the picture of the mind revives again; but we forget those that we have just left. It seems that we can think but of one place at a time. The canvas of the fancy is but of a certain extent, and if we paint one set of objects upon it, they immediately efface every other. We cannot enlarge our conceptions, we only shift our point of view. The landscape bares its bosom to the enraptured eye, we take our fill of it, and seem as if we could form no other image of beauty or grandeur. We pass one, and think no more of it: the horizon that shuts it from our sight also blots it from our memory like a dream. In traveling through a wild barren country I can form no idea of a woody and cultivated one. It appears to me that all the world must be barren, like what I see of it. In the country we forget the town, and in town we despise the country. "Beyond Hyde Park," says Sir Fopling Flutter, "all is a desert." All that part of the map that we do not see before us is a blank. The world in our conceit of it is not much bigger than a nutshell. It is not one prospect expanded into another, county joined to county, kingdom to kingdom, lands to seas, making an image voluminous and vast; the mind can form no larger idea of space than the eye can take in at a single glance. The rest is a name written in a map, a calculation of arithmetic. For instance, what is the true signification of that immense mass of territory and population known by the name of China to us? An inch of pasteboard on a wooden globe, of no more account than a China orange! Things near us are seen of the size of life; things at a distance are diminished to the size of the understanding. We measure the universe by ourselves, and even comprehend the texture of our own being only piecemeal. In this way, however, we remember an infinity of things and places. The mind is like a mechanical instrument that plays a great variety of tunes, but it must play them in succession. One idea recalls another, but it at the same time excludes all others. In trying to renew old recollections, we cannot as it were unfold the whole web of our existence; we must pick out the single threads. So in coming to a place where we have formerly lived, and with which we have intimate associations, everyone must have found that the feeling grows more vivid the nearer we approach the spot, from the mere anticipation of the actual impression: we remember circumstances, feelings, persons, faces, names, that we had not thought of for years; but for the time all the rest of the world is forgotten!

—William Hazlitt, "On Going a Journey"

X

In that great social organ which, collectively, we call literature, there may be distinguished two separate offices that may blend and often do so, but capable, severally, of a severe insulation, and naturally fitted for reciprocal repulsion. There is, first, the literature of *knowledge*, and secondly, the literature of *power*. The function of the first is to *teach*; the function of the second is to *move*; the first is a rudder, the second an oar or a sail. The first speaks to the mere discursive understanding; the second speaks ultimately, it may happen, to the higher understanding or reason, but always through affections of pleasure and sympathy. Remotely, it may travel towards an object seated in what Lord Bacon calls *dry* light; but, proximately, it does and must operate—else it ceases to be a literature of *power* —and on through that *humid* light which clothes itself in the mists and glittering *iris* of human passions, desires, and genial emotions. Men have so little reflected on the higher functions of literature as to find it a paradox if one should describe it as a mean or subordinate purpose of books to give information. But this is a paradox only in the sense which makes it honorable to be paradoxical. Whenever we talk in ordinary language of seeking information or gaining knowledge, we understand the words as connected with something of absolute novelty. But it is the grandeur of all truth which *can* occupy a very high place in human interests that it is never absolutely novel to the meanest of minds: it exists eternally by way of germ or latent principle in the lowest as in the highest, needing to be developed, but never to be planted. To be capable of transplantation is the immediate criterion of a truth that ranges on a lower scale. Besides which, there is a rarer thing than truth—namely, *power*, or deep sympathy with truth. What is the effect, for instance, upon society, of children? By the pity, by the tenderness, and by the peculiar modes of admiration, which connect themselves with the helplessness, with the innocence, and with the simplicity of children, not only are the primal affections strengthened and continually renewed, but the qualities which are dearest in the sight of heaven—the frailty, for instance, which appeals to forbearance, the innocence which symbolizes the heavenly, and the simplicity which is most alien from the worldly—are kept up in perpetual remembrance, and their ideals are continually refreshed. A purpose of the same nature is answered by the high literature, viz., the literature of power. What do you learn from *Paradise Lost?* Nothing at all. What do you learn from a cookery book? Something new, something that you did not know before, in every paragraph. But would you therefore put the wretched cookery book on a higher level of estimation than the divine poem? What you owe to Milton is not any knowledge, of which a million separate items are still but a million of advancing steps on the same earthly level; what you owe is *power*—that is, exercise and expansion to your own latent capacity of sympathy with the infinite, where every pulse and each separate influx is a step upwards, a step ascending as upon a Jacob's ladder from earth to mysterious altitudes above the earth. *All* the steps of knowledge, from first to last, carry you further on the same plane, but could never raise you one foot above your ancient level of earth: whereas the very *first* step in power is a flight—is an ascending movement into another element where earth is forgotten.

—Thomas de Quincey, "Literature of Knowledge and Literature of Power"

XI

Visible and tangible products of the Past, again, I reckon-up to the extent of three: Cities, with their Cabinets and Arsenals; then tilled Fields, to either or to both of which divisions Roads with their Bridges may belong; and thirdly—Books. In which third truly, the last invented, lies a worth far surpassing that of the two others. Wondrous indeed is the virtue of a true Book. Not like a dead city of stones, yearly crumbling, yearly needing repair; more like a tilled field, but then a spiritual field: like a spiritual tree, let me rather say, it stands from year to year, and from age to age (we have Books that already number some hundred-and-fifty human ages); and yearly comes its new produce of leaves (Commentaries, Deductions, Philosophical, Political Systems; or were it only Sermons, Pamphlets, Journalistic Essays), every one of which is talismanic and thaumaturgic, for it can persuade men. O thou who art able to write a Book, which once in the two centuries or oftener there is a man gifted to do, envy not him whom they name City-builder, and inexpressibly pity him whom they name Conqueror or City-burner! Thou too art a Conqueror and Victor: but of the true sort, namely over the Devil: thou too hast built what will outlast all marble and metal, and be a wonder-ringing City of the Mind, a Temple and Seminary and Prophetic Mount, whereto all kindreds of the Earth will pilgrim. Fool! why journeyest thou wearisomely, in thy antiquarian fervor, to gaze on the stone pyramids of Geeza, or the clay ones of Sacchara? These stand there, as I can tell thee, idle and inert, looking over the Desert, foolishly enough, for the last three thousand years: but canst thou not open thy Hebrew BIBLE, then, or even Luther's Version thereof?

—Thomas Carlyle, *Sartor Resartus*

XII

To write history respectably—that is, to abbreviate dispatches, and make extracts from speeches, to intersperse in due proportion epithets of praise and abhorrence, to draw up antithetical characters of great men, setting forth how many contradictory virtues and vices they united, and abounding in *withs* and *withouts*—all this is very easy. But to be a really great historian is perhaps the rarest of intellectual distinctions. Many scientific works are, in their kind, absolutely perfect. There are poems which we would be inclined to designate as faultless, or as disfigured only by blemishes which pass unnoticed in the general blaze of excellence. There are speeches, some speeches of Demosthenes particularly, in which it would be impossible to alter a word without altering it for the worse. But we are acquainted with no history which approaches to our notion of what a history ought to be—with no history which does not widely depart, either on the right hand or on the left, from the exact line.

The cause may easily be assigned. This province of literature is a debatable land. It lies on the confines of two distinct territories. It is under the jurisdiction of two hostile powers; and, like other districts similarly situated, it is ill-defined, ill-cultivated, and ill-regulated. Instead of being equally shared between its two rulers, the Reason and the Imagination, it falls alternately under the sole and absolute dominion of each. It is sometimes fiction. It is sometimes theory.

History, it has been said, is philosophy teaching by examples. Unhappily, what the philosophy gains in soundness and depth the examples generally lose in vividness. A perfect historian must possess an imagination sufficiently powerful to make his narrative affecting and picturesque. Yet he must control it so absolutely as to content himself with the materials which he finds, and to refrain from supplying deficiences by additions of his own. He must be a profound and ingenious reasoner. Yet he must possess sufficient self-command to abstain from casting his facts in the mold of his hypothesis. Those who can justly estimate these almost insuperable difficulties will not think it strange that every writer should have failed, either in the narrative or in the speculative department of history.

—Thomas Babington Macaulay, "History"

XIII

Knowledge is one thing, virtue is another; good sense is not conscience, refinement is not humility, nor is largeness and justness of view faith. Philosophy, however enlightened, however profound, gives no command over the passions, no influential motives, no vivifying principles. Liberal Education makes not the Christian, not the Catholic, but the gentleman. It is well to be a gentleman, it is well to have a cultivated intellect, a delicate taste, a candid, equitable, dispassionate mind, a noble and courteous bearing in the conduct of life—these are the connatural qualities of a large knowledge; they are the objects of a University; I am advocating, I shall illustrate and insist upon them; but still, I repeat, they are no guarantee for sanctity or even for conscientiousness, they may attach to the man of the world, to the profligate, to the heartless, pleasant, alas, and attractive as he shows when decked out in them. Taken by themselves, they do but seem to be what they are not; they look like virtue at a distance, but they are detected by close observers, and on the long run; and hence it is that they are popularly accused of pretense and hypocrisy, not, I repeat, from their own fault, but because their professors and their admirers persist in taking them for what they are not, and are officious in arrogating for them a praise to which they have no claim. Quarry the granite rock with razors, or moor the vessel with a thread of silk; then may you hope with such keen and delicate instruments as human knowledge and human reason to contend against those giants, the passion and the pride of man.

—John Henry Newman, *The Idea of a University*

XIV

But there is of culture another view, in which not solely the scientific passion, the sheer desire to see things as they are, natural and proper in an intelligent being, appears as the ground of it. There is a view in which all the love of our neighbor, the impulses towards action, help, and beneficence, the desire for removing human error, clearing human confusion, and diminishing human misery, the noble aspiration to leave the world better and happier than we found it—

motives eminently such as are called social—come in as part of the grounds of culture, and the main and pre-eminent part. Culture is then properly described not as having its origin in curiosity, but as having its origin in the love of perfection; it is *a study of perfection*. It moves by the force, not merely or primarily of the scientific passion for pure knowledge, but also of the moral and social passion for doing good. As, in the first view of it, we took for its worthy motto Montesquieu's words: "To render an intelligent being yet more intelligent!" so, in the second view of it, there is no better motto which it can have than these words of Bishop Wilson: "To make reason and the will of God prevail!"

Only, whereas the passion for doing good is apt to be overhasty in determining what reason and the will of God say, because its turn is for acting rather than thinking, and it wants to be beginning to act; and whereas it is apt to take its own conceptions, which proceed from its own state of development and share in all the imperfections and immaturities of this, for a basis of action; what distinguishes culture is, that it is possessed by the scientific passion as well as by the passion of doing good; that it demands worthy notions of reason and the will of God, and does not readily suffer its own crude conceptions to substitute themselves for them. And knowing that no action or institution can be salutary and stable which is not based on reason and the will of God, it is not so bent on acting and instituting, even with the great aim of diminishing human error and misery ever before its thoughts, but that it can remember that acting and instituting are of little use, unless we know how and what we ought to act and to institute.

—Matthew Arnold, "Sweetness and Light"

XV

The presence that rose thus so strangely beside the waters, is expressive of what in the ways of a thousand years men had come to desire. Hers is the head upon which all "the ends of the world are come," and the eyelids are a little weary. It is a beauty wrought out from within upon the flesh, the deposit, little cell by cell, of strange thoughts and fantastic reveries and exquisite passions. Set it for a moment beside one of those white Greek goddesses or beautiful women of antiquity, and how would they be troubled by this beauty, into which the soul with all its maladies has passed! All the thoughts and experience of the world have etched and molded there, in that which they have of power to refine and make expressive the outward form, the animalism of Greece, the lust of Rome, the mysticism of the middle ages with its spiritual ambition and imaginative loves, the return of the Pagan world, the sins of the Borgias. She is older than the rocks among which she sits; like the vampire, she has been dead many times, and learned the secrets of the grave; and has been a diver in deep seas, and keeps their fallen day about her; and trafficked for strange webs with Eastern merchants: and, as Leda, was the mother of Helen of Troy, and, as Saint Anne, the mother of Mary; and all this has been to her but as the sound of lyres and flutes, and lives only in the delicacy with which it has molded the changing lineaments, and tinged the eyelids and the hands. The fancy of a perpetual life, sweeping together ten thousand experiences, is an old one; and modern philosophy has conceived the idea of humanity as wrought upon by, and summing up in itself, all modes of thought and life. Certainly Lady Lisa might stand as the embodiment of the old fancy, the symbol of the modern idea.

—Walter Pater, *The Renaissance*

ALFRED NORTH WHITEHEAD
On Style[1]

Finally, there should grow the most austere of all mental qualities; I mean the sense for style. It is an aesthetic sense, based on admiration for the direct attainment of a foreseen end, simply and without waste. Style in art, style in literature, style in science, style in logic, style in practical execution have fundamentally the same aesthetic qualities, namely, attainment and restraint. The love of a subject in itself and for itself, where it is not the sleepy pleasure of pacing a mental quarter-deck, is the love of style as manifested in that study.

Here we are brought back to the position from which we started, the utility of education. Style, in its finest sense, is the last acquirement of the educated mind; it is also the most useful. It pervades the whole being. The administrator with a sense for style hates waste; the engineer with a sense for style economizes his material; the artisan with a sense for style prefers good work. Style is the ultimate morality of mind.

But above style, and above knowledge, there is something, a vague shape like fate above the Greek gods. That something is Power. Style is the fashioning of power, the restraining of power. But, after all, the power of attainment of the desired end is fundamental. The first thing is to get there. Do not bother about your style, but solve your problem, justify the ways of God to man, administer your province, or do whatever else is set before you.

Where, then, does style help? In this, with style the end is attained without side issues, without raising undesirable inflammations. With style you attain your end and nothing but your end. With style the effect of your activity is calculable, and foresight is the last gift of gods to men. With style your power is increased, for your mind is

1. From Chapter 1 of *The Aims of Education*, 1929.

not distracted with irrelevancies, and you are more likely to attain your object. Now style is the exclusive privilege of the expert. Whoever heard of the style of an amateur painter, of the style of an amateur poet? Style is always the product of specialist study, the peculiar contribution of specialism to culture.

J. ROBERT OPPENHEIMER
On Style[1]

The problem of doing justice to the implicit, the imponderable, and the unknown is of course not unique to politics. It is always with us in science, it is with us in the most trivial of personal affairs, and it is one of the great problems of writing and of all forms of art. The means by which it is solved is sometimes called style. It is style which complements affirmation with limitation and with humility; it is style which makes it possible to act effectively, but not absolutely; it is style which, in the domain of foreign policy, enables us to find a harmony between the pursuit of ends essential to us and the regard for the views, the sensibilities, the aspirations of those to whom the problem may appear in another light; it is style which is the deference that action pays to uncertainty; it is above all style through which power defers to reason.

1. From a speech (1948) entitled "The Open Mind," later included in a book of the same name.

WALKER GIBSON
A Note on Style and the Limits of Language[1]

Questions about style can most usefully be approached if we think of a style as the expression of a personality. I do not mean at all that our words necessarily reveal what we are "really like." I do mean that every writer and talker, more or less consciously, chooses a role which he thinks appropriate to express for a given time and situation. The personality I am expressing in this written sentence is not the same as the one I orally express to my three-year-old who at this moment is bent on climbing onto my typewriter. For each of these two situations, I choose a different "voice," a different mask, in order to accomplish what I want accomplished. There is no point in asking here which of these voices is closer to the Real Me. What may be worth asking is this: what kinds of voices, in written prose, may be said to respond most sensitively and efficiently to the sort of contemporary world that this book has been describing?

1. Conclusion of *The Limits of Language*, 1962.

First, let's be logical about it. Given the kind of dilemma with respect to knowledge and language that this book defines, what sort of style might we expect in our own time? What sort of speaking voice adopted by the writer, what mask, would be appropriate in a world where, as we have seen, the very nature of nature may be inexpressible? If we live in a pluralistic and fluxlike universe, what manner of word-man should we become in order to talk about it? Well, we might at least expect a man who knows his limits, who admits the inevitably subjective character of his wisdom. We might expect a man who knows that he has no right in a final sense to consider himself any wiser than the next fellow, including the one he is talking to. The appropriate tone, therefore, might be informal, a little tense and self-conscious perhaps, but genial as between equals. With our modern relativistic ideas about the impossibility of determining any "standard dialect" for expressing Truth in all its forms, we might expect the cautious writer to employ many dialects, to shift from formal to colloquial diction, to avoid the slightest hint of authoritarianism. The rhythm of his words will be an irregular, conversational rhythm—not the symmetrical periods of formal Victorian prose. Short sentences alternating erratically with longer sentences. Occasional sentence fragments. In sum we might expect a style rather like *this*![2]

This style, indeed, is easily recognizable and can be discovered all around us in modern prose. Thirty years ago in a book called *Modern Prose Style*, Bonamy Dobrée described it much as we have done here. "Most of us have ceased to believe, except provisionally, in truths," he wrote, "and we feel that what is important is not so much truth as the way our minds move toward truth." The consequence is a kind of self-searching need for frankness and humility on the part of the writer. "The modern prose-writer, in returning to the rhythms of everyday speech, is trying to be more honest with himself than if he used, as is too wreckingly easy, the forms and terms already published as the expression of other people's minds." Finally, in a touching sentence, "In our present confusion our only hope is to be scrupulously honest with ourselves." That was written in 1933: since then the confusion has multiplied spectacularly, while our hopes of ever being "scrupulously honest" about anything look pretty dim. Still, the relation Dobrée made, between an intellectual difficulty and a style, is essentially the relation we are making here.

The trouble with it—and a reminder of the awful complexity of

2. A few of the writer's obvious attempts to echo a conversational tone in that paragraph can be quickly summarized. Contractions (let's). Colloquialisms (well . . ., the next fellow). Some very short sentences. Capitalization in an effort to place an ironical turn on a Big Fat Abstraction (Truth)—an effort that is of course much easier to accomplish with the actual voice. Italics (*except*, like *this!*), again in mimicry of the way one speaks in conversation. And so on. The purpose of such devices, to compensate for the loss of oral intonation, is strictly speaking impossible to achieve. If only you were here I could *say* all this to you [Gibson's note].

our subject—is that sometimes this proposition simply doesn't work. Some contemporary writers, sensitively aware of the limits of language, indeed conceding them explicitly, nevertheless write in a *style* that sounds like the wisdom of Moses, or like Winston Churchill. Far from echoing the rhythms of ordinary speech, they pontificate or chant in authoritarian rhythms the assertion that one cannot be authoritarian. We have a fine example of this paradox in the paragraph by Oppenheimer that I have so much admired (page 154). Oppenheimer uses a vocabulary, sentence structure, tone, and rhythm all highly structured and formalized; there is no unbending there. The theme of his discourse—that style is "the deference that action pays to uncertainty"—seems at odds with the *personality* we hear uttering this theme. That personality, because of the way the words are chosen and arranged, appears curiously self-confident, even dictatorial, with echoes perhaps of Johnsonian prose, or Macaulay's elegant sentences. Thus the first sentence is built around a handsome triplet of alliterative abstractions ("the implicit, the imponderable, and the unknown"); the second sentence is built out of another triplet of nicely balanced clauses. The extraordinary final sentence approaches incantation in its parallel repetitions of structure. The "voice" we hear, remote indeed from ordinary conversation, seems to *know* even as it asserts its own humility. Different readers will explain all this in different ways: some will argue that the traditional manner lends sincerity and persuasiveness to the message, while others will be set off by what they consider a real discrepancy between matter and manner. We recall that the passage was taken from an address delivered at a formal occasion. I have heard Mr. Oppenheimer's platform manner described as "arrogant"; our stylistic observations might well account in part for such an impression. In any case it is clear that no easy formula—Dobrée's or anyone else's—is going to account for all the vagaries of modern prose.

Other writers in this collection will illustrate Dobrée's thesis with less embarrassment—that is, will show clear evidence of a "conversational" voice. Thus Muller:

> Emerson remarked that it is a good thing, now and then, to take a look at the landscape from between one's legs. Although this stunt might seem pointless when things are already topsy-turvy, it can be the more helpful then. One may say that what this chaotic world needs first of all is *dis*sociation; by breaking up factitious alliances and oppositions, one may get at the deep uniformities. Or...

The simplicity of the diction in that first sentence, and the absurdity of the described action, support a familiar relation of equality between the speaking voice and the reader. There is no talking down; we all know who Emerson is. (Not "That great American Transcendentalist, Ralph Waldo Emerson. . . .") "Now and then," "stunt," "topsy-turvy" contribute the colloquial touch. The slightly awkward "then" at the end of the second sentence suggests that in this particular communication formal grace would be inappropriate. But with the third sentence the writer boldly shifts his tone as his diction becomes more polysyllabic and his sentence structure more complex. "Enough of geniality," he seems to say, "you must now follow me into a serious tangle." With this abruptness, Muller is perhaps "breaking up factitious alliances" *in his style*, so that his own prose both expresses and dramatizes the point he is making.

The trick, if that is what it is, of mingling formal and colloquial vocabularly can convey a kind of ironical thrust by the writer at his own pretensions. Thus he can have it both ways—make his great assertion and kid himself for his own gall. It is a device much employed in circles that are verbally sophisticated, including academic circles. Consider an extreme example, from a professor of law at Chicago, here discussing a flexible approach to problems of judicial interpretation:

> But it leads to *good* rules of law and in the main toward flexible ones, so that most cases of a given type can come to be handled not only well but easily, and so that the odd case can normally come in also for a smidgeon of relief. The whole setup leads above all—a recognition of imperfection in language and in officer—to *on-going and unceasing judicial review of prior judicial decision* on the side of rule, tool, and technique. That, plus freedom and duty to do justice *with* the rules but *within* both them and their whole temper, that is the freedom, the leeway for own-contribution, the scope for the person, which the system offers.[3]

Here style and message work with a degree of co-operation: a call for unceasing flexibility in the operations of judicial review is expressed in an idiom that is itself almost wildly flexible. The speaker in this passage betrays the strains of an impassioned conversationalist, with his heavy reliance on italics and his interrupted sentence structures. We are buttonholed. This is a technical discussion, and most of the vocabularly has to be fairly heavy, but we have "smidgeon" and "whole setup" to cut across the formality. We have even a jazzy bit of alliteration and rhyme—"rule, tool, and technique." The "recognition of imperfection in language," therefore, which is explicitly granted by the text, is implicitly conveyed as well by the unorthodox scramblings of language. Nobody has to like this style (many are simply irritated), but at least one can see what is going on, and why.

Or consider another extreme example, from a professor of English at Wisconsin, here discussing problems of usage:

> Bad, fair, good, better, best. Only the best is Correct. No busy man can be Correct. But his wife can. That's what women are for. That's why we have women to teach English and type our letters and go to church for us and discover for us that the English say "Aren't I?" while we sinfully hunt golf-balls in the rough on Sunday and, when our partner finds two

3. From Karl N. Llewellyn, *The Common Law Tradition: Deciding Appeals*, Little, Brown, 1960 [Gibson's note].

of them, ask "Which is me?" (Webster: *colloq.*—Professor K of Harvard: I speak colloq myself, and sometimes I write it.) . . . Only a few of us today are aware of the other scales of English usage. It is our business to consciously know about their social utility.[4]

These sentences from a treatise on language admirably demonstrate that self-consciously unbuttoned informality which the subject now-adays seems to demand. To some, again, it will appear offensively "cute," idiosyncratic. Short sentences, some without predicates, sur-round one almost endless rambling sentence. The ironical capital in Correct (cf. Truth *supra*). Indifference to the rule that pronouns should have specific antecedents ("That's what women are for. That's why . . ."). Muddled number in using personal pronouns (we hunt golf balls, our partner [sing.] finds, [we] ask 'Which is me?'). Deliber-ately split infinitive in the last sentence quoted, at a point in the utterance when a conventionally formal tone has begun to enter. We may anticipate, I am sure, a time when writers will endeavor to carefully split their infinitives, at whatever cost in awkwardness, just as writers of a former generation endeavored so elaborately to avoid the "error." All this should prove to at least be amusing.

To many readers, the style displayed by a Professor Llewellyn or a Professor Joos will seem undisciplined, vulgar, and chaotic. A sign of academic deterioration. A result of wild "permissiveness" in edu-cation and in society generally. But such readers will be missing the point. There is nothing indiscriminately permissive in this style, but the writers do accept and reject different kinds of language from those accepted and rejected by traditional stylists. They express different personalities. Without insisting on the merits of these par-ticular passages, which are certainly debatable, it ought nevertheless to be clear that you do not write in this way simply by saying any-thing that occurs to you. The process of selection can be, indeed, *more* discriminating because the available supply of language and experience is larger. As this is being written, in the autumn of 1961, a mild flurry about such extensions of language is going on in the press, relating to the publication of a new edition of Webster's *New International Dictionary*. The New York *Times* has editorialized as follows:

A passel of double-domes at the G. & C. Merriam Company joint in Springfield, Mass., have been confabbing and yakking for twenty-seven years—which is not intended to infer that they have not been doing plenty work—and now they have finalized Webster's Third New International Dictionary, Unabridged, a new edition of that swell and esteemed word book.

Those who regard the foregoing paragraph as acceptable English prose will find that the new Webster's is just the dictionary for them. The words in that paragraph all are listed in the new work with no suggestion that they are anything but standard.

4. From Martin Joos, *The Five Clocks*. Copyright 1961 by Martin Joos [Gib-son's note].

Webster's has, it is apparent, surrendered to the permissive school that has been busily extending its beachhead on English instruction in the schools. This development is disastrous....

The *Times* goes on to acknowledge "the lexical explosion that has showered us with so many words in recent years," and to congratulate the Dictionary for including 100,000 new words or new definitions. "These are improvements, but they cannot outweigh the fundamental fault." Webster's has always been a "peerless authority on American English," and therefore its editors have "to some degree a public responsibility." "A new start is needed."

There is, I think, something wrong about all this. If you are acknowledging a "lexical explosion," a language changing with accelerating rapidity, then it seems rather difficult to insist at the same time on a "peerless authority." The editors of the Dictionary may have fulfilled their public responsibility by taking the only wise course—by including as many new words and definitions as they could without making "authoritative" judgments about "standard," "colloquial," and "slang." This is not to say that the modern writer ignores such distinctions; on the contrary he is sensitively aware of them as never before. But he knows, and the dictionary editors know, that no such label is good for long in a culture as volatile as this one. Yesterday's slang is today's standard, and the writer who remains resonant to these shifts has at his disposal a huge and varicolored vocabulary for his art.

The reason we call that opening paragraph in the *Times* editorial "unacceptable English" is not that it contains slang. The reason is that it contains too many kinds of slang at once, without any awareness of their differences. You do not say "passel of double-domes" unless you have some good reason for juxtaposing terms from utterly distinct language worlds. "Passel" is presumably of western-frontier origin and now has a kind of weary whimsy about it, while "double-domes" is recent, cheaply anti-intellectual, with a history something like "egghead" but without the popular acceptance of "egghead." It is conceivable that these words could be included in one sentence, but it would take more skill that the *Times* man has employed. Of course the appearance of clumsiness was just what served his purpose.

Meanwhile the writer who looks backward to "authority," who takes a static view of Standard Language, is likely to sound like the "straight" paragraphs of that editorial. The voice there is closer to a chiding or dictatorial professor than were the voices of the actual professors quoted. And when such a writer uses "modern" terms, he uses them in ways that are long overused before he gets to them— ways like "extending its beachhead on English instruction" or "lexical explosion that has showered us with so many words." It is this sort of thing that is the true vulgarity in our time.

Nevertheless our society remains generous with half-conscious concessions to the imperfections of its language. It may be, for example, that the language of the beatniks, especially their oral conventions, could be looked at in the light of such concessions. Consider just one curious symptom of jive-talk (now dated)—the suffix-plus-prefix *like*. "We came to this big town like and all the streets were like crazy, man." This attempt at rendering beat dialect is doubtless inaccurate but it should serve to make the point. That point is that the beats have (deliberately?) modified or qualified their nouns and adjectives by suggesting that they are not quite accurate, not quite the way things are. "This big town like"—it is a one-ended metaphor. Like what? We have a tenor but no vehicle, or is it a vehicle without a tenor? I have been told that many beats are determinedly anti-verbal, preferring to listen to jazz while lying on beaches in Zenlike silence. It fits. The skepticism about the validity of words that "like" implies is a peculiarly twentieth-century skepticism, it seems to me, though there may be analogies with other ages such as the seventeenth century, when scientific developments encouraged similar self-scrutinies and self-doubts. In any event the beats, in their crude and sloppy way of course, have surrounded much of their language with a metaphorical blur by using (among other things) the simple device of "like." They suggest, with this blur, their convicton of the impossibility of anybody else's doing any better with words. Only squares believe you can speak "precisely."

The complexities of experience do occasionally get faced one way or another—if not with the beats' pose of inarticulateness, then with some other pose that will serve to avoid the charge of *really knowing*. Modern novelists adopt a "point of view" which is often no point of view at all, but several points of view from which to indicate various inadequate interpretations of various fictitious characters. It is a technique that will show how two novels as apparently unlike as *The Waves*[5] * * * and Faulkner's *As I Lay Dying* belong after all to the same age. There is no narrator, no one of whom the reader might conceivably say, "There! That's the author talking." The technique is not new; there is *The Ring and the Book*, to mention one example. But the difference is that when you read *The Ring and the Book*, you feel how firmly and finally Browning is on Pompilia's "side," in spite of his wonderful multiplicity throughout that great poem. Whereas in many modern novels you scarcely know who is on anybody's side—you must simply flow in the flux. Sometimes it is so lifelike you can hardly stand it.

And of course that road—the road of chaos chaotically expressing chaos—is a dead end of imitative form where we end with a grunt, or maybe a whimper. The very point is that language will never say our experience "as is," and recognizing this truth, we have immense freedom of possibility to make, create, form what we can out of

5. A novel by Virginia Woolf, 1931.

words or out of anything else. The most elaborate of villanelles is not much further removed from Real Life than the latest Allen Ginsberg[6] poem, or a slice of Mr. Bloom's day.[7] So write a villanelle if that will meet your need. But whatever it is, there remains this simple blasphemy to be avoided, and that is the blasphemy of ignoring the limits, of assuming that one's words do indeed tell the reader what is going on. There is an important sense in which nobody knows what he is talking about.

I hope I do not except myself and everything uttered here.

6. Author of unconventional poems such as *Howl*, 1956.

7. A day in the life of Leopold Bloom, conveyed mainly through interior monologue, provides the framework of James Joyce's novel *Ulysses*, 1922.

QUESTIONS FOR STUDY, DISCUSSION, AND WRITING

1. Explain the importance of Gibson's distinction between a "speaking voice" and a "real" personality.
2. Examine several of the selections in Personal Report (pp. 1–72) or the Album of Styles (pp. 141–153) and characterize the speaking voice of each. Compare one or two of these with the "voices" of the letters (pp. 320–334) or the journals (pp. 76–85).
3. Compare Gibson's discussion of style with Ittleson and Kilpatrick's discussion of perception (pp. 267–273). To what extent are the two essays concerned with similar problems?
4. Gibson refers to Oppenheimer's definition of style (p. 154). How closely does the definition of style that Gibson implies correspond with Oppenheimer's? Where do the two differ?
5. Write two brief descriptions of the same scene (or person or object or event), using a different "voice" for each. What advantages can one "voice" have over another for handling a given subject?

On Education

THOMAS JEFFERSON
Letter to Peter Carr[1]

Paris, August 10, 1787

DEAR PETER

I have received your two letters of December the 30th and April the 18th, and am very happy to find by them, as well as by letters from Mr. Wythe,[2] that you have been so fortunate as to attract his notice and good will; I am sure you will find this to have been one of the most fortunate events of your life, as I have ever been sensible it was of mine. I enclose you a sketch of the sciences to which I would wish you to apply, in such order as Mr. Wythe shall advise; I mention also, the books in them worth your reading, which submit to his correction. Many of these are among your father's books, which you should have brought to you. As I do not recollect those of them not in his library, you must write to me for them, making out a catalogue of such as you think you shall have occasion for, in eighteen months from the date of your letter, and consulting Mr. Wythe on the subject. To this sketch, I will add a few particular observations:

1. Italian. I fear the learning this language will confound your French and Spanish. Being all of them degenerated dialects of the Latin, they are apt to mix in conversation. I have never seen a person speaking the three languages, who did not mix them. It is a delightful language, but late events having rendered the Spanish more useful, lay it aside to prosecute that.

2. Spanish. Bestow great attention on this, and endeavor to acquire an accurate knowledge of it. Our future connections with Spain and Spanish America, will render that language a valuable acquisition. The ancient history of that part of America, too, is written in that language. I send you a dictionary.

3. Moral Philosophy. I think it lost time to attend lectures on

---

1. Jefferson's nephew.
2. George Wythe, professor of law at William and Mary College.

this branch. He who made us would have been a pitiful bungler, if he had made the rules of our moral conduct a matter of science. For one man of science, there are thousands who are not. What would have become of them? Man was destined for society. His morality, therefore, was to be formed to this object. He was endowed with a sense of right and wrong, merely relative to this. This sense is as much a part of his nature, as the sense of hearing, seeing, feeling; it is the true foundation of morality, and not the το καλον,[3] truth, etc., as fanciful writers have imagined. The moral sense, or conscience, is as much a part of man as his leg or arm. It is given to all human beings in a stronger or weaker degree, as force of members is given them in a greater or less degree. It may be strengthened by exercise, as may any particular limb of the body. This sense is submitted, indeed, in some degree, to the guidance of reason; but it is a small stock which is required for this: even a less one than what we call common sense. State a moral case to a ploughman and a professor. The former will decide it as well, and often better than the latter, because he has not been led astray by artificial rules. In this branch, therefore, read good books, because they will encourage, as well as direct your feelings. The writings of Sterne, particularly, form the best course of morality that ever was written. Besides these, read the books mentioned in the enclosed paper; and, above all things, lose no occasion of exercising your dispositions to be grateful, to be generous, to be charitable, to be humane, to be true, just, firm, orderly, courageous, etc. Consider every act of this kind, as an exercise which will strengthen your moral faculties and increase your worth.

4. Religion. Your reason is now mature enough to examine this object. In the first place, divest yourself of all bias in favor of novelty and singularity of opinion. Indulge them in any other subject rather than that of religion. It is too important, and the consequences of error may be too serious. On the other hand, shake off all fears and servile prejudices, under which weak minds are servilely crouched. Fix reason firmly in her seat, and call to her tribunal every fact, every opinion. Question with boldness even the existence of a God; because, if there be one, he must more approve of the homage of reason, than that of blindfolded fear. You will naturally examine first, the religion of your own country. Read the Bible, then, as you would read Livy or Tacitus. The facts which are within the ordinary course of nature, you will believe on the authority of the writer, as you do those of the same kind in Livy and Tacitus. The testimony of the writer weighs in their favor, in one scale, and their not being against the laws of nature, does not weigh against them. But those facts in the Bible which contradict the laws of nature, must be examined with more care, and under a variety of faces. Here you must recur to

3. The beautiful.

the pretensions of the writer to inspiration from God. Examine upon what evidence his pretensions are founded, and whether that evidence is so strong, as that its falsehood would be more improbable than a change in the laws of nature, in the case he relates. For example, in the book of Joshua, we are told, the sun stood still several hours. Were we to read that fact in Livy or Tacitus, we should class it with their showers of blood, speaking of statues, beasts, etc. But it is said, that the writer of that book was inspired. Examine, therefore, candidly, what evidence there is of his having been inspired. The pretension is entitled to your inquiry, because millions believe it. On the other hand, you are astronomer enough to know how contrary it is to the law of nature that a body revolving on its axis, as the earth does, should have stopped, should not, by that sudden stoppage, have prostrated animals, trees, buildings, and should after a certain time have resumed its revolution, and that without a second general prostration. Is this arrest of the earth's motion, or the evidence which affirms it, most within the law of probabilities? You will next read the New Testament. It is the history of a personage called Jesus. Keep in your eye the opposite pretensions: 1, of those who say he was begotten by God, born of a virgin, suspended and reversed the laws of nature at will, and ascended bodily into heaven; and 2, of those who say he was a man of illegitimate birth, of a benevolent heart, enthusiastic mind, who set out without pretensions to divinity, ended in believing them, and was punished capitally for sedition, by being gibbeted, according to the Roman law, which punished the first commission of that offense by whipping, and the second by exile, or death *in furcâ*[4] . . . .

Do not be frightened from this inquiry by any fear of its consequences. If it ends in a belief that there is no God, you will find incitements to virtue in the comfort and pleasantness you feel in its exercise, and the love of others which it will procure you. If you find reason to believe there is a God, a consciousness that you are acting under his eye, and that he approves you, will be a vast additional incitement; if that there be a future state, the hope of a happy existence in that increases the appetite to deserve it; if that Jesus was also a God, you will be comforted by a belief of his aid and love. In fine, I repeat, you must lay aside all prejudice on both sides, and neither believe nor reject anything, because any other persons or description of persons, have rejected or believed it. Your own reason is the only oracle given you by heaven, and you are answerable, not for the rightness, but uprightness of the decision. I forgot to observe, when speaking of the New Testament, that you should read all the histories of Christ, as well of those whom a council of ecclesiastics have decided for us, to be Pseudo-evangelists, as those they named Evangelists. Because these Pseudo-evangelists pretended to inspiration, as

4. In the yoke, a wooden torture device placed on the neck.

much as the others, and you are to judge their pretensions by your own reason, and not by the reason of those ecclesiastics. Most of these are lost. There are some, however, still extant, collected by Fabricius, which I will endeavor to get and send you.

5. Traveling. This makes men wiser, but less happy. When men of sober age travel, they gather knowledge, which they may apply usefully for their country; but they are subject ever after to recollections mixed with regret; their affections are weakened by being extended over more objects; and they learn new habits which cannot be gratified when they return home. Young men, who travel, are exposed to all these inconveniences in a higher degree, to others still more serious, and do not acquire that wisdom for which a previous foundation is requisite, by repeated and just observations at home. The glare of pomp and pleasure is analogous to the motion of the blood; it absorbs all their affection and attention, they are torn from it as from the only good in this world, and return to their home as to a place of exile and condemnation. Their eyes are forever turned back to the object they have lost, and its recollection poisons the residue of their lives. Their first and most delicate passions are hackneyed on unworthy objects here, and they carry home the dregs, insufficient to make themselves or anybody else happy. Add to this, that a habit of idleness, an inability to apply themselves to business is acquired, and renders them useless to themselves and their country. These observations are founded in experience. There is no place where your pursuit of knowledge will be so little obstructed by foreign objects, as in your own country, nor any, wherein the virtues of the heart will be less exposed to be weakened. Be good, be learned, and be industrious, and you will not want the aid of traveling, to render you precious to your country, dear to your friends, happy within yourself. I repeat my advice, to take a great deal of exercise, and on foot. Health is the first requisite after morality. Write to me often, and be assured of the interest I take in your success, as well as the warmth of those sentiments of attachment with which I am, dear Peter, your affectionate friend.

RALPH WALDO EMERSON
The American Scholar[1]

Mr. President and Gentlemen:

I greet you on the recommencement of our literary year. Our anniversary is one of hope, and, perhaps, not enough of labor. We do not meet for games of strength or skill, for the recitation of histories, tragedies, and odes, like the ancient Greeks; for parliaments of love

1. The Phi Beta Kappa address at Harvard College, August 31, 1837.

and poesy, like the Troubadours; nor for the advancement of science, like our contemporaries in the British and European capitals. Thus far, our holiday has been simply a friendly sign of the survival of the love of letters amongst a people too busy to give to letters any more. As such it is precious as the sign of an indestructible instinct. Perhaps, the time is already come when it ought to be, and will be, something else; when the sluggard intellect of this continent will look from under its iron lids and fill the postponed expectation of the world with something better than the exertions of mechanical skill. Our day of dependence, our long apprenticeship to the learning of other lands, draws to a close. The millions that around us are rushing into life, cannot always be fed on the sere remains of foreign harvests. Events, actions arise, that must be sung, that will sing themselves. Who can doubt that poetry will revive and lead in a new age, as the star in the constellation Harp, which now flames in our zenith, astronomers announce, shall one day be the pole-star for a thousand years?

In this hope I accept the topic which not only usage but the nature of our association seem to prescribe to this day—the American Scholar. Year by year we come up hither to read one more chapter of his biography. Let us inquire what light new days and events have thrown on his character and his hopes.

It is one of those fables which out of an unknown antiquity convey an unlooked-for wisdom, that the gods, in the beginning, divided Man into men, that he might be more helpful to himself; just as the hand was divided into fingers, the better to answer its end.

The old fable covers a doctrine ever new and sublime; that there is One Man—present to all particular men only partially, or through one faculty; and that you must take the whole society to find the whole man. Man is not a farmer, or a professor, or an engineer, but he is all. Man is priest, and scholar, and statesman, and producer, and soldier. In the *divided* or social state these functions are parceled out to individuals, each of whom aims to do his stint of the joint work, whilst each other performs his. The fable implies that the individual, to possess himself, must sometimes return from his own labor to embrace all the other laborers. But, unfortunately, this original unit, this fountain of power, has been so distributed to multitudes, has been so minutely subdivided and peddled out, that it is spilled into drops, and cannot be gathered. The state of society is one in which the members have suffered amputation from the trunk, and strut about so many walking monsters—a good finger, a neck, a stomach, an elbow, but never a man.

Man is thus metamorphosed into a thing, into many things. The planter, who is Man sent out into the field to gather food, is seldom cheered by any idea of the true dignity of his ministry. He sees his bushel and his cart, and nothing beyond, and sinks into the farmer, instead of Man on the farm. The tradesman scarcely ever gives an ideal worth to his work, but is ridden by the routine of his craft, and the soul is subject to dollars. The priest becomes a form; the attorney a statute-book; the mechanic a machine; the sailor a rope of the ship.

In this distribution of functions the scholar is the delegated intellect. In the right state he is *Man Thinking*. In the degenerate state, when the victim of society, he tends to become a mere thinker, or still worse, the parrot of other men's thinking.

In this view of him, as Man Thinking, the theory of his office is contained. Him Nature solicits with all her placid, all her monitory pictures; him the past instructs; him the future invites. Is not indeed every man a student, and do not all things exist for the student's behoof? And, finally, is not the true scholar the only true master? But the old oracle said, "All things have two handles: beware of the wrong one." In life, too often, the scholar errs with mankind and forfeits his privilege. Let us see him in his school, and consider him in reference to the main influences he receives.

The first in time and the first in importance of the influences upon the mind is that of nature. Every day, the sun; and, after sunset, Night and her stars. Ever the winds blow; ever the grass grows. Every day, men and women, conversing—beholding and beholden. The scholar is he of all men whom this spectacle most engages. He must settle its value in his mind. What is nature to him? There is never a beginning, there is never an end, to the inexplicable continuity of this web of God, but always circular power returning into itself. Therein it resembles his own spirit, whose beginning, whose ending, he never can find—so entire, so boundless. Far too as her splendors shine, system on system shooting like rays, upward, downward, without center, without circumference—in the mass and in the particle, Nature hastens to render account of herself to the mind. Classification begins. To the young mind every thing is individual, stands by itself. By and by, it finds how to join two things and see in them one nature; then three, then three thousand; and so, tyrannized over by its own unifying instinct, it goes on tying things together, diminishing anomalies, discovering roots, running under ground whereby contrary and remote things cohere and flower out from one stem. It presently learns that since the dawn of history there has been a constant accumulation and classifying of facts. But what is classification but the perceiving that these objects are not chaotic, and are not foreign, but have a law which is also a law of the human mind? The astronomer discovers that geometry, a pure abstraction of the human mind, is the measure of planetary motion. The chemist finds proportions and intelligible method throughout matter; and science is nothing but the finding of analogy, identity, in the most remote parts. The ambitious soul sits down before each refractory fact; one after another reduces all strange constitutions, all new powers, to their class and their law, and goes on forever to animate the last fiber of organization, the outskirts of nature, by insight.

Thus to him, to this schoolboy under the bending dome of day, is suggested that he and it proceed from one root; one is leaf and one is flower; relation, sympathy, stirring in every vein. And what is that root? Is not that the soul of his soul? A thought too bold; a dream too wild. Yet when this spiritual light shall have revealed the law of more earthly natures—when he has learned to worship the soul, and to see that the natural philosophy that now is, is only the first gropings of its gigantic hand, he shall look forward to an ever expanding knowledge as to a becoming creator. He shall see that nature is the opposite of the soul, answering to it part for part. One is seal and one is print. Its beauty is the beauty of his own mind. Its laws are the laws of his own mind. Nature then becomes to him the measure of his attainments. So much of nature as he is ignorant of, so much of his own mind does he not yet possess. And, in fine, the ancient precept, "Know thyself," and the modern precept, "Study nature," become at last one maxim.

II. The next great influence into the spirit of the scholar is the mind of the Past—in whatever form, whether of literature, of art, of institutions, that mind is inscribed. Books are the best type of the influence of the past, and perhaps we shall get at the truth—learn the amount of this influence more conveniently—by considering their value alone.

The theory of books is noble. The scholar of the first age received into him the world around; brooded thereon; gave it the new arrangement of his mind, and uttered it again. It came into him life; it went out from him truth. It came to him short-lived actions; it went out from him immortal thoughts. It came to him business; it went from him poetry. It was dead fact; now, it is quick thought. It can stand, and it can go. It now endures, it now flies, it now inspires. Precisely in proportion to the depth of mind from which it issued, so high does it soar, so long does it sing.

Or, I might say, it depends on how far the process had gone, of transmuting life into truth. In proportion to the completeness of the distillation, so will the purity and imperishableness of the product be. But none is quite perfect. As no air-pump can by any means make a perfect vacuum, so neither can any artist entirely exclude the conventional, the local, the perishable from his book, or write a book of pure thought, that shall be as efficient, in all respects, to a remote posterity, as to contemporaries, or rather to the second age. Each age, it is found, must write its own books; or rather, each generation for the next succeeding. The books of an older period will not fit this.

Yet hence arises a grave mischief. The sacredness which attaches to the act of creation, the act of thought, is transferred to the record. The poet chanting was felt to be a divine man: henceforth the chant is divine also. The writer was a just and wise spirit: henceforward it is settled the book is perfect; as love of the hero corrupts into worship of his statue. Instantly the book becomes noxious: the guide is a tyrant. The sluggish and perverted mind of the multitude, slow to open to the incursions of Reason, having once so opened, having once received this book, stands upon it, and makes an outcry if it is disparaged. Colleges are built on it. Books are written on it by thinkers, not by Man Thinking; by men of talent, that is, who start wrong, who set out from accepted dogmas, not from their own sight of principles. Meek young men grow up in libraries, believing it their duty to accept the views which Cicero, which Locke, which Bacon, have given; forgetful that Cicero, Locke, and Bacon were only young men in libraries when they wrote these books.

Hence, instead of Man Thinking, we have the bookworm. Hence the book-learned class, who value books, as such; not as related to nature and the human constitution, but as making a sort of Third Estate with the world and the soul. Hence the restorers of readings, the emendators, the bibliomaniacs of all degrees.

Books are the best of things, well used; abused, among the worst. What is the right use? What is the one end which all means go to effect? They are for nothing but to inspire. I had better never see a book than to be warped by its attraction clean out of my own orbit, and made a satellite instead of a system. The one thing in the world, of value, is the active soul. This every man is entitled to; this every man contains within him, although in almost all men obstructed and as yet unborn. The soul active sees absolute truth and utters truth, or creates. In this action it is genius; not the privilege of here and there a favorite, but the sound estate of every man. In its essence it is progressive. The book, the college, the school of art, the institution of any kind, stop with some past utterance of genius. This is good, say they, let us hold by this. They pin me down. They look backward and not forward. But genius looks forward: the eyes of man are set in his forehead, not in his hind-head: man hopes: genius creates. Whatever talents may be, if the man create not, the pure efflux of the Deity is not his; cinders and smoke there may be, but not yet flame. There are creative manners, there are creative actions, and creative words; manners, actions, words, that is, indicative of no custom or authority, but springing spontaneous from the mind's own sense of good and fair.

On the other part, instead of being its own seer, let it receive from another mind its truth, though it were in torrents of light, without periods of solitude, inquest, and self-recovery, and a fatal disservice is done. Genius is always sufficiently the enemy of genius by over-influence. The literature of every nation bears me witness. The English dramatic poets have Shakspearized now for two hundred years.

Undoubtedly there is a right way of reading, so it be sternly sub-ordinated. Man Thinking must not be subdued by his instruments. Books are for the scholar's idle times. When he can read God directly, the hour is too precious to be wasted in other men's transcripts of their readings. But when the intervals of darkness come, as come they must—when the sun is hid and the stars withdraw their shining—we repair to the lamps which were kindled by their ray, to guide our steps to the East again, where the dawn is. We hear, that we may speak. The Arabian proverb says, "A fig tree, looking on a fig tree, becometh fruitful."

It is remarkable, the character of the pleasure we derive from the best books. They impress us with the conviction that one nature wrote and the same reads. We read the verses of one of the great English poets, of Chaucer, of Marvell, of Dryden, with the most modern joy—with a pleasure, I mean, which is in great part caused by the abstraction of all *time* from their verses. There is some awe mixed with the joy of our surprise, when this poet, who lived in some past world, two or three hundred years ago, says that which lies close to my own soul, that which I also had well-nigh thought and said. But for the evidence thence afforded to the philosophical doctrine of the identity of all minds, we should suppose some pre-established harmony, some foresight of souls that were to be, and some preparation of stores for their future wants, like the fact ob-served in insects, who lay up food before death for the young grub they shall never see.

I would not be hurried by any love of system, by any exaggeration of instincts, to underrate the Book. We all know, that as the human body can be nourished on any food, though it were boiled grass and the broth of shoes, so the human mind can be fed by any knowledge. And great and heroic men have existed who had almost no other information than by the printed page. I only would say that it needs a strong head to bear that diet. One must be an inventor to read well. As the proverb says, "He that would bring home the wealth of the Indies, must carry out the wealth of the Indies." There is then creative reading as well as creative writing. When the mind is braced by labor and invention, the page of whatever book we read becomes luminous with manifold allusion. Every sentence is doubly signifi-cant, and the sense of our author is as broad as the world. We then see, what is always true, that as the seer's hour of vision is short and rare among heavy days and months, so is its record, perchance, the least part of his volume. The discerning will read, in his Plato or Shakespeare, only that least part, only the authentic utterances of the oracle; all the rest he rejects, were it never so many times Plato's and Shakespeare's.

Of course there is a portion of reading quite indispensable to a wise man. History and exact science he must learn by laborious reading. Colleges, in like manner, have their indispensable office—to teach elements. But they can only highly serve us when they aim not to drill, but to create; when they gather from far every ray of various genius to their hospitable halls, and by the concentrated fires, set the hearts of their youth on flame. Thought and knowledge are natures in which apparatus and pretension avail nothing. Gowns and pecuniary foundations, though of towns of gold, can never countervail the least sentence or syllable of wit. Forget this, and our American colleges will recede in their public importance, whilst they grow richer every year.

III. There goes in the world a notion that the scholar should be a recluse, a valetudinarian—as unfit for any handiwork or public labor as a penknife for an axe. The so-called "practical men" sneer at speculative men, as if, because they speculate or see, they could do nothing. I have heard it said that the clergy—who are always, more universally than any other class, the scholars of their day—are addressed as women; that the rough, spontaneous conversation of men they do not hear, but only a mincing and diluted speech. They are often virtually disfranchised; and indeed there are advocates for their celibacy. As far as this is true of the studious classes, it is not just and wise. Action is with the scholar subordinate, but it is essential. Without it he is not yet man. Without it thought can never ripen into truth. While the world hangs before the eye as a cloud of beauty, we cannot even see its beauty. Inaction is cowardice, but there can be no scholar without the heroic mind. The preamble of thought, the transition through which it passes from the unconscious to the conscious, is action. Only so much do I know, as I have lived. Instantly we know whose words are loaded with life, and whose not.

The world—this shadow of the soul, or *other me*—lies wide around. Its attractions are the keys which unlock my thoughts and make me acquainted with myself. I run eagerly into this resounding tumult. I grasp the hands of those next me, and take my place in the ring to suffer and to work, taught by an instinct that so shall the dumb abyss be vocal with speech. I pierce its order; I dissipate its fear; I dispose of it within the circuit of my expanding life. So much only of life as I know by experience, so much of the wilderness have I vanquished and planted, or so far have I extended my being, my dominion. I do not see how any man can afford, for the sake of his nerves and his nap, to spare any action in which he can partake. It is pearls and rubies to his discourse. Drudgery, calamity, exasperation, want, are instructors in eloquence and wisdom. The true scholar grudges every opportunity of action past by, as a loss of power. It is the raw material out of which the intellect moulds her splendid products. A strange process too, this by which experience is converted into thought, as a mulberry leaf is converted into satin. The manufacture goes forward at all hours.

The actions and events of our childhood and youth are now matters of calmest observation. They lie like fair pictures in the air. Not so with our recent actions, with the business which we now have in hand. On this we are quite unable to speculate. Our affections as yet circulate through it. We no more feel or know it than we feel the feet, or the hand, or the brain of our body. The new deed is yet a part of life, remains for a time immersed in our unconscious life. In some contemplative hour it detaches itself from the life like a ripe fruit, to become a thought of the mind. Instantly it is raised, transfigured; the corruptible has put on incorruption. Henceforth it is an object of beauty, however base its origin and neighborhood. Observe too the impossibility of antedating this act. In its grub state, it cannot fly, it cannot shine, it is a dull grub. But suddenly, without observation, the selfsame thing unfurls beautiful wings, and is an angel of wisdom. So is there no fact, no event, in our private history, which shall not, sooner or later, lose its adhesive, inert form, and astonish us by soaring from our body into the empyrean. Cradle and infancy, school and playground, the fear of boys, and dogs, and ferules, the love of little maids and berries, and many another fact that once filled the whole sky, are gone already; friend and relative, profession and party, town and country, nation and world, must also soar and sing.

Of course, he who has put forth his total strength in fit actions has the richest return of wisdom. I will not shut myself out of this globe of action, and transplant an oak into a flowerpot, there to hunger and pine; nor trust the revenue of some single faculty, and exhaust one vein of thought, much like those Savoyards, who, getting their livelihood by carving shepherds, shepherdesses, and smoking Dutchmen, for all Europe, went out one day to the mountain to find stock, and discovered that they had whittled up the last of their pine trees. Authors we have, in numbers, who have written out their vein, and who, moved by a commendable prudence, sail for Greece or Palestine, follow the trapper into the prairie, or ramble round Algiers, to replenish their merchantable stock.

If it were only for a vocabulary, the scholar would be covetous of action. Life is our dictionary. Years are well spent in country labors; in town; in the insight into trades and manufactures; in frank intercourse with many men and women; in science; in art; to the one end of mastering in all their facts a language by which to illustrate and embody our perceptions. I learn immediately from any speaker how much he has already lived, through the poverty or the splendor of his speech. Life lies behind us as the quarry from whence we get ties and copestones for the masonry of to-day. This is the way to learn grammar. Colleges and books only copy the language which the field and the work-yard made.

But the final value of action, like that of books, and better than books, is that it is a resource. That great principle of Undulation in nature, that shows itself in the inspiring and expiring of the breath; in desire and satiety; in the ebb and flow of the sea; in day and night; in heat and cold; and, as yet more deeply ingrained in every atom and every fluid, is known to us under the name of Polarity—these "fits of easy transmission and reflection," as Newton called them, are the law of nature because they are the law of spirit.

The mind now thinks, now acts, and each fit reproduces the other. When the artist has exhausted his materials, when the fancy no longer paints, when thoughts are no longer apprehended and books are a weariness, he has always the resource to live. Character is higher than intellect. Thinking is the function. Living is the functionary. The stream retreats to its source. A great soul will be strong to live, as well as strong to think. Does he lack organ or medium to impart his truths? He can still fall back on this elemental force of living them. This is a total act. Thinking is a partial act. Let the grandeur of justice shine in his affairs. Let the beauty of affection cheer his lowly roof. Those "far from fame," who dwell and act with him, will feel the force of his constitution in the doings and passages of the day better than it can be measured by any public and designed display. Time shall teach him that the scholar loses no hour which the man lives. Herein he unfolds the sacred germ of his instinct, screened from influence. What is lost in seemliness is gained in strength. Not out of those on whom systems of education have exhausted their culture, comes the helpful giant to destroy the old or to build the new, but out of unhandselled savage nature; out of terrible Druids and Berserkers come at last Alfred and Shakespeare.

I hear therefore with joy whatever is beginning to be said of the dignity and necessity of labor to every citizen. There is virtue yet in the hoe and the spade, for learned as well as for unlearned hands. And labor is everywhere welcome; always we are invited to work; only be this limitation observed, that a man shall not for the sake of wider activity sacrifice any opinion to the popular judgments and modes of action.

I have now spoken of the education of the scholar by nature, by books, and by action. It remains to say somewhat of his duties.

They are such as become Man Thinking. They may all be comprised in self-trust. The office of the scholar is to cheer, to raise, and to guide men by showing them facts amidst appearances. He plies the slow, unhonored, and unpaid task of observation. Flamsteed and Herschel, in their glazed observatories, may catalogue the stars with the praise of all men, and the results being splendid and useful, honor is sure. But he, in his private observatory, cataloguing obscure and nebulous stars of the human mind, which as yet no man has thought of as such—watching days and months sometimes for a few facts; correcting still his old records—must relinquish display and immediate fame. In the long period of his preparation he must betray often an ignorance and shiftlessness in popular arts, incurring the disdain of the able who shoulder him aside. Long he must stammer in his speech; often forgo the living for the dead. Worse yet, he must accept—how often!—poverty and solitude. For the ease and pleasure of treading the old road, accepting the fashions, the education, the religion of society, he takes the cross of making his own, and, of course, the self-accusation, the faint heart, the frequent uncertainty and loss of time, which are the nettles and tangling vines in the way of the self-relying and self-directed; and the state of virtual hostility in which he seems to stand to society, and especially to educated society. For all this loss and scorn, what offset? He is to find consolation in exercising the highest functions of human nature. He is one who raises himself from private considerations and breathes and lives on public and illustrious thoughts. He is the world's eye. He is the world's heart. He is to resist the vulgar prosperity that retrogrades ever to barbarism, by preserving and communicating heroic sentiments, noble biographies, melodious verse, and the conclusions of history. Whatsoever oracles the human heart, in all emergencies, in all solemn hours, has uttered as its commentary on the world of actions, these he shall receive and impart. And whatsoever new verdict Reason from her inviolable seat pronounces on the passing men and events of to-day, this he shall hear and promulgate.

These being his functions, it becomes him to feel all confidence in himself, and to defer never to the popular cry. He and he only knows the world. The world of any moment is the merest appearance. Some great decorum, some fetish of a government, some ephemeral trade, or war, or man, is cried up by half mankind and cried down by the other half, as if all depended on this particular up or down. The odds are that the whole question is not worth the poorest thought which the scholar has lost in listening to the controversy. Let him not quit his belief that a popgun is a popgun, though the ancient and honorable of the earth affirm it to be the crack of doom. In silence, in steadiness, in severe abstraction, let him hold by himself; add observation to observation, patient of neglect, patient of reproach, and bide his own time—happy enough if he can satisfy himself alone that this day he has seen something truly. Success treads on every right step. For the instinct is sure, that prompts him to tell his brother what he thinks. He then learns that in going down into the secrets of his own mind he has descended into the secrets of all minds. He learns that he who has mastered any law in his private thoughts, is master to that extent of all men whose language he speaks, and of all into whose language his own can be translated. The poet, in utter solitude remembering his spontaneous thoughts and recording them, is found to have recorded that which men in crowded cities find true for them also. The orator distrusts at first the fitness of his frank confessions, his want of knowledge of the persons he addresses, until he finds that he is the complement of his hearers—that they drink his words because he fulfils for them their own nature; the deeper he dives into his privatest, secretest presentiment, to his wonder he finds this is the most acceptable, most public, and universally true. The people delight in it; the better part of every man feels, This is my music; this is myself.

In self-trust all the virtues are comprehended. Free should the scholar be—free and brave. Free even to the definition of freedom, "without any hindrance that does not arise out of his own constitution." Brave; for fear is a thing which a scholar by his very function puts behind him. Fear always springs from ignorance. It is a shame to him if his tranquillity, amid dangerous times, arise from the presumption that like children and women his is a protected class; or if he seek a temporary peace by the diversion of his thoughts from politics or vexed questions, hiding his head like an ostrich in the flowering bushes, peeping into microscopes, and turning rhymes, as a boy whistles to keep his courage up. So is the danger a danger still; so is the fear worse. Manlike let him turn and face it. Let him look into its eye and search its nature, inspect its origin—see the whelping of this lion—which lies no great way back; he will then find in himself a perfect comprehension of its nature and extent; he will have made his hands meet on the other side, and can henceforth defy it and pass on superior. The world is his who can see through its pretension. What deafness, what stone-blind custom, what overgrown error you behold is there only by sufferance—by your sufferance. See it to be a lie, and you have already dealt it its mortal blow.

Yes, we are the cowed—we the trustless. It is a mischievous notion that we are come late into nature; that the world was finished a long time ago. As the world was plastic and fluid in the hands of God, so it is ever to so much of his attributes as we bring to it. To igorance and sin, it is flint. They adapt themselves to it as they may; but in proportion as a man has any thing in him divine, the firmament flows before him and takes his signet and form. Not he is great who can alter matter, but he who can alter my state of mind. They are the kings of the world who give the color of their present thought to all nature and all art, and persuade men by the cheerful serenity of their carrying the matter, that this thing which they do is the apple which the ages have desired to pluck, now at last ripe, and inviting nations to the harvest. The great man makes the great thing. Wherever Macdonald sits, there is the head of the table.[2] Linnaeus makes botany the most alluring of studies, and wins it from the farmer and the herb-woman; Davy, chemistry; and Cuvier, fossils. The day is always his who works in it with serenity and great aims.

2. This sentence is proverbial. MacDonald is unidentified.

The unstable estimates of men crowd to him whose mind is filled with a truth, as the heaped waves of the Atlantic follow the moon.

For this self-trust, the reason is deeper than can be fathomed— darker than can be enlightened. I might not carry with me the feeling of my audience in stating my own belief. But I have already shown the ground of my hope, in adverting to the doctrine that man is one. I believe man has been wronged; he has wronged himself. He has almost lost the light that can lead him back to his prerogatives. Men are become of no account. Men in history, men in the world of to- day, are bugs, are spawn, and are called "the mass" and "the herd." In a century, in a millennium, one or two men; that is to say, one or two approximations to the right state of every man. All the rest behold in the hero or the poet their own green and crude being— ripened; yes, and are content to be less, so *that* may attain to its full stature. What a testimony, full of grandeur, full of pity, is borne to the demands of his own nature, by the poor clansman, the poor partisan, who rejoices in the glory of his chief. The poor and the low find some amends to their immense moral capacity, for their acquiescence in a political and social inferiority. They are content to be brushed like flies from the path of a great person, so that justice shall be done by him to that common nature which it is the dearest desire of all to see enlarged and glorified. They sun themselves in the great man's light, and feel it to be their own element. They cast the dignity of man from their downtrod selves upon the shoulders of a hero, and will perish to add one drop of blood to make that great heart beat, those giant sinews combat and conquer. He lives for us, and we live in him.

Men, such as they are, very naturally seek money or power; and power because it is as good as money—the "spoils," so called, "of office." And why not? for they aspire to the highest, and this, in their sleep-walking, they dream is highest. Wake them and they shall quit the false good and leap to the true, and leave governments to clerks and desks. This revolution is to be wrought by the gradual domestication of the idea of Culture. The main enterprise of the world for splendor, for extent, is the upbuilding of a man. Here are the materials strewn along the ground. The private life of one man shall be a more illustrious monarchy, more formidable to its enemy, more sweet and serene in its influence to its friend, than any kingdom in history. For a man, rightly viewed, comprehendeth the particular natures of all men. Each philosopher, each bard, each actor has only done for me, as by a delegate, what one day I can do for myself. The books which once we valued more than the apple of the eye, we have quite exhausted. What is that but saying that we have come up with the point of view which the universal mind took through the eyes of one scribe; we have been that man, and have passed on. First, one, then another, we drain all cisterns, and waxing greater by all these supplies, we crave a better and more abundant food. The man has never lived that can feed us ever. The human mind cannot be enshrined in a person who shall set a barrier on any one side to this unbounded, unboundable empire. It is one central fire, which, flaming now out of the lips of Etna, lightens the capes of Sicily, and now out of the throat of Vesuvius, illuminates the towers and vine-yards of Naples. It is one light which beams out of a thousand stars. It is one soul which animates all men.

But I have dwelt perhaps tediously upon this abstraction of the Scholar. I ought not to delay longer to add what I have to say of nearer reference to the time and to this country.

Historically, there is thought to be a difference in the ideas which predominate over successive epochs, and there are data for marking the genius of the Classic, of the Romantic, and now of the Reflective or Philosophical age. With the views I have intimated of the oneness or the identity of the mind through all individuals, I do not much dwell on these differences. In fact, I believe each individual passes through all three. The boy is a Greek; the youth, romantic; the adult, reflective. I deny not, however, that a revolution in the leading idea may be distinctly enough traced.

Our age is bewailed as the age of Introversion. Must that needs be evil? We, it seems, are critical; we are embarrassed with second thoughts; we cannot enjoy any thing for hankering to know whereof the pleasure consists; we are lined with eyes; we see with our feet; the time is infected with Hamlet's unhappiness—

> Sicklied o'er with the pale cast of thought.

It is so bad then? Sight is the last thing to be pitied. Would we be blind? Do we fear lest we should outsee nature and God, and drink truth dry? I look upon the discontent of the literary class as a mere announcement of the fact that they find themselves not in the state of mind of their fathers, and regret the coming state as untried; as a boy dreads the water before he has learned that he can swim. If there is any period one would desire to be born in, is it not the age of Revolution; when the old and the new stand side by side and admit of being compared; when the energies of all men are searched by fear and by hope; when the historic glories of the old can be compensated by the rich possibilities of the new era? This time, like all times, is a very good one, if we but know what to do with it.

I read with some joy of the auspicious signs of the coming days, as they glimmer already through poetry and art, through philosophy and science, through church and state.

One of these signs is the fact that the same movement which effected the elevation of what was called the lowest class in the state, assumed in literature a very marked and as benign an aspect. Instead of the sublime and beautiful, the near, the low, the common, was explored and poetized. That which had been negligently trodden under foot by those who were harnessing and provisioning themselves for long journeys into far countries, is suddenly found to be richer than all foreign parts. The literature of the poor, the feeling of the child, the philosophy of the street, the meaning of the household life, are the topics of the time. It is a great stride. It is a sign—is it not?—of new vigor when the extremities are made active, when currents of warm life run into the hands and the feet. I ask not for the great, the remote, the romantic; what is doing in Italy or Arabia; what is Greek art, or Provençal minstrelsy; I embrace the common, I explore and sit at the feet of the familiar, the low. Give me insight into to-day, and you may have the antique and future worlds. What would we really know the meaning of? The meal in the firkin; the milk in the pan; the ballad in the street; the news of the boat; the glance of the eye; the form and the gait of the body—show me the ultimate reason of these matters; show me the sublime presence of the highest spiritual cause lurking, as always it does lurk, in these suburbs and extremities of nature; let me see every trifle bristling with the polarity that ranges it instantly on an eternal law; and the shop, the plough, and the ledger referred to the like cause by which light undulates and poets sing—and the world lies no longer a dull miscellany and lumber-room, but has form and order; there is no trifle, there is no puzzle, but one design unites and animates the farthest pinnacle and the lowest trench.

This idea has inspired the genius of Goldsmith, Burns, Cowper, and, in a newer time, of Goethe, Wordsworth, and Carlyle. This idea they have differently followed and with various success. In contrast with their writing, the style of Pope, of Johnson, of Gibbon, looks cold and pedantic. This writing is blood-warm. Man is surprised to find that things near are not less beautiful and wondrous than things remote. The near explains the far. The drop is a small ocean. A man is related to all nature. This perception of the worth of the vulgar is fruitful in discoveries. Goethe, in this very thing the most modern of the moderns, has shown us, as none ever did, the genius of the ancients.

There is one man of genius who has done much for this philosophy of life, whose literary value has never yet been rightly estimated; I mean Emanuel Swedenborg. The most imaginative of men, yet writing with the precision of a mathematician, he endeavored to engraft a purely philosophical Ethics on the popular Christianity of his time. Such an attempt of course must have difficulty which no genius could surmount. But he saw and showed the connection between nature and the affections of the soul. He pierced the emblematic or spiritual character of the visible, audible, tangible world. Especially did his shade-loving muse hover over and interpret the lower parts of nature;

he showed the mysterious bond that allies moral evil to the foul material forms, and has given in epical parables a theory of insanity, of beasts, of unclean and fearful things.

Another sign of our times, also marked by an analogous political movement, is the new importance given to the single person. Everything that tends to insulate the individual—to surround him with barriers of natural respect, so that each man shall feel the world is his, and man shall treat with man as a sovereign state with a sovereign state—tends to true union as well as greatness. "I learned," said the melancholy Pestalozzi, "that no man in God's wide earth is either willing or able to help any other man." Help must come from the bosom alone. The scholar is that man who must take up into himself all the ability of the time, all the contributions of the past, all the hopes of the future. He must be an university of knowledges. If there be one lesson more than another which should pierce his ear, it is, The world is nothing, the man is all; in yourself is the law of all nature, and you know not yet how a globule of sap ascends; in yourself slumbers the whole of Reason; it is for you to know all; it is for you to dare all. Mr. President and Gentlemen, this confidence in the unsearched might of man belongs, by all motives, by all prophecy, by all preparation, to the American Scholar. We have listened too long to the courtly muses of Europe. The spirit of the American freeman is already suspected to be timid, imitative, tame. Public and private avarice make the air we breathe thick and fat. The scholar is decent, indolent, complaisant. See already the tragic consequence. The mind of this country, taught to aim at low objects, eats upon itself. There is no work for any but the decorous and the complaisant. Young men of the fairest promise, who begin life upon our shores, inflated by the mountain winds, shined upon by all the stars of God, find the earth below not in unison with these, but are hindered from action by the disgust which the principles on which business is managed inspire, and turn drudges, or die of disgust, some of them suicides. What is the remedy? They did not yet see, and thousands of young men as hopeful now crowding to the barriers for the career do not yet see, that if the single man plant himself indomitably on his instincts, and there abide, the huge world will come round to him. Patience, patience; with the shades of all the good and great for company; and for solace the perspective of your own infinite life; and for work the study and the communication of principles, the making those instincts prevalent, the conversion of the world. Is it not the chief disgrace in the world, not to be an unit—not to be reckoned one character—not to yield that peculiar fruit which each man was created to bear, but to be reckoned in the gross, in the hundred, or the thousand, of the party, the section, to which we belong; and our opinion predicted geographically, as the north, or the south? Not so, brothers and friends—please God, ours shall not be so. We will walk on our own feet; we will work with our own hands; we will speak our own minds. The study of letters shall be no longer a name for pity, for doubt, and for sensual indulgence. The dread of man and the love of man shall be a wall of defence and a wreath of joy around all. A nation of men will for the first time exist, because each believes himself inspired by the Divine Soul which also inspires all men.

QUESTIONS FOR STUDY, DISCUSSION, AND WRITING

1. Outline this oration, showing how its four major parts relate to the main topic. Are the parts accorded equal or different treatment, in length and detail? Why? Elaborate upon the outline, showing the main points within each part. Are the parts developed similarly or differently? Why?
2. What distinction does Emerson make between "Man thinking" and "a mere thinker"? What foundation does he provide for the distinction? What view of the nature of society does the distinction imply?
3. Why does Emerson emphasize the influence of action upon the scholar? Is there any incompatibility between an active and an intellectual life?
4. At the outset Emerson states the "doctrine of One Man" and that idea recurs several times in the work. Define the doctrine and explain its significance at each reappearance.
5. What relation exists between the "doctrine of One Man" and the idea of self-trust? In what other contexts is that doctrine, if not stated directly, an implicit governing principle?
6. Locate some of Emerson's citations of proverbs and maxims. What effects does he produce by using them? To what degree and in what ways does Emerson's style embody, apart from direct citation, the qualities of proverb and maxim?
7. Judging from this work, would Emerson agree with what Jefferson says in his *Letter to Peter Carr* (pp. 162–165) about "the moral sense"? About foreign travel in relation to education?
8. Has Emerson's thought been incorporated into or reflected by American educational practice? To what degree? In what ways? Draw upon your own experience of American schools as well as upon what you know of educational theory.

LEARNED HAND
Sources of Tolerance[1]

I am going to ask you to go with me, not into questions which have direct relation to the law or to government, but to those which concern the mental habits of our people, since these, indirectly at

1. An address delivered before the Juristic Society of the University of Pennsylvania in June 1930.

any rate, in the end determine its institutions. This is not an easy, maybe it is an impossible undertaking, but at any rate, nobody can very effectually challenge what you say about such vague things, and you are exempt from the need of citation—blessed exoneration to a judge. It may be worth discussion, if only for discussion's sake. At least it can serve to bring out differences of opinion.

By way of prelude may I then ask you for a moment to go back in our country for nearly a century and a half? We were substantially a nation of farmers; towns were few; cities, as we should now rate them, did not exist. Life was, as we like to believe, simple. Maybe it was not so in fact, for simplicity depends rather on one's inner state of mind; but at any rate it was less pressed and hurried; people did not think so much about how complicated they were, and less dissipated their attention.

The political notions of the time were divided into two contrasting groups which it has been the custom to associate with the great names of Jefferson and Hamilton. It is easy to associate Jefferson's ideas with those of Rousseau, from whom on the outside they seem to have been drawn. This, as I understand it, is wrong, but he had drunk deeply at the springs of Physiocracy, and in any event he believed in the basic virtue of mankind, once set free from artificial restraints. He found his ideal in a community of independent families, each entrenched in its farm, self-subsistent, independent, needing no regulation, and tolerant of little interference, especially by government. Those who invoke his name today must be shocked at his scorn of the mob of mechanics and artisans, whose turbulence and separation from some particular plot of earth unfitted them in his eyes for sharing in the Good Life. A nation in which information, or what passes as such, can be instantaneously sent from one end to the other, in which the craving for conformity demands uniformity in belief, which for that reason wears the same clothes, reads the same print and follows the same fashions, amusements and conventions, would have seemed to him scurvy and sordid. He would have found little in the America of today to justify that Utopia of which he had dreamed.

The extraordinary richness of his own nature, his omnivorant interest in all the activities of man, no doubt colored his picture of a life on the land; yet it also enabled him to transmute into a rosy ideal the dumb aspirations of his people, and so they looked to him for their leadership for a quarter of a century after his accession to power, and if we count Jackson as his dubious disciple, for that much longer. Clearly there was something in his outlook which responded to the needs of those among whom he lived.

Hamilton was a horse of another color, always an exotic, succeeding in his statecraft only because of the disorders which immediately followed the Revolution; whose genius needed the cloak of Washington beneath which his real work was hid for near a century. He was no Utopian; he did not believe in the perfectibility of human nature. Government was a combination of those interests in the community which collectively would be irresistible; a combination resting upon self-interest. When he secured the passage of the Constitution, it was by means of such a combination; the landed class, the manufacturers and the public creditors. In the doubtful contest for ratification, as Beard has shown, it was these votes which eventually won, and it was under the aegis of Washington that he managed to carry on for those critical eight years. With the constant movement of the frontier westward, the underlying, but less articulate, aspirations of a rural people finally asserted themselves, after Adams had run off Hamilton's momentum.

The animosity between the two men was well founded and inevitable. They represented, and we are right still to take them as our most shining examples of, two theories of human society; that which demands external control, and that which insists upon the opportunity for personal expression. Jefferson's victory seemed to him to be the sanction of all that the Revolution had implied; the liberation of a free people from the domination of greed and corruption, opening vistas of human felicity not theretofore known on earth. For its fuller expression he was willing, forced by a sad necessity, to sacrifice his constitutional scruples and forever compromise his party by the acquisition of Louisiana. To Hamilton, Jefferson's accession was the beginning of the end, the last step in a plunge towards anarchy. The squalid political quarrel for the domination of the rump of Federalism which ended in his death, had for him a deeper significance than the leadership in a party then apparently writhing to dissolution. The Eighteenth Brumaire[2] was five years past, and though the Coronation at Notre Dame was still some months away, recent events already foreshadowed it. In the final breakdown of that Jacobinism which he and his associates thought certain and early, the need would arise for some transatlantic Bonaparte to gather the shreds of society, and build a state upon surer foundations than that weak instrument in which at heart he had never really believed. To prevent Federalism, the sacred chalice, from passing into the obscene hands of a turncoat and a traitor was worth the chance that cost him his life.[3]

Each man would have said that he was the champion of liberty, and each would have been right. To one the essential condition of any tolerable life was the free expression of the individual, the power

2. Brumaire was the second month in the French revolutionary calendar. The Eighteenth Brumaire of the year VIII (Nov. 9, 1799) was the day on which Napoleon assumed supreme power of France as first Consul. His coronation at Notre Dame as emperor occurred on December 2, 1804.

3. In the presidential campaign of 1800 Hamilton supported Jefferson against Aaron Burr and subsequently lost his life in a duel with Burr arising from this political opposition.

to lead his life on his own terms, to enjoy the fruits of his industry, to garner the harvest of his hands and brain, without subtraction by a horde of office-holders, locusts who laid waste the land and spread the venal doctrine of their right to eat what others had sown, the blight, the virus, of a society of honest men, enjoying the earth which God, at least in this blessed country, had patently spread out for their satisfaction. The other saw in all this no more than the maunderings of a toxic dream. What was the assurance of man's capacity to deal with his own fate? Was it not clear that virtue and intelligence among the sons of Adam was as rare as physical prowess, indeed much rarer? Liberty could not rest upon anarchy; it was conditioned upon an ordered society, in which power should rest where power should be, with the wise and the good, who could be at least presumptively ascertained as those who in the battle of life had already given some signs of capacity. It was an empty phantom to assume some automatic regulation by which without plan and direction public affairs manage themselves. The concerns of a great people are not all individual; they have collective interests without which their life can scarcely rise above that of savages, each shifting for himself, without comfort, security, or the leisure which alone makes existence endurable. Jacobins might bawl of liberty, but really they meant no more than the tyranny of their own domination over the mob.

Placed as we now are, with an experience of over a century behind us, we can say that the future was apparently to justify Hamilton as against his great rival. Our knowledge of the ways of Nature, our command of her energies, and the materials which she has set so freely at our hands, has made it no longer possible to think of a society of families, isolated and non-communicating, each weaving its own fate independently of the rest. We have fabricated a nexus of relations which makes even rural life impossible as Jefferson understood it. The motor, the airplane, the telephone and telegraph, the radio, the railroad, the Linotype, the modern newspaper, the "movie" —and most horrible, the "talkie"—have finally destroyed it. Liberty is irretrievably gone in any sense that it was worth having to him. A farmer must have complicated machinery; he depends upon markets thousands of miles away; he will win by a crop shortage in India, and lose by a fall in industrial shares. He must "listen in" on Amos an' Andy, have camping places in the National Parks and tour in the Ford in winter. So be it; I welcome his larger life, but it has its price; he is tied to all men, as all men are tied to him, in a web whose threads no eye can follow and no fingers unravel.

Nor would there still be many, though doubtless some there are, who would deny that government must be the compromise of conflicting interests, as Hamilton supposed. While there lingers in political platforms and other declamatory compositions the notion that each man, if only he could be disabused of false doctrine, would act and vote with an enlightened eye to the public weal, few really believe it. We know well that an objective calculus of human values is impossible, and if it were available, would be so thin and speculative that men would not accept it. For any times that can count in human endeavor, we must be content with compromises in which the more powerful combination will prevail. The most we can hope is that if the maladjustment becomes too obvious, or the means too offensive to our conventions, the balance can be re-established without dissolution, a cost greater than almost any interests can justify. The method of Hamilton has had its way; so far as we can see must always have its way; in government, as in marriage, in the end the more insistent will prevails.

Liberty is so much latitude as the powerful choose to accord to the weak. So much perhaps must be admitted for abstract statement; anything short of it appears to lead to inconsistencies. At least no other formula has been devised which will answer. If a community decides that some conduct is prejudicial to itself, and so decides by numbers sufficient to impose its will upon dissenters, I know of no principle which can stay its hand. Perhaps indeed it is no more than a truism to say so; for, when we set ourselves this or that limitation, religion for example, we find that we wince in application. Who can say that the polygamy of the Mormons was not a genuine article of that faith? When we forbade it in the name of our morals, was it not an obvious subterfuge still to insist that we recognized religious freedom? Should we tolerate suttee? If we forbid birth-control in the interest of morals, is it inconceivable that we should tax celibacy? We call that conduct moral about whose effect upon our common interest we have unusually strong convictions. We do not hesitate to impose this upon those who do not share our views; and tolerance ends where faith begins. Plato may have been right about the proper relations of the sexes; we should not allow his experiment to be tried.[4] I do not see how we can set any limits to legitimate coercion beyond those which our forbearance concedes.

And yet, so phrased, we should all agree, I think, that the whole substance of liberty has disappeared. It is intolerable to feel that we are each in the power of the conglomerate conscience of a mass of Babbitts, whose intelligence we do not respect, and whose standards we may detest. Life on their terms would be impossible to endure; of their compunctions we have no guarantee. Who shall deliver us from the body of this death? Certainly there was a meaning in Jefferson's hatred of the interposition of collective pressure, though he extended it to so much of what we now accept as government. We may believe that his emphasis was wrong; that it required a great war eventually to clear away the centrifugal tendencies that underlay

4. See *The Republic*, Book V, where Socrates advocates the propagation of the human species by selective breeding.

it; but shall we not feel with him that it is monstrous to lay open the lives of each to whatever current notions of propriety may ordain? That feeling was the energy that lay back of the first ten amendments to the Constitution, which were really a part of the document itself. Impossible though they be of literal interpretation, like a statute, as counsels of moderation rather than as parts of our constituent law, they represent a mood, an attitude towards life, deep rooted in any enduring society.

Jefferson thought that they could be made to prevail by weakening the central power, but he was too astute an observer to rely upon political device alone. It was in the social, not in the political, constitution of his society that real security lay. For it was impossible to sweep a community of small eighteenth century farmers with mob hysteria. His dislike of cities was in part at any rate because they were subject to just such accesses. He did not, and he could not, see that time was to make rural life as susceptible to moral epidemics as the city mobs which he feared and mistrusted. He set his faith upon isolation and isolation in the end has failed him. The shores are no longer studded with rows of solid columns to break the waves of propaganda; they are not studded with anything whatever, and the waves sweep over them without obstacle and run far up into the land. The question I wish to put before you, which all this introduction is to prepare, is this—which I trust you will forgive me for putting in colloquial form—how far is liberty consistent with the methods of the modern "high-power" salesman? If it is not, what is to be done about it? Being Americans, we are not likely to agree that nothing can.

It has always interested me to read of the observations of those patient anthropologists who associate intimately with our cousin, the chimpanzee. I know a woman who endured the embrace of her son's pet for two hours, lest if disturbed in its caresses it might furiously strangle her. Devotion could scarcely ask more. We may learn much of ourselves from what are now, I believe, called the "conduct patterns" of the anthropoids, but it will not interest me so much as if the study could be of the herds. What I want to know is, why we have become so incurably imitative. I can improvise reasons, but you know how worthless that kind of anthropology is, so I shall spare you. But you will agree about the fact I fancy; you will agree that ideas are as infectious as bacteria and appear to run their course like epidemics. First, there is little immunity, nearly all individuals are susceptible, so that the disease spreads like a prairie fire. Next, a period where the curve of infection, as the pathologists say, remains level; this may last a long time. Last a decline of the curve which, so far as is known, nothing can check. The virus has lost its potency, or some immunity has established itself in a wholly mysterious way.

Ideas, fashions, dogmas, literary, political, scientific, and religious, have a very similar course; they get a currency, spread like wildfire, have their day and thereafter nothing can revive them. Were the old questions ever answered? Has anyone ever proved or disproved the right of secession? Most issues are not decided; their importance passes and they follow after. But in their day they rack the world they infest; men mill about them like a frantic herd: not understanding what their doctrines imply, or whither they lead. To them attach the noblest, and the meanest, motives, indifferent to all but that there is a cause to die, or to profit by. Such habits are not conducive to the life of reason; that kind of devotion is not the method by which man has raised himself from a savage. Rather by quite another way, by doubt, by trial, by tentative conclusion.

In recent times we have deliberately systematized the production of epidemics in ideas, much as a pathologist experiments with a colony of white mice, who are scarcely less protected. The science of propaganda by no means had its origin in the Great War, but that gave it a greater impetus than ever before. To the advertiser we should look for our best technique. I am told that if I see McCracken's tooth-paste often enough in street cars, on billboards and in shop windows, it makes no difference how determined I may be not to become one of McCracken's customers, I shall buy McCracken's tooth-paste sooner or later, whether I will or no; it is as inevitable as that I shut my eyes when you strike at my face. In much the same way political ideas are spread, and moral too, or for that matter, religious. You know the established way of raising money for the School of Applied and Theoretical Taxidermy. One employs a master mind in group suggestion, with lieutenants and field workers. The possible "prospects" are bombarded with a carefully planned series of what for some unknown reason is called "literature" —leaflets, pictures, pathetic appeals, masterful appeals, appeals to patriotism. Shall American animals suffer the indignity of inadequate stuffing, having themselves given their lives to the cause? Will not you as a loyal American do your bit too; they having made the last supreme sacrifice? Taxidermy is a patriotic duty; are you for taxidermy? If not, you are against it, a taxidermical outlaw at best, at worst a taxidermical Laodicean.[5] Brother, show your colors, join some group, at all costs join, be not a non-joiner, a detestable, lily-livered, half-hearted, supercilious, un-American, whom we would exile if we could and would not pass if he sought entrance.

I submit that a community used to be played on in this way, especially one so large and so homogeneous as we have become, is not a favorable soil for liberty. That plant cannot thrive in such a forcing bed; it is slow growing and needs a more equitable climate. It is the product, not of institutions, but of a temper, of an attitude towards life; of that mood that looks before and after and pines for

5. The early Christians of Laodicea were notoriously lukewarm or indifferent.

what is not. It is idle to look to laws, or courts, or principalities, or powers, to secure it. You may write into your constitutions not ten, but fifty, amendments, and it shall not help a farthing, for casuistry will undermine it as casuistry should, if it have no stay but law. It is secure only in that *constans et perpetua voluntas suum cuique tribuendi*[6]; in that sense of fair play, of give and take, of the uncertainty of human hypothesis, of how changeable and passing are our surest convictions, which has so hard a chance to survive in any times, perhaps especially in our own.

There are some who, looking on the American scene, see remedy in trying to introduce and maintain local differences. Especially in matters of government, let us be astute to preserve local autonomy, not to concentrate all power in our capital. There are reasons enough for this in any case, but as a relief from the prevalent mood it seems to me a delusion. That served very well in Jefferson's time; it will not do today. We cannot set our faces against a world enraptured with the affluence which comes from mass production; and what has served so magically in material things, is it not proved to be good for our ideas, our amusements, our morals, our religion? The heretic is odious in proportion as large industry is successful. Rapidity of communication alone makes segregation a broken reed; for men will talk with one another, visit one another, join with one another, listen collectively, look collectively, play collectively, and in the end, for aught I know, eat and sleep collectively, though they have nothing to say, nothing to do, no eyes or ears with which to enjoy or to value what they see and hear. You cannot set up again a Jeffersonian world in separate monads, each looking up to heaven. For good or evil, man, who must have lived for long in groups, likes too much the warm feeling of his mental and moral elbows in touch with his neighbors'.

Well, then, shall we surrender; shall we agree to submit to the dictation of the prevalent fashion in morals and ideas, as we do in dress? Must we capture surreptitiously such independence as we can, "bootleg" it, as it were, and let the heathen rage, the cattle mill, the air resound with imperious nostrums which will brook no dissidence? Maybe it will come to that; sometimes I wonder whether to be a foe of war, for example—which might be thought a blameless disposition—is not a stigma of degeneracy. Again I have pondered on what it is to be a Bolshevik, and once I learned. There was a time when Congress thought it could reach the salaries of my brothers and myself by an income tax, until the Supreme Court manfully came to our rescue. A judge of much experience was talking with me one day about it; I was wrong enough in my law, as it afterwards turned out, and disloyal enough in temper to my class, to say that I thought the tax valid. "Do you know anything about it?" he asked

6. "the constant and personal desire to accord to each his own."

with some asperity. "No," said I, "not a thing." "Have you ever read Taney's letter?" "No," said I again, for I was innocent of any learning. "Why, they can't do that," said he; "they can't do that, that's Bolshevism." And so it turned out, to my personal gratification, since when, freed from that Red Peril, I have enjoyed an immunity which the rest of you, alas, cannot share. Far be it from me to suggest that there are graver thrusts at the structure of society than to tax a Federal judge. Properly instructed, I have recanted my heresy, and yet there hangs about "Bolshevism" a residual vagueness, a lack of clear outline, as of a mountain against the setting sun; which only goes to show, I suppose, that a fundamentally corrupt nature can never be wholly reformed.

As I say, we may have to lie low like Bre'r Rabbit, and get our freedom as best we can, but that is the last resort. Perhaps if we cannot build breakwaters, we may be able to deepen the bottom. The Republic of Switzerland is cut into deep valleys; it has been a traditional home of freedom. Greece is made in the same way; to Greece we owe it that our civilization is not Asian. Our own country has not that protection; and in any event, of what value would it be in these later days, when Fords climb Pikes Peak and Babe Ruth is the local divinity at once in San Diego and Bangor? But what nature has not done for us, perhaps time can. I conceive that there is nothing which gives a man more pause before taking as absolute what his feelings welcome, and his mind deems plausible, than even the flicker of a recollection that something of the sort has been tried before, felt before, disputed before, and for some reason or other has now quite gone into Limbo. Historians may be dogmatists, I know, though not so often now as when history was dogma. At least you will perhaps agree that even a smattering of history and especially of letters will go far to dull the edges of uncompromising conviction. No doubt one may quote history to support any cause, as the devil quotes scripture; but modern history is not a very satisfactory side-arm in political polemics; it grows less and less so. Besides, it is not so much history one learns as the fact that one is aware that man has had a history at all. The liberation is not in the information but in the background acquired, the sense of mutability, and of the transience of what seems so poignant and so pressing today. One may take sides violently over the execution of Charles the First, but he has been dead a long while; the issue is not bitter unless we connect it with what is going on today. Many can of course do this, but that in itself requires considerable knowledge of intervening events, and those who can achieve a sustained theory are almost entitled to their partisanship, in reward of their ingenuity. After all, we can hope only for palliatives.

With history I class what in general we call the Liberal Arts, Fiction, Drama, Poetry, Biography, especially those of other countries; as far as that be possible, in other tongues. In short, I argue that the political life of a country like ours would get depth and steadiness, would tend to escape its greatest danger, which is the disposition to take the immediate for the eternal, to press the advantage of present numbers to the full, to ignore dissenters and regard them as heretics, by some adumbration of what men have thought and felt in other times and at other places. This seems to me a surer resort than liberal weeklies, societies for the promotion of cultural relations, sermons upon tolerance, American Civil Liberty Unions. I know very well how remote from the possibilities of most men anything of the kind must be, but good temper, as well as bad, is contagious. And today in America vast concourses of youth are flocking to our colleges, eager for something, just what they do not know. It makes much difference what they get. They will be prone to demand something they can immediately use; the tendency is strong to give it them; science, economics, business administration, law in its narrower sense. I submit that the shepherds should not first feed the flocks with these. I argue for the outlines of what used to go as a liberal education—not necessarily in the sense that young folks should waste precious years in efforts, unsuccessful for some reason I cannot understand, to master ancient tongues; but I speak for an introduction into the thoughts and deeds of men who have lived before them, in other countries than their own, with other strifes and other needs. This I maintain, not in the interest of that general cultural background, which is so often a cloak for the superior person, the prig, the snob and the pedant. But I submit to you that in some such way alone can we meet and master the high-power salesman of political patent medicines. I come to you, not as an advocate of education for education's sake, but as one, who like you, I suppose, is troubled by the spirit of faction, by the catch-words with the explosive energy of faith behind them, by the unwillingness to live and let live with which we are plagued. It is well enough to put one's faith in education, but the kind makes a vast difference. The principles of a common pump are in my opinion not so important politically as Keat's *Ode on a Grecian Urn*, to crib a phrase from Augustine Birrell.

May I take an illustration nearer to the field with which you are especially concerned? I venture to believe that it is as important to a judge called upon to pass on a question of constitutional law, to have at least a bowing acquaintance with Acton and Maitland, with Thucydides, Gibbon and Carlyle, with Homer, Dante, Shakespeare and Milton, with Machiavelli, Montaigne and Rabelais, with Plato, Bacon, Hume and Kant, as with the books which have been specifically written on the subject. For in such matters everything turns upon the spirit in which he approaches the questions before him. The words he must construe are empty vessels into which he can pour nearly anything he will. Men do not gather figs of thistles, nor supply institutions from judges whose outlook is limited by parish or class. They must be aware that there are before them more than verbal problems; more than final solutions cast in generalizations of universal applicability. They must be aware of the changing social tensions in every society which make it an organism; which demand new schemata of adaptation; which will disrupt it, if rigidly confined.

This is only an illustration of the much wider question of our political life at large. I submit that the aim is not so fanciful as it may seem; though at the moment I agree the outlook is not promising. Young people are not much disposed to give their time to what seems like loose browsing in the past. Though there are signs of a turn, of the significance of the insignificant, I shall try no forecast. All I want to emphasize is the political aspect of the matter, of the opportunity to preserve that spirit of liberty without which life is insupportable, and nations have never in the past been able to endure.

Jefferson is dead; time has disproved his forecasts; the society which he strove to preserve is gone to chaos and black night, as much as the empire of Genghis Khan; what has succeeded he would disown as any get of his. Yet back of the form there is still the substance, the possibility of the individual expression of life on the terms of him who has to live it. The victory is not all Hamilton's, nor can it be unless we are all to be checked as anonymous members regulated by some bureaucratic machine, impersonal, inflexible, a Chronos to devour us, its children. We shall not succeed by any attempt to put the old wine in new bottles; liberty is an essence so volatile that it will escape any vial however corked. It rests in the hearts of men, in the belief that knowledge is hard to get, that man must break through again and again the thin crust on which he walks, that the certainties of today may become the superstitions of tomorrow; that we have no warrant of assurance save by everlasting readiness to test and test again. William James was its great American apostle in modern times; we shall do well to remember him.

Surely we, the children of a time when the assumptions of even the science of our fathers have been outworn; surely we ought not to speak in apocalyptic verities, nor scourge from the temple those who do not see with our eyes. All the devices of our ingenuity, all our command over the materials of this earth, all the organization and differentiation of our industry and our social life, all our moral fetishes and exaltations, all our societies to ameliorate mankind, our hospitals, our colleges, our institutes—all these shall not save us. We shall still need some knowledge of ourselves, and where shall we better look than to the fate of those who went before? Would we hold liberty, we must have charity—charity to others, charity to ourselves, crawling up from the moist ovens of a steaming world, still carrying the passional equipment of our ferocious ancestors, emerging from black superstition amid carnage and atrocity to our perilous present. What shall it profit us, who come so by our possessions, if we have not charity?

QUESTIONS FOR STUDY, DISCUSSION, AND WRITING

1. What are the "sources of tolerance" named in the title? At what point in his address does Hand speak directly to that topic? Why does he not do so at the start?
2. What conditions, according to Hand, diminish liberty and tolerance? What proposed remedies does he consider and find insufficient?
3. To what purpose does Hand contrast Jefferson and Hamilton? What essentially is the contrast? Of what are they representative figures?
4. Consider whether, and in what ways, Hand's speech resembles a conversation, or dialogue. Is that mode of speech a suitable way of rendering the ideas he recommends? Explain.
5. Both Hand and Emerson ("The American Scholar," pp. 165–180) discuss the influence of the past and knowledge of history in forming the mind of a thinking man. Compare their views of the value and uses of that knowledge.

HERBERT GOLD

A Dog in Brooklyn, a Girl in Detroit: A Life among the Humanities

What better career for a boy who seeks to unravel the meaning of our brief span on earth than that of philosopher? We all wonder darkly, in the forbidden hours of the night, punishing our parents and building a better world, with undefined terms. Soon, however, most of us learn to sleep soundly; or we take to pills or love-making; or we call ourselves insomniacs, not philosophers. A few attempt to define the terms.

There is no code number for the career of philosophy in school, the Army, or out beyond in real life. The man with a peculiar combination of melancholic, nostalgic, and reforming instincts stands at three possibilities early in his youth. He can choose to be a hero, an artist, or a philosopher. In olden times, war, say, or the need to clean out the old west, might make up his mind for him. The old west had been pretty well cleaned up by the time I reached a man's estate, and Gary Cooper could finish the job. Heroism was an untimely option. With much bureaucratic confusion I tried a bit of heroic war, got stuck in the machine, and returned to the hectic,

Quonset campus of the G.I. Bill, burning to Know, Understand, and Convert. After a season of ferocious burrowing in books, I was ready to be a Teacher, which seemed a stern neighbor thing to Artist and Philosopher. I took on degrees, a Fulbright fellowship, a wife, a child, a head crammed with foolish questions and dogmatic answers despite the English school of linguistic analysis. I learned to smile, pardner, when I asked questions of philosophers trained at Oxford or Cambridge, but I asked them nonetheless. I signed petitions against McCarthy, wrote a novel, went on a treasure hunt, returned to my roots in the Middle West and stood rooted there, discussed the menace of the mass media, and had another child.

By stages not important here, I found myself teaching the Humanities at Wayne University in Detroit. I am now going to report a succession of classroom events which, retrospectively, seems to have determined my abandonment of formal dealing with this subject. The evidence does not, however, render any conclusion about education in the "Humanities" logically impregnable. It stands for a state of mind and is no substitute for formal argument. However, states of mind are important in this area of experience and metaexperience. However and however: it happens that most of the misty exaltation of the blessed vocation of the teacher issues from the offices of deans, editors, and college presidents. The encounter with classroom reality has caused many teachers, like Abelard meeting the relatives of Eloïse, to lose their bearings. Nevertheless this is a memoir, not a campaign, about a specific life in and out of the Humanities. Though I am not a great loss to the History of Everything in Culture, my own eagerness to teach is a loss to me.

News item of a few years ago. A young girl and her date are walking along a street in Brooklyn, New York. The girl notices that they are being followed by an enormous Great Dane. The dog is behaving peculiarly, showing its teeth and making restless movements. A moment later, sure enough, the dog, apparently maddened, leaps slavering upon the girl, who is borne to earth beneath its weight. With only an instant's hesitation, the boy jumps on the dog. Its fangs sunk in one, then in the other, the dog causes the three of them to roll like beasts across the sidewalk.

A crowd gathers at a safe distance to watch. No one interferes. They display the becalmed curiosity of teevee viewers.

A few moments later a truckdriver, attracted by the crowd, pulls his vehicle over to the curb. This brave man is the only human being stirred personally enough to leave the role of passive spectator. Instantaneously analyzing the situation, he leaps into the struggle—*attacking and beating the boy.* He has naturally assumed that the dog must be protecting an innocent young lady from the unseemly actions of a juvenile delinquent.

I recounted this anecdote in the classroom in order to introduce a course which attempted a summary experience of Humanities 610 for a monumental nine credits. There were a number of points to be made about the passivity of the crowd ("don't get involved," "not my business") and the stereotypical reaction of the truck driver who had been raised to think of man's best friend as not another human being but a dog. In both cases, addicted to entertainment and clichés, the crowd and the trucker could not recognize what was actually happening before their eyes; they responded irrelevantly to the suffering of strangers; they were not a part of the main. This led us to a discussion of the notion of "community." In a closely-knit society, the people on the street would have known the couple involved and felt a responsibility towards them. In a large city, everyone is a stranger. (Great art can give a sense of the brotherhood of men. Religion used to do this, too.) "Any questions?" I asked, expecting the authority of religion to be defended.

An eager hand shot up. Another. Another. Meditative bodies sprawled in their chairs. "Are all New Yorkers like that?" "Well, what can you do if there's a mad dog and you're not expecting it?" "Where does it say in what great book how you got to act in Brooklyn?"

I took note of humor in order to project humorousness. I found myself composing my face in the look of thought which teevee panelists use in order to project thinking. I discovered a serious point to elaborate—several. I mentioned consciousness and relevance and the undefined moral suggestion implied by the labor which produces any work of art or mind. A girl named Clotilda Adams asked me: "Why don't people try to get along better in this world?"

Somewhat digressively, we then discussed the nature of heroism, comparing the behavior of the boy and the truck driver. Both took extraordinary risks; why? We broke for cigarettes in the autumn air outside. Then, for fifty minutes more, we raised these interesting questions, referring forward to Plato, Aristotle, St. Thomas, Dostoevsky, Tolstoy, William James, and De Gaulle; and then boy, dog, girl, truck driver and crowd were left with me and the crowned ghosts of history in the deserted room while my students went on to Phys Ed, Music Appreciation, Sosh, and their other concerns. Having been the chief speaker, both dramatist and analyst, I was exalted by the lofty ideas floated up into the air around me. I was a little let down to return to our real life in which dog-eat-dog is man's closest pal. Fact. Neither glory nor pleasure nor power, and certainly not wisdom, provided the goal of my students. Not even wealth was the aim of most of them. They sought to make out, to do all right, more prideful than amorous in love, more security-hungry than covetous in status. I saw my duty as a teacher: Through the Humanities, to awaken them to the dream of mastery over the facts of our lives. I saw my duty plain: Through the Humanities, to lead them toward the exaltation of knowledge and the calm of control. I had a whole year in which to fulfill this obligation. It was a two-semester course.

Before she left the room, Clotilda Adams said, "You didn't answer my question." Fact.

Outside the university enclave of glass and grass, brick and trees, Detroit was agonizing in its last big year with the big cars. Automation, dispersion of factories, and imported automobiles were eroding a precarious confidence. Fear was spreading; soon the landlords would offer to decorate apartments and suffer the pain. Detroit remembered the war years with nostalgia. Brave days, endless hours, a three-shift clock, insufficient housing, men sleeping in the all-night, triple-feature movies on Woodward and Grand River. Though the area around the Greyhound and Trailways stations was still clotted with the hopeful out of the hill country of the mid-South and the driven from the deep South—they strolled diagonally across the boulevards, entire families holding hands—some people suspected what was already on its way down the road: twenty per cent unemployment in Detroit.

The semester continued. We churned through the great books. One could classify my students in three general groups, intelligent, mediocre, and stupid, allowing for the confusions of three general factors—background, capacity, and interest. This was how we classified the Humanities, too: ancient, medieval, and modern. It made a lot of sense, and it made me itch, scratch, and tickle. Series of three form nice distinctions. According to Jung and other authorities, they have certain mythic significances. The course was for nine credits. All the arts were touched upon. We obeyed Protagoras; man, just man, was our study. When I cited him—"the proper study of man is Man"—Clotilda Adams stirred uneasily in her seat. "By which Protagoras no doubt meant woman, too," I assured her. She rested.

Now imagine the winter coming and enduring, with explosions of storm and exfoliations of gray slush, an engorged industrial sky overhead and sinus trouble all around. The air was full of acid and a purplish, spleeny winter mist. Most of Detroit, in Indian times before the first French trappers arrived, had been a swamp and below sea level. The swamp was still present, but invisible; city stretched out in all directions, crawling along the highways. Though Detroit was choked by a dense undergrowth of streets and buildings, irrigated only by super-highways, its work was done with frantic speed. The Rouge plant roared, deafened. The assembly lines clanked to the limit allowed by the UAW. The old Hudson factory lay empty, denuded, waiting to become a parking lot. Then the new models were being introduced! Buick! Pontiac! Dodge! Ford and Chevrolet! Ford impudently purchased a huge billboard faced towards the General Motors Building on Grand Boulevard. General Motors retailiated by offering free ginger ale to all comers, and a whole bottle of Vernor's to take home if you would only consent to test-drive the new Oldsmobile, the car with the . . . I've forgotten what it had that year. All over town the automobile companies were holding revival meetings; hieratic salesmen preached to the converted and the hangers-back alike; lines at the loan companies stretched through the revolving doors and out on to the winter pavements. But many in those lines were trying to get additional financing on their last year's cars. The new models were an indifferent success despite all the uproar of display and Detroit's patriotic attention to it. Search-lights sliced up the heavens while the city lay under flu.

Teachers at Wayne University soon learn not to tease the American Automobile. *Lèse*[1] Chrysler was a moral offense, an attack on the livelihood and the sanctity of the American garage. Detroit was a town in which men looked at hub caps as men elsewhere have sometimes looked at ankles. The small foreign car found itself treated with a violent Halloween kidding-on-the-square, scratched, battered, and smeared (another Jungian series of three!). A passionate and sullen town, Detroit had no doubts about its proper business. All it doubted was everything else.

I often failed at inspiring my students to do the assigned reading. Many of them had part-time jobs in the automobile industry or its annexes. Even a Philosopher found it difficult to top the argument, "I couldn't read the book this week, I have to *work*," with its implied reproach for a scholar's leisure. But alas, many of these stricken proletarians drove freshly-minted automobiles. They worked in order to keep up the payments, racing like laboratory mice around the cage of depreciation. Certain faculty deep thinkers, addicted to broad understanding of the problems of others, argued that these students were so poor they *had* to buy new cars in order to restore their confidence. The finance companies seemed to hear their most creative expressions, not me. Deep in that long Detroit winter, I had the task of going from the pre-Socratic mystics all the way to Sartre, for nine credits. Like an audio-visual monkey, I leapt from movie projector to records to slides, with concurrent deep labor in book and tablet. We read *The Brothers Karamazov*, but knowing the movie did not give credit. We studied *The Waste Land*, and reading the footnotes did not suffice. We listened to Wanda Landowska play the harpsichord on records. We sat in the dark before a slide of Seurat's "La Grande Jatte"[2] while I explained the importance of the measles of *pointillisme* to students who only wanted to see life clear and true, see it comfortably. Clotilda Adams said that this kind of painting hurt her eyes. She said that there was too much reading for one course—

1. Injured. Cf. *lèse majesté*: injured majesty, *i.e.*, treason.
2. River park in Paris, subject of Seurat's painting.

"piling it on. This isn't the only course we take." She said that she liked music, though. Moses only had to bring the Law down the mountain to the children of Israel; I had to bring it pleasingly.

We made exegeses. I flatly turned down the request of a dean that I take attendance. As a statesmanlike compromise, I tested regularly for content and understanding.

Then, on a certain morning, I handed back some quiz papers at the beginning of class. Out on the street, a main thoroughfare through town, it was snowing; this was one of those magical days of late winter snowfall—pale, cold, clean, and the entire city momentarily muffled by the silence of snow. The room hissed with steam heat; a smell of galoshes and mackinaws arose from the class. "Let us not discuss the test—let us rise above grades. Let us try to consider nihilism as a byproduct of the Romantic revival—" I had just begun my lecture when an odd clashing, lumping noise occurred on Cass Avenue. "Eliot's later work, including *The Four Quartets*, which we will not discuss here. . . ."

But I was interrupted by a deep sigh from the class. A product of nihilism and the romantic revival? No. It was that strange tragic sigh of horror and satisfaction. Out in the street, beyond the window against which I stood, a skidding truck had sideswiped a taxi. The truckdriver had parked and gone into a drugstore. The cab was smashed like a cruller. From the door, the driver had emerged, stumbling drunkenly on the icy road, holding his head. There was blood on his head. There was blood on his hands. He clutched his temples. The lines of two-way traffic, moving very slowly in the snow and ice, carefully avoided hitting him. There were streaks of perforated and patterned snow, frothed up by tires. He was like an island around which the sea of traffic undulated in slow waves; but he was an island that moved in the sea and held hands to head. He slid and stumbled back and forth, around and about his cab in the middle of the wide street. He was in confusion, in shock. Even at this distance I could see blood on the new-fallen snow. Drivers turned their heads upon him like angry Halloween masks, but did not get involved. Snow spit at his feet.

No one in the class moved. The large window through which we gazed was like a screen, with the volume turned down by habit, by snow, by a faulty tube. As the teacher, my authority took precedence. I ran out to lead the cab driver into the building. An elderly couple sat huddled in the car, staring at the smashed door, afraid to come out the other. They said they were unhurt.

I laid the man down on the floor. He was bleeding from the head and his face was a peculiar purplish color, with a stubble of beard like that of a dead man. There was a neat prick in his forehead where the union button in his cap had been driven into the skin. I sent a student to call for an ambulance. The cab driver's color was like that of the bruised industrial sky. "You be okay till the ambulance——?"

Foolish question. No alternative. No answer.

We waited. The class was restless. When they weren't listening to me, or talking to themselves, or smudging blue books in an exam, they did not know what to do in this room devoted to the specialized absorption of ideas. Silence. Scraping of feet, crisping of paper. We watched the slow-motion traffic on the street outside.

The cab driver moved once in a rush, turning over face down against the floor, with such force that I thought he might break his nose. Then slowly, painfully, as if in a dream, he turned back and lay staring at the ceiling. His woollen lumberjack soaked up the blood trickling from one ear; the blood traveled up separated cilia of wool which drew it in with a will of their own. There was a swaying, osmotic movement like love-making in the eager little wisps of wool. An astounded ring of Humanities 610 students watched, some still holding their returned quiz papers. One girl in particular, Clotilda Adams, watched him and me with her eyes brilliant, wet and bulging, and her fist crumpling the paper. I tried by imagining it to force the ambulance through the chilled and snow-fallen city. I saw it weaving around the injured who strutted with shock over ice and drift, its single red Cyclops' eye turning, the orderlies hunched over on benches, chewing gum and cursing the driver. The ambulance did not arrive. Clotilda Adams' eye had a thick, impenetrable sheen over it. She watched from the cab driver to me as if we were in some way linked. When would the authorities get there? When the medics? There must have been many accidents in town, and heart attacks, and fires with cases of smoke inhalation.

Before the ambulance arrived, the police were there. They came strolling into the classroom with their legs apart, as if they remembered ancestors who rode the plains. Their mouths were heavy in thought. They had noses like salamis, red and mottled with fat. They were angry at the weather, at the school, at the crowd, at me, and especially at the prostrate man at our feet. He gave them a means to the creative expression of pique. (Everyone needs an outlet.)

Now Clotilda Adams took a step backward, and I recall thinking this odd. She had been treading hard near the pool of blood about the cab-driver, but when the cops strolled up, she drifted toward the outer edge of the group of students, with a sly look of caution in her downcast, sideways-cast eyes. Her hand still crisped at the returned exam paper. This sly, lid-fallen look did not do her justice. She was a hard little girl of the sort often thought to be passionate—skinny but well-breasted, a high hard rump with a narrow curve, a nervous mouth.

The two policemen stood over the body of the cab-driver. They stared at him in the classic pose—one cop with a hand resting lightly on the butt of his gun and the other on his butt, the younger cop with lips so pouted that his breath made a snuffling sound in his nose. They both had head colds. Their Ford was pulled up on the snow-covered lawn outside, with raw muddled marks of tread in the soft dirt. When the snow melted, there would be wounded streaks in the grass. The cab driver closed his eyes under the finicking, distasteful examination. At last one spoke: "See your driver's license."

The cab driver made a clumsy gesture towards his pocket. The cop bent and went into the pocket. He flipped open the wallet, glanced briefly at the photographs and cash, glanced at me, and then began lip-reading the license.

The cab-driver was in a state of shock. There was a mixture of thin and thick blood on his clothes and messing the floor. "This man is badly hurt," I said. "Can't we get him to the hospital first?"

"This is only your *driver* license," the cop said slowly, having carefully read through Color of Hair: *Brn*, Color of Eyes: *Brn*, and checked each item with a stare at the man on the floor. "Let me see your chauffeur license."

"He's badly hurt," I said. "Get an ambulance."

"Teach'," said the older cop, "you know your business? We know ours."

"It's on the way," said the other. "Didn't you call it yourself?"

"No, one of the students. . . ." I said.

He grinned with his great victory. "So—don't you trust your pupils neither?"

Shame. I felt shame at this ridicule of my authority in the classroom. A professor is not a judge, a priest, or a sea captain; he does not have the right to perform marriages on the high seas of audio-visual aids and close reasoning. But he is more than an intercom between student and fact; he can be a stranger to love for his students, but not to a passion for his subject; he is a student himself; his pride is lively. The role partakes of a certain heft and control. There is power to make decisions, power to abstain, power to bewilder, promote, hold back, adjust, and give mercy; power, an investment of pride, a risk of shame.

Clotilda Adams, still clutching her exam, stared at me with loathing. She watched me bested by the police. She barely glanced, and only contemptuously, at the man bleeding from the head on the floor. She moved slightly forward again in order to participate fully in an action which apparently had some important meaning for her. She had lost her fear of the police when she saw how we all stood with them. The limits were established.

The police were going through the cab-driver's pockets. They took out a folding pocket-knife and cast significant looks at it and at each other. It had a marbled plastic hilt, like a resort souvenir. It was attached to a key ring.

"Hey!" one said to the half-conscious man. "What's this knife for?"

"Where'd you get them keys?" the other demanded, prodding the cabbie with his toe.

"A skeleton key. These cab companies," one of the cops decided to explain to Clotilda Adams, who was standing nearby, "they get the dregs. Hillbillies, you know?"

I said nothing, found nothing to say. I now think of Lord Acton's famous law, which is accepted as true the way it was uttered. The opposite is also true—the commoner's way: Having no power corrupts; having absolutely no power corrupts absolutely.

The bleeding seemed to have stopped. The cab driver sat up, looking no better, with his bluish, greenish, drained head hanging between his knees. His legs were crumpled stiffly. He propped himself on his hands. The police shot questions at him. He mumbled, mumbled, explained, explained.

"How long you been in Detroit? How come you come out of the mountains?"

"Why you pick up this fare?"

"What makes you think Cass is a one-way street?"

Mumbling and mumbling, explaining and explaining, the cab-driver tried to satisfy them. He also said: "Hurt. Maybe you get me to the hospital, huh? Hurt real bad."

"Maybe," said one of the cops, "maybe we take you to the station house first. That boy you hit says reckless driving. I think personally you'd flunk the drunk test—what you think, Teach'?"

I sent one of the students to call for an ambulance again. In the infinitesimal pause between my suggestion and his action, an attentive reluctant expectant caesura, I put a dime in his hand for the call. One of the cops gave me that long look described by silent movie critics as the slow burn. "They drive careful," he finally said. "It's snowing. They got all that expensive equipment."

The snow had started again outside the window. The skid-marks on the lawn were covered. Though the sky was low and gray, the white sifting down gave a peaceful village glow to this industrial Detroit. Little gusts barely rattled the windows. With the class, the cops, and the driver, we were living deep within a snowy paper-weight. I felt myself moving very slowly, swimming within thick glass, like the loosened plastic figure in a paper-weight. The snow came down in large torn flakes, all over the buildings of Wayne University, grass, trees, and the pale radiance of a network of slow-motion super-highways beyond. Across the street a modern building —glass and aluminum strips—lay unfinished in this weather. Six months ago there had been a student boardinghouse on that spot, filled with the artists and the beat, the guitar-wielders and the modern dancers, with a tradition going all the way back to the Korean war. Now there were wheelbarrows full of frozen cement; there were intentions to build a Japanese garden, with Japanese proportions and imported goldfish.

My student returned from the telephone. He had reached a hospital.

The cab driver was fading away. Rootlets of shock hooded his eyes: the lid was closing shut. A cop asked him another question—what the button on his cap stood for—it was a union button—and then the man just went reclining on his elbow, he slipped slowly down, he lay in the little swamp of crusted blood on the floor. You know what happens when milk is boiled? The crust broke like the crust of boiled milk when a spoon goes into coffee. The cop stood with a delicate, disgusted grimace on his face. What a business to be in, he seemed to be thinking. In approximately ten years, at age forty-two, he could retire and sit comfortable in an undershirt, with a non-returnable can of beer, before the color TV. He could relax. He could *start* to relax. But in the meanwhile—nag, nag, nag. Drunk cabbies, goddam hillbillies. The reckless driver on the floor seemed to sleep. His lips moved. He was alive.

Then a puffing intern rushed into the room. I had not heard the ambulance. The policeman gave room and the intern kneeled. He undid his bag. The orderlies glanced at the floor and went back out for their stretcher.

I stood on one side of the body, the kneeling intern with his necklace of stethoscope, and the two meditative cops. On the other side was the group of students, and at their head, like a leader filled with wrath, risen in time of crisis, stood Clotilda Adams, still clutching her exam paper. There were tears in her eyes. She was in a fury. She had been thinking all this time, and now her thinking had issue: *rage*. Over the body she handed me a paper, crying out, "I don't think I deserved a *D* on that quiz. I answered all the questions. I can't get my credit for Philo of Ed without I get a *B* off you."

I must have looked at her with pure stupidity on my face. There is a Haitian proverb: Stupidity won't kill you, but it'll make you sweat a lot. She took the opportunity to make me sweat, took my silence for guilt, took my open-mouthed gaze for weakness. She said: "If I was a white girl, you'd grade me easier."

Guilty, a hundred years, a thousand years of it; pity for the disaster of ignorance and fear, pity for ambition rising out of ignorance; adoration of desire; trancelike response to passion—passion which justifies itself because passionate. . . . I looked at her with mixed feelings. I could not simply put her down. In order to *put down* your own mind must be made up, put down. She had beauty and dignity, stretched tall and wrathful, with teeth for biting and eyes for striking dead.

"But I know my rights," she said, "*mister*. My mother told me about your kind—lent my father money on his car and then hounded him out of town. He's been gone since fifty-three. But you can't keep us down forever, no sir, you can't always keep us down—"

She was talking and I was yelling. She was talking and yelling about injustice and I, under clamps, under ice, was yelling in a whisper about the sick man. She was blaming me for all her troubles, all the troubles she had seen, and I was blaming her for not seeing what lay before her, and we were making an appointment to meet in my office and discuss this thing more calmly, Miss Adams. Okay. All right. Later.

The police, the doctor, the orderlies, and the injured cab-driver were gone. The police car out front was gone and the snow was covering its traces. The janitor came in and swept up the bloodstains with green disinfectant powder. The frightened couple in the cab were released. They all disappeared silently into the great city, into the routine of disaster and recovery of a great city. I dismissed the class until tomorrow.

The next day I tried to explain to Miss Adams what I meant about her failing to respond adequately to the facts of our life together. Her mouth quivered. Yesterday rage; today a threat of tears. What did I mean she wasn't *adequate?* What did I know about adequate anyhow? Nothing. Just a word. Agreed, Miss Adams. I was trying to say that there were two questions at issue between us—her exam grade and her choice of occasion to dispute it. I would like to discuss each matter separately. I tried to explain why putting the two events together had disturbed me. I tried to explain the notions of empirical evidence and metaphor. Finally I urged her to have her exam looked at by the head of the department, but she refused because she knew in advance that he would support me. "White is Right," she said.

"Do you want to drop out of the class?"

"No. I'll stay," she said with a sudden patient, weary acceptance of her fate. "I'll do what I can."

"I'll do what I can too," I said.

She smiled hopefully at me. She was tuckered out by the continual alert for combat everywhere. She was willing to forgive and go easy. When she left my office, this smile, shy, pretty, and conventional, tried to tell me that she could be generous—a friend.

We had come to Thomas Hobbes and John Locke in our tour through time and the river of humanities. I pointed out that the English philosophers were noted for clarity and eloquence of style. I answered this question: The French? Isn't French noted for clarity? Yes, they too, but they were more abstract. On the whole. In general.

The class took notes on the truths we unfolded together. Spring came and the snow melted. There was that brief Detroit flowering of the new season—jasmine and hollyhocks—which, something like it, must have captivated the Frenchman Antoine de la Mothe Cadillac when he paused on the straits of Detroit in 1701. University gardeners planted grass seed where the patrol car had parked on the lawn. The new models, all except the Cadillac, were going at mean discounts.

"The 'Humanities,'" wrote Clotilda Adams in her final essay, "are a necessary additive to any teacher's development worth her 'salt' in the perilous times of today. The West and the 'Free World' must stand up to the war of ideas against the 'Iron' Curtain." This was in answer to a question about Beethoven, Goethe, and German romanticism. She did not pass the course, but she was nevertheless admitted on probation to the student teacher program because of the teacher shortage and the great need to educate our children in these perilous times. Of today.

Humanities 610 provided ballast for the ship of culture as it pitched and reeled in the heavy seas of real life; I lashed myself to the mast, but after hearing the siren song of ground course outlines, I cut myself free and leaned over the rail with the inside of my lip showing.

It would be oversimplifying to say that I left off teaching Humanities merely because of an experience. Such an argument is fit to be published under the title "I was a Teen-Age Humanities Professor." I also left for fitter jobs, more money, a different life. Still, what I remember of the formal study of Truth and Beauty, for advanced credit in education, is a great confusion of generalities, committees, conferences, audio-visual importunities, and poor contact. "Contact!" cried the desperate deans and chairmen, like radio operators in ancient war movies. And much, much discussion of how to get through to the students. How to get through? Miss Adams and Mr. Gold, cab-driver and Thomas Hobbes, policemen and the faceless student who paused an instant for a dime for the telephone—we all have to discover how relevant we are to each other. Or do we *have* to? No, we can merely perish, shot down like mad dogs or diminished into time with no more than a glimpse of the light.

Words fade; our experience does not touch; we make do with babble and time-serving. We need to learn the meaning of words, the meaning of the reality those words refer to; we must clasp reality close. We cannot flirt forever, brown-nosing or brow-beating. We must act and build out of our own spirits. How? How? We continually need new politics, new cities, new marriages and families, new ways of work and leisure. We also need the fine old ways. For me, the primitive appeal to pleasure and pain of writing stories is a possible action, is the way in and out again, as teaching was not. As a teacher, I caught my students too late and only at the top of their heads, at the raw point of pride and ambition, and I had not enough love and pressure as a teacher to open the way through their intentions to the common humanity which remains locked within. As a writer, I could hope to hit them in their bodies and needs, where lusts and ideals are murkily nurtured together, calling to the prime fears and joys directly, rising with them from the truths of innocence into the truths of experience.

The peculiar combination of ignorance and jadedness built into most institutions is a desperate parody of personal innocence, personal experience. Nevertheless, education, which means a drawing out—even formal education, a formal drawing out—is a variety of experience, and experience is the only evidence we have. After evidence comes our thinking upon it. Do the scientists, secreting their honey in distant hives, hear the barking of the black dog which follows them? Will the politicians accept the lead of life, or will they insist on a grade of *B* in Power and Dominion over a doomed race? We need to give proper answers to the proper questions.

Particular life is still the best map to truth. When we search our hearts and strip our pretenses, we all know this. Particular life—we know only what we *know*. Therefore the policemen stay with me: I have learned to despise most authority. The cab-driver remains in his sick bleeding: pity for the fallen and helpless. And I think of Clotilda Adams in her power and weakness; like the cops, she has an authority of stupidity; like the victim of an accident, she is fallen and helpless. But some place, since we persist in our cold joke against the ideal of democracy, the cops still have the right to push people around, Clotilda is leading children in the Pledge of Allegiance. We must find a way to teach better and to learn.

WILLIAM G. PERRY, JR.

Examsmanship and the Liberal Arts:
A Study in Educational Epistemology

"But sir, I don't think I really deserve it, it was mostly bull, really." This disclaimer from a student whose examination we have awarded a straight "A" is wondrously depressing. Alfred North Whitehead invented its only possible rejoinder: "Yes sir, what you wrote is nonsense, utter nonsense. But ah! Sir! It's the right *kind* of nonsense!"

Bull, in this university,[1] is customarily a source of laughter, or a problem in ethics. I shall step a little out of fashion to use the subject as a take-off point for a study in comparative epistemology. The phenomenon of bull, in all the honor and opprobrium with which it is regarded by students and faculty, says something, I think, about

1. Harvard.

our theories of knowledge. So too, the grades which we assign on examinations communicate to students what these theories may be.

We do not have to be out-and-out logical-positivists to suppose that we have something to learn about "what we think knowledge is" by having a good look at "what we do when we go about measuring it." We know the straight "A" examination when we see it, of course, and we have reason to hope that the student will understand why his work receives our recognition. He doesn't always. And those who receive lesser honor? Perhaps an understanding of certain anomalies in our customs of grading good bull will explain the students' confusion.

I must beg patience, then, both of the reader's humor and of his morals. Not that I ask him to suspend his sense of humor but that I shall ask him to go beyond it. In a great university the picture of a bright student attempting to outwit his professor while his professor takes pride in not being outwitted is certainly ridiculous. I shall report just such a scene, for its implications bear upon my point. Its comedy need not present a serious obstacle to thought.

As for the ethics of bull, I must ask for a suspension of judgment. I wish that students could suspend theirs. Unlike humor, moral commitment is hard to think beyond. Too early a moral judgment is precisely what stands between many able students and a liberal education. The stunning realization that the Harvard Faculty will often accept, as evidence of knowledge, the cerebrations of a student who has little data at his disposal, confronts every student with an ethical dilemma. For some it forms an academic focus for what used to be thought of as "adolescent disillusion." It is irrelevant that rumor inflates the phenomenon to mythical proportions. The students know that beneath the myth there remains a solid and haunting reality. The moral "bind" consequent on this awareness appears most poignantly in serious students who are reluctant to concede the competitive advantage to the bullster and who yet feel a deep personal shame when, having succumbed to "temptation," they themselves receive a high grade for work they consider "dishonest."

I have spent many hours with students caught in this unwelcome bitterness. These hours lend an urgency to my theme. I have found that students have been able to come to terms with the ethical problem, to the extent that it is real, only after a refined study of the true nature of bull and its relation to "knowledge." I shall submit grounds for my suspicion that we can be found guilty of sharing the students' confusion of moral and epistemological issues.

I

I present as my "premise," then, an amoral *fabliau*. Its hero-villain is the Abominable Mr. Metzger '47. Since I celebrate his virtuosity, I regret giving him a pseudonym, but the peculiar style of his bravado requires me to honor also his modesty. Bull in pure form is rare; there is usually some contamination by data. The community has reason to be grateful to Mr. Metzger for having created an instance of laboratory purity, free from any adulteration by matter. The more credit is due him, I think, because his act was free from premeditation, deliberation, or hope of personal gain.

Mr. Metzger stood one rainy November day in the lobby of Memorial Hall. A junior, concentrating in mathematics, he was fond of diverting himself by taking part in the drama, a penchant which may have had some influence on the events of the next hour. He was waiting to take part in a rehearsal in Sanders Theatre, but, as sometimes happens, no other players appeared. Perhaps the rehearsal had been canceled without his knowledge? He decided to wait another five minutes.

Students, meanwhile, were filing into the Great Hall opposite, and taking seats at the testing tables. Spying a friend crossing the lobby toward the Great Hall's door, Metzger greeted him and extended appropriate condolences. He inquired, too, what course his friend was being tested in. "Oh, Soc. Sci. something-or-other." "What's it all about?" asked Metzger, and this, as Homer remarked of Patroclus, was the beginning of evil for him.

"It's about Modern Perspectives on Man and Society and All That," said his friend. "Pretty interesting, really."

"Always wanted to take a course like that," said Metzger. "Any good reading?"

"Yeah, great. There's this book"—his friend did not have time to finish.

"Take your seats please" said a stern voice beside them. The idle conversation had somehow taken the two friends to one of the tables in the Great Hall. Both students automatically obeyed; the proctor put blue-books before them; another proctor presented them with copies of the printed hour-test.

Mr. Metzger remembered afterwards a brief misgiving that was suddenly overwhelmed by a surge of curiosity and puckish glee. He wrote "George Smith" on the blue book, opened it, and addressed the first question.

I must pause to exonerate the Management. The Faculty has a rule that no student may attend an examination in a course in which he is not enrolled. To the wisdom of this rule the outcome of this deplorable story stands witness. The Registrar, charged with the enforcement of the rule, has developed an organization with procedures which are certainly the finest to be devised. In November, however, class rosters are still shaky, and on this particular day another student, named Smith, was absent. As for the culprit, we can reduce his guilt no further than to suppose that he was ignorant of the rule, or, in the face of the momentous challenge before him, forgetful.

We need not be distracted by Metzger's performance on the "objective" or "spot" questions on the test. His D on these sections can be explained by those versed in the theory of probability. Our interest focuses on the quality of his essay. It appears that when Metzger's friend picked up his own blue book a few days later, he found himself in company with a large proportion of his section in having received on the essay a C +. When he quietly picked up "George Smith's" blue book to return it to Metzger, he observed that the grade for the essay was A—. In the margin was a note in the section man's hand. It read "Excellent work. Could you have pinned these observations down a bit more closely? Compare . . . in . . . pp. . . ."

Such news could hardly be kept quiet. There was a leak, and the whole scandal broke on the front page of Tuesday's *Crimson*. With the press Metzger was modest, as becomes a hero. He said that there had been nothing to it at all, really. The essay question had offered a choice of two books, Margaret Mead's *And Keep Your Powder Dry* or Geoffrey Gorer's *The American People*. Metzger reported that having read neither of them, he had chosen the second "because the title gave me some notion as to what the book might be about." On the test, two critical comments were offered on each book, one favorable, one unfavorable. The students were asked to "discuss." Metzger conceded that he had played safe in throwing his lot with the more laudatory of the two comments, "but I did not forget to be balanced."

I do not have Mr. Metzger's essay before me except in vivid memory. As I recall, he took his first cue from the name Geoffrey, and committed his strategy to the premise that Gorer was born into an "Anglo-Saxon" culture, probably English, but certainly "English speaking." Having heard that Margaret Mead was a social anthropologist, he inferred that Gorer was the same. He then entered upon his essay, centering his inquiry upon what he supposed might be the problems inherent in an anthropologist's observation of a culture which was his own, or nearly his own. Drawing in part from memories of table-talk on cultural relativity[2] and in part from creative logic, he rang changes on the relation of observer to observed, and assessed the kind and degree of objectivity which might accrue to an observer through training as an anthropologist. He concluded that the book in question did in fact contribute a considerable range of " 'objective', and even 'fresh'," insights into the nature of our culture. "At the same time," he warned, "these observations must be understood within the context of their generation by a person only partly freed from his embeddedness in the culture he is observing,

2. "An important part of Harvard's education takes place during meals in the Houses." An Official Publication [Perry's note].

and limited in his capacity to transcend those particular tendencies and biases which he has himself developed as a personality in his interaction with this culture since his birth. In this sense the book portrays as much the character of Geoffrey Gorer as it analyzes that of the American people." It is my regrettable duty to report that at this moment of triumph Mr. Metzger was carried away by the temptations of parody and added, "We are thus much the richer."

In any case, this was the essay for which Metzger received his honor grade and his public acclaim. He was now, of course, in serious trouble with the authorities.

I shall leave him for the moment to the mercy of the Administrative Board of Harvard College and turn the reader's attention to the section man who ascribed the grade. He was in much worse trouble. All the consternation in his immediate area of the Faculty and all the glee in other areas fell upon his unprotected head. I shall now undertake his defense.

I do so not simply because I was acquainted with him and feel a respect for his intelligence; I believe in the justice of his grade! Well, perhaps "justice" is the wrong word in a situation so manifestly absurd. This is a case in "equity." That is, the grade is equitable if we accept other aspects of the situation which are equally absurd. My proposition is this: if we accept as valid those C grades which were accorded students who, like Metzger's friend, demonstrated a thorough familiarity with the details of the book without relating their critique to the methodological problems of social anthropology, then "George Smith" deserved not only the same, but better.

The reader may protest that the C's given to students who showed evidence only of diligence were indeed not valid and that both these students and "George Smith" should have received E's. To give the diligent E is of course not in accord with custom. I shall take up this matter later. For now, were I to allow the protest, I could only restate my thesis: that "George Smith's" E would, in a college of liberal arts, be properly a "better" E.

At this point I need a short-hand. It is a curious fact that there is no academic slang for the presentation of evidence of diligence alone. "Parroting" won't do; it is possible to "parrot" bull. I must beg the reader's pardon, and, for reasons almost too obvious to bear, suggest "cow."

Stated as nouns, the concepts look simple enough:

> cow (pure): data, however relevant, without relevancies.
> bull (pure): relevancies, however relevant, without data.

The reader can see all too clearly where this simplicity would lead. I can assure him that I would not have imposed on him this way were I aiming to say that knowledge in this university is definable as some neuter compromise between cow and bull, some infertile hermaphrodite. This is precisely what many diligent students seem to believe: that what they must learn to do is to "find the right mean" between "amounts" of detail and "amounts" of generalities. Of course this is not the point at all. The problem is not quantitative, nor does its solution lie on a continuum between the particular and the general. Cow and bull are not poles of a single dimension. A clear notion of what they really are is essential to my inquiry, and for heuristic purposes I wish to observe them further in the celibate state.

When the pure concepts are translated into verbs, their complexities become apparent in the assumptions and purposes of the students as they write:

To cow (*v. intrans.*) or the act of cowing:

To list data (or perform operations) without awareness of, or comment upon, the contexts, frames of reference, or points of observation which determine the origin, nature, and meaning of the data (or procedures). To write on the assumption that "a fact is a fact." To present evidence of hard work as a substitute for understanding, without any intent to deceive.

To bull (*v. intrans.*) or the act of bulling:

To discourse upon the contexts, frames of reference and points of observation which would determine the origin, nature, and meaning of data if one had any. To present evidence of an understanding of form in the hope that the reader may be deceived into supposing a familiarity with content.

At the level of conscious intent, it is evident that cowing is more moral, or less immoral, than bulling. To speculate about unconscious intent would be either an injustice or a needless elaboration of my theme. It is enough that the impression left by cow is one of earnestness, diligence, and painful naiveté. The grader may feel disappointment or even irritation, but these feelings are usually balanced by pity, compassion, and a reluctance to hit a man when he's both down and moral. He may feel some challenge to his teaching, but none whatever to his one-ups-manship. He writes in the margin: "See me."

We are now in a position to understand the anomaly of custom: As instructors, we always assign bull an E, *when we detect it;* whereas we usually give cow a C, *even though it is always obvious.*

After all, we did not ask to be confronted with a choice between morals and understanding (or did we?). We evince a charming humanity, I think, in our decision to grade in favor of morals and pathos. "I simply *can't* give this student an E after he has *worked* so hard." At the same time we tacitly express our respect for the bullster's strength. We recognize a colleague. If he knows so well how to dish it out, we can be sure that he can also take it.

Of course it is just possible that we carry with us, perhaps from our own school-days, an assumption that if a student is willing to work hard and collect "good hard facts" he can always be taught to understand their relevance, whereas a student who has caught onto the forms of relevance without working at all is a lost scholar.

But this is not in accord with our experience.

It is not in accord either, as far as I can see, with the stated values of a liberal education. If a liberal education should teach students "how to think," not only in their own fields but in fields outside their own—that is, to understand "how the other fellow orders knowledge," then bulling, even in its purest form, expresses an important part of what a pluralist university holds dear, surely a more important part than the collecting of "facts that are facts" which schoolboys learn to do. Here then, good bull appears not as ignorance at all but as an aspect of knowledge. It is both relevant and "true." In a university setting good bull is therefore of more value than "facts," which, without a frame of reference, are not even "true" at all.

Perhaps this value accounts for the final anomaly: as instructors, we are inclined to reward bull highly, *where we do not detect its intent*, to the consternation of the bullster's acquaintances. And often we do not examine the matter too closely. After a long evening of reading blue books full of cow, the sudden meeting with a student who at least understands the problems of one's field provides a lift like a draught of refreshing wine, and a strong disposition toward trust.

This was, then, the sense of confidence that came to our unfortunate section man as he read "George Smith's" sympathetic considerations.

II

In my own years of watching over students' shoulders as they work, I have come to believe that this feeling of trust has a firmer basis than the confidence generated by evidence of diligence alone. I believe that the theory of a liberal education holds. Students who have dared to understand man's real relation to his knowledge have shown themselves to be in a strong position to learn content rapidly and meaningfully, and to retain it. I have learned to be less concerned about the education of a student who has come to understand the nature of man's knowledge, even though he has not yet committed himself to hard work, than I am about the education of the student who, after one or two terms at Harvard is working desperately hard and still believes that collected "facts" constitute knowledge. The latter, when I try to explain to him, too often understands me to be saying that he "doesn't *put in enough generalities*." Surely he has "put in *enough* facts."

I have come to see such quantitative statements as expressions of an entire, coherent epistemology. In grammar school the student is taught that Columbus discovered America in 1492. The *more* such items he gets "right" on a given test the more he is credited with "knowing." From years of this sort of thing it is not unnatural to develop the conviction that knowledge consists of the accretion of hard facts by hard work.

The student learns that the more facts and procedures he can get "right" in a given course, the better will be his grade. The more courses he takes, the more subjects he has "had," the more credits he accumulates, the more diplomas he will get, until, after graduate school, he will emerge with his doctorate, a member of the community of scholars.

The foundation of this entire life is the proposition that a fact is a fact. The necessary correlate of this proposition is that a fact is either right or wrong. This implies that the standard against which the rightness or wrongness of a fact may be judged exists *someplace* —perhaps graven upon a tablet in a Platonic world outside and above *this* cave of tears. In grammar school it is evident that the tablets which enshrine the spelling of a word or the answer to an arithmetic problem are visible to my teacher who need only compare my offerings to it. In high school I observe that my English teachers disagree. This can only mean that the tablets in such matters as the goodness of a poem are distant and obscured by clouds. They surely exist. The pleasing of befuddled English teachers degenerates into assessing their prejudices, a game in which I have no protection against my competitors more glib of tongue. I respect only my science teachers, authorities who *really know*. Later I learn from them that "this is only what we think *now*." But eventually, surely. . . . Into this epistemology of education, apparently shared by teachers in such terms as "credits," "semester hours" and "years of French" the student may invest his ideals, his drive, his competitiveness, his safety, his self-esteem, and even his love.

College raises other questions: by whose calendar is it proper to say that Columbus discovered America in 1492? How, when and by whom was the year 1 established in this calendar? What of other calendars? In view of the evidence for Leif Ericson's previous visit (and the American Indians), what historical ethnocentrism is suggested by the use of the word "discover" in this sentence? As for Leif Ericson, in accord with what assumptions do you order the evidence?

These questions and their answers are not "more" knowledge. They are devastation. I do not need to elaborate upon the epistemology, or rather epistemologies, they imply. A fact has become at last "an observation or an operation performed in a frame of reference." A liberal education is founded in an awareness of frame of reference even in the most immediate and empirical examination of data. Its acquirement involves relinquishing hope of absolutes and of the protection they afford against doubt and the glib-tongued competitor. It demands an ever widening sophistication about systems of thought and observation. It leads, not away from, but *through* the arts of gamesmanship to a new trust.

This trust is in the value and integrity of systems, their varied character, and the way their apparently incompatible metaphors enlighten, from complementary facets, the particulars of human experience. As one student said to me: "I used to be cynical about intellectual games. Now I want to know them thoroughly. You see I came to realize that it was only when I knew the rules of the game cold that I could tell whether what I was saying was tripe."

We too often think of the bullster as cynical. He can be, and not always in a light-hearted way. We have failed to observe that there can lie behind cow the potential of a deeper and more dangerous despair. The moralism of sheer work and obedience can be an ethic that, unwilling to face a despair of its ends, glorifies its means. The implicit refusal to consider the relativity of both ends and means leaves the operator in an unconsidered proprietary absolutism. History bears witness that in the pinches this moral superiority has no recourse to negotiation, only to force.

A liberal education proposes that man's hope lies elsewhere: in the negotiability that can arise from an understanding of the integrity of systems and of their origins in man's address to his universe. The prerequisite is the courage to accept such a definition of knowledge. From then on, of course, there is nothing incompatible between such an epistemology and hard work. Rather the contrary.

I can now at last let bull and cow get together. The reader knows best how a productive wedding is arranged in his own field. This is the nuptial he celebrates with a straight A on examinations. The masculine context must embrace the feminine particular, though itself "born of woman." Such a union is knowledge itself, and it alone can generate new contexts and new data which can unite in their turn to form new knowledge.

In this happy setting we can congratulate in particular the Natural Sciences, long thought to be barren ground to the bullster. I have indeed drawn my examples of bull from the Social Sciences, and by analogy from the Humanities. Essay-writing in these fields has long been thought to nurture the art of bull to its prime. I feel, however, that the Natural Sciences have no reason to feel slighted. It is perhaps no accident that Metzger was a mathematician. As part of my researches for this paper, furthermore, a student of considerable talent has recently honored me with an impressive analysis of the art of amassing "partial credits" on examinations in advanced physics. Though beyond me in some respects, his presentation confirmed my impression that instructors of Physics frequently honor on examinations operations structurally similar to those requisite in a good essay.

The very qualities that make the Natural Sciences fields of delight for the eager gamesman have been essential to their marvelous fertility.

III

As priests of these mysteries, how can we make our rites more precisely expressive? The student who merely cows robs himself, without knowing it, of his education and his soul. The student who only bulls robs himself, as he knows full well, of the joys of inductive discovery—that is, of engagement. The introduction of frames of reference in the new curricula of Mathematics and Physics in the schools is a hopeful experiment. We do not know yet how much of these potent revelations the very young can stand, but I suspect they may rejoice in them more than we have supposed. I can't believe they have never wondered about Leif Ericson and that word "discovered," or even about 1492. They have simply been too wise to inquire.

Increasingly in recent years better students in the better high schools and preparatory schools are being allowed to inquire. In fact they appear to be receiving both encouragement and training in their inquiry. I have the evidence before me.

Each year for the past five years all freshmen entering Harvard and Radcliffe have been asked in freshman week to "grade" two essays answering an examination question in History. They are then asked to give their reasons for their grades. One essay, filled with dates, is 99% cow. The other, with hardly a date in it, is a good essay, easily mistaken for bull. The "official" grades of these essays are, for the first (alas!) C+ "because he has worked so hard," and for the second (soundly, I think) B+. Each year a larger majority of freshmen evaluate these essays as would the majority of the faculty, and for the faculty's reasons, and each year a smaller minority give the higher honor to the essay offering data alone. Most interesting, a larger number of students each year, while not overrating the second essay, award the first the straight E appropriate to it in a college of liberal arts.

For us who must grade such students in a university, these developments imply a new urgency, did we not feel it already. Through our grades we describe for the students, in the showdown, what we believe about the nature of knowledge. The subtleties of bull are not peripheral to our academic concerns. That they penetrate to the center of our care is evident in our feelings when a student whose good work we have awarded a high grade reveals to us that he does not feel he deserves it. Whether he disqualifies himself because "there's too much bull in it," or worse because "I really don't think

I've worked that hard," he presents a serious educational problem. Many students feel this sleaziness; only a few reveal it to us.

We can hardly allow a mistaken sense of fraudulence to undermine our students' achievements. We must lead students beyond their concept of bull so that they may honor relevancies that are really relevant. We can willingly acknowledge that, in lieu of the date 1492, a consideration of calendars and of the word "discovered," may well be offered with intent to deceive. We must insist that this does not make such considerations intrinsically immoral, and that, contrariwise, the date 1492 may be no substitute for them. Most of all, we must convey the impression that we grade understanding qua understanding. To be convincing, I suppose we must concede to ourselves in advance that a bright student's understanding is understanding even if he achieved it by osmosis rather than by hard work in our course.

These are delicate matters. As for cow, its complexities are not what need concern us. Unlike good bull, it does not represent partial knowledge at all. It belongs to a different theory of knowledge entirely. In our theories of knowledge it represents total ignorance, or worse yet, a knowledge downright inimical to understanding. I even go so far as to propose that we award no more C's for cow. To do so is rarely, I feel, the act of mercy it seems. Mercy lies in clarity.

The reader may be afflicted by a lingering curiosity about the fate of Mr. Metzger. I hasten to reassure him. The Administrative Board of Harvard College, whatever its satanic reputations, is a benign body. Its members, to be sure, were on the spot. They delighted in Metzger's exploit, but they were responsible to the Faculty's rule. The hero stood in danger of probation. The debate was painful. Suddenly one member, of a refined legalistic sensibility, observed that the rule applied specifically to "examinations" and that the occasion had been simply an hour-test. Mr. Metzger was merely "admonished."

ETIENNE GILSON
Education and Higher Learning[1]

The aim and purpose of this address will be to describe the proper relationship that obtains, or should obtain, between education and higher learning. By the word "education" I intend to signify the system of schools now existing in most American and European countries, from primary schools up to universities, together with the programs and the general spirit that inspire their teaching methods.

1. An address delivered at the University of Toronto as part of the centennial celebration of St. Michael's College in 1952.

Naturally, since there is a great deal of variety within this system, my remarks will be of a general nature. They will deal with tendencies rather than with concrete facts. If and where exceptions are to be found, it should be understood beforehand that my remarks simply do not apply. If there is any truth in what I am about to say, it can be a global truth only. As to "higher learning," it will always signify that part of any complete school system that deals with liberal learning and, in consequence, with creative learning. We may have to use one or two concrete examples; yet, thus considered in its entire abstraction and generality, our problem will not be discussed in terms of any local, national, or continental situation. Even the political notions it may have to touch upon will not be borrowed from practical politics, but from political philosphy. I trust, however, that the main consequences of these reflections will not appear irrelevant to practical life. For education is a field of human activity in which it is most necessary that speculation go before action.

Let us first consider teaching as it is commonly understood in European as well as in American public schools, or even high schools, below the university level. Its object is an immediately practical one. A civilized country is made up of citizens who can read and write, perform elementary arithmetical operations, say something about the place of their own country in both space and time; last, not the least, it is made up of citizens who know enough in order to discharge one of the many functions necessary to the welfare of the community. Incidentally, this is what justifies the right of intervention by the State in matters of education, and this right extends much farther than some of us would feel willing to concede. In his encyclical letter *Repraesentanti in terra*, December 31, 1929, Pope Pius XI expressly says: "The State can demand, and therefore see to it, that all citizens be endowed with the necessary knowledge of their civic and national duties, nay, with a certain amount of intellectual, moral, and physical culture which, given the conditions prevailing in our own times, is necessarily required for the common good." Education, then, has become a public service to the full extent to which it has become a public necessity. At the same time, and to the same extent, education is tending to become more and more practical in nature, because, for the State, the common good of the body politic is a practical end. Such is the reason why our schools are progressively tending either to become vocational schools or, at least, to prepare children in view of such schools, wherein they will ultimately qualify for some specialized job.

The same remark applies even to colleges and universities. From a mere glance at their programs, it appears that their proper function is to turn out, year in, year out, the right number of trained engineers, physicians, lawyers, farmers, and businessmen necessary to the welfare of a civilized country. Professors and teachers of all types are no exceptions to the rule. Our students express themselves correctly when they say that they are looking for a teaching *job*. To teach is not to speculate, an avocation for which nobody ever was paid. To teach is to act. What do we require from future teachers at all levels? Simply that they know what they will have to teach. In many cases we content ourselves with making sure that they will be able to learn it a week ahead of their pupils. Indeed, there would be no sense in protesting against the generalized tendency that now prevails to assign useful ends to our modern system of education.

Here, however, a distinction should be made between the two notions of "practicality" and of "usefulness." Were these identical, there would be for us no problem to discuss. We could then quote with unqualified approval the forceful remarks of A. N. Whitehead on the subject.[2] "Pedants," Whitehead says, "sneer at an education which is useful. But if education is not useful, what is it? Is it a talent, to be hidden away in a napkin? Of course education should be useful, whatever your aim in life. It was useful to St. Augustine and it was useful to Napoleon. It is useful, because understanding is useful." To this, which is undoubtedly true, we nevertheless beg to add that understanding is not always useful in the same way. What Napoleon learned at the artillery school of Brienne was the art of handling guns; a useful art in its own way, to be sure, but a very practically useful one. As to what St. Augustine had learned from St. Ambrose and from Plotinus, it was infinitely more useful still, since it was the way to achieve salvation, than which nothing can be more useful to man; yet, at the same time, he had also learned that salvation was beatitude; that is, the love of truth for its own sake, than which nothing less practical and more speculative can possibly be conceived. Understanding is alway useful indeed, but when he himself wrote about the "divine beauty" of Lagrange's equations, Whitehead would have been much better understood by St. Augustine than by Napoleon. *Gaudium de veritate*, the joy born in us from the mere sight of truth: is it useful? Of course it is. But because it is an end in itself, not a means to any other end, it is not at all practical.

Seen from this precise point of view, the practical trend now prevailing in modern education raises a difficult problem. Does it provide boys and girls, students in all fields, with the proper feeling for the supreme importance of that type of knowledge which, precisely because it is not practical, might well be the most useful of all? In protesting against those who believe in the possibility of useless knowledge, Whitehead probably had in mind the distinction drawn by Cardinal Newman, whose works he knew so well, between a "liberal" education and a "useful" education. But a more careful examination of his text clearly shows that where he was writing "use-

2. A. N. Whitehead, *The Aims of Education* (Mentor Books, 1949), p. 14 [Gilson's note].

ful," what the Cardinal had in mind was "practical." In his Fifth Discourse, *On the Scope and Nature of University Education*, Newman has lovingly described what he used to call "liberal knowledge" as a knowledge "sufficient for itself, apart from every external and ulterior object."[3] To which he added that to educate for such knowledge is the true scope of a university. Even after granting to Whitehead that this knowledge is eminently useful, the fact remains that its own type of usefulness has nothing to do with practicality. How is it, then, that instead of keeping faith with Newman's ideal, the general trend of our modern school system is to stress the kind of knowledge that is not sufficient for itself, but always aims at some external and ulterior object?

Let us honestly face the difficulty. "Liberal knowledge" is not a new formula. Originally it pointed out the knowledge of the so-called "liberal arts"; that is to say, according to Cicero's own commentary, the knowledge of those arts which it is befitting for a free man to know: *artes libero dignae*. As to the other arts—namely, the mechanical ones—they were good for hand workers or, to say it more bluntly, for slaves. Of course legal slaves have long ceased to exist, yet, unless I am mistaken, more than a shade of this ancient meaning is still hovering over the language of Cardinal Newman[4] especially where he identifies "liberal knowledge" with "a gentleman's knowledge."[5] Not being myself an Englishman, I cannot pretend to know what it is to be a "gentleman." Yet I will make bold to say that, in Cardinal Newman's own mind, to study in view of becoming a skilled carpenter, a bricklayer, or even a trained mechanic would not have answered his definition of a gentleman's knowledge. When, to his own dismay, a true gentleman finds himself afflicted with a natural gift for such mechanical avocations, to resort to the British category of "hobby" is for him the only way to indulge his taste without losing his social dignity. Whatever else he may have been, the student described by Newman as a gentleman could certainly afford a university training free from immediate professional preoccupations. A truly Oxonian ideal indeed, at least as Oxford used to be in the good old times, but one which, in most parts of the world today, looks more like a dream than a reality. This gentlemanly type of education presupposes a measure of those worldly possessions which only wealthy men can afford to despise. Without in the least denying

3. Newman was well aware of this derivation as well as of its ideological implications. Speaking of the word "liberal," Newman says: "Now, first, in its grammatical sense it is opposed to *servile*; and by 'servile work' is understood, as our catechisms inform us, bodily labor, mechanical employment, and the like, in which the mind has little or no part." (*The Idea of a University*, London: Longman's, Green and Co., 1912, p. 106.) Liberal knowledge, New-

man has just observed, is "the especial property of a University and a gentleman" (p. 106). When such expressions are used in their literal meaning, "we contrast a liberal education with a commercial education or a professional" (p. 107) [Gilson's note].

4. Newman, *The Idea of a University*, pp. 107-108 [Gilson's note].

5. Newman, *The Idea of a University*, p. 111 [Gilson's note].

that modern universities are still successfully engaged in the task of turning out gentlemen, one may at least observe that the meaning of the word no longer is exactly what it used to be. In our own day, just as all women are ladies, all men are gentlemen.

The reason for this change is a political one. A democratic type of society has progressively replaced the aristocratic social order of Newman's England. This is not a question of political regimes, but rather a change in social structures, coming in the wake of political revolutions. There is no other choice than between aristocracy, which stands for inequality, and democracy, which stands for equality. Whether it calls itself a kingdom, an empire, a republic or even a democratic republic, a society remains an aristocracy to the full extent that it maintains a privileged class, be it only that of those who "have" as against those who "have not." In modern democracies, this measure is steadily becoming an always smaller and smaller one, and this fact is not without deeply affecting the nature and the spirit of their systems of education, especially with respect to their attitude toward liberal knowledge and higher learning.

From the time of its very origins, which, for Western civilization, is that of ancient Greece, free and liberal speculation has always been made possible by the existence of a leisured class whose members, if they felt so inclined, could dedicate themselves to speculative research and to contemplation. For this reason, Aristotle says, the first men to philosophize were priests. The remark clearly applies to the middle ages, when nobody could become a scholar unless he was a cleric.[6] When both in Greece and in modern societies laymen became interested in learning, the existence of lay philosophers, scientists, and scholars of any sort was made possible either because they themselves belonged to the aristocracy of their time, which was the case for Francis Bacon and for Descartes, or else because some enlightened members of that aristocracy provided them with the intellectual leisure necessary for disinterested speculation. The Florence of the Medici, Elizabethan England, the France of Louis XIV, where writers, artists, and scientists of all countries stood a fair chance of being supported by the King or by the nobility, are so many outstanding examples of what aristocratic societies can do for liberal knowledge. This type of culture was truly liberal, because it was not expected to bring about any practical results either for those who paid for it or for those who were being paid to produce it. Princes would then find it natural to favor the development of the arts and the sciences simply because they knew

6. One of the most revolutionary effects of Christianity was to call *all* men, slaves or not, ignorant or learned, to the most liberal type of knowledge, which is that of truth embraced for its own sake. Faith made it accessible to all. This is the deep-seated reason why the Catholic Church has always favored liberal studies. In as much as they are truly liberal, studies aim to lead human minds to truth enjoyed for its own sake; that is, to contemplation. And what is eternal life, if not the eternal enjoyment of absolute Truth? [Gilson's note].

that beauty and truth were good things to be enjoyed for their own sake. Artists and scientists had no idea of making a fortune out of their work. So long as their protectors gave them enough to live, they considered themselves highly privileged, as indeed they were, since they were free to live a wholly unpractical life, the only one in which they were interested.

The kind of education that befits such a type of aristocratic culture is easy to define: it is the education of the elite, by an elite, and for an elite. In such circumstances, education is the received method whereby an aristocracy recruits its future members or, at least, the competent body of citizens who, sharing in the benefits of the prevailing social system, are interested in insuring its survival. No wonder, then, that at the very times when it gave birth to a Dante, a Shakespeare, or a Descartes, Europe had practically no system of public schools; so much so, that by far the larger number of its inhabitants were illiterate. Aristocracy is a great producer of higher learning and of liberal knowledge, only it keeps it to itself; it is a spring rather than a stream.

Not so in democratic societies, whose systems of education naturally follow the rule of their political life. What they want is an education of the whole people, given by men who themselves belong among the people and, consequently, intended for the greater benefit of the people in its entirety. This time we find ourselves confronted with a powerful system of intellectual irrigation whose streams are visible everywhere; the only questions are: Where is the spring? Where are the sources? Can there still be sources in a society whose natural tendency is to universalize education and, consequently, to equalize it?

This is a genuine issue, which we must have the courage to face, not in any spirit of criticism, and still less of hostility, toward democracy, but with the sincere desire to understand its educational problems and thus throw some light on its difficulties. There are several interrelated reasons why, whereas aristocracies were more interested in creating intellectual culture than in spreading it, democracies seem to be more eager to distribute higher learning than to create it. Among these reasons there is a particularly obvious one. If our school system exists, not in view of a chosen minority, but in view of all, its average level should answer the average level of the population as a whole. Hence the unavoidable consequence that the best gifted among the pupils will be discriminated against. Nor should we imagine that creative minds will multiply in direct proportion to the growth of the school population. The reverse is much more likely to happen. In aristocratic societies, genius has often found access to higher culture, even under adverse circumstances; in democratic societies, it will have no higher culture to which to gain access. Since equality in ignorance is easier than equality in learning, each and every teacher will have to equalize his

class at the bottom level rather than at the top one, and the whole
school system will spontaneously obey the same law. It is anti-
democratic to teach all children what only some of them are able
to learn. Nay, it is anti-democratic to teach what all children can
learn by means of methods which only a minority of pupils are able
to follow. Since, as has been said, democracy stands for equality,
democratic societies have a duty to teach only what is accessible to
all and to see to it that it be made accessible to all. The overwhelming weight of their school population is therefore bound to
lower the center of gravity in their school systems. The first peril for
democracies, therefore, is to consider it their duty, in order to
educate all citizens, to teach each of them less and less and in a less
and less intelligent way.

It is not easy to say such things without sounding satirical, which
I have no intention of being. I myself am an old teacher, and I
would not let it be thought either that I am pining for a return of
our countries to some aristocratic type of society, or that, when I
remember what schools used to be around 1890, I see things
deteriorating from bad to worse. Much progress has been achieved;
the only point I am stressing is: Has there been progress all along
the line? We are teaching more and more, but are we teaching better
and better? And, if not, is it not because, confronted as they are with
the legitimate task of providing learning for all their citizens, modern
democracies have to cope with entirely new problems for which they
are not prepared? The task of turning learning into a commodity and
education into a public service is something both necessary and unheard of, for which there is no historical precedent. We should not
feel too surprised to see the democratic State handling education like
coal, hydroelectric power, or public means of transportation. The
State must control everything in order to insure the equal distribution of all necessary goods among all citizens, including even education. We do not want this progress to stop, we simply do not want
it to defeat its own purpose; and this is what the democratic State
is going to do if it does not handle learning according to its own
nature, which, because it is born of the mind, is wholly unlike any
other kind of commodity.

We have reached such a pass that pedagogical authorities are beginning to think that learning is there in view of the schools, not the
schools in view of learning.[7] This very year some schoolteachers made
once more the time-honored discovery that the spelling of their

7. A striking symptom of this disease,
and one that deserves special study, is
the present tendency of pedagogy to become an independent discipline. There
are pedagogues whose ambition it is to
teach how to teach. As often as not, such
teachers undertake to teach disciplines
which they themselves do not know, or
know imperfectly, to those who know
them. Their attitude implies that the divorce of teaching from learning is now
complete. Moreover, this also turns
teaching itself into a "servile work."
What is more, the divorce of teaching
from learning threatens our whole educational system with failure; for the
only effective pedagogical methods are
those that proceed from learning itself,
through the person of the teacher, to the
person of the pupil [Gilson's note].

mother tongue stood in need of being simplified. I need not quote the name of the country, because there is not a single language in the world whose spelling could not be made simpler than it is. The only trouble is that, in order to be perfectly simple, spelling has to be purely phonetic, in which case nobody can understand what he reads. This, however, is not my point. What I am interested in is the main rule set up by the committee on the simplification of spelling in that country. According to the school inspector who wrote the report, the committee decided either to accept, or else to reject, all suggested changes "according as they could, or could not, facilitate the teaching of the language." This curious pedagogical imperialism implies that the proper function of spelling is to be taught. Such teachers do not consider themselves the servants of learning, but its owners; so they have a full right to change it in order to facilitate their work. And indeed, why not? If all citizens have an equal right to know spelling, spelling should be made foolproof and equally available to all citizens. I am sorry to say, without any trace of irony, that this is the principle which we now apply to practically all disciplines, from spelling to metaphysics. We do not impart learning such as it is, but such as it ought to be in order to be teachable to the millions. From time to time, some simple-minded professor attempts to make his pupils understand, not himself, but that which he teaches. The rumor soon begins to spread that the poor man cannot make himself understood. So he is a bad teacher, and we turn *him* out of his class, not the pupils.

Besides the general lowering of its level, another consequence follows from this democratic treatment of education at the hands of the State; namely, its predominately practical character. Nothing is more logical; and this time, since all citizens are part and parcel of the democratic State, all we have to do is to consult ourselves in order to know its will. Time and again, we have heard fathers say with solemn gravity: "I want my son to have an education." In point of fact, we all have said it ourselves, but what we really have meant is: "I want my son to get a job." A perfectly legitimate desire indeed. At the end of their studies, good students should get jobs that will turn them into citizens equally useful to themselves, to their future families, and to their country. Since such is the wish of the vast majority of its citizens, the democratic State will naturally tend to give them what they want; that is, a sound, practical education with no frills. This is what all teaching States are now doing, and they do it pretty well. Once more, I am not criticizing; I am merely trying to observe facts, and the outstanding fact, in this case, is that what we agreed to call "liberal knowledge," precisely because it has no practical usefulness, is bound to be eliminated together with the frills. The steady decline of classical studies, in Europe as well as in America, is a clear instance of what I have in mind. Even their strongest supporters cannot pretend that classical humanities are practically useful in everyday life; those among us who try to defend them on this ground are simply betraying their cause. Even if classical humanities may be put to practical use, this cannot be the reason why they should be taught. Such an aristocratic type of education simply cannot be universalized. As a consequence, no room can be made for it in the programs of schools which must cater to all citizens. So we teach them too little, or too late, which is little better than not to teach them at all. Why complain? Liberal knowledge, Newman says, is to itself its own end; in our industrial age, contemplation is a luxury which very few States can afford to subsidize. The cold truth is that the practical uselessness which recommended liberal education to Cardinal Newman's mind today justifies its exclusion from the curriculum of our democratic schools. Even societies cannot have their cake and eat it.

Yet there should be somebody to make the cake, and it is to be feared that, unless they re-examine their own educational problem, democracies will soon find themselves with nothing to eat. First of all, democratic education rests upon the principle of equality applied to the human understanding. But this application is a fallacy of the well-known type, which consists in applying to two different orders what is true of only one of them. The notion of democracy is a social one; it expresses the common will of a people to deal with its own members as if all men were born free and equal. On the contrary, human understanding is a fact of nature, and whether we like it or not, facts of nature are not equal. Nature is not democratic. Physical and intellectual inequalities can be corrected, or compensated; the democratic State can see to it that even the less gifted among its citizens be given a fair chance to learn and to know something; it can narrow the gap that separates creative genius from merely normal intellects, and even from abnormally backward ones; above all, democracy can prevent natural inequalities from begetting social privileges sometimes worse than the natural ones; yet, when all is said and done, nature can be corrected, not suppressed. Understanding is not equal in men. Intellectual life is just what it is, not what society would like it to be. Unless democracies accept its laws just as they are, they may well turn out an always larger number of teachers, they will have less and less to teach.

We are simply forgetting that intellectual superiority and fitness for speculative knowledge are one and the same thing. In this sense, liberal knowledge is the only source of all practically useful knowledge, without any exception. Classical humanities are not the only relevant example. As a token of the general nature of the problem, I beg to quote the growing misconception of what science itself actually is. On June 16, 1952, the continental edition of the British *Daily Mail* announced to its readers that the United States had their first atom submarine "nearly ready." To this the same newspaper added the following personal comment of the President of the United States: "The day that the propellers of this new submarine first bite into the water will be the most momentous day in the field of atomic science, since the first flash of light down in the desert seven years ago." A typically democratic statement indeed, in which "science" merely means "engineering." The first flash of light in the field of atomic science did not shine in any desert seven years ago, but in the minds of Einstein and of other scientists who were speculating about the structure of matter and not looking for atom bombs or for atom submarines. True science is liberal knowledge; scientists seek after it for its own sake; engineers put it to practical use; they do not want to know in order to know, but in order to make. Yet it is a positive and well-established fact that the more speculative and liberal it is, the more fruitful scientific knowledge proves to be in its practical applications. Pasteur saved millions of human lives although he himself was not a physician. Nearer home, I do not think that Dr. Banting, who was a physician, ever intended to find a specific for diabetes; yet when he first isolated insulin, the specific was found. Science found it; medicine applied it.

If this be true, our democratic system of education now finds itself at a crossroad. It has done wonders in the past and we do not want it to undo them. There must be an education for the millions; the learning included in this type of mass education should be both practical and simple, that is to say, adapted to the general needs and to the average intellectual aptitudes of its pupils; yet, at the same time, even a thoroughly democratic system of education should not allow its ceaselessly growing body to lead its head. Unless they themselves provide, not a new aristocratic social class, but their own intellectual elite, which is something different, the social and technical progress of which our modern democratic States are so justly proud will soon come to an end. In peace and war, the powerful industrial equipment of the greatest among modern nations can be rendered obsolete at any time by the abstract speculation of some unknown scientist using a few sheets of paper and a pencil in the solitude of his own study. Nor should we forget that the times of the greatest national perils are also those when foreign scientists are no longer an available commodity.[8] This is not for democracies a

---

8. Even this very practical point is not always understood. In the Toronto *Globe and Mail*, Sept. 12, 1952, Sir Eric Rideal, a distinguished British scientist then visiting Ottawa, issued the timely warning: "You cannot trade on the originality of another country forever." If there is an obvious truth, this is one. Yet the next issue of the same paper (Sept. 13) summed up the consensus of a group of leading Canadian industrialists in this terse sentence: "Sir Eric is all wet." Their main objection was that, to carry out his suggestion "would definitely not be good for the Canadian pocketbook," the more so as "the importation of ideas is easy and there is no tax on them." This statement deserves to endure as an outstanding specimen in the history of mental parasitology. At any rate, the complete failure of Sir Eric to convey an exceedingly simple idea is enough to show that the task of importing them is not as easy as it might seem [Gilson's note].

matter of choice. None of them can hope indefinitely to consume the products of natural aristocracy without adding its own contribution to the common good. What we now need, within our present system of universal education, is another system, this time of selection, whose proper object will be not to thwart the best gifted intellects which it is our task to educate. Unless it follows such a policy, no nation can hope to prosper for a very long time. True democracy in education certainly consists in insuring the intellectual survival of even the unfit; it cannot possibly consist in preventing the natural superiority of the fittest from bearing their fruits to the greater benefit of all.

This obvious truth should not be so hard to understand. There is nothing less democratic, in the usual sense of the word, than sports and games. Championship is the triumph of carefully cultivated natural inequalities. There is no point in pretending that, in a democracy, every citizen should be able to beat Olympic records. We simply could not do it, however hard we might try, but we do not resent the fact. We do not ask our directors of athletics to prevent some students from running as fast as they can because if they did they would run faster than the others. We do not consider it democratic to set athletic standards as low as possible. On the contrary, we fully realize the fact that the exceptional performances of a few world champions act as a fruitful challenge whose effects are actually felt in all stadiums and on all athletic fields. What is democratic, here as everywhere else, is to keep both competition and selection as widely open as possible, and then to set up the highest conceivable standard as a standing invitation to all. In short, the only sound policy for any democracy is to raise the average level of its people[9] by cultivating the excellency of the best among its citizens.

What we understand so well concerning the education of the body, could we not understand concerning the education of the mind? Unless we do, we shall go on drifting along the same way which has already led us to make pedagogy the judge of learning. It can be concisely described in Shakespeare's terse words: "My foot

9. Many professors and college presidents bitterly complain about the fact that students exhibit a much more marked taste for athletics than for academic studies. I beg to suggest that the students are right on this point. To the extent that they are not "professional," sports and athletics are enjoyed for their own sake and are to themselves their own end. From this point of view, which has not escaped the perspicacity of Cardinal Newman (*op. cit.,* pp. 107-108), "manly games, or games of skill, or military prowess, though bodily, are, it seems, accounted liberal." And rightly so. But if this is true, then athletics is now the only part of our school programs which is, officially and unrestrictedly, animated by a liberal spirit. Instead of asking for less athletics, we should rather bring back to the classroom the liberal spirit which once inspired it and still inspires athletics. Our only choice, therefore, is either to eliminate from our programs everything whose practical usefulness is not perceptible to students themselves, or else to say to them frankly that practical usefulness should not be the end of their education. Where the liberal spirit still prevails, students derive as much pleasure from the classroom as from the athletic field [Gilson's note].

my tutor." High school programs adapted to the kind of pupils they receive; university programs adapted to the kind of pupils that high schools are permitted by law to provide; and no provision made for the free development of liberal knowledge under all its forms, whose creative activity is the life and blood of any system of education! Things have gone so far that I might cite several countries in which, despairing as it were of saving higher learning, their governments have erected, outside universities, new institutions specialized in research work, where scholars seek but do not teach, while university professors teach but do not seek. I beg to say that, in so far as public education is concerned, wholly to surrender to this new tendency would be nothing less than the beginning of the end. The remedy we need should not consist in killing the patient. Since it is the course of nature that education derives its substance from the creative activity of a few speculative minds, let us rather help nature to follow its course. Where there is no higher learning, the presence of creative minds becomes less probable, intellectual light ceases to shine, routine and pedantry set in, and living truths shrivel into desiccated formulas. Then we begin complaining about the general decay of studies, as if students could still take an interest in matters which, even for those who teach them, have already lost their meaning. The situation needs attention, but it is not desperate. All we have to do in order to mend it is refuse to allow our educational body to grow too big for its soul, and to remember that its soul is liberal knowledge, itself the source of higher learning.

QUESTIONS FOR STUDY, DISCUSSION, AND WRITING

1. What is Gilson's thesis concerning the correct relationship between education and higher learning?
2. What distinction does Gilson draw between "practical" and "useful"? How does that distinction help to advance his argument?
3. Part of Gilson's purpose is to detach the idea of liberal knowledge from certain political and social values historically associated with that idea. What are those values? Why does Gilson wish to detach the idea of liberal knowledge from them?
4. What consequences does Gilson see following from "the democratic treatment of education at the hands of the State"? Which of these consequences does he acknowledge as inevitable in a democracy? Which does he contend are unnecessary, and why?
5. What assumption about democratic equality in education, with respect to intelligence, does Gilson find fallacious? Do you agree? Does his analogy between education and athletics illuminate his argument? In what ways?
6. What point is Gilson making in footnote 8? How does this citation of impractical "practicality" help advance his thesis?
7. Gilson says that "Even their strongest supporters cannot pretend that classical humanities are practically useful in everyday life"

(pp. 220–221). Yet many would disagree. Develop the case that the classical humanities are practically useful in everyday life. Is the argument valid?

8. The analogy Gilson draws between education and athletics and his assertions in footnote 9 affirm a relation between liberal knowledge and the spirit of play. Explore this relation. Read Perry's "Examsmanship and the Liberal Arts" (pp. 203–213). Do Gilson and Perry agree?

GEOFFREY CROWTHER

English and American Education[1]

For the past three years I have been engaged, with my colleagues of the Central Advisory Council on Education in England, in a comprehensive study of the English educational system. I had some of my own education in the United States, and I have been a frequent visitor to America ever since. This double experience has bred in me a growing sense of astonishment that two countries which share the same language, so many of the same cultural traditions and ways of life, whose political, religious, and social aspirations are so largely identical, should have educational systems so utterly different as to provide almost no basis for a comparison between them.

That is a strong statement, and my present purpose is to try to justify it. Let me first say, however, that I have no intention whatever of trying to show that one national system is, on balance, better than the other; only that they are much more different than is usually realized.

The American and the English educational systems are different in purpose, structure, and method. Let us start with purpose. The two systems grew up in response to very different pressures and needs. In America, you have always been very conscious of the need to build up a new society. You have wanted to construct something bigger, richer, better than you have. This is said to arise from something in the American national character, but that seems to me to turn the logic upside down; it is the American national character that has arisen from the circumstances in which the American people have found themselves. From the start it was necessary to create a supply of ministers of religion, of lawyers, and of skilled artisans—I place them in the order of importance in which they were regarded at the time. Later on there came the obvious necessity of incorporating the great waves of immigrants into your society. Still later came the great task, in which you are still engaged, of

1. First presented as an address to the Conference of High School Principals and Supervisors in Baltimore, Maryland.

knitting your varied economic, social, and racial groups into the harmonious and balanced society in which the principles of democratic government can work properly.

Consciously or unconsciously, American education has at all times been designed to serve these social purposes. It has been regarded as an instrument by which society can build its own future. From its nature, it has inescapably been concerned with the rank and file of the people. Its chief concern for many generations has been to do something to the masses—and I think the word is *to*, not *for*—in the interests of the American dream.

All this, of course, is platitude in America. What may not be quite so familiar is the contrast in the historical situation in England. We have never been very conscious of the necessity to build a new society. At all relevant times we have had a fully developed society already in being. And at all relevant times we have also, I am sorry to say, been on the whole pretty satisfied with the society we have. For most of the last two hundred years, American education has been designed to do a job of construction; English education has been designed primarily for maintenance, with improvement coming second. In the very latest period, perhaps, those attitudes have started to change. As with so many aspects of education, there seem to be the first signs of a tendency to change sides. Your education is becoming socially more conservative just when ours is becoming more consciously radical.

But that is a speculation for the future, on which I will not enlarge. I am talking of the influences of the past, which have shaped the structures of today. American education has always had to concern itself with the common man in his multitudes. The concern of English education has until very recently been with the maintenance of society, in the words of the old prayer which you will often hear in school and college chapels, "that there may never be wanting a succession of persons duly qualified to serve God in church and state." This is a conception which does not necessarily embrace the education of the great mass. There is a fine, rich, broad educational tradition in England. But it is not a tradition of education, above the minimum level, for the multitude. Post-primary education has always been thought of as a privilege in England; it was not until 1944 that the principle of secondary education for all was established, and it is hardly yet fully effective.

Let me pursue this contrast a little further. Let me give you two of the consequences, of which I would guess that one will shock you, while the other may perhaps surprise you more favorably.

I will start with the shocker. The consequence of our different attitude is that the sheer size, the volume or quantity, of English education is very much smaller than American. The age at which the legal compulsion to attend school expires is still only fifteen.

Moreover, that is an effective leaving age, and more than four children out of five in fact leave school before they are sixteen. Of the sixteen-year-old age group—those between their sixteenth and seventeenth birthdays—only 22 per cent are still in full-time education. In the seventeen-year-olds, the figure falls to 13 per cent of the boys and 11 per cent of the girls. Among eighteen-year-olds, it is 8 per cent of the boys and 5.5 per cent of the girls.

What strikes Americans, I find, as even odder than these figures is the fact that we are not, as a nation, greatly disturbed by them, although many of us think they ought to be larger. But we cannot assume that public opinion is on our side. I am very doubtful whether there would be any support in public opinion for a policy of keeping the majority of children in school after sixteen, and I am certain that you would find hardly anyone in England who believes, as you do, in keeping all children at school until eighteen. Our college students represent about 3 per cent of each age group, and there is an expansion program in hand that will raise it to about 5 per cent. Anybody who suggested that we needed any more than that would meet with the strongest resistance, and not least from the universities themselves.

This attitude does not arise from any lack of love for our children. It is not because we think we can't afford it. The proportion of our national income that we spend on general welfare services—social security, health, and the like—is about the highest in the world. It is not from lack of generosity or lack of means that we confine education after the middle teens to a minority. It is because we sincerely believe that it is the right thing to do, in the interests of the children themselves. After all, there can be no absolute rules about education. Nobody believes that any child should be allowed to leave school at twelve. I do not suppose a time will ever come when, even in America, it will become legal or compulsory for everyone to stay in full-time education until twenty-five. Where you fix the age between those limits is surely a matter of judgment. And why should it be the same age for all children? Our belief in England is that, balancing what can be got out of school against what can be got out of life, the average boy or girl has probably had the optimum dose after eleven years of schooling—and do not forget that we begin, by legal compulsion, at the age of five. Eleven years, after all, is one year out of every six or seven of the average lifetime.

Now let me give you the other side of the medal. Because education after fifteen or sixteen is confined to a minority, that minority gets every assistance that the state can provide. It is nowadays, to an overwhelming extent, a minority chosen for intelligence and attainment. There are, of course, still the independent schools, where very substantial fees have to be paid. But the pressure of numbers upon them is such that a stupid boy or girl will have great difficulty getting in. And in the state schools, selection is by merit only. But once selected, a boy finds himself with his foot not so much on a ladder as an escalator. He will have the best resources of the best schools concentrated on him. If he can secure a place in a university, and that also is a matter of selection by merit, the state will pay his tuition fees and his living expenses, not only during the session but during the vacation as well. There is no such thing as working your way through college in England. We do not need a National Merit Scholarship scheme because we have one already. Nor is this a recent thing. It has been expanded in recent years, but it has always existed.

Let me move on to structure. The outstanding difference here lies in the fact that we have a very much smaller degree of local control than you do. There are about 50,000 schools boards in the United States, each of them, I suppose, more or less free to run the schools as it thinks best. That gives a total population in the average school board area of about 3500 persons. In England there are about 130 local education authorities, which gives an average population per area of about 300,000. Moreover, there are two other differences, apart from this sharp difference in size. Your school boards consist, I believe, in most states, of persons specially elected for the purpose, with no other duties. In England the schools are run by the county council, or the borough council, which is the general-purpose government of the area.

Second, your school boards raise their own money by direct taxes, or at least the greater part of it. In England about 70 per cent of the expenditure of the local education authorities is met out of grants from the central government in London. There are advantages and disadvantages in this. It means that we do not have the enormous range in standards between rich areas and poor areas that you do. It means a much greater degree of standardization of conditions of employment among the teachers, and therefore of interchangeability between school and school and between area and area. But it also inevitably means a greater degree of uniformity imposed from the center. We think our system is decentralized, because it allows much more local freedom and variety than exist in the school systems of most Continental European countries. But there is no doubt that it is much more highly centralized than the American system.

The other great difference under the heading of structure is the principle of selection upon which our system is based. All children, except the minority in fee-paying schools, go to undifferentiated schools from the age of five to the age of eleven. At eleven or thereabouts, a proportion of them, varying from area to area but averaging between 20 and 25 per cent, is selected for what we call grammar schools, which include children to the age of eighteen, though not all the pupils stay that long. The remainder go to what are called secondary modern schools, which include children to age fifteen and increasingly to sixteen, but no older.

You will see from this description that the crucial time for an English child is at the age of eleven or a little more. The selection test then applied—the famous or infamous eleven-plus examination—is supposed to be a classification purely by ability and aptitude, without any suspicion of being derogatory to those who are not selected. But, of course, everybody wants to be selected, and with the growing pressure of numbers as a result of the post-war bulge of population, the selection has been getting steadily more competitive. As the result of agitation, the Labor Party has adopted the policy of abolishing the eleven-plus examination by sending all children at that age to the same schools, the so-called comprehensive secondary schools. The Labor Party has moved toward this system in several of the areas where it controls the local council, and even in Conservative areas there is a distinct movement to experiment with systems that do not involve sending children to different schools at the age of eleven.

I have several times seen this movement quoted in America as evidence that English education is turning away from selection. I think this is a grave misunderstanding. The public objection to selection at eleven is social and political, not educational. It is an objection on the part of parents to having their children sent to different schools, not to their having different educations. And the remedies that are being applied are wholly in terms of institutions, not in terms of the education they provide. I know, for example, one large new comprehensive school built by a Labor council. Every child entering that school is tested and placed in one of fifteen "streams," differentiated by the children's intelligence and aptitude. This selection is done by the teachers; the parents have nothing to do with it; and the children are not even supposed to know which stream is which in intelligence grading. A child placed in one of the top streams will have an almost wholly different education from a child placed even in one of the middle streams. If this is not selection, I do not know the meaning of the term. But this is what we mean by a comprehensive school. Many people in England will tell you that the comprehensive school has been copied from the American comprehensive high school, some meaning it as a compliment, some as the reverse. I have often told them that they could hardly be more mistaken.

Nonselection—if that is the opposite of selection—as it is practiced in America is totally unknown in England. By nonselection I mean the principle of treating all children alike, allowing them to sort themselves out by their choice of courses, by what they find easy and difficult, or by their varying ambitions—with counseling assistance, no doubt, but without any compulsory segregations. I am sure that your system seems as odd to us as ours does to you. There is no retreat from selection in England; the only change is that a growing number of people—but still a minority—think that the selection should be within a common school, not between schools.

The differences between the two countries in educational method make an enormous subject, and I must restrict myself to four points out of many that it would be possible to make.

The first of these differences in method lies in the position of the teacher, in the relative positions of the teacher and the textbook. One of the things about American education that most strikes the English visitor is the importance you attach to textbooks. We have no parallel to that. To begin with, I do not think there are more than two or three, at most, of the local education authorities in England that tell their schools what textbooks to use. That is left to the teacher, occasionally the principal, or the head of the department in a large school. And in the higher grades, more often than not, there is not a textbook at all. A teacher will often recommend a book as covering the subject pretty well and as being useful for reference but will not make any attempt to go through it chapter by chapter.

This system places a much greater responsibility on the individual teacher, and I have often been asked in America whether we do not have a lot of trouble with it. So far as the political and social responsibility of the teacher is concerned, I cannot recall having heard of a single case arising through a teacher's being accused of using a book which seems offensive or objectionable to somebody in authority. That is partly, perhaps mainly, because our system of large authorities and rather remote and indirect public control puts the individual teacher largely out of the reach of vigilance committees, whether of parents or of the local chamber of commerce. There is also a strong tradition against anything that smacks of political interference with the schools.

Educational responsibility, however, is another matter. Quite clearly, a system like ours, which places so much responsibility on the individual teacher, cannot work well unless the average standard of intelligence, knowledge, and teaching competence is high. Up to the present, we have been able to maintain that standard. It is partly, of course, a matter of numbers. In the whole of England last year there were only some 260,000 schoolteachers. We were a little short, but 300,000 would have given us all we need. And this is in a country about one quarter the size of the United States. I do not know how many schoolteachers there are in the United States, but I am very sure it is many more than four times 300,000. I do not see how you could possibly have coped with the enormous increase in the American school population in the past forty years without being willing to take thousands of young men and women who needed close support from a textbook before they could teach. Indeed, under the pressure of rising numbers in the schools, I fear we shall find before long that we shall have to give the teacher more assistance, and that implies more external control on his teaching. This particular contrast is not, however, entirely a matter of numbers. It is partly also the result of a different tradition of teacher training, which, in England, has always laid a much greater emphasis on the content of what is to be taught than in America and much less on questions of pedagogic method.

The second difference in method is the absence in England of the course system which is so universal in your schools and colleges. Indeed, the word "course" has a wholly different meaning in the two countries. If you asked an English school child what courses he was taking, he wouldn't know what you meant. If you asked him what subjects he was taking, he would answer English, Latin, mathematics, history, and so forth. But that would not mean, as it would in America, that those were the subjects he had chosen to take. They would be the subjects that his form, or class, was taking, and therefore that he was taking with the rest of the class. Until the boy is about fifteen or sixteen, it is unlikely that he or his parents have had any say in the choice of form in which he is placed. And at no age does he have any say in deciding the curriculum of that form. At the higher ages, there is a choice between three of four different curriculums, but each curriculum has to be taken, within narrow limits, as it stands.

Here, indeed, is a contrast with the American system. Perhaps it is not quite so sharp a contrast in practice as it is in principle, as I observe that, more and more, those American boys and girls who have ambition to gain admittance to a good college find their choice of courses in high school made for them by the college entrance requirements. But there is one important consequence for teaching that is worth bringing out. In an English school, in any year but one (and that one is what we call the fifth form year, about the age of fourteen or fifteen), you can assume that the pupils who are taking a subject in one year will be taking the same subject next year. The study of a subject can therefore be planned as a continuous process over a period of years. That is what we mean when we use the word "course." We mean a whole balanced curriculum of six or seven or eight subjects, planned to continue over three or four or five years. Once a boy or girl enters on such a course, he or she will normally pursue it to the end. And all the boys and girls in a course will take substantially the same subjects, with perhaps slight options, as between a second classical or a second modern language. You will therefore understand how bewildered we are when we contemplate one of your neat, packaged, self-contained, nine-month courses, such as high school physics. It is no good asking an English schoolboy when he enters college how many years of French he has had at school. Two boys might both truthfully answer nine years. But they might mean totally different things, and neither one would mean what you thought he meant.

How, then, do we measure what a student has accomplished, if we cannot count up the number of courses he has satisfactorily taken? The answer is that we rely, to an extent wholly unknown to you, on general examinations. Every year—sometimes every term— the pupil has to take a written examination in all the subjects of the curriculum, and his further progress depends, sometimes entirely, on his performance in that examination. Most of these examinations are set and assessed within the school itself, by his own teachers. But at three crucial points in his career the examination is set and assessed by an external body. The first of these is the eleven-plus examination, which determines to which sort of secondary school the child should go. The second comes at fifteen or sixteen and is called the Ordinary Level of the General Certificate of Education, set and assessed by one of nine examining boards closely associated with the universities. This examination can be taken in any number of subjects from one upwards, but the most usual practice is to take it in from five to nine subjects. Third, there is the Adanced Level of the General Certificate of Education, which is taken at eighteen or thereabouts and which plays a large part in university entrance.

I have been describing the practice of the grammar schools; that is, the schools for the brightest 20 to 25 percent of the children. Examinations, especially written examinations, play a much smaller part in the life of the less intelligent children. Even in this case, however, they play a much larger part than they do in America; and there is a rising demand for public examinations, at lower standards of intelligence than those of the General Certificate of Education, for these less gifted children. I cannot honestly say that the children themselves clamor for examinations, but employers do, and therefore so do the parents. All the questions that Americans ask and answer in terms of the number and variety of courses a student has taken we ask and answer in terms of the examinations he has passed.

I have left to the last what is the sharpest difference of all between our two systems. This is our system of specialization, in which England is, I think, unique in the world. A student will take the examination for the Ordinary Level of the General Certificate of Education at the age of fifteen or sixteen in a wide range of subjects drawn both from the humanities and from the natural sciences. But once he has passed that examination, he will specialize. That is to say, he will devote two thirds, or perhaps even more, of his time in school to a narrow range of subjects. In one boy's case it may be physics, chemistry, and mathematics; in another's it may be chemistry and biology, or it may be history or modern languages and literature, or classical languages and philosophy. But, whatever the choice, the greater part of the pupil's attention, in the classroom and in his private study time, is given to his specialty, and he will take the advanced level examination at eighteen in his special subjects only. When he gets to the university, the specialization is even more intense. The range of subjects does not usually get any narrower, but the student gives 100 per cent of his time to it.

I have found that to Americans, and indeed to educationalists from every country in the world except England, this seems a very strange system indeed. Perhaps you will have difficulty in believing that I really mean what I say. So let me cite my own case, though it is now more than thirty years old. I was a modern languages specialist. For my last three years at school, from the age of fifteen to eighteen, I studied mostly French and German language and literature, perhaps three or four hours a week of history, and one hour of Scripture on Sundays. For another two years at Cambridge, even the history and the Scripture were cut out, and I studied French and German exclusively. Five years of my life were given to those languages. My experience was perhaps a little extreme; I think the admixture of general and contrasting subjects would nowadays, in a good school, be a little bigger. But the difference would not be great. The English boy or girl is a specialist from the age of fifteen or sixteen.

The advisory council of which I am chairman was specifically requested by the Minister of Education to review this system of specialization. We examined it most carefully and discussed it at great length, both with witnesses and among ourselves. In the end we came to the conclusion that we wanted to see it continued. We found that it was being pushed too far, and we have made a number of suggestions for removing what we think are abuses. But we have reported in favor of this system of specialization. And that is a unanimous conclusion reached by a council made up of educators of all kinds. Perhaps you will find that fact as extraordinary as the system itself, and I must try to give you some of our reasons for thinking that, in this matter, we in England are in step and the whole of the rest of the world is out of step.

Let me begin by telling you of one argument that we reject. This is the argument that every intelligent citizen, or every educated man, ought to know something about each subject in a range so wide that it compels a balanced curriculum; that no one can afford to be ignorant of history, government, science, languages, and so forth. To this, we would give our answer in two parts. First, it is true that there are certain elementary skills and knowledges that everyone must have—reading, writing, arithmetic, and several more. But these essential elements can be, and should be, provided by the age of sixteen. If you go on with them after that age, you will be wasting your time, because the knowledge you instill will be forgotten unless it can be attached to the main intellectual interest of a boy's or girl's life, which begins to emerge at about that age.

The second part of the answer is that it is only when you have got these essential elementary skills and knowledges out of the way that you can confront the real task of education. The acquisition of factual knowledge is by itself a poor test of any education and a lamentably poor test of the education of boys and girls of seventeen and eighteen. It has been said that the process of education is not to be compared to that of filling up an empty pot, but rather to that of lighting a fire. The proper test of an education is whether it teaches the pupil to think and whether it awakens his interest in applying his brain to the various problems and opportunities that life presents. If these have once been done, then factual knowledge can easily be assimilated. If these have not been done, then no amount of nodding acquaintance with widely varying fields of human knowledge will equip a boy or girl with an educated mind. We in England argue the case for specialization not primarily on the score of the information it provides but because it awakens interest, teaches clear thinking, and induces self-discipline in study.

We believe that, if you can find which of the recognized intellectual disciplines most arouses a boy's interest—and we confine his choice to five or six recognized disciplines, chosen for their intellectual content, not for their vocational value—if you can let him spend his time on what interests him, but insist that he must work hard at it, go deep into it, follow it up in the library or the laboratory, get around behind the stage scenery that defines the formal academic subject, you will really be teaching him how to use the mind that God has given him. This sort of intensive study takes a great deal of time, and that is why it can only be applied, for any one student, to a restricted range of subjects. No doubt you will say that the boy must be very narrow as a result. That may be. Are you sure that being narrow is worse than being shallow?

I find that English education has a high reputation among Americans. I am often asked, for example, whether it is not true that the eighteen-year-old boy in England is a year or two ahead of his American contemporary. I always answer that question, or assertion, by asking some others. What boy? If an English boy is still at school at eighteen, he is necessarily in the upper quartile in intelligence. Are you comparing him with the average American high school graduate, who is of average intelligence? And ahead in what? In the subjects to which he has been giving nearly all his time and attention for two years? It would be strange if he were not a long way ahead in those. Or over the whole range of a broad curriculum? He has been taught different things, by different methods, with a different purpose in view, in a different sort of school. There is no fair basis for a comparative judgment.

QUESTIONS FOR STUDY, DISCUSSION, AND WRITING

1. What three principal contrasts does Crowther draw between English and American education? Does Crowther develop each of the principal contrasts in the same manner? In the same detail? In what ways does he effect transitions from point to point within each of the principal sections? From section to section?
2. What are Crowther's sources of information? What kinds of authority does he employ to support his statements? Does he give equal weight to each kind of authority? How does he convey a sense of the kind and degree of authority in support of his statements?
3. Crowther's description of the system of American education must necessarily be general. Does it appear to be accurate? Does your own experience of American schools yield observations departing from Crowther's in particular ways? To what extent do these particular differences, if any, offer a general picture at variance with Crowther's?
4. Crowther asserts that in America education "has been regarded as an instrument by which society can build its own future" (p. 226). Find evidence to support or refute this thesis in the preceding essays of this section. Determine in what ways and to what extent the assertion fits American views of education today.

GEOFFREY CROWTHER
Two Heresies[1]

Mr. President, Regents of the University, members of the faculty, fellow graduates, ladies and gentlemen: I have been coming to Ann Arbor, on and off, for more than thirty years. I have made many friendships here. I have played some part in sending you a steady stream of graduate students from my own country. I have watched with affection and amazement the gigantic growth of this great institution. Of all the state universities of America, this is the one where I feel most at home.

Yet never in my wildest moments did I dream that I should be admitted to the dignity of becoming an honorary graduate of The University of Michigan, and I am still overwhelmed by it. It is impossible to stand here, in this great stadium, before such a gathering, surrounded as we are by the spreading buildings of a great

1. The commencement address at the University of Michigan, June 11, 1960. On this occasion Sir Geoffrey received an honorary LL.D. from the university.

campus, without feelings of deep emotion, of humility, but also of pride, to know that one is to be a member of your body. I know that in this I can speak for all my fellow honorary graduates. In the words of the Prayer Book, for being made partakers in all this, we give you most humble and hearty thanks.

On me you have conferred the supreme privilege of being permitted to address you. I would not for the world miss the honor. But it carries a very heavy burden with it. For what can be said in a commencement address that has not been said a thousand times before? Shall I extol the glories of the tradition of learning that leads from the monks' cells of the Middle Ages to the great universities of today? Those glories would gain nothing from anything I could say. Shall I sound the alarm for academic freedom? It seems to me to be in less danger today than at many other times. Should I perhaps address myself exclusively to the graduating class? Should I preach the ancient moral virtues to you? It would be an impertinence. Should I remind you of your duty to the community that has done so much for you? It would be an insult. Should I take the oldest and most shopworn theme of all, and remind you that this is a commencement, a beginning, not an ending? You wouldn't listen to me if I did. Should I try to give you the only thing that the old can give to the young—that is, the fruits of experience? But the chief thing you learn from experience is that no one will learn from other people's experience. No, members of the class of 1960, I can do nothing for you. The campuses of the country have been ringing all week long with high moral sentiments, and I haven't the heart to try to add to them.

I must presume, Mr. President, that you had some deliberate purpose in choosing for your speaker this afternoon a foreigner— and one, moreover, who has been engaged for some years past in an intensive study of the educational system of his own country. I read in that a hint that you wanted to hear something of what an American university looks like from the outside to one who has been put by chance in the position to make some comparison between American universities and those of other countries. If that is your wish, I shall try to comply.

But even then my dilemma is not quite resolved. Should I speak only of what I admire in the American university? That, indeed, would be easy. The words would come quickly to my mouth, because I spend so much of my time when I am at home in England pressing on our own universities some of your practices. I admire so much your generosity—not only your generosity of money, but your generosity of spirit, your deep sense of service to the community, the way you convince the individual—be he freshman or doctor—that you exist to serve him, not he to serve the institution. I admire the way you are forever breaking down the barriers between you and the rest of the community—not hiding behind hedges of aloofness and superiority, as too many of the academic institutions in my own country do. I admire the eagerness with which the pursuit of knowledge is carried on here. In Europe one is sometimes made to feel that the pursuit is over, that knowledge has been caught and tamed and made to live comfortably ever after. I admire the structure of graduate schools superimposed on a liberal arts college—a structure that, in my opinion, we should do well to adopt in England.

There is so much to admire. But it would be a poor compliment to you to assume that all you wanted to hear was praise. The purpose of an address, after all, is communication from one mind to another, and if I am to succeed in setting you thinking, I must give you something to think about. So, as I pondered what I would say to you this afternoon, I slowly screwed up my courage to the conviction that I can best return the compliment you pay me by telling of some of the things in the American university to which, in my opinion, you should be giving your serious critical attention. Having so often landed into trouble at home for singing the praises of the American university too loud, I had better run the risk of getting into trouble here for the opposite reason. So I determined to pick out this afternoon a couple of points on which I find myself beset with doubts. I am the more emboldened to do this because they are points which, so far as I can observe, do not seem to disturb you. That is why I gave myself the title of "Two Heresies" because I am going to challenge what is usually taken for granted.

Let me state my two heresies quite bluntly so that you will see what I am getting at, and then I will try to defend them one after the other. My first heresy is to think that there are too many college students. And my second heresy is to think that they work too hard.

When I say that there are too many college students, I don't mean here, at Michigan. There are, indeed, a goodly number here, but I would not presume to say that there are too many. There is a great deal to be said for the small college. And there is a great deal also to be said for the big college—though it is less often said. From what I know of Michigan, I would not say that it is too big—not yet. In any case, that is not my argument. I am not arguing about big colleges and small colleges. I am asking whether, in the United States, as a whole, there are not too many college students altogether—whether the proportion of the population that goes to college is not too large.

Now I know that it has always been one of the fundamental doctrines of the American people that there must be no special privileges, no select class, that every boy and girl has a right to go to college if he or she can make the grade and can find, borrow, or earn enough money to stay alive for four years. I am not challenging that great American principle. Heretic though I may be, I am not trying to preach any old-world doctrine of a privileged aristocracy. No, I am trying, now that I am to be admitted to your society, to be a good American democrat (with a small "d"). Certainly, the right exists. But then it always has existed. What is new within the past decade or so—what is new and different and doubtful—is the doctrine that almost every American boy or girl should be encouraged and assisted to claim his right. There is also a right to travel freely on the highway. But even in Michigan you can't all do it at once. Indeed, if you try to claim this right all at once the only result is that nobody gets any benefit from it. It is possible to believe passionately in the existence of a right, and yet to hope that not everyone will claim it.

Where is the process of universal education to stop? Is everyone to go to school until he is twenty-five or thirty—or thirty-five? I have had no opportunity to go back to the statistics, but my impression is that college going, as a percentage of the age group, is now in this country just about where high-school going was two generations ago. Now you know what has happened to the high school. I believe the nation-wide figure is that 85 per cent of the eighteen-year-olds are in high school. The same thing is now visibly happening to college going. If you include the junior colleges, it won't be long before the proportion reaches the halfway mark, and there is no reason to suppose that it will stop there.

In my observation most Americans seem to take it for granted that this is a good thing. Perhaps it is—but not self-evidently so. There must, after all, be a limit somewhere. There must be some age at which universal education—the keeping of everyone in school—should stop. Is it not conceivable that the limit has been reached?

Why do I say this? Chiefly because of the effect this movement towards universal college education is having on the colleges themselves. I will single out two of its effects. The first is that it must be lowering the average intellectual standard of the colleges of the country as a whole. That follows almost mathematically. If the process goes on until every boy and girl is in college, then the average standard of intelligence in the colleges in the country as a whole will be an I.Q. of exactly 100, which is a great deal lower than it has been hitherto. I am no mathematician, and it is a matter of constant surprise to me to discover that as many as half of all the people in the country are below average in intelligence. I am competently assured, however, that it is so. And what is more, that even with all the resources of modern science, there is nothing that can be done about it.

It cannot help the colleges if more and more of their students come to them not because of any genuine desire to continue their education in any real sense of the word, but because it is socially the thing to do. If this is the general picture, then colleges, like this one, which want to maintain and even improve their standards, are forced into being more and more selective. Every good college in the country is besieged by applicants and at its wit's end to know how to choose among them. I do not think that it is good for the front-rank colleges if everyone who gets in has the feeling that he has succeeded in going through the eye of the needle to get there. And I do not think it is good for the country. Thus this great democratic principle of everyone having a college education is in fact creating a new privileged class—those who manage to get a good college education.

The second consequence is this—that if nearly everybody goes to college, then increasingly all those who aspire to enter the professions or the higher ranks of business and administration—in a word all those who want to follow one of the careers for which college used to be the preparation—all these are now forced to go to a graduate school as well. Now, as I said before, I have nothing but admiration for the graduate schools. But they were never intended to serve 15 or 20 per cent of the age group. Moreover, what will happen to them when more and more of their students are there, not because they have any real interest in more study, not even because what they learn will really be useful to them, but simply because they are under some compulsion to appear better educated—which is taken to mean longer educated—than the mass, simply because they can't get the sort of job they want without a second set of letters after their names?

More and more careers, for this reason, and among the highest careers, cannot begin until the age of twenty-four—or even twenty-six or twenty-seven if there is selective service to be done. Now think what this means. I suppose one can say that active life—that is, the life of the conscious mind—begins at or about the age of six or seven when one learns to read. At the other end, retirement from gainful occupation is more and more being pushed down towards sixty. In other words, in the normal life, there are not much more than fifty years or so between infancy and retirement. Is it really good sense that for the intellectual leaders of the country—the most intelligent quarter of the whole—as many as twenty out of those fifty-plus years should be spent in learning and only a bit more than thirty in doing? Is that really a rational employment of the scarcest of all scarce resources—human talent? Isn't there something to be said for the view that there should be less preparation for life and more living? Is America right to keep its young longer and longer on the leash, and to rely for the productive work of the nation more and more on the middle-aged? Only a very rich country could do it at all. But is it a wise application of your riches? When it comes to fighting, the job has to be done by the young. Is war the only activity in which the qualities of youth are needed? Must we in everything else be studied, overtrained, and elderly?

Let me quickly turn, before the brickbats begin to fly, to my second heresy. In saying that the student of today has to work too hard, I can, I think, reasonably anticipate the sympathy of at least part of my audience. But perhaps I don't mean quite what they think I mean.

I was speaking just a moment ago of the pressure that the good colleges are under to defend their standards. It is their duty to do so. If it is a privilege to be admitted to one of these institutions of the first rank, then no student should be allowed to remain there who does not continue to measure up to the highest standards. I am not criticizing this concern for standards. Indeed, I am supporting it.

But how, by what means, have the standards been enforced and maintained? From what I see and hear, I suspect that far too many colleges are doing it by what is the easy way for them—by demanding an ever higher total of hours put in—of hours, what is more, that have to be devoted to doing what the professor says must be done. Assignments become heavier and are more rigorously enforced. I have no doubt at all that the student of today who wants to secure a good average has to work for much longer hours than he did thirty years ago, when I first knew the American colleges. I don't mean that the student of the last generation led an easy life. His mind was active for as many hours a day as now: But I do think that he didn't have his nose held so close to the grindstone of requirements. He was freer to roam and follow his fancy. Now, it seems to me, he goes very much more in harness. Indeed, I have heard the head of a famous institution—not in Michigan—openly boast that they weed out the weaklings in the first year, not by any considerations of intellectual capacity or promise, but by deliberately setting an almost impossibly heavy schedule of assigned study in order to see who can take it.

Now this all seems to me to be a mistake. Let us indeed have high standards, the highest possible. But high standards of what? Of diligence? Or of intelligence? The two are by no means the same thing. Indeed, they can be, and I suspect often are, at variance with each other, since the high intelligence, the really original mind, is likely to be the first to revolt against a drudgery which, in his case at least, is pointless and unnecessary.

Let us get back to the fundamentals. What does a university exist for? What is the purpose of education? Is it to absorb a defined quantity of instruction? Or to learn how to think? Is it to accumulate knowledge? Or to acquire understanding? No doubt you know the old comparision between the two different ways of regarding the student's mind. You can think of it either as a pitcher that has to be filled up with factual knowledge or as a fire that has to be set alight. Put it in that way, and the right choice, I think, immediately becomes clear. The proper question for educators to be asking themselves every day is not "Am I cramming my students with the proper facts?" but "Am I succeeding in setting their minds ablaze?" And we all know that what is needed for a good roaring blaze is plenty of fresh air.

Please don't misunderstand me. I am not asking for soft options. I don't want the students to live lives of leisure. I want them to be under the heaviest pressure. I want them to lead the most vigorous and rigorous lives. I want them to have to meet the severest tests. But let them be tests of intellect, of understanding, of expression, of imagination, of judgment, of purpose—and not just of the ability to stay awake.

I have one special reason for this plea. We hear a great deal nowadays of the danger of overspecialization, of the confining of the world of learning within narrow compartments which are unable, or unwilling, to say anything to each other. This is a real danger. There has been much discussion in my own country of the emergence of two cultures, the scientific and the humanitarian, which are increasingly separate from, and even hostile to, each other. I think this is an understatement of the danger. It is not two cultures with which we are threatened, but twenty-two. There is nothing in the world of learning more urgent than to find means of breaking down this separatism and moving back, so far as we can, to the time when educated men could travel in each other's territories without passports or interpreters. This is the authentic university tradition. It is indeed what the word means. Let us never forget that this great institution is a university. It ought not to be allowed to become a diversity.

Now I am simple enough to believe that the way to get a meeting of minds is to let them meet. You cannot solve the problem by prescribing courses, chemistry for the historian, or aesthetics for the engineer. You can prescribe the course all right but you can't prescribe the interest in the subject which alone makes it worthwhile. The only way you can get a real cross-fertilization between the different disciplines is to give a generous allowance of time for people of varying interests to explore each other's minds. I would plead that everyone in a university, from the freshman to the president, should make himself much less busy. He will find as a result—of this I am sure—that his mind is much more active.

I hope that I shall be forgiven for asking you to think about my two heresies. Of course, I have exaggerated them. I have been trying to use that powerful stimulus to thought, indignation. But why, after all, should I try to make you cross? There is, I repeat, so very much more to admire than to criticize. It is precisely because so much depends on the American universities that one wants to see them perfect. It is on you, more than on anyone else, that the hopes of liberal civilization in the world rest. You will remember that during the war the United States was often described as the arsenal of freedom—and how rightly. But the moral is in the long run so much more important

than the material, and what will in the end determine the shape of
the world in which our grandchildren live is not how many rockets
or space ships or tanks America can build but the ideas to which
Americans attach their faith. You attract to yourselves in your universities, and nowhere more than here in Michigan, so much of the
best in the outside world and you give it back with such generosity.
It is here that the links are forged that bind the free world together.

So you must not think of me, I hope, as a critic, or even as a candid
friend, but simply as the newest of your graduates, full of ambition
for the growth in grace and power of his Alma Mater. My prayer
for this great university is the prayer that A. C. Benson uttered for
his native country:

> Land of Hope and Glory, Mother of the Free!
> How can we extol thee, who are born of thee?
> Wider yet and wider may thy bounds be set,
> God, who made thee mighty, make thee mightier yet.

QUESTIONS FOR STUDY, DISCUSSION, AND WRITING

1. What two recommendations does Crowther make concerning
   higher education in America? Are they sound recommendations?
   Could they be put into practice? What difficulties could be anticipated?
2. A commencement address is, in certain respects, a matter of
   convention; certain things are expected of a speaker and the occasion makes some attributes of the address customary. In what
   ways are the conventions manifest in Crowther's address? Are
   there particular ways in which Crowther turns the conventions
   to advantage, using them to make his points more easily and
   effectively? Explain in detail the limitations imposed and the
   opportunities offered by the conventions.
3. What relationship to his audience does Crowther establish? Upon
   what foundation and in what order does he develop his topic?
4. This piece and the preceding one by Crowther are both addresses.
   What similarities are there in the occasions, in the relations of
   speaker to audience, in the topics chosen? What accounts for the
   differences—in the kind of thesis, in the method of development,
   in the approach to the audience, in the tone?

On Mind

Creating · Perceiving · Retaining

HENRY DAVID THOREAU
Observation

There is no such thing as pure *objective* observation. Your observation, to be interesting, *i.e.* to be significant, must be *subjective*. The sum of what the writer of whatever class has to report is simply some human experience, whether he be poet or philosopher or man of science. The man of most science is the man most alive, whose life is the greatest event. Senses that take cognizance of outward things merely are of no avail. It matters not where or how far you travel—the farther commonly the worse—but how much alive you are. If it is possible to conceive of an event outside to humanity, it is not of the slightest significance, though it were the explosion of a planet. Every important worker will report what life there is in him. It makes no odds into what seeming deserts the poet is born. Though all his neighbors pronounce it a Sahara, it will be a paradise to him; for the desert which we see is the result of the barrenness of our experience. No mere willful activity whatever, whether in writing verses or collecting statistics, will produce true poetry or science. If you are really a sick man, it is indeed to be regretted, for you cannot accomplish so much as if you were well. All that a man has to say or do that can possibly concern mankind, is in some shape or other to tell the story of his love—to sing, and, if he is fortunate and keeps alive, he will be forever in love. This alone is to be alive to the extremities. It is a pity that this divine creature should ever suffer from cold feet; a still greater pity that the coldness so often reaches to his heart. I look over the report of the doings of a scientific association and am surprised that there is so little life to be reported; I am put off with a parcel of dry technical terms. Anything living is easily and naturally expressed in popular language. I cannot help suspecting

243

that the life of these learned professors has been almost as inhuman and wooden as a rain-gauge or self-registering magnetic machine. They communicate no fact which rises to the temperature of blood-heat. It doesn't all amount to one rhyme.

GEORGE SANTAYANA
Imagination

Men are ruled by imagination: imagination makes them into men, capable of madness and of immense labors. We work dreaming. Consider what dreams must have dominated the builders of the Pyramids—dreams geometrical, dreams funereal, dreams of resurrection, dreams of outdoing the pyramid of some other Pharoah! What dreams occupy that fat man in the street, toddling by under his shabby hat and bedraggled rain-coat? Perhaps he is in love; perhaps he is a Catholic, and imagines that early this morning he has partaken of the body and blood of Christ; perhaps he is a revolutionist, with the millennium in his heart and a bomb in his pocket. The spirit bloweth where it listeth; the wind of inspiration carries our dreams before it and constantly refashions them like clouds. Nothing could be madder, more irresponsible, more dangerous than this guidance of men by dreams. What saves us is the fact that our imaginations, groundless and chimerical as they may seem, are secretly suggested and controlled by shrewd old instincts of our animal nature, and by continual contact with things. The shock of sense, breaking in upon us with a fresh irresistible image, checks wayward imagination and sends it rebounding in a new direction, perhaps more relevant to what is happening in the world outside.

When I speak of being governed by imagination, of course I am indulging in a figure of speech, in an ellipsis; in reality we are governed by that perpetual latent process within us by which imagination itself is created. Actual imaginings—the cloud-like thoughts drifting by—are not masters over themselves nor over anything else. They are like the sound of chimes in the night; they know nothing of whence they came, how they will fall out, or how long they will ring. There is a mechanism in the church tower; there was a theme in the composer's head; there is a beadle who has been winding the thing up. The sound wafted to us, muffled by distance and a thousand obstacles, is but the last lost emanation of this magical bell-ringing. Yet in our dream it is all in all; it is what first entertains and absorbs the mind. Imagination, when it chimes within us, apparently of itself, is no less elaborately grounded; it is a last symptom, a rolling echo, by which we detect and name the obscure operation that occasions it; and not this echo in its aesthetic impotence, but the whole operation whose last witness it is, receives in science the name of imagination, and may be truly said to rule the human world.

This extension of names is inevitable although unfortunate, because language and perception are poetical before they become scientific, if they ever do; as Aristotle observes that the word anger is used indifferently for two different things: dialectically, or as I call it, imaginatively, for the desire for revenge, but physically for a boiling of the humors. And utterly different as these two things are in quality, no great inconvenience results from giving them the same name, because historically they are parts of the same event. Nature has many dimensions at once, and whenever we see anything happen, much else is happening there which we cannot see. Whilst dreams entertain us, the balance of our character is shifting beneath: we are growing while we sleep. The young think in one way, the drunken in another, and the dead not at all; and I imagine—for I have imagination myself—that they do not die because they stop thinking, but they stop thinking because they die. How much veering and luffing before they make that port! The brain of man, William James used to say, has a hair-trigger organization. His life is terribly experimental. He is perilously dependent on the oscillations of a living needle, imagination, that never points to the true north.

There are books in which the footnotes, or the comments scrawled by some reader's hand in the margin, are more interesting than the text. The world is one of these books. The reciprocal interference of magnetic fields (which I understand is the latest conception of matter) may compose a marvelous moving pattern; but the chief interest to us of matter lies in its fertility in producing minds and presenting recognizable phenomena to the senses; and the chief interest of any scientific notion of its intrinsic nature lies in the fact that, if not literally true, it may liberate us from more misleading conceptions. Did we have nothing but electrical physics to think of, the nightmare would soon become intolerable. But a hint of that kind, like a hasty glance into the crater of a volcano, sends a wholesome shudder through our nerves; we realize how thin is the crust we build on, how mythical and remote from the minute and gigantic scale of nature are the bright images we seem to move among, all cut out and fitted to our human stature. Yet these bright images are our natural companions, and if we do not worship them idolatrously nor petrify them into substances, forgetting the nimble use of them in mental discourse, which is where they belong, they need not be more misleading to us, even for scientific purposes, than are words or any other symbols.

It is fortunate that the material world, whatever may be its intrinsic structure or substance, falls to our apprehension into such charming units. There is the blue vault of heaven, there are the twinkling constellations, there are the mountains, trees, and rivers, and above all those fascinating unstable unities which we call animals and persons; magnetic fields I am quite ready to believe them, for such in a vast vague way I feel them to be, but individual bodies they will remain to my sensuous imagination, and dramatic personages to my moral sense. They, too, are animate: they, too, compose a running commentary on things and on one another, adding their salacious footnotes to the dull black letter of the world. Many of them are hardly aware of their own wit; knowing they are but commentators, they are intent on fidelity and unconscious of invention. Yet against their will they gloss everything, willy-nilly we are all scholiasts together. Heaven forbid that I should depreciate this prodigious tome of nature, or question in one jot or tittle the absolute authority of its Author; but it is like an encyclopedia in an infinite number of volumes, or a directory with the addresses of everybody that ever lived. We may dip into it on occasion in search of some pertinent fact, but it is not a book to read; its wealth is infinite, but so is its monotony; it is not composed in our style nor in our language, we could not have written one line of it. Yet the briefest text invites reflection, and we may spin a little homily out of it in the vernacular for our own edification.

In the *Mahabharata*, a learned friend tells me, a young champion armed for the combat and about to rush forward between the two armies drawn up in battle array, stops for a moment to receive a word of counsel from his spiritual adviser—and that word occupies the next eighteen books of the epic; after which the battle is allowed to proceed. The Indian poets had spiritual minds, they measured things by their importance to the spirit, not to the eye. They despised verisimilitude and aesthetic proportion; they despised existence, the beauties of which they felt exquisitely nevertheless, and to which their imagination made such stupendous additions. I honor their courage in bidding the sun stand still, not that they might thoroughly vanquish an earthly enemy, but that they might wholly clarify their own soul. For this better purpose the sun need not stand still materially. For the spirit, time is an elastic thing. Fancy is quick and brings the widest vistas to a focus in a single instant. After the longest interval of oblivion and death, it can light up the same image in all the greenness of youth; and if cut short, as it were at Pompeii, in the in the midst of a word, it can, ages after, without feeling the break, add the last syllable. Imagination changes the scale of everything, and makes a thousand patterns of the woof of nature, without disturbing a single thread. Or rather—since it is nature itself that imagines—it turns to music what was only strain; as if the universal vibration, suddenly ashamed of having been so long silent and useless, had burst into tears and laughter at its own folly, and in so doing had become wise.

QUESTIONS FOR STUDY, DISCUSSION, AND WRITING

1. What effect does Santayana achieve by beginning with what he later identifies as a figure of speech, an ellipsis?
2. The language of this essay is highly figurative throughout. Find examples of the various kinds of figures of speech used. How are they appropriate to the subject? How far are they necessary to it?
3. How does analogy contribute to Santayana's definition of imagination? Why does he use the analogy between the process of imagination and the production of music, first introduced in the second paragraph, to conclude the essay? Where does it recur, directly or by implication, in the essay?
4. It is not unusual to compare the world to a book, but Santayana's comparison involves some rather special features and implications. What are these?
5. Santayana asks the reader to "consider what dreams must have dominated the builders of the Pyramids." Can dreams be said to dominate the builders of rockets and missiles? Or of research laboratories? Or do these differ fundamentally from the Pyramids? How, or why? Does Santayana's discussion illuminate, in this connection, such terms as space race and medical breakthrough?

JACOB BRONOWSKI

The Creative Mind[1]

On a fine November day in 1945, late in the afternoon, I was landed on an airstrip in Southern Japan. From there a jeep was to take me over the mountains to join a ship which lay in Nagasaki Harbor. I knew nothing of the country or the distance before us. We drove off; dusk fell; the road rose and fell away, the pine woods came down to the road, straggled on and opened again. I did not know that we had left the open country until unexpectedly I heard the ship's loudspeakers broadcasting dance music. Then suddenly I was aware that we were already at the center of damage in Nagasaki. The shadows behind me were the skeletons of the Mitsubishi factory buildings, pushed backwards and sideways as if by a giant hand. What I had thought to be broken rocks was a concrete power house with its roof punched in. I could now make out the outline of two crumpled gasometers; there was a cold furnace festooned with service pipes; otherwise nothing but cockeyed telegraph poles and loops of wire in a bare waste of ashes. I had blundered into this desolate landscape as instantly as one might wake among the mountains of the moon. The moment of recognition when I realized

1. Chapter I of *Science and Human Values*, the contents of which Bronowski sums up on p. 251.

that I was already in Nagasaki is present to me as I write, as vividly as when I lived it. I see the warm night and the meaningless shapes; I can even remember the tune that was coming from the ship. It was a dance tune which had been popular in 1945, and it was called "Is You Is Or Is You Ain't Ma Baby?"

This book, which I have called *Science and Human Values*, was born at that moment. For the moment I have recalled was a universal moment; what I met was, almost as abruptly, the experience of mankind. On an evening like that evening, some time in 1945, each of us in his own way learned that his imagination had been dwarfed. We looked up and saw the power of which we had been proud loom over us like the ruins of Nagasaki.

The power of science for good and for evil has troubled other minds than ours. We are not here fumbling with a new dilemma; our subject and our fears are as old as the tool-making civilizations. Men have been killed with weapons before now: what happened at Nagasaki was only more massive (for 40,000 were killed there by a flash which lasted seconds) and more ironical (for the bomb exploded over the main Christian community of Japan). Nothing happened in 1945 except that we changed the scale of our indifference to man; and conscience, in revenge, for an instant became immediate to us. Before this immediacy fades in a sequence of televised atomic tests, let us acknowledge our subject for what it is: civilization face to face with its own implications. The implications are both the industrial slum which Nagasaki was before it was bombed, and the ashy desolation which the bomb made of the slum. And civilization asks of both ruins: "Is You Is Or Is You Ain't Ma Baby?"

The man whom I imagine to be asking this question, wryly with a sense of shame, is not a scientist; he is civilized man. It is of course more usual for each member of civilization to take flight from its consequences by protesting that others have failed him. Those whose education and perhaps tastes have confined them to the humanities protest that the scientists alone are to blame, for plainly no mandarin ever made a bomb or an industry. The scientists say, with equal contempt, that the Greek scholars and the earnest explorers of cave paintings do well to wash their hands of blame; but what in fact are they doing to help direct the society whose ills grow more often from inaction than from error?

This absurd division reached its *reductio ad absurdum*, I think, when one of my teachers, G. H. Hardy, justified his great life work on the ground that it could do no one the least harm—or the least good. But Hardy was a mathematician; will humanists really let him opt out of the conspiracy of scientists? Or are scientists to forgive Hardy because, protest as he might, most of them learned their indispensable mathematics from his books?

There is no comfort in such bickering. When Shelley pictured science as a modern Prometheus who would wake the world to a wonderful dream of Godwin,[2] he was alas too simple. But it is as pointless to read what has happened since as a nightmare. Dream or nightmare, we have to live our experience as it is, and we have to live it awake. We live in a world which is penetrated through and through by science and which is both whole and real. We cannot turn it into a game simply by taking sides.

And this make-believe game might cost us what we value most: the human content of our lives. The scholar who disdains science may speak in fun, but his fun is not quite a laughing matter. To think of science as a set of special tricks, to see the scientist as the manipulator of outlandish skills—this is the root of the poison man-drake which flourishes rank in the comic strips. There is no more threatening and no more degrading doctrine than the fancy that somehow we may shelve the responsibility for making the decisions of our society by passing it to a few scientists armored with a special magic. This is another dream, the dream of H. G. Wells, in which the tall elegant engineers rule, with perfect benevolence, a human-ity which has no business except to be happy. To H. G. Wells this was a dream of heaven—a modern version of the idle, harp-resound-ing heaven of other childhood pieties. But in fact it is the picture of a slave society and should make us shiver whenever we hear a man of sensibility dismiss science as someone else's concern. The world today is made, it is powered by science; and for any man to abdicate an interest in science is to walk with open eyes towards slavery.

My aim in this book is to show that the parts of civilization make a whole: to display the links which give society its coherence and, more, which give it life. In particular, I want to show the place of science in the canons of conduct which it has still to perfect.

This subject falls into three parts. The first is a study of the nature of the scientific activity, and with it of all those imaginative acts of understanding which exercise *The Creative Mind*. After this it is logical to ask what is the nature of the truth, as we seek it in science and in social life and to trace the influence which this search for empirical truth has had on conduct. This influence has prompted me to call the second part *The Habit of Truth*. Last I shall study the conditions for the success of science and find in them the values of man which science would have had to invent afresh if man had not otherwise known them: the values which make up *The Sense of Human Dignity*.

This, then, is a high-ranging subject which is not to be held in the narrow limits of a laboratory. It disputes the prejudice of the humanist who takes his science sourly and, equally, the petty view

---

2. William Godwin, Shelley's father-in-law, was a philosophical anarchist who believed that men, being rational and benevolently inclined, could live in social harmony without laws or institu-tions.

which many scientists take of their own activity and that of others. When men misunderstand their own work, they cannot understand the work of others; so that it is natural that these scientists have been indifferent to the arts. They have been content, with the humanists, to think science mechanical and neutral; they could therefore justify themselves only by the claim that it is practical. By this lame criterion, they have of course found poetry and music and painting at least unreal and often meaningless. I challenge all these judgments.

There is a likeness between the creative acts of the mind in art and in science. Yet, when a man uses the word science in such a sentence, it may be suspected that he does not mean what the headlines mean by science. Am I about to sidle away to those riddles in the Theory of Numbers which Hardy loved, or to the heady speculations of astrophysicists, in order to make claims for abstract science which have no bearing on its daily practice?

I have no such design. My purpose is to talk about science as it is, practical and theoretical. I define science as the organization of our knowledge in such a way that it commands more of the hidden potential in nature. What I have in mind therefore is both deep and matter of fact; it reaches from the kinetic theory of gases to the telephone and the suspension bridge and medicated toothpaste. It admits no sharp boundary between knowledge and use. There are of course people who like to draw a line between pure and applied science; and oddly, they are often the same people who find art unreal. To them, the word useful is a final arbiter, either for or against a work; and they use this word as if it can mean only what makes a man feel heavier after meals.

There is no sanction for confining the practice of science in this or another way. True, science is full of useful inventions. And its theories have often been made by men whose imagination was directed by the uses to which their age looked. Newton turned naturally to astronomy because it was the subject of his day; and it was so because finding one's way at sea had long been a practical preoccupation of the society into which he was born. It should be added, mischievously, that astronomy also had some standing because it was used very practically to cast horoscopes. (Kepler used it for this purpose; in the Thirty Years' War, he cast the horoscope of Wallenstein which wonderfully told his character, and he predicted a universal disaster for 1643 which proved to be the murder of Wallenstein.)

In a setting which is more familiar, Faraday worked all his life to link electricity with magnetism because this was the glittering problem of his day; and it was so because his society, like ours, was on the lookout for new sources of power. Consider a more modest example today: the new mathematical methods of automatic control, a subject sometimes called cybernetics, have been developed now because this is a time when communication and control have in effect become forms of power. These inventions have been directed by social needs, and they are useful inventions; yet it was not their usefulness which dominated and set light to the minds of those who made them. Neither Newton nor Faraday, nor yet Professor Norbert Weiner, spent their time in a scramble for patents.

What a scientist does is compounded of two interests: the interest of his time and his own interest. In this his behavior is no different from any other man's. The need of the age gives its shape to scientific progress as a whole. But it is not the need of the age which gives the individual scientist his sense of pleasure and of adventure and that excitement which keeps him working late into the night when all the useful typists have gone home at five o'clock. He is personally involved in his work, as the poet is in his and as the artist is in the painting. Paints and painting, too, must have been made for useful ends; and language was developed, from whatever beginnings, for practical communication. Yet you cannot have a man handle paints or language or the symbolic concepts of physics, you cannot even have him stain a miscroscope slide, without instantly waking in him a pleasure in the very language, a sense of exploring his own activity. This sense lies at the heart of creation.

The sense of personal exploration is as urgent, and as delightful, to the practical scientist as to the theoretical. Those who think otherwise are confusing what is practical with what is humdrum. Good humdrum work without originality is done every day by every one, theoretical scientists as well as practical, and writers and painters too, as well as truck drivers and bank clerks. Of course the unoriginal work keeps the world going; but it is not therefore the monopoly of practical men. And neither need the practical man be unoriginal. If he is to break out of what has been done before, he must bring to his own tools the same sense of pride and discovery which the poet brings to words. He cannot afford to be less radical in conceiving and less creative in designing a new turbine than a new world system.

And this is why in turn practical discoveries are not made only by practical man. As the world's interest has shifted, since the Industrial Revolution, to the tapping of new springs of power, the theoretical scientist has shifted his interests too. His speculations about energy have been as abstract as once they were about astronomy; and they have been profound now as they were then, because the man loved to think. The Carnot cycle and the dynamo grew equally from this love, and so did nuclear physics and the German V weapons and Kelvin's interest in low temperatures. Man does not invent by following either use or tradition; he does not invent even a new form of communication by calling a conference of communication engineers. Who invented the television set? In any deep sense, it was Clerk Maxwell who foresaw the existence of radio waves, and

Heinrich Hertz who proved it, and J. J. Thomson who discovered the electron. This is not said in order to rob any practical man of the invention, but from a sad sense of justice; for neither Maxwell nor Hertz nor J. J. Thomson would take pride in television just now.

Man masters nature not by force but by understanding. This is why science has succeeded where magic failed: because it has looked for no spell to cast on nature. The alchemist and the magician in the Middle Ages thought, and the addict of comic strips is still encouraged to think, that nature must be mastered by a device which outrages her laws. But in four hundred years since the Scientific Revolution we have learned that we gain our ends only *with* the laws of nature; we control her only by understanding her laws. We cannot even bully nature by any insistence that our work shall be designed to give power over her. We must be content that power is the by-product of understanding. So the Greeks said that Orpheus played the lyre with such sympathy that wild beasts were tamed by the hand on the strings. They did not suggest that he got this gift by setting out to be a lion tamer.

What is the insight with which the scientist tries to see into nature? Can it indeed be called either imaginative or creative? To the literary man the question may seem merely silly. He has been taught that science is a large collection of facts; and if this is true, then the only seeing which scientists need do is, he supposes, seeing the facts. He pictures them, the colorless professionals of science, going off to work in the morning into the universe in a neutral, unexposed state. They then expose themselves like a photographic plate. And then in the darkroom or laboratory they develop the image, so that suddenly and startlingly it appears, printed in capital letters, as a new formula for atomic energy.

Men who have read Balzac and Zola are not deceived by the claims of these writers that they do no more than record the facts. The readers of Christopher Isherwood do not take him literally when he writes: "I am a camera." Yet the same readers solemnly carry with them from their school days this foolish picture of the scientist fixing by some mechanical process the facts of nature. I have had, of all people, a historian tell me that science is a collection of facts, and his voice had not even the irony of one filing cabinet reproving another.

It seems impossible that this historian had ever studied the beginnings of a scientific discovery. The Scientific Revolution can be held to begin in the year 1543 when there was brought to Copernicus, perhaps on his deathbed, the first printed copy of the book he had written about a dozen years earlier. The thesis of this book is that the earth moves around the sun. When did Copernicus go out and record this fact with his camera? What appearance in nature prompted his outrageous guess? And in what odd sense is this guess to be called a neutral record of fact?

Less than a hundred years after Copernicus, Kepler published (between 1609 and 1619) the three laws which describe the paths of the planets. The work of Newton and with it most of our mechanics spring from these laws. They have a solid, matter-of-fact sound. For example, Kepler says that if one squares the year of a planet, one gets a number which is proportional to the cube of its average distance from the sun. Does any one think that such a law is found by taking enough readings and then squaring and cubing everything in sight? If he does then, as a scientist, he is doomed to a wasted life; he has as little prospect of making a scientific discovery as an electronic brain has.

It was not this way that Copernicus and Kepler thought, or that scientists think today. Copernicus found that the orbits of the planets would look simpler if they were looked at from the sun and not from the earth. But he did not in the first place find this by routine calculation. His first step was a leap of imagination—to lift himself from the earth, and put himself wildly, speculatively into the sun. "The earth conceives from the sun," he wrote; and "the sun rules the family of stars." We catch in his mind an image, the gesture of the virile man standing in the sun, with arms outstretched, overlooking the planets. Perhaps Copernicus took the picture from the drawings of the youth with outstretched arms which the Renaissance teachers put into their books on the proportions of the body. Perhaps he knew Leonardo's drawings of his loved pupil Salai. I do not know. To me, the gesture of Copernicus, the shining youth looking outward from the sun, is still vivid in a drawing which William Blake about 1800 based on all these: the drawing which is usually called *Glad Day*.

Kepler's mind, we know, was filled with just such fanciful analogies; and we know what they are. Kepler wanted to relate the speeds of the planets to the musical intervals. He tried to fit the five regular solids into their orbits. None of these likenesses worked, and they have been forgotten; yet they have been and they remain the stepping stones of every creative mind. Kepler felt for his laws by way of metaphors, he searched mystically for likenesses with what he knew in every strange corner of nature. And when among these guesses he hit upon his laws, he did not think of their numbers as the balancing of a cosmic bank account, but as a revelation of the unity in all nature. To us, the analogies by which Kepler listened for the movement of the planets in the music of the spheres are far-fetched; but are they more so than the wild leap by which Rutherford and Bohr found a model for the atom in, of all places, the planetary system?

No scientific theory is a collection of facts. It will not even do to call a theory true or false in the simple sense in which every fact is either so or not so. The Epicureans held that matter is made of atoms two thousand years ago and we are now tempted to say that their theory was true. But if we do so, we confuse their motion of matter with our own. John Dalton in 1808 first saw the structure of matter as we do today, and what he took from the ancients was not their theory but something richer, their image: the atom. Much of what was in Dalton's mind was as vague as the Greek notion, and quite as mistaken. But he suddenly gave life to the new facts of chemistry and the ancient theory together, by fusing them to give what neither had: a coherent picture of how matter is linked and built up from different kinds of atoms. The act of fusion is the creative act.

All science is the search for unity in hidden likenesses. The search may be on a grand scale, as in the modern theories which try to link the fields of gravitation and electro-magnetism. But we do not need to be browbeaten by the scale of science. There are discoveries to be made by snatching a small likeness from the air too, if it is bold enough. In 1932 the Japanese physicist Yukawa wrote a paper which can still give heart to a young scientist. He took as his starting point the known fact that waves of light can sometimes behave as if they were separate pellets. From this he reasoned that the forces which hold the nucleus of an atom together might sometimes also be observed as if they were solid pellets. A schoolboy can see how thin Yukawa's analogy is, and his teacher would be severe with it. Yet Yukawa without a blush calculated the mass of the pellet he expected to see, and waited. He was right; his meson was found, and a range of other mesons, neither the existence nor the nature of which had been suspected before. The likeness had borne fruit.

The scientist looks for order in the appearances of nature by exploring such likenesses. For order does not display itself of itself; if it can be said to be there at all, it is not there for the mere looking. There is no way of pointing a finger or a camera at it; order must be discovered and, in a deep sense, it must be created. What we see, as we see it, is mere disorder.

This point has been put trenchantly in a fable by Professor Karl Popper. Suppose that someone wished to give his whole life to science. Suppose that he therefore sat down, pencil in hand, and for the next twenty, thirty, forty years recorded in notebook after notebook everything that he could observe. He may be supposed to leave out nothing: today's humidity, the racing results, the level of cosmic radiation and the stock market prices and the look of Mars, all would be there. He would have compiled the most careful record of nature that has ever been made; and, dying in the calm certainty of a life well spent, he would of course leave his notebooks to the Royal Society. Would the Royal Society thank him for the treasure of a lifetime of observation? It would not. It would refuse to open his notebooks at all, because it would know without looking that they contain only a jumble of disorderly and meaningless items.

Science finds order and meaning in our experience, and sets about this in quite a different way. It sets about it as Newton did in the story which he himself told in his old age, and of which the schoolbooks give only a caricature. In the year 1665, when Newton was twenty-two, the plague broke out in southern England, and the University of Cambridge was closed. Newton therefore spent the next eighteen months at home, removed from traditional learning, at a time when he was impatient for knowledge and, in his own phrase: "I was in the prime of my age for invention." In this eager, boyish mood, sitting one day in the garden of his widowed mother, he saw an apple fall. So far the books have the story right; we think we even know the kind of apple; tradition has it that it was Flower of Kent. But now they miss the crux of the story. For what struck the young Newton at the sight was not the thought that the apple must be drawn to the earth by gravity; that conception was older than Newton. What struck him was the conjecture that the same force of gravity, which reaches to the top of the tree, might go on reaching out beyond the earth and its air, endlessly into space. Gravity might reach the moon: this was Newton's new thought; and it might be gravity which holds the moon in her orbit. There and then he calculated what force from the earth would hold the moon, and compared it with the known force of gravity at tree height. The forces agreed; Newton says laconically: "I found them answer pretty nearly." Yet they agreed only nearly: the likeness and the approximation go together, for no likeness is exact. In Newton's sentence modern science is full grown.

It grows from a comparison. It has seized a likeness between two unlike appearances; for the apple in the summer garden and the grave moon overhead are surely as unlike in their movements as two things can be. Newton traced in them two expressions of a single concept, gravitation: and the concept (and the unity) are in that sense his free creation. The progress of science is the discovery at each step of a new order which gives unity to what had long seemed unlike. Faraday did this when he closed the link between electricity and magnetism. Clerk Maxwell did it when he linked both with light. Einstein linked time with space, mass with energy, and the path of light past the sun with the flight of a bullet; and spent his dying years in trying to add to these likenesses another, which would find a single imaginative order between the equations of Clerk Maxwell and his own geometry of gravitation.

When Coleridge tried to define beauty, he returned always to one deep thought: beauty, he said, is "unity in variety." Science is nothing else than the search to discover unity in the wild variety of nature—or more exactly, in the variety of our experience. Poetry, painting, the arts are the same search, in Coleridge's phrase, for unity in variety. Each in its own way looks for likenesses under the variety of human experience. What is a poetic image but the seizing and the exploration of a hidden likeness, in holding together two parts of a comparison which are to give depth each to the other? When Romeo finds Juliet in the tomb, and thinks her dead, he uses in his heart-breaking speech the words:

> Death, that hath suck'd the honey of thy breath.

The critic can only haltingly take to pieces the single shock which this image carries. The young Shakespeare admired Marlowe, and Marlowe's Faustus had said of the ghostly kiss of Helen of Troy that it sucked forth his soul. But that is a pale image; what Shakespeare has done is to fire it with the single word honey. Death is a bee at the lips of Juliet, and the bee is an insect that stings; the sting of death was a commonplace phrase when Shakespeare wrote. The sting is there, under the image; Shakespeare has packed it into the word honey; but the very word rides powerfully over its own undertones. Death is a bee that stings other people, but it comes to Juliet as if she were a flower; this is the moving thought under the instant image. The creative mind speaks in such thoughts.

The poetic image here is also, and accidentally, heightened by the tenderness which town dwellers now feel for country ways. But it need not be; there are likenesses to conjure with, and images as powerful, within the man-made world. The poems of Alexander Pope belong to this world. They are not countrified, and therefore readers today find them unemotional and often artificial. Let me then quote Pope: here he is in a formal satire face to face, towards the end of his life, with his own gifts. In eight lines he looks poignantly forward towards death and back to the laborious years which made him famous.

> Years foll'wing Years, steal something ev'ry day,
> At last they steal us from our selves away;
> In one our Frolicks, one Amusements end,
> In one a Mistress drops, in one a Friend:
> This subtle Thief of Life, this paltry Time,
> What will it leave me, if it snatch my Rhime?
> If ev'ry Wheel of that unweary'd Mill
> That turn'd ten thousand Verses, now stands still.

The human mind had been compared to what the eighteenth century called a mill, that is to a machine, before; Pope's own idol Bolingbroke had compared it to a clockwork. In these lines the likeness goes deeper, for Pope is thinking of the ten thousand Verses which he had translated from Homer: what he says is sad and just at the same time, because this really had been a mechanical and at times a grinding task. Yet the clockwork is present in the image too;

when the wheels stand still, time for Pope will stand still for ever; we feel that we already hear, over the horizon, the defiance of Faust which Goethe had not yet written—let the clock strike and stop, let the hand fall, and time be at an end.

> Werd ich zum Augenblicke sagen:
> Verweile doch! du bist so schön!
> Dann magst du mich in Fesseln schlagen,
> Dann will ich gern zugrunde gehn!
> Dann mag die Totenglocke schallen,
> Dann bist du deines Dienstes frei,
> Die Uhr mag stehn, der Zeiger fallen,
> Es sei die Zeit für mich vorbei![3]

I have quoted Pope and Goethe because their metaphor here is not poetic; it is rather a hand reaching straight into experience and arranging it with new meaning. Metaphors of this kind need not always be written in words. The most powerful of them all is simply the presence of King Lear and his Fool in the hut of a man who is shamming madness, while lightning rages outside. Or let me quote another clash of two conceptions of life, from a modern poet. In his later poems, W. B. Yeats was troubled by the feeling that in shutting himself up to write, he was missing the active pleasures of life; and yet it seemed to him certain that the man who lives for these pleasures will leave no lasting work behind him. He said this at times very simply, too:

> The intellect of man is forced to choose
> Perfection of the life, or of the work.

This problem, whether man fulfills himself in work or in play, is of course more common than Yeats allowed; and it may be more commonplace. But it is given breadth and force by the images in which Yeats pondered it.

> Get all the gold and silver that you can,
> Satisfy ambition, or animate
> The trivial days and ram them with the sun,
> And yet upon these maxims meditate:
> All women dote upon an idle man
> Although their children need a rich estate;
> No man has ever lived that had enough
> Of children's gratitude or woman's love.

The love of women, the gratitude of children: the images fix two philosophies as nothing else can. They are tools of creative thought, as coherent and as exact as the conceptual images with which science

---

3. If ever I say to the moment   Let time for me be at an end.
"Stay! You are so beautiful!"   —*Faust*, Part I, 1699-1706
Then may you clap me in chains,
Then will I gladly perish!   Faust is addressing Mephistopheles, set-
Then may the death-knell ring,   ting forth the terms of the contract, the
Then are you free from your servitude;   condition on which his soul will become
Let the clock stop, its hand fall,   the devil's.

works: as time and space, or as the proton and the neutron.

The discoveries of science, the works of art are explorations—more, are explosions, of a hidden likeness. The discoverer or the artist presents in them two aspects of nature and fuses them into one. This is the act of creation, in which an original thought is born, and it is the same act in original science and original art. But it is not therefore the monopoly of the man who wrote the poem or who made the discovery. On the contrary, I believe this view of the creative act to be right because it alone gives a meaning to the act of appreciation. The poem or the discovery exists in two moments of vision: the moment of appreciation as much as that of creation; for the appreciator must see the movement, wake to the echo which was started in the creation of the work. In the moment of appreciation we live again the moment when the creator saw and held the hidden likeness. When a simile takes us aback and persuades us together, when we find a juxtaposition in a picture both odd and intriguing, when a theory is at once fresh and convincing, we do not merely nod over someone else's work. We re-enact the creative act, and we ourselves make the discovery again. At bottom, there is no unifying likeness there until we too have seized it, we too have made it for ourselves.

How slipshod by comparison is the notion that either art or science sets out to copy nature. If the task of the painter were to copy for men what they see, the critic could make only a single judgment: either that the copy is right or that it is wrong. And if science were a copy of fact, then every theory would be either right or wrong, and would be so forever. There would be nothing left for us to say but this is so or is not so. No one who has read a page by a good critic or a speculative scientist can ever again think that this barren choice of yes or no is all that the mind offers.

Reality is not an exhibit for man's inspection, labeled: "Do not touch." There are no appearances to be photographed, no experiences to be copied, in which we do not take part. We re-make nature by the act of discovery, in the poem or in the theorem. And the great poem and the deep theorem are new to every reader, and yet are his own experiences, because he himself re-creates them. They are the marks of unity in variety; and in the instant when the mind seizes this for itself, in art or in science, the heart misses a beat.

QUESTIONS FOR STUDY, DISCUSSION, AND WRITING

1. What is Bronowski's main thesis? Through what steps does he carry the development of that thesis?
2. At the start of his essay Bronowski presents a scene of atomic devastation; toward the end he discusses poetry. Why does Bronowski concern himself with these two topics? How does he bring them into a relationship?

3. Bronowski several times repeats his definition of scientific activity. Locate each instance of repetition and explain why the definition recurs. How does each particular context clarify, modify, or extend the definition?

4. An important part of Bronowski's essay lies in his challenging and controverting of common assumptions and popular attitudes about science. Discover each such instance of challenge and explain the point Bronowski makes. Consider the relationship between this method of exposition and his main thesis.

5. To what extent does Bronowski's idea and evaluation of imagination agree with Santayana's ("Imagination," pp. 244–246)? In his last paragraph Bronowski writes, "We remake nature by the act of discovery, in the poem or in the theorem." Is that statement in accord with the view Santayana presents? Is there contradiction between Bronowski's statement that "the world today is made, it is powered by science" (p. 249) and Santayana's assertion that imagination "may be truly said to rule the human world" (p. 245)?

6. Thoreau wrote "Observation" (pp. 243–244) about a century before Bronowski wrote this piece. If Thoreau could have read "The Creative Mind," how would he have regarded it?

JOHN SELDEN
The Measure of Things

We measure from ourselves; and as things are for our use and purpose, so we approve them. Bring a pear to the table that is rotten, we cry it down, 'tis naught; but bring a medlar that is rotten, and 'tis a fine thing; and yet I'll warrant you the pear thinks as well of itself as the medlar[1] does.

We measure the excellency of other men by some excellency we conceive to be in ourselves. Nash, a poet, poor enough (as poets use to be), seeing an alderman with his gold chain, upon his great horse, by way of scorn said to one of his companions, "Do you see yon fellow, how goodly, how big he looks? Why, that fellow cannot make a blank verse."

Nay, we measure the goodness of God from ourselves; we measure his goodness, his justice, his wisdom, by something we call just, good, or wise in ourselves; and in so doing, we judge proportionally to the country-fellow in the play, who said, if he were King, he would live like a lord, and have peas and bacon every day, and a whip that cried Slash.

---

1. The medlar, a fruit like the crab apple, becomes edible only after it begins to decay.

QUESTIONS FOR STUDY, DISCUSSION, AND WRITING

1. What pattern of parallels do you discern among the three parts of Selden's statement? How does this principle of structure enforce the thesis he is setting forth?
2. Can the three paragraphs be rearranged without damage? Explain. What principle or principles appear to govern the present arrangement? Does it imply anything about value? About the kind of universe in which Selden conceives man to live?
3. Consider the three desires of the country fellow who would be king. Has Selden arranged these desires in any particular order? If so, what relation does that order bear to the order of the whole statement?

* * *

FRANCIS BACON
The Idols of the Mind[1]

There are four classes of idols which beset men's minds. To these for distinction's sake I have assigned names—calling the first class *Idols of the Tribe*; the second, *Idols of the Cave*; the third, *Idols of the Market-place*; the fourth, *Idols of the Theater*.

* * *

The Idols of the Tribe have their foundation in human nature itself, and in the tribe or race of men. For it is a false assertion that the sense of man is the measure of things. On the contrary, all perceptions, as well of the sense as of the mind, are according to the measure of the individual and not according to the measure of the universe. And the human understanding is like a false mirror, which, receiving rays irregularly, distorts and discolors the nature of things by mingling its own nature with it.

The Idols of the Cave are the idols of the individual man. For everyone (besides the errors common to human nature in general) has a cave or den of his own, which refracts and discolors the light of nature; owing either to his own proper and peculiar nature or to his education and conversation with others; or to the reading of books, and the authority of those whom he esteems and admires; or to the differences of impressions, accordingly as they take place in a mind preoccupied and predisposed or in a mind indifferent and settled; or the like * * *

There are also idols formed by the intercourse and association of men with each other, which I call Idols of the Market-place, on account of the commerce and consort of men there. For it is by

1. This selection comes from Bacon's *Novum Organum (New Instrument)*, the work that in a series of apothegms describes the method by which man is to achieve universal knowledge. The source of knowledge, says Bacon, is experience; the method, induction, the reasoning from particulars to generalities. But our inductions are confused by the false images or *idols* which beset our minds.

discourse that men associate; and words are imposed according to the apprehension of the vulgar. And therefore the ill and unfit choice of words wonderfully obstructs the understanding. Nor do the definitions or explanations wherewith in some things learned men are wont to guard and defend themselves, by any means set the matter right. But words plainly force and overrule the understanding, and throw all into confusion, and lead men away into numberless empty controversies and idle fancies.

Lastly, there are idols which have immigrated into men's minds from the various dogmas of philosophies, and also from wrong laws of demonstration. These I call Idols of the Theater; because in my judgment all the received systems[2] are but so many stage-plays, representing worlds of their own creation after an unreal and scenic fashion. Nor is it only of the systems now in vogue, or only of the ancient sects and philosophies, that I speak: for many more plays of the same kind may yet be composed and in like artificial manner set forth; seeing that errors the most widely different have nevertheless causes for the most part alike. Neither again do I mean this only of entire systems, but also of many principles and axioms in science, which by tradition, credulity, and negligence have come to be received.

But of these several kinds of idols I must speak more largely and exactly, that the understanding may be duly cautioned.

The human understanding is of its own nature prone to suppose the existence of more order and regularity in the world than it finds. And though there be many things in nature which are singular and unmatched, yet it devises for them parallels and conjugates and relatives which do not exist. Hence the fiction that all celestial bodies move in perfect circles * * *

The human understanding when it has once adopted an opinion (either as being the received opinion or as being agreeable to itself) draws all things else to support and agree with it. And though there be a greater number and weight of instances to be found on the other side, yet these it either neglects and despises, or else by some distinction sets aside and rejects; in order that by this great and pernicious predetermination the authority of its former conclusions may remain inviolate. And therefore it was a good answer that was made by one who when they showed him hanging in a temple a picture of those who had paid their vows as having escaped shipwreck, and would have him say whether he did not now acknowledge the power of the gods —"Aye," asked he again, "but where are they painted that were drowned after their vows?" And such is the way of all superstition, whether in astrology, dreams, omens, divine judgments, or the like; wherein men, having a delight in such vanities, mark the events where they are fulfilled, but where they fail, though this happen

2. Philosophical systems.

much oftener, neglect and pass them by. But with far more subtlety does this mischief insinuate itself into philosophy and the
sciences; in which the first conclusion colors and brings into conformity with itself all that come after, though far sounder and
better. Besides, independently of that delight and vanity which I
have described, it is the peculiar and perpetual error of the human
intellect to be more moved and excited by affirmatives than by nega-
tives; whereas it ought properly to hold itself indifferently disposed
towards both alike. Indeed in the establishment of any true axiom,
the negative instance is the more forcible of the two.

The human understanding is moved by those things most which
strike and enter the mind simultaneously and suddenly, and so fill
the imagination; and then it feigns and supposes all other things to
be somehow, though it cannot see how, similar to those few things
by which it is surrounded. But for that going to and fro to remote
and heterogeneous instances, by which axioms are tried as in the
fire, the intellect is altogether slow and unfit, unless it be forced
thereto by severe laws and overruling authority.

The human understanding is unquiet; it cannot stop or rest, and
still presses onward, but in vain. Therefore it is that we cannot
conceive of any end or limit to the world; but always as of necessity
it occurs to us that there is something beyond. Neither again can it
be conceived how eternity has flowed down to the present day: for
that distinction which is commonly received of infinity in time past
and in time to come can by no means hold; for it would thence follow that one infinity is greater than another, and the infinity is wasting away and tending to become finite. The like subtlety arises touching the infinite divisibility of lines, from the same inability of thought
to stop. But this inability interferes more mischievously in the discovery of causes: for although the most general principles in nature
ought to be held merely positive, as they are discovered, and cannot
with truth be referred to a cause; nevertheless the human understanding being unable to rest still seeks something prior in the order of
nature. And then it is that in struggling towards that which is further
off it falls back upon that which is more nigh at hand—namely, on
final causes[3]; which have relation clearly to the nature of man rather
than to the nature of the universe, and from this source have
strangely defined philosophy. But he is no less an unskilled and shallow philosopher who seeks causes of that which is most general, than
he who in things subordinate and subaltern omits to do so.

The human understanding is no dry light, but receives an infusion
from the will and affections[4]; whence proceed sciences which may be
called "sciences as one would." For what a man had rather were true
he more readily believes. Therefore he rejects difficult things from
impatience of research; sober things, because they narrow hope; the

3. Roughly, the purposes of God.   4. Partialities, prejudices.

deeper things of nature, from superstition; the light of experience, from arrogance and pride, lest his mind should seem to be occupied with things mean and transitory; things not commonly believed, out of deference to the opinion of the vulgar. Numberless in short are the ways, and sometimes imperceptible, in which the affections color and infect the understanding.

But by far the greatest hindrance and aberration of the human understanding proceeds from the dullness, incompetency, and deceptions of the senses; in that things which strike the sense outweigh things which do not immediately strike it, though they be more important. Hence it is that speculation commonly ceases where sight ceases, insomuch that of things invisible there is little or no observation. * * * So again the essential nature of our common air, and of all bodies less dense than air (which are very many), is almost unknown. For the sense by itself is a thing infirm and erring; neither can instruments for enlarging or sharpening the senses do much: but all the truer kind of interpretation of nature is effected by instances and experiments fit and apposite; wherein the sense decides touching the experiment only, and the experiment touching the point in nature and the thing itself.

The human understanding is of its own nature prone to abstractions and gives a substance and reality to things which are fleeting. But to resolve nature into abstractions is less to our purpose than to dissect her into parts; as did the school of Democritus, which went further into nature than the rest. Matter rather than forms[5] should be the object of our attention, its configurations and changes of configuration, and simple action, and law of action or motion; for forms are figments of the human mind, unless you will call those laws of action forms.

Such then are the idols which I call *Idols of the Tribe*; and which take their rise either from the homogeneity of the substance of the human spirit, or from its preoccupation, or from its narrowness, or from its restless motion, or from an infusion of the affections, or from the incompetency of the senses, or from the mode of impression.

The *Idols of the Cave* take their rise in the peculiar constitution, mental or bodily, of each individual; and also in education, habit, and accident. Of this kind there is a great number and variety; but I will instance those the pointing out of which contains the most important caution, and which have most effect in disturbing the clearness of the understanding.

Men become attached to certain particular sciences and speculations, either because they fancy themselves the authors and inventors thereof, or because they have bestowed the greatest pains upon

5. The *form* of a thing is its idea or essential nature, as distinguished from its *matter*.

them and become most habituated to them. But men of this kind, if they betake themselves to philosophy and contemplations of a general character, distort and color them in obedience to their former fancies; a thing especially to be noticed in Aristotle, who made his natural philosophy a mere bondservant to his logic, thereby rendering it contentious and well nigh useless. * * *

There is one principal and as it were radical distinction between different minds, in respect of philosophy and the sciences; which is this: that some minds are stronger and apter to mark the differences of things, others to mark their resemblances. The steady and acute mind can fix its contemplations and dwell and fasten on the subtlest distinctions; the lofty and discursive mind recognizes and puts together the finest and most general resemblances. Both kinds however easily err in excess, by catching the one at gradations the other at shadows.

There are found some minds given to an extreme admiration of antiquity, others to an extreme love and appetite for novelty; but few so duly tempered that they can hold the mean, neither carping at what has been well laid down by the ancients, nor despising what is well introduced by the moderns. This however turns to the great injury of the sciences and philosophy; since these affectations of antiquity and novelty are the humors of partisans rather than judgments; and truth is to be sought for not in the felicity of any age, which is an unstable thing, but in the light of nature and experience, which is eternal. These factions therefore must be abjured, and care must be taken that the intellect be not hurried by them into assent.

Contemplations of nature and of bodies in their simple form break up and distract the understanding, while contemplations of nature and bodies in their composition and configuration overpower and dissolve the understanding: a distinction well seen in the school of Leucippus and Democritus as compared with the other philosophies. For that school is so busied with the particles that it hardly attends to the structure; while the others are so lost in admiration of the structure that they do not penetrate to the simplicity of nature. These kinds of contemplation should therefore be alternated and taken by turns; that so the understanding may be rendered at once penetrating and comprehensive, and the inconveniences above mentioned, with the idols which proceed from them, may be avoided.

Let such then be our provision and contemplative prudence for keeping off and dislodging the Idols of the Cave, which grow for the most part either out of the predominance of a favorite subject, or out of an excessive tendency to compare or to distinguish, or out of partiality for particular ages, or out of the largeness or minuteness of the objects contemplated. And generally let every student of nature take this as a rule—that whatever his mind seizes and dwells upon with peculiar satisfaction is to be held in suspicion, and that so much the more care is to be taken in dealing with such questions to keep the understanding even and clear.

But the *Idols of the Market-place* are the most troublesome of all: idols which have crept into the understanding through the alliances of words and names. For men believe that their reason governs words; but it is also true that words react on the understanding; and this it is that has rendered philosophy and the sciences sophistical and inactive. Now words, being commonly framed and applied according to the capacity of the vulgar, follow those lines of division which are most obvious to the vulgar understanding. And whenever an understanding of greater acuteness or a more diligent observation would alter those lines to suit the true divisions of nature, words stand in the way and resist the change. Whence it comes to pass that the high and formal discussions of learned men end oftentimes in disputes about words and names; with which (according to the use and wisdom of the mathematicians) it would be more prudent to begin, and so by means of definitions reduce them to order. Yet even definitions cannot cure this evil in dealing with natural and material things; since the definitions themselves consist of words, and those words beget others: so that it is necessary to recur to individual instances, and those in due series and order; as I shall say presently when I come to the method and scheme for the formation of notions and axioms.

The idols imposed by words on the understanding are of two kinds. They are either names of things which do not exist (for as there are things left unnamed through lack of observation, so likewise are there names which result from fantastic suppositions and to which nothing in reality corresponds), or they are names of things which exist, but yet confused and ill-defined, and hastily and irregularly derived from realities.

* * *

Idols of the Theater, or *of Systems*, are many, and there can be and perhaps will be yet many more. For were it not that now for many ages men's minds have been busied with religion and theology; and were it not that civil governments, especially monarchies, have been averse to such novelties, even in matters speculative; so that men labor therein to the peril and harming of their fortunes —not only unrewarded, but exposed also to contempt and envy: doubtless there would have arisen many other philosophical sects like to those which in great variety flourished once among the Greeks. For as on the phenomena of the heavens many hypotheses may be constructed, so likewise (and more also) many various dogmas may be set up and established on the phenomena of philosophy. And in the plays of this philosophical theater you may observe the same thing which is found in the theater of the poets, that stories invented for the stage are more compact and elegant, and more as one would wish them to be, than true stories out of history.

In general however there is taken for the material of philosophy either a great deal out of a few things, or a very little out of many things; so that on both sides philosophy is based on too narrow a foundation of experiment and natural history, and decides on the authority of too few cases. For the rational school of philosophers snatches from experience a variety of common instances, neither duly ascertained nor diligently examined and weighed, and leaves all the rest to meditation and agitation of wit.

There is also another class of philosophers, who having bestowed much diligent and careful labor on a few experiments, have thence made bold to educe and construct systems; wresting all other facts in a strange fashion to conformity therewith.

And there is yet a third class, consisting of those who out of faith and veneration mix their philosophy with theology and traditions; among whom the vanity of some has gone so far aside as to seek the origin of science among spirits and genii. So that this parent stock of errors—this false philosophy—is of three kinds; the *sophistical*, the *empirical*, and the *superstitious*.

BENJAMIN FRANKLIN
The Convenience of Being "Reasonable"[1]

I believe I have omitted mentioning that, in my first voyage from Boston, being becalmed off Block Island, our people set about catching cod, and hauled up a great many. Hitherto I had stuck to my resolution of not eating animal food, and on this occasion I considered, with my master Tryon, the taking every fish as a kind of unprovoked murder, since none of them had, or ever could do us any injury that might justify the slaughter. All this seemed very reasonable. But I had formerly been a great lover of fish, and, when this came hot out of the frying-pan, it smelled admirably well. I balanced some time between principle and inclination, till I recollected that, when the fish were opened, I saw smaller fish taken out of their stomachs; then thought I, "if you eat one another, I don't see why we mayn't eat you." So I dined upon cod very heartily, and continued to eat with other people, returning only now and then occasionally to a vegetable diet. So convenient a thing it is to be a *reasonable creature*, since it enables one to find or make a reason for everything one has a mind to do.

1. From the *Autobiography*.

WILLIAM MARCH
The Dog and Her Rival

A dog who had been greatly loved by her master found her life less pleasant after he married. She came one night to talk things over with the mare and said, "I wish them both happiness. Perhaps it would be better if I went away, because it must grieve my master to see the way his wife humiliates me all day long."

The mare thought that would be a sensible thing to do, but the dog sighed, shook her head, and continued. "No, that would never work out, because if I disappeared without a word, the uncertainty of my fate would break my master's heart; and, besides, that wife of his would make him believe I was fickle and had abandoned him, and he'd never know how much I had suffered or how great my love was. On second thought, it might be even simpler if I took poison and died on his doorstep. That I think would be the noblest thing to do, the final proof of my love."

The mare said that such renunciation seemed a generous gesture indeed, and the dog lifted her head and stared at the moon. "I'd do it, too," she said; "I'd kill myself on my master's doorstep if only I could hear his pleas for forgiveness when he finds my body, or see him beating his worthless wife for having driven me to such an end."

Love can be the most dreadful disguise that hate assumes.

W. H. ITTELSON and F. P. KILPATRICK
Experiments in Perception

What is perception? How do we see what we see, feel what we feel, hear what we hear? We act in terms of what we perceive; our acts lead to new perceptions; these lead to new acts, and so on in the incredibly complex process that constitutes life. Clearly, then, an understanding of the process by which man becomes aware of himself and his world is basic to any adequate understanding of human behavior. But the problem of explaining how and why we perceive in the way we do is one of the most controversial fields in psychology. We shall describe here some recent experimental work which sheds new light on the problem and points the way to a new theory of perception.

The fact that we see a chair and are then able to go to the place at which we localize it and rest our bodies on a substantial object does not seem particularly amazing or difficult to explain—until we try to explain it. If we accept the prevailing current view that we can never be aware of the world as such, but only of the nervous impulses arising from the impingement of physical forces on sensory receptors, we immediately face the necessity of explaining the correspondence between what we perceive and whatever it is that is there.

An extremely logical, unbeatable—and scientifically useless—answer is simply to say there is no real world, that everything exists in the mind alone. Another approach is to postulate the existence of an external world, to grant that there is some general correspondence between that world and what we perceive and to seek some understandable and useful explanation of why that should be. Most of the prominent theories about perception have grown out of the latter approach. These theories generally agree that even though much of the correspondence may be due to learning, at some basic level there exists an absolute correspondence between what is "out there" and what is in the "mind." But there is a great deal of disagreement concerning the level at which such innately determined correspondence occurs. At one extreme are theorists who believe that the correspondence occurs at the level of simple sensations, such as color, brightness, weight, hardness, and so on, and that out of these sensations are compounded more complex awarenesses, such as the recognition of a pencil or a book. At the other extreme are Gestalt psychologists who feel that complex perceptions such as the form of an object are the result of an inherent relationship between the properties of the thing perceived and the properties of the brain. All these schools seem to agree, however, that there is some perceptual level at which exists absolute objectivity; that is, a one-to-one correspondence between experience and reality.

This belief is basic to current thinking in many fields. It underlies most theorizing concerning the nature of science, including Percy W. Bridgman's attempt to reach final scientific objectivity in the "observable operation." In psychology one is hard put to find an approach to human behavior which departs from this basic premise. But it leads to dichotomies such as organism vs. environment, subjective vs. objective. Stimuli or stimulus patterns are treated as though they exist apart from the perceiving organism. Psychologists seek to find mechanical relationships or interactions between the organism and an "objectively defined" environment. They often rule out purposes and values as not belonging in a strictly scientific psychology.

The experiments to be described here arose from a widespread and growing feeling that such dichotomies are false, and that in practice it is impossible to leave values and purposes out of consideration in scientific observation. The experiments were designed to re-examine some of the basic ideas from which these problems stem.

During the past few years Adelbert Ames, Jr., of the Institute for Associated Research in Hanover, N.H., has designed some new ways of studying visual perception. They have resulted in a new conception of the nature of knowing and of observation. This theory neither denies the existence of objects nor proposes that they exist in a given form independently, that is, apart from the perceiving organism. Instead, it suggests that the world each of us knows is a world created in large measure from our experience in dealing with the environment.

Let us illustrate this in specific terms through some of the demonstrations. In one of them the subject sits in a dark room in which he can see only two star points of light. Both are equidistant from the observer, but one is brighter than the other. If the observer closes one eye and keeps his head still, the brighter point of light looks nearer than the dimmer one. Such apparent differences are related not only to brightness but also to direction from the observer. If two points of light of equal brightness are situated near the floor, one about a foot above the other, the upper one will generally be perceived as farther away than the lower one; if they are near the ceiling, the lower one will appear farther away.

A somewhat more complex experiment uses two partly inflated balloons illuminated from a concealed source. The balloons are in fixed positions about one foot apart. Their relative sizes can be varied by means of a lever control connected to a bellows; another lever controls their relative brightness. When the size and brightness of both balloons are the same, an observer looking at them with one eye from 10 feet or more sees them as two glowing spheres at equal distances from him. If the brightnesses are left the same and the relative sizes are changed, the larger balloon appears to nearly all observers somewhat nearer. If the size lever is moved continuously, causing continuous variation in the relative size of the balloons, they appear to move dramatically back and forth through space, even when the observer watches with both eyes open. The result is similar when the sizes are kept equal and the relative brightness is varied.

With the same apparatus the effects of size and brightness may be combined so that they supplement or conflict with each other. When they supplement each other, the variation in apparent distance is much greater than when either size or brightness alone is varied. When they oppose each other, the variation is much less. Most people give more weight to relative size than to relative brightness in judging distance.

These phenomena cannot be explained by referring to "reality," because "reality" and perception do not correspond. They cannot be explained by reference to the pattern in the retina of the eye, because for any given retinal pattern there are an infinite number of brightness-size-distance combinations to which that pattern might be related. When faced with such a situation, in which an unlimited number of possibilities can be related to a given retinal pattern, the organism apparently calls upon its previous experiences and assumes that what has been most probable in the past is most probable in the immediate occasion. When presented with two star-points of different brightness, a person unconsciously "bets" or "assumes" that the two points, being similar, are probably identical (*i.e.*, of equal brightness, and therefore that the one which seems brighter must be nearer. Similarly the observed facts in the case of two star-points placed vertically one above the other suggest that when we look down we assume, on the basis of past experience, that objects in the lower part of the visual field are nearer than objects in the upper part; when we look up, we assume the opposite to be true. An analogous explanation can be made of the role of relative size as an indication of relative distance.

Why do the differences in distance seem so much greater when the relative size of two objects is varied continuously than when the size difference is fixed? This phenomenon, too, apparently is based on experience. It is a fairly common experience, though not usual, to find that two similar objects of different sizes are actually the same distance away from us. But it is rare indeed to see two stationary objects at the same distance, one growing larger and the other smaller; almost always in everyday life when we see two identical or nearly identical objects change relative size they are in motion in relation to each other. Hence under the experimental conditions we are much more likely to assume distance differences in the objects of changing size than in those of fixed size.

Visual perception involves an impression not only of *where* an object is but *what* it is. From the demonstrations already described we may guess that there is a very strong relationship between localization in space ("thereness") and the assignment of objective properties ("thatness"). This relationship can be demonstrated by a cube experiment.

Two solid white cubes are suspended on wires that are painted black so as to be invisible against a black background. One cube is about 3 feet from the observer and the other about 12 feet. The observer's head is in a headrest so positioned that the cubes are almost in line with each other but he can see both, the nearer cube being slightly to the right. A tiny metal shield is then placed a few inches in front of the left eye. It is just big enough to cut off the view of the far cube from the left eye. The result is that the near cube is seen with both eyes and the far cube with just the right eye. Under these conditions the observer can fix the position of the near cube very well, because he has available all the cues that come from the use of the two eyes. But in the case of the far cube seen with only one eye, localization is much more difficult and uncertain.

Now since the two cubes are almost in line visually, a slight movement of the head to the right will cause the inside vertical edges of the cubes to coincide. Such coincidence of edge is strongly related to an assumption of "togetherness." Hence when the subject moves his head in this way, the uncertainly located distant cube appears to have moved forward to a position even with the nearer cube. Under these conditions not only does the mislocated cube appear smaller, but it appears different in shape, that is, no longer cubical, even though the pattern cast by the cube on the retina of the eye has not changed at all.

The most reasonable explanation of these visual phenomena seems to be that an observer unconsciously relates to the stimulus pattern some sort of weighted average of the past consequences of acting with respect to that pattern. The particular perception "chosen" is the one that has the best predictive value, on the basis of previous experience, for action in carrying out the purposes of the organism. From this one may make two rather crucial deductions: (1) an unfamiliar external configuration which yields the same retinal pattern as one the observer is accustomed to deal with will be perceived as the familiar configuration; (2) when the observer acts on his interpretation of the unfamiliar configuration and finds that he is wrong, his perception will change even though the retinal pattern is unchanged.

Let us illustrate with some actual demonstrations. If an observer in a dark room looks with one eye at two lines of light which are at the same distance and elevation but of different lengths, the longer line will look nearer than the shorter one. Apparently he assumes that the lines are identical and translates the difference in length into a difference in position. If the observer takes a wand with a luminous tip and tries to touch first one line and then the other, he will be unable to do so at first. After repeated practice, however, he can learn to touch the two lines quickly and accurately. At this point he no longer sees the lines as at different distances; they now look, as they are, the same distance from him. He originally assumed that the two lines were the same length because that seemed the best bet under the circumstances. After he had tested this assumption by purposive action, he shifted to the assumption, less probable in terms of past experience but still possible, that the lines were at the same distance but of different lengths. As his assumption changed, perception did also.

There is another experiment that demonstrates these points even more convincingly. It uses a distorted room in which the floor slopes up to the right of the observer, the rear wall recedes from right to left and the windows are of different sizes and trapezoidal in shape. When an observer looks at this room with one eye from a certain point, the room appears completely normal, as if the floor were level, the rear wall at right angles to the line of sight and the windows rectangular and of the same size. Presumably the observer chooses this particular appearance instead of some other because of the assumptions he brings to the occasion. If he now takes a long stick and tries to touch the various parts of the room, he will be unsuccessful, even though he has gone into the situation knowing the true shape of the room. With practice, however, he becomes more and more successful in touching what he wants to touch with the stick. More important, he sees the room more and more in its true shape, even though the stimulus pattern on his retina has remained unchanged.

By means of a piece of apparatus called the "rotating trapezoidal window" it has been possible to extend the investigation to complex perceptual situations involving movement. This device consists of a trapezoidal surface with panes cut in it and shadows painted on it to give the appearance of a window. It is mounted on a rod connected to a motor so that it rotates at a slow constant speed in an upright position about its own axis. When an observer views the rotating surface with one eye from about 10 feet or more or with both eyes from about 25 feet or more, he sees not a rotating trapezoid but an oscillating rectangle. Its speed of movement and its shape appear to vary markedly as it turns. If a small cube is attached by a short rod to the upper part of the short side of the trapezoid, it seems to become detached, sail freely around the front of the trapezoid and attach itself again as the apparatus rotates.

All these experiments, and many more that have been made, suggest strongly that perception is never a sure thing, never an absolute revelation of "what is." Rather, what we see is a prediction—our own personal construction designed to give us the best possible bet for carrying out our purposes in action. We make these bets on the basis of our past experience. When we have a great deal of relevant and consistent experience to relate to stimulus patterns, the probability of success of our prediction (perception) as a guide to action is extremely high, and we tend to have a feeling of surety. When our experience is limited or inconsistent, the reverse holds true. According to the new theory of perception developed from the demonstrations we have described, perception is a functional affair based on action, experience and probability. The thing perceived is an inseparable part of the function of perceiving, which in turn includes all aspects of the total process of living. This view differs from the old rival theories: the thing perceived is neither just a figment of the mind nor an innately determined absolute revelation of a reality postulated to exist apart from the perceiving organism.

Object and percept are part and parcel of the same thing.

This conclusion of course has far-reaching implications for many areas of study, for some assumption as to what perception is must underly any philosophy or comprehensive theory of psychology, of science or of knowledge in general. Although the particular investigations involved here are restricted to visual perception, this is only a vehicle which carries us into a basic inquiry of much wider significance.

QUESTIONS FOR STUDY, DISCUSSION, AND WRITING

If Ittelson and Kilpatrick came in upon the following discussion in a college dormitory, what would they have to contribute to it?

"The cow is there," said Ansell, lighting a match and holding it out over the carpet. No one spoke. He waited till the end of the match fell off. Then he said again, "She is there, the cow. There, now."

"You have not proved it," said a voice.

"I have proved it to myself."

"I have proved to myself that she isn't," said the voice. "The cow is not there." Ansell frowned and lit another match.

"She's there for me," he declared. "I don't care whether she's there for you or not. Whether I'm in Cambridge or Iceland or dead, the cow will be there."

It was philosophy. They were discussing the existence of objects. Do they exist only when there is some one to look at them? or have they a real existence of their own? It is all very interesting, but at the same time it is difficult.

—E. M. Forster, *The Longest Journey*

ROBERTA WOHLSTETTER
Surprise[1]

If our intelligence system and all our other channels of information failed to produce an accurate image of Japanese intentions and capabilities, it was not for want of the relevant materials. Never before have we had so complete an intelligence picture of the enemy. And perhaps never again will we have such a magnificent collection of sources at our disposal.

Retrospect

To review these sources briefly, an American cryptanalyst, Col. William F. Friedman, had broken the top-priority Japanese diplo-

---

1. This selection is the seventh and final chapter in the author's *Pearl Harbor; Warning and Decision.*

matic code, which enabled us to listen to a large proportion of the privileged communications between Tokyo and the major Japanese embassies throughout the world. Not only did we know in advance how the Japanese ambassadors in Washington were advised, and how much they were instructed to say, but we also were listening to top-secret messages on the Tokyo-Berlin and Tokyo-Rome circuits, which gave us information vital for conduct of the war in the Atlantic and Europe. In the Far East this source provided minute details on movements connected with the Japanese program of expansion into Southeast Asia.

Besides the strictly diplomatic codes, our cryptanalysts also had some success in reading codes used by Japanese agents in major American and foreign ports. Those who were on the distribution list for MAGIC[2] had access to much of what these agents were reporting to Tokyo and what Tokyo was demanding of them in the Panama Canal Zone, in cities along the east and west coasts of the Americas from northern Canada as far south as Brazil, and in ports throughout the Far East, including the Philippines and the Hawaiian Islands. They could determine what installations, what troop and ship movements, and what alert and defense measures were of interest to Tokyo at these points on the globe, as well as approximately how much correct information her agents were sending her.

Our naval leaders also had at their disposal the results of radio traffic analysis. While before the war our naval radio experts could not read the content of any Japanese naval or military coded messages, they were able to deduce from a study of intercepted ship call signs the composition and location of the Japanese Fleet units. After a change in call signs, they might lose sight of some units, and units that went into port in home waters were also lost because the ships in port used frequencies that our radios were unable to intercept. Most of the time, however, our traffic analysts had the various Japanese Fleet units accurately pinpointed on our naval maps.

Extremely competent on-the-spot economic and political analysis was furnished by Ambassador Grew and his staff in Tokyo. Ambassador Grew was himself a most sensitive and accurate observer, as evidenced by his dispatches to the State Department. His observations were supported and supplemented with military detail by frequent reports from American naval attachés and observers in key Far Eastern ports. Navy Intelligence had men with radio equipment located along the coast of China, for example, who reported the convoy movements toward Indochina. There were also naval observers stationed in various high-tension areas in Thailand and Indochina who could fill in the local outlines of Japanese political intrigue and military planning. In Tokyo and other Japanese cities,

2. The name given to information obtained from decoded Japanese diplomatic dispatches.

it is true, Japanese censorship grew more and more rigid during 1941, until Ambassador Grew felt it necessary to disclaim any responsibility for noting or reporting overt military evidence of an imminent outbreak of war. This careful Japanese censorship naturally cut down visual confirmation of the decoded information but very probably never achieved the opaqueness of Russia's Iron Curtain.

During this period the data and interpretations of British intelligence were also available to American officers in Washington and the Far East, though the British and Americans tended to distrust each other's privileged information.

In addition to secret sources, there were some excellent public ones. Foreign correspondents for *The New York Times*, the *Herald Tribune*, and the Washington *Post* were stationed in Tokyo and Shanghai and in Canberra, Australia. Their reporting as well as their predictions on the Japanese political scene were on a very high level. Frequently their access to news was more rapid and their judgment of its significance as reliable as that of our Intelligence officers. This was certainly the case for 1940 and most of 1941. For the last weeks before the Pearl Harbor strike, however, the public newspaper accounts were not very useful. It was necessary to have secret information in order to know what was happening. Both Tokyo and Washington exercised very tight control over leaks during this crucial period, and the newsmen accordingly had to limit their accounts to speculation and notices of diplomatic meetings with no exact indication of the content of the diplomatic exchanges.

The Japanese press was another important public source. During 1941 it proclaimed with increasing shrillness the Japanese government's determination to pursue its program of expansion into Southeast Asia and the desire of the military to clear the Far East of British and American colonial exploitation. This particular source was rife with explicit signals of aggressive intent.

Finally, an essential part of the intelligence picture for 1941 was both public and privileged information on American policy and activities in the Far East. During the year the pattern of action and interaction between the Japanese and American governments grew more and more complex. At the last, it became especially important for anyone charged with the responsibility of ordering an alert to know what moves the American government was going to make with respect to Japan, as well as to try to guess what Japan's next move would be, since Japan's next move would respond in part to ours. Unfortunately our military leaders, and especially our Intelligence officers, were sometimes as surprised as the Japanese at the moves of the White House and the State Department. They usually had more orderly anticipations about Japanese policy and conduct than they had about America's. On the other hand, it was also true that State Department and White House officials were handicapped in

judging Japanese intentions and estimates of risk by an inadequate
picture of our own military vulnerability.

All of the public and private sources of information mentioned
were available to America's political and military leaders in 1941. It
is only fair to remark, however, that no single person or agency ever
had at any given moment all the signals existing in this vast information network. The signals lay scattered in a number of different
agencies; some were decoded, some were not; some traveled through
rapid channels of communication, some were blocked by technical
or procedural delays; some never reached a center of decision. But
it is legitimate to review again the general sort of picture that
emerged during the first week of December from the signals readily
at hand. Anyone close to President Roosevelt was likely to have
before him the following significant fragments.

There was first of all a picture of gathering troop and ship movements down the China coast and into Indochina. The large
dimensions of this movement to the south were established publicly
and visually as well as by analysis of ship call signs. Two changes in
Japanese naval call signs—one on November 1 and another on
December 1—had also been evaluated by Naval Intelligence as
extremely unusual and as signs of major preparations for some sort
of Japanese offensive. The two changes had interfered with the speed
of American radio traffic analysis. Thousands of interceptions after
December 1 were necessary before the new call signs could be read.
Partly for this reason American radio analysts disagreed about the
locations of the Japanese carriers. One group held that all the carriers
were near Japan because they had not been able to identify a carrier
call sign since the middle of November. Another group believed that
they had located one carrier division in the Marshalls. The probability seemed to be that the carriers, wherever they were, had gone
into radio silence; and past experience led the analysts to believe
that they were therefore in waters near the Japanese homeland,
where they could communicate with each other on wavelengths that
we could not intercept. However, our inability to locate the carriers
exactly, combined with the two changes in call signs, was itself a
danger signal.

Our best secret source, MAGIC, was confirming the aggressive
intention of the new military cabinet in Tokyo, which had replaced
the last moderate cabinet on October 17. In particular, MAGIC
provided details of some of the preparations for the move into
Southeast Asia. Running counter to this were increased troop shipments to the Manchurian border in October. (The intelligence
picture is never clear-cut.) But withdrawals had begun toward the
end of that month. MAGIC also carried explicit instructions to the
Japanese ambassadors in Washington to pursue diplomatic negotiations with the United States with increasing energy, but at the same

time it announced a deadline for the favorable conclusion of the negotiations, first for November 25, later postponed until November 29. In case of diplomatic failure by that date, the Japanese ambassadors were told, Japanese patience would be exhausted, Japan was determined to pursue her Greater East Asia policy, and on November 29 "things" would automatically begin to happen.

On November 26 Secretary Hull rejected Japan's latest bid for American approval of her policies in China and Indochina. MAGIC had repeatedly characterized this Japanese overture as the "last," and it now revealed the ambassadors' reaction of consternation and despair over the American refusal and also their country's characterization of the American Ten Point Note as an "ultimatum."

On the basis of this collection of signals, Army and Navy Intelligence experts in Washington tentatively placed D-day *for the Japanese Southeastern campaign* during the week end of November 30, and when this failed to materialize, during the week end of December 7. They also compiled an accurate list of probable British and Dutch targets and included the Philippines and Guam as possible American targets.

Also available in this mass of information, but long forgotten, was a rumor reported by Ambassador Grew in January, 1941. It came from what was regarded as a not-very-reliable source, the Peruvian embassy, and stated that the Japanese were preparing a surprise air attack on Pearl Harbor. Curiously the date of the report is coincident roughly with what we now know to have been the date of inception of Yamamoto's plan; but the rumor was labeled by everyone, including Ambassador Grew, as quite fantastic and the plan as absurdly impossible. American judgment was consistent with Japanese judgment at this time, since Yamamoto's plan was in direct contradiction to Japanese naval tactical doctrine.

Perspective

On the basis of this rapid recapitulation of the highlights in the signal picture, it is apparent that our decisionmakers had at hand an impressive amount of information on the enemy. They did not have the complete list of targets, since none of the last-minute estimates included Pearl Harbor. They did not know the exact hour and date for opening the attack. They did not have an accurate knowledge of Japanese capabilities or of Japanese ability to accept very high risks. The crucial question then, we repeat, is, If we could enumerate accurately the British and Dutch targets and give credence to a Japanese attack against them either on November 30 or December 7, why were we not expecting a specific danger to *ourselves?* And by the word "expecting," we mean expecting in the sense of taking specific alert actions to meet the contingencies of attack by land, sea, or air.

There are several answers to this question that have become apparent in the course of this study. First of all, it is much easier *after* the event to sort the relevant from the irrelevant signals. After the event, of course, a signal is always crystal clear; we can now see what disaster it was signaling, since the disaster has occurred. But before the event it is obscure and pregnant with conflicting meanings. It comes to the observer embedded in an atmosphere of "noise," *i.e.*, in the company of all sorts of information that is useless and irrelevant for predicting the particular disaster. For example, in Washington, Pearl Harbor signals were competing with a vast number of signals from the European theater. These European signals announced danger from the European theater. These European signals announced danger more frequently and more specifically than any coming from the Far East. The Far Eastern signals were also arriving at a center of decision where they had to compete with the prevailing belief that an unprotected offensive force acts as a deterrent rather than a target. In Honolulu they were competing *not* with signals from the European theater, but rather with a large number of signals announcing Japanese intentions and preparations to attack Soviet Russia rather than to move southward; here they were also competing with expectations of local sabotage prepared by previous alert situations.

In short, we failed to anticipate Pearl Harbor not for want of the relevant materials, but because of a plethora of irrelevant ones. Much of the appearance of wanton neglect that emerged in various investigations of the disaster resulted from the unconscious suppression of vast congeries of signs pointing in every direction except Pearl Harbor. It was difficult later to recall these signs since they had led nowhere. Signals that are characterized today as absolutely unequivocal warnings of surprise air attack on Pearl Harbor become, on analysis in the context of December, 1941, not merely ambiguous but occasionally inconsistent with such an attack. To recall one of the most controversial and publicized examples, the winds code,[3] both General Short and Admiral Kimmel testified that if they had had this information, they would have been prepared on the morning of December 7 for an air attack from without. The messages establishing the winds code are often described in the Pearl Harbor literature as Tokyo's declaration of war against America. If they indeed amounted to such a declaration, obviously the failure to inform Honolulu of this vital news would have been criminal negligence. On examination, however, the messages proved to be instructions for code communication after normal commercial channels had been cut. In one message the recipient was instructed on receipt of an execute to destroy all remaining codes in his possession. In another version the recipient was warned that the execute would be sent out

3. A Japanese code which, by means of specious weather information inserted in the daily Japanese-language short-wave news broadcast, signaled danger-ously deteriorated diplomatic relations between Japan and the United States, the USSR, or Great Britain.

"when relations are becoming dangerous" between Japan and three other countries. There was a different code term for each country: England, America, and the Soviet Union.

There is no evidence that an authentic execute of either message was ever intercepted by the United States before December 7. The message ordering code destruction was in any case superseded by a much more explicit code-destruction order from Tokyo that was intercepted on December 2 and translated on December 3. After December 2, the receipt of a winds-code execute for code destruction would therefore have added nothing new to our information, and code destruction in itself cannot be taken as an unambiguous substitute for a formal declaration of war. During the first week of December the United States ordered all American consulates in the Far East to destroy all American codes, yet no one has attempted to prove that this order was equivalent to an American declaration of war against Japan. As for the other winds-code message, provided an execute had been received warning that relations were dangerous between Japan and the United States, there would still have been no way on the basis of this signal alone to determine whether Tokyo was signaling Japanese intent to attack the United States or Japanese fear of an American surprise attack (in reprisal for Japanese aggressive moves against American allies in the Far East). It was only after the event that "dangerous relations" could be interpreted as "surprise air attack on Pearl Harbor."

There is a difference, then, between having a signal available somewhere in the heap of irrelevancies, and perceiving it as a warning; and there is also a difference between perceiving it as a warning, and acting or getting action on it. These distinctions, simple as they are, illuminate the obscurity shrouding this moment in history.

Many instances of these distinctions have been examined in the course of this study. We shall recall a few of the most dramatic now. To illustrate the difference between having and perceiving a signal, let us return to Colonel Fielder.[4] * * * Though he was an untrained and inexperienced Intelligence officer, he headed Army Intelligence at Pearl Harbor at the time of the attack. He had been on the job for only four months, and he regarded as quite satisfactory his sources of information and his contacts with the Navy locally and with Army Intelligence in Washington. Evidently he was unaware that Army Intelligence in Washington was not allowed to send him any "action" or policy information, and he was therefore not especially concerned about trying to read beyond the obvious meaning of any given communication that came under his eyes. Colonel Bratton, head of Army Far Eastern Intelligence in Washington, however, had a somewhat more realistic view of the extent of Colonel Fielder's knowledge. At the end of November, Colonel Bratton had learned about the

4. An officer discussed earlier in the book.

winds-code setup and was also apprised that the naval traffic analysis unit under Commander Rochefort in Honolulu was monitoring 24 hours a day for an execute. He was understandably worried about the lack of communication between this unit and Colonel Fielder's office, and by December 5 he finally felt that the matter was urgent enough to warrant sending a message directly to Colonel Fielder about the winds code. Now any information on the winds code, since it belonged to the highest classification of secret information, and since it was therefore automatically evaluated as "action" information, could not be sent through normal G-2 channels. Colonel Bratton had to figure out another way to get the information to Colonel Fielder. He sent this message: "Contact Commander Rochefort immediately thru Commandant Fourteenth Naval District regarding broadcasts from Tokyo reference weather." Signal Corps records establish that Colonel Fielder received this message. How did he react to it? He filed it. According to his testimony in 1945, it made no impression on him and he did not attempt to see Rochefort. He could not sense any urgency behind the lines because he was not expecting immediate trouble, and his expectations determined what he read. A warning signal was available to him, but he did not perceive it.

Colonel Fielder's lack of experience may make this example seem to be an exception. So let us recall the performance of Captain Wilkinson, the naval officer who headed the Office of Naval Intelligence in Washington in the fall of 1941 and who is unanimously acclaimed for a distinguished and brilliant career. His treatment of a now-famous Pearl Harbor signal does not sound much different in the telling. After the event, the signal in question was labeled "the bomb-plot message." It originated in Tokyo on September 24 and was sent to an agent in Honolulu. It requested the agent to divide Pearl Harbor into five areas and to make his future reports on ships in harbor with reference to those areas. Tokyo was especially interested in the locations of battleships, destroyers, and carriers, and also in any information on the anchoring of more than one ship at a single dock.

This message was decoded and translated on October 9 and shortly thereafter distributed to Army, Navy, and State Department recipients of MAGIC. Commander Kramer, a naval expert on MAGIC, had marked the message with an asterisk, signifying that he thought it to be of particular interest. But what was its interest? Both he and Wilkinson agreed that it illustrated the "nicety" of Japanese intelligence, the incredible zeal and efficiency with which they collected detail. The division into areas was interpreted as a device for shortening the reports. Admiral Stark was similarly impressed with Japanese efficiency, and no one felt it necessary to forward the message to Admiral Kimmel. No one read into it a specific danger to ships anchored in Pearl Harbor. At the time, this was a reasonable estimate, since somewhat similar requests for information were going to Japanese agents in Panama, Vancouver, Portland, San Diego, San Francisco, and other places. It should be observed, however, that the estimate was reasonable only on the basis of a very rough check on the quantity of espionage message passing between Tokyo and these American ports. No one in Far Eastern Intelligence had subjected the messages to any more refined analysis. An observer assigned to such a job would have been able to record an increase in the frequency and specificity of Tokyo's requests concerning Manila and Pearl Harbor in the last weeks before the outbreak of war, and he would have noted that Tokyo was not displaying the same interest in other American ports. These observations, while not significant in isolation, might have been useful in the general signal picture.

There is no need, however, to confine our examples to Intelligence personnel. Indeed, the crucial areas where the signals failed to communicate a warning were in the operational branches of the armed services. Let us take Admiral Kimmel and his reaction to the information that the Japanese were destroying most of their codes in major Far Eastern consulates and also in London and Washington. Since the Pearl Harbor attack, this information has frequently been characterized by military experts who were not stationed in Honolulu as an "unmistakable tip-off." As Admiral Ingersoll explained at the congressional hearings, with the lucidity characteristic of statements after the event:

> If you rupture diplomatic negotiations you do not necessarily have to burn your codes. The diplomats go home and they can pack up their codes with their dolls and take them home. Also, when you rupture diplomatic negotiations, you do not rupture consular relations. The consuls stay on.
> Now, in this particular set of dispatches that did not mean a rupture of diplomatic negotiations, it meant war, and that information was sent out to the fleets as soon as we got it. . . .[5]

The phrase "it meant war" was, of course, pretty vague; war in Manila, Hong Kong, Singapore, and Batavia is not war 5000 miles away in Pearl Harbor. Before the event, for Admiral Kimmel, code burning in major Japanese consulates in the Far East may have "meant war," but it did not signal danger of an air attack on Pearl Harbor. In the first place, the information that he received was not the original MAGIC. He learned from Washington that Japanese consulates were burning "almost all" of their codes, not all of them, and Honolulu was not included on the list. He knew from a local source that the Japanese consulate in Honolulu was burning secret papers (not necessarily codes), and this back-yard burning had happened three or four times during the year. In July, 1941, Kimmel had been informed that the Japanese consulates in lands neighboring Indochina had destroyed codes, and he interpreted the code burning in December as a similar attempt to protect codes in case the Americans or their British and Dutch allies tried to seize the consulates in reprisal for the southern advance. This also was a reasonable interpretation at the time, though not an especially keen one.

Indeed, at the time there was a good deal of evidence available to support all the wrong interpretations of last-minute signals, and the interpretations appeared wrong only *after* the event. There was, for example, a good deal of evidence to support the hypothesis that Japan would attack the Soviet Union from the east while the Russian Army was heavily engaged in the west. Admiral Turner, head of Navy War Plans in Washington, was an enthusiastic adherent of this view and argued the high probability of a Japanese attack on Russia up until the last week in November, when he had to concede that most of Japan's men and supplies were moving South. Richard Sorge, the expert Soviet spy who had direct access to the Japanese Cabinet, had correctly predicted the southern move as early as July, 1941, but even he was deeply alarmed during September and early October by the large number of troop movements to the Manchurian border. He feared that his July advice to the Soviet Union had been in error, and his alarm ultimately led to his capture on October 14. For at this time he increased his radio messages to Moscow to the point where it was possible for the Japanese police to pinpoint the source of the broadcasts.

It is important to emphasize here that most of the men that we have cited in our examples, such as Captain Wilkinson and Admirals Turner and Kimmel—these men and their colleagues who were involved in the Pearl Harbor disaster—were as efficient and loyal a group of men as one could find. Some of them were exceptionally able and dedicated. The fact of surprise at Pearl Harbor has never been persuasively explained by accusing the participants, individually or in groups, of conspiracy or negligence or stupidity. What these examples illustrate is rather the very human tendency to pay attention to the signals that support current expectations about enemy behavior. If no one is listening for signals of an attack against a highly improbable target, then it is very difficult for the signals to be heard.

For every signal that came into the information net in 1941 there were usually several plausible alternative explanations, and it is not surprising that our observers and analysts were inclined to select the explanations that fitted the popular hypotheses. They sometimes set down new contradictory evidence side by side with existing hypotheses, and they also sometimes held two contradictory beliefs at the same time. We have seen this happen in G-2[6] estimates for the fall of 1941. Apparently human beings have a stubborn attachment to old beliefs and an equally stubborn resistance to new material that

6. Intelligence.

will upset them.

Besides the tendency to select whatever was in accord with one's expectations, there were many other blocks to perception that prevented our analysts from making the correct interpretation. We have just mentioned the masses of conflicting evidence that supported alternative and equally reasonable hypotheses. This is the phenomenon of noise in which a signal is embedded. Even at its normal level, noise presents problems in distraction; but in addition to the natural clatter of useless information and competing signals, in 1941 a number of factors combined to raise the usual noise level. First of all, it had been raised, especially in Honolulu, by the background of previous alert situations and false alarms. Earlier alerts, as we have seen, had centered attention on local sabotage and on signals supporting the hypothesis of a probable Japanese attack on Rusisa. Second, in both Honolulu and Washington, individual reactions to danger had been numbed, or at least dulled, by the continuous international tension.

A third factor that served to increase the natural noise level was the positive effort made by the enemy to keep the relevant signals quiet. The Japanese security system was an important and successful block to perception. It was able to keep the strictest cloak of secrecy around the Pearl Harbor attack and to limit knowledge only to those closely associated with the details of military and naval planning. In the Japanese Cabinet only the Navy Minister (who was also Prime Minister) knew of the plan before the task force left its final port of departure.

In addition to keeping certain signals quiet, the enemy tried to create noise, and sent false signals into our information system by carrying on elaborate "spoofs." False radio traffic made us believe that certain ships were maneuvering near the mainland of Japan. The Japanese also sent to individual commanders false war plans for Chinese targets, which were changed only at the last moment to bring them into line with the Southeastern movement.

A fifth barrier to accurate perception was the fact that the relevant signals were subject to change, often very sudden change. This was true even of the so-called static intelligence, which included data on capabilities and the composition of military forces. In the case of our 1941 estimates of the infeasibility of torpedo attacks in the shallow waters of Pear Harbor, or the underestimation of the range and performance of the Japanese Zero, the changes happened too quickly to appear in an intelligence estimate.

Sixth, our own security system sometimes prevented the communication of signals. It confronted our officers with the problem of trying to keep information from the enemy without keeping it from each other, and, as in the case of MAGIC, they were not always successful. As we have seen, only a very few key individuals saw these secret messages, and they saw them only briefly. They had no opportunity or time to make a critical review of the material, and each one assumed that others who had seen it would arrive at identical interpretations. Exactly who those "others" were was not quite clear to any recipient. Admiral Stark, for example, thought Admiral Kimmel was reading all of MAGIC. Those who were not on the list of recipients, but who had learned somehow of the existence of the decodes, were sure that they contained military as well as diplomatic information and believed that the contents were much fuller and more precise than they actually were. The effect of carefully limiting the reading and discussion of MAGIC, which was certainly necessary to safeguard the secret of our knowledge of the code, was thus to reduce this group of signals to the point where they were scarcely heard.

To these barriers of noise and security we must add the fact that the necessarily precarious character of intelligence information and predictions was reflected in the wording of instructions to take action. The warning messages were somewhat vague and ambiguous. Enemy moves are often subject to reversal on short notice, and this was true for the Japanese. They had plans for canceling their attacks on American possessions in the Pacific up to 24 hours before the time set for attack. A full alert in the Hawaiian Islands, for example, was one condition that might have caused the Pearl Harbor task force to return to Japan on December 5 or 6. The fact that intelligence predictions must be based on moves that are almost always reversible makes understandable the reluctance of the intelligence analyst to make bold assertions. Even if he is willing to risk his reputation on a firm prediction of attack at a definite time and place, no commander will in turn lightly risk the penalties and costs of a full alert. In December, 1941, a full alert required shooting down any unidentified aircraft sighted over the Hawaiian Islands. Yet this might have been interpreted by Japan as the first overt act. At least that was one consideration that influenced General Short to order his lowest degree of alert. While the cautious phrasing in the messages to the theater is certainly understandable, it nevertheless constituted another block on the road to perception. The sentences in the final theater warnings—"A surprise aggressive move in any direction is a possibility" and "Japanese future action unpredictable but hostile action possible at any moment"—could scarcely have been expected to inform the theater commanders of any change in their strategic situation.

Last but not least we must also mention the blocks to perception and communication inherent in any large bureaucratic organization, and those that stemmed from intraservice and interservice rivalries. The most glaring example of rivalry in the Pearl Harbor case was that between Naval War Plans and Naval Intelligence. A general prejudice against intellectuals and specialists, not confined to the military but unfortunately widely held in America, also made it difficult for intelligence experts to be heard. McCollum, Bratton, Sadtler, and a few others who felt that the signal picture was ominous enough to warrant more urgent warnings had no power to influence decision. The Far Eastern code analysts, for example, were believed to be too immersed in the "Oriental point of view." Low budgets for American Intelligence departments reflected the low prestige of this activity, whereas in England, Germany, and Japan, 1941 budgets reached a height that was regarded by the American Congress as quite beyond reason.

In view of all these limitations to perception and communication, is the fact of surprise at Pearl Harbor, then, really so surprising? Even with these limitations explicitly recognized, there remains the step between perception and action. Let us assume that the first hurdle has been crossed: An available signal has been perceived as an indication of imminent danger. Then how do we resolve the next questions: What specific danger is the signal trying to communicate, and what specific action or preparation should follow?

On November 27, General MacArthur had received a war warning very similar to the one received by General Short in Honolulu. MacArthur's response had been promptly translated into orders designed to protect his bombers from possible air attack from Formosan land bases. But the orders were carried out very slowly. By December 8, Philippine time, only half of the bombers ordered to the south had left the Manila area, and reconnaissance over Formosa had not been undertaken. There was no sense of urgency in preparing for a Japanese air attack, partly because our intelligence estimates had calculated that the Japanese aircraft did not have sufficient range to bomb Manila from Formosa.

The information that Pearl Harbor had been attacked arrived at Manila early in the morning of December 8, giving the Philippine forces some 9 or 10 hours to prepare for an attack. But did an air attack on Pearl Harbor necessarily mean that the Japanese would strike from the air at the Philippines? Did they have enough equipment to mount both air attacks successfully? Would they come from Formosa or from carriers? Intelligence had indicated that they would have to come from carriers, yet the carriers were evidently off Hawaii. MacArthur's headquarters also pointed out that there had been no formal declaration of war against Japan by the United States. Therefore approval could not be granted for a counterattack on Formosan bases. Furthermore there were technical disagreements among airmen as to whether a counterattack should be mounted without advance photographic reconnaissance. While Brereton was arranging permission to undertake photographic reconnaissance, there was further disagreement about what to do with the aircraft in the meantime. Should they be sent aloft or should they be dispersed to avoid destruction in case the Japanese reached the airfields? When the Japanese bombers arrived shortly after noon, they found all the American aircraft wingtip to wingtip on the ground. Even the signal of an actual attack on Pearl Harbor was not an unambiguous signal of an attack on the Philippines, and it did not make clear what response was best.

Prospect

The history of Pearl Harbor has an interest exceeding by far any tale of an isolated catastrophe that might have been the result of negligence or stupidity or treachery, however lurid. For we have found the roots of this surprise in circumstances that affected honest, dedicated, and intelligent men. The possibility of such surprise at any time lies in the conditions of human perception and stems from uncertainties so basic that they are not likely to be eliminated, though they might be reduced.

It is only to be expected that the relevant signals, so clearly audible after an event, will be partially obscured before the event by surrounding noise. Even past diligence constructs its own background of noise, in the form of false alarms, which make less likely an alarm when the real thing arrives: the old story of "cry wolf" has a permanent relevance. A totalitarian aggressor can draw a tight curtain of secrecy about his actions and thus muffle the signals of attack. The Western democracies must interpret such signals responsibly and cautiously, for the process of commitment to war, except *in extremis*, is hedged about by the requirements of consultation. The precautions of secrecy, which are necessary even in a democracy to keep open privileged sources of information, may hamper the use of that information or may slow its transmission to those who have the power of decision. Moreover, human attention is directed by beliefs as to what is likely to occur, and one cannot always listen for the right sounds. An all-out thermonuclear attack on a Western power would be an unprecedented event, and some little time (which might be vital) would surely have to pass before that power's allies could understand the nature of the event and take appropriate action.

There is a good deal of evidence, some of it quantitative, that in conditions of great uncertainty people tend to predict that events that they want to happen actually will happen. Wishfulness in conditions of uncertainty is natural and is hard to banish simply by exhortation—or by wishing. Further, the uncertainty of strategic warning is intrinsic, since an enemy decision to attack might be reversed or the direction of the attack changed; and a defensive action can be taken only at some cost. (For example, at Pearl Harbor, flying a 360-degree reconnaissance would have meant sacrificing training, would have interrupted the high-priority shipment program to the Philippines, and would have exhausted crews and worn out equipment within a few weeks.) In general, an extraordinary state of alert that brings about a peak in readiness must be followed by a trough at a later date. In some cases the cost of the defensive actions is hard to estimate and their relevance is uncertain. Therefore the choice of action in response to strategic warning must also be uncertain. Finally, the balance of technical and military factors that might make an attack infeasible at one time can change swiftly and without notice to make it feasible at another. In our day such balances are changing with unprecedented speed.

Pearl Harbor is not an isolated catastrophe. It can be matched by many examples of effective surprise attack. The German attack on Russia in the summer of 1941 was preceded by a flood of signals, the massing of troops, and even direct warnings to Russia by the governments of the United States and the United Kingdom, both of whom had been correctly informed about the imminence of the onslaught. Yet it achieved total surprise.[7] Soviet arguments current today that Stalin and Marshal Zhukov, his Chief of the General Staff, knew and failed to act have obvious parallels with the accusations about President Roosevelt's conspiracy of silence. These Soviet reinterpretations of history aim not only to downgrade Stalin, but also to establish that Soviet leaders were not *really* surprised in 1941, and the Soviet Union can therefore count on adequate warning in any future conflict.[8] But the difficulties of discerning a surprise attack on oneself apply equally to totalitarian and democratic states.

The stunning tactical success of the Japanese attack on the British at Singapore was made possible by the deeply held British faith in the impregnability of that fortress. As Captain Grenfell put it, newspapers and statesmen like their fortresses to be impregnable. "Every fortress," he wrote, "that has come into the news in my lifetime—Port Arthur, Tsing Tao, the great French defensive system of the Maginot Line—has been popularly described as impregnable before it has been attacked. . . . One way or another it became a virtually accepted fact in Britain and the Dominions that Singapore was an impregnable bastion of Imperial security."[9] Yet the defenses of Singapore were rendered useless by military surprise in the form of an attack from an unexpected, northerly direction.

More recently, the Korean War provided some striking examples of surprise. The original North Korean attack was preceded by almost weekly maneuvers probing the border. These regular week-end pene-

---

7. I am grateful to William W. Kaufmann of the MIT Center for International Studies for permission to read his unpublished paper, "Operation Barbarossa," which deals with the background of the German surprise attack [Wohlstetter's note].

8. For a recent Russian view of the Pearl Harbor attack and its lessons on the "launching of aggression by imperialist states," see Maj. Gen. N. Pavlenko,

"Documents on Pearl Harbor," *Voenno-Istoricheskii Zhurnal (Military-Historical Journal)*, No. 1, January, 1961, pp. 85-105. I am indebted for this reference to John Thomas of the Institute of Defense Analysis and to Arnold Horelick, Soviet analyst of The RAND Corporation [Wohlstetter's note].

9. Grenfell, *Main Fleet to Singapore*, p. 64 [Wohlstetter's note].

trations built up so high a level of noise that on June 25, 1950, the actual initiation of hostilities was not distinguished from the preceding tests and false alarms. The intervention of the Chinese, at a later stage of the Korean War, was preceded by mass movements of Chinese troops and explicit warnings by the Chinese government to our own, by way of India, that this was precisely what they would do if we crossed the 38th parallel. Nonetheless, in important respects, we were surprised by the Chinese Communist forces in November, 1950.[10]

How do matters stand with reference to a future thermonuclear aggression by a totalitarian power? Would such an attack be harder or easier to conceal than the Japanese aggression against Pearl Harbor? There have been many attempts in recent years to cheer us with the thought that the H-bomb has so outmoded general war that this question may appear unimportant. However, such attempts to comfort ourselves really beg the question. The question is, Will it be possible in the future for a totalitarian power so to conceal an impending attack on the forces that we have disposed for retaliation as to have a high probability of virtually eliminating them before they receive warning or have time to respond to it? In this connection it is important to observe that there is no cause for complacency. In spite of the vast increase in expenditures for collecting and analyzing intelligence data and in spite of advances in the art of machine decoding and machine translation, the balance of advantage seems clearly to have shifted since Pearl Harbor in favor of a surprise attacker. The benefits to be expected from achieving surprise have increased enormously and the penalties for losing the initiative in an all-out war have grown correspondingly. In fact, since only by an all-out surprise attack could an attacker hope to prevent retaliation, anything less would be suicidal, assuming that some form of attack is contemplated by one major power against another.

In such a surprise attack a major power today would have advantages exceeding those enjoyed by the Japanese in 1941. It is a familiar fact that with the ever-increasing readiness of bomber and missile forces, strategic warning becomes harder and harder to obtain; and with the decrease in the flight time for delivery of massive weapons of destruction, tactical warning times have contracted from weeks to minutes. It is no longer necessary for the aggressor to undertake huge movements of troops and ships in the weeks immediately preceding an all-out war, such as we described in our account of the Japanese war plan. Manned bombers capable of delivering a blow many times more devastating then anything dreamed of by the Japanese might

10. For a succinct and lucid account, see "Strategic Surprise in the Korean War," an unpublished paper by Harvey DeWeerd of The RAND Corporation and the National Security Studies Program, University of California at Los Angeles [Wohlstetter's note].

be on their way from bases deep inside their homeland without yielding any substantial intelligence warning; they might conceivably follow routes that, by avoiding detection or at least identification among the friendly and unknown traffic appearing on radars, would be unlikely to give even any considerable tactical warning. Submarines might be kept on station several hundred miles off our coast during years of peace and might launch ballistic missiles on the receipt of a prearranged signal. Finally, intercontinental ballistic missiles might be kept for years at a high degree of readiness, and, if there were enough of them, they might be launched after simply being "counted down," with no further visible preparation. Total flight time for such rockets between continents might be less than fifteen minutes and radar warning less than that. Most important, such blows, unlike those leveled by the Japanese at Pearl Harbor, might determine the outcome not merely of a battle, but of the war itself. In short, the subject of surprise attack continues to be of vital concern. This fact has been suggested by the great debate among the powers on arms control and on the possibilities of using limitation and inspection arrangements to guard against surprise attack. The very little we have said suggests that such arrangements present formidable difficulties.

This study has not been intended as a "how-to-do-it" manual on intelligence, but perhaps one major practical lesson emerges from it. We cannot *count* on strategic warning. We *might* get it, and we might be able to take useful preparatory actions that would be impossible without it. We certainly ought to plan to exploit such a possibility should it occur. However, since we cannot rely on strategic warning, our defenses, if we are to have confidence in them, must be designed to function without it. If we accept the fact that the signal picture for impending attacks is almost sure to be ambiguous, we shall prearrange actions that are right and feasible in response to ambiguous signals, including signs of an attack that might be false. We must be capable of reacting repeatedly to false alarms without committing ourselves or the enemy to wage thermonuclear war.

It is only human to want some unique and univocal signal, to want a guarantee from intelligence, an unambiguous substitute for a formal declaration of war. This is surely the unconscious motivation of all the rewriting of Pearl Harbor history, which sees in such wavering and uncertain sources of information as the winds code and all of the various and much-argued MAGIC texts a clear statement of Japanese intent. But we have seen how drastically such an interpretation oversimplifies the task of the analyst and decisionmaker. If the study of Pearl Harbor has anything to offer for the future, it is this: We have to accept the fact of uncertainty and learn to live with it. No magic, in code or otherwise, will provide certainty. Our plans must work without it.

STANLEY MILGRAM

A Behavioral Study of Obedience[1]

This article describes a procedure for the study of destructive obedience in the laboratory. It consists of ordering a naive S to administer increasingly more severe punishment to a victim in the context of a learning experiment. Punishment is administered by means of a shock generator with 30 graded switches ranging from Slight Shock to Danger: Severe Shock. The victim is a confederate of the E. The primary dependent variable is the maximum shock the S is willing to administer before he refuses to continue further. 26 Ss obeyed the experimental commands fully, and administered the highest shock on the generator. 14 Ss broke off the experiment at some point after the victim protested and refused to provide further answers. The procedure created extreme levels of nervous tension in some Ss. Profuse sweating, trembling, and stuttering were typical expressions of this emotional disturbance. One unexpected sign of tension— yet to be explained—was the regular occurrence of nervous laughter, which in some Ss developed into uncontrollable seizures. The variety of interesting behavioral dynamics observed in the experiment, the reality of the situation for the S, and the possibility of parametric variation within the framework of the procedure, point to the fruitfulness of further study.[2]

Obedience is as basic an element in the structure of social life as one can point to. Some system of authority is a requirement of all communal living, and it is only the man dwelling in isolation who is not forced to respond, through defiance or submission, to the commands of others. Obedience, as a determinant of behavior is of particular relevance to our time. It has been reliably established that from 1933–1945 millions of innocent persons were systematically slaughtered on command. Gas chambers were built, death camps were guarded, daily quotas of corpses were produced with the same efficiency as the manufacture of appliances. These inhumane policies may have originated in the mind of a single person, but they could only be carried out on a massive scale if a very large number of persons obeyed orders.

Obedience is the psychological mechanism that links individual action to political purpose. It is the dispositional cement that binds

1. This research was supported by a grant (NSF G-17916) from the National Science Foundation. Exploratory studies conducted in 1960 were supported by a grant from the Higgins Fund at Yale University. The research assistance of Alan C. Elms and Jon Wayland is gratefully acknowledged [Milgram's note].

2. This headnote, written by the author, appeared with the article as it was originally published. S means subject; E the experimenter.

men to systems of authority. Facts of recent history and observation in daily life suggest that for many persons obedience may be a deeply ingrained behavior tendency, indeed, a prepotent impulse overriding training in ethics, sympathy, and moral conduct. C. P. Snow (1961) points to its importance when he writes:

> When you think of the long and gloomy history of man, you will find more hideous crimes have been committed in the name of obedience than have ever been committed in the name of rebellion. If you doubt that, read William Shirer's *Rise and Fall of the Third Reich.* The German Officer Corps were brought up in the most rigorous code of obedience . . . in the name of obedience they were party to, and assisted in, the most wicked large-scale actions in the history of the world [p. 24].

While the particular form of obedience dealt with in the present study has its antecedents in these episodes, it must not be thought all obedience entails acts of aggression against others. Obedience serves numerous productive functions. Indeed, the very life of society is predicated on its existence. Obedience may be ennobling and educative and refer to acts of charity and kindness, as well as to destruction.

GENERAL PROCEDURE

A procedure was devised which seems useful as a tool for studying obedience (Milgram, 1961). It consists of ordering a naive subject to administer electric shock to a victim. A simulated shock generator is used, with 30 clearly marked voltage levels that range from 15 to 450 volts. The instrument bears verbal designations that range from Slight Shock to Danger: Severe Shock. The responses of the victim, who is a trained confederate of the experimenter, are standardized. The orders to administer shocks are given to the naive subject in the context of a "learning experiment" ostensibly set up to study the effects of punishment on memory. As the experiment proceeds the naive subject is commanded to administer increasingly more intense shocks to the victim, even to the point of reaching the level marked Danger: Severe Shock. Internal resistances become stronger, and at a certain point the subject refuses to go on with the experiment. Behavior prior to this rupture is considered "obedience," in that the subject complies with the commands of the experimenter. The point of rupture is the act of disobedience. A quantitative value is assigned to the subject's performance based on the maximum intensity shock he is willing to administer before he refuses to participate further. Thus for any particular subject and for any particular experimental condition the degree of obedience may be specified with a numerical value. The crux of the study is to systematically vary the factors believed to alter the degree of obedience to the experimental commands.

The technique allows important variables to be manipulated at several points in the experiment. One may vary aspects of the source

of command, content and form of command, instrumentalities for
its execution, target object, general social setting, etc. The problem,
therefore, is not one of designing increasingly more numerous experimental conditions, but of selecting those that best illuminate the
process of obedience from the socio-psychological standpoint.

RELATED STUDIES

The inquiry bears an important relation to philosophic analyses
of obedience and authority (Arendt, 1958; Friedrich, 1958; Weber,
1947), an early experimental study of obedience by Frank (1944),
studies in "authoritarianism" (Adorno, Frenkel-Brunswik, Levinson,
& Sanford, 1950; Rokeach, 1961), and a recent series of analytic and
empirical studies in social power (Cartwright, 1959). It owes much
to the long concern with *suggestion* in social psychology, both in its
normal forms (*e.g.*, Binet, 1900) and in its clinical manifestations
(Charcot, 1881). But it derives, in the first instance, from direct
observation of a social fact; the individual who is commanded by a
legitimate authority ordinarily obeys. Obedience comes easily and
often. It is a ubiquitous and indispensable feature of social life.

Method
SUBJECTS

The subjects were 40 males between the ages of 20 and 50, drawn
from New Haven and the surrounding communities. Subjects were
obtained by a newspaper advertisement and direct mail solicitation.
Those who responded to the appeal believed they were to participate
in a study of memory and learning at Yale University. A wide range
of occupations is represented in the sample. Typical subjects were
postal clerks, high school teachers, salesmen, engineers, and laborers.
Subjects ranged in educational level from one who had not finished
elementary school, to those who had doctorate and other professional degrees. They were paid $4.50 for their participation in the
experiment. However, subjects were told that payment was simply
for coming to the laboratory, and that the money was theirs no matter what happened after they arrived. Table 1 shows the proportion
of age and occupational types assigned to the experimental
condition.

TABLE 1
DISTRIBUTION OF AGE AND OCCUPATIONAL TYPES IN THE EXPERIMENT

Occupations	20-29 years n	30-39 years n	40-50 years n	Percentage of total (Occupa-tions)
Workers, skilled and unskilled	4	5	6	37.5
Sales, business, and white-collar	3	6	7	40.0
Professional	1	5	3	22.5
Percentage of total (age)	20	40	40	

Note. Total $N = 40$.

The experiment was conducted on the grounds of Yale University in the elegant interaction laboratory. (This detail is relevant to the perceived legitimacy of the experiment. In further variations, the experiment was dissociated from the university, with consequences for performances.) The role of experimenter was played by a 31-year-old high school teacher of biology. His manner was impassive, and his appearance somewhat stern throughout the experiment. He was dressed in a gray technician's coat. The victim was played by a 47-year-old accountant, trained for the role; he was of Irish-American stock, whom most observers found mild-mannered and likable.

PROCEDURE

One naive subject and one victim (an accomplice) performed in each experiment. A pretext had to be devised that would justify the administration of electric shock by the naive subject. This was effectively accomplished by the cover story. After a general introduction on the presumed relation between punishment and learning, subjects were told:

But actually, we know *very little* about the effect of punishment on learning, because almost no truly scientific studies have been made of it in human beings.

For instance, we don't know how *much* punishment is best for learning —and we don't know how much difference it makes as to who is giving the punishment, whether an adult learns best from a younger or an older person than himself—or many things of that sort.

So in this study we are bringing together a number of adults of different occupations and ages. And we're asking some of them to be teachers and some of them to be learners.

We want to find out just what effect different people have on each other as teachers and learners, and also what effect *punishment* will have on learning in this situation.

Therefore, I'm going to ask one of you to be the teacher here tonight and the other one to be the learner.

Does either of you have a preference?

Subjects then drew slips of paper from a hat to determine who would be the teacher and who would be the learner in the experiment. The drawing was rigged so that the naive subject was always the teacher and the accomplice always the learner. (Both slips contained the word "Teacher.") Immediately after the drawing, the teacher and learner were taken to an adjacent room and the learner was strapped into an "electric chair" apparatus.

The experimenter explained that the straps were to prevent excessive movement while the learner was being shocked. The effect was to make it impossible for him to escape from the situation. An electrode was attached to the learner's wrist, and electrode paste was applied "to avoid blisters and burns." Subjects were told that the electrode was attached to the shock generator in the adjoining room.

In order to improve credibility the experimenter declared, in response to a question by the learner: "Although the shocks can be extremely painful, they cause no permanent tissue damage."

Learning task. The lesson administered by the subject was a paired-associate learning task. The subject read a series of word pairs to the learner, and then read the first word of the pair along with four terms. The learner was to indicate which of the four terms had originally been paired with the first word. He communicated his answer by pressing one of four switches in front of him, which in turn lit up one of four numbered quadrants in an answer-box located atop the shock generator.

Shock generator. The instrument panel consists of 30 lever switches set in a horizontal line. Each switch is clearly labeled with a voltage designation that ranges from 15 to 450 volts. There is a 15-volt increment from one switch to the next going from left to right. In addition, the following verbal designations are clearly indicated for groups of four switches going from left to right: Slight Shock, Moderate Shock, Strong Shock, Very Strong Shock, Intense Shock, Extreme Intensity Shock, Danger: Severe Shock. (Two switches after this last designation are simply marked XXX.)

Upon depressing a switch: a pilot light corresponding to each switch is illuminated in bright red; an electric buzzing is heard; an electric blue light, labeled "voltage energizer," flashes; the dial on the voltage meter swings to the right; various relay clicks are sounded.

The upper left-hand corner of the generator is labeled Shock Generator, Type ZLB, Dyson Instrument Company, Waltham, Mass. Output 15 Volts-450 Volts.

Details of the instrument were carefully handled to insure an appearance of authenticity. The panel was engraved by precision industrial engravers, and all components were of high quality. No subject in the experiment suspected that the instrument was merely a simulated shock generator.[3]

Sample shock. Each naive subject is given a sample shock on the shock generator, prior to beginning his run as teacher. This shock is always 45 volts, and is applied by pressing the third switch of the generator. The shock is applied to the wrist of the naive subject, and

3. A related technique, making use of a shock generator, was reported by Buss (1961) for the study of aggression in the laboratory. Despite the considerable similarity of technical detail in the experimental procedures, both investigators proceeded in ignorance of the other's work. Milgram provided plans and photographs of his shock generator, experimental procedure, and first results in a report to the National Science Founda-

tion in January, 1961. This report received only limited circulation. Buss reported his procedure 6 months later, but to a wider audience. Subsequently, technical information and reports were exchanged. The present article was first received in the Editor's office on December 27, 1961; it was resubmitted with deletions on July 27, 1962 [Milgram's note].

has its source in a 45-volt battery wired into the generator. This further convinces the subject of the authenticity of the generator.

Shock instructions. The subject is told to administer a shock to the learner each time he gives a wrong response. Moreover—and this is the key command—the subject is instructed to "move one level higher on the shock generator each time the learner flashes a wrong answer." He is also instructed to announce the voltage level before administering a shock. This serves to continually remind subjects of the increasing intensity of shocks administered to the learner.

Preliminary and regular run. Pretests revealed that the procedure of reading words and administering shocks requires some practice before it can be handled smoothly. Therefore, immediately preceding the regular run, the teacher is given a preliminary series of 10 words to read to the learner. There are 3 neutral words in the practice series (*i.e.*, words that the learner answers correctly), so that shocks are administered for 7 of the words, with the maximum shock at 105 volts (moderate shock). Almost all subjects master the procedure by the time the preliminary run is over.

Subjects are then presented with a second list, and are told that the procedure is the same as for the first list; the experimenter adds, however:

When you get to the bottom of the list, repeat it over again, and continue giving shocks, until the learner has learned all the pairs correctly.

The experimenter instructs the subject to,

start from 15 volts and increase the shock level one step each time the learner gives a wrong answer.

Feedback from the victim. In all conditions the learner gives a predetermined set of responses to the word pair test, based on a schedule of approximately three wrong answers to one correct answer. In the present experimental condition no vocal response or other sign of protest is heard from the learner until Shock Level 300 is reached. When the 300-volt shock is administered, the learner pounds on the wall of the room in which he is bound to the electric chair. The pounding can be heard by the subject. From this point on, the learner's answers no longer appear on the four-way panel.

At this juncture, subjects ordinarily turn to the experimenter for guidance. The experimenter instructs the subject to treat the absence of a response as a wrong answer, and to shock the subject according to the usual schedule. He advises the subjects to allow 5–10 seconds before considering no response as a wrong answer, and to increase the shock level one step each time the learner fails to respond correctly. The learner's pounding is repeated after the 315-volt shock is administered; afterwards he is not heard from, nor do his answers reappear on the four-way signal box.

Experimenter feedback. At various points in the experiment the subject may turn to the experimenter for advice on whether he should continue to administer shocks. Or he may indicate that he does not wish to go on. It was important to standardize the experimenter's responses to these inquiries and reactions.

If the subject indicated his unwillingness to go on, the experimenter responded with a sequence of "prods," using as many as necessary to bring the subject into line.

Prod 1: Please continue, *or* Please go on.
Prod 2: The experiment requires that you continue.
Prod 3: It is absolutely essential that you continue.
Prod 4: You have no other choice, you *must* go on.

The prods were always made in sequence: Only if Prod 1 had been unsuccessful, could Prod 2 be used. If the subject refused to obey the experimenter after Prod 4, the experiment was terminated. The experimenter's tone of voice was at all times firm, but not impolite. The sequence was begun anew on each occasion that the subject balked or showed reluctance to follow orders.

Special prods. If the subject asked if the learner was liable to suffer permanent physical injury, the experimenter said:

Although the shocks may be painful, there is no permanent tissue damage, so please go on. [Followed by Prods 2, 3, and 4 if necessary.]

If the subject said that the learner did not want to go on, the experimenter replied:

Whether the learner likes it or not, you must go on until he has learned all the word pairs correctly. So please go on. [Followed by Prods 2, 3, and 4 if necessary.]

DEPENDENT MEASURES

The primary dependent measure for any subject is the maximum shock he administers before he refuses to go any further. In principle this may vary from 0 (for a subject who refuses to administer even the first shock) to 30 (for a subject who administers the highest shock on the generator). A subject who breaks off the experiment at any point prior to administering the thirtieth shock level is termed a *defiant subject*. One who complies with experimental commands fully, and proceeds to administer all shock levels commanded, is termed an *obedient* subject.

Further records. With few exceptions, experimental sessions were recorded on magnetic tape. Occasional photographs were taken through one-way mirrors. Notes were kept on any unusual behavior occurring during the course of the experiments. On occasion, additional observers were directed to write objective descriptions of the subjects' behavior. The latency and duration of shocks were measured by accurate timing devices.

Interview and dehoax. Following the experiment, subjects were interviewed; open-ended questions, projective measures, and attitude scales were employed. After the interview, procedures were undertaken to assure that the subject would leave the laboratory in a state of well being. A friendly reconciliation was arranged between the subject and the victim, and an effort was made to reduce any tensions that arose as a result of the experiment.

Results

PRELIMINARY NOTIONS

Before giving an account of the experimental results, it is instructive to consider how persons predict others will perform when commanded to administer powerful shocks to another person. Fourteen Yale seniors, all psychology majors, were provided with a detailed description of the experimental situation. They were asked to reflect carefully on it, and to predict the behavior of 100 hypothetical subjects. More specifically, they were instructed to plot the distribution of obedience of "100 Americans of diverse occupations, and ranging in age from 20 to 50 years," who were placed in the experimental situation.

There was considerable agreement among the respondents on the expected behavior of hypothetical subjects. All respondents predicted that only an insignificant minority would go through to the end of the shock series. (The estimates ranged from 0 to 3%; *i.e.*, the most "pessimistic" member of the class predicted that of 100 persons, 3 would continue through to the most potent shock available on the shock generator—450 volts.) The class mean was 1.2%. The question was also posed informally to colleagues of the author, and the most general feeling was that few if any subjects would go beyond the designation Very Strong Shock.

RESULT OF EXPERIMENT I

Subjects accept situation. With few exceptions subjects were convinced of the reality of the experimental situation, that they were administering shocks to another person, and the most potent shocks were extremely painful. In the post-experimental interview subjects were asked: "How painful to the learner were the last few shocks that you administered to him?" Subjects were instructed to indicate their answers on a printed 14-point scale ranging from "Not at all painful" to "Extremely painful." The modal[4] response was 14 (Extremely painful), with the mean at 13.42.

Signs of extreme tension. Many subjects showed signs of nervousness in the experimental situation, and especially upon administering the more powerful shocks. In a large number of cases the degree of tension reached extremes that are rarely seen in sociopsychological laboratory studies. Subjects were observed to sweat, tremble, stutter,

4. Most frequent.

bite their lips, groan, and dig their fingernails into their flesh. These were characteristic rather than exceptional responses to the experiment.

One sign of tension was the regular occurrence of nervous laughing fits. Fourteen of the 40 subjects showed definite signs of nervous laughter and smiling. The laughter seemed entirely out of place, even bizarre. Full-blown, uncontrollable seizures were observed for 3 subjects. On one occasion we observed a seizure so violently convulsive that it was necessary to call a halt to the experiment. The subject, a 46-year-old encyclopedia salesman, was seriously embarrassed by his untoward and uncontrollable behavior. In the post-experimental interviews subjects took pains to point out that they were not sadistic types, and that the laughter did not mean they enjoyed shocking the victim.

Distribution of scores. It had been conjectured that persons would not, in general, agree to administer shocks beyond the level designated as Very Strong Shock. The distribution of maximum shocks for this experiment is shown in Table 2. The obtained distribution of scores deviates radically from the prediction.

Upon command of the experimenter, each of the 40 subjects went beyond the expected breakoff point. No subject stopped prior to administering Shock Level 20. (At this level—300 volts—the victim kicks on the wall and no longer provides answers to the teacher's multiple-choice questions.)

Of the 40 subjects, 5 refused to obey the experimental commands beyond the 300-volt level. Four more subjects administered one further shock, and then refused to go on. Two broke off at the 330-volt level, and 1 each at 345, 360, and 375 volts. Thus a total of 14 subjects defied the experimenter. It is instructive to reprint their remarks at the point of defiance, as transcribed from the tape recordings:

[0124] I think he's trying to communicate, he's knocking.... Well it's not fair to shock the guy ... these are terrific volts. I don't think this is very humane.... Oh, I can't go on with this; no, this isn't right. It's a hell of an experiment. The guy is suffering in there. No, I don't want to go on. This is crazy. [Subject refused to administer more shocks.]

[0123] He's banging in there. I'm gonna chicken out. I'd like to continue, but I can't do that to a man.... I'm sorry I can't do that to a man. I'll hurt his heart. You take your check.... No really, I couldn't do it.

These subjects were frequently in a highly agitated and even angered state. Sometimes, verbal protest was at a minimum, and the subject simply got up from his chair in front of the shock generator, and indicated that he wished to leave the laboratory.

Of the 40 subjects, 26 obeyed the orders of the experimenter to the end, proceeding to punish the victim until they reached the most potent shock available on the shock generator. At that point,

TABLE 2
DISTRIBUTION OF BREAKOFF POINTS

Verbal designation and voltage indication	Number of subjects for whom this was maximum shock
Slight Shock	
15	0
30	0
45	0
60	0
Moderate Shock	
75	0
90	0
105	0
120	0
Strong Shock	
135	0
150	0
165	0
180	0
Very Strong Shock	
195	0
210	0
225	0
240	0
Intense Shock	
255	0
270	0
285	0
300	5
Extreme Intensity Shock	
315	4
330	2
345	1
360	1
Danger: Severe Shock	
375	1
390	0
405	0
420	0
XXX	
435	0
450	26

the experimenter called a halt to the session. (The maximum shock is labeled 450 volts, and is two steps beyond the designation: Danger: Severe Shock.) Although obedient subjects continued to administer shocks, they often did so under extreme stress. Some expressed reluctance to administer shocks beyond the 300-volt level, and displayed fears similar to those who defied the experimenter; yet they obeyed.

After the maximum shocks had been delivered, and the experimenter called a halt to the proceedings, many obedient subjects heaved sighs of relief, mopped their brows, rubbed their fingers over their eyes, or nervously fumbled cigarettes. Some shook their heads, apparently in regret. Some subjects had remained calm throughout the experiment, and displayed only minimal signs of tension from beginning to end.

Discussion

The experiment yielded two findings that were surprising. The first finding concerns the sheer strength of obedient tendencies manifested in this situation. Subjects have learned from childhood that it is a fundamental breach of moral conduct to hurt another person against his will. Yet, 26 subjects abandon this tenet in following the instructions of an authority who has no special powers to enforce his commands. To disobey would bring no material loss to the subject; no punishment would ensue. It is clear from the remarks and outward behavior of many participants that in punishing the victim they are often acting against their own values. Subjects often expressed deep disapproval of shocking a man in the face of his objections, and others denounced it as stupid and senseless. Yet the majority complied with the experimental commands. This outcome was surprising from two perspectives: first, from the standpoint of predictions made in the questionnaire described earlier. (Here, however, it is possible that the remoteness of the respondents from the actual situation, and the difficulty of conveying to them the concrete details of the experiment, could account for the serious underestimation of obedience.)

But the results were also unexpected to persons who observed the experiment in progress, through one-way mirrors. Observers often uttered expressions of disbelief upon seeing a subject administer more powerful shocks to the victim. These persons had a full acquaintance with the details of the situation, and yet systematically underestimated the amount of obedience that subjects would display.

The second unanticipated effect was the extraordinary tension generated by the procedures. One might suppose that a subject would simply break off or continue as his conscience dictated. Yet, this is very far from what happened. There were striking reactions of tension and emotional strain. One observer related:

I observed a mature and initially poised businessman enter the laboratory smiling and confident. Within 20 minutes he was reduced to a twitching, stuttering wreck, who was rapidly approaching a point of nervous collapse. He constantly pulled on his earlobe, and twisted his hands. At one point he pushed his fist into his forehead and muttered: "Oh God, let's stop it." And yet he continued to respond to every word of the experimenter, and obeyed to the end.

Any understanding of the phenomenon of obedience must rest on an analysis of the particular conditions in which it occurs. The following features of the experiment go some distance in explaining the high amount of obedience observed in the situation.

1. The experiment is sponsored by and takes place on the grounds of an institution of unimpeachable reputation, Yale University. It may be reasonably presumed that the personnel are competent and reputable. The importance of this background authority is now being studied by conducting a series of experiments outside of New Haven, and without any visible ties to the university.

2. The experiment is, on the face of it, designed to attain a worthy purpose—advancement of knowledge about learning and memory. Obedience occurs not as an end in itself, but as an instrumental element in a situation that the subject construes as significant, and meaningful. He may not be able to see its full significance, but he may properly assume that the experimenter does.

3. The subject perceives that the victim has voluntarily submitted to the authority system of the experimenter. He is not (at first) an unwilling captive impressed for involuntary service. He has taken the trouble to come to the laboratory presumably to aid the experimental research. That he later becomes an involuntary subject does not alter the fact that, initially, he consented to participate without qualification. Thus he has in some degree incurred an obligation toward the experimenter.

4. The subject, too, has entered the experiment voluntarily, and perceives himself under obligation to aid the experimenter. He has made a commitment, and to disrupt the experiment is a repudiation of this initial promise of aid.

5. Certain features of the procedure strengthen the subject's sense of obligation to the experimenter. For one, he has been paid for coming to the laboratory. In part this is canceled out by the experimenter's statement that:

Of course, as in all experiments, the money is yours simply for coming to the laboratory. From this point on, no matter what happens, the money is yours.[5]

6. From the subject's standpoint, the fact that he is the teacher and the other man the learner is purely a chance consequence (it is determined by drawing lots) and he, the subject, ran the same risk as the other man in being assigned the role of learner. Since the assignment of positions in the experiment was achieved by fair means, the learner is deprived of any basis of complaint on this count. (A similar situation obtains in Army units, in which—in the

---

5. Forty-three subjects, undergraduates at Yale University, were run in the experiment without payment. The results are very similar to those obtained with paid subjects [Milgram's note].

absence of volunteers—a particularly dangerous mission may be assigned by drawing lots, and the unlucky soldier is expected to bear his misfortune with sportsmanship.)

7. There is, at best, ambiguity with regard to the prerogatives of a psychologist and the corresponding rights of his subject. There is a vagueness of expectation concerning what a psychologist may require of his subject, and when he is overstepping acceptable limits. Moreover, the experiment occurs in a closed setting, and thus provides no opportunity for the subject to remove these ambiguities by discussion with others. There are few standards that seem directly applicable to the situation, which is a novel one for most subjects.

8. The subjects are assured that the shocks administered to the subject are "painful but not dangerous." Thus they assume that the discomfort caused the victim is momentary, while the scientific gains resulting from the experiment are enduring.

9. Through Shock Level 20 the victim continues to provide answers on the signal box. The subject may construe this as a sign that the victim is still willing to "play the game." It is only after Shock Level 20 that the victim repudiates the rules completely, refusing to answer further.

These features help to explain the high amount of obedience obtained in this experiment. Many of the arguments raised need not remain matters of speculation, but can be reduced to testable propositions to be confirmed or disproved by further experiments.[6]

The following features of the experiment concern the nature of the conflict which the subject faces.

10. The subject is placed in a position in which he must respond to the competing demands of two persons: the experimenter and the victim. The conflict must be resolved by meeting the demands of one or the other; satisfaction of the victim and the experimenter are mutually exclusive. Moreover, the resolution must take the form of a highly visible action, that of continuing to shock the victim or breaking off the experiment. Thus the subject is forced into a public conflict that does not permit any completely satisfactory solution.

11. While the demands of the experimenter carry the weight of scientific authority, the demands of the victim spring from his personal experience of pain and suffering. The two claims need not be regarded as equally pressing and legitimate. The experimenter seeks an abstract scientific datum; the victim cries out for relief from physical suffering caused by the subject's actions.

12. The experiment gives the subject little time for reflection. The conflict comes on rapidly. It is only minutes after the subject has been seated before the shock generator that the victim begins his protests. Moreover, the subject perceives that he has gone through

6. A series of recently completed experiments employing the obedience paradigm is reported in Milgram (1964) [Milgram's note].

A Behavioral Study of Obedience · 303

but two-thirds of the shock levels at the time the subject's first protests are heard. Thus he understands that the conflict will have a persistent aspect to it, and may well become more intense as increasingly more powerful shocks are required. The rapidity with which the conflict descends on the subject, and his realization that it is predictably recurrent may well be sources of tension to him.

13. At a more general level, the conflict stems from the opposition of two deeply ingrained behavior dispositions: first, the disposition not to harm other people, and second, the tendency to obey those whom we perceive to be legitimate authorities.

References

Adorno, T., Else Frenkel-Brunswik, D. J. Levinson, and R. N. Sanford, *The Authoritarian Personality*. New York: Harper & Row, 1950.

Arendt, H., "What Was Authority?" In C. J. Friedrich (ed.), *Authority*. Cambridge, Mass.: Harvard University Press, 1958. Pp. 81–112.

Binet, S., *La suggestibilité*. Paris: Schleicher, 1900.

Buss, A. H., *The Psychology of Aggression*. New York: Wiley, 1961.

Cartwright, S. (ed.), *Studies in Social Power*. Ann Arbor: University of Michigan Institute for Social Research, 1959.

Chacot, J. M., *Oeuvres complètes*. Paris: Bureaux du Progrès Médical, 1881.

Frank, J. D., "Experimental Studies of Personal Pressure and Resistance." *Journal of General Psychology*, 30 (1944), 23–64.

Friedrich, C. J. (ed.), *Authority*. Cambridge, Mass.: Harvard University Press, 1958.

Milgram, S., *Dynamics of Obedience*. Washington, D.C.: National Science Foundation, January 25, 1961. (Mimeographed.)

Milgram, S., "Some Conditions of Obedience and Disobedience to Authority." *Human Relations* (1964).

Rokeach, M., "Authority, Authoritarianism, and Conformity." In I. A. Berg and B. M. Bass (eds.), *Conformity and Deviation*. New York: Harper & Row, 1961. Pp. 230–257.

Snow, C. P., "Either-or." *The Progressive*, 24 (Feburary 1961).

Weber, M., *The Theory of Social and Economic Organization*. Oxford, Eng.: Oxford University Press, 1947.

QUESTIONS FOR STUDY, DISCUSSION, AND WRITING

1. The opening paragraph states that "from 1933–1945 millions of innocent persons were systematically slaughtered on command." Does this study help to explain how that could have happened? What is the purpose of the study? What do you learn from it?
2. Does this experiment involve an actual shock to anybody?
3. What explanation is offered for the subjects' continuing the experiment even when they believed that they were inflicting intense physical pain upon the "learner"? What explains the experimenters' continuing the experiment even when they knew that they were inflicting evident psychological pain upon the subjects? How many subjects refused to complete the experiment? How many times did the experimenters find it necessary to stop the experiment?
4. Milgram points out (p. 302) that "There is, at best, ambiguity

with regard to the prerogatives of a psychologist and the corresponding rights of his subject. There is a vagueness of expectation concerning what a psychologist may require of his subject, and when he is overstepping acceptable limits." Does this study appear to bear out that observation?

5. "The orders to administer shocks are given to the naive subject in the context of a 'learning experiment' ostensibly set up to study the effects of punishment on memory" (p. 291). This sentence is in the passive voice; recast it in the active. How frequent is the passive voice in this piece of writing? Does the passive voice indicate scientific precision? Or objectivity? Or what?

6. What is a prod? A dehoax? (See pp. 296–297.) How do these terms help define the role of the experimental scientist in this study?

WILLIAM JAMES

The Ethical and Pedagogical Importance
of the Principle of Habit[1]

"Habit a second nature! Habit is ten times nature," the Duke of Wellington is said to have exclaimed; and the degree to which this is true no one probably can appreciate as well as one who is a veteran soldier himself. The daily drill and the years of discipline end by fashioning a man completely over again, as to most of the possibilities of his conduct.

"There is a story," says Prof. Huxley, "which is credible enough, though it may not be true, of a practical joker who, seeing a discharged veteran carrying home his dinner, suddenly called out, 'Attention!' whereupon the man instantly brought his hands down, and lost his mutton and potatoes in the gutter. The drill had been thorough, and its effects had become embodied in the man's nervous structure."

Riderless cavalry-horses, at many a battle, have been seen to come together and go through their customary evolutions at the sound of the bugle-call. Most domestic beasts seem machines almost pure and simple, undoubtingly, unhesitatingly doing from minute to minute the duties they have been taught, and giving no sign that the possibility of an alternative ever suggests itself to their mind. Men grown old in prison have asked to be readmitted after being once set free. In a railroad accident a menagerie-tiger, whose cage had broken open, is said to have emerged, but presently crept back again, as if too much bewildered by his new responsibilities, so that he was without difficulty secured.

Habit is thus the enormous fly-wheel of society, its most precious

1. From "Habit," Chapter 10 of *The Principles of Psychology*.

conservative agent. It alone is what keeps us all within the bounds of ordinance, and saves the children of fortune from the envious uprisings of the poor. It alone prevents the hardest and most repulsive walks of life from being deserted by those brought up to tread therein. It keeps the fisherman and the deck-hand at sea through the winter; it holds the miner in his darkness, and nails the countryman to his log-cabin and his lonely farm through all the months of snow; it protects us from invasion by the natives of the desert and the frozen zone. It dooms us all to fight out the battle of life upon the lines of our nurture or our early choice, and to make the best of a pursuit that disagrees, because there is no other for which we are fitted, and it is too late to begin again. It keeps different social strata from mixing. Already at the age of twenty-five you see the professional mannerism settling down on the young commercial traveler, on the young doctor, on the young minister, on the young counselor-at-law. You see the little lines of cleavage running through the character, the tricks of thought, the prejudices, the ways of the "shop," in a word, from which the man can by-and-by no more escape than his coat-sleeve can suddenly fall into a new set of folds. On the whole, it is best he should not escape. It is well for the world that in most of us, by the age of thirty, the character has set like plaster, and will never soften again.

If the period between twenty and thirty is the critical one in the formation of intellectual and professional habits, the period below twenty is more important still for the fixings of *personal* habits, properly so called, such as a vocalization and pronunciation, gesture, motion, and address. Hardly ever is a language learned after twenty spoken without a foreign accent; hardly ever can a youth transferred to the society of his betters unlearn the nasality and other vices of speech bred in him by the associations of his growing years. Hardly ever, indeed, no matter how much money there be in his pocket, can he even learn to *dress* like a gentleman-born. The merchants offer their wares as eagerly to him as to the veriest "swell," but he simply *cannot* buy the right things. An invisible law, as strong as gravitation, keeps him within his orbit, arrayed this year as he was the last; and how his better-clad acquaintances contrive to get the things they wear will be for him a mystery till his dying day.

The great thing, then, in all education, is to *make our nervous system our ally instead of our enemy*. It is to fund and capitalize our acquisitions, and live at ease upon the interest of the fund. *For this we must make automatic and habitual, as early as possible, as many useful actions as we can*, and guard against the growing into ways that are likely to be disadvantageous to us, as we should guard against the plague. The more of the details of our daily life we can hand over to the effortless custody of automatism, the more our higher powers of mind will be set free for their own proper work. There is no more miserable human being than one in whom nothing is habitual but indecision, and for whom the lighting of every cigar, the drinking of every cup, the time of rising and going to bed every day, and the beginning of every bit of work, are subjects of express volitional deliberation. Full half the time of such a man goes to the deciding, or regretting, of matters which ought to be so ingrained in him as practically not to exist for his consciousness at all. If there be such daily duties not yet ingrained in any one of my readers, let him begin this very hour to set the matter right.

In Professor Bain's chapter on "The Moral Habits" there are some admirable practical remarks laid down. Two great maxims emerge from his treatment. The first is that in the acquisition of a new habit, or the leaving off of an old one, we must take care to *launch ourselves with as strong and decided an initiative as possible*. Accumulate all the possible circumstances which shall re-enforce the right motives; put yourself assiduously in conditions that encourage the new way; make engagements incompatible with the old; take a public pledge, if the case allows; in short, envelop your resolution with every aid you know. This will give your new beginning such a momentum that the temptation to break down will not occur as soon as it otherwise might; and every day during which a breakdown is postponed adds to the chances of its not occurring at all.

The second maxim is: *Never suffer an exception to occur till the new habit is securely rooted in your life.* Each lapse is like the letting fall of a ball of string which one is carefully winding up; a single slip undoes more than a great many turns will wind again. *Continuity* of training is the great means of making the nervous system act infallibly right. As Professor Bain says:

"The peculiarity of the moral habits, contradistinguishing them from the intellectual acquisitions, is the presence of two hostile powers, one to be gradually raised into the ascendant over the other. It is necessary, above all things, in such a situation, never to lose a battle. Every gain on the wrong side undoes the effect of many conquests on the right. The essential precaution, therefore, is so to regulate the two opposing powers that the one may have a series of uninterrupted successes, until repetition has fortified it to such a degree as to enable it to cope with the opposition, under any circumstances. This is the theoretically best career of mental progress."

The need of securing success at the *outset* is imperative. Failure at first is apt to damp the energy of all future attempts, whereas past experiences of success nerve one to future vigor. Goethe says to a man who consulted him about an enterprise but mistrusted his own powers: "Ach! you need only blow on your hands!" And the remark illustrates the effect on Goethe's spirits of his own habitually successful career.

The question of "tapering off," in abandoning such habits as drink and opium-indulgence comes in here, and is a question about which experts differ within certain limits, and in regard to what may be best for an individual case. In the main, however, all expert opinion would agree that abrupt acquisition of the new habit is the best way, *if there be a real possibility of carrying it out.* We must be careful not to give the will so stiff a task as to insure its defeat at the very outset; but, *provided one can stand it,* a sharp period of suffering, and then a free time, is the best thing to aim at, whether in giving up a habit like that of opium, or in simply changing one's hours of rising or of work. It is surprising how soon a desire will die of inanition if it be *never* fed.

One must first learn, unmoved, looking neither to the right nor left, to walk firmly on the strait and narrow path, before one can begin "to make one's self over again." He who every day makes a fresh resolve is like one who, arriving at the edge of the ditch he is to leap, forever stops and returns for a fresh run. Without *unbroken* advance there is no such thing as *accumulation* of the ethical forces possible, and to make this possible, and to exercise us and habituate us in it, is the sovereign blessing of regular work.[2]

A third maxim may be added to the preceding pair: *Seize the very first possible opportunity to act on every resolution you make, and on every emotional prompting you may experience in the direction of the habits you aspire to gain.* It is not in the moment of their forming, but in the moment of their producing *motor effects,* that resolves and aspirations communicate the new "set" to the brain. As the author last quoted remarks:

The actual presence of the practical opportunity alone furnishes the fulcrum upon which the lever can rest, by means of which the moral will may multiply its strength, and raise itself aloft. He who has no solid ground to press against will never get beyond the stage of empty gesture-making.

No matter how full a reservoir of *maxims* one may possess, and no matter how good one's *sentiments* may be, if one have not taken advantage of every concrete opportunity to *act,* one's character may remain entirely unaffected for the better. With mere good intentions, hell is proverbially paved. And this is an obvious consequence of the principles we have laid down. A "character," as J. S. Mill says, "is a completely fashioned will"; and a will, in the sense in which he means it, is an aggregate of tendencies to act in a firm and prompt and definite way upon all the principal emergencies of life. A tendency to act only becomes effectively ingrained in

2. J. Bahnsen: "Beitäge zu Charakterologie" (1867), vol. I, p. 209 [James' note].

us in proportion to the uninterrupted frequency with which the actions actually occur, and the brain "grows" to their use. When a resolve or a fine glow of feeling is allowed to evaporate without bearing practical fruit it is worse than a chance lost; it works so as positively to hinder future resolutions and emotions from taking the normal path of discharge. There is no more contemptible type of human character than that of the nerveless sentimentalist and dreamer, who spends his life in a weltering sea of sensibility and emotion, but who never does a manly concrete deed. Rousseau, inflaming all the mothers of France, by his eloquence, to follow Nature and nurse their babies themselves, while he sends his own children to the foundling hospital, is the classical example of what I mean. But every one of us in his measure, whenever, after glowing for an abstractly formulated Good, he practically ignores some actual case, among the squalid "other particulars" of which that same Good lurks disguised, treads straight on Rousseau's path. All Goods are disguised by the vulgarity of their concomitants, in this work-a-day world; but woe to him who can only recognize them when he thinks them in their pure and abstract form! The habit of excessive novel-reading and theater-going will produce true monsters in this line. The weeping of the Russian lady over the fictitious personages in the play, while her coachman is freezing to death on his seat outside, is the sort of thing that everywhere happens on a less glaring scale. Even the habit of excessive indulgence in music, for those who are neither performers themselves nor musically gifted enough to take it in a purely intellectual way, has probably a relaxing effect upon the character. One becomes filled with emotions which habitually pass without prompting to any deed, and so the inertly sentimental condition is kept up. The remedy would be, never to suffer one's self to have an emotion at a concert, without expressing it afterward in *some* active way. Let the expression be the least thing in the world—speaking genially to one's grandmother, or giving up one's seat in a horse-car, if nothing more heroic offers—but let it not fail to take place.

These latter cases make us aware that it is not simply *particular lines* of discharge, but also *general forms* of discharge, that seem to be grooved out by habit in the brain. Just as, if we let our emotions evaporate, they get into a way of evaporating; so there is reason to suppose that if we often flinch from making an effort, before we know it the effort-making capacity will be gone; and that, if we suffer the wandering of our attention, presently it will wander all the time. Attention and effort are, as we shall see later, but two names for the same psychic fact. To what brain-processes they correspond we do not know. The strongest reason for believing that they do depend on brain-processes at all, and are not pure acts of the spirit, is just this fact, that they seem in some degree subject to the law of habit, which is a material law. As a final practical maxim, relative to these habits of the will, we may, then, offer something like this: *Keep the faculty of effort alive in you by a little gratuitous exercise every day.* That is, be systematically ascetic or heroic in little unnecessary points, do every day or two something for no other reason than that you would rather not do it, so that when the hour of dire need draws nigh, it may find you not unnerved and untrained to stand the test. Ascetism of this sort is like the insurance which a man pays on his house and goods. The tax does him no good at the time, and possibly may never bring him a return. But if the fire *does* come, his having paid it will be his salvation from ruin. So with the man who has daily inured himself to habits of concentrated attention, energetic volition, and self-denial in unnecessary things. He will stand like a tower when everything rocks around him, and when his softer fellow-mortals are winnowed like chaff in the blast.

The physiological study of mental conditions is thus the most powerful ally of hortatory ethics. The hell to be endured hereafter, of which theology tells, is no worse than the hell we make for ourselves in this world by habitually fashioning our characters in the wrong way. Could the young but realize how soon they will become mere walking bundles of habits, they would give more heed to their conduct while in the plastic state. We are spinning our own fates, good or evil, and never to be undone. Every smallest stroke of virtue or of vice leaves its never so little scar. The drunken Rip Van Winkle, in Jefferson's play, excuses himself for every fresh dereliction by saying, "I won't count this time!" Well! he may not count it, and a kind Heaven may not count it; but it is being counted none the less. Down among his nerve cells and fibres the molecules are counting it, registering and storing it up to be used against him when the next temptation comes. Nothing we ever do is, in strict scientific literalness, wiped out. Of course this has its good side as well as its bad one. As we become permanent drunkards by so many separate drinks, so we become saints in the moral, and authorities and experts in the practical and scientific spheres, by so many separate acts and hours of work. Let no youth have any anxiety about the upshot of his education, whatever the line of it may be. If he keep faithfully busy each hour of the working day, he may safely leave the final result to itself. He can with perfect certainty count on waking up some fine morning, to find himself one of the competent ones of his generation, in whatever pursuit he may have singled out. Silently, between all the details of his business, the *power of judging* in all that class of matter will have built itself up within him as a possession that will never pass away. Young people should know this truth in advance. The ignorance of it has probably engendered more discouragement and faint-heartedness in youths embarking on arduous careers than all other causes put together.

QUESTIONS FOR STUDY, DISCUSSION, AND WRITING

1. What, according to James, is the utility of habit for society? For the individual person?
2. Will conformity result from cultivating habits according to the maxims here presented?
3. James and Milgram ("A Behavioral Study of Obedience," pp. 290–303) are both psychologists. Do they appear to be working in similar ways? If dissimilar, how do you explain the difference? Is one more scientific than the other? How do the two pieces of writing compare as to subject, method of presentation, assumptions, purpose, style?
4. Compare this essay by James with his letter to his daughter (pp. 631–633). What similarities and what differences are there in content, treatment, tone? Explain these.

THOMAS DE QUINCEY
The Palimpsest of the Human Brain

You know perhaps, masculine reader, better than I can tell you, what is a *Palimpsest*. Possibly you have one in your own library. But yet, for the sake of others who may *not* know, or may have forgotten, suffer me to explain it here, lest any female reader who honors these papers with her notice should tax me with explaining it once too seldom; which would be worse to bear than a simultaneous complaint from twelve proud men that I had explained it three times too often. You, therefore, fair reader, understand that for *your* accommodation exclusively I explain the meaning of this word. It is Greek; and our sex enjoys the office and privilege of standing counsel to yours in all questions of Greek. We are, under favor, perpetual and hereditary dragomans to you. So that if, by accident, you know the meaning of a Greek word, yet by courtesy to us, your counsel learned in that matter, you will always seem *not* to know it.

A palimpsest, then, is a membrane or roll cleansed of its manuscript by reiterated successions.

What was the reason that the Greeks and the Romans had not the advantage of printed books? The answer will be, from ninety-nine persons in a hundred—Because the mystery of printing was not then discovered. But this is altogether a mistake. The secret of printing must have been discovered many thousands of times before it was used, or *could* be used. The inventive powers of man are divine; and also his stupidity is divine, as Cowper so playfully illustrates in the slow development of the *sofa*[1] through successive generations of immortal dullness. It took centuries of blockheads to

---

1. "The Sofa" is Book I of William Cowper's long poem, *The Task*.

raise a joint stool into a chair; and it required something like a miracle of genius, in the estimate of elder generations, to reveal the possibility of lengthening a chair into a *chaise-longue*, or a sofa. Yes, these were inventions that cost mighty throes of intellectual power. But still, as respects printing, and admirable as is the stupidity of man, it was really not quite equal to the task of evading an object which stared him in the face with so broad a gaze. It did not require an Athenian intellect to read the main secret of printing in many scores of processes which the ordinary uses of life were *daily* repeating. To say nothing of analogous artifices amongst various mechanic artisans, all that is essential in printing must have been known to every nation that struck coins and medals. Not, therefore, any want of a printing art—that is, of an art for multiplying impressions—but the want of a cheap material for *receiving* such impressions, was the obstacle to an introduction of printed books even as early as Pisistratus. The ancients *did* apply printing to records of silver and gold; to marble, and many other substances cheaper than gold or silver, they did *not* since each monument required a *separate* effort of inscription. Simply this defect it was of a cheap material for receiving impresses which froze in its very fountains the early resources of printing.

Some twenty years ago this view of the case was luminously expounded by Dr. Whately, and with the merit, I believe, of having first suggested it. Since then, this theory has received indirect confirmation. Now, out of that original scarcity affecting all materials proper for durable books, which continued up to times comparatively modern, grew the opening for palimpsests. Naturally, when once a roll of parchment or of vellum had done its office, by propagating through a series of generations what once had possessed an interest for *them*, but which, under changes of opinion or of taste, had faded to their feelings or had become obsolete for their undertakings, the whole *membrana* or vellum skin, the twofold product of human skill and costly material, and costly freight of thought which is carried, drooped in value concurrently—supposing that each were inalienably associated to the other. Once it had been the impress of a human mind which stamped its value upon the vellum; the vellum, though costly, had contributed but a secondary element of value to the total result. At length, however, this relation between the vehicle and its freight has gradually been undermined. The vellum, from having been the setting of the jewel, has risen at length to be the jewel itself; and the burden of thought, from having given the chief value to the vellum, has now become the chief obstacle to its value; nay, has totally extinguished its value, unless it can be dissociated from the connection. Yet, if this unlinking *can* be effected, then, fast as the inscription upon the membrane is sinking into rubbish, the membrane itself is reviving in its separate importance; and, from bearing a ministerial value, the vellum has come at last to absorb the whole value.

Hence the importance for our ancestors that the separation *should* be effected. Hence it arose in the Middle Ages as a considerable object for chemistry to discharge the writing from the roll, and thus to make it available for a new succession of thoughts. The soil, if cleansed from what once had been hot-house plants, but now were held to be weeds, would be ready to receive a fresh and more appropriate crop. In that object the monkish chemists succeeded; but after a fashion which seems almost incredible—incredible not as regards the extent of their success, but as regards the delicacy of restraints under which it moved—so equally adjusted was their success to the immediate interests of that period, and to the reversionary objects of our own. They did the thing; but not so radically as to prevent us, their posterity, from *undoing* it. They expelled the writing sufficiently to leave a field for the new manuscript, and yet not sufficiently to make the traces of the elder manuscript irrecoverable for us. Could magic, could Hermes Trismegistus, have done more? What would you think, fair reader, of a problem such as this: to write a book which should be sense for your own generation, nonsense for the next; should revive into sense for the next after that, but again become nonsense for the fourth; and so on by alternate successions sinking into night or blazing into day, like the Sicilian river Arethusa and the English river Mole, or like the undulating motions of a flattened stone which children cause to skim the breast of a river, now diving below the water, now grazing its surface, sinking heavily into darkness, rising buoyantly into light, through a long vista of alternations? Such a problem, you say, is impossible. But really it is a problem not harder apparently than to bid a generation kill, so that a subsequent generation may call back into life; bury, so that posterity may command to rise again. Yet *that* was what the rude chemistry of past ages effected when coming into combination with the reaction from the more refined chemistry of our own. Had *they* been better chemists, had *we* been worse, the mixed result—namely, that, dying for *them*, the flowers should revive for *us*—could not have been effected. They did the thing proposed to them: they did it effectually, for they founded upon it all what was wanted: and yet ineffectually, since we unraveled their work, effacing all above which they had superscribed, restoring all below which they had effaced.

Here, for instance, is a parchment which contained some Grecian tragedy—the *Agamemnon* of Aeschylus, or the *Phoenissae* of Euripides. This had possessed a value almost inappreciable in the eyes of accomplished scholars, continually growing rarer through generations. But four centuries are gone by since the destruction of the Western Empire. Christianity, with towering grandeurs of another class, has founded a different empire; and some bigoted, yet perhaps holy monk has washed away (as he persuades himself) the heathen's tragedy, replacing it with a monastic legend; which legend is disfigured with fables in its incidents, and yet in a higher sense is true, because interwoven with Christian morals, and with the sublimest of Christian revelations. Three, four, five, centuries more find man still devout as ever; but the language has become obsolete; and even for Christian devotion a new era has arisen, throwing it into the channel of crusading zeal or of chivalrous enthusiasm. The *membrana* is wanted now for a knightly romance—for *My Cid* or *Coeur de Lion*, for *Sir Tristram* or *Lybaeus Disconus*. In this way, by means of the imperfect chemistry known to the medieval period, the same roll has served as a conservatory for three separate generations of flowers and fruits, all perfectly different, and yet all specially adapted to the wants of the successive possessors. The Greek tragedy, the monkish legend, the knightly romance, each has ruled its own period. One harvest after another has been gathered into the garners of man through ages far apart. And the same hydraulic machinery has distributed, through the same marble fountains, water, milk, or wine, according to the habits and training of the generations that came to quench their thirst.

Such were the achievements of rude monastic chemistry. But the more elaborate chemistry of our own days has reversed all these motions of our simple ancestors, with results in every stage that to *them* would have realized the most fantastic amongst the promises of thaumaturgy. Insolent vaunt of Paracelsus, that he would restore the original rose or violet out of the ashes settling from its combustion—*that* is now rivaled in this modern achievement. The traces of each successive handwriting, regularly effaced, as had been imagined, have, in the inverse order, been regularly called back: the footsteps of the game pursued, wolf or stag, in each several chase, have been unlinked, and hunted back through all their doubles; and, as the chorus of the Athenian stage unwove through the antistrophe every step that had been mystically woven through the strophe, so, by our modern conjurations of science, secrets of ages remote from each other have been exorcized from the accumulated shadows of centuries. Chemistry, a witch as potent as the Erichtho of Lucan (*Pharsalia*, lib. vi or vii), has extorted by her torments, from the dust and ashes of forgotten centuries, the secrets of a life extinct for the general eye, but still glowing in the embers. Even the fable of the Phoenix, that secular bird who propagated his solitary existence, and his solitary births, along the line of centuries, through eternal relays of funeral mists, is but a type of what we have done with palimpsests. We have backed upon each phoenix in the long *regressus*, and forced him to expose his ancestral phoenix, sleeping in the ashes below his own ashes. Our good old forefathers would have been aghast at our sorceries; and, if they speculated on the propriety of burning Dr. Faustus, *us* they would have burned by acclamation. Trial there would have been none; and they could not otherwise have satisfied their horror of the brazen profligacy marking our modern magic than by plowing up the houses of all who had been parties to it, and sowing the ground with salt.

Fancy not, reader, that this tumult of images, illustrative or allusive, moves under any impulse or purpose of mirth. It is but the coruscation of a restless understanding, often made ten times more so by irritation of the nerves, such as you will first learn to comprehend (its *how* and its *why*) some stage or two ahead. The image, the memorial, the record, which for me is derived from a palimpsest as to one great fact in our human being, and which immediately I will show you, is but too repellent of laughter; or, even if laughter *had* been possible, it would have been such laughter as oftentimes is thrown off from the fields of ocean, laughter that hides, or that seems to evade, mustering tumult; foam-bells that weave garlands of phosphoric radiance for one moment round the eddies of gleaming abysses; mimicries of earthborn flowers that for the eye raise phantoms of gaiety, as oftentimes for the ear they raise the echoes of fugitive laughter, mixing with the ravings and choir-voices of an angry sea.

What else than a natural and mighty palimpsest is the human brain? Such a palimpsest is my brain; such a palimpsest, oh reader! is yours. Everlasting layers of ideas, images, feelings, have fallen upon your brain softly as light. Each succession has seemed to bury all that went before. And yet, in reality, not one has been extinguished. And, if in the vellum palimpsest, lying amongst the other *diplomata*[2] of human archives or libraries, there is anything fantastic or which moves to laughter, as oftentimes there is in the grotesque collisions of those successive themes, having no natural connection, which by pure accident have consecutively occupied the roll, yet, in our own heaven-created palimpsest, the deep memorial palimpsest of the brain, there are not and cannot be such incoherencies. The fleeting accidents of a man's life, and its external shows, may indeed be irrelate and incongruous; but the organizing principles which fuse into harmony, and gather about fixed predetermined centres, whatever heterogeneous elements life may have accumulated from without, will not permit the grandeur of human unity greatly to be violated, or its ultimate repose to be troubled, in the retrospect from dying moments, or from other great convulsions.

Such a convulsion is the struggle of gradual suffocation, as in drowning; and in the original *Opium Confessions* I mentioned a

2. Documents.

case of that nature communicated to me by a lady from her own childish experience. The lady was then still living, though of unusually great age; and I may mention that amongst her faults never was numbered any levity of principle, or carelessness of the most scrupulous veracity, but, on the contrary, such faults as arise from austerity, too harsh, perhaps, and gloomy, indulgent neither to others nor herself. And, at the time of relating this incident, when already very old, she had become religious to asceticism. According to my present belief, she had completed her ninth year when, playing by the side of a solitary brook, she fell into one of its deepest pools. Eventually, but after what lapse of time nobody ever knew, she was saved from death by a farmer, who, riding in some distant lane, had seen her rise to the surface; but not until she had descended within the abyss of death and looked into its secrets, as far, perhaps, as ever human eye *can* have looked that had permission to return. At a certain stage of this descent, a blow seemed to strike her; phosphoric radiance sprang forth from her eyeballs; and immediately a mighty theater expanded within her brain. In a moment, in the twinkling of an eye, every act, every design of her past life, lived again, arraying themselves not as a succession, but as parts of a coexistence. Such a light fell upon the whole path of her life backwards into the shades of infancy as the light, perhaps, which wrapt the destined Apostle[3] on his road to Damascus. Yet that light blinded for a season; but hers poured celestial vision upon the brain, so that her consciousness became omnipresent at one moment to every feature in the infinite review.

This anecdote was treated sceptically at the time by some critics. But, besides that it has since been confirmed by other experiences essentially the same, reported by other parties in the same circumstances, who had never heard of each other, the true point for astonishment is not the *simultaneity* of arrangement under which the past events of life, though in fact successive, had formed their dread line of revelation. This was but a secondary phenomenon; the deeper lay in the resurrection itself, and the possibility of resurrection for what had so long slept in the dust. A pall, deep as oblivion, had been thrown by life over every trace of these experiences; and yet suddenly, at a silent command, at the signal of a blazing rocket sent up from the brain, the pall draws up, and the whole depths of the theater are exposed. Here was the greater mystery. Now, this mystery is liable to no doubt; for it is repeated, and ten thousand times repeated, by opium, for those who are its martyrs.

Yes, reader, countless are the mysterious handwritings of grief or joy which have inscribed themselves successively upon the palimpsest of your brain; and, like the annual leaves of aboriginal forests, or the undissolving snows on the Himalayas, or light falling upon

3. Paul. Cf. *Acts* iv: 1-19.

light, the endless strata have covered up each other in forgetfulness. But by the hour of death, but by fever, but by the searchings of opium, all these can revive in strength. They are not dead, but sleeping. In the illustration imagined by myself from the case of some individual palimpsest, the Grecian tragedy had seemed to be displaced, but was *not* displaced, by the monkish legend; and the monkish legend had seemed to be displaced, but was *not* displaced, by the knightly romance. In some potent convulsion of the system, all wheels back into its earliest elementary stage. The bewildering romance, light tarnished with darkness, the semi-fabulous legend, truth celestial mixed with human falsehoods, these fade even of themselves as life advances. The romance has perished that the young man adored; the legend has gone that deluded the boy; but the deep, deep tragedies of infancy, as when the child's hands were unlinked for ever from his mother's neck, or his lips for ever from his sister's kisses, these remain lurking below all, and these lurk to the last.

QUESTIONS FOR STUDY, DISCUSSION, AND WRITING

1. Outline the essay, showing how De Quincey develops his subject.
2. What transitions of topic, tone, and imagery are effected in the paragraph beginning, "Fancy not, reader. . ." (p. 314)?
3. What points of correspondence does De Quincey draw from the main analogy in the essay? Are there implications of correspondence beyond those features explicitly drawn? What are they? What specific lack of correspondence does De Quincey mention?
4. Explain the following allusions and their function in the essay:
   a. "the Sicilan river Arethusa and the English river Mole" (p. 312)
   b. the "vaunt of Paracelsus" (p. 313)
   c. choral strophe and antistrophe (p. 313)
   d. "The fable of the Phoenix" (p. 313)
   e. "They are not dead, but sleeping" (p. 317)
   What have these allusions in common—in feature? in function?
5. In his closing paragraph De Quincey suggests that each human life recapitulates the stages of history, culture, and thought. Is there any validity in this notion? Can you offer any speculations to extend the notion?

Prose Forms: Letters

[In *1870* a certain Perez Cowan received this short letter:

DEAR PETER,

It is indeed sweet news. I am proud of your happiness. To Peter, and Peter's, let me give both hands. Delight has no competitor, so it is always most.

"Maggie" is a warm name. I shall like to take it.

Home is the definition of God.

EMILY

Cowan had recently married Maggie, and with customary good feeling and form for such an occasion, Emily Dickinson wrote to congratulate her friend. The familiar associations of sentiment are there: Love-Marriage-Joy-Home-Blessedness. But these sentiments are felt and expressed in so uncommon a way that the reader's start of pleasure makes him attend specially to the letter. To move from one sentiment to another ordinarily requires connected development, but here one almost feels the silences between the remark about "delight" and the compliment on the bride's name, between "home" and "definition" and "God." Cowan doubtless knew Emily Dickinson's peculiar quality of mind and personality. And he must have been unsurprised at her characteristically terse, oblique expression. The letter might have been for him as if Emily spoke these things; its whole idiom and tone seem just that personal.

The letter is probably the most directly personal gesture in written language. What the letter is about may be an extra allowance, the death of a close relative, or a purchase from a business firm. But the letter is equally about the writer of it, because he inevitably, though not always self-consciously, addresses another person to whom it matters who is speaking and how. The voice of the writer, his individuality, is important because it becomes his style, his characteristic use of the language to express that complicated thing we call his perception of experience, and to express it in a way that anticipates the expectations of his reader. When Lord Chesterfield writes to his son a letter on the art of pleasing, we hear a father's voice clearly enough, but we also hear a man whose whole way of seeing life is everywhere implied in a language that insists on the formal but reconciles it with the individual's sentiment.

317

An occasion and an exchange between two people about it: the situation is not far removed in its essentials from the abundant and accustomed experience of us all. If the occasion is something a person wants to hold for himself only, he may commit his thoughts and impressions to his journal. As soon, though, as he desires to share the occasion with another, he begins to take account of the person to whom he addresses himself. He has an audience importantly different from and importantly like himself: different in that combination of personality, temperament, taste, and judgment that makes each of them a unique person; alike in a common ground of knowledge, experience, and interests which each may reasonably assume the other to be aware of. The novelist Henry James kept very full notebooks in which his persistent concern was to clarify for himself ideas and experiences of many kinds, always in terms of his own mind's needs. But James' ideas about stoicism in the face of death in his splendid letter to Grace Norton are not set down as for a journal; he takes account of Miss Norton's situation, anticipates her frame of mind, subtly gauges her feelings about the death of a loved one. His ideas assume a shape in language that takes equal measure of him as sender and Miss Norton as receiver of the letter.

Everybody, of course, writes letters which convey things of an essentially private nature: chatty, abbreviated, "secret." But it is hard for a thoughtful adult to write even so privately without verging continually on reflection, analysis, judgment of the shared intimacies. Behind James's letter to Grace Norton there is obviously a close personal relationship that permits him to take some things for granted, to assume mutual knowledges and understanding, but also to move from these to remarks that are more impersonally true and important about death and sorrow and life. In Mrs. Banning's letter to Susan the mother and daughter are involved in a specific world of manners and morals which gives much more than a private point to the mother's first remark: "No, you can't drive to Detroit for Thanksgiving with the two boys and Ann."

When the impetus to communicate through a letter becomes less personal or private, and more "public" in its interests and its manner, the essential impetus to the essay has begun. The personal essay, especially when the author speaks unequivocally as "I," is very much like a letter in the relation of Self and Occasion. The important differences is the Other, the audience, for in the essay the audience has broadened and the common ground of fact and experience is less specific. In the essay therefore, assumptions have to be more carefully considered for their appropriateness, implications have usually to be grounded in specific facts and arguments, terms and ideas must be defined, developed, clarified, the relationships of ideas have to be spelled out rather than taken for granted. At the conclusion of Baldwin's "Stranger in the Village," we are deeply involved in his assessment of the moral meaning the black-white race dilemma poses to Americans and the world, but at the beginning of the essay, we were quickly immersed in a fascinating account of the author's experience as a lone Negro in a Swiss village. Almost imperceptibly, the limits of that very personal experience expand to a sharply critical view of a complex historical and cultural problem. Baldwin maintains the unapologetic "I" in his essay with sufficient tact not to call undue attention to himself as a private person, but rather to show the continuity of his own experience and a public problem. The first part of the essay could easily have been a letter to a friend; the latter part is sufficiently public to command that general audience to which an essay is addressed. So conscious is he of his audience that the essay defines and explains, illustrates and argues, develops and extends what, in a letter, might well have been merely asserted.

But the basic considerations remain the same: something to write about; a writer; someone to read him. All that the writer is as a person affects his mode of seeing, his consciousness of what he sees. The effect he would have on a reader disciplines that consciousness. The relationship of these three—an occasion, a self, and others—underlies the letter. It is also, with suitable adjustments in the content of the terms, the relationship which underlies the essay.]

MARGARET CULKIN BANNING: Letter to Susan

November 15, 1934

DEAR SUSAN

No, you can't drive to Detroit for Thanksgiving with the two boys and Ann. I thought that I'd better put that simple, declarative sentence at the beginning of this letter so that you wouldn't be kept in suspense even if you are put in a bad temper. I'm sorry to have to be so definite and final. I would like to leave the decision to your own judgment, but this is one of the few times when I can't do that. For the judgment of so many people, young and old, is a little askew about just such propositions as four young people motoring together for most of two days and a night without any stops except for breath and coffee.

I do agree with much of what you wrote me. It would be delightful to be there for that Thanksgiving dance and it wouldn't be expensive to carry out your plan. I quite understand that you can manage the complicated schedules all around by leaving Wednesday afternoon, driving all that night and most of Thursday, and I don't doubt that you would have a grand time until Saturday noon and all be back in college by Sunday night. Also I know that Mark is probably the best driver of all your friends and that he behaves well. His father was like that too. He was also—though this bit of history may not interest you—rather dashing in his ways, like Mark. I don't know the other boy, David, or is it Daniel? (your handwriting certainly doesn't get any better) but I'll take your word for all the sterling qualities you say he has. Nobody need argue with me about Ann, after the way she measured up to family troubles and kept gay all last summer. Even you are all that I sometimes say you are, but it doesn't affect the situation.

In fact, I think it aggravates it. Such young people as you four have no right to do things that confuse you with people who are quite different in habits and ideas of control. You write, quote, please don't say that I can't go because of the looks of the thing because that's such rubbish and not like you, unquote. You're wrong on both counts. It is not rubbish and it is like me. I get a little angry about this highhanded scrapping of the looks of things. What else have we to go by? How else can the average person form an opinion of a girl's sense of values or even of her chastity except by the looks of her conduct? If looks are so unimportant, why do you yourself spend so much time on your physical looks before you go out with strangers? In your own crowd you will go around all day wearing shorts and a sweat shirt and that eternal and dreadful red checked scarf that should be burned. But if you are going to be with people you don't know or who don't know who you are, it is different.

Then you are careful to make yourself look as if you were decently bred, as if you could read and write, and as if you had good taste in clothes and cosmetics. You wouldn't be caught wearing cheap perfume, would you? Then why do you want to wear cheap perfume on your conduct?

Looks do matter and I do not mean just hair and skin and teeth and clothes. Looks are also your social contact with the world. Suppose you take this drive. How would it look to strangers? Two young men (of marriageable age) take two young women (also of marriageable age) on a forty-hour drive. Everyone knows that many girls go on forty-hour drives with men with extremely bad results, such as overexcited emotions, reckless conduct, and road accidents. How is anyone to make a special case of you? Why should anyone? It looks as if you deliberately assumed the pathetic privileges of girls who want to be with men at any cost to their reputations.

You wrote also that you think that it is nobody's business except your own what you do, but you are wrong. This is the kind of world— and there doesn't seem to be any other—in which conduct is social as well as individual. The main point of your education, from kindergarten up, has been to make you understand that, and I don't want you to break down at this small test. Your conduct is not entirely your own business, though it begins there. Afterwards it affects other people's conduct. Other girls, seeing you go off on an unchaperoned motor jaunt, think it's all right to do the same thing. Parents doubt and wonder. Men, and even boys, grow skeptical and more careless. You confuse things by such conduct.

I must also point out, even in the face of your cool young rage, that you ask a great deal more than gasoline and company of Mark and David—who may be Daniel. An unchaperoned girl, for whom a young man is responsible to parents whom he knows and respects, is a great burden to a young man. You are—so you said yourself—decent. Mark would have you on his hands in situations when people would not know whether you are decent or not. Suppose you all had an accident. Suppose, for example, that you couldn't make this trip without a long stop, speed being so eminently respectable but stops always so questionable. If you trail into some hotel after midnight, though a tourist camp should be all any of you can afford this year, it wouldn't be so easy for either of those boys. Did it ever occur to you that there's something almost crooked in the way decent girls nowadays use the shelter of their established respectability to make things awkward for men?

There's another thing in my mind which is only partly relevant. You make no mention of it, assuming the coolest of friendly relations between the four of you. But suppose that David-Daniel (I'm beginning to love that name) found himself more excited than you anticipate by the proximity—and what proximity!—of you two good-looking girls. That happens. I seem to remember having mentioned it before. It might happen to one of those two boys. And how about you and Ann? Are you quite frank with me or yourselves? Isn't part of the lure of this trip the fact that you yourself do like Mark very much? Your plan really is to drive a car full of high explosives for forty hours, from dark to dawn, and enjoy your own daring no matter who blows up.

You wrote me that it would be such fun that you hope I'll see it your way. That's always a very disarming argument, but I think it's on my side this time. You see, if there were any necessity for this trip I would feel differently about it. If you were compelled for some real reason to travel that way, if there were a war or a *siege* to make it necessary, or if it were the only way you could see Mark for years, I would say that you could do it. But fun—that so-transient fun— of just missing being hit by a bus or finding the best hamburgers in the world at a roadside inn, or being cut in on twenty times at that Thanksgiving dance—isn't a good enough reason.

It is no fun for me either, to disappoint you like this. It isn't easy to be the person who sometimes has to try to preserve your happiness at the expense of your fun. After Thanksgiving—I know you probably can't do it until then—will you please believe that's true?

With love to you, Ann, Mark and David-Daniel,

MOTHER

LORD CHESTERFIELD: Letter to His Son

London, October 16, O.S. 1747

DEAR BOY

The art of pleasing is a very necessary one to possess, but a very difficult one to acquire. It can hardly be reduced to rules; and your own good sense and observation will teach you more of it than I can. "Do as you would be done by," is the surest method that I know of pleasing. Observe carefully what pleases you in others, and probably the same things in you will please others. If you are pleased with the complaisance and attention of others to your humors, your tastes, or your weaknesses, depend upon it, the same complaisance and attention on your part to theirs will equally please them. Take the tone of the company that you are in, and do not pretend to give it; be serious, gay, or even trifling, as you find the present humor of the company; this is an attention due from every individual to the majority. Do not tell stories in company; there is nothing more tedious and disagreeable; if by chance you know a very short story, and exceedingly applicable to the present subject of conversation, tell it in as few words as possible; and even then, throw out that you do not love to tell stories, but that the shortness of it tempted you.

Of all things banish the egotism out of your conversation, and never think of entertaining people with your own personal concerns or private affairs; though they are interesting to you, they are tedious and impertinent to everybody else; besides that, one cannot keep one's own private affairs too secret. Whatever you think your own excellencies may be, do not affectedly display them in company; nor labor, as many people do, to give that turn to the conversation, which may supply you with an opportunity of exhibiting them. If they are real, they will infallibly be discovered, without your pointing them out yourself, and with much more advantage. Never maintain an argument with heat and clamor, though you think or know yourself to be in the right; but give your opinion modestly and coolly, which is the only way to convince; and, if that does not do, try to change the conversation, by saying, with good-humor, "We shall hardly convince one another; nor is it necessary that we should, so let us talk of something else."

Remember that there is a local propriety to be observed in all companies; and that what is extremely proper in one company may be, and often is, highly improper in another.

The jokes, the *bon-mots*, the little adventures, which may do very well in one company, will seem flat and tedious, when related in another. The particular characters, the habits, the cant of one company may give merit to a word, or a gesture, which would have none at all if divested of those accidental circumstances. Here people very commonly err; and fond of something that has entertained them in one company, and in certain circumstances, repeat it with emphasis in another, where it is either insipid, or, it may be, offensive, by being ill-timed or misplaced. Nay, they often do it with this silly preamble: "I will tell you an excellent thing," or, "I will tell you the best thing in the world." This raises expectations, which, when absolutely disappointed, make the relator of this excellent thing look, very deservedly, like a fool.

If you would particularly gain the affection and friendship of particular people, whether men or women, endeavor to find out their predominant excellency, if they have one, and their prevailing weakness, which everybody has; and do justice to the one, and something more than justice to the other. Men have various objects in which they may excel, or at least would be thought to excel; and, though they love to hear justice done to them, where they know that they excel, yet they are most and best flattered upon those points where they wish to excel, and yet are doubtful whether they do or not. As for example: Cardinal Richelieu, who was undoubtedly the ablest statesman of his time, or perhaps of any other, had the idle vanity of being thought the best poet too; he envied the great Corneille his reputation, and ordered a criticism to be written upon the *Cid*. Those, therefore, who flattered skillfully, said little to him of his abilities in state affairs, or at least but *en passant*, and as it might naturally occur. But the incense which they gave him, the smoke of which they knew would turn his head in their favor, was as a *bel esprit* and a poet. Why? Because he was sure of one excellency, and distrustful as to the other.

You will easily discover every man's prevailing vanity by observing his favorite topic of conversation; for every man talks most of what he has most a mind to be thought to excel in. Touch him but there, and you touch him to the quick. The late Sir Robert Walpole (who was certainly an able man) was little open to flattery upon that head, for he was in no doubt himself about it; but his prevailing weakness was, to be thought to have a polite and happy turn to gallantry— of which he had undoubtedly less than any man living. It was his favorite and frequent subject of conversation, which proved to those who had any penetration that it was his prevailing weakness, and they applied to it with success.

Women have, in general, but one object, which is their beauty; upon which scarce any flattery is too gross for them to follow. Nature has hardly formed a woman ugly enough to be insensible to flattery upon her person; if her face is so shocking that she must, in some degree, be conscious of it, her figure and air, she trusts, make ample amends for it. If her figure is deformed, her face, she thinks, counterbalances it. If they are both bad, she comforts herself that she has graces, a certain manner, a *je ne sais quoi* still more engaging than beauty. This truth is evident from the studied and elaborate dress of the ugliest woman in the world. An undoubted, uncontested, conscious beauty is, of all women, the least sensible of flattery upon that head; she knows it is her due, and is therefore obliged to nobody for giving it her. She must be flattered upon her understanding; which, though she may possibly not doubt of herself, yet she suspects that men may distrust.

Do not mistake me, and think that I mean to recommend to you abject and criminal flattery: no; flatter nobody's vices or crimes: on the contrary, abhor and discourage them. But there is no living in the world without a complaisant indulgence for people's weaknesses, and innocent, though ridiculous vanities. If a man has a mind to be thought wiser, and a woman handsomer, than they really are, their error is a comfortable one to themselves, and an innocent one with regard to other people; and I would rather make them my friends by indulging them in it, than my enemies by endeavoring (and that to no purpose) to undeceive them.

There are little attentions, likewise, which are infinitely engaging, and which sensibly affect that degree of pride and self-love, which is inseparable from human nature, as they are unquestionable proofs of the regard and consideration which we have for the persons to whom we pay them. As, for example, to observe the little habits, the likings, the antipathies, and the tastes of those whom we would gain; and then take care to provide them with the one, and to secure them from the other; giving them, genteelly, to understand, that you had observed they liked such a dish, or such a room, for which reason you had prepared it: or, on the contrary, that having observed they had an aversion to such a dish, a dislike to such a person, etc., you had taken care to avoid presenting them. Such attention to such trifles flatters self-love much more then greater things, as it makes people think themselves almost the only objects of your thoughts and care.

These are some of the arcana necessary for your initiation in the great society of the world. I wish I had known them better at your age; I have paid the price of three and fifty years for them, and shall not grudge it if you reap the advantage. Adieu.

EMILY DICKINSON: Letters to
Thomas Wentworth Higginson

April 26, 1862

MR. HIGGINSON

Your kindness claimed earlier gratitude, but I was ill, and write to-day from my pillow.

Thank you for the surgery; it was not so painful as I supposed. I bring you others, as you ask, though they might not differ. While my thought is undressed, I can make the distinction; but when I put them in the gown, they look alike and numb.

You asked how old I was? I made no verse, but one or two, until this winter, sir.

I had a terror since September, I could tell to none; and so I sing, as the boy does of the burying ground, because I am afraid.

You inquire my books. For poets, I have Keats, and Mr. and Mrs. Browning. For prose, Mr. Ruskin, Sir Thomas Browne, and the *Revelations*. I went to school, but in your manner of the phrase had no education. When a little girl, I had a friend who taught me Immortality; but venturing too near, himself, he never returned. Soon after my tutor died, and for several years my lexicon was my only companion. Then I found one more, but he was not contented I be his scholar, so he left the land.

You ask of my companions. Hills, sir, and the sundown, and a dog large as myself, that my father bought me. They are better than beings because they know, but do not tell; and the noise in the pool at noon excels my piano.

I have a brother and sister; my mother does not care for thought, and father, too busy with his briefs to notice what we do. He buys me many books, but begs me not to read them, because he fears they joggle the mind. They are religious, except me, and address an eclipse, every morning, whom they call their "Father."

But I fear my story fatigues you. I would like to learn. Could you tell me how to grow, or is it unconveyed, like melody or witchcraft?

You speak of Mr. Whitman. I never read his book, but was told that it was disgraceful.

I read Miss Prescott's *Circumstance*, but it followed me in the dark, so I avoided her.

Two editors of journals came to my father's house this winter, and asked me for my mind, and when I asked them "why" they said I was penurious, and they would use it for the world.

I could not weigh myself, myself. My size felt small to me. I read your chapters in *The Atlantic*, and experienced honor for you. I was sure you would not reject a confiding question.

Is this, sir, what you asked me to tell you?

Your friend,
E. DICKINSON

Amherst, 1868

DEAR FRIEND

A letter always feels to me like Immortality because it is the mind alone without corporeal friend. Indebted in our talk to attitude and accent, there seems a spectral power in thought that walks alone. I would like to thank you for your great kindness, but never try to lift the words which I cannot hold.

Should you come to Amherst, I might then succeed, though gratitude is the timid wealth of those who have nothing. I am sure that you speak the truth, because the noble do, but your letters always surprise me.

My life has been too simple and stern to embarrass any. "Seen of angels," scarcely my responsibility.

It is difficult not to be fictitious in so fair a place, but tests' severe repairs are permitted all.

When a little girl I remember hearing that remarkable passage and preferring the "power," not knowing at the time that "kingdom" and "glory" were included.

You noticed my dwelling alone. To an emigrant, country is idle except it be his own. You speak kindly of seeing me; could it please your convenience to come so far as Amherst, I should be very glad, but I do not cross my father's ground to any house or town.

Of our greatest acts we are ignorant. You were not aware that you saved my life. To thank you in person has been since then one of my few requests. . . . You will excuse each that I say, because no one taught me.

EMILY DICKINSON: Letters to Mrs. Henry Hills

March, 1879

DEAR FRIEND

The only balmless wound is the departed human life we had learned to need.

For that, even Immortality is a slow solace. All other peace has many roots and will spring again.

With cheer from one who knows.

[SALUTATION OMITTED]

Vocal is but one form of remembrance, dear friend—the cherishing that is speechless is equally warm.

EMILY DICKINSON: Letter to Her Cousins

November, 1882

DEAR COUSINS

I hoped to write you before, but mother's dying almost stunned my spirit.

I have answered a few inquiries of love, but written little intuitively. She was scarcely the aunt you knew. The great mission of pain had been ratified—cultivated to tenderness by persistent sorrow, so that a larger mother died than had she died before. There was no earthly parting. She slipped from our fingers like a flake gathered by the wind, and is now part of the drift called "the infinite."

We don't know where she is, though so many tell us.

I believe we shall in some manner be cherished by our Maker— that the One who gave us this remarkable earth has the power still farther to surprise that which He has caused. Beyond that all is silence. . . .

Mother was very beautiful when she had died. Seraphs are solemn artists. The illumination that comes but once paused upon her features, and it seemed like hiding a picture to lay her in the grave; but the grass that received my father will suffice his guest, the one he asked at the altar to visit him all his life.

I cannot tell how Eternity seems. It sweeps around me like a sea. . . . Thank you for remembering me. Remembrance—mighty word.

"Thou gavest it to me from the foundation of the world."

Lovingly,
EMILY

THOMAS HENRY HUXLEY: Letter to Charles Kingsley

14 Waverly Place, Sept. 23, 1860

MY DEAR KINGSLEY

I cannot sufficiently thank you, both on my wife's account and my own, for your long and frank letter, and for all the hearty sympathy which it exhibits—and Mrs. Kingsley will, I hope, believe that we are no less sensible of her kind thought of us. To myself your letter was especially valuable, as it touched upon what I thought even more than upon what I said in my letter to you.

My convictions, positive and negative, on all the matters of which you speak, are of long and slow growth and are firmly rooted. But the great blow which fell upon me seemed to stir them to their foundation, and had I lived a couple of centuries earlier I could have fancied a devil scoffing at me and them—and asking me what profit it was to have stripped myself of the hopes and consolations of the mass of mankind? To which my only reply was and is—Oh devil! truth is better than much profit. I have searched over the grounds of my belief, and if wife and child and name and fame were all to be lost to me one after the other as the penalty, still I will not lie.

And now I feel that it is due to you to speak as frankly as you have done to me. An old and worthy friend of mine tried some three or four years ago to bring us together—because, as he said, you were the only man who would do me any good. Your letter leads me to think he was right, though not perhaps in the sense he attached to his own words.

To begin with the great doctrine you discuss. I neither deny nor affirm the immortality of man. I see no reason for believing in it, but, on the other hand, I have no means of disproving it.

Pray understand that I have no *a priori* objections to the doctrine. No man who has to deal daily and hourly with nature can trouble himself about *a priori* difficulties. Give me such evidence as would justify me in believing anything else, and I will believe that. Why should I not? It is not half so wonderful as the conservation of force, or the indestructibility of matter. Whoso clearly appreciates all that is implied in the falling of a stone can have no difficulty about any doctrine simply on account of its marvelousness.

But the longer I live, the more obvious it is to me that the most sacred act of a man's life is to say and to feel, "I believe such and such to be true." All the greatest rewards and all the heaviest penalties of existence cling about that act.

The universe is one and the same throughout; and if the condition of my success in unraveling some little difficulty of anatomy or physiology is that I shall rigorously refuse to put faith in that which does not rest on sufficient evidence, I cannot believe that the great mysteries of existence will be laid open to me on other terms.

It is no use to talk to me of analogies and probabilities. I know what I mean when I say I believe in the law of the inverse squares, and I will not rest my life and my hopes upon weaker convictions. I dare not if I would.

Measured by this standard, what becomes of the doctrine of immortality?

You rest in your strong conviction of your personal existence, and in the instinct of the persistence of that existence which is so strong in you as in most men.

To me this is as nothing. That my personality is the surest thing I know—may be true. But the attempt to conceive what it is leads me into mere verbal subtleties. I have champed up all that chaff about the ego and the non-ego, about noumena and phenomena, and all the rest of it, too often not to know that in attempting even to think of these questions, the human intellect flounders at once out of its depth.

It must be twenty years since, a boy, I read Hamilton's essay on the unconditioned, and from that time to this, ontological speculation has been a folly to me. When Mansel took up Hamilton's argument on the side of orthodoxy (!) I said he reminded me of nothing so much as the man who is sawing off the sign on which he is sitting, in Hogarth's picture. But this by the way.

I cannot conceive of my personality as a thing apart from the phenomena of my life. When I try to form such a conception I discover that, as Coleridge would have said, I only hypostatize a word, and it alters nothing if, with Fichte, I suppose the universe to be nothing but a manifestation of my personality. I am neither more nor less eternal than I was before.

Nor does the infinite difference between myself and the animals alter the case. I do not know whether the animals persist after they disappear or not. I do not even know whether the infinite difference between us and them may not be compensated by *their* persistence and *my* cessation after apparent death, just as the humble bulb of an annual lives, while the glorious flowers it has put forth die away.

Surely it must be plain that an ingenious man could speculate without end on both sides, and find analogies for all his dreams. Nor does it help me to tell me that the aspirations of mankind—that my own highest aspirations even—lead me toward the doctrine of immortality. I doubt the fact, to begin with, but if it be so even, what is this but in grand words asking me to believe a thing because I like it.

Science has taught to me the opposite lesson. She warns me to be careful how I adopt a view which jumps with my preconceptions, and to require stronger evidence for such belief than for one to which I was previously hostile.

My business is to teach my aspirations to conform themselves to fact, not to try and make facts harmonize with my aspirations.

Science seems to me to teach in the highest and strongest manner the great truth which is embodied in the Christian conception of entire surrender to the will of God. Sit down before fact as a little child, be prepared to give up every preconceived notion, follow humbly wherever and to whatever abysses nature leads, or you shall learn nothing. I have only begun to learn content and peace of mind since I have resolved at all risks to do this.

There are, however, other arguments commonly brought forward in favor of the immortality of man, which are to my mind not only delusive but mischievous. The one is the notion that the moral government of the world is imperfect without a system of future rewards and punishments. The other is: that such a system is indispensable to practical morality. I believe that both these dogmas are very mischievous lies.

With respect to the first, I am no optimist, but I have the firmest belief that the Divine Government (if we may use such a phrase to express the sum of the "customs of matter") is wholly just. The more I know intimately of the lives of other men (to say nothing of my own), the more obvious it is to me that the wicked does *not* flourish nor is the righteous punished. But for this to be clear we must bear in mind what almost all forget, that the rewards of life are contingent upon obedience to the *whole* law—physical as well as moral—and that moral obedience will not atone for physical sin, or *vice versa*.

The ledger of the Almighty is strictly kept, and every one of us has the balance of his operations paid over to him at the end of every minute of his existence.

Life cannot exist without a certain conformity to the surrounding universe—that conformity involves a certain amount of happiness in excess of pain. In short, as we live we are paid for living.

And it is to be recollected in view of the apparent discrepancy between men's acts and their rewards that Nature is juster than we. She takes into account what a man brings with him into the world, which human justice cannot do. If I, born a bloodthirsty and savage brute, inheriting these qualities from others, kill you, my fellow-men will very justly hang me, but I shall not be visited with the horrible remorse which would be my real punishment if, my nature being higher, I had done the same thing.

The absolute justice of the system of things is as clear to me as any scientific fact. The gravitation of sin to sorrow is as certain as that of the earth to the sun, and more so—for experimental proof of the fact is within reach of us all—nay, is before us all in our own lives, if we had but the eyes to see it.

Not only, then, do I disbelieve in the need for compensation, but I believe that the seeking for rewards and punishments out of this life leads men to a ruinous ignorance of the fact that their inevitable rewards and punishments are here.

If the expectation of hell hereafter can keep me from evil-doing, surely *a fortiori* the certainty of hell now will do so? If a man could be firmly impressed with the belief that stealing damaged him as much as swallowing arsenic would do (and it does), would not the dissuasive force of that belief be greater than that of any based on mere future expectations?

And this leads me to my other point.

As I stood behind the coffin of my little son the other day, with my mind bent on anything but disputation, the officiating minister read, as a part of his duty, the words, "If the dead rise not again, let us eat and drink, for tomorrow we die." I cannot tell you how inexpressibly they shocked me. Paul had neither wife nor child, or he must have known that his alternative involved a blasphemy against all that was best and noblest in human nature. I could have laughed with scorn. What! because I am face to face with irreparable loss, because I have given back to the source from whence it came, the cause of a great happiness, still retaining through all my life the blessings which have sprung and will spring from that cause, I am to renounce my manhood, and, howling, grovel in bestiality? Why, the very apes know better, and if you shoot their young, the poor brutes grieve their grief out and do not immediately seek distraction in a gorge.

Kicked into the world a boy without guide or training, or with worse than none, I confess to my shame that few men have drunk deeper of all kinds of sin than I. Happily, my course was arrested in time—before I had earned absolute destruction—and for long years I have been slowly and painfully climbing, with many a fall, towards better things. And when I look back, what do I find to have been the agents of my redemption? The hope of immortality or of future reward? I can honestly say that for these fourteen years such a consideration has not entered my head. No, I can tell you exactly what has been at work. *Sartor Resartus* led me to know that a deep sense of religion was compatible with the entire absence of theology. Secondly, science and her methods gave me a resting place independent of authority and tradition. Thirdly, love opened up to me a view of the sanctity of human nature, and impressed me with a deep sense of responsibility.

If at this moment I am not a worn-out, debauched, useless carcass of a man, if it has been or will be my fate to advance the cause of science, if I feel that I have a shadow of a claim on the love of those about me, if in the supreme moment when I looked down into my boy's grave my sorrow was full of submission and without bitterness, it is because these agencies have worked upon me, and not because I have ever cared whether my poor personality shall remain distinct for ever from the All from whence it came and whither it goes.

And thus, my dear Kingsley, you will understand what my position is. I may be quite wrong, and in that case I know I shall have to pay the penalty for being wrong. But I can only say with Luther, "*Gott helfe mir, Ich kann nichts anders.*"[1]

I know right well that 99 out of 100 of my fellows would call me atheist, infidel, and all the other usual hard names. As our laws stand, if the lowest thief steals my coat, my evidence (my opinions being known) would not be received against him.

But I cannot help it. One thing people shall not call me with justice, and that is—a liar. As you say of yourself, I too feel that I lack courage; but if ever the occasion arises when I am bound to speak, I will not shame my boy.

I have spoken more openly and distinctly to you than I ever have to any human being except my wife.

If you can show me that I err in premises or conclusion, I am ready to give up these as I would any other theories. But at any rate you will do me the justice to believe that I have not reached my conclusions without the care befitting the momentous nature of the problems involved.

And I write this the more readily to you, because it is clear to me that if that great and powerful instrument for good or evil, the Church of England, is to be saved from being shivered into fragments by the advancing tide of science—an event I should be very sorry to witness, but which will infallibly occur if men like Samuel of Oxford are to have the guidance of her destinies—it must be by the efforts of men who, like yourself, see your way to the combination of the practice of the Church with the spirit of science. Understand that all the younger men of science whom I know intimately are *essentially* of my way of thinking. (I know not a scoffer or an irreligious or an immoral man among them, but they all regard orthodoxy as you do Brahmanism.) Understand that this new school of the prophets is the only one that can work miracles, the only one that can constantly appeal to nature for evidence that it is right, and will constantly appeal to nature for evidence that it is right, and you will comprehend that it is of no use to try to barricade us with shovel hats and aprons, or to talk about our doctrines being "shocking."

I don't profess to understand the logic of yourself, Maurice, and the rest of your school, but I have always said I would swear by your truthfulness and sincerity, and that good must come of your efforts. The more plain this was to me, however, the more obvious the necessity to let you see where the men of science are driving, and it has often been in my mind to write to you before.

If I have spoken too plainly anywhere, or too abruptly, pardon me, and do the like to me.

My wife thanks you very much for your volume of sermons. Ever yours very faithfully,

T. H. Huxley

1. "God help me, I can do no other."

HENRY JAMES: Letter to Grace Norton

131 Mount Vernon St., Boston

July 28 [1883]

MY DEAR GRACE

Before the sufferings of others I am always utterly powerless, and your letter reveals such depths of suffering that I hardly know what to say to you. This indeed is not my last word—but it must be my first. You are not isolated, verily, in such states of feeling as this—that is, in the sense that you appear to make all the misery of all mankind your own; only I have a terrible sense that you give all and receive nothing—that there is no reciprocity in your sympathy —that you have all the affliction of it and none of the returns. However—I am determined not to speak to you except with the voice of stoicism. I don't know *why* we live—the gift of life comes to us from I don't know what source or for what purpose; but I believe we can go on living for the reason that (always of course up to a certain point) life is the most valuable thing we know anything about, and it is therefore presumptively a great mistake to surrender it while there is any yet left in the cup. In other words consciousness is an illimitable power, and though at times it may seem to be all consciousness of misery, yet in the way it propagates itself from wave to wave, so that we never cease to feel, and though at moments we appear to, try to, pray to, there is something that holds one in one's place, makes it a standpoint in the universe which it is probably good not to forsake. You are right in your consciousness that we are all echoes and reverberations of the *same*, and you are noble when your interest and pity as to everything that surrounds you, appears to have a sustaining and harmonizing power. Only don't, I beseech you, *generalize* too much in these sympathies and tendernesses—remember that every life is a special problem which is not yours but another's, and content yourself with the terrible algebra of your own. Don't melt too much into the universe, but be as solid and dense and fixed as you can. We all live together, and those of us who love and know, live so most. We help each other—even unconsciously, each in our own effort, we lighten the effort of others, we contribute to the sum of success, make it possible for others to live. Sorrow comes in great waves—no one can know that better than you—but it rolls over us, and though it may almost smother us it leaves us on the spot, and we know that if it is strong we are stronger, inasmuch as it passes and we remain. It wears us, uses us, but we wear it and use it in return; and it is blind, whereas we after a manner see. My dear Grace, you are passing through a darkness in which I myself in my ignorance see nothing but that you have been made wretchedly ill by it; but it is only a darkness, it is not an end, or *the* end. Don't think, don't feel, any more than you can help, don't conclude or decide—don't do anything but *wait*. Everything will pass, and serenity and *accepted* mysteries and disillusionments, and the tenderness of a few good people, and new opportunities and ever so much of life, in a word, will remain. You will do all sorts of things yet, and I will help you. The only thing is not to *melt* in the meanwhile. I insist upon the necessity of a sort of mechanical condensation—so that however fast the horse may run away there will, when he pulls up, be a somewhat agitated but perfectly identical G. N. left in the saddle. Try not to be ill—that is all; for in that there is a failure. You are marked out for success, and you must not fail. You have my tenderest affection and all my confidence. Ever your faithful friend—

HENRY JAMES

On Civilization

Manners and Marriage
Discrimination · Poverty
The Machine

JOHN STUART MILL
Civilization: Signs of the Times

The word "civilization," like many other terms of the philosophy of human nature, is a word of double meaning. It sometimes stands for *human improvement* in general, and sometimes for *certain kinds* of improvement in particular.

We are accustomed to call a country more civilized if we think it more improved; more eminent in the best characteristics of man and society; farther advanced in the road to perfection; happier, nobler, wiser. This is one sense of the word "civilization." But, in another sense, it stands for that kind of improvement only which distinguishes a wealthy and powerful nation from savages or barbarians. It is in this sense that we may speak of the vices or the miseries of civilization; and that the question has been seriously propounded, whether civilization is, on the whole, a good or an evil. Assuredly, we entertain no doubt on this point: we hold that civilization is a good; that it is the cause of much good, and not incompatible with any; but we think there is other good, much even of the highest good, which civilization in this sense does not provide for, and some which it has a tendency (though that tendency may be counteracted) to impede.

The inquiry into which these considerations would lead is calculated to throw light upon many of the characteristic features of our time. The present era[1] is pre-eminently the era of civilization in the narrow sense—whether we consider what has already been achieved, or the rapid advances making towards still greater achievements. We do not regard the age as either equally advanced or equally progressive in many of the other kinds of improvement. In some, it appears to us stationary; in some, even retrograde. Moreover, the irresistible consequences of a state of advancing civilization; the new position in which that advance has placed, and is every day more and more placing, mankind; the entire inapplicability of old rules to this new position; and the necessity, if we would either realize the benefits of the new state or preserve those of the old, that we should adopt many new rules, and new courses of action—are topics which seem to require a more comprehensive examination than they have usually received.

We shall on the present occasion use the word "civilization" only in the restricted sense; not that in which it is synonymous with improvement, but that in which it is the direct converse or contrary of rudeness or barbarism. Whatever be the characteristics of what we call savage life, the contrary of these, or the qualities which society puts on as it throws off these, constitute civilization. Thus a savage tribe consists of a handful of individuals, wandering or thinly scattered over a vast tract of country; a dense population, therefore, dwelling in fixed habitations, and largely collected together in towns and villages, we term civilized. In savage life, there is no commerce, no manufactures, no agriculture, or next to none: a country rich in the fruits of agriculture, commerce, and manufactures, we call civilized. In savage communities, each person shifts for himself: except in war (and even then very imperfectly), we seldom see any joint operations carried on by the union of many; nor do savages, in general, find much pleasure in each other's society. Wherever, therefore, we find human beings acting together for common purposes in large bodies, and enjoying the pleasures of social intercourse, we term them civilized. In savage life, there is little or no law, or administration of justice; no systematic employment of the collective strength of society to protect individuals against injury from one another: every one trusts to his own strength or cunning; and, where that fails, he is generally without resource. We accordingly call a people civilized, where the arrangements of society for protecting the persons and property of its members are sufficiently perfect to maintain peace among them; i.e., to induce the bulk of the community to rely for their security mainly upon social arrangements, and renounce for the most part, and in ordinary circumstances, the vindication of their interests (whether in the way of aggression or of defense) by their individual strength of courage.

These ingredients of civilization are various; but consideration will

1. This article was published in 1836.

satisfy us that they are not improperly classed together. History, and their own nature, alike show that they begin together, always co-exist, and accompany each other in their growth. Wherever there has arisen sufficient knowledge of arts of life, and sufficient security of property and person, to render the progressive increase of wealth and population possible, the community becomes and continues progressive in all the elements which we have just enumerated. These elements exist in modern Europe, and especially in Great Britain, in a more eminent degree, and in a state of more rapid progression, than at any other place or time. We propose to consider some of the consequences which that high and progressive state of civilization has already produced, and of the further ones which it is hastening to produce.

The most remarkable of those consequences of advancing civilization, which the state of the world is now forcing upon the attention of thinking minds, is this—that power passes more and more from individuals, and small knots of individuals, to masses; that the importance of the masses becomes constantly greater, that of individuals less.

The causes, evidences, and consequences of this law of human affairs well deserve attention.

There are two elements of importance and influence among mankind: the one is property; the other, powers and acquirements of mind. Both of these, in an early stage of civilization, are confined to a few persons. In the beginnings of society, the power of the masses does not exist, because property and intelligence have no existence beyond a very small portion of the community; and, even if they had, those who possessed the smaller portions would be, from their incapacity of co-operation, unable to cope with those who possessed the larger.

In the more backward countries of the present time, and in all Europe at no distant date, we see property entirely concentrated in a small number of hands; the remainder of the people being, with few exceptions, either the military retainers and dependants of the possessors of property, or serfs, stripped and tortured at pleasure by one master, and pillaged by a hundred. At no period could it be said that there was literally no middle class, but that class was extremely feeble, both in numbers and in power; while the laboring people, absorbed in manual toil, with difficulty earned, by the utmost excess of exertion, a more or less scanty and always precarious subsistence. The character of this state of society was the utmost excess of poverty and impotence in the masses; the most enormous importance and uncontrollable power of a small number of individuals, each of whom, within his own sphere, knew neither law nor superior.

We must leave to history to unfold the gradual rise of the trading and manufacturing classes, the gradual emancipation of the agricultural, the tumults and *bouleversements*[2] which accompanied these changes in their course, and the extraordinary alterations in institutions, opinions, habits, and the whole of social life, which they brought in their train. We need only ask the reader to form a conception of all that is implied in the words "growth of a middle class," and then to reflect on the immense increase of the numbers and property of that class throughout Great Britain, France, Germany, and other countries, in every successive generation, and the novelty of a laboring class receiving such wages as are now commonly earned by nearly the whole of the manufacturing, that is, of the most numerous, portion of the operative classes of this country—and ask himself, whether, from causes so unheard of, unheard-of effects ought not to be expected to flow. It must at least be evident, that if, as civilization advances, property and intelligence become thus widely diffused among the millions, it must also be an effect of civilization, that the portion of either of these which can belong to an individual must have a tendency to become less and less influential, and all results must more and more be decided by the movements of masses, provided that the power of combination among the masses keeps pace with the progress of their resources. And that it does so, who can doubt? There is not a more accurate test of the progress of civilization than the progress of the power of co-operation.

Consider the savage: he has bodily strength, he has courage, enterprise, and is often not without intelligence. What makes all savage communities poor and feeble? The same cause which prevented the lions and tigers from long ago extirpating the race of men—incapacity of co-operation. It is only civilized beings who can combine. All combination is compromise: it is the sacrifice of some portion of individual will for a common purpose. The savage cannot bear to sacrifice, for any purpose, the satisfaction of his individual will. His social cannot even temporarily prevail over his selfish feelings, nor his impulses bend to his calculations. Look again at the slave: he is used, indeed, to make his will give way, but to the commands of a master, not to a superior purpose of his own. He is wanting in intelligence to form such a purpose: above all, he cannot frame to himself the conception of a fixed rule; nor, if he could, has he the capacity to adhere to it. He is habituated to control, but not to self-control: when a driver is not standing over him with a whip, he is found more incapable of withstanding any temptation, or restraining any inclination, than the savage himself.

We have taken extreme cases, that the fact we seek to illustrate might stand out more conspicuously. But the remark itself applies universally. As any people approach to the condition of savages or of slaves, so are they incapable of acting in concert. Consider even war,

2. Commotions.

the most serious business of a barbarous people: see what a figure rude nations, or semi-civilized and enslaved nations, have made against civilized ones, from Marathon downwards! Why? Because discipline is more powerful than numbers, and discipline—that is, perfect co-operation—is an attribute of civilization. To come to our own times, the whole history of the Peninsular War bears witness to the incapacity of an imperfectly civilized people for co-operation. Amidst all the enthusiasm of the Spanish nation struggling against Napoléon, no one leader, military or political, could act in concert with another; no one would sacrifice one iota of his consequence, his authority, or his opinion, to the most obvious demands of the common cause: neither generals nor soldiers could observe the simplest rules of the military art. If there be an interest which one might expect to act forcibly upon the minds even of savages, it is the desire of simultaneously crushing a formidable neighbor whom none of them are strong enough to resist single-handed; yet none but civilized nations have ever been capable of forming an alliance. The native states of India have been conquered by the English, one by one; Turkey made peace with Russia in the very moment of her invasion by France; the nations of the world never could form a confederacy against the Romans, but were swallowed up in succession, some of them being always ready to aid in the subjugation of the rest. Enterprises requiring the voluntary co-operation of many persons independent of one another, in the hands of all but highly civilized nations, have always failed.

It is not difficult to see why this incapacity of organized combination characterizes savages, and disappears with the growth of civilization. Co-operation, like other difficult things, can be learnt only by practice; and, to be capable of it in great things, a people must be gradually trained to it in small. Now, the whole course of advancing civilization is a series of such training. The laborer in a rude state of society works singly; or, if several are brought to work together by the will of a master, they work side by side, but not in concert: one man digs his piece of ground; another digs a similar piece of ground close by him. In the situation of an ignorant laborer, tilling even his own field with his own hands, and associating with no one except his wife and his children, what is there that can teach him to co-operate? The division of employments; the accomplishment, by the combined labor of several, of tasks which could not be achieved by any number of persons singly—is the great school of co-operation. What a lesson, for instance, is navigation, as soon as it passes out of its first simple stage!—the safety of all constantly depending upon the vigilant performance, by each, of the part peculiarly allotted to him in the common task. Military operations, when not wholly undisciplined, are a similar school; so are all the operations of commerce and manufactures which require the employment of many hands upon the same thing at the same time. By these operations, mankind learn the value of combination; they see how much and with what ease it accomplishes, which never could be accomplished without it; they learn a practical lesson of submitting themselves to guidance, and subduing themselves to act as interdependent parts of a complex whole. A people thus progressively trained to combination by the business of their lives become capable of carrying the same habits into new things. For it holds universally, that the only mode of learning to do any thing is actually doing something of the same kind under easier circumstances. Habits of discipline, once acquired, qualify human beings to accomplish all other things for which discipline is needed. No longer either spurning control, or incapable of seeing its advantages, whenever any object presents itself which can be attained by co-operation, and which they see or believe to be beneficial, they are ripe for attaining it.

The characters, then, of a state of high civilization being the diffusion of property and intelligence, and the power of co-operation, the next thing to observe is the unexampled development which all these elements have assumed of late years.

The rapidity with which property has accumulated and is accumulating in the principal countries of Europe, but especially in this island, is obvious to every one. The capital of the industrious classes overflows into foreign countries, and into all kinds of wild speculations. The amount of capital annually exported from Great Britain alone, surpasses, probably, the whole wealth of the most flourishing commercial republics of antiquity. But this capital, collectively so vast, is mainly composed of small portions; very generally so small, that the owners cannot, without other means of livelihood, subsist on the profits of them. While such is the growth of property in the hands of the mass, the circumstances of the higher classes have undergone nothing like a corresponding improvement. Many large fortunes have, it is true, been accumulated; but many others have been wholly or partially dissipated: for the inheritors of immense fortunes, as a class, always live at least up to their incomes when at the highest; and the unavoidable vicissitudes of those incomes are always sinking them deeper and deeper into debt. A large proportion of the English landlords, as they themselves are constantly telling us, are so overwhelmed with mortgages, that they have ceased to be the real owners of the bulk of their estates. In other countries, the large properties have very generally been broken down; in France, by revolution, and the revolutionary law of inheritance; in Prussia, by successive edicts of that substantially democratic though formally absolute government.

With respect to knowledge and intelligence, it is the truism of the age, that the masses, both of the middle and even of the working classes, are treading upon the heels of their superiors.

If we now consider the progress made by those same masses in the capacity and habit of co-operation, we find it equally surprising. At what period were the operations of productive industry carried on upon any thing like their present scale? Were so many hands ever before employed at the same time, upon the same work, as now in all the principal departments of manufactures and commerce? To how enormous an extent is business now carried on by joint-stock companies!—in other words, by many small capitals thrown together to form one great one. The country is covered with associations. There are societies for political, societies for religious, societies for philanthropic purposes. But the greatest novelty of all is the spirit of combination which has grown up among the working classes. The present age has seen the commencement of benefit societies; and they now, as well as the more questionable Trades Unions, overspread the whole country. A more powerful, though not so ostensible, instrument of combination than any of these, has but lately become universally accessible—the newspaper. The newspaper carries home the voice of the many to every individual among them: by the newspaper, each learns that others are feeling as he feels; and that, if he is ready, he will find them also prepared to act upon what they feel. The newspaper is the telegraph which carries the signal throughout the country, and the flag round which it rallies. Hundreds of newspapers speaking in the same voice at once, and the rapidity of communication afforded by improved means of locomotion, were what enabled the whole country to combine in that simultaneous energetic demonstration of determined will which carried the Reform Act. Both these facilities are on the increase, every one may see how rapidly; and they will enable the people on all decisive occasions to form a collective will, and render that collective will irresistible.

To meet this wonderful development of physical and mental power on the part of the masses, can it be said that there has been any corresponding quantity of intellectual power or moral energy unfolded among those individuals or classes who have enjoyed superior advantages? No one, we think, will affirm it. There is a great increase of humanity, a decline of bigotry, as well as of arrogance and the conceit of caste, among our conspicuous classes; but there is, to say the least, no increase of shining ability, and a very marked decrease of vigor and energy. With all the advantages of this age, its facilities for mental cultivation, the incitements and the rewards which it holds out to exalted talents, there can scarcely be pointed out in the European annals any stirring times which have brought so little that is distinguished, either morally or intellectually, to the surface.

That this, too, is no more than was to be expected from the tendencies of civilization, when no attempt is made to correct them, we shall have occasion to show presently. But, even if civilization did nothing to lower the eminences, it would produce an exactly similar effect by raising the plains. When the masses become powerful, an individual, or a small band of individuals, can accomplish nothing considerable except by influencing the masses; and to do this becomes daily more difficult, from the constantly increasing number of those who are vying with one another to attract the public attention. Our position, therefore, is established, that, by the natural growth of civilization, power passes from individuals to masses, and the weight and importance of an individual, as compared with the mass, sink into greater and greater insignificance.

The change which is thus in progress, and to a great extent consummated, is the greatest ever recorded in social affairs; the most complete, the most fruitful in consequences, and the most irrevocable. Whoever can meditate on it, and not see that so great a revolution vitiates all existing rules of government and policy, and renders all practice and all predictions grounded only on prior experience worthless, is wanting in the very first and most elementary principle of statesmanship in these times.

"*Il faut*," as M. de Tocqueville has said, "*une science politique nouvelle à un monde tout nouveau.*"[3] The whole face of society is reversed; all the natural elements of power have definitely changed places; and there are people who talk of standing up for ancient institutions, and the duty of sticking to the British Constitution settled in 1688! What is still more extraordinary, these are the people who accuse others of disregarding variety of circumstances, and imposing their abstract theories upon all states of society without discrimination.

We put it to those who call themselves conservatives, whether, when the chief power in society is passing into the hands of the masses, they really think it possible to prevent the masses from making that power predominant as well in the government as elsewhere. The triumph of democracy, or, in other words, of the government of public opinion, does not depend upon the opinion of any individual, or set of individuals, that it ought to triumph, but upon the natural laws of the progress of wealth, upon the diffusion of reading, and the increase of the facilities of human intercourse. If Lord Kenyon or the Duke of Newcastle could stop these, they might accomplish something. There is no danger of the prevalence of democracy in Syria or Timbuctoo. But he must be a poor politician who does not know, that whatever is the growing power in society will force its way into the government by fair means or foul. The distribution of constitutional power cannot long continue very different from that of real power, without a convulsion; nor, if the institutions which impede the progress of democracy could be by any miracle preserved, could even they do more than render that progress a little slower. Were the constitution of Great Britain to remain henceforth unaltered, we are

3. "An entirely new world requires a new science of government."

not the less under the dominion, becoming every day more irresistible, of public opinion.

With regard to the advance of democracy, there are two different positions which it is possible for a rational person to take up, according as he thinks the masses prepared or unprepared to exercise the control which they are acquiring over their destiny, in a manner which would be an improvement upon what now exists. If he thinks them prepared, he will aid the democratic movement; or, if he deem it to be proceeding fast enough without him, he will at all events refrain from resisting it. If, on the contrary, he thinks the masses unprepared for complete control over their government—seeing at the same time, that, prepared or not, they cannot long be prevented from acquiring it—he will exert his utmost efforts in contributing to prepare them: using all means, on the one hand, for making the masses themselves wiser and better; on the other, for so rousing the slumbering energy of the opulent and lettered classes, so storing the youth of those classes with the profoundest and most valuable knowledge, so calling forth whatever of individual greatness exists or can be raised up in the country, as to create a power which might partially rival the mere power of the masses, and might exercise the most salutary influence over them for their own good. When engaged earnestly in works like these, one can understand how a rational person might think, that, in order to give more time for the performance of them, it were well if the current of democracy, which can in no sort be stayed, could be prevailed upon, for a time, to flow less impetuously. With conservatives of this sort, all democrats of corresponding enlargement of aims could fraternize as frankly and cordially as with most of their own friends; and we speak from an extensive knowledge of the wisest and most high-minded of that body, when we take upon ourselves to answer for them, that they would never push forward their own political projects in a spirit or with a violence which could tend to frustrate any rational endeavors towards the object nearest their hearts—the instruction of the understandings, and the elevation of the characters, of all classes of their countrymen.

But who is there, among the political party calling themselves conservatives, that professes to have any such object in view? Do they seek to employ the interval of respite, which they might hope to gain by withstanding democracy, in qualifying the people to wield the democracy more wisely when it comes? Would they not far rather resist any such endeavor, on the principle that knowledge is power, and that its further diffusion would make the dreaded evil come sooner? Do the leading conservatives in either house of Parliament feel that the character of the higher classes needs renovating, to qualify them for a more arduous task and a keener strife than has yet fallen to their lot? Is not the character of a Tory lord or country gentleman, or a Church-of-England parson, perfectly satisfactory to them? Is not the existing constitution of the two universities— those bodies whose especial duty it was to counteract the debilitating influence of the circumstances of the age upon individual character, and to send forth into society a succession of minds, not the creatures of their age, but capable of being its improvers and regenerators—the universities, by whom this, their especial duty, has been basely neglected, until, as is usual with all neglected duties, the very consciousness of it as a duty has faded from their remembrance —is not, we say, the existing constitution, and the whole existing system of these universities, down to the smallest of their abuses—the exclusion of Dissenters—a thing for which every Tory, though he may not, as he pretends, die in the last ditch, will at least vote in the last division? The Church, professedly the other great instrument of national culture, long since perverted (we speak of rules, not exceptions) into a grand instrument for discouraging all culture inconsistent with blind obedience to established maxims and constituted authorities—what Tory has a scheme in view for any changes in this body, but such as may pacify assailants, and make the institution wear a less disgusting appearance to the eye? What political Tory will not resist to the very last moment any alteration in that Church, which would prevent its livings from being the provision for a family, its dignities the reward of political or of private services? The Tories, those at least connected with Parliament or office, do not aim at having good institutions, or even at preserving the present ones; their object is to profit by them while they exist.

We scruple not to express our belief, that a truer spirit of conservation, as to every thing good in the principles and professed objects of our old institutions, lives in many who are determined enemies of those institutions in their present state, than in most of those who call themselves conservatives. But there are many well-meaning people who always confound attachment to an end with pertinacious adherence to any set of means by which it either is, or is pretended to be, already pursued; and have yet to learn, that bodies of men who live in honor and importance upon the pretence of fulfilling ends which they never honestly seek are the great hindrance to the attainment of those ends, and that whoever has the attainment really at heart must expect a war of extermination with all such confederacies.

Thus far as to the political effects of civilization. Its moral effects, which as yet we have only glanced at, demand further elucidation. They may be considered under two heads—the direct influence of civilization itself upon individual character, and the moral effects produced by the insignificance into which the individual falls in comparison with the masses.

One of the effects of a high state of civilization upon character is a relaxation of individual energy, or rather the concentration of it within the narrow sphere of the individual's money-getting pursuits. As civilization advances, every person becomes dependent for more and more of what most nearly concerns him, not upon his own exertions, but upon the general arrangements of society. In a rude state, each man's personal security, the protection of his family, his property, his liberty itself, depend greatly upon his bodily strength and his mental energy or cunning: in a civilized state, all this is secured to him by causes extrinsic to himself. The growing mildness of manners is a protection to him against much that he was before exposed to; while, for the remainder, he may rely with constantly increasing assurance upon the soldier, the policeman, and the judge, and (where the efficiency or purity of those instruments, as is usually the case, lags behind the general march of civilization) upon the advancing strength of public opinion. There remain, as inducements to call forth the energy of character, the desire of wealth or of personal aggrandizement, the passion of philanthropy, and the love of active virtue. But the objects to which these various feelings point are matters of choice, not of necessity; nor do the feelings act with any thing like equal force upon all minds. The only one of them which can be considered as any thing like universal is the desire of wealth; and wealth being, in the case of the majority, the most accessible means of gratifying all their other desires, nearly the whole of the energy of character which exists in highly civilized societies concentrates itself on the pursuit of that object. In the case, however, of the most influential classes—those whose energies, if they had them, might be exercised on the greatest scale and with the most considerable result—the desire of wealth is already sufficiently satisfied to render them averse to suffer pain or incur much voluntary labor for the sake of any further increase. The same classes also enjoy, from their station alone, a high degree of personal consideration. Except the high offices of the state, there is hardly any thing to tempt the ambition of men in their circumstances. Those offices, when a great nobleman could have them for asking for, and keep them with less trouble than he could manage his private estate, were, no doubt, desirable enough possessions for such persons; but when they become posts of labor, vexation, and anxiety, and, besides, cannot be had without paying the price of some previous toil, experience shows, that, among men unaccustomed to sacrifice their amusements and their ease, the number upon whom these high offices operate as incentives to activity, or in whom they call forth any vigor of character, is extremely limited. Thus it happens, that in highly civilized countries, and particularly among ourselves, the energies of the middle classes are almost confined to money-getting, and those of the higher classes are nearly extinct.

There is another circumstance to which we may trace much both of the good and of the bad qualities which distinguish our civilization from the rudeness of former times. One of the effects of civilization (not to say one of the ingredients in it) is, that the spectacle, and even the very idea, of pain, is kept more and more out of the sight of those classes who enjoy in their fulness the benefits of civilization. The state of perpetual personal conflict, rendered necessary by the circumstances of former times, and from which it was hardly possible for any person, in whatever rank of society, to be exempt, necessarily habituated every one to the spectacle of harshness, rudeness, and violence, to the struggle of one indomitable will against another, and to the alternate suffering and infliction of pain. These things, consequently, were not as revolting even to the best and most actively benevolent men of former days as they are to our own; and we find the recorded conduct of those men frequently such as would be universally considered very unfeeling in a person of our own day. They, however, thought less of the infliction of pain, because they thought less of pain altogether. When we read of actions of the Greeks and Romans, or of our own ancestors, denoting callousness to human suffering, we must not think that those who committed these actions were as cruel as we must become before we could do the like. The pain which they inflicted they were in the habit of voluntarily undergoing from slight causes: it did not appear to them as great an evil as it appears, and as it really is, to us; nor did it in any way degrade their minds. In our own time, the necessity of personal collision between one person and another is, comparatively speaking, amost at an end. All those necessary portions of the business of society which oblige any person to be the immediate agent or ocular witness of the infliction of pain are delegated by common consent to peculiar and narrow classes—to the judge, the soldier, the surgeon, the butcher, and the executioner. To most people in easy circumstances, any pain, except that inflicted upon the body by accident or disease, and upon the mind by the inevitable sorrows of life, is rather a thing known of than actually experienced. This is much more emphatically true in the more refined classes, and as refinement advances; for it is in avoiding the presence, not only of actual pain, but of whatever suggests offensive or disagreeable ideas, that a great part of refinement consists. We may remark, too, that this is possible only by a perfection of mechanical arrangements impracticable in any but a high state of civilization. Now, most kinds of pain and annoyance appear much more unendurable to those who have little experience of them than to those who have much. The consequence is, that, compared with former times, there is in the more opulent classes of modern civilized communities much more of the amiable and humane, and much less of the heroic. The heroic essentially consists in being ready, for a worthy object, to do and to suffer, but especially to do, what is painful or disagreeable; and whoever does not early learn to be capable of this will never be a great character. There has crept over the refined classes, over the whole class of gentlemen in England, a moral effeminacy, an inaptitude for every kind of struggle. They shrink from all effort, from every thing which is troublesome and disagreeable. The same causes which render them sluggish and unenterprising, make them, it is true, for the most part, stoical under inevitable evils. But heroism is an active, not a passive quality; and when it is necessary not to bear pain, but to seek it, little needs be expected from the men of the present day. They cannot undergo labor, they cannot brook ridicule, they cannot brave evil tongues: they have not hardihood to say an unpleasant thing to any one whom they are in the habit of seeing, or to face, even with a nation at their back, the coldness of some little coterie which surrounds them. This torpidity and cowardice, as a general characteristic, is new in the world; but (modified by the different temperaments of different nations) it is a natural consequence of the progress of civilization, and will continue until met by a system of cultivation adapted to counteract it.

If the source of great virtues thus dries up, great vices are placed, no doubt, under considerable restraint. The *régime* of public opinion is adverse to at least the indecorous vices; and as that restraining power gains strength, and certain classes or individuals cease to possess a virtual exemption from it, the change is highly favorable to the outward decencies of life. Nor can it be denied, that the diffusion of even such knowledge as civilization naturally brings has no slight tendency to rectify, though it be but partially, the standard of public opinion; to undermine many of those prejudices and superstitions which made mankind hate each other for things not really odious; to make them take a juster measure of the tendencies of actions, and weigh more correctly the evidence on which they condemn or applaud their fellow-creatures; to make, in short, their approbation direct itself more correctly to good actions, and their disapprobation to bad. What are the limits to this natural improvement in public opinion, when there is no other sort of cultivation going on than that which is the accompaniment of civilization, we need not at present inquire. It is enough that within those limits there is an extensive range; that as much improvement in the general understanding, softening of the feelings, and decay of pernicious errors, as naturally attends the progress of wealth and the spread of reading, suffices to render the judgment of the public upon actions and persons, so far as evidence is before them, much more discriminating and correct.

But here presents itself another ramification of the effects of civilization, which it has often surprised us to find so little attended to. The individual becomes so lost in the crowd, that, though he depends more and more upon opinion, he is apt to depend less and less upon well-grounded opinion—upon the opinion of those who know him. An established character becomes at once more difficult to gain, and more easily to be dispensed with.

It is in a small society, where everybody knows everybody, that public opinion, so far as well directed, exercises its most salutary influence. Take the case of a tradesman in a small country town. To every one of his customers he is long and accurately known: their opinion of him has been formed after repeated trials: if he could deceive them once, he cannot hope to go on deceiving them, in the quality of his goods: he has no other customers to look for if he loses these; while, if his goods are really what they profess to be, he may hope, among so few competitors, that this also will be known and recognized, and that he will acquire the character, individually and professionally, which his conduct entitles him to. Far different is the case of a man setting up in business in the crowded streets of a great city. If he trust solely to the quality of his goods, to the honesty and faithfulness with which he performs what he undertakes, he may remain ten years without a customer: be he ever so honest, he is driven to cry out on the housetops that his wares are the best of wares, past, present, and to come; while if he proclaim this, however false, with sufficient loudness to excite the curiosity of passers-by, and can give his commodities "a gloss, a salable look," not easily to be seen through at a superficial glance, he may drive a thriving trade, though no customer ever enter his shop twice. There has been much complaint of late years of growth, both in the world of trade and in that of intellect, of quackery, and especially of puffing: but nobody seems to have remarked that these are the inevitable fruits of immense competition; of a state of society, where any voice, not pitched in an exaggerated key, is lost in the hubbub. Success, in so crowded a field, depends, not upon what a person is, but upon what he seems: mere marketable qualities become the object instead of substantial ones, and a man's labor and capital are expended less in doing any thing than in persuading other people that he has done it. Our own age has seen this evil brought to its consummation. Quackery there always was; but it once was a test of the absence of sterling qualities: there was a proverb, that good wine needed no bush. It is our own age which has seen the honest dealer driven to quackery by hard necessity, and the certainty of being undersold by the dishonest. For the first time, arts for attracting public attention form a necessary part of the qualifications even of the deserving; and skill in these goes farther than any other quality towards insuring success. The same intensity of competition drives the trading public more and more to play high for success; to throw for all or nothing; and this, together with the difficulty of sure calculations in a field of commerce so widely extended, renders bankruptcy no longer disgraceful, because no longer an almost certain presumption either of dishonesty or imprudence: the discredit which it still incurs belongs to it, alas! mainly as an indication of poverty. Thus public opinion loses another of those simple criteria of desert, which, and which alone, it is capable of correctly applying; and the very cause, which has rendered it omnipotent in the gross, weakens the precision and force with which its judgment is brought home to individuals.

It is not solely on the private virtues that this growing insignificance of the individual in the mass is productive of mischief. It corrupts the very fountain of the improvement of public opinion itself; it corrupts public teaching; it weakens the influence of the more cultivated few over the many. Literature has suffered more than any other human production by the common disease. When there were few books, and when few read at all save those who had been accustomed to read the best authors, books were written with the well-grounded expectation that they would be read carefully, and, if they deserved it, would be read often. A book of sterling merit, when it came out, was sure to be heard of, and might hope to be read, by the whole reading class: it might succeed by its real excellences, though not got up to strike at once; and, even if so got up, unless it had the support of genuine merit, it fell into oblivion. The rewards were then for him who wrote *well*, not *much*; for the laborious and learned, not the crude and ill-informed writer. But now the case is reversed. "This is a reading age; and, precisely because it is so reading an age, any book which is the result of profound meditation is perhaps less likely to be duly and profitably read than at a former period. The world reads too much and too quickly to read well. When books were few, to get through one was a work of time and labor: what was written with thought was read with thought, and with a desire to extract from it as much of the materials of knowledge as possible. But when almost every person who can spell, can and will write, what is to be done? It is difficult to know what to read, except by reading every thing; and so much of the world's business is now transacted through the press, that it is necessary to know what is printed, if we desire to know what is going on. Opinion weighs with so vast a weight in the balance of events, that ideas of no value in themselves are of importance from the mere circumstance that they *are* ideas, and have a *bonâ fide* existence as such anywhere out of Bedlam. (The world, in consequence, gorges itself with intellectual food; and, in order to swallow the more, *bolts* it.) Nothing is now read slowly, or twice over. Books are run through with no less rapidity, and scarcely leave a more durable impression, than a newspaper-article. It is from this, among other causes, that so few books are produced of any value. The lioness in the fable boasted, that, though she produced only one at a birth, that one was a lion; but if each lion only counted for one, and each leveret for one, the advantage would all be on the side of the hare. When every unit is individually weak, it is only multitude that tells. What wonder that the newspapers should carry all before them? A book produces hardly a greater effect than an article, and there can be three hundred and sixty-five of these in one year. He, therefore, who should and would write a book, and write it in the proper manner of writing a book, now dashes down his first hasty thoughts, or what he mistakes for thoughts, in a periodical. And the public is in the predicament of an indolent man, who cannot bring himself to apply his mind vigorously to his own affairs, and over whom, therefore, not he who speaks most wisely, but he who speaks most frequently, obtains the influence."[4]

Hence we see that literature is becoming more and more ephemeral: books, of any solidity, are almost gone by; even reviews are not now considered sufficiently light: the attention cannot sustain itself on any serious subject, even for the space of a review-article. In the more attractive kinds of literature, novels and magazines, though the demand has so greatly increased, the supply has so outstripped it, that even a novel is seldom a lucrative speculation. It is only under circumstances of rare attraction that a bookseller will now give any thing to an author for copyright. As the difficulties of success thus progressively increase, all other ends are more and more sacrificed for the attainment of it: literature becomes more and more a mere reflection of the current sentiments, and has almost entirely abandoned its mission as an enlightener and improver of them.

There are now in this country, we may say, but two modes left in which an individual mind can hope to produce much direct effect upon the minds and destinies of his countrymen generally—as a member of Parliament, or an editor of a London newspaper. In both these capacities, much may still be done by an individual; because, while the power of the collective body is very great, the number of participants in it does not admit of much increase. One of these monopolies will be opened to competition when the newspaper-stamp is taken off; whereby the importance of the newspaper-press in the aggregate, considered as the voice of public opinion, will be increased, and the influence of any one writer in helping to form that opinion necessarily diminished. This we might regret, did we not remember to what ends that influence is now used, and is sure to be so while newspapers are a mere investment of capital for the sake of mercantile profit.

Is there, then, no remedy? Are the decay of individual energy, the weakening of the influence of superior minds over the multitude, the growth of charlatanerie, and the diminished efficacy of public opinion as a restraining power—are these the price we necessarily pay for the benefits of civilization? And can they only be avoided by checking the diffusion of knowledge, discouraging the spirit of combina-

4. From a paper by the author [Mill's note].

tion, prohibiting improvements in the arts of life, and repressing the further increase of wealth and of production? Assuredly not. Those advantages which civilization cannot give—which in its uncorrected influence it has even a tendency to destroy—may yet co-exist with civilization; and it is only when joined to civilization that they can produce their fairest fruits. All that we are in danger of losing we may preserve, all that we have lost we may regain, and bring to a perfection hitherto unknown; but not by slumbering, and leaving things to themselves, no more than by ridiculously trying our strength against their irresistible tendencies: only by establishing countertendencies, which may combine with those tendencies, and modify them.

The evils are, that the individual is lost and becomes impotent in the crowd, and that individual character itself becomes relaxed and enervated. For the first evil, the remedy is, greater and more perfect combination among individuals; for the second, national institutions of education, and forms of polity calculated to invigorate the individual character.

The former of these desiderata, as its attainment depends upon a change in the habits of society itself, can only be realized by degrees, as the necessity becomes felt; but circumstances are even now, to a certain extent, forcing it on. In Great Britain especially (which so far surpasses the rest of the Old World in the extent and rapidity of the accumulation of wealth), the fall of profits, consequent upon the vast increase of population and capital, is rapidly extinguishing the class of small dealers and small producers, from the impossibility of living on their diminished profits; and is throwing business of all kinds more and more into the hands of large capitalists, whether these be rich individuals, or joint-stock companies formed by the aggregation of many small capitals. We are not among those who believe that this progress is tending to the complete extinction of competition, or that the entire productive resources of the country will, within any assignable number of ages, if ever, be administered by, and for the benefit of, a general association of the whole community. But we believe that the multiplication of competitors in all branches of business and in all professions—which renders it more and more difficult to obtain success by merit alone, more and more easy to obtain it by plausible pretence—will find a limiting principle in the progress of the spirit of co-operation; that, in every over-crowded department, there will arise a tendency among individuals so to unite their labor or their capital, that the purchaser or employer will have to choose, not among innumerable individuals, but among a few groups. Competition will be as active as ever; but the number of competitors will be brought within manageable bounds.

Such a spirit of co-operation is most of all wanted among the intellectual classes and professions. The amount of human labor, and labor of the most precious kind, now wasted, and wasted too, in the cruelest manner, for want of combination, is incalculable. What a spectacle, for instance, does the medical profession present! One successful practitioner burthened with more work than mortal man can perform, and which he performs so summarily, that it were often better let alone: in the surrounding streets, twenty unhappy men, each of whom has been as laboriously and expensively trained as he has to do the very same thing, and is possibly as well qualified, wasting their capabilities, and starving for want of work. Under better arrangements, these twenty would form a corps of subalterns, marshaled under their more successful leader; who (granting him to be really the ablest physician of the set, and not merely the most successful impostor) is wasting time in physicking people for headaches and heartburns, which he might with better economy of mankind's resources turn over to his subordinates, while he employed his maturer powers and greater experience in studying and treating those more obscure and difficult cases upon which science has not yet thrown sufficient light, and to which ordinary knowledge and abilities would not be adequate. By such means, every person's capacities would be turned to account; and, the highest minds being kept for the highest things, these would make progress, while ordinary occasions would be no losers.

But it is in literature, above all, that a change of this sort is of most pressing urgency. There the system of individual competition has fairly worked itself out, and things can hardly continue much longer as they are. Literature is a province of exertion, upon which more, of the first value to human nature, depends, than upon any other; a province in which the highest and most valuable order of works—those which most contribute to form the opinions and shape the characters of subsequent ages—are, more than in any other class of productions, placed beyond the possibility of appreciation by those who form the bulk of the purchasers in the book-market; insomuch that, even in ages when these were a far less numerous and more select class than now, it was an admitted point, that the only success which writers of the first order could look to was the verdict of posterity. That verdict could, in those times, be confidently expected by whoever was worthy of it: for the good judges, though few in number, were sure to read every work of merit which appeared; and, as the recollection of one book was not in those days immediately obliterated by a hundred others, they remembered it, and kept alive the knowledge of it to subsequent ages. But in our day, from the immense multitude of writers (which is now not less remarkable than the multitude of readers), and from the manner in which the people of this age are obliged to read, it is difficult, for what does not strike during its novelty, to strike at all: a book either misses fire altogether, or is so read as to make no permanent impression; and the good equally with the worthless are forgotten by the next day.

For this there is no remedy, while the public have no guidance beyond booksellers' advertisements, and the ill-considered and hasty criticisms of newspapers and small periodicals, to direct them in distinguishing what is not worth reading from what is. The resource must in time be some organized co-operation among the leading intellects of the age, whereby works of first-rate merit, of whatever class, and of whatever tendency in point of opinion, might come forth, with the stamp on them, from the first, of the approval of those whose names would carry authority. There are many causes why we must wait long for such a combination; but (with enormous defects both in plan and in execution) the Society for the Diffusion of Useful Knowledge was as considerable a step towards it as could be expected in the present state of men's minds, and in a first attempt. Literature has had in this country two ages: it must now have a third. The age of patronage, as Johnson a century ago proclaimed, is gone. The age of booksellers, it has been proclaimed by Mr. Carlyle, has well nigh died out. In the first, there was nothing intrinsically base; nor, in the second, any thing inherently independent and liberal. Each has done great things: both have had their day. The time is perhaps coming, when authors, as a collective guild, will be their own patrons and their own booksellers.

* * *

With regard to the changes, in forms of polity and social arrangements, which, in addition to reforms in education, we conceive to be required for regenerating the character of the higher classes—to express them even summarily would require a long discourse. But the general idea from which they all emanate may be stated briefly. Civilization has brought about a degree of security and fixity in the possession of all advantages once acquired, which has rendered it possible for a rich man to lead the life of a Sybarite, and nevertheless enjoy throughout life a degree of power and consideration which could formerly be earned or retained only by personal activity. We cannot undo what civilization has done, and again stimulate the energy of the higher classes by insecurity of property, or danger of life or limb. The only adventitious motive it is in the power of society to hold out is reputation and consequence; and of this as much use as possible should be made for the encouragement of desert. The main thing which social changes can do for the improvement of the higher classes—and it is what the progress of democracy is insensibly but certainly accomplishing—is gradually to put an end to every kind of unearned distinction, and let the only road open to honor and ascendency be that of personal qualities.

QUESTIONS FOR STUDY, DISCUSSION, AND WRITING

1. What is the function of Mill's initial definition of civilization? Outline the major parts of his essay. Which parts are devoted to analysis of conditions, which to criticism of opinions, which to proposals for improvement?
2. At the outset Mill describes the conditions of life in a savage community. Does he seem closely familiar with life as savages live it? If an anthropologist were to prove him wrong about savage societies, what would be the impact on his argument?
3. Mill attributes the weakness of savage communities to the "same cause which prevented the lions and tigers from long ago extirpating the race of men—incapacity of cooperation" (p. 338). What view of social change does this comparison suggest?
4. At various points Mill makes it clear that he thinks the changes he describes are inevitable and irresistible. Does he indicate what the cause of the changes is? What ideas about society are implicit in his approach to these changes?
5. Discussing the future, Mill makes some optimistic predictions about the progresss of a spirit of cooperation. Looking at American society today, would you say that his predictions about competition have come true? Was his optimism justified?
6. Bettelheim ("The Imaginary Impasse," p. 452) uses "civilization" in the same sense that Mill stipulates for his discussion. How does Bettelheim's essay resemble Mill's? How does it differ?
7. Accepting the student world that you know as a civilization, describe the signs of the times. Will you want to follow Mill's organizational plan?

EDMUND WILSON
Books of Etiquette and Emily Post

Professor Arthur M. Schlesinger, the Harvard historian, has written an entertaining little treatise called *Learning How to Behave: A Historical Study of American Etiquette Books*. It is curious and rather instructive to look at the development of the United States from the point of view of the literature of etiquette. The first manuals derived from Europe and emphasized deference to rank to the point of, in one case, admonishing the young: "If thy superior be relating a story, say not, 'I have heard it before.' . . . If he tell it not right, snigger not"; but after the Revolution, and especially after the advent of Jackson, the object became not to define class differences but to provide a set of prescriptions which would show anyone how to become a gentleman. The Southerners had, however, based their practice on seventeenth-century guides which helped the planter "to model his life on that of the English landed gentry" and "provided a fairly consistent chart of behavior . . . in emulation of the ancient ideals of Christian chivalry"; and they continued to follow this code. In the period after the Civil War, when the big fortunes were being made, a fresh crop of volumes appeared which had the purpose of orienting the newly rich among the refinements and complications of calling cards and formal dinners. There was an average of five such a year, and this continued through to 1945.

The two greatest publishing successes in the department of etiquette date from the beginning of the nineteen-twenties. At this time, a Miss Lillian Eichler, an advertising copywriter, then eighteen and just out of high school, sold thousands of copies of an *Encyclopedia of Etiquette* by means of a series of advertisements with the caption "What's Wrong with This Picture?" But the book—which had been written in 1901—was by that time, it seems, obsolete (Mr. Schlesinger does not tell us in what respect), for it was returned by "droves of dissatisfied customers." The publisher then proposed to Miss Eichler that she should herself do an up-to-date book, and the result was *The Book of Etiquette*, which between 1921 and 1945 sold over a million copies. In 1922, Emily Post brought out her *Etiquette*, which by 1945 had sold more than two-thirds of a million.

An examination of these two manuals reveals fundamental differences between them and suggests that they have been appealing to two rather different publics. Miss Eichler is practical and comfortable (her book is now frankly called *Today's Etiquette*). She tells you how to teach the children table manners and how to give a dinner without servants. She makes rough tabulations of vintage wines and supplies reliable recipes for half-a-dozen well-known cocktails; she recommends, in a chapter on *The Nature and Meaning of Culture*, that one "read more than one kind of literature: not mystery stories alone, nor light fiction alone," and she lists "nine painters of undisputed glory, with whose work every person of culture should be at least familiar." The precepts are mostly appropriate for anyone of moderate income, and the whole tone is non-invidious. She makes social life sound easy and jolly. But Mrs. Post is another affair. I had had no conception of her extraordinary book till I looked into it recently, fell under its spell and read it almost through. Mrs. Post is not merely the author of a comprehensive textbook on manners: she is a considerable imaginative writer, and her book has some of the excitement of a novel. It has also the snob-appeal which is evidently an important factor in the success of a Marquand or a Galsworthy. (I should explain that the edition I read was the third printing, of 1922.)

Mrs. Post has produced a world which has its characters, its atmosphere, its drama, I was reminded, after reading *Etiquette*, of the late Scott Fitzgerald's once telling me that he had looked into Emily Post and been inspired with the idea of a play in which all the motivations should consist of trying to do the right thing. The element of dramatic conflict would be produced by setting people at cross-purposes through stalemates of good form, from which the only possible rescue would be through the intervention of some bounder as *deus ex machina* to put an end to the sufferings of the gentle-folk who had been paralyzed by Mrs. Post's principles. (There are actually novels by Howells, and even by Henry James, which very nearly fulfill this formula.) For it is true that Mrs. Post has supplied all the materials for such a drama. Her ideal gentleman-clubman and her ideal feminine house guest—described in little essays like the "characters" of La Bruyère or the *Spectator*—are models which can never deviate, and thoroughly priggish figures which would lend themselves to satirical comedy. The "considerate guest," in particular, who is always perfectly sweet to everyone and always wants to do what the others are doing, who pretends to like children and dogs and lets them "climb over her" though she loathes them, could easily be shown as a menace from whom the party would have to be saved by Mrs. Post's hideous villain: "The Guest No One Invites Again."

But Mrs. Post, in providing illustrations, has also invented types that have names, personalities and histories, and that are threaded, like the characters of Proust, in and out all through her book. These figures were originally intended merely as convenient dummies to stand in the places of hosts and guests when she was showing how the right kind of entertaining might be done on various scales by people on different income levels; but they have taken such a hold on the author that they have gratuitously been developed to exemplify, like the groups in Proust, a variety of social milieux. They do, however, all belong to Society, and the author, unlike Miss Eichler, always assumes that the reader wants to belong to Society, too.

At the top of Mrs. Post's structure, from the point of view of a wealth which is combined with "social credentials," stand the Worldlys of Great Estates (run by their butler Hastings) and the Gildings of Golden Hall. The Worldlys are a little difficult, they are constrained by the expensive habits and the inflated self-importance of the rich; but the Gildings are more human and always fun. Of Golden Hall, Mrs. Post writes: "The house is a palace, the grounds are a park. There is not only a long wing of magnificent guest rooms in the house, occupied by young girls or important older people, but there is also a guest annex, a separate building designed and run like the most luxurious country club. . . . Perfectly equipped

Turkish and Russian baths in charge of the best Swedish masseur and masseuse procurable . . . a glass-roofed and enclosed riding ring—not big enough for games of polo, but big enough to practise in winter," etc. It was after a party at Golden Hall that Mrs. Toplofty, Bobo Gilding's great-aunt, exclaimed, "How are any of us ever going to amuse any one after *this?* I feel like doing my guest rooms up in moth balls." Bobo Gilding (whose nickname is incidentally explained in a section intended to discourage what Mrs. Post calls conversational "door-slammers": "As for the name 'Bobo,' it's asinine." "Oh, it's just one of those children's names that stick sometimes for life." "Perfect rot. Ought to be called by his name.")—Bobo Gilding, on his side, does not care for his aunt's rather pompous parties, since "entering a drawing-room [for Bobo] was more suggestive of the daily afternoon tea ordeal of his early nursery days than a voluntary act of pleasure." And Mrs. Gilding (who was Lucy Wellborn) "did not care much to go either if none of her particular men friends were to be there. Little she cared to dance the cotillion with old Colonel Bluffington or to go to supper with that odious Hector Newman." Yet old Mrs. Toplofty is by no means dull, for, finding herself once at dinner "next to a man she quite openly despised, [she] said to him with apparent placidity, 'I shall not talk to you—because I don't care to. But for the sake of the hostess I shall say my multiplication tables. Twice one are two, twice two are four—' and she continued on through the tables, making him alternate them with her. As soon as she politely could, she turned to her other companion."

Lucy Gilding "smokes like a furnace and is miserable unless she can play bridge for high stakes." At her wedding, the bridesmaids were dressed "in deep shades of burnt orange and yellow, wood colored slippers and stockings, skirts that shaded from brown through orange to yellow; yellow leghorn hats trimmed with jonquils, and jonquil bouquets"; and the affair was a great success for everybody except a "distinguished uncle," with whom Mrs. Post frankly sympathizes, who declared: "I did not think it was lovely at all. Every one of the bridesmaids was so powdered and painted that there was not a sweet or fresh face among them."

The Gildings' especial friends are rich young people like the Lovejoys and the Gailys, rich bachelors like Jim Smartlington and Clubwin Doe (the former of whom was elected "with little difficulty" to Clubwin Doe's club, at the same time that young Breezy was kept out by two men who "disliked his 'manner' "). But there are also, in the higher brackets, Mr. and Mrs. Kindhart. Mrs. Kindhart, unlike Mrs. Worldly, "talks to everyone, everywhere and always." Her "position is as good as Mrs. Worldly's every bit, but perhaps she can be more relaxed." It is the Kindharts who try to be helpful at the catastrophic "bungled dinner" which is given by "you," the reader—the evening when the fire smokes and Mrs. Toplofty issues orders that the logs are to be thrown out into the yard: when the Swedish maid says "Dinner's all ready!" instead of "Dinner is served" and deals the plates out like cards and then stacks them; when the clear soup turns out a "greasy-looking brown" and the hollandaise sauce "a curdled yellow mess"—the evening after which Mrs. Toplofty, Clubwin Doe and the Worldlys and the Gildings, all of whom you invited together, will, as you well know, be telling their friends: "Whatever you do, don't dine with the Newweds unless you eat your dinner before you go, and wear black glasses so no sight can offend you." On that occasion, Mr. Kindhart is the only guest who tries to eat the soup, and Mrs. Kindhart says to you gently: "Cheer up, little girl, it doesn't really matter"—making you know for the first time "to the full how terrible the situation is." (The other guests, on this unfortunate occasion, seem to have fallen a little short of the qualities of delicacy and grace which the author has elsewhere ascribed to the truly well bred.) It was the Kindharts who gave the houseparty at informal Mountain Summit Camp which inspires Mrs. Post to one of her most memorable chapters—that party at which Mr. Kindhart points out after lunch to the guests "a dozen guides who are waiting at the boathouse" and "a small swimming pool which can be warmed artificially" for those who find the lake too cold, but at which the Worldlys strike a false note, for Mr. Worldly insists on bringing his valet, though he well knows that this was not expected, and Mrs. Worldly, at the long pine lunch-table, "looks at her napkin ring as though it were an insect"—till Mrs. Kindhart smiles and says: "I'm sorry, but I told you 'it was roughing it.' "

And then there are the Littlehouses (Mrs. Littlehouse was Sally Titherington), who, when you visit them, may "press you into service as auxiliary nurse, gardener or chauffeur," but whose "personality" is "such that there is scarcely a day in the week when the motors of the most popular of the younger set are not parked at the Littlehouse door." And, on the fringes, such occasional guests as Grace Smalltalk, who *did* write to Mrs. Norman an admirable bread-and-butter letter, and the boring Professor Bugge, who was rather a social problem till he was seated by a clever hostess next to Mrs. Entomoid. In a somewhat different category, not frowned on but not included in the Eastern set, are Mr. and Mrs. Spendeasy Western and Mr. and Mrs. Jameson Greatlake, of 24 Michigan Avenue, Chicago.

But Mrs. Post's real hero and heroine are Mr. and Mrs. Oldname. Mrs. Oldname is *"une dame élégante"*—because, as Mrs. Post tells us, there is no English word to "express the individuality of beautiful taste combined with personal dignity and grace which gives to a perfect costume an inimitable air of distinction." Her tact is unfailing and consummate: to a lady going in to dinner, she will say quietly: "Mr. Traveler, who is sitting next to you at the table, has just come back from two years alone with the cannibals." And "how does Mrs. Oldname walk? One might answer by describing how Pavlova dances. Her body is perfectly balanced, she holds herself straight, and yet nothing suggests a ramrod. She takes steps of medium length, and, like all people who move and dance well, walks from the hip, not the knee. On no account does she swing her arms, nor does she rest a hand on her hip! Nor, when walking, does she wave her hands about in gesticulation." One of the most telling of the little episodes with which Mrs. Post's commentary is interspersed is her account of a visit to the Oldnames, which has the title *The Small House of Perfection*. "A great friend of the Oldnames, but not a man who went at all into society, or considered whether people had position or not, was invited with his new wife—a woman from another State and of much wealth and discernment—to stay over a weekend at Brook Meadows." She asks her husband what sort of clothes to take, and he tells her that he has never seen Mrs. Oldname "dressed up a bit." The wife wonders whether to pack her cerise satin. The husband thinks it "much too handsome," but the wife decides to put it in. They drive up to a low, white shingled house, and the visitor notices that the flowers bordering the old-fashioned brick walk are "all of one color, all in perfect bloom." She knew no inexperienced gardener produced that apparently simple approach to a door that has been chosen as frontispiece in more than one book on Colonial architecture. The door was opened by a maid in a silver gray taffeta dress, with organdie collar, cuffs and apron, white stockings and silver buckles on black slippers, and the guest saw a quaint hall and vista of rooms that at first sight might easily be thought 'simple' by an inexpert appraiser." Mrs. Oldname herself was electrifying to the visitor of wealth from another State. To describe her as "simple," exclaims Mrs. Post, "is about as apt as to call a pearl 'simple' because it doesn't dazzle; nor was there an article in the apparently simple living-room that would be refused if it were offered to a museum." The furniture, the appointments, the other guests are filled in with glowing rapture. "That night the bride wore her cerise dress to one of the smartest dinners she ever went down to"; and when later she is alone with her husband she bursts out: "Why in the name of goodness didn't you tell me the truth about these people?" The husband misunderstands: I told you it was a little house—it was you who insisted on bringing that red dress. I told you it was much too handsome!" "Handsome!" she cries in tears. "I don't own anything half good enough to compare with the least article in this house. That 'simple' little woman, as you call her, would, I think, almost make a queen seem provincial! And as for her clothes, they are priceless—just as everything is in this little gem of a house. Why, the window curtains are as fine as the best things in my trousseau."

There is only one instance on record of anybody's scoring off the Oldnames. Mrs. Oldname had hanging in her dining-room a portrait of a Colonial officer, to which she was rather attached. One day, however, "an art critic, whose knowledge was better than his manners, blurted out, 'Will you please tell me why you have that dreadful thing in this otherwise perfect room?' Mrs. Oldname, somewhat taken aback, answered rather wonderingly: 'Is it dreadful?—Really? I have a feeling of affection for him and his dog!' The critic was merciless. 'If you call a cotton-flannel effigy a dog! And as for the figure, it is equally false and lifeless! It is amazing how anyone with your taste can bear looking at it!' In spite of his rudeness, Mrs. Oldname saw that what he said was quite true, but not until the fact had been pointed out to her. Gradually she grew to dislike the poor officer so much that he was finally relegated to the attic." It will be noted that, though the art critic carried his point, he was still guilty of a grave breach of manners.

The latest edition of Emily Post omits, as she says on the jacket, "certain non-essential customs and old-fashioned ideas," and aims to accommodate itself to the habits of later decades—including even those of the war and post-war young people—when formalities have been going by the board. The chapter, for example, which in the 1922 edition is called *The Chaperon and Other Conventions* is now headed *The Vanished Chaperon and Other Lost Conventions*. But the book is still dominated by the prestige of the Oldnames and the Gildings. Their prestige for Mrs. Post may finally have the effect of making some of her readers sympathetic toward the characters who are awful examples: the Upstarts, Mr. and Mrs. Unsuitable and that touching Mr. Richan Vulgar, who crossed the Atlantic four times a year in order to meet the smart people on shipboard and who, by capturing an innocent celebrity, attracted for a time to his table the Smartlys, the Wellborns and the Lovejoys, only to lose them every one when they found out what he was really like and took to eating their meals on deck. (The story of Mr. Richan Vulgar has been dropped from the new edition, as have also, the Unsuitables and the Upstarts, but a pathetic Miss Nobackground has appeared.) One feels, in fact, something like sadism in the whole approach of Mrs. Post. She likes to humiliate. She cannot tell us how charming Miss Wellborn is or how perfect is Mrs. Oldname's taste without putting in a little incident to show us this polish or grace making somebody else uncomfortable. Mrs. Post's popularity, I think, is partly due to precisely this.

It is obvious that the Gildings and the Oldnames do not themselves need Mrs. Post's book of etiquette; and that the ordinary amiable American, to whom Miss Eichler addresses herself, does not necessarily need to hear about either Great Estates or the Small House of Perfection. But there are people who want to believe in the existence of a social Olympus and who find here the satisfaction that is somehow derived at once from imagining the enjoyment of glamour and power and from immolating oneself before them—since the reader is let in on the lives of the dwellers in these privileged places but is constantly being reminded how desperately he should have to watch his step if he were ever admitted among them.

What you get in Emily Post, for all her concessions to the age's vulgarization, is a crude version of the social ideal to which the mass of Americans aspired after the Civil War: an ideal that was costly and glossy, smart, self-conscious and a little disgusting in a period when even Mrs. Oldname reflected the lavish Gildings in stimulating her visitors to realize that the clothes she wore were "priceless" and her tableware and furniture museum pieces. Today this ideal must be fading with the money that kept it up, but, such as it is, a great many people must still enjoy reading about it. The publishers of Mrs. Post's *Etiquette* have announced that it has sold fifty thousand copies since the beginning of this year: its biggest sale in a decade.

C. WRIGHT MILLS

Women: The Darling Little Slaves

Mlle. Simone de Beauvoir would pass judgment on institutions according to whether or not they offer concrete opportunities to individuals, and the opportunities in which she is interested are summed up in the liberty of the individual "to transcend himself, to engage in freely chosen projects."[1] It is just this humanistic liberty, she believes, that women do not have. Like many Negroes and Jews, they are judged not as individuals, but as members of a stereotyped bracket. This not only discourages their womanly efforts to become productive individuals, but more grievously, leads to their not making the effort. Accordingly, the central question to which Mlle. de Beauvoir's book is addressed is "How can a human being in woman's situation attain fulfillment?"

The difficulty in reviewing her book is that it contains so much that is interesting that one wants to summarize it at length, but it is

1. Simone de Beauvoir, *The Second Sex* (translated and edited by H. M. Parshley). New York: Alfred A. Knopf, 1953 [Mills' note].

so stimulating that one wishes to comment upon it in detail. For, by pulling out from under most of the standard arguments their assumptions of fact, Mlle. de Beauvoir has opened up the whole topic for a fresh and uninhibited argument.

I

Much of her own analysis follows vigorously upon acceptance of a radically sociological interpretation of personality and character. I will first try to summarize her point of view in five points:

(i). To the biologist, a woman is simply a female of the species. But no fact about the female fixes the meaning or sets the destiny of woman. For the body is but a limiting factor for our projects, and our projects are set not by our biology but by our values. We cannot know the nature of women apart from her situation, upon which her nature so largely depends.

The female's inferiority to the male varies according to the level of material and social technique that prevails. If her muscles are not so strong, still she is quite as capable of operating modern semiauto-matic machines. And her enslavement to the species, the burdens of maternity, are crushing only if she undergoes frequent pregnancies and if custom and economic conditions force her to constant attendance upon the young. The facts of biology themselves take on the values that we give them, and woman is a female only "to the extent that she is defined as such in her experienced situation." Anatomy is *not* destiny. And even her consciousness of her femininity does not define woman, for this consciousness is itself acquired under specific historical conditions. Like man, woman is not only a member of a species, she is an historical creation.

(ii). The little girl feels herself to be "an autonomous individual," even though she lives in the Kafka-like world of childhood. But at adolescence, when the boy "makes his way actively towards adulthood" the girl begins to wait for the man who will shape her adulthood. (328)[2] What she becomes will not depend upon her own efforts; (355) she can only become an adult by modeling herself upon men's dreams (335), and to please men she must abdicate the attempt to become an independent being (335). That is why her adolescence is so difficult. She becomes an adult only by becoming a woman, but she can become a woman only by giving up an independent existence.

(iii). "Most women are married, or have been, or plan to be, or suffer from not being." (425) For man, marriage does not prohibit real and productive activity, but woman's interests are almost necessarily divided between marriage and personal aspiration of profession; and for her these are often irreconcilable. When she finds a husband, she gives up her independent aspirations and life projects. Daily intimacy, in or out of marriage, does not necessarily lead to fellow-

2. The numbers here and hereafter refer to pages in *The Second Sex*.

ship or understanding or sympathy. In fact, marriage is in principle "obscene . . . in so far as it transforms into rights and duties those mutual relations which should be founded on a spontaneous urge."

(iv). Love, whatever it may be, is not to be had "forever after" in marriage. The truth is that eroticism is in profound tension with marital and family life. The aim of marriage is to institute the economic and reproductive functions, but love cannot be instituted; routine cannot be adventure; fidelity is not passion. "In principle marriage and love have nothing in common," (437) and the attempt to reconcile them is a *tour de force.* (439) In a well-regulated yet spontaneous life, physical love is a series of happy episodes with no external duties attached; to be authentic, love must be free: dependent upon no external constraint. (447-8) The idea of "conjugal love" is to say the least equivocal and to say the most, merely a "tender and respectful sentiment." (448)

(v). Nor does giving birth to children and rearing them provide a satisfactory solution: ". . . the mother enjoys the comforting illusion of feeling that she is a human being in herself, a value. But this is only an illusion." The meaning of pregnancy is ambiguous, woman's attitude towards it ambivalent. (497) "Mother love," which is by no means a "natural" feeling, does not imply reciprocity. "Maternity," in short, "is usually a strange mixture of narcissism, altruism, idle daydreaming, sincerity, bad faith, devotion and cynicism." (513) And, with all that, maternity is not enough: To restrict women to maternity would only perpetuate her situation of dependency and meaningless routine. Besides, after her menopause, woman still has about one-half of her adult life to live.

II

So: What should be done?

(i). Although there are genuine exceptions, women fail to gain human dignity, Mlle. de Beauvoir believes, because such dignity can only be the result of a free and independent existence, and "only independent work of her own can assure woman's genuine independence." As long as man is economically responsible for the couple, its members cannot be equal. (480) By this Mlle. de Beauvoir apparently does not mean merely that more women should go to work, but she knows that many unmarried women at work really want to escape from work by marriage, and that many unmarried women who work regard their work as a temporary burden. What she presumably means is that women, after being given identical educations as men, should become "highly trained professional women" or "highly placed women in business" with profound, permanent interests in their work.

(ii). Marriage as a "career" for women must, Mlle. de Beauvoir thinks, be "prohibited." (482) It cannot be a mutual completion if it is based, as it now generally is, upon an original mutilation. Each of the marriage partners should, as men now are, be "integrated as such in society at large." (479) And "since marriage does not generally involve physical love, it should seem reasonable to separate them quite candidly." Sexual episodes do not prevent either marriage partner from leading a joint life of amity with the other; adultery would lose its ugly character when based on liberty and sincerity rather than, as at present, on caution and hyprocrisy.

(iii). Narcissism, great loves and mystical religions—there is a chapter on each—are simply womanly ways of trying to make her prison habitable, rather than ways of escaping from it. Even love, if authentic, would require woman's economic independence: her capacity to work toward ends of her own without using man as an agent.

(iv). In the end, realization of her ideal involves not only a revolution in the relations of men and women, but in the world in which both are to live as human beings. "Only in a socialist world would woman" by work attain liberty. What Mlle. de Beauvoir wants, in short, is "what the Soviet Revolution *promised:* "women raised and trained exactly like men, working under exactly the same conditions; erotic liberty recognized by custom; the obligation of women to earn their own living; marriage a free agreement broken at will; maternity completely voluntary, with authorized birth control and abortion; married and unmarried women to have identical rights; the state to provide pregnancy leaves and to assume charge of the children," signifying not that they would be *taken away* from their parents, but that they would not be *abandoned* to them." (725)

There is no attempt to discuss the consequences of these proposals in detail as a packaged program. Yet she knows that one could not raise in our world a female human being who would be a homologue of the male human being: it would be an oddity, and she quotes Stendhal: "The forest must be planted all at once." (726) But then she falls back into a faith in social evolution which will "arrive at complete economic and social equality, which [in turn] will bring about an inner metamorphosis." (720)

III

(i). Simone de Beauvoir is well aware that when an individual is kept in a situation of inferiority, the fact is that he does become inferior. Woman, in Mlle. de Beauvoir's view, is at the center of conflicting expectations: she is a glossy little animal but also a dishwasher, an attentive mother, but also a steadfast companion. The result is slightly nervous. Under present conditions, many women are quite dreadful creatures. So are many men. Many women do not attain the dignity of the independent human being. Neither do many men. But it is about women, and the conditions that make them dreadful, that Simone de Beauvoir cries out. I agree both with her cry and with its humanistic basis. But I cannot help but feel that she often confuses the conditions of woman with the generic human condition.

In writing about the second sex she really ought to have thought more systematically about the first sex and about human beings in general. For she tends to impute to all men what is in fact true of only very few of them: a transcendent flight, a life of accomplishment. It is true that she at times recognizes that this is not so, but she does not take it into systematic account as she compares "the" situation of men with "the" situation of women. She complains that women are not free "to shape the concept of femininity." But then neither are men free to shape the concept of masculinity. Both concepts are stereotypes and both limit the human being.

(ii). "Throughout history they have always been subordinated to men," writes Mlle. de Beauvoir, to which her translator adds: "With rare exceptions, perhaps, like certain matriarchial rulers, queens, and the like," to which we must add, as a handy example: including the American suburban queens on the $10,000 to $50,000 level.

The suburban queen clings to her "dependency" because to lose them would mean to lose her privileges; and her privileges are many. The fact that she has a child or two does not to my mind eliminate the fact that she is often simply a parasite, and as a parasite an exploiter. One does not blame these privileged women. It is not their "fault" that they are incapable of making anything of their freedom.

Although she does comment on it, I do not think she takes into sufficiently systematic account the intricacy, and the various outcomes, of the power struggle between many men and women. She knows that woman, who in our epoch is losing her femininity, often wishes to retain its privileges while man wants her to retain its limitations, (719) and they are victims of each other and of the stalemate between them. But she does not stress enough the real power that many women have and use: if man is transcendent and authoritarian, woman is often manipulative: the form of power for the immanent. (393) If men command, women seduce. Resentment often causes a frigidity, real or feigned, which is often used as a feminine tool of power.

(iii). There is of course no such thing as Woman, or no such thing as The Condition of Woman. It is all the more sad that this is not concretely recognized, in an attempt to make some sort of classification of women according to their condition, because if one is not born a woman, but rather becomes one, then the woman she becomes depends quite largely on her experienced situation. Woman stands in these pages all too often as one generalized type, and the condition that makes her this type is presumed to be more or less universal in the West. The historical sketch could have provided clues to such a classification of condition and character, but it stands more or less isolated from the more general analysis. Somewhere in her book she admits about everything anyone might say, but she does not take many of them into *systematic* account—this she could only do if she worked with adequate *classifications*. In their absence she is often general in the worst sociological sense, in the sense of being unconnected with specific types of circumstances. In the end, I believe, this fault rests on a further deficiency: she does not provide appropriate classifications. Such classifications are the first and necessary step toward simplifying and hence understanding complicated subjects, and it is the only way to do justice to a complete topic without becoming vague.

Her explanations are all too often exasperatingly vague. For example, over and over again she says that the development of femininity does not depend entirely upon the physiological unfolding—which is certainly true—but "upon the subject's total attitude toward existence" (405)—which is certainly vague to the point of obscurity. Or, again, in her sympathetic account of feminine homosexuality she states that it is neither deliberate nor fated, but rather "an attitude chosen in a certain situation." (424) But what, of any human complexity, is not? And exactly what situations are most conducive to this choice on the part of exactly which types of women? We are given no systematic answers. The female is not born a woman, but becomes one; but that does not mean, as Mlle. de Beauvoir asserts, that it is "civilization as a whole" that produces her. Civilization as a whole does not produce anything. (267) After one has eliminated the explanations of woman according to biological and psychological fate— and this Mlle. de Beauvoir does well—one must *specify* the necessary and sufficient social causes which produce the various *types* of women available to our observation in different societies.

Mlle. de Beauvoir's solution to the man-woman problem, put in its briefest form, is the elimination of woman as we know her—with which one might agree, but to which one must add: and the elimination of man as we know him. There would then be male and female and each would be equally free to become an independent human being. No one can know what new types of human beings would be developed in this historically unique situation, but perhaps in sharing Mlle. de Beauvoir's passion for liberty we would all gladly forego femininity and masculinity to achieve it; and perhaps the best types would follow Coleridge's adage and become androgynous characters in an androgynous world.

In the meantime, Mlle. de Beauvoir is an idealist without being a romantic: she does not merely assert the values of some other world, but tries, quite desperately it seems to me, to develop ideas that will aid women to reshape their situation. She does not believe that people are capable of all things if they only have the will, for she knows that the will too is conditioned and sometimes determined by overwhelming conditions.

Is her book, as has been claimed, a classic?

When we call a book a "classic" we may be merely expressing approval of its excellence, or we may be saying that even after the assertions it makes are superseded, its form will remain a quite splendid cultural product. But the excellence and the readability of this book are marred by wordy portrayals of often simple and readily agreed upon points. The style is not classic, and by style I mean style of reflection as fused with style of expression. I know the easy danger of such comment, but I must say, simply, that the book is verbose, even padded; that the historical account, although at times insightful, is more often at once abstract and skimpy; and that the philosophical comments and vocabulary are more like plugs for existentialism than propositions and definitions essential to the argument. All this is the more unfortunate because the book is nevertheless indispensable reading for any woman who wishes to become more alert to her own possibilities, and for any man who wishes to understand what these possibilities might be. She has written one of those books that remind us how little we really *think* about our own personal lives and problems, and she invites us and helps us to do so.

QUESTIONS FOR STUDY, DISCUSSION, AND WRITING

1. What is Mills' main objection to Simone de Beauvoir's book? Does he give any indication of why he thinks it is important enough to review?
2. A good book review is supposed to tell its reader what the book is about and what the reviewer thinks of it. Does Mills' review pass that test? Does he seem fair to the book? What passages support your answer?
3. Is what Mills thinks about the feminine condition clear? What is his approach to the problem?

MARGARET MEAD
Each Family in a Home of Its Own[1]

The belief that every family should have a home of its own seems like a truism to which almost every American would assent without further thought. Most Americans also accept the fact that we have a housing shortage as the consequences of a failure to build in the thirties and during World War II, and of discrepancies between housing costs and wages that should somehow be reconciled.

1. A chapter from the fourth part, "The Two Sexes in Contemporary America," of *Male and Female*, 1949.

But it is important to realize that the word "family" has come to mean fewer and fewer people, the number of families has steadily increased, and so the need for housing units as distinguished from living-space has also increased by leaps and bounds. Although Southern Senators may occasionally argue against some piece of legislation for women, claiming that women's place is in the home, most legislators yield, at least nominally, to the question, "Whose home?" Women's place in the United States is no longer in the home, and her exclusion from a right that has been hers in most societies is part of our belief that every family should have its own home—with only one woman in it. Furthermore, each family should consist only of a husband, a wife, and minor children.

All other forms of living are seen as having great disadvantages. A mother-son combination is classified as bad for the son, and a failure to break the silver cord; it will spoil his life. A father-daughter household is not as disapproved, but if the girl appears marriageable, then the father may be condemned and the daughter urged to bestir herself. Brother-and-sister households, such a common refuge of the genteel poor in other ages, are also frowned upon, even where one is widowed and has children. Somebody will be said to be sacrificed to somebody else in such an arrangement. Unmarried children who are self-supporting shouldn't be clinging to the home; they should get out and get married and start homes of their own. Nor should the elderly parents of married children live in their children's homes, certainly not if they are both alive to be "company for each other," and not unless absolutely necessary when only one survives. The rigorousness of the American belief that in-laws, especially mothers-in-law, are ruinous to marriages takes little account of the loneliness of elderly people. We respect them when they "make their own lives," without, however, any social arrangements that make it possible for them to do so. The two exceptions to the insistence on the inferiority, and indeed genuine undesirability, of any other form of living-arrangement than the biological family with young or no children, are the cases of two unmarried women living together and of the divorced or widowed woman with some children who returns to the home of some relative, often an unmarried sister, or a father.[2] The proper attitude towards a woman with children to support whose husband is dead, or who is divorced, is to hope that she will marry again, and that the present living-arrangement is merely temporary. Children need a man in the home to bring them up, and are to be pitied if they haven't got a father. Grandfathers and uncles are not thought of as really good substi-

2. In 1947 one family in ten did not maintain a separate home. Of these, 2,500,000 were married couples with or without children; that is, individuals who are culturally entitled to feel that their happiness is as seriously endangered as their health would be during a famine. Three-quarters of a million were parent-child groups (nearly all mother-and-child groups) [Mead's note].

tutes. As for the households in which two unmarried women live together, they are still regarded with a tolerance that includes some of the last century's pity and absolution from blame of the woman who did not marry, but this is markedly decreasing. Young women to-day who work and share a household have to draw heavily on the housing situation or considerations of economy to justify their continuing such an arrangement. There will be doubts, perhaps fears, that at least the chances of marriage, for one if not both, are being compromised by the arrangement. Group living for men is only really tolerated in college dormitories, in armies, and in work-camps, highly patterned situations where either men are assumed to be too young to marry or their wives cannot accompany them. Men who keep house together have to fend off very heavy social doubts as to their heterosexuality. The ethics that informs all these various social disapprovals, which is expressed in private upbraiding of the one who is assumed to be selfish and attempts to rouse the one who is assumed to be suffering, is the firm American belief that one of the most henious sins is to limit other people's emotional freedom to live the good life. As the good life is defined as marriage, obviously any living-arrangement is wrong that may make any marriageable individual forgo marriage, and to benefit from such an arrangement is selfish and exploitive.

All of these attitudes and preferences add up to a world in which one should either be married, with a home of one's own, or live alone, eating in restaurants, reading all night in bed, seeing the same movies twice, dependent upon endless daily plans and initiative for companionship. Against such a background it is not surprising that Americans see one of the principal values in marriage as companionship, for we are a gregarious people, needing the presence of others to give us a full sense of ourselves. Nowhere in childhood or youth is there any training or any practice in self-sufficient isolation. Everything that a child does quietly by itself is suspect. "He is so quiet he must be up to mischief." Day-dreaming is frowned upon. People who would rather stay at home with a good book than go out with friends get poor scores on personality quizzes. Even simple sensuous pleasures, such as reading in the bath-tub on Sunday morning, are regarded as pretty self-indulgent and antisocial. Most time spent alone could be spent better if spent with others, and time and money are valuables that ought to be spent in the best way possible. The child goes from a home in which the whole family share a living-room to a school in which he studies and plays in groups, through an adolescence in which any night when he doesn't have to study he feels left out if he hasn't a date, to an adulthood in which any break in ready companionship is felt as almost unbearable. In his empty room he turns on the radio as soon as he enters, to dispel the silence. "Silence," says a generation brought up to study in groups with a radio blaring over their heads, "is embarrassing." Which is another way of saying that when one is left alone with one-self, the question "What have you done to deserve being alone?" is almost inevitable, for children who are watched if they seek isolation are also as punishment sent out of the room or to bed.

> And if you doubt what things I say,
> Suppose you make the test;
> Suppose when you've been bad someday
> And up to bed are sent away
>   From mother and the rest—
> Suppose you ask, "Who has been bad?"
>   And then you'll hear what's true;
> For the wind will moan in its ruefullest tone:
>   "Yoooooooooo!
>   "Yoooooooooo!
>   "Yoooooooooo!"[3]

Self-sought loneliness and involuntary loneliness are both unattractive and suspect. The more popular and loved one is, the more sought-after, the more selfish it becomes to sit at home with a good book, and so make at least one other person involuntarily unhappy. Good-sportsmanship, which has shifted much of its meaning in America from its traditional English content, includes never refusing to do something labelled as fun if one or more other people ask you to, on such grounds as being tired, fed-up, or even needing to study, or write letters, or mend one's stockings. Critics of Americans' need for the reassurance of other people's company often neglect to stress that in a culture like ours universally acknowledged needs also imply universal duties, and that if every one is defined as lonely when he is alone, then it is obviously every one's duty to be with some one else. So children have to have "some one to play with," adolescents have to have dates, and adults have to marry and have a home of their own.

Assured companionship and parenthood thus become the two socially desirable values that cannot be obtained outside marriage. Almost every other human need that has historically been met in the home can now be met outside it: restaurants serve food; comics, movies, and radio provide amusement, news, and gossip; there are laundries and dry-cleaners and places that mend one's socks and store one's winter coat, wash one's hair and manicure one's nails and shine one's shoes. For sex satisfaction it is no longer necessary to choose between marriage and prostitution; for most of those without religious scuples sex is available on a friendly and amateur basis and without responsibility. The automobile has made it even unnecessary for one of a pair of temporary sex partners to have an apartment. Entertaining can be done in a hotel or at a club. When one is sick, one goes to a hospital, and when one dies, one can be buried

3. From Eugene Field's "The Night Wind."

quite professionally from an undertaking establishment. A telephone service will answer one's telephone, and a shopping service do one's shopping. The old needs of food, shelter, sex, and recreation are all efficiently met outside the home—and yet more people are married to-day than ever before in the country's recorded history.

Marriage is a state towards which young Americans are propelled, and within which American women, educated to be energetic and active, try to live out the desires that have been both encouraged and muffled in them as children. Although there are other cultures in which women dominate the home more, America is conspicuous for the extent to which women have set the style of the home. This may be referred to a variety of background events: to the way in which the realm of the aesthetic was left to women during pioneer days, to the emphasis on work for every one which meant that men were too tired to spend much of their effort on the home; and, very importantly, to the division of labour among non-English-speaking immigrants. When immigrants came to this country, the husband set to work to make a living, the wife to find out how to live, and this division between making a living and a way of life, one as man's field, the other as woman's, has been intensified. Our patterns of urban life, with its highly developed transportation systems which mean that fewer and fewer men ever come home to lunch, are also one of the supporting factors in the situation. As more schools are consolidated and the distance from home is increased, and as school-lunches develop, the home with school-age children is deserted all day long, while Mother is free to study the magazines and rearrange the living-room or her knowledge of world peace or the community's school system, in between answering the telephone, waiting for the laundry-man, and doing the next errand.

So it falls to the lot of women to design the way of life of the family, consulting her husband on major issues only, simply because that is her job. Into it, during the early days of marriage and motherhood she pours all the energy that comes from a healthy well-fed active childhood. If she has had a good education and is trained for some outside work, or even possibly for a career, even more if she was successful before marriage, there is likely to be an extra bit of emphasis in the way she manages her home and her children, in her insistence on what a good mother and what a good wife she is. Sometimes she can even say frankly: "Yes, I know my child is old enough to go to school alone, but I still take her. After all, that is my justification for staying home." More often, without any articulate comment on her doubt as to whether home-making really is a full-time job, she simply puts more effort into her complex day. Here the same standards apply that apply to her husband: like him, she also must succeed, must make good, must meet higher and higher standards.

When we analyze the task of home-making in the United States to-day, in the home that is celebrated in the pages of the women's magazines and assumed in the carefully unspecific radio serials, we find some very curious contradictions. The well-equipped home—towards which all the advertisements are pointed—is a home in which everything can be done more quickly and more effortlessly, clothes get white in no time, irons press almost without your noticing it, the extra attachment on the vacuum cleaner will even brush the backs of your books, the new silver-polish keeps your silver looking like new. In fact, the American woman, and the American woman's husband, who does not escape the advertisements even if he misses the radio serials, are told how fortunate, modern, and leisurely she can be—if she simply equips her house properly. There really seems to have been a period—back in the twenties, when domestic servants were still relatively available—when a married woman who had a goodly supply of gadgets, and at least one servant, did get quite a little time to play bridge. Her image lingers on in the avid comments of professional women over fifty who still see the home-maker as having a wicked amount of leisure—especially when contrasted with the life led by the woman who must both work and discharge all the duties of the home-maker, as so many American women do, not by choice but by necessity. There was a time also when in the first fine flush of laundries and bakeries, milk deliveries and canned goods, ready-made clothes and dry-cleaning, it did look as if American life was being enormously simplified. A vacuum cleaner was a great addition to a home that kept the standards of a carpet-sweeper and a broom, laundries were a godsend to a household whose routine of sheet-changing was geared to the old-fashioned wash-tub, and bakeries to homes in which the making of bread had dominated one whole day. But just as our new medical palliatives are creating new vulnerabilities and new disease states, so the new equipment has led not to more leisure, more time to play with the baby, more time to curl up and read by an open fire, or to help with the PTA, but has merely combined with other trends in making the life of the American home-maker not easier, but more exacting. Most urban-living women do not realize that, as the Bryn Mawr report shows, housekeeping activities consumed 60.55 hours a week in a typical farm family, 78.35 in urban households in cities under 100,000, and 80.57 in households in cities of over 100,000. This was in pre-war days, and in a world that has been moving steadily towards a forty-hour week on the job.

Perhaps the most significant word in family relationships that has been invented for a very long time is the word "sitter"—the extra person who must come into the family and sit whenever the two parents go out of it together. The modern wife and mother lives alone, with a husband who comes home in the evening, and children, who as little children are on her hands twenty-four hours out of twenty-four, in a house that she is expected to run with the efficiency of a factory—for hasn't she a washing-machine and a vacuum cleaner?—and from which a great number of the compensations that once went with being a home-maker have been removed. Except in rural areas, she no longer produces, in the sense of preserving and pickling and canning. She has no orgies of house-cleaning twice a year. She doesn't give the sort of party where she is admired because of the heaps of food that she has ostentatiously prepared, but instead she is admired just in proportion to the way she "looks as if it had taken her no time at all." As our factories move toward the ideal of eliminating human labor, our home ideals have paralleled them; the successful home-maker to-day should always look as if she had neither done any work nor would have to do any; she should produce a finished effect effortlessly, even if she has to spend all day Saturday rehearsing the way in which she will serve an effortless Sunday-morning breakfast. The creativity that is expected of her is a creativity of management of an assembly-line, not of materials lovingly fashioned into food and clothes for children. She shops, she markets, she chooses, she transports, she integrates, she co-ordinates, she fits little bits of time together so as "to get through the week," and her proudest boast often has to be "It was a good week. Nothing went wrong."

The average young American woman is very cheeful over these tasks. They are a drain on her nervous energy rather than on her physical strength, time-consuming rather than back-breaking; in her incredibly clean and polished home, her kitchen where the handle of the egg-beater matches the step-ladder in color, she moves lightly, producing the miracle dishes that will make her husband and children happy and strong. Two things mar her happiness, however: the fear that even though she never has any time, she is not perhaps doing a full-time job, and the fact that although she, like her brother, was taught that the right to choose a job is every American's sacred right, she doesn't feel that she chose this one. She chose wifehood and motherhood, but she did not necessarily choose to "keep house." That, in the phrasing of contemporary America, is thrust upon her becaue she is a woman; it is not a full status to be proudly chosen, but a duty that one cannot avoid and still find happiness in marriage. Women who have jobs ask her what she is doing and she says, "Nothing," or, "Just keeping house." Eighty hours a week of work, a sitter perhaps one evening a week, great loneliness as she rushes through the work that no other woman now shares, with an eye on the children as they play, hurrying so as to look "fresh and rested" when her husband comes home.

As we have narrowed the home, excluded from it the grandmother, the unmarried sister, the unmarried daughter, and—as part of the same process of repudiating any sharing of a home with another adult—the domestic servant has vanished, we have multiplied the number of homes in which the whole life of the family has to be integrated each day, meals cooked, lunches packed, children bathed, doors locked, dogs walked, cats put out, food ordered, washing-machines set in motion, flowers sent to the sick, birthday-cakes baked, pocket-money sorted, mechanical refrigerators defrosted. Where one large pot of coffee once served a household of ten or twelve, there are three or four small pots to be made and watched and washed and polished. Each home has been reduced to the bare essentials—to barer essentials than most primitive people would consider possible. Only one woman's hands to feed the baby, answer the telephone, turn off the gas under the pot that is boiling over, soothe the older child who has broken a toy, and open both doors at once. She is a nutritionist, a child psychologist, an engineer, a production manager, an expert buyer, all in one. Her husband sees her as free to plan her own time, and envies her; she sees him as having regular hours, and envies him. To the degree to which they also see each other as the same kind of people, with the same tastes and the same preferences, each is to a degree dissatisfied and inclined to be impatient with the other's discontent.

It is not new in history that men and women have misunderstood each other's rôles or envied each other, but the significant aspect of the American scene is that there is a discrepancy between the way we bring up boys and girls—each to choose both a job and a marriage partner—and then stylize housekeeping as a price the girl pays without stylizing the job as the price the boy pays. Men are trained to want a job in a mill, or a mine, on a farm, in an office, on a newspaper, or on a ship as a sign of their maleness, their success, and to want a wife and children to crown that success; but women to-day are not given the same clear career-line—to want an apartment, or a semi-detached house, or a farm-house, or a walk-up, or some other kind of home, as their job. The American woman wants a husband, yes, children, yes, a home of her own—yes indeed, it's intolerable to live with other people! But housekeeping—she isn't sure she wouldn't rather "do something" after she gets married. A great proportion of men would like a different job—to have at least better pay, or higher status, or different working-conditions—but they are not asked to face the seeming discrepancy between being reared for a choice and reared to think that success matters, and also that love matters and that every one should marry, and yet not be able to feel that the mate one chooses and the job one does after marriage are independent. It is as if a man were to make a

set of plans for his life—to be an accountant, or a lawyer, or a pilot
—and then have to add, "Unless of course, I marry." "Why?" you
ask. "Because then I'll have to be a farmer. It's better for the
children, you know."

It is not that we have found any good substitute for the association between home-making and motherhood. Good nurseries and
schools can put children into good settings for many hours a day,
settings that are often better than the small family where two bitter little rivals may otherwise spend hours quarreling and trauma-
tizing each other. Freezers and frozen-food services and pressure
cookers make it possible to prepare meals without long hours beside
a watched pot. Hospitals do care for the very ill. But the task of
integrating the lives of little children, even with the help of nursery-
schools, kindergartens, and play-grounds, remains a full-time charge
on some woman's time. If one woman leaves the home to work,
part time or full time, another woman must replace her unless the
children are to suffer. The nursery-school is no answer for the child
with a cold, or the child who has been exposed to some contagious
disease that it has not contracted. American women have become
steadily more independent, more enterprising, more efficient, less
willing to be merely part of some on-going operation, more insistent
that when they do paid work, they work on a strictly professional
basis, with part of their personality only, and that when they keep
house they must be completely in control. But the price of this
autonomy has risen also. It is almost as if the pioneer dream, which
led Europeans of all sorts of backgrounds to become the independent American farmer, who could turn his hand to anything—and
which survives today in the perennial nostalgia for a chicken-farm,
or a business where one is one's own boss—had been transferred to
the women, who live it out in their homes, but without the full
pleasure of feeling that this is the job as well as the husband, the
routine as well as the children, that they chose.

The intensity with which the American woman with children tends
to her task of home-making includes innumerable excursions out of
the home, as consumer, as transportation officer of the family, as
responsible citizen who must protect the environment in which her
children grow up by working for better schools, better play-grounds,
better public-health regulations. To the old puritan vigour of the
pioneer woman is now added a recognition that the modern isolated
home, just because it is so isolated, is also terribly dependent upon
the community. The functions that no one woman in a home by
herself can possibly discharge must somehow be organized in the
community around her, and even so, mothers cannot get sick. When
they do, there are no adequate ordinary social ways of meeting this
major emergency in the lives of their children. But however actively

a married woman with small children takes responsibility for community work, still her life is centered in, her time filled by, her home, but principally by the children. She may importune her husband to take her out, she may complain loudly of the loneliness and the boredom of housework, but she does not complain that she has nothing to do.

It is all the harder for the mother of adolescent children when the break comes, when the children leave home for school or jobs and her task is over. Every social pressure to which she is subjected tells her that she should not spoil her children's lives, that she should let them lead their own lives, that she should make them independent and self-sufficient. Yet the more faithfully she obeys these injunctions, the more she is working herself out of a job. Some day, while she is still a young woman, she will have to face a breakfast-table with only one face across it, her husband's, and she will be alone, quite alone, in a home of their own. She is out of a job; her main justification, the work for which she "gave up everything," is gone, and yet there are still two, possibly three, meals a day to get, the door to be answered, the house to be cleaned. But there are only dishes for two and floors do not need to be polished so often when there are no children's feet to track them up. She isn't completely out of a job, but she is on the shelf, kicked upstairs, given one of those placebos by which large organizations whose employees have tenure try to disguise from the employee who is still too young to be retired the fact that he ought to be. This domestic crisis is of course much more difficult if it occurs at and is reinforced by the hormonal instability and emotional fears that surround the menopause, and combine unjustified fear of the loss of physical desire with the necessary recognition of the end of reproductivity. For married American women who have had children, the fear of loss of attractiveness and the fear of becoming emotionally unstable outweigh worries about the end of reproductivity, for they have had the one or two or three children that validate their marriages and, at least consciously, do not want more.

Meanwhile the father has been facing difficulties of his own. His rôle in the maturation of his children, especially in the maturation of his son, is to be the friendly ally of the boy, to help him cut free from his mother's apron-strings. To the extent that he sympathizes with and facilitates his son's growing desires for a job and a girl, he is a good father. He must pooh-pooh the mother's anxieties, back the boy up in minor escapades, be fraternally understanding. But to the extent that he does this he runs several risks. He relives, at least in imagination, his own budding freedom as a young adult, the freedom that he traded in so young, so willingly, for the continuous unremitting work that has kept his marriage going. Remembering, he may begin to feel that he has never really lived, that he settled down too early. This feeling may be all the stronger if it comes at a time when he realizes that further advancement in job or profession is unlikely. As long as the gradient of his life was rising, he was spurred on by the great rewards that Americans find in success. But now it will rise no further, he will instead in many cases have to work simply to hold his place, a dispiriting thought. Helping his son escape from his mother further identifies his wife for him as one from whom he has, after all, never properly escaped himself into the pleasant byways of irresponsible dalliance. Seeing his wife through his son's eyes, and through the eyes of his son's friends, he discovers a new impatience with her, as the representative of finished, self-satisfied achievement. Here he is, only in middle age, and his life is over—no new love, no new fields to conquer, only emptiness ahead. So while he is not out of a job—indeed he may often be at the height of his work-strength—the very nature of the life-cycle in America is such that he feels like an old man. He may have to fight very hard to resist the impulse to break away from it all, and he may develop serious health disturbances and die prematurely.

Superficially, the problem that faces the middle-aged couple in the home of their own is that the mother's main life-task is done while she is strong and well, and she must now find some other channel for her energies and still keep her life adjusted to the habits and needs of a husband who has lived terribly closely with her in that little self-contained home, while that husband's life-task is still going full tilt. But because of the great emphasis on Youth, because Youth is the period to which both sexes look back and age holds so few rewards, both face a deeper crisis of disappointment. The crisis may be further intensified if there are deaths of aged parents to be faced, with all the complications of the disposition of a surviving parent, long months of illness, sales of houses and furniture, all of which exacerbate the conflict about growing older. Every step of this process is made more acute by the insistence that each married couple should be self-sufficient, because many such couples have forgotten how. Yet they cannot look forward to combined homes with their married children, or with their widowed or unmarried siblings. Deeply dependent upon each other in every way, they have often become so just to the extent that the marriage is a good marriage. They have become so much like a single person that, like most individuals in America, they feel the need of others to complete themselves, to reassure them that they are good, to rid them of the self-searching that comes from being left alone and the self-reproach that attends condemning others to aloneness.

There are emerging solutions to this crisis when the children leave home. Some couples attempt a last child, for which there are even affectionate slang phrases—"little postscript," "little frost blossom" —that change the tone of the old folk-phrase "change-of-life baby." To have such a child is one way of facing the extent to which the woman's life in that home, and the marriage itself, has centered on the children. The most familiar solution is for women to make much of the independence for which they have openly yearned during the time they were tied down and go in for some active voluntary work, or even go back to the work they did before they were married. But in this event they face new hazards, especially if they have lived successfully through the instabilities of the menopause. Free of their major previous responsibilities, with twenty good years ahead of them, such women may start out on a gradient that rises steeply as they become involved in community activities or the delights of a job from which they have had a long vacation. And as it is the gradient that matters so much in America, their enthusiastic new spurt may contrast sharply with their husbands' unhappy acceptance of a plateau. A daughter's marriage and permitted absorption in grandchildren may mute the wife's energetic attitude towards her new activities, but that involves a severe problem for the husband who has to face the fact that he is a grandfather. In a country that gives so few rewards to age, who wants to be a grandfather? The woman of his unlicensed day-dreams is still a slim girl in her teens, now younger than his married daughter, who with each step that she takes towards maturity puts him more definitely out of the running.

Increasingly, the more aware middle-aged couples are treating this period seriously, assaying their personal as well as their material resources, and directing their plans not towards some dim and unhoped-for retirement, but towards the next twenty years. To the extent that both are able to re-plan their lives together, they make of the crisis a step forward rather than a step back. It is probable that society will recognize this period as a period in which professional counselling is needed as much as in adolescence. For each married couple alone in a home of their own is exposed to pressures and difficulties unknown in differently organized societies. And expressive of the shifting cycle of responsibility, the young married sons and daughters sit in their own small homes and try to decide what to do about Father and Mother. This is a question that is not answered by their all taking a house together, but by finding the parents something they can be interested in. Ideally, they will readjust their lives, live independently of their children except for grave emergencies, act as sitters, which means they go in as their children go out, and finally retire to a cottage in Florida, where their children piously hope they will have a lot of friends of their own age.

JAMES BALDWIN
Stranger in the Village

From all available evidence no black man had ever set foot in this tiny Swiss village before I came. I was told before arriving that I would probably be a "sight" for the village; I took this to mean that people of my complexion were rarely seen in Switzerland, and also that city people are always something of a "sight" outside of the city. It did not occur to me—possibly because I am an American—that there could be people anywhere who had never seen a Negro.

It is a fact that cannot be explained on the basis of the inaccessibility of the village. The village is very high, but it is only four hours from Milan and three hours from Lausanne. It is true that it is virtually unknown. Few people making plans for a holiday would elect to come here. On the other hand, the villagers are able, presumably, to come and go as they please—which they do: to another town at the foot of the mountain, with a population of approximately five thousand, the nearest place to see a movie or go to the bank. In the village there is no movie house, no bank, no library, no theater; very few radios, one jeep, one station wagon; and at the moment, one typewriter, mine, an invention which the woman next door to me here had never seen. There are about six hundred people living here, all Catholic—I conclude this from the fact that the Catholic church is open all year round, whereas the Protestant chapel, set off on a hill a little removed from the village, is open only in the summertime when the tourists arrive. There are four or five hotels, all closed now, and four or five *bistros*, of which, however, only two do any business during the winter. These two do not do a great deal, for life in the village seems to end around nine or ten o'clock. There are a few stores, butcher, baker, *épicerie*, a hardware store, and a money-changer—who cannot change travelers' checks, but must send them down to the bank, an operation which takes two or three days. There is something called the *Ballet Haus*, closed in the winter and used for God knows what, certainly not ballet, during the summer. There seems to be only one schoolhouse in the village, and this for the quite young children; I suppose this to mean that their older brothers and sisters at some point descend from these mountains in order to complete their education—possibly, again, to the town just below. The landscape is absolutely forbidding, mountains towering on all four sides, ice and snow as far as the eye can reach. In this white wilderness, men and women and children move all day, carrying washing, wood, buckets of milk or water, sometimes skiing on Sunday afternoons. All week long boys and young men are to be seen shoveling snow off the rooftops, or dragging wood down from the forest in sleds.

The village's only real attraction, which explains the tourist season, is the hot spring water. A disquietingly high proportion of these tourists are cripples, or semi-cripples, who come year after year—from other parts of Switzerland, usually—to take the waters. This lends the village, at the height of the season, a rather terrifying air of sanctity, as though it were a lesser Lourdes. There is often something beautiful, there is always something awful, in the spectacle of a person who has lost one of his faculties, a faculty he never questioned until it was gone, and who struggles to recover it. Yet people remain people, on crutches or indeed on deathbeds; and wherever I passed, the first summer I was here, among the native villagers or among the lame, a wind passed with me—of astonishment, curiosity, amusement, and outrage. That first summer I stayed two weeks and never intended to return. But I did return in the winter, to work; the village offers, obviously, no distractions whatever and has the further advantage of being extremely cheap. Now it is winter again, a year later, and I am here again. Everyone in the village knows my name, though they scarcely ever use it, knows that I come from America—though, this, apparently, they will never really believe: black men come from Africa—and everyone knows that I am the friend of the son of a woman who was born here, and that I am staying in their chalet. But I remain as much a stranger today as I was the first day I arrived, and the children shout *Neger! Neger!* as I walk along the streets.

It must be admitted that in the beginning I was far too shocked to have any real reaction. In so far as I reacted at all, I reacted by trying to be pleasant—it being a great part of the American Negro's education (long before he goes to school) that he must make people "like" him. This smile-and-the-world-smiles-with-you routine worked about as well in this situation as it had in the situation for which it was designed, which is to say that it did not work at all. No one, after all, can be liked whose human weight and complexity cannot be, or has not been, admitted. My smile was simply another unheard-of phenomenon which allowed them to see my teeth—they did not, really, see my smile and I began to think that, should I take to snarling, no one would notice any difference. All of the physical characteristics of the Negro which had caused me, in America, a very different and almost forgotten pain were nothing less than miraculous —or infernal—in the eyes of the village people. Some thought my hair was the color of tar, that it had the texture of wire, or the texture of cotton. It was jocularly suggested that I might let it all grow long and make myself a winter coat. If I sat in the sun for more than five minutes some daring creature was certain to come along and gingerly put his fingers on my hair, as though he were afraid of an electric shock, or put his hand on my hand, astonished that the color did not rub off. In all of this, in which it must be conceded there was the charm of genuine wonder and in which there were certainly no element of intentional unkindness, there was yet no suggestion that I was human: I was simply a living wonder.

I knew that they did not mean to be unkind, and I know it now; it is necessary, nevertheless, for me to repeat this to myself each time that I walk out of the chalet. The children who shout *Neger!* have no way of knowing the echoes this sound raises in me. They are brimming with good humor and the more daring swell with pride when I stop to speak with them. Just the same, there are days when I cannot pause and smile, when I have no heart to play with them; when, indeed, I mutter sourly to myself, exactly as I muttered on the streets of a city these children have never seen, when I was no bigger than these children are now: *Your* mother *was a nigger.* Joyce is right about history being a nightmare—but it may be the nightmare from which no one *can* awaken. People are trapped in history and history is trapped in them.

There is a custom in the village—I am told it is repeated in many villages—of "buying" African natives for the purpose of converting them to Christianity. There stands in the church all year round a small box with a slot for money, decorated with a black figurine, and into this box the villagers drop their francs. During the *carnaval* which precedes Lent, two village children have their faces blackened —out of which bloodless darkness their blue eyes shine like ice—and fantastic horsehair wigs are placed on their blond heads; thus disguised, they solicit among the villagers for money for the missionaries in Africa. Between the box in the church and the blackened children, the village "bought" last year six or eight African natives. This was reported to me with pride by the wife of one of the *bistro* owners and I was careful to express astonishment and pleasure at the solicitude shown by the village for the souls of black folks. The *bistro* owner's wife beamed with a pleasure far more genuine than my own and seemed to feel that I might now breathe more easily concerning the souls of at least six of my kinsmen.

I tried not to think of these so lately baptized kinsmen, of the price paid for them, or the peculiar price they themselves would pay, and said nothing about my father, who having taken his own conversion too literally never, at bottom, forgave the white world (which he described as heathen) for having saddled him with a Christ in whom, to judge at least from their treatment of him, they themselves no longer believed. I thought of white men arriving for the first time in an African village, strangers there, as I am a stranger here, and tried to imagine the astounded populace touching their hair and marveling at the color of their skin. But there is a great difference between being the first white man to be seen by Africans and being the first black man to be seen by whites. The white man takes the astonishment as tribute, for he arrives to conquer and to convert the natives, whose inferiority in relation to himself is not even to be questioned; whereas I, without a thought of conquest, find myself among a people whose culture controls me, has even, in a sense, created me, people who have cost me more in anguish and rage than they will ever know, who yet do not even know of my existence. The astonishment with which I might have greeted them, should they have stumbled into my African village a few hundred years ago, might have rejoiced their hearts. But the astonishment with which they greet me today can only poison mine.

And this is so despite everything I may do to feel differently, despite my friendly conversations with the *bistro* owner's wife, despite their three-year-old son who has at last become my friend, despite the *saluts* and *bonsoirs* which I exchange with people as I walk, despite the fact that I know that no individual can be taken to task for what history is doing, or has done. I say that the culture of these people controls me—but they can scarcely be held responsible for European culture. America comes out of Europe, but these people have never seen America, nor have most of them seen more of Europe than the hamlet at the foot of their mountain. Yet they move with an authority which I shall never have; and they regard me, quite rightly, not only as a stranger in their village but as a suspect late-comer, bearing no credentials, to everything they have—however unconsciously—inherited.

For this village, even were it incomparably more remote and incredibly more primitive, is the West, the West onto which I have been so strangely grafted. These people cannot be, from the point of view of power, strangers anywhere in the world; they have made the modern world, in effect, even if they do not know it. The most illiterate among them is related, in a way that I am not, to Dante, Shakespeare, Michelangelo, Aeschylus, Da Vinci, Rembrandt, and Racine; the cathedral at Chartres says something to them which it cannot say to me, as indeed would New York's Empire State Building, should anyone here ever see it. Out of their hymns and dances come Beethoven and Bach. Go back a few centuries and they are in their full glory—but I am in Africa, watching the conquerors arrive.

The rage of the disesteemed is personally fruitless, but it is also absolutely inevitable; this rage, so generally discounted, so little understood even among the people whose daily bread it is, is one of the things that makes history. Rage can only with difficulty, and never entirely, be brought under the domination of the intelligence and is therefore not susceptible to any arguments whatever. This is a fact which ordinary representatives of the *Herrenvolk*,[1] having never felt this rage and being unable to imagine, quite fail to understand.

1. Master race.

Also, rage cannot be hidden, it can only be dissembled. This dissembling deludes the thoughtless, and strengthens rage and adds, to rage, contempt. There are, no doubt, as many ways of coping with the resulting complex of tensions as there are black men in the world, but no black man can hope ever to be entirely liberated from this internal warfare—rage, dissembling, and contempt having inevitably accompanied his first realization of the power of white men. What is crucial here is that, since white men represent in the black man's world so heavy a weight, white men have for black men a reality which is far from being reciprocal; and hence all black men have toward all white men an attitude which is designed, really, either to rob the white man of the jewel of his naïveté, or else to make it cost him dear.

The black man insists, by whatever means he finds at his disposal, that the white man cease to regard him as an exotic rarity and recognize him as a human being. This is a very charged and difficult moment, for there is a great deal of will power involved in the white man's naïveté. Most people are not naturally reflective any more than they are naturally malicious, and the white man prefers to keep the black man at a certain human remove because it is easier for him thus to preserve his simplicity and avoid being called to account for crimes committed by his forefathers, or his neighbors. He is inescapably aware, nevertheless, that he is in a better position in the world than black men are, nor can he quite put to death the suspicion that he is hated by black men therefore. He does not wish to be hated, neither does he wish to change places, and at this point in his uneasiness he can scarcely avoid having recourse to those legends which white men have created about black men, the most usual effect of which is that the white man finds himself enmeshed, so to speak, in his own language which describes hell, as well as the attributes which lead one to hell, as being as black as night.

Every legend, moreover, contains its residuum of truth, and the root function of language is to control the universe by describing it. It is of quite considerable significance that black men remain, in the imagination, and in overwhelming numbers in fact, beyond the disciplines of salvation; and this despite the fact that the West has been "buying" African natives for centuries. There is, I should hazard, an instantaneous necessity to be divorced from this so visibly unsaved stranger, in whose heart, moreover, one cannot guess what dreams of vengeance are being nourished; and, at the same time, there are few things on earth more attractive than the idea of the unspeakable liberty which is allowed the unredeemed. When, beneath the black mask, a human being begins to make himself felt one cannot escape a certain awful wonder as to what kind of human being it is. What one's imagination makes of other people is dictated, of course, by the laws of one's own personality and it is one of the ironies of black-white relations that, by means of what the white man imagines the black man to be, the black man is enabled to know who the white man is.

I have said, for example, that I am as much a stranger in this village today as I was the first summer I arrived, but this is not quite true. The villagers wonder less about the texture of my hair than they did then, and wonder rather more about me. And the fact that their wonder now exists on another level is reflected in their attitudes and in their eyes. There are the children who make those delightful, hilarious, sometimes astonishingly grave overtures of friendship in the unpredictable fashion of children; other children, having been taught that the devil is a black man, scream in genuine anguish as I approach. Some of the older women never pass without a friendly greeting, never pass, indeed, if it seems that they will be able to engage me in conversation; other women look down or look away or rather contemptuously smirk. Some of the men drink with me and suggest that I learn how to ski—partly, I gather, because they cannot imagine what I would look like on skis—and want to know if I am married, and ask questions about my *métier*. But some of the men have accused *le sale nègre*—behind my back—of stealing wood and there is already in the eyes of some of them that peculiar, intent, paranoiac malevolence which one sometimes surprises in the eyes of American white men when, out walking with their Sunday girl, they see a Negro male approach.

There is a dreadful abyss between the streets of this village and the streets of the city in which I was born, between the children who shout *Neger!* today and those who shouted *Nigger!* yesterday— the abyss is experience, the American experience. The syllable hurled behind me today expresses, above all, wonder: I am a stranger here. But I am not a stranger in America and the same syllable riding on the American air expresses the war my presence has occasioned in the American soul.

For this village brings home to me this fact: that there was a day, and not really a very distant day, when Americans were scarcely Americans at all but discontented Europeans, facing a great unconquered continent and strolling, say, into a marketplace and seeing black men for the first time. The shock this spectacle afforded is suggested, surely, by the promptness with which they decided that these black men were not really men but cattle. It is true that the necessity on the part of the settlers of the New World of reconciling their moral assumptions with the fact—and the necessity—of slavery enhanced immensely the charm of this idea, and it is also true that this idea expresses, with a truly American bluntness, the attitude which to varying extents all masters have had toward all slaves.

But between all former slaves and slave-owners and the drama which begins for Americans over three hundred years ago at Jamestown, there are at least two differences to be observed. The American Negro slave could not suppose, for one thing, as slaves in past epochs had supposed and often done, that he would ever be able to wrest the power from his master's hands. This was a supposition which the modern era, which was to bring about such vast changes in the aims and dimensions of power, put to death; it only begins, in unprecedented fashion, and with dreadful implications, to be resurrected today. But even had this supposition persisted with undiminished force, the American Negro slave could not have used it to lend his condition dignity, for the reason that this supposition rests on another: that the slave in exile yet remains related to his past, has some means—if only in memory—of revering and sustaining the forms of his former life, is able, in short, to maintain his identity.

This was not the case with the American Negro slave. He is unique among the black men of the world in that his past was taken from him, almost literally, at one blow. One wonders what on earth the first slave found to say to the first dark child he bore. I am told that there are Haitians able to trace their ancestry back to African kings, but any American Negro wishing to go back so far will find his journey through time abruptly arrested by the signature on the bill of sale which served as the entrance paper for his ancestor. At the time—to say nothing of the circumstances—of the enslavement of the captive black man who was to become the American Negro, there was not the remotest possibility that he would ever take power from his master's hands. There was no reason to suppose that his situation would ever change, nor was there, shortly, anything to indicate that his situation had ever been different. It was his necessity, in the words of E. Franklin Frazier, to find a "motive for living under American culture or die." The identity of the American Negro comes out of this extreme situation, and the evolution of this identity was a source of the most intolerable anxiety in the minds and the lives of his masters.

For the history of the American Negro is unique also in this: that the question of his humanity, and of his rights therefore as a human being, became a burning one for several generations of Americans, so burning a question that it ultimately became one of those used to divide the nation. It is out of this argument that the venom of the epithet *Nigger!* is derived. It is an argument which Europe has never had, and hence Europe quite sincerely fails to understand how or why the argument arose in the first place, why its effects are frequently disastrous and always so unpredictable, why it refuses until today to be entirely settled. Europe's black possessions remained —and do remain—in Europe's colonies, at which remove they represented no threat whatever to European identity. If they posed any problem at all for the European conscience, it was a problem which remained comfortingly abstract: in effect, the black man, as a *man*, did not exist for Europe. But in America, even as a slave, he was an inescapable part of the general social fabric and no American could escape having an attitude toward him. Americans attempt until today to make an abstraction of the Negro, but the very nature of these abstractions reveals the tremendous effects the presence of the Negro has had on the American character.

When one considers the history of the Negro in America it is of the greatest importance to recognize that the moral beliefs of a person, or a people, are never really as tenuous as life—which is not moral—very often causes them to appear; these create for them a frame of reference and a necessary hope, the hope being that when life has done its worst they will be enabled to rise above themselves and to triumph over life. Life would scarcely be bearable if this hope did not exist. Again, even when the worst has been said, to betray a belief is not by any means to have put oneself beyond its power; the betrayal of a belief is not the same thing as ceasing to believe. If this were not so there would be no moral standards in the world at all. Yet one must also recognize that morality is based on ideas and that all ideas are dangerous—dangerous because ideas can only lead to action and where the action leads no man can say. And dangerous in this respect: that confronted with the impossibility of remaining faithful to one's beliefs, and the equal impossibility of becoming free of them, one can be driven to the most inhuman excesses. The ideas on which American beliefs are based are not, though Americans often seem to think so, ideas which originated in America. They came out of Europe. And the establishment of democracy on the American continent was scarcely as radical a break with the past as was the necessity, which Americans faced, of broadening this concept to include black men.

This was, literally, a hard necessity. It was impossible, for one thing, for Americans to abandon their beliefs, not only because these beliefs alone seemed able to justify the sacrifices they had endured and the blood that they had spilled, but also because these beliefs afforded them their only bulwark against a moral chaos as absolute as the physical chaos of the continent it was their destiny to conquer. But in the situation in which Americans found themselves, these beliefs threatened an idea which, whether or not one likes to think so, is the very warp and woof of the heritage of the West, the idea of white supremacy.

Americans have made themselves notorious by the shrillness and the brutality with which they have insisted on this idea, but they did not invent it; and it has escaped the world's notice that those very excesses of which Americans have been guilty imply a certain unprecedented uneasiness over the idea's life and power, if not, indeed, the idea's validity. The idea of white supremacy rests simply on the fact that white men are the creators of civilization (the present civilization, which is the only one that matters; all previous civilizations are simply "contributions" to our own) and are therefore civilization's guardians and defenders. Thus it was impossible for Americans to accept the black man as one of themselves, for to do so was to jeopardize their status as white men. But not so to accept him was to deny his human reality, his human weight and complexity, and the strain of denying the overwhelmingly undeniable forced Americans into rationalizations so fantastic that they approached the pathological.

At the root of the American Negro problem is the necessity of the American white man to find a way of living with the Negro in order to be able to live with himself. And the history of this problem can be reduced to the means used by Americans—lynch law and law, segregation and legal acceptance, terrorization and concession —either to come to terms with this necessity, or to find a way around it, or (most usually) to find a way of doing both these things at once. The resulting spectacle, at once foolish and dreadful, led someone to make the quite accurate observation that "the Negro-in-America is a form of insanity which overtakes white men."

In this long battle, a battle by no means finished, the unforeseeable effects of which will be felt by many future generations, the white man's motive was the protection of his identity; the black man was motivated by the need to establish an identity. And despite the terrorization which the Negro in America endured and endures sporadically until today, despite the cruel and totally inescapable ambivalence of his status in his country, the battle for his identity has long ago been won. He is not a visitor to the West, but a citizen there, an American; as American as the Americans who despise him, the Americans who fear him, the Americans who love him—the Americans who became less than themselves, or rose to be greater than themselves by virtue of the fact that the challenge he represented was inescapable. He is perhaps the only black man in the world whose relationship to white men is more terrible, more subtle, and more meaningful than the relationship of bitter possessed to uncertain possessors. His survival depended, and his development depends, on his ability to turn his peculiar status in the Western world to his own advantage and, it may be, to the very great advantage of that world. It remains for him to fashion out of his experience that which will give him sustenance, and a voice.

The cathedral at Chartres, I have said, says something to the people of this village which it cannot say to me; but it is important to understand that this cathedral says something to me which it cannot say to them. Perhaps they are struck by the power of the spires, the glory of the windows; but they have known God, after all, longer than I have known him, and in a different way, and I am terrified by the slippery bottomless well to be found in the crypt, down which heretics were hurled to death, and by the obscene, inescapable gargoyles jutting out of the stone and seeming to say that God and the devil can never be divorced. I doubt that the villagers think of the devil when they face a cathedral because they have never been identified with the devil. But I must accept the status which myth, if nothing else, gives me in the West before I can hope to change the myth.

Yet, if the American Negro has arrived at his identity by virtue of the absoluteness of his estrangement from his past, American white men still nourish the illusion that there is some means of recovering the European innocence, of returning to a state in which black men do not exist. This is one of the greatest errors Americans can make. The identity they fought so hard to protect has, by virtue of that battle, undergone a change: Americans are as unlike any other white people in the world as it is possible to be. I do not think, for example, that it is too much to suggest that the American vision of the world—which allows so little reality, generally speaking, for any of the darker forces in human life, which tends until today to paint moral issues in glaring black and white—owes a great deal to the battle waged by Americans to maintain between themselves and black men a human separation which could not be bridged. It is only now beginning to be borne in on us—very faintly, it must be admitted, very slowly, and very much against our will—that this vision of the world is dangerously inaccurate, and perfectly useless. For it protects our moral high-mindedness at the terrible expense of weakening our grasp of reality. People who shut their eyes to reality simply invite their own destruction, and anyone who insists on remaining in a state of innocence long after that innocence is dead turns himself into a monster.

The time has come to realize that the interracial drama acted out on the American continent has not only created a new black man, it has created a new white man, too. No road whatever will lead Americans back to the simplicity of this European village where white men still have the luxury of looking on me as a stranger. I am not, really, a stranger any longer for any American alive. One of the things that distinguishes Americans from other people is that no other people has ever been so deeply involved in the lives of black men, and vice versa. This fact faced, with all its implications, it can be seen that the history of the American Negro problem is not merely shameful, it is also something of an achievement. For even when the worst has been said, it must also be added that the perpetual challenge posed by this problem was always, somehow, perpetually met. It is precisely this black-white experience which may prove of indispensable value to us in the world we face today. This world is white no longer, and it will never be white again.

QUESTIONS FOR STUDY, DISCUSSION, AND WRITING

1. Baldwin begins with the narration of his experience in a Swiss village. At what point do you become aware that he is going to do more than tell the story of his stay in the village? What purpose does he make his experience serve?
2. On page 386 Baldwin says that Americans have attempted to make an abstraction of the Negro. To what degree has his purpose forced Baldwin to make an abstraction of the white man? What are the components of that abstraction?
3. What abstract argumentative thesis emerges from this essay? Many of the other essays in this section of the book (Isaacs, Sartre, Mill) deal with similarly large social questions and, therefore, in abstractions and generalizations. What is different about Baldwin's way of generalizing and abstracting?
4. Mill ("Civilization," pp. 335–353) is concerned about a threat to human individuality. Does his analysis of the problem account for the American Negro's predicament as Baldwin describes it? Does Bettelheim's ("Imaginary Impasse," pp. 452–464)?
5. Baldwin intimately relates the white man's language and legends about black men to the "laws" of the white man's personality. Bettelheim makes similar use of the myths of science fiction. This kind of inference reveals a conviction both men share about the nature of language; what is that conviction?
6. Describe some particular experience which raises a large social question or shows the working of large social forces. Does Baldwin offer any help in the problem of connecting the particular and the general?
7. Define alienation.

HAROLD R. ISAACS
Blackness and Whiteness

The entire history of Negroes in America has conspired to give them a group identity that was negative or blurred or both. When James Baldwin titles his book *Nobody Knows My Name*, he is referring to the fact that a Negro's individuality as a particular person is lost in the white world behind the identifying external mask he wears as a "Negro." This mask was fashioned out of all that went into the struggle for survival in a hostile white society. It was shaped mainly out of the myths and stereotypes created by whites for their self-appeasement and so largely accepted by blacks for their self-defense. Hence the Uncle Tom, the Sambo, the Stepin Fetchit, and all the other figures in this particular wax museum. But the problem of the Negro group identity is much more than the problem of this synthetic group personality. Nobody may know "who" the "Negro" is, but this is at least partly because the person who is a Negro has also been kept by these circumstances from knowing who he is himself. Hardly anything illustrates this more dramatically than the fact that even as "Negro" he has had enormous difficulty in deciding what to call himself, what group name to go by.

When one begins to trace the matter back in time—and it goes back nearly 200 years—one finds that the usages have varied and that preferences and arguments have swelled and swirled around a whole collection of labels: blacks, Africans, negroes (with the small "*n*"), Negroes (with the capitalisation which became general usage after a long struggle that ended only some 30 years ago and has still not ended in much of the South), Coloreds, Colored People, Colored Americans, People of Color, Ethiopians, Racemen, Negro-Saxons, African Americans, Africo-Americans, Afro-Americans, Aframericans, American Negroes, Negro Americans. Even a brief look into these differences is the beginning of discovery of some of the real inwardness of the Negro identity problem.

In the present generation, the widest common practice settled on "Negro," an embattled word which has held its own against almost constant assault. Differences, however, persist, both in opinions and usage. The term "colored" is still used almost as widely and not always interchangeably. The term "Negro" is still subject to challenge from various directions and the argument about it, kept alive by its inner essence and re-kindled by all our current events, still goes on. Black nationalists keep insisting on "Afro-American" or just plain "African." The push of this issue to the extremes of non-identity is illustrated at one end of the spectrum by the common use of the term "group" or "group man" (in which context whites would be "the majority group" or simply "the other group"), and at the other by the Black Muslims, who reject "Negro" and insist on "black" or "black men" but carry the Negro individual's identity confusion to the ultimate dramatic extreme by requiring all their followers to abandon their family names (because they all come from white origins) and to substitute the most literal symbol of non-being —the Black Muslim calls himself by a first name followed simply by "X." There is, incidentally, a long history of cults with Islamic labels among Negroes; the predecessor of the present movement, founded in 1913, required its followers to "refuse any longer to be called Negroes, black folk, colored people, or Ethiopians" but to be called "Asiatics" or "Moors" or "Moorish Americans."

* * *

The slave traders called their African cargo *negros* or simply *blacks*. Ivy reports that "negro" came to be used synonymously with *slave*. He locates an early example of this blending in a 1721 dictionary. A century later in 1819 a South Carolina court, indeed, held that the word "negro" had the fixed meaning of a "slave." This has been the most-commonly cited source for objection to the use of "Negro." It has been seen, as various writers have noted, as "a badge of shame" hopelessly freighted with its "slave origin and its consequent degradation." Closely associated with this idea and equally common as a reason for rejecting the word is the slippage of "Negro" into "nigger," the term that carries in it all the obloquy and contempt and rejection which whites have inflicted on blacks in all this time. This, many have suggested, may be "the clue to the whole business."[1]

But it becomes clear even from a brief look that there are many other clues, much more to the business than this. For Negroes the issue of the name to go by has been deeply entwined with all the deepest and unresolved issues of the flight-from-self imposed upon them by their whole history in this society, of color—that is, of relative lightness and relative darkness, of the ways in which they have related to their African origins, of all the ways in which they have striven to be both in and of the white society from which they were so consistently and so completely excluded.

The available record begins with the free Negroes who had come up out of the slave system by various means and had begun to group and assert themselves at the time of the American Revolution and the establishment of the American Republic. The 1790 census noted 59,000 free Negroes in the population and although still called "Negroes" by whites, they had begun to distinguish themselves from the slaves by using the adjective "African." This was the name they attached to the new institutions they created for themselves at this time when they found themselves excluded from the established similar institutions of the whites. Thus the African Baptist Church (1779), the first African Lodge of Masons (1787), the Free African Society (1787), the African Methodist Episcopal Church (1796) and others. The first schools established for their children

1. Roi Ottley, *New World A'Coming* (1943). Ottley goes on to remark, as have many others, that "the term nigger is used by Negroes quite freely when out of the earshot of whites, sometimes having a good deal of affectionate meaning to them." This way of turning an insulting word into something casual, light, even affectionate or humorous is a usage not uncommon in various quarters with such comparable words as *kike, wop, mick, spic.* This is a way of lightening the quality of the word, like Cyrano talking about his own nose, or saying-it-and-smiling, but it never really relieves it of its burden of contempt and self-contempt.

Even more hateful-sounding, incidentally, is the word *Nigra*, which is the way "Negro" comes out when slurred, deliberately or otherwise, in Southern accents. Negroes in Atlanta told me with much cynical amusement about a white politician seeking Negro votes in a local election who was drilled sedulously to say *Nee-gro* when talking to Negro audiences and who reverted to his more normal *Nigra* when talking to whites. The word *Negress* is almost the most objectionable of all, being strongly held to be associated with both the auction block and with animals. It may be taken as a recent sign of the times that the *Columbia Record* of Columbia, South Carolina, accepted the protest of a group of local Negro women and announced it would cease using the term *Negress*. "We were not aware that the term was offensive," the editor wrote. Columbia's other paper, *The State*, ignored the protest—*New York Amsterdam News*, April 21, 1962 [Isaacs' note].

were called "Free African Schools" in New York and elsewhere.

By 1830, however, when free Negroes met together in their urgent common interest, the adjective "African" had been replaced by "Colored." When they met in Philadelphia that year they organized the "Convention of Colored Citizens of America." In general by that time they had begun to refer to themselves as "colored people" or "people of color." Students of the period have apparently not dealt with this shift in name and I do not know what a new search through old papers would turn up on this score; but I am willing to guess that at least two sets of circumstances would be found to be part of the explanation.

The first is that in the intervening time a concerted movement had been started to get free Negroes to migrate back to Africa whereas the overwhelming majority of free Negroes, especially in the Northern cities, wanted no part of any such migration. By the process of self-purchase, manumission, and the efforts of various early abolition groups, and by natural increase, the number of free Negroes had risen by this time to 319,000, more or less evenly divided between northern and southern cities. Their freedom was tenuous and under constant threat. Their hardships attracted a certain kind of pious Northern white benevolence under which transportation back to Africa was seen as the best solution to the problem. On the other hand, the sheer existence of free Negroes was felt as a growing threat to slaveholding interests and this attracted a certain non-pious Southern malevolence which seized readily upon the same idea. These interests were wedded in 1817 in the founding of the American Colonization Society which received the ready support of certain state legislatures. Some Southern free Negroes accepted the Society's offer (in many instances manumission was made contingent upon willingness to sign up for the return to Africa) and from among these came the first boatloads of migrants who founded Liberia in 1821. By 1830 the number shipped by the Society totalled only just over 1,400. There was an independent and recurring impulse among some despairing Northern free Negroes to look to Africa as a way out of hopelessness in America, but most northern free Negroes vehemently opposed the Society's program and denounced it in strong terms, beginning in 1817 and every year thereafter in meetings in many cities. It seems reasonable to assume, therefore, that the label "African" was abandoned, at least by Northern free Negroes, because they were intent upon remaining Americans and rejected the schemes to send them, as "Africans," back to Africa.

But the choice of the term "people of color" or "colored people" to replace "African" suggests the second set of circumstances clearly involved in this change. The term "African" had been used mainly by free Negroes in the North, most of whom had gained their freedom in the early years of the Republic. The clusters of free Negroes in the South, especially those in Charleston, South Carolina and New Orleans, came out of a much older process. The first differentiation among the slaves was that made between the field hands and the house servants, and from among the latter came the issue of unions between white masters and slave women, often treated as a second family, given their freedom, means, and education. It was the descendants of such groups who developed their own special caste position (which included slaveholding of their own) and whose most visible mark of caste was their lighter color. This community in Charleston in 1790 formed not an *African* association, but the *Brown* Fellowship Society "which admitted only brown men of good character who paid an admission fee of fifty dollars."[2] In New Orleans the even older and more aristocratic mixed descendants of the older French and Spanish settlers became a distinct group in the population and were called the *gens de couleur*. It is from this term and from this group, carrying with it all the connotations of higher caste associated with non-blackness and mixed ancestry, that the vague and essentially non-descriptive term *colored* or *people of color* was derived. With its adoption by the Northern free Negroes in place of "African" during the decade before 1830, it became the term of preferred and polite usage.

Although this term became one of general use and has persisted down through time until now, it has never stood alone or uncontradicted. At the very beginning, in the 1840s and 1850s, when some of the most militant and anti-migrationalist free leaders, despairing of ever gaining a decent status in America, became advocates of migration to Africa, there was some effort made to revive the use of the term "African." Whites generally continued to use "Negro" although the abolitionist movement generally adopted "colored." Lincoln, Carl Sandburg notes in his biography, was attacked by Southern sympathizers for shifting from "negroes," a term he still used in 1859, to "colored men" in 1860 and "free Americans of African descent" in 1862. Frederick Douglass generally used "colored" in accordance with the preferred practice, but also used "Negro" and "black" as part of his effort to re-establish a sense of Negro identity. He used "Negro," he told a white audience in 1854, "precisely in the sense that you use 'Anglo-Saxon'." In referring to individual persons he continued as a rule to use "colored."

By whatever name he was called, the Negro in the closing decades of the 19th century found his status as a man and as a citizen driven lower and lower. It was at this time, in 1880, that T. Thomas Fortune came up with his effort to get Negroes and the society at large to accept the new term "Afro-American." Fortune wanted to get away from "Negro," remarks Kelly Miller, because of "the historical

2. E. Franklin Frazier, *The Negro in the United States* (New York, 1949) [Isaacs' note].

degradation and humiliation attached to it" and, it is suggested, especially to get away from "nigger." Fortune wrote: "Until we get this race designation properly fixed in the language and literature of the country, we shall be kicked and cuffed and sneered at as a common noun, sufficiently and contemptuously characterized by the vulgar term. . . ." But Fortune wanted to do a lot more than merely do away with a vulgar term. He meant his term "Afro-American" to describe the different physical type that had been created in America by mixture with the white, as "a new race in this country approximating much nearer the American than the African type." The term "Negro," he wrote, ". . . has been used to describe black people of Africa. It is not a term definitive of race affinities but of physical peculiarities of race of which color is the invariable index." For Fortune too, this strongly suggests, a critical element in choosing the name to go by was the element of color and the distinctively "Negro" physical characteristics. The term "Afro-American," despite Fortune's doughty championship and its adoption later as the name of the Baltimore *Afro-American* never gained any wide measure of acceptance among Negroes and none at all in the general currency of the language.

But the argument, largely centering on the continued use of "Negro," went on and on, acquiring peculiar force around the years of the turn of the century. Booker T. Washington advocated the use of "Negro" and opponents of the word charged this against his general posture of submission. But along came W. E. B. Du Bois, no submitter, who not only espoused "Negro" but used "black" and stressed color almost obsessively in his own special struggle for the reassertion of Negro identity. It did not matter, he pointed out, whether they were called "African" or "Ethiopian" or "colored," but what mattered was who and what you were and where you stood in the society. This was the view expressed by many other leaders over the years, although the NAACP, founded in 1909 by Du Bois and others followed the preferred usage among the middle and upper class Negroes and used "Colored." The Garvey movement a decade later did use "Negro" in its name (the United Negro Improvement Association) but much preferred "black" as a direct expression of its explicit and strong racial chauvinism.

Most of the present generation of Negro adults grew up simply accepting these confused and divided usages without questioning what they might mean. Among those I interviewed, I noticed a fairly typical cleavage: members of what one might call the more traditional middle or upper class among Negroes almost invariably used "colored" and a few had strong views on the subject ("I never class myself as 'Negro' " said an ex-college president. "I had to cease to be a 'Negro' in order to be a man.") The stronger "race man" types had opposite views. ("My father always believed we should use 'Negro' meaning black," said a noted labor leader. "As a term it has more strength than 'colored'.") More generally the younger and more sophisticated either used "Negro" alone or used it interchangeably with "colored." When asked, most of them said they were aware of the disputes over the matter but did not think them important. Most commonly, they said they thought the objection to "Negro" was its closeness to "nigger." Only a few thought there might be layers to the matter deeper than this, and they only when asked. "I hadn't thought," said a noted educator, "that any matter of color was involved in this, but it is quite possible. Some four or five years ago there was a motel sign up somewhere near here (Atlanta) which said 'for Negroes.' A taxi driver sneered as we went by it one day: 'He ought to know he won't get colored people's business with that sign.' And the fact is that the sign was changed sometime after that to 'for Colored.' "

Another well-known scholar said: "I am sure there is something about color in the use of 'Negro' and 'Colored,' though it is not always at the tip of people's consciousness."

In fact, just below the level of that more common consciousness, the issue of name-confusion is intimately locked with all the central issues of Negro identity-confusion; the flight from blackness, the flight from Negro-ness itself, the yearning to be white.

Black Stand Back

The flight from blackness and the yearning to be white have had a major part in shaping the Negro group identity down through the generations. It involved the more or less total acceptance of the white man's estimate of the black man, the more or less total rejection of self. This was a widely-shared experience and it took on many forms, but it would be hard to find a more explicit statement of it than the one made in a contribution to the argument over names in 1913 by William H. Ferris, author of a two-volume study called *The African Abroad*. Ferris had an entry of his own in the name stakes; he wanted the term *Negrosaxon* because he believed salvation for the black man lay in his complete adoption of white Anglo-Saxonism.

The Anglo-Saxon civilization is the highest and best yet evolved in the history of the human race, [he wrote. On the other hand] the word "Negro" originally referred to a native African black, who was a barbarian and a savage.... "Negro" calls up a black, kinky-haired and heavy-featured being.... [It] suggests physical and spiritual kinship to the ape, the monkey, the baboon, the chimpanzee, the orang-outang and gorilla.... It is up to the Negrosaxon or Colored man to say which badge he shall wear, the badge of monkeyhood or of manhood, the badge of brutehood and bestiality or the badge of humanity.... What causes more of a shudder of repulsion to run through the frame than the phrase "a big burly Negro ...?" The colored man who brands himself as a Negro thereby catalogues and labels himself as a being who is outside the pale of humanity.

Fortunately, Ferris goes on, most of the colored people in America were brought inside the pale of humanity by blood mixture. "While the colored people of America cannot boast of the manner in which they came by their white blood, they at least have this consolation—most of the Caucasian blood that flows in Negro-saxon veins is the blood of Southern aristocrats." Ferris believed that a full embrace of Anglo-Saxonism could save even a black man. Citing some notable examples (like Alexander Crummell and Kelly Miller), he went on:

He cannot bleach out his complexion or straighten his hair, or sharpen his nose, or thin his lips. But in mind and character and disposition he must become a black white man. After the Negro-saxon has been made over into the likeness of the white man he can hope to be made over into the image of God.

This is, of course, a familiar phenomenon which has also been called "identification with the aggressor." In wanting to become like those who have dominated, despised, and rejected them, Negroes have been behaving like members of many other dominated, despised, and rejected groups. All our various cultures and sub-cultures are filled with examples. It became part of the common experience of certain sections of the colonized peoples during the Western imperial epoch; it was even shared for quite a while by certain kinds of Chinese. In the American culture, it has been plainly visible in the experience of successive immigrant groups as they went about relating themselves to the dominant group in the society. Jews, who have been despised and rejected for a longer time than anybody, have a number of chapters of this kind in their long history. Bruno Bettelheim's interpretation of what happened to some Jews in the Nazi extermination camps suggests a recent and extreme example. More familiar and more common has been the behavior attached to the idea of "assimilation," the effort to shed all vestiges of the Jewish identity by disappearing entirely into the dominant group. The equivalent among Negroes is, of course, "passing" into the white population. But to "pass" is possible only for relatively few.[3] More generally people have to find other ways of assimilating the majority view of themselves and of expressing the self-rejection and self-hatred that follows from this. Among Negroes the forms and modes of this process are endlessly varied. One of the most pervasive of these has been the institution of color caste which raised "whiteness" to the highest value in all aspects of life. This meant everything pertaining to civilization, culture, religion, and human worth. It became among Negroes an intricate system of social, group and personal relationships based directly on degrees of relative darkness and other degrees

3. Gunnar Myrdal, *American Dilemma* (1944). Walter White, longtime secretary of the NAACP who himself had this choice, dealt with it in a novel, *Flight* (1926) [Isaacs' note].

of physical Negro-ness, the shape and kinds of features, hair, lips, and nose which were "good" if they resembled the white's, "bad" if they did not. This was carried to the point of using artificial means— hair-straighteners and skin-whiteners—in the effort to close the gap between the two.

In coming to terms with himself, every Negro individual has had in one way or another to cope with the infinity of ways in which "white" is elevated above "black" in our culture. The association of white and black with light and dark and the translation of these quantities of light into polarities of "good" and "evil" and "beauty" and "ugliness" has taken place in the conventions and languages of many cultures, but in few has this conversion of physical facts into religious and aesthetic values been worked harder than in our own.

"Black" and "White"

These concepts and usages of black evil and white goodness, of beautiful fairness and ugly blackness, are deeply imbedded in the Bible, are folded into the language of Milton and Shakespeare, indeed are laced into almost every entwining strand of the art and literature in which our history is clothed. They can be traced down the columns of any dictionary from white hope to whitewash, from the black arts to the Black Mass, from black-browed and blackhearted to blacklist and blackmail. "I am black *but* comely," sang the Shulamite maiden to the daughters of Jerusalem[4] and on that *but* hangs a whole great skein of our culture.

The Bible's central theme of good and evil is constantly represented by the symbolism of "black" and "white" and "dark" and "light." In the Scriptures the use of "black" as a negative word is consistent throughout, standing for sin, ignorance, wickedness, and evil. "My skin is black," cries Job in his great self-arraignment, using this figure to show how heavy was his burden of sin. Again in *Job*. "Let darkness and the shadow of death stain it; let a cloud dwell upon it; let the blackness of the day terrify it." Or in *Jeremiah*: "For this shall the earth mourn and the heavens above be black." And in the *Epistle of Jude* the famous phrase about "the wandering stars to whom is reserved the blackness of darkness forever."

The word "white" is apparently used a good deal less in the Bible, and less consistently. Thus "the great white throne" of God in *Revelation*, the "white raiments" of the elders in *Judges*. But "white," though most often signifying beauty, purity, and elegance, is also more rarely used—as a literally descriptive word—in connection with leprosy, and has been associated in the language with pestilence and death. More consistent is the juxtaposition of "light" and "dark," the dark being always bad and light always good, from the original creation of light to divide it from the primeval dark and to show the

4. *Song of Solomon* i.5.

way for men to see truth and good works and glory and the light of God himself: "In thy light," sang the Psalmist, "shall we see light." There can be no question that when the Lord looked upon his work and found it good, it was the light that pleased him, not the dark.

* * *

The carry-over of the Bible's imagery into the common usage, visible in Chaucer and Milton, is richly illustrated in Shakespeare, whose own impact on the English language has hardly been less great than that of the Bible itself.

> Black is the badge of hell,
> the hue of the dungeons and the suit of night.

says the King in *Love's Labour's Lost*, in a passage of raillery in which the beauty of Rosaline (French and therefore presumably brunette) is called "black as ebony" and her admirer Biron chided for loving "an Ethiope." In quite another tone, in *Macbeth*, we come on: "The devil damn thee black——," again the symbolic joining of sin, the devil, and the blackness of skin which runs continuously from Job and the prophets through centuries of our literature. (Thus Fitzgerald in *Omar Khayyam*: "For all the sin wherewith the face of man is blackened. . . .") In Shakespeare's first tragedy, *Titus Andronicus*, the villain is a black man. In *Othello* Shakespeare treats the theme with far greater subtlety. No doubt is left that Brabantio's rage is due in part to the thought that his daughter would run "to the sooty bosom of such a thing as thou," but the direct allusions to Othello's color are few. Perhaps the most ironic are those Shakespeare puts in the mouth of Othello himself, as where in the rage of his rising jealousy he says:

> Her name, that was as fresh
> As Dian's visage is now begrimed and black
> As mine own face.

and where he cries out: "Arise, black vengeance!" He looks upon the sleeping Desdemona not wanting to shed her blood,

> Nor scar that whiter skin of hers than snow
> And smooth as monumental alabaster.

When he has done the deed, the servant Emilia shrieks at him: "You the blacker devil!"

One might travel many paths into some of the mysteries of this little-studied matter, whether in other cultures, including the African, or in our own. * * * But to lead us back to the aspects of the matter that touch us here most directly let me only follow an allusion from his pages to William Blake's poem, *The Little Black Boy*—part of a collection published in 1789—in which the outlook imposed by the white society on the black child is quite neatly capsuled:

> My mother bore me in the southern wild,
> And I am black, but O! my soul is white;
> White as an angel is the English child,
> But I am black, as if bereav'd of light.
>
> My mother . . . began to say:
>
> . . . And we are put on earth a little space
> That we may learn to bear the beams of love;
> And these black bodies and this sunburnt face
> Is but a cloud, and like a shady grove.
>
> For when our souls have learn'd the heat to bear,
> The cloud will vanish; we shall hear His voice,
> Saying: "Come out from the grove, My love and care,
> And round my golden tent like lambs rejoice."
>
> Thus did my mother say, and kissed me;
> And thus I say to little English boy.
> When I from black and he from white cloud free,
> And round the tent of God like lambs we joy,
>
> I'll shade him from the heat, till he can bear
> To lean in joy upon our Father's knee;
> And then I'll stand and stroke his silver hair,
> And be like him, and he will then love me.

This raising of "white" and debasement of "black" has been marked deep on the minds of all through time and every "white" person has more or less unconsciously imbibed it as a nourishment for his self-esteem. Like the English child in Blake's poem, he was already the color of the angels, while the black man could only yearn after whiteness, whether of character, soul, or of skin, and hope that by becoming "like" the white man—whether on earth or in heaven— he would come at last to be loved. This arrangement of things was communicated to all in our culture by all its modes and means, passed by osmosis through all the membranes of class, caste, and color of relationships, caressingly and painlessly injected into our children by their school texts and, even more, their storybooks.

Consider only one contemporary example, out of the Dr. Dolittle stories, written by an Englishman, which have delighted European and American children since 1920. Dr. Dolittle, an animal doctor who travels with an entourage of a dog, a duck, a pig, an owl, a monkey, and a parrot, goes to Africa to cure monkeys of a plague. Dolittle and his animal helpers become the prisoners of a black king. In the king's garden the parrot and the monkey meet the king's son, Prince Bumpo, who is pictured as an ugly-gnome-like black man with a huge nose that covers most of his face. They hear him yearn aloud:

"If only I were a *white* prince!" The parrot promises that Dr. Dolittle will change his color if he helps them escape. To Dr. Dolittle, the unhappy prince tells his story:

Years ago I went in search of The Sleeping Beauty, whom I had read of in a book. And having traveled through the world many days, I at last found her and kissed the lady very gently to wake her—as the book said I should. 'Tis true indeed that she woke. But when she saw my face she cried out, "Oh, he's black!" And she ran away and wouldn't marry me— but went to sleep again somewhere else. So I came back, full of sadness, to my father's kingdom. Now I hear that you are a wonderful magician and have many powerful potions. So I come to you for help. If you will turn me white, so that I may go back to The Sleeping Beauty, I will give you half of my kingdom and anything besides you ask.

Bumpo refuses to settle just for blond hair and says: "I would like my eyes blue, too, but I suppose that would be very hard to do." The doctor concocts a paste which whitens Bumpo's face and keeps it that way long enough for him and his friends to escape, having first refused to give Bumpo a mirror because he knew that the medicine would wear off and that Bumpo would be "as black as ever in the morning." As they escape, the doctor says, "Poor Bumpo." The parrot says: "Oh, of course he would know we were just joking with him." The duck says: "Serve him right if he does turn black again. I hope it is a dark black." Dr. Dolittle decides that instead of apologizing he will send Bumpo some candy when he gets back home.

I do not know if Negro children have been readers of Hugh Lofting's Dolittle stories, but vast numbers of white children apparently have—it came up in the first place when a discussion of these matters in a seminar stirred the recollection of a graduate student of 30, and an indirect question brought immediate recall of the story to my own daughter, then 16. It is not hard to imagine the effect on white children who, as they chortle over the good doctor's adventures with the animals, also take in this vignette of the ugly black prince who wanted to be white in order to be loved. It takes no great art either to imagine how this tale might stab a black child or help give him all unknowingly the same love for whiteness that it nourishes in the white child.[5]

5. An example of another kind, and earlier in time, is "The Story of Two Little Lambs," in Maud Ballington Booth, *Sleepy-Time Stories* (New York, 1900).

A little white lamb strays from the flock and is lost and meets a little black lamb in the forest. Says the little black lamb: "You are what they call a White Lamb, and White Lambs have a good home and good things all the time, and they say that they have a good Shepherd; but I am only a black one . . . some day when we meet the good Shepherd (if we ever do chance to meet Him)

He will take us too, and bring us to the White Lambs' fold."

To this the white lamb replies: "I don't think He would like you very much for I have always been told that He wants His Sheep and Lambs to have very white, white wool and you are black." The Shepherd Jesus comes to recover his stray white lamb and promises that he can wash him clean and white again, and is about to leave when the little black lamb speaks up and says he wishes he was one of Jesus' lambs too. "But it's no use," he says, "for they say you only want White Sheep and

Color Caste

The imprint on Negroes of this whole system of ordering "black" and "white" has been seen and experienced by many but studied by very few. Every "black" person obviously has been called upon to reject or somehow deflect from himself the associations of evil and inferiority so powerfully attached to blackness. He has been called upon to do this, moreover, under conditions in which his ego was kept under constant assault from all the conditions of his life. That so many Negroes in every successive generation found the ego strength to meet and resist these identifications is in itself no small miracle. That a greater number accepted the white man's images as the truth about themselves is no wonder at all.

Out of this acceptance came the notions and practices of color caste among Negroes, the notions and virtue and non-virtue attached to lightness and darkness, the placing of the highest value on non-blackness. This was, as I have already remarked the basis for the separate identity of the *gens de couleur*, the underlying reason for the adoption of the term *colored*, and the starting point for the establishment of tight little groups of lighter-skinned Negro aristocrats. There is some suggestion that from the time of the forming of the "Brown Fellowship" in Charleston in 1790 until post-Civil War Reconstruction days the practice of color caste remained locked in these small communities. This seems, at least, to be the meaning of the element of surprise in an exchange of letters between Martin R. Delany (who went to Charleston from New York in 1871) to Frederick Douglass. Delany wrote indignantly to Douglass of the attitudes and practices he found among the pre-Civil War free Negroes there, bringing from Douglass an astonished and angry response:

Can it be that the colored people of South Carolina are going to make such fools of themselves. . . . Are we to have, nay have we got a caste called the *Browns* in South Carolina? . . . I certainly unite with you in your hottest denunciations of that contemptible and senseless imitation of one of the meanest feelings that ever crept into the human heart.

But color caste spread and grew, moved out into all classes among Negroes and came to shape the attitudes and personalities of all who were touched by it.[6] "Among Negroes themselves," wrote James

Lambs and cannot bear black wool, so I cannot be the sort of Lamb you want." To which Jesus replies: "Did you hear that I can wash away the stains and make my little Lamb white again?" "But, good Shepherd," interposes the little white lamb, "that Lamb has always been black. . . . It isn't your Lamb, it's quite another sort.' Jesus is sad and angry. "Who said the Black Lambs were not mine? Who said I do not want them?" So he takes up both little lambs, car-

ries them to a stream in which he washes them, "and when they came out they were both white, as white as snow. They bleated for joy and jumped around the Shepherd, and then they laid their little heads in His tender hand, and He stroked them lovingly" [Isaacs' note].

6. The yearning-after-whiteness and color caste values governed not only Negroes in the United States but throughout the Americas. James Ivy traces the matter not only through the terminolo-

Weldon Johnson in his *Autobiography of an Ex-Colored Man* (1912), "there is the peculiar inconsistency of a color question. Its existence is rarely admitted and hardly ever mentioned; it may not be too strong a statement to say that the great portion of the race is unconscious of its influence; yet this influence, though silent, is constant."

The first forthright scrutiny it ever received from scholars was in a series of investigations made in the late 1930s by a group of Negro and white social scientists led by the late E. Franklin Frazier and Charles Johnson. They showed that at all levels in the Negro population in both North and South shades of relative darkness and lightness had become tightly related to social, moral, and aesthetic judgments and affected relationships of all kinds, from playmates among children to marriage mates among adults. Until these studies appeared showing the "unimaginable bitterness and antipathies (that) rage within the veil of color," very little had ever been said in print about this pervasive fact of Negro life.

Apparently its first appearance as the central theme of a novel was in Wallace Thurman's *The Blacker the Berry* (New York, 1929) which brought out into the open, according to Langston Hughes, "a subject little dwelt upon in Negro fiction." The title comes from a folk saying often defensively on the lips of the darker-skinned, especially the women: "The blacker the berry, the sweeter the juice." Thurman's heroine Emma Lou is a dark girl whom he takes through every kind of Negro milieu, mercilessly depicting the hurts and the cruelties inflicted upon her. These begin when she is still in her cradle with the scorn and derision of relatives ("Try some lye," they would joke viciously to her mother, "it may eat it [the blackness] out. She can't look any worse!"). It goes on with the hatred of her mother who sees her daughter's darkness as her penalty for marrying a dark man of whom she was ashamed. Emma Lou goes to school in

gies used in Portuguese and Spanish but in the rich literature in both those languages.

The late Franz Fanon, a Negro of Martinique and a psycho-analyst, wrote in *Peau Blanc, Masques Noirs* (Paris, 1952) with great force and passion of the ways in which these same pressures shaped the black man who came under the domination of France.

In shapes that await someone's closer look, the matter also appears in African settings. E.g., in *Drawn in Color: African Contrasts* (New York, 1962), Noni Jabavu, daughter of a distinguished South African educator, quotes a cousin of hers: " 'Funny thing about these up-north people. All the ones who came were so *black*. . . .' We were a little taken aback, then jumped to the defense of the East Africans. . . . 'Don't talk rubbish! Haven't we got our dark-complexioned

ones?' The cousin clung to his point. . . . 'Why is it the ones who come south all happen to be this black-as-sin type?' We at once stopped laughing and winced at the idiom. We were shocked to have to admit that we had all observed it. . . . He was speaking of an ugly thing, being blunt and unashamed about the color prejudice that we all knew and felt. . . . In months to come I was to be astounded to find this same preference for copper-colored complexions lurking even among the Ugandans themselves whose own deep coloring is artistically complete and reminds you of the look of rich dark fruit when the bloom is on it. These secret dissatisfactions made me wonder if there weren't more intricacies than meet the eye in the complex attitudes about color which arouse emotions the world over" (pp. 85-86) [Isaacs' note].

Los Angeles where she hopes to find a kindlier cosmopolitanism, but she is snubbed by lighter Negroes there too. She goes to Harlem where she finds all the better jobs—even at the menial levels of restaurant work—restricted to lighter-skinned girls, and where she must even listen to the raucous taunts of hoodlums she passes on the streets, their voices carrying after her with: "Man, you know I don't haul no coal," or singing a common ditty:

> A yellow girl rides in a limousine,
> A brownskin rides a Ford,
> A black girl rides an old jackass,
> But she gets there, yes, my lord.

There are many variations on this theme, the following being one of the most common:

> White, you're right,
> Light, you can fight,
> Brown, stand around,
> Black, stand back!

Emma Lou makes a friend of a West Indian girl who is also suffering the slings and arrows of rejection as a "monkey chaser" but even here the circle is rounded for her by a West Indian landlady who turns her away because, Thurman explains, "persons of color don't associate with blacks in the Caribbean Islands she had come from." He takes us with his heroine through the common practice of skin bleaching, the use of all sorts of preparations and powders on which great fortunes were made in the ready market among dark-skinned women. She even tries arsenic wafers, which she had heard increased skin pallor, but only gets sick, and all the ointments and solutions only serve to give her rashes, burns, and irritations. In a school job, at church, she goes on seeking acceptance without finding it, and when a "yaller nigger" shows interest, she is flattered "that a man as light as he should find himself attracted to her," but then she finds she despises him for this very reason. She is drawn back to the man who had most brutally misused her, but even he, at the bottom of the pit of misfortune from which she tries vainly to lift him, feels free to step on her at will, and this finally forces her to look squarely at herself and her life. Thurman, a gifted writer who died very young, brings his dark heroine at the end to a positive affirmation of strength: "What she needed to do now was to accept her black skin as being real and unchangeable, to realize that certain things were, had been, and would be, and with this in mind to begin life anew, always fighting, not so much for acceptance by other people, but for acceptance of herself and by herself." She can do this, but only at the price of achieving a terrible hardness of spirit.

Not many other writers even yet have chosen to deal explicitly and at length with these themes of lightness and darkness in Negro life. It is deeply enfolded—indeed, often hidden—in the writing of Langston Hughes. Saunders Redding comes back to it again and again in his work, but almost always glancingly or in brief episodes through which he still manages to show how enormously important it is to him. In the first chapter of his *No Day of Triumph*, for example, he writes of his two grandmothers between whom there lay a deep abyss—"one was yellow, the other was black." He tells how as a small boy who already knew there was "a stigma attached to blackness" he realized that for his Grandma Conway blackness was not merely a *blemish* but a *taint*. Another is his poignant account of a girl, a distant relative, who never overcame the handicap of her darker color, and ended up by dissolving as a human being. In *The Third Generation* (1954) Chester Himes writes about a woman who is the product three generations removed of a union between a plantation lord and a slave. She is white in appearance and is wedded to this whiteness with an intensity that is a sickness. This is the way in which the sins of her forebears are visited upon her, for her obsession drags her, her husband, and her children into various kinds of self-destruction.

In *Proud Shoes* (1956) Pauli Murray gives us a portrait of her grandmother who was actually just such a woman, herself the daughter of a plantation owner and a slave who was mostly Cherokee Indian. She built her entire identity around these facts of her origin and her first loyalty was not only to her "whiteness" but to her "Southern aristocratic whiteness." Thus when a neighbor thinks to insult her by calling her "a half-white bastard," she retorts:

Hmph! You think I'm insulted? I'll tell anybody I'm a white man's child. A fine white man at that. A Southern aristocrat. If you want to know what I am, I'm an octoroon, that's what I am—seven eighths white. The other eighth is Cherokee Indian. I don't have one drop of colored blood in me and I don't have to mix in with good-for-nothing niggers if I don't want to.

"Anyone who has been part of a famly of mixed bloods in the United States or the West Indies," writes Miss Murray, "has lived intimately with the unremitting search for whiteness. To deny that it is part of one's heritage would be like saying one had no parents." The form it took was the unending obsession with color:

The world revolved on color and variations in color. It pervaded the air I breathed. I learned it in hundreds of ways. I picked it up from grown folks around me. I heard it in the house, on the playground, in the streets everywhere. The tide of color beat upon me ceaselessly, relentlessly.

Always, the same tune, played like a broken record, robbing one of personal identity.... It was color, color, color all the time, color, features, and hair.... Two shades lighter! Two shades darker! Dead white! Coal black! High yaller! Mariny! Good hair! Bad hair! Stringy hair! Nappy hair! Thin lips! Thick lips! Red lips! Liver lips! Blue veined! Blue gummed! Straight nosed! Flat nosed!

Brush your hair, child, don't let it get kinky. Cold-cream your face, child, don't let it get sun-burned! Don't suck your lips, child, you'll make them too niggerish! Black is evil, don't mix with mean niggers! Black is honest, you half-white bastard. I always said a little black and a little white sure to make a pretty sight! He's black as sin and evil in the bargain. The blacker the berry the sweeter the juice.

The unremitting search for "whiteness" naturally produced its counterpart in a defense by aggressive reassertion of blackness. Among the masses of black or darker people, who in the past were predominantly of the lower economic groups, elementary self-defense took the form of a strong counter-prejudice against the lighter-skinned. The popular idiom was (and still is) full of lively expression of feelings about the "yellow niggers," many of them counter-thrusting hard and deep at the assumed illegitimacy of the "yellow bastards" whether in the present or past generations. Thus "yellow" became, like "black" a fighting word in many situations and touching areas of great sensitivity and ambiguity even when used more or less lightly in the common parlance.

For a long time the defense of blackness was identified with race chauvinism and held out at the edges of Negro life. It was wrapped up with black nationalism and this was the stuff of extremism, as in the case of Marcus Garvey whose appeal in the 1920s was made to the dark and the poor against the better-off and lighter-skinned. It was, in fact, Garvey's brutal exposure of this deep cleavage which made many thoughtful Negroes realize how costly color caste had become. The beginning of the end of its most egregious forms dates from that time. Negro writers, poets, and scholars had again and again over many years tried to resist the erosions of color caste by insisting, among other things, on the virtues of blackness. W. E. B. Du Bois, himself one of the lighter Negro leaders and one of Garvey's prime foes and targets, had ceaselessly carried on a campaign on this score in all his writings. He refers caressingly always to "warm ebony" and "satin black" and "golden brown."

Color Caste Fading

But even a generation ago and longer, the sharp edge of changing circumstance was already undercutting color caste among Negroes. There was, as I have suggested, the sobering experience of Marcus Garvey's violent color chauvinism. There were also changes beginning in the Negro community which, while they came out of the common yearning to be "white"—*i.e.*, better off—in culture and mode of life, did begin to counteract the practice of assigning automatic value to degrees of actual physical whiteness. The push of rejection which had shunted so many into numbness and apathy prodded others into a fierce drive for achievement. Darker-skinned men came up from the lower economic rungs and won new status for themselves through education and financial success. This was not just a matter of a few exceptional achievers but of a sizeable class of men of the generation that grew up after the first World War followed by a still larger group of those who came up out of the depression and into the war years as they matured. As Franklin Frazier pointed out, this new class of men largely shouldered aside the older mulatto middle class. Instead of family and color, they established position and money as the chief criteria of status in the Negro community. At the same time, however, in pursuit of the prevailing color caste values by which they were still governed, such men almost invariably married lighter-skinned women. The showing of these men and the frequency of these marriages eventually had a certain taming effect on the overall expression of color caste prejudice and, more important, also began to shade down a substantial segment of the population into increasingly common shades of brown. It was already becoming bad form in many quarters even 30 years ago to express color caste prejudices openly even though they were widely held and practiced. Writing of the Negro upper crust in the 1950s, Professor Frazier said it still had an "unavowed colored snobbishness which has ceased to have much importance."[7]

In this, as in all else affecting Negro life, the pace of change quickened as we moved into the 1960s. Many of the old patterns of behavior still exist and still govern many people, but they are all but lost in the great swirl of new relationships and new attitudes. The effect is that of a kaleidoscope in which all the old images and postures are mingled with new pictures and new attitudes, and the view you get depends on where and when you look and with whom you talk at any given moment. This jumbled scene, like a vast mural with a host of sharp details, emerges so clearly and so vividly from my interviews and conversations that I turn to them now for vignettes of this process in motion. First, then, for varying views of the amount and pace of change and of the shape of the transition:

Negroes are less sensitive about color now, less self-conscious about it when they are among whites. You rarely find a Negro who does not now more easily discuss the matter. Prejudice is vanishing. You will still find it in the old strongholds of the past, in Charleston and New Orleans, a lot less still in Washington. I think this change has simply come out of the crucible of the struggle for equality in which people have learned certain elementary lessons. This is the main explanation. . . .

This is gradually melting away. You just don't hear anything any more about black, yellow, mulattos, half-whites, octoroons, the kind of terms that were fashionable 40 or 50 years ago. . . .

I hear far less about the blue-veined society among Negroes now than I used to. I don't hear references to color, except in jest. In the past to call

7. E. F. Frazier, *The Black Bourgeoisie* (1957) [Isaacs' note].

a man a "black S.O.B.," was the worst possible epithet, and not because of the S.O.B. part alone, but "black" itself was derogatory. I think there may be a difference now, an absence of emphasis of skin color rather than any new positive affirmation of the virtues of blackness. . . .

There is a lessening of color prejudice within the group. They are not as bad as they were. It's a touchy point. Negroes have not been frank on this. "Mixed blood," or "mulatto," one still doesn't know what word to use. In my upbringing, the matter of color was not to be mentioned. We could never say a man was "black" and never use the adjective "yellow" because of its connotation. "Black" was a frightening word and anyone of mixed origin would flinch at the word "yellow." Langston Hughes thought his family here, the Langstons, rejected his mother because of her color and he was always sharp on Washington's middle class because of its color snobbishness. This is changed now generally. It is still true that men select the lighter wife, the darker woman has a hard time, but not as hard as it used to be. . . .

This has changed enormously. Except that I have to say that only yesterday I visited a church in Macon, Georgia, and here were some 50 kids, all little light-colored mulatto kids. At least fifteen of them looked white, all the others were shaded up a sort of brown, but with straight hair. Only a few darker people were there. The first Congregational Church here in Atlanta used to be like that. The younger generation here is much darker. For the most part it is dark brown and black now. There are no gradations of this left in Atlanta society; a man is all right whatever his color if he has good prospects, and I think there is no disadvantage for the dark girl if she has good family. I don't get around in society much, but look at the campus queens and the drum majorettes! They have changed enormously. There are more mixed marriages. This sort of thing has been going out. . . .

I don't really know if color ideas are changing. I hear it spoken of less frequently than even ten years ago, unless I am selectively not hearing it any more. It is not uncommon now to get cases (in a clinic) based on color rejection. Any Negro family that is honest will admit that color is important in the self-image of themselves and their children. This is still prevalent although there is some evidence of change. When I was in college it was an inviolable rule that a successful man had to marry a fair woman. I don't think this trend is as marked now as it was then, 20 years ago. . . .

The change has been from shame to pride. For a long time in my life I would never admit I had a wish I wasn't colored. It was my private wish. I would feel guilty about it. As late as my college days, I would think: "O boy, if I weren't colored. . . ." I used to think that blackness, usually identified with Africa, was ugly and that Caucasian features were beautiful. I don't think that any more. I find myself wishing sometimes that I was darker. I feel myself looking at some darker people now and having a feeling of admiration, even envy, where not so long ago I would have thought they were ugly. Now in marriage the question of color would not be a problem the way it was in my younger days. . . .

Standards of beauty lie close to the core of the whole business of color caste. Negroes generally adopted the models of "white" or "Caucasian" good looks that filled the moving picture screens, billboards, newspapers, and magazines, and the greatest favor and preferment went to those Negro men and women who most closely approximated to these standards. Aggressive dark men could lift themselves above color caste discrimination by their success, but a prime reward of their success was the chance it gave them to reject dark-skinned women and to take lighter-skinned and less Negro-looking women to be their wives. This left the dark Negro woman the least desired and the least admired. She became the carrier of the heaviest part of the burden of the color caste system and that is why her status now is the real key to the extent of its passing. The evidence seems to be that her position has changed much, but still less and much more slowly than that of all the other actors in this drama.

In the 1930s, the very black and very Negro Mrs. Mary McLeod Bethune presented a new model not of beauty but of high achievement that made a considerable dent in color caste attitudes. Mrs. Bethune, daughter of ex-slaves, noted educator, frequent visitor to the Roosevelt White House, was the founder and president of the National Council of Negro Women, holder of important government posts, and a spokesman to whom everyone listened. I was told the following of her:

> Mary McLeod Bethune became the greatest Negro woman in the country and was worshipped by all and came to represent the hopes of the race. Nobody could think ill of black women after her.

Mrs. Bethune did not, of course, quite manage to cast her brighter light over *all* black women, but she did play an important role in beginning to change the perceptions of others, as in this self-examination:

> When you are ashamed of something you turn away and don't look at it or you never look deeply. When you are no longer ashamed, you look and you begin to appreciate it. When I first saw Mrs. Bethune, I thought, my God what an ugly woman! But later I could only think of what a grand lady she was. Then sometime about 1952 or so, the first time I was shockingly aware that I was thinking that a black girl I saw with kinky hair was beautiful, a girl I saw at the University of California with her hair pulled back. I saw that she was beautiful, a black girl with Negro features. In my family there was every color, from white as snow to black as coal. When I was a young fellow, I remember four or five Negro dance teachers, always pretty in the American Caucasian sense, like Lena Horne. Now I see an almost deliberate kind of native naturalness. I think of Pearl Primus, the dancer. The dark woman's disadvantage is rapidly disappearing. The number of men who would marry women darker than themselves is far greater than in my generation.

There is probably no such thing at this moment as an inclusively accurate description of this changing pattern of experience. Each individual has his own version, his own accent, agreeing with all others only that things are not as they were. Some examples:

In 1955, I heard an ad over the radio for a cosmetic: "Are you too dark to be loved?" I got sore and called the station and the girl there told me the same ad was running in my own paper, the *Afro-American*. And it was. I told the publisher I thought this sort of thing was perpetuating among Negroes the idea that a light Negro was better than a dark one. He agreed and said the language of the ad had to be changed. Here in Harlem now a dark girl would have very little to remind her of it. It is too polyglot. Now black girls figure in our cheesecake pictures as well as white or light girls. Formerly if I sent a photographer out and said get us some cheesecake, he would just automatically get as close an approximation to the Nordic as you could get. But I called our photographer in and said let's not have any of this leapfrogging over the dark person. Now you take the Press Photographer's ball, the Elks Beauty contest, you know where the judge holds his hand over the girl's head and goes by the applause, and I've seen crowds give the applause to the dark girl even though the fair girl was better looking. . . .[8]

In the old days the Negro beauty queen was indistinguishable from white. She was practically white. In the last 15 or 20 years the color ideal has been browning down and from "good hair," that is straight hair, we have now come to where Negro type of hair can be fitted into popular coiffures. The beauty queen at Howard could not be darker than brown, in some Southern schools she could be darker brown, but some other schools are worse on this than Howard. . . .

Negroes laugh about whites and sun-tan and getting their hair curled. There *is* a new appreciation of blackness, a black girl is more acceptable now than before, but she still needs white features, still has to be chiefly in the *Saturday Evening Post* style, that is closer to the white standard of beauty. But there is a certain relaxation on the item of color. A brown man will marry a black woman now where he wouldn't have 15 or 20 years ago. . . .

When I was growing up the fair-skinned girl was the more desired. Now this is not true. Brown is the color now—"I found a fine brown," a man will say. People can now find a black girl beautiful, whereas 40 years ago nobody would have. At the Comus Club dance in Brooklyn I've seen the color darkening for a long time. Thirty years ago little dark girls wouldn't come because they didn't have a good time. Now they show their dark shoulders and they're enchanting. Hair straightening is still in among women but going among men. When I was in college men used to use some gooey stuff to straighten their hair, called "Congolene." Getting your hair "conked," barbers would rub it in. You see very little of this now. . . .

The great hair question is on its way out. Some girls I know, not many, and some men, just don't bother any more about hair. They don't spend hours and weeks on it. It's getting to be the mark of a square to pay attention to hair from this point of view. This is developing this way, I notice, in musical circles and backstage in the show and art world, mostly among

8. The switch in behavior sometimes produces ironic results. In New York where hitherto lily-white enterprises have begun to open places for Negroes, they are often likely to want their new virtue to be as visible as possible. The patterns of change are infinite in their variety, but some kind of turning point was reached in this matter when a Negro model who had failed to get on a certain TV show complained to the New York State Commission on Human Rights "that she had been turned down on the basis that she 'was not colored enough.'" (*New York Amsterdam News*, April 28th, 1962) [Isaacs' note].

young people. In Harlem there's a sharp line between those who do and those who don't fiddle with their hair. For men this is 'conking,' for women 'processing.' If you conk or process your hair, you've got to keep it dry, keep out of the rain, etc. Many people just can't be bothered any more. The changes in this are mostly hidden, but they are perceptible. Ideas of beauty are changing more slowly. Look at Poitier, very black, very Negro, very beautiful. But Harry Belafonte is still the hero, girls are not putting Poitier up on their walls. The girls' ideal of beauty is still Lena Horne and Dorothy Dandridge, though we do have Pearl Bailey to give hope to little black girls who would try to bleach their skin. There is much less bleaching now. . . .

To be sure, there is an intimate entwining of all these shapes of the Negro group identity with the issue of relationship to Africa, both in the past when it was so deeply submerged and now when it has so dramatically emerged. Here is how these interactions were seen in relation to color caste, beginning with the account of a young woman who was at the time we talked just 21 and still an undergraduate at Howard University in Washington:

When I was a child in elementary school I was called "a black African" because of my color, more or less an insult. . . . When I came here (to Howard) I was very color conscious. All the queens of the courts when I first came here were light-skinned. Now we're getting away from it. Several girls my color have been elected queens of a court. At times I feel pretty bad. Recently had several isolated instances where darker girls were treated by lighter girls as though they were less of a human being, though it is never put on that basis openly. This came up in the Greek letter sororities. A dark girl has to have something special in her favor to get in, whereas a light-skinned girl just has to be light-skinned. I think we're moving away from this a good deal now. It is openly discussed, there is a greater realization of it. It is quite possible that there is a connection between this and Africa. American students used to joke about the way the Africans looked, their hair, very dark, very Negro. Now dark-skinned Negroes are just beginning to find a place in this community and so are the Africans, who are more respected now because of independence but are not really integrated as they should be. People are getting more educated, possibly realizing their common ancestral background. Some American students are getting more nationalistic about Africa and the relation between African and American students is criticized a good deal in the university paper. . . .

And some others:

I don't think Africa has anything to do with the changes that have been coming for more than a decade and even since before World War II. But I do think the emergence of Africa will accelerate the vanishing of these distinctions among Negroes. Nkrumah stands for something new in this respect too. Seeing black men in the regal majesty of dignity and power will probably wipe out whatever is left of prejudice against blackness. . . .

I think Africans are making black more acceptable. Africans with status are bound to make this difference. As African-American relations emerge, attitudes about color in America will change, both for whites and Negroes. . . .

Africa is now emerging affirmatively and blackness is benefiting from it. . . .

Color is not such a big thing for Negroes any more. As for women, the most beautiful girl I have ever seen in my whole life was a jet black girl with narrow features, slanting eyes, thick dark hair, exquisite figure, a Ga woman I saw in Accra, a school teacher. . . .

The African type is now no longer grotesque or so different. Nkrumah is seen as a handsome man, dignified, with a strong face. Only 20 years ago he wouldn't have been seen this way. The African girl here makes no effort to straighten her hair, while American girls' ideal is still the white model and they are getting closer to it with their waves and curls. Men on the other hand don't touch their hair so much now, they keep it close cropped. Only Africans let it grow long, partly out of the new pride they have in themselves.[9]

I heard a blonde Negro woman at a Nkrumah reception say: "I'm so proud of being black!" . . .

9. In her *Amsterdam News* column (May 5th, 1962) Poppy Cannon White wrote under the title "Hair and History": "Manufacturers and marketers of hair straightening preparations and even some of the beauty parlours are said to be worried about the African trends. Just the other evening on a television recital, Metropolitan Opera tenor George Shirley appeared . . . wearing white tie and tails, with his hair quite long and natural, in a manner which has already become identified with a number of leading diplomats from Africa. . . . Even more startling is a similar trend among the ladies, South African Miriam Makeba is said to have started the fashion. . . . Already there are rumors that certain style-setters are dreaming up new types of permanent waves calculated to transform straight or semi-straight hair into tight, springy twists. . . ."

But the new style obviously still had a long way to go to the more common acceptance. On the following pages of the same issue of the *Amsterdam News* were ads for "hair-weaving" ("Human hair, Color blended for Match Perfectly, Woven to your own Hair, Cannot Come Off, Defies Detection," or again: "Change your Hair-Do as easily as you change your dress . . . chignons, braids, fine curls, clusters. . . ." The new fashion in wigs in the society at large was going big in the Negro market as well. In *Ebony* the same week, May, 1962, there were twenty ads for hair preparations ("Repeated Using Results in Improved Soft-Silkened Hair") and eight for skin preparations ("Makes your skin lighter, brighter," "Lighter, lovelier skin beauty for You!") [Isaacs' note].

JEAN-PAUL SARTRE
Portrait of the Antisemite

If a man attributes all or part of his own or the country's misfortunes to the presence of Jewish elements in the French community, if he proposes remedying this state of affairs by depriving the Jews of some of their rights or by expelling or exterminating them, he is then said to hold antisemitic *opinions.*

This word *opinion* gives us food for thought. It is the word which the mistress of the house uses to end a discussion that is becoming too embittered. It suggests that all judgments are of equal value, thus reassuming and giving an inoffensive cast to thoughts by assimilating them to tastes. There are all kinds of tastes in nature, all opinions are permissible; tastes, ideas, opinions must not be discussed. In the name of democratic institutions, in the name of freedom of opinion, the antisemite claims the right to preach his anti-Jewish crusade everywhere. At the same time, used as we are since the Revolution to seeing each object in an analytical spirit, that is as if it were a whole which can be divided into its component parts, we look at people and characters as if they were mosaics, every stone of which coexists with the others without this coexistence affecting its inherent nature. Thus an antisemitic opinion appears like a molecule which can combine with any other set of molecules without changing itself. A man can be a good father and a good husband, a zealous citizen, cultured, philanthropic and an antisemite at the same time. He may like to go fishing and he may like the pleasures of love, he may be tolerant about religion, full of generous ideas about the condition of the natives of Central Africa—and still despise the Jews. If he does not like them, people say, it is because his experience has taught him that they are bad, because statistics have taught him that they are dangerous, because certain historical factors have influenced his judgment. Thus this opinion seems to be the result of external causes and those who want to study it will neglect the antisemite himself and make much of the percentage of Jews mobilized in 1914, of the percentage of Jews who are bankers, industrialists, doctors, lawyers, of the history of the Jews in France. They will succeed in laying before us a strictly objective situation determining a certain current of likewise objective opinion which they will call antisemitism, a chart of which they can draw up or the variations of which they can establish from 1890 to 1944. In this way, antisemitism seems to be both a subjective taste which combines with other tastes to form the person, and an impersonal and social phenomenon which can be expressed by means of statistics and averages, conditioned by economic, historical and political constants.

I do not say that these two concepts are necessarily contradictory. I say that they are dangerous and false. I might, strictly speaking, admit that one might have an "opinion" about the government's wine-growing policy, that is, that one might decide for this or that reason to approve or condemn the free importation of wines from Algeria. But I refuse to call an opinion a doctrine which is expressly directed toward particular persons and which tends to suppress their rights or to exterminate them. The Jew whom the antisemite wants to reach is not a schematic being defined only by his function as in administrative law, or by his position or his acts as in the legal code. He is a Jew, son of a Jew, recognizable by his physical traits, by the color of his hair, by his clothing perhaps, and they say by his character. Antisemitism is not in the category of thoughts protected by the right to freedom of opinion.

Moreover, it is much more than an idea. It is first and foremost a *passion*. Doubtless it can present itself in the form of a theoretical proposition. The "moderate" antisemite is a polite person who gently remarks: "I don't detest Jews. I simply prefer for such and such a reason that they play a lesser part in the activity of the nation." But a moment later—if you have won his confidence—he will add the following with more abandon: "You see there must be 'something' about the Jews: physically they are irritating to me." This argument, which I have heard a hundred times, is worth examining. First of all it is the result of using logic dictated by passion. For can you imagine someone saying seriously: "There must be something about tomatoes because I can't bear them." Moreover it shows that antisemitism, even in its most moderate and evolved forms, remains a syncretic totality which is expressed by statements that appear reasonable but which can lead to corporeal modifications. Some men suddenly become impotent if they find out that the woman to whom they are making love is a Jewess. Some people feel disgust for the Jew, just as some others feel disgust for the Chinaman or the Negro. Thus this revulsion is not based on something physical, since you could very well love a Jewess if you didn't know what race she belonged to, but it reaches the body through the mind; it is an involvement of the mind so deep, so complete, that it extends to the physiological as in cases of hysteria.

This involvement is not provoked by experience. I have questioned a hundred people about the reasons for their antisemitism. Most of them limit themselves to enumerating the faults which are traditionally attributed to the Jew. "I hate them because they are selfish, intriguing, hard to get rid of, oily, tactless, etc."—"But at least you do go with some Jews?"—"Indeed not!" A painter said to me: "I'm hostile to Jews because, with their critical habit of mind, they encourage our servants to become undisciplined." Here are some more precise experiences. A young actor without talent asserted that the Jews kept him from having a career in the theater by always giving him servile jobs. A young woman said to me: "I've had terrible rows with furriers, they've robbed me, they've burned the furs I entrusted to them. Well, they were all Jews." But why did she choose to hate Jews rather than furriers? Why Jews or furriers rather than such and such a Jew or such and such a furrier? Because she had a predisposition to antisemitism. A classmate of mine at the lycée told me that Jews "irritated" him because of the thousand injustices which "bejewed" social organizations committed in their favor. "A Jew got a scholarship the year I missed it and you're not going to try to make me believe that that fellow whose father came from Krakow or Lemberg understood one of Ronsard's poems or one of Virgil's eclogues better than I." But he admitted the next moment that he disdained the scholarship, that it was all a muddle and that he hadn't prepared for the competition. Thus he had two systems of interpretation to explain his failure, like an insane man who in his delirium pretends to be the King of Hungary but when suddenly put to the test admits that he is a shoemaker. His thinking moves on two planes without the least difficulty. Better still, he will succeed in justifying his past laziness by saying that it would have been too silly to prepare for an examination in which Jews are passed in preference to good Frenchmen. Moreover he was 27th on the final list. There were 26 before him, 12 of whom were accepted and 14 were not. Would he have gotten any further if Jews had been excluded altogether? And even if he had been the first of those who were not accepted, even if by eliminating one of the successful candidates he could have had his chance to be accepted, my classmate had to adopt in advance a certain idea of the Jew, of his nature, of his social role. And in order to be able to decide that among 26 more fortunate contestants it was the Jew who stole his place, he would a priori have to be the kind of person who runs his life on the basis of emotional reasoning.

It becomes obvious that no external factor can induce antisemitism in the antisemite. It is an attitude totally and freely self-chosen, a global attitude which is adopted not only in regard to Jews but in regard to men in general, to history and society; it is a passion and at the same time a concept of the world. No doubt certain characteristics are more pronounced in such and such an antisemite than in another. But they are always present together and they govern one another. It is this syncretic totality which we must now try to describe.

I stated a few minutes ago that antisemitism presents itself as a passion. Everyone has understood that it is a question of hate or anger. But ordinarily hate and anger are provoked: I hate the person who has made me suffer, the person who scorns or insults me. We have just seen that the antisemitic passion is not of such a nature: it preceded the facts which should arouse it, it seeks them out to feed upon, it must even interpret them in its own way in order to render them really offensive. And yet if you speak of the Jew to an antisemite, he evinces signs of lively irritation. If we remember, however, that we must *consent* to anger before it can manifest itself, and that we *grow* angry, to use the correct expression, we must admit that antisemitism has chosen to exist on the passionate level. It is not unusual to choose an emotional way of life rather than a reasonable one. But ordinarily one loves the *objects* of passion: women, glory, power, money. Since the antisemite has chosen hatred, we are forced to conclude that it is the emotional state that he loves. Ordinarily this kind of feeling is not pleasing: he who passionately desires a woman is passionate because of the woman and in spite of passion: one distrusts emotional reasoning which by every means aims at pointing out opinions dictated by love or jealousy or hate; one mistrusts passionate aberrations and that which has been termed monoideism. And this is what the antisemite chooses first of all. But how can one choose to reason falsely? Because one feels the nostalgia of impermeability. The rational man seeks the truth gropingly, he knows that his reasoning is only probable, that other considerations will arise to make it doubtful; he never knows too well where he's going, he is "open," he may even appear hesitant. But there are people who are attracted by the durability of stone. They want to be massive and impenetrable, they do not want to change: where would change lead them? This is an original fear of oneself and a fear of truth. And what frightens them is not the content of truth which they do not even suspect, but the very form of the true—that thing of indefinite approximation. It is as if their very existence were perpetually in suspension. They want to exist all at once and right away. They do not want acquired opinions, they want them to be innate; since they are afraid of reasoning, they want to adopt a mode of life in which reasoning and research play but a subordinate role, in which one never seeks but that which one has already found, in which one never becomes other than what one already was. Only passion can produce this. Nothing but a strong emotional bias can give instant certitude, it alone can hold reasoning within limits, it alone can remain impervious to experience and last an entire lifetime. The antisemite has chosen hate because hate is a religion: he has originally chosen to devaluate words and reasons. Since he then feels at ease, since discussions about the right of the Jew appear futile and empty to him, he has at the outset placed himself on another level. If out of courtesy he consents momentarily to defend his point of view, he lends himself without giving himself; he simply tries to project his intuitive certainty onto the field of speech.

A few moments ago I quoted some statements made by antisemites, all of them absurd: "I hate Jews because they teach indiscipline to servants, because a Jewish furrier robbed me, etc." Do not think that antisemites are completely unaware of the absurdity of these answers. They know that their statements are empty and contestable; but it amuses them to make such statements: it is their adversary whose duty it is to choose his words seriously because he believes in words. They have a *right* to play. They even like to play with speech because by putting forth ridiculous reasons, they discredit the seriousness of their interlocutor; they are enchanted with their unfairness because for them it is not a question of persuading by good argument but of intimidating or disorienting. If you insist too much they close up, they point out with one superb word that the time to argue has passed. Not that they are afraid of being convinced: their only fear is that they will look ridiculous or that their embarrassment will make a bad impression on a third party whom they want to get on their side. Thus if the antisemite is impervious, as everyone has been able to observe, to reason and experience, it is not because his conviction is so strong, but rather his conviction is strong because he has chosen to be impervious.

He has also chosen to be terrifying. One is afraid to irritate him. No one but he knows to what extremes his wayward passions will lead him: for this passion has not been provoked from the outside. He holds it well in hand, he lets himself go as much as he wants, sometimes relaxing the reins, sometimes tightening them. He is not afraid of himself: but he reads a disquieting picture in others' eyes and as he makes his statements his actions conform to this picture. This external model relieves him of the necessity of seeking his personality within himself; he has chosen to be all outside, never to examine his conscience, never to be anything but the very fear he strikes in others: he is running away from the intimate awareness that he has of himself even more than from Reason. But, you will say, what if he were only that way in regard to Jews? If he conducted himself sensibly in regard to all other matters? I answer that this is impossible: here is a fishmonger who, in 1942, irritated by the competition of two Jewish fishmongers who made a secret of their race, picked up a pen one day and denounced them. I was assured that in other respects he was kind and jovial, the best son in the world. But I don't believe it: a man who finds it natural to denounce men cannot have our concept of the humane; he does not even see those whom he aids in the same light as we do; his generosity, his kindness are not like our kindness, our generosity; one cannot localize passion.

The antisemite willingly admits that the Jew is intelligent and hard-working. He will even admit that he is inferior to him in this respect. This concession costs him little. He has put these qualities, as it were, in parentheses. Or rather, they draw their merit from the man who possesses them: the more virtues a Jew has, the more dangerous he is. As for the antisemite, he has no illusions about what he is. He considers himself an average man, modestly average, and in the last analysis a mediocre person. There is no example of an antisemite claiming individual superiority over the Jews. But do not believe for a second that this mediocrity is a cause for shame. On the contrary, he is well satisfied with it, I might even say he has chosen it. This man is afraid of any kind of solitude, that of the genius as well as that of the murderer: he is the man of the mob: no matter how short he is, he still takes the precaution of stooping for fear of standing out from the herd and of finding himself face to face with himself. If he has become an antisemite, it is because one cannot be antisemitic alone. This sentence: "I hate the Jews," is a sentence which is said in chorus; by saying it one connects oneself with a tradition and a community: that of the mediocre man. It is also well to recall that by consenting to mediocrity one is not necessarily humble, nor even modest. It is just the opposite: there is a passionate pride in being mediocre and antisemitism is an attempt to make mediocrity as such a virtue, to create an elite of the mediocre. For the antisemite, intelligence is Jewish, he can therefore disdain it in all tranquility, like all other Jewish virtues: these are all ersatz qualities which the Jews use to replace the well-balanced mediocrity which they will always lack. The true Frenchman, rooted in his province, in his country, carried along by a tradition of twenty centuries, having the advantage of ancestral wisdom, guided by proved customs, *does not need* intelligence. The basis of his virtue is the assimilation of the qualities which the work of a hundred generations has lent to objects which surround him, i.e., property. But it goes without saying that this refers to hereditary property and not to that which one buys for oneself. The antisemite misunderstands the principle of the diverse forms of modern property: money, stocks, etc. These are abstractions, things of reason which ally themselves to the abstract intelligence of the Jew. A stock belongs to no one since it can belong to everyone and then it is a sign of wealth, not a concrete piece of property. The antisemite can conceive of but one type of primitive and landowning appropriation based on a veritable magical connection with possessions, in which the object possessed and its possessor are linked by a mystical participation; he is the poet of land-holding. It transfigures the owner, endowing him with a particular and concrete sensitivity. Of course, this sensitivity is not addressed to the eternal verities, to universal values: the universal is Jewish since it has to do with the intelligence. What this subtle sense will seize upon is just what the intelligence cannot discern. In other words, the principle of antisemitism is that concrete possession of a particular object magically conveys its meaning. Maurras affirms this: a Jew will always be incapable of understanding the following line of Racine:

Dans l'Orient desert, quel devint mon ennui.[1]

And why can I, mediocre I, understand what the most shrewd, the most cultivated intelligence cannot seize? Because I *own* Racine. Racine is my language and my soil. Perhaps the Jew speaks a purer French than I, perhaps he knows the grammar and syntax better than I, perhaps he is even a writer: it doesn't matter. He has only spoken this language for twenty years, and I have spoken it for two thousand years. The correctness of his style is abstract, acquired; the mistakes in French are in conformance with the greatness of the language. Here we recognize the reasoning which Barrès used against scholarship students. Why be surprised? Aren't these Jews scholarship students? I've done nothing to deserve my superiority and I also cannot lose rank. It is bestowed once and for all: it is a *thing*.

1. "In the empty East, how great was my apathy." (*Berenice* I, iv, 234; trans. Katz.)

We begin to understand that antisemitism is not simply an "opinion" about the Jews and that it involves the entire personality of the antisemite. We are not done with him yet: for he does not limit himself to furnishing moral and political directives. He is a process of thought and a world-view all in himself. One would in fact be unable to affirm what he affirms without implicitly referring to certain intellectual principles. The Jew, he says, is entirely bad and entirely Jewish; his virtues, if any, become vices simply because they are *his* virtues, the work that comes from his hands necessarily bears his stigma: and if he builds a bridge, this bridge is bad because it is Jewish from the first span to the last. The same act committed by a Jew and by a Christian is by no means identical in the two cases. The Jew renders execrable everything he touches. The first thing the Germans did was to forbid Jews the use of swimming pools: it seemed to them that if the body of a Jew plunged into this water, it would be utterly tainted. The Jew literally sullies even the air he breathes. If we try to formulate in abstract propositions the principle referred to, this is what we would get: the whole is more than and different from the sum of all its parts; the whole determines the meaning and the true nature of the parts of which it is composed. There is not only one courageous virtue which might be indifferently a part of the Jewish or the Christian character as oxygen combines to make air either with azote or argon and combines with hydrogen to make water: but each person, with *his* courage, *his* generosity, *his* own way of thinking, of laughing, of eating and drinking, is an indivisible totality. That is to say, the antisemite has chosen to resort to the spirit of synthesis as a means of understanding the world. It is the spirit of synthesis which allows him to see himself as forming an indissoluble unity with France as a whole. It is in the name of synthesis that he denounces the purely analytical and critical intelligence of the Jew. But we must point out that for some time both the right and the left, both the traditionalists and the socialists, have brought up synthetic principles in opposition to the spirit of analysis which presided over the formation of the democratic bourgeoisie. The same principles cannot be valid for both groups. The two groups at least make different use of these principles.

Everything becomes clear if we give up expecting the Jew to behave reasonably in conformity with his interests, if we discern in him, on the contrary, a metaphysical principle which forces him *to do evil* under all circumstances, though in so doing he destroys himself. This principle, as we might expect, is magical: on the one hand it is an essence, a substantial form, and the Jew, whatever he does, cannot modify it any more than fire can keep itself from burning. And on the other hand, since the Jew must be hated and since one does not hate an earthquake or phylloxera, this virtue is also freedom. But the freedom in question is carefully limited: the Jew is free *to do evil,* not good. He has only as much free will as is necessary to bear the full responsibility of the crimes he commits, but not enough to be able to reform. Strange freedom which instead of preceding and constituting the essence, remains entirely subordinate to it, and which is but an irrational quality of it and yet remains freedom!

There is but one creature to my knowledge, as totally free and wedded to evil and that is the Spirit of Evil, Satan himself. Thus the Jew is assimilable to the spirit of evil. His will, contrary to the Kantian will,[2] is one which desires to be purely, gratuitously and universally evil, it is *the will to evil.* Evil comes to the world through him; all that is bad in society (crises, wars, famines, upheavals and revolts) is directly or indirectly imputable to the Jew. The antisemite is afraid of discovering that the world is badly made: for then things would have to be invented, modified and man would find himself once more master of his fate, filled with agonizing and infinite responsibility. He localizes all the evil of the universe in the Jew. If nations wage war, it is not due to the fact that the idea of nationalism in its present form involves imperialism and conflict of interests. No, the Jew is there breathing discord—somewhere behind all governments. If there is class struggle, it is not caused by an economic organization which leaves something to be desired: it is because Jewish ringleaders, hook-nosed agitators have seduced the workers. Thus antisemitism is primarily Manicheanism; it explains the course of the world by the struggle between the principles of Good and Evil. There is no conceivable truce between these two principles: one of them must of necessity triumph and the other be destroyed. Look at Céline[3]: his version of the universe is catastrophic; the Jew is everywhere, the earth is lost, the Aryan must not compromise, he must never make a covenant. But he must be on guard: if he breathes, already he has lost his purity, for the very air which penetrates his bronchi is contaminated. Is this not the sermon of a Cathar? If Céline was able to uphold the socialist theses of the Nazis, it was because he was paid to do so. Deep down in his heart, he did not believe in them: as far as he is concerned, there is no solution except collective suicide, non-procreation, death. Others—Maurras or the Parti Populaire Française—are less discouraging: they foresee a long and often doubtful struggle with the final triumph of good. It is Ormuzd against Ahriman.[4] The reader has understood that antisemitism does not have recourse to Manicheanism as to a secondary principle of explanation. But it is the original choice of

2. Kant's holy will always acts in harmony with the good.
3. A fascistic antisemitic author.
4. Zoroastrian gods, respectively the beneficent spirit and the source of evil.

Manicheanism which explains and conditions antisemitism. Therefore we must ask ourselves what this original choice can mean for a
man of today.

Let us compare for a moment the revolutionary idea of the class
struggle with antisemitic Manicheanism. In the eyes of the Marxist,
class struggle is in no sense the struggle between good and evil: it is
a conflict of interests between human groups. The revolutionary
adopts the proletariat's point of view firstly because it is *his* class
and secondly because it is oppressed, because it is by far the largest
class and its fate consequently tends to become fused with that of
humanity, and lastly because the consequences of his victory will
necessarily involve the suppression of classes. The aim of the
revolutionary is to change the organization of society. And in order
to do this he must of necessity destroy the old regime. But this is
not enough. First and foremost a new order must be set up. If,
assuming the impossible, the privileged class consented to cooperate
with the socialist scheme and if one had manifest proof of its good
will, there would be no valid reason to reject its co-operation. And if
it remains highly improbable that the privileged class would willingly
offer its assistance to the socialists, it is because its very position as a
privileged class prevents it from doing so and not because of any
internal demon which would force it in spite of itself to do evil. In
any case, if fractions of this class detach themselves from it and
become part of the oppressed class, they will be judged by their
actions, not by their essence. "To hell with your eternal essence,"
Politzer once said to me.

The very contrary is the case with the antisemitic Manichean.
His emphasis is on destruction. It is not a question of a conflict of
interests but of the damage that an evil power causes to society.
Behind the bitterness of the antisemite is concealed the belief that
harmony will be reestablished of itself once evil has been ejected.
His task therefore is purely negative: there is no question of building
a society but only of purifying the one that exists. Like the Good
Knight, the antisemite is sacred; but the Jew is also sacred in his
own way: sacred like the untouchables, like taboo natives. Thus the
battle is waged on a religious level and the end of the struggle can
only be an act of sacred destruction. The advantages of this position
are multiple: first of all it favors sluggishness of mind. We have seen
that the antisemite understands nothing concerning modern society,
and he would be incapable of inventing a constructive plan; his
action cannot be put on the technical level, it remains basically emotional. He prefers an explosion of rage analogous to the running
amok of the Malayans. His intellectual activity limits itself to
interpretation; in historical events he seeks the sign of the presence
of an evil power. Whence these puerile and complicated inventions
which render him comparable to the real paranoiac. The antisemite,

moreover, canalizes revolutionary thrusts toward the destruction of certain men, not institutions; an antisemitic mob would consider that it had done enough if it had massacred a few Jews and burned a few synagogues. It therefore represents a safety-valve for the ruling classes which encourage it. . . . But, above all, this naive dualism is eminently reassuring to the antisemite himself: if it is only a matter of getting rid of Evil, it means that Good is already *assumed*. There is no reason to seek it in anguish, to invent it, to debate it patiently when one has found it, to prove it in action, to verify its consequences and finally to saddle oneself with the responsibilities of the moral choice thus made. It is not by chance that the great antisemitic uprisings hide a kind of optimism: the antisemite has decided about evil so as not to have to decide about the good. The more absorbed I become in combatting Evil, the less I am tempted to question the Good . . . When he has fulfilled his mission as the sacred destroyer, the Lost Paradise will rebuild itself. For the time being the antisemite is absorbed by so many duties that he has no time to think about it: he is forever on the verge, he fights and each of his outbursts of indignation is a pretext which distracts him from the anguished search for the good.

But there is more to it and at this point we approach the domain of psychoanalysis. Manicheanism masks a profound attraction to evil. For the antisemite, evil is his lot, his "job." Others will come later who will be concerned with good, if need be. He is at the outpost of society, he turns his back on the pure virtues which he defends; he deals only with evil, his duty is to unmask it, to denounce it, to establish its dimensions. Thus we see that he is solely worried about amassing anecdotes which reveal the lewdness of the Jew, his cupidity, his ruses and his betrayals. He washes his hands in filth. One should reread Drumont's *La France Juive*: this book "characterized by high French morality" is a collection of ignoble and obscene stories. Nothing better reflects the complex nature of the antisemite: since he did not want to *choose* his own good and, for fear of being different, allowed everyone else's concept of the good to be imposed upon him, his ethics are never based on the intuition of values or on what Plato calls Love; it manifests itself only by the strictest taboos, by the severest and most gratuitous imperatives. But the thing he contemplates constantly, the thing he understands intuitively and has a taste for is evil. He can thus minutely examine to the point of obsession the description of obscene or criminal acts which trouble him and which satisfy his perverse leanings; but since, at the same time, he attributes them to these infamous Jews whom he treats with disdain he can seek gratification without compromising himself. In Berlin I knew a Protestant whose sexual desire took the form of indignation. The sight of women in bathing suits infuriated him; he welcomed this rage, spending his time in swimming pools. The antisemite does the same thing.

One of the components of his hatred is a deep sexual attraction to Jews. First of all it is curiosity fascinated by evil. But above all, I believe, it is connected with sadism. We understand nothing about antisemitism if we do not recall that the Jew, the object of such loathing, is perfectly innocent, I might even say inoffensive. The antisemite is also careful to tell us about secret Jewish organizations, of terrifying clandestine free-masonry. But if he meets a Jew face to face he is most of the time a weak individual who, ill prepared for violence, does not even succeed in defending himself. The antisemite is not aware of this individual weakness of the Jew which makes him the helpless victim of pogroms. In fact, this situation delights him. Hatred of the Jew is not comparable to the hatred which the Italians felt for the Austrians in 1830 or to that which the French felt for the Germans in 1942. In the last two cases it was a question of oppressors, of hard, cruel and strong men who possessed arms, money, power and who could do more harm to rebels than the latter could have dreamt of doing to them. The sadistic tendency was not an element of this hatred. But since evil for the antisemite is incarnate in these unarmed and harmless men, he never finds himself in the painful necessity of being heroic: it is *amusing* to be antisemitic. One can beat and torture the Jews without fear: the most they can do is to appeal to the laws of the Republic; but the laws are not hard. The sadistic attraction to the Jew which the antisemite feels is so strong that it is not unusual to see one of these sworn enemies of Israel surround himself with Jewish friends. Of course he calls them "exceptional Jews," he says: "They aren't like the others." In a prominent place in the studio of the painter whom I mentioned a little while ago and who in no way reproached the butchers of Lublin, there was a portrait of a Jew who was a dear friend of his and whom the Gestapo had executed. But such protestations of friendship are not sincere, for there is no idea in their conversation of sparing the "good Jews"; and while recognizing some virtues in those they know, they do not admit the fact that their interlocutors might also have met some who were equally good. In fact, it pleases them to protect these few people by a kind of inversion of their sadism; they like to keep before their eyes the living picture of these people whom they despise. Antisemitic women often feel a mixture of repugnance and sexual attraction for Jews. One whom I knew had intimate relations with a Polish Jew. She sometimes got into bed with him and let him caress her breasts and shoulders, but nothing more. She got enormous pleasure from the fact that he was respectful and submissive and also from the fact that she divined his violently frustrated and humiliated desire. She afterwards had normal sexual relations with other men. In the words "a beautiful Jewess" there is a specific sexual connotation, very different from that which is understood in the words "a beautiful Romanian," "a beautiful Greek woman" or "a beautiful American." The phrase "a beautiful Jewess" has a kind of flavor of rape and massacre. The beautiful Jewess is the woman whom the Czar's cossacks drag by the hair through the streets of a flaming village; and the special works devoted to descriptions of flagellation give Jewesses a place of honor. But we do not have to search through esoteric literature. From Rebecca in *Ivanhoe* down to the Jewess in "Gilles," not to leave out those of Ponson du Terrail, Jewesses have a well defined function in the most serious novels. Frequently raped or beaten, they sometimes succeed in escaping dishonor by death, but that is as it should be; those who keep their virtue are docile servants or humiliated women in love with indifferent Christians who marry Aryans. No more is needed to show the sexually symbolic importance of the Jewess in folklore.

With destruction his function, the antisemite—a sadist pure of heart—is in the depths of his soul a criminal. What he desires and prepares is the *death* of the Jew. Of course all the enemies of the Jew do not overtly demand his death, but the measures which they propose and which are all aimed at his debasement, his humiliation, his banishment, are the prerequisites of this murder which they are contemplating: they are symbolic murders. Only the antisemite has a clear conscience: he is a criminal with a worthy motive. It it not his fault after all if his mission is to destroy evil with evil; the *true* France has relegated to him its powers of supreme justice. Of course he does not have occasion to use them every day, but make no mistake: these sudden outbreaks of anger, these thunderous reproaches which he hurls against "kikes," are so many death sentences. Popular awareness divined this and invented the expression "Jew baiting." Thus the antisemite has chosen to be a criminal—a *pure* criminal: here again he evades responsibilities, he has censured his instinct for murder but he has found a way of satisfying it without admitting it to himself. He knows he is bad but since he is doing evil *for the sake of good*; since a whole people is awaiting deliverance at his hands, he considers himself a sort of bad sacred bull. By a kind of inversion of all values, examples of which we find in certain religions and, for instance, in India, where there is sacred prostitution, it is to anger, hate, pillage, murder and all forms of violence that the antisemite accords respect and enthusiasm; and at the very moment he is drunk with evil, he feels the lightness of heart and the peace afforded by a clear conscience and the satisfaction of duty well done.

The portrait is finished. If many people who willingly admit to hating the Jews do not recognize themselves, it is because they do not detest the Jews. They do not love them either. They would not do them the slightest harm but they would not raise their little fingers to protect them from violence. They are not antisemites, they are nothing, they are *no one*; and since in spite of everything, one must appear to be something, they murmur, without thinking of evil, without thinking at all, they go about repeating some formulas which they have learned and which give them the right to enter certain drawing rooms. Thus they know the delights of creating an ineffectual ripple, of having their heads crammed with an enormous affirmation which appears to them all the more respectable because they have borrowed it. Here antisemitism is but a justification; the futility of these people is, moreover, such that they willingly abandon this justification for any other one just as long as it be a "distinguished" one. For antisemitism is *distinguished*, like all the manifestations of an irrational collective soul tending to create a conservative and esoteric France. It seems to all these feather-brains that by repeating at will that the Jew injures the country, they are performing one of those initiation rites which allows them to feel themselves a part of the centers of warmth and social energy; in this sense antisemitism has retained something of the human sacrifice. It presents, too, a serious advantage for those people who recognize their profound instability and who are weary of it: it allows them to assume the appearance of passion and, as is the rule since the advent of Romanticism, to confuse passion with personality. These second-hand antisemites take on, without much cost to themselves, an aggressive personality. One of my friends often cites the example of an old cousin who came to dine with his family and about whom they said with a certain air: "Jules cannot abide the English." My friend cannot remember ever hearing anything else about Cousin Jules. But that was enough: there was a tacit agreement between Jules and his family. They ostensibly avoided talking about the English in front of him and this precaution gave him a semblance of existence in the eyes of his relatives and at the same time gave them an agreeable feeling of taking part in a sacred ceremony. And if someone, under certain specific circumstances, after careful deliberation and as it were inadvertently, made an allusion to Great Britain or its Dominions, Uncle Jules pretended to go into a fury and felt himself come to life for a moment. Everyone was happy. Many people are antisemites in the same way as Uncle Jules was an Anglophobe, and of course they have not the faintest idea what their attitude really implies. Simple reflections, reeds bent in the wind, they would certainly never have invented antisemitism if conscious antisemitism had not already existed. But they are the ones who, in all indifference, insure the survival of antisemitism and carry it forward through the generations.

We can now understand him. He is a man who is afraid. Not of the Jews of course, but of himself, of his conscience, his freedom, of his instincts, of his responsibilities, of solitude, of change, of society and the world; of everything except the Jews. He is a coward who does not want to admit his cowardice to himself; a murderer who represses and censures his penchant for murder without being able to restrain it and who nevertheless does not dare to kill except in effigy or in the anonymity of a mob; a malcontent who dares not revolt for fear of the consequences of his rebellion. By adhering to antisemitism, he is not only adopting an opinion, he is choosing himself as a person. He is choosing the permanence and the impenetrability of rock, the total irresponsibility of the warrior who obeys his leaders—and he has no leader. He chooses to acquire nothing, to deserve nothing but that everything be given him as his birthright—and he is not noble. He chooses finally, that good be ready-made, not in question, out of reach; he dare not look at it for fear of being forced to contest it and seek another form of it. The Jew is only a pretext: elsewhere it will be the Negro, the yellow race; the Jew's existence simply allows the antisemite to nip his anxieties in the bud by persuading himself that his place has always been cut out in the world, that it was waiting for him and that by virtue of tradition he has the right to occupy it. Antisemitism, in a word, is fear of man's fate. The antisemite is the man who wants to be pitiless stone, furious torrent, devastating lightning: in short, everything but a man.

QUESTIONS FOR STUDY, DISCUSSION, AND WRITING

1. According to Sartre, anti-Semitism is a passion. How does it differ from other passions? Later he classifies anti-Semitism as a his consideration of anti-Semitism?
2. What is "antisemitic Manicheanism" and how does it function in his argument?
   fear. Does this slight shift in classification accompany a shift in
3. Sartre says of the word "opinion," "It suggests that all judgments are of equal value, thus reassuming and giving an inoffensive cast to thoughts by assimilating them to tastes" (p. 411). What is the implicit distinction between thoughts and tastes? Why does the distinction matter? What are proper areas for taste? For thought?
4. What are "second-hand antisemites"? Compare the essays by Gold ("A Dog in Brooklyn," pp. 191–203) and Johnson ("On Self-Love and Indolence," pp. 616–621) on this phenomenon of "second-handedness."
5. Why does Sartre condemn anti-Semitism? How does his condemnation show that he is disturbed by the same general question that worries Agee ("Cotton," pp. 436–450) and Mill ("Civilization," pp. 335–353), all of whom discuss different particular problems?

WILLIAM O. DOUGLAS
The Six Poorest of Us[1]

The poverty of the Lurs is due partly to erosion. In Kurdistan to the north are mountain ranges practically devoid of trees; for miles and miles there is nothing but high, rolling grassland. From Kermanshah on south into Luristan one finds willow and juniper in the draws and oak on the slopes. The oaks do not form thick forests, but scattered clumps such as one sees in southwestern New Mexico and southeastern Arizona. Few are full-grown. Continuous cutting for centuries has resulted in trees that are mere bushy shoots from roots of monarchs that once commanded the range.

The grass has been so thinned by grazing that now one must take several steps between clumps. Only the thistles seem to have flourished. They stand four and five feet high in the ravines—coarse, spiny stems topped by round, blue blossoms almost as big as an orange. The scene reminded me of some overgrazed areas of our own in Oregon and Colorado.

Quick runoffs of rain and of snow water leave harsh gullies. Floods come in the spring with a mad rush, carrying topsoil with them. The water necessary for irrigation is wasted. The soil in the bottom lands is still rich, but it lacks water. Flood control and irrigation projects are needed. Protection of the ranges against overgrazing, and protection of the forests against cutting are also needed. The latter are as effective for storage of water as man-made dams. But in Luristan none of these conservation measures is in force. The wasting of resources goes on endlessly. Each year the earth is further depleted; each year the pinch of poverty is greater.

Flood control, irrigation projects, and conservation, though critical, are not the whole answer. Landownership and illiteracy are also at the bottom of the economic problems of the Lurs.

The Sagavands are often described in the chronicles of Persia as notorious highwaymen. One would not recognize them as such today. One Porsartib is their khan. Porsartib owns all the land. It lies at the head of a wide valley, fifty miles south and east of Khorramabad. There is scant water for the fields. The mountains that rim the valley on the east and west provide little moisture, except harsh runoffs in the spring. These mountains within the memory of residents of this valley were once green with oak and juniper. Now they are barren.

The tribe is sedentary—permanently settled in thirty-six villages. The menfolk gathered in a village by the road to greet me. They were in rags and tatters; their clothes more threadbare than one

1. A chapter from *Strange Lands and Friendly People*, 1951.

saw in our breadlines during the great depression. They stood huddled together, like the sheep they tend, but they held their heads with a pride despite generations of suffering and privation. These men inherited their tenancy. The entire tribe of forty-two thousand people works for Porsartib, paying one-third of the crop to him as rent. They are bound to him by debt as well. It is not extortionate debt; but it is eternal—advances to buy grain during severe winters; loans to meet the recurring emergencies of impoverished people.

Practically all the Sagavands are illiterate. Hence they have no method of escape from the system that holds them tight. Scientific agriculture, cheap means of financing, efficient methods of marketing are unknown to them. They plow with a stick pulled by a cow; they fertilize with night soil; they burn their best fertilizer—cow manure—since that is the only fuel supply they have; they reap grain with a hand sickle; they thrash it by having cows or donkeys pull a drag over it; they separate the grain from the chaff by tossing the straw in the air. This was their fathers' method. And it is likely it will be their sons'. In all the thirty-six villages there are only three schools; and these go only through the fourth grade.

There is no doctor in the entire area. Midwives with primitive methods attend to births; the umbilical cord is cut with a knife from the field. There are no medicines, no first-aid facilities. I talked with a tall, thin man with dark, deep-set eyes about the problem of medical care.

"Suppose you get a pain in your stomach, one that makes you double up. What do you do?"

He answered in a solemn voice. "If God wills it, I live."

More or less the same conditions exist among the other tribes of Lurs in this valley—the Dalvands and the Biranavands.

One August night I sat up late talking with Rustam Bahador, the khan of the Tulabi tribe, located farther to the north. Rustam Bahador owns not only the land; he owns every mud hut, every outhouse, every corral and barn in the area. He talked of the greatness of the Lurs and of their past, of the enduring qualities of his people. He emphasized the richness of their land. But this khan—rich and powerful though he is—is not leading his people out of the wilderness of ignorance and disease. I saw the villages that he owns. They have the mark of squalor on them. They have the fecal odor of the Middle East. There is no sanitation; the wells are not protected; no one is waging a campaign against flies.

Rustam Bahador—talkative, gregarious, friendly—occupies today a strong position of authority and leadership. But, like most leadership in the Middle East, it is irresponsible. He did not seem to be interested in or know anything about the central problems of agricultural production—seed selection, crossbreeding, fertilizers, irrigation, methods of plowing and cultivation, crop rotation, harvesting and thrashing. This Tulabi khan has the virtue of being a resident landlord. But the land and people he commands are merely perquisites of a feudal position.

There are not many landlords in all Persia who have a broad vision and a sense of social responsibility: Abdol Hossein Tavakoli, of Kermanshah, is one; Seyid Zia-Ed-Din of Tehran (former Prime Minister of Persia) is another. But these men are the exceptions.

One day I visited the Direkvan, Baharvand, Mir Baharvand and Papi (pronounced poppy) tribes. As I approached each village or settlement, the tribesmen tried to make a sacrifice in my honor. The Lurs are mostly too poor to kill a steer, even if they owned one; the sacrifice they usually tendered was a sheep. One day I managed to forestall it at five different places. On the sixth stop, when I visited the Papi tribe, several men had a steer tied about the ankles, preparatory to the sacrifice, and were trying to throw it. We stopped them. Beyond them, however, was another group who had four sheep in the middle of the road, ready for the sacrifice. They cut the throat of one before we had time to object. Its bright red blood streaked across the path and Ahmad Khan, their warm-hearted, friendly chief, stepped forward to greet me. And when he grasped me by the hand he put in poetic words the ultimate expression of Persian hospitality: *"Ghadam rouyeh tchashm"*—"You may walk on my eyes."

His encampment was high on slopes of the Zagros Mountains, west of Khorramabad, a thousand feet or so below Noozhian, an eight-thousand-foot pass over the range.

We sat on exquisite Persian rugs in his oblong tent of black woolen cloth. An orchestra stood on the open side of the tent. Dances went on as we sipped tea and ate melons, apples, and grapes. After a while four men seated themselves before us and played soft music. One played a long, bowl-like violin; one a flute; two played drums with their hands. And as they played they sang one of the most haunting melodies I have heard. There were seemingly endless verses ending with

> My sweetheart is Kattaneh
> I love Kattaneh
> My sweetheart is Kattaneh
> I love her dearly.

The tenderest of love songs came out of the rags and misery of the Papis. The words came almost in whispers; there was pathos in the voices; each singer poured out his heart; one middle-aged drummer had tears in his eyes. There was more than sadness in their voices; there was supplication too. It was the cry of desperately lonely people for love and affection.

Kattaneh was more than a woman; she was a symbol of justice

and mercy. All in this Papi environment that met the eye spelled poverty and suffering. The music rose above the surroundings; it was an avenue of escape from the misery of this life.

The melody has haunted me through all my travels. Goatherds in the high Himalayas of India, the miserable laborers in the date orchards of Iraq, workers in the factories of Isfahan—all these conveyed the same message through their eyes. It was a plea for love—for charity and kindness; a plea which, long neglected, turns into an orgasm of hate and revenge, producing revolution and terror.

After the singing, Ahmad Khan served lunch. There were skewers of liver, kidney, chicken, and lamb done over charcoal. They were perfectly turned by a genial male chef and removed from the fire at the peak of their flavor. We stripped the meat off with our fingers; and as we ate, the crowd of ragged human beings standing before the tent moved closer. They were so marked with poverty—their faces as well as their wretched clothes—that I felt a sharp twinge of conscience.

These morsels of rich food were drawn from the larders of the poor.

This feast was tendered by the poorest of the poor—a meal the like of which they themselves had never eaten.

And as I sat, I though of the Lurs who had died of starvation the previous winter.

And these were the people who were giving me the feast!

Not far from where I sat nine hundred Lurs out of a village of five thousand had starved to death only eight months before. The central government at last had distributed wheat; but in one village fifteen Lurs were so emaciated they died of starvation after the wheat arrived. And in the spring of this present year the Lurs in some of the villages I had visited had been so weak they could not stand for more than five minutes at a time.

I could eat no more. I motioned to two youngsters who stood in front of me to come near. They had sunken eyes and hollow cheeks. I handed first one, then the other a skewer of meat. They stripped off the delicate morsels and bolted them down. And the whole circle of hungry people moved politely nearer.

I asked my interpreter, Shahbaz, to call up at random six men among these peasants. They stood in front of me, their hands nervously twisting their gray felt skull caps. Turning to the first one I asked, "What is your name?"

"Abbas."

"What land do you own?"

"None."

"What land do you work?"

"None."

"What property do you own?"

"Four calves, ten sheep." (Skinny animals, grazed on barren tribal land.)

"How large a family do you support?"

"Five people."

I asked the other five similar questions.

Abdul. Owned no land, worked no land, owned six cows and fifteen sheep, supported a family of ten.

Emani. Owned no land; worked no land; owned four calves and twenty sheep; supported a family of two.

Hossein. Owned no land; rented wheat land from a merchant in Khorramabad and got as his share 20 per cent of the crop which last year was three hundred pounds; owned four cows and thirty sheep; supported a family of five.

Ali. Owned no land; rented wheat land from a merchant in Khorramabad and got as his share 20 per cent of the crop which last year was two hundred pounds of wheat; owned six cows and forty sheep; supported a family of two.

Taghi. Owned no land; worked no land; owned two cows and twenty sheep; supported a family of four.

I will never forget their faces. They were simple men, anxious to speak the truth, caught in a mire of poverty and squalor from which they knew not how to escape. They were eager to pour out their hearts. Their eyes searched mine, as if to obtain a promise of a new future. When I ended the conversation and turned away, the expectation and hope that had filled their faces vanished. They stood before me, ragged victims of despair.

While my questioning was going on, the elders of the tribe seated themselves on the far side of the tent. When I finished, one of them arose and came over to me. What he said was perhaps intended to save face, perhaps designed to relieve my embarrassment. He bowed graciously and then stated, "It was God's will that you should have picked the six poorest of us."

GEORGE BERNARD SHAW

The Gospel of St. Andrew Undershaft[1]

In the millionaire Undershaft I have represented a man who has become intellectually and spiritually as well as practically conscious of the irresistible natural truth which we all abhor and repudiate: to wit, that the greatest of our evils, and the worst of our crimes is poverty, and that our first duty to which every other consideration should be sacrificed, is not to be poor. "Poor but honest," "the respectable poor," and such phrases are as intolerable

1. From the preface to his play, *Major Barbara*, 1905.

and as immoral as "drunken but amiable," "fraudulent but a good after-dinner speaker," "splendidly criminal," or the like. Security, the chief pretense of civilization, cannot exist where the worst of dangers, the danger of poverty, hangs over everyone's head, and where the alleged protection of our persons from violence is only an accidental result of the existence of a police force whose real business is to force the poor man to see his children starve whilst idle people overfeed pet dogs with the money that might feed and clothe them.

It is exceedingly difficult to make people realize that an evil is an evil. For instance, we seize a man and deliberately do him a malicious injury: say, imprison him for years. One would not suppose that it needed any exceptional clearness of wit to recognize in this an act of diabolical cruelty. But in England such a recognition provokes a stare of surprise, followed by an explanation that the outrage is punishment or justice or something else that is all right, or perhaps by a heated attempt to argue that we should all be robbed and murdered in our beds if such stupid villainies as sentences of imprisonment were not committed daily. It is useless to argue that even if this were true, which it is not, the alternative to adding crimes of our own to the crimes from which we suffer is not helpless submission. Chickenpox is an evil; but if I were to declare that we must either submit to it or else repress it sternly by seizing everyone who suffers from it and punishing them by inoculation with smallpox, I should be laughed at; for though nobody could deny that the result would be to prevent chickenpox to some extent by making people avoid it much more carefully, and to effect a further apparent prevention by making them conceal it very anxiously, yet people would have sense enough to see that the deliberate propagation of smallpox was a creation of evil, and must therefore be ruled out in favor of purely humane and hygienic measures. Yet in the precisely parallel case of a man breaking into my house and stealing my wife's diamonds I am expected as a matter of course to steal ten years of his life, torturing him all the time. If he tries to defeat that monstrous retaliation by shooting me, my survivors hang him. The net result suggested by the police statistics is that we inflict atrocious injuries on the burglars we catch in order to make the rest take effectual precautions against detection; so that instead of saving our wives' diamonds from burglary we only greatly decrease our chances of ever getting them back, and increase our chances of being shot by the robber if we are unlucky enough to disturb him at his work.

But the thoughtless wickedness with which we scatter sentences of imprisonment, torture in the solitary cell and on the plank bed, and flogging, on moral invalids and energetic rebels, is as nothing compared to the silly levity with which we tolerate poverty as if it

were either a wholesome tonic for lazy people or else a virtue to be
embraced as St. Francis embraced it. If a man is indolent, let him
be poor. If he is drunken, let him be poor. If he is not a gentleman, let him be poor. If he is addicted to the fine arts or to pure
science instead of to trade and finance, let him be poor. If he
chooses to spend his urban eighteen shillings a week or his agricultural thirteen shillings a week on his beer and his family instead
of saving it up for his old age, let him be poor. Let nothing be done
for "the undeserving": let him be poor. Serve him right! Also—
somewhat inconsistently—blessed are the poor!

Now what does this Let Him Be Poor mean? It means let him
be weak. Let him be ignorant. Let him become a nucleus of disease.
Let him be a standing exhibition and example of ugliness and dirt.
Let him have rickety children. Let him be cheap and let him drag
his fellows down to his own price by selling himself to do their
work. Let his habitations turn our cities into poisonous congeries of
slums. Let his daughters infect our young men with the diseases of
the streets, and his sons revenge him by turning the nation's manhood into scrofula, cowardice, cruelty, hypocrisy, political inbecility,
and all the other fruits of oppression and malnutrition. Let the
undeserving become still less deserving; and let the deserving lay up
for himself, not treasures in heaven, but horrors in hell upon earth.
This being so, is it really wise to let him be poor? Would he not do
ten times less harm as a prosperous burglar, incendiary, ravisher
or murderer, to the utmost limits of humanity's comparatively negligible impulses in these directions? Suppose we were to abolish all
penalties for such activities, and decide that poverty is the one thing
we will not tolerate—that every adult with less than, say, £365 a
year, shall be painlessly but inexorably killed, and every hungry half-
naked child forcibly fattened and clothed, would not that be an
enormous improvement on our existing system, which has already
destroyed so many civilizations, and is visibly destroying ours in the
same way?

Is there any radicle of such legislation in our parliamentary system? Well, there are two measures just sprouting in the political
soil, which may conceivably grow to something valuable. One is the
institution of a Legal Minimum Wage. The other, Old Age Pensions. But there is a better plan than either of these. Some time
ago I mentioned the subject of Universal Old Age Pensions to my
fellow Socialist Cobden-Sanderson, famous as an artist-craftsman in
bookbinding and printing. "Why not Universal Pensions for Life?"
said Cobden-Sanderson. In saying this, he solved the industrial problem at a stroke. At present we say callously to each citizen "If you
want money, earn it" as if his having or not having it were a matter
that concerned himself alone. We do not even secure for him the
opportunity of earning it: on the contrary, we allow our industry

to be organized in open dependence on the maintenance of "a reserve army of unemployed" for the sake of "elasticity." The sensible course would be Cobden-Sanderson's: that is, to give every man enough to live well on, so as to guarantee the community against the possibility of a case of the malignant disease of poverty, and then (necessarily) to see that he earned it.

Undershaft, the hero of Major Barbara, is simply a man who, having grasped the fact that poverty is a crime, knows that when society offered him the alternative of poverty or a lucrative trade in death and destruction,[2] it offered him, not a choice between opulent villainy and humble virtue, but between energetic enterprise and cowardly infamy. His conduct stands the Kantian test, which Peter Shirley's does not.[3] Peter Shirley is what we call the honest poor man. Undershaft is what we call the wicked rich one: Shirley is Lazarus, Undershaft Dives. Well, the misery of the world is due to the fact that the great mass of men act and believe as Peter Shirley acts and believes. If they acted and believed as Undershaft acts and believes, the immediate result would be a revolution of incalculable beneficence. To be wealthy, says Undershaft, is with me a point of honor for which I am prepared to kill at the risk of my own life. This preparedness is, as he says, the final test of sincerity. Like Froissart's medieval hero, who saw that "to rob and pill was a good life" he is not the dupe of that public sentiment against killing which is propagated and endowed by people who would otherwise be killed themselves, or of the mouth-honor paid to poverty and obedience by rich and insubordinate do-nothings who want to rob the poor without courage and command them without superiority. Froissart's knight, in placing the achievement of a good life before all the other duties—which indeed are not duties at all when they conflict with it, but plain wickednesses—behaved bravely, admirably, and, in the final analysis, public-spiritedly. Medieval society, on the other hand, behaved very badly indeed in organizing itself so stupidly that a good life could be achieved by robbing and pilling. If the knight's contemporaries had been all as resolute as he, robbing and pilling would have been the shortest way to the gallows, just as, if we were all as resolute and clearsighted as Undershaft, an attempt to live by means of what is called "an independent income" would be the shortest way to the lethal chamber. But as, thanks to our political imbecility and personal cowardice (fruits of poverty, both), the best imitation of a good life now procurable is life on an independent income, all sensible people aim at securing such an income, and are, of course, careful to legalize and moralize both it and all the actions and sentiments which lead to it and support it as

2. Undershaft was a munitions manufacturer.

3. The Kantian test is to act only as you would have all others act in similar circumstances. Peter Shirley is an unemployed old man in the soup kitchen whose conscience was shaped by social-protest theories.

an institution. What else can they do? They know, of course, that they are rich because others are poor. But they cannot help that: it is for the poor to repudiate poverty when they have had enough of it. The thing can be done easily enough: the demonstrations to the contrary made by the economists, jurists, moralists and sentimentalists hired by the rich to defend them, or even doing the work gratuitously out of sheer folly and abjectness, impose only on those who want to be imposed on.

The reason why the independent income-tax payers are not solid in defence of their position is that since we are not medieval rovers through a sparsely populated country, the poverty of those we rob prevents our having the good life for which we sacrifice them. Rich men or aristocrats with a developed sense of life—men like Ruskin and William Morris and Kropotkin—have enormous social appetites and very fastidious personal ones. They are not content with handsome houses: they want handsome cities. They are not content with bediamonded wives and blooming daughters: they complain because the charwoman is badly dressed, because the laundress smells of gin, because the sempstress is anemic, because every man they meet is not a friend and every woman not a romance. They turn up their noses at their neighbors' drains, and are made ill by the architecture of their neighbors' houses. Trade patterns made to suit vulgar people do not please them (and they can get nothing else): they cannot sleep nor sit at ease upon "slaughtered" cabinet makers' furniture. The very air is not good enough for them: there is too much factory smoke in it. They even demand abstract conditions: justice, honor, a noble moral atmosphere, a mystic nexus to replace the cash nexus. Finally they declare that though to rob and pill with your own hand on horseback and in steel coat may have been a good life, to rob and pill by the hands of the policeman, the bailiff, and the soldier, and to underpay them meanly for doing it, is not a good life, but rather fatal to all possibility of even a tolerable one. They call on the poor to revolt, and, finding the poor shocked at their ungentlemenliness, despairingly revile the proletariat for its "damned wantlessness" (*verdammte Bedürfnislosigkeit*).

So far, however, their attack on society has lacked simplicity. The poor do not share their tastes nor understand their art-criticisms. They do not want the simple life, nor the esthetic life; on the contrary, they want very much to wallow in all the costly vulgarities from which the elect souls among the rich turn away with loathing. It is by surfeit and not by abstinence that they will be cured of their hankering after unwholesome sweets. What they do dislike and despise and are ashamed of is poverty. To ask them to fight for the difference between the Christmas number of the Illustrated London News and the Kelmscott Chaucer is silly: they prefer the

News. The difference between a stockbroker's cheap and dirty starched white shirt and collar and the comparatively costly and carefully dyed blue shirt of William Morris is a difference so disgraceful to Morris in their eyes that if they fought on the subject at all, they would fight in defence of the starch. "Cease to be slaves, in order that you may become cranks" is not a very inspiring call to arms; nor is it really improved by substituting saints for cranks. Both terms denote men of genius; and the common man does not want to live the life of a man of genius: he would much rather live the life of a pet collie if that were the only alternative. But he does want more money. Whatever else he may be vague about, he is clear about that. He may or may not prefer Major Barbara to the Drury Lane pantomime; but he always prefers five hundred pounds to five hundred shillings.

Now to deplore this preference as sordid, and teach children that it is sinful to desire money, is to strain towards the extreme possible limit of impudence in lying and corruption in hypocrisy. The universal regard for money is the one hopeful fact in our civilization, the one sound spot in our social conscience. Money is the most important thing in the world. It represents health, strength, honor, generosity and beauty as conspicuously and undeniably as the want of it represents illness, weakness, disgrace, meanness and ugliness. Not the least of its virtues is that it destroys base people as certainly as it fortifies and dignifies noble people. It is only when it is cheapened to worthlessness for some and made impossibly dear to others, that it becomes a curse. In short, it is a curse only in such foolish social conditions that life itself is a curse. For the two things are inseparable: money is the counter that enables life to be distributed socially: it *is* life as truly as sovereigns and bank notes are money. The first duty of every citizen is to insist on having money on reasonable terms; and this demand is not complied with by giving four men three shillings each for ten or twelve hours' drudgery and one man a thousand pounds for nothing. The crying need of the nation is not for better morals, cheaper bread, temperance, liberty, culture, redemption of fallen sisters and erring brothers, nor the grace, love and fellowship of the Trinity, but simply for enough money. And the evil to be attacked is not sin, suffering, greed, priestcraft, kingcraft, demagogy, monopoly, ignorance, drink, war, pestilence, nor any other of the scapegoats which reformers sacrifice, but simply poverty.

QUESTIONS FOR STUDY, DISCUSSION, AND WRITING

1. Cite some examples of Shaw's deliberately outrageous manner in his first paragraph. Does he ever modify this extreme manner?
2. In the second paragraph he speaks of two cases as "precisely parallel": what premise must he assume in order to say this?

How vital is this assertion to his main line of argument? What is his central assertion?

3. Explain the definition of money as life which appears in the last paragraph.

4. Outline in more neutral words and phrases than Shaw's a more conventional approach to his argument.

5. Who are Shaw's controversial antagonists? In what way is his controversial manner suited to these antagonists?

JAMES AGEE
Cotton[1]

Cotton is only one among several crops and among many labors: and all these other crops and labors mean life itself. Cotton means nothing of the sort. It demands more work of a tenant family and yields less reward than all the rest. It is the reason the tenant has the means to do the rest, and to have the rest, and to live, as a tenant, at all. Aside from a few negligibilities of minor sale and barter and of out-of-season work, it is his one possible source of money, and through this fact, though his living depends far less on money than on the manipulations of immediate nature, it has a certain royalty. It is also that by which he has all else besides money. But it is also his chief contracted obligation, for which he must neglect all else as need be; and is the central leverage and symbol of his privation and of his wasted life. It is the one crop and labor which is in no possible way useful as it stands to the tenant's living; it is among all these the one which must and can be turned into money; it is among all these the one in which the landowner is not interested; and it is among all these the one of which the tenant can hope for least, and can be surest that he is being cheated, and is always to be cheated. All other tasks are incidental to it; it is constantly on everyone's mind; yet of all of them it is the work in which the tenant has least hope and least interest, and to which he must devote the most energy. Any less involved and self-contradictory attempt to understand what cotton and cotton work "means" to a tenant would, it seems to me, be false to it. It has the doubleness that all jobs have by which one stays alive and in which one's life is made a cheated ruin, and the same sprained and twilight effect on those who must work at it: but because it is only one among the many jobs by which a tenant family must stay alive, and deflects all these others, and receives still other light from their more personal need, reward, and value, its meanings are much more complex than those of most jobs: it is a strong stale magnet among many others more weak

1. An appendix from *Let Us Now Praise Famous Men*, 1939.

and more yielding of life and hope. In the mind of one in whom all these magnetisms are daily and habituated from his birth, these meanings are one somber mull: yet all their several forces are pulling at once, and by them the brain is quietly drawn and quartered. It seems to me it is only through such a complex of meanings that a tenant can feel, toward that crop, toward each plant in it, toward all that work, what he and all grown women too appear to feel, a particular automatism, a quiet, apathetic, and inarticulate yet deeply vindictive hatred, and at the same time utter hopelessness, and the deepest of their anxieties and of their hopes: as if the plant stood enormous in the unsteady sky fastened above them in all they do like the eyes of an overseer. To do all of the hardest work of your life in service of these drawings-apart of ambiguities; and to have all other tasks and all one's consciousness stained and drawn apart in it: I can conceive of little else which could be so inevitably destructive of the appetite for living, of the spirit, of the being, or by whatever name the centers of individuals are to be called: and this very literally: for just as there are deep chemical or electric changes in all the body under anger, or love, or fear, so there must certainly be at the center of these meanings and their directed emotions; perhaps most essentially, an incalculably somber and heavy weight and dark knotted iron of subnausea at the peak of the diaphragm, darkening and weakening the whole body and being, the literal feeling by which the words a broken heart are no longer poetic, but are merely the most accurate possible description.

Yet these things as themselves are withdrawn almost beyond visibility, and the true focus and right telling of it would be in the exact textures of each immediate task.

Of cotton farming I know almost nothing with my own eyes; the rest I have of Bud Woods. I asked enough of other people to realize that every tenant differs a little in his methods, so nothing of this can be set down as "standard" or "correct"; but the dissonances are of small detail rather than of the frame and series in the year. I respect dialects too deeply, when they are used by those who have a right to them, not to be hesitant in using them, but I have decided to use some of Woods' language here. I have decided, too, to try to use my imagination a little, as carefully as I can. I must warn you that the result is sure to be somewhat inaccurate: but it is accurate anyhow to my ignorance, which I would not wish to disguise.

From the end of the season and on through the winter the cotton and the corn stand stripped and destroyed, the cotton black and brown, the corn gray and brown and rotted gold, much more shattered, the banks of woodland bare, drenched and black, the clay dirt sombered wet or hard with a shine of iron, peaceful and exhausted; the look of trees in a once full-blown country where such a burning of war has gone there is no food left even for birds and insects, all now brought utterly quiet, and the bare homes dark with dampness, under the soft and mourning midwinter suns of autumnal days, when all glows gold yet lifeless, and under constrictions of those bitter freezings when the clay is shafted and sprilled with ice, and the aching thinly drifted snows which give the land its shape, and, above all, the long, cold, silent, inexhaustible, and dark winter rains:

In the late fall or middle February this tenant, which of the three or of the millions I do not care—a man, dressed against the wet coldness, may be seen small and dark in his prostrated fields, taking down these sometimes brittle, sometimes rotted forests of last year's crops with a club or with a cutter, putting death to bed, cleaning the land: and late in February, in fulfillment of an obligation to his landlord, he borrows a second mule and, with a two-horse plow, runs up the levees,[2] that is, the terraces, which shall preserve his land; this in a softening mild brightness and odoriferousness of presaging spring, and a rustling shearing apart of the heavy land, his mules moving in slow scarce-wakened method as of work before dawn, knowing the real year's work to be not started yet, only made ready for. It is when this is done, at about the first of March, that the actual work begins, with what is planted where, and with what grade and amount of fertilizer, determined by the landlord, who will also, if he wishes, criticize, advise, and govern at all stages of planting and cultivation. But the physical work, and for that matter the knowledge by which he works, is the tenant's, and this is his tenth or his fortieth year's beginning of it, and it is of the tenant I want to tell.

How you break the land in the first place depends on whether you have one or two mules or can double up with another tenant for two mules. It is much better to broadcast if you can. With two mules you can count on doing it all in that most thorough way. But if you have only one mule you break what you have time for, more shallowly and, for the rest, you bed, that is, start the land.

To broadcast, to break the land broadcast: take a twister, which is about the same as a turning plow, and, heading the mule in concentrics the shape of the field, lay open as broad and deep a ribbon of the stiff dirt as the strength of the mule and of your own guidance can manage: eight wide by six deep with a single-horse plow, and twice that with a double, is doing well: the operation has the staggering and reeling yet steady quality of a small sailboat clambering a storm.

Where you have broadcast the land, you then lay out the furrows three and a half feet apart with a shovel plow; and put down fertilizer; and by four furrows with a turning plow, twist the dirt back over the fertilized furrow. But if, lacking mule power, you have still land

2. These farms are the width of a state and still more from the river. Is levee originally a land or a river word? It must be a river word, for terracing against erosion is recent in America. So the Mississippi has such power that men who have never seen it use its language in their work [Agee's note].

which is not broken, and it is near time to plant, you bed the rest. There are two beddings. The first is hard bedding: breaking the hard pan between the rows.

Hard bedding: set the plow parallel to the line of (last year's) stalks and along their right, follow each row to its end and up the far side. The dirt lays open always to the right. Then set the plow close in against the stalks and go around again. The stubble is cleaned out this second time round and between each two rows is a bed of soft dirt: that is to say, the hard pan is all broken. That is the first bedding.

Then drop guano along the line where the stalks were, by machine or by horn. Few tenants use the machine; most of them either buy a horn, or make it, as Woods does. It is a long tin cone, small and low, with a wood handle, and a hole in the low end. It is held in the left hand, pointed low to the furrow, and is fed in fistfuls, in a steady rhythm, from the fertilizer sack, the incipient frock, slung heavy along the right side.

After you have strowed the gyewanner you turn the dirt back over with two plowings just as before: and that is the second bedding. Pitch the bed shallow, or you won't be able to work it right.

If you have done all this right you haven't got a blemish in all your land that is not broke: and you are ready to plant.

But just roughly, only as a matter of suggestion, compute the work that has been done so far, in ten acres of land, remembering that this is not counting in ten more acres of corn and a few minor crops: how many times has this land been retraced in the rolling-gaited guidance and tensions and whippings and orderings of plowing, and with the steadily held horn, the steady arc of the right arm and right hand fisting and opening like a heart, the heavy weight of the sack at the right side?

Broadcasting, the whole unbroken plaque slivered open in rectilinear concenters, eight inches apart and six deep if with one mule, sixteen apart and twelve deep if with two: remember how much length of line is coiled in one reel or within one phonograph record: and then each furrow, each three and a half feet, scooped open with a shovel plow: and in each row the fertilizer laid: and each row folded cleanly back in four transits of its complete length: or bedding, the first bedding in four transits of each length; and then the fertilizer: and four more transits of each length: every one of the many rows of the whole of the field gone eight times over with a plow and a ninth by hand; and only now is it ready for planting.

Planting

There are three harrs you might use but the spring-toothed harr is best. The long-toothed section harrow tears your bed to pieces;

the short-toothed is better, but catches on snags and is more likely to pack the bed than loosen it. The springtooth moves lightly but incisively with a sort of knee-action sensitiveness to the modulations of the ground, and it jumps snags. You harrow just one row at a time and right behind the harrow comes the planter. The planter is rather like a tennis-court marker: a seed bin set between light wheels, with a little plow protruded from beneath it like a foot from under a hoopskirt. The little beak of the plow slits open the dirt; just at its lifted heel the seed thrills out in a spindling stream; a flat wheel flats the dirt over: a light-traveling, tender, iron sexual act entirely worthy of setting beside the die-log and the swept broad-handed arm.[3]

Depending on the moisture and the soil, it will be five days to two weeks before the cotton will show.

Cultivating begins as soon as it shows an inch.

Cultivation

Barring off: the sweepings: chopping: laying by:

The first job is barring off.

Set a five- to six-inch twister, the smallest one you have, as close in against the stalks as you can get it and not damage them, as close as the breadth of a finger if you are good at it, and throw the dirt to the middle. Alongside this plow is a wide tin defender, which doesn't allow a blemish to fall on the young plants.

Then comes the first of the four sweepings. The sweeps are blunt stocks shaped a good deal like stingrays. Over their dull foreheads and broad shoulders they neither twist nor roll the dirt, but shake it from the middle to the beds on either side. For the first sweeping you still use the defender. Use a little stock, but the biggest you dare to; probably the eighteen-inch.

Next after that comes the chopping, and with this the whole family helps down through the children of eight or seven, and by helps, I mean that the family works full time at it. Chopping is a simple and hard job, and a hot one, for by now the sun, though still damp, is very strong, hot with a kind of itchy intensity that is seldom known in northern springs. The work is, simply, thinning the cotton to a stand; hills a foot to sixteen inches apart, two to four stalks to the hill. It is done with an eight to ten-inch hoeblade. You cut the cotton flush off at the ground, bent just a little above it, with

3. I am unsure of this planting machine; I did not see one there; but what Woods described to me seemed to tally with something I had seen, and not remembered with perfect clearness, from my childhood. The die-log is still used, Woods says, by some of the older-fashioned farmers and by some negroes. I'm not very clear about it either, but I am interested because according to Woods its use goes a *way* on back. My "impression" is that it's simple enough: a hollow homemade cylinder of wood with a hole in it to regulate and direct the falling stream of seed as would be more difficult by hand [Agee's note].

a short sharp blow of the blade of which each stroke is light enough work; but multiplied into the many hundreds in each continuously added hour, it aches first the forearms, which so harden they seem to become one bone, and in time the whole spine.

The second sweeping is done with the twenty to twenty-two-inch stock you will use from now on; then comes hoeing, another job for the whole family; then you run the middles; that is, you put down soda by hand or horn or machine; soda makes the weed, guano puts on the fruit; then comes the third sweeping; and then another hoeing. The first and second sweepings you have gone pretty deep. The stuff is small and you want to give loose ground to your feed roots. The third sweeping is shallow, for the feed roots have extended themselves within danger of injury.

The fourth sweeping is so light a scraping that it is scarcely more than a ritual, like a barber's last delicate moments with his muse before he holds the mirror up to the dark side of your skull. The cotton has to be treated very carefully. By this last sweeping it is making. Break roots, or lack rain, and it is stopped dead as a hammer.

This fourth sweeping is the operation more properly known as laying by. From now on until picking time, there is nothing more a farmer can do. Everything is up to the sky, the dirt, and the cotton itself; and in six weeks now, and while the farmer is fending off such of its enemies as he can touch, and, lacking rations money to live on, is desperately seeking and conceivably finding work, or with his family is hung as if on a hook on his front porch in the terrible leisure, the cotton is making, and his year's fate is being quietly fought out between agencies over which he has no control. And in this white midsummer, while he is thus waiting however he can, and defending what little he can, these are his enemies, and this is what the cotton is doing with its time:

Each square points up. That is to say: on twig-ends, certain of the fringed leaves point themselves into the sharp form of an infant prepuce; each square points up: and opens a flat white flower which turns pink next day, purple the next, and on the next day shrivels and falls, forced off by the growth, at the base of the bloom, of the boll. The development from square to boll consumes three weeks in the early summer, ten days in the later, longer and more intense heat. The plants are well fringed with pointed squares, and young cold bolls, by the time the crop is laid by; and the blooming keeps on all summer. The development of each boll from the size of a pea to that point where, at the size of a big walnut, it darkens and dries and its white contents silently explode it, takes five to eight weeks and is by no means ended when the picking season has begun.

And meanwhile the enemies: bitterweed, ragweed, Johnson grass;

the weevil, the army worm; the slippery chances of the sky. Bitterweed is easily killed out and won't come up again. Ragweed will, with another prong every time. That weed can suck your crop to death. Johnson grass, it takes hell and scissors to control. You can't control it in the drill with your plowing. If you just cut it off with the hoe, it is high as your thumb by the next morning. The best you can do is dig up the root with the corner of your hoe, and that doesn't hold it back any too well.

There is a lot less trouble from the weevils[4] than there used to be, but not the army worms. Army worms are devils. The biggest of them get to be the size of your little finger. They eat leaves and squares and young bolls. You get only a light crop of them at first. They web up in the leaves and turn into flies, the flies lay eggs, the eggs turn into army worms by the millions and if they have got this good a start of you you can hear the sound of them eating in the whole field and it sounds like a brushfire. They are a bad menace but they are not as hard to control as the weevil. You mix arsenic poison with a sorry grade of flour and dust the plants late of an evening (afternoon) or soon of a morning (pre-morning); and the dew makes a paste of it that won't blow off.

It is only in a very unusual year that you do well with both of the most important crops, the two life mainly depends on, because they need rain and sun in such different amounts. Cotton needs a great deal less rain than corn; it is really a sun flower. If it is going to get a superflux of rain, that will best come before it is blooming; and if it has got to rain during that part of the summer when a fairsized field is blooming a bale a day, it had best rain late in the evening when the blooms are shutting or at night, not in the morning or the mid day: for then the bloom is blared out flat; rain gets in it easy and hangs on it; it shuts wet, sours, and sticks to the boll; next morning it turns red and falls. Often the boll comes off with it. But the boll that stays on is sour and rotted and good for nothing. Or to put it the other way around, it can take just one rain at the wrong time of day at the wrong time of summer to wreck you out of a whole bale.

It is therefore not surprising that they are constant readers of the sky; that it holds not an ounce of 'beauty' to them (though I know of no more magnificent skies than those of Alabama); that it is the lodestone of their deepest pieties; and that they have, also, the deep stormfear which is apparently common to all primitive peoples. Wind is as terrifying to them as cloud and lightning and thunder: and I remember how, sitting with the Woods, in an afternoon when George was away at work, and a storm was building,

---

4. If I remember rightly, people never learned any successful method against him, and it is some insect, whose name and kind I forget, who holds him in check [Agee's note].

Mrs. Gudger and her children came hurrying three quarters of a mile beneath the blackening air to shelter among company. Gudger says: "You never can tell what's in a cloud."

Picking Season

Late in August the fields begin to whiten more rarely with late bloom and more frequently with cotton and then still thicker with cotton, a sparkling ground starlight of it, steadily bursting into more and more millions of points, all the leaves seeming shrunken smaller; quite as at night the whole frontage of the universe is more and more thoroughly printed in the increasing darkness; and the wide cloudless and tremendous light holds the earth clamped and trained as beneath a vacuum bell and burningglass; in such a brilliance that half and two thirds of the sky is painful to look into; and in this white maturing oven the enlarged bolls are streaked a rusty green, then bronze, and are split and splayed open each in a loose vomit of cotton. These split bolls are now *burrs*, hard and edged as chiseled wood, pointed nearly as thorns, spread open in three and four and five gores or cells. It is slow at first, just a few dozen scattered here and there and then a few tens of dozens, and then there is a space of two or three days in which a whole field seems to be crackling open at once, and at this time it seems natural that it must be gone into and picked, but all the more temperate and experienced tenants wait a few days longer until it will be fully worth the effort: and during this bursting of bolls and this waiting, there is a kind of quickening, as if deep under the ground, of all existence, toward a climax which cannot be delayed much longer, but which is held in the tensions of this reluctance, tightening, and delay: and this can be seen equally in long, sweeping drivings of a car between these spangling fields, and in any one of the small towns or the county seats, and in the changed eyes of any one family, a kind of tightening as of an undertow, the whole world and year lifted nearly upon its crest, and soon beginning the long chute down to winter: children, and once in a while a very young or a very old woman or man, whose work is scarcely entered upon or whose last task and climax this may be, are deeply taken with an excitement and a restlessness to begin picking, and in the towns, where it is going to mean money, the towns whose existence is for it and depends on it, and which in most times of year are sunken in sleep as at the bottom of a sea: these towns are sharpening awake; even the white hot streets of a large city are subtly changed in this season: but Gudger and his wife and Ricketts and Woods, and most of the heads of the million and a quarter families who have made this and are to do the working of taking it for their own harm and another's use, they are only a little more quiet than usual, as they might be if they were waiting for a train to come in, and keep looking at the fields, and judging them; and at length one morning (the Ricketts women are already three days advanced in ragged work), Gudger says, Well:

Well; I reckin tomorrow we'd better start to picking:

And the next morning very early, with their broad hats and great sacks and the hickory baskets, they are out, silent, their bodies all slanted, on the hill: and in every field in hundreds of miles, black and white, it is the same: and such as it is, it is a joy which scarcely touches any tenant; and is worn thin and through in half a morning, and is gone for a year.

It is simple and terrible work. Skill will help you; all the endurance you can draw up against it from the roots of your existence will be thoroughly used as fuel to it: but neither skill nor endurance can make it any easier.

Over the right shoulder you have slung a long white sack whose half length trails the ground behind. You work with both hands as fast and steadily as you can. The trick is to get the cotton between your fingertips at its very roots in the burr in all three or four or five gores at once so that it is brought out clean in one pluck. It is easy enough with one burr in perhaps ten, where the cotton is ready to fall; with the rest, the fibers are more tight and tricky. So another trick is, to learn these several different shapes of burr and resistance as nearly as possible by instinct, so there will be no second trying and delay, and none left wasted in the burr; and, too, as quickly to judge what may be too rotted and dirtied to use, and what is not yet quite ready to take: there are a lot suspended between these small uncertainties, and there should be no delay, no need to use the mind's judgement, and few mistakes. Still another trick is, between these strong pulls of efficiency, proper judgement, and maximum speed, not to hurt your fingers on the burrs any worse than you can help. You would have to try hard, to break your flesh on any one burr, whether on its sharp points or its edges; and a single raindrop is only scarcely instrumental in ironing a mountain flat; but in each plucking of the hand the fingers are searched deep in along these several sharp, hard edges. In two hours' picking the hands are just well limbered up. At the end of a week you are favoring your fingers, still in the obligation of speed. The later of the three to five times over the field, the last long weeks of the season, you might be happy if it were possible to exchange them for boils. With each of these hundreds of thousands of insertions of the hands, moreover, the fingers are brought to a small point, in an action upon every joint and tendon in the hand. I suggest that if you will try, three hundred times in succession, the following exercise: touch all five fingertips as closely as possible into one point, trying meanwhile to hold loose cotton in the palm of the hand: you will see that this can very quickly tire, cramp and de-

teriorate the whole instrument, and will understand how easily
rheumatism can take up its strictures in just this place.

Meanwhile, too, you are working in a land of sunlight and heat
which are special to just such country at just that time of year:
sunlight that stands and stacks itself upon you with the serene
weight of deep sea water, and heat that makes the jointed and
muscled and fine-structured body glow like one indiscriminate oil;
and this brilliant weight of heat is piled upon you more and more
heavily in hour after hour so that it can seem you are a diving
bell whose strained seams must at any moment burst, and the eyes
are marked in stinging sweat, and the head, if your health is a little
unstable, is gently roaring, like a private blowtorch, and less gently
beating with aching blood: also the bag, which can hold a hundred
pounds, is filling as it is dragged from plant to plant, four to nine
burrs to a plant to be rifled swiftly, and the load shrugged along
another foot or two and the white row stretched ahead to a blur
and innumerably manifolded in other white rows which have not
yet been touched, and younger bolls in the cleaned row behind
already breaking like slow popcorn in the heat, and the sack still
heavier and heavier, so that it pulls you back as a beast might rather
than a mere dead weight: but it is not only this: cotton plants
are low, so that in this heat and burden of the immanent sun and
of the heavying sack you are dragging, you are continuously somewhat stooped over even if you are a child, and are bent very deep
if you are a man or a woman. A strong back is a godsend, but not
even the strongest back was built for that treatment, and there
combine at the kidneys, and rill down the thighs and up the spine
and athwart the shoulders the ticklish weakness of gruel or water,
and an aching that is increased in geometric progressions, and at
length, in the small of the spine, a literal and persistent sensation
of yielding, buckling, splintering, and breakage: and all of this,
even though the mercy of nature has hardened your flesh and has
anesthetized your nerves and your powers of reflection and of imagination, yet reaches in time the brain and the more mirror-like
nerves, and thereby is redoubled upon itself much more powerfully
than before: and this is all compounded upon you during each
successive hour of the day and during each successive day in a force
which rest and food and sleep only partly and superficially refresh:
and though, later in the season, you are relieved of the worst of
the heat, it is in exchange at the last for a coolness which many
pickers like even less well, since it so slows and chills the lubricant
garment of sweat they work in, and seriously slows and stiffens the
fingers which by then at best afford an excruciation in every touch.

The tenants' idiom has been used ad nauseam by the more unspeakable of the northern journalists but it happens to be accurate:
that picking goes on each day from can to can't: sometimes, if

there is a feeling of rush, the Ricketts continue it by moonlight. In the blasting heat of the rest of the season, unless there is a rush to beat a rain or to make up an almost completed wagonload, it is customary to quit work an hour and a half or even two hours in the worst part of the day and to sit or lie in the shade and possible draft of the hallway or porch asleep or dozing after dinner. This time narrows off as the weeks go by and a sense of rush and of the wish to be done with it grows on the pickers and is tightened through from the landlord. I have heard of tenants and pickers who have no rest-period and no midday meal,[5] but those I am acquainted with have it. It is of course no parallel in heartiness and variety to the proud and enormous meals which farm wives of the wheat country prepare for harvest hands, and which are so very zestfully regarded by some belated virgilians as common to what they like to call the American Scene. It is in fact the ordinary every day food, with perhaps a little less variety than in the earlier summer, hastily thrown together and heated by a woman who has hurried in exhausted from the field as few jumps as possible ahead of her family, and served in the dishes she hurriedly rinsed before she hurried out on the early morning as few jumps as possible behind them. When they are all done, she hurries through the dish washing and puts on her straw hat or her sunbonnet and goes on back into the field, and they are all at it in a strung-out little bunch, the sun a bitter white on their deeply bent backs, and the sacks trailing, a slow breeze idling in the tops of the pines and hickories along the far side but the leaves of the low cotton scarcely touched in it, and the whole land, under hours of heat still to go, yet listed subtly forward toward the late end of the day. They seem very small in the field and very lonely, and the motions of their industry are so small, in range, their bodies so slowly moving, that it seems less that they are so hard at work than that they are bowed over so deeply into some fascination or grief, or are as those pilgrims of Quebec who take the great flights of stairs upon their knees, slowly, a prayer spoken in each step. Ellen lies in the white load of the cotton-basket in the shade asleep; Squinchy picks the front of his dress full and takes it to his mother; Clair Bell fills a hat time after time in great speed and with an expression of delight rushes up behind her mother and dumps the cotton on all of her she can reach and goes crazy with laughter, and her mother

5. On the big plantations, where a good deal of the picking is done by day labor and is watched over by riding bosses, all the equations of speed and unresting steadiness are of course intensified; the whole nature of the work, in the men and women and their children, is somewhat altered. Yet not so much as might at first seem. A man and his family working alone are drawn narrowly together in these weeds even within themselves, and know they are being watched: from the very first, in town, their landlords are observant of which tenants bring their cotton first to gin and of who is slow and late; also, there is nearly always, in the tenant's family, the exceedingly sharp need of cottonseed money [Agee's note].

and the girls stop a minute and she is hugged, but they talk more
among themselves than the other families, they are much more
quiet than is usual to them, and Mrs. Ricketts only pauses a minute,
cleaning the cotton from her skirts and her hair and putting it in
her sack, and then she is bowed over deeply at work again. Woods
is badly slowed by weakness and by the pain in his shoulder; he welcomes any possible excuse to stop and sometimes has to pause
whether there is any excuse or not, but his wife and her mother
are both strong and good pickers, so he is able to get by without
a hired hand. Thomas is not old enough yet to be any use. Burt
too is very young for it and works only by fits and starts; little
is expected of children so small, but it is no harm what little they
do; you can't learn them too young. Junior is not very quick with
it at best. He will work for a while furiously hard, in jealousy of
Louise, and then slacken up with sore hands and begin to bully Burt.
Katy is very quick. Last summer, when she was only eight, she
picked a hundred and ten pounds in a day in a race with Flora
Merry Lee. This summer she has had runarounds and is losing two
fingernails but she is picking steadily. Pearl Woods is big for her
age and is very steadily useful. Louise is an extraordinarily steady
and quick worker for her age; she can pick a hundred and fifty
pounds in a day. The two Ricketts boys are all right when their
papa is on hand to keep them at their work; as it is, with Ricketts
at the sawmills they clown a good deal, and tease their sisters.
Mrs. Gudger picks about the average for a woman, a hundred and
fifty to two hundred pounds a day. She is fast with her fingers
until the work exhausts her; "last half of the day I just don't see
how I can keep on with it." George Gudger is a very poor picker.
When he was a child he fell in the fireplace and burnt the flesh
off the flat of both hands to the bone, so that his fingers are stiff
and slow and the best he has ever done in a day is a hundred and
fifty pounds. The average for a man is nearer two hundred and
fifty. His back hurts him badly too, so he usually picks on his
knees, the way the others pick only when they are resting. Mrs.
Ricketts used to pick three hundred and three hundred and fifty
pounds in a day but sickness has slowed her to less than two hundred
now. Mrs. Ricketts is more often than not a fantast, quite without
realizing, and in all these figures they gave me there may be inaccuracy—according to general talk surrounding the Rust machine a
hundred pounds a day is good picking—but these are their own
estimates of their own abilities, on a matter in which tenants have
some pride, and that seems to me more to the point than their
accuracy. There are sometimes shifts into gayety in the picking, or
a brief excitement, a race between two of the children, or a snake
killed; or two who sit a few moments in their sweat in the shaded
clay when they have taken some water, but they say very little to

each other, for there is little to say, and are soon back to it, and mainly, in hour upon hour, it is speechless, silent, serious, ceaseless and lonely work along the great silence of the unshaded land, ending each day in a vast blaze of dust on the west, every leaf sharpened in long knives of shadow, the clay drawn down through red to purple, and the leaves losing color, and the wild blind eyes of the cotton staring in twilight, in those odors of work done and of nature lost once more to night whose sweetness is a torture, and in the slow, loaded walking home, whose stiff and gentle motions are those of creatures just awakened.

The cotton is ordinarily stored in a small structure out in the land, the cotton house; but none of these three families has one. The Gudgers store it in one of the chambers of their barn, the Woods on their front porch, raising planks around it, the Ricketts in their spare room. The Ricketts children love to play in it, tumbling and diving and burying each other; sometimes, it is a sort of treat, they are allowed to sleep in it. Rats like it too, to make nest-es[6] in, and that draws ratsnakes. It is not around, though, for very long at a time. Each family has a sort of archaic iron beam scales, and when these scales have weighed out fourteen hundred pounds of cotton it is loaded, if possible during the first of the morning, onto the narrow and high-boarded wagon, and is taken into Cookstown to gin.

It is a long tall deep narrow load shored in with weathered wagonsides and bulged up in a high puff above these sides, and the mule, held far over to the right of the highway to let the cars go by, steps more steadily and even more slowly than ordinary, with a look almost of pomp, dragging the hearse-shaped wagon: its iron wheels on the left grince in the slags of the highway, those on the right in clay: and high upon the load, the father at the reins, the whole of the family is sitting, if it is a small family, or if it is a large, those children whose turn it is, and perhaps the mother too. The husband is dressed in the better of his work clothes; the wife, and the children, in such as they might wear to town on Saturday, or even, some of them, to church, and the children are happy and excited, high on the soft load, and even a woman is taken with it a little, much more soberly, and even the man who is driving, has in the tightness of his jaws, and in his eyes, which meet those of any stranger with the curious challenging and protective, fearful and fierce pride a poor mother shows when her child, dressed in its

---

6. Mrs. Gudger's word. Her saying of it was "rats likes it to make nest-es in." It is a common pluralization in the south. There is no Cuteness in it, of speaking by diminutives, and I wonder whether this is not Scottish dialect, and whether they, too, are not innocent of the "itsybitsying" which the middle-class literacy assumes of them. *Later*. On the proof-sheets is the following note, which I use with thanks: "Isn't it the Middle-English plural? Chaucer used it for this same word and as a usual plural ending" [Agee's note].

best, is being curiously looked at; even he who knows best of any of them, is taken with something of the same: and there is in fact about the whole of it some raw, festal quality, some air also of solemn grandeur, this member in the inconceivably huge and slow parade of mule-drawn, crawling wagons, creaking under the weight of the year's bloodsweated and prayed-over work, on all the roads drawn in, from the utmost runners and ramifications of the slender red roads of all the south and into the southern highways, a wagon every few hundred yards, crested this with a white and this with a black family, all drawn toward those little trembling lodes which are the gins, and all and in each private and silent heart toward that climax of one more year's work which yields so little at best, and nothing so often, and worse to so many hundreds of thousands:

The gin itself, too, the wagons drawn up in line, the people waiting on each wagon, the suspendered white-shirted men on the platform, the emblematic sweep of the grand-shouldered iron beam scales cradling gently on the dark doorway their design of justice, the landlords in their shirt-sleeves at the gin or relaxed in swivels beside the decorated safes in their little offices, the heavy-muscled and bloodfaced young men in baseball caps who tumble the bales with short sharp hooks, the loafers drawn into this place to have their batteries recharged in the violence that is in process here in the bare and weedy outskirts of this bare and brutal town; all this also in its hard, slack, nearly speechless, sullen-eyed way, is dancelike and triumphal: the big blank surfaces of corrugated metal, bright and sick as gas in the sunlight, square their darkness round a shuddering racket that subsumes all easy speaking: the tenant gets his ticket and his bale number, and waits his turn in the long quiet line; the wagon ahead is emptied and moves forward lightly as the mule is cut; he cuts his own load heavily under as the gin head is hoisted; he reaches up for the suction pipe and they let it down to him; he swings and cradles its voracity down through the crest of and round and round his stack of cotton, until the last lint has leapt up from the wagon bed; and all the while the gin is working in the deafening appetites of its metals, only it is his work the gin is digesting now, and standing so close in next its flank, he is intimate with this noise of great energy, cost and mystery; and out at the rear, the tin and ghostly interior of the seed shed, against whose roof and rafters a pipe extends a steady sleet of seed and upon all whose interior surfaces and all the air a dry nightmare fleece like the false snows of Christmas movies hangs shuddering as it might in horror of its just accomplished parturition: and out in front, the last of the cotton snowlike relaxing in pulses down a slide of dark iron into the compress its pure whiteness; and a few moments merely of pressure under the floor level, the air of an off-stage strangling; and the bale is lifted like a theater organ, the presses unlatched, the numbered brass tag attached, the metal ties made fast: it hangs in the light breathing of the scales, his bale, the one he has made, and a little is slivered from it, and its weight and staple length are recorded on his ginning slip, and it is caught with the hooks and tumbled out of the way, his bale of cotton, depersonalized forever now, identical with all others, which shall be melted indistinguishably into an oblivion of fabrics, wounds, bleedings, and wars; he takes his ginning slip to his land-lord, and gets his cottonseed money, and does a little buying; and gathers his family together; and leaves town. The exodus from town is even more formal than the parade in was. It has taken almost exactly eighteen minutes to gin each bale, once the waiting was over, and each tenant has done almost exactly the same amount of business afterward, and the empty, light grinding wagons are dis-tributed along the roads in a likewise exact collaboration of time and space apart, that is, the time consumed by ginning plus busi-ness, and the space apart which, in that time, a mule traverses at his classic noctambular pace. It is as if those who were drawn in full by the sun and their own effort and sucked dry at a metal heart were restored, were sown once more at large upon the slow breadths of their country, in the precisions of some mechanic and super-human hand.

That is repeated as many times as you have picked a bale. Your field is combed over three, four or five times. The height of the ginning season in that part of the country is early October, and in that time the loaded wagons are on the road before the least crack of daylight, the waiting is endless hours, and the gin is still pulsing and beating after dark. After that comes hogkilling, and the gristing of the corn and milling of the sorghum that were planted late to come ready late; and more urgent and specific meditation of whether or not to move to another man, and of whether you are to be kept; and settlement time; and the sky descends, the air becomes like dark glass, the ground stiffens, the clay honeycombs with frost, the corn and the cotton stand stripped to the naked bone and the trees are black, the odors of pork and woodsmoke sharpen all over the country, the long dark silent sleeping rains stream down in such grieving as nothing shall ever stop, and the houses are cold, fragile drums, and the animals tremble, and the clay is one shapeless sea, and winter has shut.

QUESTIONS FOR STUDY, DISCUSSION, AND WRITING

1. In his first paragraph Agee personifies cotton by alluding to its royalty: what other hints of this personification appear in this paragraph? In the same paragraph he speaks of the tenants'

"automatism" and the destruction of "the centers of individuals."
What is he asserting about the relation between cotton and the
people who raise it? What does his concluding picture of the
cotton gin add to this assertion?

2. Why would Agee's piece be a valuable document for a future
historian of the American South? How does it compare with
Cash's historical discussion of southern society ("Reconstruction
and the Southern Quandary," pp. 886–894)? Which of the two
has the larger scope?

3. Agee offers a clear, detailed description of cotton farming, yet
his language is certainly not the plain, neutral language we expect
of how-to-do-it books. Examine a fairly long passage and note
Agee's peculiarities of vocabulary and sentence structure. What
do they suggest about the man?

4. Are contemporary, urban families as dominated by their economic
function as the tenant farmers Agee describes?

WILLIAM MARCH

The Slave and the Cart Horse

A slave who had been beaten by his master came to the hut where
his wife waited for him. He lay on a pallet, while the woman took a
basin and filled it with water. He spoke after a time, answering the
question his wife did not dare ask him: "It happened while I was
working in the fields, near sunset. They had overloaded one of the
cart horses, and the poor creature was hardly able to stand up. They
were beating him with a whip, and although he was pulling with all
his strength, he wasn't able to move the load out of the ruts in the
field."

"Speak softer," said his wife. "The master might pass and hear
you."

The slave lowered his voice and continued: "So I went to the
master and told him that the horse couldn't carry such a load, and
I asked him to take some of it off."

"Speak softer," said the woman. She bent over the slave and bathed
his back with wet rags. "Speak softer. They'll whip you again if they
hear what you're saying."

The slave got up and went to the door, to see that there was nobody
outside; then he came and lay once more on the pallet. "I can't stand
to see a horse cruelly treated. Horses always seem so helpless and
pitiful to me."

When the woman spoke, her voice was so soft that it hardly carried
to her husband's ears. "You did right," she said. "Horses aren't like
us. They can't express themselves or stand up for their rights, and
they have no way of defending themselves, like we have."

Then they looked into each others' eyes and sighed, thinking how fortunate they were and how cruelly horses were used, for no man can see his own misery clearly, and that is God's great mercy to us all.

BRUNO BETTELHEIM
Imaginary Impasse[1]

Certainly the fear that ours is an age of neurosis haunts modern man, and adds to his personal unhappiness. Feeling acutely the discomforts of our civilization he grows discontented with it and often overlooks the fact that each age and society has its typical conflicts, its typical forms of discomfort and hence of neurosis. Concerned as we are with the difficulties we encounter in our civilization, we worry about those of its features that make for anxiety and mental illness. But in a hunting society it is the hunter, much as he enjoys the hunt, who worries about falling prey himself, about being hunted down. That is the price he pays for living in a society based on hunting. The farmer has different fears to mar his life; he worries about sandstorms, drought and flood. Those are discomforts that go with an agricultural way of life.

Sometimes it seems that as society evolves, every step forward may reduce old discomforts but not all the old anxieties. At the same time, each new development seems to bring new anxieties to add on to old and still active ones. These new fears coming with each higher step in social growth seem to develop in a continuum from animate to inanimate to abstract. The hunter must be wary of human enemies and wild animals; the farmer adds the vagaries of climate to his fear of hostile creatures. All these together plague modern man, whose civilization aggravates the old fear of animate and inanimate dangers by compounding them with anxieties about abstract or symbolic issues like morals.

The modern mother still has the age old fears for her own survival and the physical well being of her child; but now, much as she enjoys motherhood, she is also haunted by the fear of being a failure as a mother. In brief, whatever forms the essence of our life's activity also tends to become its most pervasive fear. In the machine age man is afraid of being robbed of his humanity by his own handiwork, the machine; witness the social fear of the evils of mass society and the psychological anxiety about losing one's identity.

As early as a century ago, a poet voiced this anxiety when confronted with the new industrial age. Heine, on visiting England, remarked: "The perfection of machinery, which is applied to every-

1. Chapter 1 of *The Informed Heart*, 1960.

thing there, and has superseded so many human functions, has for me something dismal; this artificial life on wheels, bars, cylinders, and a thousand little hooks, pins, and teeth which move almost passionately, fills me with horror. I was annoyed no less by the definiteness, the precision, the strictness, in the life of the English; for just as the machines in England seem to have the perfection of men, so the men seemed like machines. Yes, wood, iron, and brass seem to have usurped the human mind there, and to have gone almost mad from fulness of mind, while the mindless man, like a hollow ghost, exercises his ordinary duties in a machine-like fashion."

I do not know what the ancient nomad felt as he watched others settling down to agriculture in slow steps. Maybe he could not have put into similar words his feelings of anxiety as he watched those of his fellow men who gave up, for greater economic ease and security, a relative freedom to roam. But the modern Arab nomad certainly pities those who gave up their condition of freedom to settle down to the comforts that agriculture could give them. He feels that the only truly human existence is to be free as the wind. Strangely enough the desert wind, which is his symbol of freedom, is also the curse of the nomad who can scarcely protect himself against it. Still he is right; a certain bondage comes with settling down, certain freedoms and satisfactions have to be given up to win some comforts and a measure of security.

However it may have been in other times, modern man suffers from his inability to make a choice, as he sees it, between renouncing freedom and individualism, or giving up the material comforts of modern technology and the security of a collective mass society. This, as I see it, is the true conflict of our times.

Compared with this central conflict those individual neuroses based on a denial of the problem are peripheral. They are of minor importance, even though they plague many people today. Such denial may take the form of asserting individuality at all cost, as the Bohemian does, or of giving up all individuality in a wholly other directed adjustment—this "other," likely as not, being the requirements of technology and a life geared to further it.

When confronted with this seeming impasse, instead of examining to see if any new types of analysis, new techniques, new attitudes can resolve it, the Bohemian or the extremely other directed man has a tendency to deny that an impasse exists by his neurotic and essentially simple minded choice. Many who are less disturbed and less extreme try to escape it by rushing off in one single direction or an entirely different direction, in short by evasive maneuvers. Some of them, in psychoanalytic terms, are relying on repression, others are acting out or regressing, again others suffer from delusions.

Denying the Problem

Alcoholism is a graphic example of how society showed one such irrational attitude in dealing with a social impasse. Faced with the predicament of alcoholism, the U.S. decided to legislate the whole problem out of existence. Like repression on an individual basis, this denial of the complexity of the problem, and the suppression based on it, not only failed to solve the problem, but had even less desirable results. The body politic, weakened by the repressive maneuver, was invaded by criminality, violence, and sometimes even worse forms of alcoholism. Although the prohibition law was abolished, we are still not quite rid of the after effects of this attempt at a nation-wide repression, since the crime syndicates are still with us.

This example falls far short of making a difficult point about the machine age. No one yet has seriously asked that we prohibit mechanical contrivances, although repression was suggested by imaginative authors such as Butler in *Erewhon*. More often there is just a tendency to deny that the problem exists. Or else, like the person suffering addiction, our society seems to be rushing ahead unthinking into an ever greater mechanization of life, expecting more extensive technology to solve the problems it creates. Here we operate like the alcoholic who tries to escape from his hangover by going on a new binge.

Another evasive maneuver, that of escape into primitivism, is symbolized by those men of the machine age who are so discontented that they look for comfort to simpler types of civilization. These, being centered on a different life activity, do not know the dis-content of our machine-made culture. Captivated by this alone, they overlook the fact that earlier civilizations suffer, in their turn, from discontents inherent in their own mode of life.

For example, many intellectuals now look for comfort to what seem like the simple beliefs of their forefathers. In doing so, they may only acquire new fears about hell and damnation, without necessarily getting the emotional relief their forefathers got from re-vival meetings.

Nor will twentieth century man find a cozy home in an eighteenth century setting. If we are beset by the neurotic consequences of a toilet training based on the odium of dirt and smell, we will not find relief by living in the stench of dung-heaps and outhouses in a colonial Williamsburg. A restored Williamsburg, sporting modern plumbing, sewers and running water, is a nice weekend plaything but no abode for man of the technical age.[2]

Wistful side glances at the comforts of other civilizations will

2. I owe the example of Williamsburg to Daniel J. Boorstin's perceptive "Past and Present in America," *Commentary*, 25, January, 1958. Boorstin also points out that Williamsburg only became fully popular after a vast motel with a swimming pool, etc., was added [Bettelheim's note].

only distort our views, and interfere with finding a viable solution to the problems of our culture. The pleasures of hunting, diverting as they may be, will not heal the damage man can incur in a technological age. Nor will leisure time activities do away with bad features of the machine age; at best they can make us forget for stretches of time, and seduce us into avoiding the search for redress. Repeated honeymoon trips will not save a bad marriage by improving what is wrong with it, but may lead to its continuing without purpose and in growing discomfort.

The way to avoid the machine taking command is not to take more and longer vacations from a life dominated by machines, or from a machine regulated existence. The solution lies in finding ways to make this an age where humanity dominates despite the usefulness of machines, and to do this by making fullest use of their convenience. While every civilization creates its own type of discomforts and the emotional disturbances germane to it, it must also find its own solutions, both to the real needs of man and the neurotic ones typical for the age. Unless we keep this simple fact in mind, we may advocate remedies having no bearing on the special needs and stresses that ail man and society at any particular time.

To survive well under the preaching of hellfire and damnation, we need a correlary belief in revival and salvation. What is needed to survive well in the modern machine age, with its alienation of man from man and man from nature—that is the question we face in our own times. To this question I do not pretend to have discovered final answers. But the struggle to approach a solution to some of its aspects is what binds this book together.

Unwitting Bondage

In my daily work with psychotic children,[3] and in my efforts to create an institutional setting that will induce them to return to sanity, I have come face to face with this problem of how to take best advantage of all the conveniences of a technological age, of all that modern science offers toward the understanding and well being of man, and to do it without entering a bondage to science and technology.

At no time did it occur to us that we could do more or better without the "machines." On the contrary, by using them judiciously we managed to live a freer life than is possible without them. To say this may seem to belabor the obvious. After all the machine was invented to free life of bondage. But things are not quite so simple.

Whenever we introduced a new technological convenience, we had to examine its place in the life of our institution most carefully. The advantages we could enjoy from any new machine were always quite

---

3. At the Orthogenic School of the University of Chicago.

obvious; the bondage we entered by using it was much harder to assess, and much more elusive. Often we were unaware of its negative effects until after long use. By then we had come to rely on it so much, that small disadvantages that came with the use of any one contrivance seemed too trivial to warrant giving it up, or to change the pattern we had fallen into by using it. Nevertheless, when combined with the many other small disadvantages of all the other devices, it added up to a significant and undesirable change in the pattern of our life and work.

This is what I mean by "seduction." The advantages of the machines are so obvious and so desirable, that we tend to become, small step by small step, seduced into ignoring the price we pay for their unthinking use. The emphasis here is on *unthinking* use, because they all have their good uses. But the most careful thinking and planning is needed to enjoy the good use of any technical contrivance without paying a price for it in human freedom.

If an example were needed, TV is certainly a case in point. Much has been said about the contents of television programs. But my concern here is less with content and much more with what persistent watching does to a child's ability to relate to real people, to become self activating, to think on the basis of his own life experience instead of in stereotypes out of shows.

Many children, four to six years of age, communicate mainly in terms of their favorite shows and relate much better to the TV screen than to their parents. Some of them seem unable to respond any more to the simple and direct language of their parents because it sounds unimpressive compared to the suave diction and emotionally loaded idiom of TV professionals. True, for such far reaching consequences, not only the children, but their parents have to spend too much time in front of the set, or talk so little to each other that their adult conversation cannot offset the talking down or overemphatic voices of the programs.

Children who have been taught, or conditioned, to listen passively most of the day to the warm verbal communications coming from the TV screen, to the deep emotional appeal of the so-called TV personality, are often unable to respond to real persons because they arouse so much less feeling than the skilled actor. Worse, they lose the ability to learn from reality because life experiences are more complicated than the ones they see on the screen, and there is no one who comes in at the end to explain it all. The "TV child," expecting events in his own life to follow in sequence with a beginning, a middle and a predictable solution, all of it explained and made plain by one of the chief actors (as in Westerns) or by a master of ceremonies (as in comedies) ends up feeling discouraged because life is too complicated. Conditioned to being given explanations, he has not learned to puzzle for one on his own; he gets discouraged when he cannot grasp the meaning of what happens to him and is thrown back once more to find comfort in predictable stories on the screen.

If, later in life, this block of solid inertia is not removed, the emotional isolation from others that starts in front of TV may continue in school. Eventually it leads, if not to a permanent inability, then a reluctance to becoming active in learning or in relations to other people. By adolescence, this inability to relate is apt to have even more serious consequences because then the pressure of sexual emotions begins to unsettle a personality that has never learned to internalize or sublimate them, or to satisfy them through personal relations.

This being seduced into passivity and discouraged about facing life actively, on one's own, is the real danger of TV, much more than the often asinine or gruesome content of the shows. But "TV passivity" is only one aspect of the over-all "let the machines do it."

Despite all this, I am by no means suggesting that we do away with the TV sets in our homes. But if we wish to enjoy their advantages without paying too high a price, we too will have to take action. If we let our children watch TV passively we must at other times provide them with active experiences, and not just physical activity. They must be helped to experience life directly, to learn to draw conclusions and to take a stand on their own, not to accept whatever is told them as correct.

Maybe something less controversial than TV can make the point more concretely: I cannot imagine a housewife not being glad to come by a dishwashing machine. But for some couples the electric dishwasher eliminated the one thing they did together every day; one of them washed while the other dried. As one woman put it, she now enjoys not only less fatigue but a pure gift of time. Yet she added wistfully, "But it *was* cozy, just the two of us together for that little while every night, after we got the kids to bed."

This necessary chore brought husband and wife together. Obviously having a dishwasher is preferable to having to do them by hand, and more hygienic, to boot. The comfortable intimacy that went with the chore was hardly noticed until it vanished. But just as obviously, the arrival of this machine in the home meant the couple would have to find some other occasion for spending their brief while together. Only then would the machine truly add, not detract from their lives with each other. This, as I say, is obvious. But in how many families does this "obvious" become an actuality?

At the Orthogenic School we had no choice here. Prodded by necessities that grew out of our task, we found it quite possible to create and keep going, in this time and age, an institution that made use of the most up to date science and technology without entering into compromise with them. What made it easier to avoid errors was the realization that struck us again and again, of how much neurotic symptoms and their causes can tell us about what is apt to disturb the individual in a particular civilization. Realizing this helped us to eliminate from our setting such obstacles to human freedom and spontaneity.

Delusions for Moderns

While any neurotic or psychotic breakdown is rooted in the inner difficulties of man, the outer form it may take, that is the external symptoms, reflect back the nature of the society. Psychotic disturbances are particularly revealing, perhaps because of the extreme anxiety they are based on, and the total breakdown in functioning they signify and are meant to overcome. Often their exaggerations show up more clearly what ails all of us in some measure at present, and warn us of things to come. Far more than neurotic behavior, they can also inform us about which forces an age looks to for solving the difficulties it is failing to master.

In the Middle Ages when a man could not deal with the problems before him and escaped into a world of delusion, he felt possessed by devils. But once possessed, he took comfort in the thought that he might be saved by the heavenly intercession of angels or saints. At all times and in all civilizations there are persons who feel possessed or persecuted by outside forces they feel are beyond them. We recognize that this need to ascribe inner conflict to some external force arises when the individual feels he cannot solve the difficulty within his own psyche. It is less well understood that what he feels possessed by tells us a great deal about what features of society disturb him.

Sexual seduction by the devil is not often experienced unless utter chastity is required by the mores, and accepted by the individual as an inner goal to strive for. So the delusional belief that it requires a devil to seduce a woman reflects an inner standard of chastity so stringent that it takes a superhuman power (bad demons) to break it down. But the same delusion shows what forces the society looks to (good demons) for settling inner contradictions it seems unable to deal with.

In another time and age it was the great man that people turned to for solutions to their difficulties. A prevalence of the megalomanic delusion of being Napoleon, etc., tells us that an age was looking to the great man to solve its difficulties. Angels and devils were no longer superhuman, but seen in the image of man. Yet the great man is only the apotheosis of the average man. Even if a person feels "hounded" as we say, the image of his persecutor is still a dog or some other living creature. But what of a time that trusts neither angels nor great men to solve its problems, but only mechanical "brains" or guided missiles?

Modern man no longer seeks his nirvana, his escape from the

unsolvable problems of life, in heaven, but in outer space. To the extent that he relies for security on guided missiles and nuclear fusion, the fear of atomic bombs must haunt him.

What is so new in the hopes and fears of the machine age are that savior and destroyer are no longer clothed in the image of man; no longer are the figures that we imagine can save and destroy us direct projections of our human image. What we now hope will save us, is something that no longer has human qualities.[4]

This new development has other aspects. Formerly it was not just that savior and destroyer were clad in human likeness, it was also that they were conceived as supernatural or at least superior to man, never as man's servants. Machines and scientific discoveries, on the other hand, were and are conceived of as rational creations of man, existing only for man's use. The transition from the useful but mindless machine to the manipulator if not the killer of man is viewed not as a change in kind, but a change in quantity or degree.

A typical example is what (for good reasons) was first given a name in Germany: the *Karteimensch*, freely translated as punch-card-existence. The punch card, with the sorting machine that makes it useful, seems to turn each of us into a mere conglomeration of useful characteristics. Singly, or in certain combinations, these traits allow persons in control to use us first and foremost as owners of such traits, and only incidentally (if at all) as total persons.

A probably apocryphal story in *The New Yorker* illustrates the point better than any long discussion. There we are told that after a lady's subscription to a book club ran out, she discontinued it. Nevertheless she continued to get a punch card at regular intervals with the request to send in payments, though none were due. She repeatedly returned the card with notes explaining that she had dropped out and did not owe anything. Still the cards continued to come in the mail, until one day she took her son's punch and punched a few holes in the punch card. That settled it; she was no longer bothered. The machine-run organization could respond best to a machine-like reply.

This is an amusing story. But our readiness to obey requests not to fold or bend a punch card should give us pause. Most of us do not hesitate to fold or bend a personal handwritten letter; we treat the machine and its requirements with greater respect. I realize that a

4. The rational argument that the atomic bomb really can destroy, while the devil was a relatively harmless fantasy is fallacious. When the devil was real to people, he destroyed hapless victims just as the bomb does. Those burned at the stakes because they or their fellow men believed in the devil died no imaginary death; they were as dead as the victims of atomic warfare. The prophecy of the world coming to an end in the year 1000 was not only as widespread, but led to more suicides, percentage-wise, than our fear of atomic bombs destroying the world. In a religious age, man believed and feared out of religious knowledge: namely, the 1000th anniversary of Christ's birth. In a scientific age, man fears on the basis of scientific knowledge: the atomic bomb [Bettelheim's note].

valid answer is that we do not expect a machine to be able to adapt itself to human vagaries. But it still augurs poorly for a future when more and more we will have to react to punch cards and less and less to handwritten letters, inquiries or even paychecks. Not being able to react freely (with folding if we like) to such items, interferes with our general ability to react spontaneously. The more we have to keep our spontaneity in check when responding, the more extinct it may become for lack of use.

This, again, is a minor example of how a mechanical device, invented strictly to simplify tasks and save human labor, forces human beings to conform to the requirements of the machine. A change in the *degree* of difficulty in decision making seems to have changed the *nature* of the decision making process and deprived it of its human qualities. It is so much easier to route a punch card, or the number it corresponds to, than it is to direct a person. Many manipulations of men that would ordinarily arouse great resistance in the manipulator, if not open refusal, are carried out without qualms, because all the manipulator has to do is feed anonymous cards into a pre-set sorting machine. Once the cards are sorted out, it seems so simple to assign tasks to men and women whom the machine sort indicates are best suited for them. This is very different from deciding whether you, the reader, or I myself should be discharged from our jobs or sent on a difficult mission.

In a strange psychological process persons who are viewed by those in authority as numbers on punch cards, tend to view themselves as numbers rather than persons, unless they deliberately guard against it. As G. H. Mead has pointed out, the image others have of us also shapes our own image of ourselves. Psychoanalysis indicates that whatever the rational causes of an action, they also have an unconscious meaning. However rational the use of punch cards— and it is a purposeful, rational way of doing things, avoiding errors due to human shortcomings or the pressure of time—it also has irrational, unconscious effects.

Here, as in many other cases, the answer is neither to do away with the punch card and its proven advantages, nor to submit to seeing ourselves and others as the punch card describes us. The answer again is what psychoanalysis prescribes for restoring the disturbed individual to fuller human functioning: not to deny or neglect the dangers of a situation; not to run away from it by destroying it and depriving oneself of its advantages; but to realize the dangers and meet them with conscious action based on personal decision. This neutralizes the danger, and lets us enjoy the advantages of technology without letting it deprive us of our humanity.

In the same context, and again according to psychoanalytic theory, whatever the rational causes of an invention, there is also an unconscious meaning and origin.[5] If this is so, then if machines are invented for their usefulness, their invention too is unconsciously influenced by the inventor who externalizes and projects either his whole body, or isolated parts of it. Maybe with even greater specialization of the mechanical process, it will happen less and less often that the whole body and its functions or movements will be the unconscious starting point for the inventor's imagination. More and more often will an isolated part of the body or an isolated bodily function serve as the unconscious underpinning for the rational process of designing new machinery.

In modern mass production we find a human corollary. There the worker is often viewed, and views himself, as being a "cog" in the machine rather than someone who runs it. He repeats a few isolated work tasks, is theoretically unable to deal with or shape the whole productive process, never confronts the end product or end decision, or only in a manner incidental to his work.[6]

Just as modern machines can no longer be recognized as obvious extensions of our bodily organs, or as performing bodily functions more efficiently—though that may have been their origin—so in modern delusions we find more and more nonhuman projections. For example, a characteristic feature of modern insanity is the "influencing machine," a device that supposedly puts thoughts into a person's head as if they were his own, or forces him to act against his conscious will.

As one might expect, the influencing machine as a form of delusion appeared only after electrical machines were not only a basic feature of daily life, but also what many looked to as the answer to important social problems. Today, when man turns so often to the psychological skills with his personal problems, we should expect some delusions to take the form of feeling overpowered by psychological influences against one's knowledge or will. The term "brainwashing" and the widespread notion that thoughts and convictions can be put into a person's mind by psychological techniques—as well as the irrational anxiety this evokes in some people—suggest that

5. H. Sachs, "The Delay of the Machine Age," *Psychoanalytic Quarterly, 2,* 1933, pp. 404 ff [Bettelheim's note].

6. I do not know whether and to what degree automation will change this by freeing the worker from having to repeat the same task over and over again. It should certainly do away with much drudgery in the productive process. But as less of man's labor will be needed for survival, more of his time and energy will become available for other tasks. Unless he finds ways to expend this time and energy on tasks deeply meaningful to him, his personal agony will increase to the degree that less of his physical and mental energies go to assuring survival for himself and his family. It is relatively easy to find life meaningful if most of one's energy is constructively spent in securing the essentials of living for oneself and one's own. It is quite difficult to find that much meaning in less essential, or less obviously meaningful tasks. We can all derive a great deal of self respect and deep satisfaction from the knowledge that we are helping others and ourselves survive; very little meaning can be wrung from the ability to provide ourselves and others with ever less essential conveniences [Bettelheim's note].

we have reached such a point. An intensified belief in the "saving" and destructive powers of psychology has thus replaced saints, devils and even influencing machines, as the preferred content of delusional feelings of helplessness, of being overpowered and manipulated against one's will.

It can be shown that the influencing machine, too, began as a projection of the human body,[7] but the essential point is that it does not retain this image; it becomes ever more complex and the psychotic person ends up feeling controlled by mechanical devices that no longer resemble anything human or even animal-like. Thus modern man, when he is haunted, whether sane or profoundly disturbed, is no longer haunted by other men or by grandiose projections of man, but by machines. This, while at the same time relying for his protection or salvation on machines.

Machine Gods

These developments are often expressed in popular science fiction, the prefabricated daydreams of a technological age. If the machine can do so much, man by contrast can do so little. Some of the earliest philosophers recognized that if pigs and cows had gods, they would conceive them as glorified, godlike pigs or cows. The characteristics they would ascribe to them would be the ones found or desired in themselves, only magnified and made perfect. A man created in God's image, or a god created in man's image, no less than a devil created in man's image, tells us much about the fears and aspirations of man. A machine god thus tells us about the fears and aspirations of man in a machine age. If we look at science fiction in this perspective, we find it concentrating on "problems of space and time; the individual's sense of reality and identity; problems of prolonged isolation and individual existence in mortal combat with machines."[8]

Compared with other popular daydream material such as the Western—with its fantasies of sexual and aggressive desires being acted out and conflicts around them being dealt with—the modern scientific daydream, contrary to the highly developed technology we live in, deals with more primitive emotional problems. For example, space ships are completely enclosed structures in which the person is immobilized and isolated for long periods of time; all his needs are provided for, as with the human foetus. Problems of living in space, of gravity, disturbances of equilibrium, orientation, and locomotion—all these are important elements in the infant's struggles

7. See V. Tausk, "On the Origin of the 'Influencing Machine' in Schizophrenia," *The Psychoanalytic Quarterly*, 2, 1933, pp. 519 ff; M. R. Kaufman, "Some Clinical Data on Ideas of Reference," *ibid.*, 1, 1932, pp. 265 ff; L. Linn, "Some Comments on the Origin of the Influencing Machine," *Journal of the American Psychoanalytic Association*, 6, 1958, pp. 305 ff [Bettelheim's note].

8. E. P. Bernabeu, "Science Fiction," *The Psychoanalytic Quarterly*, 26, 1957, pp. 527 ff [Bettelheim's note].

with orientation, equilibrium, and movement.

Ideas about the limitless quality of space and the magnitude of once unimagined dangers also lead to feelings of insignificance and a dread of losing one's identity. It seems that if we project our wishful and anxious fantasies not on manlike objects but on complex machinery we run the risk of losing our psychological identity as man. Whether we do or not seems to depend on our ability to conjure up images that are bigger but not radically different from man.

Others who have approached the same phenomena differently have reached similar conclusions: "Comparison of these [science fiction] myths indicates that the dazzling speed of technological innovation in the present generation has psychological effects to which the rapidly increasing vogue of science fiction may give some tentative clues. In an age in which mechanical 'brains,' satellites, and flights to other planets exist, or are impending realities, the fantasies of science are vehicles for expression of far greater anxieties and more deeply regressive defenses even than those which evoked the demigods, devils, and witches of other times."[9]

I am no expert on science fiction, so I may be in error here; but it seems that this type of escape literature appeals to many educated and discriminating persons, including serious scientists. There also seems little doubt that some of the more startling of recent scientific developments were anticipated in these writings. What is interesting here is less the authors' acuteness about future scientific developments, than about the developments in man they may bring about. Apparently, authors who can anticipate new mastery over nature are also able to foresee what such progress may do to man. Or to bring it closer to what interests me here, those whose hopes lie in the extreme outposts of science are haunted by equal anxieties about how this may spell the destruction of man.

Since science fiction presents as already achieved what the authors hope for and dread about the future, the accompanying changes in man are also described as already existing. And the heroes of these stories abound in nonhuman qualities. Their depersonalization is often symbolized by their names, such as Og, or M-331, by an absence or disregard for their bodies, and by a lack of intimate human relations. More important, to the degree that the stories abound in marvels of progress, they also entail fantasies of world destruction. In some stories, after the robots or whatnot have destroyed man, they recreate him. But usually this is done synthetically, not by refashioning man in his own image, through procreation. Love relations are virtually absent; most of the heroes are basically minds without a body. Apparently science fiction writers, though motivated by a desire for scientific progress, seem to feel that the in-

9. Bernabeu, *loc. cit.* [Bettelheim's note].

herent danger of such progress is an end to our biological existence as man.

A Reasonable Thing to Do

Nevertheless, while our progress can be measured by the fact that the machine is clearly recognized as the servant of man and not his better, the fear is now widespread that it could become our master. Since this is so, we must understand those potentials within us that we project into the machine, and which could make it our master in reality as it already is in our delusions. To escape into anxious nightmares and condemn the machine will not do, whether we frighten ourselves with brave new worlds or with 1984.

The modern schizophrenic enslaved by his influencing machines is no worse nor much better off (short of access to psychotherapy) than was medieval man who felt persecuted by the devil. But we were saved from former evils not by believing in angels but by creating modern science. What we now have to face is the potential evil of the machine, though its sole origin is the image of the machine in man's mind. From this exploration we must then draw a lesson about what needs to be done to prevent the machine from overpowering us.

In closing this chapter, I want to return to some initial remarks. The seeming impasse of having to give up freedom to gain comfort, as it confronted the early farmer, is basically the same one alluded to when we moderns speak of our civilization and its discontents. We can state and accept the truism that every way of life has its own discomforts, and leave it there. We can bemoan this fact and condemn civilization. Or we can do the only reasonable thing: arrange our lives so that the comforts of civilization are so used as to reduce discontents to a minimum, while securing for each citizen the maximum possible of human satisfactions. When posed as a dilemma between freedom and bondage, the impasse is insoluble. This is how the Arab nomad poses it who can find no alternative except to choose freedom with discomfort and insecurity, or bondage with discontent and more security. And this is how modern man, worried about the machine age, about mass society and the danger of atomic destruction, still poses the problem too often.

A solution can be found only by opposing inner to outer freedom; emotional freedom to the freedom to roam or discharge aggression. The greatest danger of our machine made wealth grows out of this: that for the first time we are living in an age when material comfort is possible for almost everyone. But if this, because it is so much more available, is sought not in addition to emotional contentment but in lieu of it, then there is danger of our becoming addicted to it. We will need more and more technological progress to cover up our emotional want and discomfort. This, as I see it, is the only danger of the machine age. But it is neither necessary nor inherent in it.

QUESTIONS FOR STUDY, DISCUSSION, AND WRITING

1. What is the imaginary impasse? How does Bettelheim suggest that we deal with it?
2. On page 455 Bettelheim refers to his experience as a child psychiatrist. What does he draw from this experience that opens up his approach to the imaginary impasse and provides the crucial transition in his discussion of it?
3. On page 463 Bettelheim discusses the appeal of science fiction. How does he explain this appeal? Science fiction is a particular instance of a general theory Bettelheim holds about what makes literature effective. Working from this particular, state the general theory. What would someone holding this theory say about the prospects for the change Mill wants to see in literature ("Civilization," pp. 335–353)?
4. Does Kennedy consider King Kong ("Who Killed King Kong?," below) from a similar theoretical viewpoint? What is the difference between Kennedy's approach to King Kong and Bettelheim's to science fiction?
5. Select a movie, a television program, or a piece of popular literature of proven appeal and try to account for that appeal. What line does your explanation take if you relate the appeal to neuroses as Bettelheim does?

X. J. KENNEDY

Who Killed King Kong?

The ordeal and spectacular death of King Kong, the giant ape, undoubtedly have been witnessed by more Americans than have ever seen a performance of *Hamlet*, *Iphigenia at Aulis*, or even *Tobacco Road*. Since RKO-Radio Pictures first released *King Kong*, a quarter-century has gone by; yet year after year, from prints that grow more rain-beaten, from sound tracks that grow more tinny, ticket-buyers by thousands still pursue Kong's luckless fight against the forces of technology, tabloid journalism, and the DAR. They see him chloroformed to sleep, see him whisked from his jungle isle to New York and placed on show, see him burst his chains to roam the city (lugging a frightened blonde), at last to plunge from the spire of the Empire State Building, machine-gunned by model airplanes.

Though Kong may die, one begins to think his legend unkillable. No clearer proof of his hold upon the popular imagination may be seen than what emerged one catastrophic week in March 1955, when New York WOR-TV programmed *Kong* for seven evenings in a row (a total of sixteen showings). Many a rival network vice-president must have scowled when surveys showed that *Kong*—the 1933 B-picture—had lured away fat segments of the viewing populace from such powerful competitors as Ed Sullivan, Groucho Marx and Bishop Sheen.

But even television has failed to run *King Kong* into oblivion. Coffee-in-the-lobby cinemas still show the old hunk of hokum, with the apology that in its use of composite shots and animated models the film remains technically interesting. And no other monster in movie history has won so devoted a popular audience. None of the plodding mummies, the stultified draculas, the white-coated Lugosis[1] with their shiny pinball-machine laboratories, none of the invisible stranglers, berserk robots, or menaces from Mars has ever enjoyed so many resurrections.

Why does the American public refuse to let King Kong rest in peace? It is true, I'll admit, that *Kong* outdid every monster movie before or since in sheer carnage. Producers Cooper and Schoedsack crammed into it dinosaurs, headhunters, riots, aerial battles, bullets, bombs, bloodletting. Heroine Fay Wray, whose function is mainly to scream, shuts her mouth for hardly one uninterrupted minute from first reel to last. It is also true that *Kong* is larded with good healthy sadism, for those whose joy it is to see the frantic girl dangled from cliffs and harried by pterodactyls. But it seems to me that the abiding appeal of the giant ape rests on other foundations.

Kong has, first of all, the attraction of being manlike. His simian nature gives him one huge advantage over giant ants and walking vegetables in that an audience may conceivably identify with him. Kong's appeal has the quality that established the Tarzan series as American myth—for what man doesn't secretly image himself a huge hairy howler against whom no other monster has a chance? If Tarzan recalls the ape in us, then Kong may well appeal to that great-granddaddy primordial brute from whose tribe we have all deteriorated.

Intentionally or not, the producers of *King Kong* encourage this identification by etching the character of Kong with keen sympathy. For the ape is a figure in a tradition familiar to moviegoers: the tradition of the pitiable monster. We think of Lon Chaney in the role of Quasimodo, of Karloff in the original *Frankenstein*. As we watch the Frankenstein monster's fumbling and disastrous attempts to befriend a flower-picking child, our sympathies are enlisted with the monster in his impenetrable loneliness. And so with Kong. As he roars in his chains, while barkers sell tickets to boobs who gape at him, we perhaps feel something more deep than pathos. We begin to sense something of the problem that engaged Eugene O'Neill in *The Hairy Ape*: the dilemma of a displaced animal spirit forced to live in a jungle built by machines.

King Kong, it is true, had special relevance in 1933. Landscapes of

1. Bela Lugosi, an actor in many horror movies.

the depression are glimpsed early in the film when an impresario, seeking some desperate pretty girl to play the lead in a jungle movie, visits souplines and a Woman's Home Mission. In Fay Wray—who's been caught snitching an apple from a fruitstand—his search is ended. When he gives her a big feed and a movie contract, the girl is magic-carpeted out of the world of the National Recovery Act. And when, in the film's climax, Kong smashes that very Third Avenue landscape in which Fay had wandered hungry, audiences of 1933 may well have felt a personal satisfaction.

What is curious is that audiences of 1960 remain hooked. For in the heart of urban man, one suspects, lurks the impulse to fling a bomb. Though machines speed him to the scene of his daily grind, though IBM comptometers ("freeing the human mind from drudgery") enable him to drudge more efficiently once he arrives, there comes a moment when he wishes to turn upon his machines and kick hell out of them. He wants to hurl his combination radio-alarmclock out the bedroom window and listen to its smash. What subway commuter wouldn't love—just for once—to see the downtown express smack head-on into the uptown local? Such a wish is gratified in that memorable scene in *Kong* that opens with a wide-angle shot: interior of a railway car on the Third Avenue El. Strap-hangers are nodding, the literate refold their newspapers. Unknown to them, Kong has torn away a section of trestle toward which the train now speeds. The motorman spies Kong up ahead, jams on the brakes. Passengers hurtle together like so many peas in a pail. In a window of the car appear Kong's bloodshot eyes. Women shriek. Kong picks up the railway car as if it were a rat, flips it to the street and ties knots in it, or something. To any commuter the scene must appear one of the most satisfactory pieces of celluloid ever exposed.

Yet however violent his acts, Kong remains a gentleman. Remarkable is his sense of chivalry. Whenever a fresh boa constrictor threatens Fay, Kong first sees that the lady is safely parked, then manfully thrashes her attacker. (And she, the ingrate, runs away every time his back is turned.) Atop the Empire State Building, ignoring his pursuers, Kong places Fay on a ledge as tenderly as if she were a dozen eggs. He fondles her, then turns to face the Army Air Force. And Kong is perhaps the most disinterested lover since Cyrano: his attentions to the lady are utterly without hope of reward. After all, between a five-foot blonde and a fifty-foot ape, love can hardly be more than an intellectual flirtation. In his simian way King Kong is the hopelessly yearning lover of Petrarchan convention. His forced exit from his jungle, in chains, results directly from his single-minded pursuit of Fay. He smashes a Broadway theater when the notion enters his dull brain that the flashbulbs of photographers somehow endanger the lady. His perilous shinnying up a skyscraper to pluck Fay from her boudoir is an act of the kindliest of hearts. He's impossible to discourage even though the love of his life can't lay eyes on him without shrieking murder.

The tragedy of King Kong then, is to be the beast who at the end of the fable fails to turn into the handsome prince. This is the conviction that the scriptwriters would leave with us in the film's closing line. As Kong's corpse lies blocking traffic in the street, the enterpreneur who brought Kong to New York turns to the assembled reporters and proclaims: "That's your story, boys—it was Beauty killed the Beast!" But greater forces than those of the screaming Lady have combined to lay Kong low, if you ask me. Kong lives for a time as one of those persecuted near-animal souls bewildered in the middle of an industrial order, whose simple desires are thwarted at every turn. He climbs the Empire State Building because in all New York it's the closest thing he can find to the clifftop of his jungle isle. He dies, a pitiful dolt, and the army brass and publicity-men cackle over him. His death is the only possible outcome to as neat a tragic dilemma as you can ask for. The machine-guns do him in, while the manicured human hero (a nice clean Dartmouth boy) carries away Kong's sweetheart to the altar. O, the misery of it all. There's far more truth about upper-middle-class American life in King Kong than in the last seven dozen novels of John P. Marquand.

A Negro friend from Atlanta tells me that in movie houses in colored neighborhoods throughout the South, Kong does a constant business. They show the thing in Atlanta at least every year, presumably to the same audiences. Perhaps this popularity may simply be due to the fact that Kong is one of the most watchable movies ever constructed, but I wonder whether Negro audiences may not find some archetypical appeal in this serio-comic tale of a huge black powerful free spirit whom all the hardworking white policemen are out to kill.

Every day in the week on a screen somewhere in the world, King Kong relives his agony. Again and again he expires on the Empire State Building, as audiences of the devout assist his sacrifice. We watch him die, and by extension kill the ape within our bones, but these little deaths of ours occur in prosaic surroundings. We do not die on a tower, New York before our feet, nor do we give our lives to smash a few flying machines. It is not for us to bring to a momentary standstill the civilization in which we move. King Kong does this for us. And so we kill him again and again, in much-spliced celluloid, while the ape in us expires from day to day, obscure, in desperation.

On Literature and the Arts
Standards · Humor · Poetry

W. H. AUDEN
Reading[1]

> *A book is a mirror: if an ass peers into it, you can't expect an apostle to look out.*
>
> C. G. LICHTENBERG
>
> *One only reads well that which one reads with some quite personal purpose. It may be to acquire some power. It can be out of hatred for the author.*
>
> PAUL VALÉRY

The interests of a writer and the interests of his readers are never the same and if, on occasion, they happen to coincide, this is a lucky accident.

In relation to a writer, most readers believe in the Double Standard: they may be unfaithful to him as often as they like, but he must never, never be unfaithful to them.

To read is to translate, for no two persons' experiences are the same. A bad reader is like a bad translator: he interprets literally when he ought to paraphrase and paraphrases when he ought to interpret literally. In learning to read well, scholarship, valuable as it is, is less important than instinct; some great scholars have been poor translators.

We often derive much profit from reading a book in a different way from that which its author intended but only (once childhood is over) if we know that we are doing so.

As readers, most of us, to some degree, are like those urchins who pencil mustaches on the faces of girls in advertisements.

1. From the prologue to *The Dyer's Hand*, 1962.

One sign that a book has literary value is that it can be read in a number of different ways. Vice versa, the proof that pornography has no literary value is, that, if one attempts to read it in any other way than as a sexual stimulus, to read it, say, as a psychological case-history of the author's sexual fantasies, one is bored to tears.

Though a work of literature can be read in a number of ways, this number is finite and can be arranged in a hierarchical order; some readings are obviously "truer" than others, some doubtful, some obviously false, and some, like reading a novel backwards, absurd. That is why, for a desert island, one would choose a good dictionary rather than the greatest literary masterpiece imaginable, for, in relation to its readers, a dictionary is absolutely passive and may legitimately be read in an infinite number of ways.

We cannot read an author for the first time in the same way that we read the latest book by an established author. In a new author, we tend to see either only his virtues or only his defects and, even if we do see both, we cannot see the relation between them. In the case of an established author, if we can still read him at all, we know that we cannot enjoy the virtues we admire in him without tolerating the defects we deplore. Moreover, our judgment of an established author is never simply an aesthetic judgment. In addition to any literary merit it may have, a new book by him has a historic interest for us as the act of a person in whom we have long been interested. He is not only a poet or a novelist; he is also a character in our biography.

A poet cannot read another poet, nor a novelist another novelist, without comparing their work to his own. His judgments as he reads are of this kind: *My God! My Great-Grandfather! My Uncle! My Enemy! My Brother! My imbecile Brother!*

In literature, vulgarity is preferable to nullity, just as grocer's port is preferable to distilled water.

Good taste is much more a matter of discrimination than of exclusion, and when good taste feels compelled to exclude, it is with regret, not with pleasure.

Pleasure is by no means an infallible critical guide, but it is the least fallible.

A child's reading is guided by pleasure, but his pleasure is undifferentiated; he cannot distinguish, for example, between aesthetic pleasure and the pleasures of learning or daydreaming. In adolescence we realize that there are different kinds of pleasure, some of which cannot be enjoyed simultaneously, but we need help from others in defining them. Whether it be a matter of taste in food or taste in literature, the adolescent looks for a mentor in whose authority he can believe. He eats or reads what his mentor recommends and, inevitably, there are occasions when he has to deceive himself a little; he has to pretend that he enjoys olives or *War and Peace* a little more than he actually does. Between the ages of twenty and forty we are engaged in the process of discovering who we are, which involves learning the difference between accidental limitations which it is our duty to outgrow and the necessary limitations of our nature beyond which we cannot trespass with impunity. Few of us can learn this without making mistakes, without trying to become a little more of a universal man than we are permitted to be. It is during this period that a writer can most easily be led astray by another writer or by some ideology. When someone between twenty and forty says apropos of a work of art, "I know what I like," he is really saying "I have no taste of my own but accept the taste of my cultural milieu," because, between twenty and forty, the surest sign that a man has a genuine taste of his own is that he is uncertain of it. After forty, if we have not lost our authentic selves altogether, pleasure can again become what it was when we were children, the proper guide to what we should read.

JOSEPH CONRAD
Preface to *The Nigger of the "Narcissus"*[1]

A work that aspires, however humbly, to the condition of art should carry its justification in every line. And art itself may be defined as a single-minded attempt to render the highest kind of justice to the visible universe, by bringing to light the truth, manifold and one, underlying its every aspect. It is an attempt to find in its forms, in its colors, in its light, in its shadows, in the aspects of matter and in the facts of life, what of each is fundamental, what is enduring and essential—their one illuminating and convincing quality—the very truth of their existence. The artist, then, like the thinker or the scientist, seeks the truth and makes his appeal. Impressed by the aspect of the world the thinker plunges into ideas, the scientist into facts—whence, presently, emerging they make their appeal to those qualities of our being that fit us best for the hazardous enterprise of living. They speak authoritatively to our common-sense, to our intelligence, to our desire of peace or to our de-

---

1. *The Nigger of the "Narcissus,"* published in 1897, was Conrad's second novel. The Preface alludes in its fourth paragraph to that novel, but considered more generally it sets forth a major statement by Conrad of his conception of the art of fiction.

sire of unrest; not seldom to our prejudices, sometimes to our fears, often to our egoism—but always to our credulity. And their words are heard with reverence, for their concern is with weighty matters; with the cultivation of our minds and the proper care of our bodies: with the attainment of our ambitions: with the perfection of the means and the glorification of our precious aims.

It is otherwise with the artist.

Confronted by the same enigmatical spectacle the artist descends within himself, and in that lonely region of stress and strife, if he be deserving and fortunate, he finds the terms of his appeal. His appeal is made to our less obvious capacities: to that part of our nature which, because of the war-like conditions of existence, is necessarily kept out of sight within the more resisting and hard qualities—like the vulnerable body within a steel armor. His appeal is less loud, more profound, less distinct, more stirring—and sooner forgotten. Yet its effect endures forever. The changing wisdom of successive generations discards ideas, questions facts, demolishes theories. But the artist appeals to that part of our being which is not dependent on wisdom; to that in us which is a gift and not an acquisition—and, therefore, more permanently enduring. He speaks to our capacity for delight and wonder, to the sense of mystery surrounding our lives: to our sense of pity, and beauty, and pain: to the latent feeling of fellowship with all creation—and to the subtle but invincible, conviction of solidarity that knits together the loneliness of innumerable hearts to the solidarity in dreams, in joy, in sorrow, in aspirations, in illusions, in hope, in fear, which binds men to each other, which binds together all humanity—the dead to the living and the living to the unborn.

It is only some such train of thought, or rather of feeling, that can in a measure explain the aim of the attempt, made in the tale which follows, to present an unrestful episode in the obscure lives of a few individuals out of all the disregarded multitude of the bewildered, the simple and the voiceless. For, if there is any part of truth in the belief confessed above, it becomes evident that there is not a place of splendor or a dark corner of the earth that does not deserve, if only a passing glance of wonder and pity. The motive, then, may be held to justify the matter of the work; but this preface, which is simply an avowal of endeavor, cannot end here—for the avowal is not yet complete.

Fiction—if it at all aspires to be art—appeals to temperament. And in truth it must be, like painting, like music, like all art, the appeal of one temperament to all the other innumerable temperaments whose subtle and resistless power endows passing events with their true meaning, and creates the moral, the emotional atmosphere of the place and time. Such an appeal to be effective must be an impression conveyed through the senses; and, in fact, it cannot be made in any other way, because temperament, whether individual or collective, is not amenable to persuasion. All art, therefore, appeals primarily to the senses, and the artistic aim when expressing itself in written words must also make its appeal through the senses, if its high desire is to reach the secret spring of responsive emotions. It must strenuously aspire to the plasticity of sculpture, to the color of painting, and to the magic suggestiveness of music—which is the art of arts. And it is only through complete, unswerving devotion to the perfect blending of form and substance; it is only through an unremitting never-discouraged care for the shape and ring of sentences that an approach can be made to plasticity, to color; and the light of magic suggestiveness may be brought to play for an evanescent instant over the commonplace surface of words; of the old, old words, worn thin, defaced by ages of careless usage.

The sincere endeavor to accomplish that creative task, to go as far on that road as his strength will carry him, to go undeterred by faltering, weariness or reproach, is the only valid justification for the worker in prose. And if his conscience is clear, his answer to those who, in the fullness of a wisdom which looks for immediate profit, demand specifically to be edified, consoled, amused; who demand to be promptly improved, or encouraged, or frightened, or shocked, or charmed, must run thus: My task which I am trying to achieve is, by the power of the written word, to make you hear, to make you feel—it is, before all, to make you *see*. That—and no more, and it is everything. If I succeed, you shall find there according to your deserts: encouragement, consolation, fear, charm—all you demand and, perhaps, also that glimpse of truth for which you have forgotten to ask.

To snatch in a moment of courage, from the remorseless rush of time, a passing phase of life, is only the beginning of the task. The task approached in tenderness and faith is to hold up unquestioningly, without choice and without fear, the rescued fragment before all eyes and in the light of a sincere mood. It is to show its vibration, its color, its form; and through its movement, its form, and its color, reveal the substance of its truth—disclose its inspiring secret: the stress and passion within the core of each convincing moment. In a single-minded attempt of that kind, if one be deserving and fortunate, one may perchance attain to such clearness of sincerity that at last the presented vision of regret or pity, of terror or mirth, shall awaken in the hearts of the beholders that feeling of unavoidable solidarity; of the solidarity in mysterious origin, in toil, in joy, in hope, in uncertain fate, which binds men to each other and all mankind to the visible world.

It is evident that he who, rightly or wrongly, holds by the convictions expressed above cannot be faithful to any one of the temporary formulas of his craft. The enduring part of them—the truth which each only imperfectly veils—should abide with him as the most precious of his possessions, but they all: Realism, Romanticism, Naturalism, even the unofficial sentimentalism (which like the poor, is exceedingly difficult to get rid of), all these gods must, after a short period of fellowship, abandon him—even on the very threshold of the temple—to the stammerings of his conscience and to the outspoken consciousness of the difficulties of his work. In that uneasy solitude the supreme cry of Art for Art, itself, loses the exciting ring of its apparent immorality. It sounds far off. It has ceased to be a cry, and is heard only as a whisper, often incomprehensible, but at times and faintly encouraging.

Sometimes, stretched at ease in the shade of a roadside tree, we watch the motions of a laborer in a distant field, and after a time, begin to wonder languidly as to what the fellow may be at. We watch the movements of his body, the waving of his arms, we see him bend down, stand up, hesitate, begin again. It may add to the charm of an idle hour to be told the purpose of his exertions. If we know he is trying to lift a stone, to dig a ditch, to uproot a stump, we look with a more real interest at his efforts; we are disposed to condone the jar of his agitation upon the restfulness of the landscape; and even, if in a brotherly frame of mind, we may bring ourselves to forgive his failure. We understood his object, and, after all, the fellow has tried, and perhaps he had not the strength—and perhaps he had not the knowledge. We forgive, go on our way—and forget.

And so it is with the workman of art. Art is long and life is short, and success is very far off. And thus, doubtful of strength to travel so far, we talk a little about the aim—the aim of art, which, like life itself, is inspiring, difficult—obscured by mists. It is not in the clear logic of a triumphant conclusion; it is not in the unveiling of one of those heartless secrets which are called the Laws of Nature. It is not less great, but only more difficult.

To arrest, for the space of a breath, the hands busy about the work of the earth, and compel men entranced by the sight of distant goals to glance for a moment at the surrounding vision of form and color, of sunshine and shadows; to make them pause for a look, for a sigh, for a smile—such is the aim, difficult and evanescent, and reserved only for a very few to achieve. But sometimes, by the deserving and the fortunate, even that task is accomplished. And when it is accomplished—behold—all the truth of life is there: a moment of vision, a sigh, a smile—and the return to an eternal rest.

OSCAR WILDE

The Decay of Lying[1]

AN OBSERVATION (A DIALOGUE)

PERSONS: *Cyril and Vivian.*
SCENE: *The library of a country house in Nottinghamshire.*

CYRIL (*coming in through the open window from the terrace*). My dear Vivian, don't coop yourself up all day in the library. It is a perfectly lovely afternoon. The air is exquisite. There is a mist upon the woods, like the purple bloom upon a plum. Let us go and lie on the grass, and smoke cigarettes, and enjoy Nature.

VIVIAN. Enjoy Nature! I am glad to say that I have entirely lost that faculty. People tell us that Art makes us love Nature more than we loved her before; that it reveals her secrets to us; and that after a careful study of Corot and Constable[2] we see things in her that had escaped our observation. My own experience is that the more we study Art, the less we care for Nature. What Art really reveals to us is Nature's lack of design, her curious crudities, her extraordinary monotony, her absolutely unfinished condition. Nature has good intentions, of course, but, as Aristotle once said, she cannot carry them out. When I look at a landscape I cannot help seeing all its defects. It is fortunate for us, however, that Nature is so imperfect, as otherwise we should have had no art at all. Art is our spirited protest, our gallant attempt to teach Nature her proper place. As for the infinite variety of Nature, that is a pure myth. It is not to be found in Nature herself. It resides in the imagination, or fancy, or cultivated blindness of the man who looks at her.

CYRIL. Well, you need not look at the landscape. You can lie on the grass and smoke and talk.

VIVIAN. But Nature is so uncomfortable. Grass is hard and lumpy and damp, and full of dreadful black insects. Why, even Morris'[3] poorest workman could make you a more comfortable seat than the whole of Nature can. Nature pales before the furniture of "the street which from Oxford has borrowed its name," as the poet you love so much vilely phrased it. I don't complain. If Nature had been comfortable, mankind would never have invented architecture, and I prefer houses to the open air. In a house we all feel of the proper proportions. Everything is subordinated to us, fash-

---

1. Portions of the essay, largely topical, have been excluded.
2. Landscape painters.
3. William Morris, nineteenth-century English poet, artist, and social theorist, sought to stimulate high standards of craftsmanship and beauty in furnishings. The allusion is to the "Morris chair," from his design.

ioned for our use and our pleasure. Egotism itself, which is so necessary to a proper sense of human dignity, is entirely the result of indoor life. Out of doors one becomes abstract and impersonal. One's individuality absolutely leaves one. And then Nature is so indifferent, so unappreciative. Whenever I am walking in the park here I always feel that I am no more to her than the cattle that browse on the slope, or the burdock that blooms in the ditch. Nothing is more evident than that Nature hates Mind. Thinking is the most unhealthy thing in the world, and people die of it just as they die of any other disease. Fortunately, in England, at any rate, thought is not catching. Our splendid physique as a people is entirely due to our national stupidity. I only hope we shall be able to keep this great historic bulwark of our happiness for many years to come; but I am afraid that we are beginning to be overeducated; at least, everybody who is incapable of learning has taken to teaching —that is really what our enthusiasm for education has come to. In the meantime, you had better go back to your wearisome uncomfortable Nature, and leave me to correct my proofs.

CYRIL. Writing an article! That is not very consistent after what you have just said.

VIVIAN. Who wants to be consistent? The dullard and the doctrinaire, the tedious people who carry out their principles to the bitter end of action, to the *reductio ad absurdum* of practice. Not I. Like Emerson, I write over the door of my library the word "Whim." Besides, my article is really a most salutary and valuable warning. If it is attended to, there may be a new Renaissance of Art.

CYRIL. What is the subject?

VIVIAN. I intend to call it "The Decay of Lying: A Protest."

CYRIL. Lying! I should have thought that our politicians kept up that habit.

VIVIAN. I assure you that they do not. They never rise beyond the level of misrepresentation, and actually condescend to prove, to discuss, to argue. How different from the temper of the true liar, with his frank, fearless statements, his superb irresponsibility, his healthy, natural disdain of proof of any kind! After all, what is a fine lie? Simply that which is its own evidence. If a man is sufficiently unimaginative to produce evidence in support of a lie, he might just as well speak the truth at once. No, the politicians won't do. Something may, perhaps be urged on behalf of the Bar. The mantle of the Sophist has fallen on its members. Their feigned ardors and unreal rhetoric are delightful. They can make the worse appear the better cause, as though they were fresh from Leontine schools, and have been known to wrest from reluctant juries triumphant verdicts of acquittal for their clients, even when those clients, as often happens, were clearly and unmistakably innocent.

But they are briefed by the prosaic, and are not ashamed to appeal to precedent. In spite of their endeavors, the truth will out. Newspapers, even, have degenerated. They may now be absolutely relied upon. One feels it as one wades through their columns. It is always the unreadable that occurs. I am afraid that there is not much to be said in favor of either the lawyer or the journalist. Besides, what I am pleading for is Lying in art. Shall I read you what I have written? It might do you a great deal of good.

CYRIL. Certainly, if you give me a cigarette. Thanks. * * *

VIVIAN. (*reading in a very clear, musical voice*). "THE DECAY OF LYING: A PROTEST. One of the chief causes that can be assigned for the curiously commonplace character of most of the literature of our age is undoubtedly the decay of Lying as an art, a science, and a social pleasure. The ancient historians gave us delightful fiction in the form of fact; the modern novelist presents us with dull facts under the guise of fiction. The Blue-Book[4] is rapidly becoming his ideal both for method and manner. He has his tedious '*document humain*,' his miserable little '*coin de la création*,'[5] into which he peers with his microscope. He is to be found at the Librarie Nationale, or at the British Museum, shamelessly reading up his subject. He has not even the courage of other people's ideas, but insists on going directly to life for everything, and ultimately, between encyclopedias and personal experience, he comes to the ground, having drawn his types from the family circle or from the weekly washerwoman, and having acquired an amount of useful information from which never, even in his most meditative moments, can he thoroughly free himself.

"The loss that results to literature in general from this false ideal of our time can hardly be over-estimated. People have a careless way of talking about a 'born liar,' just as they talk about a 'born poet.' But in both cases they are wrong. Lying and poetry are arts—arts, as Plato saw, not unconnected with each other—and they require the most careful study, the most disinterested devotion. Indeed, they have their technique, just as the more material arts of painting and sculpture have, their subtle secrets of form and color, their craft-mysteries, their deliberate artistic methods. As one knows the poet by his fine music, so one can recognize the liar by his rich rhythmic utterance, and in neither case will the casual inspiration of the moment suffice. Here, as elsewhere, practice must precede perfection. But in modern days while the fashion of writing poetry has become far too common, and should, if possible, be discouraged, the fashion of lying has almost fallen into disrepute. Many a young man starts in life with a natural gift for exaggeration which,

4. A British parliamentary report, a factual document.
5. "Corner of the universe," a phrase

similar to "slice of life" to characterize realism in fiction.

if nurtured in congenial and sympathetic surroundings, or by the imitation of the best models, might grow into something really great and wonderful. But, as a rule, he comes to nothing. He either falls into careless habits of accuracy——"

CYRIL. My dear fellow!

VIVIAN. Please don't interrupt in the middle of a sentence. "He either falls into careless habits of accuracy, or takes to frequenting the society of the aged and the well-informed. Both things are equally fatal to his imagination, as indeed they would be fatal to the imagination of anybody, and in a short time he develops a morbid and unhealthy faculty of truth-telling, begins to verify all statements made in his presence, has no hesitation in contradicting people who are much younger than himself, and often ends by writing novels which are so like life that no one can possibly believe in their probability. This is no isolated instance that we are giving. It is simply one example out of many; and if something cannot be done to check, or at least to modify, our monstrous worship of facts, Art will become sterile, and Beauty will pass away from the land. * * *

The only real people are the people who never existed, and if a novelist is base enough to go to life for his personages he should at least pretend that they are creations, and not boast of them as copies. The justification of a character in a novel is not that other persons are what they are, but that the author is what he is. Otherwise the novel is not a work of art. * * * In point of fact, what is interesting about people in good society * * * is the mask that each one of them wears, not the reality that lies behind the mask. It is a humiliating confession, but we are all of us made out of the same stuff. In Falstaff there is something of Hamlet, in Hamlet there is not a little of Falstaff. The fat knight has his moods of melancholy, and the young prince his moments of coarse humor. Where we differ from each other is purely in accidentals: in personal appearance, tricks of habit, and the like. The more one analyzes people, the more all reasons for analysis disappear. Sooner or later one comes to that dreadful universal thing called human nature. Indeed, as any one who has ever worked among the poor knows only too well, the brotherhood of man is no mere poet's dream, it is a most depressing and humiliating reality; and if a writer insists upon analyzing the upper classes, he might just as well write of match-girls and costermongers at once." However, my dear Cyril, I will not detain you any further just here. I quite admit that modern novels have many good points. All I insist on is that as a class, they are quite unreadable. * * *

CYRIL. Do you object to modernity of form, then?

VIVIAN. Yes. It is a huge price to pay for a very poor result. Pure modernity of form is always somewhat vulgarizing. It cannot help being so. The public imagine that, because they are interested in their immediate surroundings, Art should be interested in them also, and should take them as her subject-matter. But the mere fact that they are interested in these things makes them unsuitable subjects for Art. The only beautiful things, as somebody once said, are the things that do not concern us. As long as a thing is useful or necessary to us, or affects us in any way, either for pain or for pleasure, or appeals strongly to our sympathies, or is a vital part of the environment in which we live, it is outside the proper sphere of art. To art's subject-matter we should be more or less indifferent. We should, at any rate, have no preferences, no prejudices, no partisan feelings of any kind. It is exactly because Hecuba is nothing to us that her sorrows are such an admirable motive for tragedy.[6] * * * Believe me, my dear Cyril, modernity of form and modernity of subject-matter are entirely and absolutely wrong. We have mistaken the common livery of the age for the vesture of the Muses, and spend our days in the sordid streets and hideous suburbs of our vile cities when we should be out on the hillside with Apollo. Certainly we are a degraded race, and have sold our birthright for a mess of facts.

CYRIL. There is something in what you say, and there is no doubt that whatever amusement we may find in reading a purely modern novel, we have rarely any artistic pleasure in re-reading it. And this is perhaps the best rough test of what is literature and what is not. If one cannot enjoy reading a book over and over again, there is no use reading it at all. But what do you say about the return to Life and Nature? This is the panacea that is always being recommended to us.

VIVIAN. I will read you what I say on that subject. The passage comes later on in the article, but I may as well give it to you now:

"The popular cry of our time is 'Let us return to Life and Nature; they will recreate Art for us, and send the red blood coursing through her veins; they will shoe her feet with swiftness and make her hand strong.' But, alas! we are mistaken in our amiable and well-meaning efforts. Nature is always behind the age. And as for Life, she is the solvent that breaks up Art, the enemy that lays waste her house."

CYRIL. What do you mean by saying that Nature is always behind the age?

VIVIAN. Well, perhaps that is rather cryptic. What I mean is this. If we take Nature to mean natural simple instinct as opposed to self-conscious culture, the work produced under this influence is always old-fashioned, antiquated, and out of date. One touch of Nature may make the whole world kin, but two touches of Nature will destroy any work of Art. If, on the other hand, we regard

6. *Hamlet* II. ii. 522-586.

Nature as the collection of phenomena external to man, people only discover in her what they bring to her. She has no suggestions of her own. Wordsworth went to the lakes, but he was never a lake poet. He found in stones the sermons he had already hidden there. He went moralizing about the district, but his good work was produced when he returned, not to Nature but to poetry. Poetry gave him "Laodamia," and the fine sonnets, and the great Ode, such as it is. Nature gave him "Martha Ray" and "Peter Bell," and the address to Mr. Wilkinson's spade.

CYRIL. I think that view might be questioned. I am rather inclined to believe in the "impulse from a vernal wood," though, of course, the artistic value of such an impulse depends entirely on the kind of temperament that receives it, so that the return to Nature would come to mean simply the advance to a great personality. You would agree with that, I fancy. However, proceed with your article.

VIVIAN. (*reading*). "Art begins with abstract decoration, with purely imaginative and pleasurable work dealing with what is unreal and nonexistent. This is the first stage. Then Life becomes fascinated with this new wonder, and asks to be admitted into the charmed circle. Art takes life as part of her rough material, recreates it, and refashions it in fresh forms, is absolutely indifferent to fact, invents, imagines, dreams, and keeps between herself and reality the impenetrable barrier of beautiful style, of decorative or ideal treatment. The third stage is when Life gets the upper hand, and drives Art out into the wilderness. This is the true decadence, and it is from this that we are now suffering.

"Take the case of the English drama. At first in the hands of the monks Dramatic Art was abstract, decorative, and mythological. Then she enlisted Life in her service, and using some of Life's external forms, she created an entirely new race of beings, whose sorrows were more terrible than any sorrow man has ever felt, whose joys were keener than lover's joys, who had the rage of the Titans and the calm of the gods, who had monstrous and marvelous sins, monstrous and marvelous virtues. To them she gave a language different from that of actual use, a language full of resonant music and sweet rhythm, made stately by solemn cadence, or made delicate by fanciful rhyme, jeweled with wonderful words, and enriched with lofty diction. She clothed her children in strange raiment and gave them masks, and at her bidding the antique world rose from its marble tomb. A new Caesar stalked through the streets of risen Rome, and with purple sail and flute-led oars another Cleopatra passed up the river to Antioch. Old myth and legend and dream took shape and substance. History was entirely re-written, and there was hardly one of the dramatists who did not recognize that the object of Art is not simple truth but complex beauty. In this they were perfectly right. Art itself is really a form of exaggeration; and selection, which is the very spirit of art, is nothing more than an intensified mode of over-emphasis.

"But Life soon shattered the perfection of the form. Even in Shakespeare we can see the beginning of the end. It shows itself by the gradual breaking up of the blank-verse in the later plays, by the predominance given to prose, and by the over-importance assigned to characterization. The passages in Shakespeare—and they are many—where the language is uncouth, vulgar, exaggerated, fantastic, obscene even, are entirely due to Life calling for an echo of her own voice, and rejecting the intervention of beautiful style, through which alone should Life be suffered to find expression. Shakespeare is not by any means a flawless artist. He is too fond of going directly to life, and borrowing life's natural utterance. He forgets that when Art surrenders her imaginative medium she surrenders everything. Goethe says, somewhere—'It is in working within limits that the master reveals himself,' and the limitation, the very condition of any art is style. However, we need not linger any longer over Shakespeare's realism. *The Tempest* is the most perfect of palinodes. All that we desired to point out was, that the magnificent work of the Elizabethan and Jacobean artists contained within itself the seeds of its own dissolution, and that, if it drew some of its strength from using life as a rough material, it drew all its weakness from using life as an artistic method. As the inevitable result of this substitution of an imitative for a creative medium, this surrender of an imaginative form, we have the modern English melodrama. The characters in these plays talk on the stage exactly as they would talk off it; they have neither aspirations nor aspirates; they are taken directly from life and reproduce its vulgarity down to the smallest detail; they present the gait, manner, costume, and accent of real people; they would pass unnoticed in a third-class railway carriage. And yet how wearisome the plays are! They do not succeed in producing even that impression of reality at which they aim, and which is their only reason for existing. As a method, realism is a complete failure.

"What is true about the drama and the novel is no less true about those arts that we call the decorative arts. The whole history of these arts in Europe is the record of the struggle between Orientalism, with its frank rejection of imitation, its love of artistic convention, its dislike to the actual representation of any object in Nature, and our own imitative spirit. Wherever the former has been paramount, as in Byzantium, Sicily, and Spain, by actual contact, or in the rest of Europe by the influence of the Crusades, we have had beautiful and imaginative work in which the visible things of life are transmuted into artistic conventions, and the things that Life has not are invented and fashioned for her delight. But wherever we have returned to Life and Nature, our work has always become vulgar, common, and uninteresting. Modern tapestry, with its aërial effects, its elaborate perspective, its broad expanses of waste sky, its faithful and laborious realism, has no beauty whatsoever. The pictorial glass of Germany is absolutely detestable. We are beginning to weave possible carpets in England, but only because we have returned to the method and spirit of the East. Our rugs and carpets of twenty years ago, with their solemn depressing truths, their inane worship of Nature, their sordid reproductions of visible objects, have become, even to the Philistine, a source of laughter. A cultured Mahomedan once remarked to us, 'You Christians are so occupied in misinterpreting the fourth commandment that you have never thought of making an artistic application of the second.' He was perfectly right, and the whole truth of the matter is this: The proper school to learn art in is not Life but Art."

And now let me read you a passage which seems to me to settle the question very completely:

"It was not always thus. We need not say anything about the poets, for they, with the unfortunate exception of Mr. Wordsworth, have been really faithful to their high mission, and are universally recognized as being absolutely unreliable. But in the works of Herodotus, who, in spite of the shallow and ungenerous attempts of modern sciolists to verify his history, may justly be called the 'Father of Lies'; in the published speeches of Cicero and the biographies of Suetonius; in Tacitus at his best; in Pliny's *Natural History*; in Hanno's *Periplus*; in all the early chronicles; in the Lives of the Saints; in Froissart and Sir Thomas Mallory; in the travels of Marco Polo; in Olaus Magnus, and Aldrovandus, and Conrad Lycosthenes, with his magnificent *Prodigiorum et Ostentorum Chronicon*; in the autobiography of Benvenuto Cellini; in the memoirs of Casanuova; in Defoe's *History of the Plague*; in Boswell's *Life of Johnson*; in Napoleon's dispatches, and in the works of our own Carlyle, whose *French Revolution* is one of the most fascinating historical novels ever written, facts are either kept in their proper subordinate position, or else entirely excluded on the general ground of dullness. Now, everything is changed. Facts are not merely finding a footing-place in history, but they are usurping the domain of Fancy, and have invaded the kingdom of Romance. Their chilling touch is over everything. They are vulgarizing mankind. The crude commercialism of America, its materializing spirit, its indifference to the poetical side of things, and its lack of imagination and of high unattainable ideals, are entirely due to that country having adopted for its national hero a man, who, according to his own confession, was incapable of telling a lie, and it is not too much to say that the story of George Washington and the cherry-tree has done more harm, and in a shorter space of time, then any other moral tale in the whole of literature."

CYRIL. My dear boy!

VIVIAN. I assure you it is the case, and the amusing part of the whole thing is that the story of the cherry-tree is an absolute myth. However, you must not think that I am too despondent about the artistic future either of America or of our own country. Listen to this:

"That some change will take place before this century has drawn to its close we have no doubt whatsoever. Bored by the tedious and improving conversation of those who have neither the wit to exaggerate nor the genius to romance, tired of the intelligent person whose reminiscences are always based upon memory, whose statements are invariably limited by probability, and who is at any time liable to be corroborated by the merest Philistine who happens to be present, Society sooner or later must return to its lost leader, the cultured and fascinating liar. Who he was who first, without ever having gone out to the rude chase, told the wondering cavemen at sunset how he had dragged the Megatherium from the purple darkness of its jasper cave, or slain the Mammoth in single combat and brought back its giant tusks, we cannot tell, and not one of our modern anthropologists, for all their much-boasted science, has had the ordinary courage to tell us. Whatever was his name or race, he certainly was the true founder of social intercourse. For the aim of the liar is simply to charm, to delight, to give pleasure. He is the very basis of civilized society, and without him a dinner party, even at the mansions of the great, is as dull as a lecture at the Royal Society, or a debate at the Incorporated Authors, or one of Mr. Burnand's farcical comedies.

"Nor will he be welcomed by society alone. Art, breaking from the prison-house of realism, will run to greet him, and will kiss his false, beautiful lips, knowing that he alone is in possession of the great secret of all her manifestations, the secret that Truth is entirely and absolutely a matter of style; while Life—poor, probable, uninteresting human life—tired of repeating herself for the benefit of Mr. Herbert Spencer, scientific historians, and the compilers of statistics in general, will follow meekly after him, and try to reproduce, in her own simple and untutored way, some of the marvels of which he talks.

"No doubt there will always be critics who, like a certain writer in the *Saturday Review*, will gravely censure the teller of fairy tales for his defective knowledge of natural history, who will measure imaginative work by their own lack of any imaginative faculty, and will hold up their inkstained hands in horror if some honest gentleman, who has never been farther than the yew-trees of his own garden, pens a fascinating book of travels like Sir

John Mandeville, or, like great Raleigh, writes a whole history of the world, without knowing anything whatsoever about the past. To excuse themselves they will try and shelter under the shield of him who made Prospero the magician, and gave him Caliban and Ariel as his servants, who heard the Tritons blowing their horns round the coral reefs of the Enchanted Isle, and the fairies singing to each other in a wood near Athens, who led the phantom kings in dim procession across the misty Scottish heath, and hid Hecate in a cave with the weird sisters. They will call upon Shakespeare— they always do—and will quote that hackneyed passage[7] about Art holding the mirror up to Nature, forgetting that this unfortunate aphorism is deliberately said by Hamlet in order to convince the bystanders of his absolute insanity in all art-matters."

CYRIL. Ahem! Another cigarette, please.

VIVIAN. My dear fellow, whatever you may say, it is merely a dramatic utterance, and no more represents Shakespeare's real views upon art than the speeches of Iago represent his real views upon morals. But let me get to the end of the passage:

"Art finds her own perfection within, and not outside of, herself. She is not to be judged by any external standard of resemblance. She is a veil, rather than a mirror. She has flowers that no forests know of, birds that no woodland possesses. She makes and unmakes many worlds, and can draw the moon from heaven with a scarlet thread. Hers are the 'forms more real than living man,' and hers the great archetypes of which things that have existence are but unfinished copies. Nature has, in her eyes, no laws, no uniformity. She can work miracles at her will, and when she calls monsters from the deep they come. She can bid the almond tree blossom in winter, and send the snow upon the ripe cornfield. At her word the frost lays its silver finger on the burning mouth of June, and the winged lions creep out from the hollows of the Lydian hills. The dryads peer from the thicket as she passes by, and the brown fauns smile strangely at her when she comes near them. She has hawk-faced gods that worship her, and the centaurs gallop at her side."

CYRIL. I like that. I can see it. Is that the end?

VIVIAN. No. There is one more passage, but it is purely practical. It simply suggests some methods by which we could revive this lost art of Lying.

CYRIL. Well, before you read it to me, I should like to ask you a question. What do you mean by saying that life, "poor, probable, uninteresting human life," will try to reproduce the marvels of art? I can quite understand your objection to art being treated as a mirror. You think it would reduce genius to the position of a cracked looking-glass. But you don't mean to say that you seriously

7. *Hamlet* III. ii. 22-27.

believe that Life imitates Art, that Life in fact is the mirror, and Art the reality?

VIVIAN. Certainly I do. Paradox though it may seem—and paradoxes are always dangerous things—it is none the less true that Life imitates art far more than Art imitates life. * * * A great artist invents a type, and Life tries to copy it, to reproduce it in a popular form, like an enterprising publisher. Neither Holbein nor Vandyck[8] found in England what they have given us. They brought their types with them, and Life with her keen imitative faculty set herself to supply the master with models. The Greeks, with their quick artistic instinct, understood this, and set in the bride's chamber the statue of Hermes or of Apollo, that she might bear children as lovely as the works of art that she looked at in her rapture or her pain. They knew that Life gains from Art not merely spirituality, depth of thought and feeling, soul-turmoil or soul-peace, but that she can form herself on the very lines and colors of art, and can reproduce the dignity of Phidias as well as the grace of Praxiteles. Hence came their objection to realism. They disliked it on purely social grounds. They felt that it inevitably makes people ugly, and they were perfectly right. We try to improve the conditions of the race by means of good air, free sunlight, wholesome water, and hideous bare buildings for the better housing of the lower orders. But these things merely produce health, they do not produce beauty. For this, Art is required, and the true disciples of the great artist are not his studio-imitators, but those who become like his works of art, be they plastic as in Greek days, or pictorial as in modern times; in a word, Life is Art's best, Art's only pupil.

As it is with the visible arts, so it is with literature. The most obvious and the vulgarest form in which this is shown is in the case of the silly boys who, after reading the adventures of Jack Sheppard or Dick Turpin, pillage the stalls of unfortunate apple-women, break into sweet-shops at night, and alarm old gentlemen who are returning home from the city by leaping out on them in suburban lanes, with black masks and unloaded revolvers. This interesting phenomenon, which always occurs after the appearance of a new edition of either of the books I have alluded to, is usually attributed to the influence of literature on the imagination. But this is a mistake. The imagination is essentially creative and always seeks for a new form. The boy-burglar is simply the inevitable result of life's imitative instinct. He is Fact, occupied as Fact usually is, with trying to reproduce Fiction, and what we see in him is repeated on an extended scale throughout the whole of life. Schopenhauer has analyzed the pessimism that characterizes modern thought, but Hamlet invented it. The world has become sad because

8. Portrait painters.

a puppet was once melancholy. The Nihilist, that strange martyr who has no faith, who goes to the stake without enthusiasm, and dies for what he does not believe in, is a purely literary product. He was invented by Tourgénieff, and completed by Dostoieffski. Robespierre came out of the pages of Rousseau as surely as the People's Palace rose out of the *débris* of a novel.[9] Literature always anticipates life. It does not copy it, but molds it to its purpose. * * *

Life holds the mirror up to Art, and either reproduces some strange type imagined by painter or sculptor, or realizes in fact what has been dreamed in fiction. Scientifically speaking, the basis of life—the energy of life, as Aristotle would call it—is simply the desire for expression, and Art is always presenting various forms through which this expression can be attained. Life seizes on them and uses them, even if they be to her own hurt. Young men have committed suicide because Rolla did so, have died by their own hand because by his own hand Werther died.[1] Think of what we owe to the imitation of Christ, of what we owe to the imitation of Caesar.

CYRIL. The theory is certainly a very curious one, but to make it complete you must show that Nature, no less than Life, is an imitation of Art. Are you prepared to prove that?

VIVIAN. My dear fellow, I am prepared to prove anything.

CYRIL. Nature follows the landscape painter then, and takes her effects from him?

VIVIAN. Certainly. Where, if not from the Impressionists, do we get those wonderful brown fogs that come creeping down our streets, blurring the gas-lamps and changing the houses into monstrous shadows? To whom, if not to them and their master, do we owe the lovely silver mists that brood over our river, and turn to faint forms of fading grace, curved bridge and swaying barge? The extraordinary change that has taken place in the climate of London during the last ten years is entirely due to this particular school of Art. You smile. Consider the matter from a scientific or a metaphysical point of view, and you will find that I am right. For what is Nature? Nature is no great mother who has borne us. She is our creation. It is in our brain that she quickens to life. Things are because we see them, and what we see, and how we see it, depends on the Arts that have influenced us. To look at a thing is very different from seeing a thing. One does not see anything until one sees its beauty. Then, and then only does it come into existence. At present, people see fogs, not because there are fogs, but because poets and painters have taught them the mysteri-

9. The People's Palace was erected in Victorian London to provide a theater for the working class. Wilde claims that it was inspired by a fictional prototype just as (he asserts) the character of Robespierre, who rose to power in the French Revolution's Reign of Terror, was formed from the writings of Jean Jacques Rousseau.

1. Fictional heroes.

ous loveliness of such effects. There may have been fogs for centuries in London. I dare say there were. But no one saw them, and so we do not know anything about them. They did not exist until Art had invented them. Now, it must be admitted, fogs are carried to excess. They have become the mere mannerisms of a clique, and the exaggerated realism of their method gives dull people bronchitis. Where the cultured catch an effect, the uncultured catch cold. And so, let us be humane, and invite Art to turn her wonderful eyes elsewhere. She has done so already, indeed. That white quivering sunlight that one sees now in France, with its strange blotches of mauve, and its restless violet shadows, is her latest fancy, and, on the whole, Nature reproduces it quite admirably. Where she used to give us Corots and Daubignys, she gives us now exquisite Monets and entrancing Pisaros. Indeed, there are moments, rare, it is true, but still to be observed from time to time, when Nature becomes absolutely modern. Of course she is not always to be relied upon. The fact is that she is in this unfortunate position: Art creates an incomparable and unique effect, and, having done so, passes on to other things. Nature, upon the other hand, forgetting that imitation can be made the sincerest form of insult, keeps on repeating this effect until we all become absolutely wearied of it. Nobody of any real culture, for instance, ever talks nowadays about the beauty of a sunset. Sunsets are quite old-fashioned. They belong to the time when Turner was the last note in art. To admire them is a distinct sign of provincialism of temperament. Upon the other hand they go on. Yesterday evening Mrs. Arundel insisted on my going to the window, and looking at the glorious sky, as she called it. Of course I had to look at it. She is one of those absurdly pretty Philistines, to whom one can deny nothing. And what was it? It was simply a very second-rate Turner, a Turner of a bad period, with all the painter's worst faults exaggerated and over-emphasized. * * * But have I proved my theory to your satisfaction?

CYRIL. You have proved it to my dissatisfaction, which is better. But even admitting this strange imitative instinct in Life and Nature, surely you would acknowledge that Art expresses the temper of its age, the spirit of its time, the moral and social conditions that surround it, and under whose influence it is produced.

VIVIAN. Certainly not! Art never expresses anything but itself. This is the principle of my new aesthetics; and it is this, more than that vital connection between form and substance, on which Mr. Pater dwells, that makes music the type of all the arts. Of course, nations and individuals, with that healthy natural vanity which is the secret of existence, are always under the impression that it is of them that the Muses are talking, always trying to find in the calm dignity of imaginative art some mirror of their own turbid passions, always forgetting that the singer of life is not Apollo, but Marsyas.[2] Remote from reality, and with her eyes turned away from the shadows of the cave, Art reveals her own perfection, and the wondering crowd that watches the opening of the marvelous, many-petalled rose fancies that it is its own history that is being told to it, its own spirit that is finding expression in a new form. But it is not so. The highest art rejects the burden of the human spirit, and gains more from a new medium or a fresh material than she does from any enthusiasm for art, or from any great awakening of the human consciousness. She develops purely on her own lines. She is not symbolic of any age. It is the ages that are her symbols.

Even those who hold that Art is representative of time and place and people, cannot help admitting that the more imitative an art is, the less it represents to us the spirit of its age. The evil faces of the Roman emperors look out at us from the foul porphyry and spotted jasper in which the realistic artists of the day delighted to work, and we fancy that in those cruel lips and heavy sensual jaws we can find the secret of the ruin of the Empire. But it was not so. The vices of Tiberius could not destroy that supreme civilization, any more than the virtues of the Antonines could save it. It fell for other, for less interesting reasons. The sibyls and prophets of the Sistine may indeed serve to interpret for some that new birth of the emancipated spirit that we call the Renaissance; but what do the drunken boors and brawling peasants of Dutch art tell us about the great soul of Holland? The more abstract, the more ideal an art is, the more it reveals to us the temper of its age. If we wish to understand a nation by means of its art, let us look at its architecture or its music.

CYRIL. I quite agree with you there. The spirit of an age may be best expressed in the abstract ideal arts, for the spirit itself is abstract and ideal. Upon the other hand, for the visible aspect of an age, for its look, as the phrase goes, we must, of course, go to the arts of imitation.

VIVIAN. I don't think so. After all, what the imitative arts really give us are merely the various styles of particular artists, or of certain schools of artists. Surely you don't imagine that the people of the Middle Ages bore any resemblance at all to the figures on mediaeval stained glass, or in mediaeval stone and wood carving, or on mediaeval metal-work, or tapestries, or illuminated MSS. They were probably very ordinary-looking people with nothing grotesque, or remarkable, or fantastic in their appearance. The Middle Ages, as we know them in art, are simply a definite form of

---

2. In Greek mythology, Marsyas, presumptuously rivaling the god Apollo, was defeated by the god in a musical contest and flayed alive. Here Wilde presents Marsyas as typifying the false notion of art, and Apollo the true.

style, and there is no reason at all why an artist with this style should not be produced in the nineteenth century. No great artist ever sees things as they really are. If he did, he would cease to be an artist. * * * The fact is that we look back on the ages entirely through the medium of Art, and Art, very fortunately, has never once told us the truth.

CYRIL. But modern portraits by English painters, what of them? Surely they are like the people they pretend to represent?

VIVIAN. Quite so. They are so like them that a hundred years from now no one will believe in them. The only portraits in which one believes are portraits where there is very little of the sitter and a very great deal of the artist. Holbein's drawings of the men and women of his time impress us with a sense of their absolute reality. But this is simply because Holbein compelled life to accept his conditions, to restrain itself within his limitations, to reproduce his type, and to appear as he wished it to appear. It is style that makes us believe in a thing—nothing but style. Most of our modern portrait painters are doomed to absolute oblivion. They never paint what they see. They paint what the public sees, and the public never sees anything.

CYRIL. Well, after that, I think I should like to hear the end of your article.

VIVIAN. With pleasure. * * * "What we have to do, what at any rate it is our duty to do, is to revive this old art of Lying. Much, of course, may be done, in the way of educating the public, by amateurs in the domestic circle, at literary lunches, and at afternoon teas. But this is merely the light and graceful side of lying, such as was probably heard at Cretan dinner parties. There are many other forms. Lying for the sake of gaining some immediate personal advantage, for instance—lying with a moral purpose, as it is usually called—though of late it has been rather looked down upon, was extremely popular with the antique world. Athena laughs when Odysseus tells her 'his words of sly devising,' as Mr. William Morris phrases it, and the glory of mendacity illumines the pale brow of the stainless hero of Euripidean tragedy, and sets among the noble women of the past the young bride of one of Horace's most exquisite odes. Later on, what at first had been merely a natural instinct was elevated into a self-conscious science. Elaborate rules were laid down for the guidance of mankind, and an important school of literature grew up round the subject. Indeed, when one remembers the excellent philosophical treatise of Sanchez[3] on the whole question, one cannot help regretting that no one has ever thought of publishing a cheap and condensed edition of the works of that great casuist. A short

---

3. Thomas Sanchez (1550-1610), Spanish Jesuit and moralist, whose works include treatment of the morality of equivocation.

primer, 'When to Lie and How,' if brought out in an attractive and not too expensive a form, would, no doubt, command a large sale, and would prove of real practical service to many earnest and deep-thinking people. Lying for the sake of the improvement of the young, which is the basis of home education, still lingers amongst us, and its advantages are so admirably set forth in the early books of Plato's *Republic* that it is unnecessary to dwell upon them here. It is a mode of lying for which all good mothers have peculiar capabilities, but it is capable of still further development, and has been sadly overlooked by the School Board. Lying for the sake of a monthly salary is, of course, well known in Fleet Street,[4] and the profession of a political leader-writer is not without its advantages. But it is said to be a somewhat dull occupation, and it certainly does not lead to much beyond a kind of ostentatious obscurity. The only form of lying that is absolutely beyond reproach is Lying for its own sake, and the highest development of this is, as we have already pointed out, Lying in Art. Just as those who do not love Plato more than Truth cannot pass beyond the threshold of the Academe, so those who do not love Beauty more than Truth never know the inmost shrine of Art. The solid, stolid British intellect lies in the desert sands like the Sphinx in Flaubert's marvelous tale, and fantasy, *La Chimère*, dances round it, and calls to it with her false, flute-toned voice. It may not hear her now, but surely some day, when we are all bored to death with the commonplace character of modern fiction, it will hearken to her and try to borrow her wings.

"And when that day dawns, or sunset reddens, how joyous we shall all be! Facts will be regarded as discreditable, Truth will be found mourning over her fetters, and Romance, with her temper of wonder, will return to the land. The very aspect of the world will change to our startled eyes. Out of the sea will rise Behemoth and Leviathan, and sail round the high-pooped galleys, as they do on the delightful maps of those ages when books on geography were actually readable. Dragons will wander about the waste places, and the phoenix will soar from her nest of fire into the air. We shall lay our hands upon the basilisk, and see the jewel in the toad's head. Champing his gilded oats, the Hippogriff will stand in our stalls, and over our heads will float the Blue Bird, singing of beautiful and impossible things, of things that are lovely and that never happen, of things that are not and that should be. But before this comes to pass, we must cultivate the lost art of Lying."

CYRIL. Then we must certainly cultivate it at once. But in order to avoid making any error, I want you to tell me briefly the doctrines of the new aesthetics.

VIVIAN. Briefly, then, they are these. Art never expresses any-

---

4. The London street where most British newspapers have offices.

thing but itself. It has an independent life, just as Thought has, and develops purely on its own lines. It is not necessarily realistic in an age of realism, nor spiritual in an age of faith. So far from being the creation of its time, it is usually in direct opposition to it, and the only history that it preserves for us is the history of its own progress. Sometimes it returns upon its footsteps, and revives some antique form, as happened in the archaistic movement of late Greek Art, and in the pre-Raphaelite movement of our own day. At other times it entirely anticipates its age, and produces in one century work that it takes another century to understand, to appreciate, and to enjoy. In no case does it reproduce its age. To pass from the art of a time to the time itself is the great mistake that all historians commit.

The second doctrine is this. All bad art comes from returning to Life and Nature, and elevating them into ideals. Life and Nature may sometimes be used as a part of Art's rough material, but before they are of any real service to art they must be translated into artistic conventions. The moment Art surrenders its imaginative medium it surrenders everything. As a method, Realism is a complete failure, and the two things that every artist should avoid are modernity of form and modernity of subject-matter. To us, who live in the nineteenth century, any century is a suitable subject for art except our own. The only beautiful things are the things that do not concern us. It is, to have the pleasure of quoting myself, exactly because Hecuba is nothing to us that her sorrows are so suitable a motive for a tragedy. Besides, it is only the modern that ever becomes old-fashioned. M. Zola sits down to give us a picture of the Second Empire. Who cares for the Second Empire now? It is out of date. Life goes faster than Realism, but Romanticism is always in front of Life.

The third doctrine is that Life imitates Art far more than Art imitates Life. This results not merely from Life's imitative instinct, but from the fact that the self-conscious aim of Life is to find expression, and that Art offers it certain beautiful forms through which it may realize that energy. It is a theory that has never been put forward before, but it is extremely fruitful, and throws an entirely new light upon the history of Art.

It follows, as a corollary from this, that external Nature also imitates Art. The only effects that she can show us are effects that we have already seen through poetry, or in paintings. This is the secret of Nature's charm, as well as the explanation of Nature's weakness.

The final revelation is that Lying, the telling of beautiful untrue things, is the proper aim of Art. But of this I think I have spoken at sufficient length. And now let us go out on the terrace, where "droops the milk-white peacock like a ghost," while the evening star "washes the dusk with silver." At twilight nature becomes a wonderfully suggestive effect, and is not without loveliness, though perhaps its chief use is to illustrate quotations from the poets. Come! We have talked long enough.

QUESTIONS FOR STUDY, DISCUSSION, AND WRITING

1. In "The Decay of Lying" Wilde advances a number of rather unusual ideas about Art and Nature. How does the dialogue form facilitate his task? How are the two speakers differentiated?
2. What, according to Vivian, is the real relation between Nature and Art? What proofs does he bring forward in support of his thesis? How persuasive are they? Indicate some further proofs or present the counterargument.
3. What illustrations from present-day life might Vivian give of his doctrine that Life imitates Art? What place might television and advertising, business and fashion have in his argument?
4. What objections has Vivian to realism in literature? Upon what assumptions does he hold realism to rest, and what refutation of those assumptions does he offer?
5. Vivian says of the realistic novelist that "he has not even the courage of other peoples' ideas" (p. 477). From what does the humor of his statement derive? Give other instances of Wilde's humor.
6. Vivian says that life is "tired of repeating herself for the benefit of Mr. Herbert Spencer, scientific historians, and the compilers of statistics in general" (p. 483). Does Spencer's essay on style, "Force in Words" (pp. 90–94), give some indication of what Vivian means? Explain.
7. What merit has Wilde's suggestion that Nature is a product of our imagination? Compare Santayana's "Imagination" (pp. 244–246) and Bronowski's "The Creative Mind" (pp. 247–258).

WILLIAM BUTLER YEATS
Letter to Sean O'Casey

April 20, 1928

MY DEAR CASEY

I had looked forward with great hope and excitement to reading your play,[1] and not merely because of my admiration for your work, for I bore in mind that the Abbey[2] owed its recent prosperity to you. If you had not brought us your plays just at that moment I doubt if it would now exist. I read the first act with admiration, I thought it was the best first act you had written, and told a friend that you had surpassed yourself. The next night I read the second and third acts, and to-night I have read the fourth. I am sad and discouraged; you have no subject. You were interested in the Irish Civil War, and at

1. *The Silver Tassie.*
2. The Dublin theatre where O'Casey's works were first presented.

every moment of those plays wrote out of your own amusement with life or your sense of its tragedy; you were excited, and we all caught your excitement; you were exasperated almost beyond endurance by what you had seen or heard, as a man is by what happens under his window, and you moved us as Swift moved his contemporaries.

But you are not interested in the great war; you never stood on its battlefields or walked its hospitals, and so write out of your opinions. You illustrate those opinions by a series of almost unrelated scenes, as you might in a leading article; there is no dominating character, no dominating action, neither psychological unity nor unity of action; and your great power of the past has been the creation of some unique character who dominated all about him and was himself a main impulse in some action that filled the play from beginning to end.

The mere greatness of the world war has thwarted you; it has refused to become mere background, and obtrudes itself upon the stage as so much dead wood that will not burn with the dramatic fire. Dramatic action is a fire that must burn up everything but itself; there should be no room in a play for anything that does not belong to it; the whole history of the world must be reduced to wallpaper in front of which the characters must pose and speak.

Among the things that dramatic action must burn up are the author's opinions; while he is writing he has no business to know anything that is not a portion of that action. Do you suppose for one moment that Shakespeare educated Hamlet and King Lear by telling them what he thought and believed? As I see it, Hamlet and Lear educated Shakespeare, and I have no doubt that in the process of that education he found out that he was an altogether different man to what he thought himself, and had altogether different beliefs. A dramatist can help his characters to educate him by thinking and studying everything that gives them the language they are groping for through his hands and eyes, but the control must be theirs, and that is why the ancient philosophers thought a poet or dramatist Daimon-possessed.

This is a hateful letter to write, or rather to dictate—I am dictating to my wife—and all the more so, because I cannot advise you to amend the play. It is all too abstract, after the first act; the second act is an interesting technical experiment, but it is too long for the material; and after that there is nothing. I can imagine how you have toiled over this play. A good scenario writes itself, it puts words into the mouths of all its characters while we sleep, but a bad scenario exacts the most miserable toil. I see nothing for it but a new theme, something you have found and no newspaper writer has ever found. What business have we with anything but the unique?

Put the dogmatism of this letter down to splenetic age and forgive it.

W B Y

FINLEY PETER DUNNE
On Books

"Ivry time I pick up me mornin' paper to see how th' scrap come out at Batthry D," said Mr. Dooley, "th' first thing I r-run acrost is somethin' like this: 'A hot an' handsome gift f'r Christmas is Lucy Ann Patzooni's "Jims iv Englewood Thought" '; or 'If ye wud delight th' hear-rt iv yer child, ye'll give him Dr. Harper's monymental histhry iv th' Jewish thribes fr'm Moses to Dhryfuss' or 'Ivrybody is r-readin' Roodyard Kiplin's "Busy Pomes f'r Busy People." ' Th' idee iv givin' books f'r Christmas prisints whin th' stores are full iv tin hor-rns an' dhrums an' boxin' gloves and choo-choo ca-ars! People must be crazy."

"They ar-re," said Mr. Hennessy. "My house is so full iv books ye cudden't tur-rn around without stumblin' over thim. I found th' life iv an ex-convict, the 'Prisoner iv Zinders,' in me high hat th' other day, where Mary Ann was hidin' it fr'm her sister. Instead iv th' childher fightin' an' skylarkin' in th' evenin', they're settin' around th' table with their noses glued into books. Th' ol' woman doesn't read, but she picks up what's goin' on. 'Tis 'Honoria, did Lor-rd What's-his-name marry th' fair Aminta?' or 'But that Lady Jane was a case.' An' so it goes. There's no injymint in th' house, an' they're usin' me cravats f'r bookmarks."

" 'Tis all wrong," said Mr. Dooley. "They're on'y three books in th' wurruld worth readin'—Shakespeare, th' Bible, an' Mike Ahearn's histhry iv Chicago. I have Shakespeare on thrust, Father Kelly r-reads th' Bible f'r me, an' I didn't buy Mike Ahearn's histhry because I seen more thin he cud put into it. Books is th' roon iv people, specially novels. Whin I was a young man, th' parish priest used to preach again thim; but nobody knowed what he meant. At that time Willum Joyce had th' on'y library in th' Sixth Wa-ard. Th' mayor give him th' bound volumes iv th' council proceedings, an' they was a very handsome set. Th' on'y books I seen was th' kind that has th' life iv th' pope on th' outside an' a set iv dominos on th' inside. They're good readin'. Nawthin' cud be better f'r a man whin he's tired out afther a day's wurruk thin to go to his library an' take down wan iv th' gr-reat wurruks iv lithratchoor an' play a game iv dominos f'r th' dhrinks out iv it. Anny other kind iv r-readin', barrin' th' newspapers, which will niver hurt anny onedycated man, is desthructive iv morals.

"I had it out with Father Kelly th' other day in this very matther. He was comin' up fr'm down town with an ar-rmful iv books f'r prizes at th' school. 'Have ye th' Key to Heaven there?' says I. 'No,' says he, 'th' childher that'll get these books don't need no key. They go in under th' turn-stile,' he says, laughin'. 'Have ye th' Lives iv th' Saints, or the Christyan Dooty, or th' Story iv Saint Rose iv Lima?' I says. 'I have not,' says he. 'I have some good story books. I'd rather th' kids'd r-read Charrles Dickens than anny iv th' tales iv thim holy men that was burned in ile or et up be lines,' he says. 'It does no good in these degin'rate days to prove that th' best that can come to a man f'r behavin' himsilf is to be cooked in a pot or di-gisted be a line,' he says. 'Ye're wrong,' says I. 'Beg-gin' ye're riv'rince's pardon, ye're wrong,' I says. 'What ar-re ye goin' to do with thim young wans? Ye're goin' to make thim near-sighted an' round-shouldered,' I says. 'Ye're goin' to have thim believe that, if they behave thimsilves an' lead a virchous life, they'll marry rich an' go to Congress. They'll wake up some day, an' find out that gettin' money an behavin' ye'ersilf don't always go together,' I says. 'Some iv th' wickedest men in th' wur-ruld have marrid rich,' I says. 'Ye're goin' to teach thim that a man doesn't have to use an ax to get along in th' wur-ruld. Ye're goin' to teach thim that a la-ad with a curlin' black mustache an' smokin' a cigareet is always a villyan, whin he's more often a barber with a lar-rge family. Life, says ye! There's no life in a book. If ye want to show thim what life is, tell thim to look around thim. There's more life on a Saturdah night in th' Ar-rchy Road thin in all th' books fr'm Shakespeare to th' rayport iv th' drainage thrustees. No man,' I says, 'iver wrote a book if he had annything to write about, except Shakespeare an' Mike Ahearn. Shakespeare was all r-right. I niver read anny of his pieces, but they sound good; an' I know Mike Ahearn is all r-right.' "

"What did he say?" asked Mr. Hennessy.

"He took it all r-right," said Mr. Dooley. "He kind o' grinned, an' says he: 'What ye say is thrue, an' it's not thrue,' he says. 'Books is f'r thim that can't injye thimsilves in anny other way,' he says. 'If ye're in good health, an' ar-re atin' three squares a day, an' not ayether sad or very much in love with ye'er lot, but just lookin' on an' not carin' a'—he said rush—'not carin' a rush, ye don't need books,' he says. 'But if ye're a down-spirited thing an' want to get away an' can't, ye need books. 'Tis betther to be comfortable at home thin to go to th' circus, an' 'tis betther to go to th' circus thin to r-read anny book. But 'tis betther to r-read a book thin to want to go to th' circus an' not be able to,' he says. 'Well,' says I, 'whin I was growin' up, half th' congregation heard mass with their prayer books tur-rned upside down, an' they were as pious as anny. Th' Apostles' Creed niver was as con-vincin' to me afther I larned to r-read it as it was whin I cudden't read it, but believed it."

ANATOLE FRANCE
Children's Playthings

I have just had the pleasure of reading some children's tales, *La Comédie des jouets*,[1] which M. Camille Lemonnier has given us. M. Camille Lemonnier has taken his place in the front rank of Belgian men of letters. He writes real romances in a language full of savor. He is a natural story-teller who pleases the Parisians as well as the people of Brussels. I knew from his books that he adored the various aspects of life, and that his artistic dreams have eagerly pursued the infinite forms of beings. I discover to-day that he sometimes amuses himself with children's playthings, and this taste inspires me with new sympathies for him. I am his well-wisher because of his poetic interpretations of playthings, and also because he possesses the mystic sense. Without the smallest effort he is able to give life and animation to his Jumping Jacks and his Punches. He reveals the spiritual nature of Father Christmas, who reappears every year covered with frost in the grocer's shop. At the breath of his thought a forest, which really consists of only six trees painted green, with chips for foliage, stretches forth every night out of its deal box, and becomes a haunt of shadow, mystery, and terror. That is what pleases and touches me. For, like him, I practice the fetishism of lead soldiers, Noah's arks, and wooden sheepfolds. Think of it, this fetishism is the last that is left us. When humanity felt itself young, it gave souls to all things. That charming faith departed little by little, and to-day our modern thinkers no longer perceive souls in this disenchanted universe. At least M. Camille Lemonnier and I have a profound belief left us: we believe in the souls of toys.

For my own part, I do not hesitate to formulate my creed. I believe in the immortal soul of Punch. I believe in the majesty of marionettes and dolls.

Doubtless there is nothing human according to the flesh in those little personages of wood or cardboard, but there is in them something divine, however little it may be. They do not live as we do, but still they live. They live the life of the immortal gods.

If I were a scholar I should endeavor to build up their symbolism, as Guigniant, following Creutzer, attempted to establish the symbolism of the divinities of ancient Greece. Assuredly dolls and marionettes are very tiny gods; but they are gods all the same.

For, look you: they are like the lesser idols of antiquity. They bear even a still closer resemblance to those ruder figures by which savages attempt to show the invisible. And what should they be like if not idols, since they are themselves idols? Theirs is an absolutely

1. *The Toy Comedy.*

religious function. They bring to little children the only vision of the divine which would be intelligible to them. They represent all the religion that is accessible to tender years. They are the cause of our earliest dreams. They inspire our first fears and our first hopes. Pierrot and Punch contain as much divine anthropomorphism as brains, as yet scarce fashioned though terribly active, can conceive. They are the Hermes and the Zeus of our babies. And every doll is to this day a Proserpine, a Cora,[2] for our little girls. I would have these words taken in their most literal sense. Children are born religious. M. Hovelacque and his municipal council do not perceive a god anywhere. Children see them everywhere. Their interpretation of nature is mystic and religious. I will even say that they have more relations with gods than with men, and this proposition will not appear strange if we remember that since the divine is the unknown, the idea of the divine is the first which must engage the attention of growing thought.

Children are religious, but that does not mean that they are spiritual. Spirituality is the supreme elegance of intelligence on the down grade. Humanity began with fetishism, and children begin humanity anew. They are profound fetishists. What have I said? Little children go back farther than humanity itself. They reproduce not only the ideas of the men of the Stone Age, but even the ideas of animals. And these, be sure of it, are also religious ideas. St. Francis of Assisi, in his beautiful mystic soul, recognized the piety of animals. You need not watch a dog for long to realize that his soul is full of sacred terrors. The faith of a dog, like that of a child, is a pronounced fetishism. It would be impossible to remove from a dog's mind the belief that the moon is divine.

Since children, then, are born religious, they worship their toys. They ask of their toys what men have always asked of the gods: joy and forgetfulness, the revelation of mysterious harmonies, the secret of being. Toys, like the gods, inspire terror and love. Are not the dolls, whom the ancient Greeks called their Nymphs, the divine virgins of early childhood? The devils who pop out of boxes, do they not, like the Greek Gorgon or the Christian Beelzebub, represent the sympathetic alliance between visible ugliness and moral evil? It is true that children are familiar with their gods, but have men never blasphemed theirs? Children sometimes break their dolls, but what symbols has not humanity broken? The child, like the man, continually changes his ideal. His gods are always imperfect because they necessarily proceed from himself.

I will go further. I will show that this religious character, inherent in all toys, and above all in anthropomorphic toys, is implicitly recognized not only by all children, but even by those adults who

2. Hermes, Zeus, and Proserpine (also called Cora) are deities in classical mythology.

still preserve the simplicity of childhood. Those who are good enough to read me know my respect for sacred things. I can say, without fear of being suspected of any irreverence, that even to-day entirely puerile images take their place in the ceremonies of the Church, and that innocent and pious souls ingenuously associate actual toys with the mysteries of worship. Are not the shops of the Rue Saint-Sulpice full of liturgical dolls? And what are the Bethlehems that are put in the churches during Christmas time but pious toys? Not a week ago, in a chapel opened by the English Catholics in the Étoile district, I saw the scene of the Nativity represented in the apse by modeled and painted figures. Gentle women came and knelt before them. With joy they recognized the grotto of Bethlehem, the Holy Virgin, St. Joseph, and the little Jesus opening His arms to the world from His cradle. Prostrate at the feet of the Child-God, the three wise men presented gold, frankincense, and myrrh. Melchior could be recognized by his white beard, Gaspar by his youthful air, and the good Balthazar by the naïve expression on his ebony countenance. The latter was smiling under his enormous turban. O the candor of the good negro! Imperishable sweetness of Uncle Tom! None of the figures were bigger than my hand. Shepherds and shepherdesses as large as a finger occupied the approaches to the grotto. There were also camels and camel-drivers, a bridge over a stream, and a house with glass windows which were lit up at night by tiny candles. The scene answered exactly to the aesthetic needs of a litle girl of six years old. During the time that I remained in the church, I heard the sounds of a musical box which aided contemplation.

Thus the innocent ladies were deeply affected by this pretty pastoral. In order to be able to impart such emotions, it is necessary that these half-comic, half-sacred images must have a soul, a little doll's soul. It would be ungracious for me to sneer at an ingenuousness which I myself shared: those worthy souls who knelt and yearned before the dolls seemed to me quite charming. And if I point out the elements of fetishism that entered into the composition of their orthodoxy, it is not with any intention of depreciating such an alloy. I hold with that generous chief of positivism, M. Pierre Laffite, that the creed of fetishism has good in it, and, indeed, I do not believe that there is any true religion which has not a litle fetishism. I go further: every deep human feeling leads back to that ancient religion of men. Look at gamblers or lovers: they must have fetishes.

I have just shown you the doll in the sanctuary. I shall not have much difficulty in showing it to you also on the threshold of the museum. It belongs at once to the invisible gods, and to the museums. Because the toy is religious, it is artistic. I beg you to regard that proposition as demonstrated. The creeds and the arts come from the same inspiration. From the infant laboriously arranging his lead soldiers on a table, to the venerable M. Ravaisson enthusiastically grouping the Venus Victrix and the Borghese Achilles in his studio at the Louvre, there is but a shade of difference. The principle of the two actions is precisely the same. Every little raga-muffin who grasps his toys is already an aesthete.

It is quite true to say that the doll is the rough draft of the statue. The learned M. Edmond Pottier hesitates before certain little figures from the Necropolis of Myrrhina, not knowing whether he has before him a doll or an idol. The dolls which the little girls pressed against their hearts in the days of beauty in holy Hellas have perished; they were made of wax, and have been melted by the sun. They have not survived the charming arms which, after having carried them, opened in love or closed in despair, and then froze in death. I regret those waxen dolls; I imagine the genius of Greece must have given beauty to their fragility. Those that remain to us are made of baked earth; they are poor little dolls found in the tombs of children. Their frail limbs are jointed like the arms and legs of marionettes. That is another special characteristic that ought to be considered.

If the doll precedes sculpture by its form, it owes several other precious properties to the suppleness of its joints. The child com-municates gestures and attitudes to it, the child makes it act, and speaks for it. And there you have the theatre created!

Who was it that said, "Dolls and songs, almost all Shakespeare is in them"?

RALPH WALDO EMERSON
An Evening of Dance[1]

I saw in Boston Fanny Elssler in the ballet of *Nathalie*. She must show, I suppose, the whole compass of her instrument, and add to her softest graces of motion or "the wisdom of her feet," the feats of the rope-dancer and tumbler; and perhaps on the whole the beauty of the exhibition is enhanced by this that is strong and strange, as when she stands erect on the extremities of her toes or on one toe, or "performs the impossible" in attitude. But the chief beauty is in the extreme grace of her movement, the variety and nature of her attitude, the winning fun and spirit of all her little coquetries, the beautiful erectness of her body, and the freedom and determination which she can so easily assume, and, what struck me much, the air of perfect sympathy with the house, and that mixture of deference and conscious superiority which puts her in perfect spirits and equality to her part. When she curtsies, her sweet and slow and prolonged salaam which descends and still descends whilst

1. From Emerson's *Journals*.

the curtain falls, until she seems to have invented new depths of grace and condescension, she earns well the profusion of bouquets of flowers which are hurled on to the stage.

As to the morals, as it is called, of this exhibition, that lies wholly with the spectator. The basis of this exhibition, like that of every human talent, is moral, is the sport and triumph of health or the virtue of organization. Her charm for the house is that she dances for them or they dance in her, not being (fault of some defect in their forms and educations) able to dance themselves. We must be expressed. Hence all the cheer and exhilaration which the spectacle imparts and the intimate property which each beholder feels in the dancer, and the joy with which he hears good anecdotes of her spirit and her benevolence. They know that such surpassing grace must rest on some occult foundations of inward harmony.

But over and above her genius for dancing are the incidental vices of this individual, her own false taste or her meretricious arts to please the groundlings and which must displease the judicious. The immorality the immoral will see; the very immoral will see that only; the pure will not heed it—for it is not obtrusive—perhaps will not see it at all. I should not think of danger to young women stepping with their father or brother out of happy and guarded parlors into this theatre to return in a few hours to the same; but I can easily suppose that it is not the safest resort for college boys who have left metaphysics, conic sections, or Tacitus to see these tripping satin slippers, and they may not forget this graceful, silvery swimmer when they have retreated again to their baccalaureate cells.

It is a great satisfaction to see the best in each kind, and as a good student of the world, I desire to let pass nothing that is excellent in its own kind unseen, unheard.

E. M. FORSTER
Not Listening to Music

Listening to music is such a muddle that one scarcely knows how to start describing it. The first point to get clear in my own case is that during the greater part of every performance I do not attend. The nice sounds make me think of something else. I wool-gather most of the time, and am surprised that others don't. Professional critics can listen to a piece as consistently and as steadily as if they were reading a chapter in a novel. This seems to me an amazing feat, and probably they only achieve it through intellectual training; that is to say, they find in the music the equivalent of a plot; they are following the ground bass or expecting the theme to re-enter in the dominant, and so on, and this keeps them on the rails. But I fly off every minute: after a bar or two I think how musical I am, or of something smart I might have said in conversation; or I wonder what the composer—dead a couple of centuries—can be feeling as the flames on the altar still flicker up; or how soon an H.E. bomb[1] would extinguish them. Not to mention more obvious distractions: the tilt of the soprano's chin or chins; the antics of the conductor, that impassioned beetle, especially when it is night time and he waves his shards; the affection of the pianist when he takes a top note with difficulty, as if he too were a soprano; the backs of the chairs; the bumps on the ceiling; the extreme physical ugliness of the audience. A classical audience is surely the plainest collection of people anywhere assembled for any common purpose; contributing my quota, I have the right to point this out. Compare us with a gang of navvies or with an office staff, and you will be appalled. This, too, distracts me.

What do I hear during the intervals when I do attend? Two sorts of music. They melt into each other all the time, and are not easy to christen, but I will call one of them "music that reminds me of something," and the other "music itself." I used to be very fond of music that reminded me of something, and especially fond of Wagner. With Wagner I always knew where I was; he never let the fancy roam; he ordained that one phrase should recall the ring, another the sword, another the blameless fool and so on; he was as precise in his indications as an oriental dancer. Since he is a great poet, that did not matter, but I accepted his leitmotiv system much too reverently and forced it onto other composers whom it did not suit, such as Beethoven and Franck. I thought that music must be the better for having a meaning. I think so still, but am less clear as to what "a meaning" is. In those days it was either a non-musical object, such as a sword or a blameless fool, or a non-musical emotion, such as fear, lust, or resignation. When music reminded me of something which was not music, I supposed it was getting me somewhere. "How like Monet!" I thought when listening to Debussy, and "How like Debussy!" when looking at Monet. I translated sounds into colours, saw the piccolo as apple-green, and the trumpets as scarlet. The arts were to be enriched by taking in one another's washing.

I still listen to some music this way. For instance, the slow start of Beethoven's Seventh Symphony invokes a gray-green tapestry of hunting scenes, and the slow movement of his Fourth Piano Concerto (the dialogue between piano and orchestra) reminds me of the dialogue between Orpheus and the Furies in Gluck. The climax of the first movement of the Appassionata (the "più allegro") seems to me sexual, although I can detect no sex in the Kreutzer, nor have I come across anyone who could, except Tolstoy. That disappointing

1. A high explosive.

work, Brahms' Violin Concerto, promises me clear skies at the opening, and only when the violin has squealed up in the air for page after page is the promise falsified. Wolf's "Ganymed" does give me sky—stratosphere beyond stratosphere. In these cases and in many others music reminds me of something non-musical, and I fancy that to do so is part of its job. Only a purist would condemn all visual parallels, all emotional labelings, all programs.

Yet there is a danger. Music that reminds does open the door to that imp of the concert hall, inattention. To think of a gray-green tapestry is not very different from thinking of the backs of the chairs. We gather a superior wool from it, still we do wool-gather, and the sounds slip by blurred. The sounds! It is for them that we come, and the closer we can get up against them the better. So I do prefer "music itself" and listen to it and for it as far as possible. In this connection, I will try to analyze a mishap that has recently overtaken the Coriolanus Overture. I used to listen to the Coriolanus for "itself," conscious when it passed of something important and agitating, but not defining further. Now I learn that Wagner, endorsed by Sir Donald Tovey, has provided it with a Program: the opening bars indicate the hero's decision to destroy the Volscii, then a sweet tune for female influence, then the dotted-quaver-restlessness of indecision. This seems indisputable, and there is no doubt that this was, or was almost, Beethoven's intention. All the same, I have lost my Coriolanus. Its largeness and freedom have gone. The exquisite sounds have been hardened like a road that has been tarred for traffic. One has to go somewhere down them, and to pass through the same domestic crisis to the same military impasse, each time the overture is played.

Music is so very queer that an amateur is bound to get muddled when writing about it. It seems to be more "real" than anything, and to survive when the rest of civilization decays. In these days I am always thinking of it with relief. It can never be ruined or nationalized. So that the music which is untrammeled and untainted by reference is obviously the best sort of music to listen to; we get nearer the center of reality. Yet though it is untainted, it is never abstract; it is not like mathematics, even when it uses them. The Goldberg Variations, the last Beethoven Sonata, the Franck Quartet, the Schumann Piano Quintet and the Fourth Symphonies of Tchaikovsky and of Brahms certainly have a message. Though what on earth is it? I shall get tied up trying to say. There's an insistence in music—expressed largely through rhythm; there's a sense that it is trying to push across at us something which is neither an esthetic pattern nor a sermon. That's what I listen for specially.

So music that is itself seems on the whole better than music that reminds. And now to end with an important point: my own performances upon the piano. These grow worse yearly, but never will

I give them up. For one thing, they compel me to attend—no wool-gathering or thinking myself clever here—and they drain off all non-musical matter. For another thing, they teach me a little about construction. I see what becomes of a phrase, how it is transformed or returned, sometimes bottom upward, and get some notion of the relation of keys. Playing Beethoven, as I generally do, I grow familiar with his tricks, his impatience, his sudden softnesses, his dropping of a tragic theme one semitone, his love, when tragic, for the key of C minor, and his aversion to the key of B major. This gives me a physical approach to Beethoven which cannot be gained through the slough of "appreciation." Even when people play as badly as I do, they should continue: it will help them to listen.

QUESTIONS FOR STUDY, DISCUSSION, AND WRITING

1. Forster carries his discussion of listening to music through three stages. What are they? Where in the essay is each introduced? Where does Forster make it clear that the first two stages resemble each other?
2. What devices of language and attitude does Forster use to establish an informal, relaxed approach to his topic? Does he appear to be addressing himself to a particular kind of audience? Explain.
3. What is "music itself"? By what means does Forster seek to define it?
4. Early in the essay Forster says that it seems to him an "amazing feat" that professional critics can listen to music "as consistently and steadily as if they were reading a chapter in a novel." What does this indicate as to Forster's view of the novel? Is he being ironical?
5. What does playing the piano teach Forster about listening to music? The closing paragraph, on playing and listening, suggests a similar relationship between writing and reading. Following Forster's strategy of organization, write a brief essay on "Not Reading a Novel," "Not Looking at Pictures," "Not Going to a Lecture," or "Not Studying an Assignment."

KENNETH CLARK

The Blot and the Diagram

I have been told to "look down from a high place over the whole extensive landscape of modern art." We all know how tempting high places can be, and how dangerous. I usually avoid them myself. But if I must do as I am told, I shall try to find out why modern art has taken its peculiar form, and to guess how long that form will continue.

I shall begin with Leonardo da Vinci, because although all processes are gradual, he does represent one clearly marked turning point in the history of art. Before that time, the painters' intentions were quite simple; they were first of all to tell a story, secondly to make the invisible visible, and thirdly to turn a plain surface into a decorated surface. Those are all very ancient aims, going back to the earliest civilizations, or beyond; and for three hundred years painters had been instructed how to carry them out by means of a workshop tradition. Of course, there had been breaks in that tradition—in the fourth century, maybe, and towards the end of the seventh century; but broadly speaking, the artist learnt what he could about the technique of art from his master in his workshop, and then set up shop on his own and tried to do better.

As is well known, Leonardo had a different view of art. He thought that it involved both science and the pursuit of some peculiar attribute called beauty or grace. He was, by inclination, a scientist: he wanted to find out how things worked, and he believed that this knowledge could be stated mathematically. He said "Let no one who is not a mathematician read my works," and he tried to relate this belief in measurement to his belief in beauty. This involved him in two rather different lines of thought, one concerned with magic—the magic of numbers—the other with science. Ever since Pythagoras had discovered that the musical scale could be stated mathematically, by means of the length of the strings, etc., and so had thrown a bridge between intellectual analysis and sensory perception, thinkers on art had felt that it should be possible to do the same for painting. I must say that their effort had not been very rewarding; the modulus, or golden section, and the logarithmic spiral of shells are practically the only undisputed results. But Leonardo lived at a time when it was still possible to hope great things from perspective, which should not only define space, but order it harmoniously; and he also inherited a belief that ideal mathematical combinations could be derived from the proportions of the human body. This line of thought may be called the *mystique* of measurement. The other line may be called *the use* of measurement. Leonardo wished to state mathematically various facts related to the act of seeing. How do we see light passing over a sphere? What happens when objects make themselves perceptible on our retina? Both these lines of thought involved him in drawing diagrams and taking measurements, and for this reason were closely related in his mind. No painter except perhaps Piero della Francesca has tried more strenuously to find a mathematical statement of art, nor has had a greater equipment for doing so.

But Leonardo was also a man of powerful and disturbing imagination. In his notebooks, side by side with his attempts to achieve *order* by mathematics, are drawings and descriptions of the most violent scenes of *disorder* which the human mind can conceive—battles, deluges, eruptions. And he included in his treatise on painting advice on how to develop this side of the artistic faculty also. The passages in which he does so have often been quoted, but they are so incredibly foreign to the whole Renaissance idea of art, although related to a remark in Pliny,[1] that each time I read them, they give me a fresh surprise. I will, therefore, quote them again.

I shall not refrain from including among these precepts a new and speculative idea, which although it may seem trivial and almost laughable, is none the less of great value in quickening the spirit of invention. It is this: that you should look at certain walls stained with damp or at stones of uneven color. If you have to invent some setting you will be able to see in these the likeness of divine landscapes, adorned with mountains, ruins, rocks, woods, great plains, hills and valleys in great variety; and then again you will see there battles and strange figures in violent action, expressions of faces and clothes and an infinity of things which you will be able to reduce to their complete and proper forms. In such walls the same thing happens as in the sound of bells, in whose strokes you may find every named word which you can imagine.

Later he repeats this suggestion in slightly different form, advising the painter to study not only marks on walls, but also "the embers of the fire, or clouds or mud, or other similar objects from which you will find most admirable ideas . . . because from a confusion of shapes the spirit is quickened to new inventions."

I hardly need to insist on how relevant these passages are to modern painting. Almost every morning I receive cards inviting me to current exhibitions, and on the cards are photographs of the works exhibited. Some of them consist of blots, some of scrawls, some look like clouds, some like embers of the fire, some are like mud—some of them are mud; a great many look like stains on walls, and one of them, I remember, consisted of actual stains on walls, photographed and framed. Leonardo's famous passage has been illustrated in every particular. And yet I doubt if he would have been satisfied with the results, because he believed that we must somehow unite the two opposite poles of our faculties. Art itself was the connection between the diagram and the blot.

Now in order to prevent the impression that I am taking advantage of a metaphor, as writers on art are often bound to do, I should explain how I am going to use these words. By "diagram" I mean a rational statement in a visible form, involving measurements, and usually done with an ulterior motive. The theorem of Pythagoras is proved by a diagram. Leonardo's drawings of light striking a sphere are diagrams; but the works of Mondrian, although made up of straight lines, are not diagrams, because they are not done in order to prove or measure some experience, but to please the eye. That they look like diagrams is due to influences which I will examine later. But diagrams can exist with no motive other than their own perfection, just as mathematical propositions can.

1. Roman naturalist, first century A.D.

By "blots" I mean marks or areas which are not intended to convey information, but which, for some reason, seem pleasant and memorable to the maker, and can be accepted in the same sense by the spectator. I said that these blots were not intended to convey information, but of course they do, and that of two kinds. First, they tell us through association, about things we had forgotten; that was the function of Leonardo's stains on walls, which as he said, quickened the spirit of invention, and it can be the function of man-made blots as well; and secondly a man-made blot will tell us about the artist. Unless it is made entirely accidentally, as by spilling an inkpot, it will be a commitment. It is quite difficult to make a non-committal blot. Although the two are connected, I think we can distinguish between analogy blots and gesture blots.

Now let me try to apply this to modern art. Modern art is not a subject on which one can hope for a large measure of agreement, but I hope I may be allowed two assumptions. The first is that the kind of painting and architecture which we call, with varying inflections of the voice, "modern," is a true and vital expression of our own day; and the second assumption is that it differs radically from any art which has preceded it. Both these assumptions have been questioned. It has been said that modern art is "a racket" engineered by art dealers, who have exploited the incompetence of artists and the gullibility of patrons, that the whole thing is a kind of vast and very expensive practical joke. Well, fifty years is a long time to keep up a hoax of this kind, and during these years modern art has spread all over the free world and created a complete international style. I don't think that any honest-minded historian, whether he liked it or not, could pretend that modern art was the result of an accident or a conspiracy. The only doubt he could have would be whether it is, so to say, a long-term or a short-term movement. In the history of art there are stylistic changes which appear to develop from purely internal causes, and seem almost accidental in relation to the other circumstances of life and society. Such, for example, was the state of art in Italy (outside Venice) from about 1530 to 1600. When all is said about the religious disturbances of the time, the real cause of the Mannerist style was the domination of Michelangelo, who had both created an irresistible style and exhausted its possibilities. It needed the almost equally powerful pictorial imagination of Caravaggio to produce a counter-infection, which could spread from Rome to Spain and the Netherlands and prepare the way for Rembrandt. I can see nothing in the history of man's spirit to account for this episode. It seems to me to be due to an internal and specifically artistic chain of events which are easily related to one another, and comprehensible within the general framework of European art. On the other hand, there are events in the history of art which go far beyond the interaction of styles and which evidently reflect a change in the whole condition of the human spirit. Such an event took place towards the end of the fifth century, when the Hellenistic-Roman style gradually became what we call Byzantine; and again in the early thirteenth century, when the Gothic cathedrals shot up out of the ground. In each case the historian could produce a series of examples to prove that the change was inevitable. But actually, it was nothing of the sort; it was wholly unpredictable; and was part of a complete spiritual revolution.

Whether we think that modern art represents a transformation of style or a change of spirit depends to some extent on my second assumption, that it differs radically from anything which has preceded it. This too has been questioned; it has been said that Léger is only a logical development of Poussin, or Mondrian of Vermeer.[2] And it is true that the element of design in each has something in common. If we pare a Poussin down to its bare bones, there are combinations of curves and cubes which are the foundations of much classical painting, and Léger had the good sense to make use of them. Similarly, in Vermeer there is a use of rectangles, large areas contrasted with very narrow ones, and a feeling for shallow recessions, which became the preferred theme of Mondrian. But such analogies are trifling compared with the differences. Poussin was a very intelligent man who thought deeply about his art, and if anyone had suggested to him that his pictures were praiseworthy solely on account of their construction, he would have been incredulous and affronted.

So let us agree that the kind of painting and architecture which we find most representative of our times—say, the painting of Jackson Pollock and the architecture of the Lever building—is deeply different from the painting and architecture of the past; and is *not* a mere whim of fashion, but the result of a great change in our ways of thinking and feeling.

How did this great change take place and what does it mean? To begin with, I think it is related to the development upon which all industrial civilization depends, the differentiation of function. Leonardo was exceptional, almost unique in his integration of functions —the scientific and the imaginative. Yet he foreshadowed more than any other artist their disintegration, by noting and treating in isolation the diagrammatic faculty and the blot-making faculty. The average artist took the unity of these faculties for granted. They were united in Leonardo, and in lesser artists, by *interest* or *pleasure in the thing seen*. The external object was like a magnetic pole which drew the two faculties together. At some point the external object became a negative rather than a positive charge. Instead of drawing together the two faculties, it completely dissociated them; architec-

---

2. Léger and Mondrian: French and Dutch modern painters, respectively. Poussin, French, and Vermeer, Dutch, were both seventeenth-century painters.

ture went off in one direction with the diagram, painting went in the other direction with the blot.

This disintegration was related to a radical change in the philosophy of art. We all know that such changes, however harmless they sound when first enunciated, can have drastic consequences in the world of action. Rulers who wish to maintain the *status quo* are well advised to chop off the heads of all philosophers. What Hilaire Belloc called the "remote and ineffectual don" is more dangerous than the busy columnist with his eye on the day's news. The revolution in our ideas about the nature of painting seems to have been hatched by a don who was considered remote and ineffectual even by Oxford standards—Walter Pater. It was he (inspired, I believe, by Schopenhauer) who first propounded the idea of the aesthetic sensation, intuitively perceived.

In its primary aspect [Pater said] a great picture has no more difficult message for us than an accidental play of sunlight and shadow for a few moments on the wall or floor; in itself, in truth, a space of such fallen light, caught, as in the colors of an Eastern carpet, but refined upon and dealt with more subtly and exquisitely than by nature itself.

It is true that his comparison with an Eastern carpet admits the possibility of "pleasant sensations" being arranged or organized; and Pater confirms this need for organization a few lines later, when he sets down his famous dictum that "all art constantly aspires towards the condition of music." He does not believe in blots uncontrolled by the conscious mind. But he is very far from the information-giving diagram.

This belief that art has its origin in our intuitive rather than our rational faculties, picturesquely asserted by Pater, was worked out historically and philosophically, in the somewhat wearisome volumes of Benedetto Croce, and owing to his authoritative tone, he is usually considered the originator of a new theory of aesthetics. It was, in fact, the reversion to a very old idea. Long before the Romantics had stressed the importance of intuition and self-expression, men had admitted the Dionysiac nature of art. But philosophers had always assumed that the frenzy of inspiration must be controlled by law and by the intellectual power of putting things into harmonious order. And this general philosophic concept of art as a combination of intuition and intellect had been supported by technical necessities. It was necessary to master certain laws and to use the intellect in order to build the Gothic cathedrals, or set up the stained glass windows of Chartres or cast the bronze doors of the Florence Baptistry. When this bracing element of craftsmanship ceased to dominate the artist's outlook, as happened soon after the time of Leonardo, new scientific disciples had to be invented to maintain the intellectual element in art. Such were perspective and anatomy. From a purely artistic point of view, they were unneccessary. The Chinese produced some of the finest landscapes ever painted, without any systematic knowledge of perspective. Greek figure sculpture reached its highest point before the study of anatomy had been systematized. But from the Renaissance onwards, painters felt that these two sciences made their art intellectually respectable. They were two ways of connecting the diagram and the blot.

In the nineteenth century, belief in art as a scientific activity declined, for a quantity of reasons. Science and technology withdrew into specialization. Voltaire's efforts to investigate the nature of heat seem to us ludicrous; Goethe's studies of botany and physics a waste of a great poet's time. In spite of their belief in inspiration, the great Romantics were aware of the impoverishment of the imagination which would take place when science had drifted out of reach, and both Shelley and Coleridge spent much time in chemical experiments. Even Turner, whose letters reveal a singular lack of analytic faculty, annotated Goethe's theories of color, and painted two pictures to demonstrate them. No good. The laws which govern the movement of the human spirit are inexorable. The enveloping assumption, within which the artist has to function, was that science was no longer approachable by any but the specialist. And gradually there grew up the idea that all intellectual activities were hostile to art.

I have mentioned the philosophic development of this view of Croce. Let me give one example of its quiet acceptance by the official mind. The British Council sends all over the world, even to Florence and Rome, exhibitions of children's art—the point of these children's pictures being that they have no instruction of any kind, and do not attempt the troublesome task of painting what they see. Well, why not, after all? The results are quite agreeable—sometimes strangely beautiful; and the therapeutic effect on the children is said to be excellent. It is like one of those small harmless heresies which we are shocked to find were the object of persecution by the Mediaeval Church. When, however, we hear admired modern painters saying that they draw their inspiration from the drawings of children and lunatics, as well as from stains on walls, we recognize that we have accomplices in a revolution.

The lawless and intuitive character of modern art is a familiar theme and certain historians have said that it is symptomatic of a decline in Western civilization. This is journalism—one of those statements that sound well to-day and nonsense to-morrow. It is obvious that the development of physical science in the last hundred years has been one of the most colossal efforts the human intellect has ever made. But I think it is also true that human beings can produce, in a given epoch, only a certain amount of creative energy, and that this is directed to different ends and different times —music in the eighteenth century is the obvious example; and I believe that the dazzling achievements of science during the last seventy years have deflected far more of those skills and endowments which go to the making of a work of art than is usually realized. To begin with, there is the sheer energy. In every molding of a Renaissance palace we are conscious of an immense intellectual energy, and it is the absence of this energy in the nineteenth-century copies of Renaissance buildings which makes them seem so dead. To find a form with the same vitality as a window molding of the Palazzo Farnese I must wait till I get back into an aeroplane, and look at the relation of the engine to the wing. That form is alive, not (as used to be said) because it is functional—many functional shapes are entirely uninteresting—but because it is animated by the breath of modern science.

The deflections from art to science are the more serious because these are not, as used to be supposed, two contrary activities, but in fact draw on many of the same capacities of the human mind. In the last resort each depends on the imagination. Artist and scientist alike are both trying to give concrete form to dimly apprehended ideas. Dr. Bronowski has put it very well: "All science is the search for unity in hidden likenesses, and the starting point is an image, because then the unity is before our mind's eye." Even if we no longer have to pretend that a group of stars looks like a plough or a bear, our scientists still depend on humanly comprehensible images, and it is striking that the valid symbols of our time, invented to embody some scientific truth, have taken root in the popular imagination. Do those red and blue balls connected by rods really resemble a type of atomic structure? I am too ignorant to say. I accept the symbol just as an early Christian accepted the Fish or the Lamb, and I find it echoed or even (it would seem) anticipated in the work of modern artists like Kandinsky and Miró.

Finally, there is the question of popular interest and approval. We have grown accustomed to the idea that artists can work in solitude and incomprehension; but that was not the way things happened in the Renaissance or the seventeenth century, still less in ancient Greece. The pictures carried through the streets by cheering crowds, the *Te Deum* sung on completion of a public building—all this indicates a state of opinion in which men could undertake great works of art with a confidence quite impossible to-day. The research scientist, on the other hand, not only has millions of pounds worth of plant and equipment for the asking, he has principalities and powers waiting for his conclusions. He goes to work, as Titian once did, confident that he will succeed because the strong tide of popular admiration is flowing with him.

But although science has absorbed so many of the functions of art and deflected (I believe) so many potential artists, it obviously cannot be a *substitute* for art. Its mental process may be similar, but its ends are different. There have been three views about the purpose of art. First that it aims simply at imitation; secondly that it should influence human conduct; and thirdly that it should produce a kind of exalted happiness. The first view, which was developed in ancient Greece, must be reckoned one of the outstanding failures of Greek thought. It is simply contrary to experience, because if the visual arts aimed solely at imitating things they would be of very little importance; whereas the Greeks above all people knew that they were important, and treated them as such. Yet such was the prestige of Greek thought that this theory of art was revived in the Renaissance, in an uncomfortable sort of way, and had a remarkable recrudescence in the nineteenth century. The second view, that art should influence conduct and opinions, is more respectable, and held the field throughout the Middle Ages; indeed the more we learn about the art of the past and motives of those who commissioned it, the more important this particular aim appears to be; it still dominated art theory in the time of Diderot. The third view, that art should produce a kind of exalted happiness, was invented by the Romantics at the beginning of the nineteenth century (well, perhaps *invented* by Plotinus, but given currency by the Romantics), and gradually gained ground until by the end of the century it was believed in by almost all educated people. It has held the field in Western Europe till the present day. Leaving aside the question which of these theories is correct, let me ask which of them is most likely to be a helpful background to art (for that is all that a theory of aesthetics can be) in an age when science has such an overwhelming domination over the human mind. The first aim must be reckoned *by itself* to be pointless, since science has now discovered so many ways of imitating appearances, which are incomparably more accurate and convincing than even the most realistic picture. Painting might defend itself against the daguerreotype, but not against Cinerama.

The popular application of science has also, it seems to me, invalidated the second aim of art, because it is quite obvious that no picture can influence human conduct as effectively as a television advertisement. It is quite true that in totalitarian countries artists are still instructed to influence conduct. But that is either due to technical deficiencies, as in China, where in default of T.V., broadsheets and posters are an important way of communicating with an illiterate population; or, in Russia, to a philosophic time-lag. The fact is that very few countries have had the courage to take Plato's advice and exclude works of art altogether. They have, therefore, had to invent some excuse for keeping them on, and the Russians are still using the pretext that paintings and sculpture can influence people in favor of socialist and national policies, although it must have dawned on them that these results can be obtained far more effectively by the cinema and television.

So it seems to me that of these three possible purposes of art—imitation, persuasion, or exalted pleasure—only the third still holds good in an age of science; and it must be justified very largely by the fact that it is a feeling which is absent from scientific achievements—although mathematicians have told us that it is similar to the feeling aroused by their finest calculations. We might say that in the modern world the art of painting is defensible only in so far as it is complementary to science.

We are propelled in the same direction by another achievement of modern science, the study of psychology. That peeling away of the psyche, which was formerly confined to spiritual instructors, or the great novelists, has become a commonplace of conversation. When a good, solid, external word like Duty is turned into a vague, uneasy, internal word like Guilt, one cannot expect artists to take much interest in good, solid, external objects. The artist has always been involved in the painful process of turning himself inside out, but in the past his inner convictions have been of such a kind that they can, so to say, re-form themselves round an object. But, as we have seen, even in Leonardo's time, there were certain obscure needs and patterns of the spirit, which could discover themselves only through less precise analogies—the analogies provided by stains on walls or the embers of a fire. Now, I think that in this inward-looking age, when we have become so much more aware of the vagaries of the spirit, and so respectful of the working of the unconscious, the artist is more likely to find his point of departure in analogies of this kind. They are more exciting because they, so to say, take us by surprise, like forgotten smells; and they seem to be more profound because the memories they awaken have been deeply buried in our minds. Whether Jung is right in believing that this free, undirected, illogical form of mental activity will allow us to pick up, like a magic radio station, some deep memories of our race which can be of universal interest, I do not know. The satisfaction we derive from certain combinations of shape and color does seem to be inexplicable even by the remotest analogies, and may perhaps involve inherited memories. It is not yet time for the art-historian to venture in to that mysterious jungle. I must, however, observe that our respect for the unconscious mind not only gives us an interest in analogy blots, but in what I called "gesture blots" as well. We recognize how free and forceful such a communication can be, and this aspect of art has become more important in the last ten years. An apologist of modern art has said: "What we want to know is not what the world looks like, but what we mean to each other." So the gesture blot becomes a sort of ideogram, like primitive Chinese writing. Students of Zen assure us it is a means of communication more direct and complete than anything which our analytic system can achieve. Almost 2,000 years before Leonardo looked for images in blots, Lao-tzu had written:

> The Tao is something blurred and indistinct.
> How indistinct! How blurred!
> Yet within are images,
> How blurred! How indistinct!
> Yet within are things.

I said that when the split took place between our faculties of measurement and intuition, *architecture* went off with the diagram. Of course architecture had always been involved with measurement and calculation, but we tend to forget how greatly it was also involved with the imitation of external objects. "The question to be determined," said Ruskin, "is whether architecture is a frame for the sculpture, or the sculpture an ornament of the architecture." And he came down on the first alternative. He thought that a building became architecture only in so far as it was a frame for figurative sculpture. I wonder if there is a single person alive who would agree with him. And yet Ruskin had the most sensitive eye and the keenest analytic faculty that has ever been applied to architecture. Many people disagreed with him in his own day; they thought that sculpture should be subordinate to the total design of the building. But that anything claiming to be architecture could dispense with ornament altogether never entered anyone's head till a relatively short time ago.

A purely diagrammatic architecture is only about thirty years older than a purely blottesque painting; yet it has changed the face of the world and produced in every big city a growing uniformity. Perhaps because it is a little older, perhaps because it seems to have a material justification, we have come to accept it without question. People who are still puzzled or affronted by action painting are proud of the great steel and glass boxes which have arisen so miraculously in the last ten years. And yet these two are manifestations of the same state of mind. The same difficulties of function, the same deflection from the external object, and the same triumph of science. Abstract painting and glass box architecture are related in two different ways. There is the direct relationship of style—the kind of relationship which painting and architecture had with one another in the great consistent ages of art like the 13th and 17th centuries. For modern architecture is not simply functional; at its best it has a style which is almost as definite and as arbitrary as Gothic. And this leads me back to my earlier point: that diagrams can be drawn in order to achieve some imagined perfection, similar to that of certain mathematical propositions. Thirty years after Pater's famous dictum, painters in Russia, Holland, and France began to put into practice the theory that "all art constantly aspires to the condition of music"; and curiously enough this Pythagorean mystique of measurements produced a style—the style which reached its purest expression in the Dutch painter, Mondrian. And through the influence of the Bauhaus, this became the leading style of modern architecture.

The other relationship between contemporary architecture and painting appears to be indirect and even accidental. I am thinking of the visual impact when the whole upper part of a tall glass building mirrors the clouds or the dying embers of a sunset, and so becomes a frame for a marvelous, moving Tachiste[3] picture. I do not think that future historians of art will find this accidental at all, but will see it as the culmination of a long process beginning in the Romantic period, in which, from Wordsworth and De Quincey onwards, poets and philosophers recognized the movement of clouds as the symbol of a newly discovered mental faculty.

Such, then, would be my diagnosis of the present condition of art. I must now, by special request, say what I think will happen to art in the future. I think that the state of affairs which I have called the blot and the diagram will last for a long time. Architecture will continue to be made up of glass boxes and steel grids, without ornament of any kind. Painting will continue to be subjective and arcane, an art of accident rather than rule, of stains on walls rather than of calculation, of inscape rather than of external reality.

This conclusion is rejected by those who believe in a social theory of art. They maintain that a living art must depend on the popular will, and that neither the blot nor the diagram is popular; and, since those who hold a social theory of art are usually Marxists, they point to Soviet Russia as a country where all my conditions obtain—differentiation of function, the domination of science and so forth—and yet what we call modern art has gained no hold. This argument does not impress me. There is of course, nothing at all in the idea that Communist doctrines inevitably produce social realism. Painting in Yugoslavia, in Poland and Hungary is in the same modern idiom as painting in the United States, and shows remarkable vitality. Whereas the official social realism of the U.S.S.R., except for a few illustrators, lacks life or conviction, and shows no evidence of representing the popular will. In fact Russian architecture has already dropped the grandiose official style, and I am told that this is now taking place in painting also. In spite of disapproval amounting to persecution, experimental painters exist and find buyers.

I doubt if the Marxists are even correct in saying that the blot and the diagram are not popular. The power, size, and splendor of, say, the Seagram building in New York makes it as much the object of pride and wonder as great architecture was in the past. And one of

---

3. A method of nonrepresentational contemporary painting which exploits the quality of freely flowing oil paint for its own sake.

the remarkable things about Tachisme is the speed with which it has spread throughout the world, not only in sophisticated centers, but in small local art societies. It has become as much an international style as Gothic in the 14th and Baroque in the 17th centuries. I recently visited the exhibition of a provincial academy in the north of England, a very respectable body then celebrating its hundred and fiftieth anniversary. A few years ago it had been full of Welsh mountain landscapes, and scenes of streets and harbors, carefully delineated. Now practically every picture was in the Tachiste style, and I found that many of them were painted by the same artists, often quite elderly people, who had previously painted the mountains and streets. As works of art, they seemed to me neither better nor worse. But I could not help thinking that they must have been less trouble to do, and I reflected that the painters must have had a happy time releasing the Dionysiac elements in their natures. However, we must not be too cynical about this. I do not believe that the spread of action painting is due solely to the fact that it is easy to do. Cubism, especially synthetic Cubism, also looks easy to do, and never had this immense diffusion. It remained the style of a small élite of professional painters and specialized art lovers; whereas Tachisme has spread to fabrics, to the decoration of public buildings, to the backgrounds of television programs, to advertising of all kinds. Indeed the closest analogy to action painting is the most popular art of all—the art of jazz. The trumpeter who rises from his seat as one possessed, and squirts out his melody like a scarlet scrawl against a background of plangent dashes and dots, is not as a rule performing for a small body of intellectuals.

Nevertheless, I do not think that the style of the blot and the diagram will last forever. For one thing, I believe that the imitation of external reality is a fundamental human instinct which is bound to reassert itself. In his admirable book on sculpture called *Aratra Pentelici*, Ruskin describes an experience which many of us could confirm. "Having been always desirous," he says,

that the education of women should begin in learning how to cook, I got leave, one day, for a little girl of eleven years old to exchange, much to her satisfaction, her schoolroom for the kitchen. But as ill fortune would have it, there was some pastry toward, and she was left unadvisedly in command of some delicately rolled paste; whereof she made no pies, but an unlimited quantity of cats and mice....

Now [he continues] you may read the works of the gravest critics of art from end to end; but you will find, at last, they can give you no other true account of the spirit of sculpture than that it is an irresistible human instinct for the making of cats and mice, and other imitable living creatures, in such permanent form that one may play with the images at leisure.

I cannot help feeling that he was right. I am fond of works of art, and I collect them. But I do not want to hang them on the wall simply in order to get an electric shock every time that I pass them.

I want to hold them, and turn them round and re-hang them—in short, to play with the images at leisure. And, putting aside what may be no more than a personal prejudice, I rather doubt if an art which depends solely on the first impact on our emotions is permanently valid. When the shock is exhausted, we have nothing to occupy our minds. And this is particularly troublesome with an art which depends so much on the unconscious, because, as we know from the analysis of dreams, the furniture of our unconscious minds is even more limited, repetitive, and commonplace than that of our conscious minds. The blots and stains of modern painting depend ultimately on the memories of things seen, memories sunk deep in the unconscious, overlaid, transformed, assimilated to a physical condition, but memories none the less. *Ex nihilo nihil fit.* It is not possible for a painter to lose contact with the visible world.

At this point the apes have provided valuable evidence. There is no doubt that they are Tachiste painters of considerable accomplishment. I do not myself care for the work of Congo the chimp, but Sophie, the Rotterdam gorilla, is a charming artist, whose delicate traceries remind me of early Paul Klee. As you know, apes take their painting seriously. The patterns they produce are not the result of mere accident, but of intense, if short-lived, concentration, and a lively sense of balance and space-filling. If you compare the painting of a young ape with that of a human child of relatively the same age, you will find that in the first, expressive, pattern-making stage, the ape is superior. Then, automatically and inexorably the child begins to draw *things*—man, house, truck, etc. This the ape never does. Of course his Tachiste paintings are far more attractive than the child's crude conceptual outlines. But they cannot develop. They are monotonous and ultimately rather depressing.

The difference between the child and the ape does not show itself in aesthetic perception, or in physical perception of any kind, but in the child's power to form a concept. Later, as we know, he will spend his time trying to adapt his concept to the evidence of physical sensation; in that struggle lies the whole of style. But the concept —the need to draw a line round his thought—comes first. Now it is a truism that the power to form concepts is what distinguishes man from the animals; although the prophets of modern society, Freud, Jung, D. H. Lawrence, have rightly insisted on the importance of animal perceptions in balanced human personality, the concept-forming faculty has not declined in modern man. On the contrary, it is the basis of that vast scientific achievement which, as I said earlier, seems almost to have put art out of business.

Now, if the desire to represent external reality depended solely on an interest in visual sensation, I would agree that it might disappear from art and never return. But if, as the evidence of children and monkeys indicates, it depends primarily on the formation of concepts, which are then modified by visual sensation, I think it is bound to return. For I consider the human faculty of forming concepts at least as "inalienable" as "life, liberty, and the pursuit of happiness. . . ."

I am not, of course, suggesting that the imitation of external reality will ever again become what it was in European art from the mid-17th to the late 19th centuries. Such a subordination of the concept to the visual sensation was altogether exceptional in the history of art. Much of the territory won by modern painting will, I believe, be held. For example, freedom of association, the immediate passage from one association to another—which is so much a part of Picasso's painting and Henry Moore's sculpture, is something which has existed in music since Wagner and in poetry since Rimbaud and Mallarmé. (I mean existed consciously; of course it underlies all great poetry and music.) It need not be sacrificed in a return to external reality. Nor need the direct communication of intuition, through touch and an instinctive sense of materials. This I consider pure gain. In the words of my original metaphor, both the association blot and the gesture blot can remain. But they must be given more nourishment: they must be related to a fuller knowledge of the forms and structures which impress us most powerfully, and so become part of our concept of natural order. At the end of the passage in which Leonardo tells the painter that he can look for battles, landscapes, and animals in the stains on walls, he adds this caution, "But first be sure that you know all the members of all things you wish to depict, both the members of the animals and the members of landscapes, that is to say of rocks, plants, and so forth." It is because one feels in Henry Moore's sculpture this knowledge of the members of animals and plants, that his work, even at its most abstract, makes an impression on us different from that of his imitators. His figures are not merely pleasing examples of design, but seem to be a part of nature, "rolled round in Earth's diurnal course with rocks and stones and trees."

Those lines of Wordsworth lead me to the last reason why I feel that the intuitive blot and scribble may not dominate painting forever. Our belief in the whole purpose of art may change. I said earlier that we now believe it should aim at producing a kind of exalted happiness: this really means that art becomes an end in itself. Now it is an incontrovertible fact of history that the greatest art has always been *about* something, a means of communicating some truth which is assumed to be more important than the art itself. The truths which art has been able to communicate have been of a kind which could not be put in any other way. They have been ultimate truths, stated symbolically. Science has achieved its triumph precisely by disregarding such truths, by not asking unanswerable questions, but sticking to the question "how." I confess it looks to me as if we shall have to wait a long time before there is some new belief which requires expression through art rather than through statistics or equations. And until this happens, the visual arts will fall short of the greatest epochs, the ages of the Parthenon, the Sistine Ceiling, and Chartres Cathedral.

I am afraid there is nothing we can do about it. No amount of goodwill and no expenditure of money can affect that sort of change. We cannot even dimly foresee when it will happen or what form it will take. We can only be thankful for what we have got—a vigorous, popular, decorative art, complementary to our architecture and our science, somewhat monotonous, somewhat prone to charlatanism, but genuinely expressive of our time.

QUESTIONS FOR STUDY, DISCUSSION, AND WRITING

1. What definition does Clark give of his central metaphor, "the blot and the diagram"? Are "blot" and "diagram" the equivalents of "art" and "science"? Explain.
2. What distinction does Clark make between "analogy (or association) blot" and "gesture blot"? What importance does the distinction have for his discussion of modern painting?
3. In what ways, according to Clark, is the place of science in the modern world similar to the place occupied by science in the past? What past functions of art has science assumed? To what extent does Clark consider the situation satisfactory? What defects does he mention?
4. How does Clark show "blot" painting and "diagram" architecture to be related? Is architecture today an art or a science? How scientific is painting?
5. Clark points out that "the closest analogy to action painting is the most popular art of all—the art of jazz" (p. 515). Is there any jazz analogous to "diagram"? Explain.
6. Study closely some examples of advertising layout. To what extent do they appear influenced by "blot"? Is there influence of "diagram" in any? Are any exemplary of "blot" and "diagram" in harmony?
7. On page 510 Clark quotes Bronowski with approval. What points of agreement are there between this essay and Bronowski's "The Creative Mind" (pp. 247–258)?
8. What extensions into other disciplines can be made of Clark's blot-diagram antithesis? Does it apply in literature? In psychology?
9. Why, according to Clark, will man's concept-forming nature eventually bring about a change of style in art?

LESTER D. LONGMAN
Criteria in Criticism of Contemporary Art

What we value in art today is not clear. We have systematically depreciated all the qualities which are discriminated in standard aesthetic theory as perennially desirable. Respectable critics agree fairly well in their approval of trends and general classes of objects, but are vague or negligent in considering the qualities which might sustain a work of art after interest in an approved trend or class of objects declines. As a result, it is virtually impossible to predict a critic's opinion of a particular contemporary work of art even when one knows the critic well. This is especially obvious when the artist is relatively unknown and when he can't be clearly classified.

As recently as twenty-five years ago this was not true. When we knew the critic, we knew that he would commend a work of art for its pictorial design, its technical virtuosity, its social commentary, its truth to medium, its functional utility, its humanistic insight, or some similiar virtue conceived to transcend the enthusiasms of the moment. Today, however, any clear criterion seems dogmatic. Confronted with what appears to be the only alternative, we prefer anarchy in criticism.

A major cause of this anarchy seems to be that critics no longer respect the independence of their profession. In theory, a criticism is a judicial appraisal, which is as detached and objective as possible, viewing the work from a more comprehensive perspective than that of the artist. Now, however, critics seem to be entangled with the artists themselves in a common syndrome of preoccupations and involvements. They pronounce their opinions from within the same charmed circle of shared experiences, enjoying the same emotional commitments and the same prestige of an *avant-garde* status, desiring no larger frame of reference, and using the same prejudicial or equivocal terminology. The psychology of the perpetual revolutionary holds tightly in its grip both artist and critic. Hence, neither can afford to consult tradition, consider the more permanent values, or even be unambiguous in view of the certainty of continuous change.

For the critic this is a form of abdication, a renunciation of the art of criticism. What he writes may still be interesting, just as what the artist paints may still be interesting—so long as the current mood persists; but he should be detached enough to observe that in the long run more is required of the artist than to be representative of his time, and more is required of himself than sophisticated involvement in the passions of the moment. One remembers the infatuations to which many critics succumbed in the recent past—to surrealism, to social realism, to regionalism, to cubism, etc. We bought for museums and gave prizes to the right kind of art, that which was then new and respectable. With the passage of time our enthusiasms were dissipated, and now much that was exciting while *à la mode* seems grotesquely lifeless for lack of those more permanent aesthetic values which would sustain it. A work of art is one thing, an historical artifact quite another, and the critic's function is to distinguish between them at a moment when the rest of us are lost in excited admiration of the latest vogue.

At the present time the criteria of value which seem to enjoy the highest prestige in the world of art are originality and its corollaries, contemporaneity and irrationality. They would be inadequate to define permanent aesthetic value, unless their usual connotations are greatly altered; but they point to art which we consider "vital" and "modern" and, in our zest, credulity, and infatuation with their style, we scarcely miss what we doubt could be attained in any case. And with our psychology of permanent revolution, the critic who stands aside from the enthusiasms of the day, as in any kind of revolution, finds doubt identified with black reaction: he who is not with us is against us.

Originality is the paramount value today. The term "beauty" has been abandoned, or at most restricted to one kind of aesthetic value like that of Greek art of the fifth and fourth centuries. The general quality of beauty is now designated by the term "originality," much as the surrealists deliberately extended the term "marvelous" to make it synonymous with the beautiful. This usage is bound to generate inconsistencies and non sequiturs, since in aesthetic value neither the new nor the old is inherently superior. We all recognize this in other contexts than a discussion of modern art. Why, then, in modern art does the new seem to have a built-in superiority over the old?

In part, no doubt, it results from our addiction to the religion of progress. We normally prefer new models of every product and assume the new is the better, as frequently it is in the realm of technology where progress is most conspicuous. This is especially true in America. In Rome a large exhibition of contemporary art may contain work in every style since Courbet, with no apparent feeling that older styles are disqualified because they are outmoded. It may also be due to an unconscious analogy with science, where the new is usually superior because of the cumulative character of scientific knowledge. Although there is no parallel in art to this unilinear progress in the evolution of science, in this age of science we can hardly avoid, in any area of activity, the dynamic and pervasive influence of scientific modes of thought.

Strangely enough, this admiration of the latest model is inconsistently reversed when the same critic turns to historic styles. In that case the older object is normally considered superior unless there is incontestable evidence to the contrary. An archaizing Hellenistic sculpture rises immensely in esteem and monetary value if it is proved to be Greek of the transitional period. And "improvements" to pictures introduced by later repaintings are removed, layer by layer, in order to arrive at the superior, older version. Occasionally in this process the original turns out to be rather commonplace, the improvements having been made by a more accomplished artist; nevertheless the older one is preferred. Such an inconsistency should make more obvious the elementary principle that neither the new nor the old in art is valuable artistically because of its age.

In science the new unseats the old when validated by standard procedures of experimental verifications. While there is no analogue in art to this kind of progress, we act as though new work discredits that which went before as soon as it becomes widespread. *Success* is progress. Thus, there can be no such thing as decline or retrogression in the history of art. Even in Late Minoan or West Christian art, historians condemn examples which are *retardataire*[1] in the story of that which succeeds. It is reassuring that no currently successful movement in modern art can possibly represent a general decline. Such reasoning saves us from a morbid concern about the ultimate significance of widespread contemporary styles; although we may sometimes wonder why we now relegate to museum basements much of the art of the nineteenth century, which was international in style and at the time widely approved by cultural authorities. We used to base an adverse judgment of this art on aesthetic and a-historical grounds, but could not do so if originality is beauty and success is the measure of merit. At one time sentimental naturalism was original and it soon became a very successful international style.

In line with this reasoning, the most original artist would be the one with most imitators. We could have no other way to recognize him or to judge an artist's achievement. Thus Michelangelo's art was very original during his life time, but El Greco's would not be until nearly three hundred years after his death; and the significance of a contemporary artist with a following could not be doubted. Such a view seems over-simplified. Avoiding the complexities of aesthetic judgment, it contents itself with historic importance as an agreeably simple substitute.

The current concept of originality in art raises another kind of semantic problem. Again by analogy with science, we tend to apply the term "originality" to those cases which exhibit a new general principle which can be phrased in words, like a new scientific theory. We may coin a word ending in "ism" to designate the new con-

1. Appearing late.

cept. The aesthetic value of a given painting is then determined by the degree to which its character incorporates the values ascribed to the general principle or "ism"; and critics may be content to stop the inquiry at this point, being unaccustomed or unable to judge a work of art on grounds different from those which evaluate the class as a whole. A work of art, however, is not essentially an illustration of an idea; and its originality does not consist of mere conceptual innovation. On the contrary, one may be exceptionally original while working in any established style, for there is an infinite number of possible variations in any general style of expression, and the differential of originality between the most significant and the most negligible example is also infinite.

As historians, we recognize this on many occasions. We do not lament the similarities between Simone Martini and Duccio, Van der Weyden and the Van Eycks, the early Titian and Giorgione, Leonardo and Verrocchio. Although Luini and Gaddi could not do so, it was possible in principle for followers of Leonardo and Giotto to equal or surpass them while continuing to work in the same style. We do not reprove Rouault for imitating Gothic glass, Picasso for imitating Pompeian murals or African sculpture, or Matisse for imitating Persian art; and if David and Canova are not universally admired, it would be an error of judgment to say that it was because they imitated Hellenistic sculpture. In theory, Rembrandt might have had a follower whose work surpassed his own. Indeed, such an imitator could still arise, reviving with exciting new content the same general style, unless art be wholly conditioned by the historical context, and this our concept of originality does not permit. We accept complete historical determinism only when convenient to advocate a prejudice; at other times the complete autonomy of the artist's imagination is a more useful rationalization. The judicious position is that a stylistic revival, incorporating content with which we are concerned today, is always theoretically possible, even when it seems empirically unlikely.

Our inconsistency in believing in originality and simultaneously in historical determinism in modern art leads us to an excessive devaluation of historic art and of many traditional values. Artists and critics of modern art have little time for the Metropolitan Museum. Visiting it for serious study would be like reading a novel in a foreign language, something the average educated man does only occasionally. The greater the artist the less he should fear the weight of tradition; it is the minor artist who escapes its burden by cavalierly declaring that one cannot "revive the past." Rouault, Matisse, and Picasso have proved the value of trying. Michelangelo's generation created a great new art while believing it was engaged in reviving classical forms; and we can see now that David's generation made something new and timely in spite of its very serious intention to imitate. It is so certain that one cannot really revive the past that one need never fear to try.

The identification of originality with ideological innovation is discredited in practice by our esteem for the successive works of major artists. Should Titian have contented himself with one reclining Venus because his first version made the essential point? Or should he have avoided the subject altogether after seeing Giorgione's *Sleeping Venus,* to which he could add only a corollary? Perugino and Botticelli may have painted too many Madonnas, but was one enough? If originality is measured by innovations, Mondrian could have made his point with one painting about 1921, after which his originality could be seriously questioned. Are we misguided to buy and hang on the walls of museums the repetitious variations of an artist's major themes?

It would seem so when we note how artists strain today for the kind of originality which can be classified by a new term, and when we see them abetted in this error by the critics. An artist who strives to be himself will turn out as original as he can be, and the one who succeeds in the long view of history was certainly thinking about something else than originality while he worked. Such an observation is not likely, however, to deter the artist who is anxious to be "modern." He struggles so hard to find a new method that the methodology itself may become the content, for one paints what one is thinking about. He and his fellow artists, eyeing one another in the labor of their lonely battles, end up being eccentric in much the same way. Or he may imitate a recent innovator like Klee or Kandinsky, rather than an older one like Degas or Cézanne; it is no less imitation, but current critical opinion will illogically allow him to retain the eulogistic vocabulary of innovation in speaking about his work.

Another result of our exaltation of the original is an excessive esteem for an art that is disaffected. When every artist and critic feels obliged to become a pioneer of a new movement, they reinforce their efforts by depreciating salutary as well as moribund conventions. David was perhaps the last major artist to glorify the prevailing social ideology; thereafter the history of art is, increasingly as the generations pass in review, a history of rebels against the status quo. Admittedly, the principle of alienation from one's fellows can and has produced great artists; but it has not been the usual pattern in history and we normally (and inconsistently) commend the great painters and sculptors of all periods before the French Revolution for their achievements in faithfully symbolizing the prevailing thought of the ruling classes and intellectuals of their day. We try to explain away the inconsistency by a semantic manipulation, by claiming that the few rebels among us are the true representatives of our time—thus they are both the pioneers of a future culture and simultaneously the "true" spokesmen of the dominant culture against which they rebel.

Our inordinate emphasis on the aesthetic value of originality also leads to excessive tolerance in criticism. If the cardinal virtue of the artist is invention of the new, that of the critic must be to recognize it immediately. What can one say of a critic more reprehensible than that he did not recognize a certain original artist while he lived? Lurid examples of such failures by the distinguished critics over the past hundred years are constantly held up to ridicule to keep alive the awful moral. Who can forget what was said of the Impressionists during the 1870's? Have we overdone it, playing safe by praising every eccentric effort? I am told that in an old movie the Marx Brothers had to play the part of surgeons. They busied themselves rushing around with their tools and equipment and endlessly washing and rewashing their hands and arms clear up to the armpits. Finally someone had the courage to challenge them, saying, "Why don't you get down to business; you guys must be crazy." Whereupon Groucho replied, "That's what they said about Pasteur."

Even our extraordinary critical tolerance is no guarantee that the original artist of our time will be caught in the ample net. For in one respect it may not be ample enough. The majority of critics are expecting to find the true pioneers within the compass of styles approved by the recognized art authorities—representatives of certain art museums, editors of art magazines, certain writers on contemporary movements, and a selection of college professors—in short the representatives of official taste, the vanguard *pompiers*,[2] all of whom have entrenched interests interweaving financial and psychological commitments, and who could not easily change their minds on fundamental matters. Unfortunately, it was the same class of officials who made all the flagrant errors of the recent past. Will history repeat itself? Are they perhaps again united in dramatic error? If not, who are the Bouguereaus[3] of our generation, highly venerated by authorities today and destined tomorrow to be relegated to museum basements? Or have such egregious errors ceased? We claim the artists who are right are rebels and are few. Can, then, the critics who are right be the official arbiters of taste and their legions of complacent followers who uphold the *status quo*. Where are the rebel critics?

Turning now to the criterion of contemporaneity, which naturally follows from our emphasis upon originality in art, as we have noted an artist who struggles unsuccessfully to be original may be commended by critics if he works within a style of very recent

2. Philistines, conventional or old-fashioned persons.

3. Adolphe-William Bouguereau was a nineteenth-century French academic painter acclaimed by the critics in his lifetime and forgotten today.

vintage which the leading authorities consider truly contemporary. Many critics believe that abstract expressionism or action painting is the true mode of contemporaneity, or that some mystical determinism will force it upon the future. They proclaim certain artists superior and genuinely progressive abstractionists and others inferior and derivative. The evidence of current critical writing and statements by leading artists suggest that we ordinarily base such judgments upon spontaneous acts of intuition, whose authority rests upon eloquence and office. To believe them is an act of faith in dogma. There are high priests, each with a magic talisman of ineffable sensibility, and from the offices for which they are paid they pronounce aesthetic decrees supported by casually eloquent rationalizations. The rest of us play the game of follow the leader, with the hope that the blind are not leading the blind down a path to ultimate disillusionment and the dark laughter of another generation.

Who, in fact, is qualified to define the content of the term "contemporaneity" for our time? Historians say that the post-impressionists expressed the *Zeitgeist* of the late nineteenth century, but at that time they were scarcely known. Most critics and artists, including even Van Gogh, would have pointed to Bouguereau as typically contemporaneous. Such a view is still reasonable. Either it is no virtue to be contemporaneous, which seems likely, or it is not possible to define contemporaneity, which also seems likely. How often, on the other hand, have we heard it said that a serious artist today has the *obligation* to express our time, and that the important artists are those who do? As a result, many try to conform to what they consider the most respectable version of contemporaneity, which leads them away from those personal concerns which alone can make their art persuasive and enduring.

The current use of the term "contemporaneity" to refer to art not representative of one's time but "ahead of it," introduces semantic confusion to promote a cause. We must question whether any artist can succeed in being contemporaneous in this sense by deliberately trying to, and whether any critic can identify the contemporaneous artist while he lives. How can either one predict what the *Zeitgeist* requires of him, or travel ahead of others over the horizon of time merely by taking thought? Such pretense demeans the critic's art, for it can be no more than special pleading disguised as prophecy, and it is irrelevant to aesthetic judgment.

If, on the other hand, to be contemporaneous means to reflect one's time in the most literal sense, then no one can avoid doing so. Everyone today, no matter how he paints or what his critical judgments may be, is reflecting our time in some aspect—Norman Rockwell and Grandma Moses no less than Picasso and Dali or Kline and Barnett Newman, and everyone in equal measure. Thus, in this case, too, the problem of aesthetic evaluation remains to be solved on other grounds.

One hears sometimes from reputable critics that representation is dead, and that it takes abstraction to express contemporaneity. It is true, of course, that those abstract artists who have made a gesture toward reviving representation have ordinarily been unable to carry it far, being content to suggest enigmatically a human figure or part thereof. To be more explicit one must be more sure of what one means to say about the nature of a human being, and must be willing to take the consequences of not being ambiguous. Very few are ready for this at present. We will know how to do it when someone does it, and then it will not look so difficult.

In principle, one might have claimed at any time in history that representation had reached its end and had said all it was capable of saying. Could Giotto's admiring followers have foreseen the images created by Michelangelo, and could Michelangelo's benumbed imitators foretell the vision of Rembrandt? It seems likely that representational forms may be eloquently significant in any age and that their potential variability is unlimited, just as there is no imaginable limit to the number and variety of forms and faces and personalities of human being themselves. Were artists and critics certain of this today many of them would be freed from the needless tensions produced by the contemporaneity complex.

Our emphasis upon originality as the central criterion of aesthetic merit encourages a corollary stress upon irrationality as a value. The surrealists seem to have left their mark upon us when they said that rational thought during the creative act may alter the result, but cannot augment the aesthetic quality of the work of art. Every serious artist knows from personal experience that this is not true. On the other hand original work cannot be produced by pure calculation, and hence cannot be fully accounted for by the critic. In this sense its value is not rational. It does not follow, however, that one can most likely produce something original by using irrational methods of working and by exploiting equivocal and enigmatic content. It is easy to see why we are intrigued by this non sequitur, in a time when the sensitive intellectual is certain of nothing except the appropriateness of uncertainty, and when he fears the creeping mechanization of life. To him, art which is systematically irrational will seem "vitally contemporaneous." The time will come, of course, when this point of view is out of date and today's paintings and sculpture will be judged by the more perennial aesthetic values. A responsible critic interested in judicial appraisals will be *avant-garde* in recognizing this now.

At the moment, however, critics of prestige imitate the artists they admire in their apotheosis of the irrational, assuming like the surrealists that rational criticism only illuminates the inconsequential and does not touch the aesthetic. If this were true, even criticism in the limited sense of "verbal equivalents expressed in poetic form" would be impossible, for one can never know the intent of the artist if it be wholly irrational. Such criticism is often met in journalistic literature, but with increasing frequency the critic is following the complete logic of his premises. He stops trying to uncover and paraphrase the intent of the artist. He writes instead a poetic arrangement of words and ideas which the work of art suggests at least to him, and which fits into and tends to complete and perfect his own notion of the spiritually contemporaneous. By implication, anyone else has an equal right to do the same, hoping that literary distinction may suffice to replace the judicial objectivity which eludes our grasp. Any question regarding the accuracy, the truth, or even the appropriateness of such "criticism" would be meaningless. Thus in criticism, as in art itself, the door is wide open to sensationalism and to anarchy. The critic, now an artist with words, inspired by objects conventionally labelled art, pours out a poem distinguished, he hopes, by originality and spiritual contemporaneity. Like the artist, he is inspired by the Dionysiac muses of mystery, magic, mysticism and enigma, of virtuosity, vitality, violence and obscurity. He, too, would be a pioneering artist and share the same motivations and prejudices. He would ride side by side with the artist upon the wave of the future. This is both safer for the moment and more fun than to stand aside and view the artist in the light of a larger perspective and more constant norms, in an effort to predict how his work will stand the test of time.

Meanwhile the *avant-garde* artist, more learned than inspired, profiting by a capacity for intellectual discrimination unusual among the artists of history, emulates the condition of the critic, painting repetitious non-verbal "criticism" of what he considers the well-established doctrines of our mass culture. His work often seems to need and indeed may have clever verbal texts, either supplied in the catalogue or volubly to the critic himself, to be passed on to eager, sympathetic artists and intellectuals in search of what is expected of them. Thus artists disarm critics by assimilating them, rendering them harmless and gaining their cooperation. And critics write poetic descriptions which are inspired by paintings, but which make no claim to genuine relevance—in other words, poetry which has not yet been painted but soon may be.

We do, of course, on occasion use terms like vitality, conviction, and sincerity to describe work which we intuitively approve. But these terms are ambiguous and mercurial. One can be meaninglessly vital; one can be as convinced of error as of truth; and one may also be sincerely insincere. Every critic must have been deluded at one time or another by the apparent vitality, sincerity, and conviction of a dedicated abstract artist. He may have questioned the artist's sense of design and been reminded that a painting which seems well-designed by current taste is already dead, and that it is a signal virtue for a painting to have a built-in non-art quality; later it will *become* art. Did the technical inadequacy of the artist disturb him? If so, he may have forgotten that good technique is merely being able to say what one wants to say, and that each picture requires and generates its own technique; otherwise it couldn't be original enough to merit our attention. Was the content apparently vacuous? Perhaps he failed to understand its private symbolism and cosmic import. The artist is able to explain at length with indubitable sincerity and conviction. A tolerant critic in such a case may fear to chance an error.

How disillusioning, then, if one discovers later that the artist had been deceiving himself, that he admits to having been an opportunist with one eye on the dealer's prejudice, or that of the museum director, the exhibition jury, or art editor—all of whom expect the sincere artist to work in a variation on an approved manner—to be original, but not too original. In art, the *avant-garde* artist may be a typical "organization man." He may sincerely misunderstand his own motives, conforming to prevailing official taste with the utmost conviction. And, at the same time, for years he may employ the eulogistic vocabulary of individualism and freedom of expression to describe his principles and his work. The critic is in no position to illuminate his true condition for, unlike the psychoanalyst, he shares the same couch with the artist.

Our confusion in criticism is also compounded by our indulgence in semantic transformations, by which terms lose their pristine meaning through a process of intentional forfeiture. Our purpose is to rationalize our prejudices, as when a tyranny claims to be another form of democracy, or slavery is pronounced a form of freedom after the yoke ceases to be felt about the neck. Thus, both terms are rendered useless if we accept the partial truth that abstraction is but another form of representation, or vice versa. "Humanism" is surely broad enough when used to designate those works of art which interpret the condition of man; it becomes useless if extended to designate, as well, all works which manifest the condition of the artist who made them.

Even the term "irrational" may be destroyed by extention, as when we equate it with the accidental. To say that creative art is irrational in nature is not to admit that it is accidental, even though at times a quality is found by accident. Jumping to this conclusion, however, dadaistic artists in large numbers endeavor to create art by contriving accidents and critics are prepared to judge it good if the accidents are fortunate. In the process, art becomes anonymous and the values once attributed to self-expression are lost. It follows, too, that art cannot in any sense be taught, although we still get paid for going through the motions. And, finally, the respectability of this art of anonymity justifies the serious consideration which we give to paintings made by chimpanzees and parrots, to whom as to humans fortunate accidents may happen.

Because in most artistic excellence there is an element of originality, we let the part stand for the whole and equate these terms to the detriment of both. Because in originality there is an element of the irrational we often equate these terms, and all that is irrational becomes original. Because in the irrational there may be an element of the accidental—at least there is no evident casual determinism at work—we equate these terms. And thus, at length, the beautiful in art becomes the accidental; and to be consistent we are obliged to hang the work of a chimpanzee or parrot and consider it for prizes—except when the authorities announce in advance that the exhibition is open only to humans for reasons of space limitations. One beholds this state of affairs as did the peasant who looked for the first time at a camel and said: "It isn't true." And one is reminded of Verdi's reputed remark: "Let us return to old times and that will be progress." It undoubtedly would be although, of course, this is not enough to ask in an age of restless vitality and rich endowment.

We need to re-examine the adequacy of the criteria of originality, contemporaneity, and irrationality by which we judge the merits of contemporary art. We need to stop misusing terms for the purpose of advocacy. And the critic needs to divorce himself from the enticing world of involvements, enthusiasms, and commitments enjoyed by the artist, in order that he may repair his damaged vocabulary, view the scene from a larger and more enduring perspective, and revive his power to make judicial appraisals based upon clear and independent reasoning.

QUESTIONS FOR STUDY, DISCUSSION, AND WRITING

1. Outline Longman's essay. What is his thesis concerning the criteria prevailing in contemporary art criticism? Concerning the role of the art critic? What criteria does he discuss, and in what order? Which criterion is dominant? What is Longman's main argumentative strategy in presenting his case against the validity or adequacy of these criteria?

2. What causes, in Longman's view, help bring about the great value placed upon originality in art? Which of these involve a transference of ideas from other phenomena to art? Which such transferences does Longman consider faulty? What distinction does he draw between new work in science and new work in art?

3. What specific inconsistencies does Longman point to as incurred by the criterion of originality? What results from the application of this criterion does Longman specially deprecate? What does the anecdote about the Marx Brothers illustrate?

4. Why does Longman object to "contemporaneity" as a criterion for art? What confusions does the term entail? How is it used as a term of advocacy, to promote a cause?
5. Does Longman deny that irrationality is a component in art? Explain.
6. "In art, the avant-garde artist may be a typical 'organization man' " (p. 528). Explain Longman's meaning.
7. What relationships does Longman indicate between aberrancies in contemporary art criticism and other characteristics of modern life?
8. Both Longman and Clark ("The Blot and the Diagram," p. 516) mention painting by chimpanzees. Compare their attitudes toward the phenomenon and what it signifies.
9. Does Longman's essay constitute an attack upon modern art? Explain.

HENRI BERGSON

The Comic in General; the Comic Element in Forms and Movements[1]

What does laughter mean? What is the basal element in the laughable? What common ground can we find between the grimace of a merry-andrew,[2] a play upon words, an equivocal situation in a burlesque and a scene of high comedy? What method of distillation will yield us invariably the same essence from which so many different products borrow either their obtrusive odor or their delicate perfume? The greatest of thinkers, from Aristotle downwards, have tackled this little problem, which has a knack of baffling every effort, of slipping away and escaping only to bob up again, a pert challenge flung at philosophic speculation.

Our excuse for attacking the problem in our turn must lie in the fact that we shall not aim at imprisoning the comic spirit within a definition. We regard it, above all, as a living thing. However trivial it may be, we shall treat it with the respect due to life. We shall confine ourselves to watching it grow and expand. Passing by imperceptible gradations from one form to another, it will be seen to achieve the strangest metamorphoses. We shall disdain nothing we have seen. Maybe we may gain from this prolonged contact, for the matter of that, something more flexible than an abstract definition—a practical, intimate acquaintance, such as springs from a long companionship. And maybe we may also find that, unintentionally, we have made an acquaintance that is useful. For the comic spirit has a logic of its own, even in its wildest eccentricities. It has a method in its madness. It dreams, I admit,

1. From the opening section of Bergson's essay "Laughter."
2. A clown.

but it conjures up in its dreams visions that are at once accepted and understood by the whole of a social group. Can it then fail to throw light for us on the way that human imagination works, and more particularly social, collective, and popular imagination? Begotten of real life and akin to art, should it not also have something of its own to tell us about art and life?

At the outset we shall put forward three observations which we look upon as fundamental. They have less bearing on the actually comic than on the field within which it must be sought.

I

The first point to which attention should be called is that the comic does not exist outside the pale of what is strictly *human*. A landscape may be beautiful, charming and sublime, or insignificant and ugly; it will never be laughable. You may laugh at an animal, but only because you have detected in it some human attitude or expression. You may laugh at a hat, but what you are making fun of, in this case, is not the piece of felt or straw, but the shape that men have given it—the human caprice whose mold it has assumed. It is strange that so important a fact, and such a simple one too, has not attracted to a greater degree the attention of philosophers. Several have defined man as "an animal which laughs." They might equally well have defined him as an animal which is laughed at; for if any other animal, or some lifeless object, produces the same effect, it is always because of some resemblance to man, of the stamp he gives it or the use he puts it to.

Here I would point out, as a symptom equally worthy of notice, the *absence of feeling* which usually accompanies laughter. It seems as though the comic could not produce its disturbing effect unless it fell, so to say, on the surface of a soul that is thoroughly calm and unruffled. Indifference is its natural environment, for laughter has no greater foe than emotion. I do not mean that we could not laugh at a person who inspires us with pity, for instance, or even with affection, but in such a case we must, for the moment, put our affection out of court and impose silence upon our pity. In a society composed of pure intelligences there would probably be no more tears, though perhaps there would still be laughter; whereas highly emotional souls, in tune and unison with life, in whom every event would be sentimentally prolonged and re-echoed, would neither know nor understand laughter. Try, for a moment, to become interested in everything that is being said and done; act, in imagination, with those who act, and feel with those who feel; in a word, give your sympathy its widest expansion: as though at the touch of a fairy wand you will see the flimsiest of objects assume importance, and a gloomy hue spread over everything. Now step aside, look upon life as a disinterested spectator: many a drama will turn into a comedy. It is enough for us to stop our ears to the sound of music in a room, where dancing is going on, for the dancers at once to appear ridiculous. How many human actions would stand a similar test? Should we not see many of them suddenly pass from grave to gay, on isolating them from the accompanying music of sentiment? To produce the whole of its effect, then, the comic demands something like a momentary anesthesia of the heart. Its appeal is to intelligence, pure and simple.

This intelligence, however, must always remain in touch with other intelligences. And here is the third fact to which attention should be drawn. You would hardly appreciate the comic if you felt yourself isolated from others. Laughter appears to stand in need of an echo. Listen to it carefully: it is not an articulate, clear, well-defined sound; it is something which would fain be prolonged by reverberating from one to another, something beginning with a crash, to continue in successive rumblings, like thunder in a mountain. Still, this reverberation cannot go on for ever. It can travel within as wide a circle as you please: the circle remains, none the less, a closed one. Our laughter is always the laughter of a group. It may, perchance, have happened to you, when seated in a railway carriage or at *table d'hôte,* to hear travelers relating to one another stories which must have been comic to them, for they laughed heartily. Had you been one of their company, you would have laughed like them, but, as you were not, you had no desire whatever to do so. A man who was once asked why he did not weep at a sermon when everybody else was shedding tears replied: "I don't belong to the parish!" What that man thought of tears would be still more true of laughter. However spontaneous it seems, laughter always implies a kind of secret freemasonry, or even complicity, with other laughers, real or imaginary. How often has it been said that the fuller the theatre, the more uncontrolled the laughter of the audience! On the other hand, how often has the remark been made that many comic effects are incapable of translation from one language to another, because they refer to the customs and ideas of a particular social group! It is through not understanding the importance of this double fact that the comic has been looked upon as a mere curiosity in which the mind finds amusement, and laughter itself as a strange, isolated phenomenon, without any bearing on the rest of human activity. Hence those definitions which tend to make the comic into an abstract relation between ideas: "an intellectual contrast," "a patent absurdity," etc., definitions which, even were they really suitable to every form of the comic, would not in the least explain why the comic makes us laugh. How, indeed, should it come about that this particular logical relation, as soon as it is perceived, contracts, expands and shakes our limbs, whilst all other relations leave the body unaffected? It is not from this point of view that we shall approach the problem. To understand laughter, we must put it back into its natural environment, which is society, and above all must we determine the utility of its functions, which is a social one. Such, let us say at once, will be the leading idea of all our investigations. Laughter must answer to certain requirements of life in common. It must have a *social* signification.

Let us clearly mark the point towards which our three preliminary observations are converging. The comic will come into being, it appears, whenever a group of men concentrate their attention on one of their number, imposing silence on their emotions and calling into play nothing but their intelligence. What, now, is the particular point on which their attention will have to be concentrated, and what will here be the function of intelligence? To reply to these questions will be at once to come to closer grips with the problem. But here a few examples have become indispensable.

II

A man, running along the street, stumbles and falls; the passersby burst out laughing. They would not laugh at him, I imagine, could they suppose that the whim had suddenly seized him to sit down on the ground. They laugh because his sitting down is involuntary. Consequently, it is not his sudden change of attitude that raises a laugh, but rather the involuntary element in this change— his clumsiness, in fact. Perhaps there was a stone on the road. He should have altered his pace or avoided the obstacle. Instead of that, through lack of elasticity, through absentmindedness and a kind of physical obstinacy, *as a result, in fact, of rigidity or of momentum,* the muscles continued to perform the same movement when the circumstances of the case called for something else. That is the reason of the man's fall, and also of the people's laughter.

Now, take the case of a person who attends to the petty occupations of his everyday life with mathematical precision. The objects around him, however, have all been tampered with by a mischievous wag, the result being that when he dips his pen into the inkstand he draws it out all covered with mud, when he fancies he is sitting down on a solid chair he finds himself sprawling on the floor, in a word his actions are all topsy-turvy or mere beating the air, while in every case the effect is invariably one of momentum. Habit has given the impulse: what was wanted was to check the movement or deflect it. He did nothing of the sort, but continued like a machine in the same straight line. The victim, then, of a practical joke is in a position similar to that of a runner who falls—he is comic for the same reason. The laughable element in both cases consists of a certain *mechanical inelasticity,* just where one would expect to find the wideawake adaptability and the living pliableness of a human being. The only difference in the two cases is that the former happened of itself, whilst the latter was obtained artificially. In the first instance, the passer-by does nothing but look on, but in the second the mischievous wag intervenes.

All the same, in both cases the result has been brought about by an external circumstance. The comic is therefore accidental: it remains, so to speak, in superficial contact with the person. How is it to penetrate within? The necessary conditions will be fulfilled when mechanical rigidity no longer requires for its manifestation a stumbling-block which either the hazard of circumstance or human knavery has set in its way, but extracts by natural processes, from its own store, an inexhaustible series of opportunities for externally revealing its presence. Suppose, then, we imagine a mind always thinking of what it has just done and never of what it is doing, like a song which lags behind its accompaniment. Let us try to picture to ourselves a certain inborn lack of elasticity of both senses and intelligence, which brings it to pass that we continue to see what is no longer visible, to hear what is no longer audible, to say what is no longer to the point: in short, to adapt ourselves to a past and therefore imaginary situation, when we ought to be shaping our conduct in accordance with the reality which is present. This time the comic will take up its abode in the person himself; it is the person who will supply it with everything—matter and form, cause and opportunity. Is it then surprising that the absentminded individual—for this is the character we have just been describing—has usually fired the imagination of comic authors? When La Bruyère[3] came across this particular type, he realized, on analyzing it, that he had got hold of a recipe for the wholesale manufacture of comic effects. As a matter of fact he overdid it, and gave us far too lengthy and detailed a description of *Ménalque*, coming back to his subject, dwelling and expatiating on it beyond all bounds. The very facility of the subject fascinated him. Absentmindedness, indeed, is not perhaps the actual fountain-head of the comic, but surely it is contiguous to a certain stream of facts and fancies which flows straight from the fountain-head. It is situated, so to say, on one of the great natural watersheds of laughter.

Now, the effect of absentmindedness may gather strength in its turn. There is a general law, the first example of which we have just encountered, and which we will formulate in the following terms: when a certain comic effect has its origin in a certain cause, the more natural we regard the cause to be, the more comic shall we find the effect. Even now we laugh at absentmindedness when presented to us as a simple fact. Still more laughable will be the absentmindedness we have seen springing up and growing before our very eyes, with whose origin we are acquainted and whose life-history we can reconstruct. To choose a definite example: suppose

3. Seventeenth-century French moralist, a writer of "characters"; his *Ménalque* describes the absent-minded man.

a man has taken to reading nothing but romances of love and chivalry. Attracted and fascinated by his heroes, his thoughts and intentions gradually turn more and more towards them, till one fine day we find him walking among us like a somnambulist. His actions are distractions. But then his distractions can be traced back to a definite, positive cause. They are no longer cases of *absence* of mind, pure and simple; they find their explanation in the *presence* of the individual in quite definite, though imaginary, surroundings. Doubtless a fall is always a fall, but it is one thing to tumble into a well because you were looking anywhere but in front of you, it is quite another thing to fall into it because you were intent upon a star. It was certainly a star at which Don Quixote was gazing. How profound is the comic element in the over-romantic, Utopian bent of mind! And yet, if you reintroduce the idea of absentmindedness, which acts as a go-between you will see this profound comic element uniting with the most superficial type. Yes, indeed, these whimsical wild enthusiasts, these madmen who are yet so strangely reasonable, excite us to laugher by playing on the same chords within ourselves, by setting in motion the same inner mechanism, as does the victim of a practical joke or the passer-by who slips down in the street. They, too, are runners who fall and simple souls who are being hoaxed—runners after the ideal who stumble over realities, child-like dreamers for whom life delights to lie in wait. But, above all, they are past-masters in absentmindedness, with this superiority over their fellows that their absentmindedness is systematic and organized around one central idea, and that their mishaps are also quite coherent, thanks to the inexorable logic which reality applies to the correction of dreams, so that they kindle in those around them, by a series of cumulative effects, a hilarity capable of unlimited expansion.

Now, let us go a little further. Might not certain vices have the same relation to character that the rigidity of a fixed idea has to intellect? Whether as a moral kink or a crooked twist given to the will, vice has often the appearance of a curvature of the soul. Doubtless there are vices into which the soul plunges deeply with all its pregnant potency, which it rejuvenates and drags along with it into a moving circle of reincarnations. Those are tragic vices. But the vice capable of making us comic is, on the contrary, that which is brought from without, like a ready-made frame into which we are to step. It lends us its own rigidity instead of borrowing from us our flexibility. We do not render it more complicated; on the contrary, it simplifies us. Here, as we shall see later on in the concluding section of this study, lies the essential difference between comedy and drama. A drama, even when portraying passions or vices that bear a name, so completely incorporates them in the person that their names are forgotten, their general characteristics effaced, and we no longer think of them at all, but rather of the person in whom they are assimilated; hence, the title of a drama can seldom be anything else than a proper noun. On the other hand, many comedies have a common noun as their title: *l'Avare*, *le Joueur*, etc. Were you asked to think of a play capable of being called *le Jaloux*, for instance, you would find that *Sganarelle* or *George Dandin* would occur to your mind, but not *Othello*: *le Jaloux* could only be the title of a comedy.[4] The reason is that, however intimately vice, when comic, is associated with persons, it none the less retains its simple, independent existence, it remains the central character, present though invisible, to which the characters in flesh and blood on the stage are attached. At times it delights in dragging them down with its own weight and making them share in its tumbles. More frequently, however, it plays on them as on an instrument or pulls the strings as though they were puppets. Look closely: you will find that the art of the comic poet consists in making us so well acquainted with the particular vice, in introducing us, the spectators, to such a degree of intimacy with it, that in the end we get hold of some of the strings of the marionette with which he is playing, and actually work them ourselves; this it is that explains part of the pleasure we feel. Here, too, it is really a kind of automatism that makes us laugh—an automatism, as we have already remarked, closely akin to mere absentmindedness. To realize this more fully, it need only be noted that a comic character is generally comic in proportion to his ignorance of himself. The comic person is unconscious. As though wearing the ring of Gyges with reverse effect, he becomes invisible to himself while remaining visible to all the world. A character in a tragedy will make no change in his conduct because he will know how it is judged by us; he may continue therein even though fully conscious of what he is and feeling keenly the horror he inspires in us. But a defect that is ridiculous, as soon as it feels itself to be so, endeavors to modify itself or at least to appear as though it did. Were Harpagon[5] to see us laugh at his miserliness, I do not say that he would get rid of it, but he would either show it less or show it differently. Indeed, it is in this sense only that laughter "corrects men's manners." It makes us at once endeavor to appear what we ought to be, what some day we shall perhaps end in being.

It is unnecessary to carry this analysis any further. From the runner who falls to the simpleton who is hoaxed, from a state of being hoaxed to one of absentmindedness, from absentmindedness to wild enthusiasm, from wild enthusiasm to various distortions of

---

4. *L'Avare* (*The Miser*) is a play by Molière, and *le Joueur* (*The Gamester*) was the work of his successor, Jean-Francois Regnard. Molière's *Sganarelle* and *George Dandin* have jealous husbands as their chief comic figures, so that *le Jaloux* (*The Jealous Man*) would be a suitable title for either play.

5. The miser of Molière's *l'Avare*.

character and will, we have followed the line of progress along which the comic becomes more and more deeply imbedded in the person, yet without ceasing, in its subtler manifestations, to recall to us some trace of what we noticed in its grosser forms, an effect of automatism and of inelasticity. Now we can obtain a first glimpse —a distant one, it is true, and still hazy and confused—of the laughable side of human nature and of the ordinary function of laughter.

What life and society require of each of us is a constantly alert attention that discerns the outlines of the present situation, together with a certain elasticity of mind and body to enable us to adapt ourselves in consequence. *Tension* and *elasticity* are two forces, mutually complementary, which life brings into play. If these two forces are lacking in the body to any considerable extent, we have sickness and infirmity and accidents of every kind. If they are lacking in the mind, we find every degree of mental deficiency, every variety of insanity. Finally, if they are lacking in the character, we have cases of the gravest inadaptability to social life, which are the sources of misery and at times the causes of crime. Once these elements of inferiority that affect the serious side of existence are removed—and they tend to eliminate themselves in what has been called the struggle for life—the person can live, and that in common with other persons. But society asks for something more; it is not satisfied with simply living, it insists on living well. What it now has to dread is that each one of us, content with paying attention to what affects the essentials of life, will, so far as the rest is concerned, give way to the easy automatism of acquired habits. Another thing it must fear is that the members of whom it is made up, instead of aiming after an increasingly delicate adjustment of wills which will fit more and more perfectly into one another, will confine themselves to respecting simply the fundamental conditions of this adjustment: a cut-and-dried agreement among the persons will not satisfy it, it insists on a constant striving after reciprocal adaptation. Society will therefore be suspicious of all *inelasticity* of character, of mind and even of body, because it is the possible sign of a slumbering activity as well as of an activity with separatist tendencies, that inclines to swerve from the common center round which society gravitates: in short, because it is the sign of an eccentricity. And yet, society cannot intervene at this stage by material repression, since it is not affected in a material fashion. It is confronted with something that makes it uneasy, but only as a symptom—scarcely a threat, at the very most a gesture. A gesture, therefore, will be its reply. Laughter must be something of this kind, a sort of *social gesture*. By the fear which it inspires, it restrains eccentricity, keeps constantly awake and in mutual contact certain activities of a secondary order which might retire into their shell and go to sleep, and in short, softens down whatever the surface of the social body may retain of mechanical inelasticity. Laughter, then, does not belong to the province of esthetics alone, since unconsciously (and even immorally in many particular instances) it pursues a utilitarian aim of general improvement. And yet there is something esthetic about it, since the comic comes into being just when society and the individual, freed from the worry of self-preservation, begin to regard themselves as works of art. In a word, if a circle be drawn round those actions and dispositions—implied in individual or social life—to which their natural consequences bring their own penalties, there remains outside this sphere of emotion and struggle—and within a neutral zone in which man simply exposes himself to man's curiosity—a certain rigidity of body, mind and character that society would still like to get rid of in order to obtain from its members the greatest possible degree of elasticity and sociability. This rigidity is the comic, and laughter is its corrective.

Still, we must not accept this formula as a definition of the comic. It is suitable only for cases that are elementary, theoretical and perfect, in which the comic is free from all adulteration. Nor do we offer it, either, as an explanation. We prefer to make it, if you will, the *leitmotiv* which is to accompany all our explanations. We must ever keep it in mind, though without dwelling on it too much, somewhat as a skilful fencer must think of the discontinuous movements of the lesson whilst his body is given up to the continuity of the fencing-match. We will now endeavor to reconstruct the sequence of comic forms, taking up again the thread that leads from the horseplay of a clown up to the most refined effects of comedy, following this thread in its often unforeseen windings, halting at intervals to look around, and finally getting back, if possible, to the point at which the thread is dangling and where we shall perhaps find—since the comic oscillates between life and art—the general relation that art bears to life.

QUESTIONS FOR STUDY, DISCUSSION, AND WRITING

1. What three conditions does Bergson say are necessary to the appearance of comic effect? Does Bergson contradict himself when he says that the appeal of the comic "is to intelligence, pure and simple" but that a definition of the comic as "an abstract relation between ideas" is inadequate? Explain his point.
2. According to what principle does Bergson arrange his examples of the comic in section II of the essay? How are the examples differentiated, and what are they said to have in common?
3. What relationships exist between sections I and II of the essay?
4. What, according to Bergson, is the social function of laughter?
5. One stage of Bergson's analysis of comic effect concerns the practical joke. What considerations might inhibit laughter at this

kind of joke? Compare Leacock's attitude toward the practical
joke ("Humor as I See It," below) and Twain's view as reported
by Brooks ("Mark Twain's Humor," p. 560).
6. Bergson refers to Don Quixote as exemplary of comic romantic
idealism. If you know the work referred to, you know that the
Don is not solely comic. Why? What considerations might inhibit,
or replace, laughter as romantic idealism?
7. Does Bergson's analysis explain the comic effect of animated
movie cartoons, often violent and preposterous? How? What qualities of film comedy in general does Bergson's discussion illuminate?

STEPHEN LEACOCK

Humor as I See It

It is only fair that I should be allowed a few pages to myself to
put down some things that I really think. Once I might have taken
my pen in hand to write about humor with the confident air of
an acknowledged professional.

But that time is past. Such claim as I had has been taken from
me. In fact I stand unmasked. An English reviewer writing in a
literary journal, the very name of which is enough to put contradiction to sleep, has said of my writing, "What is there, after all, in
Professor Leacock's humor but a rather ingenious mixture of hyperbole and myosis?"

The man was right. How he stumbled upon this trade secret, I
do not know. But I am willing to admit, since the truth is out, that
it has long been my custom in preparing an article of a humorous
nature to go down to the cellar and mix up half a gallon of myosis
with a pint of hyperbole. If I want to give the article a decidedly
literary character, I find it well to put in about half a pint of
paresis. The whole thing is amazingly simple.

But I only mention this by way of introduction and to dispel
any idea that I am conceited enough to write about humor, with
the professional authority of Ella Wheeler Wilcox writing about
love, or Fred Astaire talking about dancing.

All that I dare claim is that I have as much sense of humor as
other people. And, oddly enough, I notice that everybody else makes
this same claim. Any man will admit, if need be, that his sight is
not good, or that he cannot swim, or shoots badly with a rifle, but
to touch upon his sense of humor is to give him a mortal affront.

"No," said a friend of mine the other day, "I never go to Grand
Opera," and then he added with an air of pride—"You see, I have
absolutely no ear for music."

"You don't say so!" I exclaimed.

"None!" he went on. "I can't tell one tune from another. I don't know *Home, Sweet Home* from *God Save the King.* I can't tell whether a man is tuning a violin or playing a sonata."

He seemed to get prouder and prouder over each item of his own deficiency. He ended by saying that he had a dog at his house that had a far better ear for music than he had. As soon as his wife or any visitor started to play the piano the dog always began to howl—plaintively, he said, as if it were hurt. He himself never did this.

When he had finished I made what I thought a harmless comment.

"I suppose," I said, "that you find your sense of humor deficient in the same way: the two generally go together."

My friend was livid with rage in a moment.

"Sense of humor!" he said. "My sense of humor! Me without a sense of humor! Why, I suppose I've a keener sense of humor than any man, or any two men, in this city!"

From that he turned to bitter personal attack. He said that my sense of humor seemed to have withered altogether.

He left me, still quivering with indignation.

Personally, however, I do not mind making the admission, however damaging it may be, that there are certain forms of so-called humor, or, at least, fun, which I am quite unable to appreciate. Chief among these is that ancient thing called the Practical Joke.

"You never knew McGann, did you?" a friend of mine asked me the other day. When I said, "No, I had never known McGann," he shook his head with a sigh, and said:

"Ah, you should have known McGann. He had the greatest sense of humor of any man I ever knew—always full of jokes. I remember one night at the boarding house where we were, he stretched a string across the passageway and then rang the dinner bell. One of the boarders broke his leg. We nearly died laughing."

"Dear me!" I said. "What a humorist! Did he often do things like that?"

"Oh, yes, he was at them all the time. He used to put tar in the tomato soup, and beeswax and tin-tacks on the chairs. He was full of ideas. They seemed to come to him without any trouble."

McGann, I understand, is dead. I am not sorry for it. Indeed I think that for most of us the time has gone by when we can see the fun of putting tacks on chairs, or thistles in beds, or live snakes in people's boots.

To me it has always seemed that the very essence of good humor is that it must be without harm and without malice. I admit that there is in all of us a certain vein of the old original demoniacal humor or joy in the misfortune of another which sticks to us like our original sin. It ought not to be funny to see a man, especially a fat and pompous man, slip suddenly on a banana skin. But it is. When a skater on a pond who is describing graceful circles and showing off before the crowd, breaks through the ice and gets a ducking, everybody shouts with joy. To the original savage, the cream of the joke in such cases was found if the man who slipped broke his neck, or the man who went through the ice never came up again. I can imagine a group of prehistoric men standing round the ice-hole where he had disappeared and laughing till their sides split. If there had been such a thing as a prehistoric newspaper, the affair would have been headed up: *"Amusing Incident. Unknown Gentleman Breaks Through Ice and Is Drowned."*

But our sense of humor under civilization has been weakened. Much of the fun of this sort of thing has been lost on us.

Children, however, still retain a large share of this primitive sense of enjoyment.

I remember once watching two little boys making snow-balls at the side of the street and getting ready a little store of them to use. As they worked there came along an old man wearing a silk hat, and belonging by appearance to the class of "jolly old gentlemen." When he saw the boys his gold spectacles gleamed with kindly enjoyment. He began waving his arms and calling, "Now, then, boys, free shot at me! free shot!" In his gaiety he had, without noticing it, edged himself over the sidewalk on to the street. An express cart collided with him and knocked him over on his back in a heap of snow. He lay there gasping and trying to get the snow off his face and spectacles. The boys gathered up their snow-balls and took a run towards him. "Free shot!" they yelled. "Soak him! Soak him!"

I repeat, however, that for me, as I suppose for most of us, it is a prime condition of humor that it must be without harm or malice, nor should it convey even incidentally any real picture of sorrow or suffering or death. There is a great deal in the humor of Scotland (I admit its general merit) which seems to me, not being a Scotchman, to sin in this respect. Take this familiar story (I quote it as something already known and not for the sake of telling it).

A Scotchman had a sister-in-law—his wife's sister—with whom he could never agree. He always objected to going anywhere with her, and in spite of his wife's entreaties always refused to do so. The wife was taken mortally ill and as she lay dying, she whispered, "John, ye'll drive Janet with you to the funeral, will ye no?" The Scotchman, after an internal struggle, answered, "Margaret, I'll do it for ye, but it'll spoil my day."

Whatever humor there may be in this is lost for me by the actual and vivid picture that it conjures up—the dying wife, the darkened room and the last whispered request.

No doubt the Scotch see things differently. That wonderful people—whom personally I cannot too much admire—always seem to me to prefer adversity to sunshine, to welcome the prospect of a pretty general damnation, and to live with grim cheerfulness within the very shadow of death. Alone among the nations they have converted the devil—under such names as Old Horny—into a familiar acquaintance not without a certain grim charm of his own. No doubt also there enters into their humor something of the original barbaric attitude towards things. For a primitive people who saw death often and at first hand, and for whom the future world was a vivid reality, that could be *felt*, as it were, in the midnight forest and heard in the roaring storm—for such a people it was no doubt natural to turn the flank of terror by forcing a merry and jovial acquaintance with the unseen world. Such a practice as a wake, and the merrymaking about the corpse, carry us back to the twilight of the world, with the poor savage in his bewildered misery, pretending that his dead still lived. Our funeral with its black trappings and its elaborate ceremonies is the lineal descendant of a merrymaking. Our undertaker is, by evolution, a genial master of ceremonies, keeping things lively at the death-dance. Thus have the ceremonies and the trappings of death been transformed in the course of ages till the forced gaiety is gone, and the black hearse and the gloomy mutes betoken the cold dignity of our despair.

But I fear this article is getting serious. I must apologize.

I was about to say, when I wandered from the point, that there is another form of humor which I am also quite unable to appreciate. This is that particular form of story which may be called, par excellence, the English Anecdote. It always deals with persons of rank and birth, and, except for the exalted nature of the subject itself, is, as far as I can see, absolutely pointless.

This is the kind of thing that I mean.

"His Grace the Fourth Duke of Marlborough was noted for the open-handed hospitality which reigned at Blenheim, the family seat, during his régime. One day on going in to luncheon it was discovered that there were thirty guests present, whereas the table only held covers for twenty-one. 'Oh, well,' said the Duke, not a whit abashed, 'some of us will have to eat standing up.' Everybody, of course, roared with laughter."

My only wonder is that they didn't kill themselves with it. A mere roar doesn't seem enough to do justice to such a story as this.

The Duke of Wellington has been made the storm-center of three generations of wit of this sort. In fact the typical Duke of Wellington story had been reduced to a thin skeleton such as this:

"A young subaltern once met the Duke of Wellington coming out of Westminster Abbey. 'Good morning, your Grace,' he said, 'rather a wet morning.' 'Yes,' said the Duke, with a very rigid bow, 'but it was a damn sight wetter, sir, on the morning of Waterloo.' The young subaltern, rightly rebuked, hung his head."

Nor is it only the English who sin in regard to anecdotes.

One can indeed make the sweeping assertion that the telling of stories as a mode of amusing others, ought to be kept within strict limits. Few people realize how extremely difficult it is to tell a story so as to reproduce the real fun of it—to "get it over" as the actors say. The mere "facts" of a story seldom make it funny. It needs the right words, with every word in its proper place. Here and there, perhaps once in a hundred times, a story turns up which needs no telling. The humor of it turns so completely on a sudden twist or incongruity in the dénouement of it that no narrator however clumsy can altogether fumble it.

Take, for example, this well known instance—a story which, in one form or other, everybody has heard.

"George Grossmith, the famous comedian, was once badly run down and went to consult a doctor. It happened that the doctor, though, like everybody else, he had often seen Grossmith on the stage, had never seen him without his make-up and did not know him by sight. He examined his patient, looked at his tongue, felt his pulse and tapped his lungs. Then he shook his head. 'There's nothing wrong with you, sir,' he said, 'except that you're run down from overwork and worry. You need rest and amusement. Take a night off and go and see George Grossmith at the Savoy.'

" 'Thank you,' said the patient, 'I *am* George Grossmith.' "

Let the reader please observe that I have purposely told this story all wrongly, just as wrongly as could be, and yet there is something left of it. Will the reader kindly look back to the beginning of it and see for himself just how it ought to be narrated and what obvious error has been made. If he has any particle of the artist in his make-up, he will see at once that the story ought to begin:

"One day a very haggard and nervous-looking patient called at the office of a fashionable doctor, etc., etc."

In other words, the chief point of the joke lies in keeping it concealed till the moment when the patient says, "Thank you, I am George Grossmith." But the story is such a good one that it cannot be completely spoiled even when told wrongly. This particular anecdote has been variously told of George Grossmith, Coquelin, Joe Jefferson, John Hare, Cyril Maude, and about sixty others. And I have noticed that there is a certain type of man who, on hearing this story about Grossmith, immediately tells it all back again, putting in the name of somebody else, and goes into new fits of laughter over it, as if the change of name made it brand new.

But few people, I repeat, realize the difficulty of reproducing a humorous or comic effect in its original spirit.

"I saw Harry Lauder last night," said Griggs, a Stock-Exchange friend of mine, as we walked up town together the other day. "He came onto the stage in kilts" (here Griggs started to chuckle) "and he had a slate under his arm" (here Griggs began to laugh quite heartily), "and he said, 'I always like to carry a slate with me' (of course he said it in Scotch, but I can't do the Scotch the way he does it) 'just in case there might be any figures I'd be wanting to put down'" (by this time Griggs was almost suffocated with laughter)—"and he took a little bit of chalk out of his pocket, and he said" (Griggs was now almost hysterical), "'I like to carry a wee bit chalk along because I find the slate is'" (Griggs was now faint with laughter), "'the slate is—is—not much good without the chalk.'"

Griggs had to stop, with his hand to his side and lean against a lamp post. "I can't, of course, do the Scotch the way Harry Lauder does it," he repeated.

Exactly. He couldn't do the Scotch and he couldn't do the rich mellow voice of Mr. Lauder and the face beaming with merriment, and the spectacles glittering with amusement, and he couldn't do the slate, nor the "wee bit chalk"—in fact he couldn't do any of it. He ought merely to have said "Harry Lauder," and leaned up against a post and laughed till he had got over it.

Yet in spite of everything, people insist on spoiling conversation by telling stories. I know nothing more dreadful at a dinner table than one of these amateur raconteurs—except perhaps, two of them. After about three stories have been told, there falls on the dinner table an uncomfortable silence, in which everybody is aware that everybody else is trying hard to think of another story, and is failing to find it. There is no peace in the gathering again till some man of firm and quiet mind turns to his neighbor and says—"But after all there is no doubt that whether we like it or not prohibition is coming." Then everybody in his heart says, Thank Heaven! and the whole tableful are happy and contented again, till one of the story tellers "thinks of another," and breaks loose.

Worst of all perhaps is the modest story teller who is haunted by the idea that one has heard his story before. He attacks you after this fashion:

"I heard a very good story the other day on the steamer going to Bermuda"—then he pauses with a certain doubt in his face—"but perhaps you've heard this?"

"No, no, I've never been to Bermuda. Go ahead."

"Well, this is a story that they tell about a man who went down to Bermuda one winter to get cured of rheumatism—but you've heard this?"

"No, no."

"Well, he had rheumatism pretty bad and he went to Bermuda to get cured of it. And so when he went into the hotel he said to the clerk at the desk—but, perhaps you know this."

"No, no, go right ahead."

"Well, he said to the clerk I want a room that looks out over the sea—but perhaps—"

Now the sensible thing to do is to stop the narrator right at this point. Say to him quietly and firmly, "Yes, I have heard that story. I always liked it ever since it came out in *Titbits* in 1878, and I read it every time I see it. Go on and tell it to me and I'll sit back with my eyes closed and enjoy it."

No doubt the story-telling habit owes much to the fact that ordinary people, quite unconsciously, rate humor very low: I mean, they underestimate the difficulty of "making humor." It would never occur to them that the thing is hard, meritorious and dignified. Because the result is gay and light, they think the process must be. Few people would realize that it is much harder to write one of Owen Seaman's "funny" poems in *Punch* than to write one of the Archbishop of Canterbury's sermons. Mark Twain's *Huckleberry Finn* is a greater work than Kant's *Critique of Pure Reason*, and Charles Dickens' creation of Mr. Pickwick did more for the elevation of the human race—I say it in all seriousness—than Cardinal Newman's *Lead, Kindly Light, Amid the Encircling Gloom.* Newman only cried out for light in the gloom of a sad world. Dickens gave it.

But the deep background that lies behind and beyond what we call humor is revealed only to the few who, by instinct or by effort, have given thought to it. The world's humor, in its best and greatest sense, is perhaps the highest product of our civilization. One thinks here not of the mere spasmodic effects of the comic artist or the blackface expert of the vaudeville show, but of the really great humor which, once or twice in a generation at best, illuminates and elevates our literature. It is no longer dependent upon the mere trick and quibble of words, or the odd and meaningless incongruities in things that strike us as "funny." Its basis lies in the deeper contrasts offered by life itself: the strange incongruity between our aspiration and our achievement, the eager and fretful anxieties of to-day that fade into nothingness to-morrow, the burning pain and the sharp sorrow that are softened in the gentle retrospect of time, till as we look back upon the course that has been traversed we pass in view the panorama of our lives, as people in old age may recall, with mingled tears and smiles, the angry quarrels of their childhood. And here, in its larger aspect, humor is blended with pathos till the two are one, and represent, as they have in every age, the mingled heritage of tears and laughter that is our lot on earth.

WILLIAM EDWARD WILSON
Madeline among the Midshipmen

One night not long ago, I found myself remembering for the first time in years a gruff and briny old sea-dog I served under for a while in the Second World War. I had been reading the poems of Percy Bysshe Shelley, and it was the "Hymn to Intellectual Beauty" that brought my old skipper to mind.

No finer officer than this Captain, U.S.N., ever sailed the seas, I am sure, but when I knew him he was Head of the Department of English, History, and Government at the United States Naval Academy. At the Academy, the Department of E., H., and G. is appropriately known as "the Bull Department," and I was assigned to it early in the war when BuPers decided I was more expendable with a book in my hand than while conning an LST. Why the Captain was assigned to that Department I do not know, unless it was because he had once read "A Dissertation on Roast Pig."

"You ever read that thing about roast pork?" he always asked new-comers to the Department, as a test of their backgrounds in literature. "I thought it was a pretty good yarn when I was a Midshipman."

I admired the Captain. Indeed, I was grateful that he was my first skipper on shore duty, because he gave a salty atmosphere to Mahan Hall and almost justified the Academy's ironclad rule that we must think of walls as bulkheads, floors as decks, drinking fountains as scuttlebutts, and ourselves as Naval officers. Still, with all the ribbons on his broad chest, the Captain had never fought the campaign of iambic pentameter nor the battle of the synecdoche, nor had he navigated any closer to the main current of English Literature than Charles Lamb's little eddy about roast pig. It was therefore inevitable that the day he discovered Shelley in the Plebe reading assignments he blew all his stacks at once.

When he came steaming across the gangway to the Lit Deck in Mahan Hall that day, the Lit textbook in his hand and his eyes ablaze, we officers of the Lit Detail were so startled that we knocked over a half dozen chairs coming to attention.

"Ten*shun!*" shouted the Chairman of the Lit Detail, a Lieutenant, U.S.N.R., recently surfaced from the Harvard Graduate School; but we were already standing and as stiff as *rigor mortis*.

"What is *this* doing in here?" the Captain roared; and as he spoke he pounded the Lit text so hard with his fist that he knocked it out of his own hand.

The Chairman of the Lit Detail leaped to pick the book up.

"Find that fellow Shelley for me," the Captain commanded. "That thing about beauty."

Later, the Chairman of the Lit Detail said it was like looking for hay in a haystack. But he took a long shot and returned the book to the Captain opened to "Hymn to Intellectual Beauty."

The Captain scanned the page till he found the lines he wanted.

"Now, hear this!" he bellowed, and began to read to us in a high falsetto, which he obviously intended to sound effeminate but which sounded, instead, more like a bosun with laryngitis:

"Sudden, thy shadow fell on me; I shrieked and clasped my hands with ecstasy."

Snapping the book shut, the Captain then glowered at each of us in turn, as if to ferret out any concealed admiration for the lines he had read. If there was any such admiration in that complement of men, it was not exposed. The officers of the Lit Detail, every man-jack of them—and the majority held Ph.D.'s in English—looked as if they had never before heard of Percy Bysshe Shelley.

When he was satisfied with his inspection, the Captain proceeded to a pronouncement.

"That Shelley fellow was a *sissy!* Strike the poem off the reading list."

"Aye, aye, sir!" said the Chairman of the Lit Detail.

The Captain warped his majestic hull around toward the door, but there he stopped, caught in the backwash of an afterthought.

"Belay that," he said, turning to the Chairman. "Not just that thing about beauty. Strike off everything in the book by that fellow. No Shelley. Understand?"

"But, sir—" the Chairman began.

"*All* of it!" the Captain shouted. "No Shelley! Won't do for Midshipmen. Can't have them exposed to that kind of bilge." He gave his falsetto a try again. "*Shrieking* and *clasping* his hands!" But he still sounded like a bosun in sick bay. "I might have known it when I saw the fellow's name on the list. *Percy*—!"

"Please let us keep 'Ode to the West Wind,' Captain," the Chairman of the Lit Detail pleaded. "In a way, sir, it's a nautical poem. That is, it's about the weather."

The Captain shook his head.

"Won't do!" he said. 'That one too! *All* of them! After all, there's a war on. Throw them *all* out! Understand? *Shrieking* and all that bilge! *Percy*—! Percy Bysshe—! Percy *Bosh*, I say!"

So, that year at the United States Naval Academy, Nineteenth Century English Poetry was taught with no mention of Percy Bysshe Shelley. To quiet my conscience in the matter, I tried to believe that a whole class of officers in the U. S. Navy would be manlier than their comrades in Blue and Gold because they had never heard of him. At least, if they ever encountered Beauty and recognized it and *shrieked*, they would have no one to blame but themselves.

We did retain Keats in the Plebe syllabus that year, however, probably because the Captain never had the stomach for looking into "The Eve of St. Agnes" after he jettisoned Shelley. At the time, I was sure that if he had known what was going on in Madeline's bedroom on St. Agnes Eve and heard the commotion it caused in my Plebe class John Keats would have gone over the side too.

At the Naval Academy, the teaching method is somewhat different from the method practiced in most institutions of so-called higher learning. Or so it was during the war. Every Midshipman had to have a grade in the instructor's grade book for every day, and for that reason you had very little time for shilly-shallying around with superfluous things like ideas. You got each Midshipman on his feet in the course of the fifty-minute period, asked him a question that he would find it hard to answer equivocally, jotted a numerical grade in your grade book, and proceeded to the next man. According to Academy Regs, you said, "That is well," at the end of each recitation, whether all was well or not; and it was a good idea to observe this rule because, if you didn't, your Midshipman would remain standing at attention, as solemn as a ninepin, even after you had called on someone else.

When I came to "The Eve of St. Agnes" in the Lit syllabus, I was pleased to note that there were forty-two stanzas in the poem. There were twenty-one Plebes in my Lit class. That meant two stanzas per Plebe. At the rate of a minute per stanza, I would have eight minutes left over for teaching.

We cast off to a good start with Keats's poem. I gave the class the poop about the legend of St. Agnes Eve, made sure they had the word on the rivalry between Madeline's family and Porphyro's, ran them through a drill in pronouncing Porphyro as *Porphyro* and not *Proffero*, and together we convoyed that amorous young man through the "dusky galleries" of Madeline's castle and into Madeline's bedroom, where, as Keats put it, he "took covert, pleased amain." That phrase caused a little difficulty, but I persuaded my future officers and gentlemen that *Porphyro*, being himself a gentleman if not a Naval officer, only hid in a corner of Madeline's room and did not take to the covers of her sack.

Then came Madeline's turn. All innocence, but eagerness too, "St. Agnes' charméd maid" climbed the marble stairs, lighting her way with a candle, and finally hove to at the door of her room, where Porphyro was hiding.

"Then what happened?" I asked the Plebe I had brought to attention to sound off on Stanzas 23 and 24.

The Plebe hesitated, and I thought he looked puzzled. But it was hard to tell. Most Plebes looked puzzled aboard the Bull Department.

"Well, sir," he said, finally, "when Madeline opened her bedroom door, a big animal ran out."

I could not have been more startled if the Engineering Department (known as "Steam") had blown out a boiler under my classroom windows, as indeed they were in the habit of doing from time to time.

"A big *what?*" I said.

"A big animal, sir."

I tried to think of all the things cluttering Madeline's bedroom that St. Agnes Eve. There was a table covered with cloth of woven crimson, gold, and jet. There were candied apple, quince, and plum and lucent syrops, tinct with cinnamon. And of course there was Porphyro. But I could recall no animals, large or small on the loose in the girl's chamber.

"I think you must be mistaken," I said.

"It's in the book, sir," the Plebe replied, solemnly. "May I show you?"

In the Navy, if it's in the book it's so. In my place, even the Captain would have had to give that Plebe a 4.0 for the day if he proved himself right.

"Very well," I said. "Find it in the book and read it to me."

The Plebe opened his book to Stanza 23 and read the first line.

"*Out went the taper as she hurried in.* . . . . That's a large tropical animal found mainly in South America, sir," he said. "I looked it up."

Five minutes later, Steam was sending over a man to ask *us* to pipe down.

The Captain never heard about this interpretation of Keats in my classroom, and at the time I was grateful. Maybe, though, it would have been all right if he had. On second thought, I believe he would have approved of Madeline's bedroom. After all, he liked animals in literature. It was only Beauty and that sort of bilge that he disapproved of.

SAMUEL L. CLEMENS

Fenimore Cooper's Literary Offenses

The Pathfinder *and* The Deerslayer *stand at the head of Cooper's novels as artistic creations. There are others of his works which contain parts as perfect as are to be found in these, and scenes even more thrilling. Not one can be compared with either of them as a finished whole.*

*The defects in both of these tales are comparatively slight.
They were pure works of art.*

PROF. LOUNSBURY

*The five tales reveal an extraordinary fullness of invention.
. . . One of the very greatest characters in fiction, Natty
Bumppo. . . . The craft of the woodsman, the trick of the
trapper, all the delicate art of the forest, were familiar to
Cooper from his youth up.*

PROF. BRANDER MATTHEWS

*Cooper is the greatest artist in the domain of romantic
fiction yet produced by America.*

WILKIE COLLINS

It seems to me that it was far from right for the Professor of English Literature in Yale, the Professor of English Literature in Columbia, and Wilkie Collins to deliver opinions on Cooper's literature
without having read some of it. It would have been much more
decorous to keep silent and let persons talk who have read Cooper.

Cooper's art has some defects. In one place in *Deerslayer*, and in
the restricted space of two-thirds of a page, Cooper has scored 114
offenses against literary art out of a possible 115. It breaks the
record.

There are nineteen rules governing literary art in the domain of
romantic fiction—some say twenty-two. In *Deerslayer*, Cooper violated eighteen of them. These eighteen require:

1. That a tale shall accomplish something and arrive somewhere.
But the *Deerslayer* tale accomplishes nothing and arrives in the air.

2. They require that the episodes of a tale shall be necessary parts
of the tale, and shall help to develop it. But as the *Deerslayer*
tale is not a tale, and accomplishes nothing and arrives nowhere,
the episodes have no rightful place in the work, since there was
nothing for them to develop.

3. They require that the personages in a tale shall be alive, except
in the case of corpses, and that always the reader shall be able to
tell the corpses from the others. But this detail has often been overlooked in the *Deerslayer* tale.

4. They require that the personages in a tale, both dead and alive,
shall exhibit a sufficient excuse for being there. But this detail also
has been overlooked in the *Deerslayer* tale.

5. They require that when the personages of a tale deal in conversation, the talk shall sound like human talk, and be talk such as
human beings would be likely to talk in the given circumstances,
and have a discoverable meaning, also a discoverable purpose, and
a show of relevancy, and remain in the neighborhood of the subject
in hand, and be interesting to the reader, and help out the tale, and
stop when the people cannot think of anything more to say. But

this requirement has been ignored from the beginning of the *Deer-slayer* tale to the end of it.

6. They require that when the author describes the character of a personage in his tale, the conduct and conversation of that personage shall justify said description. But this law gets little or no attention in the *Deerslayer* tale, as Natty Bumppo's case will amply prove.

7. They require that when a personage talks like an illustrated gilt-edged, tree-calf, hand-tooled, seven-dollar Friendship's Offering[1] in the beginning of a paragraph he shall not talk like a negro minstrel in the end of it. But this rule is flung down and danced upon in the *Deerslayer* tale.

8. They require that crass stupidities shall not be played upon the reader as "the craft of the woodsman, the delicate art of the forest," by either the author or the people in the tale. But this rule is persistently violated in the *Deerslayer* tale.

9. They require that the personages of a tale shall confine themselves to possibilities and let miracles alone; or if they venture a miracle, the author must so plausibly set it forth as to make it look possible and reasonable. But these rules are not respected in the *Deerslayer* tale.

10. They require that the author shall make the reader feel a deep interest in the personages of his tale and in their fate; and that he shall make the reader love the good people in the tale and hate the bad ones. But the reader of the *Deerslayer* tale dislikes the good people in it, is indifferent to the others, and wishes they would all get drowned together.

11. They require that the characters in a tale shall be so clearly defined that the reader can tell beforehand what each will do in a given emergency. But in the *Deerslayer* this rule is vacated.

In addition to these large rules there are some little ones. These require that the author shall:

12. Say what he is proposing to say, not merely come near it.
13. Use the right word, not its second cousin.
14. Eschew surplusage.
15. Not omit necessary details.
16. Avoid slovenliness of form.
17. Use good grammar.
18. Employ a simple and straightforward style.

Even these seven are coldly and persistently violated in the *Deerslayer* tale.

Cooper's gift in the way of invention was not a rich endowment; but such as it was he liked to work it; he was pleased with the effects, and indeed he did some quite sweet things with it. In his little box of stage-properties he kept six or eight cunning devices, tricks,

---

1. A book of conventional and polite sentiments and verse. Tree-calf is a pol-ished calfskin binding, stained with tree-like designs.

artifices for his savages and woodsmen to deceive and circumvent each other with, and he was never so happy as when he was working these innocent things and seeing them go. A favorite one was to make a moccasined person tread in the tracks of the moccasined enemy, and thus hide his own trail. Cooper wore out barrels and barrels of moccasins in working that trick. Another stage-property that he pulled out of his box pretty frequently was his broken twig. He prized his broken twig above all the rest of his effects, and worked it the hardest. It is a restful chapter in any book of his when somebody doesn't step on a dry twig and alarm all the reds and whites for two hundred yards around. Every time a Cooper person is in peril, and absolute silence is worth four dollars a minute, he is sure to step on a dry twig. There may be a hundred handier things to step on, but that wouldn't satisfy Cooper. Cooper requires him to turn out and find a dry twig; and if he can't do it, go and borrow one. In fact, the Leatherstocking series ought to have been called the Broken Twig Series.

I am sorry there is not room to put in a few dozen instances of the delicate art of the forest, as practiced by Natty Bumppo and some of the other Cooperian experts. Perhaps we may venture two or three samples. Cooper was a sailor—a naval officer; yet he gravely tells us how a vessel, driving toward a lee shore in a gale, is steered for a particular spot by her skipper because he knows of an *undertow* there which will hold her back against the gale and save her. For just pure woodcraft, or sailorcraft, or whatever it is, isn't that neat? For several years Cooper was daily in the society of artillery, and he ought to have noticed that when a cannon-ball strikes the ground it either buries itself or skips a hundred feet or so; skips again a hundred feet or so—and so on, till finally it gets tired and rolls. Now in one place he loses some "females"—as he always calls women—in the edge of a wood near a plain at night in a fog, on purpose to give Bumppo a chance to show off the delicate art of the forest before the reader. These mislaid people are hunting for a fort. They hear a cannon-blast, and a cannon-ball presently comes rolling into the wood and stops at their feet. To the females this suggests nothing. The case is very different with the admirable Bumppo. I wish I may never know peace again if he doesn't strike out promptly and *follow the track* of that cannon-ball across the plain through the dense fog and find the fort. Isn't it a daisy? If Cooper had any real knowledge of Nature's way of doing things, he had a most delicate art in concealing the fact. For instance: one of his acute Indian experts, Chingachgook (pronounced Chicago, I think), has lost the trail of a person he is tracking through the forest. Apparently that trail is hopelessly lost. Neither you nor I could ever have guessed out the way to find it. It was very different with Chicago. Chicago was not stumped for long. He turned a running stream out of its course and there in the slush in its old bed, were that person's moccasin tracks. The current did not wash them away, as it would have done in all other like cases—no, even the eternal laws of Nature have to vacate when Cooper wants to put up a delicate job of wood-craft on the reader.

We must be a little wary when Brander Matthews tells us that Cooper's books "reveal an extraordinary fullness of invention." As a rule, I am quite willing to accept Brander Matthews' literary judg-ments and applaud his lucid and graceful phrasing of them; but that particular statement needs to be taken with a few tons of salt. Bless your heart, Cooper hasn't any more invention than a horse; and I don't mean a high-class horse, either; I mean a clotheshorse. It would be very difficult to find a really clever "situation" in Coo-per's books, and still more difficult to find one of any kind which he has failed to render absurd by his handling of it. Look at the epi-sodes of "the caves"; and at the celebrated scuffle between Maqua and those others on the tableland a few days later; and at Hurry Harry's queer water-transit from the castle to the ark; and at Deer-slayer's half-hour with his first corpse; and at the quarrel between Hurry Harry and Deerslayer later; and at—but choose for yourself; you can't go amiss.

If Cooper had been an observer his inventive faculty would have worked better; not more interestingly, but more rationally, more plausibly. Cooper's proudest creations in the way of "situations" suffer noticeably from the absence of the observer's protecting gift. Cooper's eye was splendidly inaccurate. Cooper seldom saw anything correctly. He saw nearly all things as through a glass eye, darkly. Of course a man who cannot see the commonest little everyday matters accurately is working at a disadvantage when he is construct-ing a "situation." In the *Deerslayer* tale Cooper has a stream which is fifty feet wide where it flows out of a lake; it presently narrows to twenty as it meanders along for no given reason, and yet when a stream acts like that it ought to be required to explain itself. Fourteen pages later the width of the brook's outlet from the lake has suddenly shrunk thirty feet, and become "the narrowest part of the stream." This shrinkage is not accounted for. The stream has bends in it, a sure indication that it has alluvial banks and cuts them; yet these bends are only thirty and fifty feet long. If Cooper had been a nice and punctilious observer he would have noticed that the bends were oftener nine hundred feet long than short of it.

Cooper made the exit of that stream fifty feet wide, in the first place, for no particular reason; in the second place, he narrowed it to less than twenty to accommodate some Indians. He bends a "sap-ling" to the form of an arch over this narrow passage, and conceals six Indians in its foliage. They are "laying" for a settler's scow or ark which is coming up the stream on its way to the lake; it is being hauled against the stiff current by a rope whose stationary end is anchored in the lake; its rate of progress cannot be more than a mile an hour. Cooper describes the ark, but pretty obscurely. In the matter of dimensions "It was little more than a modern canal-boat." Let us guess, then, that it was about one hundred and forty feet long. It was of "greater breadth than common." Let us guess, then, that it was about sixteen feet wide. This leviathan had been prowling down bends which were but a third as long as itself, and scraping between banks where it had only two feet of space to spare on each side. We can not too much admire this miracle. A low-roofed log dwelling occupies "two-thirds of the ark's length"—a dwelling ninety feet long and sixteen feet wide, let us say—a kind of vestibule train. The dwelling has two rooms—each forty-five feet long and sixteen feet wide, let us guess. One of them is the bedroom of the Hutter girls, Judith and Hetty; the other is the parlor in the daytime, at night it is papa's bedchamber. The ark is arriving at the stream's exit now, whose width has been reduced to less than twenty feet to accommodate the Indians—say to eighteen. There is a foot to spare on each side of the boat. Did the Indians notice that there was going to be a tight squeeze there? Did they notice that they could make money, by climbing down out of that arched sapling and just stepping aboard when the ark scraped by? No, other Indians would have noticed these things, but Cooper's Indians never notice anything. Cooper thinks they are marvelous creatures for noticing, but he was almost always in error about his Indians. There was seldom a sane one among them.

The ark is one hundred and forty feet long; the dwelling is ninety feet long. The idea of the Indians is to drop softly and secretly from the arched sapling to the dwelling as the ark creeps along under it at the rate of a mile an hour, and butcher the family. It will take the ark a minute and a half to pass under. It will take the ninety-foot dwelling a minute to pass under. Now, then, what did the six Indians do? It would take you thirty years to guess, and even then you would have to give it up, I believe. Therefore, I will tell you what the Indians did. Their chief, a person of quite extraordinary intellect for a Cooper Indian, warily watched the canal-boat as it squeezed along under him, and when he had got his calculations fined down to exactly the right shade, as he judged, he let go and dropped. And missed the house! That is actually what he did. He missed the house, and landed in the stern of the scow. It was not much of a fall, yet it knocked him silly. He lay there unconscious. If the house had been ninety-seven feet feet long he would have made the trip. The fault was Cooper's, not his. The error lay in the construction of the house. Cooper was no architect.

There still remained in the roost five Indians. The boat has passed under and is now out of their reach. Let me explain what the five did—you would not be able to reason it out for yourself. No. 1 jumped for the boat, but fell in the water astern of it. Then No. 2 jumped for the boat, but fell in the water still farther astern of it. Then No. 3 jumped for the boat, and fell a good way astern of it. Then No. 4 jumped for the boat, and fell in the water away astern. Then even No. 5 made a jump for the boat—for he was a Cooper Indian. In the matter of intellect, the difference between a Cooper Indian and the Indian that stands in front of the cigar-shop is not spacious. The scow episode is really a sublime burst of invention; but it does not thrill, because the inaccuracy of the details throws a sort of air of fictitiousness and general improbability over it. This comes of Cooper's inadequacy as an observer.

The reader will find some examples of Cooper's high talent for inaccurate observation in the account of the shooting-match in *The Pathfinder.*

A common wrought nail was driven lightly into the target, its head having been first touched with paint.

The color of the paint is not stated—an important omission, but Cooper deals freely in important omissions. No, after all, it was not an important omission; for this nail-head is a *hundred yards* from the marksmen, and could not be seen by them at that distance, no matter what its color might be. How far can the best eyes see a common house-fly? A hundred yards? It is quite impossible. Very well; eyes that cannot see a house-fly that is a hundred yards away cannot see an ordinary nail-head at that distance, for the size of the two objects is the same. It takes a keen eye to see a fly or a nail-head at fifty yards, one hundred and fifty feet. Can the reader do it?

The nail was lightly driven, its head painted, and game called. Then the Cooper miracles began. The bullet of the first marksman chipped an edge of the nail-head; the next man's bullet drove the nail a little way into the target—and removed all the paint. Haven't the miracles gone far enough now? Not to suit Cooper; for the purpose of this whole scheme is to show off his prodigy, Deerslayer-Hawkeye-Long-Rifle-Leatherstocking-Pathfinder-Bumppo before the ladies.

"Be all ready to clench it, boys!" cried out Pathfinder, stepping into his friend's tracks the instant they were vacant. "Never mind a new nail; I can see that, though the paint is gone, and what I can see I can hit at a hundred yards, though it were only a mosquito's eye. Be ready to clench!"

The rifle cracked, the bullet sped its way, and the head of the nail was buried in the wood, covered by the piece of flattened lead.

There, you see, is a man who could hunt flies with a rifle, and command a ducal salary in a Wild West show to-day if we had him back with us.

The recorded feat is certainly surprising just as it stands; but it is not surprising enough for Cooper. Cooper adds a touch. He has made Pathfinder do this miracle with another man's rifle; and not only that, but Pathfinder did not have even the advantage of loading it himself. He had everything against him, and yet he made that impossible shot; and not only made it, but did it with absolute confidence, saying, "Be ready to clench." Now a person like that would have undertaken that same feat with a brickbat, and with Cooper to help he would have achieved it, too.

Pathfinder showed off handsomely that day before the ladies. His very first feat was a thing which no Wild West show can touch. He was standing with the group of marksmen, observing—a hundred yards from the target, mind; one Jasper raised his rifle and drove the center of the bull's-eye. Then the Quartermaster fired. The target exhibited no result this time. There was a laugh. "It's a dead miss," said Major Lundie. Pathfinder waited an impressive moment or two; then said, in that calm, indifferent, know-it-all way of his, "No, Major, he has covered Jasper's bullet, as will be seen if anyone will take the trouble to examine the target."

Wasn't it remarkable? How *could* he see that little pellet fly through the air and enter that distant bullet-hole? Yet that is what he did; for nothing is impossible to a Cooper person. Did any of those people have any deep-seated doubts about this thing? No; for that would imply sanity, and these were all Cooper people.

The respect for Pathfinder's skill and for his *quickness and accuracy of sight* [italics are mine] was so profound and general, that the instant he made this declaration the spectators began to distrust their own opinions, and a dozen rushed to the target in order to ascertain the fact. There, sure enough, it was found that the Quartermaster's bullet had gone through the hole made by Jasper's, and that, too, so accurately as to require a minute examination to be certain of the circumstance, which, however, was soon clearly established by discovering one bullet over the other in the stump against which the target was placed.

They made a "minute" examination; but never mind, how could they know that there were two bullets in that hole without digging the latest one out? for neither probe nor eyesight could prove the presence of any more than one bullet. Did they dig? No; as we shall see. It is the Pathfinder's turn now; he steps out before the ladies, takes aim, and fires.

But alas! here is a disappointment; an incredible, an unimaginable disappointment—for the target's aspect is unchanged; there is nothing there but that same old bullet-hole!

"If one dared to hint at such a thing," cried Major Duncan, "I should say that the Pathfinder has *also* missed the target!"

As nobody had missed it yet, the "also" was not necessary; but never mind about that, for the Pathfinder is going to speak.

"No, no, Major," said he, confidently, "that would be a risky declaration. I didn't load the piece, and can't say what was in it; but if it was lead, you will find the bullet driving down those of the Quartermaster and Jasper, else is not my name Pathfinder."

A shout from the target announced the truth of this assertion.

Is the miracle sufficient as it stands? Not for Cooper. The Pathfinder speaks again, as he "now slowly advances toward the stage occupied by the females":

"That's not all, boys, that's not all; if you find the target touched at all, I'll own to a miss. The Quartermaster cut the wood, but you'll find no wood cut by that last messenger."

The miracle is at last complete. He knew—doubtless saw—at the distance of a hundred yards—that his bullet had passed into the hole *without fraying the edges*. There were now three bullets in that one hole—three bullets embedded processionally in the body of the stump back of the target. Everybody knew this—somehow or other—and yet nobody had dug any of them out to make sure. Cooper is not a close observer, but he is interesting. He is certainly always that, no matter what happens. And he is more interesting when he is not noticing what he is about than when he is. This is a considerable merit.

The conversations in the Cooper books have a curious sound in our modern ears. To believe that such talk really ever came out of people's mouths would be to believe that there was a time when time was of no value to a person who thought he had something to say; when it was the custom to spread a two-minute remark out to ten; when a man's mouth was a rolling-mill, and busied itself all day long in turning four-foot pigs of thought into thirty-foot bars of conversational railroad iron by attenuation; when subjects were seldom faithfully stuck to, but the talk wandered all around and arrived nowhere; when conversations consisted mainly of irrelevancies, with here and there a relevancy, a relevancy with an embarrassed look, as not being able to explain how it got there.

Cooper was certainly not a master in the construction of dialogue. Inaccurate observation defeated him here as it defeated him in so many other enterprises of his. He even failed to notice that the man who talks corrupt English six days in the week must and will talk it on the seventh, and can't help himself. In the *Deerslayer* story he lets Deerslayer talk the showiest kind of book-talk sometimes, and at other times the basest of base dialects. For instance, when some one asks him if he has a sweetheart, and if so, where she abides, this is his majestic answer:

"She's in the forest—hanging from the boughs of the trees, in a soft rain —in the dew on the open grass—the clouds that float about in the blue heaven—the birds that sing in the woods—the sweet springs where I slake my thirst—and in all the other glorious gifts that come from God's Providence!"

And he preceded that, a little before, with this:

"It consarns me as all things that touches a fri'nd consarns a fri'nd."

And this another of his remarks:

"If I was Injun born, now, I might tell of this, or carry in the scalp and boast of the explite afore the whole tribe; or if my inimy had only been a bear"—[and so on].

We cannot imagine such a thing as a veteran Scotch Commander-in-Chief comporting himself in the field like a windy melodramatic actor, but Cooper could. On one occasion Alice and Cora were being chased by the French through a fog in the neighborhood of their father's fort:

"*Point de quartier aux coquins!*" cried an eager pursuer, who seemed to direct the operations of the enemy.
"Stand firm and be ready, my gallant 60ths!" suddenly exclaimed a voice above them; "wait to see the enemy; fire low, and sweep the glacis."
"Father! father!" exclaimed a piercing cry from out the mist; "it is I! Alice! thy own Elsie! spare, O! save your daughters!"
"Hold" shouted the former speaker, in the awful tones of parental agony, the sound reaching even to the woods, and rolling back in solemn echo. "Tis she! God has restored me my children! Throw open the sallyports; to the field, 60ths, to the field! pull not a trigger, lest ye kill my lambs! Drive off these dogs of France with your steel!"

Cooper's word-sense was singularly dull. When a person has a poor ear for music he will flat and sharp right along without knowing it. He keeps near the tune, but it is *not* the tune. When a person has a poor ear for words, the result is a literary flatting and sharping; you perceive what he is intending to say, but you also perceive that he doesn't *say* it. This is Cooper. He was not a word-musician. His ear was satisfied with the *approximate* word. I will furnish some circumstantial evidence in support of this charge. My instances are gathered from half a dozen pages of the tale called *Deerslayer*. He uses "verbal" for "oral"; "precision" for "facility"; "phenomena" for "marvels"; "necessary" for "predetermined"; "unsophisticated" for "primitive"; "preparation" for "expectancy"; "rebuked" for "subdued"; "dependent on" for "resulting from"; "fact" for "condition"; "fact" for "conjecture"; "precaution" for "caution"; "explain" for "determine"; "mortified" for "disappointed"; "meretricious" for "factitious"; "materially" for "considerably"; "decreasing" for "deepening"; "increasing" for "disappearing"; "embedded" for "enclosed"; "treacherous" for "hostile"; "stood" for "stooped"; "softened" for "replaced"; "rejoined" for "remarked"; "situation" for "condition"; "different" for "differing"; "insensible" for "unsentient"; "brevity" for "celerity"; "distrusted" for "suspicious"; "mental imbecility" for "imbecility"; "eyes" for "sight"; "counteracting" for "opposing"; "funeral obsequies" for "obsequies."

There have been daring people in the world who claimed that Cooper could write English, but they are all dead now—all dead but Lounsbury. I don't remember that Lounsbury makes the claim in so many words, still he makes it, for he says the *Deerslayer* is a "pure work of art." Pure, in that connection, means faultless—faultless in all details—and language is a detail. If Mr. Lounsbury had only compared Cooper's English with the English which he writes himself—but it is plain that he didn't; and so it is likely that he imagines until this day that Cooper's is as clear and compact as his own. Now I feel sure, deep down in my heart, that Cooper wrote about the poorest English that exists in our language, and that the English of *Deerslayer* is the very worst that even Cooper ever wrote.

I may be mistaken, but it does seem to me that *Deerslayer* is not a work of art in any sense; it does seem to me that it is destitute of every detail that goes to the making of a work of art; in truth, it seems to me that *Deerslayer* is just simply a literary *delirium tremens*.

A work of art? It has no invention; it has no order, system, sequence, or result; it has no life-likeness, no thrill, no stir, no seeming of reality; its characters are confusedly drawn, and by their acts and words they prove that they are not the sort of people the author claims that they are; its humor is pathetic; its pathos is funny; its conversations are—oh! indescribable; its love scenes odious; its English a crime against the language.

Counting these out what is left is Art. I think we must all admit that.

QUESTIONS FOR STUDY, DISCUSSION, AND WRITING

1. Do Clemens' remarks on Cooper follow any particular order? Explain.
2. Why does Clemens specify that nineteen rules govern romantic fiction (allowing that some say twenty-two)? Might the number really be larger, or smaller? What effect does he seek by particularizing Cooper's violation of eighteen of the rules? Does that list resemble any sort of document known to you? Why is the form, "They require that . . .", repeated? What is the effect of variations within that form?
3. Why does Clemens repeatedly allude to Cooper's "delicate art of the forest"? Give further examples of the technique of repetition, explaining the purpose in each case.
4. Where in the essay is exaggeration evident? Does the exaggeration enhance or detract from the essay as a piece of literary criticism? Why do you suspect that Clemens' criticism is imperfect?

VAN WYCK BROOKS

Mark Twain's Humor[1]

And now we are ready for Mark Twain's humor. We recall how reluctant Mark Twain was to adopt the humorist's career and how, all his life, he was in revolt against a role which, as he vaguely felt, had been thrust upon him: that he considered it necessary to publish his *Joan of Arc* anonymously is only one of many proofs of a lifelong sense that Mark Twain was an unworthy double of Samuel Langhorne Clemens. His humorous writing he regarded as something external to himself, as something other than artistic self-expression; and it was in consequence of pursuing it, we have divined, that he was arrested in his moral and aesthetic development. We have seen, on the other hand, that he adopted his career because his humor was the only writing he did in Nevada that found an appreciative audience and that, as a result of his decision, he obtained from the American public the prodigious and permanent approval which his own craving for success and prestige had driven him to seek. Here, then, are the facts our discussion of Mark Twain's humor will have to explain. We must see what that humor was, and what produced it, and why in following it he violated his own nature and at the same time achieved such ample material rewards.

It was in Nevada and California that Mark Twain's humor, of which we have evidences during the whole of his adolescence, came to the front; and it is a notable fact that almost every man of a literary tendency who was brought into contact with those pioneer conditions became a humorist. The "funnyman" was one of the outstanding pioneer types; he was, indeed, virtually the sole representative of the republic of letters in the old West. Artemus Ward, Orpheus C. Ker, Petroleum Nasby, even Bret Harte, sufficiently remind us of this fact. Plainly, pioneer life had a sort of chemical effect on the creative mind, instantly giving it a humorous cast. Plainly, also, the humorist was a type that pioneer society required in order to maintain its psychic equilibrium. Mr. Paine[2] seems to have divined this in his description of Western humor. "It is a distinct product," he says. "It grew out of a distinct condition—the battle with the frontier. The fight was so desperate, to take it seriously was to surrender. Women laughed that they might not weep; men, when they could no longer swear. 'Western humor' was the result. It is the freshest, wildest humor in the world, but there is tragedy behind it."

Perhaps we can best surprise the secret of this humor by noting

1. Chapter 9 of *The Ordeal of Mark Twain*, 1920.   2. Albert Bigelow Paine, Twain's biographer and editor.

Mark Twain's instinctive reaction to the life in Nevada. It is evident that in many ways, and in spite of his high spirits and high hopes, he found that life profoundly repugnant to him: he constantly confesses in his diary and letters to the misery it involved. "I do *hate* to go back to the Washoe," he writes, after a few weeks of respite from mining. "We fag ourselves completely out every day." He describes Nevada as a place where the devil would feel homesick: "I heard a gentleman say, the other day, that it was the 'd——dest country under the sun'—and that comprehensive conception I fully subscribe to. It never rains here, and the dew never falls. No flowers grow here, and no green thing gladdens the eye.... Our city lies in the midst of a desert of the purest—most unadulterated and uncompromising—*sand*." And as with the setting, so with the life. "High-strung and neurotic," says Mr. Paine, "the strain of newspaper work and the tumult of the Comstock had told on him": more than once he found it necessary—this young man of twenty-eight—"to drop all work and rest for a time at Steamboat Springs, a place near Virginia City, where there were boiling springs and steaming fissures in the mountain-side, and a comfortable hotel." That he found the pace in California just as difficult we have his own testimony; with what fervor he speaks of the "d——n San Francisco style of wearing out life," the "careworn or eager, anxious faces" that made his brief escape to the Sandwich Islands—"God, what a contrast with California and the Washoe!"—ever sweet and blessed in his memory. Never, in short, was a man more rasped by any social situation than was this young "barbarian," as people have called him, by what people also call the free life of the West. We can see this in his profanity, which also, like his humor, came to the front in Nevada and remained one of his prominent traits through life. We remember how "mad" he was, "clear through," over the famous highway robbery episode: he was always half-seriously threatening to kill people; he threatened to kill his best friend, Jim Gillis. "To hear him denounce a thing," says Mr. Paine, "was to give one the fierce, searching delight of galvanic waves"; naturally, therefore, no one in Virginia, according to one of the Gillis brothers, could "resist the temptation of making Sam swear." Naturally; but from all this we observe that Mark Twain was living in a state of chronic nervous exasperation.

Was this not due to the extraordinary number of repressions the life of pioneering involved? It was, of course, in one sense, a free life. It was an irresponsible life, it implied a break with civilization, with domestic, religious and political ties. Nothing could be freer in that sense than the society of the gold-seekers in Nevada and California as we find it pictured in *Roughing It*. Free as that society was, however, scarcely any normal instinct could have been expressed or satisfied in it. The pioneers were not primitive men, they were civilized men, often of gentle birth and education, men for whom civilization had implied many restraints, to be sure, but innumerable avenues also of social and personal expression and activity to which their natures were accustomed. In escaping responsibility, therefore, they had only placed themselves in a position where their instincts were blocked on every side. There were so few women among them, for instance, that their sexual lives were either starved or debased; and children were as rare as the "Luck" of Roaring Camp,[3] a story that shows how hysterical, in consequence of these and similar conditions, the mining population was. Those who were accustomed to the exercise of complex tastes and preferences found themselves obliged to conform to a single monotonous routine. There were criminal elements among them, too, which kept them continually on their guard, and at best they were so diverse in origin that any real community of feeling among them was virtually impossible. In becoming pioneers they had, as Mr. Paine says, to accept a common mold; they were obliged to surrender their individuality, to conceal their differences and their personal pretensions under the mask of a rough good-fellowship that found expression mainly in the nervously and emotionally devastating terms of the saloon, the brothel and the gambling-hall. Mark Twain has described for us the "gallant host" which peopled this hectic scene, that army of "erect, bright-eyed, quick-moving, strong-handed young giants—the very pick and choice of the world's glorious ones." Where are they now? he asks in *Roughing It.* "Scattered to the ends of the earth, or prematurely aged or decrepit—or shot or stabbed in street affrays—or dead of disappointed hopes and broken hearts—all gone, or nearly all, victims devoted upon the altar of the golden calf." We could not have a more conclusive proof of the atrophying effects upon human nature which this old Nevada life entailed.

Innumerable repressions, I say, produced the fierce intensity of that life, which burnt itself out so quickly. We can see this, indeed, in the fact that it was marked by an incessant series of eruptions. The gold-seekers had come of their own volition, they had to maintain an outward equilibrium, they were sworn, as it were, to a conspiracy of masculine silence regarding these repressions, of which, in fact, in the intensity of their mania, they were scarcely aware. Nevertheless, the human organism will not submit to such conditions without registering one protest after another; accordingly, we find that in the mining-camps the practical joke was, as Mr. Paine says, "legal tender," profanity was almost the normal language, and murder was committed at all hours of the day and night. Mark Twain records that in Virginia City murders were so common that they were scarcely worth more than a line or two in the newspaper, and "almost every

---

3. By Bret Harte. "Luck" is a foundling, the only baby in the mining community of Roaring Camp.

man" in the town, according to one of his old friends, "had fought with pistols either impromptu or premeditated duels." We have just noted that for Mark Twain this life was a life of chronic nervous exasperation. Can we not say now that, in a lesser degree, it was a life of chronic exasperation for all the pioneers?

But why? What do we mean when we speak of repressions? We mean that individuality, the whole complex of personal desires, tastes and preferences, is inhibited from expressing itself, from registering itself. The situation of the pioneers was, humanly speaking, an impossible one. But, victims as they were of their own thirst for gold, they could not withdraw from it, and their masculine pride prevented them even from openly complaining of it or criticizing it. In this respect, as I have already observed, their position was precisely parallel to that of soldiers in the trenches; and, like the soldiers in the trenches, they were always on the verge of laughter, which philosophers generally agree in calling a relief from restraint.

We are now in a position to understand why all the writers who were subjected to these conditions became humorists. The creative mind is the most sensitive mind, the most highly individualized, the most complicated in its range of desires: consequently, in circumstances where individuality cannot register itself, it undergoes the most general and the most painful repression. The more imaginative a man was, the more he would naturally have felt himself restrained and chafed by such a life as that of the gold-seekers. He, like his comrades, was under the necessity of making money, of succeeding—the same impulse had brought him there that had brought every one else; we know how deeply Mark Twain felt this obligation, an obligation that prevented him from attempting to pursue the artistic life directly because that life was despised and because the pursuit of it would have required just those expressions of individuality that pioneer life rendered impossible. On the other hand, sensitive as he was, he instinctively recoiled from violence of all kinds and was thus inhibited by his own nature from obtaining those outlets in practical jokes, impromptu duels and murder to which his companions constantly resorted. Mr. Paine tells us that Mark Twain never "cared for" duels and "discouraged" them, and that he "seldom indulged physically" in practical jokes. In point of fact, he abhorred them. "When grown-up people indulge in practical jokes," he wrote, forty years later, in his autobiography, "the fact gauges them. They have lived narrow, obscure and ignorant lives, and at full manhood they still retain and cherish a job-lot of leftover standards and ideals that would have been discarded with their boyhood if they had then moved out into the world and a broader life. There were many practical jokers in the new Territory." After all those years he had not outgrown his instinctive resentment against the assault to which his dignity had had to submit. To Mark Twain, in short, the life of the gold-fields was a life of almost infinite repression: the fact, as we have seen, that he became a universal butt proves in itself how large an area of individuality he was obliged to subject to the censorship of public opinion if he was to fulfill his pledge and win success in Nevada.

Here we have the psychogenesis of Mark Twain's humor. An outlet of some kind his prodigious energy was bound to have, and this outlet, since he had been unable to throw himself whole-heartedly into mining, had to be one which, in some way, however obliquely, expressed the artist in him. That expression, nevertheless, had also to be one which, far from outraging public opinion, would win its emphatic approval. Mark Twain was obliged to remain a "good fellow" in order to succeed, in order to satisfy his inordinate will-to-power; and we have seen how he acquiesced in the suppression of all those manifestations of his individuality—his natural freedom of sentiment, his love of reading, his constant desire for privacy—that struck his comrades as "different" or "superior." His choice of a pen-name, as we have noticed, proves how urgently he felt the need of a "protective coloration" in this society where the writer was a despised type. Too sensitive to relieve himself by horseplay, he had what one might call a preliminary recourse in his profanity, those "scorching, singeing blasts" he was always directing at his companions; and that this in a measure appeased him we can see from Mr. Paine's remark that his profanity seemed "the safety-valve of his high-pressure intellectual engine. . . . When he had blown off he was always calm, gentle, forgiving and even tender." We can best see his humor, then, precisely as Mr. Paine seems to see it in the phrase, "Men laughed when they could no longer swear"—as the expression, in short, of a psychic stage one step beyond the stage where he could find relief in swearing, as a harmless "moral equivalent," in other words, of those acts of violence which his own sensitiveness and his fear of consequences alike prevented him from committing. By means of ferocious jokes—and most of Mark Twain's early jokes are ferocious to a degree that will hardly be believed by any one who has not examined them critically—he could vent his hatred of pioneer life and all its conditions, those conditions that were thwarting his creative life; he could, in this vicarious manner, appease the artist in him, while at the same time keeping on the safe side of public opinion, since the very act of transforming his aggressions into jokes rendered them innocuous. And what made this a relief to him made it also popular. According to Freud, whose investigations in this field are perhaps the most enlightening we have, the pleasurable effect of humor consists in affording "an economy of expenditure in feeling." It requires an infinitely smaller psychic effort to expel one's spleen in a verbal joke than in a practical joke or a murder, the common method among the pioneers, and it is vastly safer—a fact that instantly explains the function of the humorist in pioneer society and the immense success of Mark Twain. By means of those jokes of his—("men were killed every week," says Mr. Paine, of one little contest of wit in which he engaged, "for milder things than the editors had spoken each of the other")—his comrades were able, without transgressing the law and the conventions, to vent their own exasperation with the conditions of their life, to vent the mutual hatred, the destructive desires that were buried under the attitude of good-fellowship imposed by the exigencies of their work. And as for Mark Twain himself, the protective coloration that enabled him to maintain his standing in pioneer society ended by giving him the position which he craved, the position of an acknowledged leader.

For, as I have said, Mark Twain's early humor was of a singular ferocity. The titles of his Western sketches reveal their general character: *The Dutch Nick Massacre, A New Crime, Lionizing Murderers, The Killing of Julius Caesar "Localized," Cannibalism in the Cars.* He is obsessed with the figure of the undertaker and his labors, and it would be a worthy task for some zealous aspirant for the doctor's degree to enumerate the occasions when Mark Twain uses the phrase "I brained him on the spot" or some equivalent. "If the desire to kill and the opportunity to kill came always together," says Pudd'nhead Wilson, expressing Mark Twain's own frequent mood, "who would escape hanging?" His early humor, in short, was almost wholly aggressive. It began with a series of hoaxes, "usually intended," says Mr. Paine, "as a special punishment of some particular individual or paper or locality; but victims were gathered wholesale in their seductive web." He was "unsparing in his ridicule of the Governor, the officials in general, the legislative members, and of individual citizens." He became known, in fact, as "a sort of general censor," and the officials, the corrupt officials—we gather that they were all corrupt, except his own painfully honest brother Orion—were frankly afraid of him. "He was very far," said one of his later friends, "from being one who tried in any way to make himself popular." To be sure he was! He was very far even from trying to be a humorist!

Do we not recall the early youth of that most unhumorous soul Henrik Ibsen, who, as an apothecary's apprentice in a little provincial town, found it impossible, as he wrote later, "to give expression to all that fermented in me except by mad, riotous pranks, which brought down upon me the ill-will of all the respectable citizens, who could not enter into that world which I was wrestling with alone"? Any young man with a highly developed individuality would have reacted in the same way; Mark Twain had committed the same "mad, riotous pranks" in his own childhood, and with the same effect upon the respectable citizens of Hannibal: if he had been as conscious as Ibsen and had not been obliged to make terms with his environment, his antagonism would ultimately have taken the form, not of humor, but of satire also. For it began as satire. He had the courage of a kind heart, the most humane of souls: to that extent the poet was awake in him. His attacks on corrupt officials were no more vehement than his pleas on behalf of the despised Chinese, who were cuffed and maltreated and swindled by the Californians. In these attacks and these pleas alike he was venting the humane desires of the pioneers themselves: that is the secret of his "daily philippics." San Francisco was "weltering in corruption," and the settlers instinctively loathed this condition of things almost as much as did Mark Twain himself. But they could not seriously undertake to reform it because this corruption was an inevitable part of a social situation that made their own adventure, their own success as gambling miners, possible. The desire to change and reform the situation was checked in the individual by a counter-desire for unlimited material success that throve on the very moral and political disorder against which all but his acquisitive instincts rebelled. And satire, a true campaign of satire, would naturally have tended towards a reorientation of society that would have put an end to the conditions under which the miners flourished, not as human beings, but as seekers of wealth. Consequently, while they admired Mark Twain's vehemence and felt themselves relieved through it—a relief they expressed in their "storms of laughter and applause," they could not permit it beyond a certain point. Mark Twain had been compelled to leave Nevada to escape the legal consequences of a duel. He had gone to San Francisco, where he had immediately engaged in such a crusade of "muck-raking" that the officials "found means," as Mr. Paine says, "of making the writer's life there difficult and comfortless." As a matter of fact, "only one of the several severe articles he wrote criticizing officials and institutions seems to have appeared," the result being that he lost all interest in his work on the San Francisco papers. When, on the other hand, he wrote about San Francisco as a correspondent for his paper in the rival community in Nevada, it was, we are told, "with all the fierceness of a flaming indignation long restrained." His impulse, his desire, we see, was not that of the "humorist," it was that of the satirist; but whether in Nevada or in California, he was prohibited, on pain of social extinction, from expressing himself directly regarding the life about him. Satire, in short, had become for him as impossible as murder: he was obliged to remain a humorist.

In a pamphlet published in the eighties, a certain phrenologist, "Professor" Beall, found the trait of secretiveness very strongly indicated in Mark Twain's "slow, guarded manner of speech." Such testimony perhaps has little value, yet it seems to throw some light on the famous Mark Twain "drawl," which he had inherited indeed, but which people say he also cultivated. Perhaps we can understand also why it is that half the art of American humor consists in "keeping one's face straight." These humorists of ours do not know themselves how much they are concealing; and they would be as surprised as anybody to learn that they are a kind of social revolutionists who lack the audacity to admit it.

Mark Twain, once committed to the pursuit of success, was obliged, as I say, to remain a humorist whether he would or no. When he went East to carry on his journalistic career, the publishers of *The Galaxy*, to which he became a regular contributor, specifically asked him to conduct a "humorous department"; and after the success of *The Innocents Abroad* his publisher, Bliss, we find, "especially suggested and emphasized a humorous work—that is to say, a work humorously inclined." We have already seen in a previous chapter, that whatever was true of the pioneer society on the Pacific slope was essentially true also of the rest of the American population during the Gilded Age, that the business men of the East were in much the same case as the pioneers of the West. The whole country, in fact, was as thirsty for humor as it was for ice-water. Mark Twain's humor fulfilled during its generation a national demand as universal in America as the demand fulfilled in Russia by Dostoievsky, in France by Victor Hugo, in England by Dickens; and we have at last begun to approach the secret of this fact.

I have spoken of the homogeneity of the American people during the Gilded Age. Howells has already related this to the phenomenon of Mark Twain's humor. "We are doubtless," he says, "the most thoroughly homogeneous folk that ever existed as a great nation. In our phrase, we have somehow all 'been there.' When [our humor] mentions hash we smile because we have each somehow known the cheap boarding-house or restaurant; when it alludes to putting up stoves in the fall, each of us feels the grime and rust of the pipes on his hands." We smile *because!* In that "because" we have the whole story of Mark Twain's success. The "cheap boarding-house," where every one has to pretend that he loves all his neighbors, is the scene of many restraints and many irritations; and as for the grime and rust of stovepipes, that is a sensation very far from pleasant. Sensitive men, constrained by love and duty to indulge in these things, have been known more than once to complain about them; they have even been known, if the truth were told, to cry bloody murder. That was Mark Twain's habitual reaction, as we can see from the innumerable sketches in which he wades knee-deep in the blood of chambermaids, barbers, lightning-rod men, watchmakers and other perpetrators of the small harassments of life. Mark Twain was more exasperated by these annoyances of everyday life than most people are, because he was more sensitive; but most people are exasperated by them also, and, as Howells says, all the

American people of Mark Twain's time were exasperated by the same annoyances. They were more civilized individually, in short, than the primitive environment to which they had to submit: and Mark Twain's humor gave them, face to face as they were with these annoyances, the same relief it had given the miners in the West, afforded them, that is to say, the same "economy of expenditure in feeling." We "smile because" that humor shows us that we are all in the same boat; it relieves us from the strain of being unique and solitary sufferers and enables us to murder our tormentors in our imaginations alone, thus absolving us from the odious necessity of shedding the blood our first impulse prompts us to shed. Howells says that "we have somehow all 'been there,'" a phrase which he qualifies by adding that the typical American of the last generation was "the man who has risen." The man who has "risen" is the man who has become progressively aware of civilization; and the demands of the typical American of Mark Twain's time, the demands he made upon his environment, had become, *pari passu*, progressively more stringent, while the environment itself remained, perforce, just as barbarous and corrupt and "annoying" as ever. But why perforce? Because it was "good for business"; it was the environment favorable for a regime of commercial exploitation. Was not the "man who has risen," the typical American, himself a business man?

Now, we have already seen that this process of "rising in the world," of succeeding in business, is usually attained at the cost of a certain suppression of individuality. The social effect of the stimulation of the acquisitive instinct in the individual is a general "leveling down," and this is universally conceded to have been characteristic of the epoch of industrial pioneering. The whole nation was practically organized—by a sort of common consent—on the plan of a vast business establishment, under a majority rule inalterably opposed to all the inequalities of differentiation and to a moral and aesthetic development in the individual that would have retarded or compromised the success of the business regime. We can see, therefore, that if Mark Twain's humor was universally popular, it was because it contributed to the efficiency of this regime, because it helped to maintain the psychic equilibrium of the business man, throughout the United States, precisely as at first it had helped to maintain the psychic equilibrium of the Western pioneer.

As a matter of fact, Mark Twain has often been called the "business man's writer." In that humor of his, as in no other literature, the "strong, silent man," who is the archetype of the business world, sees an aid rather than a menace to his practical efficiency. But why does he find it an aid and not a menace? Let us put the question the other way and ask why, in other forms of literature, he finds a menace and not an aid? The acquisitive and the creative instincts are, as we know, diametrically opposed, and, as we also know, all manifestations of the creative spirit require an emotional effort, a psychic cooperation, on the part of the reader or the spectator. This accounts for the business man's proverbial dislike of the artist. Every sort of spiritual expansion, intellectual interest, emotional freedom implies a retardation of the business man's mental machinery, a retardation of the "strenuous life," the life of pure action; and the business man shuns everything that distracts him, stimulates him to think or to feel. Such things are bad for business! On the other hand, he welcomes everything that simplifies his course, everything that helps him to cut short his impulses of admiration and sympathy, everything that prevents his mind from opening and responding to the complications and the implications of the spiritual and intellectual life. And this is precisely what Mark Twain's humor does. It is just as "irreverent" as the Boston Brahmins thought, when they gave Mark Twain a seat below the salt: it degrades, "takes down," punctures, ridicules as pretentious and absurd everything of a spiritual, aesthetic and intellectual nature the recognition of which, the participation in which, would retard the smooth and simple operation of the business man's mind. Mark Twain, as we shall presently see, enables the business man to laugh at art, antiquity, chivalry, beauty and return to his desk with an infinitely intensified conceit of his own worthiness and well-being. That is one aspect of his humor. In another aspect, he releases, in a hundred murderous fantasies of which I have mentioned several, all the spleen which the business life, with its repression of individuality, involves. Finally, in his books about childhood, he enables the reader to become "a boy again, just for a day," to escape from the emotional stress of maturity to a simpler and more primitive moral plane. In all these respects, Mark Twain's humor affords that "economy of expenditure in feeling" which, as we now perceive, the business man requires as much as the pioneer.

Glance, now, at a few examples of Mark Twain's humor: let us see whether they corroborate this argument.

In A *Tramp Abroad*, Mark Twain, at the opera in Mannheim, finds himself seated directly behind a young girl:

How pretty she was, and how sweet she was! I wished she would speak. But evidently she was absorbed in her own thoughts, her own young-girl dreams, and found a dearer pleasure in silence. But she was not dreaming sleepy dreams—no, she was awake, alive, alert, she could not sit still a moment. She was an enchanting study. Her gown was of a soft white silky stuff that clung to her round young figure like a fish's skin, and it was rippled over with the gracefullest little fringy films of lace; she had deep, tender eyes, with long, curved lashes; and she had peachy cheeks, and a dimpled chin, and such a dear little dewy rosebud of a mouth; and she was so dove-like, so pure, and so gracious, so sweet and bewitching. For long hours I did mightily wish she would speak. And at last she did; the red lips parted, and out leaped her thought—and with such a guileless and pretty enthusiasm, too: "Auntie, I just *know* I've got five hundred fleas on me!"

This bit of humor is certainly characteristic of its author. What is its tendency, as the psychologists say? Mark Twain has, one observes, all the normal emotions of a man confronted with a pretty girl: he has them indeed so strongly that he cannot keep his mind on the "business in hand," which happens to be the opera. He finds himself actually, prevented as he is from expressing himself in any direct way, drifting into a rhapsody about this girl! What does he do then? He suddenly dashes a pailful of cold water over the beautiful vision, cuts it short by a turn of the mind so sharp, so vulgar indeed, that the vision itself evaporates in a sudden jet of acrid steam. That young girl will no longer disturb the reader's thoughts! She has vanished as utterly as a butterfly under a barrel of quicklime. Beauty is undone and trampled in the dust, but the practical man is enabled to return to the "business in hand" with a soul purified of all troubling emotions.

Another example, the famous "oesophagus" hoax in the opening paragraph of A *Double-Barrelled Detective Story:*

It was a crisp and spicy morning in early October. The lilacs and labur-nums, lit with the glory-fires of autumn, hung burning and flashing in the upper air, a fairy bridge provided by kind nature for the wingless wild things that have their home in the tree-tops and would visit together; the larch and the pomegranate flung their purple and yellow flames in brilliant broad splashes along the slanting sweep of woodland, the sensuous fra-grance of innumerable deciduous flowers rose upon the swooning atmos-phere, far in the empty sky a solitary oesophagus slept upon motionless wing; everywhere brooded stillness, serenity, and the peace of God.

We scarcely need Mr. Paine's assurance that "the warm light and luxury of this paragraph are facetious. The careful reader will note that its various accessories are ridiculously associated, and only the most careless reader will accept the oesophagus as a bird." Mark Twain's sole and wilful purpose, one observes, is to disturb the con-templation of beauty, which requires an emotional effort, to degrade beauty and thus divert the reader's feeling for it.

To degrade beauty, to debase distinction and thus to simplify the life of the man with an eye single to the main chance—that, one would almost say, is the general tendency of Mark Twain's humor. Mr. Ludwig Lewisohn is of another opinion. This humor, he says, is "directed against pretentiousness and falseness. It 'takes them down a peg.'" But it "takes down" real superiority, too. In almost every one of Mark Twain's sallies, as any one can see who examines them, he burns the house down in order to roast his pig—he destroys, that is to say, an entire complex of legitimate pretensions for the sake of puncturing a single sham. And, as a rule, even the "shams" are not shams at all; they are manifestations of just that personal, aesthetic or moral distinction which any but a bourgeois democracy would seek in every way to cherish. Consider, for example, the value assailed in Mark Twain's famous speech on General Grant and his big toe. The effect of this humorous assault on the dignity of Grant was to reduce him not to the human but to the common level, to puncture the reluctant reverence of the groundlings for moral elevation in itself, and the success of that audacious venture, its success even with General Grant himself, was the final proof of the universal acquiescence of a race of pioneers in a democratic regime opposed, in the name of business, to the recognition of any superior value in the individual. And we may add that it would hardly have been possible if Grant himself had not gone the way of all flesh and become a business man.

The supreme example of Mark Twain's humor in this kind is *A Connecticut Yankee.* "It was another of my surreptitious schemes for extinguishing knighthood by making it grotesque and absurd," says the Yankee. "Sir Ozana's saddle was hung about with leather hat-boxes, and every time he overcame a wandering knight he swore him into my service and fitted him with a plug and made him wear it." Mark Twain's contemporaries, Howells among them, liked to imagine that in this fashion he was exposing shams and pretensions; but unhappily for this argument knighthood in the classic sense had long been extinct when Mark Twain undertook his doughty attack upon it, and it had no modern equivalent. To exalt the plug above the plume was a very easy conquest for our humorist; it was for this reason, and not, as Mark Twain fancied, from any snobbish self-sufficiency, that the English public failed to be abashed by the book. In this respect, at least, *A Connecticut Yankee* was an assault, not upon a corrupt social institution, but upon the principle of beauty, an assault, moreover, committed in the very name of the shrewd pioneer business man.

How easy it is now to understand the prodigious success of *The Innocents Abroad,* appearing as it did precisely at the psychological moment, at the close of the Civil War, at the opening of the epoch of industrial pioneering, at the hour when the life of business had become obligatory upon almost every American! How easy it is to understand why it was so generally used as a guidebook by Americans traveling in Europe! Setting out only to ridicule the sentimental pretensions of the author's pseudo-cultivated fellow-countrymen, it ridiculed in fact everything of which the author's totally uncultivated fellow-countrymen were ignorant, everything for which they wished just such an excuse to be ignorant where knowledge would have contributed to a personal development that was incompatible with success in business, a knowledge that would have involved an expenditure in thought and feeling altogether too costly for the mind that was fixed upon the main chance. It attacked not only the illegitimate pretensions of the human spirit but the legitimate pretensions also. It expressly made the American business man as good as Titian and a little better: it made him feel that art and history and all the great, elevated, admirable, painful discoveries of human-kind were not worth wasting one's emotions over. It exempted the Holy Land, to be sure. But the popular Biblical culture of the nineteenth century was notoriously, as Matthew Arnold pointed out, the handmaid of commercial philistinism; and besides, ancient Palestine was hardly a rival, as Europe was, of modern America. There was something to be said, it is true, for *The Innocents Abroad*. "I find your people—your best people, I suppose they are—very nice, very intelligent, very pleasant—only talk about Europe," says a traveling Englishman in one of Howells's novels. "They talk about London, and about Paris, and about Rome; there seems to be quite a passion for Italy; but they don't seem interested in their own country. I can't make it out." It was true; and no doubt Mark Twain's dash of cold water had its salutary effect. The defiant Americanism of *The Innocents Abroad* marked, almost as definitely as Whitman's *Leaves of Grass*, the opening of the national conscious-ness of which every one hopes such great things in the future. But, unlike *Leaves of Grass*, having served to open this national con-sciousness, it served also to postpone its fruition. Its whole tendency ran precisely counter to Whitman's, in sterilizing, that is to say, instead of promoting, the creative impulses in the individual. It buttressed the feeble confidence of our busy race in a commercial civilization so little capable of commanding the true allegiance of men that they could not help anxiously asking every traveling foreigner's opinion of it. Here we have the measure of its influence both for good and for evil. It was good in so far as it helped to con-centrate the American mind on the destinies of America; it was evil, and it was mainly evil, in so far as the book contributed to a national self-complacency, to the prevailing satisfaction of Americans with a banker's paradise in which, as long as it lasts, the true destinies of America will remain unfulfilled.

So much for the nature and the significance of Mark Twain's humor. I think we can understand now the practical success it brought him. And are we not already in a position to see why the role of humorist was foreign to his nature, why he was reluctant to adopt it, why he always rebelled against it, and why it arrested his own development? For obviously the making of the humorist was the undoing of the artist. It meant the suppression of his aesthetic desires, the degradation of everything in his own nature upon which the creative instinct feeds. How can a man forever check his natural impulses without in the end becoming the victim of his own habit?

I have spoken of A *Connecticut Yankee*. We know how Mark Twain loved the tales of Sir Thomas Malory: they were to him a lifelong passion and delight. As for "knightly trappings," he adored them: think of his love for gorgeous costumes, of the pleasure he found in dressing up for charades, of the affection with which he wrote *The Prince and the Pauper!* When, therefore, in his valiant endeavor to "extinguish knighthood," he sent Sir Ozana about the country laying violent hands on wandering knights and clapping plug hats on their heads he was doing something that was very agreeable indeed to the complacent American business man, agreeable to the business man in himself, but in absolute violation of his own spirit. That is why his taste remained infantile, why he continued to adore "knightly trapping" instead of developing to a more advanced aesthetic stage. His feeling for Malory, we are told, was one of "reverence," but the reverence which he felt can be justly measured by the irreverence with which he acted. One cannot degrade the undegradable, one can actually degrade only oneself; and the result of perpetually "taking things down" is that one remains "down" oneself, and beauty becomes more and more inaccessibly "up." That is why, in the presence of art, Mark Twain always felt, as he said, "like a barkeeper in heaven." In destroying what he was constrained to consider the false pretensions of others, he destroyed also the legitimate pretensions of his own soul. Thus his humor, which had originally served him as a protective coloration, ended by stunting and thwarting his creative life and leaving Mark Twain a scarred child.

He had, to the end, the intuition of another sort of humor. "Will a day come," asks Satan, in *The Mysterious Stranger*, "when the race will detect the funniness of these juvenilities and laugh at them —and by laughing at them destroy them? For your race, in its poverty, has unquestionably one really effective weapon—laughter. Power, money, persuasion, supplication, persecution—these can lift at a colossal humbug—push it a little—weaken it a little, century by century; but only laughter can blow it to rags and atoms at a blast . . . . As a race, do you ever use it at all? No; you lack sense and the courage." It was satire that he had in mind when he wrote these lines, the great purifying force with which nature had endowed him, but of the use of which his life had deprived him. How many times he confessed that it was he who lacked the "courage"! How many times we have seen that if he lacked the courage it was because, quite literally, he lacked the "sense," the consciousness, that is to say, of his own powers, of his proper function! Satire necessitates, above all, a supreme degree of moral maturity, a supreme sense of proportion, a free individual position. As for Mark Twain, by reacting immediately to every irritating stimulus he had literally sworn and joked away the energy, the indignation, that a free life would have enabled him to store up, the energy that would have made him not the public ventilator that he became but the regenerator he was meant to be. Mr. Paine speaks of his "high-pressure intellectual engine." Let us follow the metaphor by saying that Mark Twain permitted the steam in his system to escape instead of harnessing it till the time was ripe to "blow to rags and atoms" that world of humbug against which he chafed all his life. But he had staked everything upon the dream of happiness; and humor, by affording him an endless series of small assuagements, enabled him to maintain that equilibrium. "I am tired to death all the time," he wrote in 1895, out of the stress of his financial anxieties. With that in mind we can appreciate the unconscious irony in Mr. Paine's comment: "Perhaps, after all, it was his comic outlook on things in general that was his chief lifesaver."

QUESTIONS FOR STUDY, DISCUSSION, AND WRITING

1. What conditions in frontier life explain, according to Brooks, the necessity for and popularity of humorous writings? What account does he give of the function of humor in the more settled, business-oriented East? Indicate how the idea of repression becomes an explanatory element in each case.
2. How did Twain's personality cast him in the role of humorist? With what other impulses in Twain was this role in conflict? Show how Brooks has made this idea of internal conflict the thesis and organizing principle of his essay.
3. What distinction does Brooks draw between humor and satire? Why, according to Brooks, did Twain become and remain a humorist, not a satirist?
4. Brooks says (p. 567) that "half the art of American humor consists in 'keeping one's face straight.' " Are there examples of that technique in "Fenimore Cooper's Literary Offenses" (pp. 549–559)? To what other elements in that essay are Brooks' remarks on Twain applicable?
5. What evidence from Clemens' writing in "Overland Stage-Coaching" (pp. 39–44) might Brooks draw upon to support or illustrate his remarks about Twain? Write a brief essay showing whether and how Brooks' essay seems applicable to "Overland Stage-Coaching."

JAMES B. GREENOUGH and GEORGE L. KITTREDGE

Language Is Poetry[1]

When we examine the dictionary of any highly developed language like English, we are impressed not only with the enormous extent of the vocabulary, but with its infinite variety. There are plain words for common things (as *bread*, *stone*, *house*, *child*, *horse*) and simple physical acts (as *eat*, *drink*, *run*, *climb*); *there*

1. Chapter 2 of *Words and Their Ways in English Speech*, 1900. Some of the authors' footnotes have been omitted.

are formal or dignified or poetical words for equally simple conceptions (like *residence, progeny, quaff, masticate*); there are vague words (like *thing, affair, matter, act, do*) and scientific terms of rigid exactness (like *oxygen, atmosphere, chloride, carbon, inoculate*); there are abstract terms for mental and moral qualities (as *sagacity, carelessness, probity, honor*) and adjectives describing persons who exemplify these qualities (as *sagacious, careless, honest, honorable*); there are words of a distinctly undignified character (like *chum, crank, bamboozle, blubber, bawl, fizzle*), others so dignified as to be uncommon in familiar talk (as *remunerative, emolument, eleemosynary, recalcitrant*) or so high-sounding as hardly to be allowable even in elaborate writing (as *exacerbate, cachinnation, adumbrate*), there are words which have poetical associations (as *golden, roseate, silver-tongued, gambol, soaring, eterne*), and others so prosaic that every poet avoids them (as *fry, exchequer, discount, cross-question, extra, medium, miscellaneous*); there are words so technical as to be understood by specialists only (as *electrolysis, cotyledon, ontology, quaternions*), and others so childish as to be confined to the dialect of the nursery (as *naughty, mammy, dad, dolly*.)

Frequently, too, we find a number of different words ("synonyms," we call them) for what is essentially the same idea[2]: *ask, request, beseech, pray, beg, petition, supplicate, entreat, implore, solicit, crave, importune; angry, wrathful, incensed, irritated, vexed, resentful, enraged, furious, indignant, exasperated, irate, hot, infuriated; join, unite, associate, unify, link, connect, couple, combine*.[3]

The same marvelous variety shows itself when we study the different meanings of a single word. Thus *figure* may be equally well applied to a persons's form, a polygon, a numerical sign, an elaborate drawing or picture in a book, a metaphor or simile; *energy* may be used in a general sense or in the technical language of science ("the conservation of *energy*"); *property* may be a quality, one's possessions, or (in theatrical language) a thing or utensil used in setting the stage; *character* may refer to one's personal qualities, or it may denote a mark or sign in writing or printing, or it may be colloquially used for an eccentric person.

The question is immediately suggested: Whence does a nation provide itself with this enormous mass of words, with their multifarious meanings so aptly differentiated as to express all the aspects of any conception that can occur to the mind of civilized man?

2. So-called synonyms almost always differ from each other in some shade of meaning, or in emphasis, or at all events in their connotations [Greenough and Kittredge's note].

3. The reader may easily multiply examples by collecting, for instance, the synonyms for *awkward, beautiful, healthy, strange, throw, go, law, sin, people, custom* [Greenough and Kittredge's note].

In the first place, no people is perfectly homogenous, and this is strikingly true of the English nation, which is "Saxon and Norman and Dane," as Tennyson wrote, and Celtic as well. Each component part of the population contributes its proportion of words, small or large, but always characteristic, and distinct in many particulars from the contributions of all the rest. Then, too, all cultivated languages have borrowed much from outside nations with whom they have come in contact in war or trade or literature. Our own language, as we shall see, has enriched itself in this way from every quarter of the globe.

The varied materials thus brought together are constantly subjected to what may be called mechanical processes of growth. Every language has its machinery of prefixes and suffixes and compounds, by means of which a single word may become the center of a considerable group of related terms: as, *true, tru-th, tru-ly, un-true, un-tru-ly, tru-th-ful, tru-th-ful-ness*, etc.

But these causes are not sufficient to explain the richness and complexity of our speech. Such a result was achieved only when this great mass of variously derived material had been subjected for centuries to the language-making instinct; that is, to the poetic faculty of man. The dictum that "all language is poetry," then, if properly understood, goes far toward answering the question with which we are concerned.

The essentially poetical or figurative character of language may easily be seen by comparing a number of passages from the poets with ordinary prosaic expressions.

When Wordsworth writes, in "Laodamia,"

> The gods approve,
> The *depth*, and not the tumult of the soul,

the imaginative power of his phrasing at once appeals to us. If, however, we compare such common expressions as "He was *deeply* moved," "*profoundly* affected," "from the *bottom* of my heart," we recognize the same figure of speech. In other words, the poetical history of Wordsworth's line goes back to that unknown time when some primitive poet, without knowing that he was talking poetry, first applied to the emotions words which in their literal sense were only applicable to the physical conception of *depth*. As time has passed, the primitive metaphor has grown so familiar that it has ceased to be a metaphor. It has become merely an ordinary meaning of a group of common words. The modern poet, perceiving the imaginative significance of this usage, elaborated the figure it embodied, phrased it anew with conscious literary art, and thus, in an instant, restored it to its full poetic rights. Similarly, we may compare with "the *tumult* of the soul," such prose expressions as "his mind was *disturbed*," "his *agitation* was painful to witness," "the *violence* of his *emotion*"—each of which, though no longer felt as figurative, embodies a metaphor precisely similar to Wordsworth's.[4] We are not at this moment concerned with the ethical or philosophical contents of Wordsworth's line, for these might have been stated, with perfect accuracy, in the plainest terms, but merely with the poetical language in which he clothed his thought.

When Banquo says to Macbeth that the witches' salutation "might yet *enkindle* him unto the crown," we perceive that *enkindle* is used metaphorically. So, also, when Macbeth declares

I have no *spur*
To *prick* the sides of my intent.

But we feel the figure less vividly in such a phrase as "*fired* with ambition," and in the terms *instigation* and *incentive* we are not conscious of any metaphor whatever. Yet *instigation* comes from a root which means "to goad," and *incentive* means literally "that which sets the tune" (from L. *in* and *canere*, "to sing"); so that both these words were, in their first application to "motives" or "promptings," quite as poetical as either *enkindle* or *spur*.

The ordinary processes by which words change their meanings are, then, essentially the same as the devices of poetry; or, to express the fact more accurately, the figurative language of poetry differs from the speech of common life mainly in employing fresher figures, or in revivifying those which have lost their freshness from age and constant use.

Language is fossil poetry which is constantly being worked over for the uses of speech. Our commonest words are worn-out metaphors.

Thus, *depend* is literally "to hang from" (L. *dependo*); *egregious* means "selected from the [common] herd" (L. *e*, "from," and *grex, gregis*, "herd"); *spoil* means "to strip," i.e. "to strip off the armor, etc., of a slain or defeated enemy"; *front* means "forehead" (L. *frons, frontis*); to fret is originally "to eat up," "to devour" (A.S. *fretan, for-*, "away," and *etan*, "eat")—compare "gnawing anxiety"; *precocious* means "too early ripe" (L. *praecox*, from *prae-*, "before," and *coquo*, "to cook," "to ripen"); to thrill is literally "to bore," "to pierce," and is related to *drill* (the same word is seen in *nostril*, formerly *nosethril*); *sullen* means at first "solitary" and comes (through the French) from L. *solus*, "alone," (whence our adjective *sole*).

Such illustrations might be multiplied indefinitely. Indeed, almost every word that we shall have occasion to study will serve

---

4. *Disturb* is to "drive asunder in disorder," from L. *dis-*, "apart," and *turba*, "disorder," "a riotous crowd." *Agitation* comes from L. *agito*, "to drive to and fro." *Violence* is from *vis*, "force." *Emotion* is the "act of moving (one) away," "disturbance (of mind)" [Greenough and Kittredge's note].

as an example, for the processes that we are considering go on incessantly so long as a language is alive. We shall find that there is no device which we are accustomed to call poetical, no similitude so slight, no metaphor so strained or so commonplace, that language has not seized upon it to make new forms of expression as the needs of advancing thought required them. Even when the resultant words appear intensely prosaic, the processes that created them are identical with those of artistic poetry.

This important truth may be further illustrated in the growth of words from a single root.

The Indo-European family of languages (to which belong Sanskrit, Greek, Latin, English, and many other tongues) had a simple linguistic form (a "root") PET, which signified "rapid motion across the field of vision." This root is clearly seen in the Latin verb *peto*. Since such motion is produced either by *falling* or by *flying*, words with these meanings have been formed from the root PET in various languages of our family. But such motion may include also the idea of "intentional direction." Hence other words from the same root have acquired the sense of "aim," and, by the transference from actual to figurative aim, the meanings (originally metaphorical) of "seek" and "ask." All three senses, "aim," "seek," and "ask," are found in the Latin verb *peto*. Thus from this one root PET, we have, by various differentiations of meaning, such words[5] as the following:

Latin *penna*, "a means of flying," "a wing," "a feather"—whence, through the French, the English *pen*, originally applied to a quill used for writing, but now extended to other devices (steel pen, gold pen, stylographic pen, etc.).

Greek πτῶσις (*ptôsis*), "a falling"—then, figuratively, "a case" in grammar (since the genitive, dative, and other so-called "oblique" cases were conceived as *falling away from* the nominative, which was fancifully called the "upright case").

im-petus, "a force of forward movement"—first literal, then figurative.

ap-petite, "a craving" (of body or mind).

re-peat, "to go back *to get* something," "to take up a thing a second time."

petition, "a seeking," "a request."

com-petition, "a seeking together"—then, especially, "rivalry" (in modern times applied especially to commercial rivalry).

petulant, "butting" (as goats do), "attacking"—then figuratively, for "ill-humored," "irritable."

Another root, PU, meant "clean," and thence came the Latin adjectives *putus*, "clean," and *purus*, "clear." From *putus* arose a verb *puto*, "to clean." In a vine-bearing country, *cleaning* is particularly "pruning," and from that idea, specially applied in surgery, we get *amputation*. In mercantile language "to clean up accounts" (*putare rationes*) became a common expression for "reckoning,"

5. These words are built up by the mechanical means of word-formations developed in the various languages [Greenough and Kittredge's note].

and finally "accounts" (*rationes*) was dropped, and *puto* was used for "reckon" in general (as in *computation*). From "reckon" we pass easily to "think,"[6] and this becomes the ruling sense of *puto* (as in the adjective *putative*). From the same mercantile dialect comes *imputo*, "reckon in," "credit or charge to the account of," whence we get *imputation*. From "considering" or "turning back to observe" (cf. *re-gard*, *re-spect*, both meaning originally "to look back") we get the word *reputation*; and *deputation* is derived from another idea of "consideration carried out in *resolve*." Thus from a root signifying originally "clean," the imagination of the race, utilizing the mechanical means which the laws of derivation and composition afford, has gradually formed a group of words of the most varied meaning. Vine-dressing, surgery, mathematics, commerce, and politics are all included within this circle, and one word (*reputation*) is general enough to apply to all men.

Finally we may establish the poetical character of language by a striking and conclusive test. Literature has been attentively studied, as *literature*, for hundreds and even thousands of years. Hence there has grown up among scholars a set of technical terms —the names of the so-called "figures of speech"—which designate what are commonly regarded as the ornaments or devices that characterize the poetical style as opposed to the speech of everyday life. Yet it is easy to see that all of these "figures" are perfectly familiar in our ordinary talk. *Metaphor*, the most important of all figures, we have already considered. It occurs everywhere, and one can hardly utter a sentence without employing it. Every occupation of mankind, every subject (however remote) that engages man's attention, has furnished us with metaphorical expressions. We shall have occasion to return to this point again and again. For the present we may pass to other figures, making a selection from those comprised in the list commonly printed in works on grammar or rhetoric.

Simile is involved in the great class of English adjectives that end in *-ly*, which is an abraded form of *like*. Thus a "*manly* boy" is a boy who is "*like* a man" in certain traits of character. So *cowardly*, *ruffianly*, *saintly*, *homely* ("like home," and so "ordinary," "commonplace," with a further development of meaning in America to "hard-featured," "plain"). Still clearer cases of simile are the more recent adjectives compounded with *like*: as *childlike*, *lionlike*, *birdlike*, *homelike*, etc.

Metonymy is the figure by which a thing is designated, not by its own name, but by the name of something that resembles or suggests it—as in Tennyson's "the bright death" for "the keen fatal knife," or Horace's *Pontica pinus* for "ship of wood from Pontus."

6. Compare the provincial use of *I reckon* for "I think," in both England and America [Greenough and Kittredge's note].

This "figure" is so common in ordinary speech that it seldom attracts our attention. Thus we say *irons* for "fetters," *glasses* for "spectacles," or "drinking-glasses," *the knife* for "surgery," *canvas* for "sails," *style* (from L. *stilus*, a writing implement) for "manner of writing," *bill-boes* for "shackles" (from *Bilbao*, in Spain, famous for its iron and steel), and so on. Many of the words thus treated are perfectly prosaic, but the process is the same as that of poetry. A man's *linen* or *flannels* are just as much metonymy as Milton's "nodding horror" for the branches of a thick and dismal forest.

Synecodoche (the part for the whole, the genus for the species, or *vice versa*) is seen in "sixty *head*" (of cattle), "fifty *sail*" (of ships), "a *bottomry* bond," "a *poll* tax," a *rumshop*, a *gin-palace*, a *cutthroat* for a "murderer," a *hangman* for an "executioner."

Antonomasia, or the use of a person's name for any one who resembles him, is very common; a *Solomon*, a *Shylock*, "a *Daniel* come to judgment," a *Maecenas*, "a regular *Nero*," "a *Roland* for an *Oliver*."

Hyperbole is natural in unstudied speech: "I beg a *thousand* pardons," "scared to *death*," "I'd give the *world* to see him." Expressions of approval and disapproval are especially affected by hyperbole ("good for nothing," "a magnificent idea"), and the language of schoolgirls is proverbially made up of it: "thanks awfully," "extravagantly fond," "tremendously angry," "immensely obliged."

Antithesis is frequent in the commonest expressions, as: "up and down," "hither and yon," "this way and that." So, "Napoleon the Little," "Prince and Peasant."

Alliteration, a favorite poetic fancy, is found in such phrases as, "tit for tat," "blind as a bat," "spick and span," "the seven senses," "neck or nothing," "rough and ready."

Onomatopoeia has given rise to such words as *whiz, buzz, chickadee, bobolink*, and countless others. Many of them are humorous, and not a few are slangy.

Irony appears in "a *pretty* how-d'ye-do!" "Here's richness!" and other colloquialisms. Horace's "splendide mendax"[7] is called a poetical *oxymoron*, but such phrases as "a magnificent failure," "a beautiful imbroglio," "to swim like a stone," show the same figure—the joining of two inconsistent words to produce a peculiar rhetorical effect.

Catachresis, as it is called by the pedantic grammarians—that is, an "abuse" of language consisting in the employment of a harsh metaphor—is not peculiar to the poets. A well-known writer has ventured "He *spasmed* to him," to express the act of a boy making signs to another by contortion of the face. This is not likely to become good English, but it might easily become slang,

7. "Finely false."

and "misuses of language" quite as extraordinary have often made their way into our vocabulary. "To *jockey* a confiding partner" is an example. A *chaush* is a Turkish official interpreter; in 1609, a particular *chaush* is said to have distinguished himself by swindling a number of merchants in London; hence *chouse* for "defraud"— a sufficiently good instance of *catachresis* in its origin.

Litotes, or understatement, is found in all languages, but is heard particularly in New England provincialisms, as well as in slang. It comes partly from euphemism, and partly from caution or hesitation. Thus we have "the late unpleasantness" for the Civil War, "no conjuror" for a stupid person, "pretty well" and "so-so" for "in good health." The sarcastic *rather!* may be compared.

Periphrasis, like litotes, is a favorite means of avoiding plain language: "he came to grief," "I hope nothing will happen to him," "I am inclined to think your accounts are not very accurate," will serve as examples.

Pleonasm, or the practice of saying the same thing twice over in the same expression, is a universal characteristic of speech: as "go back again," "reared up," "go away from here," "he fell down and jumped up again." Excessive pleonasm is of course objectionable, but it is idle for the purist to object to such idiomatic phrases as those which we have just cited. They are of the very fiber of language. As well complain of "John! John!" or "no! no!" on the ground that one *John* or one *no* would suffice. The double comparative ("*most unkindest* cut of all"), formerly in good usage, is an excellent example of pleonasm.[8] The same tendency may be seen in such compounds as *inexsuperabilis*.[9]

Thus we have subjected the principle that "language is poetry" to a variety of tests. We have compared specific passages of poetry with ordinary phraseology, and have found a similar metaphorical character in both. We have observed the imaginative nature of the development of many meanings from a simple root-idea. We have recognized the existence of many so-called "figures of speech" in the commonest locutions of everyday life. We may feel certain, therefore, that the principle is a sound one, and may utilize it whenever it appears to be useful in our further study of English words.

8. Many forms which appear to be units are really instances of "double comparison." Thus *nearer* is *near* (comparative of *nigh*) with a comparative suffix *-er* added. Similarly *farther*, *nethermost*, *uppermost*, and so on. Compare the incorrect *furtherer* and *furtherest*, which are simply examples of the same tendency that have not had the fortune to gain admittance to good linguistic society [Greenough and Kittredge's note].

9. Insurmountable. Since *superabilis* and *exsuperabilis* both mean surmountable, the *ex-* is pleonastic.

QUESTIONS FOR STUDY, DISCUSSION, AND WRITING

1. What several causes contribute to the variety and complexity of language? What main principle do Greenough and Kittredge

present, and in what ways do they develop and support their thesis?

2. Select a short passage of poetry and show whether the language vivifies or restores the figurative force of ordinary prosaic expressions.

3. Show whether the following group of words exemplifies the principle adumbrated in this essay: respect, suspect, inspector, expectations, spectacular.

4. Give a further example, for each class set out in the essay, of "figures of speech" in ordinary talk.

5. In their own writing Greenough and Kittredge frequently exemplify the principle they are discussing. Explain the full meaning of: "Language is fossil poetry" (p. 577); "the growth of words from a single root" (p. 578); "-ly, which is an abraded form of like" (p. 579). Give further instances of the same. Should this occurrence be expected? Explain.

ARCHIBALD MacLEISH
Why Do We Teach Poetry?

1

There is something about the art of poetry which induces a defensive posture. Even in the old days when the primacy of poetry was no more challenged than the primacy of Heaven, which is now also challenged, the posture was habitual. If you published your reflections on the art in those days you called them a *Defense*. Today when the queen of sciences is Science, you do not perhaps employ that term but you mean it. It is not that the gentlemen at the long table in the Faculty Club whose brains have been officially cleared to serve as depositories of scientific secrets of the eighth and thirteenth classes are patronizing in their manner. They are still gentlemen and therefore still modest no matter how great their distinction or how greatly certified. But one knows one's place. One knows that whereas the teachers of science meet to hear of new triumphs which the newspapers will proudly report, the teachers of poetry meet to ask old questions—which no one will report: such questions as, why teach poetry anyway in a time like this?

It is a relief in this general atmosphere to come upon someone who feels no defensiveness whatever: who is perfectly certain that poetry ought to be taught now as at any other time and who is perfectly certain also that he knows why. The paragon I have in mind is a young friend of mine, a devoted teacher, who was recently made headmaster of one of the leading American preparatory schools, and who has been taking stock, for some time past, of his curriculum and his faculty. Poetry, as he sees it, ought to be taught "as a most essential form of human expression as well as a carrier throughout the ages of some of the most important values in our heritage." What troubles him is that few teachers, at least in the schools he knows, seem to share his conviction. He is not too sure that teachers themselves have "an abiding and missionary faith in poetry" which would lead them to see it as a great clarifier—a "human language" capable of competing with the languages and mathematics and science.

But though teachers lack the necessary faith, the fault, as my young friend sees it, is not wholly theirs. The fault is the fault of modern criticism, which has turned poetry into something he calls "poetry itself"—meaning, I suppose, poetry for poetry's sake. "Poetry itself" turns out to be poetry with its meanings distilled away, and poetry with its meanings distilled away is difficult if not impossible to teach in a secondary school—at least *his* secondary school. The result is that secondary school teachers have gone back, as to the lesser of two evils, to those historical and anecdotal practices sanctified by American graduate schools in generations past. They teach "poets and not poetry." With the result that "students become acquainted with poets from Homer to MacLeish" (quite a distance no matter how you measure it!) "but the experience doesn't necessarily leave them with increased confidence in what poetry has to offer." I can well believe it.

The reason why modern criticism has this disastrous effect, the reason why it produces "an almost morbid apathy toward 'content' or 'statement of idea,' " is its excessive "preoccupation with aesthetic values." Modern criticism insists that poems are primarily works of art; and when you insist that poems are primarily works of art you cannot, in my friend's view, teach them as carriers "throughout the ages of some of the most important values in our heritage." What is important about Homer and Shakespeare and the authors of the Bible is that they were "realists with great vision . . . whose work contains immensely valuable constructions of the meaning of life"; and if you talk too much about them as artists, those constructions of the meaning of life get lost.

Now this, you will observe, is not merely another walloping of the old horse who was once called the New Criticism. It goes a great deal farther. It is a frontal attack upon a general position maintained by many who never accepted the New Criticism or even heard of it. It is an attack upon those who believe—as most poets, I think, have believed—that a poem *is* primarily a work of art and must be read as a work of art if it is to be read at all. It is a high-minded and disinterested attack delivered for the noblest of purposes, but an attack notwithstanding—and an effective one. What it contends is that an approach to poetry which insists that a poem is a work of art blocks off what the poem has to say, whereas what the poem has to say is the principal reason for teaching it. What the argument comes down to, in other words, is the proposition that it is a mistake, in teaching poetry, to insist that poetry is art, because, if you do so insist, you will not be able to bring your students to the meaning of the poem, the idea of the poem, what the poem has to tell them about man and world and life and death—and it is for these things the teaching of the poem is important.

Now, I can understand this argument and can respect the reasons for making it. Far too many of those who define poetry in exclusively artistic terms use their definition as a limiting and protective statement which relieves them of all obligation to drive the poem's meanings beyond the meanings of the poem: beyond the mere translation of the symbols and metaphors and the classical or other references—the whole apparatus of *explication du texte*. Far too many, indeed, of those who have to do with literature generally in our time, and particularly with modern literature, consider that meanings in any but a literary (which includes a Freudian) sense are not only outside, but beneath, their proper concern—that the intrusion of questions of morality and religion into the world of art is a kind of trespass and that works of literary art not only should but *can* be studied in a moral vacuum. Literature in the hands of such teachers is well on the way to becoming again that "terrible queen" which the men of the nineties raised above life and which Yeats, when he outgrew the men of the nineties, rejected.

But although I can understand this argument, and although I can respect its reasons, and although I believe it raises a true issue and an important issue, I cannot accept it; for it rests, or seems to me to rest, on two quite dubious assumptions. The first is the assumption, familiar in one form or another to all of us, that the "idea" of a work of art is somehow separable from the work of art itself. The most recent—and most egregious—expression of this persistent notion comes from a distinguished Dean of Humanities in a great institution of learning who is reported by *The New York Times* to have argued in a scholarly gathering that "the idea which the reader derives from Ernest Hemingway's *The Old Man and The Sea* comes after the reader has absorbed some 60,000 words. This takes at least an hour. . . . A similar understanding could come after a few minutes study of a painting by a skillful artist." Precisely, one imagines, as the Doré illustrations gave one the "idea" of the *Inferno* in a few easy looks!

2

It is the second assumption, however, which divides me most emphatically from my young friend. For the second assumption seems to be that *unless* idea and work of art are distinguished from each other in the teaching of a poem, the idea—and so the effectiveness of the teaching—will be lost. At this point my friend and I part company. I am ready, and more than ready, to agree that it is for the meanings of life that one reads (and teaches) poetry. But I am unable to see how there can be a distinction between a poem as a conveyer of such meanings and a poem as a work of art. In brief, the distinction between art and knowledge which is made throughout my friend's argument seems to me wholly without foundation. That it is a distinction almost universally recognized in our epoch I know well enough. Science makes it. Poetry makes it. And the world agrees with both. "Whatever can be *known*," says Bertrand Russell, "can be known by means of science." Poetry, say its profesors, has no "messages" to deliver. And no one dissents from either. The exclusive proprietary right of science to know and to communicate knowledge is not only commonly recognized in our civilization: in a very real sense it is our civilization. For the characteristic of our civilization—that which distinguishes it from the civilizations which have preceded it—is the characteristic which knowledge-by-science has conferred upon it: its abstractness.

But though the agreement is general, the proposition is not one I can accept. I argue that the apologists for science are not justified in claiming, nor the apologists for poetry in admitting, the sole right of science to know. I insist that poetry is also capable of knowledge; that poetry, indeed, is capable of a kind of knowledge of which science is not capable; that it is capable of that knowledge *as poetry*; and that the teaching of poetry as poetry, the teaching of poem as work of art, is not only not incompatible with the teaching of poetry as knowledge but is, indeed, the only possible way of teaching poetry as knowledge.

To most of us, brought up as we have been in the world of abstractions which science has prepared for us, and in the kind of school which that world produces—schools in which almost all teaching is teaching of abstractions—the notion of poetry as knowledge, the notion of art as knowledge, is a fanciful notion. Knowledge by abstraction we understand. Science can abstract ideas about apple from apple. It can organize those ideas into knowledge about apple. It can then, by some means, introduce that knowledge into our heads—possibly because our heads are abstractions also. But poetry, we know, does not abstract. Poetry presents. Poetry presents the thing as the thing. And that it should be possible to *know* the thing *as the thing it is*—to *know* apple *as* apple—this we do not understand; this, the true child of the time will assure you, cannot be done. To the true child of abstraction you can't know apple as apple. You can't know tree as tree. You can't know man as man. All you can *know* is a world dissolved by analyzing intellect into abstraction—not a world composed by imaginative intellect into itself. And the result, for the generations of abstraction, is that neither poetry nor art can be a means to knowledge. To inspiration, yes; poetry can undoubtedly lead to that—whatever it is. To revelation, perhaps: there may certainly be moments of revelation in poetry. But to knowledge, no. The only connection between poetry and knowledge we can see is the burden of used abstractions—adages and old saws—which poetry, some poetry, seems to like to carry—adages most of which we knew before and some of which aren't even true.

But if all this is so, what then is the "experience of art"—the "experience of poetry"—which all of us who think about these things at all have known? What is the experience of *realization* which comes over us with those apples on a dish of Cézanne's or those three pine trees? What is the experience of realization which comes over us with Debussy's *Nuages?* What is the experience of realization which comes over us when Coleridge's robin sits and sings

> Betwixt the tufts of snow on the bare branch
> Of mossy apple-tree, while the night thatch
> Smokes in the sun thaw; . . .

or when his eave-drops fall

> Heard only in the trances of the blast,
> Or if the secret ministry of frost
> Shall hang them up in silent icicles,
> Quietly shining to the quiet Moon.

And if all this is so, why does one of the most effective of modern definitions of poetry (Arnold's in his letter to Maurice de Guérin) assign to that art the peculiar "power of so dealing with *things* as to awaken in us a wonderfully full, new and intimate sense of them and of our relation with them"?

The answer is, of course, that the children of abstraction are wrong—and are impoverished by their error, as our entire time is impoverished by it. They are wrong on both heads. They are wrong when they think they *can* know the world through its abstractions: nothing can be known through an abstraction but the abstraction itself. They are wrong also when they think they *cannot* know the world as the world: the whole achievement of art is a demonstration to the contrary. And the reason they are wrong on both heads is the reason given, quite unintentionally, by Matthew Arnold. They are wrong because they do not realize that all true knowledge is a matter of relation: that we *really* know a thing only when we are filled with "a wonderfully full, new and intimate sense of it" and, above all, of "our relation with" it. This sense—this *knowledge* in the truest meaning of the word knowledge—art can give but abstraction cannot.

There are as many proofs as there are successful works of art. Take, for obvious example, that unseen mysterious phenomenon, the wind. Take any attempt, by the familiar processes of abstraction, to "know" the wind. Put beside those two familiar lines of George Meredith:—

> Mark where the pressing wind shoots javelin-like
> Its skeleton shadow on the broad-backd wave!

What will be the essential difference between the two? Will it not be that the first, the analytical, statement is or attempts to be a wholly objective statement made without reference to an observer (true everywhere and always), whereas an observer—*one's self* as observer!—is involved in the second? And will not the consequential difference be that a relation involving one's self is created by the second but not by the first? And will not the end difference be that the second, but not the first, will enable us to know the thing itself— to know what the thing is *like*?

It would be quite possible, I suppose, to semanticize this difference between knowledge by poetry and knowledge by abstraction out of existence by demonstrating that the word, know, is being used in two different senses in the two instances, but the triumph would be merely verbal, for the difference is real. It is indeed the realest of all differences, for what it touches is the means by which we come at reality. How are we to find the knowledge of reality in the world without, or in the shifting, flowing, fluid world within? Is all this a task for the techniques of abstraction—for science as it may be or as it is? Is it through abstraction alone that we are to find what is real in our experience of our lives—and so, conceivably, what is real in ourselves? Or do we need another and a different way of knowing —a way of knowing which will make that world out there, this world in here, available to us, not by translating them into something else —into abstractions of quantity and measure—but by bringing us ourselves to confront them as they are—man and tree face to face in the shock of recognition, man and love face to face?

The question, I beg you to see, is not what we *ought* to do. There is no ought. A man can "live" on abstractions all his life if he has the stomach for them, and many of us have—not the scientists only, but great numbers of the rest of us in this contemporary world, men whose days are a web of statistics, and names, and business deals, held together by the parentheses of a pair of commuting trains with three Martinis at the close. The question is not what we ought to do. The question is what we have the choice of doing—what alternatives are open to us. And it is here and in these terms that the issue presents itself to the teacher of poetry.

3

Colleges and universities do not exist to impose duties but to reveal choices. In a civilization like ours in which one choice has all but overwhelmed the other, a civilization dominated by abstraction, in which men are less and less able to deal with their experience of the world or of themselves unless experience and self have first been translated into abstract terms—a civilization like a foreign language —in such a civilization the need for an understanding of the alternative is urgent. What must be put before the generation of the young is the possibility of a knowledge of experience *as* experience, of self *as* self; and that possibility only the work of art, only the poem, can reveal. That it is so rarely, or so timidly, presented in our schools is one of the greatest failures of our educational system. Young men and young women graduate from American schools and colleges by the hundreds of thousands every year to whom science is the only road to knowledge, and to whom poetry is little more than a subdivision of something called "literature"—a kind of writing printed in columns instead of straight across the page and primarily intended to be deciphered by girls, who don't read it either.

This sort of thing has consequences. Abstractions are wonderfully clever tools for taking things apart and for arranging things in patterns but they are very little use in putting things together and no use at all when it comes to determining what things are *for*. Furthermore, abstractions have a limiting, a dehumanizing, a dehydrating effect on the relation to things of the man who must live with them. The result is that we are more and more left, in our scientific society, without the means of knowledge of ourselves as we truly are or of our experience as it actually is. We have the tools, all the tools—we are suffocating in tools—but we cannot find the actual wood to work or even the actual hand to work it. We begin with one abstraction (something we think of as ourselves) and a mess of other abstractions (standing for the world) and we arrange and rearrange the counters, but who we are and what we are doing we simply do not know— above all what we are doing. With the inevitable consequence that we do not know either what our purpose is or our end. So that when the latest discoveries of the cyclotron are reported we hail them with the cry that we will now be able to control nature better than ever before—but we never go on to say for what purpose, to what end, we will control her. To destroy a city? To remake a world?

It was something of this kind, I imagine, that Adlai Stevenson had in mind when he startled a Smith Commencement last spring by warning his newly graduated audience of prospective wives that the "typical Western man—or typical Western husband—operates well in the realm of means, as the Roman did before him. But outside his specialty, in the realm of ends he is apt to operate poorly or not at all. . . . The neglect of the cultivation of more mature values," Mr. Stevenson went on, "can only mean that his life, and the life of the society he determines, will lack valid purpose, however busy and even profitable it may be."

As he has so often done before, Mr. Stevenson there found words for an uneasiness which has been endemic but inarticulate in the American mind for many years—the sense that we are getting nowhere far too fast and that, if something doesn't happen soon, we may arrive. But when he came to spell out the causes for "the neglect of the cultivation of more mature values" Mr. Stevenson failed, or so it seems to me, to identify the actual villain. The contemporary environment in America, he told his young listeners, is "an environment in which 'facts,' the data of the senses, are glorified and value judgments are assigned inferior status as 'mere matters of opinion.' It is an environment in which art is often regarded as an adornment of civilization rather than a vital element of it, while philosophy is not only neglected but deemed faintly disreputable because 'it never gets you anywhere.'" It is true that philosophy is neglected, and even truer that art is regarded in this country generally as it seems to be regarded by the automobile manufacturers of Detroit: as so much enamel paint and chromium to be applied for allegedly decorative purposes to the outside of a car which would run better without it. But the explanation is not, I think, that we set facts—even facts in quotation marks—above values, or that we glorify the data of the senses, unless one means by that latter phrase not what the senses tell us of the world we live in but what the statistics that can be compiled out of the data of the senses would tell us if we were ever in touch with our senses.

In few civilizations have the senses been less alive than they are with us. Look at the cities we build and occupy—but look at them! —the houses we live in, the way we hold ourselves and move; listen to the speaking voices of the greater part of our women. And in no civilization, at least in recorded time, have human beings been farther from the *facts* if we mean by that word, facets of reality. Our indifference to ends is the result of our obsession with abstractions rather than facts: with the ideas of things rather than with things. For there can be no concern for ends without a hunger for reality. And there can be no hunger for reality without a sense of the real. And there can be no sense of the real in the world which abstraction creates, for abstraction is incapable of the real; it can neither lay hold of the real itself nor show us where to find it. It cannot, that is to say, create the *relation* between reality and ourselves which makes *knowledge* of reality possible, for neither reality nor ourselves exist in abstraction. Everything in the world of abstraction is object. And, as George Buttrick[1] pointedly says, *we* are not objects: we are subjects.

1. Professor Emeritus and Preacher to the University, Harvard.

4

But all this is a negative way of saying what a defender of poetry should not be afraid of saying positively. Let me say it. We have lost our concern with ends because we have lost our touch with reality and we have lost our touch with reality because we are estranged from the means to reality which is the poem—the work of art. To most members of our generation this would seem an extravagant statement but it is not extravagant in fact and would not have seemed so in another time. In ancient China the place of poetry in men's lives was assumed as matter of course; indeed, the polity was based on it. The three hundred and five odes or songs which make up the Song-word Scripture survived to the fourth century B.C., when Confucius is said to have collected them because they were part of the government records preserved in the Imperial Archive. For thousands of years the examinations for the Chinese civil service were examinations in poetry, and there is no record that the results were more disappointing to the throne than examinations of a different character might have been. Certainly there is no record that a Chinese civil servant ever attempted to deny an honor student in a military academy his commission in the imperial army or navy because he was friendly with his own mother![2] Idiocies which the study of science and of other abstractions in contemporary institutions of naval education in the United States seem to nourish were apparently cauterized from the mind by the reading of poems.

It was not for nothing that Confucius told his disciples that the three hundred and five songs of the Song-word Scripture could be boiled down to the commandment: "Have no twisty thoughts." You cannot have twisty thoughts if you are real and if you are thinking about real things. But if a mother is merely a biological event to you and if you yourself are merely a military event called an admiral, anything may happen: you may make your country ridiculous, humiliate a promising boy, and deprive the navy of a good officer, all in the twisted belief that you are being a wise man and a patriot.

One can see, not only in the three hundred and five songs, but in Chinese poetry of other periods, what Confucius meant. Consider two Chinese poems of the second century B.C. and the sixth of our era, both written by Emperors. The first is a poem of grief—of the sense of loss of someone loved: a poem therefore of that inward world of feeling, of emotion, which seems to us most nearly ourselves and which, because it is always in flux, always shifting and changing and flowing away, is, of all parts of our experience of our lives, most difficult to know. We cannot know it through science. We cannot

---

2. MacLeish alludes to an incident in the news of the time: a graduating midshipman at the U.S. Naval Academy was refused a commission because of his mother's political associations.

know it by knowing things *about* it—even the shrewdest and most intelligent things, helpful though they may be to us in other ways. We cannot know it either by merely feeling it—by uttering its passing urgencies, crying out "I love" meaning "I think of myself as loving" or sobbing "I grieve" meaning "I think of myself as grieving." How then can we know it?

The Emperor Wu-ti wrote (this is Arthur Waley's beautiful translation):

> The sound of her silk skirt has stopped.
> On the marble pavement dust grows.
> Her empty room is cold and still.
> Fallen leaves are piled against the doors.
> Longing for that lovely lady
> How can I bring my aching heart to rest?

Four images, one of sound, two of sight, one of feeling, each like a note plucked on a stringed instrument. Then a question like the chord the four would make together. And all at once we *know*. We know this grief which no word could have described, which any abstraction the mind is capable of would have destroyed. But we know more than this grief: we know our own—or will when it shall visit us—and so know something of ourselves.

The second is a poem of that emotion, that feeling, which is even more difficult to know than grief itself. The second is a poem of delight: youth and delight—the morning of the world—the emotion, of all emotions, most difficult to stop, to hold, to see. "Joy whose hand is ever at his lips bidding adieu." How would you *know* delight in yourself and therefore yourself delighting? Will the psychiatrists tell you? Is there a definition somewhere in the folios of abstraction by which we attempt to live which will capture it for you? The Emperor Ch'ien Wen-ti (again Waley's translation) knew that there is only one mirror which will hold that vanishing smile: the mirror of art, the mirror of the poem:

> A beautiful place is the town of Lo-yang:
> The big streets are full of spring light
> The lads go driving out with harps in their hands:
> The mulberry girls go out to the fields with their baskets
> Golden whips glint at the horses' flanks,
> Gauze sleeves brush the green boughs.
> Racing dawn the carriages come home—
> And the girls with their high baskets full of fruit.

In this world within, you see, this world which is ourselves, there is no possibility of knowing by abstracting the meaning out—or what we hope will be the meaning. There we must know things *as* themselves and it must be *we* who know them. Only art, only poetry, can bring about that confrontation, because only art, only poetry, can show us what we are and ourselves confronting it. To be ignorant of poetry is to be ignorant therefore of the one means of reaching the world of our experience of the world. And to be ignorant of *that* world is to be ignorant of who and what we are. And to be ignorant of who and what we are is to be incapable of reality no matter what tools we have, or what intelligence, or what skills. It is this incapacity, this impotence, which is the tragedy of the time we live in. We are spiritually impotent because we have cut ourselves off from the poem. And the crowning irony is that it is only in the poem that we can know how impotent we have become.

Why do we teach poetry in this scientific age? To present the great alternative not to science but to that knowledge by abstraction which science has imposed. And what is this great alternative? Not the "messages" of poems, their interpreted "meanings," for these are abstractions also—abstractions far inferior to those of science. Not the explications of poetic texts, for the explication of a poetic text which goes no farther ends only in abstraction.

No, the great alternative is the poem as itself, the poem as a poem, the poem as a work of art—which is to say, the poem in the context in which alone the work of art exists: the context of the world, of the man and of the thing, of the infinite relationship which is our lives. To present the great alternative is to present the poem not as a message in a bottle, and not as an object in an uninhabited landscape, but as an action in the world, an action in which we ourselves are actors and our lives are known.

QUESTIONS FOR STUDY, DISCUSSION, AND WRITING

1. What two approaches to the teaching and study of poetry does MacLeish examine and reject? Why does he reject them? Indicate the main features of his own position. Does he set forth this position in a single thesis sentence anywhere in the essay?

2. Does MacLeish believe that we pay too much attention nowadays to fact, and therefore not enough to the finer things of life, such as poetry?

3. In the course of the essay MacLeish asks the reader to "look at the cities we build and occupy" and to "listen to the speaking voices of the greater part of our women" (p. 589). He implies that the cities and the voices are ugly. Is it the function of a city to be beautiful, or of women's voices to be graceful? Explain.

4. At the start of section 3 MacLeish writes: "Colleges and universities do not exist to impose duties but to reveal choices" (p. 587). Does the statement square with your experience? Perhaps you are now in a required writing course; is there any choice there? (You might begin by asking yourself why you are in the writing course; carry the question beyond the answer "because it's required.") Write an essay, developing your view of the matter.

ROGER ASCHAM
The Wind[1]

The wind is sometime plain up and down, which is commonly most
certain, and requireth least knowledge, wherein a mean shooter, with
mean gear, if he can shoot home, may make best shift. A side wind
trieth an archer and good gear very much. Sometime it bloweth
aloft, sometime hard by the ground; sometime it bloweth by blasts,
and sometime it continueth all in one; sometime full side wind,
sometime quarter with him, and more; and likewise against him, as a
man with casting up light grass, or else if he take good heed, shall
sensibly learn by the experience. To see the wind with a man his eyes
it is unpossible, the nature of it is so fine and subtile; yet this experience of the wind had I once myself, and that was in the great snow
that fell four years ago. I rode in the high way betwixt Topcliff-
upon-Swale and Boroughbridge, the way being somewhat trodden
before, by wayfaring men; the fields on both sides were plain, and
lay almost yard-deep with snow; the night afore had been a little frost,
so that the snow was hard and crusted above; that morning the sun
shone bright and clear, the wind was whistling aloft, and sharp,
according to the time of the year; the snow in the high way lay loose
and trodden with horses' feet; so as the wind blew, it took the
loose snow with it, and made it so slide upon the snow in the field,
which was hard and crusted by reason of the frost over night, that
thereby I might see very well the whole nature of the wind as it blew
that day. And I had a great delight and pleasure to mark it, which
maketh me now far better to remember it. Sometime the wind would
be not past two yards broad, and so it would carry the snow as far as I
could see. Another time the snow would blow over half the field at
once. Sometime the snow would tumble softly; by and by it would
fly wonderful fast. And this I perceived also, that the wind goeth by
streams, and not whole together. For I should see one stream within
a score on me; then the space of two score, no snow would stir; but,
after so much quantity of ground, another stream of snow, at the
same very time, should be carried likewise, but not equally, for the
one would stand still, when the other flew apace and so continue
sometime swiftlier, sometime slowlier, sometime broader, sometime
narrower, as far as I could see. Nor it flew not straight, but sometime
it crooked this way, sometime that way, and sometime it ran round
about in a compass. And sometime the snow would be lift clean
from the ground up to the air, and by and by it would be all clapt to
the ground, as though there had been no wind at all, straightway it

---

1. From Ascham's *Toxophilus: A Treatise on the Art of Shooting with the Bow*
(1545).

would rise and fly again. And that which was the most marvel of all, at one time two drifts of snow flew, the one out of the west into the east, the other out of the north into the east. And I saw two winds, by reason of the snow, the one cross over the other, as it had been two high ways. And, again, I should hear the wind blow in the air, when nothing was stirred at the ground. And when all was still where I rode, not very far from me the snow should be lifted wonderfully. This experience made me more marvel at the nature of the wind, than it made me cunning in the knowledge of the wind; but yet thereby I learned perfectly that it is no marvel at all though men in wind lose their length in shooting, seeing so many ways the wind is so variable in blowing.

ROBERT FROST

Education by Poetry: A Meditative Monologue[1]

I am going to urge nothing in my talk. I am not an advocate. I am going to consider a matter, and commit a description. And I am going to describe other colleges than Amherst. Or, rather say all that is good can be taken as about Amherst; all that is bad will be about other colleges.

I know whole colleges where all American poetry is barred—whole colleges. I know whole colleges where all contemporary poetry is barred.

I once heard of a minister who turned his daughter—his poetry-writing daughter—out on the street to earn a living, because he said there should be no more books written; God wrote one book, and that was enough. (My friend George Russell, "Æ", has read no literature, he protests, since just before Chaucer.)

That all seems sufficiently safe, and you can say one thing for it. It takes the onus off the poetry of having to be used to teach children anything. It comes pretty hard on poetry, I sometimes think, what it has to bear in the teaching process.

Then I know whole colleges where, though they let in older poetry, they manage to bar all that is poetical in it by treating it as something other than poetry. It is not so hard to do that. Their reason I have often hunted for. It may be that these people act from a kind of modesty. Who are professors that they should attempt to deal with a thing as high and as fine as poetry? Who are *they*? There is a certain manly modesty in that.

That is the best general way of settling the problem; treat all poetry as if it were something else than poetry, as if it were syntax, language, science. Then you can even come down into the American

1. An address given at Amherst College in 1930.

and into the contemporary without any special risk.

There is another reason they have, and that is that they are, first and foremost in life, markers. They have the marking problem to consider. Now, I stand here a teacher of many years' experience and I have never complained of having had to mark. I had rather mark anyone for anything—for his looks, carriage, his ideas, his correctness, his exactness, anything you please—I would rather give him a mark in terms of letters, A, B, C, D, than have to use adjectives on him. We are all being marked by each other all the time, classified, ranked, put in our place, and I see no escape from that. I am no sentimentalist. You have got to mark, and you have got to mark, first of all, for accuracy, for correctness. But if I am going to give a mark, that is the least part of my marking. The hard part is the part beyond that, the part where the adventure begins.

One other way to rid the curriculum of the poetry nuisance has been considered. More merciful than the others it would neither abolish nor denature the poetry, but only turn it out to disport itself, with the plays and games—in no wise discredited, though given no credit for. Any one who liked to teach poetically could take his subject, whether English, Latin, Greek or French, out into the no-where along with the poetry. One side of a sharp line would be left to the rigorous and righteous; the other side would be assigned to the flowery where they would know what could be expected of them. Grade marks where more easily given, of course, in the courses concentrating on correctness and exactness as the only forms of honesty recognized by plain people; a general indefinite mark of X in the courses that scatter brains over taste and opinion. On inquiry I have found no teacher willing to take position on either side of the line, either among the rigors or among the flowers. No one is willing to admit that his discipline is not partly in exactness. No one is willing to admit that his discipline is not partly in taste and enthusiasm.

How shall a man go through college without having been marked for taste and judgment? What will become of him? What will his end be? He will have to take continuation courses for college graduates. He will have to go to night schools. They are having night schools now, you know, for college graduates. Why? Because they have not been educated enough to find their way around in contemporary literature. They don't know what they may safely like in the libraries and galleries. They don't know how to judge an editorial when they see one. They don't know how to judge a political campaign. They don't know when they are being fooled by a metaphor, an analogy, a parable. And metaphor is, of course, what we are talking about. Education by poetry is education by metaphor.

Suppose we stop short of imagination, initiative, enthusiasm, inspiration and originality—dread words. Suppose we don't mark in such things at all. There are still two minimal things, that we have got to take care of, taste and judgment. Americans are supposed to have more judgment than taste, but taste is there to be dealt with. That is what poetry, the only art in the colleges of arts, is there for. I for my part would not be afraid to go in for enthusiasm. There is the enthusiasm like a blinding light, or the enthusiasm of the deafening shout, the crude enthusiasm that you get uneducated by poetry, outside of poetry. It is exemplified in what I might call "sunset raving." You look westward toward the sunset, or if you get up early enough, eastward toward the sunrise, and you rave. It is oh's and ah's with you and no more.

But the enthusiasm I mean is taken through the prism of the intellect and spread on the screen in a color, all the way from hyperbole at one end—or overstatement, at one end—to understatement at the other end. It is a long strip of dark lines and many colors. Such enthusiasm is one object of all teaching in poetry. I heard wonderful things said about Virgil yesterday, and many of them seemed to me crude enthusiasm, more like a deafening shout, many of them. But one speech had range, something of overstatement, something of statement, and something of understatement. It had all the colors of an enthusiasm passed through an idea.

I would be willing to throw away everything else but that: enthusiasm tamed by metaphor. Let me rest the case there. Enthusiasm tamed to metaphor, tamed to that much of it. I do not think anybody ever knows the discreet use of metaphor, his own and other people's, the discreet handling of metaphor, unless he has been properly educated in poetry.

Poetry begins in trivial metaphors, petty metaphors, "grace" metaphors, and goes on to the profoundest thinking that we have. Poetry provides the one permissible way of saying one thing and meaning another. People say, "Why don't you say what you mean?" We never do that, do we, being all of us too much poets. We like to talk in parables and in hints and in indirections—whether from diffidence or some other instinct.

I have wanted in late years to go further and further in making metaphor the whole of thinking. I find some one now and then to agree with me that all thinking, except mathematical thinking, is metaphorical, or all thinking except scientific thinking. The mathematical might be difficult for me to bring in, but the scientific is easy enough.

Once on a time all the Greeks were busy telling each other what the All was—or was like unto. All was three elements, air, earth, and water (we once thought it was ninety elements; now we think it is only one). All was substance, said another. All was change, said a third. But best and most fruitful was Pythagoras' comparison of the universe with number. Number of what? Number of feet, pounds, and seconds was the answer, and we had science and all that has followed in science. The metaphor has held and held, breaking down only when it came to the spiritual and psychological or the out of the way places of the physical.

The other day we had a visitor here, a noted scientist, whose latest word to the world has been that the more accurately you know where a thing is, the less accurately you are able to state how fast it is moving. You can see why that would be so, without going back to Zeno's problem of the arrow's flight. In carrying numbers into the realm of space and at the same time into the realm of time you are mixing metaphors, that is all, and you are in trouble. They won't mix. The two don't go together.

Let's take two or three more of the metaphors now in use to live by. I have just spoken of one of the new ones, a charming mixed metaphor right in the realm of higher mathematics and higher physics: that the more accurately you state where a thing is, the less accurately you will be able to tell how fast it is moving. And, of course everything is moving. Everything is an event now. Another metaphor. A thing, they say, is an event. Do you believe it is? Not quite. I believe it is almost an event. But I like the comparison of a thing with an event.

I notice another from the same quarter. "In the neighborhood of matter space is something like curved." Isn't that a good one! It seems to me that that is simply and utterly charming—to say that space is something like curved in the neighborhood of matter. "Something like."

Another amusing one is from—what is the book?—I can't say it now; but here is the metaphor. Its aim is to restore you to your ideas of free will. It wants to give you back your freedom of will. All right, here it is on a platter. You know that you can't tell by name what persons in a certain class will be dead ten years after graduation, but you can tell actuarially how many will be dead. Now, just so this scientist says of the particles of matter flying at a screen, striking a screen; you can't tell what individual particles will come, but you can say in general that a certain number will strike in a given time. It shows, you see, that the individual particle can come freely. I asked Bohr about that particularly, and he said, "Yes, it is so. It can come when it wills and as it wills; and the action of the individual particle is unpredictable. But it is not so of the action of the mass. There you can predict." He says, "That gives the individual atom its freedom, but the mass its necessity."

Another metaphor that has interested us in our time and has done all our thinking for us is the metaphor of evolution. Never mind going into the Latin word. The metaphor is simply the metaphor of the growing plant or of the growing thing. And somebody very brilliantly, quite a while ago, said that the whole universe, the whole of everything, was like unto a growing thing. That is all. I know the

metaphor will break down at some point, but it has not failed everywhere. It is a very brilliant metaphor, I acknowledge, though I myself
get too tired of the kind of essay that talks about the evolution of
candy, we will say, or the evolution of elevators—the evolution of
this, that, and the other. Everything is evolution. I emancipate myself by simply saying that I didn't get up the metaphor and so am not
much interested in it.

What I am pointing out is that unless you are at home in the
metaphor, unless you have had your proper poetical education in the
metaphor, you are not safe anywhere. Because you are not at ease with
figurative values: you don't know the metaphor in its strength and its
weakness. You don't know how far you may expect to ride it and
when it may break down with you. You are not safe in science; you are
not safe in history. In history, for instance—to show that is the same
in history as elsewhere—I heard somebody say yesterday that Aeneas
was to be likened unto (those words, "likened unto"!) George
Washington. He was that type of national hero, the middle-class man,
not thinking of being a hero at all, bent on building the future, bent
on his children, his descendants. A good metaphor, as far as it goes,
and you must know how far. And then he added that Odysseus
should be likened unto Theodore Roosevelt. I don't think that is so
good. Someone visiting Gibbon at the point of death, said he was the
same Gibbon as of old; still at his parallels.

Take the way we have been led into our present position morally,
the world over. It is by a sort of metaphorical gradient. There is a
kind of thinking—to speak metaphorically—there is a kind of thinking you might say was endemic in the brothel. It is always there.
And every now and then in some mysterious way it becomes epidemic in the world. And how does it do so? By using all the good
words that virtue has invented to maintain virtue. It uses honesty,
first—frankness, sincerity—those words; picks them up, uses them.
"In the name of honesty, let us see what we are." You know. And
then it picks up the word joy. "Let us in the name of joy, which is
the enemy of our ancestors, the Puritans . . . Let us in the name of
joy, which is the enemy of the kill-joy Puritan . . . " You see. "Let
us," and so on. And then, "In the name of health . . . " Health is
another good word. And that is the metaphor Freudianism trades on,
mental health. And the first thing we know, it has us all in up to the
top knot. I suppose we may blame the artists a good deal, because
they are great people to spread by metaphor. The stage too—the
stage is always a good intermediary between the two worlds, the under
and the upper, if I may say so without personal prejudice to the stage.

In all this, I have only been saying that the devil can quote
Scripture, which simply means that the good words you have lying
around the devil can use for his purposes as well as anybody else.
Never mind about my morality. I am not here to urge anything. I

don't care whether the world is good or bad—not on any particular day.

Let me ask you to watch a metaphor breaking down here before you.

Somebody said to me a little while ago, "It is easy enough for me to think of the universe as a machine, as a mechanism."

I said, "You mean the universe is like a machine?"

He said, "No. I think it is one . . . Well, it is like . . ."

"I think you mean the universe is like a machine."

"All right. Let it go at that."

I asked him, "Did you ever see a machine without a pedal for the foot, or a lever for the hand, or a button for the finger?"

He said "No—no."

I said, "All right. Is the universe like that?"

And he said, "No. I mean it is like a machine, only . . ."

". . . it is different from a machine," I said.

He wanted to go just that far with that metaphor and no further. And so do we all. All metaphor breaks down somewhere. That is the beauty of it. It is touch and go with the metaphor, and until you have lived with it long enough you don't know when it is going. You don't know how much you can get out of it and when it will cease to yield. It is a very living thing. It is as life itself.

I have heard this ever since I can remember, and ever since I have taught: the teacher must teach the pupil to think. I saw a teacher once going around in a great school and snapping pupils' heads with thumb and finger and saying, "Think." That was when thinking was becoming the fashion. The fashion hasn't yet quite gone out.

We still ask boys in college to think, as in the nineties, but we seldom tell them what thinking means; we seldom tell them it is just putting this and that together; it is saying one thing in terms of another. To tell them is to set their feet on the first rung of a ladder the top of which sticks through the sky.

Greatest of all attempts to say one thing in terms of another is the philosophical attempt to say matter in terms of spirit, or spirit in terms of matter, to make the final unity. That is the greatest attempt that ever failed. We stop just short there. But it is the height of poetry, the height of all thinking, the height of all poetic thinking, that attempt to say matter in terms of spirit and spirit in terms of matter. It is wrong to call anybody a materialist simply because he tries to say spirit in terms of matter, as if that were a sin. Materialism is not the attempt to say all in terms of matter. The only materialist —be he poet, teacher, scientist, politician, or statesman—is the man who gets lost in his material without a gathering metaphor to throw it into shape and order. He is the lost soul.

We ask people to think, and we don't show them what thinking is. Somebody says we don't need to show them how to think; bye and

bye they will think. We will give them the forms of sentences and, if they have any ideas, then they will know how to write them. But that is preposterous. All there is to writing is having ideas. To learn to write is to learn to have ideas.

The first little metaphor . . . Take some of the trivial ones. I would rather have trivial ones of my own to live by than the big ones of other people.

I remember a boy saying, "He is the kind of person that wounds with his shield." That may be a slender one, of course. It goes a good way in character description. It has poetic grace. "He is the kind that wounds with his shield."

The shield reminds me—just to linger a minute—the shield reminds me of the inverted shield spoken of in one of the books of the *Odyssey*, the book that tells about the longest swim on record. I forget how long it lasted—several days, was it?—but at last as Odysseus came near the coast of Phoenicia, he saw it on the horizon "like an inverted shield."

There is a better metaphor in the same book. In the end Odysseus comes ashore and crawls up the beach to spend the night under a double olive tree, and it says, as in a lonely farmhouse where it is hard to get fire—I am not quoting exactly—where it is hard to start the fire again if it goes out, they cover the seeds of fire with ashes to preserve it for the night, so Odysseus covered himself with the leaves around him and went to sleep. There you have something that gives you character, something of Odysseus himself. "Seeds of fire." So Odysseus covered the seeds of fire in himself. You get the greatness of his nature.

But these are slighter metaphors than the ones we live by. They have their charm, their passing charm. They are as it were the first steps toward the great thoughts, grave thoughts, thoughts lasting to the end.

The metaphor whose manage we are best taught in poetry—that is all there is of thinking. It may not seem far for the mind to go but it is the mind's furthest. The richest accumulation of the ages is the noble metaphors we have rolled up.

I want to add one thing more that the experience of poetry is to anyone who comes close to poetry. There are two ways of coming close to poetry. One is by writing poetry. And some people think I want people to write poetry, but I don't; that is, I don't necessarily. I only want people to write poetry if they want to write poetry. I have never encouraged anybody to write poetry that did not want to write it, and I have not always encouraged those who did want to write it. That ought to be one's own funeral. It is a hard, hard life, as they say.

(I have just been to a city in the West, a city full of poets, a city they have made safe for poets. The whole city is so lovely that you do

not have to write it up to make it poetry; it is ready-made for you. But, I don't know—the poetry written in that city might not seem like poetry if read outside of the city. It would be like the jokes made when you were drunk; you have to get drunk again to appreciate them.)

But as I say, there is another way to come close to poetry, fortunately, and that is in the reading of it, not as linguistics, not as history, not as anything but poetry. It is one of the hard things for a teacher to know how close a man has come in reading poetry. How do I know whether a man has come close to Keats in reading Keats? It is hard for me to know. I have lived with some boys a whole year over some of the poets and I have not felt sure whether they have come near what it was all about. One remark sometimes told me. One remark was their mark for the year; had to be—it was all I got that told me what I wanted to know. And that is enough, if it was the right remark, if it came close enough. I think a man might make twenty fool remarks if he made one good one some time in the year. His mark would depend on that good remark.

The closeness—everything depends on the closeness with which you come, and you ought to be marked for the closeness, for nothing else. And that will have to be estimated by chance remarks, not by question and answer. It is only by accident that you know some day how near a person has come.

The person who gets close enough to poetry, he is going to know more about the word *belief* than anybody else knows, even in religion nowadays. There are two or three places where we know belief outside of religion. One of them is at the age of fifteen to twenty, in our self-belief. A young man knows more about himself than he is able to prove to anybody. He has no knowledge that anybody else will accept as knowledge. In his foreknowledge he has something that is going to believe itself into fulfilment, into acceptance.

There is another belief like that, the belief in someone else, a relationship of two that is going to be believed into fulfilment. That is what we are talking about in our novels, the belief of love. And disillusionment that the novels are full of is simply the disillusionment from disappointment in that belief. That belief can fail, of course.

Then there is a literary belief. Every time a poem is written, every time a short story is written, it is written not by cunning, but by belief. The beauty, the something, the little charm of the thing to be, is more felt than known. There is a common jest, one that always annoys me, on the writers, that they write the last end first, and then work up to it; that they lay a train toward one sentence that they think is pretty nice and have all fixed up to set like a trap to close with. No, it should not be that way at all. No one who has ever come close to the arts has failed to see the difference between things written that way, with cunning and device, and the kind that are believed into existence, that begin in something more felt than known. This you can realize quite as well—not quite as well, perhaps, but nearly as well—in reading as you can in writing. I would undertake to separate short stories on that principle; stories that have been believed into existence and stories that have been cunningly devised. And I could separate the poems still more easily.

Now I think—I happen to think—that those three beliefs that I speak of, the self-belief, the love-belief, and the art-belief, are all closely related to the God-belief, that the belief in God is a relationship you enter into with Him to bring about the future.

There is a national belief like that, too. One feels it. I have been where I came near getting up and walking out on the people who thought that they had to talk against nations, against nationalism, in order to curry favor with internationalism. Their metaphors are all mixed up. They think that because a Frenchman and an American and an Englishman can all sit down on the same platform and receive honors together, it must be that there is no such thing as nations. That kind of bad thinking springs from a source we all know. I should want to say to anyone like that: "Look! First I want to be a person. And I want you to be a person, and then we can be as interpersonal as you please. We can pull each other's noses—do all sorts of things. But, first of all, you have got to have the personality. First of all, you have got to have the nations and then they can be as international as they please with each other."

I should like to use another metaphor on them. I want my palette, if I am a painter, I want my palette on my thumb or on my chair, all clean, pure, separate colors. Then I will do the mixing on the canvas. The canvas is where the work of art is, where we make the conquest. But we want the nations all separate, pure, distinct, things as separate as we can make them; and then in our thoughts, in our arts, and so on, we can do what we please about it.

But I go back. There are four beliefs that I know more about from having lived with poetry. One is the personal belief, which is a knowledge that you don't want to tell other people about because you cannot prove that you know. You are saying nothing about it till you see. The love belief, just the same, has that same shyness. It knows it cannot tell; only the outcome can tell. And the national belief we enter into socially with each other, all together, party of the first part, party of the second part, we enter into that to bring the future of the country. We cannot tell some people what it is we believe, partly, because they are too stupid to understand and partly because we are too proudly vague to explain. And anyway it has got to be fulfilled, and we are not talking until we know more, until we have something to show. And then the literary one in every work of art, not of cunning and craft, mind you, but of real art; that believing the thing into existence, saying as you go more than you even hoped you were going to be able to say, and coming with surprise to an end that you foreknew only with some sort of emotion. And then finally the relationship we enter into with God to believe the future in—to believe the hereafter in.

QUESTIONS FOR STUDY, DISCUSSION, AND WRITING

1. In what way does the subtitle describe this essay? Is it rambling? Is it unified?
2. How can the "poetry nuisance" be gotten out of the curriculum? Does Frost think it ought to stay in? Why?
3. What is meant by "enthusiasm passed through an idea" and "enthusiasm tamed to metaphor" (p. 596)? What sort of metaphors does Frost use in those phrases, and what do they imply?
4. What does Frost mean when he says "unless you have had your proper poetical education in the metaphor, you are not safe anywhere" (p. 598)? Indicate some of the metaphors Frost examines in this essay. From what fields are they drawn? What does he say about each? Nominate some further metaphors—from politics, science, sociology, or anything else—and analyze them. To what extent are they useful? Do they have a breaking point? How might they mislead beyond the breaking point?
5. Is the reason Frost gives for knowing poetry similar to, or very different from, the reason MacLeish gives in "Why Do We Teach Poetry?" (pp. 582–592)? Explain.
6. Frost admires a speech that has "range, something of overstatement, something of statement, and something of understatement." Is this spectrum visible in Frost's own speech? Show where and how.

Prose Forms: Characters

[One of the oldest activities of the human mind is to give a concrete shape to an abstract idea. The legends and myths about ancient gods and heroes make concrete a whole complex of historical and cultural ideas. The symbolisms of a church, the allegory of Bunyan's The Pilgrim's Progress, and even the church or school pageant where children act the parts of "Truth" or "Friendliness"—these are all, in their various ways, illustrative of the effort significantly to relate ideas in the mind and the particular realities that the senses are familiar with in everyday experience. What it means to be a "good student" becomes clearer if Mary Brown's accomplishments are called to mind. What one learns in a sociology course about the problems of minorities in urban centers gains greater authority during field work among those groups. The specific conduct of Germany in World War II would doubtless help more than mere points of theoretical ethics to understand why the idea that "might makes right" is false and dangerous.

Although much that a man understands, or how he understands, begins in abstractions and large general ideas, his desire to communicate with another person immediately raises the necessity for points of reference to the realities of concrete experience. To make his ideas clear and forceful to an audience, he will often convey the ideas in forms of concrete particulars. Like the novelist or the dramatist, he will show, rather than tell, if what he wants to define or explain is to be communicated simply and directly. To say a certain character is vile may be clear enough if the novelist writes what in effect is an essay explaining and specifying the ideas of vileness. But how much more effective and compelling it is to create a set of circumstances in which the character shows by his speech, his behavior, his thoughts that he is unquestionably vile.

Perhaps something of this difference between showing and telling was in the mind of the Greek philosopher Theophrastus when he developed for his students a set of explicatory descriptions called Characters to pinpoint the essential characteristics of certain types of people. Theophrastus chose to show, not tell abstractly, what the several foibles of men are. Not that dealing directly with abstractions is without merit; there are many subjects—and occasions—when to do so is entirely appropriate and effective. But because the mind is specially receptive to the concrete, the ends of communication are often better served by engaging the reader's mind with concrete particulars than by inviting his mind to analyze the abstract descriptively.

Once given Theophrastus' simple definition of flattery, the reader is made to realize immediately what a person must be like whose behavior represents it. From "flattery" to "flatterer" is a direct movement from a broad abstract conception to a narrower one. But Theophrastus shows the flatterer behaving in very particular ways. The reader overhears his remarks to someone whose favor he courts; his stance as he walks and talks is clearly visible; the very scene of his behavior is particularized in the number of people present, the apples and pears he buys. And yet it is not that singular person, John Jones flatterer, described to the reader; it is the essential character of any flatterer, but set out so concretely that the reader feels as if the John Jones, flatterer, whom he knows is in the writer's mind. The universal or general idea is preserved, but its content is explored through representative particulars drawn from a common body of fact and experience shared by the writer and the reader.

In some of the characters of John Earle a critical accent is more explicit than in those of Theophrastus. In "A Young Man" Earle offers a set of specific conditions, beliefs, actions which characterize the type of the young man. But it is clear that Earle believes the conditions of youth are not particularly happy and agreeable, whether or not the youth himself realizes this. This attitude toward youth is not asserted overtly; it is apparent in the way Earle describes a characteristic, as in the matter of youth's virtue: "He is free from many vices, by being not grown to the performance, and is only more virtuous out of weakness." Exposition of the idea of "young man" moves toward a proposition about that idea; there is a subject, and a thesis. The conditions of the essay begin to be manifest.

The character conventionally concerns itself with a single idea, usually a single aspect of the moral nature of men. The writer's intent is to define that idea and to substantiate its truth through observations of concrete experience. Because it invites both its writer and its reader to attend carefully to men and their behavior, the character requires intensive powers of observation, generalization, and judgment. And because it points to, rather than analyzes, its matter, the character is brief. The form becomes, then, a singularly helpful way of forcing the writer to answer the question "What do you mean by that idea?" with a brief and definitive adjustment of abstracts and concretes. In its conception and method the character represents one of the fundamental processes that define the essay: communicating thought and experience by appealing to the deep instinct of the mind for a significant relation between ideas about experience and experience itself. Practice in writing characters gives a concrete and easily accessible shape to one's ideas, and therefore can be a model discipline for skill and effectiveness with the essay.]

JOSEPH ADDISON: A Salamander

There is a species of women whom I shall distinguish by the name of salamanders. Now a salamander is a kind of heroine in chastity, that treads upon fire and lives in the midst of flames without being hurt. A salamander knows no distinction of sex in those she converses with, grows familiar with a stranger at first sight, and is not so narrow-spirited as to observe whether the person she talks to be in breeches or petticoats. She admits a male visitant to her bedside, plays with him a whole afternoon at piquet, walks with him two or three hours by moonlight, and is extremely scandalized at the unreasonableness of a husband or the severity of a parent, that would debar the sex from such innocent liberties. Your salamander is therefore a perpetual declaimer against jealousy, an admirer of the French good breeding, and a great stickler for freedom in conversation. In short, the salamander lives in an invincible state of simplicity and innocence. Her constitution is preserved in a kind of natural frost. She wonders what people mean by temptations, and defies mankind to do their worst. Her chastity is engaged in a constant ordeal, or fiery trial: like good queen Emma, the pretty innocent walks blindfolded among burning plowshares, without being scorched or singed by them.

JOHN EARLE: A Child

Is a man in a small letter, yet the best copy of Adam before he tasted of Eve or the apple; and he is happy whose small practice in the world can only write his character. He is nature's fresh picture newly drawn in oil, which time, and much handling, dims and defaces. His soul is yet a white paper unscribbled with observations of the world, wherewith, at length, it becomes a blurred note-book. He is purely happy because he knows no evil, nor hath made means by sin to be acquainted with misery. He arrives not at the mischief of being wise, nor endures evils to come, by foreseeing them. He kisses and loves all, and, when the smart of the rod is past, smiles on his beater. Nature and parents alike dandle him, and tice him on with a bait of sugar to a draft of wormwood. He plays yet, like a young prentice the first day, and is not come to his task of melancholy. All the language he speaks yet is tears, and they serve him well enough to express his necessity. His hardest labor is his tongue, as if he were loath to use so deceitful an organ; and he is best company with it when he can but prattle. We laugh at his foolish sports, but his game is our earnest; and his drums, rattles and hobbyhorses, but the emblems and mocking of man's business. His father hath writ him as his own little story, wherein he reads those days of his life that he cannot remember, and sighs to see what innocence he hath outlived. The elder he grows, he is a stair lower from God; and, like his first father, much worse in his breeches. He is the Christian's example, and the old man's relapse; the one imitates his pureness, and the other falls into his simplicity. Could he put off his body with his little coat, he had got eternity without a burden, and exchanged but one heaven for another.

JOHN EARLE: A Young Man

He is now out of nature's protection, though not yet able to guide himself; but let loose to the world and fortune, from which the weakness of his childhood preserved him; and now his strength exposes him. He is, indeed, just of age to be miserable, yet in his own conceit first begins to be happy; and he is happier in this imagination, and his misery not felt is less. He sees yet but the outside of the world and men, and conceives them, according to their appearing, glitter, and out of this ignorance believes them. He pursues all vanities for happiness, and enjoys them best in this fancy. His reason serves, not to curb but understand his attitude, and prosecute the motions thereof with a more eager earnestness. Himself is his own temptation, and needs not Satan, and the world will come hereafter. He leaves repentance for gray hairs, and performs it in being covetous. He is mingled with the vices of the age as the fashion and custom, with which he longs to be acquainted, and sins to better his understanding. He conceives his youth as the season of his lust, and the hour wherein he ought to be bad; and because he would not lose his time, spends it. He distastes religion as a sad thing, and is six years elder for a thought of heaven. He scorns and fears, and yet hopes for old age, but dares not imagine it with wrinkles. He loves and hates with the same inflammation, and when the heat is over is cool alike to friends and enemies. His friendship is seldom so steadfast, but that lust, drink or anger may overturn it. He offers you his blood to-day in kindness, and is ready to take yours to-morrow. He does seldom any thing which he wishes not to do again, and is only wise after a misfortune. He suffers much for his knowledge, and a great deal of folly it is makes him a wise man. He is free from many vices, by being not grown to the performance, and is only more virtuous out of weakness. Every action is his danger, and every man his ambush. He is a ship without pilot or tackling, and only good fortune may steer him. If he scape this age, he has scaped a tempest, and may live to be a man.

JOHN EARLE: A Plausible Man

Is one that would fain run an even path in the world, and jut against no man. His endeavor is not to offend, and his aim the general opinion. His conversation is a kind of continued compliment, and his life a practice of manners. The relation he bears to others, a kind of fashionable respect, not friendship but friendliness, which is equal to all and general, and his kindnesses seldom exceed courtesies. He loves not deeper mutualities, because he would not take sides, nor hazard himself on displeasures, which he principally avoids. At your first acquaintance with him he is exceedingly kind and friendly, and at your twentieth meeting after but friendly still. He has an excellent command over his patience and tongue, especially the last, which he accommodates always to the times and persons, and speaks seldom what is sincere, but what is civil. He is one that uses all companies, drinks all healths, and is reasonable cool in all religions. He considers who are friends to the company, and speaks well where he is sure to hear of it again. He can listen to a foolish discourse with an applausive attention, and conceal his laughter at nonsense. Silly men much honor and esteem him, because by his fair reasoning with them as with men of understanding, he puts them into an erroneous opinion of themselves, and makes them forwarder thereafter to their own discovery. He is one rather well thought on than beloved, and that love he has is more of whole companies together than any one in particular. Men gratify him notwithstanding with a good report, and whatever vices he has besides, yet having no enemies, he is sure to be an honest fellow.

JOHN EARLE: A Coward

Is the man that is commonly most fierce against the coward, and laboring to take off this suspicion from himself; for the opinion of valor is a good protection to those that dare not use it. No man is valianter than he is in civil company, and where he thinks no danger may come on it, and is the readiest man to fall upon a drawer and those that must not strike again: wonderful exceptious and choleric where he sees men are loth to give him occasion, and you cannot pacify him better than by quarreling with him. The hotter you grow, the more temperate man is he; he protests he always honored you, and the more you rail upon him, the more he honors you, and you threaten him at last into a very honest quiet man. The sight of a sword wounds him more sensibly than the stroke, for before that come he is dead already. Every man is his master that dare beat him, and every man dares that knows him. And he that dare do this is the only man can do much with him; for his friend he cares not for, as a man that carries no such terror as his enemy, which for this cause only is more potent with him of the two: and men fall out with him of purpose to get courtesies from him, and be bribed again to a reconcilement. A man in whom no secret can be bound up, for the apprehension of each danger loosens him, and makes him bewray both the room and it. He is a Christian merely for fear of hell-fire; and if any religion could fright him more, would be of that.

THOMAS FULLER: The Harlot

The Harlot is one that herself is both merchant and merchandise, which she selleth for profit, and hath pleasure given her into the bargain, and yet remains a great loser. To describe her is very difficult; it being hard to draw those to the life, who never sit still: she is so various in her humors and mutable, it is almost impossible to character her in fixed posture; yea, indeed, some cunning harlots are not discernible from honest women. Solomon saith, "She wipeth her mouth"; and who can distinguish betwixt that which was never foul, and that which is cleanly wiped?

SAMUEL JOHNSON: Tetrica

. . . . . Tetrica came forth into the world, in which she endeavored to force respect by haughtiness of mein and vehemence of language; but having neither birth, beauty, nor wit, in any uncommon degree, she suffered such mortifications from those who thought themselves at liberty to return her insults, as reduced her turbulence to cooler malignity, and taught her to practice her arts of vexation only when she might hope to tyrannize without resistance. She continued from her twentieth to her fifty-fifth year to torment all her inferiors, with so much diligence that she has formed a principle of disapprobation, and finds in every place something to grate her mind, and disturb her quiet.

If she takes the air, she is offended with the heat or cold, the glare of the sun, or the gloom of the clouds; if she makes a visit, the room in which she is to be received is too light or too dark, or furnished with something which she cannot see without aversion. Her tea is never of the right sort; the figures on the china give her disgust. Where there are children, she hates the gabble of brats; where there are none, she cannot bear a place without some cheerfulness and rattle. If many servants are kept in a house, she never fails to tell how Lord Lavish was ruined by a numerous retinue; if few, she relates the story of a miser that made his company wait on themselves. She quarreled with one family, because she had an unpleasant view from their windows; with another, because the squirrel leaped within two yards of her; and with a third, because she could not bear the noise of the parrot.

Of milliners and mantua-makers she is the proverbial torment. She compels them to alter their work, then to unmake it, and contrive it after another fashion; then changes her mind, and likes it better as it was at first; then will have a small improvement. Thus she proceeds till no profit can recompense the vexation; they at last leave the clothes at her house and refuse to serve her. Her maid, the only being that can endure her tyranny, professes to take her own course, and hear her mistress talk. Such is the consequence of peevishness; it can be borne only when it is despised.

THOMAS OVERBURY: A Fair and Happy Milkmaid

Is a country wench, that is so far from making herself beautiful by art, that one look of hers is able to put all face-physic out of countenance. She knows a fair look is but a dumb orator to commend virtue, therefore minds it not. All her excellencies stand in her so silently, as if they had stolen upon her without her knowledge. The lining of her apparel (which is herself) is far better than the outsides of tissue; for though she be not arrayed in the spoil of the silk-worm, she is decked in innocency, a far better wearing. She doth not, with lying long abed, spoil both her complexion and conditions; nature hath taught her, too immoderate sleep is rust to the soul: she rises therefore with chanticleer, her dame's cock, and at night makes the lamb her curfew. In milking a cow, and straining the teats through her fingers, it seems that so sweet a milk-press makes the milk the whiter or sweeter; for never came almond glove or aromatic ointment on her palm to taint it. The golden ears of corn fall and kiss her feet when she reaps them, as if they wished to be bound and led prisoners by the same hand that felled them. Her breath is her own, which scents all the year long of June, like a new made haycock. She makes her hand hard with labor, and her heart soft with pity: and when winter evenings fall early (sitting at her merry wheel), she sings a defiance to the giddy wheel of fortune. She doth all things with so sweet a grace, it seems ignorance will not suffer her to do ill, being her mind is to do well. She bestows her year's wages at next fair; and in choosing her garments, counts no bravery in the world, like decency. The garden and the bee-hive are all her physic and chirurgery, and she lives the longer for it. She dares go alone, and unfold sheep in the night, and fears no manner of ill, because she means none: yet to say truth, she is never alone, for she is still accompanied with old songs, honest thoughts, and prayers, but short ones; yet they have their efficacy, in that they are not palled with ensuing idle cogitations. Lastly, her dreams are so chaste, that she dare tell them;

only a Friday's dream is all her superstition: that she conceals for fear of anger. Thus lives she, and all her care is that she may die in the spring-time, to have store of flowers stuck upon her winding sheet.

THEOPHRASTUS: The Flatterer

Flattery is a cringing sort of conduct that aims to promote the advantage of the flatterer. The flatterer is the kind of man who, as he walks with an acquaintance, says: "Behold! how the people gaze at you! There is not a man in the city who enjoys so much notice as yourself. Yesterday your praises were the talk of the Porch. While above thirty men were sitting there together and the conversation fell upon the topic: 'Who is our noblest citizen?' they all began and ended with your name." As the flatterer goes on talking in this strain he picks a speck of lint from his hero's cloak; or if the wind has lodged a bit of straw in his locks, he plucks it off and says laughingly, "See you? Because I have not been with you these two days, your beard is turned gray. And yet if any man has a beard that is black for his years, it is you."

While his patron speaks, he bids the rest be silent. He sounds his praises in his hearing and after the patron's speech gives the cue for applause by "Bravo!" If the patron makes a stale jest, the flatterer laughs and stuffs his sleeve into his mouth as though he could not contain himself.

If they meet people on the street, he asks them to wait until the master passes. He buys apples and pears, carries them to his hero's house and gives them to the children, and in the presence of the father, who is looking on, he kisses them, exclaiming: "Bairns of a worthy sire!" When the patron buys a pair of shoes, the flatterer observes: "The foot is of a finer pattern than the boot"; if he calls on a friend, the flatterer trips on ahead and says: "You are to have the honor of his visit"; and then turns back with, "I have announced you." Of course he can run and do the errands at the market in a twinkle.

Amongst guests at a banquet he is the first to praise the wine and, doing it ample justice, he observes: "What a fine cuisine you have!" He takes a bit from the board and exclaims: "What a dainty morsel this is!" Then he inquires whether his friend is chilly, asks if he would like a wrap put over his shoulders, and whether he shall throw one about him. With these words he bends over and whispers in his ear. While his talk is directed to the rest, his eye is fixed on his patron. In the theatre he takes the cushions from the page and himself adjusts them for the comfort of the master. Of his hero's house he says: "It is well built"; of his farm: "It is well tilled"; and of his portrait: "It is a speaking image."

ON ETHICS
Moral Traits · Advice · Judgment

LA ROCHEFOUCAULD
Bravery and Cowardice

Perfect bravery and total cowardice are two extremes only rarely to be met. Between them lies a vast territory where will be found every variation and degree of courage. These are as diverse as are men's faces or their feelings. There are soldiers who will readily risk their lives early in the engagement, but who will lose heart later in the day. There are others who are satisfied when they have upheld their honor in the eyes of the world, and who will scarcely advance beyond this. Some are not uniformly masters of their fears: some are susceptible to the contagion of panic: others advance to the attack because they dare not stay behind. There are men who, becoming gradually accustomed to smaller perils, are reinforced in their courage and enabled to confront greater ones. Some are brave with a sword, but frightened by musket fire; others can face bullets but fear steel. All these various forms of courage have this in common: that whereas darkness increases fear, it also hides both good and bad deeds, so that a soldier has greater opportunities for caution by night. There is another aspect of self-protection which is of more general application: no man is ever as totally brave as he would be, were he quite certain of surviving the day. The fear of death, in fact, diminishes valor.

ROBERT LYND
On Not Being a Philosopher

"Have you read Epictetus lately?" "No, not lately." "Oh, you ought to read him. Tommy's been reading him for the first time, and is fearfully excited." I caught this scrap of dialogue from the next table in the lounge of an hotel. I became interested, curious, for I had never read Epictetus, though I had often looked at his works on the shelf—perhaps I had even quoted him—and I wondered if here at last was the book of wisdom that I had been looking for at intervals ever since I was at school. Never have I lost my early faith that wisdom is to be found somewhere in a book—to be picked up as easily as a shell from the sand. I desire wisdom as keenly as Solomon did, but it must be wisdom that can be obtained with very little effort—wisdom that can be caught almost by infection. I have no time or energy for the laborious quest of philosophy. I wish the philosophers to perform the laborious quest and, at the end of it, to feed me with the fruits of their labors; just as I get eggs from the farmer, apples from the fruit-grower, medicines from the chemist, so do I expect the philosopher to provide me with wisdom at the cost of a few shillings. That is why at one time I read Emerson and, at another, Marcus Aurelius. To read them, I hoped, was to become wise by reading. But I did not become wise. I agreed with them while I read them, but, when I had finished reading, I was still much the same man that I had been before, incapable of concentrating on the things on which they said I should concentrate or of not being indifferent to the things to which they said I should not be indifferent. Still, I have never lost faith in books, believing that somewhere printed matter exists from which I shall be able to absorb philosophy and strength of character while smoking in an armchair. It was in this mood that I took down Epictetus after hearing the conversation in the hotel lounge.

I read him, I confess, with considerable excitement. He is the kind of philosopher I like, not treating life as if at its finest it were an argument conducted in difficult jargon, but discussing, among other things, how men should behave in the affairs of ordinary life. Also, I agreed with nearly everything he said. Indifference to pain, death, poverty—yes, that is eminently desirable. Not to be troubled about anything over which one has no control, whether the oppression of tyrants or the peril of earthquakes—on the necessity of this also, Epictetus and I are as one. Yet, close as is the resemblance between our opinions, I could not help feeling, as I read, that Epictetus was wise in holding his opinions and that I, though holding the same opinions, was far from wise. For, indeed, though I held the same opinions for purposes of theory, I could not entertain them for a moment for purposes of conduct. Death, pain, and poverty are to me very real evils, except when I am in an armchair reading a book by a philosopher. If an earthquake happened while I was reading a book of philosophy, I should forget the book of philosophy and think only of the earthquake and how to avoid tumbling walls and chimneys. This, though I am the staunchest possible admirer of Socrates, Pliny, and people of that sort. Sound though I am as an armchair philosopher, at a crisis I find that both the spirit and the flesh are weak.

Even in the small things of life I cannot comfort myself like a philosopher of the school of Epictetus. Thus, for example, when he advises us how to "eat acceptably to the gods" and bids us to this end to be patient even under the most incompetent service at our meals, he commends a spiritual attitude of which my nature is incapable. "When you have asked for warm water," he says, "and the slave does not heed you; or if he does heed you but brings tepid water; or if he is not even to be found in the house, then to refrain from anger and not to explode, is not this acceptable to the gods? . . . Do you not remember over whom you rule—that they are kinsmen, that they are brothers by nature, and they are the offspring of Zeus?" That is all perfectly true, and I should like very much to be a man who could sit in a restaurant, smiling patiently and philosophically while the waiter brought all the wrong things or forgot to bring anything at all. But in point of fact bad waiting irritates me. I dislike having to ask three times for the wine-list. I am annoyed when, after a quarter of an hour's delay, I am told that there is no celery. It is true that I do not make a scene on such occasions. I have not enough courage for that. I am as sparing of objurgations as a philosopher, but I suspect that the scowling spirit within me must show itself in my features. Certainly, I do not think of telling myself: "This waiter is my kinsman; he is the offspring of Zeus." Besides, even if he were, why should the offspring of Zeus wait so badly? Epictetus never dined at the ———— Restaurant. And yet his patience might have served him even there. If so, what a difference between Epictetus and me! And, if I cannot achieve his imperturbability in so small affairs as I have mentioned, what hope is there of my being able to play the philosopher in presence of tyrants and earthquakes?

Again, when Epictetus expresses his opinions on material possessions and counsels us to be so indifferent to them that we should not object to their being stolen, I agree with him in theory and yet in practice I know I should be unable to obey him. There is nothing more certain than that a man whose happiness depends on his possessions is not happy. I am sure a wise man can be happy on a pittance. Not that happiness should be the aim of life, according to Epictetus or myself. But Epictetus at least holds up an ideal of imperturbability, and he assures us that we shall achieve this if we care so little for material things that it does not matter to us whether somebody steals them or not. "Stop admiring your clothes," he bids us, "and you are not angry at the man who steals them." And he goes on persuasively concerning the thief: "*He* does not know wherein the true good of man consists, but fancies that it consists in having fine clothes, the very same fancy that you also entertain. Shall he not come, then, and carry them off?" Yes, logically I suppose he should, and yet I cannot feel so at the moment at which I find that a guest at a party has taken my new hat and left his old one in its place. It gives me no comfort to say to myself: "*He* does not know wherein the true good of man consists, but fancies that it consists in having my hat." Nor should I dream of attempting to console a guest at a party in my own house with such philosophy in similar circumstances. It is very irritating to lose a new hat. It is very irritating to lose anything at all, especially if one thinks it has been taken on purpose. I feel that I could imitate Epictetus if I lived in a world in which nothing happened. But in a world in which things disappear through loss, theft, and "pinching," and in which bad meals are served by bad waiters in many of the restaurants, and a thousand other disagreeable things happen, an ordinary man might as well set out to climb the Himalayas in walking shoes as attempt to live the life of a philosopher at all hours.

In spite of this, however, most of us cannot help believing that the philosophers were right—right when they proclaimed, amid all their differences, that most of the things we bother about are not worth bothering about. It is easier to believe that oneself is a fool than that Socrates was a fool, and yet, if he was not right, he must have been the greatest fool who ever lived. The truth is, nearly everybody is agreed that such men as Socrates and Epictetus were right in their indifference to external things. Even men earning £10,000 a year and working for more would admit this. Yet, while admitting it, most of us would be alarmed if one of our dearest friends began to put the philosophy of Epictetus into practice too literally. What we regard as wisdom in Epictetus we should look on as insanity in an acquaintance. Or, perhaps, not in an acquaintance, but at least in a near relation. I am sure that if I became as indifferent to money and comfort and all external things as Epictetus, and reasoned in his fashion with a happy smile about property and thieves, my relations would become more perturbed than if I became a successful company promoter with the most materialistic philosophy conceivable. Think, for example, of the reasoning of Epictetus over the thief who stole his iron lamp:

He bought a lamp for a very high price; for a lamp he became a thief, for a lamp he became faithless, for a lamp he became bestial. This is what seemed to him to be profitable!

The reasoning is sound, yet neither individually nor as a society do we live in that contempt of property on which it is based. A few saints do, but even they are at first a cause of great concern to their friends. When the world is normally cheerful and comfortable, we hold the paradoxical belief that the philosophers were wise men, but that we should be fools to imitate them. We are convinced that, while philosophers are worth reading, material things are worth bothering about. It is as though we enjoyed wisdom as a spectacle—a delightful spectacle on a stage which it would be unseemly for the audience to attempt to invade. Were the Greeks and the Romans made differently? Did the admirers of Socrates and Epictetus really attempt to become philosophers, or were they like ourselves, hopeful of achieving wisdom, not by practice but through a magic potion administered by a wiser man than they? To become wise without effort—by listening to a voice, by reading a book—it is at once the most exciting and the most soothing of dreams. In such a dream I took down Epictetus. And, behold, it was only a dream.

QUESTIONS FOR STUDY, DISCUSSION, AND WRITING

1. *What relation to his audience does Lynd seek to establish? How does he achieve it?*
2. *What is funny about Lynd's juxtaposing the advice of Epictetus with his own feelings about restaurant service? Are there other instances of a similar effect in the essay? Is the resulting tone sardonic? Cynical? Contemptuous of philosophy?*
3. *Lynd in his closing paragraph (p. 615) writes, "we hold the paradoxical belief that the philosophers were wise men, but that we should be fools to imitate them." Does he seek to explain the paradox? Can you offer an explanation for it? What is the significance of the "when" clause in the earlier part of that sentence?*
4. *Lynd in his opening paragraph (p. 613) writes, "Still, I have never lost faith in books, believing that somewhere printed matter exists from which I shall be able to absorb philosophy and strength of character while smoking in an armchair." In the light of the whole essay, how is that statement to be taken?*
5. *To what degree does Lynd's essay exhibit the ideal of imperturbability he admires in philosophy? Explain.*
6. *Is there some pursuit, activity, ideal that you admire but do not seek to practice? Write an essay explaining your attitude.*

SAMUEL JOHNSON

On Self-love and Indolence[1]

—Steriles transmisimus annos,
Haec aevi mihi prima dies, haec limina vitae.

STAT. [I. 362]

—Our barren years are past;
Be this of life the first, of sloth the last.

ELPHINSTON

No weakness of the human mind has more frequently incurred animadversion, than the negligence with which men overlook their

1. *The Rambler,* No. 15, Tuesday, September 10, 1751.

own faults, however flagrant, and the easiness with which they pardon them, however frequently repeated.

It seems generally believed, that, as the eye cannot see itself, the
mind has no faculties by which it can contemplate its own state,
and that therefore we have not means of becoming acquainted with
our real characters; an opinion which, like innumerable other postulates, an inquirer finds himself inclined to admit upon very little
evidence, because it affords a ready solution of many difficulties. It
will explain why the greatest abilities frequently fail to promote the
happiness of those who possess them; why those who can distinguish
with the utmost nicety the boundaries of vice and virtue, suffer
them to be confounded in their own conduct; why the active and
vigilant resign their affairs implicitly to the management of others;
and why the cautious and fearful make hourly approaches toward
ruin, without one sigh of solicitude or struggle for escape.

When a position teems thus with commodious consequences, who
can without regret confess it to be false? Yet it is certain that de-
claimers have indulged a disposition to describe the dominion of
the passions as extended beyond the limits that nature assigned.
Self-love is often rather arrogant than blind; it does not hide our
faults from ourselves, but persuades us that they escape the notice
of others, and disposes us to resent censures lest we would confess
them to be just. We are secretly conscious of defects and vices which
we hope to conceal from the public eye, and please ourselves with
innumerable impostures, by which, in reality, no body is deceived.

In proof of the dimness of our internal sight, or the general
inability of man to determine rightly concerning his own character,
it is common to urge the success of the most absurd and incredible
flattery, and the resentment always raised by advice, however soft,
benevolent, and reasonable. But flattery, if its operation be nearly
examined, will be found to owe its acceptance not to our ignorance
but knowledge of our failures, and to delight us rather as it consoles
our wants than displays our possessions. He that shall solicit the
favor of his patron by praising him for qualities which he can find
in himself, will be defeated by the more daring panegyrist who en-
riches him with adscititious excellence. Just praise is only a debt,
but flattery is a present. The acknowledgment of those virtues on
which conscience congratulates us, is a tribute that we can at any
time exact with confidence, but the celebration of those which we
only feign, or desire without any vigorous endeavors to attain them,
is received as a confession of sovereignty over regions never conquered, as a favorable decision of disputable claims, and is more welcome as it is more gratuitous.

Advice is offensive, not because it lays us open to unexpected regret, or convicts us of any fault which had escaped our notice, but
because it shows us that we are known to others as well as to our-

selves; and the officious monitor is persecuted with hatred, not because his accusation is false, but because he assumes that superiority which we are not willing to grant him, and has dared to detect what we desired to conceal.

For this reason advice is commonly ineffectual. If those who follow the call of their desires, without inquiry whither they are going, had deviated ignorantly from the paths of wisdom, and were rushing upon dangers unforeseen, they would readily listen to information that recalls them from their errors, and catch the first alarm by which destruction or infamy is denounced. Few that wander in the wrong way mistake it for the right; they only find it more smooth and flowery, and indulge their own choice rather than approve it: therefore few are persuaded to quit it by admonition or reproof, since it impresses no new conviction, nor confers any powers of action or resistance. He that is gravely informed how soon profusion will annihilate his fortune, hears with little advantage what he knew before, and catches at the next occasion of expense, because advice has no force to suppress his vanity. He that is told how certainly intemperance will hurry him to the grave, runs with his usual speed to a new course of luxury, because his reason is not invigorated, nor his appetite weakened.

The mischief of flattery is, not that it persuades any man that he is what he is not, but that it suppresses the influence of honest ambition, by raising an opinion that honor may be gained without the toil of merit; and the benefit of advice arises commonly, not from any new light imparted to the mind, but from the discovery which it affords of the publick suffrages. He that could withstand conscience, is frighted at infamy, and shame prevails where reason was defeated.

As we all know our own faults, and know them commonly with many aggravations which human perspicacity cannot discover, there is, perhaps, no man, however hardened by impudence or dissipated by levity, sheltered by hypocrisy, or blasted by disgrace, who does not intend some time to review his conduct, and to regulate the remainder of his life by the laws of virtue. New temptations indeed attack him, new invitations are offered by pleasure and interest, and the hour of reformation is always delayed; every delay gives vice another opportunity of fortifying itself by habit; and the change of manners, though sincerely intended and rationally planned, is referred to the time when some craving passion shall be fully gratified, or some powerful allurement cease its importunity.

Thus procrastination is accumulated on procrastination, and one impediment succeeds another, till age shatters our resolution, or death intercepts the project of amendment. Such is often the end of salutary purposes, after they have long delighted the imagination, and appeased that disquiet which every mind feels from known mis-conduct, when the attention is not diverted by business or by pleasure.

Nothing surely can be more unworthy of a reasonable nature, than to continue in a state so opposite to real happiness, as that all the peace of solitude and felicity of meditation, must arise from reso-lutions of forsaking it. Yet the world will often afford examples of men, who pass months and years in a continual war with their own convictions, and are daily dragged by habit or betrayed by passion into practices, which they closed and opened their eyes with pur-poses to avoid; purposes which, though settled on conviction, the first impulse of momentary desire totally overthrows.

The influence of custom is indeed such that to conquer it will require the utmost efforts of fortitude and virtue, nor can I think any man more worthy of veneration and renown, than those who have burst the shackles of habitual vice. This victory however has different degrees of glory as of difficulty; it is more heroic as the objects of guilty gratification are more familiar, and the recurrence of solicita-tion more frequent. He that from experience of the folly of ambi-tion resigns his offices, may set himself free at once from temptation to squander his life in courts, because he cannot regain his former station. He who is enslaved by an amorous passion, may quit his tyrant in disgust, and absence will without the help of reason over-come by degrees the desire of returning. But those appetites to which every place affords their proper object, and which require no preparatory measures or gradual advances, are more tenaciously adhesive; the wish is so near the enjoyment, that compliance often precedes consideration, and before the powers of reason can be sum-moned, the time for employing them is past.

Indolence is therefore one of the vices from which those whom it once infects are seldom reformed. Every other species of luxury oper-ates upon some appetite that is quickly satiated, and requires some concurrence of art or accident which every place will not supply; but the desire of ease acts equally at all hours, and the longer it is indulged in the more increased. To do nothing is in every man's power; we can never want an opportunity of omitting duties. The lapse to indolence is soft and imperceptible, because it is only a mere cessation of activity; but the return to diligence is difficult, because it implies a change from rest to motion, from privation to reality.

—*Facilis descensus Averni:*
Noctes atque dies patet atri janua Ditis:
Sed revocare gradum, superasque evadere ad auras,
Hoc opus, hic labor est.—

[VIR. *Aeneid* VI. 126]

> The gates of *Hell* are open night and day;
> Smooth the descent, and easy is the way:
> But, to return, and view the chearful skies;
> In this, the task and mighty labour lies.
>
> DRYDEN

Of this vice, as of all others, every man who indulges it is conscious; we all know our own state, if we could be induced to consider it; and it might perhaps be useful to the conquest of all these ensnarers of the mind, if at certain stated days life was reviewed. Many things necessary are omitted, because we vainly imagine that they may be always performed, and what cannot be done without pain will for ever be delayed if the time of doing it be left unsettled. No corruption is great but by long negligence, which can scarcely prevail in a mind regularly and frequently awakened by periodical remorse. He that thus breaks his life into parts, will find in himself a desire to distinguish every stage of his existence by some improvement, and delight himself with the approach of the day of recollection, as of the time which is to begin a new series of virtue and felicity.

QUESTIONS FOR STUDY, DISCUSSION, AND WRITING

1. What observation upon human experience does the essay set out to explore?
2. What facts of moral behavior does Johnson say can be explained on the theory that the mind cannot know its own state, that a man cannot know his own real character? Why, if the theory explains so much, does Johnson reject it?
3. To what does Johnson ascribe the success of flattery and the resentment raised by advice? How does this explanation serve to support his assertion that men are commonly aware of their own real character?
4. What explanation does Johnson give for advice being "commonly ineffectual"? When advice does produce an effect, how, according to Johnson, does it operate?
5. Does Johnson attempt to explain why, if men have accurate self-knowledge, defects in character are not straightway corrected?
6. Why does Johnson consider indolence especially pernicious? What practical counsel does he offer for overcoming it?
7. Parallelism is a marked feature of Johnson's style. Find examples of: (a) paired words or phrases within a clause, (b) parallel clauses within a sentence, and (c) similarly formed sentences within a paragraph. What relation holds between parallel syntactic structures and the over-all purpose of the essay? What devices does Johnson use to offset a rigid, overwrought parallelism?

LIONEL TRILLING
The Morality of Inertia

A theological seminary in New York planned a series of lectures on "The Literary Presentations of Great Moral Issues," and invited me to give one of the talks. Since I have a weakness for the general subject, I was disposed to accept the invitation. But I hesitated over the particular instance, for I was asked to discuss the moral issues in *Ethan Frome*. I had not read Edith Wharton's little novel in a good many years, and I remembered it with no pleasure or admiration. I recalled it as not at all the sort of book that deserved to stand in a list which included *The Brothers Karamazov* and *Billy Budd, Foretopman*. If it presented a moral issue at all, I could not bring to mind what that issue was. And so I postponed my acceptance of the invitation and made it conditional upon my being able to come to terms with the subject assigned to me.

Ethan Frome, when I read it again, turned out to be pretty much as I had recalled it, not a great book or even a fine book, but a factitious book, perhaps even a cruel book. I was puzzled to understand how it ever came to be put on the list, why anyone should want to have it discussed as an example of moral perception. Then I remembered its reputation, which, in America, is very considerable. It is sometimes spoken of as an American classic. It is often assigned to high-school and college students as a text for study.

But the high and solemn repute in which it stands is, I am sure, in large part a mere accident of American culture. *Ethan Frome* appeared in 1911, at a time when, to a degree that we can now only wonder at, American literature was committed to optimism, cheerfulness, and gentility. What William Dean Howells called the "smiling aspects of life" had an importance in the literature of America some fifty years ago which is unmatched in the literature of any other time and place. It was inevitable that those who were critical of the prevailing culture and who wished to foster in America higher and more serious literature should put a heavy stress upon the grimmer aspects of life, that they should equate the smiling aspects with falsehood, the grimmer aspects with truth. For these devoted people, sickened as they were by cheerfulness and hope, the word "stark" seemed to carry the highest possible praise a critical review or a blurb could bestow, with "relentless" and "inevitable" as its proper variants. *Ethan Frome* was admired because it was "stark"—its action, we note, takes place in the New England village of Starkville—and because the fate it describes is *relentless* and *inevitable*.

No one would wish to question any high valuation that may be given to the literary representation of unhappy events—except, perhaps, as the high valuation may be a mere cliché of an intellectual class, except as it is supposed to seem the hallmark of the superior sensibility and intelligence of that class. When it is only this, we have the right, and the duty, to look sniffishly at starkness, and relentlessness, and inevitability, to cock a skeptical eye at grimness. And I am quite unable to overcome my belief that *Ethan Frome* enjoys its high reputation because it still satisfies our modern snobbishness about tragedy and pain.

We can never speak of Edith Wharton without some degree of respect. She brought to her novels a strong if limited intelligence, notable powers of observation, and a genuine desire to tell the truth, a desire which in some part she satisfied. But she was a woman in whom we cannot fail to see a limitation of heart, and this limitation makes itself manifest as a literary and moral deficiency of her work, and of *Ethan Frome* especially. It appears in the deadness of her prose, and more flagrantly in the suffering of her characters. Whenever the characters of a story suffer, they do so at the behest of their author—the author is responsible for their suffering and must justify his cruelty by the seriousness of his moral intention. The author of *Ethan Frome*, it seemed to me as I read the book again to test my memory of it, could not lay claim to any such justification. Her intention in writing the story was not adequate to the dreadful fate she contrived for her characters. She indulges herself by what she contrives—she is, as the phrase goes, "merely literary." This is not to say that the merely literary intention does not make its very considerable effects. There is in *Ethan Frome* an image of life-in-death, of hell-on-earth, which is not easily forgotten: the crippled Ethan, and Zeena, his dreadful wife, and Matty, the once charming girl he had loved, now bedridden and querulous with pain, all living out their death in the kitchen of the desolate Frome farm—a perpetuity of suffering memorializes a moment of passion. It is terrible to contemplate, it is unforgettable, but the mind can do nothing with it, can only endure it.

My new reading of the book, then, did not lead me to suppose that it justified its reputation, but only confirmed my recollection that *Ethan Frome* was a dead book, the product of mere will, of the cold hard literary will. What is more, it seemed to me quite unavailable for any moral discourse. In the context of morality, there is nothing to say about *Ethan Frome*. It presents no moral issue at all.

For consider the story it tells. A young man of good and gentle character is the only son of a New England farm couple. He has some intellectual gifts and some desire to know the world, and for a year he is happy attending a technical school. But his father is incapacitated by a farm accident, and Ethan dutifully returns to manage the failing farm and saw mill. His father dies; his mother loses her mental faculties, and during her last illness she is nursed by a female relative whom young Ethan marries, for no other reason than that he is bemused by loneliness. The new wife, Zeena, immediately becomes a shrew, a harridan and a valetudinarian—she lives only to be ill. Because Zeena now must spare herself, the Fromes take into their home a gentle and charming young girl, a destitute cousin of the wife. Ethan and Matty fall in love, innocently but deeply. The wife, perceiving this, plans to send the girl away, her place to be taken by a servant whose wages the husband cannot possibly afford. In despair at the thought of separation Matty and Ethan attempt suicide. They mean to die by sledding down a steep hill and crashing into a great elm at the bottom. Their plan fails: both survive the crash, Ethan to be sorely crippled, Matty to be bedridden in perpetual pain. Now the wife Zeena surrenders her claim to a mysterious pathology and becomes the devoted nurse and jailer of the lovers. The terrible tableau to which I have referred is ready for inspection.

It seemed to be that it was quite impossible to talk about this story. This is not to say that the story is without interest as a story, but what interest it may have does not yield discourse, or at least not moral discourse.

But as I began to explain to the lecture committee why I could not accept the invitation to lecture about the book, it suddenly came over me how very strange a phenomenon the book made— how remarkable it was that a story should place before us the dreadful image of three ruined and tortured lives, showing how their ruin came about, and yet propose no moral issue of any kind. And if *issue* seems to imply something more precisely formulated than we have a right to demand of a story, then it seemed to me no less remarkable that the book had scarcely any moral reverberation, that strange and often beautiful sound we seem to hear generated in the air by a tale of suffering, a sound which is not always music, which does not always have a "meaning," but which yet entrances us, like the random notes of an Aeolian harp, or merely the sound of the wind in the chimney. The moral sound that *Ethan Frome* makes is a dull thud. And this seemed to me so remarkable, indeed, that in the very act of saying why I could not possibly discuss *Ethan Frome*, I found the reason why it must be discussed.

It is, as I have suggested, a very great fault in *Ethan Frome* that it presents no moral issue, sets off no moral reverberation. A certain propriety controls the literary representation of human suffering. This propriety dictates that the representation of pain may not be, as it were, gratuitous; it must not be an end in itself. The naked act of representing, or contemplating, human suffering is a self-indulgence, and it may be a cruelty. Between a tragedy and a spectacle in the Roman circus there is at least this much similarity, that the pleasure both afford derives from observing the pain of others. A tragedy is always on the verge of cruelty. What saves it from the actuality of cruelty is that it has an intention beyond itself. This intention may be so simple a one as that of getting us to do something practical about the cause of the suffering or to help actual sufferers, or at least to feel that we should; or it may lead us to look beyond apparent causes to those which the author wishes us to think of as more real, such as Fate, or the will of the gods, or the will of God; or it may challenge our fortitude or intelligence or piety.

A sense of the necessity of some such intention animates all considerations of the strange paradox of tragedy. Aristotle is concerned to solve the riddle of how the contemplation of human suffering can possibly be pleasurable, of why its pleasure is permissible. He wanted to know what literary conditions were needed to keep a tragedy from being a display of horror. Here it is well to remember that the Greeks were not so concerned as we have been led to believe to keep all dreadful things off the stage—in the presentation of Aristotle's favorite tragedy, the audience saw Jocasta hanging from a beam, it saw the representation of Oedipus's bloody eye-sockets. And so Aristotle discovered, or pretended to discover, that tragedy did certain things to protect itself from being merely cruel. It chose, Aristotle said, a certain kind of hero; he was of a certain social and moral stature; he had a certain degree of possibility of free choice; he must justify his fate, or seem to justify it, by his moral condition, being neither wholly good nor wholly bad, having a particular fault that collaborates with destiny to bring about his ruin. The purpose of all these specifications for the tragic hero is to assure us that we observe something more than mere passivity when we witness the hero's suffering, that the suffering has, as we say, some meaning, some show of rationality.

Aristotle's theory of tragedy has had its way with the world to an extent which is perhaps out of proportion to its comprehensiveness and accuracy. Its success is largely due to its having dealt so openly with the paradox of tragedy. It serves to explain away any guilty feelings that we may have at deriving pleasure from suffering.

But at the same time that the world has accepted Aristotle's theory of tragedy, it has also been a little uneasy about some of its implications. The element of the theory that causes uneasiness in modern times is the matter of the stature of the hero. To a society based in egalitarian sentiments, the requirement that the hero be a man of rank seems to deny the presumed dignity of tragedy to men of lesser status. And to a culture which questions the freedom of the will, Aristotle's hero seems to be a little beside the point. Aristotle's prescription for the tragic hero is clearly connected with his definition, in his *Ethics,* of the nature of an ethical action. He tells us that a truly ethical action must be a free choice between two alternatives. This definition is then wonderfully complicated by a further requirement—that the moral man must be so trained in making the right choice that he makes it as a matter of habit, makes it, as it were, instinctively. Yet it *is* a choice, and reason plays a part in its making. But we, of course, don't give to reason the same place in the moral life that Aristotle gave it. And in general, over the last hundred and fifty years, dramatists and novelists have tried their hand at the representation of human suffering without the particular safeguards against cruelty which Aristotle perceived, or contrived. A very large part of the literature of Western Europe may be understood in terms of an attempt to invert or criticize the heroic prescription of the hero, by burlesque and comedy, or by the insistence on the commonplace, the lowering of the hero's social status and the diminution of his power of reasoned choice. The work of Fielding may serve as an example of how the mind of Europe has been haunted by the great image of classical tragedy, and how it has tried to lay that famous ghost. When Fielding calls his hero Tom Jones, he means that his young man is not Orestes or Achilles; when he calls him a foundling, he is suggesting that Tom Jones is not, all appearances to the contrary notwithstanding, Oedipus.

Edith Wharton was following where others led. Her impulse in conceiving the story of Ethan Frome was not, however, that of moral experimentation. It was, as I have said, a purely literary impulse, in the bad sense of the word "literary." Her aim is not that of Wordsworth in any of his stories of the suffering poor, to require of us that we open our minds to a realization of the kinds of people whom suffering touches. Nor is it that of Flaubert in *Madame Bovary*, to wring from solid circumstances all the pity and terror of an ancient tragic fable. Nor is it that of Dickens or Zola, to shake us with the perception of social injustice, to instruct us in the true nature of social life and to dispose us to indignant opinion and action. These are not essentially literary intentions; they are moral intentions. But all that Edith Wharton has in mind is to achieve that grim tableau of which I have spoken, of pain and imprisonment, of life-in-death. About the events that lead up to this tableau, there is nothing she finds to say, nothing whatever. The best we can conclude of the meaning of her story is that it might perhaps be a subject of discourse in the context of rural sociology—it might be understood to exemplify the thesis that love and joy do not flourish on poverty-stricken New England farms. If we try to bring it into the context of morality, its meaning goes no further than certain cultural considerations—that is, to people who like their literature to show the "smiling aspects of life," it may be thought to say, "This is the aspect that life really has, as grim as this"; while to people who repudiate a literature that represents only the smiling aspects of life it says, "How intelligent and how brave you are to be able to understand that life is as grim as this." It is really not very much to say.

And yet there is in *Ethan Frome* an idea of considerable importance. It is there by reason of the author's deficiencies, not by reason of her powers—because it suits Edith Wharton's rather dull intention to be content with telling a story about people who do not make moral decisions, whose fate cannot have moral reverberations. The idea is this: that moral inertia, the *not* making of moral decisions, constitutes a large part of the moral life of humanity.

This isn't an idea that literature likes to deal with. Literature is charmed by energy and dislikes inertia. It characteristically represents morality as positive action. The same is true of the moral philosophy of the West—has been true ever since Aristotle defined a truly moral act by its energy of reason, of choice. A later development of this tendency said that an act was really moral only if it went against the inclination of the person performing the act: the idea was parodied as saying that one could not possibly act morally to one's friends, only to one's enemies.

Yet the dull daily world sees something below this delightful preoccupation of literature and moral philosophy. It is aware of the morality of inertia, and of its function as a social base, as a social cement. It knows that duties are done for no other reason than that they are said to be duties; for no other reason, sometimes, than that the doer has not really been able to conceive of any other course, has, perhaps, been afraid to think of any other course. Hobbes said of the Capitol geese that saved Rome by their cackling that they were the salvation of the city, not because they were they but there. How often the moral act is performed not because we are we but because we are there! This is the morality of habit, or the morality of biology. This is Ethan Frome's morality, simple, unquestioning, passive, even masochistic. His duties as a son are discharged because he is a son; his duties as a husband are discharged because he is a husband. He does nothing by moral election. At one point in his story he is brought to moral crisis—he must choose between his habituated duty to his wife and his duty and inclination to the girl he loves. It is quite impossible for him to deal with the dilemma in the high way that literature and moral philosophy prescribe, by reason and choice. Choice is incompatible with his idea of his existence; he can only elect to die.

Literature, of course, is not wholly indifferent to what I have called the morality of habit and biology, the morality of inertia. But literature, when it deals with this morality, is tempted to qualify its dullness by endowing it with a certain high grace. There is never any real moral choice for the Félicité of Flaubert's story "A Simple Heart." She is all pious habit of virtue, and of blind, unthinking, unquestioning love. There are, of course, actually such people as

Félicité, simple, good, loving—quite stupid in their love, not choosing where to bestow it. We meet such people frequently in literature, in the pages of Balzac, Dickens, Dostoievski, Joyce, Faulkner, Hemingway. They are of a quite different order of being from those who try the world with their passion and their reason; they are by way of being saints, of the less complicated kind. They do not really exemplify what I mean by the morality of inertia. Literature is uncomfortable in the representation of the morality of inertia or of biology, and overcomes its discomfort by representing it with the added grace of that extravagance which we denominate saintliness.

But the morality of inertia is to be found in very precise exemplification in one of Wordsworth's poems. Wordsworth is pre-eminent among the writers who experimented in the representation of new kinds and bases of moral action—he has a genius for imputing moral existence to people who, according to the classical morality, should have no moral life at all. And he has the courage to make this imputation without at the same time imputing the special grace and interest of saintliness. The poem I have in mind is ostensibly about a flower, but the transition from the symbol to the human fact is clearly, if awkwardly, made. The flower is a small celandine, and the poet observes that it has not, in the natural way of flowers, folded itself against rough weather:

> But lately, one rough day, this Flower I passed
> And recognized it, though in altered form,
> Now standing as an offering to the blast,
> And buffeted at will by rain and storm.
>
> I stopped, and said with inly-muttered voice,
> It doth not love the shower nor seek the cold;
> This neither is its courage nor its choice,
> But its necessity in being old.

Neither courage nor choice, but necessity: it cannot do otherwise. Yet it acts as if by courage and choice. This is the morality imposed by brute circumstance, by biology, by habit, by the unspoken social demand which we have not the strength to refuse, or, often, to imagine refusing. People are scarcely ever praised for living according to this morality—we do not suppose it to be a morality at all until we see it being broken.

This is morality as it is conceived by the great mass of people in the world. And with this conception of morality goes the almost entire negation of any connection between morality and destiny. A superstitious belief in retribution may play its part in the thought of simple people, but essentially they think of catastrophes as fortuitous, without explanation, without reason. They live in the moral universe of the Book of Job. In complex lives, morality does in some part determine destiny; in most lives it does not. Between the moral life of Ethan and Matty and their terrible fate we cannot make any reasonable connection. Only a moral judgment cruel to the point of insanity could speak of it as anything but accidental.

I have not spoken of the morality of inertia in order to praise it but only to recognize it, to suggest that when we keep our minds fixed on what the great invigorating books tell us about the moral life, we obscure the large bulking dull mass of moral fact. Morality is not only the high, torturing dilemmas of Ivan Karamazov and Captain Vere. It is also the deeds performed without thought, without choice, perhaps even without love, as Zeena Frome ministers to Ethan and Matty. The morality of inertia, of the dull, unthinking round of duties, may, and often does, yield the immorality of inertia; the example that will most readily occur to us is that of the good simple people, so true to their family responsibilities, who gave no thought to the concentration camps in whose shadow they lived. No: the morality of inertia is not to be praised, but it must be recognized. And Edith Wharton's little novel must be recognized for bringing to our attention what we, and literature, so easily forget.

QUESTIONS FOR STUDY, DISCUSSION, AND WRITING

1. Why does Trilling not embark at once upon his stated topic, the morality of inertia? At what point in his essay does he begin direct discussion of that idea?
2. What explanation does Trilling present for the success and repute of Ethan Frome? What are his objections to the novel?
3. To what purposes does Trilling introduce and examine Aristotle's theory of tragedy?
4. How does Trilling define the morality of inertia? To what idea or ideas of morality does it appear to be contrasted?
5. Trilling conceives that "the morality of habit" is incompatible with choice. Are habit and choice necessarily exclusive of each other? Consider whether Johnson's discussion of the formation of habits (pp. 618–620) or James' essay on habit (pp. 304–309) suggest possible relationships between habit and choice.
6. What is Trilling's attitude toward the morality of inertia? How is that attitude conveyed explicitly in statement? Implicitly in tone?
7. Trilling says of the morality of inertia that "this is morality as it is conceived by the great mass of people in the world" (p. 627). Does it seem to be Trilling's conception of morality? Is it yours? How valid is the assertion? How can you test its validity?

W. H. AUDEN
Pride[1]

He who despises himself, nevertheless esteems himself as a self-despiser. (NIETZSCHE.) A vain person is always vain *about* something.

1. From "Hic et Ille" (This and That), in *The Dyer's Hand,* 1962.

He overestimates the importance of some quality or exaggerates the degree to which he possesses it, but the quality has some real importance and he does possess it to some degree. The fantasy of overestimation or exaggeration makes the vain person comic, but the fact that he cannot be vain about nothing makes his vanity a venial sin, because it is always open to correction by appeal to objective fact.

A proud person, on the other hand, is not proud *of* anything, he *is* proud, he exists proudly. Pride is neither comic nor venial, but the most mortal of all sins because, lacking any basis in concrete particulars, it is both incorrigible and absolute: one cannot be more or less proud, only proud or humble.

Thus, if a painter tries to portray the Seven Deadly Sins, his experience will furnish him readily enough with images symbolic of Gluttony, Lust, Sloth, Anger, Avarice, and Envy, for all these are qualities of a person's relations to others and the world, but no experience can provide an image of Pride, for the relation it qualifies is the subjective relation of a person to himself. In the seventh frame, therefore, the painter can only place, in lieu of a canvas, a mirror.

JOHN DONNE
Tentation

After wee have parled with a tentation,[1] debating whether we should embrace it or no, and entertain'd some discourse with it, though some tendernesse, some remorse, make us turn our back upon it, and depart a little from it, yet the arrow overtakes us; some *reclinations*, some *retrospects* we have, a little of *Lot's wife*[2] is in us, a little *sociablenesse*, and *conversation*, a little point of *honour*, not to be false to former promises, a little *false gratitude*, and thankfulnesse, in respect of former obligations, a little of the *compassion* and *charity* of Hell, that another should not be miserable, for want of *us*, a little of this, which is but the good nature of the *Devill*, arrests us, stops us, fixes us, till the arrow, the tentation shoot us in the back, even when wee had a purpose of departing from that sin, and kils us over again.

1. Parleyed, spoken with a temptation.
2. Fleeing from the burning Sodom, she looked back upon the city. Genesis xix. 17-26.

QUESTIONS FOR STUDY, DISCUSSION, AND WRITING

1. Analyze this single-sentence passage, determining its syntax. What are the subject, predicate, and object? How many main or independent clauses are there? Which clauses and phrases are modifiers?
2. What metaphors does Donne use?

3. Taking syntax and metaphorical content together, indicate the effects Donne achieves in this sentence. Does it convey a sense of motion, speedy or lingering? What scene or scenes are pictured? What use is made of the sense of touch? How does the presentation of physical sensation work to convey Donne's statement about the operation of temptation?

ABRAHAM LINCOLN

Letter to James M. Cutts, Jr.[1]

Executive Mansion
Washington, Oct. 26, 1863

CAPT. JAMES M. CUTTS.

Although what I am now to say is to be, in form, a reprimand, it is not intended to add a pang to what you have already suffered

1. This reprimand may have been delivered to Captain Cutts in a personal interview. Never published by Nicolay and Hay for obvious reasons, a portion was, however, incorporated in their footnote to Lincoln's letter to William G. Anderson, October 31, 1840, as an unidentified bit of advice "given many years afterward to a young officer condemned to be court-martialed for quarreling" (NH, I, 152).

The court-martial trial on June 30, 1863, of Captain James Madison Cutts, Jr., brother of Stephen A. Douglas' second wife, on the charge of "conduct unbecoming an officer and a gentleman," involved three subordinate specifications: (1) that Cutts had used unbecoming language in addressing Captain Charles G. Hutton, aide-de-camp to General Burnside, when Hutton attempted to take over Cutts' desk; (2) that Cutts had sent a written communication to Major William Cutting derogatory to the accomplishments of Captain Hutton as an officer; and (3) that the said "*James M. Cutts* . . . did, on or about the 10th day of April, 1863, while occupying room No. 79, Burnet House, Cincinnati, Ohio, on the afternoon of said day, attempt to look through the key-hole of room No. 80 of said house, occupied by a gentleman and his wife, and did, in the evening of said day, at about half past eleven o'clock, after said lady had retired to her room, and while her husband was in the corridor below, said lady being at the time partly undressed, previous to retiring, take a valise or portmanteau from his room and . . . placing himself thereon, did look through the Venetian blind or transom light in or over the door into said room and at said lady while undressing. . . ." (AGO *General Orders No. 330*, October 8, 1863). To the first

and second specifications Cutts pleaded not guilty; to the third, he acknowledged the facts" with deep regret," and pleaded guilty. The court found him guilty on all three specifications and sentenced him to be dismissed from the service.

In connection with this episode, John Hay's *Diary* on July 18 records Lincoln's humorous remark that Cutts "should be elevated to the peerage for it with the title of Count Peeper." Lincoln's pun and allusion were probably suggested by the name of the Swedish minister, Edward Count Piper.

Tried before the same court-martial, Captain Hutton was found guilty of having sent Captain Cutts a challenge to a duel, but was sentenced merely to a presidential reprimand. Major Cutting was found not guilty of the charge of having carried the challenge from Hutton to Cutts.

Lincoln approved the proceedings in the cases of Cutting and Cutts, but in view of Cutts' previous good character . . . and gallant conduct in battle" remitted the sentence after reprimand. (*General Orders No. 330*). The proceedings in the case of Captain Hutton, Lincoln disapproved, because "The penalty fixed by the 25th Article of War for the offence of which the accused is found guilty, viz., sending a challenge to another officer, is cashiering, and admits of no alternative. . . . The President directs that Captain Hutton be dismissed the service of the United States from the 28th day of September, 1863." (*Ibid.*). Hutton was reappointed, however, as of October 30, 1863, and served throughout the war. [This note comes from *The Collected Works of Abraham Lincoln*, Roy P. Basler, ed., Marion Dolores Pratt and Lloyd A. Dunlap, asst. eds., Vol. VI.]

upon the subject to which it relates. You have too much of life yet before you, and have shown too much of promise as an officer, for your future to be lightly surrendered. You were convicted of two offences. One of them, not of great enormity, and yet greatly to be avoided, I feel sure you are in no danger of repeating. The other you are not so well assured against. The advice of a father to his son "Beware of entrance to a quarrel, but being in, bear it that the opposed may beware of thee,"[2] is good, and yet not the best. Quarrel not at all. No man resolved to make the most of himself, can spare time for personal contention. Still less can he afford to take all the consequences, including the vitiating of his temper, and the loss of self-control. Yield larger things to which you can show no more than equal right; and yield lesser ones, though clearly your own. Better give your path to a dog, than be bitten by him in contesting for the right. Even killing the dog would not cure the bite.

In the mood indicated deal henceforth with your fellow men, and especially with your brother officers; and even the unpleasant events you are passing from will not have been profitless to you.

2. Polonius to Laertes, *Hamlet* I, iii, 65-67.

WILLIAM JAMES
Letter to Peg[1]

Villa Luise
Bad-Nauheim, May 26, 1900

DARLING PEG—Your letter came last night and explained sufficiently the cause of your long silence. You have evidently been in a bad state of spirits again, and dissatisfied with your environment; and I judge that you have been still more dissatisfied with the inner state of trying to consume your own smoke, and grin and bear it, so as to carry out your mother's behests made after the time when you scared us so by your inexplicable tragic outcries in those earlier letters. Well! I believe you have been trying to do the manly thing under difficult circumstances, but one learns only gradually to do the *best* thing; and the best thing for you would be to write at least weekly, if only a post-card, and say just how things are going. If you are in bad spirits, there is no harm whatever in communicating that fact, and defining the character of it, or describing it as exactly as you like. The bad thing is to pour out the *contents* of one's bad spirits on others and leave them with it, as it were, on their hands, as if it was for them to do something about it. That was what you did in your other letter which alarmed us so, for your shrieks of

1. Peg is James' thirteen-year-old daughter who was then living with family friends in England and experiencing some home-sickness.

anguish were so excessive, and so unexplained by anything you told us in the way of facts, that we didn't know but what you had suddenly gone crazy. That is the *worst* sort of thing you can do. The middle sort of thing is what you do this time—namely, keep silent for more than a fortnight, and when you do write, still write rather mysteriously about your sorrows, not being quite open enough.

Now, my dear little girl, you have come to an age when the inward life develops and when some people (and on the whole those who have most of a destiny) find that all is not a bed of roses. Among other things there will be waves of terrible sadness, which last sometimes for days; and dissatisfaction with one's self, and irritation at others, and anger at circumstances and stony insensibility, etc., etc., which taken together form a melancholy. Now, painful as it is, this is sent to us for an enlightenment. It always passes off, and we learn about life from it, and we ought to learn a great many good things if we react on it rightly. [*From margin.*] (For instance, you learn how good a thing your home is, and your country, and your brothers, and you may learn to be more considerate of other people, who, you now learn, may have their inner weaknesses and sufferings, too.) Many persons take a kind of sickly delight in hugging it; and some sentimental ones may even be proud of it, as showing a fine sorrowful kind of sensibility. Such persons make a regular habit of the luxury of woe. That is the worst possible reaction on it. It is usually a sort of disease, when we get it strong, arising from the organism having generated some poison in the blood; and we mustn't submit to it an hour longer than we can help, but jump at every chance to attend to anything cheerful or comic or take part in anything active that will divert us from our mean, pining inward state of feeling. When it passes off, as I said, we know more than we did before. And we must try to make it last as short a time as possible. The worst of it often is that, while we are in it, we don't *want* to get out of it. We hate it, and yet we prefer staying in it—that is a part of the disease. If we find ourselves like that, we must make ourselves do something different, go with people, speak cheerfully, set ourselves to some hard work, make ourselves sweat, etc.; and that is the good way of reacting that makes of us a valuable character. The disease makes you think of *yourself* all the time; and the way out of it is to keep as busy as we can thinking of *things* and of *other people* —no matter what's the matter with our self.

I have no doubt you are doing as well as you know how, darling little Peg; but we have to learn everything, and I also have no doubt that you'll manage it better and better if you ever have any more of it, and soon it will fade away, simply leaving you with more experience. The great thing for you *now*, I should suppose, would be to enter as friendlily as possible into the interest of the Clarke children. If you like them, or acted as if you liked them, you needn't trouble about the question of whether they like you or not. They probably will, fast enough; and if they don't, it will be their funeral, not yours. But this is a great lecture, so I will stop. The great thing about it is that it is all true.

FRANCIS BACON

Of Simulation and Dissimulation

Dissimulation is but a faint kind of policy or wisdom; for it asketh a strong wit and a strong heart to know when to tell truth, and to do it. Therefore it is the weaker sort of politics[1] that are the great dissemblers.

Tacitus saith, *Livia sorted well with the arts of her husband and dissimulation of her son;* attributing arts or policy to Augustus, and dissimulation to Tiberius. And again, when Mucianus encourageth Vespasian to take arms against Vitellius, he saith, *We rise not against the piercing judgment of Augustus, nor the extreme caution or closeness of Tiberius.*[2] These properties, of arts or policy and dissimulation or closeness, are indeed habits and faculties several, and to be distinguished. For if a man have that penetration of judgment as he can discern what things are to be laid open, and what to be secreted, and what to be shewed at half lights, and to whom and when, (which indeed are arts of state and arts of life, as Tacitus well calleth them), to him a habit of dissimulation is a hinderance and a poorness. But if a man cannot obtain to that judgment, then it is left to him generally to be close, and a dissembler. For where a man cannot choose or vary in particulars, there it is good to take the safest and wariest way in general; like the going softly, by one that cannot well see. Certainly the ablest men that ever were have had all an openness and frankness of dealing; and a name of certainty and veracity; but then they were like horses well managed; for they could tell passing well when to stop or turn; and at such times when they thought the case indeed required dissimulation, if then they used it, it came to pass that the former opinion spread abroad of their good faith and clearness of dealing made them almost invisible.

There be three degrees of this hiding and veiling of a man's self. The first, Closeness, Reservation, and Secrecy; when a man leaveth himself without observation, or without hold to be taken, what he is. The second, Dissimulation, in the negative; when a man lets fall signs and arguments, that he is not that he is. And the third,

1. Politicians.
2. The Roman historian Tacitus here speaks of the plottings of Livia, wife of the emperor Augustus Caesar and mother of his successor Tiberius; and of the Roman official Mucianus, who in 69 A.D. supported Vespasian in his successful struggle against Vitellius to gain the imperial throne.

Simulation, in the affirmative; when a man industriously and expressly feigns and pretends to be that he is not.

For the first of these, Secrecy; it is indeed the virtue of a confessor.[3] And assuredly the secret man heareth many confessions. For who will open himself to a blab or babbler? But if a man be thought secret, it inviteth discovery; as the more close air sucketh in the more open; and as in confession the revealing is not for worldly use, but for the ease of a man's heart, so secret men come to the knowledge of many things in that kind; while men rather discharge their minds than impart their minds. In few words, mysteries are due to secrecy. Besides (to say truth) nakedness is uncomely, as well in mind as body; and it addeth no small reverence to men's manners and actions, if they be not altogether open. As for talkers and futile persons, they are commonly vain and credulous withal. For he that talketh what he knoweth, will also talk what he knoweth not. Therefore set it down, *that an habit of secrecy is both politic and moral*. And in this part, it is good that a man's face give his tongue leave to speak. For the discovery of a man's self by the tracts of his countenance is a great weakness and betraying; by how much it is many times more marked and believed than a man's words.

For the second, which is Dissimulation; it followeth many times upon secrecy by a necessity; so that he that will be secret must be a dissembler in some degree. For men are too cunning to suffer a man to keep an indifferent carriage between both, and to be secret, without swaying the balance on either side. They will so beset a man with questions, and draw him on, and pick it out of him, that, without an absurd silence, he must shew an inclination one way; or if he do not, they will gather as much by his silence as by his speech. As for equivocations, or oraculous speeches, they cannot hold out for long. So that no man can be secret, except he give himself a little scope of dissimulation; which is, as it were, but the skirts or train of secrecy.

But for the third degree, which is Simulation and false profession; that I hold more culpable, and less politic; except it be in great and rare matters. And therefore a general custom of simulation (which is this last degree) is a vice, rising either of a natural falseness or fearfulness, or of a mind that hath some main faults, which because a man must needs disguise, it maketh him practice simulation in other things, lest his hand should be out of ure.[4]

The great advantages of simulation and dissimulation are three. First, to lay asleep opposition, and to surprise. For where a man's intentions are published, it is an alarum to call up all that are against them. The second is, to reserve to a man's self a fair retreat. For if a man engage himself by a manifest declaration, he must go through or take a fall. The third is, the better to discover the mind

---

3. One to whom confession is made.   4. Practice.

of another. For to him that opens himself men will hardly shew themselves adverse; but will (fair) let him go on, and turn their freedom of speech to freedom of thought. And therefore it is a good shrewd proverb of the Spaniard, *Tell a lie and find a troth.* As if there were no way of discovery but by simulation. There be also three disadvantages, to set it even. The first, that simulation and dissimulation commonly carry with them a shew of fearfulness, which in any business doth spoil the feathers of round flying up to the mark.[5] The second, that it puzzleth and perplexeth the conceits of many, that perhaps would otherwise co-operate with him; and makes a man walk almost alone to his own ends. The third and greatest is, that it depriveth a man of one of the most principal instruments for action; which is trust and belief. The best composition and temperature is to have openness in fame and opinion; secrecy in habit; dissimulation in seasonable use; and a power to feign, if there be no remedy.

5. Conceptions, thoughts.

QUESTIONS FOR STUDY, DISCUSSION, AND WRITING

1. Explain Bacon's distinction, drawn in the first two paragraphs, between dissembling, on the one hand, and, on the other, arts and policy. How does this opening prepare the way for the remainder of the essay?
2. How is the word "dissimulation" as used in the third paragraph and thereafter to be distinguished from its use in the first two paragraphs?
3. What are the three degrees of hiding of a man's self? According to what principles does Bacon arrange these degrees? What accounts for his according unequal amounts of space to the exposition of them?
4. Make a close analysis of Bacon's closing paragraph, indicating the ways Bacon achieves symmetry, balance. How does that effect contribute to his tone and purpose? What elements in the paragraph offset a mere symmetry?
5. In what connection and to what purpose does Bacon use the following expressions? Explain the image or allusion in each:
   a. "like the going softly, by one that cannot well see" (p. 633)
   b. "like horses well managed; for they could tell passing well when to stop or turn" (p. 633)
   c. "as the more close air sucketh in the more open" (p. 634)
   d. "it is good that a man's face give his tongue leave to speak" (p. 634)
   e. "he must go through or take a fall" (p. 634)
   f. "fearfulness, which in any business doth spoil the feathers of round flying up to the mark" (p. 635)
6. Bacon would allow "simulation and false profession" in "great and rare matters." Would you? Give an example of such matters. Write a brief essay explaining your position.

7. What view of the world underlies Bacon's essay? Write an essay showing what Bacon's assumptions about the world seem to be. Be careful to show how you draw upon the essay to find out Bacon's assumptions.

STEPHEN POTTER

The Game Itself[1]

"East wind dhu blëow
En-tout-cas dhu gëow."
ESSEX SAYING

Some Basic Plays

"How to win Games Without Being Able to Play Them." Reduced to the simplest terms, that is the formula, and the student must not at first try flights too far away from this basic thought.

To begin with, let him, say, carry on the "flurry" motive. Let him aim at tension. Let him, for instance, invent some "train which he would rather like to catch if the game was over by then," but "doesn't want to hurry."

Sportsmanship Play

Remember the slogan: "THE GOOD GAMESMAN IS THE GOOD SPORTSMAN." The use of sportsmanship is, of course, most important. In general, with the athletic but stupid player, ex-rowing or ex-boxing, perhaps, who is going to take it out of you, by God, if he suspects you of being unsporting, extreme sportingness is the thing, and the instant waiving of any rule which works in your favor is the procedure.

On the other hand, playing against the introvert crusty cynical type, remember that sportingness will be wasted on him. There must be no unsportingness on your part, of course; but a keen knowledge of little-known rules and penalties will cause him to feel he is being beaten at his own game. (See under "Croquet, rulesmanship in.")

When questioned about the etiquette of gamesmanship—so important for the young player—I talk about Fidgets. If your adversary is nervy, and put off by the mannerisms of his opponent, it is unsporting, and therefore not gamesmanship, to go in, e.g., for a loud noseblow, say, at billiards, or to chalk your cue squeakingly, when he is either making or considering a shot.

On the other hand, a basic play, in perfect order, can be achieved by, say, whistling fidgetingly *while playing yourself*. And I once converted two down into two up when playing golf against P. Beard,

1. Chapter III of *The Theory and Practice of Gamesmanship or the Art of Winning Games Without Actually Cheating,* 1947.

known also as the leader of an orchestra, by constantly whistling a phrase from the Dorabella Variation with one note—always the same note—wrong.[2]

A good general attack can be made by talking to your opponent about his own job, in the character of the kind of man who always tries to know more about your own profession than you know yourself.

Playing-For-Fun Play

The good gamesman, like the good sportsman, never plays for large sums of money. But something can usually be made out of the situation if your opponent expresses a wish to play for the "usual half-crown," or a wish not to do so. It is obviously easy for the gamesman to make his opponent feel awkward by countering his suggestion that they should play for stakes with a frank, "Come, let's play for the fun of the game." Alternatively, if your opponent refuses your offer to play for half a crown here is a neat counter:

LAYMAN: Half a crown on it? No, I'm not particularly anxious to play for money. What *is* the point? If one starts worrying about the pennies...
GAMESMAN: Exactly. If money is important to you, much better not.
LAYMAN: But I meant——
GAMESMAN (*friendly*): Of course.

Nice Chapmanship

A bitter subject which may be introduced here revolves round the huge question of nice chapmanship and its uses. (I refuse to use the hideous neologism "nicemanship" which I see much in evidence lately.)

Here is the general principle: that Being a Nice Chap in *certain circumstances* is valuable when playing against extremely young, public schooly players who are genuinely nice. A train of thought can be started in their minds to the effect that "it would be rather a rotten trick to beat old G. by too much." Thereby that fatal "letting up" is inaugurated which can be the undoing of so many fine players. R. Lodge, at sixty-five, always said that he had never been beaten, in a key match, by any decently brought up boy under twenty-five, and that he would always "feel 'em out of their phizzes."

2. It may be worth recalling that Elgar himself, when playing croquet against fellow-musicians, made use of the Horn *motiv* from the *Ring*:

He would whistle this correctly except for the second note, substituting for A some inappropriate variant, often a

slightly flattened D sharp, *sliding* up to it, from the opening note of the phrase:

A voice from the past indeed. Yet have any of our modern experts in the music ploy really improved on this phrase, devised before Gamesmanship was formulated or even described? [Potter's note.]

Audience Play

Nice chapmanship is, of course, closely associated with sports-manship, especially in its relation to the question of playing or not playing to the audience. There is obviously some value in a good hearty "Have it again" early in the game (of darts, for instance), or the lawn tennis ball slammed into the net after the doubtful decision, especially if this is done so that your opponent can see through the ploy[3] but the onlookers cannot.

But the experienced gamesman knows that if he is playing to a small audience he must make up his mind whether he is going to play *to* the audience, or whether he is going to retire behind an impersonal mask of modesty.

In general, the rule holds—LET YOUR ATTITUDE BE THE ANTITHESIS OF YOUR OPPONENT'S; and let your manner of emphasizing this different attitude put him in the wrong.

For example, if your opponent is a great showman, assume (e.g., at snooker) an air of modesty anonymity; be appreciative, even, of his antics; then quietly play your shot, so that the audience begins to say, "I prefer G.'s game. He gets on with it, anyhow."

Per contra, when in play against a dour opponent, who studiously avoids all reaction to the audience, implying that "this is a match"— *then*, by all means be the "chap who doesn't care a damn" ... though "Of course—sh!—old L. is taking this devilish seriously so I must keep a straight face."

(There is some danger of counter-gamesmanship here. The layman, if he is wise, will pursue his poker-faced policy and you may find your assumption of ill-suppressed gaiety wearing thin. I have myself experienced a partial paralysis in this situation.)

So much for some of the principal general ploys. Now for some common technical phrases.

Ruggership and Ruggership Counter-Play

Under the heading of "Ruggership" comes all that great inter-play of suggestion summarized in the phrase "Of course, this isn't my game," with the implication that "this game is rather an amusing game, but not grand, dangerous and classical like my game . . ." If "my game" is rugger or polo or tennis (see under "Tennis players, how to press home advantage of, over lawn tennis players"), then very good work can be done with this gambit.

But it has severe weaknesses, and a promising gamesman in his second year may be able to counter with some such simple enquiry as this:

COUNTER-GAMESMAN (*with interest*): When did you *last play* rugger?
GAMESMAN: Oh! How long since actually playing? I wonder.... I was talking to Leggers the other day——

---

3. Sub-plays, or individual maneuvers of a gambit, are usually referred to as "ploys." It is not known why this is [Potter's note].

COUNTER-GAMESMAN: Yes, but how long is it since you played yourself? I mean what date, roughly, was it when you last held a ball in your hand?

GAMESMAN (*hard-pressed*): 1913.

COUNTER-GAMESMAN: A bit of a time. But that, I imagine, is one of the grand things about rugger. If you've ever kicked a rugger ball, at a prep school or home club, you feel that you're a rugger player for the rest of your life.

Much exaggerated praise has been churned out in honor of gamesmanship and its part in the building of the British character. Still, if we study the records, they do reveal not a little of courage in the overcoming of apparently hopeless odds. I am thinking, of course, of G. Tearle—not the actor, but the croquet-player. And, indeed, some of the prettiest effects of gamesmanship are to be seen when an expert in, say, croquet, plays golf, it may be, off the same handicap, against a real expert in, say, rugger—a man who really has played rugger, twice capped for England. The rugger man certainly starts with a tremendous advantage. His name is a legend, his game is glorious. Croquet is considered, by the lay world, to be piddling. The two meet on the common ground of golf; and even golf, to the rugger man, is considered fairly piddling. Yet I have seen Tearle not only break down this view *but reverse it*, so that in the end the Rugger international would sometimes even be heard claiming that he came from croquet people, but that his character "was not suited to the game."

Tearle by long practice actually made capital out of croquet. And let me add that Tearle's triumph demonstrates once again that it is in these long-drawn-out reversal tactics that training and the proper diet stand you in such good stead.

Counterpoint

This phrase, now used exclusively in music, originally stood for Number Three of the general Principles of Gamesmanship. "PLAY AGAINST YOUR OPPONENT'S TEMPO." This is one of the oldest of gambits and is now almost entirely used in the form "My Slow to your Fast." E.g., at billiards, or snooker, or golf especially, against a player who makes a great deal of "wanting to get on with the game," the technique is (1) to agree (Jeffreys always adds here "as long as we don't hurry on the shot"); (2) to hold things up by fifteen to twenty disguised pauses. Peg-top tees for golf were introduced by Samuel in '33 for this use. The technique is to tee the ball, frame up for the shot, and then at the last moment stop, pretend to push the peg a little further in or pull it a little furher out, and then start all over again. At the next hole vary this with Samuel's "Golden Perfecto" peg tee, made in such a way that the ball, after sitting still in the cup for two to three seconds, rolls off. (Fig. 1.)

Through the green, the usual procedure is to frame up for the shot and then decide on another club at the last moment.

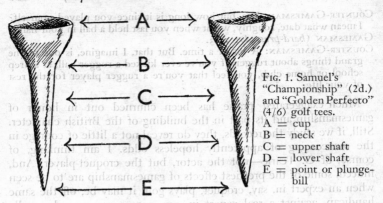

Fig. 1. Samuel's "Championship" (2d.) and "Golden Perfecto" (4/6) golf tees.
A = cup
B = neck
C = upper shaft
D = lower shaft
E = point or plunge-bill

NOTE—*Do not attempt to irritate partner by spending too long looking for your lost ball.* This is unsporting. But good gamesmanship which is also very good sportsmanship can be practiced if the gamesman makes a great and irritatingly prolonged parade of spending extra time looking for his *opponent's* ball.

At billiards, the custom of arranging to be summoned to the telephone on fake calls, so as to break your opponent's concentration, is out of date now and interesting only as a reminder of the days when "couriers" were paid to gallup up to the old billiard halls for the same purpose. In snooker, the usual practice is to walk quickly up to the table, squat half down on the haunches to look at sight-lines, move to the other end of the table to look at sight-lines of balls which may come in to play later on in the break which you are supposed to be planning. Decide on the shot. Frame up for it, and then at the last moment see some obvious red shot which you had "missed," and which your opponent and everybody else will have noticed before you moved to the table, and which they know is the shot you are going to play in the end anyhow.

For chess tempos see "Chess, tempi."

"My To-morrow's Match"

In a Key Friendly, or any individual match which you are particularly anxious to win, the best general approach (Rule IV) is the expression of anxiety *to play to-day, because of the match to-morrow.* Construct a story that you are playing A. J. du C. Masterman.[4] Or perhaps the name should be A. C. Swinburne (your opponent will feel he has vaguely heard of this name). Go on to say (if the game is golf)—"Do you mind if I practice using my Number One iron to-day"—(no need to use it or even have one)—"as I want to know whether to take it to-morrow?" Take one practice shot after having picked up your ball, at a lost hole. Seek the advice of oppo-

4. Names impress according to the square of their initials [Potter's note].

nent. Ask him "What *he* would do if he found himself playing against a *really* long driver, like A. C. Swinburne."

Game Leg (Also Known as "Crocked Ankle Play," or "Gamesman's Leg"[5])

"Limpmanship," as it used to be called, or the exact use of minor injury, not only for the purpose of getting out of, but for actually winning difficult contests, is certainly as old as the mediaeval tourneys, the knightly combats, of ancient chivalry. Yet, nowadays, no device is more clumsily used, no gambit more often muffed. "I hope I shall be able to give you a game," says the middle-aged golfer to his young opponent, turning his head from side to side and hunching up his shounders. "My back was a bit seized up yesterday . . . this wind." How wretchedly weak. "O.K. My youth *versus* your age," says the young counter-gamesman to himself, and rubs this thought in with a variety of subsequent slanting references: "You ought to take it easy, for a week or two," etc. No, if use the hackneyed ankle gambit you must, let the injury be the result of a campaign in one of the wars, or a quixotic attempt to stop a runaway horse, at least.

But, here as so often, it is the *reply*, the counter, wherein the ploy of the gamesman can be used to best effect. Indeed, there is nothing prettier than the right use of an opponent's injury. There is the refusal to be put off even if the injury is genuine. There is the adoption of a game which, though apparently ignoring and indeed even favoring your opponent's disability, will yet benefit you in the end. In their own different ways, the "Two F's," Frier and Frith-Morteroy, were the greatest masters of the art of "Countering the Crock." No one who heard them will ever forget their apologies for sending a short one to the man with the twisted ankle, their excuses for the accidental lob in the sun against an opponent with sensitive eyes. But the Frith-Morteroy counter, though not for beginners, has more of grace, and needs more of explanation. Let it be lawn tennis—Frith's game. Frith against "Novice Gamesman," we will call him.

Novice Gamesman is limping slightly. "Hopes he can give F.-M. a game, but his rugger knee has just been prodded back into place by old Coutts of Welbeck Street." Right. F.-M. is full of sympathy. F.-M. sends not a single short one. In fact he does nothing whatever. His supporters become anxious—and then—during, say, the *first* game of the *second* set, while they are changing sides Frith is heard to say (on arriving at point K—see Fig. 2) "Ooo!" sharply.

NOVICE GAMESMAN: What's that?
FRITH-MORTEROY: Nothing. Nothing. I thought——
N. G. (*further away*): What did you say?
F.-M.: Nothing.

5. Usually shortened now into "Game Leg" [Potter's note].

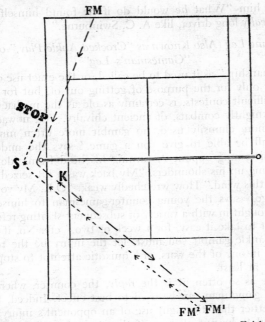

FIG. 2. Diagram of tennis court to show Frith-Morteroy's path of changing, and the position S from which he makes his "echo" attack, in Morteroy Counter Game Leg play. Point K on the line FM-FM¹ is the position from which the demi-cry is made. At point S, on the line FM², the full cry is made. "Stop" marks the usual position for the actual verbal interchange or "parlette."

The game continues. But at that next cross over, Frith says "Ow!" (point S, Fig. 2). He pauses a minute, and stands as if lost in thought.

N. G.: What's up?

F.-M.: Nothing. Half a moment.

N. G.: Something wrong?

F.-M. (*rubs his chest with his knuckles*): No. No. It's only the old pump.

N. G.: Pump?

F.-M.: Yes. The ancient ticker.

N. G.: What—heart?

F.-M.: I'm supposed not to be using it full out at the moment. Only a temporary thing.

N. G.: Good Lord.

F.-M.: It's all right now!

N. G.: Good.

F.-M.: Couple of crocks!

N. G.: Well. Shall we get on?

"*Couple* of crocks." Observe the triple thrust against the Novice Gamesman. (1) Frith establishes the fact that he, also, labors under a handicap; (2) the atmosphere which Novice Gamesman has built up with so much restraint, but so much labor—the suggestion of silent suffering—is the precise climate in which Frith is now going to prosper, and (3)—most important of all—Frith has won the gamesmanship part of the contest already, set and match, by sportingly waiting, say twenty-five minutes, before revealing his own somewhat worse disability. Novice Gamesman having mentioned his rugger knee—a stale type of infliction anyhow—is made to look a fool and a fusser. More, he is made to look unsporting.

I believe it is true to say that once Frith-Morteroy had achieved this position, he was never known to lose a game. He made a special study of it—and I believe much of his spare time was spent reading the medical books on the subject of minor cardiac weaknesses.

Jack Rivers Opening

After this most successful of basic plays, may I dare to end this chapter with a very simple but favorite gambit of my own?

I call it the Jack Rivers Opening. I have written elsewhere of the sporting-unsporting approach, always to be revered as the parent of modern gamesman play. But if sporting-unsporting is vaguely regarded as a thing of the past, the gamesman knows that it is a habit of thought still rooted in many British players.

Perhaps the most difficult type for the gamesman to beat is the man who indulges in pure play. He gets down to it, he gets on with it, he plays each shot according to its merits, and his own powers, without a trace of exhibitionism, and no by-play whatever. In golf, croquet or ping-pong—golf especially—he is liable to wear you down by playing the "old aunty" type of game.

My only counter to this, which some have praised, is to invent, early in the game or before it has started, an imaginary character called "Jack Rivers." I speak of his charm, his good looks, his fine war record and his talent for games—and, "by the way, he is a first-class pianist as well." Then, a little later: "I like Jack Rivers's game," I say. "He doesn't care a damn whether he wins or loses so long as he has a good match."

Some such rubbish as this, although at first it may not be effective, often wears down the most successfully cautious opponent, *if the method is given time to soak in*. Allow your opponent to achieve a small lead, perhaps, by his stone-walling methods; and the chances are that—even if he has only been hearing about Jack Rivers for thirty minutes—he will begin to think: "Well, perhaps I am being a bit of a stick-in-the-mud." He feels an irrational desire to play up to what appears to be your ideal of a good fellow. After all, he remembers, hadn't he been once chaffed for breaking a window with a cricketball when he was on holiday at Whitby? He himself was a bit mad once. Soon he is throwing away point after point by adopting a happy-go-lucky, hit-or-miss method which doesn't suit his game in the least.

Meanwhile *you* begin to play with pawky steadiness, and screen this fact by redoubling your references to Jack Rivers. You talk of the way in which Jack, too, loved to open his shoulders for a mighty smite, landing him in trouble as often as not; but the glorious thing about him was that he didn't care two hoots for that . . . and so long as he had a good smack, and a good game . . ., etc.

So much for the Principal Plays, in gamesmanship. Now for the other gambits which must be brought into play as the game progresses.

JOHN RUSKIN
Traffic[1]

My good Yorkshire friends, you asked me down here among your hills that I might talk to you about this Exchange you are going to build: but earnestly and seriously asking you to pardon me, I am going to do nothing of the kind. I cannot talk, or at least can say very little, about this same Exchange. I must talk of quite other things, though not willingly; I could not deserve your pardon, if, when you invited me to speak on one subject, I willfully spoke on another. But I cannot speak, to purpose, of anything about which I do not care; and most simply and sorrowfully I have to tell you, in the outset, that I do *not* care about this Exchange of yours.

If, however, when you sent me your invitation, I had answered, "I won't come, I don't care about the Exchange of Bradford," you would have been justly offended with me, not knowing the reasons of so blunt a carelessness. So I have come down, hoping that you will patiently let me tell you why, on this, and many other such occasions, I now remain silent, when formerly I should have caught at the opportunity of speaking to a gracious audience.

In a word, then, I do not care about this Exchange—because *you* don't; and because you know perfectly well I cannot make you. Look at the essential circumstances of the case, which you, as business men, know perfectly well, though perhaps you think I forget them. You are going to spend £30,000, which to you, collectively, is nothing; the buying a new coat is, as to the cost of it, a much more important matter of consideration to me than building a new Exchange is to you. But you think you may as well have the right thing for your money. You know there are a great many odd styles of architecture about; you don't want to do anything ridiculous; you hear of me, among others, as a respectable architectural man-milliner:

1. An address delivered in the Bradford Town Hall, Yorkshire, in 1866.

and you send for me, that I may tell you the leading fashion; and what is, in our shops, for the moment, the newest and sweetest thing in pinnacles.

Now, pardon me for telling you frankly, you cannot have good architecture merely by asking people's advice on occasion. All good architecture is the expression of national life and character; and it is produced by a prevalent and eager national taste, or desire for beauty. And I want you to think a little of the deep significance of this word "taste"; for no statement of mine has been more earnestly or oftener controverted than that good taste is essentially a moral quality. "No," say many of my antagonists, "taste is one thing, morality is another. Tell us what is pretty: we shall be glad to know that: but preach no sermons to us."

Permit me, therefore, to fortify this old dogma of mine somewhat. Taste is not only a part and an index of morality; it is the ONLY morality. The first, and last, and closest trial question to any living creature is, "What do you like?" Tell me what you like, and I'll tell you what you are. Go out into the street, and ask the first man or woman you meet, what their "taste" is; and if they answer candidly, you know them, body and soul. "You, my friend in the rags, with the unsteady gait, what do *you* like?" "A pipe, and a quartern of gin." I know you. "You, good woman, with the quick step and tidy bonnet, what do you like?" "A swept hearth, and a clean tea-table; and my husband opposite me, and a baby at my breast." Good, I know you also. "You, little girl with the golden hair and the soft eyes, what do you like?" "My canary, and a run among the wood hyacinths." "You, little boy with the dirty hands, and the low forehead, what do you like?" "A shy at the sparrows, and a game at pitch-farthing." Good; we know them all now. What more need we ask?

"Nay," perhaps you answer; "we need rather to ask what these people and children do, than what they like. If they *do* right, it is no matter that they like what is wrong; and if they *do* wrong, it is no matter that they like what is right. Doing is the great thing; and it does not matter that the man likes drinking, so that he does not drink; nor that the little girl likes to be kind to her canary, if she will not learn her lessons; nor that the little boy likes throwing stones at the sparrows, if he goes to the Sunday school." Indeed, for a short time, and in a provisional sense, this is true. For if, resolutely, people do what is right, in time they come to like doing it. But they only are in a right moral state when they *have* come to like doing it; and as long as they don't like it, they are still in a vicious state. The man is not in health of body who is always thirsting for the bottle in the cupboard, though he bravely bears his thirst; but the man who heartily enjoys water in the morning and wine in the evening, each in its proper quantity and time. And the entire object of true education is to make people not merely *do* the right things, but *enjoy* the right things—not merely industrious, but to love industry—not merely learned, but to love knowledge—not merely pure, but to love purity—not merely just, but to hunger and thirst after justice.

But you may answer or think, "Is the liking for outside ornaments—for pictures, or statues, or furniture, or architecture—a moral quality?" Yes, most surely, if a rightly set liking. Taste for *any* pictures or statues is not a moral quality, but taste for good ones is. Only here again we have to define the word "good." I don't mean by "good," clever—or learned—or difficult in the doing. Take a picture by Teniers, of sots quarreling over their dice; it is an entirely clever picture; so clever that nothing in its kind has ever been done equal to it; but it is also an entirely base and evil picture. It is an expression of delight in the prolonged contemplation of a vile thing, and delight in that is an "unmannered," or "immoral" quality. It is "bad taste" in the profoundest sense—it is the taste of the devils. On the other hand, a picture of Titian's, or a Greek statue, or a Greek coin, or a Turner landscape, expresses delight in the perpetual contemplation of a good and perfect thing. That is an entirely moral quality—it is the taste of the angels. And all delight in art, and all love of it, resolve themselves into simple love of that which deserves love. That deserving is the quality which we call "loveliness"—(we ought to have an opposite word, hateliness, to be said of the things which deserve to be hated), and it is not an indifferent nor optional thing whether we love this or that; but it is just the vital function of all our being. What we *like* determines what we *are*, and is the sign of what we are; and to teach taste is inevitably to form character. As I was thinking over this, in walking up Fleet Street the other day, my eye caught the title of a book standing open in a bookseller's window. It was—*On the Necessity of the Diffusion of Taste among all Classes.* "Ah," I thought to myself, "my classifying friend, when you have diffused your taste, where will your classes be? The man who likes what you like, belongs to the same class with you, I think. Inevitably so. You may put him to other work if you choose; but, by the condition you have brought him into, he will dislike the other work as much as you would yourself. You get hold of a scavenger, or a costermonger, who enjoyed the *Newgate Calendar* for literature, and "Pop goes the Weasel" for music. You think you can make him like Dante and Beethoven? I wish you joy of your lessons; but if you do, you have made a gentleman of him: he won't like to go back to his costermongering."

And so completely and unexceptionally is this so, that, if I had time to-night, I could show you that a nation cannot be affected by any vice, or weakness, without expressing it, legibly, and for ever, either in bad art, or by want of art; and that there is no national virtue, small or great, which is not manifestly expressed in all the art which circumstances enable the people possessing that virtue to produce. Take, for instance, your great English virtue of enduring and patient courage. You have at present in England only one art of any consequence—that is, iron-working. You know thoroughly well how to cast and hammer iron. Now, do you think in those masses of lava which you build volcanic cones to melt, and which you forge at the mouths of the Infernos you have created; do you think, on those iron plates, your courage and endurance are not written for ever—not merely with an iron pen, but on iron parchment? And take also your great English vice—European vice—vice of all the world— vice of all other worlds that roll or shine in heaven, bearing with them yet the atmosphere of hell—the vice of jealousy, which brings competition into your commerce, treachery into your councils, and dishonor into your wars—that vice which has rendered for you, and for your next neighboring nation, the daily occupations of existence no longer possible, but with the mail upon your breasts and the sword loose in its sheath; so that, at last, you have realized for all the multitudes of the two great peoples who lead the so-called civilization of the earth—you have realized for them all, I say, in person and in policy, what was once true only of the rough Border riders of your Cheviot hills—

> They carved at the meal
> With gloves of steel,
> And they drank the red wine through the helmet barr'd;

do you think that this national shame and dastardliness of heart are not written as legibly on every rivet of your iron armor as the strength of the right hands that forged it? Friends, I know not whether this thing be the more ludicrous or the more melancholy. It is quite unspeakably both. Suppose, instead of being now sent for by you, I had been sent for by some private gentleman, living in a suburban house, with his garden separated only by a fruit-wall from his next door neighbor's; and he had called me to consult with him on the furnishings of his drawing-room. I begin looking about me, and find the walls rather bare; I think such and such a paper might be desirable—perhaps a little fresco here and there on the ceiling—a damask curtain or so at the windows. "Ah," says my employer, "damask curtains, indeed! That's all very fine, but you know I can't afford that kind of thing just now!" "Yet the world credits you with a splendid income!" "Ah, yes," says my friend, "but do you know, at present, I am obliged to spend it nearly all in steel-traps?" "Steel-traps! for whom?" "Why, for that fellow on the other side the wall, you know: we're very good friends, capital friends; but we are obliged to keep our traps set on both sides of the wall; we could not possibly keep on friendly terms without them, and our spring guns. The worst of it is, we are both clever fellows enough; and there's never a day passes that we don't find out a new trap, or a new gun-barrel, or something; we spend about fifteen millions a year each in our traps, take it altogether; and I don't see how we're to do with less." A highly comic state of life for two private gentlemen! but for two nations, it seems to me, not wholly comic? Bedlam would be comic, perhaps, if there were only one madman in it; and your Christmas pantomime is comic, when there is only one clown in it; but when the whole world turns clown, and paints itself red with its own heart's blood instead of vermilion, it is something else than comic, I think.

Mind, I know a great deal of this is play, and willingly allow for that. You don't know what to do with yourselves for a sensation: fox-hunting and cricketing will not carry you through the whole of this unendurably long mortal life: you liked pop-guns when you were schoolboys, and rifles and Armstrongs are only the same things better made: but then the worst of it is, that what was play to you when boys, was not play to the sparrows; and what is play to you now, is not play to the small birds of State neither; and for the black eagles,[2] you are somewhat shy of taking shots at them, if I mistake not.

I must get back to the matter in hand, however. Believe me, without farther instance, I could show you, in all time, that every nation's vice, or virtue, was written in its art: the soldiership of early Greece; the sensuality of late Italy; the visionary religion of Tuscany; the splendid human energy and beauty of Venice. I have no time to do this to-night (I have done it elsewhere before now); but I proceed to apply the principle to ourselves in a more searching manner.

I notice that among all the new buildings which cover your once wild hills, churches and schools are mixed in due, that is to say, in large proportion, with your mills and mansions; and I notice also that the churches and schools are almost always Gothic, and the mansions and mills are never Gothic. Will you allow me to ask precisely the meaning of this? For, remember, it is peculiarly a modern phenomenon. When Gothic was invented, houses were Gothic as well as churches; and when the Italian style superseded the Gothic, churches were Italian as well as houses. If there is a Gothic spire to the cathedral of Antwerp, there is a Gothic belfry to the Hôtel de Ville at Brussels; if Inigo Jones builds an Italian Whitehall, Sir Christopher Wren builds an Italian St. Paul's. But now you live under one school of architecture, and worship under another. What do you mean by doing this? Am I to understand that you are thinking of changing your architecture back to Gothic; and that you

2. Apparently an allusion to the emblem of Prussia, pursuing at the time a militaristic policy under Bismarck.

treat your churches experimentally, because it does not matter what mistakes you make in a church? Or am I to understand that you consider Gothic a pre-eminently sacred and beautiful mode of building, which you think, like the fine frankincense, should be mixed for the tabernacle only, and reserved for your religious services? For if this be the feeling, though it may seem at first as if it were graceful and reverent, you will find that, at the root of the matter, it signifies neither more nor less than that you have separated your religion from your life.

For consider what a wide significance this fact has; and remember that it is not you only, but all the people of England, who are behaving thus just now.

You have all got into the habit of calling the church "the house of God." I have seen, over the doors of many churches, the legend actually carved, "*This* is the house of God, and this is the gate of heaven." Now, note where that legend comes from, and of what place it was first spoken.[3] A boy leaves his father's house to go on a long journey on foot, to visit his uncle: he has to cross a wild hill-desert; just as if one of your own boys had to cross the wolds of Westmoreland, to visit an uncle at Carlisle. The second or third day your boy finds himself somewhere between Hawes and Brough, in the midst of the moors, at sunset. It is stony ground, and boggy; he cannot go one foot farther that night. Down he lies, to sleep, on Wharnside, where best he may, gathering a few of the stones together to put under his head; so wild the place is, he cannot get anything but stones. And there, lying under the broad night, he has a dream; and he sees a ladder set up on the earth, and the top of it reaches to heaven, and the angels of God are ascending and descending upon it. And when he wakes out of his sleep, he says, "How dreadful is this place; surely, this is none other than the house of God, and this is the gate of heaven." This PLACE, observe; not this church; not this city; not this stone, even, which he puts up for a memorial—the piece of flint on which his head has lain. But this *place*; this windy slope of Wharnside; this moorland hollow, torrent-bitten, snow-blighted; this *any* place where God lets down the ladder. And how are you to know where that will be? or how are you to determine where it may be, but by being ready for it always? Do you know where the lightning is to fall next? You *do* know that, partly; you can guide the lightning; but you cannot guide the going forth of the Spirit, which is as that lightning when it shines from the east to the west.

But the perpetual and insolent warping of that strong verse to serve a merely ecclesiastical purpose, is only one of the thousand instances in which we sink back into gross Judaism. We call our churches "temples." Now, you know, or ought to know, they are

3. Told of Jacob and his vision, Genesis xxviii. 10-22.

not temples. They have never had, never can have, anything what-ever to do with temples. They are "synagogues"—"gathering places"—where you gather yourselves together as an assembly; and by not calling them so, you again miss the force of another mighty text—"Thou, when thou prayest, shalt not be as the hypocrites are; for they love to pray standing in the *churches*" [we should translate it], "that they may be seen of men. But thou, when thou prayest, enter into thy closet, and when thou hast shut thy door, pray to thy Father"—which is, not in chancel nor in aisle, but "in secret."

Now, you feel, as I say this to you—I know you feel—as if I were trying to take away the honor of your churches. Not so; I am trying to prove to you the honor of your houses and your hills; I am trying to show you—not that the Church is not sacred—but that the whole Earth is. I would have you feel, what careless, what constant, with infectious sin there is in all modes of thought, where-by, in calling your churches only "holy," you call your hearts and homes profane; and have separated yourselves from the heathen by casting all your household gods to the ground, instead of rec-ognizing, in the places of their many and feeble Lares, the presence of your One and Mighty Lord and Lar.

"But what has all this to do with our Exchange?" you ask me, impatiently. My dear friends, it has just everything to do with it; on these inner and great questions depend all the outer and little ones; and if you have asked me down here to speak to you, because you had before been interested in anything I have written, you must know that all I have yet said about architecture was to show this. The book I called *The Seven Lamps* was to show that certain right states of temper and moral feeling were the magic powers by which all good architecture, without exception, had been produced. *The Stones of Venice* had, from beginning to end, no other aim than to show that the Gothic architecture of Venice had arisen out of, and indicated in all its features, a state of pure national faith, and of domestic virtue; and that its Renaissance architecture had arisen out of, and all its features indicated, a state of concealed national infidelity, and of domestic corruption. And now, you ask me what style is best to build in; and how can I answer, knowing the meaning of the two styles, but by another question—do you mean to build as Christians or as Infidels? And still more—do you mean to build as honest Christians or as honest Infidels? as thor-oughly and confessedly either one or the other? You don't like to be asked such rude questions. I cannot help it; they are of much more importance than this Exchange business; and if they can be at once answered, the Exchange business settles itself in a mo-ment. But, before I press them farther, I must ask leave to explain one point clearly. In all my past work, my endeavor has been to show that good architecture is essentially religious—the production of a faithful and virtuous, not of an infidel and corrupted people. But in the course of doing this, I have had also to show that good architecture is not *ecclesiastical*. People are so apt to look upon religion as the business of the clergy, not their own, that the moment they hear of anything depending on "religion," they think it must also have depended on the priesthood; and I have had to take what place was to be occupied between these two errors, and fight both, often with seeming contradiction. Good architecture is the work of good and believing men; therefore, you say, at least some people say, "Good architecture must essentially have been the work of the clergy, not of the laity." No—a thousand times no; good architecture has always been the work of the commonalty, *not* of the clergy. What, you say, those glorious cathedrals—the pride of Europe—did their builders not form Gothic architecture? No; they corrupted Gothic architecture. Gothic was formed in the baron's castle, and the burgher's street. It was formed by the thoughts, and hands, and powers of free citizens and soldier kings. By the monk it was used as an instrument for the aid of his superstition: when that superstition became a beautiful madness, and the best hearts of Europe vainly dreamed and pined in the cloister, and vainly raged and perished in the crusade—through that fury of perverted faith and wasted war, the Gothic rose also to its loveliest, most fantastic, and finally, most foolish dreams; and, in those dreams, was lost.

I hope, now, that there is no risk of your misunderstanding me when I come to the gist of what I want to say to-night—when I repeat, that every great national architecture has been the result and exponent of a great national religion. You can't have bits of it here, bits there—you must have it everywhere or nowhere. It is not the monopoly of a clerical company—it is not the exponent of a theological dogma—it is not the hieroglyphic writing of an initiated priesthood; it is the manly language of a people inspired by resolute and common purpose, and rendering resolute and common fidelity to the legible laws of an undoubted God.

Now there have as yet been three distinct schools of European architecture. I say, European, because Asiatic and African architectures belong so entirely to other races and climates, that there is no question of them here; only, in passing, I will simply assure you that whatever is good or great in Egypt, and Syria, and India, is just good or great for the same reasons as the buildings on our side of the Bosphorus. We Europeans, then, have had three great religions: the Greek, which was the worship of the God of Wisdom and Power; the Mediaeval, which was the worship of the God of Judgment and Consolation; the Renaissance, which was the worship of the God of Pride and Beauty: these three we have had—they are past—and now, at last, we English have got a fourth religion, and a God of our own, about which I want to ask you. But I must explain these three old ones first.

I repeat, first, the Greeks essentially worshipped the God of Wisdom; so that whatever contended against their religion—to the Jews a stumbling-block—was, to the Greeks—*Foolishness.*

The first Greek idea of deity was that expressed in the word, of which we keep the remnant in our words "*Di-*urnal" and "*Di-*vine" —the god of *Day,* Jupiter the revealer. Athena is his daughter, but especially daughter of the Intellect, springing armed from the head. We are only with the help of recent investigation beginning to penetrate the depth of meaning couched under the Athenaic symbols: but I may note rapidly, that her aegis, the mantle with the serpent fringes, in which she often, in the best statues, is represented as folding up her left hand for better guard, and the Gorgon on her shield, are both representative mainly of the chilling horror and sadness, (turning men to stone, as it were,) of the outmost and superficial spheres of knowledge—that knowledge which separates, in bitterness, hardness, and sorrow, the heart of the full-grown man from the heart of the child. For out of imperfect knowledge spring terror, dissension, danger, and disdain; but from perfect knowledge, given by the full-revealed Athena, strength and peace, in sign of which she is crowned with the olive spray, and bears the resistless spear.

This, then, was the Greek conception of purest Deity, and every habit of life, and every form of his art developed themselves from the seeking this bright, serene, resistless wisdom; and setting himself, as a man, to do things evermore rightly and strongly;[4] not with any ardent affection or ultimate hope; but with a resolute and continent energy of will, as knowing that for failure there was no consolation, and for sin there was no remission. And the Greek architecture rose unerring, bright, clearly defined, and self-contained.

Next followed in Europe the great Christian faith, which was essentially the religion of Comfort. Its great doctrine is the remission of sins; for which cause it happens, too often, in certain phases of Christianity, that sin and sickness themselves are partly glorified, as if, the more you had to be healed of, the more divine was the healing. The practical result of this doctrine, in art, is a continual contemplation of sin and disease, and of imaginary states of purification from them; thus we have an architecture conceived in a mingled sentiment of melancholy and aspiration, partly severe, partly luxuriant, which will bend itself to every one of our needs, and

4. It is an error to suppose that the Greek worship, or seeking, was chiefly of Beauty. It was essentially of Rightness and Strength, founded on Forethought: the principal character of Greek art is not beauty, but Design: and the Dorian Apollo-worship and Athenian Virgin-worship are both expressions of adoration of divine Wisdom and Purity. Next to these great deities rank, in power over the national mind, Dionysus and Ceres, the givers of human strength and life; then, for heroic example, Hercules. There is no Venus-worship among the Greeks in the great times: and the Muses are essentially teachers of truth, and of its harmonies [Ruskin's note].

every one of our fancies, and be strong or weak with us, as we are strong or weak ourselves. It is, of all architecture, the basest, when base people build it—of all, the noblest, when built by the noble.

And now note that both these religions—Greek and Mediaeval —perished by falsehood in their own main purpose. The Greek religion of Wisdom perished in a false philosophy—"Oppositions of science, falsely so called." The Mediaeval religion of Consolation perished in false comfort; in remission of sins given lyingly. It was the selling of absolution that ended the Mediaeval faith; and I can tell you more, it is the selling of absolution which, to the end of time, will mark false Christianity. Pure Christianity gives her remission of sins only by *ending* them; but false Christianity gets her remission of sins by *compounding for* them. And there are many ways of compounding for them. We English have beautiful little quiet ways of buying absolution, whether in low Church or high, far more cunning than any of Tetzel's trading.[5]

Then, thirdly, there followed the religion of Pleasure, in which all Europe gave itself to luxury, ending in death. First, *bals masqués* in every saloon, and then guillotines in every square. And all these three worships issue in vast temple building. Your Greek worshipped Wisdom, and built you the Parthenon—the Virgin's temple. The Mediaeval worshipped Consolation, and built you Virgin temples also—but to our Lady of Salvation. Then the Revivalist worshipped beauty, of a sort, and built you Versailles, and the Vatican. Now, lastly will you tell me what *we* worship, and what *we* build?

You know we are speaking always of the real, active, continual, national worship; that by which men act while they live; not that which they talk of when they die. Now, we have, indeed, a nominal religion, to which we pay tithes of property and sevenths of time; but we have also a practical and earnest religion, to which we devote nine-tenths of our property and six-sevenths of our time. And we dispute a great deal about the nominal religion; but we are all unanimous about this practical one, of which I think you will admit that the ruling goddess may be best generally described as the "Goddess of Getting-on," or "Britannia of the Market." The Athenians had an "Athena Agoraia," or Minerva of the Market; but she was a subordinate type of their goddess, while our Britannia Agoraia is the principal type of ours. And all your great architectural works are, of course, built to her. It is long since you built a great cathedral; and how you would laugh at me, if I proposed building a cathedral on the top of one of these hills of yours, taking it for an Acropolis! But your railroad mounds, prolonged masses of Acropolis; your railroad stations, vaster than the Parthenon, and innumerable; your chimneys, how much more mighty and costly than cathedral spires!

5. The traffic in indulgences done by the German monk Tetzel is regarded as one of the immediate causes of the Protestant Reformation.

your harbor-piers; your warehouses; your exchanges!—all these are built to your great Goddess of "Getting-on;" and she has formed, and will continue to form, your architecture, as long as you worship her; and it is quite vain to ask me to tell you how to build to *her*; you know far better than I.

There might, indeed, on some theories, be a conceivably good architecture for Exchanges—that is to say if there were any heroism in the fact or deed of exchange, which might be typically carved on the outside of your building. For, you know, all beautiful architecture must be adorned with sculpture or painting; and for sculpture or painting, you must have a subject. And hitherto it has been a received opinion among the nations of the world that the only right subjects for either, were *heroisms* of some sort. Even on his pots and flagons, the Greek put a Hercules slaying lions, or an Apollo slaying serpents, or Bacchus slaying melancholy giants, and earthborn despondencies. On his temples, the Greeks put contests of great warriors in founding states, or of gods with evil spirits. On his house and temple alike, the Christian put carvings of angels conquering devils; or of hero-martyrs exchanging this world for another; subject inappropriate, I think, to our manner of exchange here. And the Master of Christians not only left his followers without any orders as to the sculpture of affairs of exchange on the outside of buildings, but gave some strong evidence of his dislike of affairs of exchange within them.[6] And yet there might surely be a heroism in such affairs; and all commerce become a kind of selling of doves, not impious. The wonder has always been great to me, that heroism has never been supposed to be in anywise consistent with the practice of supplying people with food, or clothes; but rather with that of quartering oneself upon them for food, and stripping them of their clothes. Spoiling of armor is an heroic deed in all ages; but the selling of clothes, old, or new, has never taken any color of magnanimity. Yet one does not see why feeding the hungry and clothing the naked should ever become base businesses, even when engaged in on a large scale. If one could contrive to attach the notion of conquest to them anyhow? so that, supposing there were anywhere an obstinate race, who refused to be comforted, one might take some pride in giving them compulsory comfort; and as it were, "occupying a country" with one's gifts, instead of one's armies? If one could only consider it as much a victory to get a barren field sown, as to get an eared field stripped; and contend who should build villages, instead of who should "carry" them. Are not all forms of heroism, conceivable in doing these serviceable deeds? You doubt who is strongest? It might be ascertained by push of spade, as well as push of sword. Who is wisest? There are witty things to be thought of in planning other

6. A reference to Jesus' casting the moneychangers out of the Temple (Matthew xxi. 12-13).

business than campaigns. Who is bravest? There are always the elements to fight with, stronger than men; and nearly as merciless. The only absolutely and unapproachably heroic element in the soldier's work seems to be—that he is paid little for it—and regularly: while you traffickers, and exchangers, and others occupied in presumably benevolent business, like to be paid much for it—and by chance. I never can make out how it is that a knight-errant does not expect to be paid for his trouble, but a pedlar-errant always does; that people are willing to take hard knocks for nothing, but never to sell ribands cheap; that they are ready to go on fervent crusades to recover the tomb of a buried God, never on any travels to fulfill the orders of a living God; that they will go anywhere barefoot to preach their faith, but must be well bribed to practice it, and are perfectly ready to give the Gospel gratis, but never the loaves and fishes. If you chose to take the matter up on any such soldierly principle, to do your commerce, and your feeding of nations, for fixed salaries; and to be as particular about giving people the best food, and the best cloth, as soldiers are about giving them the best gunpowder, I could carve something for you on your exchange worth looking at. But I can only at present suggest decorating its frieze with pendant purses; and making its pillars broad at the base, for the sticking of bills. And in the innermost chambers of it there might be a statute of Britannia of the Market, who may have, perhaps advisably, a partridge for her crest, typical at once of her courage in fighting for noble ideas; and of her interest in game; and round its neck the inscription in golden letters, "Perdix fovit quae non peperit."[7] Then, for her spear, she might have a weaver's beam; and on her shield, instead of her Cross, the Milanese boar, semi-fleeced, with the town of Gennesaret proper, in the field and the legend, "In the best market," and her corslet, of leather, folded over her heart in the shape of a purse, with thirty slits in it for a piece of money to go in at, on each day of the month. And I doubt not but that people would come to see your exchange, and its goddess, with applause.

Nevertheless, I want to point out to you certain strange characters in this goddess of yours. She differs from the Greek and Mediaeval dieties essentially in two things—first, as to the continuance of her presumed power; secondly, as to the extent of it.

I. As to the Continuance.

The Greek Goddess of Wisdom gave continual increase of wisdom, as the Christian Spirit of Comfort (or Comforter) continual increase of comfort. There was no question, with these, of any limit or cessation of function. But with your Agora Goddess, that is just

7. Jeremiah xvii. 11 (best in Septuagint and Vulgate). "As the partridge, fostering what she brought not forth, so he that getteth riches, not by right, shall leave them in the midst of his days, and at his end shall be a fool" [Ruskin's note].

the most important question. Getting on—but where to? Gathering together—but how much? Do you mean to gather always—never to spend? If so, I wish you joy of your goddess, for I am just as well-off as you, without the trouble of worshipping her at all. But if you do not spend, somebody else will—somebody else must. And it is because of this (among many other such errors) that I have fearlessly declared your so-called science of Political Economy to be no science; because, namely, it has omitted the study of exactly the most important branch of the business—the study of *spending*. For spend you must, and as much as you make, ultimately. You gather corn: will you bury England under a heap of grain; or will you, when you have gathered, finally eat? You gather gold: will you make your house-roofs of it, or pave your streets with it? That is still one way of spending it. But if you keep it, that you may get more, I'll give you more; I'll give you all the gold you want—all you can imagine—if you can tell me what you'll do with it. You shall have thousands of gold pieces; thousands of thousands—millions—mountains, of gold: where will you keep them? Will you put an Olympus of silver upon a golden Pelion—make Ossa like a wart? Do you think the rain and dew would then come down to you, in the streams from such mountains, more blessedly than they will down the mountains which God has made for you, of moss and whinstone? But it is not gold that you want to gather! What is it? greenbacks? No; not those neither. What is it then—is it ciphers after a capital I? Cannot you practice writing ciphers, and write as many as you want? Write ciphers for an hour every morning, in a big book, and say every evening, I am worth all those noughts more than I was yesterday. Won't that do? Well, what in the name of Plutus is it you want? Not gold, not greenbacks, not ciphers after a capital I? You will have to answer, after all, "No; we want, somehow or other, money's *worth*." Well, what is that? Let your Goddess of Getting-on discover it, and let her learn to stay therein.

II. But there is yet another question to be asked respecting this Goddess of Getting-on. The first was of the continuance of her power; the second is of its extent.

Pallas and the Madonna were supposed to be all the world's Pallas, and all the world's Madonna. They could teach all men, and they could comfort all men. But, look strictly into the nature of the power of your Goddess of Getting-on; and you will find she is the Goddess—not of everybody's getting on—but only of somebody's getting on. This is a vital, or rather deathful, distinction. Examine it in your own ideal of the state of national life which this Goddess is to evoke and maintain. I asked you what it was, when I was last here;[8] you have never told me. Now, shall I try to tell you?

Your ideal of human life then is, I think, that it should be passed

8. *Two Paths* [Ruskin's note].

in a pleasant undulating world, with iron and coal everywhere underneath it. On each pleasant bank of this world is to be a beautiful mansion, with two wings; and stables, and coachhouses; a moderately sized park; a large garden and hot-houses; and pleasant carriage drives through the shrubberies. In this mansion are to live the favored votaries of the Goddess; the English gentleman, with his gracious wife, and his beautiful family; always able to have the boudoir and the jewels for the wife, and the beautiful ball dresses for the daughters, and hunters for the sons, and a shooting in the Highlands for himself. At the bottom of the bank, is to be the mill; not less than a quarter of a mile long, with a steam engine at each end, and two in the middle, and a chimney three hundred feet high. In this mill are to be in constant employment from eight hundred to a thousand workers, who never drink, never strike, always go to church on Sunday, and always express themselves in respectful language.

Is not that, broadly, and in the main features, the kind of thing you propose to yourselves? It is very pretty indeed, seen from above; not at all so pretty, seen from below. For, observe, while to one family this diety is indeed the Goddess of Getting-on, to a thousand families she is the Goddess of *not* Getting-on. "Nay," you say, "they have all their chance." Yes, so has every one in a lottery, but there must always be the same number of blanks. "Ah! but in a lottery it is not skill and intelligence which take the lead, but blind chance." What then! do you think the old practice, that "they should take who have the power, and they should keep who can," is less iniquitous, when the power has become power of brains instead of fist? and that, though we may not take advantage of a child's or a woman's weakness, we may of a man's foolishness? "Nay, but finally, work must be done, and some one must be at the top, some one at the bottom." Granted, my friends. Work must always be, and captains of work must always be; and if you in the least remember the tone of any of my writings, you must know that they are thought unfit for this age, because they are always insisting on need of government, and speaking with scorn of liberty. But I beg you to observe that there is a wide difference between being captains or governors of work, and taking the profits of it. It does not follow, because you are general of an army, that you are to take all the treasure, or land, it wins (if it fight for treasure or land); neither, because you are king of a nation, that you are to consume all the profits of the nation's work. Real kings, on the contrary, are known invariably by their doing quite the reverse of this—by their taking the least possible quantity of the nation's work for themselves. There is no test of real kinghood so infallible as that. Does the crowned creature live simply, bravely, unostentatiously? probably he *is* a King. Does he cover his body with jewels, and his table with delicates? in all probability he is *not* a King. It is possible he may be, as Solomon was; but that is when the nation shares his splendor with him. Solomon made gold, not only to be in his own palace as stones, but to be in Jerusalem as stones. But, even so, for the most part, these splendid kinghoods expire in ruin, and only the true kinghoods live, which are of royal laborers governing loyal laborers; who, both leading rough lives, establish the true dynasties. Conclusively you will find that because you are king of a nation, it does not follow that you are to gather for yourself all the wealth of that nation; neither, because you are king of a small part of the nation, and lord over the means of its maintenance—over field, or mill, or mine, are you to take all the produce of that piece of the foundation of national existence for yourself.

You will tell me I need not preach against these things, for I cannot mend them. No, good friends, I cannot; but you can, and you will; or something else can and will. Do you think these phenomena are to stay always in their present power or aspect? All history shows, on the contrary, that to be the exact thing they never can do. Change *must* come; but it is ours to determine whether change of growth, or change of death. Shall the Parthenon be in ruins on its rock, and Bolton priory in its meadow, but these mills of yours be the consummation of the buildings of the earth, and their wheels be as the wheels of eternity? Think you that "men may come, and men may go," but—mills—go on for ever? Not so; out of these, better or worse shall come; and it is for you to choose which.

I know that none of this wrong is done with deliberate purpose. I know, on the contrary, that you wish your workmen well; that you do much for them, and that you desire to do more for them, if you saw your way to it, safely. I know that many of you have done, and are every day doing, whatever you feel to be in your power; and that even all this wrong and misery are brought about by a warped sense of duty, each of you striving to do his best, without noticing that this best is essentially and centrally the best for himself, not for others. And all this has come of the spreading of that thrice accursed, thrice impious doctrine of the modern economist, that, "To do the best for yourself, is finally to do the best for others." Friends, our great Master said not so; and most absolutely we shall find this world is not made so. Indeed, to do the best for others, is finally to do the best for ourselves; but it will not do to have our eyes fixed on that issue. The Pagans had got beyond that. Hear what a Pagan says of this matter; hear what were, perhaps, the last written words of Plato, if not the last actually written, (for this we cannot know), yet assuredly in fact and power his parting words—in which, endeavoring to give full crowning and harmonious close to all his thoughts, and to speak the sum of them by the imagined sentence of the Great Spirit, his strength and his heart fail him, and the words cease, broken off for ever. It is the close of the dialogue called "Critias," in which he describes, partly from real tradition, partly in ideal dream, the early state of Athens; and the genesis, and order, and religion, of the fabled isle of Atlantis; in which genesis he conceives the same first perfection and final degeneracy of man, which in our own Scriptural tradition is expressed by saying that the Sons of God intermarried with the daughters of men, for he supposes the earliest race to have been indeed the children of God; and to have corrupted themselves, until "their spot was not the spot of his children." And this, he says, was the end; that indeed "through many generations, so long as the God's nature in them yet was full, they were submissive to the sacred laws, and carried themselves lovingly to all that had kindred with them in divineness; for their uttermost spirit was faithful and true, and in every wise great; so that, in all meekness of wisdom, they dealt with each other, and took all the chances of life; and despising all things except virtue, they cared little what happened day by day, and bore *lightly the burden* of gold and of possessions; for they saw that, if only their common love and virtue increased, all these things would be increased together with them; but to set their esteem and ardent pursuit upon material possession, would be to lose that first, and their virtue and affection together with it. And by such reasoning, and what of the divine nature remained in them, they gained all this greatness of which we have already told; but when the God's part of them faded and became extinct, being mixed again and again, and effaced by the prevalent mortality; and the human nature at last exceeded, they then became unable to endure the courses of fortune; and fell into shapelessness of life, and baseness in the sight of him who could see, having lost everything that was fairest of their honor; while to the blind hearts which could not discern the true life, tending to happiness, it seemed that they were then chiefly noble and happy, being filled with all iniquity of inordinate possession and power. Whereupon, the God of Gods, whose Kinghood is in laws, beholding a once just nation thus cast into misery, and desiring to lay such punishment upon them as might make them repent into restraining, gathered together all the gods into his dwelling place, which from heaven's centre overlooks whatever has part in creation; and having assembled them, he said"——

The rest is silence. So ended are the last words of the chief wisdom of the heathen, spoken of this idol of riches; this idol of yours; this golden image, high by measureless cubits, set up where your green fields of England are furnace-burnt into the likeness of the plain of Dura: this idol, forbidden to us, first of all idols, by our own Master and faith; forbidden to us also by every human lip that has ever, in any age or people, been accounted of as able to speak according to the purposes of God. Continue to make that forbidden deity your principal one, and soon no more art, no more science, no more pleasure will be possible. Catastrophe will come; or, worse than catastrophe, slow mouldering and withering into Hades. But if you can fix some conception of a true human state of life to be striven for—life for all men as for yourselves—if you can determine some honest and simple order of existence; following those trodden ways of wisdom, which are pleasantness, and seeking her quiet and withdrawn paths, which are peace; then, and so sanctifying wealth into "commonwealth," all your art, your literature, your daily labors, your domestic affection, and citizen's duty, will join and increase into one magnificent harmony. You will know then how to build, well enough; you will build with stone well, but with flesh better; temples not made with hands, but riveted of hearts; and that kind of marble, crimson-veined, is indeed eternal.

QUESTIONS FOR STUDY, DISCUSSION, AND WRITING

1. What does the title mean?
2. What special relation to his audience does Ruskin establish at the outset? To what purpose? Is this relation changed or modified later in the discourse?
3. What is Ruskin's main thesis concerning taste and morality? In what ways does he explain and seek to demonstrate it? Is the idea persuasive? Why, or why not?
4. Ruskin asserts that ironworking was the foremost art of Britain in his day and that it manifested itself in the national character. In what two main respects did he hold that it did so? Make a similar analysis of art and American national life at present.
5. What is Ruskin's objection to the building of Gothic churches?
6. On page 649 Ruskin adapts the biblical story of Jacob's sojourn and dream to the conditions of his discourse. Explain in detail how he accomplishes this. What other instances of biblical allusion and adaptation are there in the work? How is this matter related to Ruskin's main thesis and purpose in the work?
7. Why does Ruskin picture the grotesque statue of "the Goddess of Getting-on" and the scene of the mill-owner's house and factory? What place have these architectural designs in the development of the discourse?
8. How does the Goddess of Getting-on differ from other deities?
9. Does Ruskin's discourse suggest any contemporary parallels? Has it any relevance to our own social, economic, aesthetic, and religious circumstances? Develop your response in an essay.

JAMES THURBER
The Bear Who Let It Alone

In the words of the Far West there once lived a brown bear who could take it or let it alone. He would go into a bar where they sold mead, a fermented drink made of honey, and he would have just two drinks. Then he would put some money on the bar and say, "See what the bears in the back room will have," and he would go home. But finally he took to drinking by himself most of the day. He would reel home at night, kick over the umbrella stand, knock down the bridge lamps, and ram his elbows through the windows. Then he would collapse on the floor and lie there until he went to sleep. His wife was greatly distressed and his children were very frightened.

At length the bear saw the error of his ways and began to reform. In the end he became a famous teetotaller and a persistent temperance lecturer. He would tell everybody that came to his house about the awful effects of drink, and he would boast about how strong and well he had become since he gave up touching the stuff. To demonstrate this, he would stand on his head and on his hands and he would turn cartwheels in the house, kicking over the umbrella stand, knocking down the bridge lamps, and ramming his elbows through the windows. Then he would lie down on the floor, tired by his healthful exercise, and go to sleep. His wife was greatly distressed and his children were very frightened.

Moral: You might as well fall flat on your face as lean over too far backward.

DONALD HALL
A Hundred Thousand Straightened Nails

When I was growing up, I spent every summer helping out on my grandparents' farm. My grandfather was a great storyteller and told me anecdotes to go with every face whose portrait hung in the farmhouse gallery, those long rows of silhouettes, daguerreotypes, tinted photographs and snapshots which my grandmother kept in the parlor and the sitting room. The portraits had names which I recognized on headstones when we visited graveyards. Though I loved the bright flowery borders and the white paint of the farmhouse, and though I loved our haying in the dry heat of the fields, I was always aware that New Hampshire was more dead than alive. Walking in the dense woods, I learned to be careful not to fall into the cellar holes.

If I was morbid, it was not my grandfather's fault. He was interested only in lively stories about the dead, and he lived so completely in the dramatic scenes of his memory that everything was continually present to him. My grandmother was occasionally elegiac, but not enough to influence me. When I was nine I saw my Great-Aunt Nannie, blind and insane, dying for one long summer on a cot in the parlor, yet my own lamentation for the dead and the past had begun even earlier. Many of my grandfather's stories were symptoms, to me and not to him, of the decay of New Hampshire; a story might include a meadow where the farm boys had played baseball, or a wood through which a railroad had once run.

I found myself, too, taking some of the characters in his stories at a value different from his. So many of them lived a half-life, a life of casual waste. He often talked about Washington Woodward, who was a cousin of ours. I knew Washington well, yet my image of him was a mixture of what I had observed and what my grandfather had told me. The whole farm was composed of things which Washington had made or at least repaired, so there was no end of devices to remind my grandfather of a story about him. Most of them were funny, for Washington was eccentric, yet after I had finished laughing, even perhaps when I lay in bed at night and thought over what had happened in the day, the final effect of the stories was not comic. I turned Washington into a sign of the dying place. I loved him, and I could feel his affection for me. Yet when I thought of the disease that afflicted New Hampshire, I knew that my grandfather's face was the exception to disease. The face of sickness was the mouth and moving beard, the ingenious futility of Washington Woodward.

This was a paradox, for Washington hated corruption and spied it everywhere like a prophet. Yet unlike a prophet he retired from corruption to the hills, meditated it, and never returned to denounce it. He bought a few acres high up New Canada Road, on Ragged Mountain, in 1895. He lived there alone, with few forays into the world, for the more than fifty years until he died.

I have seen pictures of him, in the farmhouse gallery, taken when he was a young man. He was short and muscular of body, handsome and stern, with a full black mustache over a downcurved mouth. I remembered him only as old, for even in my first memories he must have been sixty. The image I retained had him bent nearly double from the waist, with quick bright eyes and his mouth jiggling his beard in an incessant monotone.

When Washington was young, my grandfather told me, he was already the misanthrope who would exile himself. He had been the youngest of eleven children in a family related to my grandmother. His father, everyone admits, was lazy and mean. Their house burned down, and the children were boarded with various relatives. Washington was only six but already embittered and even surly when he came to live with the Kenestons. My grandmother was a baby. He stayed until he was twelve, and he always looked back to those years as a golden age; my grandmother's family was the great exception to the misanthropic rule. To my grandmother, he was an older brother; when she nursed him during illnesses late in his life, she was remembering someone who had been kind to her when she was as dependent as he had become.

He would never have left the Keneston house of his own will. When Washington was twelve, his father drove into the farmyard on his broken-down wagon and called for him until he came out of the barn where he had been wandering with little Katie. Washington knew the sort of man his father was, but he knew that sons obeyed fathers. When he had reached the wagon his father told him to lift a hundred-pound sack of grain out onto the ground, and then back into the wagon again. When he did it without straining, his father said, "You're big enough to work. Get packed up. You're coming home."

Washington ran away four years later and set up on his own as a hired hand and an odd-jobber. He was a hard worker and skillful. The best thing about him was his pride in good work. By the time he was twenty-five, he had repaired or built everything but a locomotive. Give him a forge and some scraps of old iron, my grandfather said, and he could make a locomotive too. I knew him to shoe a horse, install plumbing, dig a well, make a gun, build a road, lay a dry stone wall, do the foundation and frame of a house, invent a new kind of trap for beavers, manufacture his own shotgun shells, grind knives and turn a baseball bat on a lathe. The bat was made out of rock maple, and so heavy that I could barely lift it to my shoulders when he made it for my thirteenth birthday. The trouble was that he was incredibly slow. He was not interested in your problems, but in the problems of the job itself. He didn't care if it took him five weeks to shingle an outhouse that plumbing was going to outmode in a year. This was one outhouse that would *stay* shingled, although the shingles might protect only the spiders and the mother cat.

His slowness cost him money, but money did not matter to him. He did not even call it an abomination like drinking, cardplaying, smoking, swearing, lipstick and dancing; he simply did not think of it. He needed no more for supper than bread and milk. Did anyone else? If he didn't care about money, he cared about people sticking to their word; he cared about honor, whether it concerned his pay or the hour at which he was to finish a job. Once a deacon of the church asked Washington to fix the rickety wheels of a carriage. Washington told him it would be four dollars, and he spent six full days at the forge strengthening the wheels and adding supports until the axles would have carried five tons of hay, much less the deacon and his thin wife. But the deacon said, when the carriage was delivered, that four dollars was too much, and that three dollars was what the job was worth. Washington refused to take anything, and he never sat in his pew again, for if deacons cheated, churches were corrupt. He read his Bible by himself.

During all his years of solitude, he was extraordinarily sociable whenever he saw his family, as if the taciturnity he had assumed with his solitude was unnatural. He stored up, alone in his shack, acres of volubility which the sight of a relative discovered. If I remarked to him that an apple he had given me was a good apple, he might say, "Well, I remember; that apple came from the tree by the woodchuck hole in the northeast corner that leans toward the south; though it don't lean too much; down in that patch there; it's from a splice, that branch is, from a big tree, high as a house, on John Wentworth's land; his orchard behind his cowbarn beside the saphouse; well, the tree, old John Wentworth's been dead twenty years' tree, was always a good one for apples, big and meaty with plenty of juice to them; and one summer about 1919, no, 1920 I guess, I was working up to John's; I was fixing some sap pails had leaks and I shingled the icehouse, the back of it, where you couldn't see from the road but it was about gone; I'd done the front before and I told him the back would need doing; I was there as much as two months, ten weeks I guess; and it come apple time while I was there, and I helped him picking and he come up here and helped me; and I had my few trees up here, not so many as now, not half so many, as I reckon it, and one time I was mending a water pipe that fed the horse trough, it had come loose, and John didn't have no more solder, so I had to come all the way back to the shop; and as I was going I stopped to look at the tree, the big one, and I thought about asking John if I could splice off a limb as part pay; well, I never did get back that day because I saw a deer in the peas when I got here. . . ." And then he would tell how he waited for the deer and shot him, and what he had done with the pelt, and what John Wentworth had said to him when he asked for the limb, and how he had spliced it to his own tree, and on and on until, if the body had been strong enough, Washington would have talked out the whole contents of his mind. Scratch him anywhere and you touched his autobiography. Any detail was sufficiently relevant if it kept the tongue moving and the silence broken. My grandfather's many memories, on the other hand, were separated into stories with just enough irrelevant material of the past to keep them circumstantial; they had form, and you knew when he had come to a stopping point. Washington was a talking machine capable of producing the recall of every sensation, every motive, of a lifetime; and all the objects of his world could serve him like Proust's *madeleine*.[1]

It was not the past that interested him, but talking. If he had known about contemporary politics, he would have been willing to use it as his pretext for speech; but in the pursuit of independence

1. A small rich cake, the taste of which sets off a flood of memories of his childhood and early life in the mind of the hero of Proust's novel *Remembrance of Things Past*.

he had cut himself off from everything but his daily sensations. The talking was the same when he was young and when he was old. When we visited him at his shack, he would invariably trot alongside the car or buggy as we left, jogging a hundred yards farther with the story he couldn't end. My mother remembers from her girlhood, and I from twenty-five years later, how my grandparents would go to bed while he was talking, and how he would drone on for hours in the dark. When he was old and sick, he would talk in his chair in the kitchen while they read in the living room. Sometimes he would laugh a little and pause, as he reached a brief resting space in his unfinishable monologue. My grandmother learned to say, "Is that so?" whenever there was a pause. My grandfather swore that she could do it in her sleep.

Washington always wore the same costume in the years I knew him. The only thing that ever differed about his appearance was his beard, for he shaved in the summer and let his hair grow for warmth in the winter. He wore heavy brown overalls, patched and stitched, and a lighter brown workshirt stitched so extensively that the cloth had nearly vanished under the coarse stitches; over these he wore a light, nondescript workcoat, and in winter a thick, ancient overcoat with safety pins instead of buttons. He often spent his evenings sewing by the light of a candle until his eyes hurt.

Washington had built his shack on the slope of Ragged Mountain on the western, downward side of New Canada Road, two miles up from U.S. 3 by the road, but half a mile as the crow flies. He had a small pasture for cattle, a hen yard, geese wandering loose, a good orchard of various apple trees and other northern fruits, and at various times he kept pigs, goats, ducks and a dog. His shack was small, and it had grown smaller inside every year. Layers of things saved grew inward from the walls until Washington could barely move inside it. A tiny path among the boxes and animal pelts led from the door to a cross path from an iron stove to a Morris chair. Washington slept upright in the chair every night.

If he found a board in a ditch as he walked home from the day's work, and if the board had a bent nail in it, he would hammer the nail out of the board with a rock and take it home. If the board would make kindling or if it was strong enough to build with, he would take it along too. He would straighten the nail with a hammer on the anvil at his lean-to shop and put it in a box with other nails of the same dimensions. He might have to move a dozen other boxes to find the right one, but he would know where it was. It wasn't that he was a miser, because he cared nothing for the money he saved by collecting used nails. And when he died he did not, like the misers reported in the newspapers, leave a hundred thousand dollars in the back of a mirror; he left a hundred thousand straightened nails. He saved the nails because it was a sin to allow good material to go to waste. Everyone knows the story about the box of pieces of string, found in an old attic, labeled "String too short to be saved."

Besides nails, Washington kept a complete line of hardware and parts: clasps, hinges, brackets, braces, hoe handles, axe heads and spare rungs for ladders. He also saved elk, moose, bear, beaver, fox and deer pelts. On the wall beside the door were his rifle and shotgun and boxes of shells and cartridges. He was a good shot and a patient hunter. Until he was old he shot a big buck every year and ate nothing but venison until the bones were bare. Once a year, in the early fall, he had my grandmother bake him a woodchuck in her big oven. Only when his legs were so bad that he did not dare to wait out an animal, for fear that he would not be able to move after being still, did the woodchucks and hedgehogs manage to eat his peas and his apples and in this way avenge their ancestors.

He ate one kind of food exclusively until he finished his supply of it. Often it would be nothing but oatmeal for a week. Again he would buy two dozen loaves of stale bread and eat nothing else until the last moldy crust was gone. I remember him eating his way through a case of corn flakes; and when the woodchucks had eaten his garden, one winter, he ate a case of canned peas. It was no principle with him, but simply the easiest thing to do. When he was old and sick, living a winter in the rocking chair in my grandmother's kitchen beside Christopher, the canary, he bought his own food and kept it separately, in a cardboard box beside him. At this time he had a run on graham crackers. He did not eat on any schedule, and sometimes my grandparents would wake up in the middle of the night to hear him gumming a cracker, his false teeth lost in the darkness of a Mason jar.

When he was younger he must have been nearly self-sufficient. For much of each year he would refuse outside jobs from anyone, unless my grandfather particularly needed a mowing machine fixed or a scythe handle made when the store was out of them. And often he wouldn't take any money from my grandfather, although my grandmother would try to pay him in disguise with shirts and canned vegetables and pies. To pay the taxes on his land he worked a few days a year on the county road gang, repairing the dirt roads that laced the hills and connected the back farms with the main road in the valley. For clothing he had his gifts, and I know that he once made himself a coat out of fur he had trapped. For food he had all the game he shot, and he kept potatoes and apples and carrots and turnips in a lean-to (the food covered with burlap a foot thick to keep it from freezing) beside his shack, and he canned on his small stove dozens of jars of peas, tomatoes, corn and wax beans.

When he took an outside job or made a little money by peddling patent medicines like Quaker Oil or Rawleigh's Salve, he might buy himself a candy bar or five postcards or a pad of paper, or he might give it away. When my mother and her sister were at college, they sometimes had a letter from Washington with a nickel carefully wrapped inside. The patent medicines were before my time, and my grandfather told me about them. Washington would occasionally fill a large basket with his vials and jars, cut himself a walking stick, and set out to peddle on the back roads. He would sleep in barns, barter for his food, and return after a week with a pocketful of change. A room on the second floor of the farmhouse was always full of cases marked in the trade name of a cough syrup or a tonic. Everyone in the family sniffed up drops of Quaker Oil to stop sneezing, or ate a few drops on a lump of sugar for coughing.

Washington worked hard at tending his trees and garden and animals, and when he was through with his chores he invented more work for himself. He spent considerable time and energy at what I could only call his hobby. He moved big rocks. His ingenuity, which was always providing him with the creation of new, usually trivial tools (tools which took him four days to make and which simplified a fifteen-minute job), invented a massive instrument of three tall pine logs and an arrangement of pulleys. It looked like the tripod of a camera, but the camera would have been as big as a Model A. By means of this engine, he was able to move huge rocks; I don't know how he moved the whole contraption after the rock was lifted, though when I was a boy I must have heard detailed descriptions of a hundred rock-moves. (I was another who learned to shut the door between his ears and his brain.) He moved any rock for whose displacement he could find an excuse: small boulders that obstructed his fields; rocks near the house whose appearance offended him; rocks beside the road into which a car might sometime, possibly, crash; rocks, even, in the way of other people's cows in other people's pastures. When he was old and couldn't use the machine any more, it weathered beside the front door of his shack, and when he died someone took it away for the pine.

It was the cows he was thinking of, not the farmers, when he moved rocks in a pasture. However seriously he meant it, he often indicated that, except for his family and one or two others, humanity was morally inferior to animals; at least to the animals which were, like his family, his own creatures. He had developed a gorgeous line of cattle, out of a combination of devotion and shrewd trading. It was when I knew him that he had Phoebe, the last beast that he truly loved. Phoebe was a Holstein, a prodigy among milkers and the only cow in the world who thought she was a collie dog. Treated like a house pet from birth, she acted like one with Washington. She came frisking to him when he called her, romped with him, and all but whined when she couldn't follow him into the shack and curl her great bulk at his feet. Washington fed her apples and peas in the pod while he ate stale bread. She slept on the other side of a plank wall from him, so that he could hear any irregularity in her breathing. He washed her every day. When she was old and lame, Washington invented a rig like his rock-mover to help her stand or lie down. He nursed her when she was sick, and he was caressing her when she died.

My grandfather told me about an earlier pet, Old Duke the ox. Washington taught Old Duke to shake hands and roll over. He made a cart and a sled which Old Duke could pull, and it would take him a whole forenoon to drive the two and a half miles from his shack to the farmhouse. The only time Washington ever showed romantic interest in a woman was when a young girl named Esther Dodge helped out at the farm one harvest. Washington paid court by asking Esther, a pretty red-cheeked country girl as my mother remembers her, to go for a ride behind Old Duke. Esther would only go if the girls, my ten-year-old mother and her younger sister Caroline, could come along, and they giggled all the way.

When Washington was seventy-eight, Anson Buck found him in a coma one morning when he came to deliver a package on his R.F.D. route. Anson carried him into the back seat and drove fourteen miles to the hospital at Franklin, where they operated. When he recovered, he went back to his shack. One day the following December, my grandmother made some mince pies and decided to send one to Wash. She flagged down a young lumberman as he passed by in his blue 1934 Chevrolet and asked him to leave it off on his way up New Canada to work. He was back almost as soon as he left, saying, "He's looney. Old Wash is looney." After Great-Aunt Nannie, no such announcement was liable to surprise my grandmother. She called "Yoo-hoo" to the barn and told my grandfather what had happened. The lumberman drove them to the shack.

They found Washington sitting on the floor of his cabin between his sleeping chair and his cold stove, which my grandfather said hadn't been lit all night. Washington didn't seem to notice that they were there but kept on talking as they had heard him talk before they entered. What he said was incoherent at first, but they could tell that it was about building a road, about white hogs and about two ladies. He allowed himself to be helped over the thick snow into the Model A and driven back to the house.

Washington told his story for many days, over and over, until my grandparents finally understood its sequence. My grandfather told me all about it the next summer. The night before he was found, Wash said, he took a walk to look at a timber lot of my grandfather's north of his shack. (His legs were so bad that he never walked any farther than his well that winter; the timber was three-quarters of a mile away.) When he got there he saw a whole crowd of people working, though it was nearly dark, and they were cutting a big new road. They had bulldozers, which were white, and a big herd of white horses. He walked up to some of the people and tried to talk to them, but they acted as if they couldn't see him, and they were jabbering in a language he couldn't make out, but it wasn't Canuck. He walked away from the crowd and climbed a little rise, and when he looked down on the other side of the rise to a cleared field he saw about a hundred hogs, all pure white. In front of them were the biggest sow and the biggest boar he had ever seen, both pure white, and they were mating. Washington started to walk down the hill and he stubbed his boot on the nose of a horse that was sticking up through the snow. He and the horse fell in the snow, down and down, until the people lifted them up on the huge piece of chicken wire that was underneath the snow. Then two women among the people took him back to his cabin and stayed there all night with him. He watched, all night long, the tips of their hats against the background of starlight from the cracks in the cabin walls. Though he asked them questions, they never answered.

The doctor came and listened to Washington and gave him morphine. When he woke up he seemed fine except that he kept on with his story. My grandfather told him that there was no road going into his timber lot, and Washington was only indignant. After a week he began to ask visitors about the road, and they all told him there wasn't any, and he stopped telling the story. In the spring he paid a boy with a flivver to drive him past the place so that he could see with his own eyes.

He never had delusions again. Perhaps he had left his cabin for water and had fallen in the snow when his legs failed him. Perhaps he had crawled for an hour in pain through all that whiteness back to his shack where he had talked to the boxes all night. By April he was back at his cabin again, and that summer he was eighty years old.

He died in a state nursing home. My grandfather and I went to see him a month before he died, and his cheeks were flushed above the white beard, and his eyes shone while he preformed his monologue. He joked with us and showed us the sores on his legs. He displayed me to his nurses and to the silent old men in the room with him. It was a little like all the other times I had met him, yet seeing him ready to die I was all the more impressed by the waste of him —the energy, the ingenuity, the strength to do what he wanted— as he lay frail and bearded in a nightgown provided by the legislature. The waste that he hated, I thought, was through him like blood in his veins. He had saved nails and wasted life. He had lived alone, but if he was a hermit he was neither religious nor philosophical. His fanaticisms, which might have been creative, were as petulant as his break from the church. I felt that he was intelligent, or it would not have mattered, but I had no evidence to support my conviction. His only vision was a delusion of white hogs. He worked hard all his life at being himself, but there were no principles to examine when his life was over. It was as if there had been a moral skeleton which had lacked the flesh of the intellect and the blood of experience. The life that he could recall totally was not worth recalling; it was a box of string too short to be saved.

Standing beside him in the nursing home, I saw ahead for one moment into the residue, five years from then, of Washington Woodward's life: the shack has caved in and his straightened nails have rusted into the dirt of Ragged Mountain; though the rocks stay where he moved them, no one knows how they got there; his animals are dead and their descendants have made bad connections; his apple trees produce small and sour fruits; the best built hayracks rot under rotting sheds; in New Hampshire the frost tumbles the cleverest wall; those who knew him best are dead or dying, and his gestures have assumed the final waste of irrelevance.

THOMAS BABINGTON MACAULAY
Boswell[1]

The Life of Johnson is assuredly a great, a very great work. Homer is not more decidedly the first of heroic poets, Shakespeare is not more decidedly the first of dramatists, Demosthenes is not more decidedly the first of orators, than Boswell is the first of biographers. He has no second. He has distanced all his competitors so decidedly that it is not worth while to place them. Eclipse is first, and the rest nowhere.

We are not sure that there is in the whole history of the human intellect so strange a phenomenon as this book. Many of the greatest men that ever lived have written biography. Boswell was one of the smallest men that ever lived, and he has beaten them all. He was, if we are to give any credit to his own account or to the united testimony of all who knew him, a man of the meanest and feeblest intellect. Johnson described him as a fellow who had missed his only chance of immortality by not having been alive when the Dunciad was written. Beauclerk used his name as a proverbial expression for a bore. He was the laughing-stock of the whole of that brilliant society which has owed to him the greater part of its fame. He was always laying himself at the feet of some eminent man, and begging to be spit upon and trampled upon. He was always earning some ridiculous nickname, and then "binding it as a crown unto him," not merely in metaphor, but literally. He exhibited himself, at the Shakespeare Jubilee, to all the crowd which filled Stratford-on-Avon, with a placard round his hat bearing the inscription of Corsica Bos-

1. From a review of Croker's edition (1831) of Boswell's *Life of Johnson*.

well.[2] In his Tour he proclaimed to all the world that at Edinburgh he was known by the appellation of Paoli Boswell. Servile and impertinent, shallow and pedantic, a bigot and a sot, bloated with family pride, and eternally blustering about the dignity of a born gentleman, yet stooping to be a tale-bearer, an eavesdropper, a common butt in the taverns of London, so curious to know everybody who was talked about, that, Tory and high Churchman as he was, he maneuvered, we have been told, for an introduction to Tom Paine, so vain of the most childish distinctions, that when he had been to court, he drove to the office where his book was printing without changing his clothes, and summoned all the printer's devils to admire his new ruffles and sword; such was this man, and such he was content and proud to be. Everything which another man would have hidden, everything the publication of which would have made another man hang himself, was matter of gay and clamorous exultation to his weak and diseased mind. What silly things he said, what bitter retorts he provoked, how at one place he was troubled with evil presentiments which came to nothing, how at another place, on waking from a drunken doze, he read the prayerbook and took a hair of the dog that had bitten him, how he went to see men hanged and came away maudlin, how he added five hundred pounds to the fortune of one of his babies because she was not scared at Johnson's ugly face, how he was frightened out of his wits at sea, and how the sailors quieted him as they would have quieted a child, how tipsy he was at Lady Cork's one evening and how much his merriment annoyed the ladies, how impertinent he was to the Duchess of Argyle and with what stately contempt she put down his impertinence, how Colonel Macleod sneered to his face at his impudent obtrusiveness, how his father and the very wife of his bosom laughed and fretted at his fooleries, all these things he proclaimed to all the world, as if they had been subjects for pride and ostentatious rejoicing. All the caprices of his temper, all the illusions of his vanity, all his hypochondriac whimsies, all his castles in the air, he displayed with a cool self-complacency, a perfect unconsciousness that he was making a fool of himself, to which it is impossible to find a parallel in the whole history of mankind. He has used many people ill; but assuredly he has used nobody so ill as himself.

That such a man should have written one of the best books in the world is strange enough. But this is not all. Many persons who have conducted themselves foolishly in active life, and whose conversation has indicated no superior powers of mind, have left us valuable works. Goldsmith was very justly described by one of his contemporaries as an inspired idiot, and by another as a being

Who wrote like an angel, and talked like poor Poll.

2. Boswell traveled on the Continent in 1765-1766 and was introduced to General Paoli, leader of the resistance to French power in Corsica. Boswell sympathized with the Corsican cause and paraded his sentiments.

La Fontaine was in society a mere simpleton. His blunders would not come in amiss among the stories of Hierocles.[3] But these men attained literary eminence in spite of their weaknesses. Boswell attained it by reason of his weaknesses. If he had not been a great fool, he would never have been a great writer. Without all the qualities which made him the jest and the torment of those among whom he lived, without the officiousness, the inquisitiveness, the effrontery, the toad-eating,[4] the insensibility to all reproof, he never could have produced so excellent a book. He was a slave, proud of his servitude, a Paul Pry, convinced that his own curiosity and garrulity were virtues, an unsafe companion who never scrupled to repay the most liberal hospitality by the basest violation of confidence, a man without delicacy, without shame, without sense enough to know when he was hurting the feelings of others or when he was exposing himself to derision; and because he was all this, he has, in an important department of literature,[5] immeasurably surpassed such writers as Tacitus, Clarendon, Alfieri, and his own idol Johnson.

Of the talents which ordinarily raise men to eminence as writers, Boswell had absolutely none. There is not in all his books a single remark of his own on literature, politics, religion, or society, which is not either commonplace or absurd. His dissertations on hereditary gentility, on the slave-trade, and on the entailing of landed estates, may serve as examples. To say that these passages are sophistical would be to pay them an extravagant compliment. They have no pretence to argument, or even to meaning. He has reported innumerable observations made by himself in the course of conversation. Of those observations we do not remember one which is above the intellectual capacity of a boy of fifteen. He has printed many of his own letters, and in these letters he is always ranting or twaddling. Logic, eloquence, wit, taste, all those things which are generally considered as making a book valuable, were utterly wanting to him. He had, indeed, a quick observation and a retentive memory. These qualities, if he had been a man of sense and virtue, would scarcely of themselves have sufficed to make him conspicuous; but, because he was a dunce, a parasite, and a coxcomb, they have made him immortal.

Those parts of his book which, considered abstractedly, are most utterly worthless, are delightful when we read them as illustrations of the character of the writer. Bad in themselves, they are good dramatically, like the nonsense of Justice Shallow, the clipped English of Dr. Caius, or the misplaced consonants of Fluellen.[6] Of all confessors, Boswell is the most candid. Other men who have pretended to lay open their own hearts, Rousseau, for example, and Lord Byron,

---

3. A fourth-century Roman versifier, author of *Facetiae (Jests)*.
4. Obsequiousness, servile flattery.
5. Biography.

6. Comic characters in Shakespeare's *Henry IV Part Two*, *The Merry Wives of Windsor*, and *Henry V*, respectively.

have evidently written with a constant view to effect, and are to be then most distrusted when they seem to be most sincere. There is scarcely any man who would not rather accuse himself of great crimes and of dark and tempestuous passions than proclaim all his little vanities and wild fancies. It would be easier to find a person who would avow actions like those of Caesar Borgia or Danton, than one who would publish a daydream like those of Alnaschar and Malvolio.[7] Those weaknesses which most men keep covered up in the most secret places of the mind, not to be disclosed to the eye of friendship or of love, were precisely the weaknesses which Boswell paraded before all the world. He was perfectly frank, because the weakness of his understanding and the tumult of his spirits prevented him from knowing when he made himself ridiculous. His book resembles nothing so much as the conversation of the inmates of the Palace of Truth.

His face is great; and it will, we have no doubt, be lasting, but it is fame of a peculiar kind, and indeed marvelously resembles infamy. We remember no other case in which the world has made so great a distinction between a book and its author. In general, the book and the author are considered as one. To admire the book is to admire the author. The case of Boswell is an exception, we think the only exception, to this rule. His work is universally allowed to be interesting, instructive, eminently original: yet it has brought him nothing but contempt. All the world reads it: all the world delights in it: yet we do not remember ever to have read or ever to have heard any expression of respect and admiration for the man to whom we owe so much instruction and amusement. While edition after edition of his book was coming forth, his son, as Mr. Croker tells us, was ashamed of it, and hated to hear it mentioned. This feeling was natural and reasonable. Sir Alexander saw that, in proportion to the celebrity of the work, was the degradation of the author. The very editors of this unfortunate gentleman's books have forgotten their allegiance, and, like those Puritan casuists who took arms by the authority of the king against his person, have attacked the writer while doing homage to the writings. Mr. Croker, for example, has published two thousand five hundred notes on the life of Johnson, and yet scarcely ever mentions the biographer whose performance he has taken such pains to illustrate without some expression of contempt.

An ill-natured man Boswell certainly was not. Yet the malignity of the most malignant satirist could scarcely cut deeper than his thoughtless loquacity. Having himself no sensibility to derision and contempt, he took it for granted that all others were equally callous.

7. Caesar Borgia was a Renaissance prince, infamous for treachery and cruelty, and Danton was a leader in the Terror during the French Revolution. Malvolio, a character in Shakespeare's *Twelfth Night*, and Alnaschar, a figure in the *Arabian Nights*, are both noted for foolish vanity and ludicrous fantasies.

He was not ashamed to exhibit himself to the whole world as a common spy, a common tattler, a humble companion without the excuse of poverty, and to tell a hundred stories of his own pertness and folly, and of the insults which his pertness and folly brought upon him. It was natural that he should show little discretion in cases in which the feelings or the honor of others might be concerned. No man, surely, ever published such stories respecting persons whom he professed to love and revere. He would infallibly have made his hero as contemptible as he has made himself, had not his hero really possessed some moral and intellectual qualities of a very high order. The best proof that Johnson was really an extraordinary man is that his character, instead of being degraded, has, on the whole, been decidedly raised by a work in which all his vices and weaknesses are exposed more unsparingly than they ever were exposed by Churchill or by Kenrick.[8]

8. The one a satiric poet and the other an irritable scholar, contemporaries of Johnson who attacked him in verse and biography.

QUESTIONS FOR STUDY, DISCUSSION, AND WRITING

1. *In what ways does Macaulay use contrast, antithesis, to carry out his characterization of Boswell? What major contrast is central to the sketch, its organizing principle? With what other writers is Boswell compared, and to what purposes? To what extent and in what particular ways does antithesis appear in the construction of the paragraphs?*
2. *Indicate several instances of repetition of sentence structure. What effects does Macaulay seek with such repetition? How does he vary from it, and with what results?*
3. *What, according to Macaulay, are the defects in Boswell's personal character that contribute to the excellence of his writing?*
4. *What particulars of Macaulay's characterization are discernible in these two extracts from Boswell's* Life of Johnson:

The heterogeneous composition of human nature was remarkably exemplified in Johnson. His liberality in giving his money to persons in distress was extraordinary. Yet there lurked about him a propensity to paltry saving. One day I owned to him that "I was occasionally troubled with a fit of narrowness." "Why, sir," said he, "so am I. But I do not tell it." He has now and then borrowed a shilling of me; and when I asked for it again, seemed to be rather out of humor. A droll little circumstance once occurred: As if he meant to reprimand my minute exactness as a creditor, he thus addressed me—"Boswell, lend me sixpence—*not to be repaid.*"

I have no minute of any interview with Johnson till Thursday, May 15th, when I find what follows:

BOSWELL. "I wish much to be in Parliament, sir." JOHNSON. "Why, sir, unless you come resolved to support any administration, you would be the worse for being in Parliament, because you would be obliged to live more expensively." BOSWELL. "Perhaps, sir, I should be the less happy for being in Parliament. I never would sell my vote, and I should be vexed if things went wrong." JOHNSON. "That's cant, sir. It would not vex you more in the house than in the gallery; public affairs vex no man." BOSWELL. "Have not they vexed yourself a little, sir? Have not you been vexed by all the turbulence of this reign, and by that absurd vote in the House of Commons, 'That the influence of the Crown has increased, is increasing, and ought to be diminished?'" JOHNSON. "Sir, I have never slept an hour less nor eat an ounce less meat. I would have knocked the factious dogs on the head, to be sure; but I was not vexed." BOSWELL. "I declare, sir, upon my honor, I did imagine I was vexed, and took a pride in it; but it was, perhaps, cant; for I own I neither ate less nor slept less." JOHNSON. "My dear friend, clear your *mind* of cant. You may *talk* as other people do; you may say to a man, 'Sir, I am your most humble servant.' You are *not* his most humble servant. You may say, 'These are bad times; it is a melancholy thing to be reserved to such times.' You don't mind the times. You tell a man, 'I am sorry you had such bad weather the last day of your journey, and were so much wet.' You don't care sixpence whether he is wet or dry. You may *talk* in this manner; it is a mode of talking in society; but don't *think* foolishly."

THE BOOK OF SAMUEL

Thou Art the Man[1]

And it came to pass, after the year was expired, at the time when kings go forth to battle, that David sent Joab, and his servants with him, and all Israel; and they destroyed the children of Ammon, and beseiged Rabbah. But David tarried still at Jerusalem.

And it came to pass in an eveningtide, that David arose from off his bed, and walked upon the roof of the king's house: and from the roof he saw a woman washing herself; and the woman was very beautiful to look upon. And David sent and enquired after the woman. And one said, Is not this Bathsheba, the daughter of Eliam, the wife of Uriah the Hittite? And David sent messengers, and took her; and she came in unto him, and he lay with her; for she was purified from her uncleanness: and she returned unto her house. And the woman conceived, and sent and told David, and said, I am with child.

And David sent to Joab, saying, Send me Uriah the Hittite. And Joab sent Uriah to David. And when Uriah was come unto him, David demanded of him how Joab did, and how the people did, and how the war prospered. And David said to Uriah, Go down to thy house, and wash thy feet. And Uriah departed out of the king's

1. II Samuel xi and 1-xii. 7.

house, and there followed him a mess of meat from the king. But Uriah slept at the door of the king's house with all the servants of his lord, and went not down to his house. And when they had told David, saying, Uriah went not down unto his house, David said unto Uriah, Camest thou not from thy journey? why then didst thou not go down unto thine house? And Uriah said unto David, The ark, and Israel, and Judah, abide in tents; and my lord Joab, and the servants of my lord, are encamped in the open fields; shall I then go into mine house, to eat and to drink, and to lie with my wife? as thou livest, and as thy soul liveth, I will not do this thing. And David said to Uriah, Tarry here to day also, and to morrow I will let thee depart. So Uriah abode in Jerusalem that day, and the morrow. And when David had called him, he did eat and drink before him; and he made him drunk: and at even he went out to lie on his bed with the servants of his lord, but went not down to his house.

And it came to pass in the morning, that David wrote a letter to Joab, and sent it by the hand of Uriah. And he wrote in the letter, saying, Set ye Uriah in the forefront of the hottest battle, and retire ye from him, that he may be smitten, and die. And it came to pass, when Joab observed the city, that he assigned Uriah unto a place where he knew that valiant men were. And the men of the city went out, and fought with Joab: and there fell some of the people of the servants of David; and Uriah the Hittite died also. Then Joab sent and told David all the things concerning the war; and charged the messenger, saying, When thou hast made an end of telling the matters of the war unto the king, and if so be that the king's wrath arise, and he say unto thee, Wherefore approached ye so nigh unto the city when ye did fight? knew ye not that they would shoot from the wall? Who smote Abimelech the son of Jerubbesheth? did not a woman cast a piece of millstone upon him from the wall, that he died in Thebez? why went ye nigh the wall? then say thou, Thy servant Uriah the Hittite is dead also.

So the messenger went, and came and shewed David all that Joab had sent him for. And the messenger said unto David, Surely the men prevailed against us, and came out unto us into the field, and we were upon them even unto the entering of the gate. And the shooters shot from off the wall upon thy servants; and some of the king's servants be dead, and thy servant Uriah the Hittite is dead also. Then David said unto the messenger, Thus shalt thou say unto Joab, Let not this thing displease thee, for the sword devoureth one as well as another: make thy battle more strong against the city, and overthrow it: and encourage thou him.

And when the wife of Uriah heard that Uriah her husband was dead, she mourned for her husband. And when the mourning was past, David sent and fetched her to his house, and she became his wife, and bare him a son. But the thing that David had done displeased the Lord.

And the Lord sent Nathan unto David. And he came unto him, and said unto him, There were two men in one city; the one rich, and the other poor. The rich man had exceeding many flocks and herds: but the poor man had nothing, save one little ewe lamb, which he had bought and nourished up: and it grew up together with him, and with his children; it did eat of his own meat, and drank of his own cup, and lay in his bosom, and was unto him as a daughter. And there came a traveller unto the rich man, and he spared to take of his own flock and of his own herd, to dress for the wayfaring man that was come unto him; but took the poor man's lamb, and dressed it for the man that was come to him. And David's anger was greatly kindled against the man; and he said to Nathan, As the Lord liveth, the man that hath done this thing shall surely die: and he shall restore the lamb fourfold, because he did this thing, and because he had no pity.

And Nathan said to David, Thou art the man.

EDITH HAMILTON
Xenophon[1]

To turn from Thucydides to Xenophon is a pleasant, but surprising, experience. The lives of the two men overlapped, although Xenophon was much the younger. Both were Athenians and soldiers; both lived through the war and saw the defeat of Athens.[2] Yet they inhabited different worlds; worlds so different, they seem to have no connection with each other. Thucydides' world was a place racked and ruined and disintegrated by war, where hope was gone and happiness was unimaginable. Xenophon's was a cheerful place with many nice people in it and many agreeable ways of passing the time. There was hunting, for instance. He writes a charming essay about it: of the delights of the early start, in winter over the snow, to track the hare with hounds as keen for the chase as their masters; in spring "when the fields are so full of wildflowers, the scent for the dogs is poor"; or a deer may be the quarry, first-rate sport; or a wild boar, dangerous, but delightfully exciting. Such rewards, too, as the hunter has: he keeps strong and young far longer than other men; he is braver, and even more trustworthy—although why that should be our author does not trouble to explain. A hunting man just is better than one who does not hunt and that is all there is to it. Ask any fox-hunting squire in English literature.

1. Chapter 10 in *The Greek Way*, 1930. The preceding chapter deals with Thucydides.

2. Sparta conquered Athens in 404 B.C., after twenty-seven years of war.

Hunting is a good, healthy, honest pleasure, and a young man is lucky if he takes to it. It will save him from city vices and incline him to love virtue.

At what period in Thucydides' history were the Athenians going a hunting, one wonders. Did that man of tragic vision ever watch a hunt? Did he ever listen to stories about the size of the boar that had been killed? Was he ever at a dinner-party where any stories were told over the wine? The imagination fails before the attempt to put him there, even if Socrates had been a guest as he was at a dinner Xenophon went to and reported. It followed more closely, we must suppose, the fashion of the day for such parties than did Plato's famous supper at Agathon's house, where conversation was the only entertainment. Agathon's guests were the elite of Athens and wanted lofty discourse for their diversion. The guests at Xenophon's dinner, except for himself and Socrates, were ordinary people who would quickly have been bored by the speeches in the *Symposium*. But no one could possibly have been bored at the party Xenophon describes. It was from first to last a most enjoyable occasion. There was some good talk at the table, of course—Socrates would see to that; and now and then the discourse turned to matters sober enough to have engaged even Thucydides' attention. But for the most part, it was lighthearted as befitted a good dinner. There was a great deal of laughter when, for instance, Socrates defended his flat nose as being preferable to a straight one, and when a man newly married refused the onions. There was music, too, and Socrates obliged with a song, to the delighted amusement of the others. A pleasant interlude was afforded by a happy boy, and Xenophon's description reveals his power of keen observation and quick sympathy. The lad had been invited to come with his father, a great honor, but he had just won the chief contest for boys at the principal Athenian festival. He sat beside his father, regarded very kindly by the company. They tried to draw him out, but he was too shy to speak a word until someone asked him what he was most proud of, and someone else cried, "Oh, his victory, of course." At this he blushed and blurted out, "No—I'm not." All were delighted to have him finally say something and they encouraged him. "No? Of what are you proudest, then?" "Of my father," he said, and pressed closer to him. It is an attractive picture of Athenian boyhood in the brilliant, corrupt city where Thucydides could find nothing good.

As was usual, entertainment had been provided for the guests. A girl did some diverting and surprising feats. The best turn was when she danced and kept twelve hoops whirling in the air, catching and throwing them in perfect time with the music. Watching her with great attention Socrates declared that he was forced to conclude, "Not only from this girl, my friends, but from other things, too, that a woman's talent is not at all inferior to a man's." A pleasant thing to know, he added, if any of them wanted to teach something to his wife. A murmur passed around the table: "Xanthippe"; and one of the company ventured, "Why do not you, then, teach good temper to yours?" "Because," Socrates retorted, "my great aim in life is to get on well with people, and I chose Xanthippe because I knew if I could get on with her I could with anyone." The explanation was unanimously voted satisfactory.

A little desultory talk followed that finally turned upon exercise, and Socrates said, to the intense delight of all, that he danced every morning in order to reduce. "It's true," one of the others broke in. "I found him doing it and I thought he'd gone mad. But he talked to me and I tell you he convinced me. When I went home—will you believe it? I did not dance; I don't know how; but I waved my arms about." There was a general outcry, "O, Socrates, let us see you, too."

By this time the dancing girl was turning somersaults and leaping headfirst into a circle formed by swords. This displeased Socrates. "No doubt it is a wonderful performance," he conceded. "But pleasure? In watching a lovely young creature exposing herself to to danger like that? I don't find it agreeable." The others agreed, and a pantomime between the girl and her partner, a graceful boy, was quickly substituted: "The Rescue of the Forsaken Ariadne by Bacchus." It was performed to admiration. Not a word was spoken by the two actors, but such was their skill that by gestures and dancing they expressed all the events and emotions of the story with perfect clarity to the spectators. "They seemed not actors who had learned their parts, but veritable lovers." With that the party broke up, Socrates walking home with the nice boy and his father. Of himself Xenophon says nothing throughout the essay except at the very beginning when he explains that he was one of the guests and decided to give an account of the dinner because he thought what honorable and virtuous men did in their hours of amusement had its importance. One can only regret that so few Greek writers agreed with him.

Another pleasant picture he gives of domestic Athens has an interest not only as a period piece but because it shows a glimpse of that person so elusive in all periods, the woman of ancient Greece. A man lately married talks about his wife. She was not yet fifteen, he says, and had been admirably brought up "to see as little, and hear as little, and ask as few questions as possible." The young husband had the delightful prospect of inscribing on this blank page whatever he chose. There was no doubt in his mind what he should start with. "Of course," Xenophon reports him as saying, "I had to give her time to grow used to me; but when we had reached a point where we could talk easily together, I told her she had great responsibilities. I took up with her what I expected of her as a housekeeper. She said wonderingly, 'But my mother told me I was of no consequence, only you. All I had to do, she said, was to be sensible and careful.' " Her husband was quick to seize the cue. Kindly but weightily he explained to the young thing that her life henceforth was to be a perpetual exercise in carefulness and good sense. She would have to keep stock of everything brought into the house; oversee all the work that went on; superintend the spinning, the weaving, the making of clothes; train the new servants and nurse the sick. At this point the girl's spirits seem to have risen a little for she murmured that she thought she would like to take care of sick people. But her husband kept steadily on. Of course she would stay indoors. He himself enjoyed starting the day with a long ride into the country—very healthful as well as very pleasant. But for a woman to be roaming abroad was most discreditable. However, she could get plenty of exercise, at the loom, or making beds, or supervising the maids. Kneading bread was said to be as good exercise as one could find. All that sort of thing would improve her health and help her complexion—very important in keeping herself attractive to her husband. Artificial substitutes were no good: husbands always knew when their wives painted, and they never liked it; white and red stuff on the face was disgusting when a man was aware of it, as a husband must be. The essay ends happily with the declaration, "Ever since, my wife has done in all respects just as I taught her."

It is as hard to fit the dutiful young wife and the happily important husband and their immaculate household into Thucydides' Athens as it is to put Thucydides himself at the table beside Socrates watching the girl with the hoops. There is no use trying to make a composite picture out of Xenophon and Thucydides. The only result would be to lose the truth on each side. Thucydides' truth was immeasurably more profound. In life's uneasy panorama he could discover unchanging verities. He could probe to the depths in the never varying evils of human nature. In Sparta's victory over Athens he saw what the decision of war was worth as a test of values, and that war would forever decide matters of highest importance to the world if men continued to be governed by greed and the passion for power. What he knew was truth indeed, with no shadow of turning and inexpressibly sad.

But Xenophon's truths were true, too. There were pleasant parties and well-ordered homes and nice lads and jolly hunters in war-wracked Greece. History never takes account of such pleasantries, but they have their importance. The Greek world would have gone insane if Thucydides' picture had been all-inclusive. Of course, Xenophon's mind was on an altogether lower level. Eternal truths were not in his line. The average man in Periclean Athens can be seen through Xenophon's eyes as he cannot be through Thucydides' or Plato's. In Xenophon there are no dark, greed-ridden schemers such as Thucydides saw in Athens; neither are there any Platonic idealists. The people in his books are ordinary, pleasant folk, not given to extremes in any direction and convincingly real, just as Xenophon himself is. Here is a picture he draws of one of them:

He said that he had long realized that "unless we know what we ought to do and try our best to do it God has decided that we have no right to be prosperous. If we are wise and do take pains he makes some of us prosperous, although not all. So to start with, I reverence him and then do all I can to be worthy when I pray to be given health and strength of body and the respect of the Athenians and the affection of my friends and an increase of wealth—with honor, and safety in war—with honor."

These eminently sensible aspirations strike a true Greek note. The man who uttered them and the man who recorded them were typical Athenian gentlemen. What Xenophon was comes through clearly in his writings—a man of good will and good sense, kindly, honest, pious; intelligent, too, interested in ideas, not the purely speculative kind, rather those that could be made to work toward some rational, practical good. His friends were like him, they were representative Athenians of the better sort.

In another way, too, Xenophon represented his times. His life shows the widely separated interests and varied occupations which made the Periclean Athenians different from other men. As a young man he came to Athens from his father's estate in Attica, to be educated out of country ways; he joined the circle around Socrates, where young and old alike were, as Plato puts it, "possessed and maddened with the passion for knowledge," or, as he himself states, "wanting to become good and fine men and learn their duty to their family, their servants, their friends and their country." The Socrates he listened to did not, like Plato's Socrates, discourse upon "the glorious sights of justice and wisdom and truth the enraptured soul beholds, shining in pure light," or anything like that. This Socrates was a soberly thinking man, distinguished for common sense, and in Xenophon's record of him, the *Memorabilia*, what he chiefly does for his young friends is to give them practical advice on how to manage their affairs. A budding officer is told the way to make his men efficient soldiers; a conscientious lad, burdened with many female relatives, is shown how they can be taught to support themselves, and so on, while Xenophon listens entranced by such serviceable wisdom. How long Xenophon lived this delightful life of conversation is not known, but he was still young when he left it for the very opposite kind of life, that of a soldier. He was truly a man of his times, when poets and dramatists and historians were soldiers and generals and explorers.

In his campaigns he traveled far and saw the great world. He also got enough money to live on for the rest of his days by capturing and holding for ransom a rich Persian noble. Then he went back to Greece—but to Sparta, not Athens. Curiously, although he has left in his *Anabasis* an unsurpassed picture of what the democratic ideal can accomplish, he was himself no democrat. He came of a noble family and all his life kept the convictions of his class. He always loved Sparta and distrusted Athens. Even so, in the great crisis of his life, when he and his companions faced imminent destruction, he acted like a true Athenian, who knew what freedom was and what free men could achieve. When the Ten Thousand elected him general in order to get them out of their terrible predicament, he never tried out any Spartan ideas on them. He became as democratic a leader as there could possibly be of the freest democracy conceivable. The fact that the astonishing success which resulted had no permanent effect upon his point of view should not be surprising; a converted aristocrat is a rare figure in history. Xenophon never went back to Athens; indeed, a few years after his return to Greece he was fighting on the Spartan side against her and was declared an exile. The Spartans gave him an estate in the pleasant country near Olympia, where he lived for many years, riding and hunting and farming, a model country gentleman. Here he wrote a great many books on subjects as far apart as the dinner Socrates attended and the proper management of the Athenian revenues. With two or three exceptions the writings are quite pedestrian; sensible, straightforward, clearly written, but no more. There are a few sentences, however, scattered through them which show a surprising power of thought and far-reaching vision. Although, or perhaps because, he had fought much, he believed that peace should be the aim of all states. Diplomacy, he says, is the way to settle disputes, not war. He urges Athens to use her influence to maintain peace, and he suggests making Delphi a meeting place for the nations, where they can talk out their differences. "He who conquers by force," he says, "may fancy that he can continue to do so, but the only conquests that last are when men willingly submit to those who are better than themselves. The only way really to conquer a country is through generosity." The world has not yet caught up with Xenophon.

His best book, however, the book he really lives by, is on war. It is, of course, the *Anabasis*, the "Retreat of the Ten Thousand," a great story, and of great importance for our knowledge of the Greeks. No other piece of writing gives so clear a picture of Greek individualism, that instinct which was supremely characteristic of ancient Greece and decided the course of the Greek achievement. It was the cause, or the result, as one chooses to look at it, of the Greek love for freedom. A Greek had a passion for being left free to live his life in his own way. He wanted to act by himself and think for himself. It did not come natural to him to turn to others for direction; he depended upon his own sense of what was right and true. Indeed, there was no generally acknowledged source of direction anywhere in Greece except the oracles, difficult to reach and still more difficult to understand. Athens had no authoritarian church, or state either, to formulate what a man should believe and to regulate the details of how he should live. There was no agency or institution to oppose his thinking in any way he chose on anything whatsoever. As for the state, it never entered an Athenian's head that it could interfere with his private life: that it could see, for instance, that his children were taught to be patriotic, or limit the amount of liquor he could buy, or compel him to save for his old age. Everything like that a citizen of Athens had to decide himself and take full responsibility for.

The basis of the Athenian democracy was the conviction of all democracies—that the average man can be depended upon to do his duty and to use good sense in doing it. *Trust the individual* was the avowed doctrine in Athens, and expressed or unexpressed it was common to Greece. Sparta we know as the exception, and there must have been other backwaters; nevertheless, the most reactionary Greek might at any time revert to type. It is on record that Spartan soldiers abroad shouted down an unpopular officer; threw stones at a general whose orders they did not approve; in an emergency, put down incompetent leaders and acted for themselves. Even the iron discipline of Sparta could not completely eradicate the primary Greek passion for independence. "A people ruling," says Herodotus, "—the very name of it is so beautiful." In Aeschylus' play about the defeat of the Persians at Salamis, the Persian queen asks, "Who is set over the Greeks as despots?" and the proud answer is, "They are the slaves and vassals of no man." Therefore, all Greeks believed, they conquered the slave-subjects of the Persian tyrant. Free men, independent men, were always worth inexpressibly more than men submissive and controlled.

Military authorities have never advocated this point of view, but how applicable it is to soldiers, too, is shown for all time by the *Anabasis*. The Ten Thousand got back safely after one of the most perilous marches ever undertaken just because they were not a model, disciplined army but a band of enterprising individuals.

The epic of the Retreat begins in a camp beside a little town in Asia not far from Babylon. There, more than ten thousand Greeks were gathered. They had come from different places: one of the leaders was from Thessaly; another from Boeotia; the commander-in-chief was a Spartan; on his staff was a young civilian from Athens named Xenophon. They were soldiers of fortune, a typical army of mercenaries who had gone abroad because there was no hope of employment at home. Greece was not at war for the moment. A

Spartan peace was over the land. It was the summer of 401, three years after the fall of Athens.

Persia, however, was a hotbed of plots and counterplots that were bringing a revolution near. The late king's two sons were enemies, and the younger planned to take the throne from his brother. This young man was Cyrus, named for the great Cyrus, the conqueror of Babylon a hundred and fifty years earlier. His namesake is famous for one reason only: because when he marched into Persia Xenophon joined his army. If that had not happened he would be lost in the endless list of little Asiatic royalties forever fighting for no purpose of the slightest importance to the world. As it is, he lives in Xenophon's pages, gay and gallant and generous; careful for his soldiers' welfare; sharing their hardships; always first in the fighting; a great leader.

The Ten Thousand had enlisted under his banner with no clear idea of what they were to do beyond the matter of real importance, get regular pay and enough food. They earned their share of both in the next few months. They marched from the Mediterranean through sandy deserts far into Asia Minor living on the country, which generally meant a minimum of food and occasionally none at all. There was a large Asiatic contingent, a hundred thousand strong at the least, but they play very little part in the *Anabasis*. The Greeks are the real army Cyrus depends upon. As Xenophon tells the story they won the day for him when he met the king's forces. The battle of Cunaxa was a decisive victory for Cyrus. Only, he himself was dead, killed in the fighting as he struck at his brother and wounded him. With his death the reason for the expedition ceased to exist. The Asiatic forces melted away. The little Greek army was alone in the heart of Asia, in an unknown country swarming with hostile troops, with no food, no ammunition, and no notion how to get back. Soon there were no leaders either. The chief officers went to a conference with the Persians under a safe-conduct. Their return, eagerly awaited, was alarmingly delayed; and all eyes were watching for them when in the distance a man, one man all alone, was seen advancing very slowly, a Greek by his dress. They ran to meet him and caught him as he fell dying, terribly wounded. He could just gasp out that all the others were dead, assassinated by the Persians.

That was a terrible night. The Persian plan was clear. In their experience leaderless men were helpless. Kill the officers and the army would be a lot of sheep waiting to be slaughtered. The only thing wrong with the idea was that this was a Greek army.

Xenophon, all his friends dead, wandered away from the horrified camp, found a quiet spot and fell asleep. He dreamed a dream. He saw the thunderbolt of Zeus fall on his home and a great light shine forth, and he awoke with the absolute conviction that Zeus had chosen him to save the army. On fire with enthusiasm, he called a council of the under officers who had not gone to the conference. There, young and a civilian, he stood up and addressed them, hardened veterans all. He told them to throw off despair and "show some superiority to misfortune." He reminded them that they were Greeks, not to be cowed by mere Asiatics. Something of his own fire was communicated to them. He even got them laughing. One man who stubbornly objected to everything and would talk only of their desperate case, Xenophon advised reducing to the ranks and using to carry baggage; he would make an excellent mule, he told his appreciative audience. They elected him unanimously to lead the rear, and then had the general assembly sounded so that he could address the soldiers. He gave them a rousing talk. Things were black and might seem hopeless to others, but they were Greeks, free men, living in free states, born of free ancestors. The enemy they had to face were slaves, ruled by despots, ignorant of the very idea of freedom. "They think we are defeated because our officers are dead and our good old general Clearchus. But we will show them that they have turned us all into generals. Instead of one Clearchus they have ten thousand Clearchuses against them." He won them over and that very morning the ten thousand generals started the march back.

They had only enemies around them, not one man they could trust as a guide, and there were no maps in those days and no compasses. One thing only they were sure of: they could not go back by the way they had come. Wherever they had passed the food was exhausted. They were forced to turn northward and follow the course of the rivers up to the mountains where the Tigris and the Euphrates rise, through what is to-day the wilds of Kurdistan and the highlands of Georgia and Armenia, all inhabited by savage mountain tribes. These were their only source of provisions. If they could not conquer their strongholds and get at their stores they would starve. Mountain warfare of the most desperate character awaited them, waged by an enemy who knew every foot of the country, who watched for them on the heights above narrow valleys and rolled masses of rocks down on them, whose sharpshooters attacked them hidden in thickets on the opposite bank of some torrential icy river while the Greeks searched desperately for a ford. As they advanced ever higher into the hills, they found bitter cold and deep snow, and their equipment was designed for the Arabian desert.

Probably anyone to-day considering their plight would conclude that their only chance of safety would lie in maintaining strict discipline, abiding by their excellent military tradition, and obeying their leaders implicitly. The chief leaders, however, were dead; mountain fighting against savages was not a part of their military tradition; above all, being Greeks, they did not incline to blind obedience in desperate circumstances. In point of fact, the situation which confronted them could be met only by throwing away the rules and regulations that had been drilled into them. What they needed was to draw upon all the intelligence and power of initiative every man of them possessed.

They were merely a band of mercenaries, but they were Greek mercenaries and the average of intelligence was high. The question of discipline among ten thousand generals would otherwise certainly have been serious and might well have proved fatal, but, no less than our westward-faring pioneer ancestors who resembled them, they understood the necessity of acting together. Not a soldier but knew what it would mean to have disorder added to the perils they faced. Their discipline was a voluntary product, but it worked. When the covered wagons made their way across America any leader that arose did so by virtue of superior ability, which men in danger always follow willingly. The leaders of the Ten Thousand got their posts in the same way. The army was keen to perceive a man's quality and before long the young civilian Xenophon was practically in command.

Each man, however, had a share in the responsibility. Once when Xenophon sent out a reconnoitering force to find a pass through the mountains, he told them, "Every one of you is the leader." At any crisis an assembly was held, the situation explained and full discussion invited. "Whoever has a better plan, let him speak. Our aim is the safety of all and that is the concern of all." The case was argued back and forth, then put to the vote and the majority decided. Incompetent leaders were brought to trial. The whole army sat as judges and acquitted or punished. It reads like a caricature, but there has never been a better vindication of the average man when he is up against it. The ten thousand judges, which the ten thousand generals turned into on occasion, never, so far as Xenophon's record goes, passed an unjust sentence. On one occasion Xenophon was called to account for striking a soldier. " 'I own that I did so,' he said. 'I told him to carry to camp a wounded man, but I found him burying him still alive. I have struck others, too, half-frozen men who were sinking down in the snow to die, worn-out men lagging behind where the enemy might catch them. A blow would often make them get up and hasten. Those I have given offense to now accuse me. But those I have helped, in battle, on the march, in cold, in sickness, none of them speak up. They do not remember. And yet surely it is better—and happier, too— to remember a man's good deeds than his evil deeds.' Upon this," the narrative goes on, "the assembly, calling the past to mind, rose up and Xenophon was acquitted."

This completely disarming speech for the defense shows how well

Xenophon knew the way to manage men. There is wounded feeling in his words, but no anger, no resentment, above all, no self-righteousness. Those listening were convinced by his frankness of his honesty; reminded, without a suggestion of boasting, how great his services had been; and given to understand that far from claiming to be faultless, he appealed to them only to remember his deserts as well as his mistakes. He understood his audience and the qualities a leader must have, at least any leader who would lead Greeks. In a book he wrote on the education of the great Cyrus he draws a picture of the ideal general which, absurd as it is when applied to an Oriental monarch, shows to perfection the Greek idea of the one method that will make men who are worth anything independent, self-reliant men, willing to follow another man. "The leader," he writes, "must himself believe that willing obedience always beats forced obedience, and that he can get this only by really knowing what should be done. Thus he can secure obedience from his men because he can convince them that he knows best, precisely as a good doctor makes his patients obey him. Also he must be ready to suffer more hardships than he asks of his soldiers, more fatigue, greater extremes of heat and cold. 'No one,' Cyrus always said, 'can be a good officer who does not undergo more than those he commands.' " However that may be, it is certain that the inexperienced civilian Xenophon was could have won over the Ten Thousand in no other way. He was able to convince them that he knew best and they gave up their own ideas and followed him willingly.

He showed them too that even if they made him their leader, it was share and share alike between him and the army. On one occasion when he was riding up from his post in the rear to consult with the van, and the snow was deep and the marching hard, a soldier cried to him, "Oh, it's easy enough for you on horseback." Xenophon leaped from his horse, flung the man aside and marched in his place.

Always, no matter how desperate things seemed, the initiative which only free men can be counted on to develop got them through. They abandoned their baggage by common consent and threw away their loot. "We will make the enemy carry our baggage for us," they said. "When we have conquered them we can take what we want." Early in the march they were terribly harassed by the Persian cavalry because they had none of their own. The men of Rhodes could throw with their slings twice as far as the Persians. They set them on baggage mules, directed them to aim at the riders, but spare their mounts and bring them back, and from that time on the Persians kept them in horses. If they needed ammunition they sent bowmen who could shoot farther than the foe to draw down showers of arrows that fell short and could be easily collected. One way or another they forced the Persians into service. When they got to the hills they discarded the tactics they had been trained in. They gave up the solid line, the only formation they knew, and the army advanced by columns, sometimes far apart. It was merely common sense in the rough broken country, but that virtue belongs peculiarly to men acting for themselves. The disciplined military mind has never been distinguished for it.

So, always cold and sometimes freezing, always hungry and sometimes starving, and always, always fighting, they held their own. No one by now had any clear idea where in the world they were. One day, Xenophon, riding in the rear, putting his horse up a steep hill, heard a great noise in front. A tumult was carried back to him by the wind, loud cries and shouting. An ambush, he thought, and calling to the others to follow at full speed, he drove his horse forward. No enemy was on the hilltop; only the Greeks. They were standing, all faced the same way, with tears running down their faces, their arms stretched out to what they saw before them. The shouting swelled into a great roar, "The sea! The sea!"

They were home at last. The sea was home to a Greek. It was the middle of January. They had left Cunaxa on the seventh of September. In four months they had marched well on to two thousand miles in circumstances never surpassed before or since for hardship and danger.

The *Anabasis* is the story of the Greeks in miniature. Ten thousand men, fiercely independent by nature, in a situation where they were a law unto themselves, showed that they were pre-eminently able to work together and proved what miracles of achievement willing co-operation can bring to pass. The Greek state, at any rate the Athenian state, which we know best, showed the same. What brought the Greeks safely back from Asia was precisely what made Athens great. The Athenian was a law unto himself, but his dominant instinct to stand alone was counterbalanced by his sense of overwhelming obligation to serve the state. This was his own spontaneous reaction to the facts of his life, nothing imposed upon him from outside. The city was his defense in a hostile world, his security, his pride, too, the guarantee to all of his worth as an Athenian.

Plato said that men could find their true moral development only in service to the city. The Athenian was saved from looking at his life as a private affair. Our word "idiot" comes from the Greek name for the man who took no share in public matters. Pericles in the funeral oration reported by Thucydides says:

We are a free democracy, but we are obedient. We obey the laws, more especially those which protect the oppressed, and the unwritten laws whose transgression brings acknowledged shame. We do not allow absorption in our own affairs to interfere with participation in the city's. We differ from other states in regarding the man who holds aloof from public life as useless, yet we yield to none in independence of spirit and complete self-reliance.

This happy balance was maintained for a very brief period. No doubt at its best it was as imperfect as the working out of every lofty idea in human terms is bound to be. Even so, it was the foundation of the Greek achievement. The creed of democracy, spiritual and political liberty for all, and each man a willing servant of the state, was the conception which underlay the highest reach of Greek genius. It was fatally weakened by the race for money and power in the Periclean age; the Peloponnesian War destroyed it and Greece lost it forever. Nevertheless, the ideal of free individuals unified by a spontaneous service to the common life was left as a possession to the world, never to be forgotten.

QUESTIONS FOR STUDY, DISCUSSION, AND WRITING

1. Hamilton's account of Xenophon has two main parts, a description of his life and writings in Greece and of his conduct during the Persian campaign. How does the characterization of Xenophon in Greece prepare for or illuminate his actions as commander of the Ten Thousand? What qualities in Xenophon are emphasized in this portrayal? Show some of the details selected to point up Xenophon's character.

2. What contrasts does Hamilton draw between the attitudes and interests of Xenophon and Thucydides? What implications for the writing and study of history are there in these contrasts? Compare your conclusions with E. H. Carr's discussion of the nature of historical fact ("The Historian and His Facts," pp. 920–937).

3. What does Xenophon's description of the dinner party indicate of the life of ancient Greece? Which details seem peculiar to that time and place? Which appear perennial, details that might be matched in accounts of comparable dinner parties at any time or place?

4. Does the account Xenophon gives of Socrates accord with that given by Plato? To what extent can the two accounts be reconciled?

5. In the closing paragraph of his essay "On Not Being a Philosopher" (p. 615), Lynd asks some questions about the attitude of the Greeks toward their philosophers. What answers does the account Xenophon gives of himself and other young men in the company of Socrates provide?

6. In what ways does Hamilton demonstrate that the Greek ideal of liberty combined personal independence with willing service to the state. to the common good? Compare Santayana's account, "Classic Liberty" (pp. 1150–1153).

7. Write an account of an incident in your own experience (comparable to Xenophon's dinner party) as if you were going to include it in a history of your own time. Take into account the results of your thinking about Questions 2 and 3, above.

On Government

Prince or President · Conflict
Democracy · Law

NICCOLÒ MACHIAVELLI
The Morals of the Prince[1]

*On Things for Which Men, and Particularly Princes, Are Praised
or Blamed*

We now have left to consider what should be the manners and
attitudes of a prince toward his subjects and his friends. As I know
that many have written on this subject I feel that I may be held
presumptuous in what I have to say, if in my comments I do not
follow the lines laid down by others. Since, however, it has been
my intention to write something which may be of use to the understanding reader, it has seemed wiser to me to follow the real truth
of the matter rather than what we imagine it to be. For imagination
has created many principalities and republics that have never been
seen or known to have any real existence, for how we live is so
different from how we ought to live that he who studies what ought
to be done rather than what is done will learn the way to his downfall rather than to his preservation. A man striving in every way
to be good will meet his ruin among the great number who are
not good. Hence it is necessary for a prince, if he wishes to remain
in power, to learn how not to be good and to use his knowledge
or refrain from using it as he may need.

Putting aside then the things imagined as pertaining to a prince
and considering those that really do, I will say that all men, and particularly princes because of their prominence, when comment is
made of them, are noted as having some characteristics deserving

1. Chapters 15-18 of *The Prince*.

either praise or blame. One is accounted liberal, another stingy, to use a Tuscan term—for in our speech avaricious *(avaro)* is applied to such as are desirous of acquiring by rapine whereas stingy *(misero)* is the term used for those who are reluctant to part with their own—one is considered bountiful, another rapacious; one cruel, another tender-hearted; one false to his word, another trustworthy; one effeminate and pusillanimous, another wild and spirited; one humane, another haughty; one lascivious, another chaste; one a man of integrity and another sly; one tough and another pliant; one serious and another frivolous; one religious and another skeptical, and so on. Everyone will agree, I know, that it would be a most praiseworthy thing if all the qualities accounted as good in the above enumeration were found in a Prince. But since they cannot be so possessed nor observed because of human conditions which do not allow of it, what is necessary for the prince is to be prudent enough to escape the infamy of such vices as would result in the loss of his state; as for the others which would not have that effect, he must guard himself from them as far as possible but if he cannot, he may overlook them as being of less importance. Further, he should have no concern about incurring the infamy of such vices without which the preservation of his state would be difficult. For, if the matter be well considered, it will be seen that some habits which appear virtuous, if adopted would signify ruin, and others that seem vices lead to security and the well-being of a prince.

Generosity and Meanness

To begin then with the first characteristic set forth above, I will say that it would be well always to be considered generous, yet generosity used in such a way as not to bring you honor does you harm, for if it is practiced virtuously and as it is meant to be practiced it will not be publicly known and you will not lose the name of being just the opposite of generous. Hence to preserve the reputation of being generous among your friends you must not neglect any kind of lavish display, yet a prince of this sort will consume all his property in such gestures and, if he wishes to preserve his reputation for generosity, he will be forced to levy heavy taxes on his subjects and turn to fiscal measures and do everything possible to get money. Thus he will begin to be regarded with hatred by his subjects and should he become poor he will be held in scant esteem; having by his prodigality given offense to many and rewarded only a few, he will suffer at the first hint of adversity, and the first danger will be critical for him. Yet when he realizes this and tries to reform he will immediately get the name of being a miser. So a prince, as he is unable to adopt the virtue of generosity without danger to himself, must, if he is a wise man, accept with indifference the name of miser. For with the passage of time he will be regarded as increasingly generous when it is seen that, by virtue of his parsimony, his income suffices for him to defend himself in wartime and undertake his enterprises without heavily taxing his people. For in that way he practices generosity towards all from whom he refrains from taking money, who are many, and stinginess only toward those from whom he withholds gifts, who are few.

In our times we have seen great things accomplished only by such as have had the name of misers; all others have come to naught. Pope Julius made use of his reputation for generosity to make himself Pope but later, in order to carry on his war against the King of France, he made no effort to maintain it; and he has waged a great number of wars without having had recourse to heavy taxation because his persistent parsimony has made up for the extra expenses. The present King of Spain, had he had any reputation for generosity, would never have carried through to victory so many enterprises.

A prince then, if he wishes not to rob his subjects but to be able to defend himself and not to become poor and despised nor to be obliged to become rapacious, must consider it a matter of small importance to incur the name of miser, for this is one of the vices which keep him on his throne. Some may say Caesar through generosity won his way to the purple, and others either through being generous or being accounted so have risen to the highest ranks. But I will answer by pointing out that either you are already a prince or you are on the way to becoming one and in the first case generosity is harmful while in the second it is very necessary to be considered open-handed. Caesar was seeking to arrive at the domination of Rome but if he had survived after reaching his goal and had not moderated his lavishness he would certainly have destroyed the empire.

It might also be objected that there have been many princes, accomplishing great things with their armies, who have been acclaimed for their generosity. To which I would answer that the prince either spends his own (or his subjects') money or that of others; in the first case he must be very sparing but in the second he should overlook no aspect of open-handedness. So the prince who leads his armies and lives on looting and extortion and booty, thus handling the wealth of others, must indeed have this quality of generosity for otherwise his soldiers will not follow him. You can be very free with wealth not belonging to yourself or your subjects, in the fashion of Cyrus, Caesar, or Alexander, for spending what belongs to others rather enhances your reputation than detracts from it; it is only spending your own wealth that is dangerous. There is nothing that consumes itself as does prodigality; even as you practice it you lose the faculty of practicing it and either you become poor and despicable or, in order to escape poverty, rapacious and unpopular. And among the things a prince must guard against is precisely the danger of becoming an object either of contempt or of hatred. Generosity leads you to both these evils, wherefore it is wiser to accept the name of miserly, since the reproach it brings is without hatred, than to seek a reputation for generosity and thus perforce acquire the name of rapacious, which breeds hatred as well as infamy.

Cruelty and Clemency and Whether It Is Better to Be Loved or Feared

Now to continue with the list of characteristics. It should be the desire of every prince to be considered merciful and not cruel, yet he should take care not to make poor use of his clemency. Cesare Borgia was regarded as cruel, yet his cruelty reorganized Romagna and united it in peace and loyalty. Indeed, if we reflect, we shall see that this man was more merciful than the Florentines who, to avoid the charge of cruelty, allowed Pistoia to be destroyed.[2] A prince should care nothing for the accusation of cruelty so long as he keeps his subjects united and loyal; by making a very few examples he can be more truly merciful than those who through too much tender-heartedness allow disorders to arise whence come killings and rapine. For these offend an entire community, while the few executions ordered by the prince affect only a few individuals. For a new prince above all it is impossible not to earn a reputation for cruelty since new states are full of dangers. Virgil indeed has Dido apologize for the inhumanity of her rule because it is new, in the words:

> *Res dura et regni novitas me talia cogunt*
> *Moliri et late fines custode tueri.*[3]

Nevertheless a prince should not be too ready to listen to talebearers nor to act on suspicion, nor should he allow himself to be easily frightened. He should proceed with a mixture of prudence and humanity in such a way as not to be made incautious by overconfidence nor yet intolerable by excessive mistrust.

Here the question arises; whether it is better to be loved than feared or feared than loved. The answer is that it would be desirable to be both but, since that is difficult, it is much safer to be feared than to be loved, if one must choose. For on men in general this observation may be made: they are ungrateful, fickle, and deceitful, eager to avoid dangers, and avid for gain, and while you are useful to them they are all with you, offering you their blood, their property,

---

2. By unchecked rioting between opposing factions (1502).

3. ". . . my cruel fate / And doubts attending an unsettled state / Force me to guard my coast from foreign foes —
DRYDEN.

their lives, and their sons so long as danger is remote, as we noted above, but when it approaches they turn on you. Any prince, trusting only in their words and having no other preparations made, will fall to his ruin, for friendships that are bought at a price and not by greatness and nobility of soul are paid for indeed, but they are not owned and cannot be called upon in time of need. Men have less hesitation in offending a man who is loved than one who is feared, for love is held by a bond of obligation which, as men are wicked, is broken whenever personal advantage suggests it, but fear is accompanied by the dread of punishment which never relaxes.

Yet a prince should make himself feared in such a way that, if he does not thereby merit love, at least he may escape odium, for being feared and not hated may well go together. And indeed the prince may attain this end if he but respect the property and the women of his subjects and citizens. And if it should become necessary to seek the death of someone, he should find a proper justification and a public cause, and above all he should keep his hands off another's property, for men forget more readily the death of their father than the loss of their patrimony. Besides, pretexts for seizing property are never lacking, and when a prince begins to live by means of rapine he will always find some excuse for plundering others, and conversely pretexts for execution are rarer and are more quickly exhausted.

A prince at the head of his armies and with a vast number of soldiers under his command should give not the slightest heed if he is esteemed cruel, for without such a reputation he will not be able to keep his army united and ready for action. Among the marvelous things told of Hannibal is that, having a vast army under his command made up of all kinds and races of men and waging war far from his own country, he never allowed any dissension to arise either as between the troops and their leaders or among the troops themselves, and this both in times of good fortune and bad. This could only have come about through his most inhuman cruelty which, taken in conjunction with his great valor, kept him always an object of respect and terror in the eyes of his soldiers. And without the cruelty his other characteristics would not have achieved this effect. Thoughtless writers have admired his actions and at the same time deplored the cruelty which was the basis of them. As evidence of the truth of our statement that his other virtues would have been insufficient let us examine the case of Scipio, an extraordinary leader not only in his own day but for all recorded history. His army in Spain revolted and for no other reason than because of his kind-heartedness, which had allowed more license to his soldiery than military discipline properly permits. His policy was attacked in the Senate by Fabius Maximus, who called him a corrupter of the Roman arms. When the Locrians had been mishandled by one of his lieutenants, his easy-going nature prevented him from avenging them or disciplining his officer, and it was apropos of this incident that one of the senators remarked, wishing to find an excuse for him, that there were many men who knew better how to avoid error themselves than to correct it in others. This characteristic of Scipio would have clouded his fame and glory had he continued in authority, but as he lived under the government of the Senate, its harmful aspect was hidden and it reflected credit on him.

Hence, on the subject of being loved or feared I will conclude that since love depends on the subjects, but the prince has it in his own hands to create fear, a wise prince will rely on what is his own, remembering at the same time that he must avoid arousing hatred, as we have said.

In What Manner Princes Should Keep Their Word

How laudable it is for a prince to keep his word and govern his actions by integrity rather than trickery will be understood by all. Nonetheless we have in our times seen great things accomplished by many princes who have thought little of keeping their promises and have known the art of mystifying the minds of men. Such princes have won out over those whose actions were based on fidelity to their word.

It must be understood that there are two ways of fighting, one with laws and the other with arms. The first is the way of men, the second is the style of beasts, but since very often the first does not suffice it is necessary to turn to the second. Therefore a prince must know how to play the beast as well as the man. This lesson was taught allegorically by the ancient writers who related that Achilles and many other princes were brought up by Chiron the Centaur, who took them under his discipline. The clear significance of this half-man and half-beast preceptorship is that a prince must know how to use either of these two natures and that one without the other has no enduring strength. Now since the prince must make use of the characteristics of beasts he should choose those of the fox and the lion, though the lion cannot defend himself against snares and the fox is helpless against wolves. One must be a fox in avoiding traps and a lion in frightening wolves. Such as choose simply the rôle of a lion do not rightly understand the matter. Hence a wise leader cannot and should not keep his word when keeping it is not to his advantage or when the reasons that made him give it are no longer valid. If men were good, this would not be a good precept, but since they are wicked and will not keep faith with you, you are not bound to keep faith with them.

A prince has never lacked legitimate reasons to justify his breach of faith. We could give countless recent examples and show how any number of peace treaties or promises have been broken and rendered meaningless by the faithlessness of princes, and how success has fallen to the one who best knows how to counterfeit the fox. But it is necessary to know how to disguise this nature well and how to pretend and dissemble. Men are so simple and so ready to follow the needs of the moment that the deceiver will always find some one to deceive. Of recent examples I shall mention one. Alexander VI did nothing but deceive and never thought of anything else and always found some occasion for it. Never was there a man more convincing in his asseverations nor more willing to offer the most solemn oaths nor less likely to observe them. Yet his deceptions were always successful for he was an expert in this field.

So a prince need not have all the aforementioned good qualities, but it is most essential that he appear to have them. Indeed, I should go so far as to say that having them and always practising them is harmful, while seeming to have them is useful. It is good to appear clement, trustworthy, humane, religious, and honest, and also to be so, but always with the mind so disposed that, when the occasion arises not to be so, you can become the opposite. It must be understood that a prince and particularly a new prince cannot practise all the virtues for which men are accounted good, for the necessity of preserving the state often compels him to take actions which are opposed to loyalty, charity, humanity, and religion. Hence he must have a spirit ready to adapt itself as the varying winds of fortune command him. As I have said, so far as he is able, a prince should stick to the path of good but, if the necessity arises, he should know how to follow evil.

A prince must take great care that no word ever passes his lips that is not full of the above mentioned five good qualities, and he must seem to all who see and hear him a model of piety, loyalty, integrity, humanity, and religion. Nothing is more necessary than to seem to possess this last quality, for men in general judge more by the eye than the hand, as all can see but few can feel. Everyone sees what you seem to be, few experience what you really are and these few do not dare to set themselves up against the opinion of the majority supported by the majesty of the state. In the actions of all men and especially princes, where there is no court of appeal, the end is all that counts. Let a prince then concern himself with the acquisition or the maintenance of a state; the means employed will always be considered honorable and praised by all, for the mass of mankind is always swayed by appearances and by the outcome of an enterprise. And in the world there is only the mass, for the few find their place only when the majority has no base of support.

JOHN WINTHROP
Speech to the General Court[1]

I suppose something may be expected from me, upon this charge that is befallen me, which moves me to speak now to you; yet I intend not to intermeddle in the proceedings of the court, or with any of the persons concerned therein. Only I bless God, that I see an issue of this troublesome business. I also acknowledge the justice of the court, and, for mine own part, I am well satisfied, I was publicly charged, and I am publicly and legally acquitted, which is all I did expect or desire. And though this be sufficient for my justification before men, yet not so before the God, who hath seen so much amiss in my dispensations (and even in this affair) as calls me to be humble. For to be publicly and criminally charged in this court, is matter of humiliation, (and I desire to make a right use of it) notwithstanding I be thus acquitted. If her father had spit in her face, (saith the Lord concerning Miriam), should she not have been ashamed seven days?[2] Shame had lien upon her, whatever the occasion had been. I am unwilling to stay you from your urgent affairs, yet give me leave (upon this special occasion) to speak a little more to this assembly. It may be of some good use, to inform and rectify the judgments of some of the people, and may prevent such distempers as have arisen amongst us. The great questions that have troubled the country, are about the authority of the magistrates and the liberty of the people. It is yourselves who have called us to this office, and being called by you, we have our authority from God, in way of an ordinance, such as hath the image of God eminently stamped upon it, the contempt and violation whereof hath been vindicated with examples of divine vengeance, I entreat you to consider, that when you choose magistrates, you take them from among yourselves, men subject to like passions as you are. Therefore when you see infirmities in us, you should reflect upon your own, and that would make you bear the more with us, and not be severe censurers of the failings of your magistrates, when you have continual experience of the like infirmities in yourselves and others. We account him a good servant, who breaks not his covenant. The covenant between you and us is the oath you have taken of us, which is to this purpose, that we shall govern you and judge your causes by the rules of God's laws and our own, according to our best skill. When you agree with a workman to build you a ship or house, etc., he undertakes as well for

---

1. Winthrop, who had been found innocent of exceeding his authority as a magistrate, gave this speech to the General Court of Massachusetts Bay Colony on July 3, 1645.

2. See Numbers xii. 1-15.

his skill as for his faithfulness, for it is his profession, and you pay him for both. But when you call one to be a magistrate, he doth not profess nor undertake to have sufficient skill for that office, nor can you furnish him with gifts, etc., therefore you must run the hazard of his skill and ability. But if he fail in faithfulness, which by his oath he is bound unto, that he must answer for. If it fall out that the case be clear to common apprehension, and the rule clear also, if he transgress here, the error is not in the skill, but in the evil of the will: it must be required of him. But if the case be doubtful, or the rule doubtful, to men of such understanding and parts as your magistrates are, if your magistrates should err here, yourselves must bear it.

For the other point concerning liberty, I observe a great mistake in the country about that. There is a twofold liberty, natural (I mean as our nature is now corrupt) and civil or federal. The first is common to man with beasts and other creatures. By this, man, as he stands in relation to man simply, hath liberty to do what he lists; it is a liberty to evil as well as to good. This liberty is incompatible and inconsistent with authority, and cannot endure the least restraint of the most just authority. The exercise and maintaining of this liberty makes men grow more evil, and in time to be worse than brute beasts: *omnes sumus licentia deteriores.*[3] This is that great enemy of truth and peace, that wild beast, which all the ordinances of God are bent against, to restrain and subdue it. The other kind of liberty I call civil or federal, it may also be termed moral, in reference to the covenant between God and man, in the moral law, and the politic covenants and constitutions, amongst men themselves. This liberty is the proper end and object of authority, and cannot subsist without it; and it is a liberty to that only which is good, just, and honest. This liberty you are to stand for, with the hazard (not only of your goods, but) of your lives, if need be. Whatsoever crosseth this, is not authority, but a distemper thereof. This liberty is maintained and exercised in a way of subjection to authority; it is of the same kind of liberty wherewith Christ hath made us free. The woman's own choice makes such a man her husband; yet being so chosen, he is her lord, and she is to be subject to him, yet in a way of liberty, not of bondage; and a true wife accounts her subjection her honor and freedom, and would not think her condition safe and free, but in her subjection to her husband's authority. Such is the liberty of the church under the authority of Christ, her king and husband; his yoke is so easy and sweet to her as a bride's ornaments; and if through forwardness or wantonness, etc., she shake it off, at any time, she is at no rest in her spirit, until she take it up again; and whether her lord smiles upon her, and embraceth her in his arms, or whether he frowns, or rebukes,

3. "We all become meaner through selfish liberty."

or smites her, she apprehends the sweetness of his love in all, and is refreshed, supported, and instructed by every such dispensation of his authority over her. On the other side, ye know who they are that complain of this yoke and say, let us break their bands, etc., we will not have this man to rule over us. Even so, brethren, it will be between you and your magistrates. If you stand for your natural corrupt liberties, and will do what is good in your own eyes, you will not endure the least weight of authority, but will murmur, and oppose, and be always striving to shake off that yoke; but if you will be satisfied to enjoy such civil and lawful liberties, such as Christ allows you, then will you quietly and cheerfully submit unto that authority which is set over you, in all the administrations of it, for your good. Wherein, if we fail at any time, we hope we shall be willing (by God's assistance) to hearken to good advice from any of you, or in any other way of God; so shall your liberties be preserved, in upholding the honor and power of authority amongst you.

QUESTIONS FOR STUDY, DISCUSSION, AND WRITING

1. What is Winthrop's distinction between "skill" and "will"? What connection has this with the two kinds of liberty he discusses?
2. Does Winthrop use the two extended analogies of the workman and the marriage partners in the same way and for the same purpose? Explain.
3. In what ways might Lincoln's definition of liberty (p. 709) be considered a refinement of Winthrop's?

DESIDERIUS ERASMUS
The Arts of Peace[1]

Although the writers of antiquity divided the whole theory of state government into two sections, war and peace, the first and most important objective is the instruction of the prince in the matter of ruling wisely during times of peace, in which he should strive his utmost to preclude any future need for the science of war. In this matter it seems best that the prince should first know his own kingdom. This knowledge is best gained from a study of geography and history and from frequent visits through his provinces and cities. Let him first be eager to learn the location of his districts and cities, with their beginnings, their nature, institutions, customs, laws, annals, and privileges. No one can heal the body until he is thoroughly conversant with it. No one can properly till a field which he does not understand. To be sure, the tyrant takes great

1. From *The Education of a Christian Prince*.

care in such matters, but it is the spirit, not the act, which singles out the good prince. The physician studies the functions of the body so as to be more adept in healing it; the poisoning assassin, to more surely end it! Next, the prince should love the land over which he rules just as a farmer loves the fields of his ancestors or as a good man feels affection toward his household. He should make it his especial interest to hand it over to his successor, whosoever he may be, better than he received it. If he has any children, devotion toward them should urge him on; if he has no family, he should be guided by devotion to his country; and he should always keep kindled the flame of love for his subjects. He should consider his kingdom as a great body of which he is the most outstanding member and remember that they who have entrusted all their fortunes and their very safety to the good faith of one man are deserving of consideration. He should keep constantly in mind the example of those rulers to whom the welfare of their people was dearer than their own lives; for it is obviously impossible for a prince to do violence to the state without injuring himself.

In the second place the prince will see to it that he is loved by his subjects in return, but in such a way that his authority is no less strong among them. There are some who are so stupid as to strive to win good will for themselves by incantations and magic rings, when there is no charm more efficacious than good character itself; nothing can be more lovable than that, for, as this is a real and immortal good, so it brings a man true and undying good will. The best formula is this: let him love, who would be loved, so that he may attach his subjects to him as God has won the peoples of the world to Himself by His goodness.

They are also wrong who win the hearts of the masses by largesses, feasts, and gross indulgence. It is true that some popular favor, instead of affection, is gained by these means, but it is neither genuine nor permanent. In the meanwhile the greed of the populace is developed, which, as happens, after it has reached large proportions thinks nothing is enough. Then there is an uprising, unless complete satisfaction is made to their demands. By this means your people are not won, but corrupted. And so by this means the average prince is accustomed to win his way into the hearts of the people after the fashion of these foolish husbands who beguile their wives with blandishments, gifts, and complaisance, instead of winning their love by their character and good actions. So at length it comes about that they are not loved; instead of a thrifty and well mannered wife they have a haughty and intractable one; instead of an obedient spouse they find one who is quarrelsome and rebellious. Or take the case of those unhappy women who desperately try to arouse love in their husbands' hearts by giving them drugs, with the result that they have madmen instead of sane lovers.

The wife should first learn the ways and means of loving her husband and then let him show himself worthy of her love. And so with the people—let them become accustomed to the best, and let the prince be the source of the best things. Those who begin to love through reason, love long.

In the first place, then, he who would be loved by his people should show himself a prince worthy of love; after that it will do some good to consider how best he may win his way into their hearts. The prince should do this first so that the best men may have the highest regard for him and that he may be accepted by those who are lauded by all. They are the men he should have for his close friends; they are the ones for his counselors; they are the ones on whom he should bestow his honors and whom he should allow to have the greatest influence with him. By this means everyone will come to have an excellent opinion of the prince, who is the source of all good will. I have known some princes who were not really evil themselves who incurred the hatred of the people for no other reason than that they granted too much liberty to those whom universal public sentiment condemned. The people judged the character of the prince by these other men.

For my part, I should like to see the prince born and raised among those people whom he is destined to rule, because friendship is created and confirmed most when the source of good will is in nature itself. The common people shun and hate even good qualities which they are unknown to them, while evils which are familiar are sometimes loved. This matter at hand has a twofold advantage to offer, for the prince will be more kindly disposed toward his subjects and certainly more ready to regard them as his own. The people on their part will feel more kindness in their hearts and be more willing to recognize his position as prince. For this reason I am especially opposed to the accepted [idea of] alliances of the princes with foreign, particularly with distant, nations.

The ties of birth and country and a mutual spirit of understanding, as it were, have a great deal to do with establishing a feeling of good will. A goodly part of this feeling must of necessity be lost if mixed marriages confuse that native and inborn spirit. But when nature has laid a foundation of mutual affection, then it should be developed and strengthened by every other means. When the opposite situation is presented, then even greater energy must be employed to secure this feeling of good will by mutual obligations and a character worthy of commendation. In marriage, the wife at first yields entirely to the husband, and he makes a few concessions to her and indulges her whims until, as they come really to know one another, a firm bond unites them; so it should be in the case of a prince selected from a foreign country. Mithridates learned the languages of all the peoples over whom he ruled, and they were said to be twenty in number. Alexander the Great, however barbarous the peoples with whom he was dealing, at once used to imitate their ways and customs and by this method subtly worked himself into their good graces. Alcibiades has been praised for the same thing. Nothing so alienates the affections of his people from a prince as for him to take great pleasure in living abroad, because then they seem to be neglected by him to whom they wish to be most important. The result of this is that the people feel that they are not paying taxes to a prince (since the moneys are spent elsewhere and totally lost as far as they are concerned) but that they are casting spoils to foreigners. Lastly, there is nothing more harmful and disastrous to a country, nor more dangerous for a prince, than visits to far-away places, especially if these visits are prolonged; for it was this, according to the opinion of everyone, that took Philip from us and injured his kingdom no less than the war with the Gelrii, which was dragged out for so many years. The king bee is hedged about in the midst of the swarm and does not fly out and away. The heart is situated in the very middle of the body. Just so should a prince always be found among his own people.

There are two factors, as Aristotle tells us in his *Politics*, which have played the greatest roles in the overthrow of empires. They are hatred and contempt. Good will is the opposite of hatred; respected authority, of contempt. Therefore it will be the duty of the prince to study the best way to win the former and avoid the latter. Hatred is kindled by an ugly temper, by violence, insulting language, sourness of character, meanness, and greediness; it is more easily aroused than allayed. A good prince must therefore use every caution to prevent any possibility of losing the affections of his subjects. You may take my word that whoever loses the favor of his people is thereby stripped of a great safeguard. On the other hand, the affections of the populace are won by those characteristics which, in general, are farthest removed from tyranny. They are clemency, affability, fairness, courtesy, and kindliness. This last is a spur to duty, especially if they who have been of good service to the state, see that they will be rewarded at the hands of the prince. Clemency inspires to better efforts those who are aware of their faults, while forgiveness extends hope to those who are now eager to make recompense by virtuous conduct for the shortcomings of their earlier life and provides the steadfast with a happy reflection on human nature. Courtesy everywhere engenders love—or at least assuages hatred. This quality in a great prince is by far the most pleasing to the masses.

Contempt is most likely to spring from a penchant for the worldly pleasures of lust, for excessive drinking and eating, and for fools and clowns—in other words, for folly and idleness. Authority is gained by the following varied characteristics: in the first place wisdom, then integrity, self-restraint, seriousness, and alertness. These are the things by which a prince should commend himself, if he would be respected in his authority over his subjects. Some have the absurd idea that if they make the greatest confusion possible by their appearance, and dress with pompous display, they must be held in high esteem among their subjects. Who thinks a prince great just because he is adorned with gold and precious stones? Everyone knows he has as many as he wants. But in the meanwhile what else does the prince expose except the misfortunes of his people, who are supporting his extravagance to their great cost? And now lastly, what else does such a prince sow among his people, if not the seeds of all crime? Let the good prince be reared in such a manner and [continue to] live in such a manner that from the example of his life all the others (nobles and commoners alike) may take the model of frugality and temperance. Let him so conduct himself in the privacy of his home as not to be caught unawares by the sudden entrance of anyone. And in public it is unseemly for a prince to be seen anywhere, unless always in connection with something that will benefit the people as a whole. The real character of the prince is revealed by his speech rather than by his dress. Every word that is dropped from the lips of the prince is scattered wide among the masses. He should exercise the greatest care to see that whatever he says bears the stamp of [genuine] worth and evidences a mind becoming a good prince.

Aristotle's advice on this subject should not be overlooked. He says that a prince who would escape incurring the hatred of his people and would foster their affection for him should delegate to others the odious duties and keep for himself the tasks which will be sure to win favor. Thereby a great portion of any unpopularity will be diverted upon those who carry out the administration, and especially will it be so if these men are unpopular with the people on other grounds as well. In the matter of benefits, however, the genuine thanks redound to the prince alone. I should like to add also that gratitude for a favor will be returned twofold if it is given quickly, with no hesitation, spontaneously, and with a few words of friendly commendation. If anything must be refused, refusal should be affable and without offense. If it is necessary to impose a punishment, some slight diminution of the penalty prescribed by law should be made, and the sentence should be carried out as if the prince were being forced [to act] against his own desires.

It is not enough for the prince to keep his own character pure and uncorrupted for his state. He must give no less serious attention, in so far as he can, to see that every member of his household —his nobles, his friends, his ministers, and his magistrates—follows his example. They are one with the prince, and any hatred that is aroused by their vicious acts rebounds upon the prince himself.

But, someone will say, this supervision is extremely difficult to accomplish. It will be easy enough if the prince is careful to admit only the best men into his household, and if he makes them understand that the prince is most pleased by that which is best for the people. Otherwise it too often turns out that, due to the disregard of the prince in these matters or even his connivance in them, the most criminal men (hiding under cover of the prince) force a tyranny upon the people, and while they appear to be carrying out the affairs of the prince, they are doing the greatest harm to his good name. What is more, the condition of the state is more bearable when the prince himself is wicked than when he has evil friends; we manage to bear up under a single tyrant. Somehow or other the people can sate the greed of one man without difficulty: it is not a matter of great effort to satisfy the wild desires of just one man or to appease the vicious fierceness of a single individual, but to content so many tyrants is a heavy burden. The prince should avoid every novel idea in so far as he is capable of doing so; for even if conditions are bettered thereby, the very innovation is a stumbling block. The establishment of a state, the unwritten laws of a city, or the old legal code are never changed without great confusion. Therefore, if there is anything of this sort that can be endured, it should not be changed but should either be tolerated or happily diverted to a better function. As a last resort, if there is some absolutely unbearable condition, the change should be made, but [only] gradually and by a practiced hand.

The end which the prince sets for himself is of the greatest consequence, for if he shows little wisdom in its selection he must of necessity be wrong in all his plans. The cardinal principle of a good prince should be not only to preserve the present prosperity of the state but to pass it on more prosperous than when he received it. To use the jargon of the Peripatetics, there are three kinds of "good"—that of the mind, that of the body, and the external good. The prince must be careful not to evaluate them in reverse order and judge the good fortune of his state mainly by the external good, for these latter conditions should only be judged good in so far as they relate to the good of the mind and of the body; that is, in a word, the prince should consider his subjects to be most fortunate not if they are very wealthy or in excellent bodily health but if they are most honorable and self-controlled, if they have as little taste for greed and quarreling as could be hoped for, and if they are not at all factious but live in complete accord with one another. He must also beware of being deceived by the false names of the fairest things, for in this deception lies the fountainhead from which spring practically all the evils that abound in the world. It is no true state of happiness in which the people are given over to idleness and wasteful extravagance, any more than it is true liberty for everyone to be allowed to do as he pleases. Neither is it a state of servitude to live according to the letter of just laws. Nor is that a peaceful state in which the populace bows to every whim of the prince; but rather is it peaceful when it obeys good laws and a prince who has a keen regard for the authority of the laws. Equity does not lie in giving everyone the same reward, the same rights, the same honor; as a matter of fact, that is sometimes a mark of the greatest unfairness.

A prince who is about to assume control of the state must be advised at once that the main hope of a state lies in the proper education of its youth. This Xenophon wisely taught in his *Cyropaedia*. Pliable youth is amenable to any system of training. Therefore the greatest care should be exercised over public and private schools and over the education of the girls, so that the children may be placed under the best and most trustworthy instructors and may learn the teachings of Christ and that good literature which is beneficial to the state. As a result of this scheme of things, there will be no need for many laws or punishments, for the people will of their own free will follow the course of right.

Education exerts such a powerful influence, as Plato says, that a man who has been trained in the right develops into a sort of divine creature, while on the other hand, a person who has received a perverted training degenerates into a monstrous sort of savage beast. Nothing is of more importance to a prince than to have the best possible subjects.

The first effort, then, is to get them accustomed to the best influences, because any music has a soothing effect to the accustomed ear, and there is nothing harder than to rid people of those traits which have become second nature to them through habit. None of those tasks will be too difficult if the prince himself adheres to the best manners. It is the essence of tyranny, or rather trickery, to treat the common citizen as animal trainers are accustomed to treat a savage beast: first they carefully study the way in which these creatures are quieted or aroused, and then they anger them or quiet them at their pleasure. This Plato has painstakingly pointed out. Such a course is an abuse of the emotions of the masses and is no help to them. However, if the people prove intractable and rebel against what is good for them, then you must bide your time and gradually lead them over to your end, either by some subterfuge or by some helpful pretence. This works just as wine does, for when that is first taken it has no effect, but when it has gradually flowed through every vein it captivates the whole man and holds him in its power.

If sometimes the whirling course of events and public opinion beat the prince from his course, and he is forced to obey the [exigencies of the] time, yet he must not cease his efforts as long as he is able to renew his fight, and what he has not accomplished by one method he should try to effect by another.

QUESTIONS FOR STUDY, DISCUSSION, AND WRITING

1. Early in the essay Erasmus analogizes the relation of prince to people to that of a physician to the body, a farmer to a field, a husband to a wife. Why does he develop this last analogy more fully than the others and use it again later? How does his use of analogy differ from Winthrop's (pp. 697–699)?
2. On page 702 Erasmus lists the "varied characteristics" by which authority is gained. Why does he put wisdom "in the first place"? Is there any significance to the order in which he places the other characteristics?
3. Erasmus says that "the real character of the prince is revealed by his speech rather than by his dress." Would this be equally true of people other than princes? How can both speech and dress reveal character?
4. Compare Erasmus' ideal prince with Machiavelli's. What is the significance of the title, "The Arts of Peace"?
5. Is the advice to "avoid every novel idea" (p. 704) sound? To what does "novelty" apply in this context? How would Erasmus counter the charge that such a policy might lead to stagnation and corruption in government?
6. Why does Erasmus find it necessary to qualify so carefully what he means by "prosperity" (p. 704)? How does his definition differ from more commonly accepted ones today?
7. "Equity does not lie in giving everyone the same reward, the same rights, the same honor; as a matter of fact, that is sometimes a mark of the greatest unfairness" (p. 705). How does this implied definition of "equity" jibe with the statement in the Declaration of Independence that "all men are created equal" and "are endowed by their Creator with certain unalienable Rights" (pp. 748–749)?
8. How far do leading political figures today correspond to Erasmus' ideal prince?

ABRAHAM LINCOLN
Second Inaugural Address

At this second appearing to take the oath of the presidential office, there is less occasion for an extended address than there was at the first. Then a statement, somewhat in detail, of a course to be pursued, seemed fitting and proper. Now, at the expiration of four years, during which public declarations have been constantly called forth on every point and phase of the great contest which still absorbs the attention, and engrosses the energies of the nation, little that is new could be presented. The progress of our arms, upon which all else chiefly depends, is as well known to the public as to myself; and it is, I trust, reasonably satisfactory and encouraging to all. With high hope for the future, no prediction in regard to it is ventured.

On the occasion corresponding to this four years ago, all thoughts were anxiously directed to an impending civil war. All dreaded it—all sought to avert it. While the inaugural address was being delivered from this place, devoted altogether to *saving* the Union without war, insurgent agents were in the city seeking to *destroy* it without war—seeking to dissolve the Union, and divide effects, by negotiation. Both parties deprecated war; but one of them would *make* war rather than let the nation survive; and the other would *accept* war rather than let it perish. And the war came.

One-eighth of the whole population were colored slaves, not distributed generally over the Union, but localized in the Southern part of it. These slaves constituted a peculiar and powerful interest. All knew that this interest was, somehow, the cause of the war. To strengthen, perpetuate, and extend this interest was the object for which the insurgents would rend the Union, even by war; while the government claimed no right to do more than to restrict the territorial enlargement of it. Neither party expected for the war, the magnitude, or the duration, which it has already attained. Neither anticipated that the *cause* of the conflict might cease with, or even before, the conflict itself should cease. Each looked for an easier triumph, and a result less fundamental and astounding. Both read the same Bible, and pray to the same God; and each invokes His aid against the other. It may seem strange that any men should dare to ask a just God's assistance in wringing their bread from the sweat of other men's faces[1]; but let us judge not that we be not judged.[2] The prayers of both could not be answered; that of neither has been answered fully. The Almighty has His own purposes. "Woe unto the world because of offenses! for it must needs be that offenses come; but woe to that man by whom the offense cometh!"[3] If we shall suppose that American slavery is one of those offenses which, in the providence of God, must needs come, but which, having continued through His appointed time, He now wills to remove, and that He gives to both North and South, this terrible war, as the woe due to those by whom the offense came, shall we discern therein any departure from those divine attributes which the believers in a Living God always ascribe to Him? Fondly do we hope—fervently do we pray—that this mighty scourge of war may speedily pass away. Yet, if God wills that it continue, until all the wealth piled by the bondman's two hundred and fifty years of unrequited toil shall be sunk, and until every drop of blood drawn

---

1. See Genesis iii. 19.
2. See Matthew vii. 1.

3. See Matthew xviii. 7.

with the lash, shall be paid by another drawn with the sword, as was said three thousand years ago, so still it must be said "the judgments of the Lord are true and righteous altogether."[4]

With malice toward none; with charity for all; with firmness in the right, as God gives us to see the right, let us strive on to finish the work we are in; to bind up the nation's wounds; to care for him who shall have borne the battle, and for his widow, and his orphan —to do all which may achieve and cherish a just, and a lasting peace, among ourselves, and with all nations.

4. See Psalms xix. 9.

JAMES THURBER
The Rabbits Who Caused All the Trouble

Within the memory of the youngest child there was a family of rabbits who lived near a pack of wolves. The wolves announced that they did not like the way the rabbits were living. (The wolves were crazy about the way they themselves were living, because it was the only way to live.) One night several wolves were killed in an earthquake and this was blamed on the rabbits, for it is well known that rabbits pound on the ground with their hind legs and cause earthquakes. On another night one of the wolves was killed by a bolt of lightning and this was also blamed on the rabbits, for it is well known that lettuce-eaters cause lightning. The wolves threatened to civilize the rabbits if they didn't behave, and the rabbits decided to run away to a desert island. But the other animals, who lived at a great distance, shamed them, saying, "You must stay where you are and be brave. This is no world for escapists. If the wolves attack you, we will come to your aid, in all probability." So the rabbits continued to live near the wolves and one day there was a terrible flood which drowned a great many wolves. This was blamed on the rabbits, for it is well known that carrot-nibblers with long ears cause floods. The wolves descended on the rabbits, for their own good, and imprisoned them in a dark cave, for their own protection.

When nothing was heard about the rabbits for some weeks, the other animals demanded to know what had happened to them. The wolves replied that the rabbits had been eaten and since they had been eaten the affair was a purely internal matter. But the other animals warned that they might possibly unite against the wolves unless some reason was given for the destruction of the rabbits. So the wolves gave them one. "They were trying to escape," said the wolves, "and, as you know, this is no world for escapists."

Moral: Run, don't walk, to the nearest desert island.

ABRAHAM LINCOLN
Liberty[1]

The world has never had a good definition of the word liberty, and the American people, just now, are much in want of one. We all declare for liberty; but in using the same *word* we do not all mean the same *thing*. With some the word liberty may mean for each man to do as he pleases with himself, and the product of his labor; while with others the same word may mean for some men to do as they please with other men, and the product of other men's labor. Here are two, not only different, but incompatible things, called by the same name—liberty. And it follows that each of the things is, by the respective parties, called by two different and incompatible names—liberty and tyranny.

The shepherd drives the wolf from the sheep's throat, for which the sheep thanks the shepherd as a *liberator*, while the wolf denounces him for the same act as the destroyer of liberty, especially as the sheep was a black one. Plainly the sheep and the wolf are not agreed upon a definition of the word liberty; and precisely the same difference prevails today among us human creatures, even in the North, and all professing to love liberty. Hence we behold the processes by which thousands are daily passing from under the yoke of bondage, hailed by some as the advance of liberty, and bewailed by others as the destruction of all liberty. Recently, as it seems, the people of Maryland have been doing something to define liberty; and thanks to them that, in what they have done, the wolf's dictionary has been repudiated.

1. From an address at the Sanitary Fair, Baltimore, Maryland, April 18, 1864.

QUESTIONS FOR STUDY, DISCUSSION, AND WRITING

1. How does the analogy of the sheep and the wolf in the second paragraph correspond to the two conceptions of liberty Lincoln has given in the first paragraph? Is the analogy exact?
2. How does the choice of that particular analogy reveal Lincoln's own attitude toward liberty? What connotations do we usually associate with the wolf who attacks the sheep?
3. How is Lincoln's definition of liberty applicable to the situation he talks about in his Second Inaugural Address?
4. Is "liberty" like the "key words"—words which reflect changes in a society through changes in their meaning—that Williams talks about (pp. 881–886)?
5. Compare Lincoln's use of figurative language here with E. B. White's (p. 767). What are the significant similarities and differences?

JONATHAN SWIFT

A Modest Proposal

FOR PREVENTING THE CHILDREN OF POOR PEOPLE IN IRELAND
FROM BEING A BURDEN TO THEIR PARENTS OR COUNTRY,
AND FOR MAKING THEM BENEFICIAL TO THE PUBLIC

It is a melancholy object to those who walk through this great town or travel in the country, when they see the streets, the roads, and cabin doors, crowded with beggars of the female-sex, followed by three, four, or six children, all in rags and importuning every passenger for an alms. These mothers, instead of being able to work for their honest livelihood, are forced to employ all their time in strolling to beg sustenance for their helpless infants, who, as they grow up, either turn thieves for want of work, or leave their dear native country to fight for the Pretender in Spain, or sell themselves to the Barbadoes.[1]

I think it is agreed by all parties that this prodigious number of children in the arms, or on the backs, or at the heels of their mothers, and frequently of their fathers, is in the present deplorable state of the kingdom a very great additional grievance; and therefore whoever could find out a fair, cheap, and easy method of making these children sound, useful members of the commonwealth would deserve so well of the public as to have his statue set up for a preserver of the nation.

But my intention is very far from being confined to provide only for the children of professed beggars; it is of a much greater extent, and shall take in the whole number of infants at a certain age who are born of parents in effect as little able to support them as those who demand our charity in the streets.

As to my own part, having turned my thoughts for many years upon this important subject, and maturely weighed the several schemes of other projectors, I have always found them grossly mistaken in their computation. It is true, a child just dropped from its dam may be supported by her milk for a solar year, with little other nourishment; at most not above the value of two shillings, which the mother may certainly get, or the value in scraps, by her lawful occupation of begging; and it is exactly at one year old that I propose to provide for them in such a manner as instead of being a charge upon their parents or the parish, or wanting food and raiment for the rest of their lives, they shall on the contrary contribute to the feeding, and partly to the clothing, of many thousands. There is likewise another great advantage in my scheme, that it

1. That is, bind themselves to work for a period of years, in order to pay for their transportation to a colony.

will prevent those voluntary abortions, and that horrid practice of women murdering their bastard children, alas, too frequent among us, sacrificing the poor innocent babes, I doubt, more to avoid the expense than the shame, which would move tears and pity in the most savage and inhuman breast.

The number of souls in this kingdom being usually reckoned one million and a half, of these I calculate there may be about two hundred thousand couple whose wives are breeders; from which number I subtract thirty thousand couples who are able to maintain their own children, although I apprehend there cannot be so many under the present distresses of the kingdom; but this being granted, there will remain an hundred and seventy thousand breeders. I again subtract fifty thousand for those women who miscarry, or whose children die by accident or disease within the year. There only remain an hundred and twenty thousand children of poor parents annually born. The question therefore is, how this number shall be reared and provided for, which, as I have already said, under the present situation of affairs, is utterly impossible by all the methods hitherto proposed. For we can neither employ them in handicraft or agriculture; we neither build houses (I mean in the country) nor cultivate land. They can very seldom pick up a livelihood by stealing till they arrive at six years old, except where they are of towardly parts; although I confess they learn the rudiments much earlier, during which time they can however be looked upon only as probationers, as I have been informed by a principal gentleman in the county of Cavan, who protested to me that he never knew above one or two instances under the age of six, even in a part of the kingdom so renowned for the quickest proficiency in that art.

I am assured by our merchants that a boy or a girl before twelve years old is no salable commodity; and even when they come to this age they will not yield above three pounds, or three pounds and half a crown at most on the Exchange; which cannot turn to account either to the parents or the kingdom, the charge of nutriment and rags having been at least four times that value.

I shall now therefore humbly propose my own thoughts, which I hope will not be liable to the least objection.

I have been assured by a very knowing American of my acquaintance in London, that a young healthy child well nursed is at a year old a most delicious, nourishing, and wholesome food, whether stewed, roasted, baked, or boiled; and I make no doubt that it will equally serve in a fricassee or a ragout.

I do therefore humbly offer it to public consideration that of the hundred and twenty thousand children, already computed, twenty thousand may be reserved for breed, whereof only one fourth part to be males, which is more than we allow to sheep, black cattle, or swine; and my reason is that these children are seldom the fruits of marriage, a circumstance not much regarded by our savages, therefore one male will be sufficient to serve four females. That the remaining hundred thousand may at a year old be offered in sale to the persons of quality and fortune through the kingdom, always advising the mother to let them suck plentifully in the last month, so as to render them plump and fat for a good table. A child will make two dishes at an entertainment for friends; and when the family dines alone, the fore or hind quarter will make a reasonable dish, and seasoned with a little pepper or salt will be very good boiled on the fourth day, especially in winter.

I have reckoned upon a medium that a child just born will weigh twelve pounds, and in a solar year if tolerably nursed increaseth to twenty-eight pounds.

I grant this food will be somewhat dear, and therefore very proper for landlords, who, as they have already devoured most of the parents, seem to have the best title to the children.

Infant's flesh will be in season throughout the year, but more plentiful in March, and a little before and after. For we are told by a grave author, an eminent French physician,[2] that fish being a prolific diet, there are more children born in Roman Catholic countries about nine months after Lent than at any other season; therefore, reckoning a year after Lent, the markets will be more glutted than usual, because the number of popish infants is at least three to one in this kingdom; and therefore it will have one other collateral advantage, by lessening the number of Papists among us.

I have already computed the charge of nursing a beggar's child (in which list I reckon all cottagers, laborers, and four fifths of the farmers) to be about two shillings per annum, rags included; and I believe no gentleman would repine to give ten shillings for the carcass of a good fat child, which, as I have said, will make four dishes of excellent nutritive meat, when he hath only some particular friend or his own family to dine with him. Thus the squire will learn to be a good landlord, and grow popular among the tenants; the mother will have eight shillings net profit, and be fit for work till she produces another child.

Those who are more thrifty (as I must confess the times require) may flay the carcass; the skin of which artificially dressed will make admirable gloves for ladies, and summer boots for fine gentlemen.

As to our city of Dublin, shambles may be appointed for this purpose in the most convenient parts of it, and butchers we may be assured will not be wanting; although I rather recommend buying the children alive, and dressing them hot from the knife as we do roasting pigs.

A very worthy person, a true lover of his country, and whose

2. Rabelais.

virtues I highly esteem, was lately pleased in discoursing on this matter to offer a refinement upon my scheme. He said that many gentlemen of this kingdom, having of late destroyed their deer, he conceived that the want of venison might be well supplied by the bodies of young lads and maidens, not exceeding fourteen years of age nor under twelve, so great a number of both sexes in every county being now ready to starve for want of work and service; and these to be disposed of by their parents, if alive, or otherwise by their nearest relations. But with due deference to so excellent a friend and so deserving a patriot, I cannot be altogether in his sentiments; for as to the males, my American acquaintance assured me from frequent experience that their flesh was generally tough and lean, like that of our schoolboys, by continual exercise, and their taste disagreeable; and to fatten them would not answer the charge. Then as to the females, it would, I think with humble submission, be a loss to the public, because they soon would become breeders themselves: and besides, it is not improbable that some scrupulous people might be apt to censure such a practice (although indeed very unjustly) as a little bordering upon cruelty; which, I confess, hath always been with me the strongest objection against any project, how well soever intended.

But in order to justify my friend, he confessed that this expedient was put into his head by the famous Psalmanazar, a native of the island Formosa, who came from thence to London above twenty years ago, and in conversation told my friend that in his country when any young person happened to be put to death, the executioner sold the carcass to persons of quality as a prime dainty; and that in his time the body of a plump girl of fifteen, who was crucified for an attempt to poison the emperor, was sold to his Imperial Majesty's prime minister of state, and other great mandarins of the court, in joints from the gibbet, at four hundred crowns. Neither indeed can I deny that if the same use were made of several plump young girls in this town, who without one single groat to their fortunes cannot stir abroad without a chair, and appear at the playhouse and assemblies in foreign fineries which they never will pay for, the kingdom would not be the worse.

Some persons of a desponding spirit are in great concern about that vast number of poor people who are aged, diseased, or maimed, and I have been desired to employ my thoughts what course may be taken to ease the nation of so grievous an encumbrance. But I am not in the least pain upon that matter, because it is very well known that they are every day dying and rotting by cold and famine, and filth and vermin, as fast as can be reasonably expected. And as to the younger laborers, they are now in almost as hopeful a condition. They cannot get work, and consequently pine away for want of nourishment to a degree that if at any time they are accidentally hired to common labor, they have not strength to perform it; and thus the country and themselves are happily delivered from the evils to come.

I have too long digressed, and therefore shall return to my subject. I think the advantages by the proposal which I have made are obvious and many, as well as of the highest importance.

For first, as I have already observed, it would greatly lessen the number of Papists, with whom we are yearly overrun, being the principal breeders of the nation as well as our most dangerous enemies; and who stay at home on purpose to deliver the kingdom to the Pretender, hoping to take their advantage by the absence of so many good Protestants, who have chosen rather to leave their country than to stay at home and pay tithes against their conscience to an Episcopal curate.

Secondly, the poorer tenants will have something valuable of their own, which by law may be made liable to distress, and help to pay their landlord's rent, their corn and cattle being already seized and money a thing unknown.

Thirdly, whereas the maintenance of an hundred thousand children, from two years old and upwards, cannot be computed at less than ten shillings a piece per annum, the nation's stock will be thereby increased fifty thousand pounds per annum, besides the profit of a new dish introduced to the tables of all gentlemen of fortune in the kingdom who have any refinement in taste. And the money will circulate among ourselves, the goods being entirely of our own growth and manufacture.

Fourthly, the constant breeders, besides the gain of eight shillings sterling per annum by the sale of their children, will be rid of the charge of maintaining them after the first year.

Fifthly, this food would likewise bring great custom to taverns, where the vintners will certainly be so prudent as to procure the best receipts for dressing it to perfection, and consequently have their houses frequented by all the fine gentlemen, who justly value themselves upon their knowledge in good eating; and a skillful cook, who understands how to oblige his guests, will contrive to make it as expensive as they please.

Sixthly, this would be a great inducement to marriage, which all wise nations have either encouraged by rewards or enforced by laws and penalties. It would increase the care and tenderness of mothers toward their children, when they were sure of a settlement for life to the poor babes, provided in some sort by the public, to their annual profit instead of expense. We should see an honest emulation among the married women, which of them could bring the fattest child to the market. Men would become as fond of their wives during the time of their pregnancy as they are now of their mares in foal, their cows in calf, or sows when they are ready to farrow;

nor offer to beat or kick them (as is too frequent a practice) for fear of a miscarriage.

Many other advantages might be enumerated. For instance, the addition of some thousand carcasses in our exportation of barreled beef, the propagation of swine's flesh, and improvement in the art of making good bacon, so much wanted among us by the great destruction of pigs, too frequent at our tables, which are no way comparable in taste or magnificence to a well-grown, fat, yearling child, which roasted whole will make a considerable figure at a lord mayor's feast or any other public entertainment. But this and many others I omit, being studious of brevity.

Supposing that one thousand families in this city would be constant customers for infants' flesh, besides others who might have it at merry meetings, particularly weddings and christenings, I compute that Dublin would take off annually about twenty thousand carcasses, and the rest of the kingdom (where probably they will be sold somewhat cheaper) the remaining eighty thousand.

I can think of no one objection that will possibly be raised against this proposal, unless it should be urged that the number of people will be thereby much lessened in the kingdom. This I freely own, and it was indeed one principal design in offering it to the world. I desire the reader will observe, that I calculate my remedy for this one individual kingdom of Ireland and for no other that ever was, is, or I think ever can be upon earth. Therefore let no man talk to me of other expedients: of taxing our absentees at five shillings a pound: of using neither clothes nor household furniture except what is of our own growth and manufacture: of utterly rejecting the materials and instruments that promote foreign luxury: of curing the expensiveness of pride, vanity, idleness, and gaming in our women: of introducing a vein of parsimony, prudence, and temperance: of learning to love our country, in the want of which we differ even from Laplanders and the inhabitants of Topinamboo[3]: of quitting our animosities and factions, nor acting any longer like the Jews, who were murdering one another at the very moment their city was taken: of being a little cautious not to sell our country and conscience for nothing: of teaching landlords to have at least one degree of mercy toward their tenants: lastly, of putting a spirit of honesty, industry, and skill into our shopkeepers; who, if a resolution could now be taken to buy only our native goods, would immediately unite to cheat and exact upon us in the price, the measure, and the goodness, nor could ever yet be brought to make one fair proposal of just dealing, though often and earnestly invited to it.[4]

Therefore I repeat, let no man talk to me of these and the like

3. A district in Brazil.
4. Swift himself has made these various proposals in previous works.

expedients, till he hath at least some glimpse of hope that there will ever be some hearty and sincere attempt to put them in practice.

But as to myself, having been wearied out for many years with offering vain, idle, visionary thoughts, and at length utterly despairing of success, I fortunately fell upon this proposal, which, as it is wholly new, so it hath something solid and real, of no expense and little trouble, full in our own power, and whereby we can incur no danger in disobliging England. For this kind of commodity will not bear exportation, the flesh being of too tender a consistence to admit a long continuance in salt, although perhaps I could name a country which would be glad to eat up our whole nation without it.

After all, I am not so violently bent upon my own opinion as to reject any offer proposed by wise men, which shall be found equally innocent, cheap, easy, and effectual. But before something of that kind shall be advanced in contradiction to my scheme, and offering a better, I desire the author or authors will be pleased maturely to consider two points. First, as things now stand, how they will be able to find food and raiment for an hundred thousand useless mouths and backs. And secondly, there being a round million of creatures in human figure throughout this kingdom, whose sole subsistence put into a common stock would leave them in debt two millions of pounds sterling, adding those who are beggars by profession to the bulk of farmers, cottagers, and laborers, with their wives and children who are beggars in effect; I desire those politicians who dislike my overture, and may perhaps be so bold to attempt an answer, that they will first ask the parents of these mortals whether they would not at this day think it a great happiness to have been sold for food at a year old in the manner I prescribe, and thereby have avoided such a perpetual scene of misfortunes as they have since gone through by the oppression of landlords, the impossibility of paying rent without money or trade, the want of common sustenance, with neither house nor clothes to cover them from the inclemencies of the weather, and the most inevitable prospect of entailing the like or greater miseries upon their breed forever.

I profess, in the sincerity of my heart, that I have not the least personal interest in endeavoring to promote this necessary work, having no other motive than the public good of my country, by advancing our trade, providing for infants, relieving the poor, and giving some pleasure to the rich. I have no children by which I can propose to get a single penny; the youngest being nine years old, and my wife past childbearing.

QUESTIONS FOR STUDY, DISCUSSION, AND WRITING

1. This essay has been called one of the best examples of sustained irony in the English language. Irony is difficult to handle because

there is always the danger that the reader will miss the irony and take what is said literally. What does Swift do to try to prevent this? In answering this question, consider such matters as these: Is the first sentence of the essay ironic? At what point do you begin to suspect that Swift is using irony? What further evidence accumulates to make you certain that Swift is being ironic?

2. What is the speaker like? How are his views and character different from Swift's? Is the character of the speaker consistent? What is the purpose of the essay's final sentence?

3. Why does Swift use such phrases as "just dropt from its dam," "whose wives are breeders," "one fourth part to be males"?

4. Does the essay shock you? Was it Swift's purpose to shock you?

5. What is the main target of Swift's attack? What subsidiary targets are there? Does Swift offer any serious solutions for the problems and conditions he is describing?

6. What devices of argument, apart from the use of irony, does Swift use that could be successfully applied to other subjects?

THOMAS JEFFERSON

Slaves and Taxes[1]

On Friday, July 12, the committee appointed to draw the articles of Confederation reported them, and, on the 22d, the House resolved themselves into a committee to take them into consideration. On the 30th and 31st of that month, and 1st of the ensuing, those articles were debated which determined the proportion, or quota, of money which each state should furnish to the common treasury, and the manner of voting in Congress. The first of these articles was expressed in the original draught in these words.

Art. XI. All charges of war and all other expenses that shall be incurred for the common defence, or general welfare, and allowed by the United States assembled, shall be defrayed out of a common treasury, which shall be supplied by the several colonies in proportion to the number of inhabitants of every age, sex, and quality, except Indians not paying taxes, in each colony, a true account of which, distinguishing the white inhabitants, shall be triennially taken and transmitted to the Assembly of the United States.

Mr. Chase moved that the quotas should be fixed, not by the number of inhabitants of every condition, but by that of the "white inhabitants." He admitted that taxation should be always in proportion to property, that this was, in theory, the true rule; but that, from a variety of difficulties, it was a rule which could never be adopted in practice. The value of the property in every State, could never be estimated justly and equally. Some other measure

1. From Jefferson's *Autobiography*. The selection reports on debates in the   Second Continental Congress in July, 1776.

for the wealth of the State must therefore be devised, some standard referred to, which would be more simple. He considered the number of inhabitants as a tolerably good criterion of property, and that this might always be obtained. He therefore thought it the best mode which we could adopt, with one exception only: he observed that negroes are property, and as such, cannot be distinguished from the lands or personalities held in those States where there are few slaves; that the surplus of profit which a Northern farmer is able to lay by, he invests in cattle, horses, etc., whereas a Southern farmer lays out the same surplus in slaves. There is no more reason, therefore, for taxing the Southern States on the farmer's head, and on his slave's head, than the Northern ones on their farmer's heads and the heads of their cattle; that the method proposed would, therefore, tax the Southern States according to their numbers and their wealth conjunctly, while the Northern would be taxed on numbers only: that negroes, in fact, should not be considered as members of the State, more than cattle, and that they have no more interest in it.

Mr. John Adams observed that the numbers of people were taken by this article, as an index of the wealth of the State, and not as subjects of taxation; that, as to this matter, it was of no consequence by what name you called your people, whether by that of freemen or of slaves; that in some countries the laboring poor were called freemen, in others they were called slaves; but that the difference as to the state was imaginary only. What matters it whether a landlord, employing ten laborers on his farm, gives them annually as much money as will buy them the necessaries of life, or gives them those necessaries at short hand? The ten laborers add as much wealth annually to the State, increase its exports as much in the one case as the other. Certainly five hundred freemen produce no more profits, no greater surplus for the payment of taxes, than five hundred slaves. Therefore, the State in which are the laborers called freemen, should be taxed no more than that in which are those called slaves. Suppose, by an extraordinary operation of nature or of law, one-half the laborers of a State could in the course of one night be transformed into slaves; would the State be made the poorer or the less able to pay taxes? That the condition of the laboring poor in most countries, that of the fishermen particularly of the Northern States, is as abject as that of slaves. It is the number of laborers which produces the surplus for taxation, and numbers, therefore, indiscriminately, are the fair index of wealth; that it is the use of the word "property" here, and its application to some of the people of the State, which produces the fallacy. How does the Southern farmer procure slaves? Either by importation or by purchase from his neighbor. If he imports a slave, he adds one to the number of laborers in his country, and proportionably to its profits and abilities to pay taxes; if he buys from his neighbor, it is only a transfer of a laborer from one farm to another, which does not change the annual produce of the State, and therefore, should not change its tax: that if a Northern farmer works ten laborers on his farm, he can, it is true, invest the surplus of ten men's labor in cattle; but so may the Southern farmer, working ten slaves; that a State of one hundred thousand freemen can maintain no more cattle, than one of one hundred thousand slaves. Therefore, they have no more of that kind of property; that a slave may indeed, from the custom of speech, be more properly called the wealth of his master, than the free laborer might be called the wealth of his employer; but as to the State, both were equally its wealth, and should, therefore, equally add to the quota of its tax.

Mr. Harrison proposed, as a compromise, that two slaves should be counted as one freeman. He affirmed that slaves did not do as much work as freemen, and doubted if two effected more than one; that this was proved by the price of labor; the hire of a laborer in the Southern colonies being from £8 to £12, while in the Northern it was generally £24.

Mr. Wilson said, that if this amendment should take place, the Southern colonies would have all the benefit of slaves, whilst the Northern ones would bear the burden: that slaves increase the profits of a State, which the Southern States mean to take to themselves; that they also increase the burden of defense, which would of course fall so much the heavier on the Northern: that slaves occupy the places of freemen, and eat their food. Dismiss your slaves, and freemen will take their places. It is our duty to lay every discouragement on the importation of slaves; but this amendment would give the *jus trium liberorum*[1] to him who would import slaves: that other kinds of property were pretty equally distributed through all the colonies: there were as many cattle, horses and sheep, in the North as the South, and South as the North; but not so as to slaves: that experience has shown that those colonies have been always able to pay most, which have the most inhabitants, whether they be black or white; and the practice of the Southern colonies has always been to make every farmer pay poll taxes upon all his laborers, whether black or white. He acknowledges, indeed, that freemen work the most; but they consume the most also. They do not produce a greater surplus for taxation. The slave is neither fed nor clothed so expensively as a freeman. Again, white women are exempted from labor generally, but negro women are not. In this, then, the Southern States have an advantage as the article now stands. It has sometimes been said, that slavery is necessary, because the commodities they raise

2. Right of three freemen.

would be too dear for market if cultivated by freemen; but now it is said that the labor of the slave is the dearest.

Mr. Payne urged the original resolution of Congress, to proportion the quotas of the States to the number of souls.

Dr. Witherspoon was of opinion, that the value of lands and houses was the best estimate of the wealth of a nation, and that it was practicable to obtain such a valuation. This is the true barometer of wealth. The one now proposed is imperfect in itself, and unequal between the States. It has been objected that negroes eat the food of freemen, and, therefore, should be taxed; horses also eat the food of freemen; therefore they also should be taxed. It has been said too, that in carrying slaves into the estimate of the taxes the State is to pay, we do no more than those States themselves do, who always take slaves into the estimate of the taxes the individual is to pay. But the cases are not parallel. In the Southern colonies slaves pervade the whole colony; but they do not pervade the whole continent. That as to the original resolution of Congress, to proportion the quotas according to the souls, it was temporary only, and related to the moneys heretofore emitted: whereas we are now entering into a new compact, and therefore stand on original ground.

August 1. The question being put, the amendment proposed was rejected by the votes of New Hampshire, Massachusetts, Rhode Island, Connecticut, New York, New Jersey, and Pennsylvania, against those of Delaware, Maryland, Virginia, North and South Carolina. Georgia was divided.

JOHN DOS PASSOS
Fighting Bob[1]

La Follette was born in the town limits of Primrose; he worked on a farm in Dane County, Wisconsin, until he was nineteen.

At the university of Wisconsin he worked his way through. He wanted to be an actor, studied elocution and Robert Ingersoll and Shakespeare and Burke;

(who will ever explain the influence of Shakespeare in the last century, Marc Antony over Caesar's bier, Othello to the Venetian Senate and Polonius, everywhere Polonius?)

riding home in a buggy after commencement he was Booth and Wilkes writing the Junius papers and Daniel Webster and Ingersoll defying God and the togaed great grave and incorruptible as statues magnificently spouting through the capitoline centuries;

1. From *The 42nd Parallel* (1930).

he was the star debater in his class,
and won an interstate debate with an oration on the character
of Iago.

He went to work in a law office and ran for district attorney. His
schoolfriends canvassed the county riding round evenings. He bucked
the machine and won the election.

It was the revolt of the young man against the state republican
machine

and Boss Keyes the postmaster in Madison who ran the county
was so surprised he about fell out of his chair.

That gave La Follette a salary to marry on. He was twenty-five
years old.

Four years later he ran for congress; the university was with him
again; he was the youngsters' candidate. When he was elected he
was the youngest representative in the house

He was introduced round Washington by Philetus Sawyer the
Wisconsin lumber king who was used to stacking and selling politicians the way he stacked and sold cordwood.

He was a Republican and he'd bucked the machine. Now they
thought they had him. No man could stay honest in Washington.

Booth[2] played Shakespeare in Baltimore that winter. Booth never
would go to Washington on account of the bitter memory of his
brother. Bob La Follette and his wife went to every performance.

In the parlor of the Plankinton Hotel in Milwaukee during the
state fair, Boss Sawyer the lumber king tried to bribe him to influence his brother-in-law who was presiding judge over the prosecution of the Republican state treasurer;

Bob La Follette walked out of the hotel in a white rage. From
that time it was war without quarter with the Republican machine
in Wisconsin until he was elected governor and wrecked the Republican machine;

this was the tenyears war that left Wisconsin the model state
where the voters, orderloving Germans and Finns, Scandinavians
fond of their own opinion, learned to use the new leverage, direct
primaries, referendum and recall.

La Follette taxed the railroads

John C. Payne[3] said to a group of politicians in the lobby of the
Ebbitt House in Washington "La Follette's a damn fool if he thinks
he can buck a railroad with five thousand miles of continuous track,

2. Edwin Booth, brother of Lincoln's
assassin.

3. Apparently a slip for Henry C.
Payne, lobbyist for the St. Paul road

and packing interests. The incident is
chronicled by Belle Case La Follette and
Fola La Follette in their *Robert M. La
Follette* (New York, 1953), Vol. I, p. 82.

he'll find he's mistaken . . . We'll take care of him when the time comes."

But when the time came the farmers of Wisconsin and the young lawyers and doctors and businessmen just out of school
    took care of him
    and elected him governor three times
    and then to the United States Senate,

where he worked all his life making long speeches full of statistics, struggling to save democratic government, to make a farmers' and small businessmen's commonwealth, lonely with his back to the wall, fighting corruption and big business and high finance and trusts and combinations of combinations and the miasmic lethargy of Washington.

He was one of "the little group of wilful men expressing no opinion but their own"
    who stood out against Woodrow Wilson's armed ship bill that made war with Germany certain; they called it a filibuster but it was six men with nerve straining to hold back a crazy steamroller with their bare hands;
    the press pumped hatred into its readers against La Follette,
    the traitor,
    they burned him in effigy in Illinois;
    in Wheeling they refused to let him speak.

In nineteen twentyfour La Follette ran for president and without money or political machine rolled up four and a half million votes
    but he was a sick man, incessant work and the breathed out air of committee rooms and legislative chambers choked him
    and the dirty smell of politicians,
    and he died,
    an orator haranguing from the capitol of a lost republic;
    but we will remember
    how he sat firm in March nineteen seventeen while Woodrow Wilson was being inaugurated for the second time, and for three days held the vast machine at deadlock.[4] They wouldn't let him speak; the galleries glared hatred at him; the senate was a lynching party,
    a stumpy man with a lined face, one leg stuck out in the aisle and his arms folded and a chewed cigar in the corner of his mouth
    and an undelivered speech on his desk,
    a wilful man expressing no opinion but his own.

4. President Wilson submitted the Armed-ship bill to the 64th Congress only a few days before its automatic termination on March 4, 1917. The bill would have enabled the President to supply merchant ships with defensive arms. La Follette saw the bill as leading the U.S. into World War I and was instrumental in preventing it from coming to a vote.

QUESTIONS FOR STUDY, DISCUSSION, AND WRITING

1. What has guided Dos Passos in his selection of the particular things about La Follette that he includes? Why, for example, does he gives illustrations of La Follette's interest in Shakespeare?
2. What were the chief influences in La Follette's education?
3. Why does Dos Passos devote so little space to La Follette's Senate career?
4. What connotations would usually attach to the phrase "the little group of wilful men expressing no opinion but their own"? What is its effect in the context in which Dos Passos places it?
5. What impression of La Follette does Dos Passos wish to create? Write a brief sketch of La Follette using only the information given by Dos Passos, but attempting to create a different impression.

MURRAY KEMPTON

Father and Sons: The Reuther Boys

I'll be back, you sons of bitches; I'll be back and organize this plant.

EMIL MAZEY, upon ejection from the Briggs
Motor Corporation, December 1, 1936

The trouble with you, Reuther, is that you're still young and full of piss and vinegar.

ARNOLD LENZ, plant manager, Flint Chevrolet,
to Roy Reuther, March, 1937

Valentine Reuther's father brought him from Imperial Germany when he was nine years old out of that variety of impulses which were at the bottom of the historic quarrel of one Germany with the other—distaste for the army, distaste for the empire, distaste for Bismarck.

They settled in Wheeling, West Virginia, late in the eighties. Almost before Valentine had grown up, he went to work in the breweries, almost as determined an occupational terminus for the immigrant German as the dress shop for the immigrant Jew, the trolley car for the Irish, the open ditch for the Italian.

In the beginning, he earned $1.50 a day driving a brewery wagon. He spent some of it on courses from the International Correspondence Schools. After awhile this devotion to self-help qualified Valentine Reuther to be secretary of his AFL brewery workers' local. He earned a wage large enough for marriage for a man of moderate appetites. Valentine Reuther's four sons came close together—first Ted, then Walter in 1907, then Roy in 1909, and last of all Victor. At the time Roy was born, Valentine Reuther had climbed off his brewery wagon to become an organizer for his union and the rest of the AFL in the Ohio Valley. But this elevation brought no marked change in social status; his was a routine of close rations and prolonged trips from home.

When Roy was a little boy, he used to cry in the night because of his father's long absences; and Valentine Reuther was then quietly and easily reconciled to abandoning the road and confining his efforts for the world he wanted to Wheeling. But it was an entirely geographical compromise. Valentine Reuther never had to struggle with his natural impulses. He was a German working man; and so he had at once a sense of family and helped his union and voted Socialist and was happy and uncomplicated in all these processes.

He ran for Congress as a Socialist; he was president of the Ohio Valley AFL and he hoped for greater things from his sons. But Valentine Reuther inhabited a quiet pond of the American dream. He distrusted glittering success and glaring failure alike; vagabondage was as distasteful to him as any other kind of conspicuous consumption. And so he wanted his sons to be more successful than he had been, but in a fashion in no wise pretentious. The Germany of the last century had conditioned even its rebels to order and social stratification and to the idea that there are levels of achievement and that the good artisan should have pride of place.

Valentine Reuther taught his boys that each must have a trade. Walter would be a machinist, and Roy an electrician, and Victor seemed to hold promise as a plumber. Ted alone among them could expect to wear a white collar; he went into an office after he left high school. There was in their adolescence no rebellion, no slamming of doors, no apparent alienation. Their mother felt very deep the impress of German Protestantism; they were so faithful at Sunday School that each of their chests was heavy with the attendance pin and its ladder of bars certifying seven years without a Sunday missed.

In high school, the Reuther boys accepted with no sign of dissatisfaction the course in self-improvement their father prescribed for them. He would send them to the town library after school. On Sunday afternoons in winter, they would go to their bedroom and split into two-man teams to debate pacifism, capital punishment, or women in industry—what Valentine Reuther called "social questions"—while their father sat in a corner and graded them on how well they had organized and presented their material.

On Sunday afternoons in summer, this uncomplained-of regimen eased, and the Reuther boys would polish the family car and drive their parents to the public picnic grounds. They were adolescents of the twenties, a decade when by popular recollection the family was turning upon itself; it was a civil war which passed them by. Improvement of oneself and one's world was a basic goal in the home where the Reuthers grew up, but they appear to have shown little sense that their parents were old-fashioned or that there was an outside world with newer, easier standards than those by which Valentine Reuther ordered his life.

Roy is the only one of them who can recollect any temptation to live by the dictates of simple enjoyment. He was talented enough at track and basketball to consider a career as an athletic instructor; but his father told him that this was "rah-rah" stuff and brought him easily back to the family pattern. Roy and Victor finished high school in Wheeling. Walter had dropped out when he was sixteen to become an apprentice toolmaker. After three years he was a master mechanic and unemployed, having lost his last job for agitating against Sunday work.

And so he went, as all good unattached toolmakers seemed to go, to Detroit. For Detroit was the golden city of the twenties, a haven of promise for factory workers dreaming of a hundred-dollar-a-week pay check. It was a city of native immigrants, wandering prospectors, floaters, all drawn by Henry Ford's five-dollar-a-day base rate, which the imagination of ordinary men could so easily multiply through repetition to ten dollars or even fifteen dollars a day. The workers came there like pretty girls to Hollywood, clustering outside the works gates on rumors that so-and-so was hiring, husbanding themselves with odd jobs, and always waiting for the great chance that would open to them when they were taken on the assembly line. The old toolmakers had come early; the tide of migrants into Detroit in the twenties was of the untrained, drawn by Ford's promise to pay five dollars a day for skills that were minimal if they could be called skills at all.

Walter Reuther was not like most of these men, who had come to Detroit as though to Canaan and found it very much like the homes they had left behind, only noisier and less open and so much more cruel. The world is especially round to the unskilled. The dollar came only a little faster and a lot more painfully in Detroit than in most other places. But its workers did not study their failure and their loss and draw any large social judgments from them. They would sum up this latest piece of deception with some bit of pith about life in the harsher plants ("If poison fails, try Briggs") and wash it down with a boilermaker and go home to sleep off their exhaustion. Detroit was after all the last Klondike; no other delusive promise seemed to shimmer with a sheen making it worthwhile to move along.

* * *

Detroit's patron was Henry Ford, a man of strange terrors with a little boy's awe and affection for the tough and the violent. He did not want his hands to smoke or drink or skip church, but he hired gangsters to supervise them and keep them docile and pure of heart. He was the Don Quixote of an heraldic legend of self-interest; his Sancho Panza was an old navy saloon fighter named Harry Bennett, hired by Ford with the simple, direct question: "Can you shoot?" and master of his plant police and the police of Detroit and the state of Michigan as well.

Ford believed, in all matters except faith and morals, that if a man did not take care of himself, no one else should take care of him. All over America men read of his banner wage and trooped to Detroit. Once there, the fortunate among them worked the twelve-hour shift in his River Rouge plant eight months a year and were laid off four months for the model changeover, year after year, in the best of times. But that was their problem and not his.

Henry Ford delighted in visiting Bennett's office at the Rouge to take target practice; together they inhabited a swarm-haunted fortress from the Middle Ages where the show of violence was never hidden and where Bennett used his fists freely on his fellow executives and where they passed the compliment on to their inferiors. They ruled by whim and iron. In the spring of 1927, Ford discontinued the Model T and closed his works to retool for the Model A. For most of that year, 60,000 unemployed Detroit auto workers awaited the reopening of the golden door. They came back to be rehired according to custom as new employees, the young and the old each taking his place again at five dollars a day.

The executives had gotten rich too fast, and the production hands were broke too often. There was no ease and peace and quiet in Detroit; the classes hated one another, but in a way they were quite alike. They were at once careless and uncertain of the morrow; they were alike violent, brawling, and unconscious of any meaning in their lives. Communication in the city of the puritan Henry Ford was habitually conducted in language barely printable. Its typical citizens drank too much and wasted their substance and lost their jobs and went hungry and got them back and ate fairly well up on the hog and wondered all the while why it was so different from what they had expected.

If they were executives at Ford, they did things they were ashamed to do; but, as Bennett says, "they knew what side their bread was buttered on and did as they were told." Since they could not consciously hate themselves, they hated Henry Ford and one another. If they were only production hands at Ford, they spent their blood on the lines and too much of their wages in gin mills and made up bitter saws and longed for home. When the depression came and the jobs were gone, nearly a third of them went back to Mississippi or Missouri or Pennsylvania or took to the road that might lead them to some new, though no more promising, home.

Walter Reuther does not appear to have wondered; he was like neither the executives nor the men with whom he worked. From

the very beginning, his life in Detroit was unusual for its stability
and for what was even a moderate success. He began on the night
shift at Briggs. Before very long, his skill told, and he was able to
transfer to Ford with a higher rating, and after a while he was a
foreman. He went to Dearborn High School, and thereafter to
Wayne University, where, instead of engineering, he studied the
social sciences.

The difference between him and the others is framed best in
one of Reuther's own favorite memories of those days. Every afternoon when he came on, his predecessor on shift would ask him how
the ball game was going. Reuther never knew and always forgot
to find out. At last his shopmate suspended his inquiries with the
final judgment: "Reuther, you're the dumbest bastard I ever knew."
Reuther replied by asking, "Do you know the name of your
Congressman?" His mate answered that of course he didn't, and
Reuther returned a triumphant "Then you're the dumbest bastard
I've ever known."

Walter Reuther has a special affection for making a point, and
his zeal in this pursuit occasionally takes him into areas of platform
reminiscence which sound suspiciously like apocrypha. He has of
late been accustomed to cap this anecdote with a sequel. Fourteen
years after their last argument, he says he was inspecting a CIO
picketline and encountered his old detractor on gloomy parade.

"How're you doing?" Reuther chirped. "Not so good, Reuther,"
the picket replied and took off his cap to display a lump the size
of an egg, the consequence of conflict with the police. Reuther observed it without comment. At last his old shopmate asked, "Aren't
you going to say you're sorry for me?" And Reuther says he
answered, "No, I'm not sorry for you. If you'd known who your
Congressman was back then, you wouldn't have a lump on your
head now." Reuther and the ordinary auto worker have happily
reconciled their differences. But, even so, when Reuther tells that
story, his audience must have a hard time escaping a faint chill
at the back and a sense that to accept Walter Reuther is to expect
a comfort sometimes frigid.

Back in the twenties, when so few men were reputed to be
like their fathers, Walter Reuther had no ideals of which his father
could not entirely approve. Henry Ford's ban on smoking in or
about Highland Park was no deprivation to him. He saved his
money; he was a model workman; and he was a Socialist accepting his father's assurance that Detroit's chills and fevers were the
ordained results of private enterprise. If the union had never come,
no one can be sure that this revolutionary would not today be a
foreman at River Rouge, living as he does now and earning not too
much less than he makes as president of the United Auto Workers
and Congress of Industrial Organizations. Even his tireless talking

about the union did not cost him his job at Ford until very late in 1932; unlike so many of the others, he was able to work right into the trough of the depression and even save money. The Reuther boys were very normal except for their socialist bug. And there is something excessively normal about sons who acquire the parental bug.

Victor Reuther had taken Walter's path to Detroit late in the twenties. They went to Wayne together and worked in the auto plants and tried to build a fire there. But their efforts made little early mark. For Detroit was as quiet inside as it was noisy on the surface. Its residents managed at once to seem heavy with social portent and to make few social motions. There was a general assumption that if the revolution came at all, it would come to Detroit first. Yet, rough, disinherited, and ready for violence though Detroit's workers seemed, there had not been a union in its factories since they were carriage works before World War I.

In this context, Walter Reuther seemed clearly out of step in all he said and did. He was a Socialist when many of his shop-mates voted for Herbert Hoover. He was talking about a union through the boom and into the bust, when few of them would listen. He was working in the depression, when few of them could find jobs. In 1932, he campaigned for Norman Thomas and Detroit's auto workers voted for Franklin D. Roosevelt.

His passion for the 1932 Socialist campaign cost him his job at Ford. The politics which was one of his differences from ordinary men had thus put an end to the job security which was another difference and left Walter Reuther for once like so many of the rest—out of work in a crash town.

Ford's 1927 shift to the Model A had given Detroit a taste of depression. The 1929 bust laid it lower than any city of comparable size in the United States. It was beggared by the collapse of the auto industry which had made it rich. In 1929, there were nearly half a million persons employed in Michigan car factories; two years later there were barely 250,000. By 1932 Ford was producing almost alone among Detroit's giants, and the bulk of its orders were coming from the Soviet Union. The machine was coughing everywhere else; in Detroit, it was almost silent.

There were whole city blocks without light or artificial heat. Families missed their rent or mortgage payments. But no bank or landlord dared to evict them; to leave a house vacant was to risk its being stripped of its wires, its plumbing, and even its wood-work for fuel. At the onset of spring in 1932, Detroit's Welfare Department was the entire support of an estimated 250,000 persons. So many families had their water turned off that the schools instituted compulsory weekly showers for their pupils; in some neighborhoods, there were no graduation exercises because the graduates had no proper clothes for them.

The old values were melting and property laws breaking up. At one moment that spring, the city administration was so sunk in debt that grocers refused to accept nine million dollars of its welfare scrip. Mayor Frank Murphy called their representatives in to report that five stores had been entered and stripped the night before. The police had kept that fact out of the papers; but, once it became known, he could not guarantee an unrifled stock of groceries in Detroit. The storekeepers capitulated, and some time later Frank Murphy found the bank credit to honor his scrip.

* * *

But the revolution did not come and there was only one damp run of it. One February day in 1932, ten thousand persons, led by Communists, marched on River Rouge and were beaten back by the Dearborn police, first with fire hoses and then with bullets. When they had gone, Harry Bennett was stretched unconscious from a shower of rocks, and four demonstrators were dead. It was the disparity in casualties to be expected on the barricades in Detroit, and there were no further trials of physical strength.

Herbert Hoover came to Detroit that fall struggling for re-election. A hundred thousand people came out to see him. He drove past them through block after block of total, ghastly silence. The Secret Service speeded up his cortege; Detroit was as usual assumed to be the rim of violence, and no one was sure that even the President of the United States was immune from its buried passions.

Walter Reuther had his father's answer to all these terrors. Roy Reuther remembers Walter coming back to Wheeling in the summer of 1932 in a car covered with Thomas stickers and organizing a Socialist campaign meeting. A purpose was, as always, Walter Reuther's greatest pleasure. The Thomas campaign was as much his concept of a proper vacation pursuit as the family debate had been his idea of the best of possible Sunday afternoons.

He was not yet, of course, in step with history; in Wheeling, he had no trouble persuading Roy to vote for Thomas. All his arts could not persuade even Roy, then and there, to join the Socialist Party. But Roy came back to Detroit with his brothers; and before very long he had joined the Party too. Except for Ted, who was now in business in Wheeling, the Reuthers had all followed their father.

* * *

The Reuther boys had an hereditary faith in unions as instruments for social revolt. But the icons of their father's home were not labor leaders like Samuel Gompers and William Green but political figures like Eugene V. Debs and Robert M. La Follette. Debs might have known ease as president of one of those steam-driven, low-pressure railroad unions; he had chosen instead a course which made him a Socialist and destroyed him at last in prison for opposing World War I. Valentine Reuther approved every step along this, his personal saint's, path. Even as an AFL organizer, he had believed, with Debs, that Samuel Gompers was dissipating the large to grasp at the small.

The AFL national leadership had seemed to him narrow and petty and unconscious of its historic function, and Debs had seemed a knight with no dress on his shield and no dust on his plumes and no less glorious because his reward was of the future. Valentine Reuther was a German trade unionist of the nineties; to a German trade unionist, no little victory of his union was as anything set next to the vision of ultimate victory for all the workers. If the Reuther boys took from his house any vision of themselves grown up, it was an image of Debs renewed, not of Gompers repeated.

In November of 1932, Detroit inflicted impartial neglect upon Herbert Hoover and Norman Thomas alike. The auto workers, in bad times as in good, had shown no disposition to indulge the revolutionary politics which so many men hoped or feared was their potential. But very soon there were fresh alarms: the auto workers went on strike at Briggs, the place they had described so often in their bars as at once more certain and less comfortable than poison. Reporters came in from all around the country to watch what could be the onset of revolution.

But Detroit did not blow up. The Briggs strikers discovered in mid-passage that their leaders were Communists and threw them out. Briggs, of course, rewarded this demonstration of loyalty to American institutions by freezing and finally breaking their strike. But Walter and Victor were not around for the death of the Briggs strike. They had become infected with the auto worker's old impulse to wander.

Walter Reuther could not find a new job. He and Victor were so certain that this was no Paris Commune[1] upon which they were trembling that they decided to go to Europe. Walter had a bank account large enough to pay their passage and, with his customary knack for the act of good fortune, withdrew it the day before the beginning of the runs which were to make Detroit the cradle of the 1933 banking crisis.

He and Victor were still asleep on their departure day when Roy arose for his duties at the Briggs strike kitchen. He shook hands with them both and said good-by; he would not see them again for almost three years. They were already at sea when the police broke up the Briggs picket line, pushed Roy into an iron

1. The revolutionary socialist government of Paris, March-May, 1871.

fence, and gave him the scar he still carries on his ankle.

The NRA[2] came and passed. At its outset, the AFL had recruited 100,000 auto workers, all assuming, in John L. Lewis' phrase, that Franklin D. Roosevelt wanted them to join a union. By 1936, the AFL lost 90 percent of these newcomers. There had been a successful strike in 1934 at the Autolite Company in Toledo, Ohio; there was another, less successful, at Chevrolet in Cleveland in 1935; but these were at the industry's fringe; its major bastions remained untroubled.

In Roosevelt's third year, Detroit appeared, if anything, less vulnerable to the unions than it had on the day of his inauguration. The industry was functioning again, and its fearsome, lowering army of unemployed had begun to diminish. Emil Mazey,[3] a volunteer union organizer, was enduring the life the Reuthers might have known if they had been in Detroit.

"I couldn't exist with the violin," Mazey says now, "so I went to Gulf Refining in nineteen thirty-four. They had a strike in Cleveland. I watched it. We were making eighty-one dollars a month; after the strike, we made a few motions at the company and they gave us twenty to forty-five dollars a month more.

"I thought after that I could get the men to go AFL, but they sort of let me down and I got fired. After that I hung around the Y awhile and read on the bulletin board that Rotary Steel wanted people, so a bunch of us from the Y went up there and hired on. After a little while I got the boys from the Y to form an independent union and we went up to the AFL office to see if they'd take us in. The AFL didn't care much, and nothing happened, and after a while, I got fired there too.

"That didn't leave much but Briggs, so I ended up there in April of nineteen thirty-six. We did a little organizing and in the month of November, we had fifty-one sit-down strikes. They must have figured it was me giving them the trouble, because on December the first, nineteen thirty-six, a couple of plant guards took me off the line and threw me out in the street.

"They roughed me up pretty good and I got up and said: 'All right, you sons of bitches, I'll be back; I'll be back and organize this plant.'

"The next day, they fired my father and my brother for being related to me; they even tried to fire another fellow whose name was spelt like mine until he convinced them he wasn't a relative. But, after that, my brother and the old man joined the union, so I at least organized my own family."

Emil Mazey's was the course of the unpaid labor agitator in

2. The National Recovery Act, passed in 1933, declared unconstitutional by the U. S. Supreme Court in 1935, aimed to reduce cutthroat competition in industry and thus help the nation to recover from the depression.

3. Mazey had come to the United States from Hungary as a violinist.

Detroit in the early thirties, first let down by his own, then thrown down by the AFL, then thrown out by the company. Walter and Victor Reuther returned to that life from the Soviet Union by way of India, Japan, and a Pacific freighter, late in 1935.

Walter caught on at General Motors Ternstedt on Detroit's West Side. By now he was blacklisted and had to assume a new name to get his job. Even under this disguise, he made enough of a nuisance of himself to be fired before long, and thereafter settled down in the cold to supervise the six AFL auto locals on the West Side. When he showed up for the auto union convention in South Bend, Indiana, all six aggregated fewer than eighty members.

* * *

On the surface at least, the worst recollections of the depression had been buried. There was little talk of boom, but there appeared to be a growing sense that before long things might be as they were when people thought they had been so much happier than they really had been. Yet all that summer things were happening to foreshadow the flame which burst upon Detroit in the summer of 1937. First of all, the UAW was beginning to win recruits. There were not many of them, but they were the ordinary auto workers from whom the Reuthers had until then seemed so different.

The most important new arrival was the Chrysler independent union, which came into the UAW led by Richard Frankensteen, a raucus, fleshy giant who had been a tackle for the University of Dayton and had come to Chrysler to start at the bottom and had been anchored there by the depression. Frankensteen and the other Chrysler leaders had no ideological eccentricities and no spiritual ties except with Father Coughlin,[4] the witch doctor from the Shrine of the Little Flower. Frankensteen was glad to use Coughlin; Frankensteen would have used Mephistopheles if the imps would pay union dues.

The qualities of sin and virtue were mixed in Richard Frankensteen as they are in most men, and far more evenly than they are ever likely to be in Walter Reuther. Labor spying was one of Detroit's staple industries in those days; General Motors alone was spending for private detectives a sum more than twice as large as its president's salary. The way a Chrysler spy once deceived Richard Frankensteen was a gauge of his difference from Walter Reuther.

The Chrysler local was always shorthanded, and in 1936 Frankensteen was rejoiced by the tireless assistance of a young man named John Andrews. Andrews was valuable for more than his devotion to the union. He was a delightful companion with a

---

4. Priest and pastor of the Shrine of the Little Flower in Royal Oak, Michigan, Father Coughlin regularly broad-cast sermons that were venomously anti-Roosevelt, anti-Communist, and anti-Semitic.

millionaire uncle of abiding benevolence; and Andrews and Frankensteen were accustomed to relax together on week ends in the company of Andrew's uncle, never stinting a desire and never paying a check. Then, in 1937, Frankensteen learned from a Senate committee that John Andrews and his rich uncle had both been private detectives for Chrysler. The company had been buying the drinks, and his companions had been taking down his unguarded observations on union business for transmittal to Chrysler.

Dick Frankensteen had been hooked, but he had been hooked in the auto worker's fashion——with a few drinks and the image of a rich uncle, one of those successful men he wanted so much to be like. And so his followers could not blame him for being taken that way; they had but to assess the lure and their own incapacity to resist it, Calvinism being a minor element in the auto worker's philosophy.

Walter Reuther could hardly have been captured, even temporarily, with a tender of good fellowship from a private detective posing as a capitalist. The only feasible distraction for him would have been the loan of a home power lathe, a subtlety beyond the imagination of the corporations. They were different men. But Dick Frankensteen had his uses, for he was like the men in the plants, capable of violent activity between long periods of sloth, roaring in the short and slumbrous in the long, never mad at anyone for more than a little while.

Frankensteen brought along enough followers to make him the UAW's Detroit organizer. His time came very soon and blazed fleetingly, and after that he was hammering a cold anvil until, bored and empty, he left for good a life that seemed routine thereafter. For, unlike Walter Reuther, he was a man only for the sudden shock and the reeling crisis; but, together, for a little while they made the Detroit revolution.

The revolution began in the fall of 1936 in little, undisciplined strikes, which annoyed the industry more than they scared it. Briggs was the worst; but its wave of sit-down strikes ebbed, and on December 1st, Emil Mazey was out in the street and the season of peace, if not good will, was presumed to be at hand.

And then suddenly Walter Reuther won a big plant. His West Side local struck the Kelsey-Hayes Wheel Company in December. The strikers did a thing Detroit labor had never done before: they seized the administration offices, fortified the plant, and sat there, an army of occupation, for nine days, until the company gave in and accepted the union. Detroit's now quiet, now fitful quarrel had passed to a military phase. The Kelsey-Hayes strikers were captained by a young man named George Edwards, lately out of the Harvard Business School, and he fought like a line officer. The reports on the capture of Kelsey-Hayes were in the language of war:

"That morning we barricaded the Kelsey gates. The main gates were blocked by a solid, three-foot-high wall of steel, formed from a dozen carefully placed steel containers. We loaded each container with a couple of tons of hub-castings, and behind the barricade we set a dolly-load of eighteen-inch T irons."

They sat thus impregnable while Walter Reuther haggled with their company's displaced officers. Victor Reuther made hideous the noon outside with his sound truck; and one of the union delegates observed that this was the voice of Walter's brother. Someone brought in a Detroit paper with its picture of Roy Reuther stirring up Flint.

"Jesus Christ," said a Kelsey-Hayes official, the first of his breed to feel the sense of encirclement, "how many of you bastards are there?" The Reuther boys, in whom profanity does not spring naturally and who husband it for great occasions, are a bottomless inspiration for it in others.

But Kelsey-Hayes was not a major salient. The auto union's fate rested with Roy Reuther and the others who sat on the main line at Flint, the capital of General Motors and the company town of 150,000 persons where Chevrolets were made. There the union's organizers moved delicately among a very few who could be trusted, a few more who belonged to the enemy, and a great many who only stood and watched.

Every social war is a battle beween the very few on both sides who care and who fire their shots across a crowd of spectators. The ordinary Flint auto worker might well have voted for the union, granted the chance for the peaceful proceedings of a National Labor Relations Board election, but he would not risk his job for it. Peaceful proceedings were very far from Flint. The men who worked in Chevrolet were completely conscious of the dangers of public affirmation. In the beginning most of them stayed outside the union.

* * *

A combat officer on such a field must depend not on the mass but on a small, mobile, and itself dubious force of the dedicated. He must live by crisis and choose the moments when he is bold and his enemies indecisive and the army of neutrals can be moved his way by tidal shock. The sit-down strike was a military action, and Roy Reuther was a battalion commander.

The ground upon which he fought was clustered all about Flint—the two Fisher Body plants, the ramparts of Chevrolet where 14,000 people worked, the Buick and Cadillac enclaves. Chevrolet held the key to the citadel, but at first it seemed beyond assault. Whatever strength the union had was in Fisher Number One, where the bodies were made for Cadillacs, Buicks, and Oldsmobiles. The first battle was there. Late in December, Cleveland Fisher, the Chevrolet center, went on strike. If the UAW could stop Flint Fisher One, it could tie up 80 per cent of GM's production.

The war for Flint began on December 30, 1936, when 3,000 men sat down in Fisher Number One. They started in a carnival mood. On New Year's Eve, a foreman brought in liquor; two prostitutes came across the lines; the casual and the neutral began drifting out; by dawn fewer than a hundred men remained. The dedicated thereafter threw out their guests, sent for reinforcements, banned all whisky, and settled down to the sit-down strike's unaccustomed discipline for the next six weeks.

They slept in unfinished bodies or made their beds of car-cushion wadding and labeled them "Hotel Astor" or "Hotel Sloan," the latter for the chairman of the board of General Motors. A group of them took a vow not to shave until the strike was over; but they were required to take a shower every day. Each afternoon they swept up their garbage and saw it carried away by GM's disposal crew. They ran a daily inspection of quarters for cleanliness. Hour after hour, in groups, they practiced throwing car hinges at a piece of beaverboard to train themselves to repel invaders. But when they walked out, they left the company's property otherwise intact, except for the gougings of someone's file on a few car bodies, an act which Bud Simons, a Communist activist inside the plant, described in terms of the outraged morality of these incendiaries: "Only a stoolie would have done such a disgusting thing."

Every night they braced for a counterattack that never came. GM was trying the courts and the governor and the state police and every device but an invasion in force. None of their rulers could quite muster the decision to challenge the auto workers with the heavy battalions which might have broken them. But they were under siege. Outside their gates Flint was angry and restive; four-fifths of its workers were jobless, a majority not by choice. Late in January, GM announced a back-to-work movement. Governor Murphy was a bending reed; an unfavorable court decision could be deferred no longer; its certain consequence would be an injunction ordering Fisher Number One purged of its trespassers. The strike was not going well; it could be saved only by some stroke of strength and passion. The only worthwhile target was Chevrolet.

But Flint was quiet when GM reopened its unstruck plants on January 24, 1937. The company had redoubled its guards in and about the Chevrolet works. This ground, unhealthy in December, seemed deadly in January.

The union's leaders huddled in their headquarters the night of January 27th and surveyed their unpromising situation. Chevrolet Plant Number Four, where the engines were made, was the only operation worth stopping; the UAW's resources there were terribly small; there were, in fact, only fifty trustworthy men in all Flint Chevrolet. Roy Reuther had a fresh shirt sitting on his desk. He reached over and drew out its cardboard backing and, with a blue pencil, commenced to sketch a diagram of their objective: Chevvy Number Four, the main target, and Chevrolet Number Nine to its right, and Chevrolets Six and Eight, where the few sure believers were, just above that.

It was a diagram of battle undreamed of at the University of Wisconsin, unthought of even at Brookwood Labor College.[5] Their only chance, said Roy Reuther, was in a diversion. The union would call in its noncoms and announce a plan to capture Chevrolet Number Nine, just across the way from Number Four. The Pinkertons could be expected to inform the company of this schedule and GM would strip its other plants of guards to protect the threatened point. And, while the battle was on and the UAW's partisans were diverting the enemy in Number Nine, twenty-five of the union's most trusted bravoes would attempt the seizure of Chevrolet Number Four.

On January 29th, Chevrolet Works Manager Arnold Lenz, alerted as expected, showed up with all his guards to meet the decoy invasion as it came. They fought in clouds of gas, the guards with blackjacks, the strikers with oil pumps, for the forty minutes which Roy Reuther thought his auxiliaries would need to raid and subdue Chevrolet Four.

Roy Reuther had sent a call for fireworks outside Chevrolet Nine. Victor was on the street with his sound truck and Walter with his Kelsey-Hayes shock troops to lend color to Roy's diversion. The windows of Number Nine were clouded; the crowd outside could see only the shadows of struggling men. Once someone broke a window and they could see the tear-gas smoke seeping out and they knew the battle was going badly. A few members of Walter Reuther's legion set up a clamor to charge the gates. He grabbed the loudest of them and knocked him out to quiet him. Walter Reuther knew, in the hot moments as in the cold, the sacrifices required of men assigned to serve as a diversion.

But, by now, a skeleton crew of foremen was all that was left to fight for General Motors inside Chevrolet Four. There was no one else there except neutrals and UAW partisans. Roy Reuther's squad subdued it quickly, marching through with their wrenches, calling out their friends, cowing the undecided. As the battle for Chevrolet Nine swirled toward its predestined end, there was a sudden silence from Chevrolet Four; and the pickets outside understood that GM's main engine plant had been halted.

---

5. At Wisconsin, the Department of Economics under John R. Commons had developed a leading school of labor and industrial relations. Brookwood Labor College, now defunct, was a Socialist school in upper New York state affiliated with trade unions.

The battalion in Chevrolet Nine executed an orderly withdrawal. The new garrison in Number Four was throwing up its barricade —gondolas loaded with 8,000 pounds of stock and piled one on top of the other against the great doors. Joe Sayen, a Chevrolet Four worker thereafter unheard upon any great stage again, climbed the spiked fence outside Chevrolet and told the pickets that the bastions had fallen:

"We want the whole world to know what we are fighting for. We are fighting for freedom and life and liberty. This is our great opportunity. What if we should be defeated? What if we should be killed? We have only one life. That is all we can lose and we might as well die like heroes than like slaves."

For his little while, the auto worker was speaking a language beyond the dreams of the Reuther boys, his words like those Shakespeare put into the mouth of the tailor called to the wars: "By my troth I care not; a man can die but once; we owe God a death; . . . and let it go which way it will, he that dies this year is quit for the next."

The seizure of Chevrolet Four meant the end of the GM strike; the company recognized that it had lost the ascendancy; John Lewis came in to invest the men in its plants with his own heroic effrontery, to strut and fret and wangle a settlement. The union had won very little on paper. Outsiders wondered if it had won anything at all. But the men in the plants knew that this was a victory; it was summed up for them in the words of a striker who announced that he would slug the first foreman who looked cock-eyed at him.

On February 11, 1937, they marched out in the twilight, down Chevrolet Avenue, the beards still on so many of their faces, the cigars in their mouths, the confetti sifting down from the gates of Chevrolet Four, on into the center of Flint, and no one who watched them could doubt who the winners were.

The fire they had set would blaze through Detroit for two more months. Briggs had its sit-down in February. Emil Mazey settled it in the early hours of the morning. "I came out of the personnel office at four A.M. and climbed on a barrel and made a soapbox speech and told the boys we'd won."

* * *

The sit-down strike was the most orderly of armed insurrections. Its general use as a technique explains better than any other factor why Detroit's great change was so free of blood. Once a union seized a plant, the risk of property damage from evicting the strikers so inhibited the employer and the authorities that their tenure was apt to be peaceful. By this challenge to total war, the unions seem to have avoided the risks of limited conflict; the bloodiest labor struggle of 1937 was the CIO Little Steel strike, where the union abstained from the sit-down and relied on the traditional walkout.

Industry deserves some credit for all this order in disorder, if only because it never thought of any general technique for meeting the challenge of the sit-downs. The solitary contribution of American productive genius to defense against the sit-down strike was the invention of Howard Keele, a vice president of the Fansteel Corporation. Keele devised a platform upon which Chicago police could be wheeled into action and from which they could pour tear-gas bombs into the second barricade of Fansteel's sit-downers. Keele had began as an instructor in English at the University of Illinois, a fact which may serve as some counter to the theory that in the thirties all scholars in the humanities chose the improper side of the barricades.

During the March fires of 1937, Dick Frankensteen, age 32, roared through Detroit like a great bellows; Walter Reuther, 30, hurled his implacable voice at employers bruised in pride and helpless to avenge themselves. Victor Reuther, 26, moved his sound truck from command post to command post. Emil Mazey, 23, was president of a local union with 2,000 members. Roy Reuther, 28, could never go to sleep in his Flint Hotel without expecting to awake to a telephone ringing its summons to go to some GM plant at once; the line had been struck again.

GM's Arnold Lenz spoke for all the Detroit that was passing when he growled at Roy Reuther one afternoon, "The trouble with you, Reuther, and all you fellows, is that you are young and full of piss and vinegar." Arnold Lenz had a dim sense that he was fighting youth and the future. Even to him it must have seemed, as it did to the Reuthers then, a future without the limits of compromise.

General Motors fought with the same desperate sense even after the Flint strike was settled, as though every inch given was so much more surrendered from the last ditch. It was hard to believe that men who would seize your property and fight you like soldiers dug in on the high ground had any intention but your total destruction.

The most articulate citizens of Detroit thought then that the United Auto Workers was something more than a union, that it was in fact a revolutionary army whose final destination was the conquest of all power for labor. Through the next thirteen years, every action of the union and every counteraction of its industry reflected the illusion of fundamental revolution which had infected Detroit in March of 1937. Until 1950, every strike had its mood of basic crisis; the union and the company alike talked as though very life hung on its decision.

But there was only one March of 1937. When it had passed, the passion lifted from Detroit as suddenly as it had come. The city would never be exactly as it had been; but it would be settled and normal in its fashion. The men who had barricaded themselves in the fortresses of their proprietors had wanted something badly enough to face death for it. But they had not wanted to be masters. They had asked only to be equals.

The striker who had affirmed his resolve to slug any foreman who looked cross-eyed at him in the future had not been offended by the fact of the foreman's existence as an institution. He had accepted the system and was demanding only a measure of amenity in its confines.

Through the spring of 1937 there was a cooling and a settling in Detroit and the limits of its great insurrection began to appear. They were limits detectable mostly to the vision of hindsight. Walter Reuther was only the most articulate of a number of UAW leaders who remained certain for a while longer that the politics, the economics, the culture, the whole future of Detroit and ultimately of this country belonged to these emancipated auto workers, whose vision had no bounds, and whose passions would not slack.

That summer of 1937, the UAW entered its own candidate for mayor of Detroit; Walter Reuther, Dick Frankensteen, and four others ran for the City Council under the unashamed label of a labor slate. The politicians beat them with unexpected ease. And that same summer, Henry Ford braced to resistance. He alone remained unbeaten and almost undamaged among the rulers of Detroit. He fought the union as he always had, with spies and blackjacks and blacklists, and he stopped its revolution cold.

One day near early summer, Walter Reuther, Dick Frankensteen, and a group of other UAW organizers walked near the overpass at Ford's River Rouge works to distribute union leaflets. Harry Bennett met them in force; Frankensteen later testified that fully fifty Ford service men assaulted him and Reuther. Frankensteen, with the ill-considered vanity of an old football player, made an effort to defend himself. Reuther only covered his face with his hands and let them take him; false pride was not one of Walter Reuther's problems. Afterward he described it all to the National Labor Relations Board in cold, sparse, exact terms:

"Seven times they raised me off the concrete and threw me down on it. They pinned my arms and shot short jabs to my face. I was punched and dragged by my feet to the stairway. I grabbed the railing and they wrenched me loose. I was thrown down the first flight of iron steps. Then they kicked me down the other flight of steps until I found myself on the ground where I was beaten and kicked. . . . At that time girls and women who came from Detroit with circulars tried to get off the streetcars, and so the men seemed to lose interest in me."

It all sounded so terribly matter of fact, as though circumstance were a minor condition beside Walter Reuther's need to function. He had worked fifteen months in a Soviet factory; Rouge was only the hottest of the plant gates at which he was pummeled; in 1948, when he seemed to have reached a stable plane, he was shot by some still unknown fugitive from Detroit's days of wrath. All that has happened has made no more change in him that if it had never happened. The Soviet experience did not exalt him beyond reason; the Rouge beating did not reduce him to the rhetoric of self-pity; even the shotgun did not alter his will to function.

The 1948 shooting almost tore his right arm off; it was only saved by an intricate operation on the radial nerves. A little while after he left the hospital bed, a visitor found him pacing the floor, talking as always, but with pain in the set of his mouth and sweat on his forehead. It was a sight so discomforting that his visitor begged Reuther to sit down and be quiet.

"Don't you see," said Walter Reuther, "that I've got to live with this thing?"

Every new circumstance was a thing that he would live with, and that must not damage, divert, or alter him. Edward Levinson, then publicity director of the UAW, drove him from Detroit to New York for a union board meeting on December 7, 1941. Reuther was then chairman of the UAW's housing committee, and a report on its work was his chief assignment at the meeting. There was no radio in the car; they arrived at their hotel to find the newsboys holding up the extras reporting Japan's attack on Pearl Harbor.

It was a moment in history. Levinson's first instinct was to rush from the car up to Times Square and see how New York was taking it. The flat voice of Walter Reuther came up from the back seat:

"Well, Eddie, this means we'll have to rewrite the report. We'd better go and wash up and I'll see you in the room in twenty minutes."

For Walter Reuther never felt the impulse to lose himself in any tide of history; every exterior crash seemed to break upon the rock of his will to independent function. Yet this was a will detached from circumstance but not blind to it. If his world changed, he would live with the change.

And back in that summer of 1937, he recognized that circumstances were not what they had seemed only last March, and that he must live with a new state of things. The men for whom he had bled at the Rouge looked at his scars without interest; the politicians had beaten him for the City Council. March had been only a flash fire. The revolution would move no longer at the double-quick. He and Roy and Victor could not again be captains in a war of movement; what stretched ahead was a stewardship that would seem routine more often than it seemed electric.

Once, not very long ago, Walter Reuther had wanted much more; he had thought of the union as an instrument to reshape America sharp and fast. Now the surge of that promise was over, and he was left with the ebb. For the auto worker had now won most of what had seemed to him worth the chance of disaster: security on his job, higher wages, shorter hours, and the sense that he was no less human that his foreman. The union was important in his life, but it was not the only thing. All the diversions which turn men away from further assault upon the heights were at work now. There was nothing on the heights which seemed to the auto worker worth an immediate, desperate, dangerous grasp.

His institution would not change for Walter Reuther, and so Walter Reuther changed for it. He began by leaving the Socialist Party in the late thirties, quietly and without pain; he was on his way to becoming a rock of stability. It was a change not easy for many of the UAW's founding field commanders, and they lost their offices or wandered away for want of the will or the capacity to deal with the new condition.

* * *

The change in Walter Reuther, if it can be called a change, must have begun very soon after the sit-downs, but it did not show itself to the clouded eye. Detroit had been very briefly a pillar of flame, but its vision would not soon leave the minds of those who had so long believed the labor movement could be the cleansing agent of the social revolution and who had clutched that belief through numberless discouragements from the manners, the barnacled social vision, and the soggy prose of the leaders of the American Federation of Labor.

They had watched the flames of Detroit for the emergence of a new sort of labor leader—a walking sword conscious of the mission of which his profession had been by tradition but semi-conscious and ready to thrust through to an America whose old rulers would be overthrown and whose old oppressed would be finally triumphant. With the cooling of the fires of 1937, every UAW figure except those of the Reuthers appeared to their anxious eyes disappointingly like the old-fashioned labor professional.

The Reuthers alone in Detroit seemed to speak with a confident voice of labor's wider destiny. They spoke of co-operatives and labor parties and labor control of industry and the revolutionary aspirations of the workers of Asia. And they were figures of history with a growing army behind them. If figures of history could speak with the tongue of the scorned and lonely left of Valentine Reuther, there was cause to hope that history might be going Valentine Reuther's way.

In the very late thirties, none of the Reuthers was a national officer of the auto workers' union, which was itself just a fragment of the labor movement. Yet even then, except for John Lewis, Philip Murray, and Harry Bridges, Walter Reuther was better known to the public at large than anyone in the CIO. All over America, there were people who thought of him, young, purposeful, and sure of his destiny, as a symbol of a unionism that promised everything.

To them Walter Reuther appeared like some Archangel Michael; but there were others to his acquaintance to whom he appeared, as Michael had to Lucifer, as an abhorrent shape and who wished he would be hence. The burning of incense and the singing of hosannas around Walter Reuther was a natural source of discomfort to his colleagues in the UAW who ranked him in office but trailed so far behind him in public excitement.

And the old rulers of Detroit, dislocated and sore in bones and pride, heard the rattle of the tumbrels in his speeches and thought they detected a young man after the jugular. There must be men of property who fairly long for the knife at their throats; there are certainly men without security who seek always for someone to thrust the knife for them; and it took both groups a long while to be disappointed in Walter Reuther.

They watched with fear and fascination his rise in the auto union, feeling each beat of its conventions—turning now for him and now against him—as though the balance of all life hung on those delegates hoarsely shouting their votes and their locals' numbers. And yet, when Walter Reuther had become president of the auto workers, none of his upward steps seemed as periled and as faltering as they had at the time he took them. With hindsight his progress seemed assured from the beginning, as though nature had intended him to succeed Henry Ford as the first citizen of a Detroit which, however unchecked its own passions, must always have a household god who neither smokes nor drinks.

And all of it had been so little the result of the primary qualities which the public assigned to Walter Reuther. It had been so little a progress of rhetoric; Reuther remained, as always, available for discourse to the laity on elevating social subjects as other men are available for poker or drinks around the corner. But rhetoric was only his pleasure. Reality of function was his pursuit and his true passion.

Those made timid and those exalted by his image could wake together in the fifties to find that Walter Reuther was not a barnburner after all. Valentine Reuther did not bring his boys up to burn barns. Walter Reuther was, in fact, rather conservative and unexpectedly normal in his lack of the impulse to destruction. The auto workers, for all their flash of fundamental challenge, were with time more conservative and more normal than anyone could have believed seventeen years ago. For even in Detroit, men do not march long under wild flags. And if Walter Reuther had summoned his troops to any wild flags, they would have been his troops no longer.

There had been a few desperate hours after 1937. Ford had hung on until 1941, and had surrendered only to the last of the sit-down strikes. When it was over, he gave the union a little more than it asked with the expectation that these incursors would commence to fight among themselves for the spoils and after a while go away. But it was Henry Ford who went away at last. After his death, the service men departed and were replaced, to a degree at least, by college boys who put away the Anglo-Saxon diction of the middle thirties and fought their skirmishes with Walter Reuther through the soft fog which is the uniform of the labor relations man's language. And Harry Bennett, an obsolete model, retired to his residence near Lake Michigan.

General Motors cherished the hope that the new order would pass and carried that hope through a one-hundred-and-seven-day strike in 1946, a quiet affair but no less passionate for its lack of violence. That strike ended with the assumption that Detroit's two great powers would glare at one another for the predictable future through an armed truce broken biennially by a marathon strike.

But then Charles E. Wilson, president of General Motors, and Walter Reuther suddenly shook hands across Detroit's wall. In 1950, GM agreed to give the auto union a five-year contract, keying its wages to the cost of living, guaranteeing its members a yearly increase reflecting their company's technological progress. The other companies trooped to follow; there has not been a major auto strike in Detroit since that spring.

When Walter Reuther came to Detroit, he entered an industrial dictatorship. Each auto worker was alone and fragmented; his future did not extend beyond the spring layoff, and the foreman was his master in fact. In 1937, the Reuther boys were commanders at war with the whole order of society in Detroit; it did not seem possible that their war could end with quarter. But today Detroit is quiet; it moves not, nor shakes, nor seems pregnant with violence as it once did. There has come upon it the peace of understanding. An auto worker earns a minimum of $84 a week; he has a pension and a paid vacation and the automatic assurance that his wages will move up and up; he is in short the unexpected inhabitant of an industrial democracy.

This miracle accomplished by the rabble captained by Roy, exhorted by Victor, and maneuvered by Walter Reuther is no less a miracle for being not quite the sort expected of them. Walter Reuther and the auto makers of Detroit, who seemed so irreconcilable, have ended by sharing a common response to the moments of passion in their lives. They alike understand the necessity of living with things as they are.

* * *

So much has happened to the Reuther boys—some of it heroic, some of it almost tragic, all of it rather fantastic—that it is surprising how little it has done to them. They have had adventures, but they were not raised to be adventurers. They were raised to follow a trade and be a credit to their home. Of all the heritage their father passed on to them from the Eugene Debs who was his hero, he passed on most the notion that it is better to rise with your class than from it.

There are limitations to that portion of Valentine Reuther's estate. A man ingrained with its vision is not apt to be exalted, to dare everything for great and distant passions, or to enjoy tumult for its own sake, for the class from which Walter Reuther came is not long committed to any of these diversions. But those are also its virtues; in spite of Deb's own tragedy, his heritage encompasses the normal and the unalienated.

The Reuther boys saw life in the ideal image of their father's house and their father's aspirations; they did not seek their revolution on their father's grave. And so, through all the tombstones of the thirties, they have walked unchanged and unafflicted, because they were very normal young men caught in a wild circumstance and glad to pass through it to normality again.

THOMAS JEFFERSON
Original Draft of the Declaration of Independence

A Declaration of the Representatives of the UNITED STATES OF AMERICA, in General Congress assembled.

When in the course of human events it becomes necessary for a people to advance from that subordination in which they have hitherto remained, & to assume among the powers of the earth the equal & independant station to which the laws of nature & of nature's god entitle them, a decent respect to the opinions of mankind requires that they should declare the causes which impel them to the change.

We hold these truths to be sacred & undeniable; that all men are created equal & independant, that from that equal creation they derive rights inherent & inalienable, among which are the preservation of life, & liberty, & the spirit of happiness; that to secure these ends, governments are instituted among men, deriving their just powers from the consent of the governed; that whenever any form of government shall become destructive of these ends, it is the right of the people to alter or to abolish it, & to institute new government, laying it's foundation on such principles & organising it's powers in such form, as to them shall seem most likely to effect their safety & happiness. prudence indeed will dictate that governments long established should not be changed for light & transient causes: and accordingly all experience hath shewn that mankind are more disposed to suffer while evils are sufferable, than to right themselves by abolishing the forms to which they are accustomed. but when a long train of abuses & usurpations, begun at a distinguished period, & pursuing invariably the same object, evinces a design to subject them to arbitrary power, it is their right, it is their duty, to throw off such government & to provide new guards for their future security. such has been the patient sufferance of these colonies; & such is now the necessity which constrains them to expunge their former systems of government. the history of his present majesty, is a history of unremitting injuries and usurpations, among which no one fact stands single or solitary to contradict the uniform tenor of the rest, all of which have in direct object the establishment of an absolute tyranny over these states. to prove this, let facts be submited to a candid world, for the truth of which we pledge a faith yet unsullied by falsehood.

he has refused his assent to laws the most wholesome and necessary for the public good:

he has forbidden his governors to pass laws of immediate & pressing importance, unless suspended in their operation till his assent should be obtained; and when so suspended, he has neglected utterly to attend to them.

he has refused to pass other laws for the accommodation of large districts of people unless those people would relinquish the right of representation, a right inestimable to them, & formidable to tyrants alone:[1]

he has dissolved Representative houses repeatedly & continually, for opposing with manly firmness his invasions on the rights of the people:

he has refused for a long space of time to cause others to be elected, whereby the legislative powers, incapable of annihilation, have returned to the people at large for their exercise, the state remaining in the mean time exposed to all the dangers of invasion from without, &, convulsions within:

1. At this point in the manuscript a strip containing the following clause is inserted: "He called together legislative bodies at places unusual, unco[mfortable, & distant from] the depository of their public records for the sole purpose of fatiguing [them into compliance] with his measures:" Missing parts in the Library of Congress text are supplied from the copy made by Jefferson for George Wythe. This copy is in the New York Public Library. The fact that this passage was omitted from John Adams's transcript suggests that it was not a part of Jefferson's original rough draft.

he has suffered the administration of justice totally to cease in some of these colonies, refusing his assent to laws for establishing judiciary powers:

he has made our judges dependant on his will alone, for the tenure of their offices, and amount of their salaries:

he has erected a multitude of new offices by a self-assumed power, & sent hither swarms of officers to harrass our people & eat out their substance:

he has kept among us in times of peace standing armies & ships of war:

he has affected to render the military, independent of & superior to the civil power:

he has combined with others to subject us to a jurisdiction foreign to our constitutions and unacknoledged by our laws; giving his assent to their pretended acts of legislation, for quartering large bodies of armed troops among us;

> for protecting them by a mock-trial from punishment for any murders they should commit on the inhabitants of these states;

> for cutting off our trade with all parts of the world;

> for imposing taxes on us without our consent;

> for depriving us of the benefits of trial by jury

he has endeavored to prevent the population of these states; for that purpose obstructing the laws for naturalization of foreigners; refusing to pass others to encourage their migrations hither; & raising the conditions of new appropriations of lands;

> for transporting us beyond seas to be tried for pretended offences:

> for taking away our charters & altering fundamentally the forms of our governments;

> for suspending our own legislatures & declaring themselves invested with power to legislate for us in all cases whatsoever:

he has abdicated government here, withdrawing his governors, & declaring us out of his allegiance & protection:

he has plundered our seas, ravaged our coasts, burnt our towns & destroyed the lives of our people:

he is at this time transporting large armies of foreign mercenaries to compleat the works of death, desolation & tyranny, already begun with circumstances of cruelty & perfidy unworthy the head of a civilized nation:

he has endeavored to bring on the inhabitants of our frontiers the merciless Indian savages, whose known rule of warfare is an undistinguished destruction of all ages, sexes, & conditions of existence:

he has incited treasonable insurrections of our fellow-citizens, with the allurements of forfeiture & confiscation of our property: he has waged cruel war against human nature itself, violating it's most sacred rights of life & liberty in the persons of a distant people who never offended him, captivating & carrying them into slavery in another hemisphere, or to incur miserable death in their transportation thither. this piratical warfare, the opprobrium of *infidel* powers, is the warfare of the CHRISTIAN king of Great Britain. determined to keep open a market where MEN should be bought & sold; he has prostituted his negative for suppressing every legislative attempt to prohibit or to restrain this execrable commerce: and that this assemblage of horrors might want no fact of distinguished die, he is now exciting those very people to rise in arms among us, and to purchase that liberty of which *he* has deprived them, by murdering the people upon whom *he* also obtruded them; thus paying off former crimes committed against the *liberties* of one people, with crimes which he urges them to commit against the *lives* of another.

in every stage of these oppressions we have petitioned for redress in the most humble terms; our repeated petitions have been answered by repeated injury. a prince whose character is thus marked by every act which may define a tyrant, is unfit to be the ruler of a people who mean to be free. future ages will scarce believe that the hardiness of one man, adventured within the short compass of twelve years only, on so many acts of tyranny without a mask, over a people fostered & fixed in principles of liberty.

Nor have we been wanting in attentions to our British brethren. we have warned them from time to time of attempts by their legislature to extend a jurisdiction over these our states. we have reminded them of the circumstances of our emigration & settlement here, no one of which could warrant so strange a pretension: that these were effected at the expence of our own blood & treasure, unassisted by the wealth or the strength of Great Britain: that in constituting indeed our several forms of government, we had adopted one common king, thereby laying a foundation for perpetual league & amity with them; but that submission to their [Parliament, was no Part of our Constitution, nor ever in Idea, if History may be][2] credited: and we appealed to their native justice & magnanimity, as to the ties of our common kindred to disavow these usurpations which were likely to interrupt our correspondence & connection. they too have been deaf to the voice of justice & of consanguinity, & when occasions have been given them, by the regular course of their laws, of removing from their councils the disturbers of our

2. An illegible passage is supplied from John Adams' transcription.

harmony, they have by their free election re-established them in power. at this very time too they are permitting their chief magistrate to send over not only soldiers of our common blood, but Scotch & foreign mercenaries to invade & deluge us in blood. these facts have given the last stab to agonizing affection, and manly spirit bids us to renounce for ever these unfeeling brethren. we must endeavor to forget our former love for them, and to hold them as we hold the rest of mankind, enemies in war, in peace friends. we might have been a free & a great people together; but a communication of grandeur & of freedom it seems is below their dignity. be it so, since they will have it: the road to glory & happiness is open to us too; we will climb it in a separate state, and acquiesce in the necessity which pronounces our everlasting Adieu!

We therefore the representatives of the United States of America in General Congress assembled do, in the name & by authority of the good people of these states, reject and renounce all allegiance & subjection to the kings of Great Britain & all others who may hereafter claim by, through, or under them; we utterly dissolve & break off all political connection which may have heretofore subsisted between us & the people or parliament of Great Britain; and finally we do assert and declare these colonies to be free and independant states, and that as free & independant states they shall hereafter have power to levy war, conclude peace, contract alliances, establish commerce, & to do all other acts and things which independant states may of right do. And for the support of this declaration we mutually pledge to each other our lives, our fortunes, & our sacred honour.

THOMAS JEFFERSON and OTHERS

The Declaration of Independence

In Congress, July 4, 1776
The unanimous Declaration of the
thirteen united States of America

When in the Course of human events it becomes necessary for one people to dissolve the political bands which have connected them with another, and to assume among the powers of the earth, the separate and equal station to which the Laws of Nature and of Nature's God entitle them, a decent respect to the opinions of mankind requires that they should declare the causes which impel them to the separation.

We hold these truths to be self-evident, that all men are created equal, that they are endowed by their Creator with certain unalienable Rights, that among these are Life, Liberty and the pursuit of Happiness. That to secure these rights, Governments are instituted among Men, deriving their just powers from the consent of the governed, That whenever any Form of Government becomes destructive of these ends, it is the Right of the People to alter or to abolish it, and to institute new Government, laying its foundation on such principles and organizing its powers in such form, as to them shall seem most likely to affect their Safety and Happiness. Prudence, indeed, will dictate that Governments long established should not be changed for light and transient causes; and accordingly all experience hath shewn that mankind are more disposed to suffer, while evils are sufferable, than to right themselves by abolishing the forms to which they are accustomed. But when a long train of abuses and usurpations, pursuing invariably the same Object evinces a design to reduce them under absolute Despotism, it is their right, it is their duty, to throw off such Government, and to provide new Guards for their future security. Such has been the patient sufferance of these Colonies; and such is now the necessity which constrains them to alter their former Systems of Government. The history of the present King of Great Britain is a history of repeated injuries and usurpations, all having in direct object the establishment of an absolute Tyranny over these States. To prove this, let Facts be submitted to a candid world.

He has refused his Assent to Laws, the most wholesome and necessary for the public good.

He has forbidden his Governors to pass laws of immediate and pressing importance, unless suspended in their operation till his Assent should be obtained; and when so suspended, he has utterly neglected to attend to them.

He has refused to pass other Laws for the accommodation of large districts of people, unless those people would relinquish the right of Representation in the Legislature, a right inestimable to them and formidable to tyrants only.

He has called together legislative bodies at places unusual, uncomfortable, and distant from the depository of their Public Records, for the sole purpose of fatiguing them into compliance with his measures.

He has dissolved Representative Houses repeatedly, for opposing with manly firmness his invasions on the rights of the people.

He has refused for a long time, after such dissolutions, to cause others to be elected; whereby the Legislative Powers, incapable of Annihilation, have returned to the People at large for their exercise; the State remaining in the mean time exposed to all the dangers of invasion from without, and convulsions within.

He has endeavored to prevent the population of these States; for that purpose obstructing the Laws for Naturalization of Foreigners; refusing to pass others to encourage their migration hither, and raising the conditions of new Appropriations of Lands.

He has obstructed the Administration of Justice, by refusing his Assent to Laws for establishing Judiciary Powers.

He has made Judges dependent on his Will alone, for the tenure of their offices, and the amount and payment of their salaries.

He has erected a multitude of New Offices, and sent hither swarms of Officers to harass our people, and eat out their substance.

He has kept among us, in times of peace, Standing Armies without the Consent of our legislatures.

He has affected to render the Military independent of and superior to the Civil Power.

He has combined with others to subject us to a jurisdiction foreign to our constitution, and unacknowledged by our laws; giving his Assent to their Acts of pretended Legislation: For quartering large bodies of armed troops among us: For protecting them, by a mock Trial, from punishment for any Murders which they should commit on the Inhabitants of these States: For cutting off our Trade with all parts of the world: For imposing Taxes on us without our Consent: For depriving us in many cases, of the benefits of Trial by Jury; For transporting us beyond Seas to be tried for pretended offenses: for abolishing the free System of English Laws in a neighboring Province, establishing therein an Arbitrary government, and enlarging its Boundaries so as to render it at once an example and fit instrument for introducing the same absolute rule into these Colonies: For taking away our Charters, abolishing our most valuable Laws and altering fundamentally the Forms of our Governments: For suspending our own Legislatures, and declaring themselves invested with power to legislate for us in all cases whatsoever.

He has abdicated Government here, by declaring us out of his Protection and waging War against us.

He has plundered our seas, ravaged our Coasts, burnt our towns, and destroyed the lives of our people.

He is at this time transporting large Armies of foreign Mercenaries to complete the works of death, desolation and tyranny, already begun with circumstances of Cruelty & Perfidy scarcely paralleled in the most barbarous ages, and totally unworthy the Head of a civilized nation.

He has constrained our fellow Citizens taken Captive on the high Seas to bear Arms against their Country, to become the executioners of their friends and Brethren, or to fall themselves by their Hands.

He has excited domestic insurrections amongst us, and has endeavored to bring on the inhabitants of our frontiers, the merciless Indian Savages, whose known rule of warfare, is an undistinguished destruction of all ages, sexes, and conditions.

In every stage of these Oppressions We have Petitioned for Redress in the most humble terms: Our repeated Petitions have been answered only by repeated injury. A Prince, whose character is thus marked by every act which may define a Tyrant, is unfit to be the ruler of a free people.

Nor have We been wanting in attention to our British brethren. We have warned them from time to time of attempts by their legislature to extend an unwarrantable jurisdiction over us. We have reminded them of the circumstances of our emigration and settlement here. We have appealed to their native justice and magnanimity, and we have conjured them by the ties of our common kindred to disavow these usurpations, which would inevitably interrupt our connections and correspondence. They too have been deaf to the voice of justice and of consanguinity. We must, therefore, acquiesce in the necessity, which denounces our Separation, and hold them, as we hold the rest of mankind, Enemies in War, in Peace Friends.

We, THEREFORE, the Representatives of the UNITED STATES OF AMERICA, in General Congress, Assembled, appealing to the Supreme Judge of the world for the rectitude of our intentions, do, in the Name, and by Authority of the good People of these Colonies, solemnly publish and declare, That these United Colonies are, and of Right ought to be FREE AND INDEPENDENT STATES; that they are Absolved from all Allegiance to the British Crown, and that all political connection between them and the State of Great Britain, is and ought to be totally dissolved; and that as Free and Independent States, they have full Power to levy War, conclude Peace, contract Alliances, establish Commerce, and to do all other Acts and Things which Independent States may of right do. And for the support of this Declaration, with a firm reliance on the protection of Divine Providence, we mutually pledge to each other our Lives, our Fortunes, and our sacred Honor.

QUESTIONS FOR STUDY, DISCUSSION, AND WRITING

1. The Declaration of Independence was addressed to several audiences: the king of Great Britain, the people of Great Britain, the people of America, and the world at large. Show ways in which the final draft was adapted for its several audiences.
2. Examine the second paragraph of each version closely. How have the revisions in the final version increased its effectiveness over the first draft?
3. The Declaration has often been called a classic example of deductive argument: setting up general statements, relating particular cases to them, and drawing conclusions. Trace this pattern through the document, noting the way each part is developed. Would the document have been as effective if the long middle part had either come first or been left out entirely? Explain.
4. Find the key terms and phrases of the Declaration (such as "these

truths . . . self-evident," "created equal," "unalienable rights," and so on) and determine how fully they are defined by the contexts in which they occur. Why are no formal definitions given for them?

5. *The signers of the Declaration appeal both to general principles and to factual evidence in presenting their case. Which of the appeals to principle could still legitimately be made today by a nation eager to achieve independence? In other words, how far does the Declaration reflect unique events of history and how far does it reflect universal aspirations and ideals?*

ROGER WILLIAMS

Letter to the Town of Providence, January 1655

That ever I should speak or write a tittle, that tends to such an infinite liberty of conscience, is a mistake, and which I have ever disclaimed and abhorred. To prevent such mistakes, I shall at present only propose this case: There goes many a ship to sea, with many hundred souls in one ship, whose weal or woe is common, and is a true picture of a commonwealth, or a human combination or society. It hath fallen out sometimes, that both papists and protestants, Jews and Turks, may be embarked in one ship; upon which supposal I affirm, that all the liberty of conscience, that ever I pleaded for, turns upon these two hinges—that none of the papists, protestants, Jews, or Turks, be forced to come to the ship's prayers or worship, nor compelled from their own particular prayers or worship, if they practice any. I further add, that I never denied, that notwithstanding this liberty, the commander of this ship ought to command the ship's course, yea, and also command that justice, peace and sobriety, be kept and practiced, both among the seamen and all the passengers. If any of the seamen refuse to perform their services, or passengers to pay their freight; if any refuse to help, in person or purse, towards the common charges or defense; if any refuse to obey the common laws and orders of the ship, concerning their common peace or preservation; if any shall mutiny and rise up against their commanders and officers; if any should preach or write that there ought to be no commanders or officers, because all are equal in Christ, therefore no masters nor officers, no laws nor orders, nor corrections nor punishments; I say, I never denied, but in such cases, whatever is pretended, the commander or commanders may judge, resist, compel and punish such transgressors, according to their deserts and merits. This if seriously and honestly minded, may, if it so please the Father of lights, let in some light to such as willingly shut not their eyes.

I remain studious of your common peace and liberty.

JAMES MADISON

The Merits of a Republic[1]

To the People of the State of New York

Among the numerous advantages promised by a well-constructed Union, none deserves to be more accurately developed than its tendency to break and control the violence of faction. The friend of popular governments never finds himself so much alarmed for their character and fate, as when he contemplates their propensity to this dangerous vice. He will not fail, therefore, to set a due value on any plan which, without violating the principles to which he is attached, provides a proper cure for it. The instability, injustice, and confusion introduced into the public councils have, in truth, been the mortal diseases under which popular governments have everywhere perished; as they continue to be the favorite and fruitful topics from which the adversaries to liberty derive their most specious declamations. The valuable improvements made by the American constitutions on the popular models, both ancient and modern, cannot certainly be too much admired; but it would be an unwarrantable partiality, to contend that they have as effectually obviated the danger on this side, as was wished and expected. Complaints are everywhere heard from our most considerate and virtuous citizens, equally the friends of public and private faith, and of public and personal liberty, that our governments are too unstable, that the public good is disregarded in the conflicts of rival parties, and that measures are too often decided, not according to the rules of justice and the rights of the minor party, but by the superior force of an interested and overbearing majority. However anxiously we may wish that these complaints had no foundation, the evidence of known facts will not permit us to deny that they are in some degree true. It will be found, indeed, on a candid review of our situation, that some of the distresses under which we labor have been erroneously charged on the operation of our governments; but it will be found, at the same time, that other causes will not alone account for many of our heaviest misfortunes; and, particularly, for that prevailing and increasing distrust of public engagements, and alarm for private rights, which are echoed from one end of the continent to the other. These must be chiefly, if not wholly, effects of the unsteadiness and injustice with which a factious spirit has tainted our public administrations.

By a faction, I understand a number of citizens, whether amounting to a majority or minority of the whole, who are united and actuated by some common impulse of passion, or of interest,

1. From *The Federalist*, No. 10.

adverse to the rights of other citizens, or to the permanent and aggregate interests of the community.

There are two methods of curing the mischiefs of faction: the one, by removing its causes; the other, by controlling its effects.

There are again two methods of removing the causes of faction: the one, by destroying the liberty which is essential to its existence; the other, by giving to every citizen the same opinions, the same passions, and the same interests.

It could never be more truly said than of the first remedy, that it was worse than the disease. Liberty is to faction what air is to fire, an ailment without which it instantly expires. But it could not be less folly to abolish liberty, which is essential to political life, because it nourishes faction, than it would be to wish the annihilation of air, which is essential to animal life, because it imparts to fire its destructive agency.

The second expedient is as impracticable as the first would be unwise. As long as the reason of man continues fallible, and he is at liberty to exercise it, different opinions will be formed. As long as the connection subsists between his reason and his self-love, his opinions and his passions will have a reciprocal influence on each other; and the former will be objects to which the latter will attach themselves. The diversity in the faculties of men, from which the rights of property originate, is not less an insuperable obstacle to a uniformity of interests. The protection of these faculties is the first object of government. From the protection of different and unequal faculties of acquiring property, the possession of different degrees and kinds of property immediately results; and from the influence of these on the sentiments and views of the respective proprietors, ensues a division of the society into different interests and parties.

The latent causes of faction are thus sown in the nature of man; and we see them everywhere brought into different degrees of activity, according to the different circumstances of civil society. A zeal for different opinions concerning religion, concerning government, and many other points, as well of speculation as of practice; an attachment to different leaders ambitiously contending for preeminence and power; or to persons of other descriptions whose fortunes have been interesting to the human passions, have, in turn, divided mankind into parties, inflamed them with mutual animosity, and rendered them much more disposed to vex and oppress each other than to co-operate for their common good. So strong is this propensity of mankind to fall into mutual animosities, that where no substantial occasion presents itself, the most frivolous and fanciful distinctions have been sufficient to kindle their unfriendly passions and excite their most violent conflicts. But the most common and durable source of factions has been the various and unequal distribution of property. Those who hold and those who are without property have ever formed distinct interests in society. Those who are creditors, and those who are debtors, fall under a like discrimination. A landed interest, a manufacturing interest, a mercantile interest, a moneyed interest, with many lesser interests, grow up of necessity in civilized nations, and divide them into different classes, actuated by different sentiments and views. The regulation of these various and interfering interests forms the principal task of modern legislation, and involves the spirit of party and faction in the necessary and ordinary operations of the government.

No man is allowed to be a judge in his own cause, because his interest would certainly bias his judgment, and, not improbably, corrupt his integrity. With equal, nay with greater reason, a body of men are unfit to be both judges and parties at the same time; yet what are many of the most important acts of legislation, but so many judicial determinations, not indeed concerning the rights of single persons, but concerning the rights of large bodies of citizens? And what are the different classes of legislators but advocates and parties to the causes which they determine? Is a law proposed concerning private debts? It is a question to which the creditors are parties on one side and the debtors on the other. Justice ought to hold the balance between them. Yet the parties are, and must be, themselves the judges; and the most numerous party, or, in other words, the most powerful faction must be expected to prevail. Shall domestic manufactures be encouraged, and in what degree, by restrictions on foreign manufactures? are questions which would be differently decided by the landed and the manufacturing classes, and probably by neither with a sole regard to justice and the public good. The apportionment of taxes on the various descriptions of property is an act which seems to require the most exact impartiality; yet there is, perhaps, no legislative act in which greater opportunity and temptation are given to a predominant party to trample on the rules of justice. Every shilling with which they overburden the inferior number, is a shilling saved to their own pockets.

It is in vain to say that enlightened statesmen will be able to adjust these clashing interests, and render them all subservient to the public good. Enlightened statesmen will not always be at the helm. Nor, in many cases, can such an adjustment be made at all without taking into view indirect and remote considerations, which will rarely prevail over the immediate interest which one party may find in disregarding the rights of another or the good of the whole.

The inference to which we are brought is, that the *causes* of faction cannot be removed, and that relief is only to be sought in the means of controlling its *effects*.

If a faction consists of less than a majority, relief is supplied by the republican principle, which enables the majority to defeat its sinister views by regular vote. It may clog the administration, it may convulse the society; but it will be unable to execute and mask its violence under the forms of the Constitution. When a majority is included in a faction, the form of popular government, on the other hand, enables it to sacrifice to its ruling passion or interest both the public good and the rights of other citizens. To secure the public good and private rights against the danger of such a faction, and at the same time to preserve the spirit and the form of popular government, is then the great object to which our inquiries are directed. Let me add that it is the great desideratum by which this form of government can be rescued from the opprobrium under which it has so long labored, and be recommended to the esteem and adoption of mankind.

By what means is this object attainable? Evidently by one of two only. Either the existence of the same passion or interest in a majority at the same time must be prevented, or the majority, having such coexistent passion or interest, must be rendered, by their number and local situation, unable to concert and carry into effect schemes of oppression. If the impulse and the opportunity be suffered to coincide, we well know that neither moral nor religious motives can be relied on as an adequate control. They are not found to be such on the injustice and violence of individuals, and lose their efficacy in proportion to the number combined together, that is, in proportion as their efficacy becomes needful.

From this view of the subject it may be concluded that a pure democracy, by which I mean a society consisting of a small number of citizens, who assemble and administer the government in person, can admit of no cure for the mischiefs of faction. A common passion or interest will, in almost every case, be felt by a majority of the whole; a communication and concert result from the form of government itself; and there is nothing to check the inducements to sacrifice the weaker party or an obnoxious individual. Hence it is that such democracies have ever been spectacles of turbulence and contention; have ever been found incompatible with personal security or the rights of property; and have in general been as short in their lives as they have been violent in their deaths. Theoretic politicians, who have patronized this species of government, have erroneously supposed that by reducing mankind to a perfect equality in their political rights, they would, at the same time, be perfectly equalized and assimilated in their possessions, their opinions, and their passions.

A republic, by which I mean a government in which the scheme of representation takes place, opens a different prospect, and promises the cure for which we are seeking. Let us examine the points in which it varies from pure democracy, and we shall comprehend both the nature of the cure and the efficacy which it must derive from the Union.

The two great points of difference between a democracy and a republic are: first, the delegation of the government, in the latter, to a small number of citizens elected by the rest; secondly, the greater number of citizens, and greater sphere of country, over which the latter may be extended.

The effect of the first difference is, on the one hand, to refine and enlarge the public views, by passing them through the medium of a chosen body of citizens, whose wisdom may be best discern the true interest of their country, and whose patriotism and love of justice will be least likely to sacrifice it to temporary or partial considerations. Under such a regulation, it may well happen that the public voice, pronounced by the representatives of the people, will be more consonant to the public good than if pronounced by the people themselves, convened for the purpose. On the other hand, the effect may be inverted. Men of factious tempers, of local prejudices, or of sinister designs, may, by intrigue, by corruption, or by other means, first obtain the suffrages, and then betray the interests, of the people. The question resulting is, whether small or extensive republics are more favorable to the election of proper guardians of the public weal; and it is clearly decided in favor of the latter by two obvious considerations:

In the first place, it is to be remarked that, however small the republic may be, the representatives must be raised to a certain number, in order to guard against the cabals of a few; and that, however large it may be, they must be limited to a certain number, in order to guard against the confusion of a multitude. Hence, the number of representatives in the two cases not being in proportion to that of the two constituents, and being proportionally greater in the small republic, it follows that, if the proportion of fit characters be not less in the large than in the small republic, the former will present a greater option, and consequently a greater probability of a fit choice.

In the next place, as each representative will be chosen by a greater number of citizens in the large than in the small republic, it will be more difficult for unworthy candidates to practise with success the vicious arts by which elections are too often carried; and the suffrages of the people being more free, will be more likely to centre in men who possess the most attractive merit and the most diffusive and established characters.

It must be confessed that in this, as in most other cases, there is a mean, on both sides of which inconveniences will be found to lie. By enlarging too much the number of electors, you render the representative too little acquainted with all their local circumstances and lesser interests; as by reducing it too much, you render him unduly attached to these, and too little fit to comprehend and pursue great and national objects. The federal Constitution forms a happy combination in this respect; the great and aggregate interests being referred to the national, the local and particularly to the State legislatures.

The other point of difference is, the greater number of citizens and extent of territory which may be brought within the compass of republican than of democratic government; and it is this circumstance principally which renders factious combinations less to be dreaded in the former than in the latter. The smaller the society, the fewer probably will be the distinct parties and interests composing it; the fewer the distinct parties and interests, the more frequently will a majority be found of the same party; and the smaller the number of individuals composing a majority, and the smaller the compass within which they are placed, the more easily will they concert and execute their plans of oppression. Extend the sphere, and you take in a greater variety of parties and interests; you make it less probable that a majority of the whole will have a common motive to invade the rights of other citizens; or if such a common motive exists, it will be more difficult for all who feel it to discover their own strength, and to act in unison with each other. Besides other impediments, it may be remarked that, where there is a consciousness of unjust or dishonorable purposes, communication is always checked by distrust in proportion to the number whose concurrence is necessary.

Hence, it clearly appears, that the same advantage which a republic has over a democracy, in controlling the effects of faction, is enjoyed by a large over a small republic,—is enjoyed by the Union over the States composing it. Does the advantage consist in the substitution of representatives whose enlightened views and virtuous sentiments render them superior to local prejudices and to schemes of injustice? It will not be denied that the representation of the Union will be most likely to possess these requisite endowments. Does it consist in the greater security afforded by a greater variety of parties, against the event of any one party being able to outnumber and oppress the rest? In an equal degree does the increased variety of parties comprised within the Union, increase this security. Does it, in fine, consist in the greater obstacles opposed to the concert and accomplishment of the secret wishes of an unjust and interested majority? Here, again, the extent of the Union gives it the most palpable advantage.

The influence of factious leaders may kindle a flame within their particular States, but will be unable to spread a general conflagration through the other States. A religious sect may degenerate into a political faction in a part of the Confederacy; but the variety of sects dispersed over the entire face of it must secure the national councils against any danger from that source. A rage for paper money, for an abolition of debts, for an equal division of property, or for any other improper or wicked project, will be less apt to pervade the whole body of the Union than a particular member of it; in the same proportion as such a malady is more likely to taint a particular county or district, than an entire State.

In the extent and proper structure of the Union, therefore, we behold a republican remedy for the diseases most incident to republican government. And according to the degree of pleasure and pride we feel in being republicans, ought to be our zeal in cherishing the spirit and supporting the character of Federalists.

QUESTIONS FOR STUDY, DISCUSSION, AND WRITING

1. Outline Madison's essay. What does the structure of the essay suggest about Madison's purpose? What has guided him in the order in which he treats his major points? Has he left out any important considerations?
2. This piece has sometimes been titled "The Control of Faction." Is the present title preferable? Explain.
3. Does Madison seem to view his audience as hostile, skeptical, neutral, or sympathetic? Explain.
4. Examine Madison's definition of "faction." What would happen if one or another of the clauses in the definition were left out?
5. What is the relationship between Madison's definition of faction and his distinction between a democracy and a republic?
6. Discuss the relative merits of a democracy and a republic. What is the place of factions in each form of government?
7. Compare Madison's view of the role of minorities with Lippmann's in "The Indispensable Opposition" (pp. 761–767).

CARL BECKER

Democracy[1]

Democracy, like liberty or science or progress, is a word with which we are all so familiar that we rarely take the trouble to ask what we mean by it. It is a term, as the devotees of semantics say, which has no "referent"—there is no precise or palpable thing or object which we all think of when the word is pronounced. On the contrary, it is a word which connotes different things to different people, a kind of conceptual Gladstone bag which, with a little manipulation, can be made to accommodate almost any collection of social facts we may wish to carry about in it. In it we can as easily pack a dictatorship as any other form of government. We have only to stretch the concept to include any form of government supported by a majority of the people, for whatever reasons

1. From Lecture I, "The Ideal," in *Modern Democracy*, 1941.

and by whatever means of expressing assent, and before we know it the empire of Napoleon, the Soviet regime of Stalin, and the Fascist systems of Mussolini and Hitler are all safely in the bag. But if this is what we mean by democracy, then virtually all forms of government are democratic, since virtually all governments, except in times of revolution, rest upon the explicit or implicit consent of the people. In order to discuss democracy intelligently it will be necessary, therefore, to define it, to attach to the word a sufficiently precise meaning to avoid the confusion which is not infrequently the chief result of such discussions.

All human institutions, we are told, have their ideal forms laid away in heaven, and we do not need to be told that the actual institutions conform but indifferently to these ideal counterparts. It would be possible then to define democracy either in terms of the ideal or in terms of the real form—to define it as government of the people, by the people, for the people; or to define it as government of the people, by the politicians, for whatever pressure groups can get their interests taken care of. But as a historian I am naturally disposed to be satisfied with the meaning which, in the history of politics, men have commonly attributed to the word—a meaning, needless to say, which derives partly from the experience and partly from the aspirations of mankind. So regarded, the term democracy refers primarily to a form of government, and it has always meant government by the many as opposed to government by the one— government by the people as opposed to government by a tyrant, a dictator, or an absolute monarch. This is the most general meaning of the word as men have commonly understood it.

In this antithesis there are, however, certain implications, always tacitly understood, which give a more precise meaning to the term. Peisistratus, for example, was supported by a majority of the people, but his government was never regarded as a democracy for all that. Caesar's power derived from a popular mandate, conveyed through established republican forms, but that did not make his government any the less a dictatorship. Napoleon called his government a democratic empire, but no one, least of all Napoleon himself, doubted that he had destroyed the last vestiges of the democratic republic. Since the Greeks first used the term, the essential test of democratic government has always been this: the source of political authority must be and remain in the people and not in the ruler. A democratic government has always meant one in which the citizens, or a sufficient number of them to represent more or less effectively the common will, freely act from time to time, and according to established forms, to appoint or recall the magistrates and to enact or revoke the laws by which the community is governed. This I take to be the meaning which history has impressed upon the term democracy as a form of government.

WALTER LIPPMANN
The Indispensable Opposition

Were they pressed hard enough, most men would probably confess that political freedom—that is to say, the right to speak freely and to act in opposition—is a noble ideal rather than a practical necessity. As the case for freedom is generally put today, the argument lends itself to this feeling. It is made to appear that, whereas each man claims his freedom as a matter of right, the freedom he accords to other men is a matter of toleration. Thus, the defense of freedom of opinion tends to rest not on its substantial, beneficial, and indispensable consequences, but on a somewhat eccentric, a rather vaguely benevolent, attachment to an abstraction.

It is all very well to say with Voltaire, "I wholly disapprove of what you say, but will defend to the death your right to say it," but as a matter of fact most men will not defend to the death the rights of other men: if they disapprove sufficiently what other men say, they will somehow suppress those men if they can.

So, if this is the best that can be said for liberty of opinion, that a man must tolerate his opponents because everyone has a "right" to say what he pleases, then we shall find that liberty of opinion is a luxury, safe only in pleasant times when men can be tolerant because they are not deeply and vitally concerned.

Yet actually, as a matter of historic fact, there is a much stronger foundation for the great constitutional right of freedom of speech, and as a matter of practical human experience there is a much more compelling reason for cultivating the habits of free men. We take, it seems to me, a naïvely self-righteous view when we argue as if the right of our opponents to speak were something that we protect because we are magnanimous, noble, and unselfish. The compelling reason why, if liberty of opinion did not exist, we should have to invent it, why it will eventually have to be restored in all civilized countries where it is now suppressed, is that we must protect the right of our opponents to speak because we must hear what they have to say.

We miss the whole point when we imagine that we tolerate the freedom of our political opponents as we tolerate a howling baby next door, as we put up with the blasts from our neighbor's radio because we are too peaceable to heave a brick through the window. If this were all there is to freedom of opinion, that we are too good-natured or too timid to do anything about our opponents and our critics except to let them talk, it would be difficult to say whether we are tolerant because we are magnanimous or because we are lazy, because we have strong principles or because we lack serious convictions, whether we have the hospitality of an inquiring mind or the indifference of an empty mind. And so, if we truly wish to understand why freedom is necessary in a civilized society, we must begin by realizing that, because freedom of discussion improves our own opinions, the liberties of other men are our own vital necessity.

We are much closer to the essence of the matter, not when we quote Voltaire, but when we go to the doctor and pay him to ask us the most embarrassing questions and to prescribe the most disagreeable diet. When we pay the doctor to exercise complete freedom of speech about the cause and cure of our stomachache, we do not look upon ourselves as tolerant and magnanimous, and worthy to be admired by ourselves. We have enough common sense to know that if we threaten to put the doctor in jail because we do not like the diagnosis and the prescription it will be unpleasant for the doctor, to be sure, but equally unpleasant for our own stomachache. That is why even the most ferocious dictator would rather be treated by a doctor who was free to think and speak the truth than by his own Minister of Propaganda. For there is a point, the point at which things really matter, where the freedom of others is no longer a question of their right but of our own need.

The point at which we recognize this need is much higher in some men than in others. The totalitarian rulers think they do not need the freedom of an opposition: they exile, imprison, or shoot their opponents. We have concluded on the basis of practical experience, which goes back to Magna Carta and beyond, that we need the opposition. We pay the opposition salaries out of the public treasury.

In so far as the usual apology for freedom of speech ignores this experience, it becomes abstract and eccentric rather than concrete and human. The emphasis is generally put on the right to speak, as if all that mattered were that the doctor should be free to go out into the park and explain to the vacant air why I have a stomachache. Surely that is a miserable caricature of the great civic right which men have bled and died for. What really matters is that the doctor should tell *me* what ails me, that I should listen to him; that if I do not like what he says I should be free to call in another doctor; and that then the first doctor should have to listen to the second doctor; and that out of all the speaking and listening, the give-and-take of opinions, the truth should be arrived at.

This is the creative principle of freedom of speech, not that it is a system for the tolerating of error, but that it is a system for finding the truth. It may not produce the truth, or the whole truth all the time, or often, or in some cases ever. But if the truth can be found, there is no other system which will normally and habitually find so much truth. Until we have thoroughly understood this principle, we shall not know why we must value our liberty, or how we can protect and develop it.

Let us apply this principle to the system of public speech in a totalitarian state. We may, without any serious falsification, picture a condition of affairs in which the mass of the people are being addressed through one broadcasting system by one man and his chosen subordinates. The orators speak. The audience listens but cannot and dare not speak back. It is a system of one-way communication; the opinions of the rulers are broadcast outwardly to the mass of the people. But nothing comes back to the rulers from the people except the cheers; nothing returns in the way of knowledge of forgotten facts, hidden feelings, neglected truths, and practical suggestions.

But even a dictator cannot govern by his own one-way inspiration alone. In practice, therefore, the totalitarian rulers get back the reports of the secret police and of their party henchmen down among the crowd. If these reports are competent, the rulers may manage to remain in touch with public sentiment. Yet that is not enough to know what the audience feels. The rulers have also to make great decisions that have enormous consequences, and here their system provides virtually no help from the give-and-take of opinion in the nation. So they must either rely on their own intuition, which cannot be permanently and continually inspired, or, if they are intelligent despots, encourage their trusted advisers and their technicians to speak and debate freely in their presence.

On the walls of the houses of Italian peasants one may see inscribed in large letters the legend, "Mussolini is always right." But if that legend is taken seriously by Italian ambassadors, by the Italian General Staff, and by the Ministry of Finance, then all one can say is heaven help Mussolini, heaven help Italy, and the new Emperor of Ethiopia.

For at some point, even in a totalitarian state, it is indispensable that there should exist the freedom of opinion which causes opposing opinions to be debated. As time goes on, that is less and less easy under a despotism; critical discussion disappears as the internal opposition is liquidated in favor of men who think and feel alike. That is why the early successes of despots, of Napoleon I and of Napoleon III, have usually been followed by an irreparable mistake. For in listening only to his yes men—the others being in exile or in concentration camps, or terrified—the despot shuts himself off from the truth that no man can dispense with.

We know all this well enough when we contemplate the dictatorships. But when we try to picture our own system, by way of contrast, what picture do we have in our minds? It is, is it not, that anyone may stand up on his own soapbox and say anything he pleases, like the individuals in Kipling's poem[1] who sit each in his

1. "L'Envoi."

separate star and draw the Thing as they see it for the God of Things as they are. Kipling, perhaps, could do this, since he was a poet. But the ordinary mortal isolated on his separate star will have an hallucination, and a citizenry declaiming from separate soapboxes will poison the air with hot and nonsensical confusion.

If the democratic alternative to the totalitarian one-way broadcasts is a row of separate soapboxes, than I submit that the alternative is unworkable, is unreasonable, and is humanly unattractive. It is above all a false alternative. It is not true that liberty has developed among civilized men when anyone is free to set up a soapbox, is free to hire a hall where he may expound his opinions to those who are willing to listen. On the contrary, freedom of speech is established to achieve its essential purpose only when different opinions are expounded in the same hall to the same audience.

For, while the right to talk may be the beginning of freedom, the necessity of listening is what makes the right important. Even in Russia and Germany a man may still stand in an open field and speak his mind. What matters is not the utterance of opinions. What matters is the confrontation of opinions in debate. No man can care profoundly that every fool should say what he likes. Nothing has been accomplished if the wisest man proclaims his wisdom in the middle of the Sahara Desert. This is the shadow. We have the substance of liberty when the fool is compelled to listen to the wise man and learn; when the wise man is compelled to take account of the fool, and to instruct him; when the wise man can increase his wisdom by hearing the judgment of his peers.

That is why civilized men must cherish liberty—as a means of promoting the discovery of truth. So we must not fix our whole attention on the right of anyone to hire his own hall, to rent his own broadcasting station, to distribute his own pamphlets. These rights are incidental; and though they must be preserved, they can be preserved only by regarding them as incidental, as auxiliary to the substance of liberty that must be cherished and cultivated.

Freedom of speech is best conceived, therefore, by having in mind the picture of a place like the American Congress, an assembly where opposing views are represented, where ideas are not merely uttered but debated, or the British Parliament, where men who are free to speak are also compelled to answer. We may picture the true condition of freedom as existing in a place like a court of law, where witnesses testify and are cross-examined, where the lawyer argues against the opposing lawyer before the same judge and in the presence of one jury. We may picture freedom as existing in a forum where the speaker must respond to questions; in a gathering of scientists where the data, the hypothesis, and the conclusion are submitted to men competent to judge them; in a reputable newspaper which not only will publish the opinions of those who disagree but will re-examine its own opinion in the light of what they say.

Thus the essence of freedom of opinion is not in mere toleration as such, but in the debate which toleration provides: it is not in the venting of opinion, but in the confrontation of opinion. That this is the practical substance can readily be understood when we remember how differently we feel and act about the censorship and regulation of opinion purveyed by different media of communication. We find then that, in so far as the medium makes difficult the confrontation of opinion in debate, we are driven towards censorship and regulation.

There is, for example, the whispering campaign, the circulation of anonymous rumors by men who cannot be compelled to prove what they say. They put the utmost strain on our tolerance, and there are few who do not rejoice when the anonymous slanderer is caught, exposed, and punished. At a higher level there is the moving picture, a most powerful medium for conveying ideas, but a medium which does not permit debate. A moving picture cannot be answered effectively by another moving picture; in all free countries there is some censorship of the movies, and there would be more if the producers did not recognize their limitations by avoiding political controversy. There is then the radio. Here debate is difficult: it is not easy to make sure that the speaker is being answered in the presence of the same audience. Inevitably, there is some regulation of the radio.

When we reach the newspaper press, the opportunity for debate is so considerable that discontent cannot grow to the point where under normal conditions there is any disposition to regulate the press. But when newspapers abuse their power by injuring people who have no means of replying, a disposition to regulate the press appears. When we arrive at Congress we find that, because the membership of the House is so large, full debate is impracticable. So there are restrictive rules. On the other hand, in the Senate, where the conditions of full debate exist, there is almost absolute freedom of speech.

This shows us that the preservation and development of freedom of opinion are not only a matter of adhering to abstract legal rights, but also, and very urgently, a matter of organizing and arranging sufficient debate. Once we have a firm hold on the central principle, there are many practical conclusions to be drawn. We then realize that the defense of freedom of opinion consists primarily in perfecting the opportunity for an adequate give-and-take of opinion; it consists also in regulating the freedom of those revolutionists who cannot or will not permit or maintain debate when it does not suit their purposes.

We must insist that free oratory is only the beginning of free speech; it is not the end, but a means to an end. The end is to find the truth. The practical justification of civil liberty is not that self-expression is one of the rights of man. It is that the examination of opinion is one of the necessities of man. For experience tells us that it is only when freedom of opinion becomes the compulsion to debate that the seed which our fathers planted has produced its fruit. When that is understood, freedom will be cherished not because it is a vent for our opinions but because it is the surest method of correcting them.

The unexamined life, said Socrates, is unfit to be lived by man. This is the virtue of liberty, and the ground on which we may best justify our belief in it, that it tolerates error in order to serve the truth. When men are brought face to face with their opponents, forced to listen and learn and mend their ideas, they cease to be children and savages and begin to live like civilized men. Then only is freedom a reality, when men may voice their opinions because they must examine their opinions.

The only reason for dwelling on all this is that if we are to preserve democracy we must understand its principles. And the principle which distinguishes it from all other forms of government is that in a democracy the opposition not only is tolerated as constitutional but must be maintained because it is in fact indispensable.

The democratic system cannot be operated without effective opposition. For, in making the great experiment of governing people by consent rather than by coercion, it is not sufficient that the party in power should have a majority. It is just as necessary that the party in power should never outrage the minority. That means that it must listen to the minority and be moved by the criticisms of the minority. That means that its measures must take account of the minority's objections, and that in administering measures it must remember that the minority may become the majority.

The opposition is indispensable. A good statesman, like any other sensible human being, always learns more from his opponents than from his fervent supporters. For his supporters will push him to disaster unless his opponents show him where the dangers are. So if he is wise he will often pray to be delivered from his friends, because they will ruin him. But, though it hurts, he ought also to pray never to be left without opponents; for they keep him on the path of reason and good sense.

The national unity of a free people depends upon a sufficiently even balance of political power to make it impracticable for the administration to be arbitrary and for the opposition to be revolutionary and irreconcilable. Where that balance no longer exists, democracy perishes. For unless all the citizens of a state are forced by circumstances to compromise, unless they feel that they can affect policy but that no one can wholly dominate it, unless by habit and necessity they have to give and take, freedom cannot be maintained.

QUESTIONS FOR STUDY, DISCUSSION, AND WRITING

1. What is Lippmann's reason for dividing the essay into three parts? What is the purpose of the third part?
2. What is the importance of Lippmann's distinction between "free oratory" and "free speech" (p. 766)?
3. What does Lippmann mean when he says that the point at which we recognize the need for the freedom of others "is much higher in some men than in others" (p. 762)? Does this assertion in any way weaken his argument?
4. Why has Lippmann discussed motion pictures but not literature (p. 765)? How sound is his view that the motion picture is "a medium which does not permit debate"? Does literature permit debate?
5. What does Lippmann mean by his statement that "the usual apology for freedom of speech . . . becomes abstract and eccentric rather than concrete and human" (p. 762)? Why has he chosen these particular words to contrast the "usual apology" with his own view? Is his argument "concrete and human"?
6. Thurber's rabbits (p. 708) listened to their opposition—that is, "the other animals, who lived at a great distance"—and were annihilated. Does Thurber's fable suggest any necessary qualification for Lippmann's thesis concerning the value of the opposition? Explain.
7. Lippmann's essay was written before the term "brainwashing" was in common use. If he were writing the essay today, how might he take account of this term?

E. B. WHITE

Democracy

July 3, 1943

We received a letter from the Writers' War Board the other day asking for a statement on "The Meaning of Democracy." It presumably is our duty to comply with such a request, and it is certainly our pleasure.

Surely the Board knows what democracy is. It is the line that forms on the right. It is the don't in don't shove. It is the hole in the stuffed shirt through which the sawdust slowly trickles; it is the dent in the high hat. Democracy is the recurrent suspicion that more than half of the people are right more than half of the time. It is the feeling of privacy in the voting booths, the feeling of communion in the libraries, the feeling of vitality everywhere. Democracy is a letter to the editor. Democracy is the score at the beginning of the ninth. It is an idea which hasn't been disproved yet, a song the words of which have not gone bad. It's the mustard on the hot dog and the cream in the rationed coffee. Democracy is a request from a War Board, in the middle of a morning in the middle of a war, wanting to know what democracy is.

QUESTIONS FOR STUDY, DISCUSSION, AND WRITING

1. White's piece is dated July 3, 1943, the middle of World War II. How did the occasion shape what White says about democracy?
2. Look up "democracy" in a standard desk dictionary. Of the several meanings given, which one best applies to Becker's definition (p. 760)? Does more than one apply to White's?
3. How does Becker's language differ from White's? What does the difference suggest about the purposes and audiences of the two men?
4. Translate White's definition into non-metaphorical language. (For example, "It is the line that forms on the right" might be translated by "It has no special privileges.") Determine what is lost in the translation, or, in other words, what White has gained by using figurative language.

WILLIAM MARCH
The Farmer and the Mink

A farmer caught the mink who was raiding his chicken roost and brought him to trial. The mink, acting in his own defense, asked that the indictment be read to him, and the judge said, "You are charged with destroying the farmer's hens. How do you plead?"

The mink said, "I plead innocent, for I have not destroyed the farmer's hens, as he maintains." He pointed to the six fat pullets that lay on the table as evidence. "The farmer has accused me of destroying his hens," he went on, "and yet he offers in evidence, to make a case against me, the very hens he charges me with having destroyed."

The judge nodded, and the mink continued rapidly: "To sum up, it seems to me the farmer's case comes to this: if I *destroyed* his hens, as he charges, then he has no evidence against me since the evidence, being destroyed, no longer exists; if, on the other hand, the evidence I am said to have destroyed is *still* in existence, then obviously I could not have *destroyed* it, and I am innocent."

The judge, impressed by the mink's reasoning, dismissed the case.

At once the farmer got up in protest. "But everybody knows the mink destroyed my hens!" he said. "I came into court seeking justice. Everybody knows I have not received it."

The judge said: "This court isn't interested in what you're saying. Our concern here is to administer the law."

OLIVER WENDELL HOLMES, JR.

United States *v.* Schwimmer[1]

[Citizenship was denied to a woman of fifty who stated in her application that she would not take up arms for this country. Against her willingness to swear allegiance and do everything (except go to war) that a citizen might be called upon to do, the Naturalization Act of 1906 was quoted. This law required applicants to "support and defend the Constitution and the laws of the United States against all enemies" and to satisfy the court of their attachment to the principles of the Constitution.

The [U. S.] District Court doubted that this person held those principles dear. On the other hand, the Circuit Court of Appeals held that women were considered incapable of bearing arms. But the Department of Justice appealed, arguing that Mrs. Schwimmer's incapacity because of her sex was immaterial; her attitude toward the Government's defense "with its necessary influence on others" was the vital matter: "In time of war she would be a menace to the country. If every citizen believed as she does and acted as she will we would have no Constitution and no Government."

Six Justices of the Supreme Court accepted that view. This self-described uncompromising pacifist, who classed herself with male conscientious objectors and asserted she had no sense of nationalism, was said by Mr. Justice Butler to be lacking in "that attachment to the principles of the Constitution of which the applicant is required to give affirmative evidence by the Naturalization Act." He held it a fundamental duty to defend the Government by force of arms; it was important to find out whether an alien applying for citizenship held beliefs opposed to the discharge of that duty: "The influence of conscientious objectors against the use of military force in defense of the principles of our Government is apt to be more detrimental than their mere refusal to bear arms. The fact that, by reason of sex, age or other cause, they may be unfit to serve does not lessen their purpose or power to influence others."

In dissenting Justice Holmes was supported by Justice Brandeis (Mr. Justice Sanford agreed with the reasoning of the Circuit Court of Appeals).]

The applicant seems to be a woman of superior character and intelligence, obviously more than ordinarily desirable as a citizen of the United States. It is agreed that she is qualified for citizenship except so far as the views set forth in a statement of facts "may show that the applicant is not attached to the principles of the Constitution of the United States and well disposed to the good order and happiness of the same, and except in so far as the same may

1. *United States* v. *Schwimmer*, 279 U.S. 644, 653 (1928). From *The Dissenting Opinions of Mr. Justice Holmes*, edited by Alfred Lief. The introductory note is by Mr. Lief.

show that she cannot take the oath of allegiance without a mental reservation."

The views referred to are an extreme opinion in favor of pacifism and a statement that she would not bear arms to defend the Constitution. So far as the adequacy of her oath is concerned I hardly can see how it is affected by the statement, inasmuch as she is a woman over fifty years of age, and would not be allowed to bear arms if she wanted to. And as to the opinion, the whole examination of the applicant shows that she holds none of the now-dreaded creeds but thoroughly believes in organized government and prefers that of the United States to any other in the world.

Surely it cannot show lack of attachment to the principles of the Constitution that she thinks it can be improved. I suppose that most intelligent people think that it might be. Her particular improvement looking to the abolition of war seems to me not materially different in its bearing on this case from a wish to establish cabinet government as in England, or a single house, or one term of seven years for the President. To touch a more burning question, only a judge mad with partisanship would exclude because the applicant thought that the Eighteenth Amendment should be repealed.

Of course the fear is that if a war came the applicant would exert activities such as were dealt with in *Schenck* v. *United States*.[2] But that seems to me unfounded. Her position and motives are wholly different from those of Schenck. She is an optimist and states in strong and, I do not doubt, sincere words her belief that war will disappear and that the impending destiny of mankind is to unite in peaceful leagues.

I do not share that optimism nor do I think that a philosophic view of the world would regard war as absurd. But most people who have known it regard it with horror, as a last resort, and even if not yet ready for cosmopolitan efforts, would welcome any practicable combinations that would increase the power on the side of peace.

The notion that the applicant's optimistic anticipations would make her a worse citizen is sufficiently answered by her examination, which seems to me a better argument for her admission than any I can offer. Some of her answers might excite popular prejudice, but if there is any principle of the Constitution that more imperatively calls for attachment than any other it is the principle of free thought—not free thought for those who agree with us but freedom for the thought that we hate. I think that we should adhere to that principle with regard to admission into, as well as to life within, this country.

2. Fomenting insubordination in the military and naval forces, obstructing the recruiting and enlistment services, by speech or written document.

And recurring to the opinion that bars this applicant's way, I would suggest that the Quakers have done their share to make the country what it is, that many citizens agree with the applicant's belief and that I had not supposed hitherto that we regretted our inability to expel them because they believe more than some of us do in the teachings of the Sermon on the Mount.

QUESTIONS FOR STUDY, DISCUSSION, AND WRITING

1. Which is more convincing, Holmes' reasoning or the reasoning of the Circuit Court of Appeals?
2. Would Holmes have felt the same way about the case if Schwimmer had been a man of military age instead of a woman in her fifties?
3. Why does Holmes bring in the reference to the Eighteenth Amendment?
4. What is the purpose and effect of the last one-sentence paragraph?
5. Compare Holmes' attitude toward liberty of conscience with that of Roger Williams (p. 752). What might Williams' judgment of the Schwimmer case be?

FELIX FRANKFURTER

Haley v. Ohio[1]

[In this case, Justice Frankfurter cast the deciding vote to help form the necessary majority for reversing a conviction in a state court because of the methods used by the police in securing the confession on which it was based. His opinion explaining why he did so illustrates dramatically the extent to which it continues to be true that whether a conviction will be upset depends on the way the Justices see the circumstances in the particular case.

Arrested on Friday evening for the murder of a storekeeper, Haley, a fifteen-year-old Negro, was questioned for five hours during the night, without counsel or family being present, and was not brought before a magistrate until Tuesday. His mother was not allowed to see him until Thursday. Said Justice William O. Douglas for the Court: "A 15-year-old lad, questioned through the dead of night by relays of police, is a ready victim of the inquisition. Mature men possibly might stand the ordeal from midnight to 5 A.M. But we cannot believe that a lad of tender years is a match for the police in such a contest. He needs counsel and support if he is not to become the victim first of fear, then of panic. He needs someone on whom to lean lest the overpowering presence of the law, as he knows it, crush him. No friend stood at the side of this 15-year-old boy as the police, working in relays, questioned him hour after hour, from midnight until dawn. No lawyer stood guard to make sure that the police went so far and no farther, to see to it that they stopped short of the point where

1. *Haley v. Ohio*, 332 U.S. 596, 601 (1948). From *The Constitutional World of Mr. Justice Frankfurter*, ed. Samuel J. Konefsky. The introductory note is by Mr. Konefsky.

he became the victim of coercion." Chief Justice Vinson and Justices Reed, Jackson, and Burton dissented.

Mr. Justice Frankfurter's concurring opinion said in part:]

In a recent series of cases, beginning with *Brown* v. *Mississippi*, 297 U.S. 278, the Court has set aside convictions coming here from State courts because they were based on confessions admitted under circumstances that offended the requirements of the "due process" exacted from the States by the Fourteenth Amendment. If the rationale of those cases ruled this, we would dispose of it *per curiam*[2] with the mere citation of the cases. They do not rule it. Since at best this Court's reversal of a State court's conviction for want of due process always involves a delicate exercise of power and since there is sharp division as to the propriety of its exercise in this case, I deem it appropriate to state as explicitly as possible why, although I have doubts and difficulties, I cannot support affirmance of the conviction.

The doubts and difficulties derive from the very nature of the problem before us. They arise frequently when this Court is obliged to give definiteness to "the vague contours" of Due Process or, to change the figure, to spin judgment upon State action out of that gossamer concept. Subtle and even elusive as its criteria are, we cannot escape that duty of judicial review. The nature of the duty, however, makes it especially important to be humble in exercising it. Humility in this context means an alert self-scrutiny so as to avoid infusing into the vagueness of a Constitutional command one's merely private notions. Like other mortals, judges, though unaware, may be in the grip of prepossessions. The only way to relax such a grip, the only way to avoid finding in the Constitution the personal bias one has placed in it, is to explore the influences that have shaped one's unanalyzed views in order to lay bare prepossessions.

A lifetime's preoccupation with criminal justice, as prosecutor, defender of civil liberties and scientific student, naturally leaves one with views. Thus, I disbelieve in capital punishment. But as a judge I could not impose the views of the very few States who through bitter experience have abolished capital punishment upon all the other States, by finding that "due process" proscribes it. Again, I do not believe that even capital offenses by boys of fifteen should be dealt with according to the conventional criminal procedure. It would, however, be bald judicial usurpation to hold that States violate the Constitution in subjecting minors like Haley to such a procedure. If a State, consistently with the Fourteenth Amendment, may try a boy of fifteen charged with murder by the ordinary criminal procedure, I cannot say that such a youth is never capable of that free choice of action which, in the eyes of the law,

2. "Through the court"—that is, by a decision rendered without elaborate discussion.

makes a confession "voluntary."

But whether a confession of a lad of fifteen is "voluntary" and as such admissible, or "coerced" and thus wanting in due process, is not a matter of mathematical determination. Essentially it invites psychological judgment—a psychological judgment that reflects deep, even if inarticulate, feelings of our society. Judges must divine that feeling as best they can from all the relevant evidence and light which they can bring to bear for a confident judgment of such an issue, and with every endeavor to detach themselves from their merely private views. . . .

While the issue thus formulated appears vague and impalpable, it cannot be too often repeated that the limitations which the Due Process Clause of the Fourteenth Amendment placed upon the methods by which the States may prosecute for crime cannot be more narrowly conceived. This Court must give the freest possible scope to States in the choice of their methods of criminal procedure. But these procedures cannot include methods that may fairly be deemed to be in conflict with deeply rooted feelings of the community. . . . Of course this is a most difficult test to apply, but apply it we must, warily, and from case to case.

This brings me to the precise issue on the record before us. Suspecting a fifteen-year-old boy of complicity in murder resulting from attempted robbery, at about midnight the police took him from his home to police headquarters. There he was questioned for about five hours by at least five police officers who interrogated in relays of two or more. About five o'clock in the morning this procedure culminated in what the police regarded as a confession, whereupon it was formally reduced to writing. During the course of the interrogation the boy was not advised that he was not obliged to talk, that it was his right if he chose to say not a word, nor that he was entitled to have the benefit of counsel or the help of his family. Bearing upon the safeguards of these rights, the Chief of Police admitted that while he knew that the boy "had a right to remain mute and not answer any questions" he did not know that it was the duty of the police to apprise him of that fact. Unquestionably, during this whole period he was held incommunicado. Only after the nightlong questioning had resulted in disclosures satisfactory to the police and as such to be documented, was there read to the boy a clause giving the conventional formula about his constitutional right to make or withhold a statement and stating that if he makes it, he makes it of his "own free will." Do these uncontested facts justify a State court in finding that the boy's confession was "voluntary," or do the circumstances by their very nature preclude a finding that a deliberate and responsible choice was exercised by the boy in the confession that came at the end of five hours' questioning?

The answer, as has already been intimated, depends on an evaluation of psychological factors, or, more accurately stated, upon the pervasive feeling of society regarding such psychological factors. Unfortunately, we cannot draw upon any formulated expression of the existence of such feeling. Nor are there available experts on such matters to guide the judicial judgment. Our Constitutional system makes it the Court's duty to interpret those feelings of society to which the Due Process Clause gives legal protection. Because of their inherent vagueness the tests by which we are to be guided are most unsatisfactory, but such as they are we must apply them.

The Ohio courts have in effect denied that the very nature of the circumstances of the boy's confession precludes a finding that it was voluntary. Their denial carries great weight, of course. It requires much to be overborne. But it does not end the matter. Against it we have the judgment that comes from judicial experience with the conduct of criminal trials as they pass in review before this Court. An impressive series of cases in this and other courts admonishes of the temptations to abuse of police endeavors to secure confessions from suspects, through protracted questioning, carried on in secrecy, with the inevitable disquietude and fears police interrogations naturally engender in individuals questioned while held incommunicado, without the aid of counsel and unprotected by the safeguards of a judicial inquiry. Disinterested zeal for the public good does not assure either wisdom or right in the methods it pursues. A report of President Hoover's National Commission on Law Observance and Enforcement gave proof of the fact, unfortunately, that these potentialities of abuse were not the imaginings of mawkish sentimentality, nor their tolerance desirable or necessary for a stern policy against crime. Legislation throughout the country reflects a similar belief that detention for purposes of eliciting confessions through secret, persistent, long-continued interrogation violates sentiments deeply embedded in the feelings of our people. . . .

It is suggested that Haley's guilt could easily have been established without the confession elicited by the sweating process of the night's secret interrogation. But this only affords one more proof that in guarding against misuse of the law enforcement process the effective detection of crime and the prosecution of criminals are furthered and not hampered. Such constitutional restraints of decency derive from reliance upon the resources of intelligence in dealing with crime and discourage the too easy temptations of unimaginative crude force, even when such force is not brutally employed. . . .

It would disregard standards that we cherish as part of our faith in the strength and well-being of a rational, civilized society to hold that a confession is "voluntary" simply because the confession is the product of a sentient choice. "Conduct under duress involves a choice," . . . and conduct devoid of physical pressure but not leaving a free exercise of choice is the product of duress as much so as choice reflecting physical constraint.

Unhappily we have neither physical nor intellectual weights and measures by which judicial judgment can determine when pressures in securing a confession reach the coercive intensity that calls for the exclusion of a statement so secured. Of course, the police meant to exercise pressure upon Haley to make him talk. That was the very purpose of their procedure. In concluding that the pressures that were exerted in this case to make a lad of fifteen talk when the Constitution gives him the right to keep silent, and when the situation was so contrived that appreciation of his rights and thereby the means of asserting them were effectively withheld from him by the police, I do not believe I express a merely personal bias against such a procedure. Such a finding, I believe, reflects those fundamental notions of fairness and justice in the determination of guilt or innocence which lie embedded in the feelings of the American people and are enshrined in the Due Process Clause of the Fourteenth Amendment. To remove the inductment to resort to such methods this Court has repeatedly denied use of the fruits of illicit methods.

Accordingly, I think Haley's confession should have been excluded and the conviction based upon it should not stand.

QUESTIONS FOR STUDY, DISCUSSION, AND WRITING

1. What essential differences are there between this case and the *Rosika Schwimmer* case in the kind of issue involved? Could any of the general principles stated or implied by Holmes be applied to the Haley case?
2. Why does Frankfurter have "doubts and difficulties" in taking the stand he does? What specific facts in the case weighed most heavily with him when he arrived at his opinion?
3. How does Frankfurter distinguish between a "Constitutional command" and "one's merely private notions"?
4. What definition of "voluntary" does Frankfurter give? How does he develop it?
5. Frankfurter nowhere gives a formal definition of "due process." What can be deduced about that concept from his use of the term?
6. What does Frankfurter mean by the "deeply rooted feelings of the community"? What other examples of such feelings might be given?
7. Compare Frankfurter's last sentence with Holmes' last sentence. What can be deduced from the sentences about Holmes and Frankfurter as writers, judges, and men? What other support for the deductions can be found elsewhere in the two pieces?

TALBOT SMITH

Salmon *v.* Bagley Laundry Company[1]

[Mrs. Salmon was employed by the defendant laundry, her job being to feed clothes into a mangle and to fold them when they came out.

On the day in question, Mrs. Salmon began work at 8:00 A.M. and worked until the morning rest period which began at 9:20 A.M. She and other employees then went to a nearby restaurant where she had coffee. On returning from the restaurant and on ascending the step outside the front door of the laundry, which step was on the laundry's premises, she slipped and injured her left wrist.

Prior to the plaintiff's injury, a contract had been negotiated by her union, providing for the ten-minute rest period in the morning and another in the afternoon. During these times employees were permitted to leave the laundry for a coffee-break. When the coffee-break period arrived, a whistle would blow and the employees could go out for coffee or take care of other personal wants. No deduction of wages was made during the period. Prior to the inauguration of the ten-minute rest period under the contract, the employees were permitted, at their own discretion, but with the consent of the employer, to go out of the laundry to get coffee and sandwiches, as the laundry did not provide such facilities. The main purpose in selecting a particular time for the rest period, was to eliminate the previous confusion arising from departure from the laundry by employees at irregular periods.

The application by Mrs. Salmon for workmen's compensation for her injuries sustained in the manner above described was granted by Workmen's Compensation Commission, which said: "It is our opinion that plaintiff sustained an accidental injury while performing an act which was beneficial to her employer, incident to and within the ambit of her employment and conclusive of the proposition that her injury arose out of and in the course of her employment." The defendant employer and its insurance company appealed from the workmen's compensation award for Mrs. Salmon. A majority of the (Michigan) Supreme Court reversed the Workmen's Compensation Commission. Justice Smith dissented.

The majority held that the basic question was whether Mrs. Salmon's injuries arose out of and in the course of her employment. The court went on to say: "The right to control or direct an employee is an essential element in determining whether the relationship of employer and employee exists." The court concluded that in the case of Mrs. Salmon, the right to control the actions or activities of the employees during the noon hour lunch period or coffee-break was absent. In the instant case plaintiff had the option of leaving the laundry for coffee or remaining within the building for a rest period. During this period her employer had no control over her actions, nor can it be said that she was actively engaged in rendering a service to her employer. The fact that she was paid during this 10-minute interval has no bearing upon whether her injury arose out of and during the course of her employment. During this period plaintiff was exercising a privilege common to all employees of the defendant company. The facts in this case do not warrant a finding that her injury arose out of and during the course of her employment. Excerpts from Justice Smith's dissent follow:]

1. 344 Mich. 471 (1955).

. . . The fundamental issue posed by this simple case is so sweeping that we may be justified in casting a glance backward before we begin to appraise the present. It was the combination of the mechanization of industry and the development of the corporate device which brought together large masses of people and great pools of capital. As a result, we have been showered with blessings of a material nature. But it must never be forgotten that there is a poor relation in the back room, a tragic by-product of our progress, the injured worker, sometimes grotesque, sometimes severely crippled. His number is appalling. Somers' recent treatise *Workmen's Compensation* contains in readily available form the summaries, respecting disabling work injuries, of the United States Bureau of Labor Statistics, expressed by the authors in the following language (p. 2):

> Another way of putting it would be that one American worker will have been killed or crippled every three minutes. Another will have been injured every 11 seconds.
>
> Multiply the daily casualty list by the 260 days which constitute an average American work year and you arrive at the annual human toll which modern industry exacts: about 16,000 fatalities, 91,000 permanent disabilities—of which some 1600 are "total" such as paraplegia, broken backs, blindness, or double amputations, the others representing loss, or loss of use of, an arm, a leg, an eye, a finger or part thereof—and nearly two million temporary disabilities.

What have we done about this injured worker? It is clear what we have done. First of all, we no longer shoulder him aside and leave him to his own devices. Rejected also is the theory of the handout. What we have given him is called "compensation," which, though modest, was to be certain and speedy, and the reason we gave it was because of widespread dissatisfaction with the application of common-law tort theories to the injuries of workmen. The common law, in truth, was almost helpless to meet the challenge of the industrial age. "To speak of the common-law personal injury action as a remedy for the problem was to jest with serious subjects, to give a stone to one who asks for bread," said the supreme court of Wisconsin in *Borgnis* v. *Falk Company*, 147 Wis. 327, 348. Why was the common law helpless in this situation? Largely because the courts looked to tort concepts, developed in strikingly dissimilar situations, for precedent. At the risk of oversimplifying a most complex matter we observe that fault and negligence, in the ordinary tort law sought to be applied by the early courts, were personal. How, then, could the employer be forced to answer for the injury? He (as distinguished from the early master who worked shoulder to shoulder with his apprentice and servant) usually was not even in the plant at the time of the injury. . . .

The atmosphere, in brief, was one of sorrow and frustration. The industrial revolution had arrived and with it had come mechanization. But the machine was as contemptuous of human flesh as it was of impersonal steel. The face of the courts was turned, turned by what was thought to be precedent and *stare decisis*.[1] Our sons cried out.

Our answer was given in the form of the great workmen's compensation acts, humanitarian measures which, all courts agree, are to be construed liberally (e.g., *Adkins v. Rives Plating Corp.*, 338 Mich. 265) to accomplish their healing mission of solace and relief . . .

. . . How is it possible, under an act passed "to ameliorate a social condition—not to define a situation or fix a liability by adherence to the old common law," an act to be construed both reasonably and liberally, how is it possible that the laundress before us, injured on the employer's premises during the working day, in an activity sanctioned by contract and paid for by her employer, can find herself without recovery? In reply we are told that the employer lacked "control" over her at the time she was hurt.

From whence comes this requirement of "control"? There is nothing in the act fixing liability in such terms. It comes from the law of torts. It is blood brother to contributory negligence, assumption of risk, the fellow-servant rule[2] and the other tort concepts which were utilized so effectively in the common-law courts to bar employees' recovery; so effectively, in fact, that this act was passed in response to peremptory and overwhelming public demand. I cannot agree that we should import this tort concept into this great remedial statute. It is foreign to the purposes of the act. . . .

Consider the application of the control test to the facts before us. The claimant, when she came to work that morning, was concededly an employee. As such, in the normal situation, and we find nothing in this record to indicate otherwise, she comes to work when the employer says to come. She goes when he says to go. She stops at his command. She performs her routine tasks as he directs them to be performed. If her work is unsatisfactory, or business is "slack" she is free, even requested, to seek employment elsewhere. She is dependent, economically, upon her wage, and she earns it from her employer by doing his bidding. In all of this I find complete control, if we require such. Now, when did this control cease? When she went for coffee? (Even the mechanics of the coffee break, as we gather them from the record, demonstrate the plenary control exercised. A whistle blew. Production stopped. The machines were shut down. The front door was thrown open [in the winter] and those who wished went for coffee. Another whistle, the doors were closed, and the rest period was at a close. I have difficulty in saying that

1. "To stand by decided matters"; the policy of judge and lawyers to "follow precedent."

2. The rule exempting an employer from liability for injuries suffered by an employee if these were caused by the negligence of another employee (the first employee's fellow servant).

all of this is not control. Even from whistle to whistle there is at least a smell of control.)

To repeat, there was indisputably an employment relation until the coffee whistle blew. All tests, even control, could lead only to such conclusion. Was this employment relation suspended at the blast of the whistle because of lack of "control"?

If so, it is well to observe that we have, throughout the working day, not continuous employment, but a checkerboard of legal relationships. The workman comes to his job. At that point he is an employee. He turns from the lathe to blow his nose. Plainly the board of directors does not 'control' this operation. He is no longer an employee. He returns to the work assigned. Once again he is an employee. He goes to the toilet. He returns. He takes the coffee break. Again, he loses his employment status.

I must reject the checkerboard resulting from the application of the control concept. It must be apparent that the answer to our problem is not to be found in the ancient and dubious concept of control, lifted from the law of torts . . .

. . . The act provides, very simply, that injuries suffered in the course of employment be recompensed . . . Do, then, the words "course of employment" include the coffee break described?

The question can, consistently with the purpose of the act, as described in *Mackin* v. *Detroit Timken Axle Company*, be answered only in the affirmative. The manufacture of the product involves a series of casualties and deaths. The cost of the product must bear the burden, thus spreading the burden among the consumers rather than concentrating it on the helpless family unit involved. The words "course of employment" in our act include the coffee break simply because the product, which must shoulder the burdens of injuries in its manufacture, is made by a human being. He brings to his work all of his human characteristics, his frailties as well as his virtues. We cannot, either actually or legally, make the precise excisions of the surgeon. We cannot remove from him, and put to work for his employer, only his strength. His strength goes hand in hand with his temper. It is impossible for us to employ only the grace and charm of the female worker. We hire as well her lively curiosity. We collect these people by the hundreds, even thousands, and we put them to work, sometimes amid noise and vibration, sometimes in smoke and steam. They get tired. They get hungry. They get thirsty. They have to go to the toilet. The day wears on and tempers grow short. Relief is sought in horseplay. Trips to the water cooler and coffee urn grow in number and duration. This is the course of employment. "Course of employment" is not a sterile form of words. It is descriptive of life in the industrial age. These human deviations from the course of the automaton do not suspend the employer-employee relationship. They are not departures from employment, but the very substance of it. They are the inevitable concomitants of the working relationship and conditions which produce the product. Its cost must reflect the fatigue, the irritations, and sometimes the blood that went into it. It is here that we find the explanation for the horseplay cases, the curiosity cases, and the assault cases. Such problems will cease with the arrival of automation.

I take it to be clear, then, that the course of employment of a human being . . . includes not only his repetitive acts at the machine to which he is assigned, but includes, as well, his ministrations to his human needs. . . .

Here, then, is the reason for the compensation award: His injury was suffered during his working day while he was doing a natural thing, a thing which an employee, while working, might reasonably do. The fundamental inquiry is whether or not the act in question, either because of its nature, or local custom, or contractual provision, is reasonably to be regarded as part of the on-the-job activities of the human being involved, a part of his normal and reasonable sphere of activities. If so, it takes place "in the course of his employment." . . .

TALBOT SMITH

The Philosophy of Dissent as Applied to the Courts[1]

I am honored, indeed, to be asked to speak to this group. I know that among your members have been some of the greatest spirits of our times, men like Thomas Jefferson and Horace Mann. Even today I note in the audience the faces of men and women who are famed throughout our great community for their good works and great courage. It is, for me, a rare privilege to be in such company.

My subject is: "The Philosophy of Dissent as Applied to the Courts." This is a wonderful title. I like that word "philosophy." A less pretentious title—perhaps a more accurate title—would be "Dissenting Opinions: Their Purposes and Effect." Whatever the title, we are looking at a minor aspect of the judicial process, a small segment of the pie, yet a complete analysis of even this segment would transcend the limits of my time and my capacity, to say nothing of the limits of your patience.

First, let's brush aside one common cause of misunderstanding. I fancy every one of you has met somewhere the naive idea that when judges differ on a given case, this proves that some of these judges are incompetent, or maybe that all of them are incompetent.

1. An address delivered to the Layman's League, Church of Our Father, Detroit, Michigan, March 27, 1956.

That is, if they all knew the law, they would all come up with the same conclusion. That some judges are incompetent, one can hardly doubt, for the judicial branch, like the legislative branch and the executive branch, is staffed by men, not by angels, and we haven't yet discovered a method of selecting judges that guarantees 100 percent exclusion of the incompetent.

I assume then, that some judges are incompetent, but the question before us is whether disagreement among the judges (who deal with a given case) is proof that some of these judges are incompetent. To put it another way, the question is whether incompetence is the cause of disagreement. My answer to these questions is NO. Of course, in the nature of things, it may sometimes happen that incompetence is the cause of disagreement. But this is the very unusual situation. Let us here deal with the normal, not the abnormal.

Excluding that particular, and particularly regrettable situation, we must start, in any study of dissent, with an abstraction based upon a generalization. It is a striking fact that the more fundamental a document, be it law or constitution, the vaguer, necessarily, must be its terms. The great fundamental charters which govern our lives are phrased in the broadest possible terminology. They speak of such things as "life, liberty, and the pursuit of happiness." Did you ever try defining one of these terms? They say thou shalt not "covet thy neighbor's wife." They say that no citizen shall be subject to "unlawful search and seizure." Parse these phrases as you will, and you come back, again and again, to the inescapable fact that the document is general, not specific. It treats of concepts—not fact situations.

So, we start with generalizations. Add to these generalizations, now, a somewhat different, though closely related consideration: The obstructions involved in speech itself. It was one of our great dissenting Justices, Holmes, who reminded us that a word is a transparent vessel, into which one can pour any shade of meaning, from the pastel to the violent. What coloring will the crystal take from the hands of the judge? Let me give you an example: Consider as simple a word as the word "search." We all know what a search is. As children we took part in them, and as adults we have sought, in turn, for our own children as the evening drew near. Suppose, now, that you receive a letter describing some business proposition which is secret. Your home is broken into by certain officials and the letter found and read. I suppose we would all agree that there has been an unlawful search. But suppose, instead, information concerning the business transaction is obtained by tapping your telephone wires. Has your home been searched? What meaning will a Supreme Court apply to the word? What factors will influence the Court in the choice made? Possibly we may be able to answer that question with a little more understanding when we get through.

We start, then, our analysis of the dissenting opinion with the observation that words are weak vehicles for the transportation of ideas. They are inherently passive, inherently inert. That, of course, is not peculiar to words used in the courts. It is also true as to words used in the churches.

But we in the law have an additional element of doubt, an additional element of confusion injected into our problem by the principle of *stare decisis*. *Stare decisis* is simply the Latin way of saying "to follow precedent." If, however, precedent is to be blindly followed, much injustice may be done because of changed social conditions.

But, on the other hand, if precedent is to be ignored, our people may awake some morning to find that, unexpectedly, and without warning, rules of conduct and principles upon which they have risked their possibly slender store of assets, intangible as well as tangible, have been repudiated and abandoned. This, indeed, is one of the most difficult problems facing the courts. *Stare decisis* represents "an element of continuity in the law, and is rooted in the psychologic need to satisfy reasonable expectations." Yet it is not, as Justice Brandeis observed, a universal, inexorable command, and "whether it shall be followed, or departed from, is a question entirely within the discretion of the court."

Again, you see, we have introduced into the law an unknown, what the scientists call an X-factor, a factor as to the application of which the minds of reasonable men might well differ, differ to the point where conclusions honestly reached by the one judge will be unacceptable to his fellows, who honestly differ.

But we must examine still another prolific cause of disagreement among judges. It was eloquently pointed out by Mr. Justice Douglas a number of years ago that all legislation of major importance has marked advocates and antagonists. The law, as it finally emerges from the legislative halls, usually represents a compromise, or series of compromises. At times the meaning of one clause or paragraph will seem to be at complete variance with that of another. You see, what happened in that case was that both sides won in the law that finally emerged. Or, as sometimes happens, neither side may win. A law may be passed in which some important ingredient is completely missing. One side couldn't get its provision in, so they saw to it that the other side didn't get its in, either.

Now, in all of these cases the court must make a decision when the case comes before it. This means that the controversy which divided the legislators is merely transferred from the halls of the legislature to the chambers of the courts. The law is there before us. It must be given some kind of effect. How will it be interpreted? At that point, you will find the justices passing on the case responding to the same stimuli that prompted the legislators. To some, the solution indicated by the bill as a whole will be socialism of the worst kind, which I now understand is called "creeping socialism," while to others the solution indicated will be the only solution which will carry out the obvious intent of the bill as a whole.

Where we finally arrive, at this phase of our discussion, is to a realization that the dissenting opinion does not necessarily involve incompetence, it does not necessarily involve bias, it does not necessarily turn on technical differences, or even on conflicting legal authorities. It involves a determination of social and moral values. The court may split because some of its members are convinced, for instance that *stare decisis* shall, under today's social conditions, apply; the others reply, with Holmes, that "it is revolting to have no better reason for a rule of law or interpretation than that it was laid down in the time of Henvy IV," and that "it is still more revolting if the grounds upon which it was laid down have vanished long since, and the rule simply exists as a blind imitation of the past." The court may split, in still other cases, because of varying social standards, resulting in widely differing views as to the "liberality" of interpretation. One group will interpret the law grudgingly, in a frigid atmosphere, walking with hesitant steps down the new path. Another group, with equal honesty, will embrace the law eagerly, pushing it to its farthest limits of construction in order to accomplish its beneficent purpose. Again, the situation is ripe for dissent.

In all of these cases note what we have in essence: A deep-seated, well-marked cleavage in fundamental human values, in which all the human characteristics play their part. It is not incompetence which divides the justices of our highest courts, but competence and convictions. These human values which are being weighed are weighed by the judges in their individual scales. It is not a mathematical, but a moral process. It has, even, its elements of relativity, for I think it was another great Justice, Cardozo, who asked, in effect, whether the sins of the weak and the helpless should be weighed in the same scales as the sins of the strong and the powerful. The answer to that one may at times be reached, but only on your knees.

The ground, then, as I said, is ripe for dissent. The words are slippery and ambiguous, the dead hand of the past tries to lay hold on the problems, the organized forces of society with all their pressures, obvious and hidden, blunt and subtle, move into the considerations. What is the Justice to do? Will he pour into the transparent vessels (the words before him) the color poured by the majority?

At this point the most powerful forces of the profession and society come into operation. There is said to be a real public need for stability—stability in the family, in the churches and schools, and above all in the unchanging immutable law. How can you have stability if you forsake *stare decisis?* There is said, also, to be a real professional need for certainty, in the law above all else, since it rules and governs our lives. And how can you have certainty if one judge says: This is just not true! If these considerations rooted in the past, in old decisions, in older social values and morals, are taken at their face value the matter is closed. For there is no doubt that a powerful dissent so weakens the majority opinion that it often collapses after a few years; and there is no doubt that the same dissent casts much uncertainty upon the prevailing opinion. Why? Because it was meant to. That is why it was written.

The dissent, then, as Chief Justice Hughes once put it, "is an appeal to the brooding spirit of the law, to the intelligence of a future day, when a later decision may possibly correct the error into which the dissenting judge believes the court to have been betrayed." It might be interjected, as well, that in many cases the dissenting opinion has, in truth, later become the law. And even in those cases where it has not, it exerts a powerful influence on the development of the law, for it points out, often with pronounced vigor, weaknesses in the majority opinion which simply cannot stand the searching spotlight of professional and public opinion.

Here then, we are faced with a basic, fundamental, human issue, not peculiar to the courts or, indeed, to the churches: How much room is there, in our society, for re-examination of principles, for unsettling the settled past? If the world of 1920 had been the best of all possible worlds, we would still have the stain of child labor on our souls. If the world of 1930 had been the best of all possible worlds, we would today be without our great advances in the field of human needs. We grow. We live by growing. Our society must represent an adjustment of competing needs, the old and the new, a reconciliation of opposing views. It must, as well, find room, not only in its mind, but in its heart, for the new and the untried. The law must, from time to time, be revised to meet the changing needs of our people. The responsibility is on the courts, as the third co-ordinate branch of government, to correct what time and experience have shown to be its own mistakes, to modify its views as the needs of our people change, and as the social conscience is quickened. The modification is all the more imperative because of one characteristic of the judicial opinion which is not completely understood by many of our people: The fact that a judicial opinion becomes the law of the land. It decides, not only the case before the court at that time, but it serves as well as precedent for all *similar* cases. Thus when the child labor law was declared unconstitutional by the Supreme Court of the United States, it affected not only the few children involved in the test case then before the courts, but it affected the lives of every child in this nation, from North to South, from East to West. I will digress slightly to repeat to you the most devastating commentary, in my judgment, that was ever made concerning that opinion. It consists only of four lines. It goes something like this:

> The golf course lies beside the mill
> And on a summer day
> The happy children, at their looms,
> Can see the men at play.[2]

Similarly, when the Supreme Court recently ruled that segregation was unconstitutional, it affected not only the few young men and women in the cases then before the Court, but equally all men, women, and children of Negro parentage in this country.

But I said that the opinion was precedent for all *similar* cases. Here we must observe one of the most striking features of the dissent: It emphasizes the outstanding, significant, characteristics of the case, and thus serves as a guide to our people, in recognizing the dissimilarities in tomorrow's case. In that way, our people are encouraged to bring before our Supreme Court cases which might otherwise never reach us, for the parties would say—"What's the use? The Court has already ruled on the matter." So, I feel it is a superficial and trivial comment to say that dissents will destroy confidence in the courts, because confidence comes not from hiding cleavages in thought, and principle, but in exposing and exploring them. People lack confidence only in what they don't understand.

I find from all of this more than a suggestion. I find from it a duty—a duty to speak, to speak, if need be, by way of dissent. The voice may be the voice of one Justice standing alone. If so, it is all the more important that he speak, for it is important to our people to know that the individual, standing alone, still counts. What he believes, counts, though he numbers but one. What he says, counts, whether he is right or wrong. Once we stifle the voice of the individual in the shout of the pack, we have stifled a part of our freedom, merged ourselves, as well as our voices, in the mob. Let those who will, counsel caution and silence, the need for certainty and stability. There can be no silence while wrongs done our people cry for relief. And as for stability, the only real stability is that of the grave. Permit me to bring my thoughts closer to you: We all live by visions, whether they are good or evil.

I want to put before you a vision: The Judge our people should have. He who listens with his heart, as well as his head. The Judge who weighs the sins of the malevolent, the sins of the wise, the sins of the crafty on different scales than the sins of the helpless and

---

2. Smith is apparently quoting from memory Sarah N. Cleghorn's poem:
The golf links lie so near the mill
That almost every day
The laboring children can look out
And see the men at play.

the weak. The Judge who sees the bench as an altar, rather than a counter, or a ladder. The Judge who respects the mother's need, and the dignity of her barely coherent pleas for mercy for the boy who has taken the wrong turn in the road, the girl on whom society has turned its back. The Judge who can hear the faint whisper of the fatherless above the roar of industry.

This judge often seems to walk alone. Never, for him, will come the cheers of the crowds. Those who remember him control no crowds, no airways. But though he signs alone, in his dissents, he is not alone. He walks with a great unseen host. Cardozo, Holmes, and Brandeis sometimes fall in step with him in his solitary vigils through the dark thoughts pressed upon him. Far from being alone, he is attended night and day by those powerful forces of good which so long for expression in all, but find it, for reasons beyond human control, in so few.

There you see: The dissenting Justice and the philosophy of his "dissent."

QUESTIONS FOR STUDY, DISCUSSION, AND WRITING

1. Apart from the first paragraph, what has Smith done to adapt his speech to his audience of nonlawyers?
2. What does Smith mean by the "philosophy of dissent"? Is his philosophy applicable only to dissent? (Consider the fact that in the Schwimmer case Holmes was writing a dissenting opinion, while in the Haley case Frankfurter spoke for the majority.)
3. Smith refers to the "brooding spirit of the law." How does this conception differ from that of the law as a collection of rules or statutes written down in books?
4. Smith refers to Holmes' statement that "a word is a transparent vessel, into which one can pour any shade of meaning, from the pastel to the violent." How does the quotation seem characteristic of Holmes as he reveals himself in his opinion on the Schwimmer case (pp. 769–770)? How does Smith use the reference in his own speech? Is this an accurate account of the way language works?
5. What evidences of Smith's philosophy in action can be detected in his dissenting opinion in Salmon v. Bagley Laundry Company (pp. 776–780)?
6. How does Smith develop his "vision" of the ideal judge? Why does he use the metaphors of the altar, the counter, and the ladder? If the judge "weighs the sins of the malevolent, the sins of the wise, the sins of the crafty on different scales than the sins of the helpless and the weak," what happens to the concept of "equal justice"? Can justice be "equal"?
7. What parallels may be drawn between Smith's philosophy of dissent and Lippmann's arguments for the indispensable opposition (pp. 761–768)?

Prose Forms: Apothegms

[At the beginning of Bacon's essay "Of Truth," jesting Pilate asks, "What is truth?" and does not stay for an answer. Perhaps Pilate asked in jest because he thought the question foolish; perhaps because he thought an answer impossible. Something of Pilate's skepticism is in most of us, but something too of a belief that there is truth, even if—as the history of philosophy teaches us—determining its nature may be enormously difficult. We readily assume some things to be true even if we hesitate to say what ultimately is Truth.

The test of truth most often is an appeal to the observed facts of experience. The observation of experience yields knowledge; the generalized statement of that knowledge yields a concept of the experience; the concise, descriptive form in which that concept is expressed we call variously, apothegm, proverb, maxim, or aphorism. Thus Sir James Mackintosh can speak of apothegms as "the condensed good sense of nations," because the apothegm conveys the distilled observations of men about their own persistent conduct. To hear the familiar "Absence makes the heart grow fonder" is to be reminded of a general truth which you and the world acknowledge. It does not matter that the equally familiar "Out of sight, out of mind" seems to contradict the other saying; both are true but applicable to different situations. Both statements are immediately recognizable as true and neither requires to be argued for, representing as they do the collective experience of mankind intelligently observed.

Not everyone is as astute an observer as the writer of apothegms and maxims, of course, but everyone is presumably capable of perceiving their rightness. What we perceive first is the facts to which the saying applies. When Franklin says "An empty bag cannot stand upright" (in 1740 he obviously had in mind a cloth bag), we acknowledge that this is the condition of the empty bag—and of ourselves when we are empty. Or when La Rochefoucauld says "We are all strong enough to endure the misfortunes of others," he too observes a condition that exists among men.

Many aphoristic assertions claim their validity primarily in descriptive terms. But the descriptive is in most apothegms and maxims ims is joined to a normative "ought" and the sayings therefore convey admonitions about and judgments of the conditions they describe.

"Waste not, want not" is a simple illustration of this use of fact to admonish. Mark Twain assumes as observed fact the value of illusions, and goes on to offer a warning: "Don't part with your illusions. When they are gone you may still exist, but you have ceased to live." The condition of "ought" need not always be admonitory; it may be the implied judgment in La Rochefoucauld's assertion that "It is the habit of mediocre minds to condemn all that is beyond their grasp." The judgment is explicit in Franklin's "Fish and visitors stink in three days." And Bierce's definitions of ordinary words are not specifications of meanings in the way of ordinary dictionaries, but critical concepts of the experiences to which the words point.

"Wisdom" or "good sense," then, is the heart of the apothegm or maxim, the conjunction of "is" and "ought" in an assertion of universal truth. Unlike ordinary assertions of fact or opinion usually concerned with particular rather than universal experience, the wise saying is complete in its brevity. Before the ordinary assertion is allowed to hold, we require that the assumptions on which it rests, the implications it carries, the critical concepts and terms it contains, be examined closely and explored or justified. If someone says that the modern college student wants most to succeed materially in life, we want to be satisfied about what constitutes "modern," which college students (and where) are referred to, what else is involved in the comparative "most," what specifically is meant by "materially." But the apothegm assumes facts widely known and accepted, and in its judgments invokes values or attitudes readily intelligible to the great majority. It is the truth as most men experience it.

In a sense, every writer's concern is ultimately with truth. Certainly the essayist is directly concerned, in his definition and ordering of ideas, to say what is true and, somehow, to say it "new." Much of what he says is of the nature of assertion about particular experience; he must therefore be at pains to handle such matters as assumptions and logical proofs carefully and deliberately. But he cannot always be starting from scratch, not daring to assume anything, trusting no certain knowledge or experience or beliefs held in common with his fellows. Careful he must be, but also aware that available to him, in addition to methods of logical analysis and proof, rules of evidence, and the other means to effective exposition, is the whole memory and record of the vast experience of the race contained in a people's apothegms and aphorisms. In them is a treasury of truths useful to many demands of clarity and precision. And in them, too, is a valuable lesson in the way a significantly large body of experience— direct, in a person's day-to-day encounters; indirect, in his study of all forms of history—can be observed, conceptualized, and then expressed in an economy of language brief in form, comprehensive in meaning, and satisfyingly true.]

W. H. AUDEN: Apothegms

Some books are undeservedly forgotten; none are undeservedly remembered.

You do not educate a person's palate by telling him that what he has been in the habit of eating—watery, overboiled cabbage, let us say—is disgusting, but by persuading him to try a dish of vegetables which have been properly cooked. With some people, it is true, you seem to get quicker results by telling them—"Only vulgar people like overcooked cabbage; the best people like cabbage as the Chinese cook it"—but the results are less likely to be lasting.

No poet or novelist wishes he were the only one who ever lived, but most of them wish they were the only one alive, and quite a number fondly believe their wish has been granted.

The integrity of a writer is more threatened by appeals to his social conscience, his political or religious convictions, than by appeals to his cupidity. It is morally less confusing to be goosed by a traveling salesman than by a bishop.

Only a minor talent can be a perfect gentleman; a major talent is always more than a bit of a cad. Hence the importance of minor writers—as teachers of good manners. Now and again, an exquisite minor work can make a master feel thoroughly ashamed of himself.

Narcissus does not fall in love with his reflection because it is beautiful, but because it is *his*. If it were his beauty that enthralled him, he would be set free in a few years by its fading.

"After all," sighed Narcissus the hunchback, "on *me* it looks good."

Our sufferings and weaknesses, in so far as they are personal, *our* sufferings, *our* weaknesses, are of no literary interest whatsoever. They are only interesting in so far as we can see them as typical of the human condition. A suffering, a weakness, which cannot be expressed as an aphorism should not be mentioned.

The same rules apply to self-examination as apply to confession to a priest: *be brief, be blunt, be gone*. Be brief, be blunt, forget. The scrupuland is a nasty specimen.

In a state of panic, a man runs round in circles by himself. In a state of joy, he links hands with others and they dance round in a circle together.

A sense of humor develops in a society to the degree that its members are simultaneously conscious of being each a unique person and of being all in common subjection to unalterable laws.

Among those whom I like or admire, I can find no common denominator, but among those whom I love, I can: all of them make me laugh.

If Homer had tried reading the *Iliad* to the gods on Olympus, they would either have started to fidget and presently asked if he hadn't got something a little lighter, or, taking it as a comic poem, would have roared with laughter or possibly, even, reacting like ourselves to a tear-jerking movie, have poured pleasing tears.

AMBROSE BIERCE: *from* The Devil's Dictionary

abdication, *n.* An act whereby a sovereign attests his sense of the high temperature of the throne.

abscond, *v.i.* To "move in a mysterious way," commonly with the property of another.

absent, *adj.* Peculiarly exposed to the tooth of detraction; vilified; hopelessly in the wrong; superseded in the consideration and affection of another.

accident, *n.* An inevitable occurrence due to the action of immutable natural laws.

accordion, *n.* An instrument in harmony with the sentiments of an assassin.

achievement, *n.* The death of endeavor and the birth of disgust.

admiration, *n.* Our polite recognition of another's resemblance to ourselves.

alone, *adj.* In bad company.

applause, *n.* The echo of a platitude.

ardor, *n.* The quality that distinguishes love without knowledge.

bore, *n.* A person who talks when you wish him to listen.

cemetery, *n.* An isolated suburban spot where mourners match lies, poets write at a target and stone-cutters spell for a wager. The inscription following will serve to illustrate the success attained in these Olympian games:

His virtues were so conspicuous that his enemies, unable to overlook them, denied them, and his friends, to whose loose lives they were a rebuke, represented them as vices. They are here commemorated by his family, who shared them.

childhood, *n.* The period of human life intermediate between the idiocy of infancy and the folly of youth—two removes from the sin of manhood and three from the remorse of age.

Christian, *n.* One who believes that the New Testament is a divinely inspired book admirably suited to the spiritual needs of his neighbor. One who follows the teachings of Christ in so far as they are not inconsistent with a life of sin.

compulsion, *n.* The eloquence of power.

congratulation, *n.* The civility of envy.

conservative, *n.* A statesman who is enamored of existing evils, as distinguished from the Liberal, who wishes to replace them with others.

consult, *v.t.* To seek another's approval of a course already decided on.

contempt, *n.* The feeling of a prudent man for an enemy who is too formidable safely to be opposed.

coward, *n.* One who in a perilous emergency thinks with his legs.

debauchee, *n.* One who has so earnestly pursued pleasure that he has had the misfortune to overtake it.

destiny, *n.* A tyrant's authority for crime and a fool's excuse for failure.

diplomacy, *n.* The patriotic art of lying for one's country.

distance, *n.* The only thing that the rich are willing for the poor to call theirs and keep.

duty, *n.* That which sternly impels us in the direction of profit, along the line of desire.

education, *n.* That which discloses to the wise and disguises from the foolish their lack of understanding.

erudition, *n.* Dust shaken out of a book into an empty skull.

extinction, *n.* The raw material out of which theology created the future state.

faith, *n.* Belief without evidence in what is told by one who speaks without knowledge, of things without parallel.

genealogy, *n.* An account of one's descent from an ancestor who did not particularly care to trace his own.

ghost, *n.* The outward and visible sign of an inward fear.

habit, *n.* A shackle for the free.

heaven, *n.* A place where the wicked cease from troubling you with talk of their personal affairs, and the good listen with attention while you expound your own.

historian, *n.* A broad-gauge gossip.

hope, *n.* Desire and expectation rolled into one.

hypocrite, *n.* One who, professing virtues that he does not respect, secures the advantage of seeming to be what he despises.

impiety, *n.* Your irreverence toward my deity.

impunity, *n.* Wealth.

language, *n.* The music with which we charm the serpents guarding another's treasure.

logic, *n.* The art of thinking and reasoning in strict accordance with the limitations and incapacities of the human misunderstanding. The basic of logic is the syllogism, consisting of a major and a minor premise and a conclusion—thus:

Major Premise: Sixty men can do a piece of work sixty times as quickly as one man.

Minor Premise: One man can dig a post-hole in sixty seconds; therefore—

Conclusion: Sixty men can dig a post-hole in one second.

This may be called the syllogism arithmetical, in which, by

combining logic and mathematics, we obtain a double certainty and are twice blessed.

love, *n.* A temporary insanity curable by marriage or by removal of the patient from the influences under which he incurred the disorder. This disease, like *caries* and many other ailments, is prevalent only among civilized races living under artificial conditions; barbarous nations breathing pure air and eating simple food enjoy immunity from its ravages. It is sometimes fatal, but more frequently to the physician than to the patient.

miracle, *n.* An act or event out of the order of nature and unaccountable, as beating a normal hand of four kings and an ace with four aces and a king.

monkey, *n.* An arboreal animal which makes itself at home in genealogical trees.

mouth, *n.* In man, the gateway to the soul; in woman, the outlet of the heart.

non-combatant, *n.* A dead Quaker.

platitude, *n.* The fundamental element and special glory of popular literature. A thought that snores in words that smoke. The wisdom of a million fools in the diction of a dullard. A fossil sentiment in artificial rock. A moral without the fable. All that is mortal of a departed truth. A demi-tasse of milk-and-morality. The Pope's-nose of a featherless peacock. A jelly-fish withering on the shore of the sea of thought. The cackle surviving the egg. A dessicated epigram.

pray, *v.* To ask that the laws of the universe be annulled in behalf of a single petitioner confessedly unworthy.

presidency, *n.* The greased pig in the field game of American politics.

prude, *n.* A bawd hiding behind the back of her demeanor.

rapacity, *n.* Providence without industry. The thrift of power.

reason, *v.i.* To weigh probabilities in the scales of desire.

religion, *n.* A daughter of Hope and Fear, explaining to Ignorance the nature of the Unknowable.

resolute, *adj.* Obstinate in a course that we approve.

retaliation, *n.* The natural rock upon which is reared the Temple of Law.

saint, *n.* A dead sinner revised and edited.

The Duchess of Orleans relates that the irreverent old calumniator, Marshal Villeroi, who in his youth had known St. Francis de Sales, said, on hearing him called saint: "I am delighted to hear that Monsieur de Sales is a saint. He was fond of saying indelicate things, and used to cheat at cards. In other respects he was a perfect gentleman, though a fool."

valor, *n.* A soldierly compound of vanity, duty and the gambler's hope:

"Why have you halted?" roared the commander of a division at Chickamauga, who had ordered a charge; "move forward, sir, at once."

"General," said the commander of the delinquent brigade, "I am persuaded that any further display of valor by my troops will bring them into collision with the enemy."

WILLIAM BLAKE: Proverbs of Hell

In seed time learn, in harvest teach, in winter enjoy.
Drive your cart and your plough over the bones of the dead.
The road of excess leads to the palace of wisdom.
Prudence is a rich, ugly old maid courted by Incapacity.
He who desires but acts not, breeds pestilence.
The cut worm forgives the plough.
Dip him in the river who loves water.
A fool sees not the same tree that a wise man sees.
He whose face gives no light, shall never become a star.
Eternity is in love with the productions of time.
The busy bee has no time for sorrow.
The hours of folly are measur'd by the clock; but of wisdom, no clock can measure.
All wholesome food is caught without a net or a trap.
Bring out number, weight, and measure in a year of dearth.
No bird soars too high, if he soars with his own wings.
A dead body revenges not injuries.
The most sublime act is to set another before you.
If the fool would persist in his folly he would become wise.
Folly is the cloak of knavery.
Shame is Pride's cloak.
Prisons are built with stones of Law, brothels with bricks of Religion.
The pride of the peacock is the glory of God.
The lust of the goat is the bounty of God.
The wrath of the lion is the wisdom of God.
The nakedness of woman is the work of God.
Excess of sorrow laughs. Excess of joy weeps.
The roaring of lions, the howling of wolves, the raging of the stormy sea, and the destructive sword are portions of eternity too great for the eye of man.
The fox condemns the trap, not himself.
Joys impregnate. Sorrows bring forth.
Let man wear the fell of the lion, woman the fleece of the sheep.
The bird a nest, the spider a web, man friendship.
The selfish, smiling fool, and the sullen, frowning fool shall be both thought wise, that they may be a rod.
What is now proved was once only imagin'd.

The rat, the mouse, the fox, the rabbit watch the roots; the lion, the tiger, the horse, the elephant watch the fruits.

The cistern contains: the fountain overflows.

One thought fills immensity.

Always be ready to speak your mind, and a base man will avoid you.

Everything possible to be believ'd is an image of truth.

The eagle never lost so much time as when he submitted to learn of the crow.

The fox provides for himself; but God provides for the lion.

Think in the morning. Act in the noon. Eat in the evening. Sleep in the night.

He who has suffer'd you to impose on him, knows you.

As the plough follows words, so God rewards prayers.

The tigers of wrath are wiser than the horses of instruction.

Expect poison from the standing water.

You never know what is enough unless you know what is more than enough.

Listen to the fool's reproach! it is a kingly title!

The eyes of fire, the nostrils of air, the mouth of water, the beard of earth.

The weak in courage is strong in cunning.

The apple tree never asks the beech how he shall grow; nor the lion, the horse, how he shall take is prey.

The thankful receiver bears a plentiful harvest.

If others had not been foolish, we should be so.

The soul of sweet delight can never be defil'd.

When thou seest an eagle, thou seest a portion of Genius; lift up thy head!

As the caterpillar chooses the fairest leaves to lay her eggs on, so the priest lays his curse on the fairest joys.

To create a little flower is the labor of ages.

Damn braces. Bless relaxes.

The best wine is the oldest, the best water the newest.

Prayers plough not! Praises reap not!

Joys laugh not! Sorrows weep not!

The head Sublime, the heart Pathos, the genitals Beauty, the hands and feet Proportion.

As the air to a bird or the sea to a fish, so is contempt to the contemptible.

The crow wish'd everything was black, the owl that everything was white.

Exuberance is Beauty.

If the lion was advised by the fox, he would be cunning.

Improvement makes straight roads; but the crooked roads without improvement are roads of Genius.

Sooner murder an infant in its cradle than nurse unacted desires.

Where man is not, nature is barren.
Truth can never be told so as to be understood, and not be believ'd.
Enough! or Too much.

SAMUEL L. CLEMENS: *from* Pudd'nhead Wilson's Calendars

Training is everything. The peach was once a bitter almond; cauliflower is nothing but cabbage with a college education.

As to the Adjective: when in doubt, strike it out.

Noise proves nothing. Often a hen who has merely laid an egg cackles as if she had laid an asteroid.

Everything human is pathetic. The secret source of Humor itself is not joy but sorrow. There is no humor in heaven.

We should be careful to get out of an experience only the wisdom that is in it—and stop there; lest we be like the cat that sits down on a hot stove-lid. She will never sit down on a hot stove-lid again, and that is well; but also she will never sit down on a cold one any more.

Truth is stranger than Fiction, but it is because Fiction is obliged to stick to possibilities; Truth isn't.

Man is the Only Animal that blushes. Or needs to.

When people do not respect us we are sharply offended; yet deep down in his private heart no man much respects himself.

There are several good protections against temptations but the surest is cowardice.

It takes your enemy and your friend, working together, to hurt you to the heart, the one to slander you and the other to get the news to you.

Let me make the superstitions of a nation and I care not who makes its laws or its songs either.

True irreverence is disrespect for another man's god.

Don't part with your illusions. When they are gone you may still exist but you have ceased to live.

Every one is a moon and has a dark side which he never shows to anybody.

BENJAMIN FRANKLIN: *from* Poor Richard's Almanack

Light purse, heavy heart.   1733
He's a fool that makes his doctor his heir.
Love well, whip well.
Hunger never saw bad bread.
Fools make feasts, and wise men eat 'em.
He that lies down with dogs, shall rise up with fleas.
He is ill clothed, who is bare of virtue.
There is no little enemy.

Without justice courage is weak.   1734
Where there's marriage without love, there will be love without
marriage.
Do good to thy friend to keep him, to thy enemy to gain him.
He that cannot obey, cannot command.
Marry your son when you will, but your daughter when you can.

Approve not of him who commends all you say.   1735
Necessity never made a good bargain.
Be slow in chusing a friend, slower in changing.
Three may keep a secret, if two of them are dead.
Deny self for self's sake.
To be humble to superiors is duty, to equals courtesy, to inferiors
nobleness.

Fish and visitors stink in three days.   1736
Do not do that which you would not have known.
Bargaining has neither friends nor relations.
Now I've a sheep and a cow, every body bids me good morrow.
God helps them that help themselves.
He that speaks much, is much mistaken.
God heals, and the doctor takes the fees.

There are no ugly loves, nor handsome prisons.   1737
Three good meals a day is bad living.

Who has deceiv'd thee so oft as thyself?   1738
Read much, but not many books.
Let thy vices die before thee.

He that falls in love with himself, will have no rivals.   1739
Sin is not hurtful because it is forbidden, but it is forbidden
because it's hurtful.

An empty bag cannot stand upright.   1740

Learn of the skilful: he that teaches himself, hath a fool for his
master.   1741

Death takes no bribes. 1742

An old man in a house is a good sign. 1744
Fear God, and your enemies will fear you.

He's a fool that cannot conceal his wisdom. 1745
Many complain of their memory, few of their judgment.

When the well's dry, we know the worth of water. 1746
The sting of a reproach is the truth of it.

Write injuries in dust, benefits in marble. 1747
Nine men in *ten* are suicides.
A man in a passion rides a mad horse. 1749

He is a governor that governs his passions, and he is a servant
that serves them. 1750
Sorrow is good for nothing but sin.

Calamity and prosperity are the touchstones of integrity. 1752
Generous minds are all of kin.

Haste makes waste. 1753

The doors of wisdom are never shut. 1755

The way to be safe, is never to be secure. 1757

WILLIAM HAZLITT: *from* Characteristics

1. Of all virtues, magnamity is the rarest. There are a hundred persons of merit for one who willingly acknowledges it in another.

13. Some people tell us all the harm—others as carefully conceal
all the good they hear of us.

15. The silence of a friend commonly amounts to treachery. His
not daring to say anything in our behalf implies a tacit censure.

23. Envy is a littleness of soul, which cannot see beyond a certain
point, and if it does not occupy the whole space, feels itself excluded.

27. Those who are the most distrustful of themselves, are the
most envious of others; as the most weak and cowardly are the
most revengeful.

38. The wish is often "father to the thought"; but we are quite
as apt to believe what we dread as what we hope.

45. Nothing is more successful with women than that sort of condescending patronage of the sex, which goes by the general name
of gallantry. It has the double advantage of imposing on their weakness and flattering their pride. By being indiscriminate, it tantalizes and keeps them in suspense; and by making a profession of

an extreme deference for the sex in general, naturally suggests the reflection, what a delightful thing must be to gain the exclusive regard of a man who has so high an opinion of what is due to the female character. It is possible for a man, by talking of what is *feminine* or *unfeminine*, *vulgar* or *genteel*, by saying *how shocking such an article of dress is*, or that *no lady ought to touch a particular kind of food*, fairly to starve or strip a whole circle of simpletons half-naked, by mere dint of impertinence, and an air of commonplace assurance. How interesting to be acquainted with a man whose every thought turns upon the sex! How charming to make a conquest of one who sets up for a consummate judge of female perfections!

46. We like characters and actions which we do not approve. There are amiable vices and obnoxious virtues, on the mere principle that our sympathy with a person who yields to obvious impulses (however prejudicial) is itself agreeable, while to sympathize with exercises of self-denial or fortitude, is a painful effort. Virtue costs the spectator, as well as the performer, something. We are touched by the immediate motives of actions, we judge of them by the consequences. We like a convivial character better than an abstemious one, because the idea of conviviality in the first instance is pleasanter than that of sobriety. For the same reason, we prefer generosity to justice, because the imagination lends itself more easily to an ebullition of feeling, than to the suppression of it on remote and abstract principles; and we like a good-natured fool, or even knave better than the severe professors of wisdom and morality. Cato, Brutus, etc. are characters to admire and applaud, rather than to love or imitate.

49. We may observe persons who seem to have a peculiar delight in the *disagreeable*. They catch all sorts of uncouth tones and gestures, the manners and dialect of clowns and hoydens, and aim at vulgarity as others ape gentility. (This is what is often understood by a love of low life.) They say all sorts of disagreeable things without meaning or feeling what they say. What startles or shocks other people is to them an amusing excitement, a fillip to their constitutions; and from the bluntness of their perceptions and a certain wilfulness of spirit, not being able to enter into the refined and pleasurable, they make a merit of being insensible to everything of the kind. Masculine women, for instance, are those who, not being possessed of the charms and delicacy of the sex, affect a superiority over it by throwing aside all decorum.

57. The surest way to make ourselves agreeable to others is by seeming to think them so. If we appear fully sensible of their good qualities, they will not complain of the want of them in us.

59. Silence is one great art of conversation. He is not a fool who knows when to hold his tongue; and a person may gain credit for

sense, eloquence, wit, who merely says nothing to lessen the opinion which others have of these qualities in themselves.

61. A man who is always defending his friends from the most trifling charges, will be apt to make other people their enemies.

64. We do not like our friends the worse because they sometimes give us an opportunity to rail at them heartily. Their faults reconcile us to their virtues. Indeed, we never have much esteem or regard, except for those that we can afford to speak our minds of freely; whose follies vex us in proportion to our anxiety for their welfare, and who have plenty of redeeming points about them to balance their defects. When we "spy abuses" of this kind, it is a wiser and more generous proceeding to give vent to our impatience and ill-humor, than to brood over it, and let it, by sinking into our minds, poison the very sources of our goodwill.

85. The public have neither shame nor gratitude.

89. It is wonderful how soon men acquire talents for offices of trust and importance. The higher the situation, the higher the opinion it gives us of ourselves; and as is our confidence, so is our capacity. We *assume* an equality with circumstances.

101. Cunning is the art of concealing our own defects, and discovering other people's weaknesses. Or it is taking advantages of others which they do not suspect, because they are contrary to propriety and the settled practice. We feel no inferiority to a fellow who picks our pockets; though we feel mortified at being overreached by trick and cunning. Yet there is no more reason for it in the one case than in the other. Any one may win at cards by cheating—*till he is found out*. We have been playing against odds. So any one may deceive us by lying, or take an unfair advantage of us, who is not withheld by a sense of shame or honesty from doing so.

105. The error in the reasonings of Mandeville, Rochefoucauld, and others, is this: they first find out that there is something mixed in the motives of all our actions, and they then proceed to argue, that they must all arise from one motive, *viz.* self-love. They make the exception the rule. It would be easy to reverse the argument, and prove that our most selfish actions are disinterested. There is honor among thieves. Robbers, murderers, etc. do not commit those actions, from a pleasure in pure villainy, or for their own benefit only, but from a mistaken regard to the welfare or good opinion of those with whom they are immediately connected.

108. True modesty and true pride are much the same thing. Both consist in setting a just value on ourselves—neither more nor less. It is a want of proper spirit to fancy ourselves inferior to others in those things in which we really excel them. It is conceit and want of common-sense to arrogate a superiority over others, without the most well-founded pretensions.

115. We do not hate those who injure us, if they do not at the same time wound our self-love. We can forgive any one sooner than those who lower us in our own opinion. It is no wonder, therefore, that we as often dislike others for their virtues as for their vices. We naturally hate whatever makes us despise ourselves.

127. We as often repent the good we have done as the ill.

131. The fear of punishment may be necessary to the suppression of vice; but it also suspends the finer motives to virtue.

134. Vulgar prejudices are those which arise out of accident, ignorance, or authority. Natural prejudices are those which arise out of the constitution of the human mind itself.

138. Most codes of morality proceed on a supposition of *Original Sin;* as if the only object was to coerce the headstrong propensities to vice, and there were no natural disposition to good in the mind, which it was possible to improve, refine, and cultivate.

139. This *negative* system of virtue leads to a very low style of moral sentiment. It is as if the highest excellence in a picture was to avoid gross defects in drawing; or in writing, instances of bad grammar. It ought surely to be our aim in virtue, as well as in other things, "to snatch a grace beyond the reach of art."

142. When the imagination is continually led to the brink of vice by a system of terror and denunciations, people fling themselves over the precipice from the mere dread of falling.

145. Honesty is one part of eloquence. We persuade others by being in earnest ourselves.

LA ROCHEFOUCAULD: *from* Maxims

Our virtues are mostly but vices in disguise.

14. Men not only forget benefits received and injuries endured; they even come to dislike those to whom they are indebted, while ceasing to hate those others who have done them harm. Diligence in returning good for good, and in exacting vengeance for evil, comes to be a sort of servitude which we do not readily accept.

19. We are all strong enough to endure the misfortunes of others.

20. The steadiness of the wise man is only the art of keeping his agitations locked within his breast.

25. Firmer virtues are required to support good fortune than bad.

28. Jealousy is, in its way, both fair and reasonable, since its intention is to preserve for ourselves something which is ours, or which we believe to be ours; envy, on the other hand, is a frenzy which cannot endure contemplating the possessions of others.

31. Were we faultless, we would not derive such satisfaction from remarking the faults of others.

38. Our promises are made in hope, and kept in fear.

50. A man convinced of his own merit will accept misfortune as an honor, for thus can he persuade others, as well as himself, that he is a worthy target for the arrows of fate.

56. To achieve a position in the world a man will do his utmost to appear already arrived.

59. There is no accident so disastrous that a clever man cannot derive some profit from it: nor any so fortunate that a fool cannot turn it to his disadvantage.

62. Sincerity comes from an open heart. It is exceedingly rare; what usually passes for sincerity is only an artful pretense designed to win the confidence of others.

67. Grace is to the body what sense is to the mind.

71. When two people have ceased to love, the memory that remains is almost always one of shame.

72. Love, to judge by most of its effects, is closer to hatred than to friendship.

75. Love, like fire, needs constant motion; when it ceases to hope, or to fear, love dies.

78. For most men the love of justice is only the fear of suffering injustice.

79. For a man who lacks self-confidence, silence is the wisest course.

83. What men have called friendship is only a social arrangement, a mutual adjustment of interests, an interchange of services given and received; it is, in sum, simply a business from which those involved purpose to derive a steady profit for their own self-love.

89. Everyone complains of his memory, none of his judgment.

90. In daily life our faults are frequently more pleasant than our good qualities.

93. Old people love to give good advice: it compensates them for their inability nowadays to set a bad example.

119. We are so accustomed to adopting a mask before others that we end by being unable to recognize ourselves.

122. If we master our passions it is due to their weakness, not our strength.

133. The only good copies are those which point the absurdity of bad originals.

134. We are never so ridiculous through what we are as through what we pretend to be.

138. We would rather speak ill of ourselves than not at all.

144. We do not like to give praise, and we never do so without reasons of self-interest. Praise is a cunning, concealed and delicate form of flattery which, in different ways, gratifies both the giver and the receiver; the one accepts it as the reward for merit; the

other bestows it to display his sense of justice and his powers of discernment.

146. We usually only praise that we may be praised.

149. The refusal to accept praise is the desire to be praised twice over.

150. The wish to deserve the praise we receive strengthens our virtues; and praise bestowed upon wit, courage and beauty contributes to their increase.

160. Splendid though an action may be, it should not be regarded as great unless it be the effect of a great design.

167. Avarice, more than open-handedness, is the opposite of economy.

170. When a man's behavior is straightforward, sincere and honest it is hard to be sure whether this is due to rectitude or cleverness.

176. In love there are two sorts of constancy: the one comes from the perpetual discovery of new delights in the beloved: the other, from the self-esteem which we derive from our own fidelity.

180. Our repentance is less a regret for the evil we have done than a precaution against the evil that may be done to us.

185. Evil, like good, has its heroes.

186. Not all who have vices are contemptible: all without a trace of virtue are.

190. Only great men are marked with great faults.

192. When our vices depart from us, we flatter ourselves that it is we who have rid ourselves of them.

200. Virtue would not go so far did vanity not keep her company.

205. Virtue, in women, is often love of reputation and fondness for tranquillity.

216. Perfect valor is to behave, without witnesses, as one would act were all the world watching.

218. Hypocrisy is the tribute that vice pays to virtue.

230. Nothing is as contagious as example, and we never perform an outstandingly good or evil action without its producing others of its sort. We copy goodness in the spirit of emulation, and wickedness owing to the malignity of our nature which shame holds in check until example sets it free.

237. No man should be praised for his goodness if he lacks the strength to be bad: in such cases goodness is usually only the effect of indolence or impotence of will.

259. The pleasure of love is in loving: and there is more joy in the passion one feels than in that which one inspires.

264. Pity is often only the sentiment of our own misfortunes felt in the ills of others. It is a clever pre-science of the evil times upon which we may fall. We help others in order to ensure their help in similar circumstances; and the kindnesses we do them are,

if the truth were told, only acts of charity towards ourselves invested against the future.

276. Absence diminishes small loves and increases great ones, as the wind blows out the candle and blows up the bonfire.

277. Women frequently believe themselves to be in love even when they are not: the pursuit of an intrigue, the stimulus of gallantry, the natural inclination towards the joys of being loved, and the difficulty of refusal, all these combine to tell them that their passions are aroused when in fact it is but their coquetry at play.

375. It is the habit of mediocre minds to condemn all that is beyond their grasp.

376. True friendship destroys envy, as true love puts an end to coquetry.

378. We give advice but we do not inspire behavior.

392. One should treat one's fate as one does one's health; enjoy it when it is good, be patient with it when it is poorly, and never attempt any drastic cure save as an ultimate resort.

399. There is a form of eminence which is quite independent of our fate; it is an air which distinguishes us from our fellow men and makes us appear destined for great things; it is the value which we imperceptibly attach to ourselves; it is the quality which wins us the deference of others; more than birth, honours or even merit, it gives us ascendancy.

417. In love, the person who recovers first recovers best.

423. Few people know how to be old.

467. Vanity leads us to act against our inclinations more often than does reason.

479. Only people who are strong can be truly gentle: what normally passes for gentleness is mere weakness, which quickly turns sour.

483. Vanity, rather than malice, is the usual source of slander.

540. Hope and fear are inseparable. There is no hope without fear, nor any fear without hope.

576. We always discover, in the misfortunes of our dearest friends, something not altogether displeasing.

597. No man can be sure of his own courage until he has stared danger in the face.

617. How can we expect another to keep our secret, if we cannot keep it ourself?

BLAISE PASCAL: *from* Pensées

When we wish to correct with advantage, and to show another that he errs, we must notice from what side he views the matter, for on that side it is usually true, and admit that truth to him, but reveal to him the side on which it is false. He is satisfied with that, for he sees that he was not mistaken, and that he only failed to see all sides. Now, no one is offended at not seeing everything; but one does not like to be mistaken, and that perhaps arises from the fact that man naturally cannot see everything, and that naturally he cannot err in the side he looks at, since the perceptions of our senses are always true.

Certain authors, speaking of their works, say, "My book," "My commentary," "My history," etc. They resemble middle-class people who have a house of their own, and always have "My house" on their tongue. They would do better to say, "Our book," "Our commentary," "Our history," etc., because there is in them usually more of other people's than their own.

Weariness. Nothing is so insufferable to man as to be completely at rest, without passions, without business, without diversion, without study. He then feels his nothingness, his forlornness, his insufficiency, his dependence, his weakness, his emptiness. There will immediately arise from the depth of his heart weariness, gloom, sadness, fretfulness, vexation, despair.

Diversion. As men are not able to fight against death, misery, ignorance, they have taken it into their heads, in order to be happy, not to think of them at all.

The great and the humble have the same misfortunes, the same griefs, the same passions; but the one is at the top of the wheel, and the other near the center, and so less disturbed by the same revolutions.

Children are astonished to see their comrades respected.

I can well conceive a man without hands, feet, head (for it is only experience which teaches us that the head is more necessary than feet). But I cannot conceive man without thought; he would be a stone or a brute.

The strength of a man's virtue must not be measured by his efforts, but by his ordinary life.

Man is neither angel nor brute, and the unfortunate thing is that he who would act the angel acts the brute.

All the principles of skeptics, stoics, atheists, etc., are true. But their conclusions are false, because the opposite principles are also true.

If it is an extraordinary blindness to live without investigating what we are, it is a terrible one to live an evil life, while believing in God.

Experience makes us see an enormous difference between piety and goodness.

GEORGE BERNARD SHAW: *from* The Revolutionist's
Handbook (*in* Man and Superman)

Democracy

If the lesser mind could measure the greater as a footrule can
measure a pyramid, there would be finality in universal suffrage.
As it is, the political problem remains unsolved.

Democracy substitutes selection by the incompetent many for
appointment by the corrupt few.

Democratic republics can no more dispense with national idols
than monarchies with public functionaries.

Government presents only one problem: the discovery of a trustworthy anthropometric method.

Liberty and Equality

He who confuses political liberty with freedom and political equality with similarity has never thought for five minutes about either.

Nothing can be unconditional: consequently nothing can be free.

Liberty means responsibility. That is why most men dread it.

The duke inquires contemptuously whether his gamekeeper is the
equal of the Astronomer Royal; but he insists that they shall both
be hanged equally if they murder him.

The notion that the colonel need be a better man than the
private is as confused as the notion that the keystone need be stronger than the coping stone.

Where equality is undisputed, so also is subordination.

Equality is fundamental in every department of social organization.

The relation of superior to inferior excludes good manners.

Education

When a man teaches something he does not know to somebody
else who has no aptitude for it, and gives him a certificate of proficiency, the latter has completed the education of a gentleman.

A fool's brain digests philosophy into folly, science into superstition, and art into pedantry. Hence University education.

The best brought-up children are those who have seen their
parents as they are. Hypocrisy is not the parent's first duty.

The vilest abortionist is he who attempts to mould a child's character.

At the University every great treatise is postponed until its author attains impartial judgment and perfect knowledge. If a horse could wait as long for its shoes and would pay for them in advance, our blacksmiths would all be college dons.

He who can, does. He who cannot, teaches.

A learned man is an idler who kills time with study. Beware of his false knowledge: it is more dangerous than ignorance.

Activity is the only road to knowledge.

Every fool believes what his teachers tell him, and calls his credulity science or morality as confidently as his father called it divine revelation.

No man fully capable of his own language ever masters another.

No man can be a pure specialist without being in the strict sense an idiot.

Do not give your children moral and religious instruction unless you are quite sure they will not take it too seriously. Better be the mother of Henri Quatre and Nell Gwynne than of Robespierre and Queen Mary Tudor.

Virtues and Vices

No specific virtue or vice in a man implies the existence of any other specific virtue or vice in him, however closely the imagination may associate them.

Virtue consists, not in abstaining from vice, but in not desiring it.

Self-denial is not a virtue: it is only the effect of prudence on rascality.

Obedience simulates subordination as fear of the police simulates honesty.

Disobedience, the rarest and most courageous of the virtues, is seldom distinguished from neglect, the laziest and commonest of the vices.

Vice is waste of life. Poverty, obedience, and celibacy are the canonical vices.

Economy is the art of making the most of life.

The love of economy is the root of all virtue.

Greatness

Greatness is only one of the sensations of littleness.

In heaven an angel is nobody in particular.

Greatness is the secular name for Divinity: both mean simply what lies beyond us.

If a great man could make us understand him, we should hang him.

We admit that when the divinity we worshipped made itself visible and comprehensible we crucified it.

To a mathematician the eleventh means only a single unit: to the bushman who cannot count further than his ten fingers it is an incalculable myriad.

The difference between the shallowest routineer and the deepest thinker appears, to the latter, trifling; to the former, infinite.

In a stupid nation the man of genius becomes a god: everybody worships him and nobody does his will.

The Perfect Gentleman

The fatal reservation of the gentleman is that he sacrifices everything to his honor except his gentility.

A gentleman of our days is one who has money enough to do what every fool would do if he could afford it: that is, consume without producing.

The true diagnostic of modern gentility is parasitism.

No elaboration of physical or moral accomplishment can atone for the sin of parasitism.

A modern gentleman is necessarily the enemy of his country. Even in war he does not fight to defend it, but to prevent his power of preying on it from passing to a foreigner. Such combatants are patriots in the same sense as two dogs fighting for a bone are lovers of animals.

The North American Indian was a type of the sportsman warrior gentleman. The Periclean Athenian was a type of the intellectually and artistically cultivated gentleman. Both were political failures. The modern gentleman, without the hardihood of the one or the culture of the other, has the appetite of both put together. He will not succeed where they failed.

He who believes in education, criminal law, and sport, needs only property to make him a perfect modern gentleman.

Gambling

The most popular method of distributing wealth is the method of the roulette table.

The roulette table pays nobody except him that keeps it. Nevertheless a passion for gaming is common, though a passion for keeping roulette tables is unknown.

Gambling promises the poor what Property performs for the rich: that is why the bishops dare not denounce it fundamentally.

On History
Men · Events · Philosophies

THOMAS JEFFERSON
George Washington[1]

I think I knew General Washington intimately and thoroughly; and were I called on to delineate his character, it should be in terms like these.

His mind was great and powerful, without being of the very first order; his penetration strong, though not so acute as that of a Newton, Bacon, or Locke; and as far as he saw, no judgment was ever sounder. It was slow in operation, being little aided by invention or imagination, but sure in conclusion. Hence the common remark of his officers, of the advantage he derived from councils of war, where hearing all suggestions, he selected whatever was best; and certainly no general ever planned his battles more judiciously. But if deranged during the course of the action, if any member of his plan was dislocated by sudden circumstances, he was slow in re-adjustment. The consequence was, that he often failed in the field, and rarely against an enemy in station, as at Boston and York. He was incapable of fear, meeting personal dangers with the calmest unconcern. Perhaps the strongest feature in his character was prudence, never acting until every circumstance, every consideration, was maturely weighed; refraining if he saw a doubt, but, when once decided, going through with his purpose, whatever obstacles opposed. His integrity was most pure, his justice the most inflexible I have ever known, no motives of interest or consanguinity, of friendship or hatred, being able to bias his decision. He was, indeed, in every sense of the words, a wise, a good, and a great man. His temper was naturally irritable and high toned; but reflection and

1. From a letter written in 1814 to a Doctor Jones, who was writing a history and wanted to know about Washington's role in the Federalist-Republican controversy.

809

resolution had obtained a firm and habitual ascendency over it. If ever, however, it broke its bonds, he was most tremendous in his wrath. In his expenses he was honorable, but exact; liberal in contributions to whatever promised utility; but frowning and unyielding on all visionary projects, and all unworthy calls on his charity. His heart was not warm in its affections; but he exactly calculated every man's value, and gave him a solid esteem proportioned to it. His person, you know, was fine, his stature exactly what one would wish, his deportment easy, erect and noble; the best horseman of his age, and the most graceful figure that could be seen on horseback. Although in the circle of his friends, where he might be unreserved with safety, he took a free share in conversation, his colloquial talents were not above mediocrity, possessing neither copiousness of ideas, nor fluency of words. In public, when called on for a sudden opinion, he was unready, short and embarrassed. Yet he wrote readily, rather diffusely, in an easy and correct style. This he had acquired by conversation with the world, for his education was merely reading, writing and common arithmetic, to which he added surveying at a later day. His time was employed in action chiefly, reading little, and that only in agriculture and English history. His correspondence became necessarily extensive, and, with journalizing his agricultural proceedings, occupied most of his leisure hours within doors. On the whole, his character was, in its mass, perfect, in nothing bad, in few points indifferent; and it may truly be said, that never did nature and fortune combine more perfectly to make a man great, and to place him in the same constellation with whatever worthies have meritied from man an everlasting remembrance. For his was the singular destiny and merit, of leading the armies of his country successfully through an arduous war, for the establishment of its independence; of conducting its councils through the birth of a government, new in its forms and principles, until it had settled down into a quiet and orderly train; and of scrupulously obeying the laws through the whole of his career, civil and military, of which the history of the world furnishes no other example.

* * * I am satisfied the great body of republicans think of him as I do. We were, indeed, dissatisfied with him on his ratification of the British treaty. But this was short lived. We knew his honesty, the wiles with which he was encompassed, and that age had already begun to relax the firmness of his purposes; and I am convinced he is more deeply seated in the love and gratitude of the republicans, than in the Pharisaical homage of the federal monarchists. For he was no monarchist from preference of his judgment. The soundness of that gave him correct views of the rights of man, and his severe justice devoted him to them. He has often declared to me that he considered our new Constitution as an experiment on the practicability of republican government, and with what dose of liberty man could be trusted for his own good; that he was determined the experiment should have a fair trial, and would lose the last drop of his blood in support of it. And these declarations he repeated to me the oftener and more pointedly, because he knew my suspicions of Colonel Hamilton's views, and probably had heard from him the same declarations which I had, to wit, "that the British constitution, with its unequal representation, corruption and other existing abuses, was the most perfect government which had ever been established on earth, and that a reformation of those abuses would make it an impracticable government." I do believe that General Washington had not a firm confidence in the durability of our government. He was naturally distrustful of men, and inclined to gloomy apprehensions; and I was ever persuaded that a belief that we must at length end in something like a British constitution, had some weight in his adoption of the ceremonies of levees, birthdays, pompous meetings with Congress, and other forms of the same character, calculated to prepare us gradually for a change which he believed possible, and to let it come on with as little shock as might be to the public mind.

These are my opinions of General Washington which I would vouch at the judgment seat of God, having been formed on an acquaintance of thirty years. I served with him in the Virginia legislature from 1769 to the Revolutionary war, and again, a short time in Congress, until he left us to take command of the army. During the war and after it we corresponded occasionally, and in the four years of my continuance in the office of Secretary of State, our intercourse was daily, confidential and cordial. After I retired from that office, great and malignant pains were taken by our federal monarchists, and not entirely without effect, to make him view me as a theorist, holding French principles of government, which would lead infallibly to licentiousness and anarchy. And to this he listened the more easily, from my known disapprobation of the British treaty. I never saw him afterwards, or these malignant insinuations should have been dissipated before his just judgment, as mists before the sun. I felt on his death, with my countrymen, that "verily a great man hath fallen this day in Israel."

NATHANIEL HAWTHORNE

Abraham Lincoln[1]

Of course, there was one other personage, in the class of statesmen, whom I should have been truly mortified to leave Washington without seeing; since (temporarily, at least, and by force of circumstances)

1. From an article in *The Atlantic Monthly,* July, 1862.

he was the man of men. But a private grief had built up a barrier about him, impeding the customary free intercourse of Americans with their chief magistrate; so that I might have come away without a glimpse of his very remarkable physiognomy, save for a semi-official opportunity of which I was glad to take advantage. The fact is, we were invited to annex ourselves, as supernumeraries, to a deputation that was about to wait upon the President, from a Massachusetts whip factory, with a present of a splendid whip.

Our immediate party consisted only of four or five (including Major Ben Perley Poore, with his note-book and pencil), but we were joined by several other persons, who seemed to have been lounging about the precincts of the White House, under the spacious porch, or within the hall, and who swarmed in with us to take the chances of a presentation. Nine o'clock had been appointed as the time for receiving the deputation, and we were punctual to the moment; but not so the President, who sent us word that he was eating his breakfast, and would come as soon as he could. His appetite, we were glad to think, must have been a pretty fair one; for we waited about half an hour in one of the antechambers, and then were ushered into a reception-room, in one corner of which sat the Secretaries of War and of the Treasury, expecting, like ourselves, the termination of the Presidential breakfast. During this interval there were several new additions to our group, one or two of whom were in a working-garb, so that we formed a very miscellaneous collection of people, mostly unknown to each other, and without any common sponsor, but all with an equal right to look our head servant in the face.

By and by there was a little stir on the staircase and in the passage-way, and in lounged a tall, loose-jointed figure, of an exaggerated Yankee port and demeanor, whom (as being about the homeliest man I ever saw, yet by no means repulsive or disagreeable) it was impossible not to recognize as Uncle Abe.

Unquestionably, Western man though he be, and Kentuckian by birth, President Lincoln is the essential representative of all Yankees, and the veritable specimen, physically, of what the world seems determined to regard as our characteristic qualities. It is the strangest and yet the fittest thing in the jumble of human vicissitudes, that he, out of so many millions, unlooked for, unselected by any intelligible process that could be based upon his genuine qualities, unknown to those who chose him, and unsuspected of what endowments may adapt him for his tremendous responsibility, should have found the way open for him to fling his lank personality into the chair of state—where, I presume, it was his first impulse to throw his legs on the council-table, and tell the Cabinet Ministers a story. There is no describing his lengthy awkwardness, nor the uncouthness of his movement; and yet it seemed as if I had been in the habit of seeing him daily, and had shaken hands with him a thousand times in some village street; so true was he to the aspect of the pattern American, though with a certain extravagance which, possibly, I exaggerated still further by the delighted eagerness with which I took it in. If put to guess his calling and livelihood, I should have taken him for a country school-master as soon as anything else. He was dressed in a rusty black frock coat and pantaloons, unbrushed, and worn so faithfully that the suit had adapted itself to the curves and angularities of his figure, and had grown to be an outer skin of the man. His hair was black, still unmixed with gray, stiff, somewhat bushy, and had apparently been acquainted with neither brush nor comb that morning, after the disarrangement of the pillow; and as to a nightcap, Uncle Abe probably knows nothing of such effeminacies. His complexion is dark and sallow, betokening, I fear, a insalubrious atmosphere around the White House; he has thick black eyebrows and an impending brow; his nose is large, and the lines about his mouth are very strongly defined.

The whole physiognomy is as coarse a one as you would meet anywhere in the length and breadth of the States; but, withal, it is redeemed, illuminated, softened, and brightened by a kindly though serious look out of his eyes, and an expression of homely sagacity, that seems weighted with rich results of village experience. A great deal of native sense; no bookish cultivation, no refinement; honest at heart, and thoroughly so, and yet, in some sort, sly—at least, endowed with a sort of tact and wisdom that are akin to craft, and would impel him, I think, to take an antagonist in flank, rather than to make a bull-run at him right in front. But, on the whole, I like this sallow, queer, sagacious visage, with the homely human sympathies that warmed it; and, for my small share in the matter, would as lief have Uncle Abe for a ruler as any man whom it would have been practicable to put in his place.

Immediately on his entrance the President accosted our member of Congress, who had us in charge, and, with a comical twist of his face, made some jocular remark about the length of his breakfast. He then greeted us all round, not waiting for an introduction, but shaking and squeezing everybody's hand with the utmost cordiality, whether the individual's name was announced to him or not. His manner towards us was wholly without pretence, but yet had a kind of natural dignity, quite sufficient to keep the forwardest of us from clapping him on the shoulder and asking him for a story. A mutual acquaintance being established, our leader took the whip out of its case, and began to read the address of presentation. The whip was an exceedingly long one, its handle wrought in ivory (by some artist in the Massachusetts State Prison, I believe), and ornamented with a medallion of the President, and other equally beautiful devices; and along its whole length there was a succession of golden bands and ferrules. The address was shorter than the whip, but equally well made, consisting chiefly of an explanatory description of these artistic designs, and closing with a hint that the gift was a suggestive and emblematic one, and that the President would recognize the use to which such an instrument should be put.

This suggestion gave Uncle Abe rather a delicate task in his reply, because, slight as the matter seemed, it apparently called for some declaration, or intimation, or faint foreshadowing of policy in reference to the conduct of the war, and the final treatment of the Rebels. But the President's Yankee aptness and not-to-be-caughtness stood him in good stead, and he jerked or wiggled himself out of the dilemma with an uncouth dexterity that was entirely in character; although, without his gesticulation of eye and mouth—and especially the flourish of the whip, with which he imagined himself touching up a pair of fat horses—I doubt whether his words would be worth recording, even if I could remember them. The gist of the reply was, that he accepted the whip as an emblem of peace, not punishment; and, this great affair over, we retired out of the presence in high good humor, only regretting that we could not have seen the President sit down and fold up his legs (which is said to be a most extraordinary spectacle), or have heard him tell one of those delectable stories for which he is so celebrated. A good many of them are afloat upon the common talk of Washington, and are certainly the aptest, pithiest, and funniest little things imaginable; though, to be sure, they smack of the frontier freedom, and would not always bear repetition in a drawing-room, or on the immaculate page of the *Atlantic*.[2]

Good Heavens! what liberties have I been taking with one of the potentates of the earth, and the man on whose conduct more important consequences depend than on that of any other historical personage of the century! But with whom is an American citizen entitled to take a liberty, if not with his own chief magistrate? However, lest the above allusions to President Lincoln's little peculiarities (already well known to the country and to the world) should be misinterpreted, I deem it proper to say a word or two in regard to him, of unfeigned respect and measurable confidence. He is evidently a man of keen faculties, and, what is still more to the purpose, of powerful character. As to his integrity, the people have that intuition of it which is never deceived. Before he actually entered upon his great office, and for a considerable time afterwards, there is no reason to suppose that he adequately estimated the gigantic task about to be imposed on him, or, at least, had any distinct idea how it was to be managed;

---

2. This passage was one of those omitted from the article as originally published, and the following note was appended to explain the omission, which had been indicated by a line of points:

"We are compelled to omit two or three pages, in which the author describes the interview, and gives his idea of the personal appearance and deportment of the President. The sketch appears to have been written in a benign spirit, and perhaps conveys a not inaccurate impression of its august subject; but it lacks *reverence*, and it pains us to see a gentleman of ripe age, and who has spent years under the corrective influence of foreign institutions, falling into the characteristic and most ominous fault of Young America."

and I presume there may have been more than one veteran politician who proposed to himself to take the power out of President Lincoln's hands into his own, leaving our honest friend only the public responsibility for the good or ill success of the career. The extremely imperfect development of his statesmanly qualities, at that period, may have justified such designs. But the President is teachable by events, and has now spent a year in a very arduous course of education; he has a flexible mind, capable of much expansion, and convertible towards far loftier studies and activities than those of his early life; and if he came to Washington a backwoods humorist, he has already transformed himself into as good a statesman (to speak moderately) as his prime minister.[3]

3. Presumably the Secretary of State, William H. Seward.

QUESTIONS FOR STUDY, DISCUSSION, AND WRITING

1. In one sentence summarize Hawthorne's attitude toward Lincoln in the first seven paragraphs.
2. What is the basic pattern of the opening sentence of the fifth paragraph? Find other examples of this pattern. What is their total impact on Hawthorne's description?
3. In his final paragraph Hawthorne seeks to prevent misunderstanding by stressing his respect for and confidence in Lincoln. Is there anything in the paragraph which runs counter to that expression? To what effect?
4. In the footnote to the seventh paragraph the editor of The Atlantic Monthly explains his omission of the first seven paragraphs. On the evidence of this statement what sort of a person does the editor seem to be? Is there anything in the omitted paragraphs that would tend to justify his decision? Is the full description superior to the last paragraph printed alone? Explain.
5. Describe someone you know with a strong personality that has contrasting characteristics.

DOUGLAS SOUTHALL FREEMAN

Over the River[1]

Every soldier had been hoping "Old Jack's" return would not be far distant. Tuesday morning, May 5, after Jackson had agreed that

1. From "Promotion for Rodes and for Jackson," Chapter XXXVI of *Lee's Lieutenants*, Vol. II, 1943.

In his notes Freeman uses short or cue titles, as follows: *Cooke's Jackson* for J. E. Cooke, *Stonewall Jackson, A Military Biography* (edition of 1866); *Dabney* for R. L. Dabney, *Life and Campaigns of Lieut.-Gen. Thomas J. Jackson; Mrs. Jackson* for Mary Anna Jackson, *Memoirs of Stonewall Jack-*

son; *McGuire* for Hunter H. McGuire and George L. Christian, *The Confederate Cause and Conduct in the War between the States; Owen* for W. M. Owen, *In Camp and Battle with the Washington Artillery of New Orleans; O. R.* for *Official Records of the Union and Confederate Armies; Pendleton* for Susan P. Lee, *Memoirs of William Nelson Pendleton; R. E. Lee* for D. S. Freeman, *R. E. Lee.*

"all things work together for good," he welcomed Chaplain Lacy, who arrived at 10 o'clock to conduct bedside worship and to give the General the satisfacton of discussing religion. Jackson asked that Lacy come every morning at the same hour, but he had made up his mind that he ought not to gratify his wish of having Lacy go with him to Ashland. He explained to the chaplain: "It would be setting an example of self-gratification to the troops, and you had better stay at your post of duty. I have always tried to set the troops a good example."[2] Meantime, he could enjoy to the limit of his strength the privilege of Lieutenant Smith, who was of his same Presbyterian faith and was minded to the ministry.

That morning or the next, Jackson took occasion to expound one of his favorite views—that the Bible supplied rules for every action of life. He had contended many times that if an army rested on the Sabbath, it could cover more ground in a given week than if it marched all seven days. Now he argued that the Bible was rich in lessons for each exigency of a soldier's life. For instance—and he turned to Smith with a smile, "Can you tell me where the Bible gives Generals a model for their official reports of battles?

Smith answered that he never had consulted Holy Writ to find examples of battle reports.

"Nevertheless," Jackson insisted, "there are such: and excellent models, too." He went on: "Look, for instance, at the narrative of Joshua's battle with the Amalekites; there you have one. It had clearness, brevity, fairness, modesty; and it traces the victory to its right source, the blessing of God."[3] Lee's battle, as well as Joshua's, came in for discussion, but not with any excited concern that day on the part of the wounded man. When someone told him that Hooker had entrenched North of Chancellorsville and seemed to be inviting attack there, comment was brief: "That is bad; very bad."[4] Beyond that, Jackson expressed no doubt of the result. As hopefully as the day began, it ended, but to the accompaniment of a hard, chilling rain.[5]

Light rain was falling on the morning of the 6th when, in the Wilderness North of Chancellorsville, the pickets sent back word that the enemy, whom Lee intended that day to attack, had crossed during the night to the north side of the Rappahannock. If anything of this was said to Jackson, there is no record of his observations. He passed that day, Wednesday, as he had spent Tuesday with no symptoms of other involvement, and with some delectable discourse on theology. Did Dr. McGuire suppose, Jackson asked, that the sufferers of the New Testament, who had received the healing touch

2. *Pendleton,* 271 [This and all the other footnotes are Freeman's].

3. This and the references in these pages to other phases of Jackson's religious experience at this time, merely are paraphrased from *Dabney,* 715 ff. Joshua's battle with the Amalekites is described in *Exodus* xvii, 8 ff.

4. *Dabney,* 715.

5. *Hotchkiss' MS Diary,* 187.

of Jesus, ever were afflicted afterward with the same disease? Mc-Guire had no opinion. Jackson was firm in his conviction that one healed by the Saviour of any malady never would suffer from it again. "Oh, for infinite power!" Jackson exclaimed.

For a time he was silent, and then he asked of Smith, "Where were the headquarters of Christianity after the crucifixion?"

Smith could answer that as readily as he could describe the road to Yerby's or tell a stranger how to get to Moss Neck. Jerusalem, said Smith, remained for a time the chief seat of the church; but after the dispersion of the disciples, by reason of persecution, the Christians had no home city until they established Antioch, Iconium, Rome and Alexandria as centers of influence.

That was fair enough as answer for most men, but the wounded Cromwell of the South, a military realist, would not have it so: "Why do you say, 'centers of influence'? Is not 'headquarters' a better term?" That reiterated, he urged Smith to proceed with the account of the manner in which those cities had become headquarters of the faith.

Smith hesitated to deliver to a wounded soldier a discourse on church history, and before he answered, he looked inquiringly at McGuire. An encouraging nod was assurance that Jackson might be helped, rather than hurt by learning more about the divisional headquarters of Christendom. Smith must have thanked inwardly his instructors and his good memory, because he was able without hesitation or vagueness to explain, in the approving words of Dr. Dabney, "how the Apostles were directed by Divine Providence, seemingly, to plant their most flourishing churches, at an early period, in these great cities, which were rendered by their political, commercial and ethnical relations, 'headquarters' of influence for the whole civilized world."[6]

Jackson was loath to have the explanation end without supporting topographical data. He wanted, especially, to know where Iconium was, and he bade Smith "get the map" and point out the place to him, just as Jed. Hotchkiss, a year before, had made clear to him, after some effort, that Fisher's Gap and Swift Run Gap were *not* the same pass.

Smith deferentially suggested that perhaps no map at hand would show Iconium. "Yes, sir," Jackson corrected, "you will find it in the atlas which is in my old trunk." To satisfy his chief, Smith is said to have examined the trunk[7] and, when he did not find the atlas, to have asked if it might be in Jackson's portable desk. "Yes," said Jackson, "you are right, I left it in my desk," and he mentioned the shelf, but by this time his attention was lagging. Exhaustion was creeping

6. *Dabney,* 720.
7. The text follows Dabney, but W. N. Pendleton, in an order of Apr. 15, 1863, for a reduction in the baggage of officers, remarked: "General Jackson takes no trunk himself, and allows none in his Corps" (*Owen,* 210).

over him. "Mr. Smith," he said, once more the General, "I wish you would examine into that matter . . . and report to me."[8]

Despite weariness at the end, this theological meat helped to make a day of consistent and encouraging gain. Ere its close, Chaplain Lacy went to Army Headquarters to request the detail of Dr. S. B. Morrison of Early's Division, who had been the General's family physician and was, besides, a kinsman of Mrs. Jackson's. He would be an excellent medical counsellor and a relief chief nurse in the place of Dr. McGuire, who could not endure much longer his vigils at the bedside.

With word that Dr. Morrison would be sent as soon as practicable, Lacy in due time returned. The chaplain brought also a thoughtful message from General Lee: "Give [General Jackson] my affectionate regards, and tell him to make haste and get well, and come back to me as soon as he can. He has lost his left arm; but I have lost my right arm."[9] This, of course, was gratifying to Jackson and was perhaps the most pleasant incident of the day.[1]

That night, Wednesday, May 6, Dr. McGuire was so weary that instead of trying to stay awake by the General's side, he decided he would sleep on a couch in Jackson's room and would leave the patient in the care of Jim. The General's body servant, who was sponsor of many picturesque stories about his master, was devoted to Jackson and was quite competent to act as assistant nurse. With Dr. McGuire on the couch and Jim silent in the chair, Jackson went to sleep without difficulty.

About 1:00 A.M. Thursday, May 7, the General was awakened by nausea. As quietly as he could, be aroused Jim and told the Negro to get a wet towel and to apply it to his stomach. Jim was vaguely conscious that this was the wrong thing to do. Might he not wake Dr. McGuire and ask him? Jackson refused: The doctor had been very tired; let him sleep; get the towel. Obediently Jim went out, wet a towel thoroughly in cold water, and helped in applying it to the General's stomach.

The cold and the dampness did no good. Paroxysms in the right side were added to the nausea. Moment by moment, pain increased until it almost passed endurance. The General's frame was shaken but his resolution was firm: he would not wake the sleeping surgeon if he could endure till morning. Soon Jackson observed, though without panic, that the pain was sharpened every time he drew breath. Agonizing as that was, he held out until the gray of dawn and the first stir out of doors. Then he had to permit Jim to awaken McGuire.

---

8. *Dabney,* 720-21. There is some doubt concerning the time of this curious incident, but the 6th, rather than the 8th, seems the more probable date.

9. *Dabney,* 716.
1. *Dabney,* 715; *Hotchkiss' MS Diary,* 187.

In a moment the tall young physician with his long face and his understanding eye was by the bedside. He listened intently to the General's breathing and he examined the painful area of the chest. All too readily, McGuire became convinced of what the patient himself may have suspected: Jackson was developing pneumonia.

Hope and planning and confident expectation now were halted. Instead of an early removal to Ashland, a peaceful convalescence at Lexington and a prompt return to the head of the Second Corps, there must be a sterner battle there in the cottage at Chandlers'. If it was won, Chancellorsville was a double victory. Were the battle lost—were it possible, even, to think that Jackson might not recover —then the North would be repaid for all the boys who had been slain or maimed there in the Wilderness of Spotsylvania, where the burnt forest still smoked and the dead lay unburied.

Jackson was not afraid. He did not believe pneumonia would kill him. Judgment, confidence, faith, ambition—something had convinced him that he had more work to do. Attack, then, the disease that was assailing him! Preliminary to cupping, which would bring more blood to the affected member, Jackson was given morphia.

This of course made him less sensitive to his pain but it threw him quickly into a stupor. From that hour, the personality of Jackson, as his officers knew it, seemed in a haze, obscured, uncertain. He began to mutter and occasionally he used connected sentences, but it was difficult to tell whether he was rational or was babbling. His attendants disagreed, at least in retrospect, regarding his consciousness at particular moments. What seemed to one auditor the expression of clear religious faith seemed to another hearer the uncontrolled expression of the formal words the General had loved and learned. In the first offthrust of reason, he seemed to be carried back again to the attack on Hooker's right. "Major Pendleton," he exclaimed, "send in and see if there is higher ground back of Chancellorsville."[2]

About noon, when the doctors had done what they could for him, he asked for a glass of lemonade. This, after some whispering and considerable delay, was brought him by Smith. The General sipped it and then said quickly: "You did not mix this, it is too sweet; take it back."

He was correct in saying that Smith had not prepared the beverage, but had he known by whose anxious hands it had been prepared,

---

2. *Dabney*, 715. In *Pendleton*, 271, on the authority of Chaplain Lacy, Jackson is quoted as saying: "I must find out whether there is high ground between Chancellorsville and the river.... Push up the columns.... Hasten the columns. ... Pendleton, you take charge of that. ...Where's Pendleton? ... Tell him to push up the columns." It is necessary to give warning that Jackson's delirious and semi-conscious remarks during his illness did not have anything that approximated the order and the dramatic quality assigned them in some of the contemporary accounts. Mrs. Jackson, *op. cit.*, 451, undoubtedly stated the fact correctly when she said: "From the time I reached him he was too ill to notice or talk much, and he lay most of the time in a semi-conscious state; but when aroused, he recognized those about him and consciousness would return."

he would have been less critical. Soon he was aware of another presence in the room. There by his bed, white-faced but composed, was his wife. He stirred himself to greet her and he found words to express his thankfulness that she had come, but so deeply was he under his opiate that he dropped off again quickly. When she spoke or ministered to him he was able to show by smile or glance that he knew her. At length, looking steadfastly at her he observed the emotion she was trying to conceal. With an effort, but seemingly in full command of his faculties, he said, "My darling, you must cheer up and not wear a long face. I love cheerfulness and brightness in a sickroom."[3]

Had he known all she had endured, he would have been proud that she held back her tears. On Sunday morning, May 3, after family worship at Dr. Hoge's home in Richmond, she had been told as gently as possible that the evening before her husband had been wounded severely but, it was hoped, not dangerously. Her instant wish, of course, was to hasten to him. That was impossible. North of Richmond, railway service was suspended because of Stoneman's raid; private travel over more than forty-five miles of road was dangerous until the Federal cavalry were driven back. Communication by telegraph and by mail was uncertain. It was Tuesday before Mrs. Jackson's brother Joseph, who left the General Sunday, got to Richmond and told her the circumstances of the wounding and of the operation.

This report increased her solicitude. She begged to be permitted to start immediately and to take her chances of eluding the enemy; but she received word that the railroad company expected at any time to reopen the line to Guiney's. Thursday, this was done. The she started on the first passenger train that left Richmond.

As soon as she arrived, she sensed danger. All that could be said for her encouragement by the staff officer who met her was that the General was doing "pretty well." When she reached the house, Mrs. Chandler greeted her with womanly understanding and invited her to rest there until the surgeons, who were then "dressing the General's wounds" were ready for her to see her husband.

Mrs. Jackson could not sit still. She went out on the long porch[4] and walked up and down and waited, as it seemed to her, for hours.

At length she noticed men digging in the family graveyard at no great distance from the house. As she watched, she saw them bring to the surface a coffin which was being exhumed for shipment elsewhere. Horrified, Mrs. Jackson asked whose was the body. It was,

3. *Mrs. Jackson*, 451. From noon, Thursday, May 7, Mrs. Jackson, though she wrote years afterward, is the fullest authority on the General's illness. She made some errors, confused certain events and omitted a few incidents, but she did not yield to the temptation, as more than one of the other first-hand authorities did, of "dressing up" every occurrence in the sickroom.

4. Which was on the level of the basement—*Mrs. Pendleton's MS Statement.*

she was told, that of General Paxton, of whose death she had not heard. A scene of 1861 flashed over her: "My husband's own neighbor and friend! and I knew the young wife, and remembered how I had seen her weeping bitterly as she watched his departure from her in those first days of the war, when all our hearts were well-nigh bursting with foreboding and dread. Now the cruel war had done its worst for *her*, and she was left widowed, and her children fatherless."[5] No wonder, when Mrs. Jackson was assigned the task of preparing her husband's lemonade, as a means of occupying her unhappy mind, she spoiled it with too much sugar![6]

He was trying to tell her something else: "I know you would gladly give your life for me, but I am perfectly resigned. Do not be sad; I hope I *may* yet recover. Pray for me, but always remember in your prayers to use the petition, 'Thy will be done.' "[7] Although he dozed off again then, every time he opened his eyes and saw her, he would murmur, "My darling . . . . you are very much loved" or "You are one of the most precious little wives in the world."[8] He seemed able to look at her and to speak to her without emotional strain, but more than once, when she asked, "Shall I bring in the baby for you to see?" he answered, "Not yet; wait till I feel better." The last time he had seen the child, spring was coming to the valley of the Massaponax and the peach trees had been blooming.

About 2:00 P.M., Dr. Samuel B. Morrison arrived and came at once to the General. As the surgeon leaned over him, Jackson opened his eyes, recognized Morrison, smiled and said simply: "That's an old, familiar face."[9] Morrison and McGuire now held a consultation and decided that if Mrs. Jackson was to be gratified in her wish to attend the General, she must have some capable, cheerful friend to help with the baby, who had not yet been weaned. Mrs. Jackson agreed to this and asked that Mrs. Moses D. Hoge of Richmond be asked to come. For their own part, the surgeons determined that they could call from the capital its most distinguished authority on pneumonia, Dr. David Tucker. To summon him and to escort Mrs. Hoge to Guiney's, Lieutenant Smith was sent to the city on the next train.[1] Mrs. Hoge was one of the wisest of women and would strengthen the young wife.

Jackson all the while seemed half asleep, half delirious. He continued able to rouse himself when called but he had to ask Mrs. Jackson to speak distinctly, so that he could hear every word.[2] When left alone, his mind would turn to the battlefield. More than once he seemed to be thinking of his troops as weary at the end of a long conflict. He wanted the commissary at hand, wanted the soldiers fed. "Tell Major Hawks to send forward provisions to the men." The

5. *Mrs. Jackson*, 449-50.
6. *Dabney*, 716-17.
7. *McGuire*, 227.
8. *Mrs. Jackson*, 451.

9. *Dabney*, 717; *Mrs. Jackson*, 453.
1. *Dabney*, 717-18.
2. *Mrs. Jackson*, 451.

name stuck in his mind . . . . "Major Hawks . . . Major Hawks" he muttered.[3]

Despite his delirium, the doctors did not feel discouraged. When the cool evening closed in rain,[4] they could not dispute the nature and progress of the malady, but they believed he was holding his own against it. There were some reasons for thinking him better,[5] though these may have been nothing more than the effect of the opiates the surgeons continued to administer. At bedtime, Morrison took his seat by Jackson to watch and to give the medicines. The doctor had little to do. Jackson lay in stupor but kept a grip on himself. Once, during the night, when the doctor offered him a draught and asked, "Will you take this, General?" Jackson seemed almost to reprimand with a terse answer—"Do your duty!" As Morrison paused, uncertain what Jackson meant, the General said again, "Do your duty!"[6]

Friday, May 8, the anniversary of the Battle of McDowell, dawned cool and misty.[7] Among the camps, there was profound concern. For the first time, men seriously were asking. Was "Old Jack" in danger? How could the Army do without him? For a year, a rounded year that very day, his name had been the symbol of victory. Others had failed or had fallen; he had defied rout and death. Many who had seen him in battle, those blue eyes ablaze, had shared Dick Taylor's belief that the bullet which could kill "Stonewall" never had been moulded. The enemy had not struck him down; his own troops had; and if they, even they, had not been able to slay him, could pneumonia? Veterans of the old Army of the Valley, in particular, argued and wondered or feared and prayed. In the name of all of them General Lee was to speak when he said, "Surely, General Jackson must recover; God will not take him from us, now that we need him so much."[8]

In the cottage at Chandlers', that Friday, some of the surgeons were not so sure. Dr. Tucker had not yet arrived from Richmond, but Surgeons Breckinridge and Smith, men of high repute in the Army Medical Corps, had come at Dr. McGuire's request for consultation. These three and Dr. Morrison made as thorough an examination as Jackson's condition allowed. The wounds appeared to be doing well. Although the discharge had diminished, healing was continuing. Pain in the side no longer was troubling the patient.

The ominous condition was his difficult breathing and his great exhaustion. Of his sense of weakness, Jackson spoke; but when Dr. Breckinridge expressed hope that a blister would help, Jackson voiced

3. *Mrs. Jackson,* 452; *Dabney,* 719. Again it must be noted that these remarks cannot be given their proper sequence, but apparently they were spoken on Thursday and not, as usually stated, on Sunday.

4. *Hotchkiss' MS Diary,* 189.
5. *McGuire,* 227.
6. *Dabney,* 718-19.
7. *Hotchkiss' MS Diary,* 189.
8. *Cf.* 2 *R. E. Lee,* 562. This remark was made Sunday, May 10.

his own confidence in that treatment and maintained that he would get well.[9] Later in the day, Dr. Morrison had to express a fear that the disease might not be overcome. To this, Jackson listened without emotion, and then, rallying his mind and tongue, he said deliberately: "I am not afraid to die; I am willing to abide by the will of my Heavenly Father. But I do not believe that I shall die at this time; I am persuaded the Almighty has yet a work for me to perform."[1] The General demanded that Dr. McGuire be summoned to pass on Dr. Morrison's opinion; and even after his own Medical Director admitted doubt concerning the outcome, Jackson still insisted that he would recover. He had a restless night, but he did not appear to be shaken in his confidence that he would beat his new adversary.

Out of doors, the brightest day of a changeable May week was Saturday, the 9th.[2] It found Jackson's breathing apparently less difficult and his pain diminished. His weakness manifestly was worse.[3] He still observed intermittently what was going on in his sick room, and he noticed dimly that to the intelligent faces of the doctors around his bed, another had been added—that of David Tucker, the Richmond authority on pneumonia, who at length had arrived. Jackson did not remark at the moment how many consultants had been summoned. Later in the day he said slowly to McGuire: "I see from the number of physicians that you think my condition dangerous, but I thank God, if it is His will, that I am ready to go."[4] Ready though he was, he still was determined to fight for recovery. He asked to see his baby and, when she came, he beamed at her in no spirit of farewell. With his splinted hand, which the child did not seem to fear, he caressed her. "Little comforter . . . little comforter," he murmured.[5]

In the afternoon, he bade his attendants summon Chaplain Lacy. At the time, the lungs of Jackson were so nearly filled that his breathing was difficult again. Such respiration as he had was shallow and cruelly fast. For these reasons, Mrs. Jackson and the physicians tried to dissuade him from conversing with Lacy. The General would not be balked. He must see the Chaplain. It was important. His attendants yielded. Tucker Lacy came in as if for another of the theological discussions in which Jackson delighted. This time the General had a more practical question of religion: Was Lacy working to promote Sunday observance by the Army in the manner previously enjoined on him? Lacy was able to report that he was. Jackson was pleased and relieved, but as the subject was one regarding which he had positive convictions, he tried to explain them once again,

9. *McGuire*, 227.
1. These sentences are put in quotations because Dr. Dabney, *op. cit.*, 719, insisted that Jackson used "precisely these words." Further, Dr. Dabney insisted that Jackson distinguished with care and purpose between "my Heavenly

Father," when speaking of his own relationship to God, and "the Almighty" when he referred to the divine plan.
2. *Hotchkiss' MS Diary*, 189.
3. *Dabney*, 721; *McGuire*, 227.
4. *McGuire*, 227.
5. *Ibid.*

slowly and painfully, to the Chaplain.[6] When Lacy at length arose, he offered to remain with the General on the Sabbath Day; but Jackson insisted that Lacy go to second corps headquarters and preach, as usual, to the soldiers.[7]

Evening came, clear and warm. A week before, at that very hour, Jackson had been driving furiously through the Wilderness and, looking backward at the sunset skies, he had wished for an hour more of daylight.[8] Now, what was it he desired as he lay there and lifted his arm above his head again, in his familiar gesture, and shut his eyes and seemed to pray?[9] Was it for another day of life—for recovery—for opportunity, with blazing batteries and the cheering line of his veterans, to drive Hooker into the river? He talked more of battle than of anything else and he commanded and exhorted— "Order A. P. Hill to prepare for action . . . Pass the infantry to the front."[1] Most of his other words were confused or unintelligible.

Now, again, into the deepening silence, came the voice of Mrs. Jackson: Might she read to him some of the Psalms of consolation? He shook his head vaguely; he was suffering too much, he said, to be able to listen. No sooner had he spoken than his disciplined conscience stirred and smote him even in his stupor. Would he not heed the Psalms, the Word of God? "Yes," he corrected himself, "we must never refuse that." He managed to add briefly: "Get the Bible and read them."

She brought the book and in her soft voice read. He tried to fix his attention on the promises of the Most High but he grew weary. "Sing to me," he said presently, and when she asked what she should sing, he bade her choose the most spiritual of the hymns. The brave woman thus far had endured the emotional strain but she was afraid to trust her voice alone on the hymns beloved by the man she loved. Her brother Joseph—the Lieutenant Morrison who had been with Jackson in the Wilderness—was there at the cottage. Would he help her? He came. She got the hymn book. Together in the dim light of the room, brother and sister sat by the bed and sang . . . to the ominous accompaniment of Jackson's wild breathing.

"Sing, 'Shew Pity, Lord,' " Jackson gasped.

They knew what he wanted—Dr. Watts's rendering of part of the Fifty-first Psalm, which was marked "A penitent pleading for pardon"—

> Shew pity, Lord; O Lord, forgive;
> Let a repenting rebel live;
> Are not thy mercies large and free?
> May not a sinner trust in thee?[2]

6. *Mrs. Jackson*, 453; *Dabney*, 721.
7. *Mrs. Jackson*, 453.
8. *Cooke's Jackson*, 419.
9. *McGuire*, 227, with no certainty concerning the hour this occurred.
1. See *supra*, p. 671, n. 119.

2. In Winchell's *Watts*, this is assigned the tunes German, Bath and Limehouse; but Dr. Dabney, *op cit.*, 722, stated that it was sung to the tune Old Hundred.

Doubtless, as it was written, they sang it through its sixth and last verse:

> Yet save a trembling sinner, Lord,
> Whose hope, still hov'ring round thy word,
> Would light on some sweet promise there,
> Some sure support against despair.

"The singing," Mrs. Jackson said afterward, "had a quieting effect, and he seemed to rest in perfect peace."[3] When Dr. Morrison hinted again, later in the evening, that the end might not be far distant, the spirit of the soldier asserted itself once more. "I don't think so," said Jackson; "I think I will be better by morning."[4]

Determined as he was to fight on, he lost ground as the night passed and, half conscious, he seemed to get no relief except from cold sponging of his face and forehead.[5] As he appeared to be sinking steadily, one of the physicians tried to get him to take a drink of brandy. Jackson tasted it but refused to do more. "It tastes like fire," he said, "and cannot do me any good."[6]

The soft spring night ended at last in warmth and promise of sunshine.[7] It was the 10th of May. Two years ago that day at Harpers Ferry, when he was a Colonel of Virginia Volunteers, he had named as Surgeon the man who now was leaning over him. Orders had been issued also, May 10, 1861, for regimental commanders to superintend the drill of their regiments. Captains had been directed to inspect their companies before marching them to dress parade.[8]

Jackson's mind then had been intent on training the superb raw manpower he had. Plans he had been maturing to increase the artillery of his command.[9] A year later, May 10, 1862, as a Major General in the Provisional Army of the Confederacy, he had been in pursuit of Milroy after the action at McDowell, and he had been writing Ewell: "My troops are in advance. Should circumstances justify it, I will try, through God's blessing, to get in Banks' rear . . . "[1] In Richmond, on the 10th of May, 1862, there had been rejoicing over the brief telegram he had sent on the 9th to the Adjutant General: "God blessed our arms with victory at McDowell yesterday."[2] Was all that ended now—McDowell, Front Royal, Winchester, Cross Keys, Port Republic, Cedar Mountain, Groveton, Harpers Ferry—those battles of his own and all those he had fought with Lee? It was Sunday; was the day to witness the last contest? In his mind there was contention—muttered references again to A. P. Hill, orders to Major Hawks, directions for the battle.

Mrs. Jackson slipped out of the room. If he observed her departure, he said nothing. Breathing hard, he lay there and said nothing.

3. *Mrs. Jackson*, 473.
4. *Dabney*, 719.
5. *Dabney*, 722.
6. *Mrs. Jackson*, 454.
7. *Hotchkiss' MS Diary*.

8. *Calendar Confederate Papers*, 286.
9. *O. R.*, 2, 823-24.
1. *O. R.*, 12, pt. 3, p. 386.
2. *O. R.*, 12, pt. 1, p. 470.

Jim sat drowsily by. One of the surgeons helplessly watched. Minutes passed in silence. Presently, as the morning light grew brighter, Mrs. Jackson came back. The others left the chamber. Alone, she sat down by him. On her face were the marks of an emotional battle, but he was calm. Long before, he had told her that he did not fear to die but that he hoped he would "have a few hours' preparation before entering into the presence of his Maker and Redeemer." Now she felt she had to discharge the hard, hard duty that remark imposed.

Her voice came to him on the border of the far country. He stirred in evidence that he heard it but at first he could not arouse himself. She was talking to him: "Do you know the doctors say, you must very soon be in Heaven?"

He said nothing. She repeated it, and added: "Do you not feel willing to acquiesce in God's allotment, if He wills you to go today?"

Again she had to ask him the same question. Slowly the words and their import sank into his mind. He opened his eyes and looked at her. "I prefer it," he said slowly and with much difficulty. If he could focus his eyes to see her expression, he must have noticed that she seemed uncertain whether he was babbling or knew what he was saying. More carefully he framed the syllables: "I prefer it."

"Well," she said, incredibly keeping her self-control, "before this day closes, you will be with the blessed Saviour in His glory."

He steadied himself for the effort of speech and said deliberately, "I will be an infinite gainer to be translated."[3]

She talked with him further and asked his wishes about many things, but she could not hold his attention.[4] Nor did he appear to be convinced that his end actually was at hand. The man who had beaten off all the foe's attacks at Groveton was not of the spirit to believe that even the Last Enemy could rout him.

After Mrs. Jackson conversed with him, the surgeons must have made their examinations, but they did not attempt to dress his wounds. He was disturbed as little as possible. About 11 A.M.—the day continued warm and beautiful—he was aroused again by Mrs. Jackson. This time she was kneeling by his bed and was telling him again that before the sun went down he would be in Heaven. Often, in battle, he had met on their way to the rear unnerved men who had told of calamity and death at the front. He had rebuked them; he could not fail now to chide even her. Full consciousness seemed to return. Clearly he said: "Oh, no! you are frightened, my child; death is not so near; I may yet get well."

3. *Dabney*, 722-23.

4. Mrs. Jackson wrote as if all the wishes expressed by Jackson were voiced in a single interview which occurred in the early morning. Dr. McGuire mentioned a second conversation at 11 A.M. The sole way to reconcile the difference between Mrs. Jackson's account and the earlier narrative of Dr. McGuire is to assume that Mrs. Jackson forgot, after thirty years, that she had the second and longer conversation with her husband later in the morning.

With this she threw herself on the bed and in a flood of tears told him that the doctors said there was no hope for him. He listened and seemed to reflect, and then he asked her to call Dr. McGuire.

Almost on the instant, the man who so often had come to his campfire to report the wounded and the dead, was at his command. "Doctor," said Jackson, still distinctly, "Anna informs me that you have told her that I am to die today; is it so?"

As gently and as sympathetically as was possible, McGuire replied that medicine had done its utmost.

Again Jackson seemed to ponder. He turned his eyes from McGuire's face to the ceiling and gazed upward for a few moments. In battle, when orders were well executed or some shining deed was performed, he often would say, "Good, good"; but now he thought the orders of Higher Command had been given, his response was stronger: "Very good; very good; it is all right."[5] With that he turned to the weeping woman and tried to comfort her. Much he had to tell her, he said, but he was too weak.[6] After a struggle, she undertook to inquire what he desired for himself and for her and the baby? Should she go back to her father when it was all over? she asked.

"You have a kind and good father," he said, scarcely conscious, "but there is no one so kind and good as your Heavenly Father."[7]

Where did he wish to be buried?

He did not seem to be interested. "Charlotte," she understood him to say, and she inquired again. "Charlottesville," he said half consciously.

There was no reason for that, no association other than that of names. She prompted him: Did he wish to be buried in Lexington?

"Yes," he answered, "in Lexington, and in my own plot," but he spoke of it casually, as if it scarcely mattered.[8]

In accordance with the customs of the day, it seemed proper that he say farewell to his child. Mrs. Hoge accordingly brought in the baby, with the nurse. Jackson recognized the child at once and seemed far more pleased to see her than to talk of funerary details. His face, now emaciated and strangely ascetic in appearance, lighted up with a smile. "Little darling," he said, . . . "sweet one!" The baby smiled back and did not seem in any way frightened. She alone, of all the company, was the embodiment of life without knowledge or fear of death. Through the fog of morphia and weakness he played with her and called her endearing names until he sank back into the unconscious.[9]

5. *McGuire*, 228.
6. *Ibid.*
7. It is possible that he made this re-mark in the first conversation of the morning with Mrs. Jackson, cf. *McGuire*, 227-28, but the probabilities would seem

to favor the discussion of all the family arrangements at one time.
8. *Mrs. Jackson*, 456. Dabney said, *op. cit.*, 723, "his tune expressed rather acquiescence than lively interest."
9. *Mrs. Jackson*, 456.

When next he aroused, "Sandie" Pendleton in his martial gray was standing by his bed—"Sandie" who had so much of his unvoiced affection and soldierly admiration. The presence of the young soldier brought Jackson back for an instant to a world of camps and sinning soldiers. "Who is preaching at headquarters today?" he asked. Pendleton told him that Lacy was,[1] but he thoughtfully refrained from reminding Jackson that the Chaplain was there by the General's own forgotten order. Jackson was gratified that the men were to hear so eminent a preacher. Still more was Jackson pleased when "Sandie" told him that the whole army was praying for him. "Thank God," he murmured, "they are very kind . . ." Presently he spoke again. "It is the Lord's Day . . . . My wish is fulfilled. I have always desired to die on Sunday."[2]

"Sandie" went out to weep and not to weep alone. Everyone was in tears. The faithful Jim was overwhelmed. Not one of the doctors, looking at Jackson and listening to the struggle for breath, dared hope that the General could live even till night, but Dr. McGuire thought he should stimulate Jackson with some brandy. The next time the man on the bed seemed conscious, McGuire asked him to drink from the glass. Jackson shook his head: "It will only delay my departure, and do no good; I want to preserve my mind, if possible, to the last."[3] Once more he slipped back into the land of far and near, where faces change instantly and scenes melt one into another. He murmured again, gave orders, sat at mess with his staff, was back in Lexington with his little family, was fighting, was praying.

From another world came presently the voice of McGuire, with kindly but solemn warning that the sands were running low. It was 1:30: Jackson might not have more than two hours to live.

Feebly but firmly the assurance was given: "Very good; it is all right!"[4]

More there was in the same mutter—Hill, Hawks, orders to the infantry—and then a long, long silence, such a silence as might have come that May night the previous year when he had pushed the Stonewall Brigade forward toward Winchester and had halted and heard only the breath of his companions, and then had seen the fire of the Federal sharpshooters run along the hillside. Great events had been impending then. Long marches and hard battles and wide streams had been ahead. Now . . . the clock striking three, the spring sunshine in the room, the rustle of new leaves in the breeze, peace and the end of a Sabbath Day's journey. Fifteen minutes more; breathing now was in the very throat; and then from

---

1. Lacy's text that day was, "And we know that all things work together for good. . . ." *Romans* viii, 28. *Hotchkiss' MS Diary,* 189.

2. *McGuire,* 228.
3. *McGuire,* 228.
4. *McGuire,* 228.

the bed, clearly, quietly, cheerfully. "Let us cross over the river, and rest under the shade of the trees."[5]

5. *McGuire*, 229. In this final quotation, McGuire's words are followed. The verb is "cross" over the river. Many of the early authorities insisted that the verb was "pass."

HENRY DAVID THOREAU

The Battle of the Ants[1]

One day when I went out to my wood-pile, or rather my pile of stumps, I observed two large ants, the one red, the other much larger, nearly half an inch long, and black, fiercely contending with one another. Having once got hold they never let go, but struggled and wrestled and rolled on the chips incessantly. Looking farther, I was surprised to find that the chips were covered with such combatants, that it was not a *duellum*, but a *bellum*, a war between two races of ants, the red always pitted against the black, and frequently two red ones to one black. The legions of these Myrmidons covered all the hills and vales in my wood-yard, and the ground was already strewn with the dead and dying, both red and black. It was the only battle which I have ever witnessed, the only battle-field I ever trod while the battle was raging; internecine war; the red republicans on the one hand, and the black imperialists on the other. On every side they were engaged in deadly combat, yet without any noise that I could hear, and human soldiers never fought so resolutely. I watched a couple that were fast locked in each other's embraces, in a little sunny valley amid the chips, now at noonday prepared to fight till the sun went down, or life went out. The smaller red champion had fastened himself like a vice to his adversary's front, and through all the tumblings on that field never for an instant ceased to gnaw at one of his feelers near the root, having already caused the other to go by the board; while the stronger black one dashed him from side to side, and, as I saw on looking nearer, had already divested him of several of his members. They fought with more pertinacity than bulldogs. Neither manifested the least disposition to retreat. It was evident that their battle-cry was "Conquer or die." In the meanwhile there came along a single red ant on the hillside of this valley, evidently full of excitement, who either had despatched his foe, or had not yet taken part in the battle; probably the latter, for he had lost none of his limbs; whose mother had charged him to return with his shield or upon it. Or perchance he was some Achilles, who had nourished his wrath apart, and had now

1. From "Brute Neighbors," Chapter XII of *Walden*.

come to avenge or rescue his Patroclus.[2] He saw this unequal combat from afar—for the blacks were nearly twice the size of the red—he drew near with rapid pace till he stood on his guard within half an inch of the combatants; then, watching his opportunity, he sprang upon the black warrior, and commenced his operations near the root of his right fore leg, leaving the foe to select among his own members; and so there were three united for life, as if a new kind of attraction had been invented which put all other locks and cements to shame. I should not have wondered by this time to find that they had their respective musical bands stationed on some eminent chip, and playing their national airs the while, to excite the slow and cheer the dying combatants. I was myself excited somewhat even as if they had been men. The more you think of it, the less the difference. And certainly there is not the fight recorded in Concord history, at least, if in the history of America, that will bear a moment's comparison with this, whether for the numbers engaged in it, or for the patriotism and heroism displayed. For numbers and for carnage it was an Austerlitz or Dresden.[3] Concord Fight! Two killed on the patriots' side, and Luther Blanchard wounded! Why here every ant was a Buttrick—"Fire! for God's sake fire!"—and thousands shared the fate of Davis and Hosmer. There was not one hireling there. I have no doubt that it was a principle they fought for, as much as our ancestors, and not to avoid a three-penny tax on their tea; and the results of this battle will be as important and memorable to those whom it concerns as those of the battle of Bunker Hill, at least.

I took up the chip on which the three I have particularly described were struggling, carried into my house, and placed it under a tumbler on my window-sill, in order to see the issue. Holding a microscope to the first-mentioned red ant, I saw that, though he was assiduously gnawing at the near fore leg of his enemy, having severed his remaining feeler, his own breast was all torn away, exposing what vitals he had there to the jaws of the black warrior, whose breastplate was apparently too thick for him to pierce; and the dark carbuncles of the sufferer's eyes shone with ferocity such as war only could excite. They struggled half an hour longer under the tumbler, and when I looked again the black soldier had severed the heads of his foes from their bodies, and the still living heads were hanging on either side of him like ghastly trophies at his saddle-bow, still apparently as firmly fastened as ever, and he was endeavoring with feeble struggles, being without feelers, and with only the remnant of a leg, and I know not how many other wounds, to divest himself of them; which at length, after half an hour more, he accomplished. I

2. A Greek warrior in the *Iliad*, whose death Achilles avenges.
3. Bloody Napoleonic victories.

raised the glass, and he went off over the window-sill in that crippled state. Whether he finally survived that combat, and spent the remainder of his days in some Hôtel des Invalides, I do not know; but I thought that his industry would not be worth much thereafter. I never learned which party was victorious, nor the cause of the war, but I felt for the rest of that day as if I had my feelings excited and harrowed by witnessing the struggle, the ferocity and carnage, of a human battle before my door.

Kirby and Spence tell us that the battles of ants have long been celebrated and the date of them recorded, though they say that Huber[4] is the only modern author who appears to have witnessed them. "Aeneas Sylvius," say they, "after giving a very circumstantial account of one contested with great obstinacy by a great and small species on the trunk of a pear tree," adds that " 'this action was fought in the pontificate of Eugenius the Fourth, in the presence of Nicholas Pistoriensis, an eminent lawyer, who related the whole history of the battle with the greatest fidelity.' A similar engagement between great and small ants is recorded by Olaus Magnus, in which the small ones, being victorious, are said to have buried the bodies of their own soldiers, but left those of their giant enemies a prey to the birds. This event happened previous to the expulsion of the tyrant Christiern the Second from Sweden." The battle which I witnessed took place in the Presidency of Polk, five years before the passage of Webster's Fugitive-Slave Bill.

4. Kirby and Spence were nineteenth-century American entomologists; Huber was a great Swiss entomologist.

QUESTIONS FOR STUDY, DISCUSSION, AND WRITING

1. Thoreau uses the Latin word *bellum* to describe the struggle of the ants and he quickly follows this with a reference to the *Myrmidons* of Achilles. What comparison is implicit here? Find further examples of it. This passage comes from a chapter entitled "Brute Neighbors"; how does this comparison amplify the meaning of that title?

2. Goetsch ("Warfare and Hunting," pp. 1043–1047) and Thoreau both discuss ants. Choose a sentence from each which reveals the writer's viewpoint or purpose. What are the viewpoints or purposes?

3. Thoreau obviously joins the lower form of life—the ant—with man. Does this reflect what Bury (pp. 909–920) calls a Darwinistic or genetic approach to history?

4. Describe the life, or part of the life, of an animal so that, while remaining faithful to the facts as you understand them, your description opens outward as do those of Thoreau, Stewart ("Vulture Country," pp. 1036–1043), and Goetsch ("Warfare and Hunting," pp. 1043–1047) and speaks not only of the animal but of man, society, or nature.

JAMES ANTHONY FROUDE
Defeat of the Armada[1]

In the gallery at Madrid there is a picture, painted by Titian, representing the Genius of Spain coming to the delivery of the afflicted Bride of Christ. Titian was dead, but the temper of the age survived, and in the study of that great picture you will see the spirit in which the Spanish nation had set out for the conquest of England. The scene is the seashore. The Church a naked Andromeda,[2] with disheveled hair, fastened to the trunk of an ancient disbranched tree. The cross lies at her feet, the cup overturned, the serpents of heresy biting at her from behind with uplifted crests. Coming on before a leading breeze is the sea monster, the Moslem fleet, eager for their prey; while in front is Perseus, the Genius of Spain, banner in hand, with the legions of the faithful laying not raiment before him, but shield and helmet, the apparel of war for the Lady of Nations to clothe herself with strength and smite her foes.

In the Armada the crusading enthusiasm had reached its point and focus. England was the stake to which the Virgin, the daughter of Sion,[3] was bound in captivity. Perseus had come at last in the person of the Duke of Medina Sidonia, and with him all that was best and brightest in the countrymen of Cervantes, to break her bonds and replace her on her throne. They had sailed into the channel in pious hope, with the blessed banner waving over their heads.

To be the executor of the decrees of Providence is a lofty ambition, but men in a state of high emotion overlook the precautions which are not to be dispensed with even on the sublimest of errands. Don Quixote, when he set out to redress the wrongs of humanity, forgot that a change of linen might be necessary and that he must take money with him to pay his hotel bills. Philip II, in sending the Armada to England, and confident in supernatural protection, imagined an unresisted triumphal procession. He forgot that contractors might be rascals, that water four months in the casks in a hot climate turned putrid, and that putrid water would poison his ships' companies, though his crews were companies of angels. He forgot that the servants of the evil one might fight for their mistress after all, and that he must send adequate supplies of powder, and, worst forgetfulness of all, that a great naval expedition required a leader who understood his business. Perseus, in the shape of the Duke of Medina Sidonia, after a week of disastrous battles, found

---

1. From *English Seamen in the XVIth Century*.
2. In Greek mythology Andromeda was a maiden rescued by Perseus from a sea-serpent.
3. The hill in Jerusalem on which the temple was built.

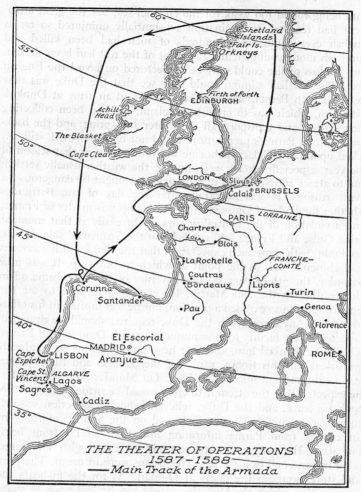

THE THEATER OF OPERATIONS
1587–1588
—— *Main Track of the Armada*

himself at the end of it in an exposed roadstead, where he ought never to have been, nine-tenths of his provisions thrown overboard as unfit for food, his ammunition exhausted by the unforeseen demands upon it, the seamen and soldiers harassed and dispirited, officers the whole week without sleep, and the enemy, who had hunted him from Plymouth to Calais, anchored within half a league of him.

Still, after all his misadventures, he had brought the fleet, if not to the North Foreland, yet within a few miles of it, and to outward appearance not materially injured. Two of the galleons had been taken; a third, the *Santa Aña*, had strayed; and his galleys had left him, being found too weak for the channel sea; but the great arma ment had reached its destination substantially uninjured so far as English eyes could see. Hundreds of men had been killed and hundreds more wounded, and the spirit of the rest had been shaken. But the loss of life could only be conjectured on board the English fleet. The English admiral could only see that the Duke was now in touch with Parma.[4] Parma, they knew, had an army at Dunkirk with him, which was to cross to England. He had been collecting men, barges, and transports all the winter and spring, and the back ward state of Parma's preparations could not be anticipated, still less relied upon. The Calais anchorage was unsafe; but at that season of the year, especially after a wet summer, the weather usually settled; and to attack the Spaniards in a French port might be dangerous for many reasons. It was uncertain after the day of the Barricades whether the Duke of Guise or Henry of Valois was master of France, and a violation of the neutrality laws might easily at that moment bring Guise and France into the field on the Spaniards' side. It was, no doubt, with some such expectation that the Duke and his advisers had chosen Calais as the point at which to bring up. It was now Saturday, the 7th of August. The governor of the town came off in the evening to the *San Martin*. He expressed surprise to see the Spanish fleet in so exposed a position, but he was profuse in his offers of service. Anything which the Duke required should be provided, especially every facility for communicating with Dunkirk and Parma. The Duke thanked him, said that he supposed Parma to be already embarked with his troops, ready for the passage, and that his own stay in the roads would be but brief. On Monday morning at latest he expected that the attempt to cross would be made. The governor took his leave, and the Duke, relieved from his anxieties, was left to a peaceful night. He was disturbed on the Sunday morning by an express from Parma informing him that, so far from being embarked, the army could not be ready for a fortnight. The barges were not in condition for sea. The troops were in camp. The arms and stores were on the quays at Dunkirk. As for the fly-boats and ammunition which the Duke had asked for, he had none to spare. He had himself looked to be supplied from the Armada. He promised to use his best expedition, but the Duke, meanwhile, must see to the safety of the fleet.

Unwelcome news to a harassed landsman thrust into the position of an admiral and eager to be rid of his responsibilities. If by evil fortune the northwester should come down upon him, with the shoals and sandbanks close under his lee, he would be in a bad way. Nor was the view behind him calculated for comfort. There lay the enemy almost within gunshot, who, though scarcely more than half his numbers, had hunted him like a pack of bloodhounds, and,

4. The Duke of Parma, Spanish governor in the Netherlands.

worse than all, in double strength; for the Thames squadron—three Queen's ships and thirty London adventurers—under Lord H. Seymour and Sir John Hawkins, had crossed in the night. There they were between him and Cape Grisnez, and the reinforcements meant plainly enough that mischief was in the wind.

After a week so trying the Spanish crews would have been glad of a Sunday's rest if they could have had it; but the rough handling which they had gone through had thrown everything into disorder. The sick and wounded had to be cared for, torn rigging looked to, splintered timbers mended, decks scoured, and guns and arms cleaned up and put to rights. And so it was that no rest could be allowed; so much had to be done, and so busy was every one, that the usual rations were not served out and the Sunday was kept as a fast. In the afternoon the stewards went ashore for fresh meat and vegetables. They came back with their boats loaded, and the prospect seemed a little less gloomy. Suddenly, as the Duke and a group of officers were watching the English fleet from the *San Martin's* poop deck, a small smart pinnace, carrying a gun in her bow, shot out from Howard's lines, bore down on the *San Martin*, sailed round her, sending in a shot or two as she passed, and went off unhurt. The Spanish officers could not help admiring such airy impertinence. Hugo de Monçada sent a ball after the pinnace, which went through her mainsail, but did no damage, and the pinnace again disappeared behind the English ships.

So a Spanish officer describes the scene. The English story says nothing of the pinnace; but she doubtless came and went as the Spaniard says, and for sufficient purpose. The English, too, were in straits, though the Duke did not dream of it. You will remember that the last supplies which the Queen had allowed to the fleet had been issued in the middle of June. They were to serve for a month, and the contractors were forbidden to prepare more. The Queen had clung to her hope that her differences with Philip were to be settled by the Commission at Ostend; and she feared that if Drake and Howard were too well furnished they would venture some fresh rash stroke on the coast of Spain, which might mar the negotiations. Their month's provisions had been stretched to serve for six weeks, and when the Armada appeared but two full days' rations remained. On these they had fought their way up Channel. Something had been brought out by private exertion on the Dorsetshire coast, and Seymour had, perhaps, brought a little more. But they were still in extremity. The contractors had warned the Government that they could provide nothing without notice, and notice had not been given. The adventurers were in better state, having been equipped by private owners. But the Queen's ships in a day or two more must either go home or their crews would be starving. They had been on reduced rations for near two months. Worse than that, they were still poisoned by the sour beer. The Queen had changed her mind so often, now ordering the fleet to prepare for sea, then recalling her instructions and paying off the men, that those whom Howard had with him had been enlisted in haste, had come on board as they were, and their clothes were hanging in rags on them. The fighting and the sight of the flying Spaniards were meat and drink, and clothing too, and had made them careless of all else. There was no fear of mutiny; but there was a limit to the toughest endurance. If the Armada was left undisturbed a long struggle might be still before them. The enemy would recover from its flurry, and Parma would come out from Dunkirk. To attack them directly in French waters might lead to perilous complications, while delay meant famine. The Spanish fleet had to be started from the roads in some way. Done it must be, and done immediately.

Then, on that same Sunday afternoon a memorable council of war was held in the *Ark's* main cabin. Howard, Drake, Seymour, Hawkins, Martin Frobisher, and two or three others met to consult, knowing that on them at that moment the liberties of England were depending. Their resolution was taken promptly. There was no time for talk. After nightfall a strong flood tide would be setting up along shore to the Spanish anchorage. They would try what could be done with fire ships, and the excursion of the pinnace, which was taken for bravado, was probably for a survey of the Armada's exact position. Meantime eight useless vessels were coated with pitch—hulls, spars, and rigging. Pitch was poured on the decks and over the sides, and parties were told off to steer them to their destination and then fire and leave them.

The hours stole on, and twilight passed into dark. The night was without a moon. The Duke paced his deck late with uneasy sense of danger. He observed lights moving up and down the English lines, and imagining that the *endemoniada gente*—the infernal devils— might be up to mischief, ordered a sharp look-out. A faint westerly air was curling the water, and towards midnight the watchers on board the galleons made out dimly several ships which seemed to be drifting down upon them. Their experience since the action off Plymouth had been so strange and unlooked for that anything unintelligible which the English did was alarming.

The phantom forms drew nearer, and were among them when they broke into a blaze from water-line to truck, and the two fleets were seen by the lurid light of the conflagration; the anchorage, the walls and windows of Calais, and the sea shining red as far as eye could reach, as if the ocean itself was burning. Among the dangers which they might have to encounter, English fireworks had been especially dreaded by the Spaniards. Fire ships—a fit device of heretics—had worked havoc among the Spanish troops, when the bridge was blown up, at Antwerp. They imagined that similar infernal machines were approaching the Armada. A capable commander would have sent a few launches to grapple the burning hulks, which of course were now deserted, and tow them out of harm's way. Spanish sailors were not cowards, and would not have flinched from duty because it might be dangerous; but the Duke and Diego Florez lost their heads again. A signal gun from the *San Martin* ordered the whole fleet to slip their cables and stand out to sea.

Orders given in panic are doubly unwise, for they spread the terror in which they originate. The danger from the fire ships was chiefly from the effect on the imagination, for they appear to have drifted by and done no real injury. And it speaks well for the seamanship and courage of the Spaniards that they were able, crowded together as they were, at midnight and in sudden alarm to set their canvas and clear out without running into one another. They buoyed their cables, expecting to return for them at daylight, and with only a single accident, to be mentioned directly, they executed successfully a really difficult maneuver.

The Duke was delighted with himself. The fire ships burned harmlessly out. He had baffled the inventions of the *endemoniada gente*. He brought up a league outside the harbour, and supposed that the whole Armada had done the same. Unluckily for himself, he found it at daylight divided into two bodies. The *San Martin* with forty of the best appointed of the galleons were riding together at their anchors. The rest, two thirds of the whole, having no second anchors ready, and inexperienced in Channel tides and currents, had been lying to. The west wind was blowing up. Without seeing where they were going they had drifted to leeward, and were two leagues off, towards Gravelines, dangerously near the shore. The Duke was too ignorant to realise the full peril of his situation. He signaled to them to return and rejoin him. As the wind and tide stood it was impossible. He proposed to follow them. The pilots told him that if he did the whole fleet might be lost on the banks. Towards the land the look of things was not more encouraging.

One accident only had happened the night before. The *Capitana* galleass, with Don Hugo de Monçada and eight hundred men on board, had fouled her helm in a cable in getting under way and had become unmanageable. The galley slaves disobeyed orders, or else Don Hugo was as incompetent as his commander-in-chief. The galleass had gone on the sands, and as the tide ebbed had fallen over on her side. Howard, seeing her condition, had followed her in the *Ark* with four or five other of the Queen's ships, and was furiously attacking her with his boats, careless of neutrality laws. Howard's theory was, as he said, to pluck the feathers one by one from the Spaniard's wing, and here was a feather worth picking up. The galleass was the most splendid vessel of her kind afloat, Don Hugo one of the greatest of Spanish grandees.

Howard was making a double mistake. He took the galleass at last after three hours' fighting. Don Hugo was killed by a musket ball. The vessel was plundered, and Howard's men took possession, meaning to carry her away when the tide rose. The French authorities ordered him off, threatening to fire upon him; and after wasting the forenoon, he was obliged at last to leave her where she lay. Worse than this, he had lost three precious hours, and had lost along with them, in the opinion of the Prince of Parma, the honors of the great day.

Drake and Hawkins knew better than to waste time plucking single feathers. The fire ships had been more effective than they could have dared to hope. The enemy was broken up. The Duke was shorn of half his strength, and the Lord had delivered him into their hand. He had got under way, still signaling wildly, and uncertain in which direction to turn. His uncertainties were ended for him by seeing Drake bear down upon him with the whole English fleet, save those which were loitering about the galleass. The English had now the advantage of numbers. The superiority of their guns he knew already, and their greater speed allowed him no hope to escape a battle. Forty ships alone were left to him to defend the banner of the crusade and the honor of Castile; but those forty were the largest and most powerfully armed and manned that he had, and on board them were Oquendo, De Leyva, Recalde, Bretandona, the best officers in the Spanish navy next to the lost Don Pedro.

It was now or never for England. The scene of the action which was to decide the future of Europe was between Calais and Dunkirk, a few miles off shore, and within sight of Parma's camp. There was no more maneuvering for the weather-gage, no more fighting at long range. Drake dashed straight upon his prey as the falcon swoops upon its quarry. A chance had fallen to him which might never return; not for the vain distinction of carrying prizes into English ports, not for the ray of honor which would fall on him if he could carry off the sacred banner itself and hang it in the Abbey at Westminster, but a chance so to handle the Armada that it should never be seen again in English waters, and deal such a blow on Philip that the Spanish Empire should reel with it. The English ships had the same superiority over the galleons which steamers have now over sailing vessels. They had twice the speed; they could lie two points nearer to the wind. Sweeping round them at cable's length, crowding them in one upon the other, yet never once giving them a chance to grapple, they hurled in their cataracts of round shot. Short as was the powder supply, there was no sparing it that morning. The hours went on, and still the battle raged, if battle it could be called where the blows were all dealt on one side and the suffering was all on the other. Never on sea or land did the Spaniards show themselves worthier of their great name than on that day. But from the first they could do nothing. It was said afterwards in Spain that the Duke showed the white feather, that he charged his pilot to keep him out of harm's way, that he shut himself up in his cabin, buried in woolpacks, and so on. The Duke had faults enough, but poltroonery was not one of them. He, who till he entered the English Channel had never been in action on sea or land, found himself, as he said, in the midst of the most furious engagement recorded in the history of the world. As to being out of harm's way, the standard at his masthead drew the hottest of the fire upon him. The *San Martin's* timbers were of oak and a foot thick, but the shot, he said, went through them enough to shatter a rock. Her deck was a slaughterhouse; half his company were killed or wounded, and no more would have been heard or seen of the *San Martin* or her commander had not Oquendo and De Leyva pushed in to the rescue and enabled him to creep away under their cover. He himself saw nothing more of the action after this. The smoke, he said, was so thick that he could make out nothing, even from his masthead. But all round it was but a repetition of the same scene. The Spanish shot flew high, as before, above the low English hulls, and they were themselves helpless butts to the English guns. And it is noticeable and supremely creditable to them that not a single galleon struck her colors. One of them, after a long duel with an Englishman, was on the point of sinking. An English officer, admiring the courage which the Spaniards had shown, ran out upon his bowsprit, told them that they had done all which became men, and urged them to surrender and save their lives. For answer they cursed the English as cowards and chickens because they refused to close. The officer was shot. His fall brought a last broadside on them, which finished the work. They went down, and the water closed over them. Rather death to the soldiers of the Cross than surrender to a heretic.

The deadly hail rained on. In some ships blood was seen streaming out of the scupper-holes. Yet there was no yielding; all ranks showed equal heroism. The priests went up and down in the midst of the carnage, holding the crucifix before the eyes of the dying. At midday Howard came up to claim a second share in a victory which was no longer doubtful. Towards the afternoon the Spanish fire slackened. Their powder was gone, and they could make no return to the cannonade which was still overwhelming them. They admitted freely afterwards that if the attack had been continued but two hours more they must all have struck or gone ashore. But the English magazines were empty also; the last cartridge was shot away, and the battle ended from mere inability to keep it up. It had been fought on both sides with peculiar determination. In the English there was the accumulated resentment of thirty years of menace to their country and their creed, with the enemy in tangible shape at last to be caught and grappled with; in the Spanish, the sense that if their cause had not brought them the help they looked for from above, the honor and faith of Castile should not suffer in their hands.

It was over. The English drew off, regretting that their thrifty mistress had limited their means of fighting for her, and so obliged them to leave their work half done. When the cannon ceased the wind rose, the smoke rolled away, and in the level light of the sunset they could see the results of the action.

A galleon in Recalde's squadron was sinking with all hands. The *San Philip* and the *San Matteo* were drifting dismasted towards the Dutch coast, where they were afterwards wrecked. Those which were left with canvas still showing were crawling slowly after their comrades who had not been engaged, the spars and rigging so cut up that they could scarce bear their sails. The loss of life could only be conjectured, but it had been obviously terrible. The nor'-wester was blowing up and was pressing the wounded ships upon the shoals, from which, if it held, it seemed impossible in their crippled state they would be able to work off.

In this condition Drake left them for the night, not to rest, but from any quarter to collect, if he could, more food and powder. The snake had been scotched, but not killed. More than half the great fleet were far away, untouched by shot, perhaps able to fight a second battle if they recovered heart. To follow, to drive them on the banks if the wind held, or into the North Sea, anywhere so that he left them no chance of joining hands with Parma again, and to use the time before they had rallied from his blows, that was the present necessity. His own poor fellows were famished and in rags; but neither he nor they had leisure to think of themselves. There was but one thought in the whole of them, to be again in chase of the flying foe. Howard was resolute as Drake. All that was possible was swiftly done. Seymour and the Thames squadron were to stay in the straits and watch Parma. From every obtainable source food and powder were collected for the rest—far short in both ways of what ought to have been, but, as Drake said, "we were resolved to put on a brag and go on as if we needed nothing." Before dawn the admiral and he were again off on the chase.

The brag was unneeded. What man could do had been done, and the rest was left to the elements. Never again could Spanish seamen be brought to face the English guns with Medina Sidonia to lead them. They had a fool at their head. The Invisible Powers in whom they had been taught to trust had deserted them. Their confidence was gone and their spirit broken. Drearily the morning broke on the Duke and his consorts the day after the battle. The Armada had collected in the night. The nor'-wester had freshened to a gale, and they were labouring heavily along, making fatal leeway towards the shoals.

It was St. Lawrence's Day, Philip's patron saint, whose shoulder-bone he had lately added to the treasures of the Escurial; but St. Lawrence was as heedless as St. Dominic. The *San Martin* had but six fathoms under her. Those nearer to the land signaled five, and right before them they could see the brown foam of the breakers curling over the sands, while on their weather-beam, a mile distant and clinging to them like the shadow of death, were the English ships which had pursued them from Plymouth like the dogs of the Furies. The Spanish sailors and soldiers had been without food since the evening when they anchored at Calais. All Sunday they had been at work, no rest allowed them to eat. On the Sunday night they had been stirred out of their sleep by the fire ships. Monday they had been fighting, and Monday night committing their dead to the sea. Now they seemed advancing directly upon inevitable destruction. As the wind stood there was still room for them to wear and thus escape the banks, but they would then have to face the enemy, who seemed only refraining from attacking them because whle they continued on their present couse the winds and waves would finish the work without help from man. Recalde, De Leyva, Oquendo, and other officers were sent for to the *San Martin* to consult. Oquendo came last. "Ah, Señor Oquendo," said the Duke as the heroic Biscayan stepped on board, "que haremos?" (what shall we do?) "Let your Excellency bid load the guns again," was Oquendo's gallant answer. It could not be. De Leyva himself said that the men would not fight the English again. Florez advised surrender. The Duke wavered. It was said that a boat was actually lowered to go off to Howard and make terms, and that Oquendo swore that if the boat left the *San Martin* on such an errand he would fling Florez into the sea. Oquendo's advice would have, perhaps, been the safest if the Duke could have taken it. There were still seventy ships in the Armada little hurt. The English were "bragging," as Drake said, and in no condition themselves for another serious engagement. But the temper of the entire fleet made a courageous course impossible. There was but one Oquendo. Discipline was gone. The soldiers in their desperation had taken the command out of the hands of the seamen. Officers and men alike abandoned hope, and, with no human prospect of salvation left to them, they flung themselves on their knees upon the decks and prayed the Almighty to have pity on them. But two weeks were gone since they had knelt on those same decks on the first sight of the English shore to thank Him for having brought them so far on an enterprise so glorious. Two weeks; and what weeks! Wrecked, torn by cannon shot, ten thousand of them dead or dying—for this was the estimated loss by battle—the survivors could now but pray to be delivered from a miserable death by the elements. In cyclones the wind often changes suddenly back from north-west to west, from west to south. At that moment, as if in answer to their petition, one of these sudden shifts of wind saved them from the immediate peril. The gale backed round to S.S.W., and ceased to press them on the shoals. They could ease their sheets, draw off into open water, and steer a course up the middle of the North Sea.

So only that they went north, Drake was content to leave them unmolested. Once away into the high latitudes they might go where they would. Neither Howard nor he, in the low state of their own magazines, desired any unnecessary fighting. If the Armada turned back they must close with it. If it held its present course they must follow it till they could be assured it would communicate no more for that summer with the Prince of Parma. Drake thought they would perhaps make for the Baltic or some port in Norway. They would meet no hospitable reception from either Swedes or Danes, but they would probably try. One only imminent danger remained to be provided against. If they turned into the Forth, it was still possible for the Spaniards to redeem their defeat, and even yet shake Elizabeth's throne. Among the many plans which had been formed for the invasion of England, a landing in Scotland had long been the favorite. Guise had always preferred Scotland when it was intended that Guise should be the leader. Santa Cruz had been in close correspondence with Guise on this very subject, and many officers in the Armada must have been acquainted with Santa Cruz's views. The Scotch Catholic nobles were still savage at Mary Stuart's execution and had the Armada anchored in Leith Roads with twenty thousand men, half a million ducats, and a Santa Cruz at its head, it might have kindled a blaze at that moment from John o'Groat's Land to the Border.[5]

But no such purpose occurred to the Duke of Medina Sidonia. He probably knew nothing at all of Scotland or its parties. Among the many deficiencies which he had pleaded to Philip as unfitting him for the command, he had said that Santa Cruz had acquaintances among the English and Scotch peers. He had himself none. The small information which he had of anything did not go beyond his orange gardens and his tunny fishing. His chief merit was that he was conscious of his incapacity; and, detesting a service into which he had been fooled by a hysterical nun, his only anxiety was to carry home the still considerable fleet which had been trusted to him without further loss. Beyond Scotland and the Scotch isles there was the open ocean, and in the open ocean there were no sandbanks and no English guns. Thus, with all sail set he went on before the wind. Drake and Howard attended him till they had seen him past the Forth, and knew then that there was no more to fear. It was time to see to the wants of their own poor fellows, who had endured so patiently and fought so magnificently. On the 13th of August they

5. From the north of Scotland to the English border.

saw the last of the Armada, turned back, and made their way to the Thames.

But the story has yet to be told of the final fate of the great "enterprise of England" (the "empresa de Inglaterra"), the object of so many prayers, on which the hopes of the Catholic world had been so long and passionately fixed. It had been ostentatiously a religious crusade. The preparations had been attended with peculiar solemnities. In the eyes of the faithful it was to be the execution of Divine justice on a wicked princess and a wicked people. In the eyes of millions whose convictions were less decided it was an appeal to God's judgment to decide between the Reformation and the Pope. There was an appropriateness, therefore, if due to accident, that other causes besides the action of man should have combined in its overthrow.

The Spaniards were experienced sailors; a voyage round the Orkneys and round Ireland to Spain might be tedious, but at that season of the year need not have seemed either dangerous or difficult. On inquiry, however, it was found that the condition of the fleet was seriously alarming. The provisions placed on board at Lisbon had been found unfit for food, and almost all had been thrown into the sea. The fresh stores taken in at Corunna had been consumed, and it was found that at the present rate there would be nothing left in a fortnight. Worse than all, the water-casks refilled there had been carelessly stowed. They had been shot through in the fighting and were empty; while of clothing or other comforts for the cold regions which they were entering no thought had been taken. The mules and horses were flung overboard and Scotch smacks, which had followed the retreating fleet, reported that they had sailed for miles through floating carcasses.

The rations were reduced for each man to a daily half-pound of biscuit, a pint of water, and a pint of wine. Thus, sick and hungry, the wounded left to the care of a medical officer, who went from ship to ship, the subjects of so many prayers were left to encounter the climate of the North Atlantic. The Duke blamed all but himself; he hanged one poor captain for neglect of orders, and would have hanged another had he dared; but his authority was gone. They passed the Orkneys in a single body. They then parted, it was said in a fog; but each commander had to look out for himself and his men. In many ships water must be had somewhere, or they would die. The *San Martin*, with sixty consorts, went north to the sixtieth parallel. From that height the pilots promised to take them down clear of the coast. The wind still clung to the west, each day blowing harder than the last. When they braced round to it their wounded spars gave way. Their rigging parted. With the greatest difficulty they made at last sufficient offing, and rolled down somehow out of sight of land, dipping their yards in the enormous seas. Of the rest, one or two went down among the Western Isles and became wrecks there, their crews, or part of them, making their way through Scotland to Flanders. Others went north to Shetland or the Faroe Islands. Between thirty or forty were tempted in upon the Irish coasts. There were Irishmen in the fleet, who must have told them that they would find the water there for which they were perishing, safe harbors, and a friendly Catholic people; and they found either harbors which they could not reach or sea-washed sands and reefs. They were all wrecked at various places between Donegal and the Blaskets. Something like eight thousand half-drowned wretches struggled on shore alive. Many were gentlemen, richly dressed, with velvet coats, gold chains, and rings. The common sailors and soldiers had been paid their wages before they started, and each had a bag of ducats lashed to his waist when he landed through the surf. The wild Irish of the coast, tempted by the booty, knocked unknown numbers of them on the head with their battle-axes, or stripped them naked and left them to die of the cold. On one long sand strip in Sligo an English officer counted eleven hundred bodies, and he heard that there were as many more a few miles distant.

The better educated of the Ulster chiefs, the O'Rourke and O'Donnell, hurried down to stop the butchery and spare Ireland the shame of murdering helpless Catholic friends. Many—how many cannot be said—found protection in their castles. But even so it seemed as if some inexorable fate pursued all who had sailed in that doomed expedition. Alonzo de Leyva, with half a hundred young Spanish nobles of high rank who were under his special charge, made his way in a galleass into Killibeg. He was himself disabled in landing. O'Donnell received and took care of him and his companions. After remaining in O'Donnell's castle for a month he recovered. The weather appeared to mend. The galleass was patched up, and De Leyva ventured an attempt to make his way in her to Scotland. He had passed the worst danger, and Scotland was almost in sight; but fate would have its victims. The galleass struck a rock off Dunluce and went to pieces, and Don Alonzo and the princely youths who had sailed with him were washed ashore all dead, to find an unmarked grave in Antrim.

Most pitiful of all was the fate of those who fell into the hands of the English garrisons in Galway and Mayo. Galleons had found their way into Galway Bay—one of them had reached Galway itself—the crews half dead with famine and offering a cask of wine for a cask of water. The Galway townsmen were human, and tried to feed and care for them. Most were too far gone to be revived, and died of exhaustion. Some might have recovered, but recovered they would be a danger to the State. The English in the West of

Ireland were but a handful in the midst of a sullen, half conquered population. The ashes of the Desmond rebellion were still smoking, and Dr. Sanders and his Legatine Commission were fresh in immediate memory. The defeat of the Armada in the Channel could only have been vaguely heard of. All that English officers could have accurately known must have been that an enormous expedition had been sent to England by Philip to restore the Pope; and Spaniards, they found, were landing in thousands in the midst of them with arms and money; distressed for the moment, but sure, if allowed time to get their strength again, to set Connaught in a blaze. They had no fortresses to hold so many prisoners, no means of feeding them, no men to spare to escort them to Dublin. They were responsible to the Queen's Government for the safety of the country. The Spaniards had not come on any errand of mercy to her or hers. The stern order went out to kill them all wherever they might be found, and two thousand or more were shot, hanged, or put to the sword. Dreadful! Yes, but war itself is dreadful and has its own necessities.

The sixty ships which had followed the *San Martin* succeeded at last in getting round Cape Clear, but in a condition scarcely less miserable than that of their companions who had perished in Ireland. Half their companions died—died of untended wounds, hunger, thirst, and famine fever. The survivors were moving skeletons, more shadows and ghosts than living men, with scarce strength left them to draw a rope or handle a tiller. In some ships there was no water for fourteen days. The weather in the lower latitudes lost part of its violence, or not one of them would have seen Spain again. As it was they drifted on outside Scilly and into the Bay of Biscay, and in the second week of September they dropped in one by one. Recalde, with better success than the rest, made Corunna. The Duke, not knowing where he was, found himself in sight of Corunna also. The crew of the *San Martin* were prostrate, and could not work her in. They signaled for help, but none came, and they dropped away to leeward to Bilboa. Oquendo had fallen off still farther to Santander, and the rest of the sixty arrived in the following days at one or other of the Biscay ports. On board them, of the thirty thousand who had left those shores but two months before in high hope and passionate enthusiasm, nine thousand only came back alive—if alive they could be called. It is touching to read in a letter from Bilboa of their joy at warm Spanish sun, the sight of the grapes on the white walls, and the taste of fresh home bread and water again. But it came too late to save them, and those whose bodies might have rallied died of broken hearts and disappointed dreams. Santa Cruz's old companions could not survive the ruin of the Spanish navy. Recalde died two days after he landed at Bilboa. Santander was Oquendo's home. He had a wife and children there, but he refused to see them, turned his face to the wall, and died too. The common seamen and soldiers were too weak to help themselves. They had to be left on board the poisoned ships till hospitals could be prepared to take them in. The authorities of Church and State did all that men could do; but the case was past help, and before September was out all but a few hundred needed no further care.

Philip, it must be said for him, spared nothing to relieve the misery. The widows and orphans were pensioned by the State. The stroke which had fallen was received with a dignified submission to the inscrutable purposes of Heaven. Diego Florez escaped with a brief imprisonment at Burgos. None else were punished for faults which lay chiefly in the King's own presumption in imagining himself the instrument of Providence.

The Duke thought himself more sinned against than sinning. He did not die, like Recalde or Oquendo, seeing no occasion for it. He flung down his command and retired to his palace at St. Lucan; and so far was Philip from resenting the loss of the Armada on its commander, that he continued him in his governorship of Cadiz, where Essex found him seven years later, and where he ran from Essex as he had run from Drake.

The Spaniards made no attempt to conceal the greatness of their defeat. Unwilling to allow that the Upper Powers had been against them, they set it frankly down to the superior fighting powers of the English.

The English themselves, the Prince of Parma said, were modest in their victory. They thought little of their own gallantry. To them the defeat and destruction of the Spanish fleet was a declaration of the Almighty in the cause of their country and the Protestant faith. Both sides had appealed to Heaven, and Heaven had spoken.

It was the turn of the tide. The wave of the reconquest of the Netherlands ebbed from that moment. Parma took no more towns from the Hollanders. The Catholic peers and gentlemen of England, who had held aloof from the Established Church, waiting *ad illud tempus* for a religious revolution, accepted the verdict of Providence. They discovered that in Anglicanism they could keep the faith of their fathers, yet remain in communion with their Protestant fellow-countrymen, use the same liturgy, and pray in the same temples. For the first time since Elizabeth's father broke the bonds of Rome the English became a united nation, joined in loyal enthusiasm for the Queen, and were satisfied that thenceforward no Italian priest should tithe or toll in her dominions.

But all that, and all that went with it, the passing from Spain to England of the sceptre of the seas, must be left to other lectures, or other lecturers who have more years before them than I. My own theme has been the poor Protestant adventurers who fought through that perilous week in the English Channel and saved their country and their country's liberty.

QUESTIONS FOR STUDY, DISCUSSION, AND WRITING

1. In his last sentence Froude says that his theme has been the English seamen. Yet in these climactic pages he has paid much more direct attention to the Spanish seamen. How does this emphasis develop his theme?
2. Froude's emphasis on the Spaniards gives him the opportunity to stress their confidence in providence and, therefore, the disappointment of that confidence. What larger issues does he thus introduce into his narrative of the battle? What is the tide that turns in the next to last paragraph?
3. Froude's approach to his theme has the potential disadvantage of encouraging partisan or nationalistic disparagement of the Spanish efforts. How does he guard against this?
4. Does Froude anywhere endorse English Anglicanism as superior to defeated Spanish Catholicism?

FRANCIS PARKMAN

La Salle Begins Anew, 1681[1]

HIS CONSTANCY—HIS PLANS—HIS SAVAGE ALLIES—HE BECOMES
SNOW-BLIND—NEGOTIATIONS—GRAND COUNCIL—LA SALLE'S ORATORY
—MEETING WITH TONTY—PREPARATION—DEPARTURE

In tracing the adventures of Tonty and the rovings of Hennepin, we have lost sight of La Salle, the pivot of the enterprise. Returning from the desolation and horror in the valley of the Illinois, he had spent the winter at Fort Miami, on the St. Joseph, by the borders of Lake Michigan. Here he might have brooded on the redoubled ruin that had befallen him: the desponding friends, the exulting foes; the wasted energies, the crushing load of debt, the stormy past, the black and lowering future. But his mind was of a different temper. He had no thought but to grapple with adversity, and out of the fragments of his ruin to build up the fabric of success.

He would not recoil; but he modified his plans to meet the new contingency. His white enemies had found, or rather, perhaps, had made, a savage ally in the Iroquois. Their incursions must be stopped, or his enterprise would come to nought; and he thought he saw the means by which this new danger could be converted into a source of strength. The tribes of the West, threatened by the common enemy, might be taught to forget their mutual animosities,

1. This and the following selection are Chapters 19 and 20 of *La Salle and the Discovery of the Great West*.

and join in a defensive league, with La Salle at its head. They might be colonized around his fort in the valley of the Illinois, where, in the shadow of the French flag, and with the aid of French allies, they could hold the Iroquois in check, and acquire in some measure the arts of a settled life. The Franciscan friars could teach them the Faith; and La Salle and his associates could supply them with goods, in exchange for the vast harvest of furs which their hunters could gather in these boundless wilds. Meanwhile, he would seek out the mouth of the Mississippi; and the furs gathered at his colony in the Illinois would then find a ready passage to the markets of the world. Thus might this ancient slaughter-field of warring savages be redeemed to civilization and Christianity; and a stable settlement, half-feudal, half-commercial, grow up in the heart of the western wilderness. This plan was but a part of the original scheme of his enterprise, adapted to new and unexpected circumstances; and he now set himself to its execution with his usual vigor, joined to an address that, when dealing with Indians, never failed him.

There were allies close at hand. Near Fort Miami were the huts of twenty-five or thirty savages, exiles from their homes, and strangers in this western world. Several of the English colonies, from Virginia to Maine, had of late years been harassed by Indian wars; and the Puritans of New England, above all, had been scourged by the deadly outbreak of King Philip's war. Those engaged in it had paid a bitter price for their brief triumphs. A band of refugees, chiefly Abenakis and Mohegans, driven from their native seats, had roamed into these distant wilds, and were wintering in the friendly neighborhood of the French. La Salle soon won them over to his interests. One of their number was the Mohegan hunter, who for two years had faithfully followed his fortunes, and who had been four years in the West. He is described as a prudent and discreet young man, in whom La Salle had great confidence, and who could make himself understood in several western languages, belonging, like his own, to the great Algonquin tongue. This devoted henchman proved an efficient mediator with his countrymen. The New England Indians, with one voice, promised to follow La Salle, asking no recompense but to call him their chief, and yield to him the love and admiration which he rarely failed to command from this hero-worshipping race.

New allies soon appeared. A Shawanoe chief from the valley of the Ohio, whose following embraced a hundred and fifty warriors, came to ask the protection of the French against the all-destroying Iroquois. "The Shawanoes are too distant," was La Salle's reply; "but let them come to me at the Illinois, and they shall be safe." The chief promised to join him in the autumn, at Fort Miami, with all his band. But, more important than all, the consent and cooperation of the Illinois must be gained; and the Miamis, their neighbors, and of late their enemies, must be taught the folly of their league with the Iroquois, and the necessity of joining in the new confederation. Of late, they had been made to see the perfidy of their dangerous allies. A band of the Iroquois, returning from the slaughter of the Tamaroa Illinois, had met and murdered a band of Miamis on the Ohio, and had not only refused satisfaction, but had entrenched themselves in three rude forts of trees and brushwood in the heart of the Miami country. The moment was favorable for negotiating; but, first, La Salle wished to open a communication with the Illinois, some of whom had begun to return to the country they had abandoned. With this view, and also, it seems, to procure provisions, he set out on the first of March, with his lieutenant, La Forest, and fifteen men.

The country was sheeted in snow, and the party journeyed on snow-shoes; but, when they reached the open prairies, the white expanse glared in the sun with so dazzling a brightness that La Salle and several of the men became snow-blind. They stopped and encamped under the edge of a forest; and here La Salle remained in darkness for three days, suffering extreme pain. Meanwhile, he sent forward La Forest, and most of the men, keeping with him his old attendant Hunaut. Going out in quest of pine-leaves—a decoction of which was supposed to be useful in cases of snow-blindness—this man discovered the fresh tracks of Indians, followed them, and found a camp of Outagamies, or Foxes, from the neighborhood of Green Bay. From them he heard welcome news. They told him that Tonty was safe among the Pottawattamies, and that Hennepin had passed through their country on his return from among the Sioux.

A thaw took place; the snow melted rapidly; the rivers were opened; the blind men began to recover; and, launching the canoes which they had dragged after them, the party pursued their way by water. They soon met a band of Illinois. La Salle gave them presents, condoled with them on their losses, and urged them to make peace and alliance with the Miamis. Thus, he said, they could set the Iroquois at defiance; for he himself, with his Frenchmen and his Indian friends, would make his abode among them, supply them with goods, and aid them to defend themselves. They listened, well pleased, promised to carry his message to their countrymen, and furnished him with a large supply of corn. Meanwhile, he had rejoined La Forest, whom he now sent to Michillimackinac to await Tonty, and tell him to remain there till he, La Salle, should arrive.

Having thus accomplished the objects of his journey, he returned to Fort Miami, whence he soon after ascended the St. Joseph to the village of the Miami Indians, on the portage, at the head of the Kankakee. Here he found unwelcome guests. These were three Iroquois warriors, who had been for some time in the place, and who, as he was told, had demeaned themselves with the insolence of conquerors, and spoken of the French with the utmost contempt. He hastened to confront them, rebuked and menaced them, and told them that now, when he was present, they dared not repeat the calumnies which they had uttered in his absence. They stood abashed and confounded, and during the following night secretly left the town and fled. The effect was prodigious on the minds of the Miamis, when they saw that La Salle, backed by ten Frenchmen, could command from their arrogant visitors a respect which they, with their hundreds of warriors had wholly failed to inspire. Here at the outset, was an augury full of promise for the approaching negotiations.

There were other strangers in the town—a band of eastern Indians, more numerous than those who had wintered at the fort. The greater number were from Rhode Island, including, probably, some of King Philip's warriors; others were from New York, and others again from Virginia. La Salle called them to a council, promised them a new home in the West, under the protection of the Great King, with rich lands, an abundance of game, and French traders to supply them with the goods which they had once received from the English. Let them but help him to make peace between the Miamis and the Illinois, and he would insure for them a future of prosperity and safety. They listened with open ears, and promised their aid in the work of peace.

On the next morning, the Miamis were called to a grand council. It was held in the lodge of their chief, from which the mats were removed, that the crowd without might hear what was said. La Salle rose and harangued the concourse. Few men were so skilled in the arts of forest rhetoric and diplomacy. After the Indian mode, he was, to follow his chroniclers, "the greatest orator in North America." He began with a gift of tobacco, to clear the brains of his auditory; next, for he had brought a canoe-load of presents to support his eloquence, he gave them cloth to cover their dead, coats to dress them, hatchets to build a grand scaffold in their honor, and beads, bells, and trinkets of all sorts, to decorate their relatives at a grand funeral feast. All this was mere metaphor. The living, while appropriating the gifts to their own use, were pleased at the compliment offered to their dead; and their delight redoubled as the orator proceeded. One of their great chiefs had lately been killed; and La Salle, after a eulogy of the departed, declared that he would now raise him to life again; that is, that he would assume his name and give support to his squaws and children. This flattering announcement drew forth an outburst of applause; and when, to confirm his words, his attendants placed before them a huge pile of coats, shirts, and hunting-knives, the whole assembly exploded in yelps of admiration.

Now came the climax of the harangue, introduced by a farther present of six guns.

"He who is my master, and the master of all this country, is a mighty chief, feared by the whole world; but he loves peace, and the words of his lips are for good alone. He is called the King of France, and he is the mightiest among the chiefs beyond the great water. His goodness reaches even to your dead, and his subjects come among you to raise them up to life. But it is his will to preserve the life he has given: it is his will that you should obey his laws, and make no war without the leave of Onontio, who commands in his name at Quebec, and who loves all the nations alike, because such is the will of the Great King. You ought, then, to live at peace with your neighbors, and above all with the Illinois. You have had causes of quarrel with them; but their defeat has avenged you. Though they are still strong, they wish to make peace with you. Be content with the glory of having obliged them to ask for it. You have an interest in preserving them; since, if the Iroquois destroy them, they will next destroy you. Let us all obey the Great King, and live together in peace, under his protection. Be of my mind, and use these guns that I have given you, not to make war, but only to hunt and to defend yourselves."

So saying, he gave two belts of wampum to confirm his words; and the assembly dissolved. On the following day, the chiefs again convoked it, and made their reply in form. It was all that La Salle could have wished. "The Illinois is our brother, because he is the son of our Father, the Great King." "We make you the master to our beaver and our lands, of our minds and our bodies." "We cannot wonder that our brothers from the East wish to live with you. We should have wished so too, if we had known what a blessing it is to be the children of the Great King." The rest of this auspicious day was passed in feasts and dances, in which La Salle and his Frenchmen all bore part. His new scheme was hopefully begun. It remained to achieve the enterprise, twice defeated, of the discovery of the mouth of the Mississippi, that vital condition of his triumph, without which all other success was meaningless and vain.

To this end, he must return to Canada, appease his creditors, and collect his scattered resources. Towards the end of May, he set out in canoes from Fort Miami, and reached Michillimackinac after a prosperous voyage. Here, to his great joy, he found Tonty and Zenobe Membré, who had lately arrived from Green Bay. The meeting was one at which even his stoic nature must have melted. Each had for the other a tale of disaster; but, when La Salle recounted the long succession of his reverses, it was with the tranquil tone and cheerful look of one who relates the incidents of an ordinary journey. Membré looked on him with admiration. "Any one else," he says, "would have thrown up his hand and abandoned the enterprise; but, far from this, with a firmness and constancy that never had its equal, I saw him more resolved than ever to continue his work and push forward his discovery."

Without loss of time, they embarked together for Fort Frontenac, paddled their canoes a thousand miles, and safely reached their destination. Here, in this third beginning of his enterprise, La Salle found himself beset with embarrassments. Not only was he burdened with the fruitless costs of his two former efforts, but the heavy debts which he had incurred in building and maintaining Fort Frontenac had not been wholly paid. The fort and the seigniory were already deeply mortgaged; yet, through the influence of Count Frontenac, the assistance of his secretary, Barrois, a consummate man of business, and the support of a wealthy relative, he found means to appease his creditors and even to gain fresh advances. To this end, however, he was forced to part with a portion of his monopolies. Having first made his will at Montreal, in favor of a cousin who had befriended him, he mustered his men, and once more set forth, resolved to trust no more to agents, but to lead on his followers, in a united body, under his own personal command.

At the beginning of autumn, he was at Toronto, where the long and difficult portage to Lake Simcoe detained him a fortnight. He spent a part of it in writing an account of what had lately occurred to a correspondent in France, and he closes his letter thus: "This is all I can tell you this year. I have a hundred things to write, but you could not believe how hard it is to do it among Indians. The canoes and their lading must be got over the portage, and I must speak to them continually, and bear all their importunity, or else they will do nothing I want. I hope to write more at leisure next year, and tell you the end of this business, which I hope will turn out well: for I have M. de Tonty, who is full of zeal; thirty Frenchmen, all good men, without reckoning such as I cannot trust; and more than a hundred Indians, some of them Shawanoes, and others from New England, all of whom know how to use guns."

It was October before he reached Lake Huron. Day after day, and week after week, the heavy-laden canoes crept on along the lonely wilderness shores, by the monotonous ranks of bristling moss-bearded firs; lake and forest, forest and lake; a dreary scene haunted with yet more dreary memories—disasters, sorrows, and deferred hopes; time, strength, and wealth spent in vain; a ruinous past and a doubtful future; slander, obloquy, and hate. With unmoved heart, the patient voyager held his course, and drew up his canoes at last on the beach at Fort Miami.

The Success of La Salle, 1681-1682

HIS FOLLOWERS—THE CHICAGO PORTAGE—DESCENT OF THE
MISSISSIPPI—THE LOST HUNTER—THE ARKANSAS—THE TAENSAS—
THE NATCHEZ—HOSTILITY—THE MOUTH OF THE MISSISSIPPI—
LOUIS XIV PROCLAIMED SOVEREIGN OF THE GREAT WEST

The season was far advanced. On the bare limbs of the forest
hung a few withered remnants of its gay autumnal livery; and the
smoke crept upward through the sullen November air from the
squalid wigwams of La Salle's Abenaki and Mohegan allies. These,
his new friends, were savages whose midnight yells had startled the
border hamlets of New England; who had danced around Puritan
scalps, and whom Puritan imaginations painted as incarnate fiends.
La Salle chose eighteen of them, whom he added to the twenty-
three Frenchmen who remained with him, some of the rest having
deserted and others lagged behind. The Indians insisted on taking
their squaws with them. These were ten in number, besides three
children; and thus the expedition included fifty-four persons, of
whom some were useless, and others a burden.

On the 21st of December, Tonty and Membré set out from Fort
Miami with some of the party in six canoes, and crossed to the little
river Chicago. La Salle, with the rest of the men, joined them a few
days later. It was the dead of winter, and the streams were frozen.
They made sledges, placed on them the canoes, the baggage, and a
disabled Frenchman; crossed from the Chicago to the northern
branch of the Illinois, and filed in a long procession down its frozen
course. They reached the site of the great Illinois village, found it
tenantless, and continued their journey, still dragging their canoes,
till at length they reached open water below Lake Peoria.

La Salle had abandoned for a time his original plan of building
a vessel for the navigation of the Mississippi. Bitter experience had
taught him the difficulty of the attempt, and he resolved to trust
to his canoes alone. They embarked again, floating prosperously
down between the leafless forests that flanked the tranquil river;
till, on the sixth of February, they issued upon the majestic bosom
of the Mississippi. Here, for the time, their progress was stopped;
for the river was full of floating ice. La Salle's Indians, too, had
lagged behind; but, within a week, all had arrived, the navigation
was once more free, and they resumed their course. Towards evening, they saw on their right the mouth of a great river; and the
clear current was invaded by the headlong torrent of the Missouri,
opaque with mud. They built their campfires in the neighboring
forest; and at daylight, embarking anew on the dark and mighty
stream, drifted swiftly down towards unknown destinies. They

passed a deserted town of the Tamaroas; saw, three days after, the mouth of the Ohio;[2] and, gliding by the wastes of bordering swamp, landed on the twenty-fourth of February near the Third Chickasaw Bluffs. They encamped, and the hunters went out for game. All returned, excepting Pierre Prudhomme; and, as the others had seen fresh tracks of Indians, La Salle feared that he was killed. While some of his followers built a small stockade fort on a high bluff by the river, others ranged the woods in pursuit of the missing hunter. After six days of ceaseless and fruitless search, they met two Chickasaw Indians in the forest; and, through them, La Salle sent presents and peace-messages to that warlike people, whose villages were a few days' journey distant. Several days later, Prudhomme was found, and brought in to the camp, half-dead. He had lost his way while hunting; and, to console him for his woes, La Salle christened the newly built fort with his name, and left him, with a few others, in charge of it.

Again they embarked; and, with every stage of their adventurous progress, the mystery of this vast New World was more and more unveiled. More and more they entered the realms of spring. The hazy sunlight, the warm and drowsy air, the tender foliage, the opening flowers, betokened the reviving life of Nature. For several days more they followed the writhings of the great river, on its tortuous course through wastes of swamp and canebrake, till on the thirteenth of March they found themselves wrapped in a thick fog. Neither shore was visible; but they heard on the right the booming of an Indian drum and the shrill outcries of the war-dance. La Salle at once crossed to the opposite side, where, in less than an hour, his men threw up a rude fort of felled trees. Meanwhile, the fog cleared; and, from the farther bank, the astonished Indians saw the strange visitors at their work. Some of the French advanced to the edge of the water, and beckoned them to come over. Several of them approached, in a wooden canoe, to within the distance of a gun-shot. La Salle displayed the calumet, and sent a Frenchman to meet them. He was well received; and, the friendly mood of the Indians being now apparent, the whole party crossed the river.

On landing, they found themselves at a town of the Kappa band of the Arkansas, a people dwelling near the mouth of the river which bears their name. "The whole village," writes Membré to his superior, "came down to the shore to meet us, except the women, who had run off. I cannot tell you the civility and kindness we received from these barbarians, who brought us poles to make huts, supplied us with firewood during the three days we were among them, and took turns in feasting us. But, my Reverend Father, this gives no idea of the good qualities of these savages, who are gay, civil, and free-hearted. The young men, though the most alert and

2. Called by Membré the Ouabache (Wabash) [Parkman's note].

spirited we had seen, are nevertheless so modest that not one of them would take the liberty to enter our hut, but all stood quietly at the door. They are so well formed that we were in admiration at their beauty. We did not lose the value of a pin while we were among them."

Various were the dances and ceremonies with which they entertained the strangers, who, on their part, responded with a solemnity which their hosts would have liked less, if they had understood it better. La Salle and Tonty, at the head of their followers, marched to the open area in the midst of the village. Here, to the admiration of the gazing crowd of warriors, women, and children, a cross was raised bearing the arms of France. Membré, in canonicals, sang a hymn; the men shouted *Vive le Roi*; and La Salle, in the king's name, took formal possession of the country. The friar, not, he flatters himself, without success, labored to expound by signs the mysteries of the Faith; while La Salle, by methods equally satisfactory, drew from the chief an acknowledgment of fealty to Louis XIV.[3]

After touching at several other towns of this people, the voyagers resumed their course, guided by two of the Arkansas; passed the sites, since become historic, of Vicksburg and Grand Gulf; and, about three hundred miles below the Arkansas, stopped by the edge of a swamp on the western side of the river.[4] Here, as their two guides told them, was the path to the great town of the Taensas. Tonty and Membré were sent to visit it. They and their men shouldered their birch canoe through the swamp, and launched it on a lake which had once formed a portion of the channel of the river. In two hours, they reached the town; and Tonty gazed at it with astonishment. He had seen nothing like it in America: large square dwellings, built of sun-baked mud mixed with straw, arched over with a dome-shaped roof of canes, and placed in regular order around an open area. Two of them were larger and better than the rest. One was the lodge of the chief; the other was the temple, or house of the sun. They entered the former, and found a single room, forty feet square, where, in the dim light—for there was no opening but the door—the chief sat awaiting them on a sort of bedstead, three of his wives at his side, while sixty old men, wrap-

3. The nation of the Arkanseas, Alkansas, or Arkansas, dwelt on the west bank of the Mississippi, near the mouth of the Arkansas. They were divided into four tribes, living for the most part in separate villages. Those first visited by La Salle were the Kappas, or Quapaws, a remnant of whom still subsists. The others were the Topingas, or Tongengas; the Torimans; and the Osotouoy, or Sauthouie [Parkman's note].

According to Charlevoix who saw them in 1721, they were regarded as the tallest and best-formed Indians in America, and were known as *les Beaux Hommes*. Graier says that they once lived on the Ohio.

4. In Tensas County, Louisiana. Tonty's estimates of distance are here much too low. They seem to be founded on observations of latitude, without reckoning the windings of the river. It may interest sportsmen to know that the party killed several large alligators, on their way. Membré is much astonished that such monsters should be born of eggs, like chickens [Parkman's note].

ped in white cloaks woven of mulberry-bark, formed his divan. When he spoke, his wives howled to do him honor; and the assembled councillors listened with the reverence due to a potentate for whom, at his death, a hundred victims were to be sacrificed. He received the visitors graciously, and joyfully accepted the gifts which Tonty laid before him. This interview over, the Frenchmen repaired to the temple, wherein were kept the bones of the departed chiefs. In construction, it was much like the royal dwelling. Over it were rude wooden figures, representing three eagles turned towards the east. A strong mud wall surrounded it, planted with stakes, on which were stuck the skulls of enemies sacrificed to the Sun; while before the door was a block of wood, on which lay a large shell surrounded with the braided hair of the victims. The interior was rude as a barn, dimly lighted from the doorway, and full of smoke. There was a structure in the middle which Membré thinks was a kind of altar; and before it burned a perpetual fire, fed with three logs laid end to end, and watched by two old men devoted to this sacred office. There was a mysterious recess, too, which the strangers were forbidden to explore, but which, as Tonty was told, contained the riches of the nation, consisting of pearls from the Gulf, and trinkets obtained, probably through other tribes, from the Spaniards and other Europeans.

The chief condescended to visit La Salle at his camp; a favor which he would by no means have granted, had the visitors been Indians. A master of ceremonies and six attendants preceded him, to clear the path and prepare the place of meeting. When all was ready, he was seen advancing, clothed in a white robe, and preceded by two men bearing white fans, while a third displayed a disk of burnished copper, doubtless to represent the Sun, his ancestor, or, as others will have it, his elder brother. His aspect was marvellously grave, and he and La Salle met with gestures of ceremonious courtesy. The interview was very friendly; and the chief returned well pleased with the gifts which his entertainer bestowed on him, and which, indeed, had been the principal motive of his visit.

On the next morning, as they descended the river, they saw a wooden canoe full of Indians; and Tonty gave chase. He had nearly overtaken it, when more than a hundred men appeared suddenly on the shore, with bows bent to defend their countrymen. La Salle called out to Tonty to withdraw. He obeyed; and the whole party encamped on the opposite bank. Tonty offered to cross the river with a peace-pipe, and set out accordingly with a small party of men. When he landed, the Indians made signs of friendship by joining their hands—a proceeding by which Tonty, having but one hand, was somewhat embarrassed; but he directed his men to respond in his stead. La Salle and Membré now joined him, and went with the Indians to their village, three leagues distant. Here they spent the night. "The Sieur de la Salle," write Membré, "whose very air, engaging manners, tact, and address attract love and respect alike, produced such an effect on the hearts of these people that they did not know how to treat us well enough."

The Indians of this village were the Natchez; and their chief was brother of the great chief, or Sun, of the whole nation. His town was several leagues distant, near the site of the city of Natchez; and thither the French repaired to visit him. They saw what they had already seen among the Taensas—a religious and political despotism, a privileged caste descended from the sun, a temple, and a sacred fire.[5] La Salle planted a large cross, with the arms of France attached, in the midst of the town; while the inhabitants looked on with a satisfaction which they would hardly have displayed, had they understood the meaning of the act.

The French next visited the Coroas, at their village, two leagues below; and here they found a reception no less auspicious. On the thirty-first of March, as they approached Red River, they passed in the fog a town of the Oumas; and, three days later, discovered a party of fishermen, in wooden canoes, among the canes along the margin of the water. They fled at sight of the Frenchmen. La Salle sent men to reconnoitre, who, as they struggled through the marsh, were greeted with a shower of arrows; while, from the neighboring village of the Quinipissas,[6] invisible behind the canebrake, they heard the sound of an Indian drum and the whoops of the mustering warriors. La Salle, anxious to keep the peace with all the tribes along the river, recalled his men, and pursued his voyage. A few leagues below, they saw a cluster of Indian lodges on the left bank, apparently void of inhabitants. They landed, and found three of them filled with corpses. It was a village of the Tangibao, sacked by their enemies only a few days before.

And now they neared their journey's end. On the sixth of April, the river divided itself into three broad channels. La Salle followed that of the West, and D'Autray that of the east; while Tonty took the middle passage. As he drifted down the turbid current, between the low and marshy shores, the brackish water changed to brine, and the breeze grew fresh with the salt breath of the sea. Then

5. The Natchez and the Taensas, whose habits and customs were similar, did not, in their social organization, differ radically from other Indians. The same principle of clanship, or *totemship*, so widely spread, existed in full force among them, combined with their religious ideas, and developed into forms of which no other example, equally distinct, is to be found. (For Indian clanship, see *The Jesuits in North America*, Introduction.) Among the Natchez and Taensas, the principal clan formed a ruling caste; and its chiefs had the attributes of demi-gods. As descent was through the female, the chief's son never succeeded him, but the son of one of his sisters; and as she, by the usual totemic law, was forced to marry in another clan —that is, to marry a common mortal— her husband, though the destined father of a demi-god, was treated by her as little better than a slave. She might kill him, if he proved unfaithful; but he was forced to submit to her infidelities in silence [Parkman's note].

6. In St. Charles County, on the left bank, not far above New Orleans [Parkman's note].

the broad bosom of the great Gulf opened on his sight, tossing its restless billows, limitless, voiceless, lonely as when born of chaos, without a sail, without a sign of life.

La Salle, in a canoe, coasted the marshy borders of the sea; and then the reunited parties assembled on a spot of dry ground, a short distance above the mouth of the river. Here a column was made ready, bearing the arms of France, and inscribed with the words,

Louis Le Grand, Roy de France et de Navarre, regne; le Neuvième Avril, 1682

The Frenchmen were mustered under arms; and, while the New England Indians and their squaws looked on in wondering silence, they chanted the *Te Deum*, the *Exaudiat*, and the *Domine salvum fac Regem*. Then, amid volleys of musketry and shouts of *Vive le Roi*, La Salle planted the column in its place, and, standing near it, proclaimed in a loud voice,

"In the name of the most high, mighty, invincible, and victorious Prince, Louis the Great, by the grace of God King of France and of Navarre, Fourteenth of that name, I, this ninth day of April, one thousand six hundred and eighty-two, in virtue of the commission of his Majesty, which I hold in my hand, and which may be seen by all whom it may concern, have taken, and do now take, in the name of his Majesty and of his successors to the crown, possession of this country of Louisiana, the seas, harbors, ports, bays, adjacent straits, and all the nations, peoples, provinces, cities, towns, villages, mines, minerals, fisheries, streams, and rivers, within the extent of the said Louisiana, from the mouth of the great river St. Louis, otherwise called the Ohio, . . . as also along the river Colbert, or Mississippi, and the rivers which discharge themselves thereinto, from its source beyond the country of the Nadouessioux . . . as far as its mouth at the sea, or Gulf of Mexico, and also to the mouth of the River of Palms, upon the assurance we have had from the natives of these countries, that we are the first Europeans who have descended or ascended the said river Colbert; hereby protesting against all who may hereafter undertake to invade any or all of these aforesaid countries, peoples, or lands, to the prejudice of the rights of his Majesty, acquired by the consent of the nations dwelling herein. Of which, and of all else that is needful, I hereby take to witness those who hear me, and demand an act of the notary here present."

Shouts of *Vive le Roi* and volleys of musketry responded to his words. Then a cross was planted beside the column, and a leaden plate buried near it, bearing the arms of France, with a Latin inscription, *Ludovicus Magnus regnat.*[7] The weather-beaten voyagers joined their voices in the grand hymn of the *Vexilla Regis:*

7. "Louis the Great rules."

> The banners of Heaven's King advance,
> The mystery of the Cross shines forth;

and renewed shouts of *Vive le Roi* closed the ceremony.

On that day, the realm of France received on parchment a stupendous accession. The fertile plains of Texas; the vast basin of the Mississippi, from its frozen northern springs to the sultry borders of the Gulf; from the woody ridges of the Alleghanies to the bare peaks of the Rocky Mountains—a region of savannahs and forests, suncracked deserts, and grassy prairies, watered by a thousand rivers, ranged by a thousand warlike tribes, passed beneath the sceptre of the Sultan of Versailles; and all by virtue of a feeble human voice, inaudible at half a mile.

DANIEL DEFOE

The Coming of the Plague to London[1]

But I must go back again to the beginning of this surprizing time. While the fears of the people were young, they were increased strangely by several odd accidents, which put altogether, it was really a wonder the whole body of the people did not rise as one man and abandon their dwellings, leaving the place as a space of ground designed by Heaven for an Akeldama,[2] doomed to be destroyed from the face of the earth, and that all that would be found in it would perish with it. I shall name but a few of these things; but sure they were so many, and so many wizards and cunning people propagating them, that I have often wondered there was any (women especially) left behind.

In the first place, a blazing star or comet appeared for several months before the plague, as there did the year after another, a little before the fire. The old women and the phlegmatic hypochondriac part of the other sex, whom I could almost call old women too, remarked (especially afterward, though not till both those judgments were over) that those two comets passed directly over the city, and that so very near the houses that it was plain they imported something peculiar to the city alone; that the comet before the pestilence was of a faint, dull, languid color, and its motion very heavy solemn, and slow; but that the comet before the fire was bright and sparkling, or, as others said, flaming, and its motion swift and furious; and that accordingly one foretold a heavy judgment, slow but severe, terrible and frightful, as was the plague;

---

1. From *A Journal of the Plague Year*. Defoe was a young child at the time of the plague (1664-1665) so, although he might have had a strong general recollection of it, he could not have been the narrator in the journal.

2. The field of blood, the potter's field bought with Judas' thirty pieces of silver. Matthew xxvii. 8.

but the other foretold a stroke, sudden, swift, and fiery as the conflagration. Nay, so particular some people were, that as they looked upon that comet preceding the fire, they fancied that they not only saw it pass swiftly and fiercely, and could perceive the motion with their eye, but even they heard it; that it made a rushing, mighty noise, fierce and terrible, though at a distance, and but just perceivable.

I saw both these stars, and, I must confess, had so much of the common notion of such things in my head, that I was apt to look upon them as the forerunners and warnings of God's judgments; and especially when, after the plague had followed the first, I yet saw another of the like kind, I could not but say God had not yet sufficiently scourged the city.

But I could not at the same time carry these things to the height that others did, knowing, too, that natural causes are assigned by the astronomers for such things, and that their motions and even their revolutions are calculated, or pretended to be calculated, so that they cannot be so perfectly called the forerunners or foretellers, much less the procurers, of such events as pestilence, war, fire, and the like.

But let my thoughts and the thoughts of the philosophers be, or have been, what they will, these things had a more than ordinary influence upon the minds of the common people, and they had almost universal melancholy apprehensions of some dreadful calamity and judgment coming upon the city; and this principally from the sight of this comet, and the little alarm that was given in December by two people dying at St. Giles's, as above.

The apprehensions of the people were likewise strangely increased by the error of the times, in which, I think, the people, from what principle I cannot imagine, were more addicted to prophecies and astrological conjurations, dreams and old wives' tales than ever they were before or since. Whether this unhappy temper was originally raised by the follies of some people who got money by it, that is to say, by printing predictions and prognostications, I know not; but certain it is, books frighted them terribly, such as Lilly's *Almanack*, Gadbury's *Astrological Predictions*, *Poor Robin's Almanack*, and the like; also several pretended religious books, one entitled, *Come Out of Her, My People, Lest You Be Partaker of Her Plagues*; another called *Fair Warning*; another, *Britain's Remembrancer*; and many such, all, or most part of which, foretold, directly or covertly, the ruin of the city. Nay, some were so enthusiastically[3] bold as to run about the streets with their oral predictions, pretending they were sent to preach to the city; and one in particular, who, like Jonah to Nineveh, cried in the street, "Yet forty days, and London shall be destroyed." I will not be positive

3. Fanatically.

whether he said yet forty days or yet a few days. Another ran about naked, except a pair of drawers about his waist, crying day and night, like a man that Josephus mentions, who cried, "Woe to Jerusalem!" a little before the destruction of that city. So this poor naked creature cried, "Oh, the great and the dreadful God!" and said no more, but repeated those words continually, with a voice and countenance full of horror, a swift pace, and nobody could ever find him to stop or rest, or take any sustenance, at least that ever I could hear of. I met this poor creature several times in the streets, and would have spoke to him, but he would not enter into speech with me or any one else, but held on his dismal cries continually.

These things terrified the people to the last degree, and especially when two or three times, as I have mentioned already, they found one or two in the bills dead of the plague at St. Giles's.[4]

Next to these publick things were the dreams of old women, or, I should say, the interpretation of old women upon other people's dreams; and these put abundance of people even out of their wits. Some heard voices warning them to be gone, for that there would be such a plague in London, so that the living would not be able to bury the dead. Others saw apparitions in the air; and I must be allowed to say of both, I hope without breach of charity, that they heard voices that never spake, and saw sights that never appeared, but the imagination of the people was really turned wayward and possessed. And no wonder, if they who were poring continually at the clouds saw shapes and figures, representations and appearances, which had nothing in them but air and vapour. Here they told us they saw a flaming sword held in a hand coming out of a cloud, with a point hanging directly over the city. There they saw hearses and coffins in the air carrying to be buried. And there again, heaps of dead bodies lying unburied, and the like, just as the imagination of the poor terrified people furnished them with matter to work upon.

> So hypochondriac fancies represent
> Ships, armies, battles in the firmament;
> Till steady eyes the exhalations solve,
> And all to its first matter, cloud, resolve.

I could fill this account with the strange relations such people gave every day of what they had seen; and every one was so positive of their having seen what they pretended to see, that there was no contradicting them without breach of friendship, or being accounted rude and unmannerly on the one hand, and profane and impenetrable on the other. One time before the plague was begun (otherwise than as I have said in St. Giles's), I think it was in March, seeing a crowd of people in the street, I joined with them to satisfy my curiosity, and found them all staring up into the air to see

4. London parish church.

what a woman told them appeared plain to her, which was an angel clothed in white, with a fiery sword in his hand, waving it or brandishing it over his head. She described every part of the figure to the life, shewed them the motion and the form, and the poor people came into it so eagerly, and with so much readiness, "Yes, I see it all plainly," says one. "There's the sword as plain as can be." Another saw the angel. One saw his very face, and cried out what a glorious creature he was! One saw one thing, and one another. I looked as earnestly as the rest, but perhaps not with so much willingness to be imposed upon; and I said, indeed, that I could see nothing but a white cloud, bright on one side by the shining of the sun upon the other part. The woman endeavoured to shew it me, but could not make me confess that I saw it, which, indeed, if I had I must have lied. But the woman, turning upon me, looked in my face, and fancied I laughed, in which her imagination deceived her too, for I really did not laugh, but was very seriously reflecting how the poor people were terrified by the force of their own imagination. However, she turned from me, called me profane fellow and a scoffer; told me that it was a time of God's anger, and dreadful judgments were approaching, and that despisers such as I should wander and perish.

The people about her seemed disgusted as well as she; and I found there was no persuading them that I did not laugh at them, and that I should be rather mobbed by them than be able to undeceive them. So I left them; and this appearance passed for as real as the blazing star itself.

Another encounter I had in the open day also; and this was in going through a narrow passage from Petty France into Bishopsgate Churchyard, by a row of alms-houses. There are two churchyards to Bishopsgate church or parish; one we go over to pass from the place called Petty France into Bishopsgate Street, coming out just by the church door; the other is on the side of the narrow passage where the alms-houses are on the left; and a dwarf-wall with a palisado on it on the right hand, and the city wall on the other side more to the right.

In this narrow passage stands a man looking through between the palisadoes into the burying-place, and as many people as the narrowness of the passage would admit to stop, without hindering the passage of others, and he was talking mighty eagerly to them, and pointing now to one place, then to another, and affirming that he saw a ghost walking upon such a gravestone there. He described the shape, the posture, and the movement of it so exactly that it was the greatest matter of amazement to him in he world that everybody did not see it as well as he. On a sudden he would cry, "There it is; now it comes this way." Then, " 'Tis turned back;" till at length he persuaded the people into so firm a belief of it.

that one fancied he saw it, and another fancied he saw it; and thus he came every day making a strange hubbub, considering it was in so narrow a passage, till Bishopsgate clock struck eleven, and then the ghost would seem to start, and, as if he were called away, disappeared on a sudden.

I looked earnestly every way, and at the very moment that this man directed but could not see the least appearance of anything; but so positive was this poor man, that he gave the people the vapors[5] in abundance, and sent them away trembling and frighted, till at length few people that knew of it cared to go through that passage, and hardly anybody by night on any account whatever.

This ghost, as the poor man affirmed, made signs to the houses, and to the ground, and to the people, plainly intimating, or else they so understanding it, that abundance of the people should come to be buried in that churchyard, as indeed happened; but that he saw such aspects I must acknowledge I never believed, nor could I see anything of it myself, though I looked most earnestly to see it if possible.

These things serve to shew how far the people were really overcome with delusions; and as they had a notion of the approach of a visitation, all their predictions ran upon a most dreadful plague, which should lay the whole city, and even the kingdom, waste, and should destroy almost all the nation, both man and beast.

To this, as I said before, the astrologers added stories of the conjunction of planet in a malignant manner and with a mischievous influence, one of which conjunctions was to happen, and did happen, in October, and the other in November; and they filled the people's heads with predictions on these signs of the heavens, intimating that those conjunctions foretold drought, famine, and pestilence. In the two first of them, however, they were entirely mistaken, for we had no droughty season, but in the beginning of the year a hard frost, which lasted from December almost to March, and after that moderate weather, rather warm than hot, with refreshing winds, and, in short, very seasonable weather, and also several very great rains.

Some endeavors were used to suppress the printing of such books as terrified the people, and to frighten the dispersers of them, some of whom were taken up; but nothing was done in it, as I am informed, the Government being unwilling to exasperate the people, who were, as I may say, all out of their wits already.

Neither can I acquit those ministers that in their sermons rather sank than lifted up the hearts of their hearers. Many of them no doubt did it for the strengthening the resolution of the people, and especially for quickening them to repentance; but it certainly answered not their end, at least not in proportion to the injury

5. Morbid state of depression.

it did another way; and indeed, as God Himself through the whole Scriptures rather draws to Him by invitations and calls to turn to Him and live, than drives us by terror and amazement, so I must confess I thought the ministers should have done also, imitating our blessed Lord and Master in this, that His whole Gospel is full of declarations from heaven of God's mercy, and His readiness to receive penitents and forgive them, complaining, "Ye will not come unto Me that ye may have life," and that therefore His Gospel is called the Gospel of Peace and the Gospel of Grace.

But we had some good men, and that of all persuasions and opinions, whose discourses were full of terror, who spoke nothing but dismal things; and as they brought the people together with a kind of horror, sent them away in tears, prophesying nothing but evil tidings, terrifying the people with the apprehensions of being utterly destroyed, not guiding them, at least not enough, to cry to heaven for mercy.

It was, indeed, a time of very unhappy breaches among us in matters of religion. Innumerable sects and divisions and separate opinions prevailed among the people. The Church of England was restored, indeed, with the restoration of the monarchy, about four years before, but the ministers and preachers of the Presbyterians and Independents, and of all the other sorts of professions, had begun to gather separate societies and erect altar against altar, and all those had their meetings for worship apart, as they have now, but not so many then, the Dissenters being not thoroughly formed into a body as they are since, and those congregations which were thus gathered together were yet but few. And even those that were, the Government did not allow, but endeavoured to suppress them and shut up their meetings.

But the visitation reconciled them again, at least for a time, and many of the best and most valuable ministers and preachers of the Dissenters were suffered to go into the churches where the incumbents were fled away, as many were, not being able to stand it; and the people flocked without distinction to hear them preach, not much enquiring who or what opinion they were of. But after the sickness was over, that spirit of charity abated; and every church being again supplied with their own ministers, or others presented where the minister was dead, things returned to their old channel again.

One mischief always introduces another. These terrors and apprehensions of the people led them into a thousand weak, foolish, and wicked things, which they wanted not a sort of people really wicked to encourage them to; and this was running about to fortune-tellers, cunning-men, and astrologers to know their fortune, or, as it is vulgarly expressed, to have their fortunes told them, their nativities calculated, and the like; and this folly presently made the town swarm with a wicked generation of pretenders to magick, to the *black art*, as they called it, and I know not what; nay, to a thousand worse dealings with the devil than they were really guilty of. And this trade grew so open and so generally practised that it became common to have signs and inscriptions set up at doors: "Here lives a fortune-teller," "Here lives an astrologer," "Here you may have your nativity calculated," and the like; and Friar Bacon's brazenhead, which was the usual sign of these people's dwellings, was to be seen almost in every street, or else the sign of Mother Shipton, or of Merlin's head, and the like.[6]

With what blind, absurd, and ridiculous stuff these oracles of the devil pleased and satisfied the people I really know not, but certain it is that innumerable attendants crowded about their doors every day. And if but a grave fellow in a velvet jacket, a band, and a black cloak, which was the habit those quack-conjurers generally went in, was but seen in the streets, the people would follow them in crowds, and ask them questions as they went along.

I need not mention what a horrid delusion this was, or what it tended to; but there was no remedy for it till the plague itself put an end to it all, and, I suppose, cleared the town of most of those calculators themselves. One mischief was, that if the poor people asked these mock astrologers whether there would be a plague or no, they all agreed in general to answer "Yes," for that kept up their trade. And had the people not been kept in a fright about that, the wizards would presently have been rendered useless, and their craft had been at an end. But they always talked to them of such-and-such influences of the stars, of the conjunctions of such-and-such planets, which must necessarily bring sickness and distempers, and consequently the plague. And some had the assurance to tell them the plague was begun already, which was too true, though they that said so knew nothing of the matter.

The ministers, to do them justice, and preachers of most sorts that were serious and understanding persons, thundered against these and other wicked practices, and exposed the folly as well as the wickedness of them together, and the most sober and judicious people despised and abhorred them. But it was impossible to make any impression upon the middling people and the working laboring poor; their fears were predominant over all their passions, and they threw away their money in a most distracted manner upon those whimsies. Maidservants especially, and men-servants, were the chief of their customers, and their question generally was, after the first

6. Roger Bacon: a medieval philosopher supposed to have been a magician. Ursula Shipton: a prophetess of fifteenth and sixteenth centuries. Merlin: an Arthurian sorcerer.

demand of "Will there be a plague?" I say, the next question was, "Oh, sir! for the Lord's sake, what will become of me? Will my mistress keep me, or will she turn me off? Will she stay here, or will she go into the country? And if she goes into the country, will she take me with her, or leave me here to be starved and undone?" And the like of men-servants.

The truth is, the case of poor servants was very dismal, as I shall have occasion to mention again by and by, for it was apparent a prodigious number of them would be turned away, and it was so. And of them abundance perished, and particularly of those that these false prophets had flattered with hopes that they should be continued in their services, and carried with their masters and mistresses into the country; and had not publick charity provided for these poor creatures, whose number was exceeding great, and in all cases of this nature must be so, they would have been in the worst condition of any people in the city.

These things agitated the minds of the common people for months, while the first apprehensions were upon them, and while the plague was not, as I may say, yet broken out. But I must also not forget that the more serious part of the inhabitants behaved after another manner. The Government encouraged their devotion, and appointed publick prayers and days of fasting and humiliation, to make publick confession of sin and implore the mercy of God to avert the dreadful judgment which hung over their heads: and it is not to be expressed with what alacrity the people of all persuasions embraced the occasion; how they flocked to the churches and meetings, and they were all so thronged that there was often no coming near, no, not to the very doors of the largest churches. Also there were daily prayers appointed morning and evening at several churches, and days of private praying at other places; at all which the people attended, I say, with an uncommon devotion. Several private families also, as well of one opinion as of another, kept family fasts, to which they admitted their near relations only. So that, in a word, those people who were really serious and religious applied themselves in a truly Christian manner to the proper work of repentance and humiliation, as a Christian people ought to do.

Again, the publick shewed that they would bear their share in these things; the very Court, which was then gay and luxurious, put on a face of just concern for the publick danger. All the plays and interludes which, after the manner of the French Court, had been set up and began to increase among us, were forbid to act; the gaming tables, publick dancing rooms, and music houses, which multiplied and began to debauch the manners of the people, were shut up and suppressed; and the jack-puddings, merry-andrews, puppet-shows, rope-dancers, and suchlike doings, which had bewitched the poor common people, shut up their shops, finding indeed no trade; for the minds of the people were agitated with other things, and a kind of sadness and horror at these things sat upon the countenances even of the common people. Death was before their eyes, and everybody began to think of their graves, not of mirth and diversions.

But even those wholesome reflections, which, rightly managed, would have most happily led the people to fall upon their knees, make confession of their sins, and look up to their merciful Saviour for pardon, imploring His compassion on them in such a time of their distress, by which we might have been as a second Nineveh, had a quite contrary extream in the common people, who, ignorant and stupid in their reflections as they were brutishly wicked and thoughtless before, were now led by their fright to extreams of folly; and, as I have said before that they ran to conjurers and witches, and all sorts of deceivers, to know what should become of them (who fed their fears, and kept them always alarmed and awake on purpose to delude them and pick their pockets), so they were as mad upon their running after quacks and mountebanks and every practising old woman for medicines and remedies, storing themselves with such multitudes of pills, potions, and preservatives, as they were called, that they not only spent their money, but even poisoned themselves beforehand for fear of the poison of the infection, and prepared their bodies for the plague instead of preserving them against it. On the other hand, it is incredible, and scarce to be imagined, how the posts of houses and corners of streets were plastered over with doctors' bills and papers of ignorant fellows, quacking and tampering in physick and inviting the people to come to them for remedies, which was generally set off with such flourishes as these, *viz.*: "INFALLIBLE preventive pills against the plague." "NEVER-FAILING preservatives against the infection." "SOVEREIGN cordials against the corruption of the air." "EXACT regulations for the conduct of the body in case of an infection." "Antipestilential pills." "INCOMPARABLE drink against the plague, never found out before." "An UNIVERSAL remedy for the plague." "The ONLY TRUE plague-water." "The ROYAL ANTIDOTE against all kinds of infection;" and such a number more that I cannot reckon up; and if I could, would fill a book of themselves to set them down.

Others set up bills to summon people to their lodgings for directions and advice in the case of infection. These had specious titles also, such as these:

An eminent High Dutch physician, newly come over from Holland, where he resided during all the time of the great plague last year in Amsterdam, and cured multitudes of people that actually had the plague upon them.

An Italian gentlewoman just arrived from Naples, having a choice secret to prevent infection, which she found out by her great experience, and did wonderful cures with it in the late plague there, wherein there died 20,000 in one day.

An ancient gentlewoman, having practiced with great success in the late plague in this city, anno 1636, gives her advice only to the female sex. To be spoke with, &c.

An experienced physician, who has long studied the doctrine of antidotes against all sorts of poison and infection, has, after forty years' practice, arrived to such skill as may, with God's blessing, direct persons how to prevent their being touched by any contagious distemper whatsoever. He directs the poor gratis.

I take notice of these by way of specimen. I could give you two or three dozen of the like and yet have abundance left behind. 'Tis sufficient from these to apprise any one of the humour of those times, and how a set of thieves and pickpockets not only robbed and cheated the poor people of their money, but poisoned their bodies with odious and fatal preparations; some with mercury, and some with other things as bad, perfectly remote from the thing pretended to, and rather hurtful than serviceable to the body in case an infection followed.

I cannot omit a subtility of one of those quack operators, with which he gulled the poor people to crowd about him, but did nothing for them without money. He had, it seems, added to his bills, which he gave about the streets, this advertisement in capital letters, *viz.*, "He gives advice to the poor for nothing."

Abundance of poor people came to him accordingly, to whom he made a great many fine speeches, examined them of the state of their health and of the constitution of their bodies, and told them many good things for them to do, which were of no great moment. But the issue and conclusion of all was, that he had a preparation which if they took such a quantity of every morning, he would pawn his life they should never have the plague; no, though they lived in the house with people that were infected. This made the people all resolve to have it; but then the price of that was so much, I think 'twas half-a-crown. "But sir," says one poor woman, "I am a poor almswoman, and am kept by the parish, and your bills say you give the poor your help for nothing." "Ay, good woman," says the doctor, "so I do, as I published there. I give my advice to the poor for nothing, but not my physick." "Alas, sir!" says she, "that is a snare laid for the poor, then; for you give them advice for nothing; that is to say, you advise them gratis, to buy your physick for their money; so does every shopkeeper with his wares." Here the woman began to give him ill words, and stood at his door all that day, telling her tale to all the people that came, till the doctor, finding she turned away his customers, was obliged to call her upstairs again and give her his box of physick for nothing, which perhaps, too, was good for nothing when she had it.

But to return to the people, whose confusions fitted them to be imposed upon by all sorts of pretenders and by every mountebank. There is no doubt but these quacking sort of fellows raised great gains out of the miserable people, for we daily found the crowds that ran after them were infinitely greater, and their doors were more thronged than those of Dr Brooks, Dr Upton, Dr Hodges, Dr Berwick, or any, though the most famous men of the time. And I was told that some of them got five pounds a day by their physick.

But there was still another madness beyond all this, which may serve to give an idea of the distracted humour of the poor people at that time, and this was their following a worse sort of deceivers than any of these; for these petty thieves only deluded them to pick their pockets and get their money, in which their wickedness, whatever it was, lay chiefly on the side of the deceivers deceiving, not upon the deceived. But in this part I am going to mention it lay chiefly in the people deceived, or equally in both, and this was in wearing charms, philtres, exorcisms, amulets, and I know not what preparations, to fortify the body with them against the plague; as if the plague was not the hand of God, but a kind of a possession of an evil spirit, and that it was to be kept off with crossings, signs of the zodiac, papers tied up with so many knots, and certain words or figures written on them, as particularly the word Abracadabra, formed in triangle or pyramid, thus:

ABRACADABRA
ABRACADABR
ABRACADAB   Others had the Jesuits'
ABRACADA   mark in a cross: I H
ABRACAD   S.
ABRACA
ABRAC   Others nothing but this
ABRA   mark, thus:
ABR
AB
A

I might spend a great deal of time in my exclamations against the follies, and indeed the wickedness, of those things in a time of such danger, in a matter of such consequences as this, of a national infection. But my memorandums of these things relate rather to take notice only of the fact, and mention only that it was so. How the poor people found the insufficiency of those things, and how many of them were afterwards carried away in the dead-carts and thrown into the common graves of every parish with these hellish charms and trumpery hanging about their necks, remains to be spoken of as we go along.

All this was the effect of the hurry the people were in, after the first notion of the plague being at hand was among them, and which may be said to be from about Michaelmas, 1664, but more particularly after the two men died in St. Giles's, in the beginning of December; and again, after another alarm in February. For when the plague evidently spread itself, they soon began to see the folly of trusting to those unperforming creatures who had gulled them of their money; and then their fears worked another way, namely, to amazement and stupidity, not knowing what course to take or what to do either to help or relieve themselves. But they ran about from one neighbor's house to another, and even in the streets, from one door to another, with repeated cries of, "Lord, have mercy upon us! What shall we do?"

Indeed, the poor people were to be pitied in one particular thing, in which they had little or no relief, and which I desire to mention with a serious awe and reflection, which perhaps every one that reads this may not relish, namely, that whereas death now began not, as we may say, to hover over every one's head only, but to look into their houses and chambers, and stare in their faces. Though there might be some stupidity and dullness of the mind, and there was so, a great deal, yet there was a great deal of just alarm sounded into the very inmost soul, if I may so say, of others. Many consciences were awakened; many hard hearts melted into tears; many a penitent confession was made of crimes long concealed. [It] would wound the soul of any Christian to have heard the dying groans of many a despairing creature, and none durst come near to comfort them. Many a robbery, many a murder, was then confessed aloud, and nobody surviving to record the accounts of it. People might be heard, even into the streets as we passed along, calling upon God for mercy, through Jesus Christ, and saying "I have been a thief," "I have been an adulterer," "I have been a murderer," and the like, and none durst stop to make the least enquiry into such things or to administer comfort to the poor creatures that in the anguish both of soul and body thus cried out. Some of the ministers did visit the sick at first and for a little while, but it was not to be done; it would have been present death to have gone into some houses. The very buriers of the dead, who were the hardenedest creatures in town, were sometimes beaten back and so terrified that they durst not go into houses where the whole families were swept away together, and where the circumstances were more particularly horrible, as some were; but this was, indeed, at the first heat of the distemper.

Time enured them to it all, and they ventured everywhere afterwards without hesitation.

CHARLES WILLIAMS
Salem[1]

The history of the Salem witches deserves to be noticed separately, not so much because of its process as because of its end. It was not altogether a coincidence that the end of the trial came so near the pacification in the whole general war;[2] men's beliefs were already shaken, and the Salem conclusion is likely to have affected minds in England at least. It is a smaller coincidence, but one that should not be forgotten, that this particular end should come at a place called Salem.[3]

The facts themselves are nothing new. One of the most horrible themes of the whole history is the conflict, as it were, between children and the accused. Children had been supposed to be a particular prey. In a book by a certain Ignatius Lupo published at Bergamo in 1648, or a little earlier, the question was raised why God allowed the deaths of so many children at the hands of witches. Lupo fell back on His inscrutable wisdom and goodness. But the answer was only pious and the problem oppressed many. All over Europe the attack of Goetia[4] had been felt to be aimed at children, either to pervert or to kill. The authors of the *Malleus*[5] had imagined a kind of destruction of all Christendom by such means; with the dwindling of the generations, and with the increase of the abhorred conventicles in every generation, the number of the faithful would diminish and perhaps disappear. But also, imaginatively, there was that old junction of opposites—the supreme supernatural malice and the semblance at least of natural innocence. The very appearance of a natural child was clearly the thing in all the world most unlike the body of evil, especially of aged evil, which was a witch, and most provocative to it. Was it wonderful that the witch should desire to destroy it?

As it were by diabolical intervention, the children retaliated. In England, in France, in Germany, in Spain, in New England, the clear voices of children gave evidence against their neighbors, their friends, their kindred, their parents. Yes, those small voices said, they had been at the Sabbath; yes, they had helped to cook the food; yes, they had seen so-and-so there and so-and-so and such-a-one; yes, they had given themselves to the devil, or had not; yes, father or mother or brother had said or done this or the other. And then mostly they vanish—scourged three times naked around the

---

1. Chapter 12 of *Witchcraft* (1941).
2. The centuries-old war between humane religion and the destructive obsession with the works of the devil as manifest in witchcraft.

3. An old name for Jerusalem.
4. The religion and discipline of witchcraft, sorcery, and so forth.
5. *Malleus Maleficiarum*, a fifteenth-century treatise on sorcery.

stake, or shut up in a convent, or driven away from their homes, or even, like Jennet Device, living a quite ordinary life after their month of exhibition, until, in turn, a boy's voice pipes up with the same accusation against them which had come against others from their own younger lips.

Such had been the history, but the war was, at least for a while, to cease; the children of Salem were to be among the last who had the opportunity to testify: Elizabeth Parris, nine years old, daughter of the Reverend Samuel Parris, minister of Salem, and Abigail Williams, eleven years old, her cousin; Anne Putnam, twelve years old, daughter of Thomas Putnam, the parish clerk, and others, but it was those three with whom the thing began, for they were seen "to creep into holes and under chairs, put themselves into odd postures, make antic gestures, and utter loud outcries." It was a land where everything was immediately translated into terms of God; that is, no doubt, proper, but then they must be His terms and not ours—the terms He deigns to apply, not the terms we force on Him. And this, it seems, is the use of all science—to discover His own terms. The minister and the family prayed and asked serious questions; the children responded. Names were heard—Tituba, the old Indian servant of the minister; Sarah Good, Sarah Osburn, two very old, very poor members of the congregation. Warrants were issued, and the three were arrested.

It is more than possible that the whole thing had begun with Tituba, that it was she whose tales, or other than tales, had thrilled, excited, and provoked the children. If so, the reveries of her race returned on her from her pupils. When the three prisoners were examined in turn Tituba was quicker than the other two to see what was expected or to confess what had happened. She put all the blame on the other women; there had been four of them and a man; they had said to her: "Hurt the children or we will do worse to you." She added: "Last night there was an appearance that said: 'Hurt the children.'" What was it like? "Like a hog and sometimes like a great dog." She said they had all gone to the meeting: "We see nothing but are there presently." She told of the familiars[6] the other women had. Sarah Good had a little yellow bird, which was seen afterwards by the afflicted children. "What hath Sarah Osburn?" "Yesterday she had a thing like a woman with two legs and wings." This also the afflicted Abigail found that she had seen. "What else have you see with Osburn?" "Another thing, hairy; it goes upright like a man; it hath only two legs." The man with the four women went, she thought, in black clothes; he was a tall man with white hair.

Sarah Good at first refused to admit any guilt. The children were ordered to look at her, when they all found themselves tormented.

6. Familiars were usually animals inhabited by a spirit who was attached to a witch in the dual role of servant and master.

This was the great dramatic thrill of the examinations. There stood the children, and if any of the prisoners moved a limb they cried out accordingly: if a hand, they were pinched; if a foot, they were stamped on; if the body, they were crushed. "Why do you torment them?" the court asked Good. She denied it; she said: "What do I know? You bring others here, and now you charge me with it."

"Why, who was it?"

"I do not know, but it was some you brought into the meeting-house with you."

"We brought you into the meeting-house."

"But you brought in two more."

At last she said yes; Osburn had done it. All three were remitted to prison. Sarah Osburn died there. The others in due course were put to death.

It appeared, however, that there were more. Two more certainly; Good and Tituba had both testified to it. There were, walking about the meeting-house, two beings, either the hairy winged things going on legs that Tituba had seen, familiars of witches, or perhaps the witches themselves. Here again is that curious horror in which it can be believed that a man or a woman can be in one place and yet in another place. Two women might be in their own houses, at their own work, and yet walking also in the meeting-house; or they might even be sitting in that very meeting-house, orthodox, pious, attentive, shocked, and yet they might be walking about in it, tormenting the children, evil and restless, like the Devil, in dry places. There were, though the Salem magistrates may not have known it, thousands of stories—of how a woman would be seemingly asleep by her husband's side, and yet it was but a shape that slept there, for the woman herself was away at the Sabbath. Crudely, it was said to be the familiar or some other devil who put on the identity, but it seems sometimes as if this were but a manner of speech; as if the witch body shed itself or multiplied itself,[7] and went as it would and stayed as it would; so that no-one could know to whom they spoke, whether to the witch or her shape; and in those places and times no-one could know, till confession, who was the witch. Who, of all the women in Salem, were the two? Everyone looked and shrank and wondered. And the afflicted children were still afflicted before them all.

From that moment the panic spread. More were arrested, and more in danger. Sarah Good was hanged: when she came to the scaffold, one of the ministers, Mr. Nicholas Noyes, of First Church, Salem, urged her to confess, and she refused. He said: "I know you are a witch"; she answered: "I am no more a witch

7. Golden-thighed Pythagoras is said to have lectured in two cities at the same time; it is an ancient dream of power [Williams' note].

than you are a wizard, and if you take away my life, God will give you blood to drink."

The afflicted children continued to testify; there entered into the cases what was called "spectral evidence," a declaration by the witness that he or she could see that else invisible shape before them, perhaps hurting them. It was a very ancient tendency of witnesses, and it had occurred in a number of trials in Europe. "Many a man hath verily believed he hath seen a spirit externally before him when it hath been only an internal image dancing in his own brain," wrote Francis Hutchinson in 1720 in the chapter of his *Historical Essay concerning Witchcraft* which deals with the Salem trials; and to the objection that "God would not allow such horrors" he answers, in a sentence worthy to be recollected continually: "Hath God anywhere promised that he will save credulous men from being deceived because otherwise the blood of the innocent man will be in danger?" The children at Salem supplied all that credulity needed. At the trial of Martha Carrier they declared that "the black man" was present in the court. Martha Carrier was another of those parents who were convicted on the evidence of her own children. Four of them were taken to prison, and Sarah Carrier, a child of seven, was examined.

"How long has thou been a witch?"

"Ever since I was six years old."

"How old are you now?"

"Near eight years old; brother Richard says I shall be eight years old in November next."

"Who made you a witch?"

"My mother; she made me set my hand to a book."

"How did you set your hand to it?"

"I touched it with my fingers, and the book was red; the paper of it was white."

She went on to say that her mother had "baptized" her with the words: "Thou art mine for ever and ever, Amen"; and had sent her to afflict folks by pinching them. She added that her mother, while confined, had come to her in the shape of a black cat. "The cat told me so, that she was my mother." And the cat carried the child "in her spirit" to afflict. She confirmed other testimony that Martha was she to whom the Devil had promised that she should be Queen of Hell.

The black man was also seen to be spectrally present at the execution of the Reverend George Burroughs. Burroughs had been a a minister in Salem, but had left the village for another pastorate. He was, however, arrested on a warrant from Boston and on the 4th May brought back to Salem to be tried. At the trial Ann Putnam (it may be remembered that she was twelve years old) testified as follows:

"On the 8th day of May, at evening, I saw the apparition of Mr. George Burroughs, who grievously tortured me, and urged me to write in his book, which I refused. He then told me that his two first wives would appear to me presently, and tell me a great many lies, but I should not believe them.

"Then immediately appeared to me the forms of two women in winding sheets, and napkins about their heads, at which I was greatly affrighted; and they turned their faces towards Mr. Burroughs, and looked very red and angry, and told him that he had been a cruel man to them, and that their blood did cry for vengeance against him; and also told him that they should be clothed with white robes in heaven, when he should be cast into hell; and immediately he vanished away. And, as soon as he was gone, the two women turned their heads toward me, and looked as pale as a white wall; and told me that they were Mr. Burroughs' two first wives, and that he had murdered them. And one of them told me that she was his first wife, and he stabbed her under the left arm and put a piece of sealing-wax on the wound. And she pulled aside the winding-sheet and showed me the place; and also told me that she was in the house where Mr. Parris now lives, when it was done.

"And the other told me that Mr. Burroughs and that wife which he hath now, killed her in the vessel, as she was coming to see her friends, because they would have one another. And they both charged me that I should tell these things to the magistrates before Mr. Burroughs' face; and, if he did not own them, they did not know but they should appear there. This morning, also, Mrs. Lawson and her daughter Ann appeared to me, whom I knew, and told me Mr. Burroughs murdered them. This morning also appeared to me another woman in a winding-sheet, and told me that she was Goodman Fuller's first wife, and Mr. Burroughs killed her because there was some difference between her husband and him."

Other evidence proved that he was the "devil" of the coven; it was he who had seduced many to join, and who summoned the witches to their meeting with the sound of a trumpet. He preached at the meetings and was present when they "had a Sacrament at a house in the village, and they had Red Bread and Red Drink." One of the witnesses said she had been taken up by Burroughs "into a very high mountain, where he showed her mighty and glorious kingdoms." These however, like her great Exemplar, she refused. During the examinations the sufferers cried out that he was biting them, and there were seen on their flesh the prints of teeth, "just such a set of teeth as G.B.'s . . . which could be distinguished from those of other men." His unusual strength was also brought in evidence against him. Eventually he was found guilty. At his execution he made a prayer and made an address to the crowd of such ardent devotion that it seems to have shaken many.

But "the accusers said the black man stood and dictated to him. As soon as he was turned off, Mr. Cotton Mather, being mounted upon a horse, addressed himself to the people, partly to declare that he (Mr. Burroughs) was no ordained minister, and partly to possess the people of his guilt, saying that the Devil had often been transformed into an angel of light; and this somewhat appeased the people, and the executions went on."

By now the whole tale had been reaffirmed: the coven, the meeting, the infernal sacrament, the book of signatures, the devil-master and his deputy, familiars, charms, deaths, and destructions. By now also the usual witnesses appeared. The general informer was in this case a man called Joseph Ring, and he was the subject of much admiration on the part of the great Mr. Cotton Mather when he wrote of the affair in his *Wonders of the Invisible World*. "This man has been strangely carried about, by demons, from one witch-meeting to another, for near two years together." He was visited by unknown shapes, and was for a long while made dumb by the Devils, though at the time of the trials released. There often came to him a man with a book for him to sign, but he always refused. "Once, with the book, there was a pen offered him, and an inkhorn, with liquor in it that seemed like blood; but he never touched it." Mr. Ring was thus able to recognize whom he chose, as he chose. He was wasted in Salem; he would have done better in London, a few years earlier, under Titus Oates.

At Andover, a town near at hand, there were the beginnings of a similar outbreak. The wife of a certain Joseph Ballard fell ill and her husband, believing her to be bewitched, sent to Salem for some of the accusers (there were by now others than the afflicted children), some who had the power to see the spectral evidence, to come and say who was oppressing the sick woman. They came and did as they were asked; they were thrown into fits, and cried out that they saw such a one sitting on the invalid's head and such a one on her lower parts. More than Mrs. Ballard fell ill. "Many parents believed their children to be witches; many husbands their wives." The accusers, the witch-finders, were taken about; and their capacity also spread. Others, especially the young people of Andover, "had the same spectral sight." Presently more than fifty of the inhabitants were accused and under suspicions. A magistrate of the place, who had granted warrants for the arrest of thirty or forty, hesitated, for some reason, to grant more. A cry against him was immediately begun; it was said that the spirits of those he had himself killed, some eight or nine, were floating over him in the air. His wife was also "cried out on." He took warning in time; husband and wife fled together.

But another of the accused acted differently. He was then living at Boston, "a worthy gentleman," and his name had been mentioned by the witch-finders at Andover. He was not in immediate danger; he had time to act; he did act. He procured a writ against the accusers for defamation of character, and set the damages at a thousand pounds. This writ he gave to some of his friends who were going to Andover, and charged them to procure certain proof of the slanders, "in doing which their business was perceived." The knowledge wonderfully quenched zeal; the accusers saw *his* spectre at least no more; then other rumours began to dwindle; the accusations at Andover generally ceased. It is unfortunate that no-one had taken the same course with Matthew Hopkins in England.

At Salem there was an incident which showed the determination of the mob to have its panic appeased by death. Rebecca Nurse was a woman of seventy, the mother of a large family, a respected member of the Church, and of some social position. She was a little deaf; she was ill when she was arrested, but she was brought to examination in the usual way, and she maintained her defense with dignity. Asked, "Do you think that these suffer against their wills?" she answered "I do not think these suffer against their wills." A paper testifying to her upright character and signed by thirty-nine acquaintances was handed in. The jury pronounced her guiltless. There was an immediate hubbub in the court. The accusers cried out; the affiliated children screamed. The judges exclaimed against the verdict. One said they would have her indicted over again. Another directed the attention of the jury to a phrase used by the accused: when Deliverance Hobbs, who had been a witch and had confessed, came to give evidence, Rebecca Nurse was heard to say: "What, do these persons give in evidence against me now? they used to come amongst us." The jury asked leave to withdraw again. The foreman was still troubled and went back into court to ask the prisoner what she meant by the words. But she was hard of hearing and most unhappy; the court was noisy; she did not hear him. He went out again, and the jury found her guilty. Afterwards she was told what had happened; she said that all she had meant was that Goodwife Hobbs and her daughter had been her fellow prisoners. The governor, perhaps upon hearing of this declaration, issued a reprieve, but there was a fresh outcry and he withdrew it. She was executed on the 19th July.

It was, however, at her trial that the first fault was made by the accusers. They cried out on Mr. Willard. Now Mr. Willard was a minister, of the Old South Church, Boston; he appears to have displayed some hesitation about accepting all the evidence. But he was too great a man for the accusers of Salem to be allowed to reach; whoever spoke was hastily hushed, pushed out of court, and "it was told about that she was mistaken in the person."

The modification of the panic seems to have begun in a similar rashness—when the wife of the Reverend John Hale, of Beverly, was accused. This happened in October, and the Reverend John Hale found it impossible to believe. He began to stand out; others joined him. The Governor also took action; he refused to allow any more spectral evidence; he ordered the special court which had been sitting to cease from witchcraft trials. By November the accusers found the tales falling harmless. They fell into fits at the sight of an old woman on a bridge, but she was not arrested; they had visions of three persons sitting on a sick person till she died, but bond was accepted for all three. By the next May all those who were still prisoners were released; it is said there were about a hundred and fifty, though another two hundred had been accused. Twenty during the year of panic had been executed, nineteen hanged and one (the famous Giles Corey) pressed to death for refusing to plead. Two had died in prison. Eight were under condemnation when they were released. This release so moved the chief judge that he protested loudly: "We were in a way to have cleared the land of them; who it is that obstructs the cause of justice I know not; the Lord be merciful to this country!"

But the affair did not end there. It was followed by the operation of some of the Salem people against their minister Mr. Parris, and of the declaration of others against themselves. Few trials have had such a conclusion. In April 1963, before the final release had taken place, eight men of Salem drew up a paper which they read to Mr. Parris. It accused him of credulity, lack of charity, and the practice of unwarrantable methods; it said they seriously feared to be accused as the Devil's instruments, since they had seen those better than themselves accused; they said that his continual dwelling on the mystery of iniquity working among them all "was not profitable but offensive." For this reason they had preferred to withdraw from communion with the church at Salem village. Mr. Parris in his reply acknowledged his faults and changed his opinions. He lamented the beginning of the terror in his own household; he said that "God hath been righteously spitting in my face: Numbers xii. 14. And I desire to lie low under all this reproach and to lay my hand on my mouth." He allowed that "God sometimes suffers the Devil, as of late, to afflict in shape of not only innocent but pious persons; or so to delude the senses of the afflicted, that they strongly conceit their hurt is from such persons, when it is not."

This, of course, was fatal to any accusation based on spectral evidence. It had been maintained long ago by the authors of the *Malleus* that the apparent good might be evil. But only here and there had any intellect maintained that the apparent evil might be good. Yet one can hardly imagine Satan's kingdom by halves; if he can deceive, he can deceive. Mr. Parris, to do him justice, saw the difficulty at last: God had suffered them to be deluded—"but how far on the one side or the other is much above me to say."

The opposition, however, were unsatisfied. They did not think it above them to say that Mr. Parris and his side had been deluded throughout. The other churches of the district made some attempt to compose the difference and failed. In 1695 the congregation was demanding the minister's withdrawal, and in another two years the dispute had to be put to arbitration. In the paper put in by attorneys on behalf of the village Mr. Parris was flatly accused of having "dealt with them that have a familiar spirit," in so far as he had inquired of the afflicted children; it came near the old problem of using sorcery to cure sorcery. This, and his preaching such "scandalous immoralities," his "believing the Devil's accusations"—"by these practices and principles" he had been "the beginner and procurer of the sorest afflictions not to this village only but to this whole country." The petition ended:

"We, the subscribers, in behalf of ourselves, and of several others of the same mind with us (touching these things) having some of us had our relations by these practices taken off by an untimely death; others have been imprisoned, and suffered in our persons, reputations, and estates; submit the whole to your honors' decision, to determine whether we are or ought to be any ways obliged to honor, respect and support such an instrument of our miseries; praying God to guide your honors to act herein as may be for his glory, and the future settlement of our village in amity and unity."

To this attack the minister was compelled to yield; he actually left the village and went elsewhere; it was not perhaps unjustified. But though it exhibited regret and determination in the townsmen, it could not exhibit repentance. One at least of the afflicted children made some motion towards such a greater acknowledgement. Anne Putnam, in 1706, was received into the Church at the age of twenty-six. But the events of 1692 had not been forgotten; either by her own will or under the direction of others, she produced a Confession. It read as follows:

"I desire to be humbled before God for that sad and humbling providence that befell my father's family in the year about '92; that I being then in my childhood, should by such providence be made an instrument for the accusing of several persons of a grievous crime, whereby their lives were taken away from them, whom now I have just grounds and good reason to believe they were innocent persons; and that it was a great delusion of Satan that deceived me in that sad time, whereby I justly fear I have been instrumental, with others, though ignorantly and unwittingly, to bring upon myself and this land the guilt of innocent blood; though what was said or done by me against any person I can truly and uprightly say, before God and man, I did it not out of any anger, malice or ill-will to any person, for I had no such thing against one of them; but what I did was ignorantly, being deluded by Satan. And particularly, as I was a chief instrument of accusing of Goodwife Nurse and her two sisters, I desire to lie in the dust, and to be humbled for it, in that I was a cause, with others, of so sad a calamity to them and their families; for which cause I desire to lie in the dust, and earnestly beg forgiveness of God, and from all those unto whom I have given just cause of sorrow and offense, whose relations were taken away or accused."

But the unique thing in all the history was the action of one of the judges and of the jurors. Judge Sewall, who had taken an active part, could not content himself with blaming Mr. Parris or the Devil or the Providence of God. He stood up one day in Old South Church, in Boston; he handed up a paper, before all the congregation, to be read from the pulpit; he remained standing upright while it was read. It confessed his error and his fault; it implored the forgiveness of God; it entreated the prayers of the Church to avert the anger of God from his country, his family and himself. He continued to observe privately an annual day of fasting and prayer. The actual document does not remain. But the Confession of the twelve jurors does remain.[8]

"We, whose names are under written, being in the year 1692 called to serve as jurors in court at Salem on trial of many, who were by some suspected guilty of doing acts of witchcraft upon the bodies of sundry persons:

"We confess that we ourselves were not capable to understand, nor able to withstand, the mysterious delusions of the powers of darkness, and prince of the air; but were, for want of knowledge in ourselves, and better information from others, prevailed with to take up with such evidence against the accused, as, on further consideration and better information, we justly fear was insufficient for the touching the lives of any (Deut. xvii. 6) whereby we fear we have been instrumental, with others, though ignorantly and unwittingly, to bring upon ourselves and this people of the Lord the guilt of innocent blood; which sin the Lord saith, in scripture, he would not pardon (2 Kings xxiv. 4), that is, we suppose, in regard of his temporal judgements. We do therefore hereby signify to all in general (and to the surviving sufferers in special) our deep sense of, and sorrow for, our errors, in acting on such evidence to the condemning of any person; and do hereby declare, that we justly fear that we were

8. Taken from *More Wonders of the Invisible World* (1700), a collection made by Robert Calafe, an opponent of Cotton Mather's. It was ordered to be burnt by Increase Mather [Williams' note].

sadly deluded and mistaken; for which we are much disquieted and distressed in our minds; and do therefore humbly beg forgiveness, first of God for Christ's sake, for this our error; and pray that God would not impute the guilt of it to ourselves, nor others; and we also pray that we may be considered candidly, and aright, by the living sufferers, as being then under the power of a strong and general delusion, utterly unacquainted with, and not experienced in, matters of that nature.

"We do heartily ask forgiveness of you all, whom we have justly offended; and do declare, according to our present minds, we would none of us do such things again on such grounds for the whole world; praying you to accept of this in way of satisfaction for our offense, and that you would bless the inheritance of the Lord, that he may be entreated for the land.

Foreman, Thomas Fisk,	Th. Pearly, sen.
William Fisk,	John Peabody,
John Bachelor,	Thomas Perkins,
Thomas Fisk, jun.	Samuel Sayer,
John Dane,	Andrew Eliot,
Joseph Evelith,	Henry Herrick, sen."

If it had not been for the Salem jury (and for the Supreme Court of the Inquisition in Spain), the Church of God would not, through those centuries, have made a much better showing than the most malicious of those against whom they set themselves. The century that followed, during which on the whole the panics ceased, would have owed that appeasement rather to the growing scepticism than to any more holy impulse. All that certainly was a part of the change. But, coming when and where it did, the repentance of the Salem jurors on the edge of Christendom seems to carry with it an efficacious grace. Salem has been too long remembered for its witches and its trials; it ought to be remembered for its reparation. In that, in those thirteen good and Christian men—twelve jurors and one judge— by whom it was accomplished it may be thought that our Lord saw Satan, as lightning, fall from heaven.

RAYMOND WILLIAMS
Key Words[1]

In the last decades of the eighteenth century, and in the first half of the nineteenth century, a number of words, which are now of capital importance, came for the first time into common English use, or, where they had already been generally used in the language,

1. From the "Preface" to *Culture and Society*, 1958.

acquired new and important meanings. There is in fact a general pattern of change in these words, and this can be used as a special kind of map by which it is possible to look again at those wider changes in life and thought to which the changes in language evidently refer.

Five words are the key points from which this map can be drawn. They are *industry, democracy, class, art* and *culture.* The importance of these words, in our modern structure of meanings, is obvious. The changes in their use, at this critical period, bear witness to a general change in our characteristic ways of thinking about our common life: about our social, political and economic institutions; about the purposes which these institutions are designed to embody; and about the relations to these institutions and purposes of our activities in learning, education and the arts.

The first important word is *industry,* and the period in which its use changes is the period which we now call the Industrial Revolution. *Industry,* before this period, was a name for a particular human attribute, which could be paraphrased as "skill, assiduity, perseverance, diligence." This use of *industry* of course survives. But, in the last decades of the eighteenth century, *industry* came also to mean something else; it became a collective word for our manufacturing and productive institutions, and for their general activities. Adam Smith, in *The Wealth of Nations* (1776), is one of the first writers to use the word in this way, and from his time the development of this use is assured. *Industry,* with a capital letter, is thought of as a thing in itself—an institution, a body of activities—rather than simply a human attribute. *Industrious,* which described persons, is joined, in the nineteenth century, by *industrial,* which describes the institutions. The rapid growth in importance of these institutions is seen as creating a new system, which in the 1830s is first called *Industrialism.* In part, this is the acknowledgement of a series of very important technical changes, and of their transforming effect on methods of production. It is also, however, an acknowledgement of the effect of these changes on society as a whole, which is similarly transformed. The phrase *Industrial Revolution* amply confirms this, for the phrase, first used by French writers in the 1820s, and gradually adopted, in the course of the century, by English writers, is modelled explicitly on an analogy with the French Revolution of 1789. As that had transformed France, so this has transformed England; the means of change are different, but the change is comparable in kind: it has produced, by a pattern of change, a new society.

The second important word is *democracy,* which had been known, from the Greek, as a term for "government by the people," but which only came into common English use at the time of the American and French Revolutions. Weekley, in *Words Ancient and Modern,* writes:

It was not until the French Revolution that *democracy* ceased to be a mere literary word, and became part of the political vocabulary.

In this he is substantially right. Certainly, it is in reference to America and France that the examples begin to multipy, at the end of the eighteenth century, and it is worth noting that the great majority of these examples show the word being used unfavorably: in close relation with the hated *Jacobinism*, or with the familiar *mob-rule*. England may have been (the word has so many modern definitions) a democracy since Magna Carta, or since the Commonwealth, or since 1688, but it certainly did not call itself one. *Democrats*, at the end of the eighteenth and the beginning of the nineteenth centuries, were seen, commonly, as dangerous and subversive mob agitators. Just as *industry* and its derived words record what we now call the Industrial Revolution, so *democracy* and *democrat*, in their entry into ordinary speech, record the effects, in England, of the American and French Revolutions, and a crucial phase of the struggle, at home, for what we would now call democratic representation.

Industry, to indicate an institution, begins in about 1776; *democracy*, as a practical word, can be dated from about the same time. The third word, *class*, can be dated, in its most important modern sense, from about 1772. Before this, the ordinary use of *class*, in English, was to refer to a division or group in schools and colleges: "the usual Classes in Logick and Philosophy." It is only at the end of the eighteenth century that the modern structure of *class*, in its social sense, begins to be built up. First comes *lower classes*, to join *lower orders*, which appears earlier in the eighteenth century. Then, in the 1790s, we get *higher classes*; *middle classes* and *middling classes* follow at once; *working classes* in about 1815; *upper classes* in the 1820s. *Class prejudice, class legislation, class consciousness, class conflict* and *class war* follow in the course of the nineteenth century. The *upper middle classes* are first heard of in the 1890s; the *lower middle class* in our own century.

It is obvious, of course, that this spectacular history of the new use of *class* does not indicate the *beginning* of social divisions in England. But it indicates, quite clearly, a change in the character of these divisions, and it records, equally clearly, a change in attitudes towards them. *Class* is a more indefinite word than *rank*, and this was probably one of the reasons for its introduction. The structure then built on it is in nineteenth-century terms: in terms, that is to say, of the changed social structure, and the changed social feelings, of an England which was passing through the Industrial Revolution, and which was at a crucial phase in the development of political democracy.

The fourth word, *art*, is remarkably similar, in its pattern of change, to *industry*. From its original sense of a human attribute, a "skill" it had come, by the period with which we are concerned, to be a kind of institution, a set body of activities of a certain kind. An *art* had formerly been any human skill; but *Art*, now, signified a particular group of skills, the "imaginative" or "creative" arts. *Artist* had meant a skilled person, as had *artisan*; but *artist* now referred to these selected skills alone. Further, and most significantly, *Art* came to stand for a special kind of truth, "imaginative truth," and *artist* for a special kind of person, as the words *artistic* and *artistical*, to describe human beings, new in the 1840s, show. A new name, *aesthetics*, was found to describe the judgment of art, and this, in its turn, produced a name for a special kind of person—*aesthete*. *The arts*—literature, music, painting, sculpture, theatre—were grouped together, in this new phrase, as having something essentially in common which distinguished them from other human skills. The same separation as had grown up between *artist* and *artisan* grew up between *artist* and *craftsman*. *Genius*, from meaning "a characteristic disposition," came to mean "exalted ability," and a distinction was made between it and *talent*. As *art* had produced *artist* in the new sense, and *aesthetics aesthete*, so this produced *a genius*, to indicate a special kind of person. These changes, which belong in time to the period of the other changes discussed, form a record of a remarkable change in ideas of the nature and purpose of art, and of its relations to other human activities and to society as a whole.

The fifth word, *culture*, similarly changes, in the same critical period. Before this period, it had meant, primarily, the "tending of a natural growth," and then, by analogy, a process of human training. But this latter use, which had usually been a culture *of* something, was changed, in the nineteenth century, to *culture* as such, a thing in itself. It came to mean, first, "a general state or habit of the mind," having close relations with the idea of human perfection. Second, it came to mean "the general state of intellectual development, in a society as a whole." Third, it came to mean "the general body of the arts." Fourth, later in the century, it came to mean "a whole way of life, material, intellectual and spiritual." It came also, as we know, to be a word which often provoked either hostility or embarrassment.

The development of *culture* is perhaps the most striking among all the words named. It might be said, indeed, that the questions now concentrated in the meanings of the word *culture* are questions directly raised by the great historical changes which the changes in *industry*, *democracy* and *class*, in their own way, represent, and to which the changes in *art* are a closely related response. The development of the word *culture* is a record of a number of important and continuing reactions to these changes in our social, economic and political life, and may be seen, in itself, as a special kind of map by means of which the nature of the changes can be explored.

I have stated, briefly, the fact of the changes in these important words. As a background to them I must also draw attention to a number of other words which are either new, or acquired new meanings, in this decisive period. Among the new words, for example, there are *ideology, intellectual, rationalism, scientist, humanitarian, utilitarian, romanticism, atomistic; bureaucracy, capitalism, collectivism, commercialism, communism, doctrinaire, equalitarian, liberalism, masses, mediaeval* and *mediaevalism, operative* (noun), *primitivism, proletariat* (a new word for "mob"), *socialism, unemployment; cranks, highbrow, isms* and *pretentious*. Among words which then acquired their now normal modern meanings are *business* (= trade), *common* (= vulgar), *earnest* (derisive), *Education* and *educational, getting-on, handmade, idealist* (= visionary), *Progress, rank-and-file* (other than military), *reformer* and *reformism, revolutionary* and *revolutionize, salary* (as opposed to "wages"), *Science* (= natural and physical sciences), *speculator* (financial), *solidarity, strike* and *suburban* (as a description of attitudes). The field which these changes cover is again a field of general change, introducing many elements which we now point to as distinctively modern in situation and feeling. It is the relations within this general pattern of change which it will be my particular task to describe.

The word which more than any other comprises these relations is *culture*, with all its complexity of idea and reference. My overall purpose in the book is to describe and analyse this complex, and to give an account of its historical formation. Because of its very range of reference, it is necessary, however, to set the enquiry from the beginning on a wide basis. I had originally intended to keep very closely to *culture* itself, but, the more closely I examined it, the more widely my terms of reference had to be set. For what I see in the history of this word, in its structure of meanings, is a wide and general movement in thought and feeling. I shall hope to show this movement in detail. In summary, I wish to show the emergence of *culture* as an abstraction and an absolute: an emergence which, in a very complex way, merges two general responses—first, the recognition of the practical separation of certain moral and intellectual activities from the driven impetus of a new kind of society; second, the emphasis of these activities, as a court of human appeal, to be set over the processes of practical social judgment and yet to offer itself as a mitigating and rallying alternative. But, in both these senses, culture was not a response to the new methods of production, the new *Industry*, alone. It was concerned, beyond these, with the new kinds of personal and social relationship: again, both as a recognition of practical separation and as an emphasis of alternatives. The idea of *culture* would be simpler if it had been a response to industrialism alone, but it was also, quite evidently, a response to the new political and social developments, to *Democracy*. Again, in relation to this, it is a complex and radical response to the new problems of social class. Further, while these responses define bearings, in a given external area that was surveyed, there is also, in the formation of the meanings of *culture*, an evident reference back to an area of personal and apparently private experience, which was notably to affect the meaning and practice of art. These are the first stages of the formulations of the idea of culture, but its historical development is at least as important. For the recognition of a separate body of moral and intellectual activities, and the offering of a court of human appeal, which comprise the early meanings of the word, are joined, and in themselves changed, by the growing assertion of a whole way of life, not ony as a scale of integrity, but as a mode of interpreting all our common experience, and, in this new interpretation, changing it. Where *culture* meant a state or habit of the mind, or the body of intellectual and moral activities, it means now, also a whole way of life. This development, like each of the original meanings and the relations between them, is not accidental, but general and deeply significant. . . .

QUESTIONS FOR STUDY, DISCUSSION, AND WRITING

1. Williams *believes that the five words he has chosen are key words. For a period of several days record sentences and phrases in which you hear the words used. Then review your list to see if the words form a pattern or structure of meaning. In other words, determine on your own evidence what, if anything, the words are key to.*
2. On *page* 885 *Williams lists a number of similar words. Why has he chosen these five instead of some others? Examine three or four of the others before answering.*
3. What *are the five key words to your world? Do they form a pattern?*

W. J. CASH
Reconstruction and the Southern Quandary[1]

It had been obvious from the first, of course, that the South's most pressing internal need was for money. To get money, then, it had turned with absorbing passion to the extension of the only practice which, in its experience, had yielded it: the cultivation of cotton. In the years from 1875 to 1890 it would double its annual production of the staple; and in the next decade it would triple it.

---

1. From "Of Quandary—and the Birth of a Dream," Chapter 2 of *The Mind of the South*, 1941.

But so far from affording the expected relief, cotton, always fickle and dangerous, was developing now into a Fata Morgana, the pursuit of which was actually bearing the South deeper and deeper into trouble.

To grasp the fact here in its fullness, we have to notice first just where and how this increase in production was achieved. Some little part of it is explained by the opening of new lands westward of the limit reached by the plantation in the days before the war. Possibly a greater part is accounted for by the adoption here and there of more intensive methods on the old plantation lands. But the greatest part represented the calling into use of those old lands which in the antebellum South had been adjudged as of no worth for the growing of the fiber; the progressive passage of the culture into the fringes, the contained areas, and the upland borders of the original plantation country; the lands, that is, of the yeoman farmers and, to a large extent, of the poor whites.

But these lands, you will recall, were relatively, and often absolutely, poor lands. And cotton is a voracious plant. To grow it here at all would require fertilizers, and in growing quantities. Moreover, the conversion of the yeomen and the poor whites to cotton culture meant that, in greater or less measure, they ceased to be self-sufficient in food; they no longer produced provender enough at home to take care of themselves and their animals from crop to crop, and must, therefore, somehow manage to secure it from outside.

To this it is to be added also that cotton had long ago begun to exhaust even those plantation lands which had once seemed so eternally fecund; and that now perhaps the greater part of them were demanding fertilization almost as necessitously as those of the very poor whites. And on these plantation units, with from twenty-five to five hundred human mouths and half a dozen to a hundred mules to be fed from crop to crop, plantation units which had never been even remotely self-sufficient in this respect and which were still less so as time went on, the amount of aliment which had to be got from without was staggering.

But in the nature of the case virtually none of the farmers and none of the poor whites were in any position to finance for themselves these needs. Having to have fertilizers and food, they had to have credit. Nor was the condition of at least nine out of every ten planters any better. The financing of the plantation had always been too much for the individual planter. Even in the happiest days before the Civil War, all but the wealthiest and the most thrifty had been dependent upon the services of the cotton factor, a sort of combination banker, merchant, and sales agent located in the central markets for the staple.

Now, however, to make the circle complete, most of these great factors were bankrupt. And with them had disappeared also the whole credit machinery of the Old South. Of the few banks the region had been able to show, there was scarcely a single solvent one left. And nowhere were there sufficient aggregations of capital to set up a proper banking system anew.

To meet this situation, then, to provide the credit which had to be found, to set the farmers and the poor whites up at cotton farming, to relieve the paralysis of the plantations, there sprang into existence one of the worst systems ever developed: that of the supply merchants.

From one standpoint this system may be said to have been most admirably contrived, for it brought the available resources of the South to focus on the purpose with great effectiveness. Under it practically every man who could lay hands on from a few hundred to a few thousand dollars and persuade the wholesale houses in the North to extend him credit was soon or late borne almost irresistibly by the prospect of its rewards into establishing shop and holding himself out to supply guano and bread to two or three, a dozen, or a hundred of his neighbors, according to his resources. So thoroughly were such poor hoards of mobile capital as could be found in the South captured for the end that by the 1800's almost every crossroad was provided with at least one such banker-merchant, and every village had from two to half a score. Thus the necessary credit was achieved, as it could not, perhaps, have been achieved in any other manner.

The evil thing was the price which had to be paid. Virtual monopolists in relation to their own particular groups of clients (for though they were numerous, they were nevertheless not numerous enough, for a long time at any rate, for competition to be of any considerable importance), these new masters of Southern economics were not slow to see that it was in their power to exact whatever rate of payment they pleased. Moreover, they themselves were subjected to harsh terms by the Yankee dealers, and the risks they took were great. And so they fastened upon the unfortunate Southern cotton-grower terms which are almost without a parallel for rigor. Specifically, what he had to submit to in order to get credit from this source was the following: first, he gave a mortgage on the projected crop; next, he usually, if not strictly always, gave a mortgage on the land on which the crop was to be grown—often on all his lands and chattels—and finally, he undertook to pay charges which, what with "time prices," interest rates, and so on, commonly averaged in most districts from 40 per cent to 80 per cent.

In sum, the growing of cotton in the South was saddled with a crushing burden, with such a burden as no agricultural product could be expected to bear and still afford a decent return for the producer.

But this is as yet only half the tale. Despite this handicap, the

South might still have had some hope in cotton; if only the price of the fiber had held up to the high levels prevailing in the first decade after the war. But of course it didn't. The swift extension we have been looking at speedily brought on a condition bordering upon, and often falling into, a glut in the world market. As early as 1878 the price had dropped to ten cents. And in the next twenty years, the general trend was fatally downward, until in 1898 it plunged to below five cents—the lowest level in history. For all the period from the late 1870's to the early 1900's there was not a year in which the average return per acre was more than fifteen dollars; and there were years in which the return for great areas of the South was hardly more than half that.

The sociological and psychological consequences of this situation were varied and far-reaching. But the first thing we have to observe is that it brings us fully into that major change at which I have glanced already: the turning back of the South on the road to aristocracy, and the beginning of decay, in planter and the superior sort of yeoman, of the actual content of the pattern at the same time when the legend of its full and inalienable inheritance was being finally elaborated.

For here, you see, was created a world in which the hard, energetic, horse-trading type of man was remorselessly indicated for survival— even more remorselessly, indeed, than in the old days when the plantation was flinging out over the backcountry, and land-speculation and wildcat finance were the prevailing order. To have any fair chance of coping with the new exigencies, that is, these Southerners were almost irresistibly summoned back upon the old backcountry heritage which had been progressively falling out of view in the last decades prior to the war.

All the elaborately built-up pattern of leisure and hedonistic *drift;* all the slow, cool, gracious and graceful gesturing of movement —which, if it had never been generally and fully established in sober reality, had nevertheless subsisted as an ideal and a tendency—was plainly marked out for abandonment as incompatible with success. And along with it, the vague largeness of outlook which was so essentially a part of the same aristocratic complex; the *magnanimity* in the old-fashioned sense of the word, with its contempt for mere money-grubbing, and its positive pride in a certain looseness of attention to affairs, in scorn for thrifty detail; the careless tolerance of inefficiency and humane aversion for the role of harsh taskmaster, which had gone so far by 1858 that Olmsted estimated that, on some plantations, a Negro did no more than a third of the work done by a hired farm-hand in New York State.

To make certain of getting the last penny of the possible returns with the fewest possible hands and the least expenditure of labor costs, and to make these meager returns perform the feat of meeting all the charges I have indicated, paying taxes, allowing for the replacement of draft animals every five or six years, maintaining the necessary equipment, and leaving something over to provide for his own family: such was the goal imperatively laid down by circumstances for the man of any considerable holdings.

And so he must give himself to business with a single-minded devotion which had not been the fashion in his country since the days when his sires wrested the earth from the forest with ax and brawn. More, if he were the greater sort of yeoman or the lesser sort of planter, then, always in the first case and very often in the latter, he must himself, along with all his sons, set hand to the plow. And whether his status was great or small, he must generally be out of bed before sun-up, pounding on the doors of his tenants, routing them out from the oldest crone to the child just able to toddle, and hurrying them into the field while the dawn was still only a promise in the east. And having got them there, he must stand over them all day, lashing them with his tongue (and sometimes with the whip itself; for, especially in the deeper South, its use on the Negro was far from having disappeared with the formal disestablishment of slavery), until darkness made further effort impossible.

But this was no more, perhaps, than barely to penetrate the essential shell of aristocracy. There was that here which went deeper and struck into the core of the gentlemanly ideal.

For even after the Southern landowner had complied with the conditions I recite, his troubles were often a long way from being solved. In many instances he was still short of the achievement of bare survival on any terms. And in what was perhaps the majority of cases, he came unavoidably to some such impasse as this: that either he was going to have to deny his children the toys they clamored for at Christmas; to turn a deaf ear to the pleas of his womenfolk for a new coat for winter, a new hat at Easter, a new piano for the parlor, a new coat of paint for the drab nakedness of the house, and, almost certainly, to son Will's ambition to go to college; to resign himself and his family to an unending prospect of accumulating shabbiness and frustrated desire—in many and many a case, indeed, actually to seeing himself reduced to sending his children to school barefoot or all but barefoot in winter, and even to setting his daughters to work in the fields like those of any European peasant or any black man— or he was going to have to trade in the need of his neighbor and to stint and cheat his laborers, the tenants and the sharecroppers.

One might have thought at first glance that the latter could hardly be done. Merely to feed and clothe and house them after any decent standard, and to make that add up to the whole of that portion of their product to which they were legally entitled—there was little room for the profits of skulduggery in this; for so it was likely to turn out naturally, and in the hands of the most honest and generous of men. But that phrase: "any decent standard," is an exceedingly elastic one, of course. And if the standard here was already the standard inherited from slavery, still, given the will, it could be made leaner yet.

The old monotonous, pellagra-and-rickets-breeding diet had at least been abundant? Strip it rigidly to fatback, molasses, and corn-bread, dole it out with an ever stingier hand, and particularly in winter when there was no work to be done in the fields; blind your eyes to peaked faces, seal up your ears to hungry whines. New houses must be built now and then? Abandon altogether the standard of the old slave-cabin (which had been at best both solid and more or less tight), and take up in its place the poor white standard at its worst: upend green-pine clapboards into a flimsy box—clapboards which, drying and shrinking, would leave wide slits in the wall for slashing wind and wet. But even a nigger had to have a suit of over-alls once in a while? Not at all: put him in guano-sacking and meal-bagging instead. And as for shoes—why, the damn rascal had a pair year before last; if he was fool enough to wear them every day, let him go without.

Add that, under the prevailing system, the landowner commonly had all sales of the product, all settlements, the entire financing and bookkeeping of the unit, entirely in his hands; that he had usually to deal only with the most abject ignorance in his dependents; that his power was inevitably such that he could easily cow or crush any recalcitrant into submission—and the picture is finished.

Few peoples can ever have been confronted with a crueler dilemma than were these planters and labor-employing yeomen of the South. And for none, surely, has the pressure against the maintenance of honor and *noblesse oblige*—the temptation to let go of aristocratic values and fall back to more primitive and brutal standards—been more tremendous.

But let us take care to see the result here in perspective. I must not seem to suggest universal and head-long retreat, any uniform and sudden emptying out of the stuff of aristocracy from the South.

So far as that great body of men on whom the complex had never been able to stamp itself save superficially and secondarily—those men in whom it had always been impotent against the old horse-trading instinct and the hard core of the *nouveau*—so far as these were concerned, the process, indeed, tended to be comparatively rapid and simple. Faced with the logic of circumstances, they did not tarry long in coming to terms with it, in making themselves as hard as their individual situations ordained. And some of the worst of them even began before long (without in the least mitigating their asser-tion of and their belief in their gentility, and often without even putting aside the old naïve habit of noble profession) to find positive delight in the exercise, positive pride in the reputation, of their hardness.

But elsewhere: To begin with, there were those long-realized aristocrats whom I have called the Virginians—a group which, though it does not entirely fit within the frame I have set up here, may, for practical purposes, be treated just as though it did. Typically, they neither could nor would meet the demands of the times. There were men within the fold, certainly, who could and did meet them in their entirety and at their worst. There were, again, individuals of unusual latent energy, who, while holding more or less fast to the better part of their heritage, managed to ride triumphantly through by sheer force. And to this it must be added also that there was in evidence from an early time some normal human tendency (which we shall see emerging more sharply later on) on the part of the young and more malleable to move toward adaptation: some tendency toward immediate and direct decay.

But typically, as I say, they were too firmly bound within their pattern, were at once too soft and too fine. Decay, as it came to them, came rather obliquely than directly; came, for long at least, and ironically, not so much through any even partial surrender to the demands made upon them as through the inevitable consequences of their failure and their refusal thus to surrender. Many of them fell into bankruptcy and found themselves reduced, like their forerunners for whom the cotton frontier of old had been too much, to keeping school or inn. And if the majority survived, they commonly survived to a steadily declining estate.

And flowing with and out of this came terror, defeatism, apathy, the will to escape. A growing inclination to withdraw themselves altogether from the struggle, from a world grown too dangerous; to shut away the present and abandon the future; here to flee to the inglorious asylum of a political sinecure, as likely as not created expressly for the case; there to retreat behind their own barred gates and hold commerce with none save the members of their own caste. A growing tendency to dissociate their standards wholly from reality, and convert them from living principles of action into mere eidolons.[2]

But it is not only the Virginians with whom we have to do. Of the *nouveaux* of the Old South, not a few were so far gone in the dawdling habit, so far removed from the nimble diligence of their sires, that they also could not encounter the requirements of the hour and went much the same way taken by their models.

And beyond these were hundreds of others: the flower of those planters and yeomen in whom the notions of aristocracy had fallen

2. Plato's word for the material appearances of the absolutes (cf. Bacon's term, "*idols of the mind*").

on the immensely receptive ground of the old native integrity and decency; hundreds of others who, able and consenting (however reluctantly) to put away languor and ease, to accommodate themselves to the reigning exigencies in every humane and honorable respect, yet, to their everlasting glory, set their faces against them on the inhumane and dishonorable side.

Some of them simply refused to compromise at all: not only would not stint and cheat their dependents, but even clung to the better part of magnanimity; managed somehow to reconcile the assiduous practice of thrift with the maintenance of the old liberal-handed spirit toward the available means; and, in a word, declined to make themselves stingy or mean or petty in any fashion whatever. They wore their patches, they carried lean jowls, they denied themselves and their families, and, if must be, they paid the penalty of economic ruin or decay (and, for all their superior energy, it was so in many a case) with high pride, unflinching and undismayed.

And if, under the law of averages for human nature, the majority of even the better sort did inevitably compromise, then they compromised by iotas and jots—fell back by inches. They compromised no more than was required if they were to avoid extinction. And they did it with reluctance and with genuine grief. They fought valiantly to hold on to the essence of the heritage and strove earnestly to keep alive and potent in their increasingly restless sons a notion of honor distinctly bearing the aristocratic impress, and not altogether without success.

Yet, when all this is said—by token of it, in truth—the central fact stands fast: slowly here, rapidly there, more superficially in the one case, more fundamentally in another, directly or indirectly, the South was slipping back from the gains it had made: was receding avoidlessly and forever from the aristocratic goal of the *ancien régime*. And the old primary, simple, back-country heritage of the vast body of Southerners was swinging continuously up from the obscurity which had sometime engulfed it, toward the mastery of the field again.

On the more superficial side, the change wrote itself unmistakably in the final extinction, along in the early 1890's (at a time, that is, when general violence and, in certain ways at least, the romantic spirit were rolling up to new heights), of the formal duel; the universal enactment of laws against it.

And on the more important side, it wrote itself just as decisively in a gathering tendency toward a more ruthless enunciation, even by good men, of the old brutal individualistic doctrine—which yet was never felt as conflicting with humane profession and notions of paternalistic right and duty—that every man was, in economics at any rate, absolutely responsible for himself, and that whatever he got in this world was exactly what he deserved.

QUESTIONS FOR STUDY, DISCUSSION, AND WRITING

1. Describe the working of the cotton economy according to Cash. What is its relevance to his thesis?
2. How does Cash move from economics to morality?
3. What does each of the four last paragraphs add to the summary description of this large social change?
4. How might Freeman's Jackson ("Over the River," pp. 815–829) be seen as a happy combination of aristocratic values and back-country heritage?

HANNAH ARENDT
Denmark and the Jews[1]

At the Wannsee Conference,[2] Martin Luther, of the Foreign Office, warned of great difficulties in the Scandinavian countries, notably in Norway and Denmark. (Sweden was never occupied, and Finland, though in the war on the side of the Axis, was one country the Nazis never even approached on the Jewish question. This surprising exception of Finland, with some two thousand Jews, may have been due to Hitler's great esteem for the Finns, whom perhaps he did not want to subject to threats and humiliating blackmail.) Luther proposed postponing evacuations from Scandinavia for the time being, and as far as Denmark was concerned, this really went without saying, since the country retained its independent government, and was respected as a neutral state, until the fall of 1943, although it, along with Norway, had been invaded by the German Army in April, 1940. There existed no Fascist or Nazi movement in Denmark worth mentioning, and therefore no collaborators. In Norway, however, the Germans had been able to find enthusiastic supporters; indeed, Vidkun Quisling, leader of the pro-Nazi and anti-Semitic Norwegian party, gave his name to what later became known as a "quisling government." The bulk of Norway's seventeen hundred Jews were stateless, refugees from Germany; they were seized and interned in a few lightning operations in October and November, 1942. When Eichmann's office ordered their deportation to Auschwitz, some of Quisling's own men resigned their government posts. This may not have come as a surprise to Mr. Luther and the Foreign Office, but what was much more serious, and certainly totally unexpected, was that Sweden immediately offered asylum, and even Swedish nationality, to all who were persecuted. Dr. Ernst von Weizsäcker, Undersecretary of State of the Foreign Office, who received the proposal, refused to discuss it, but the offer

---

1. From "Deportations from Western Europe—France, Belgium, Holland, Denmark, Italy," Chapter X of *Eich-* *mann in Jerusalem,* 1963.
2. A meeting of German officials on "the Jewish question."

helped nevertheless. It is always relatively easy to get out of a country illegally, whereas it is nearly impossible to enter the place of refuge without permission and to dodge the immigration authorities. Hence, about nine hundred people, slightly more than half of the small Norwegian community, could be smuggled into Sweden.

It was in Denmark, however, that the Germans found out how fully justified the Foreign Offices's apprehensions had been. The story of the Danish Jews is *sui generis*, and the behavior of the Danish people and their government was unique among all the countries in Europe—whether occupied, or a partner of the Axis, or neutral and truly independent. One is tempted to recommend the story as required reading in political science for all students who wish to learn something about the enormous power potential inherent in non-violent action and in resistance to an opponent possessing vastly superior means of violence. To be sure, a few other countries in Europe lacked proper "understanding of the Jewish question," and actually a majority of them were opposed to "radical" and "final" solutions. Like Denmark, Sweden, Italy, and Bulgaria proved to be nearly immune to anti-Semitism, but of the three that were in the German sphere of influence, only the Danes dared speak out on the subject to their German masters. Italy and Bulgaria sabotaged German orders and indulged in a complicated game of double-dealing and double-crossing, saving their Jews by a tour de force of sheer ingenuity, but they never contested the policy as such. That was totally different from what the Danes did. When the Germans approached them rather cautiously about introducing the yellow badge, they were simply told that the King would be the first to wear it, and the Danish government officials were careful to point out that anti-Jewish measures of any sort would cause their own immediate resignation. It was decisive in this whole matter that the Germans did not even succeed in introducing the vitally important distinction between native Danes of Jewish origin, of whom there were about sixty-four hundred, and the fourteen hundred German Jewish refugees who had found asylum in the country prior to the war and who now had been declared stateless by the German government. This refusal must have surprised the Germans no end, since it appeared so "illogical" for a government to protect people to whom it had categorically denied naturalization and even permission to work. (Legally, the prewar situation of refugees in Denmark was not unlike that in France, except that the general corruption in the Third Republic's civil services enabled a few of them to obtain naturalization papers, through bribes or "connections," and most refugees in France could work illegally, without a permit. But Denmark, like Switzerland, was no country *pour se débrouiller*[3].) The Danes, however, explained to the German

3. For wangling—using bribery to circumvent bureaucratic regulations.

officials that because the stateless refugees were no longer German citizens, the Nazis could not claim them without Danish assent. This was one of the few cases in which statelessness turned out to be an asset, although it was of course not statelessness per se that saved the Jews but, on the contrary, the fact that the Danish government had decided to protect them. Thus, none of the preparatory moves, so important for the bureaucracy of murder, could be carried out, and operations were postponed until the fall of 1943.

What happened then was truly amazing; compared with what took place in other European countries, everything went topsy-turvey. In August, 1943—after the German offensive in Russia had failed, the Afrika Korps had surrendered in Tunisia, and the Allies had invaded Italy—the Swedish government canceled its 1940 agreement with Germany which had permitted German troops the right to pass through the country. Thereupon, the Danish workers decided that they could help a bit in hurrying things up; riots broke out in Danish shipyards, where the dock workers refused to repair German ships and then went on strike. The German military commander proclaimed a state of emergency and imposed martial law, and Himmler thought this was the right moment to tackle the Jewish question, whose "solution" was long overdue. What he did not reckon with was that—quite apart from Danish resistance—the German officials who had been living in the country for years were no longer the same. Not only did General von Hannecken, the military commander, refuse to put troops at the disposal of the Reich plenipotentiary, Dr. Werner Best; the special S.S. units (*Einsatz-kommandos*) employed in Denmark very frequently objected to "the measures they were ordered to carry out by the central agencies"—according to Best's testimony at Nuremberg. And Best himself, an old Gestapo man and former legal adviser to Heydrich, author of a then famous book on the police, who had worked for the military government in Paris to the entire satisfaction of his superiors, could no longer be trusted, although it is doubtful that Berlin ever learned the extent of his unreliability. Still, it was clear from the beginning that things were not going well, and Eichmann's office sent one of its best men to Denmark—Rolf Günther, whom no one had ever accused of not possessing the required "ruthless toughness." Günther made no impression on his colleagues in Copenhagen, and now von Hannecken refused even to issue a decree requiring all Jews to report for work.

Best went to Berlin and obtained a promise that all Jews from Denmark would be sent to Theresienstadt[4] regardless of their category—a very important concession, from the Nazis' point of view. The night of October 1 was set for their seizure and immediate

4. A camp for certain classes of prisoners who were to receive special treatment.

departure—ships were ready in the harbor—and since neither the Danes nor the Jews nor the German troops stationed in Denmark could be relied on to help, police units arrived from Germany for a door-to-door search. At the last moment, Best told them that they were not permitted to break into apartments, because the Danish police might then interfere, and they were not supposed to fight it out with the Danes. Hence they could seize only those Jews who voluntarily opened their doors. They found exactly 477 people, out of a total of more then 7,800, at home and willing to let them in. A few days before the date of doom, a German shipping agent, Georg F. Duckwitz, having probably been tipped off by Best himself, had revealed the whole plan to Danish government officials, who, in turn, had hurriedly informed the heads of the Jewish community. They, in marked contrast to Jewish leaders in other countries, had then communicated the news openly in the synagogues on the occasion of the New Year services. The Jews had just time enough to leave their apartments and go into hiding, which was very easy in Denmark, because, in the words of the judgment, "all sections of the Danish people, from the King down to simple citizens," stood ready to receive them.

They might have remained in hiding until the end of the war if the Danes had not been blessed with Sweden as a neighbor. It seemed reasonable to ship the Jews to Sweden, and this was done with the help of the Danish fishing fleet. The cost of transportation for people without means—about a hundred dollars per person—was paid largely by wealthy Danish citizens, and that was perhaps the most astounding feat of all, since this was a time when Jews were paying for their own deportation, when the rich among them were paying fortunes for exit permits (in Holland, Slovakia, and, later, in Hungary) either by bribing the local authorities or by negotiating "legally" with the S.S., who accepted only hard currency and sold exit permits, in Holland, to the tune of five or ten thousand dollars per person. Even in places where Jews met with genuine sympathy and a sincere willingness to help, they had to pay for it, and the chances poor people had of escaping were nil.

It took the better part of October to ferry all the Jews across the five to fifteen miles of water that separates Denmark from Sweden. The Swedes received 5,919 refugees, of whom at least 1,000 were of German origin, 1,310 were half-Jews, and 686 were non-Jews married to Jews. (Almost half the Danish Jews seem to have remained in the country and survived the war in hiding.) The non-Danish Jews were better off than ever before, they all received permission to work. The few hundred Jews whom the German police had been able to arrest were shipped to Theresienstadt. They were old or poor people, who either had not received the news in time or had not been able to comprehend its meaning. In the ghetto, they enjoyed greater privileges than any other group because of the never-ending "fuss" made about them by Danish institutions and private persons. Forty-eight persons died, a figure that was not particularly high, in view of the average age of the group. When everything was over, it was the considered opinion of Eichmann that "for various reasons the action against the Jews in Denmark has been a failure," whereas the curious Dr. Best declared that "the objective of the operation was not to seize a great number of Jews but to clean Denmark of Jews, and this objective has now been achieved."

Politically and psychologically, the most interesting aspect of this incident is perhaps the role played by the German authorities in Denmark, their obvious sabotage of orders from Berlin. It is the only case we know of in which the Nazis met with *open* native resistance, and the result seems to have been that those exposed to it changed their minds. They themselves apparently no longer looked upon the extermination of a whole people as a matter of course. They had met resistance based on principle, and their "toughness" had melted like butter in the sun, they had even been able to show a few timid beginnings of genuine courage. That the ideal of "toughness," except, perhaps, for a few half-demented brutes, was nothing but a myth of self-deception, concealing a ruthless desire for conformity at any price, was clearly revealed at the Nuremberg Trials, where the defendants accused and betrayed each other and assured the world that they "had always been against it" or claimed, as Eichmann was to do, that their best qualities had been "abused" by their superiors. (In Jerusalem, he accused "those in power" of having abused his "obedience." "The subject of a good government is lucky, the subject of a bad government is unlucky. I had no luck.") The atmosphere had changed, and although most of them must have known that they were doomed, not a single one of them had the guts to defend the Nazi ideology. Werner Best claimed at Nuremberg that he had played a complicated double role and that it was thanks to him that the Danish officials had been warned of the impending catastrophe; documentary evidence showed, on the contrary, that he himself had proposed the Danish operation in Berlin, but he explained that this was all part of the game. He was extradited to Denmark and there condemned to death, but he appealed the sentence, with surprising results; because of "new evidence," his sentence was commuted to five years in prison, from which he was released soon afterward. He must have been able to prove to the satisfaction of the Danish court that he really had done his best.

MARTIN GANSBERG

38 Who Saw Murder Didn't Call the Police[1]

For more than half an hour 38 respectable, law-abiding citizens in Queens watched a killer stalk and stab a woman in three separate attacks in Kew Gardens.

Twice their chatter and the sudden glow of their bedroom lights interrupted him and frightened him off. Each time he returned, sought her out, and stabbed her again. Not one person telephoned the police during the assault; one witness called after the woman was dead.

That was two weeks ago today.

Still shocked is Assistant Chief Inspector Frederick M. Lussen, in charge of the borough's detectives and a veteran of 25 years of homicide investigations. He can give a matter-of-fact recitation on many murders. But the Kew Gardens slaying baffles him—not because it is a murder, but because the "good people" failed to call the police.

"As we have reconstructed the crime," he said, "the assailant had three chances to kill this woman during a 35-minute period. He returned twice to complete the job. If we had been called when he first attacked, the woman might not be dead now."

This is what the police say happened beginning at 3:20 A.M. in the staid, middle-class, tree-lined Austin Street area:

Twenty-eight-year-old Catherine Genovese, who was called Kitty by almost everyone in the neighborhood, was returning home from her job as manager of a bar in Hollis. She parked her red Fiat in a lot adjacent to the Kew Gardens Long Island Rail Road Station, facing Mowbray Place. Like many residents of the neighborhood, she had parked there day after day since her arrival from Connecticut a year ago, although the railroad frowns on the practice.

She turned off the lights of her car, locked the door, and started to walk the 100 feet to the entrance of her apartment at 82-70 Austin Street, which is in a Tudor building, with stores on the first floor and apartments on the second.

The entrance to the apartment is in the rear of the building because the front is rented to retail stores. At night the quiet neighborhood is shrouded in the slumbering darkness that marks most residential areas.

Miss Genovese noticed a man at the far end of the lot, near a seven-story apartment house at 82-40 Austin Street. She halted.

1. This account appeared in *The New York Times* on Friday, March 27, 1964.

Then, nervously, she headed up Austin Street toward Lefferts Boulevard, where there is a call box to the 102nd Police Precinct in nearby Richmond Hill.

She got as far as a street light in front of a bookstore before the man grabbed her. She screamed. Lights went on in the 10-story apartment house at 82-67 Austin Street, which faces the bookstore. Windows slid open and voices punctuated the early-morning stillness.

Miss Genovese screamed: "Oh, my God, he stabbed me! Please help me! Please help me!"

From one of the upper windows in the apartment house, a man called down: "Let that girl alone!"

The assailant looked up at him, shrugged, and walked down Austin Street toward a white sedan parked a short distance away. Miss Genovese struggled to her feet.

Lights went out. The killer returned to Miss Genovese, now trying to make her way around the side of the building by the parking lot to get to her apartment. The assailant stabbed her again.

"I'm dying!" she shrieked. "I'm dying!"

Windows were opened again, and lights went on in many apartments. The assailant got into his car and drove away. Miss Genovese staggered to her feet. A city bus, O-10, the Lefferts Boulevard line to Kennedy International Airport, passed. It was 3:35 A.M.

The assailant returned. By then, Miss Genovese had crawled to the back of the building, where the freshly painted brown doors to the apartment house held out hope for safety. The killer tried the first door; she wasn't there. At the second door, 82-62 Austin Street, he saw her slumped on the floor at the foot of the stairs. He stabbed her a third time—fatally.

It was 3:50 by the time the police received their first call, from a man who was a neighbor of Miss Genovese. In two minutes they were at the scene. The neighbor, a 70-year-old woman, and another woman were the only persons on the street. Nobody else came forward.

The man explained that he had called the police after much deliberation. He had phoned a friend in Nassau County for advice and then he had crossed the roof of the building to the apartment of the elderly woman to get her to make the call.

"I didn't want to get involved," he sheepishly told the police.

Six days later, the police arrested Winston Moseley, a 29-year-old business-machine operator, and charged him with the homicide. Moseley had no previous record. He is married, has two children and owns a home at 133-19 Sutter Avenue, South Ozone Park, Queens. On Wednesday, a court committed him to Kings County Hospital for psychiatric observation.

When questioned by the police, Moseley also said that he had slain Mrs. Annie May Johnson, 24, of 146-12 133d Avenue, Jamaica, on Feb. 29 and Barbara Kralik, 15, of 174-17 140th Avenue, Springfield Gardens, last July. In the Kralik case, the police are holding Alvin L. Mitchell, who is said to have confessed that slaying.

The police stressed how simple it would have been to have gotten in touch with them. "A phone call," said one of the detectives, "would have done it." The police may be reached by dialing "0" for operator or SPring 7-3100.

Today witnesses from the neighborhood, which is made up of one-family homes in the $35,000 to $60,000 range with the exception of the two apartment houses near the railroad station, find it difficult to explain why they didn't call the police.

A housewife, knowingly if quite casual, said, "We thought it was a lover's quarrel." A husband and wife both said, "Frankly, we were afraid." They seemed aware of the fact that events might have been different. A distraught woman, wiping her hands in her apron, said, "I didn't want my husband to get involved."

One couple, now willing to talk about that night, said they heard the first screams. The husband looked thoughtfully at the bookstore where the killer first grabbed Miss Genovese.

"We went to the window to see what was happening," he said, "but the light from our bedroom made it difficult to see the street." The wife, still apprehensive, added: "I put out the light and we were able to see better."

Asked why they hadn't called the police, she shrugged and replied: "I don't know."

A man peeked out from a slight opening in the doorway to his apartment and rattled off an account of the killer's second attack. Why hadn't he called the police at the time? "I was tired," he said without emotion. "I went back to bed."

It was 4:25 A.M. when the ambulance arrived to take the body of Miss Genovese. It drove off. "Then," a solemn police detective said, "the people came out."

QUESTIONS FOR STUDY, DISCUSSION, AND WRITING

The Danes faced a moral problem and, although it was a much easier one, so did the people in Kew Gardens. Why didn't they call the police? Do the pieces in this book by Herbert Gold, Samuel Johnson, Stanley Milgram, and Jean-Paul Sartre offer any help in answering this question?

STANLEY MILGRAM
and PAUL HOLLANDER

The Murder They Heard

Catherine Genovese, coming home from a night job in the early hours of an April morning, was stabbed repeatedly and over an extended period of time. Thirty-eight residents of a respectable New York City neighborhood admit to having witnessed at least a part of the attack but not one of them went to her aid or even so much as called the police until after she was dead.

We are all certain that we would have done better. Our indignation toward the residents of Kew Gardens swells to a sense of outrage. The crime, or more precisely, the lack of civic response to it, was so vile that Senator Russell of Georgia read *The New York Times* account of it into the *Congressional Record*. The fact that it *was* Senator Russell is an indication of the complex social reactions touched off by this neighborhood tragedy.

It is noteworthy, first, that anger is directed, not toward the crime, nor the criminal, but toward those who failed to halt the criminal's actions. It is a curious shift, reminiscent of recent trends in moralizing about the Nazi era. Writers once focused on the sins of the Nazis; it is now more fashionable to discuss the complicity of their victims. The event is significant, also, for the way it is being exploited. Senator Russell is but one case in point. In his home state, several brutal murders of Negroes have taken place before large crowds of unprotesting white onlookers, but the Senator has never felt called upon to insert reports of *these* brutalities into the *Record*. The crime against Miss Genovese no longer exists in and of itself. It is rapidly being assimilated to the uses and ideologies of the day.

For example, the Kew Gardens incident has become the occasion for a general attack on the city. It is portrayed as callous, cruel, indifferent to the needs of the people, and wholly inferior to the small town in the quality of its personal relationships. The abrasiveness of urban life cannot be argued; it is not true, however, that personal relationships are necessarily inferior in the city. They are merely organized on a different principle. Urban friendships and associations are not primarily formed on the basis of physical proximity. A person with numerous close friends in different parts of the city may not know the occupant of an adjacent apartment. Some hold this to be an advantage of the city: men and women can conduct lives unmonitored by the constant scrutiny of neighbors. This does not mean that a city dweller has fewer friends than does a villager, or knows fewer persons who will come to his aid;

however, it does mean that his allies are not constantly at hand. Miss Genovese required immediate aid from those physically present; her predicament was desperate and not typical of the occasions when we look for the support of friends. There is no evidence that the city had deprived Miss Genovese of human associations, but the friends who might have rushed to her side were miles from the scene of her tragedy.

A truly extraordinary aspect of the case is the general readiness to forget the man who committed a very foul crime. This is typical of social reactions in present-day America. It begins to seem that everyone, having absorbed a smattering of sociology, looks at once beyond the concrete case in an eager quest for high-sounding generalizations that imply an enlightened social vista. What gets lost in many of these discussions—and what needs at least a partial restoration—is the notion that people may occasionally be responsible for what they do, even if their acts are criminal. In our righteous denunciation of the thirty-eight witnesses we should not forget that they did not commit the murder; they merely failed to prevent it. It is no more than clear thinking to bear in mind the moral difference.

A related and equally confusing error is to infer ethical values from the actual behavior of people in concrete situations. For example, in the case of Miss Genovese we must ask: did the witnesses remain passive because they thought it was the right thing to do, or did they refrain from action *despite* what they thought or felt they should do? We cannot take it for granted that people always do what they consider right. It would be more fruitful to inquire why, in general and in this particular case, there is so marked a discrepancy between values and behavior. What makes people choose a course of action that probably shames them in retrospect? How do they become reduced to resignation, acquiescence and helplessness?

Those who vilify the residents of Kew Gardens measure them against the standard of their own ability to formulate high-minded moral prescriptions. Bt that is hardly a fair standard. It is entirely likely that many of the witnesses, at the level of stated opinion, feel quite as strongly as any of us about the moral requirement of aiding a helpless victim. They too, in general terms, know what *ought* to be done, and can state their values when the occasion arises. This has little, if anything, to do with actual behavior under the press of circumstances.

Furthermore, we must distinguish between the facts of the murder as finally known and reported in the press and the events of the evening as they were experienced by the Kew Gardens residents. We can now say that if the police had been called after the first attack, the woman's life might have been saved, and we tend to judge the inaction of the Kew Gardens residents in the light of this lost possibility. That is natural, perhaps, but it is unrealistic. If those men and women had had as clear a grasp of the situation as we have now, the chances are that many of them would have acted to save Miss Genovese's life. What they had, instead, were fragments of an ambiguous, confusing and doubtless frightening episode—one, moreover, that seemed totally incongruous in a respectable neighborhood. The very lack of correspondence between the violence of the crime and the character of the neighborhood must have created a sense of unreality which inhibited rational action. A lesser crime, one more in character with the locale—say, after-hours rowdiness from a group of college students—might have led more readily to a call for the police.

The incongruity, the sheer improbability of the event predisposed many to reject the most extreme interpretation: that a young woman was in fact being murdered outside the window. How much more probable, not to say more consoling, was the interpretation that a drunken party was sounding off, that two lovers were quarreling, or that youths were playing a nasty prank. Bruno Bettleheim, in *The Informed Heart*, describes how resistant many German Jews were to the signs around them of impending disaster. Given any possibility for fitting events into an acceptable order of things, men are quick to seize it. It takes courage to perceive clearly and without distortion. We cannot justly condemn all the Kew Gardens residents in the light of a horrible outcome which only the most perspicacious could have foreseen.

Why didn't the group of onlookers band together, run out into the street, and subdue the assailant? Aside from the fact that such organization takes time, and that the onlookers were not in communication (who in such a community knows his neighbor's phone number?), there is another factor that would render such action almost impossible. Despite our current fears about the contagion of violence in the mass media, the fact remains that the middle-class person is totally unequipped to deal with its actual occurrence. More especially, he is unable to use personal violence, either singly or collectively, even when it is required for productive and socially valued ends.

More generally, modern societies are so organized as to discourage even the most beneficial, spontaneous group action. This applies with particular sharpness to the law-abiding, respectable segments of the population—such as the people of Kew Gardens—who have most thoroughly accepted the admonition: "do not take the law into your own hands." In a highly specialized society such people take it for granted that certain functions and activities—from garbage collection to fire protection, from meat certification to the control of criminals—are taken care of by specially trained people.

The puzzle in the case under consideration is the reluctance to supply to the police even the barest information which it was essential they have if they were to fulfill their acknowledged functions.

Many facts of the case have not been made public, such as the quality of the relationship between Miss Genovese and the community, the extent to which she was recognized that night, and the number of persons who knew her. It is known that her cries for help were not directed to a specific person: they were general. But only individuals can act, and as the cries were not specifically directed, no particular person felt a special responsibility. The crime and the failure of community response seem absurd to us. At the time, it may well have seemed equally absurd to the Kew Gardens residents that not one of the neighbors would have called the police. A collective paralysis may have developed from the belief of each of the witnesses that someone else must surely have taken that obvious step.

If we ask why they did not call the police, we should also ask what were the alternatives. To be sure, phoning from within an apartment was the most prudent course of action, one involving the minimum of both physical inconvenience and personal involvement with a violent criminal. And yet, one has to assume that in the minds of many there lurked the alternative of going down to the street and defending the helpless woman. This, indeed, might have been felt as the ideal response. By comparison, a mere phone call from the safety of home may have seemed a cowardly compromise with what should be done. As often happens, the ideal solution was difficult, probably dangerous; but, as also happens, the practical, safe alternative may have seemed distasteful in the light of the ideal. Awareness of an ideal response often paralyzes a move toward the less than ideal alternative. Rather than accept the belittling second-best, the person so beset prefers to blot out the whole issue. Therefore, he pretends that there is nothing to get upset about. Probably it was only a drunken brawl.

The symbolic significance of "the street" for the middle-class mentality may have some relevance to the case. Although it cannot explain in full the failure to grab the telephone and call the police, it may account in part for the inertia and indifference. For the middle-class resident of a big city the street and what happens on the street are often symbolic of all that is vulgar and perilous in life. The street is the antithesis of privacy, security, and the support one derives from contemplating and living amidst prized personal possessions. The street represents the world of pushing and shoving crowds, potentially hostile strangers, sweat, dust, and noise. Those who spend much time on the street have nothing better to do and nowhere better to go: the poor, the foot-loose, the drifters, juvenile delinquents. Therefore, the middle-class person seeks almost automatically to disengage himself from the life of the street; he is on it only from necessity, rarely for pleasure. Such considerations help explain the genesis of attitudes that prevented the witnesses from making the crucial phone call. The tragic drama was taking place on the street, hence hardly relevant to their lives; in fact, in some ways radically opposed to their outlook and concerns.

In an effort to make the strongest possible case against the Kew Gardens citizens, the press has ignored actual dangers of involvement, even at the level of calling the police. They have treated the "fears" of the residents as foolish rationalizations, utterly without basis. In doing so they have conveniently forgotten instances in which such involvement did not turn out well for the hero. One spectacular case in the early fifties, amply publicized by the press, concerned the misfortune of Arnold Schuster. While riding in the subway this young Brooklyn man spotted Willie Sutton, an escaped criminal. He reported this information to the police, and it led to Sutton's arrest. Schuster was proclaimed a hero, but before a month was up Schuster was dead—murdered in reprisal for his part in Sutton's recapture. Schuster had done nothing more than phone the police.

The fact is that there *are* risks even in minimal forms of involvement, and it is dishonest to ignore them. One becomes involved with the police, with the general agents of publicity that swarm to such events, and possibly with the criminal. If the criminal is not caught immediately, there is the chance that he will learn who called the police (which apartment did they enter first, whose pictures are in the papers, etc.) and may fear that the caller can identify him. The caller, then, is of special concern to the criminal. If a trial is held, the person who telephoned is likely to be a witness. Even if he is jailed, the criminal may have underworld friends who will act to avenge him. One is a responsible citizen and a worthy human being, not because of the absence of risk but because one acts in the face of it.

In seeking explanations for their inaction, we have not intended to defend, certainly not to excuse, Kew Gardens' passive witnesses. We have sought, rather, to put ourselves in their place, to try to understand their response. The causes we have suggested are in no way sufficient reason for inaction. Perhaps we should have started with a more fundamental question: Why should anyone have gone to the aid of the victim? Why should anyone have taken the trouble to call the police? The answer must be that it is a matter of common decency to help those who are in distress. It is a humane and compassionate requirement in the relations between people. Yet how generally is it observed? In New York City it is not at all unusual to see a man, sick with alcohol, lying in a doorway; he does not command the least attention or interest from those who pass by. The trouble here, as in Kew Gardens, is that the individual does not perceive that his interests are identified with others or with the community at large. And is such a perception possible? What evidence is there in the American community that collective interests have priority over personal advantage?

There are, of course, practical limitations to the Samaritan impulse in a major city. If a citizen attended to every needy person, if he were sensitive to and acted on every altruistic impulse that was evoked in the city, he could scarcely keep his own affairs in order. A calculated and strategic indifference is an unavoidable part of life in our cities, and it must be faced without sentimentality or rage. At most, each of us can resolve to extend the range of his responsibilities in some perceptible degree, to rise a little more adequately to moral obligations. City life is harsh; still, we owe it to ourselves and our fellows to resolve that it be no more harsh than is inevitable.

JOHN STEINBECK
Battle Scene

You can't see much of a battle. Those paintings reproduced in history books which show long lines of advancing troops, close massed, and being received by massed defending troops, are either idealized or else times and battles have changed. The account in the morning papers of the battle of yesterday was not seen by the correspondent, but was put together from reports.

What the correspondent really saw was dust and the nasty burst of shells, low bushes and slit trenches. He lay on his stomach, if he had any sense, and watched ants crawling among the little sticks on the sand dune, and his nose was so close to the ants that their progress was interfered with by it.

Then he saw an advance. Not straight lines of men marching into cannon fire, but little groups scuttling like crabs from bits of cover to other cover, while the high chatter of machine guns sounded, and the deep proom of shellfire.

Perhaps the correspondent scuttled with them and hit the ground again. His report will be of battle plan and tactics, of taken ground or lost terrain, of attack and counterattack. But these are some of the things he probably really saw:

He might have seen the splash of dirt and dust that is a shell burst, and a small Italian girl in the street with her stomach blown out, and he might have seen an American soldier standing over a twitching body, crying. He probably saw many dead mules, lying on their sides, reduced to pulp. He saw the wreckage of houses, with torn beds hanging like shreds out of the spilled hole in a plaster wall. There were red carts and the stalled vehicles of refugees who did not get away.

The stretcher-bearers come back from the lines, walking in off step, so that the burden will not be jounced too much, and the blood dripping from the canvas, brother and enemy in the stretchers, so long as they are hurt. And the walking wounded coming back with shattered arms and bandaged heads, the walking wounded struggling painfully to the rear.

He would have smelled the sharp cordite in the air and the hot reek of blood if the going has been rough. The burning odor of dust will be in his nose and the stench of men and animals killed yesterday and the day before. Then a whole building is blown up and an earthy, sour smell comes from its walls. He will smell his own sweat and the accumulated sweat of an army. When his throat is dry he will drink warm water from his canteen, which tastes of disinfectant.

While the correspondent is writing for you of advances and retreats, his skin will be raw from the woolen clothes he has not taken off for three days, and his feet will be hot and dirty and swollen from not having taken off his shoes for days. He will itch from last night's mosquito bites and from today's sand-fly bites. Perhaps he will have a little sand-fly fever, so that his head pulses and a red rim comes into his vision. His head may ache from the heat and his eyes burn with the dust. The knee that was sprained when he leaped ashore will grow stiff and painful, but it is no wound and cannot be treated.

"The 5th Army advanced two kilometers," he will write, while the lines of trucks churn the road to deep dust and truck drivers hunch over their wheels. And off to the right the burial squads are scooping slits in the sandy earth. Their charges lie huddled on the ground and before they are laid in the sand, the second of the two dog tags is detached so that you know that that man with that army serial number is dead and out of it.

These are the things he sees while he writes of tactics and strategy and names generals and in print decorates heroes. He takes a heavily waxed box from his pocket. That is his dinner. Inside there are two little packets of hard cake which have the flavor of dog biscuits. There is a tin can of cheese and a roll of vitamin-charged candy, an envelope of lemon powder to make the canteen water taste less bad and a tiny package of four cigarettes.

That is dinner, and it will keep him moving for several more hours and keep his stomach working and his heart pumping. And if the line has advanced beyond him while he eats, dirty, buglike children will sidle up to him cringing and sniffling, their noses ringed with flies, and these children will whine for one of the hard biscuits and some of the vitamin candy. They will cry for candy: "Caramela—caramela—caramela—O.K., O.K., shank you, good-by." And if he gives the candy to one, the ground will spew up more dirty, buglike children, and they will scream shrilly, "Caramela—caramela." The correspondent will get the communiqué and will write your morning dispatch on his creaking, dust-filled portable, "General Clark's 5th Army advanced two kilometers against heavy artillery fire yesterday."

T. E. LAWRENCE
Fact and Truth[1]

Remember that the manner is greater than the matter, so far as modern history is concerned. One of the ominous signs of the times is that the public can no longer read history. The historian is retired into a shell to study the whole truth; which means that he learns to attach insensate importance to documents. The documents are liars. No man ever yet tried to write down the entire truth of any action in which he has been engaged. All narrative is parti-pris. And to prefer an ancient written statement to the guiding of your instinct through the maze of related facts, is to encounter either banality or unreadableness. We know too much, and use too little knowledge.

1. From a 1927 letter to Lionel Curtis.

J. B. BURY
Darwinism and History

1. Evolution, and the principles associated with the Darwinian theory, could not fail to exert a considerable influence on the studies connected with the history of civilized man. The speculations which are known as "philosophy of history," as well as the sciences of anthropology, ethnography, and sociology (sciences which though they stand on their own feet are for the historian auxiliary), have been deeply affected by these principles. Historiographers, indeed, have with few exceptions made little attempt to apply them; but the growth of historical study in the nineteenth century has been determined and characterized by the same general principle, which has underlain the simultaneous developments of the study of nature, namely the *genetic* idea. The "historical" conception of nature, which has produced the history of the solar system, the story of the earth, the genealogies of telluric organisms, and has revolutionized natural science, belongs to the same order of thought as the conception of

human history as a continuous, genetic, causal process—a conception which has revolutionized historical research and made it scientific. Before proceeding to consider the application of evolutional principles, it will be pertinent to notice the rise of this new view.

2. With the Greeks and Romans history had been either a descriptive record or had been written in practical interests. The most eminent of the ancient historians were pragmatical; that is, they regarded history as an instructress in statesmanship, or in the art of war, or in morals. Their records reached back such a short way, their experience was so brief, that they never attained to the conception of continuous process, or realized the significance of time; and they never viewed the history of human societies as a phenomenon to be investigated for its own sake. In the middle ages there was still less chance of the emergence of the ideas of progress and development. Such notions were excluded by the fundamental doctrines of the dominant religion which bounded and bound men's minds. As the course of history was held to be determined from hour to hour by the arbitrary will of an extra-cosmic person, there could be no self-contained causal development, only a dispensation imposed from without. And as it was believed that the world was within no great distance from the end of this dispensation, there was no motive to take much interest in understanding the temporal, which was to be only temporary.

The intellectual movements of the fifteenth and sixteenth centuries prepared the way for a new conception, but it did not emerge immediately. The historians of the Renaissance period simply reverted to the ancient pragmatical view. For Machiavelli, exactly as for Thucydides and Polybius, the use of studying history was instruction in the art of politics. The Renaissance itself was the appearance of a new culture, different from anything that had gone before; but at the time men were not conscious of this; they saw clearly that the traditions of classical antiquity had been lost for a long period, and they were seeking to revive them, but otherwise they did not perceive that the world had moved, and that their own spirit, culture, and conditions were entirely unlike those of the thirteenth century. It was hardly till the seventeenth century that the presence of a new age, as different from the middle ages as from the ages of Greece and Rome, was fully realized. It was then that the triple division of ancient, medieval, and modern was first applied to the history of western civilization. Whatever objections may be urged against this division, which has now become almost a category of thought, it marks a most significant advance in man's view of his own past. He has become conscious of the immense changes in civilization which have come about slowly in the course of time, and history confronts him with a new aspect. He has to explain how those changes have been produced, how the transformations were effected. The appearance of this problem was almost simultaneous with the rise of rationalism, and the great historians and thinkers of the eighteenth century, such as Montesquieu, Voltaire, Gibbon, attempted to explain the movement of civilization by purely natural causes. These brilliant writers prepared the way for the genetic history of the following century. But in the spirit of the *Aufklärung*, that eighteenth-century Enlightenment to which they belonged, they were concerned to judge all phenomena before the tribunal of reason; and the apotheosis of "reason" tended to foster a certain superior *a priori* attitude, which was not favorable to objective treatment and was incompatible with a "historical sense." Moreover the traditions of pragmatical historiography had by no means disappeared.

3. In the first quarter of the nineteenth century the meaning of genetic history was fully realized. "Genetic" perhaps is as good a word as can be found for the conception which in this century was applied to so many branches of knowledge in the spheres both of nature and of mind. It does not commit us to the doctrine proper of evolution, nor yet to any teleological hypothesis such as is implied in "progress." For history it meant that the present condition of the human race is simply and strictly the result of a causal series (or set of causal series)—a continuous succession of changes, where each state arises causally out of the preceding; and that the business of historians is to trace this genetic process, to explain each change, and ultimately to grasp the complete development of the life of humanity. Three influential writers, who appeared at this stage and helped to initiate a new period of research, may specially be mentioned. Ranke in 1824 definitely repudiated the pragmatical view which ascribes to history the duties of an instructress, and with no less decision renounced the function, assumed by the historians of the *Aufklärung*, to judge the past; it was his business, he said, merely to show how things really happened. Niebuhr was already working in the same spirit and did more than any other writer to establish the principle that historical transactions must be related to the ideas and conditions of their age. Savigny about the same time founded the "historical school" of law. He sought to show that law was not the creation of an enlightened will, but grew out of custom and was developed by a series of adaptations and rejections, thus applying the conception of evolution. He helped to diffuse the notion that all the institutions of a society or a nation are as closely inter-connected as the parts of a living organism.

4. The conception of the history of man as a causal development meant the elevation of historical inquiry to the dignity of a science. Just as the study of bees cannot become scientific so long as the student's interest in them is only to procure honey or to derive moral lessons from the labors of "the little busy bee," so the history of human societies cannot become the object of pure scientific inves-

tigation so long as man estimates its value in pragmatical scales. Nor can it become a science until it is conceived as lying entirely within a sphere in which the law of cause and effect has unreserved and unrestricted dominion. On the other hand, once history is envisaged as a causal process, which contains within itself the explanation of the development of man from his primitive state to the point which he has reached, such a process necessarily becomes the object of scientific investigation and the interest in it is scientific curiosity.

At the same time, the instruments were sharpened and refined. Here Wolf, a philologist with historical instinct, was a pioneer. His *Prolegomena to Homer* (1795) announced new modes of attack. Historical investigation was soon transformed by the elaboration of new methods.

5. "Progress" involves a judgment of value, which is not involved in the conception of history as a genetic process. It is also an idea distinct from that of evolution. Nevertheless it is closely related to the ideas which revolutionized history at the beginning of the last century; it swam into men's ken simultaneously; and it helped effectively to establish the notion of history as a continuous process and to emphasize the significance of time. Passing over earlier anticipations, I may point to a *Discours* of Turgot (1750), where history is presented as a process in which "the total mass of the human race" "marches continually though sometimes slowly to an ever increasing perfection." That is a clear statement of the conception which Turgot's friend Condorcet elaborated in the famous work, published in 1795,[1] *Esquisse d'un tableau historique des progrés de l'esprit humain*.[2] This work first treated with explicit fullness the idea to which a leading role was to fall in the ideology of the nineteenth century. Condorcet's book reflects the triumphs of the *Tiers état*,[3] whose growing importance had also inspired Turgot; it was the political changes in the eighteenth century which led to the doctrine, emphatically formulated by Condorcet, that the masses are the most important element in the historical process. I dwell on this because, though Condorcet had no idea of evolution, the predominant importance of the masses was the assumption which made it possible to apply evolutional principles to history. And it enabled Condorcet himself to maintain that the history of civilization, a progress still far from being complete, was a development conditioned by general laws.

6. The assimilation of society to an organism, which was a governing notion in the school of Savigny, and the conception of progress, combined to produce the idea of an organic development, in which the historian has to determine the central principle or leading character. This is illustrated by the apotheosis of democracy in Tocqueville's

---

1. Written in 1793 in prison before he took poison [Bury's note].
2. *Sketch for a Historical Picture of the Progress of the Human Mind.*

3. Third estate, representatives of the common people in the prerevolutionary Estates-General.

Démocratie en Amérique, where the theory is maintained that "the gradual and progressive development of equality is at once the past and the future of the history of men." The same two principles are combined in the doctrine of Spencer (who held that society is an organism, though he also contemplated its being what he calls a "super-organic aggregate"),[4] that social evolution is a progressive change from militarism to industrialism.

7. The idea of development assumed another form in the speculations of German idealism. Hegel conceived the successive periods of history as corresponding to the ascending phases or ideas in the self-evolution of his Absolute Being. His *Lectures on the Philosophy of History* were published in 1837 after his death. His philosophy had a considerable effect, direct and indirect, on the treatment of history by historians, and although he was superficial and unscientific himself in dealing with historical phenomena, he contributed much towards making the idea of historical development familiar. Ranke was influenced, if not by Hegel himself, at least by the Idealistic philosophies of which Hegel's was the greatest. He was inclined to conceive the stages in the process of history as marked by incarnations, as it were, of ideas, and sometimes speaks as if the ideas were independent forces, with hands and feet. But while Hegel determined his ideas by *a priori* logic, Ranke obtained his by induction—by a strict investigation of the phenomena; so that he was scientific in his method and work, and was influenced by Hegelian prepossessions only in the kind of significance which he was disposed to ascribe to his results. It is to be noted that the theory of Hegel implied a judgment of value; the movement was a progress towards perfection.

8. In France, Comte approached the subject from a different side, and exercised, outside Germany, a far wider influence than Hegel. The 4th volume of his *Cours de philosophie positive,* which appeared in 1839, created sociology and treated history as a part of this new science, namely as "social dynamics." Comte sought the key for unfolding historical development, in what he called the social-psychological point of view, and he worked out the two ideas which had been enunciated by Condorcet: that the historian's attention should be directed not, as hitherto, principally to eminent individuals, but to the collective behavior of the masses, as being the most important element in the process; and that, as in nature, so in history, there are general laws, necessary and constant, which condition the development. The two points are intimately connected, for it is only

4. A society presents suggestive analogies with an organism, but it certainly is not an organism, and sociologists who draw inferences from the assumption of its organic nature must fall into error. A vital organism and a society are radically distinguished by the fact that the individual components of the former, namely the cells, are morphologically as well as functionally differentiated, whereas the individuals which compose a society are morphologically homogeneous and only functionally differentiated. The resemblances and the differences are worked out in E. de Majewski's striking book, *La Science de la Civilisation,* Paris, 1908 [Bury's note].

when the masses are moved into the foreground that regularity, uniformity, and law can be conceived as applicable. To determine the social-psychological laws which have controlled the development is, according to Comte, the task of sociologists and historians.

9. The hypothesis of general laws operative in history was carried further in a book which appeared in England twenty years later and exercised an influence in Europe far beyond its intrinsic merit, Buckle's *History of Civilization in England* (1857-61). Buckle owed much to Comte, and followed him, or rather outdid him, in regarding intellect as the most important factor conditioning the upward development of man, so that progress, according to him, consisted in the victory of the intellectual over the moral laws.

10. The tendency of Comte and Buckle to assimilate history to the sciences of nature by reducing it to general "laws," derived stimulus and plausibility from the vista offered by the study of statistics, in which the Belgian Quetelet, whose book *Sur l'homme* appeared in 1835, discerned endless possibilities. The astonishing uniformities which statistical inquiry disclosed led to the belief that it was only a question of collecting a sufficient amount of statistical material, to enable us to predict how a given social group will act in a particular case. Bourdeau, a disciple of this school, looks forward to the time when historical science will become entirely quantitative. The actions of prominent individuals, which are generally considered to have altered or determined the course of things, are obviously not amenable to statistical computation or explicable by general laws. Thinkers like Buckle sought to minimize their importance or explain them away.

11. These indications may suffice to show that the new efforts to interpret history which marked the first half of the nineteenth century were governed by conceptions closely related to those which were current in the field of natural science and which resulted in the doctrine of evolution. The genetic principle, progressive development, general laws, the significance of time, the conception of society as an organic aggregate, the metaphysical theory of history as the self-evolution of spirit—all these ideas show that historical inquiry had been advancing independently on somewhat parallel lines to the sciences of nature. It was necessary to bring this out in order to appreciate the influence of Darwinism.

12. In the course of the dozen years which elapsed between the appearances of *The Origin of Species*[5] (observe that the first volume of Buckle's work was published just two years before) and of *The Descent of Man* (1871), the hypothesis of Lamarck that man is the co-descendant with other species of some lower extinct form was admitted to have been raised to the rank of an established fact by

5. 1859 [Bury's note].

most thinkers whose brains were not working under the constraint of theological authority.

One important effect of the discovery of this fact (I am not speaking now of the Darwinian explanation) was to assign to history a definite place in the coordinated whole of knowledge, and relate it more closely to other sciences. It had indeed a defined logical place in systems such as Hegel's and Comte's; but Darwinism certified its standing convincingly and without more ado. The prevailing doctrine that man was created *ex abrupto* had placed history in an isolated position, disconnected with the sciences of nature. Anthropology, which deals with the animal *anthropos*, now comes into line with zoology, and brings it into relation with history.[6] Man's condition at the present day is the result of a series of transformations, going back to the most primitive phase of society, which is the ideal (unattainable) beginning of history. But that beginning had emerged without any breach of continuity from a development which carries us back to a quadrimane ancestor, still further back (according to Darwin's conjecture) to a marine animal of the ascidian type, and then through remoter periods to the lowest form of organism. It is essential in this theory that though links have been lost there was no break in the gradual development; and this conception of a continuous progress in the evolution of life, resulting in the appearance of uncivilized Anthropos, helped to reinforce, and increase a belief in, the conception of the history of civilized Anthropos as itself also a continuous progressive development.

13. Thus the diffusion of the Darwinian theory of the origin of man, by emphasizing the idea of continuity and breaking down the barriers between the human and animal kingdoms, has had an important effect in establishing the position of history among the sciences which deal with telluric development. The perspective of history is merged in a larger perspective of development. As one of the objects of biology is to find the exact steps in the genealogy of man from the lowest organic form, so the scope of history is to determine the stages in the unique causal series from the most rudimentary to the present state of human civilization.

It is to be observed that the interest in historical research implied by this conception need not be that of Comte. In the Positive Philosophy history is part of sociology; the interest in it is to discover

6. It is to be observed that history is (not only different in scope but) not coextensive with anthropology *in time*. For it deals only with the development of man in societies, whereas anthropology includes in its definition the proto-anthropic period when *anthropos* was still non-social, whether he lived in herds like the chimpanzee, or alone like the male ourang-outang. (It has been well shown by Majewski that congregations—herds, flocks, packs, etc.—of animals are not *societies;* the characteristic of a society is differentiation of function. Bee hives, ant hills, may be called quasi-societies; but in their case the classes which perform distinct functions are morphologically different.) [Bury's note].

the sociological laws. In the view of which I have just spoken, history is permitted to be an end in itself; the reconstruction of the genetic process is an independent interest. For the purpose of the reconstruction, sociology, as well as physical geography, biology, psychology, is necessary; the sociologist and the historian play into each other's hands; but the object of the former is to establish generalizations; the aim of the latter is to trace in detail a singular causal sequence.

14. The success of the evolutional theory helped to discredit the assumption or at least the invocation of transcendent causes. Philosophically of course it is compatible with theism, but historians have for the most part desisted from invoking the naive conception of a "god in history" to explain historical movements. A historian may be a theist; but, so far as his work is concerned, this particular belief is otiose. Otherwise indeed (as was remarked above) history could not be a science; for with a *deus ex machina* who can be brought on the stage to solve difficulties scientific treatment is a farce. The transcendent element had appeared in a more subtle form through the influence of German philosophy. I noticed how Ranke is prone to refer to ideas as if they were transcendent existences manifesting themselves in the successive movements of history. It is intelligible to speak of certain ideas as controlling, in a given period—for instance, the idea of nationality; but from the scientific point of view, such ideas have no existence outside the minds of individuals and are purely psychical forces; and a historical "idea," if it does not exist in this form, is merely a way of expressing a synthesis of the historian himself.

15. From the more general influence of Darwinism on the place of history in the system of human knowledge, we may turn to the influence of the principles and methods by which Darwin explained development. It had been recognized even by ancient writers (such as Aristotle and Polybius) that physical circumstances (geography, climate) were factors conditioning the character and history of a race or society. In the sixteenth century Bodin emphasized these factors, and many subsequent writers took them into account. The investigations of Darwin, which brought them into the foreground, naturally promoted attempts to discover in them the chief key to the growth of civilization. Comte had expressly denounced the notion that the biological methods of Lamarck could be applied to social man. Buckle had taken account of natural influences, but had relegated them to a secondary plane, compared with psychological factors. But the Darwinian theory made it tempting to explain the development of civilization in terms of "adaptation to environment," "struggle for existence," "natural selection," "survival of the fittest," etc.[7]

7. Recently O. Seeck has applied these principles to the decline of Graeco-Roman civilization in his *Untergang* *der antiken Welt*, 2 vols., Berlin, 1895, 1901 [Bury's note].

The operation of these principles cannot be denied. Man is still an animal, subject to zoological as well as mechanical laws. The dark influence of heredity continues to be effective; and psychical development had [has?] begun in lower organic forms—perhaps with life itself. The organic and the social struggles for existence are manifestations of the same principle. Environment and climatic influence must be called in to explain not only the differentiation of the great racial sections of humanity, but also the varieties within these sub-species and, it may be, the assimilation of distinct varieties. Ritter's *Anthropogeography* has opened a useful line of research. But on the other hand, it is urged that, in explaining the course of history, these principles do not take us very far, and that it is chiefly for the primitive ultra-prehistoric period that they can account for human development. It may be said that, so far as concerns the actions and movements of men which are the subject of recorded history, physical environment has ceased to act mechanically, and in order to affect their actions must affect their wills first; and that this psychical character of the causal relations substantially alters the problem. The development of human societies, it may be argued, derives a completely new character from the dominance of the conscious psychical element, creating as it does new conditions (inventions, social institutions, etc.) which limit and counteract the operation of natural selection, and control and modify the influence of physical environment. Most thinkers agree now that the chief clues to the growth of civilization must be sought in the psychological sphere. Imitation, for instance, is a principle which is probably more significant for the explanation of human development than natural selection. Darwin himself was conscious that his principles had only a very restricted application in this sphere, as is evident from his cautious and tentative remarks in the 5th chapter of his *Descent of Man*. He applied natural selection to the growth of the intellectual faculties and of the fundamental social instincts, and also to the differentiation of the great races or "sub-species" (Caucasian, African, etc.) which differ in anthropological character.[8]

16. But if it is admitted that the governing factors which concern the student of social development are of the psychical order, the preliminary success of natural science in explaining organic evolution by general principles encouraged sociologists to hope that social evolution could be explained on general principles also. The idea of Condorcet, Buckle, and others, that history could be assimilated to the

8. Darwinian formulae may be suggestive by way of analogy. For instance, it is characteristic of social advance that a multitude of inventions, schemes and plans are framed which are never carried out, similar to, or designed for the same end as, an invention or plan which is actually adopted because it has chanced to suit the particular conditions of the hour (just as the works accomplished by an individual statesman, artist or savant are usually only a residue of the numerous projects conceived by his brain). This process in which so much abortive production occurs is analogous to elimination by natural selection [Bury's note].

natural sciences was powerfully reinforced, and the notion that the actual historical process, and every social movement involved in it, can be accounted for by sociological generalizations, so-called "laws," is still entertained by many, in one form or another. Dissentients from this view do not deny that the generalizations at which the sociologist arrives by the comparative method, by the analysis of social factors, and by psychological deduction may be an aid to the historian; but they deny that such uniformities are laws or contain an explanation of the phenomena. They can point to the element of chance coincidence. This element must have played a part in the events of organic evolution, but it has probably in a larger measure helped to determine events in social evolution. The collision of two unconnected sequences may be fraught with great results. The sudden death of a leader or a marriage without issue, to take simple cases, has again and again led to permanent political consequences. More emphasis is laid on the decisive actions of individuals, which cannot be reduced under generalizations and which deflect the course of events. If the significance of the individual will had been exaggerated to the neglect of the collective activity of the social aggregate before Condorcet, his doctrine tended to eliminate as unimportant the roles of prominent men, and by means of this elimination it was possible to found sociology. But it may be urged that it is patent on the face of history that its course has constantly been shaped and modified by the wills of individuals,[9] which are by no means always the expression of the collective will; and that the appearance of such personalities at the given moments is not a necessary outcome of the conditions and cannot be deduced. Nor is there any proof that, if such and such an individual had not been born, some one else would have arisen to do what he did. In some cases there is no reason to think that what happened need ever have come to pass. In other cases it seems evident that the actual change was inevitable, but in default of the man who initiated and guided it, it might have been postponed, and, postponed or not, might have borne a different cachet. I may illustrate by an instance which has just come under my notice. Modern painting was founded by Giotto, and the Italian expedition of Charles VIII, near the close of the sixteenth century, introduced into France the fashion of imitating Italian painters. But for Giotto and Charles VIII, French painting might have been very different. It may be said that "if Giotto had not appeared, some other great initiator would have played a role analogous to his, and that without Charles VIII there would have been the commerce with Italy, which in the long run would have sufficed to place France in relation with

9. We can ignore here the metaphysical question of freewill and determinism. For the character of the individual's brain depends in any case on ante-natal accidents and coincidences, and so it may be said that the role of individuals ultimately depends on chance—the accidental coincidence of independent sequences [Bury's note].

Italian artists. But the equivalent of Giotto might have been deferred for a century and probably would have been different; and commercial relations would have required ages to produce the *rayonnement imitatif* of Italian art in France, which the expedition of the royal adventurer provoked in a few years."[1] Instances furnished by political history are simply endless. Can we conjecture how events would have moved if the son of Philip of Macedon had been an incompetent? The aggressive action of Prussia which astonished Europe in 1740 determined the subsequent history of Germany; but that action was anything but inevitable; it depended entirely on the personality of Frederic the Great.

Hence it may be argued that the action of individual wills is a determining and disturbing factor, too significant and effective to allow history to be grasped by sociological formulae. The types and general forms of development which the sociologist attempts to disengage can only assist the historian in understanding the actual course of events. It is in the special domains of economic history and *Kulturgeschichte* which have come to the front in modern times that generalization is most fruitful, but even in these it may be contended that it furnishes only partial explanations.

17. The truth is that Darwinism itself offers the best illustration of the insufficiency of general laws to account for historical development. The part played by coincidence, and the part played by individuals—limited by, and related to general social conditions—render it impossible to deduce the course of the past history of man or to predict the future. But it is just the same with organic development. Darwin (or any other zoologist) could not deduce the actual course of evolution from general principles. Given an organism and its environment, he could not show that it must evolve into a more complex organism of a definite predetermined type; knowing what it has evolved into, he could attempt to discover and assign the determining causes. General principles do not account for a particular sequence; they embody necessary conditions; but there is a chapter of accidents too. It is the same in the case of history.

* * *

20. The men engaged in special historical researches—which have been pursued unremittingly for a century past, according to scientific methods of investigating evidence (initiated by Wolf, Niebuhr, Ranke)—have for the most part worked on the assumptions of genetic history or at least followed in the footsteps of those who fully grasped the genetic point of view. But their aim has been to collect and sift evidence, and determine particular facts; comparatively few have given serious thought to the lines of research and the speculations which have been considered in this paper. They

1. I have taken this example from G. Tarde's *La logique sociale* (p. 403), Paris, 1904, where it is used for quite a different purpose [Bury's note].

have been reasonably shy of compromising their work by applying theories which are still much debated and immature. But historiography cannot permanently evade the questions raised by these theories. One may venture to say that no historical change or transformation will be fully understood until it is explained how social environment acted on the individual components of the society (both immediately and by heredity), and how the individuals reacted upon their environment. The problem is psychical, but it is analogous to the main problem of the biologist.

QUESTIONS FOR STUDY, DISCUSSION, AND WRITING

1. What is the genetic idea of history? What does the last paragraph add to the definition given at the outset?
2. At the end of his first paragraph Bury sets forth a two-part organization—"applications of evolutional principles" and "rise of this view." Where is the point of transition between the two parts? How does he subdivide the first part? What is the central problem which concerns him in the second part?
3. Several times Bury defines the genetic idea of history by referring to another, antithetical idea of history. What name does he give the antithetical idea? What other names would be appropriate?
4. Carr's essay (below) was written a half-century later on more or less the same subject as Bury. Does Carr feel the same antithesis between these two ideas of history? What historical generalization about the writing of history would explain your answer to this question?
5. Would Beadle (pp. 1015–1030) agree with Bury that the problem he defines for the historian "is analogous to the main problem of the biologist"?

EDWARD HALLETT CARR
The Historian and His Facts[1]

What is history? Lest anyone think the question meaningless or superfluous, I will take as my text two passages relating respectively to the first and second incarnations of *The Cambridge Modern History*. Here is Acton in his report of October 1896 to the Syndics of the Cambridge University Press on the work which he had undertaken to edit:

It is a unique opportunity of recording, in the way most useful to the greatest number, the fullness of the knowledge which the nineteenth century is about to bequeath.... By the judicious division of labor we should be able to do it, and to bring home to every man the last document, and the ripest conclusions of international research.

1. Chapter I of *What is History?*, 1961.

Ultimate history we cannot have in this generation; but we can dispose of conventional history, and show the point we have reached on the road from one to the other, now that all information is within reach, and every problem has become capable of solution.[2]

And almost exactly sixty years later Professor Sir George Clark, in his general introduction to the second *Cambridge Modern History*, commented on this belief of Acton and his collaborators that it would one day be possible to produce "ultimate history," and went on:

Historians of a later generation do not look forward to any such prospect. They expect their work to be superseded again and again. They consider that knowledge of the past has come down through one or more human minds, has been "processed" by them, and therefore cannot consist of elemental and impersonal atoms which nothing can alter.... The exploration seems to be endless, and some impatient scholars take refuge in scepticism, or at least in the doctrine that, since all historical judgments involve persons and points of view, one is as good as another and there is no "objective" historical truth.[3]

Where the pundits contradict each other so flagrantly the field is open to enquiry. I hope that I am sufficiently up-to-date to recognize that anything written in the 1890's must be nonsense. But I am not yet advanced enough to be committed to the view that anything written in the 1950's necessarily makes sense. Indeed, it may already have occurred to you that this enquiry is liable to stray into something even broader than the nature of history. The clash between Acton and Sir George Clark is a reflection of the change in our total outlook on society over the interval between these two pronouncements. Acton speaks out of the positive belief, the clear-eyed self-confidence of the later Victorian age; Sir George Clark echoes the bewilderment and distracted scepticism of the beat generation. When we attempt to answer the question, What is history?, our answer, consciously or unconsciously, reflects our own position in time, and forms part of our answer to the broader question, what view we take of the society in which we live. I have no fear that my subject may, on closer inspection, seem trivial. I am afraid only that I may seem presumptuous to have broached a question so vast and so important.

The nineteenth century was a great age for facts. "What I want," said Mr. Gradgrind in *Hard Times*, "is Facts.... Facts alone are wanted in life." Nineteenth-century historians on the whole agreed with him. When Ranke in the 1830's, in legitimate protest against moralizing history, remarked that the task of the historian was "simply to show how it really was [*wie es eigentlich gewesen*]" this not very profound aphorism had an astonishing success. Three

2. *The Cambridge Modern History: Its Origin, Authorship and Production* (Cambridge University Press, 1907), pp. 10-12 [This and the following footnotes are Carr's].

3. *The New Cambridge Modern History*, I (Cambridge University Press, 1957), pp. xxiv-xxv.

generations of German, British, and even French historians marched into battle intoning the magic words, *"Wie es eigentlich gewesen"* like an incantation—designed, like most incantations, to save them from the tiresome obligation to think for themselves. The Positivists, anxious to stake out their claim for history as a science, contributed the weight of their influence to this cult of facts. First ascertain the facts, said the positivists, then draw your conclusions from them. In Great Britain, this view of history fitted in perfectly with the empiricist tradition which was the dominant strain in British philosophy from Locke to Bertrand Russell. The empirical theory of knowledge presupposes a complete separation between subject and object. Facts, like sense-impressions, impinge on the observer from outside, and are independent of his consciousness. The process of reception is passive: having received the data, he then acts on them. *The Shorter Oxford English Dictionary*, a useful but tendentious work of the empirical school, clearly marks the separateness of the two processes by defining a fact as "a datum of experience as distinct from conclusions." This is what may be called the common-sense view of history. History consists of a corpus of ascertained facts. The facts are available to the historian in documents, inscriptions, and so on, like fish on the fishmonger's slab. The historian collects them, takes them home, and cooks and serves them in whatever style appeals to him. Acton, whose culinary tastes were austere, wanted them served plain. In his letter of instructions to contributors to the first *Cambridge Modern History* he announced the requirement "that our Waterloo must be one that satisfies French and English, German and Dutch alike; that nobody can tell, without examining the list of authors where the Bishop of Oxford laid down the pen, and whether Fairbairn or Gasquet, Liebermann or Harrison took it up."[4] Even Sir George Clark, critical as he was of Acton's attitude, himself contrasted the "hard core of facts" in history with the "surrounding pulp of disputable interpretation"[5]—forgetting perhaps that the pulpy part of the fruit is more rewarding than the hard core. First get your facts straight, then plunge at your peril into the shifting sands of interpretation—that is the ultimate wisdom of the empirical, common-sense school of history. It recalls the favorite dictum of the great liberal journalist C. P. Scott: "Facts are sacred, opinion is free."

Now this clearly will not do. I shall not embark on a philosophical discussion of the nature of our knowledge of the past. Let us assume for present purposes that the fact that Caesar crossed the Rubicon and the fact that there is a table in the middle of the room are facts of the same or of a comparable order, that both these facts enter our consciousness in the same or in a comparable

4. Acton: *Lectures on Modern History* (London: Macmillan & Co., 1906), p. 318.

5. Quoted in *The Listener* (June 19, 1952), p. 992.

manner, and that both have the same objective character in relation to the person who knows them. But, even on this bold and not very plausible assumption, our argument at once runs into the difficulty that not all facts about the past are historical facts, or are treated as such by the historian. What is the criterion which distinguishes the facts of history from other facts about the past?

What is a historical fact? This is a crucial question into which we must look a little more closely. According to the common-sense view, there are certain basic facts which are the same for all historians and which form, so to speak, the backbone of history—the fact, for example, that the Battle of Hastings was fought in 1066. But this view calls for two observations. In the first place, it is not with facts like these that the historian is primarily concerned. It is no doubt important to know that the great battle was fought in 1066 and not in 1065 or 1067, and that it was fought at Hastings and not at Eastbourne or Brighton. The historian must not get these things wrong. But when points of this kind are raised, I am reminded of Housman's remark that "accuracy is a duty, not a virtue."[6] To praise a historian for his accuracy is like praising an architect for using well-seasoned timber or properly mixed concrete in his building. It is a necessary condition of his work, but not his essential function. It is precisely for matters of this kind that the historian is entitled to rely on what have been called the "auxiliary sciences" of history—archaeology, epigraphy, numismatics, chronology, and so forth. The historian is not required to have the special skills which enable the expert to determine the origin and period of a fragment of pottery or marble, or decipher an obscure inscription, or to make the elaborate astronomical calculations necessary to establish a precise date. These so-called basic facts which are the same for all historians commonly belong to the category of the raw materials of the historian rather than of history itself. The second observation is that the necessity to establish these basic facts rests not on any quality in the facts themselves, but on an *a priori* decision of the historian. In spite of C. P. Scott's motto, every journalist knows today that the most effective way to influence opinion is by the selection and arrangement of the appropriate facts. It used to be said that facts speak for themselves. This is, of course, untrue. The facts speak only when the historian calls on them: It is he who decides to which facts to give the floor, and in what order or context. It was, I think, one of Pirandello's characters who said that a fact is like a sack—it won't stand up till you've put something in it. The only reason why we are interested to know that the battle was fought at Hastings in 1066 is that historians regard it as a major historical event. It is

6. M. Manilius: *Astronomicon: Liber Primus*, 2nd ed. (Cambridge University Press, 1937), p. 87.

the historian who has decided for his own reasons that Caesar's crossing of that petty stream, the Rubicon, is a fact of history, whereas the crossing of the Rubicon by millions of other people before or since interests nobody at all. The fact that you arrived in this building half an hour ago on foot, or on a bicycle, or in a car, is just as much a fact about the past as the fact that Caesar crossed the Rubicon. But it will probably be ignored by historians. Professor Talcott Parsons once called science "a selective system of cognitive orientations to reality."[7] It might perhaps have been put more simply. But history is, among other things, that. The historian is necessarily selective. The belief in a hard core of historical facts existing objectively and independently of the interpretation of the historian is a preposterous fallacy, but one which it is very hard to eradicate.

Let us take a look at the process by which a mere fact about the past is transformed into a fact of history. At Stalybridge Wakes in 1850, a vendor of gingerbread, as the result of some petty dispute, was deliberately kicked to death by an angry mob. Is this a fact of history? A year ago I should unhesitatingly have said "no." It was recorded by an eyewitness in some little-known memoirs;[8] but I had never seen it judged worthy of mention by any historian. A year ago Dr. Kitson Clark cited it in his Ford lectures in Oxford.[9] Does this make it into a historical fact? Not, I think, yet. Its present status, I suggest, is that it has been proposed for membership of the select club of historical facts. It now awaits a seconder and sponsors. It may be that in the course of the next few years we shall see this fact appearing first in footnotes, then in the text, of articles and books about nineteenth-century England, and that in twenty or thirty years' time it may be a well established historical fact. Alternatively, nobody may take it up, in which case it will relapse into the limbo of unhistorical facts about the past from which Dr. Kitson Clark has gallantly attempted to rescue it. What will decide which of these two things will happen? It will depend, I think, on whether the thesis or interpretation in support of which Dr. Kitson Clark cited this incident is accepted by other historians as valid and significant. Its status as a historical fact will turn on a question of interpretation. This element of interpretation enters into every fact of history.

May I be allowed a personal reminiscence? When I studied ancient history in this university many years ago, I had as a special subject "Greece in the period of the Perisan Wars." I collected fifteen or twenty volumes on my shelves and took it for granted

7. Talcott Parsons and Edward A. Shils: *Toward a General Theory of Action*, 3rd ed. (Cambridge, Mass.: Harvard University Press, 1954), p. 167.

8. Lord George Sanger: *Seventy Years*

a Showman (London: J. M. Dent & Sons, 1926), pp. 188-9.

9. These will shortly be published under the title *The Making of Victorian England*.

that there, recorded in these volumes, I had all the facts relating to my subject. Let us assume—it was very nearly true—that those volumes contained all the facts about it that were then known, or could be known. It never occurred to me to enquire by what accident or process of attrition that minute selection of facts, out of all the myriad facts that must have once been known to somebody, had survived to become *the* facts of history. I suspect that even today one of the fascinations of ancient and mediaeval history is that it gives us the illusion of having all the facts at our disposal within a manageable compass: the nagging distinction between the facts of history and other facts about the past vanishes because the few known facts are all facts of history. As Bury, who had worked in both periods, said "the records of ancient and mediaeval history are starred with lacunae."[1] History has been called an enormous jig-saw with a lot of missing parts. But the main trouble does not consist of the lacunae. Our picture of Greece in the fifth century B.C. is defective not primarily because so many of the bits have been accidentally lost, but because it is, by and large, the picture formed by a tiny group of people in the city of Athens. We know a lot about what fifth-century Greece looked like to an Athenian citizen; but hardly anything about what it looked like to a Spartan, a Corinthian, or a Theban—not to mention a Persian, or a slave or other non-citizen resident in Athens. Our picture has been preselected and predetermined for us, not so much by accident as by people who were consciously or unconsciously imbued with a particular view and thought the facts which supported that view worth preserving. In the same way, when I read in a modern history of the Middle Ages that the people of the Middle Ages were deeply concerned with religion, I wonder how we know this, and whether it is true. What we know as the facts of mediaeval history have almost all been selected for us by generations of chroniclers who were professionally occupied in the theory and practice of religion, and who therefore thought it supremely important, and recorded everything relating to it, and not much else. The picture of the Russian peasant as devoutly religious was destroyed by the revolution of 1917. The picture of mediaeval man as devoutly religious, whether true or not, is indestructible, because nearly all the known facts about him were preselected for us by people who believed it, and wanted others to believe it, and a mass of other facts, in which we might possibly have found evidence to the contrary, has been lost beyond recall. The dead hand of vanished generations of historians, scribes, and chroniclers has determined beyond the possibility of appeal the pattern of the past. "The history we read," writes Professor Barraclough, himself trained as a mediaevalist, "though based on facts, is, strictly speak-

1. John Bagnell Bury: *Selected Essays* (Cambridge University Press, 1930, p. 52.)

ing, not factual at all, but a series of accepted judgments."[2]

But let us turn to the different, but equally grave, plight of the modern historian. The ancient or mediaeval historian may be grateful for the vast winnowing process which, over the years, has put at his disposal a manageable corpus of historical facts. As Lytton Strachey said in his mischievous way, "ignorance is the first requisite of the historian, ignorance which simplifies and clarifies, which selects and omits."[3] When I am tempted, as I sometimes am, to envy the extreme competence of colleagues engaged in writing ancient or mediaeval history, I find consolation in the reflection that they are so competent mainly because they are so ignorant of their subject. The modern historian enjoys none of the advantages of this built-in ignorance. He must cultivate this necessary ignorance for himself—the more so the nearer he comes to his own times. He has the dual task of discovering the few significant facts and turning them into facts of history, and of discarding the many insignificant facts as unhistorical. But this is the very converse of the nineteenth-century heresy that history consists of the compilation of a maximum number of irrefutable and objective facts. Anyone who succumbs to this heresy will either have to give up history as a bad job, and take to stamp-collecting or some other form of antiquarianism, or end in a madhouse. It is this heresy, which during the past hundred years has had such devastating effects on the modern historian, producing in Germany, in Great Britain, and in the United States a vast and growing mass of dry-as-dust factual histories, of minutely specialized monographs, of would-be historians knowing more and more about less and less, sunk without trace in an ocean of facts. It was, I suspect, this heresy—rather than the alleged conflict between liberal and Catholic loyalties—which frustrated Acton as a historian. In an early essay he said of his teacher Döllinger: "He would not write with imperfect materials, and to him the materials were always imperfect."[4] Acton was surely here pronouncing an anticipatory verdict on himself, on that strange phenomenon of a historian whom many would regard as the most distinguished occupant the Regius Chair of Modern History in this university has ever had—but who wrote no history. And Acton wrote his own epitaph in the introductory note to the first volume of the *Cambridge Modern History*, published just after his death, when he lamented that the requirements pressing on the historian "threaten to turn him from a man of letters into

2. Geoffrey Barraclough: *History in a Changing World* (London; Basil Blackwell & Mott, 1955), p. 14.

3. Lytton Strachey: Preface to *Eminent Victorians*.

4. Quoted in George P. Gooch: *History and Historians in the Nineteenth Century* (London: Longmans, Green & Company, 1952), p. 385. Later Acton said of Döllinger that "it was given him to form his philosophy of history on the largest induction ever available to man" (*History of Freedom and Other Essays* [London: Macmillan & Co., 1907], p. 435).

the compiler of an encyclopedia."[5] Something had gone wrong. What had gone wrong was the belief in this untiring and unending accumulation of hard facts as the foundation of history, the belief that facts speak for themselves and that we cannot have too many facts, a belief at that time so unquestioning that few historians then thought it necessary—and some still think it unnecessary today —to ask themselves the question: What is history?

The nineteenth-century fetishism of facts was completed and justified by a fetishism of documents. The documents were the Ark of the Covenant in the temple of facts. The reverent historian approached them with bowed head and spoke of them in awed tones. If you find it in the documents, it is so. But what, when we get down to it, do these documents—the decrees, the treaties, the rent-rolls, the blue books, the official correspondence, the private letters and diaries—tell us? No document can tell us more than what the author of the document thought—what he thought had happened, what he thought ought to happen or would happen, or perhaps only what he wanted others to think he thought, or even only what he himself thought he thought. None of this means anything until the historian has got to work on it and deciphered it. The facts, whether found in documents or not, have still to be processed by the historian before he can make any use of them: the use he makes of them is, if I may put it that way, the processing process.

Let me illustrate what I am trying to say by an example which I happen to know well. When Gustav Stresemann, the Foreign Minister of the Weimar Republic, died in 1929, he left behind him an enormous mass—30 boxes full—of papers, official, semi-official, and private, nearly all relating to the six years of his tenure of office as Foreign Minister. His friends and relatives naturally thought that a monument should be raised to the memory of so great a man. His faithful secretary Bernhardt got to work; and within three years there appeared three massive volumes, of some 600 pages each, of selected documents from the 300 boxes, with the impressive title *Stresemann's Vermächtnis*.[6] In the ordinary way the documents themselves would have moldered away in some cellar or attic and disappeared for ever; or perhaps in a hundred years or so some curious scholar would have come upon them and set out to compare them with Bernhardt's text. What happened was far more dramatic. In 1945 the documents fell into the hands of the British and the American governments, who photographed the lot and put the photostats at the disposal of scholars in the Public Record Office in London and in the National Archives in Washington, so that, if we have sufficient patience and curiosity,

5. *The Cambridge Modern History*, I (1902), p. 4.
6. *Stresemann's Legacy.*

we can discover exactly what Bernhardt did. What he did was neither very unusual nor very shocking. When Stresemann died, his Western policy seemed to have been crowned with a series of brilliant successes—Locarno, the admission of Germany to the League of Nations, the Dawes and Young plans and the American loans, the withdrawal of allied occupation armies from the Rhineland. This seemed the important and rewarding part of Stresemann's foreign policy; and it was not unnatural that it should have been over-represented in Bernhardt's selection of documents. Stresemann's Eastern policy, on the other hand, his relations with the Soviet Union, seemed to have led nowhere in particular; and, since masses of documents about negotiations which yielded only trivial results were not very interesting and added nothing to Stresemann's reputation, the process of selection could be more rigorous. Stresemann in fact devoted a far more constant and anxious attention to relations with the Soviet Union, and they played a far larger part in his foreign policy as a whole, than the reader of the Bernhardt selection would surmise. But the Bernhardt volumes compare favorably, I suspect, with many published collections of documents on which the ordinary historian implicitly relies.

This is not the end of my story. Shortly after the publication of Bernhardt's volumes, Hitler came into power. Stresemann's name was consigned to oblivion in Germany, and the volumes disappeared from circulation: many, perhaps most, of the copies must have been destroyed. Today *Stresemanns Vermächtnis* is a rather rare book. But in the West Stresemann's reputation stood high. In 1935 an English publisher brought out an abbreviated translation of Bernhardt's work—a selection from Bernhardt's selection; perhaps one third of the original was omitted. Sutton, a well-known translator from the German, did his job competently and well. The English version, he explained in the preface, was "slightly condensed, but only by the omission of a certain amount of what, it was felt, was more ephemeral matter . . . of little interest to English readers or students."[7] This again is natural enough. But the result is that Stresemann's Eastern policy, already under-represented in Bernhardt, recedes still further from view, and the Soviet Union appears in Sutton's volumes merely as an occasional and rather unwelcome intruder in Stresemann's predominantly Western foreign policy. Yet it is safe to say that, for all except a few specialists, Sutton and not Bernhardt—and still less the documents themselves—represents for the Western world the authentic voice of Stresemann. Had the documents perished in 1945 in the bombing, and had the remaining Bernhardt volumes disappeared, the authenticity and authority of Sutton would never have been questioned. Many printed collections

---

7. *Gustav Stresemann: His Diaries, Letters, and Papers* (London: Macmillan & Co.; 1935), I.

of documents gratefully accepted by historians in default of the originals rest on no securer basis than this.

But I want to carry the story one step further. Let us forget about Bernhardt and Sutton, and be thankful that we can, if we choose, consult the authentic papers of a leading participant in some important events of recent European history. What do hte papers tell us? Among other things they contain records of some hundreds of Stresemann's conversations with the Soviet ambassador in Berlin and of a score or so with Chicherin.[8] These records have one feature in common. They depict Stresemann as having the lion's share of the conversations and reveal his arguments as invariably well put and cogent, while those of his partner are for the most part scanty, confused, and unconvincing. This is a familiar characteristic of all records of diplomatic conversations. The documents do not tell us what happened, but only what Stresemann thought had happened. It was not Sutton or Bernhardt, but Stresemann himself, who started the process of selection. And, if we had, say, Chicherin's records of these same conversations, we should still learn from them only what Chicherin thought, and what really happened would still have to be reconstructed in the mind of the historian. Of course, facts and documents are essential to the historian. But do not make a fetish of them. They do not by themselves constitute history; they provide in themselves no ready-made answer to this tiresome question: What is history?

At this point I should like to say a few words on the question of why nineteenth-century historians were generally indifferent to the philosophy of history. The term was invented by Voltaire, and has since been used in different senses; but I shall take it to mean, if I use it at all, our answer to the question: What is history? The nineteenth century was, for the intellectuals of Western Europe, a comfortable period exuding confidence and optimism. The facts were on the whole satisfactory; and the inclination to ask and answer awkward questions about them was correspondingly weak. Ranke piously believed that divine providence would take care of the meaning of history if he took care of the facts; and Burckhardt with a more modern touch of cynicism observed that "we are not initiated into the purposes of the eternal wisdom." Professor Butterfield as late as 1931 noted with apparent satisfaction that "historians have reflected little upon the nature of things and even the nature of their own subject."[9] But my predecessor in these lectures, Dr. A. L. Rowse, more justly critical, wrote of Sir Winston Churchill's *The World Crisis*—his book about the First World War— that, while it matched Trotsky's *History of the Russian Revolution* in personality, vividness, and vitality, it was inferior in one respect: it

---

8. Soviet foreign minister 1918–28 [Editor's note].

9. Herbert Butterfield: *The Whig In-*

terpretation of History (London: George Bell & Sons, 1931), p. 67.

had "no philosophy of history behind it."[1] British historians refused to be drawn, not because they believed that history had no meaning, but because they believed that its meaning was implicit and self-evident. The liberal nineteenth-century view of history had a close affinity with the economic doctrine of *laissez-faire*—also the product of a serene and self-confident outlook on the world. Let everyone get on with his particular job, and the hidden hand would take care of the universal harmony. The facts of history were themselves a demonstration of the supreme fact of a beneficent and apparently infinite progress towards higher things. This was the age of innocence, and historians walked in the Garden of Eden, without a scrap of philosophy to cover them, naked and unashamed before the god of history. Since then, we have known Sin and experienced a Fall; and those historians who today pretend to dispense with a philosophy of history are merely trying, vainly and self-consciously, like members of a nudist colony, to recreate the Garden of Eden in their garden suburb. Today the awkward question can no longer be evaded. * * *

During the past fifty years a good deal of serious work has been done on the question: What is history? It was from Germany, the country which was to do so much to upset the comfortable reign of nineteenth-century liberalism, that the first challenge came in the 1880's and 1890's to the doctrine of the primacy and autonomy of facts in history. The philosophers who made the challenge are now little more than names: Dilthey is the only one of them who has recently received some belated recognition in Great Britain. Before the turn of the century, prosperity and confidence were still too great in this country for any attention to be paid to heretics who attacked the cult of facts. But early in the new century, the torch passed to Italy, where Croce began to propound a philosophy of history which obviously owed much to German masters. All history is "contemporary history," declared Croce,[2] meaning that history consists essentially in seeing the past through the eyes of the present and in the light of its problems, and that the main work of the historian is not to record, but to evaluate; for, if he does not evaluate, how can he know what is worth recording? In 1910 the American philosopher, Carl Becker, argued in deliberately provocative language that "the facts of history do not exist for any historian till he creates them."[3] These challenges were for the moment little noticed. It was only after 1920 that Croce began to have a consid-

---

1. Alfred L. Rowse: *The End of an Epoch* (London: Macmillan & Co., 1947), pp. 282-3.
2. The context of this celebrated aphorism is as follows: "The practical requirements which underlie every historical judgment give to all history the character of 'contemporary history,' because, however remote in time events

thus recounted may seem to be, the history in reality refers to present needs and present situations wherein those events vibrate" (Benedetto Croce: *History as the Story of Liberty* [London: George Allen & Unwin, 1941], p. 19).
3. *Atlantic Monthly* (October 1928), p. 528.

erable vogue in France and Great Britain. This was not perhaps because Croce was a subtler thinker or a better stylist than his German predecessors, but because, after the First World War, the facts seemed to smile on us less propitiously than in the years before 1914, and we were therefore more accessible to a philosophy which sought to diminish their prestige. Croce was an important influence on the Oxford philosopher and historian Collingwood, the only British thinker in the present century who has made a serious contribution to the philosophy of history. He did not live to write the systematic treatise he had planned; but his published and unpublished papers on the subject were collected after his death in a volume entitled *The Idea of History*, which appeared in 1945.

The views of Collingwood can be summarized as follows. The philosophy of history is concerned neither with "the past by itself" nor with "the historian's thought about it by itself," but with "the two things in their mutual relations." (This dictum reflects the two current meanings of the word "history"—the enquiry conducted by the historian and the series of past events into which he enquires.) "The past which a historian studies is not a dead past, but a past which in some sense is still living in the present." But a past act is dead, *i.e.* meaningless to the historian, unless he can understand the thought that lay behind it. Hence "all history is the history of thought," and "history is the re-enactment in the historian's mind of the thought whose history he is studying." The reconstitution of the past in the historian's mind is dependent on empirical evidence. But it is not in itself an empirical process, and cannot consist in a mere recital of facts. On the contrary, the process of reconstitution governs the selection and interpretation of the facts: this, indeed, is what makes them historical facts. "History," says Professor Oakeshott, who on this point stands near to Collingwood, "is the historian's experience. It is 'made' by nobody save the historian: to write history is the only way of making it."[4]

This searching critique, though it may call for some serious reservations, brings to light certain neglected truths.

In the first place, the facts of history never come to us "pure," since they do not and cannot exist in a pure form: they are always refracted through the mind of the recorder. It follows that when we take up a work of history, our first concern should be not with the facts which it contains but with the historian who wrote it. Let me take as an example the great historian in whose honor and in whose name these lectures were founded. Trevelyan, as he tells us in his autobiography, was "brought up at home on a somewhat exuberantly Whig tradition"[5]; and he would not, I hope, disclaim the title if I described him as the last and not the least of the great English

---

4. Michael Oakeshott: *Experience and Its Modes* (Cambridge University Press, 1933), p. 99.

5. G. M. Trevelyan: *An Autobiography* (London: Longmans, Green & Company, 1949), p. 11.

liberal historians of the Whig tradition. It is not for nothing that he traces back his family tree, through the great Whig historian George Otto Trevelyan, to Macaulay, incomparably the greatest of the Whig historians. Dr. Trevelyan's finest and maturest work *England under Queen Anne* was written against that background, and will yield its full meaning and significance to the reader only when read against that background. The author, indeed, leaves the reader with no excuse for failing to do so. For if, following the technique of connoisseurs of detective novels, you read the end first, you will find on the last few pages of the third volume the best summary known to me of what is nowadays called the Whig interpretation of history; and you will see that what Trevelyan is trying to do is to investigate the origin and development of the Whig tradition, and to roof it fairly and squarely in the years after the death of its founder, William III. Though this is not, perhaps, the only conceivable interpretation of the events of Queen Anne's reign, it is a valid and, in Trevelyan's hands, a fruitful interpretation. But, in order to appreciate it at its full value, you have to understand what the historian is doing. For if, as Collingwood says, the historian must re-enact in thought what has gone on in the mind of his *dramatis personae*, so the reader in his turn must re-enact what goes on in the mind of the historian. Study the historian before you begin to study the facts. This is, after all, not very abstruse. It is what is already done by the intelligent undergraduate who, when recommended to read a work by that great scholar Jones of St. Jude's, goes round to a friend at St. Jude's to ask what sort of chap Jones is, and what bees he has in his bonnet. When you read a work of history, always listen out for the buzzing. If you can detect none, either you are tone deaf or your historian is a dull dog. The facts are really not at all like fish on the fishmonger's slab. They are like fish swimming about in a vast and sometimes inaccessible ocean; and what the historian catches will depend partly on chance, but mainly on what part of the ocean he chooses to fish in and what tackle he chooses to use—these two factors being, of course, determined by the kind of fish he wants to catch. By and large, the historian will get the kind of facts he wants. History means interpretation. Indeed, if, standing Sir George Clark on his head, I were to call history "a hard core of interpretation surrounded by a pulp of disputable facts," my statement would, no doubt, be one-sided and misleading, but no more so, I venture to think, than the original dictum.

The second point is the more familiar one of the historian's need of imaginative understanding for the minds of the people with whom he is dealing, for the thought behind their acts: I say "imaginative understanding," not "sympathy," lest sympathy should be supposed to imply agreement. The nineteenth century was weak in

mediaeval history, because it was too much repelled by the superstitious beliefs of the Middle Ages and by the barbarities which
they inspired, to have any imaginative understanding of mediaeval
people. Or take Burckhardt's censorious remark about the Thirty
Years' War: "It is scandalous for a creed, no matter whether it is
Catholic or Protestant, to place its salvation above the integrity of
the nation."[6] It was extremely difficult for a nineteenth-century liberal historian, brought up to believe that it is right and praiseworthy to kill in defense of one's country, but wicked and wrong-
headed to kill in defense of one's religion, to enter into the state of
mind of those who fought the Thirty Years' War. This difficulty is
particularly acute in the field in which I am now working. Much of
what has been written in English-speaking countries in the last ten
years about the Soviet Union, and in the Soviet Union about the
English-speaking countries, has been vitiated by this inability to
achieve even the most elementary measure of imaginative understanding of what goes on in the mind of the other party, so that the
words and actions of the other are always made to appear malign,
senseless, or hypocritical. History cannot be written unless the historian can achieve some kind of contact with the mind of those about
whom he is writing.

The third point is that we can view the past, and achieve our
understanding of the past, only through the eyes of the present.
The historian is of his own age, and is bound to it by the conditions
of human existence. The very words which he uses—words like
democracy, empire, war, revolution—have current connotations
from which he cannot divorce them. Ancient historians have taken
to using words like *polis* and *plebs* in the original, just in order to
show that they have not fallen into this trap. This does not help
them. They, too, live in the present, and cannot cheat themselves
into the past by using unfamiliar or obsolete words, any more than
they would become better Greek or Roman historians if they delivered their lectures in a *chlamys* or a *toga*. The names by which successive French historians have described the Parisian crowds which
played so prominent a role in the French revolution—*les sans-
culottes, le peuple, la canaille, les bras-nus*—are all, for those who
know the rules of the game, manifestos of a political affiliation and
of a particular interpretation. Yet the historian is obliged to
choose: the use of language forbids him to be neutral. Nor is it a
matter of words alone. Over the past hundred years the changed
balance of power in Europe has reversed the attitude of British historians to Frederick the Great. The changed balance of power within
the Christian churches between Catholicism and Protestantism has
profoundly altered their attitude to such figures as Loyola, Luther,

---

6. Jacob Burckhardt: *Judgments on History and Historians* (London: S. J.   Reginald Saunders & Company, 1958), p. 179.

and Cromwell. It requires only a superficial knowledge of the work of French historians of the last forty years on the French revolution to recognize how deeply it has been affected by the Russian revolution of 1917. The historian belongs not to the past but to the present. Professor Trevor-Roper tells us that the historian "ought to love the past."[7] This is a dubious injunction. To love the past may easily be an expression of the nostalgic romanticism of old men and old societies, a symptom of loss of faith and interest in the present or future.[8] *Cliché* for *cliché*, I should prefer the one about freeing oneself from "the dead hand of the past." The function of the historian is neither to love the past nor to emancipate himself from the past, but to master and understand it as the key to the understanding of the present.

If, however, these are some of the sights of what I may call the Collingwood view of history, it is time to consider some of the dangers. The emphasis on the role of the historian in the making of history tends, if pressed to its logical conclusion, to rule out any objective history at all: history is what the historian makes. Collingwood seems indeed, at one moment, in an unpublished note quoted by his editor, to have reached this conclusion:

St. Augustine looked at history from the point of view of the early Christian; Tillemont, from that of a seventeenth-century Frenchman; Gibbon, from that of an eighteenth-century Englishman; Mommsen, from that of a nineteenth-century German. There is no point in asking which was the right point of view. Each was the only one possible for the man who adopted it.[9]

This amounts to total scepticism, like Froude's remark that history is "a child's box of letters with which we can spell any word we please."[1] Collingwood, in his reaction against "scissors-and-paste history," against the view of history as a mere compilation of facts, comes perilously near to treating history as something spun out of the human brain, and leads back to the conclusion referred to by Sir George Clark in the passage which I quoted earlier, that "there is no 'objective' historical truth." In place of the theory that history has no meaning, we are offered here the theory of an infinity of meanings, none any more right than any other—which comes to much the same thing. The second theory is surely as untenable as the first. It does not follow that, because a mountain appears to take on different shapes from different angles of vision, it has objectively either no shape at all or an infinity of shapes. It does not follow

7. Introduction to Burckhardt: *Judgments on History and Historians,* p. 17.

8. Compare Nietzsche's view of history: "To old age belongs the old man's business of looking back and casting up his accounts, of seeking consolation in the memories of the past, in historical culture" (*Thoughts Out of Season* [London: Macmillan & Co., 1909], II, pp. 65-6).

9. Robin G. Collingwood: *The Idea of History* (London: Oxford University Press; 1946), p. xii.

1. James Anthony Froude: *Short Studies on Great Subjects* (1894), I, p. 21.

that, because interpretation plays a necessary part in establishing the facts of history, and because no existing interpretation is wholly objective, one interpretation is as good as another, and the facts of history are in principle not amenable to objective interpretation. I shall have to consider at a later stage what exactly is meant by objectivity in history.

But a still greater danger lurks in the Collingwood hypothesis. If the historian necessarily looks at his period of history through the eyes of his own time, and studies the problems of the past as a key to those of the present, will he not fall into a purely pragmatic view of the facts, and maintain that the criterion of a right interpretation is its suitability to some present purpose? On this hypothesis, the facts of history are nothing, interpretation is everything. Nietzsche had already enunciated the principle: "The falseness of an opinion is not for us any objection to it. . . . The question is how far it is life-furthering, life-preserving, species-preserving, perhaps species-creating."[2] The American pragmatists moved, less explicitly and less wholeheartedly, along the same line. Knowledge is knowledge for some purpose. The validity of the knowledge depends on the validity of the purpose. But, even where no such theory has been professed, the practice has often been no less disquieting. In my own field of study, I have seen too many examples of extravagant interpretation riding roughshod over facts, not to be impressed with the reality of this danger. It is not surprising that perusal of some of the more extreme products of Soviet and anti-Soviet schools of historiography should sometimes breed a certain nostalgia for that illusory nineteenth-century heaven of purely factual history.

How then, in the middle of the twentieth century, are we to define the obligation of the historian to his facts? I trust that I have spent a sufficient number of hours in recent years chasing and perusing documents, and stuffing my historical narrative with properly footnoted facts, to escape the imputation of treating facts and documents too cavalierly. The duty of the historian to respect his facts is not exhausted by the obligation to see that his facts are accurate. He must seek to bring into the picture all known or knowable facts relevant, in one sense or another, to the theme on which he is engaged and to the interpretation proposed. If he seeks to depict the Victorian Englishman as a moral and rational being, he must not forget what happened at Stalybridge Wakes in 1850. But this, in turn, does not mean that he can eliminate interpretation, which is the life-blood of history. Laymen—that is to say, non-academic friends or friends from other academic disciplines—sometimes ask me how the historian goes to work when he writes history. The commonest assumption appears to be that the historian divides his work into two sharply distinguishable phases or periods. First, he

2. Froude: *Beyond Good and Evil*, Ch. i.

spends a long preliminary period reading his source and filling his notebooks with facts: then, when this is over, he puts away his sources, takes out his notebooks, and writes his book from beginning to end. This is to me an unconvincing and unplausible picture. For myself, as soon as I have got going on a few of what I take to be the capital sources, the itch becomes too strong and I begin to write— not necessarily at the beginning, but somewhere, anywhere. Thereafter, reading and writing go on simultaneously. The writing is added to, subtracted from, re-shaped, cancelled, as I go on reading. The reading is guided and directed and made fruitful by the writing: the more I write, the more I know what I am looking for, the better I understand the significance and relevance of what I find. Some historians probably do all this preliminary writing in their head without using pen, paper, or typewriter, just as some people play chess in their heads without recourse to board and chess-men: this is a talent which I envy, but cannot emulate. But I am convinced that, for any historian worth the name, the two processes of what economists call "input" and "output" go on simultaneously and are, in practice, parts of a single process. If you try to separate them, or to give one priority over the other, you fall into one of two heresies. Either you write scissors-and-paste history without meaning or significance; or you write propaganda or historical fiction, and merely use facts of the past to embroider a kind of writing which has nothing to do with history.

Our examination of the relation of the historian to the facts of history finds us, therefore, in an apparently precarious situation, navigating delicately between the Scylla of an untenable theory of history as an objective compilation of facts, of the unqualified primacy of fact over interpretation, and the Charybdis of an equally untenable theory of history as the subjective product of the mind of the historian who establishes the facts of history and masters them through the process of interpretation, between a view of history having the center of gravity in the past and the view having the center of gravity in the present. But our situation is less precarious than it seems. We shall encounter the same dichotomy of fact and interpretation again in these lectures in other guises—the particular and the general, the empirical and the theoretical, the objective and the subjective. The predicament of the historian is a reflection of the nature of man. Man, except perhaps in earliest infancy and in extreme old age, is not totally involved in his environment and unconditionally subject to it. On the other hand, he is never totally independent of it and its unconditional master. The relation of man to his environment is the relation of the historian to his theme. The historian is neither the humble slave, nor the tyrannical master, of his facts. The relation between the historian and his facts is one of equality, of give-and-take. As any working historian knows, if he stops to reflect what he is doing as he thinks and writes, the historian is engaged on a continuous process of molding his facts to his interpretation and his interpretation to his facts. It is impossible to assign primacy to one over the other.

The historian starts with the provisional selection of facts and a provisional interpretation in the light of which that selection has been made—by others as well as by himself. As he works, both the interpretation and the selection and ordering of facts undergo subtle and perhaps partly unconscious changes through the reciprocal action of one or the other. And this reciprocal action also involves reciprocity between present and past, since the historian is part of the present and the facts belong to the past. The historian and the facts of history are necessary to one another. The historian without his facts is rootless and futile; the facts without their historian are dead and meaningless. My first answer therefore to the question, What is history?, is that it is a continuous process of interaction between the historian and his facts, an unending dialogue between the present and the past.

QUESTIONS FOR STUDY, DISCUSSION, AND WRITING

1. Carr begins with a question but does not answer it until the last sentence. What are the main steps of the discussion leading to his answer? The answer takes the form of a definition: which is the most important of the defining words?
2. In what sense is Steinbeck (p. 907) "saying the same thing" as Carr? What are the differences? What are the advantages of each man's approach to historical fact?
3. In his discussion of the facts of history, Carr distinguishes between a "mere fact about the past" and a "fact of history." Into which category should the following go? (a) the murder of Catherine Genovese (see pp. 899–907); (b) the FitzGerald contraction (p. 987); (c) Stonewall Jackson's lemonade (p. 819); (d) Bruno Bettelheim's encounter with the infirmary guard (pp. 50–52).
4. Carr says, "the facts of history never come to us 'pure,' since they do not and cannot exist in a pure form: they are always refracted through the mind of the recorder" (p. 931). Freeman (pp. 815–829) records facts which do not seem central to his subject. What are some of these facts? It would follow from Carr's statement that if such facts are refracted, their refraction might tell something about the nature of the refracting medium, the historian's mind, his interests and convictions. What do the peripheral facts he records reveal about Freeman?
5. If you were commissioned to write a history of the semester or of a particular group during the semester, what would be your most important "facts of history"?

On Science

Aims · Perspectives · Applications

CHARLES SANDERS PEIRCE

The Fixation of Belief[1]

That which determines us, from given premises, to draw one inference rather than another, is some habit of mind, whether it be constitutional or acquired. The habit is good or otherwise, according as it produces true conclusions from true premises or not; and an inference is regarded as valid or not, without reference to the truth or falsity of its conclusion specially, but according as the habit which determines it is such as to produce true conclusions in general or not. The particular habit of mind which governs this or that inference may be formulated in a proposition whose truth depends on the validity of the inferences which the habit determines; and such a formula is called a *guiding principle* of inference. Suppose, for example, that we observe that a rotating disk of copper quickly comes to rest when placed between the poles of a magnet, and we infer that this will happen with every disk of copper. The guiding principle is, that what is true of one piece of copper is true of another. Such a guiding principle with regard to copper would be much safer than with regard to many other substances—brass, for example.

A book might be written to signalize all the most important of these guiding principles of reasoning. It would probably be, we must confess, of no service to a person whose thought is directed wholly to practical subjects, and whose activity moves along thoroughly-beaten paths. The problems which present themselves to such a mind are matters of routine which he has learned once for all to handle in learning his business. But let a man venture into an

1. The first in a series of papers, published by Peirce in *The Popular Science Monthly*, 1877-1878. "Illustrations of the Logic of Science,"

unfamiliar field, or where his results are not continually checked by experience, and all history shows that the most masculine intellect will ofttimes lose his orientation and waste his efforts in directions which bring him no nearer to his goal, or even carry him entirely astray. He is like a ship in the open sea, with no one on board who understands the rules of navigation. And in such a case some general study of the guiding principles of reasoning would be sure to be found useful.

The subject could hardly be treated, however, without being first limited; since almost any fact may serve as a guiding principle. But it so happens that there exists a division among facts, such that in one class are all those which are absolutely essential as guiding principles, while in the others are all which have any other interest as objects of research. This division is between those which are necessarily taken for granted in asking whether a certain conclusion follows from certain premises, and those which are not implied in that question. A moment's thought will show that a variety of facts are already assumed when the logical question is first asked. It is implied, for instance, that there are such states of mind as doubt and belief—that a passage from one to the other is possible, the object of thought remaining the same, and that this transition is subject to some rules which all minds are alike bound by. As these are facts which we must already know before we can have any clear conception of reasoning at all, it cannot be supposed to be any longer of much interest to inquire into their truth or falsity. On the other hand, it is easy to believe that those rules of reasoning which are deduced from the very idea of the process are the ones which are the most essential; and, indeed, that so long as it conforms to these it will, at least, not lead to false conclusions from true premises. In point of fact, the importance of what may be deduced from the assumptions involved in the logical question turns out to be greater than might be supposed, and this for reasons which it is difficult to exhibit at the outset. The only one which I shall here mention is, that conceptions which are really products of logical reflection, without being readily seen to be so, mingle with our ordinary thoughts, and are frequently the causes of great confusion. This is the case, for example, with the conception of quality. A quality as such is never an object of observation. We can see that a thing is blue or green, but the quality of being blue and the quality of being green are not things which we see; they are products of logical reflection. The truth is, that common-sense, or thought as it first emerges above the level of the narrowly practical, is deeply imbued with that bad logical quality to which the epithet *metaphysical* is commonly applied; and nothing can clear it up but a severe course of logic.

We generally know when we wish to ask a question and when we wish to pronounce a judgment, for there is a dissimilarity between the sensation of doubting and that of believing.

But this is not all which distinguishes doubt from belief. There is a practical difference. Our beliefs guide our desires and shape our actions. The Assassins, or followers of the Old Man of the Mountain, used to rush into death at his least command, because they believed that obedience to him would insure everlasting felicity. Had they doubted this, they would not have acted as they did. So it is with every belief, according to its degree. The feeling of believing is a more or less sure indication of there being established in our nature some habit which will determine our actions. Doubt never has such an effect.

Nor must we overlook a third point of difference. Doubt is an uneasy and dissatisfied state from which we struggle to free ourselves and pass into the state of belief; while the latter is a calm and satisfactory state which we do not wish to avoid, or to change to a belief in anything else.[2] On the contrary, we cling tenaciously, not merely to believing, but to believing just what we do believe.

Thus, both doubt and belief have positive effects upon us, though very different ones. Belief does not make us act at once, but puts us into such a condition that we shall behave in a certain way, when the occasion arises. Doubt has not the least effect of this sort, but stimulates us to action until it is destroyed. This reminds us of the irritation of a nerve and the reflex action produced thereby; while for the analogue of belief, in the nervous system, we must look to what are called nervous associations—for example, to that habit of the nerves in consequence of which the smell of a peach will make the mouth water.

The irritation of doubt causes a struggle to attain a state of belief. I shall term this struggle *inquiry*, though it must be admitted that this is sometimes not a very apt designation.

The irritation of doubt is the only immediate motive for the struggle to attain belief. It is certainly best for us that our beliefs should be such as may truly guide our actions so as to satisfy our desires; and this reflection will make us reject any belief which does not seem to have been so formed as to insure this result. But it will only do so by creating a doubt in the place of that belief. With the doubt, therefore, the struggle begins, and with the cessation of doubt it ends. Hence, the sole object of inquiry is the settlement of opinion. We may fancy that this is not enough for us, and that we seek, not merely an opinion, but a true opinion. But put this fancy to the test, and it proves groundless; for as soon as a firm belief is reached we are entirely satisfied, whether the belief be true or false. And it is clear that nothing out of the sphere

2. I am not speaking of secondary effects occasionally produced by the in- terference of other impulses [Peirce's note].

of our knowledge can be our object, for nothing which does not affect the mind can be the motive for a mental effort. The most that can be maintained is, that we seek for a belief that we shall *think* to be true. But we think each one of our beliefs to be true, and, indeed, it is mere tautology to say so.

That the settlement of opinion is the sole end of inquiry is a very important proposition. It sweeps away, at once, various vague and erroneous conceptions of proof. A few of these may be noticed here.

1. Some philosophers have imagined that to start an inquiry it was only necessary to utter a question or set it down upon paper, and have even recommended us to begin our studies with questioning everything! But the mere putting of a proposition into the interrogative form does not stimulate the mind to any struggle after belief. There must be a real and living doubt, and without this all discussion is idle.

2. It is a very common idea that a demonstration must rest on some ultimate and absolutely indubitable propositions. These, according to one school, are first principles of a general nature; according to another, are first sensations. But, in point of fact, an inquiry, to have that completely satisfactory result called demonstration, has only to start with propositions perfectly free from all actual doubt. If the premises are not in fact doubted at all, they cannot be more satisfactory than they are.

3. Some people seem to love to argue a point after all the world is fully convinced of it. But no further advance can be made. When doubt ceases, mental action on the subject comes to an end; and, if it did go on, it would be without a purpose.

If the settlement of opinion is the sole object of inquiry, and if belief is of the nature of a habit, why should we not attain the desired end, by taking any answer to a question which we may fancy, and constantly reiterating it to ourselves, dwelling on all which may conduce to that belief, and learning to turn with contempt and hatred from anything which might disturb it? This simple and direct method is really pursued by many men. I remember once being entreated not to read a certain newspaper lest it might change my opinion upon free-trade. "Lest I might be entrapped by its fallacies and misstatements," was the form of expression. "You are not," my friend said, "a special student of political economy. You might, therefore, easily be deceived by fallacious arguments upon the subject. You might, then, if you read this paper, be led to believe in protection. But you admit that free-trade is the true doctrine; and you do not wish to believe what is not true." I have often known this system to be deliberately adopted. Still oftener, the instinctive dislike of an undecided state of mind, exaggerated into a vague dread of doubt, makes men cling spasmodically to the views they already take. The man feels that, if he only holds to his belief without wavering, it will be entirely satisfactory. Nor can it be denied that a steady and immovable faith yields great peace of mind. It may, indeed, give rise to inconveniences, as if a man should resolutely continue to believe that fire would not burn him, or that he would be eternally damned if he received his *ingesta* otherwise than through a stomach-pump. But then the man who adopts this method will not allow that its inconveniences are greater than its advantages. He will say, "I hold steadfastly to the truth, and the truth is always wholesome." And in many cases it may very well be that the pleasure he derives from his calm faith overbalances any inconveniences resulting from its deceptive character. Thus, if it be true that death is annihilation, then the man who believes that he will certainly go straight to heaven when he dies, provided he have fulfilled certain simple observances in this life, has a cheap pleasure which will not be followed by the least disappointment. A similar consideration seems to have weight with many persons in religious topics, for we frequently hear it said, "Oh, I could not believe so-and-so, because I should be wretched if I did." When an ostrich buries its head in the sand as danger approaches, it very likely takes the happiest course. It hides the danger, and then calmly says there is no danger; and, if it feels perfectly sure there is none, why should it raise its head to see? A man may go through life, systematically keeping out of view all that might cause a change in his opinions, and if he only succeeds—basing his method, as he does, on two fundamental psychological laws—I do not see what can be said against his doing so. It would be an egotistical impertinence to object that his procedure is irrational, for that only amounts to saying that his method of settling belief is not ours. He does not propose to himself to be rational, and, indeed, will often talk with scorn of man's weak and illusive reason. So let him think as he pleases.

But this method of fixing belief, which may be called the method of tenacity, will be unable to hold its ground in practice. The social impulse is against it. The man who adopts it will find that other men think differently from him, and it will be apt to occur to him, in some saner moment, that their opinions are quite as good as his own, and this will shake his confidence in his belief. This conception, that another man's thought or sentiment may be equivalent to one's own, is a distinctly new step, and a highly important one. It arises from an impulse too strong in man to be suppressed, without danger of destroying the human species. Unless we make ourselves hermits, we shall necessarily influence each other's opinions; so that the problem becomes how to fix belief, not in the individual merely, but in the community.

Let the will of the state act, then, instead of that of the individual. Let an institution be created which shall have for its object to keep correct doctrines before the attention of the people, to reiterate them perpetually, and to teach them to the young; having at the same time power to prevent contrary doctrines from being taught, advocated, or expressed. Let all possible causes of a change of mind be removed from men's apprehensions. Let them be kept ignorant, lest they should learn of some reason to think otherwise than they do. Let their passions be enlisted, so that they may regard private and unusual opinions with hatred and horror. Then, let all men who reject the established belief be terrified into silence. Let the people turn out and tar-and-feather such men, or let inquisitions be made into the manner of thinking of suspected persons, and, when they are found guilty of forbidden beliefs, let them be subjected to some signal punishment. When complete agreement could not otherwise be reached, a general massacre of all who have not thought in a certain way has proved a very effective means of settling opinion in a country. If the power to do this be wanting, let a list of opinions be drawn up, to which no man of the least independence of thought can assent, and let the faithful be required to accept all these propositions, in order to segregate them as radically as possible from the influence of the rest of the world.

This method has, from the earliest times, been one of the chief means of upholding correct theological and political doctrines, and of preserving their universal or catholic character. In Rome, especially, it has been practiced from the days of Numa Pompilius[3] to those of Pius Nonus.[4] This is the most perfect example in history; but wherever there is a priesthood—and no religion has been without one—this method has been more or less made use of. Wherever there is an aristocracy, or a guild, or any association of a class of men whose interests depend or are supposed to depend on certain propositions, there will be inevitably found some traces of this natural product of social feeling. Cruelties always accompany this system; and when it is consistently carried out, they become atrocities of the most horrible kind in the eyes of any rational man. Nor should this occasion surprise, for the officer of a society does not feel justified in surrendering the interests of that society for the sake of mercy, as he might his own private interests. It is natural, therefore, that sympathy and fellowship should thus produce a most ruthless power.

In judging this method of fixing belief, which may be called the method of authority, we must, in the first place, allow its immeasurable mental and moral superiority to the method of tenacity. Its

---

3. The legendary second king of Rome (715-672 B.C.), supposed to be the founder of nearly all the early religious institutions of Rome.

4. Pope, 1846-1878, foe of modernism, proclaimer of the important dogma of the Immaculate Conception, first pope to be regarded infallible.

success is proportionately greater; and, in fact, it has over and over again worked the most majestic results. The mere structures of stone which it has caused to be put together—in Siam, for example, in Egypt, and in Europe—have many of them a sublimity hardly more than rivaled by the greatest works of Nature. And, except the geological epochs, there are no periods of time so vast as those which are measured by some of these organized faiths. If we scrutinize the matter closely, we shall find that there has not been one of their creeds which has remained always the same; yet the change is so slow as to be imperceptible during one person's life, so that individual belief remains sensibly fixed. For the mass of mankind, then, there is perhaps no better method than this. If it is their highest impulse to be intellectual slaves, then slaves they ought to remain.

But no institution can undertake to regulate opinions upon every subject. Only the most important ones can be attended to, and on the rest men's minds must be left to the action of natural causes. This imperfection will be no source of weakness so long as men are in such a state of culture that one opinion does not influence another—that is, so long as they cannot put two and two together. But in the most priestridden states some individuals will be found who are raised above that condition. These men possess a wider sort of social feeling; they see that men in other countries and in other ages have held to very different doctrines from those which they themselves have been brought up to believe; and they cannot help seeing that it is the mere accident of their having been taught as they have, and of their having been surrounded with the manners and associations they have, that has caused them to believe as they do and not far differently. And their candor cannot resist the reflection that there is no reason to rate their own views at a higher value than those of other nations and other centuries; and this gives rise to doubts in their minds.

They will further perceive that such doubts as these must exist in their minds with reference to every belief which seems to be determined by the caprice either of themselves or of those who originated the popular opinions. The willful adherence to a belief, and the arbitrary forcing of it upon others, must, therefore, both be given up, and a new method of settling opinions must be adopted, which shall not only produce an impulse to believe, but shall also decide what proposition it is which is to be believed. Let the action of natural preferences be unimpeded, then, and under their influence let men, conversing together and regarding matters in different lights, gradually develop beliefs in harmony with natural causes. This method resembles that by which conceptions of art have been brought to maturity. The most perfect example of it is to be found in the history of metaphysical philosophy. Systems of this sort have not usually rested upon any observed facts, at least not in any great degree. They have been chiefly adopted because their fundamental propositions seemed "agreeable to reason." This is an apt expression; it does not mean that which agrees with experience, but that which we find ourselves inclined to believe. Plato, for example, finds it agreeable to reason that the distances of the celestial spheres from one another should be proportional to the different lengths of strings which produce harmonious chords. Many philosophers have been led to their main conclusions by considerations like this; but this is the lowest and least developed form which the method takes, for it is clear that another man might find Kepler's theory, that the celestial spheres are proportional to the inscribed and circumscribed spheres of the different regular solids, more agreeable to *his* reason. But the shock of opinions will soon lead men to rest on preferences of a far more universal nature. Take, for example, the doctrine that man only acts selfishly—that is, from the consideration that acting in one way will afford him more pleasure than acting in another. This rests on no fact in the world, but it has had a wide acceptance as being the only reasonable theory.

This method is far more intellectual and respectable from the point of view of reason than either of the others which we have noticed. But its failure has been the most manifest. It makes of inquiry something similar to the development of taste; but taste, unfortunately, is always more or less a matter of fashion, and accordingly metaphysicians have never come to any fixed agreement, but the pendulum has swung backward and forward between a more material and a more spiritual philosophy, from the earliest times to the latest. And so from this, which has been called the *a priori* method, we are driven, in Lord Bacon's phrase, to a true induction. We have examined into this *a priori* method as something which promised to deliver our opinions from their accidental and capricious element. But development, while it is a process which eliminates the effect of some casual circumstances, only magnifies that of others. This method, therefore, does not differ in a very essential way from that of authority. The government may not have lifted its finger to influence my convictions; I may have been left outwardly quite free to choose, we will say, between monogamy and polygamy, and, appealing to my conscience only, I may have concluded that the latter practice is in itself licentious. But when I come to see that the chief obstacle to the spread of Christianity among a people of as high culture as the Hindus has been a conviction of the immorality of our way of treating women, I cannot help seeing that, though governments do not interfere, sentiments in their development will be very greatly determined by accidental causes. Now, there are some people, among whom I must suppose that my reader is to be found, who, when they see that any belief of theirs is determined by any circumstance extraneous to the facts, will from that moment not merely admit in words that that belief is doubtful, but will experience a real doubt of it, so that it ceases to be a belief.

To satisfy our doubts, therefore, it is necessary that a method should be found by which our beliefs may be caused by nothing human, but by some external permanency—by something upon which our thinking has no effect. Some mystics imagine that they have such a method in a private inspiration from on high. But that is only a form of the method of tenacity, in which the conception of truth as something public is not yet developed. Our external permanency could not be external, in our sense, if it was restricted in its influence to one individual. It must be something which affects, or might affect, every man. And, though these affections are necessarily as various as are individual conditions, yet the method must be such that the ultimate conclusion of every man shall be the same. Such is the method of science. Its fundamental hypothesis, restated in more familiar language, is this: There are real things, whose characters are entirely independent of our opinions about them; those realities affect our senses according to regular laws, and, though our sensations are as different as our relations to the objects, yet, by taking advantage of the laws of perception, we can ascertain by reasoning how things really are, and any man, if he have sufficient experience and reason enough about it, will be led to the one true conclusion. The new conception here involved is that of reality. It may be asked how I know that there are any realities. If this hypothesis is the sole support of my method of inquiry, my method of inquiry must not be used to support my hypothesis. The reply is this: (1) If investigation cannot be regarded as proving that there are real things, it at least does not lead to a contrary conclusion; but the method and the conception on which it is based remain ever in harmony. No doubts of the method, therefore, necessarily arise from its practice, as is the case with all the others. (2) The feeling which gives rise to any method of fixing belief is a dissatisfaction at two repugnant propositions. But here already is a vague concession that there is some *one* thing to which a proposition should conform. Nobody, therefore, can really doubt that there are realities, or, if he did, doubt would not be a source of dissatisfaction. The hypothesis, therefore, is one which every mind admits. So that the social impulse does not cause me to doubt it. (3) Everybody uses the scienctific method about a great many things, and only ceases to use it when he does not know how to apply it. (4) Experience of the method has not led me to doubt it, but, on the contrary, scientific investigation has had the most wonderful triumphs in the way of settling opinion. These afford the explanation of my not doubting the method or the hypothesis which it supposes; and not having any doubt, nor believing that anybody else whom I could influence has, it would be the merest babble for me to say more about it. If there be anybody with a living doubt upon the subject, let him consider it.

To describe the method of scientific investigation is the object of this series of papers. At present I have only room to notice some points of contrast between it and other methods of fixing belief.

This is the only one of the four methods which presents any distinction of a right and a wrong way. If I adopt the method of tenacity and shut myself out from all influences, whatever I think necessary to doing this is necessary according to that method. So with the method of authority: the state may try to put down heresy by means which, from a scientific point of view, seem very ill-calculated to accomplish its purposes; but the only test *on that method* is what the state thinks, so that it cannot pursue the method wrongly. So with the *a priori* method. The very essence of it is to think as one is inclined to think. All metaphysicians will be sure to do that, however they may be inclined to judge each other to be perversely wrong. The Hegelian system recognizes every natural tendency of thought as logical, although it is certain to be abolished by counter-tendencies. Hegel thinks there is a regular system in the succession of these tendencies, in consequence of which, after drifting one way and the other for a long time, opinion will at last go right. And it is true that metaphysicians get the right ideas at last; Hegel's system of Nature represents tolerably the science of that day; and one may be sure that whatever scientific investigation has put out of doubt will presently receive *a priori* demonstration on the part of the metaphysicians. But with the scientific method the case is different. I may start with known and observed facts to proceed to the unknown; and yet the rules which I follow in doing so may not be such as investigation would approve. The test of whether I am truly following the method is not an immediate appeal to my feelings and purposes, but, on the contrary, itself involves the application of the method. Hence it is that bad reasoning as well as good reasoning is possible; and this fact is the foundation of the practical side of logic.

It is not to be supposed that the first three methods of settling opinion present no advantage whatever over the scientific method. On the contrary, each has some peculiar convenience of its own. The *a priori* method is distinguished for its comfortable conclusions. It is the nature of the process to adopt whatever belief we are inclined to, and there are certain flatteries to the vanity of man which we all believe by nature, until we are awakened from our pleasing dream by some rough facts. The method of authority will always govern the mass of mankind; and those who wield the various forms of organized force in the state will never be convinced that dangerous reasoning ought not to be suppressed in some way. If liberty of speech is to be untrammeled from the grosser forms of constraint, then uniformity of opinion will be secured by a moral terrorism to which the respectability of society will give its thorough approval. Following the method of authority is the path of peace. Certain non-conformities are permitted; certain others (considered unsafe) are forbidden. These are different in different countries and in different ages; but, wherever you are, let it be known that you seriously hold a tabooed belief, and you may be perfectly sure of being treated with a cruelty less brutal but more refined than hunting you like a wolf. Thus, the greatest intellectual benefactors of mankind have never dared, and dare not now, to utter the whole of their thought; and thus a shade of *prima facie* doubt is cast upon every proposition which is considered essential to the security of society. Singularly enough, the persecution does not all come from without; but a man torments himself and is oftentimes most distressed at finding himself believing propositions which he has been brought up to regard with aversion. The peaceful and sympathetic man will, therefore, find it hard to resist the temptation to submit his opinions to authority. But most of all I admire the method of tenacity for its strength, simplicity, and directness. Men who pursue it are distinguished for their decision of character, which becomes very easy with such a mental rule. They do not waste time in trying to make up their minds what they want, but, fastening like lightning upon whatever alternative comes first, they hold to it to the end, whatever happens, without an instant's irresolution. This is one of the splendid qualities which generally accompany brilliant, unlasting success. It is impossible not to envy the man who can dismiss reason, although we know how it must turn out at last.

Such are the advantages which the other methods of settling opinion have over scientific investigation. A man should consider well of them; and then he should consider that, after all, he wishes his opinions to coincide with the fact, and that there is no reason why the results of these three methods should do so. To bring about this effect is the prerogative of the method of science. Upon such considerations he has to make his choice—a choice which is far more than the adoption of any intellectual opinion, which is one of the ruling decisions of his life, to which, when once made, he is bound to adhere. The force of habit will sometimes cause a man to hold on to old beliefs, after he is in a condition to see that they have no sound basis. But reflection upon the state of the case will overcome these habits, and he ought to allow reflection its full weight. People sometimes shrink from doing this, having an idea that beliefs are wholesome which they cannot help feeling rest on nothing. But let such persons suppose an analogous though different case from their own. Let them ask themselves what they would say to a reformed Mussulman who should hesitate to give up his old notions in regard to the relations of the sexes; or to a reformed Catholic who should still shrink from reading the Bible. Would they not say that these persons ought to consider the matter fully, and clearly understand the new doctrine, and then ought to embrace it, in its entirety? But, above all, let it be considered that what is more wholesome than any particular belief is integrity of belief, and that to avoid looking into the support of any belief from a fear that it may turn out rotten is quite as immoral as it is disadvantageous. The person who confesses that there is such a thing as truth, which is distinguished from falsehood simply by this, that if acted on it will carry us to the point we aim at and not astray, and then, though convinced of this, dares not know the truth and seeks to avoid it, is in a sorry state of mind indeed.

Yes, the other methods do have their merits: a clear logical conscience does cost something—just as any virtue, just as all that we cherish, costs us dear. But we should not desire it to be otherwise. The genius of a man's logical method should be loved and reverenced as his bride, whom he has chosen from all the world. He need not contemn the others; on the contrary, he may honor them deeply, and in doing so he only honors her the more. But she is the one that he has chosen, and he knows that he was right in making that choice. And having made it, he will work and fight for her, and will not complain that there are blows to take, hoping that there may be as many and as hard to give, and will strive to be the worthy knight and champion of her from the blaze of whose splendors he draws his inspiration and his courage.

QUESTIONS FOR STUDY, DISCUSSION, AND WRITING

1. Why does Peirce distinguish between doubt and belief on p. 540?
2. What are the four methods of inquiry? Which of the four most closely describes the development of Peirce's argument?
3. Would Peirce restrict application of the method of science to the natural sciences? Would he consider as scientific Milgram's "Behavioral Study of Obedience" (pp. 290–304)? Arendt's study of "Denmark and the Jews" (pp. 894–898)?
4. On p. 947 Peirce sharply distinguishes between the a priori method and the method of science. Consider Platt's discussion ("Style in Science," pp. 973–984); would he agree with Peirce's sharp distinction?
5. In the next-to-last paragraph the last sentence separates the subject noun from its verb by six clauses. Does Peirce gain or lose by this? Explain.

6. *This essay says little about religion directly, yet many of Peirce's remarks implicitly convey a decided attitude toward the subject. What is that attitude, and in which passages is it most clearly conveyed?*

THOMAS HENRY HUXLEY
The Method of Scientific Investigation

The method of scientific investigation is nothing but the expression of the necessary mode of working of the human mind. It is simply the mode at which all phenomena are reasoned about, rendered precise and exact. There is no more difference, between the mental operations of a man of science and those of an ordinary person, than there is between the operations and methods of a baker or of a butcher weighing out his goods in common scales, and the operations of a chemist in performing a difficult and complex analysis by means of his balance and finely graduated weights. It is not that the action of the scales in the one case, and the balance in the other, differ in the principles of their construction or manner of working; but the beam of one is set on an infinitely finer axis than the other, and of course turns by the addition of a much smaller weight.

You will understand this better, perhaps, if I give you some familiar example. You have all heard it repeated, I dare say, that men of science work by means of induction and deduction, and that by the help of these operations, they, in a sort of sense, wring from Nature certain other things, which are called natural laws, and causes, and that out of these, by some cunning skill of their own, they build up hypotheses and theories. And it is imagined by many that the operations of the common mind can be by no means compared with these processes, and that they have to be acquired by a sort of special apprenticeship to the craft. To hear all these large words, you would think that the mind of a man of science must be constituted differently from that of his fellow men; but if you will not be frightened by terms, you will discover that you are quite wrong, and that all these terrible apparatus are being used by yourselves every day and every hour of your lives.

There is a well-known incident in one of Molière's plays, when the author makes the hero express unbounded delight on being told that he had been talking prose during the whole of his life. In the same way I trust that you will take comfort, and be delighted with yourselves, on the discovery that you have been acting on the principles of inductive and deductive philosophy during the same period. Probably there is not one here who has not in the course of the day had occasion to set in motion a complex train of reasoning, of the very same kind, though differing of course in degree, as that which a scientific man goes through in tracing the causes of natural phenomena.

A very trivial circumstance will serve to exemplify this. Suppose you go into a fruiterer's shop, wanting an apple—you take up one, and, on biting it, you find it is sour; you look at it, and see that it is hard and green. You take up another one, and that too is hard, green, and sour. The shopman offers you a third; but, before biting it, you examine it, and find that it is hard and green, and you immediately say that you will not have it, as it must be sour, like those you have already tried.

Nothing can be more simple than that, you think; but if you will take the trouble to analyze and trace out into its logical elements what has been done by the mind, you will be greatly surprised. In the first place, you have performed the operation of induction. You found that, in two experiences, hardness and greenness in apples went together with sourness. It was so in the first case, and it was confirmed by the second. True, it is a very small basis, but still it is enough to make an induction from; you generalize the facts, and you expect to find sourness in apples where you get hardness and greenness. You found upon that a general law, that all hard and green apples are sour; and that, so far as it goes, is a perfect induction. Well, having got your natural law in this way, when you are offered another apple which you find is hard and green, you say, "All hard and green apples are sour; this apple is hard and green, therefore this apple is sour." That train of reasoning is what logicians call a syllogism, and has all its various parts and terms—its major premise, its minor premise, and its conclusion. And, by the help of further reasoning, which, if drawn out, would have to be exhibited in two or three other syllogisms, you arrive at your final determination, "I will not have that apple." So that, you see, you have, in the first place, established a law by induction, and upon that you have founded a deduction, and reasoned out the special conclusion of the particular case. Well now, suppose, having got your law, that at some time afterwards, you are discussing the qualities of apples with a friend: you will say to him, "It is a very curious thing but I find that all hard and green apples are sour!" Your friend says to you, "But how do you know that?" You at once reply, "Oh, because I have tried them over and over again, and have always found them to be so." Well, if we were talking science instead of common sense, we should call that an experimental verification. And, if still opposed, you go further, and say, "I have heard from the people in Somersetshire and Devonshire, where a large number of apples are grown, that they have observed the same thing. It is also found to be the case in Normandy, and in North

America. In short, I find it to be the universal experience of mankind wherever attention has been directed to the subject." Whereupon, your friend, unless he is a very unreasonable man, agrees with you, and is convinced that you are quite right in the conclusion you have drawn. He believes, although perhaps he does not know he believes it, that the more extensive verifications are—that the more frequently experiments have been made, and results of the same kind arrived at—that the more varied the conditions under which the same results are attained, the more certain is the ultimate concluson, and he disputes the question no further. He sees that the experiment has been tried under all sorts of conditions, as to time, place, and people, with the same result; and he says with you, therefore, that the law you have laid down must be a good one, and he must believe it.

In science we do the same thing; the philosopher exercises precisely the same faculties, though in a much more delicate manner. In scientific inquiry it becomes a matter of duty to expose a supposed law to every possible kind of verification, and to take care, moreover, that this is done intentionally, and not left to a mere accident, as in the case of the apples. And in science, as in common life, our confidence in a law is in exact proportion to the absence of variation in the result of our experimental verifications. For instance, if you let go your grasp of an article you may have in your hand, it will immediately fall to the ground. That is a very common verification of one of the best established laws of nature—that of gravitation. The method by which men of science establish the existence of that law is exactly the same as that by which we have established the trivial proposition about the sourness of hard and green apples. But we believe it in such an extensive, thorough, and unhesitating manner because the universal experience of mankind verifies it, and we can verify it ourselves at any time; and that is the strongest possible foundation on which any natural law can rest.

So much, then, by way of proof that the method of establishing laws in science is exactly the same as that pursued in common life. Let us now turn to another matter (though really it is but another phase of the same question), and that is the method by which, from the relations of certain phenomena, we prove that some stand in the position of causes towards the others.

I want to put the case clearly before you, and I will therefore show you what I mean by another familiar example. I will suppose that one of you, on coming down in the morning to the parlor of your house, finds that a teapot and some spoons which had been left in the room on the previous evening are gone—the window is open, and you observe the mark of a dirty hand on the window frame, and perhaps, in addition to that, you notice the impress of a hobnailed shoe on the gravel outside. All these phenomena have struck your attention instantly, and before two seconds have passed you say, "Oh, somebody has broken open the window, entered the room, and run off with the spoons and the teapot!" That speech is out of your mouth in a moment. And you will probably add, "I know he has; I am quite sure of it!" You mean to say exactly what you know; but in reality you are giving expression to what is, in all essential particulars, an hypothesis. You do not *know* it at all; it is nothing but an hypothesis rapidly framed in your own mind. And it is an hypothesis founded on a long train of inductions and deductions.

What are those inductions and deductions, and how have you got at this hypothesis? You have observed, in the first place, that the window is open; but by a train of reasoning involving many inductions and deductions, you have probably arrived long before at the general law—and a very good one it is—that windows do not open of themselves; and you therefore conclude that something has opened the window. A second general law that you have arrived at in the same way is, that teapots and spoons do not go out of a window spontaneously, and you are satisfied that, as they are not now where you left them, they have been removed. In the third place, you look at the marks on the window sill, and the shoe-marks outside, and you say say that in all previous experience the former kind of mark has never been produced by anything else but the hand of a human being; and the same experience shows that no other animal but man at present wears shoes with hobnails in them such as would produce the marks in the gravel. I do not know, even if we could discover any of those "missing links" that are talked about, that they would help us to any other conclusion! At any rate the law which states our present experience is strong enough for my present purpose. You next reach the conclusion that as these kinds of marks have not been left by any other animals than men, or are liable to be formed in any other way than by a man's hand and shoe, the marks in question have been formed by a man in that way. You have, further, a general law, founded on observation and experience, and that, too is, I am sorry to say, a very universal and unimpeachable one—that some men are thieves; and you assume at once from all these premises—and that is what constitutes your hypothesis—that the man who made the marks outside and on the window sill, opened the window, got into the room, and stole your teapot and spoons. You have now arrived at a *vera causa*[1]; you have assumed a cause which, it is plain, is competent to produce all the phenomena you have observed. You can explain all these phenomena only by the hypothesis of a thief. But that is a hypothetical conclusion, of the justice of which you have no absolute proof at all; it is only rendered highly probable by a series of inductive and deductive reasonings.

1. True cause.

I suppose your first action, assuming that you are a man of ordinary common sense, and that you have established this hypothesis to your own satisfaction, will very likely be to go off for the police, and set them on the track of the burglar, with the view to the recovery of your property. But just as you are starting with this object, some person comes in, and on learning what you are about, says, "My good friend, you are going on a great deal too fast. How do you know that the man who really made the marks took the spoons? It might have been a monkey that took them and the man may have merely looked in afterwards." You would probably reply, "Well, that is all very well, but you see it is contrary to all experience of the way teapots and spoons are abstracted; so that, at any rate, your hypothesis is less probable than mine." While you are talking the thing over in this way, another friend arrives, one of that good kind of people that I was talking of a little while ago. And he might say, "Oh, my dear sir, you are certainly going on a great deal too fast. You are most presumptuous. You admit that all these occurrences took place when you were fast asleep, at a time when you could not possibly have known anything about what was taking place. How do you know that the laws of Nature are not suspended during the night? It may be that there has been some kind of supernatural interference in this case." In point of fact, he declares that your hypothesis is one of which you cannot at all demonstrate the truth, and that you are by no means sure that the laws of Nature are the same when you are asleep as when you are awake.

Well, now, you cannot at the moment answer that kind of reasoning. You feel that your worthy friend has you somewhat at a disadvantage. You will feel perfectly convinced in your own mind, however, that you are quite right, and you say to him, "My good friend, I can only be guided by the natural probabilities of the case, and if you will be kind enough to stand aside and permit me to pass, I will go and fetch the police." Well, we will suppose that your journey is successful, and that by good luck you meet with a policeman; that eventually the burglar is found with your property on his person, and the marks correspond to his hand and to his boots. Probably any jury would consider those facts a very good experimental verification of your hypothesis, touching the cause of the abnormal phenomena observed in your parlor, and would act accordingly.

Now, in this suppositious case, I have taken phenomena of a very common kind, in order that you might see what are the different steps in an ordinary process of reasoning, if you will only take the trouble to analyze it carefully. All the operations I have described, you will see, are involved in the mind of any man of sense in leading him to a conclusion as to the course he should take in order to make good a robbery and punish the offender. I say that you are led, in that case, to your conclusion by exactly the same train of reasoning as that which a man of science pursues when he is endeavoring to discover the origin and laws of the most occult phenomena. The process is, and always must be, the same; and precisely the same mode of reasoning was employed by Newton and Laplace in their endeavors to discover and define the causes of the movements of the heavenly bodies as you, with your own common sense, would employ to detect a burglar. The only difference is that the nature of the inquiry being more abstruse, every step has to be most carefully watched, so that there may not be a single crack or flaw in your hypothesis. A flaw or crack in many of the hypotheses of daily life may be of little or no moment as affecting the general correctness of the conclusions at which we may arrive; but, in a scientific inquiry, a fallacy, a great or small, is always of importance, and is sure to be in the long run constantly productive of mischievous, if not fatal results.

Do not allow yourselves to be misled by the common notion that an hypothesis is untrustworthy simply because it is an hypothesis. It is often urged, in respect to some scientific conclusion, that, after all, it is only an hypothesis. But what more have we to guide us in nine-tenths of the most important affairs of daily life than hypotheses, and often very ill-based ones? So that in science, where the evidence of a hypothesis is subjected to the most rigid examination, we may rightly pursue the same course. You may have hypotheses and hypotheses. A man may say, if he likes, that the moon is made of green cheese: that is an hypothesis. But another man, who has devoted a great deal of time and attention to the subject, and availed himself of the most powerful telescopes and the results of the observations of others, declares that in his opinion it is probably composed of materials very similar to those of which our own earth is made up: and that is also only an hypothesis. But I need not tell you that there is an enormous difference in the value of the two hypotheses. That one which is based on sound scientific knowledge is sure to have a corresponding value; and that which is a mere hasty random guess is likely to have but little value. Every great step in our progress in discovering causes has been made in exactly the same way as that which I have detailed to you. A person observing the occurrence of certain facts and phenomena asks, naturally enough, what process, what kind of operation known to occur in Nature applied to the particular case, will unravel and explain the mystery? Hence you have the scientific hypothesis; and its value will be proportionate to the care and completeness with which its basis has been tested and verified. It is in these matters as in the commonest affairs of practical life: the guess of the fool will be folly, while the guess of the wise man will contain wisdom. In all cases, you see that the value of the result depends on the patience and faithfulness with which the investigator applies to his hypothesis every possible kind of verification.

DONALD FLEMING

Charles Darwin, the Anaesthetic Man

Here are three voices from Victorian England.

"What do I know of tastes and fancies? What escape have I had from problems that could be demonstrated, and realities that could be grasped? If I had been stone blind; if I had groped my way by my sense of touch, and had been free, while I knew the shapes and surfaces of things, to exercise my fancy somewhat, in regard to them; I should have been a million times wiser, happier, more loving, more contented, more innocent and human in all good respects, than I am with the eyes I have."—"I never knew you were unhappy."—"I always knew it."

I became persuaded, that my love of mankind, and of excellence for its own sake, had worn itself out. For I now saw, what I had always before received with incredulity—that the habit of analysis has a tendency to wear away the feelings. I was left stranded at the commencement of my voyage, with a well-equipped ship and a rudder, but no sail. The fountains of vanity and ambition seemed to have dried up within me, as completely as those of benevolence. I frequently asked myself if I could go on living.

I have tried lately to read Shakespeare, and found it so intolerably dull that it nauseated me. I have also almost lost my taste for pictures or music. I am glad you were at the *Messiah*, but I dare say I should find my soul too dried up to appreciate it; and then I should feel very flat, for it is a horrid bore to feel as I constantly do, that I am a withered leaf for every subject except Science. The loss of these tastes is a loss of happiness. My mind seems to have become a kind of machine for grinding general laws out of large collections of facts. It sometimes makes me hate Science.

The first speaker is Louisa in Dickens' *Hard Times* of 1854.[1] The second is John Stuart Mill in his *Autobiography* of 1873, describing a crisis that he passed through in the winter of 1826-27.[2] The third is Charles Darwin in a letter of 1868 and his autobiography of 1876.[3] Most historians would say that Dickens is validated by Mill and Darwin. One might argue instead that

1. Conflated and abbreviated from Bk. I, ch. xv, and Bk. II, ch. xii. The most stimulating analysis of *Hard Times*, by which I have been greatly influenced, is by F. R. Leavis in *The Great Tradition* (London, 1948) [Fleming's note].

2. Conflated, abbreviated, and rearranged from *Autobiography*, ed. John J. Coss (New York, 1924), pp. 96-99 [Fleming's note].

3. Conflated, abbreviated, and rearranged from Francis Darwin, ed., *The Life and Letters of Charles Darwin* (London, 1887), III, 92; and *The Autobiography of Charles Darwin, 1809-1882*, ed. Nora Barlow (London, 1958), pp. 138-139 [Fleming's note].

recollections of the inner life have to be validated by art in their representative historical character. One thing is certain, when the same theme reverberates upon itself from life to art and back again, the historian had better pay attention.

The common predicament of the fictional Louisa and the real Mill and Darwin may be described as the dissociation of knowledge and sensibility; fact and affect. They know but cannot feel and are afraid to feel and fearful of not feeling—joyless, parched, and worn-out. I am tired, says the young Louisa, "I have been tired a long time" (Bk. I, ch. iii). Louisa's state of exhaustion is the product of her father Thomas Gradgrind's fact-system of education. "Facts alone are wanted in life. Plant nothing else, and root out everything else" (Bk. I, ch. i). Over against the Gradgrinds of Coketown Dickens put the orphan circus-girl Sissy Jupe, lamentably brought up on the "destructive nonsense" of *A Thousand and One Nights* and other fairy tales and predictably unable to see why she cannot have flowers on carpets for the fancy of it, where they would get crushed if real and if not real have no business being there. " 'They wouldn't crush or wither, if you please, Sir. They would be pictures of what was very pretty and pleasant, and I would fancy—' 'Ay, ay, ay. But you musn't fancy' " (Bk. I, ch. ii). Sissy is an emblem of the circus acrobats from whom she came, with their emotional abundance and immediacy of feeling and their power of taking up easy attitudes and dispensing ease to others—artists who stacked themselves up in pyramids to lift the people of Coketown clean out of the Flood of Facts. The Gradgrinds are Utilitarians, Political Economists, Statisticians; in Dickens's terrible figure, dustmen raising clouds of dust to stifle feeling. The circus people are human beings fulfilling the human condition. In the end only Sissy Jupe can nurse Louisa into humanness.

John Stuart Mill was dusty from the cradle. He was a product of the same philosophy of education that Dickens satirized in *Hard Times*, Benthamite Utilitarianism (*Autobiography*, pp. 27-36). James Mill, the father, was a man of more spacious views than Thomas Gradgrind; and more than this, he had a not merely ideal but felt aversion from pain and suffering. Religion to him was intolerable as postulating an omnipotent and benevolent god as the ground of such evil. He was, his son thought, a man of deep feelings who could not imagine they would be in short supply with anybody else. Education was needed as a bridle upon them and could never lack for a mount to rein in. For this reason it did not occur to him to make good in his education of his son the characteristic Benthamite undervaluation of poetry and imagination. Bentham himself had said, notoriously, that "all poetry is misrepresentation," to which the younger Mill enters the odd demurrer that the old man did not really mean that *poetry* was misrepresentation but merely anything at all that was "more oratorical in its character than a sum in arithmetic" (*Autobiography*, p. 78). Which clears that up. John Stuart Mill as a boy actually did read some poetry—including Pope's *Essay on Man*—but he was like his preceptors in not being able to connect this with the real business of life, to beat abuses over the head with facts. So the boy grew up, speculatively benevolent to all mankind but mainly speculative, and headed straight for deadness of the heart.

When the doldrums had come and withered him up and he had no wind to puff his sails, he tried to find help in Byron, but that was no good—"Harold and Manfred[4] had the same burden on them which I had" (*Autobiography*, p. 103). The true medicine was Wordsworth, who dealt in "states of feeling, and of thought colored by feeling, under the excitement of beauty"—"they seemed to be the very culture of the feelings, which I was in quest of" (*Autobiography*, p. 104). The lesson that Wordsworth drove home to Mill about the necessity of poetry and art as "instruments of human culture," the best means to cultivation of the "passive susceptibilities," he tried to pass on in turn to other Utilitarians, most notably the young Radical politician J. A. Roebuck, already a lover of music, painting, and Byronic poetry, but like the rest unable to see that these things had any value as "aids in the formation of character" (*Autobiography*, pp. 105-107). Cultivation of the feelings through the imagination, Roebuck told him, was "only cultivating illusions." Mill thought that underneath, Roebuck was like his own father, endowed with "quick and strong sensibilities" but "more susceptible to the painful sympathies than to the pleasurable" and seeking to deaden his feelings rather than stir them up. If what John Stuart Mill had to say in praise of poetry could give offense to Utilitarians, his mature view on the role of music would have been more alarming still: it surpassed all other arts in "exciting enthusiasm; in winding up to a high pitch those feelings of an elevated kind which are already in the character, but to which this excitement gives a glow and a fervor, which, though transitory at its utmost height, is precious for sustaining them at other times" (*Autobiography*, p. 101). This exaltation of irresponsible excitement was like ushering an obscene force out of nightmares into the hard clear daytime of Benthamism— a fund of free-floating emotional energy, unexpended and unspoken-for, mere dangerous potentiality declining to be trussed up and handed over to any determinate end. The cure that Wordsworth had commenced, Mill's only love Helen Taylor completed—a Shelley among women in feeling, he said, a veritable Mill in liberation from superstition, as he might have added, and one integral

---

4. The brooding heroes of Byron's *Childe Harold's Pilgrimage* and *Manfred*, respectively.

being, who gave proof that Mill to be a whole man would not have to give up his father's warfare upon religion and all other forms of acquiescence in the evil of the world.

I

Louisa Gradgrind and John Stuart Mill after many vain attempts passed through the door of feeling into life. Charles Darwin traced the opposite course from a carefree youth to a desiccated old age when many doors that gave upon the world of art and feeling had slammed upon him (Darwin, *Autobiography*). From the time of his mother's death when he was only eight, the young Darwin had his whole being in the immense shadow of his father—340 pounds the last time they dared to weigh him, with an almost Johnsonian force of personality to match—but the latter never tried to mold him to order or sought to impose his own conviction that religious belief was unworthy of an intelligent man. Darwin as a young man responded to this permissive environment by displaying a catholic enthusiasm for life. His chief pleasure, indeed passion, was hunting, and he got plenty of it in, the anthem in King's Chapel made him shiver with delight, he loved Raphael and Sebastian del Piombo, Handel's *Messiah* and Maria Malibran, Shakespeare and Milton, Wordsworth and Coleridge, and fine scenery into the bargain. He was bored by long stretches of his education but was always permitted to move on to something else and some other prospective career. He began by preparing to be a physician like his father, but between the tedium of the lectures and the horror of operations before chloroform, of which the memory hounded him "for many a long year," he decided to call it a bad job, and Dr. Darwin acquiesced. He himself avoided being present at surgery and could not bear the sight of blood. Their next idea was the clergy, which would never have been the father's choice for himself but anything sooner than an idle sporting life, and the son thought it would be all right if he got a country living with a continual round of hunting and natural history, punctuated by a few sermons. Dogma was no problem. All 39 Articles[5] went down smoothly. It never struck him at the time, he later wrote, "how illogical it was to say that I believed in what I could not understand and what is in fact unintelligible." That was later. On the great voyage of the *Beagle*, Darwin passed among his shipmates for naïvely religious and given to crediting the letter of the Bible in a way that was already old-fashioned. If this was mere habit, he several times in the course of the expedition felt an experiential influx of "the sublime"—"the higher feelings of wonder, admiration, and devotion," which bore irresistible testimony to God and the immortality of the soul (*Autobiography*, p. 91). Once he stood upon the summit of the Andes and surveyed the magnificent

5. The basic statement of faith for the Church of England.

prospect all around and felt "as if his nerves had become fiddle-strings, and had all taken to rapidly vibrating" (*Life and Letters,* III, 54). But he felt "most sublime" of all in the rain-forests of Brazil, corresponding to the jungle red in tooth and claw of the homekeeping Tennyson but to Darwin on the spot a source of incommunicable delight, more gorgeous even than the landscapes of Claude Lorrain—his own comparison. Under the spell of the sublime Darwin did not see the jungle as an arena of combat to be shunned by sensitive men but as an occasion for rejoicing and deep assent to the universe. The thing that made him cringe was the uneven contest between slaves and their masters. "The remembrance," his son says, "of screams, or other sounds heard in Brazil, where he was powerless to interfere with what he believed to be the torture of a slave, haunted him for years, especially at night" (*Life and Letters,* III, 200). With these deep echoes resounding through his spirit and the queer fauna of oceanic islands teasing his brain, Darwin returned to England in 1836. In the course of the next two years he thought a good deal about religion, found that he could less and less imagine any evidence that would persuade him of the truth of Christianity, and came to think that even if true it was a "damnable doctrine" for condemning to eternal punishment unbelievers like his father and elder brother (*Autobiography,* pp. 86-87). In theory, and more or less in practice, this left open the question whether Darwin might still be able to salvage some kind of theism from the ruins of his now exploded orthodoxy. He had already gone far enough in unconventionality to make his father advise him to keep any future wife in the dark.

It was pertinent advice. In the same period when he began to find revealed religion wanting, Darwin was also canvassing in the abstract whether to get married or not. One credit item for getting married ran that a wife would be something to play with and better than a dog anyhow. Marriage it was, but marriage to a commonplace woman, deeply though not illiberally religious; no Helen Taylor to energize and set him free and add her strength to his own. It is clear that in the midst of her tender care for him, Emma Darwin was not above administering the most loving possible pinpricks on the subject of religion; for Darwin did not take his father's advice but told her everything. One gets the impression that she was always checking herself bravely on the verge of lamenting her husband's unregenerate state and professing not quite to believe that he really wasn't religious and she of course was just a poor muddle-headed little woman and he musn't mind her but had he thought of *this* argument for religion (*Autobiography,* pp. 235-238). He says, in point of fact, in his autobiography of 1876, that on the whole he did still believe in a sort of God, though not the God of the Christians, when he wrote the *Origin of Species* (*Autobiography*, p. 93). Total unbelief did not come till later.

This progression from naïve faith to abandonment of religion was one of the ground-notes of his private experience, always with the added dimension of flying in the face of his wife's desires for him. They were undergoing divergent evolution. The other ground-note was his estrangement from the arts. The history of this, not the fact itself but the stages by which it was accomplished, is difficult to pin down. Darwin says in his autobiography that "up to the age of 30," which would bring him to the year of his marriage, "or beyond," he loved poetry and specifically Milton, Gray, Bryon, Wordsworth, Coleridge, Shelley, and Shakespeare (p. 138). Now for many years he had not been able to "endure" a line of poetry and Shakespeare least of all. His old taste for pictures and music had equally deserted him. "Music generally sets me thinking too energetically on what I have been at work on, instead of giving me pleasure" (p. 138). The only art works that meant anything to him in his prime were novels read aloud by his womenfolk and stipulated to have happy endings, dear lovable women in them, and no aftertaste. Of these he says with characteristic precision of speech that they were a "wonderful relief" to him (pp. 138-139). He took novels as a sedative to put his jangling nerves and churning thoughts to sleep. Great novels making great demands he did not relish. As his contemporary George Eliot went on making her tragic vision more intense and her art more powerful, she continually declined in Darwin's favor (*Life and Letters*, II, 305; III, 40).

With this falling away from great art, Darwin associated a general loss of power to feel intensely. He had experienced a decline in his fondness for fine scenery, which he says in 1876 has lasted longer than any other source of aesthetic gratification but "does not cause me the exquisite delight which it formerly did" (*Autobiography*, p. 138). Worse still, he thought he had lost the power of loving friends deeply. "Whilst I was young and strong I was capable of very warm attachments, but of late years, though I still have very friendly feelings towards many persons, I have lost the power of becoming deeply attached to anyone, not even so deeply to my good and dear friends Hooker and Huxley, as I should formerly have been" (*Autobiography*, p. 115). He took no pleasure in this stripping bare of his personality, so that the thinking machine cast off the flesh that clothed it. "The loss of these tastes is a loss of happiness, and may possibly be injurious to the intellect, and more probably to the moral character, by enfeebling the emotional part of our nature."

II

Why did Darwin experience this atrophy of the aesthetic instincts? At least once he implied that he saw himself as Blake and Wordsworth might have seen him, murdering to dissect, a type of the analytical man who set the atomizing vision of science above the integrating vision of art. "At last I fell fast asleep on the grass, and awoke with a chorus of birds singing around me, and squirrels running up the trees, and some woodpeckers laughing, and it was as pleasant and rural a scene as ever I saw, and I did not care one penny how any of the beasts or birds had been formed" (*Life and Letters*, II, 114). This was written on the only kind of vacation from science that he ever permitted himself, an occasional short visit to a hydropathic establishment to repair the "horrid state" of his stomach induced by steady work. Once he was out from under the burden of science, he could see nature whole again and recover the posture of Wordsworth. But he always buckled his burden back on and headed for the dark tunnel of ratiocination that blotted out the light of common day. He was ratifying out of his own experience the teaching of the poets, Wordsworth, Blake, and Keats, but not Shelley, that a man could not run with them and see as they did and be a scientist too—unweave the rainbow and still expect the heart to leap up at the sight. It was an antinomy that John Stuart Mill declined to be impaled upon. He knew, he said, that clouds are "vapor of water, subject to all the laws of vapors in a state of suspension," but he knew equally that they were objects of beauty lit up by the sun, not either-or but both together (*Autobiography*, p. 107).

The healing and integral nature that Mill submitted to but Darwin put from himself dwelt in the domesticated landscapes of England. As a young man Darwin had gone voyaging on the *Beagle* into some of the most untamed landscapes in the world—from the bleak arid plains of Patagonia, too dour for human comfort, to the "great wild, untidy, luxuriant hothouse" of the Brazilian forest, which overshot the mark in the opposite direction.[6] These landscapes from another world—he so describes them, as the nearest thing to visiting another planet—Darwin could never put out of mind. They stood for a quite determinate thing in his life-history; his most powerful experience of "the sublime." This old category, rendered classic by Longinus and refurbished in the eighteenth century by numerous hands, including Edmund Burke, is the most common piece of aesthetic terminology in Darwin's writings from youth into age.[7] He was still puzzling over the exact

6. *Journal of Researches into the Geology and Natural History of the various countries visited by H. M. S. Beagle* (London, 1839), pp. 590, 604 [Fleming's note].

7. On the concept of the sublime, see Marjorie Hope Nicolson, *Mountain Gloom and Mountain Glory* (Ithaca, N.Y., 1959) [Fleming's note].

signification of it and simultaneously throwing it about with abandon in the 1870's. The two things in his experience which had the most power to trigger an access of sublimity were scenic grandeur, as in mountains and forests, and great music, always epitomized for him by the *Messiah*. "I felt glad I was alone," he said, on top of the Andes, "it was like watching a thunderstorm, or hearing a chorus of the *Messiah* in full orchestra" (*Beagle*, p. 394). What did the Hallelujah Chorus and the view from the Andes have in common? What did Darwin mean by "the sublime"? He never did give a straightforward definition, but one thing is clear. The sublime was associated by Darwin with an upwelling from the depths of the spirit that appeared to set reason aside and prevail over it. This, at any rate, was in keeping with Longinus' formula that the sublime is above and beyond the mere "persuasive"—compelling assent by no logical sequence of propositions but by immediate conviction. No wonder Darwin's sublime encompassed powerful incitements to religion. Sublime scenery as he witnessed it on his voyage around the world induced in him reverence, devotion, and worship. Great art by association with scenic grandeur, scenic grandeur with religion, and all three with the sublime, became part of a single universe of experience. "The state of mind," he says, "which grand scenes formerly excited in me, and which was intimately connected with a belief in God, did not essentially differ from that which is often called the sense of sublimity" and brings to mind "the powerful though vague and similar feelings excited by music" (*Autobiography*, p. 91-92). And again: music arouses the feelings of tenderness and love "which readily pass into devotion."[8] The mature Darwin moved away from art because he was continually moving away from religion.

The mainspring of Darwin's aversion from religion is unmistakable. He saw in religion what James and John Stuart Mill saw, assent to the evil of the world and acquiescence in it. To understand the form in which Darwin chiefly apprehended evil, it is necessary to juxtapose the peculiarities of his personal situation with the character of the age he lived in. As a boy he was encouraged by his father's example to hate the sight of blood and the practice of bleeding. As a medical student in Edinburgh, he had felt a "vivid" distress in walking the wards and rushed away in horror from blundering operations. From soon after his marriage till his death more than forty years later, he was a chronic sufferer from headaches, nausea, and stomach upsets. He had always been sensitive to pain. Now he came to live with it as an evil immediately perceived from within. It was all the more an evil for the monumental circumscription of pain that was going forward in Darwin's own lifetime. This took the double form of efforts at the

8. *The Descent of Man* (London, 1871), II, 335 [Fleming's note].

mitigation or removal of pain and the pursuit of new occasions for sympathy with it. Darwin witnessed the introduction of anaesthesia and modern narcotics, the abolition of slavery and serfdom in the Western world, and the birth of organized movements for kindness to animals and children. The "blessed discovery" of chloroform, by which he had out five "grinders" at one time and hardly felt a thing, made him very happy for his children's sake (*Life and Letters*, I, 385). On the evils of slavery, always linked in his mind with the screams heard in Brazil and for ever after in his own nightmares, he was absolutely intransigent. Affection for Asa Gray did not keep him from saying plainly that people in England would never see anything to choose between North and South till the Northern cause was indissolubly bound up with abolition; and the only harsh words he is ever known to have addressed to any of his children were spoken to a son who appeared to be apologizing for the brutal conduct of the infamous Governor Eyre in Jamaica (*Life and Letters*, II, 377; III, 52-53). He was almost equally incensed about cruelty to animals, now first looming up as an unpardonable offense against civilization.

His concern for animals effected a powerful conjunction between the assault on pain and the accomplishment of Darwin's life-work. The discovery in animals of a whole new realm of objects to be felt for, sentimentalized over, and safeguarded from harm was a fundamental, and may have been a necessary, part of the environment in which the doctrine of evolution was established. It was no accident that Darwin lived in an age when Sir Edwin Landseer and Rosa Bonheur were among the most widely admired painters and the organized movement for kindness to animals got under way. It was no accident either that the people portrayed by his contemporary Dickens in *Hard Times* as having found the secret of being fully human were circus performers living on easy terms of companionability with learned dogs and horses and actually constituting with them a single economic and social unit. Darwin and all England with him, and a good deal of the rest of the civilized world besides, were conditioned as never before to accept their kinship with animals. The strategy of a man like Bishop Wilberforce, who tried to undermine the doctrine of evolution by seizing upon the postulated link to animals, could hardly have been more inept. The great apes no doubt were not very widely kept or loved in England, and it would have been better if Darwin had been able to say that men were descended from horses or dogs or better still the Monarch of the Glen,[9] but the general idea of welcoming man's poor relations into the fold of human sympathies had already pre-

9. A painting of a noble stag (1851) by Landseer, widely popular in Victorian England.

vailed. When Darwin sprang from his carriage and fiercely berated a stranger for beating a horse, he was enacting one of the principal reasons for his inevitable triumph over his critics (*Life and Letters*, II, 200).

Not surprisingly, he took an equivocal position on the one matter where the current was superficially flowing in the other direction from the awakening of tenderness: the mushrooming recourse to vivisection by scientific investigators. Darwin did not deny that, properly guarded against abuse, it had an essential role to play in physiology. That did not change the fact that the practice made him personally "sick with horror" and he could not speak too harshly of men who engaged in it out of a "mere damnable and detestable curiosity" (*Life and Letters*, II, 200-201). As a result of these profoundly divided feelings, he initially lent his countenance to the disastrous view that moderate restraints upon vivisection by Parliament would be desirable, only to find that the restraints actually imposed (in 1876) were not moderate and not desirable. Yet even in retreat from his earlier position that legislation could do some good and no harm, he was motivated by his aversion from pain. Vivisection, humanely managed by the conscience of the investigator, would have to be tolerated precisely because it might produce new "remedies for pain and disease" in men and animals alike. He would sanction even pain to put pain to flight.

The raw sensitivity to pain which made Darwin a man of his age, and the fellow-feeling with animals which helped to make him the great vindicator of evolution, afford a clue to his alienation from the best literature of his time, symbolized in his not-so-joking remark that there ought to be a law against novels with unhappy endings. The power which great tragic novels have to raise a storm in the spirit that can never be laid again—their permanent heightening of sensitivity—he could not bear but sought instead for a dampening of consciousness by literature that left no trace behind; ephemeral and conducive to repose. He was in the position of James Mill and J. A. Roebuck, who felt so deeply that they could not imagine that others would experience a dearth of feeling and for themselves wished rather to hold it in check. In the circumstances Darwin could not possibly enter into the younger Mill's vindication of art as an emotional stimulus to the unfeeling. Darwin was trying to cut down on his emotional intake; and according to his own testimony, had considerable success in weaning himself from the rich diet of his youth and learning to feel more dimly. His turning away from art was both a means to this success and a token of it. It was a token as well of the fires within him that he was conscious of having to bank down.

Intense feeling was undesirable in Darwin's own experience as

exacerbating his already keen sensitivities. It was or could be undesirable in a cosmic view as well. Therein lay a tremendous
ambiguity at the very heart of Darwin's position. Natural selection
itself proceeds by pain, suffering, frustration, and unfulfillment—
the whole gamut that failure of promise encompasses. Any good
that comes of it, comes by evil. Darwin could not deny, in fact he
had to insist, that failure was stalking the world and performing
grim labors. If the grim labors were to slacken or failure not to take
its toll, natural selection would be by so much impeded. Darwin
points in the Descent of Man to many dysgenic factors in civilized
life by which those who would otherwise go under in the struggle
for survival and procreation are kept afloat by the rest, often at the
direct expense of the latter: exemption of the physically inferior
from warfare, with conscription of the strongest young men to die in
battle and leave few or no heirs behind them; public assistance to
the poor; organized solicitude for the "imbecile" and "maimed";
and universal extension of medical benefits, so that to take only
one example, thousands of people who would have succumbed to
smallpox by reason of their weak constitutions have been spared to
become fathers of the race.[1] Except for the policy on conscription,
which is partly pragmatic as well as compassionate, all of these
dysgenic factors arise out of tenderness for the weak. The implication
is clear that tenderness has become a clog upon evolution. It was
not always thus. Darwin in the Descent of Man can be seen looking
wistfully back to some indistinct but shining age in the past, a
moment of poise between two extremes, when men had learned
to value social solidarity but had not yet confused this with tenderness for what he calls "the imbecile, the maimed, and other useless
members of society" (Descent of Man, I, 103). One catches a
momentary glimpse of Darwin's Wagnerian or Carlylean self peeping shyly out from under his invalid's cloak, where such things are
often most at home, and yearning for the brave old forest days
when the world was bathed in a stern but golden light and men
were faithful to comrades, obedient to leaders, and strangers to
pity. Good actions were those requiring "self-sacrifice, self-command,
and the power of endurance" to further the ends of the tribe rather
than the happiness of the individual members (Descent of Man,
I, 95). Darwin hints that the light that shone in other days might
come again if men would take as their object, not the furtherance
of individual happiness, but the promotion of the "general good,"
defined as "the means by which the greatest possible number of
individuals can be reared in full vigor and health, with all their

1. *Descent of Man*, 2d ed. (London, 1874), cited from 2-volume edition (London, 1888), I, 206-207. The entire argument, except for conscription, in 1st ed. (London, 1871), I, 167-170. Unless otherwise indicated references will be to the latter edition [Fleming''s note].

faculties perfect, under the conditions to which they are exposed" (*Descent of Man*, I, 98). But, he adds, rather delightfully, such a procedure might "perhaps require some limitation on account of political ethics."

III

Darwin remained in his central being a deeply sensitive man, shrinking back from the spectacle of pain in other creatures, and wishing to offer some alleviation. What could this consistently be for the great proponent of natural selection? One answer was to refrain from positive acts of cruelty oneself and try to get others to refrain. More profoundly, Darwin's answer consisted in his repudiation of religion. This is the animus behind his unflagging interest in the theological interpretation of his doctrines. If natural selection were to be construed, as his great friend Asa Gray in America urged, as God's instrument of continuous creation, then there was an overmastering Will in the world that pain and evil should exist, if only to some further end. They were not mere existents, they were existents willed from on high. This to the shrinking and wincing Darwin was an intolerable conception of the universe, shared by all religions alike. People kept telling him that to conjoin belief in God with belief in natural selection merely went to deepen their faith and enlarge the consolations of religion.[2] To him, a God that dwelt in natural selection would be the worst of all possible Gods. For the proprietor of the universe to have to seek for a mere preponderance of good over evil in the world that he made, which was the best that could be said for any progress attained by natural selection, was monstrous in Darwin's eyes. He did not want a *God* that had to proceed by Benthamite calculus and either did not know how or did not care enough to decree uncontaminated good. In a sense, he belonged, with the Mills, to a class of God-deniers who were yearning after a better God than God. How high their standard was in these matters can be judged from the fact that Darwin thought there was a decided over-balance of happiness as against misery among sentient beings. He expressly says that the world is on the whole a good world—for "if all the individuals of any species were habitually to suffer to an extreme degree they would neglect to propagate their kind," but we have no evidence of this (*Autobiography*, pp. 88-90). Yet much intermittent suffering does occur; and this is sufficient in Darwin's opinion to condemn the idea of an "intelligent first cause" beyond any appeal to the admittedly greater quantity of habitual happiness. Moreover, he says that even if we are willing (as he was not) to accept the traditional Christian view that all evils suffered by men

---

2. See, *e.g.*, Mrs. Boole to Darwin, *ca.* 1867; *Life and Letters*, III, 63-65 [Fleming's note].

can be discounted as opportunities for spiritual improvement, the pain experienced by animals would remain an unanswerable reproach to any deity that presided over it: "the number of men in the world is as nothing compared with that of all other sentient beings, and these often suffer greatly without any moral improvement. A being so powerful and so full of knowledge as a God who could create the universe, is to our finite minds omnipotent and omniscient, and it revolts our understanding to suppose that his benevolence is not unbounded, for what advantage can there be in the sufferings of millions of the lower animals throughout almost endless time?" (*Autobiography*, p. 90). After God was discarded by Darwin, the suffering of the world remained undiminished; but he rightly intuited that modern man would rather have senseless suffering than suffering warranted to be intelligible because willed from on high. Darwin gave to his fellow men the best though terrible gift and comfort that he could devise: the assurance that the evil of the world was like the world itself, brute and ungrounded and ready to be stamped by each man with his own meaning and no other.

Here Darwin was sitting in judgment upon the tradition of natural theology, which sought to confer upon the universe the character of a work of art from the hand of the Great Artist; and more than this, sought to lend a common affective tone, a unifying vision of beauty, harmony, and fostering influences, to the universal landscape, so that all partial evils were lost in a greater good. This impulse to make a willed unity of disparate elements, to fuse parts into an emotional whole, is almost diagnostic for the artist's temperament. Natural selection was precisely the denial of nature as a planned work of art and an effort to dissipate the pleasing affective tone that natural theologians tried to lend it. It would be tempting to say that Darwin turned against works of art because he had determined to smash the greatest of all. At some deep level this may have operated; but we are on safer ground if, while recognizing the profound consonance between his revulsion from art and his repudiation of natural theology, we emphasize Darwin's resolve not to be an accomplice in the evil of the world by assenting to God's dominion.

We are brought round again to Darwin's experience of the sublime and the triple conjunction in this thought of scenic grandeur, music, and religion: all standing in common for the uncontrollable motions in the spirit and cutting adrift from reason which Darwin associated with the intimations of divinity which came to him in the Brazilian forest. He had to believe for his own comfort and the comfort of others that the instruction of the sublime in behalf of religion was false. Just so, the surges of feeling that music could arouse were capable of arming men for battle, but equally without any real bearing upon the right and reason of their cause. The dominion of art, as of religion, is the dominion of the irrational. The association can be documented from both ends of Darwin's career. At twenty-nine, he spoke of getting up close to a painting and being laid open by the "peculiar smell," presumably varnish, to the "old irrational ideas" that "thrilled across me" as an under-graduate in the Fitzwilliam Museum at Cambridge.[3] Thirty-six years later, in a moment of deep revelation in the *Descent of Man*, he touched in immediate succession upon the gusts of emotion that whip through a crowd of African Negroes, the excited chat-tering of monkeys, and the "sensations and ideas" aroused in modern man by music, which appear "from their vagueness, yet depth, like mental reversions to the emotions and thoughts of a long-past age."[4] Communion with primitive man and subhuman relatives of man and reversion through music to the dawn of history—it is an evocation in time and place of all occasions where feeling may be expected to prevail over reason or not even encounter any reason to put to rout. Response to music, like response to religion, does not give true evidence of anything except a will toward illusion. Music "arouses dormant sentiments of which we had not conceived the possibility, and do not know the meaning; or, as Richter says, tells us of things we have not seen and shall not see."[5] We are here in the general vicinity of Bentham's dictum that art is lies and has the power to certify lies and make them pass for truth. It was among the most terrible indictments that a man like Darwin could imagine, whose most distinctive quality was an instinct for truth-telling which has hardly ever been surpassed—has there ever been another scientist who included in his great book all the arguments against it that he could think of? He could only be true to himself by resisting the access of illusion wherever it tried to creep in.

In his resolve to be one of the great Truth-Bearers, Darwin strove to perfect himself as a fact-and-dust man, more abundant in learn-ing and insight, more generous in spirit, and more divided than Thomas Gradgrind, but endeavoring to stand for the same thing and indeed opening out cosmic vistas for application of the Grad-grind philosophy. To deal, not in apt caricatures upon historical men, but in real men of heroic stature, Darwin was a kind of

3. Entry of 12 Aug. 1838 in the un-published Notebook "M" in Cambridge University Library. I owe this quotation to the kindness of Dr. Sydney Smith of St. Catharine's College, Cambridge [Fleming's note].

4. *Descent of Man* (London, 1888), II, 364-365. Negroes omitted in 1st ed.; relevant passage, II, 336 [Fleming's note].

5. *Descent of Man* (London, 1871), II, 336; the entire passage, including the quotation from Richter, quoted from Herbert Spencer. Cf. footnote 6 below [Fleming's note].

successor to the seventeenth-century Puritans with their terror of the imagination. To those who would resist its wiles, the Puritans held out in compensation the prospect of a sober and godly life. Redemption they could not promise. So too with Darwin. In repelling illusion, he was taking the only compassion upon his fellow-men that he could contrive and bestowing upon them the best though somber good that their situation permitted. The chief lie of lying religion for him was that evil could have been inflicted from on high instead of simply occurring. If, by access to the sublime, he should assent to this lie, his act of charity to mankind for uncovering the harsh necessity of natural selection would fall to the ground. Love of mankind and love of the truth combined with fear of religion to make Darwin suspicious of art, a type of the anaesthetic man, both in the literal sense of "not feeling" and in the derivative sense of taking steps to repress the pain that he was capable of feeling.

IV

His own anaesthetic state was mirrored forth in his scientific view of the world. As he had cut art out of his own life, so he left it out of his evolutionary scheme for mankind in the *Descent of Man*. In his only direct confrontation with Herbert Spencer, they took diametrically opposite views on the cosmic role of music. Spencer held that music followed speech in the evolutionary sequence as an "idealized language of emotion" and has been continually reacting upon ordinary language in the form of vocal modulation to produce a kind of running "commentary of the emotions upon the propositions of the intellect."[6] Men not only understand each other, they *feel* for each other to the extent that this language of emotions is perfected. Spencer looks to the day when perfection will be attained. We may expect, he says, that the language of feelings will ultimately enable men to partake "completely" of one another's emotions. It is a prospect of universal good-will born of music and fed by music. For Darwin the role of music in the history of the world has long since been outworn.[7] He held, in direct contradiction to Spencer, that music preceded speech and gave birth to it. Once this occurred, music had outlived its cosmic function except as a means of courtship among birds. In the life of men, music is now a mere epiphenomenon, a froth on the surface of life: "neither the enjoyment not the capacity of producing musical notes are faculties of the least direct use to man in reference to his ordinary habits of life" (*Descent of Man*, II, 333). He even went on to say that this useless attribute "must be ranked among the most

6. Herbert Spencer, "The Origin and Function of Music" (1857); in *Essays, Scientific, Political, and Speculative* (New York, 1891), II, 419, 422 [Fleming's note].

7. *Descent of Man* (London, 1888), II, 355-367; slightly amended from 1st ed., II, 330-337 [Fleming's note].

mysterious" with which man is endowed. Here, in his eagerness to put down the pretensions of music, Darwin was underestimating the power of his own teaching. He had supplied a perfectly plausible account of the *emergence* of poetry, singing, dancing, and love of ornamentation, as rooted in sexual selection. He had even assigned to music in the distant past the tremendous cosmic function of generating language. What he had failed to do was to suggest of what use the fine arts might be in the present and for the long future; why in their "mysterious" way they should stubbornly endure and grow more potent instead of shrivelling up into rudimentary organs like the appendix.

Historical circumstances conspired to make Darwin's great refusal of significance to the arts less glaring. He died in 1882, before the major works of prehistoric sculpture and painting had been authenticated. Though engraved pieces of bone were being uncovered by Edouard Lartet from the early 1860's forward, Sir Charles Lyell in his *Antiquity of Man* of 1863 always meant by "work of art" an artifact; and the incredible cave paintings of Altamira, though actually discovered at the end of the '70's, were not given a clean bill of authenticity by the principal skeptic till 1902. Darwin did refer in the second and last edition of the *Descent* in 1874 to the discovery by Lartet of two flutes made of bone, but these did not have the power to project artistic expression into the very center of prehistoric life as the great mural paintings did.[8] If one could imagine a slight speeding up in the history of archaeology—which is probably excluded by the fact that the cave paintings required for their acceptance at true value precisely the steeping of an entire generation in Darwinism—Darwin would have been confronted with a grave spiritual crisis. If driven to it, he would not have been at a loss to imagine a cosmic function for art. That was the trouble. He had a solution all too ready at hand but one that would have been intolerable to him as a human being. The iron band that clamped art, sublimity, and religion together in his own experience would have meant that the obvious way to build art into his system would be to assign a powerful role to religion as a constructive force in the development of mankind. Despite one or two equivocal tributes to religion as the mainstay of morality but also superstition, the last thing that Darwin wanted to do was to attribute any lasting evolutionary significance to it.

John Stuart Mill, if he had been charged with drawing up an evolutionary scheme, would not have lain under the same inhibition. For him the arts energized indeterminately, they did not confine him to a single channel and that unwelcome, or make him "recreant" to his prior commitments, but infused these with emo-

8. *Descent of Man* (London, 1888), II, 362 [Fleming's note].

tional gratification without in any way pitching him into the arms of religion (*Autobiography*, p. 101). He was not turned about in his course but sped rejoicing on his way. That was part of what Dickens had been trying to say about Louisa Gradgrind. By openness to works and endeavors of the imagination, she would have been "wiser, happier, more loving, more contented, more innocent and human" and persuaded that life was "worth the pain and trouble of a contest." But even at the end of the book, when she had begun to be human, she continued to lead the same domestic life as before. She did not find a new calling but new courage and zest to prosecute the old. Significantly, Dickens nowhere attributes to her any yearning after religion or ultimate conversion to it. The instrument of her redemption, Sissy Jupe, is like Mill's Helen Taylor in not even proffering solicitations to conversion.

Darwin was menaced by conversion from within and without. That was the irreducible difference between him and his wife, with her discreet endeavors at bringing him around and silent dissent from his deepening unbelief; and that, above all, was the menace of art. *He* would be turned about by art, manacled to religion, and diverted from his role in history. For the humane import of the doctrine of evolution through natural selection was to lop off the Godhead and show how biological order could be generated without a divine fiat. He could only keep upon his course and be the fit author of his own revolution by burking the evolutionary significance of the arts.

It was an omission that has never been fully repaired. Only one voice since Darwin has spoken with comparable force to the biological situation of man; and though Sigmund Freud took ample account of the arts as a fundamental human activity, he failed equally with Darwin to attribute to them any desirable function in evolution. With some qualifications, he tended to regard the arts as a strategy of concealment by which men attempted to evade the truth about their own nature, to wrap it up in symbols. If Freud had believed with Eugene O'Neill and others in the healing and saving power of illusion, he might have seen in this an aid to survival and increment of fitness. On the contrary, he regarded art as being in this character regressive, a means of turning away from reality to the pleasure principle. It was his own office to make men behold the truth about themselves in its naked aspect with a steady and unflinching regard; and health of mind lay in the scrutiny. Freud could not correct the bias in Darwin. They were as one in their mistrust of the arts as fostering illusion. As their common heirs, we still lack a universally compelling vision of science and art as reenforcing each other and flourishing together, not as truth locked in battle with illusion but as clarity of intellect joined to warmth of feeling.

JOHN RADER PLATT
Style in Science

All scientists are not alike. Look at any laboratory or university science department. Professor Able is the kind of man who seizes an idea as a dog seizes a stick, all at once. As he talks you can see him stop short, with the chalk in his fingers, and then almost jump with excitement as the insight grips him. His colleague, Baker, on the other hand, is a man who comes to understand an idea as a worm might understand the same stick, digesting it a little at a time, drawing his conclusions cautiously, and tunneling slowly through it from end to end and back again.

Which of these methods is likely to make the greater contribution to science? There are drawbacks to both. Able is volatile. He may drop his idea as rapidly as he acquired it. In a short time he can race through a forest of ideas and leave all his colleagues breathless behind, including Baker. Baker is scornful of such a procedure, perhaps a little envious. He can never try so many ideas, though in the end each one he tries becomes part of him, each one tested in every aspect.

Or consider another pair of scientific minds, whose contrasted inner workings are revealed by their contrasted footnote habits.

Charlson is the one who discovers everything for himself. He dislikes reading other men's efforts because they stale the fresh springs of his thought. Though he is famous to the world, his scientific enemies are numbered by the dozens because he never bothered to look up their prior parallelisms and dim anticipations. So he left out all the references that would have been their tendril grasps on fame. Rumors of plagiarism are heard at the Society meetings.

Doctor Doggett, instead, is footnote-happy. No historical cranny is safe. He pries out the foreshadowings, the counterarguments, and the misprints. If he makes a creative contribution himself it is lost among the references, for there are more lines of footnotes than there are of text. Yet he gathers a thousand strands together and may find distant connections which pass unnoticed by other men.

Will it be Doggett or Charlson who makes the great discovery?

This is a question we could pursue through the whole academic alphabet, contrasting the syndromes and merits of the types of scientific personality. Simply as writers, one man is dull, one witty; one verbose, another terse. This man's equations lie like boulders on the page, that man's like a fog. It is amusing to see how the differences show through the attempted impersonality of scientific verbiage.

But we soon realize that the question of relative merit hinges on a more fundamental question: Is personality significant for science? We often hear the arguments for scientific determinism, which is the belief that scientific discoveries are somewhat like the measles, breaking out everywhere at once when the time is ripe. If this is so, is not one man in a given field as likely as another to make an important discovery? Does it make any difference to knowledge who invents a thing first, or what kind of mind and style he has?

If we look at some examples from the history of science with this problem in mind, I think we will see that personality does indeed make a difference. The two aspects interpenetrate. To a remarkable extent the discovery ripe to be born selects one discoverer from among the contestants, picking out the master of a line of thought and method essential to its birth. But equally remarkable is the extent to which the undetermined and peculiar stamp of his parenthood is embedded forever in the body of pure knowledge.

The evidence for scientific determinism—with its lesser emphasis on personality—is the familiar catalogue of the instances of multiple discovery. The great cases of this kind were the simultaneous and independent discovery of the calculus by Newton and Leibnitz three centuries ago, and the simultaneous Darwin and Wallace discoveries of natural selection in the last century. Hundreds of lesser examples could be listed. Each idea, with variations, is found and found again. Patent lawyers make their living from such competition.

Independent discoveries are sometimes only months or weeks apart, especially today in the fields crowded with first-rate competitors. In physics, for example, the synchrocyclotron was invented simultaneously in the United States and in Russia. Independent communications from this country and from Germany announced the current theoretical "shell model" of atomic nuclei in the very same issue of the *Physical Review*. The race for priority hinges on days, and the Saturday afternoon Letter-to-the-Editor becomes a regular event.

Such examples make scientific developments appear almost inevitable, maturing like dandelions on both sides of company fences and national ones, to the despair of Congressmen and drug houses. The reason for this is that discoveries have preconditions that must be met. Once these are met, even a non-genius may make a discovery if he is playing with the right apparatus and tries everything. To a certain extent, science is successful because it is a code of rules that enables ordinary brains with ordinary motivations to set up, one step at a time, the necessary preconditions.

Some are mechanical. Take the discoveries of electrons and of

X-rays, which occurred within two years of each other in the 1890's. Both required the application of a high voltage to a good vacuum. This in turn required the knowledge of direct current electricity, a good cheap high-voltage generator, and a good cheap vacuum pump, with an electric motor drive for convenience. All these are late-nineteenth-century items. The incandescent lamp, not a discovery but an invention, had similar preconditions; but it could be made with a lower voltage and a poorer vacuum, and so was invented a few years earlier.

This is not to say that these discoveries could have been predicted. No one foresaw that such phenomena existed. But if anything were there to be found with that apparatus, it must have been found *then*. The discoveries were made by highly competent experimenters; yet within a few years almost any intelligent student might have made them independently, while experimenters ten times as competent could scarcely have set the dates of discovery earlier by as much as two decades. In present times, the anti-proton could be predicted, and planned for at Berkeley, years in advance; and then discovered almost as soon as the apparatus was designed, finished, and turned on. We can see why one celebrated physicist said that half of his success consisted in knowing what to order and where to order it.

There are also intellectual conditions that must be met, before a discovery can be made or appreciated or understood. The brilliant idea requires intellectual groundwork and, what is equally important, a scientific community ready for the novelty. It is just as sure a recipe for failure to have the right idea fifty years too soon as five years too late. William James might have been advising young men in any science when he said: Decide what important thing will be done in the next twenty years; then do it.

Occasionally, untimely ideas do get preserved to be marveled at. In mathematics, Fermat's Last Theorem still tantalizes us; and Hamilton's Quaternions, which were thought by his contemporaries to indicate mild insanity, were simply premature by two or three generations.

Abbé Mendel, father of genetics, actually bred his sweet peas decades too soon. His contribution was finally disinterred at the time when it could be understood. Roentgen made the discovery of X-rays in a momentary lapse from a lifelong study of crystals, which was no doubt equally painstaking and inspired but is almost unremembered because it was fifty years too early. Sometimes even a short time makes a great difference in the response to a new idea. Stories persist that the equations of quantum mechanics were derived by this man or that but were rejected by editors only a year or two before Schrödinger got his version accepted and won a Nobel prize.

We may speculate on how many good scientists may have died mute, inglorious, and bitter because their work was too advanced to be understood. This is the standard defense of the ill-prepared and the crackpot. Yet the failure to recognize a brilliant man is only partly due to the stupidity or stubbornness of the scientific community; it is also partly his own fault.

For brilliance has an obligation not only to create but also to communicate. A scientist can not really go "voyaging through strange seas of thought alone." The more penetrating eye will see him to be surrounded by a cloud of witnesses. He takes from others; he gives to others. He must address the problems of his time. He must translate his thoughts into the language of his contemporaries. He must scatter them abroad for interaction. A thought which has not penetrated to other minds will die unfruitful.

As a result, the scientist can hardly be recognized posthumously, like the artist or poet. He is much less independent, much more bound to the current needs and purposes of the scientific community. His achievement of thought needs to be at the same time an achievement of communication and leadership which must be acknowledged by the group—by at least one editor!—before its intellectual viability fades away.

It is a perishable achievement. Not many of us know who first cut the trees or cleared the land beside our houses. The scientific explorer, like the wilderness explorer, exists to be superseded. Wandering at random, he finds a first, clumsy way to the new goal. The more important the goal, the greater the speed with which his path is by-passed by short-cuts, ridden over by electronic computing machines, and obliterated by the marching masses of Ph.D.'s. His hesitations, his sextant readings, the art and intuition by which he avoided this pitfall or that rabbit track—these make dull hard reading after a few years, for they apply to a world of difficulties which, because of his very efforts, has vanished and can scarcely be reconstructed. But such a man is properly contemptuous of the incoherent genius whose ravishing discoveries are too strange and vague to be communicable.

Determinism also plays a more intimate role. Not only is the time of a discovery approximately determined, it seems that the personality of the discoverer may to some extent be determined. To find America, we must have a fifteenth-century Western sea captain, uncommercial, convinced, dogged, persuasive, with delusions of grandeur—whether his name is Columbus or something else.

To see this principle in science, we must concentrate on two components of personality which I shall call method and style. By method, I mean the type of a scientist's intuition, his normally preferred method of attack. One man loves most to design and build apparatus, a glorified instrument maker. Another is a human measuring engine who can turn out more data or more precise data than anyone else. Some like to improve on other men's experiments in familiar fields, others prefer wild and novel experiments of their own at the limit of the possible. In these differences, one major axis of variation ought to be especially emphasized. It is the difference between the generally inductive and the generally deductive types of mind.

In an inductive mind, the internal monologue might go somewhat as follows: "Now here's a funny result. It doesn't fit in at all with Smollengoble's theorem! Yes, the apparatus is okay. Didn't I see last month where someone else had trouble with that theorem? But he had lower pressure. If we increased the pressure, would it go farther in the same direction?"

The general from the particular. This is the man who covers his laboratory walls with graphs of his data and squints at them every morning before he turns on his power supply, wondering if those deviations are experimental error or a real effect. There is something of this turn of mind in all of us. A talented few, like the master organic chemists, develop it until they can play their residues and hunches as a virtuoso plays the violin.

The deductive genius may be tone deaf to such music. His passion is not for the uncertain new order but for elegance and clarity in the old. At his highest pinnacle, he is the Euclid or Maxwell who stands and looks back after a period of growth and sees that a few simple postulates will unite a whole body of separate rules into a symmetrical system.

Like the inductive mind, he sees patterns, but in a different medium. Perhaps when he closes his eyes by the fire he stares into a magnificent void where the luminous theorems move and intersect and enclose each other an he leaps up shouting, "I have it! I have it!" However jumbled his desk may be, there is some distant region of the spirit where his files are clearly labeled and his papers have been written in a neat hand on one side only and are stapled into bundles with their edges straight—the great plan encompassing every particular in every pigeonhole. There is something of this, too, in all of us.

One of these minds anticipates, the other reconstructs. Inductive steps must come before deductive ones. So in each subject area there is a time when one method is most appropriate. Then it exhausts its material, at least for the moment, and recedes as the important discoveries begin to fall to another kind of mental machine. A field of knowledge has a curve of growth and a morphology, branches and stem—a beginning, a middle, and an end. Different talents are needed in the gardeners at different times. Those with a green thumb must plant, while others with a sure balance climb ladders later for the fruit.

Take the discovery of the law of gravitation. First there is visual observation and instrumentation, from the ancients to Tycho Brahe's quadrant and his tables of years of nights of measurement. Then there are the rule-makers, from the Ptolemaic astronomers to Kepler, who asked how all this would look from the nearest star and searched Tycho's tables for regularities, boiling the regularities down to his three laws of planetary motion.

Wandering in and out of the procession are the speculators— Lucretius, Copernicus—who animate the mixture with their lively controversies. At one side are the auxiliaries: Archimedes on conic sections; the navigators, defining the shape and size of the earth; Galileo, hurling balls and abstracting from them that ingenious invention, the ideal free body.

What a preparation for Newton! It might be compared to some Biblical prophecy in its visions and connections and anticipations across the milleniums. These are the shoulders of giants, with linked arms—not merely a human pyramid, but the braced and giant framework of knowledge itself.

The main line of development in scientific theory follows this sequence of work methods: observation, rule of thumb, speculation, synthesis. Naturally the methods of work are not perfectly separated in time nor even in the individual scientists. Every research man must be capable of performing all the functions in some degree—especially the speculative function—if he is to be worth his scientific salt. He may even have several highly developed talents, like Newton. This should not blind us to the big difference in the different mental processes, even such as that between the maker of the important little first syntheses—frequently an experimenter—and the maker of final grand syntheses who often shows a native distaste for the raw and original datum.

To see the historical necessity that selects these types, let us try a thought experiment on history. Consider what would have happened if the minds of Newton and Kepler had been interchanged. The slightest acquaintance with the work of either man will show that Newton's mind was not the one to unravel Tycho's data, and Kepler's was not the one to do Newton's necessary preliminary work of discovering the calculus. Not that it would have been absolutely impossible; only that it would have been slow and burdensome for either mind to try to use intuition methods like the other, and that they would have turned aside soon and wisely to more congenial discoveries.

A mature research worker needs to seek out tasks which he can undertake best with his mental gifts at his moment of history. A Maxwell in the eighteenth century could not have united electricity and magnetism but would have had to work on, let us say, astronomy, while the Franklins did the groundwork of electricity. Maxwell in the nineteenth century could and did perfect electricity but would have been lost in atomic spectra, where a Kepler kind of mind was needed. A Maxwell today might find chemistry or field-theory almost ripe for his talents, but would probably be foolish to go back to the well-plowed area of electricity unless he proposed to make a still larger synthesis, or a synthesis from a completely new point of view.

The time sequence of work methods is never perfectly clear-cut, however; in a single field the different types of talent co-exist and make simultaneous contributions. For the different types of talent need each other. Inductive and deductive, intuitive and classical, are the two halves of a pair of scissors and cut only when they are opposed. Each work method produces its own peculiar excesses which must be seen from another viewpoint before their deformity can be recognized.

The inductive mind often goes too far. Not having the advantage of the grand synthesis, it does not know where to stop. Searching for important relations, it finds unimportant ones. Experimental error may be turned into law, or clear disproof dismissed as experimental error.

Pythagoras' useful relation between the sides of triangles seems to have been associated in his own enthusiasm with the lengths of musically harmonious strings, and so with the harmonies of the universe and the music of the spheres. This goes too far, but it is not all nonsense: the lengths of harmonious strings do indeed have simple numerical ratios.

The first regularity of planets which Kepler thought he found was that they moved on spheres circumscribed and inscribed in five vast regular polyhedrons in the heavens. This is not all nonsense: the regular spacing of the orbits is a main feature of several recent cosmologies.

Such jumps "beyond Reason" need to be continuously criticized by the deductive and classical mind. Yet the inductive mind is like a sentry who must be forgiven for firing at an occasional shadow provided he always fires toward the enemy.

The sin of the deductive mind is that it derides and suppresses those inductive jumps that later prove to be right about as harshly as those that prove to be wrong. Newton rejected Huygens' and Hooke's wave theory of light which swept out Newton's own ideas a hundred years later. An esteemed critic showed that Balmer's formula, the first real regularity found in atomic spectra, must be a mathematical accident. De Broglie's paper, which contained the first germ of quantum mechanics, was widely regarded as nonsense.

Still, this conservatism has a good result. The success of an innovator is meted out in proportion to his scientific persuasiveness, his patience in amassing crucial observations, like Darwin, to show that the old faith is unjustified. It is not the moment of insight but the moment of acceptance that marks a firm step forward. Scientific growth is by conflict. The truth is found only in the heat of controversy as each man is forced to defend his thesis: the classicist his sufficiency, the innovator his necessity.

The historical counterpoint between the inductive and deductive mind is useful even in its subtler manifestations. It provides an unspectacular tension which is a major force in keeping science balanced. Each creative worker lives in a steady stream of deductive criticism—normally, in fact, self-criticism—curbing and channeling his intuitive impulses.

It is not so much that his little daily jumps and inferences must not violate "reason" as that they must satisfy more delicate canons of scientific good taste. How many readings or decimal places to take; what precautions; how ignorant or speculative to show oneself at various stages of scientific friendship; how soon to publish; and so on. A large part of the training of science students is really devoted to instilling this code of scientific manners.

The code is a balance of opposites. A man may acquire deductive good manners at the expense of some of his inductive hope, faith, and fire; fanning the fire may soften in turn the rigor of his self-criticism. Some individuals and groups try to solve the problem by separating the two processes, starting with an idea stage in which the imaginaton runs wild and free, followed by an analytical stage in which the ideas are critically selected and combined. The genius is the one who can maximize both elements and maintain at the time the fiercest productivity and the most exacting standards.

Likewise for a successful scientific group, the curbing of inductive jumps by the canons of taste must be neither too rigid nor too loose. The scissors will not cut if the blades are locked or if they are wobbly. The rigor of editors is needed to restrict the wilder flights as much as the zeal of speculators is needed to keep knowledge alive. Science cannot be fruitful where publishers indulge unready authors, wild fancies, and incompetent techniques; nor where hoary academic despots hold the seats of power and press the young men to a mold two generations old. But neither side can afford to be dogmatic, for it is only in the light of the syntheses of a succeeding generation that we can look back and be certain what was excess of speculation and what was excess of repression.

These remarks have perhaps conveyed some idea of the depth to which scientific determinism goes. A social necessity fixes not only the timing of a discovery but the work methods of the discoverer; it affects the heat of the controversies engendered, and where science is successful it sets the canons of taste which determine whether the discovery is accepted or rejected at a given stage of proof.

Nevertheless, all is not fixed. If we move about inside this framework we can now begin to see the ornaments and gargoyles added, unnecessarily and delightfully and sometimes unexpectedly, by exuberant craftsmen, shaped by personality above and beyond strict scientific need.

For one thing, each person has his own combination of fields of interest. A scientist trained in one subject often makes spectacular contributions when his novel outlook and work methods are turned into another field. Think of the special approach of Helmholtz, the physiologist turned physicist; or of Pasteur, the chemist, among the diseases.

Personality also enters through language, with its hidden assumptions. Without Newton himself, we might never have had "force" or "mass" in the equations of motion; or they might have had very different definitions and emphases. Philosophers have pulled and hauled at them for centuries; the difficulties were ineradicable, because these symbols were written from the beginning in the Newtonian equations that worked. The Father of Physics has imprinted "force" and "mass," like intellectual genes, into every cell of the physical sciences today.

Kepler, on the other hand, seems to have eschewed, largely on aesthetic grounds, the anthropomorphic concept of "force" between heavenly bodies. In this question of taste, he anticipates Einstein. If history had put the Kepler mind in the Newton body, it might have delayed the discovery of universal gravitation, which would have been difficult for Kepler—but it might have accelerated the discovery of general relativity.

Terminology is often chained to such initial biases. Franklin's choice of the arithmetic terms "positive" and "negative" to designate the two supplementary types of electricity still plagues our thinking and may have delayed who knows what happier synthesis.

The idiosyncrasies of taste and choice, of abilities and workmanship, embellish and modify a discovery. The work method is determined; the style is not. Any physical law is exhibited in many places and forms and may be found by single experiments on hundreds of compounds or by hundreds of experiments on a grain of sand. And the discoverer may be an exhibitionist, or a conservative; an equation maker, or a model maker; he may want priority, or certainty. He may succeed by testing everything to destruction, at unusual temperatures and pressures; or by exploring his materials with nothing but a beam of light. He may be guided by shrewd and almost superstitious hunches, that only fluorocarbons will give him clear-cut answers, or density-matrix methods, or Drosophila, or sweet peas.

Sometimes the effects of such variations are profound indeed. There is one instance where a vast intellectual development has been hung on the deficiencies of a single piece of apparatus. We might not believe that electrons are in atoms except for some equipment assembled in 1898 by Zeeman in Holland, with which he found that the spectrum lines of atoms were broadened and polarized by a magnetic field. This "Zeeman effect" was explained by Lorentz on the assumption that the atoms contained the newly discovered corpuscles called electrons. Later, Bohr continued to assume this in his atomic theory; and whole-electrons-in-atoms passed on into the quantum mechanics that we now use.

But meanwhile, what of the Zeeman effect? If Zeeman had had a better spectrograph or had improved his apparatus before publishing his first results, he would have reported what a college senior can discover now; that each of his broadened spectrum lines is really a complex array of many lines, with every array different. Neither Lorentz nor anyone else would then have believed that there were intact electrons, all alike, inside the atom; perhaps fractional ones would have been assumed. The Bohr atom would have been different, or impossible. Quantum mechanics as we know it might never have appeared. No doubt some other theoretical system would have been produced in its place, but by now, after fifty years, its practitioners would speak a language incomprehensible or perhaps unbelievable to our best physicists. (The scientists will not find it any easier to talk to scientists they meet from another planet than laymen will.)

If a piece of apparatus can shape a field of knowledge, a brilliant scientist may also have a great personal effect. Many of the peculiarities of modern physics seem to have this individual stamp. Bohr, de Broglie, Schrödinger, Heisenberg, Dirac—each is responsible for some aspect of the synthesis of atomic structure which is quantum mechanics. Yet their approaches are very different: Bohr with his electron-orbits in space; de Broglie with his almost mystical waves; Heisenberg with his matrices and strict operationalism; Dirac with his formalism. If we had lost one of these, it would not have affected our ability to predict experimental results, which is often said to be the aim of science; but it would have been a great loss indeed to our understanding.

And a great change. Without Bohr himself, would the earlier ideas of an atom as a vibrating jelly have been strangely modified by some other young pseudo-Bohr in the 1910's to explain the spectra and win the day? Without the particular style of a particular man, Dirac, we might have had formalism of a sort, but probably not the chaste, terse, awful elegance that now strikes fear and admiration into the graduate students.

The work of Willard Gibbs in chemical thermodynamics may be the most individual tour de force of all. Somewhat cut off in late-nineteenth-century America from the larger body of European theoretical physicists and chemists, he evolved an unusual kind of thinking; perhaps as an island population evolves aberrant species when cut off from the mainland. His equations show no trace of the mechanical particles bombarding the walls of a box which still dominated the thought of European scientists. He produced a theory without "forces" and without imaginary models of what was happening in the box, using simply relations among the things oberved on the outside, such as temperature, pressure, and volume. And he combined these with a logical absolute, a naked and apparently vulnerable assertion about entropy.

True, this was not completely alien to contemporary style. Differential equations like his were the admired mathematical form in other areas. There had been some interest in the physical power of syllogisms; and Mach and Einstein were shortly to remove "force" from motion and from gravitation and to assert other logical absolutes. But taken together and applied to chemistry, what a change! Small wonder that nobody noticed him but Maxwell. Small wonder that the best science students still go blank and dumb, and the little philosophy major at the back of the room suddenly begins to get the right answers, when they come to this part of the course. It hurts a three-dimensional man to see temperature computed from a syllogism.

It seems probable to me that if Gibbs had lived in England or Germany this fusion of ideas might not have occurred until at least a generation later. By that time chemical thinking would have been set in another mold, and chemistry today would be a different thing.

There are many lessons, for our culture, for our teachers, and for our scientists, to be learned from examining closely the interplay of the Great Man aspect of history with the Determinist aspect. It is exhibited in the microcosm of the scientific world in a relatively simple form in which the casual intellectual strands are rather easy to trace. The general cultural or political historian might find this limited but precisely known area a good testing ground for theories of history.

I think he would conclude, as I have here, that the nature of the achievements of a large competing scientific group is determined by the group and its history, and depends little on the behavior of individual discoverers. We can almost write down equations for the speed and scope of advance in some departments of knowledge. But the pressure of scientific determinism becomes weak and random as we approach the great unitary syntheses. For they are not only discoveries. They are also artistic creations, shaped by the taste and style of a single hand.

QUESTIONS FOR STUDY, DISCUSSION, AND WRITING

1. What is the relation between the first seven paragraphs and the eighth? Are the first seven necessary to the argument? If not, do they serve another function? What happens in the ninth?
2. On page 983 Platt speaks of a "competing scientific group." Find examples of competition in his essay. What sort of competition does it seem to be? What regulates it?
3. On page 980 Platt says, "Still this conservatism has a good result." What is the good result and what has it to do with style?
4. What does Platt mean by the classicist's "sufficiency" and the innovator's "necessity" (p. 980)?
5. While Platt never explicitly defines style, he does imply a definition. Where is the implied definition most clearly evident? Oppenheimer ("On Style," p. 154) and Whitehead ("On Style," p. 153) do give explicit definitions of style. How do they compare with Platt's implicit definition?
6. Many people talk about style (e.g., sports editors, sociologists, and, of course, fashion editors). Define style and explain its role in some nonaesthetic and nonscientific activity.

A. S. EDDINGTON

The Downfall of Classical Physics[1]

The Structure of the Atom

Between 1905 and 1908 Einstein and Minkowski introduced fundamental changes in our ideas of time and space. In 1911 Rutherford introduced the greatest change in our idea of matter since the time of Democritus. The reception of these two changes was curiously different. The new ideas of space and time were regarded on all sides as revolutionary; they were received with the greatest enthusiasm by some and the keenest opposition by others. The new idea of matter underwent the ordinary experience of scientific discovery; it gradually proved its worth, and when the evidence became overwhelmingly convincing it quietly supplanted previous theories. No great shock was felt. And yet when I hear to-day protests against the Bolshevism of modern science and regrets for the old-established order, I am inclined to think that Rutherford, not Einstein, is the real villain of the piece. When we compare the

1. Chapter I of *The Nature of the Physical World*, 1929.

universe as it is now supposed to be with the universe as we had ordinarily preconceived it, the most arresting change is not the rearrangement of space and time by Einstein but the dissolution of all that we regard as most solid into tiny specks floating in void. That gives an abrupt jar to those who think that things are more or less what they seem. The revelation by modern physics of the void within the atom is more disturbing than the revelation by astronomy of the immense void of interstellar space.

The atom is as porous as the solar system. If we eliminated all the unfilled space in a man's body and collected his protons and electrons into one mass, the man would be reduced to a speck just visible with a magnifying glass.

This porosity of matter was not foreshadowed in the atomic theory. Certainly it was known that in a gas like air the atoms are far separated, leaving a great deal of empty space; but it was only to be expected that material with the characteristics of air should have relatively little substance in it, and "airy nothing" is a common phrase for the insubstantial. In solids the atoms are packed tightly in contact, so that the old atomic theory agreed with our preconceptions in regarding solid bodies as mainly substantial without much interstice.

The electrical theory of matter which arose towards the end of the nineteenth century did not at first alter this view. It was known that the negative electricity was concentrated into unit charges of very small bulk; but the other constituent of matter, the positive electricity, was pictured as a sphere of jelly of the same dimensions as the atom and having the tiny negative charges embedded in it. Thus the space inside a solid was still for the most part well filled.

But in 1911 Rutherford showed that the positive electricity was also concentrated into tiny specks. His scattering experiments proved that the atom was able to exert large electrical forces which would be impossible unless the positive charge acted as a highly concentrated source of attraction; it must be contained in a nucleus minute in comparison with the dimensions of the atom. Thus for the first time the main volume of the atom was entirely evacuated, and a "solar system" type of atom was substituted for a substantial "billiard-ball." Two years later Niels Bohr developed his famous theory on the basis of the Rutherford atom, and since then rapid progress has been made. Whatever further changes of view are in prospect, a reversion to the old substantial atoms is unthinkable.

The accepted conclusion at the present day is that all varieties of matter are ultimately composed of two elementary constituents —protons and electrons. Electrically these are the exact opposites of one another, the proton being a charge of positive electricity and the electron a charge of negative electricity. But in other respects their properties are very different. The proton has 1840 times the mass of the electron, so that nearly all the mass of matter is due to its constituent protons. The proton is not found unadulterated except in hydrogen, which seems to be the most primitive form of matter, its atom consisting of one proton and one electron. In other atoms a number of protons and a lesser number of electrons are cemented together to form a nucleus; the electrons required to make up the balance are scattered like remote satellites of the nucleus, and can even escape from the atom and wander freely through the material. The diameter of an electron is about 1/50,000 of the diameter of an atom; that of the nucleus is not very much larger; an isolated proton is supposed to be much smaller still.

Thirty years ago there was much debate over the question of ether-drag—whether the earth moving round the sun drags the ether with it. At that time the solidity of the atom was unquestioned, and it was difficult to believe that matter could push its way through the ether without disturbing it. It was surprising and perplexing to find as the result of experiments that no convection of the ether occurred. But we now realize that the ether can slip through the atoms as easily as through the solar system, and our expectation is all the other way.

We shall return to the "solar system" atom in later chapters. For the present the two things which concerns us are (1) its extreme emptiness and (2) the fact that it is made up of electrical charges.

Rutherford's nuclear theory of the atom is not usually counted as one of the scientific revolutions of the present century. It was a far-reaching discovery, but a discovery falling within the classical scheme of physics. The nature and significance of the discovery could be stated in plain terms, i.e. in terms of conceptions already current in science. The epithet "revolutionary" is usually reserved for two great modern developments—the Relativity Theory and the Quantum Theory. These are not merely new discoveries as to the content of the world; they involve changes in our mode of thought about the world. They cannot be stated immediately in plain terms because we have first to grasp new conceptions undreamt of in the classical scheme of physics.

I am not sure that the phrase "classical physics" has ever been closely defined. But the general idea is that the scheme of natural law developed by Newton in the *Principia* provided a pattern which all subsequent developments might be expected to follow. Within the four corners of the scheme great changes of outlook were possible; the wave-theory of light supplanted the corpuscular theory; heat was changed from substance (caloric) to energy of motion; electricity from continuous fluid to nuclei of strain in the ether. But this was all allowed for in the elasticity of the original scheme. Waves, kinetic energy, and strain already had their place in the scheme; and the application of the same conceptions to account for a wider range of phenomena was a tribute to the comprehensiveness of Newton's original outlook.

We have now to see how the classical scheme broke down.

The FitzGerald Contraction

We can best start from the following fact. Suppose that you have a rod moving at very high speed. Let it first be pointing transverse to its line of motion. Now turn it through a right angle so that it is along the line of motion. The rod contracts. It is shorter when it is along the line of motion than when it is across the line of motion.

This contraction, known as the FitzGerald contraction, is exceedingly small in all ordinary circumstances. It does not depend at all on the material of the rod but only on the speed. For example, if the speed is 19 miles a second—the speed of the earth round the sun—the contraction of length is 1 part in 200,000,000, or 2½ inches in the diameter of the earth.

This is demonstrated by a number of experiments of different kinds of which the earliest and best known is the Michelson-Morley experiment first performed in 1887, repeated more accurately by Morley and Miller in 1905, and again by several observers within the last year or two. I am not going to describe these experiments except to mention that the convenient way of giving your rod a large velocity is to carry it on the earth which moves at high speed round the sun. Nor shall I discuss here how complete is the proof afforded by these experiments. It is much more important that you should realize that the contraction is just what would be expected from our current knowledge of a material rod.

You are surprised that the dimensions of a moving rod can be altered merely by pointing it different ways. You expect them to remain unchanged. But which rod are you thinking of? * * * If you are thinking of continuous substance, extending in space because it is the nature of substance to occupy space, then there seems to be no valid cause for a change of dimensions. But the scientific rod is a swarm of electrical particles rushing about and widely separated from one another. The marvel is that such a swarm should tend to preserve any definite extension. The particles, however, keep a certain average spacing so that the whole volume remains practically steady; they exert electrical forces on one another, and the volume which they fill corresponds to a balance between the forces drawing them together and the diverse motions tending to spread them apart. When the rod is set in motion these electrical forces change. Electricity in motion constitutes an electric current. But electric currents give rise to forces of a different type from those due to electricity at rest, viz. magnetic forces. Moreover these forces arising from the motion of electric charges will naturally be of different intensity in the directions along and across the line of motion.

By setting in motion the rod with all the little electric charges contained in it we introduce new magnetic forces between the particles. Clearly the original balance is upset, and the average spacing between the particles must alter until a new balance is found. And so the extension of the swarm of particles—the length of the rod—alters.

There is really nothing mysterious about the FitzGerald contraction. It would be an unnatural property of a rod pictured in the old way as continuous substance occupying space in virtue of its substantiality; but it is an entirely natural property of a swarm of particles held in delicate balance by electromagnetic forces, and occupying space by buffeting away anything that tries to enter. Or you may look at it this way: your expectation that the rod will keep its original length presupposes, of course, that it receives fair treatment and is not subjected to any new stresses. But a rod in motion is subjected to a new magnetic stress, arising not from unfair outside tampering but as a necessary consequence of its own electrical constitution; and under this stress the contraction occurs. Perhaps you will think that if the rod were rigid enough it might be able to resist the compressing force. That is not so; the FitzGerald contraction is the same for a rod of steel and for a rod of india-rubber; the rigidity and the compressing stress are bound up with the constitution in such a way that if one is large so also is the other. It is necessary to rid our minds of the idea that this failure to keep a constant length is an imperfection of the rod; it is only imperfect as compared with an imaginary "something" which has not this electrical constitution—and therefore is not material at all. The FitzGerald contraction is not an imperfection but a fixed and characteristic property of matter, like inertia.

We have here drawn a qualitative inference from the electrical structure of matter; we must leave it to the mathematician to calculate the quantitative effect. The problem was worked out by Lorentz and Larmor about 1900. They calculated the change in the average spacing of the particles required to restore the balance after it had been upset by the new forces due to the change of motion of the charges. This calculation was found to give precisely the FitzGerald contraction, i.e., the amount already inferred from the experiments above mentioned. Thus we have two legs to stand on. Some will prefer to trust the results because they seem to be well established by experiment; others will be more easily persuaded by the knowledge that the FitzGerald contraction is a necessary consequence of the scheme of electromagnetic laws universally accepted since the time of Maxwell. Both experiments and theories sometimes go wrong; so it is just as well to have both alternatives.

Consequences of the Contraction

This result alone, although it may not quite lead you to the theory of relativity, ought to make you uneasy about classical physics. The physicist when he wishes to measure a length—and he cannot get far in any experiment without measuring a length—takes a scale and turns it in the direction needed. It never occurred to him that in spite of all precautions the scale would change length when he did this; but unless the earth happens to be at rest a change must occur. The constancy of a measuring scale is the rock on which the whole structure of physics has been reared; and that rock has crumbled away. You may think that this assumption cannot have betrayed the physicist very badly; the changes of length cannot be serious or they would have been noticed. Wait and see.

Let us look at some of the consequences of the FitzGerald contraction. First take what may seem to be a rather fantastic case. Imagine you are on a planet moving very fast indeed, say 161,000 miles a second. For this speed the contraction is one-half. Any solid contracts to half its original length when turned from across to along the line of motion. A railway journey between two towns which was 100 miles at noon is shortened to 50 miles at 6 P.M. when the planet has turned through a right angle. The inhabitants copy Alice in Wonderland; they pull out and shut up like a telescope.

I do not know of a planet moving at 161,000 miles a second, but I could point to a spiral nebula far away in space which is moving at 1000 miles a second. This may well contain a planet and (speaking unprofessionally) perhaps I shall not be taking too much licence if I place intelligent beings on it. At 1000 miles a second the contraction is not large enough to be appreciable in ordinary affairs; but it is quite large enough to be appreciable in measurements of scientific or even of engineering accuracy. One of the most fundamental procedures in physics is to measure lengths with a scale moved about in any way. Imagine the consternation of the physicists on this planet when they learn that they have made a mistake in supposing that their scale is a constant measure of length. What a business to go back over all the experiments ever performed, apply the corrections for orientation of the scale at the time, and then consider *de novo* the inferences and system of physical laws to be deduced from the amended data! How thankful our own physicists ought to be that they are not in this runaway nebula but on a decently slow-moving planet like the earth!

But stay a moment. Is it so certain that we are on a slow-moving planet? I can imagine the astronomers in that nebula observing far away in space an insignificant star attended by an insignificant planet called Earth. They observe too that it is moving with the huge velocity of 1000 miles a second; because naturally if we see them receding from us at 1000 miles a second they will see us receding from them at 1000 miles a second. "A thousand miles a second!" exclaim the nebular physicists. "How unfortunate for the poor physicists on the Earth! The FitzGerald contraction will be quite appreciable, and all their measures with scales will be seriously wrong. What a weird system of laws of Nature they will have deduced, if they have over-looked this correction!"

There is no means of deciding which is right—to which of us the observed relative velocity of 1000 miles a second *really* belongs. Astronomically the galaxy of which the earth is a member does not seem to be more important, more central, than the nebula. The presumption that it is we who are the more nearly at rest has no serious foundation; it is mere self-flattery.

"But," you will say, "surely if these appreciable changes of length occurred on the earth, we should detect them by our measurements." That brings me to the interesting point. We could not detect them by any measurement; they may occur and yet pass quite unnoticed. Let me try to show how this happens.

This room, we will say, is traveling at 161,000 miles a second vertically upwards. That is my statement, and it is up to you to prove it wrong. I turn my arm from horizontal to vertical and it contracts to half its original length. You don't believe me? Then bring a yard-measure and measure it. First, horizontally, the result is 30 inches; now vertically, the result is 30 half-inches. You must allow for the fact that an inch-division of the scale contracts to half an inch when the yard-measure is turned vertically.

"But we can see that your arm does not become shorter; can we not trust our own eyes?"

Certainly not, unless you remember that when you got up this morning your retina contracted to half its original width in the vertical direction; consequently it is now exaggerating vertical distances to twice the scale of horizontal distances.

"Very well," you reply, "I will not get up. I will lie in bed and watch you go through your performance in an inclined mirror. Then my retina will be all right, but I know I shall see no contraction."

But a moving mirror does not give an undistorted image of what is happening. The angle of reflection of light is altered by motion of a mirror, just as the angle of reflection of a billiard-ball would be altered if the cushion were moving. If you will work out by the ordinary laws of optics the effect of moving a mirror at 161,000 miles a second, you will find that it introduces a distortion which just conceals the contraction of my arm.

And so on for every proposed test. You cannot disprove my assertion, and, of course, I cannot prove it; I might equally well have chosen and defended any other velocity. At first this seems to contradict what I told you earlier—that the contraction had been proved and measured by the Michelson-Morley and other experiments—but there is really no contradiction. They were all *null* experiments, just as your experiment of watching my arm in an inclined mirror was a null experiment. Certain optical or electrical consequences of the earth's motion were looked for of the same type as the distortion of images by a moving mirror; these would have been observed unless a contraction occurred of just the right amount to compensate them. They were not observed; therefore the compensating contraction had occurred. There was just one alternative; the earth's true velocity through space might happen to have been nil. This was ruled out by repeating the experiment six months later, since the earth's motion could not be nil on both occasions. Thus the contraction was demonstrated and its law of dependence on velocity verified. But the actual amount of contraction on either occasion was unknown, since the earth's true velocity (as distinct from its orbital velocity with respect to the sun) was unknown. It remains unknown because the optical and electrical effects by which we might hope to measure it are always compensated by the contraction.

I have said that the constancy of a measuring scale is the rock on which the structure of physics has been reared. The structure has also been supported by supplementary props because optical and electrical devices can often be used instead of material scales to ascertain lengths and distances. But we find that all these are united in a conspiracy not to give one another away. The rock has crumbled and simultaneously all the other supports have collapsed.

Frames of Space

We can now return to the quarrel between the nebular physicists and ourselves. One of us has a large velocity and his scientific measurements are seriously affected by the contraction of his scales. Each has hitherto taken it for granted that it is the other fellow who is making the mistake. We cannot settle the dispute by appeal to experiment because in every *experiment* the mistake introduces two errors which just compensate one another.

It is a curious sort of mistake which always carries with it its own compensation. But remember that the compensation only applies to phenomena actually observed or capable of observation. The compensation does not apply to the intermediate part of our deduction—that system of inference from observation which forms the classical physical theory of the universe.

Suppose that we and the nebular physicists survey the world, that is to say we allocate the surrounding objects to their respective positions in space. One party, say the nebular physicists, has a large velocity; their yard-measures will contract and become less than a yard when they measure distances in a certain direction; consequently they will reckon distances in that direction too great. It does not matter whether they use a yard-measure, or a theodolite, or merely judge distances with the eye; all methods of measurement must agree. If motion caused a disagreement of any kind, we should be able to determine the motion by observing the amount of disagreement; but, as we have already seen, both theory and observation indicate that there is complete compensation. If the nebular physicists try to construct a square they will construct an oblong. No test can ever reveal to them that it is not a square; the greatest advance they can make is to recognize that there are people in another world who have got it into their heads that it is an oblong, and they may be broadminded enough to admit that this point of view, absurd as it seems, is really as defensible as their own. It is clear that their whole conception of space is distorted as compared with ours, and ours is distorted as compared with theirs. We are regarding the same universe, but we have arranged it in different spaces. The original quarrel as to whether they or we are moving with the speed of 1000 miles a second has made so deep a cleavage between us that we cannot even use the same space.

Space and time are words conveying more than one meaning. Space is an empty void; or it is such and such a number of inches, acres, pints. Time is an ever-rolling stream; or it is something signaled to us by wireless. The physicist has no use for vague conceptions; he often has them, alas! but he cannot make real use of them. So when he speaks of space it is always the inches or pints that he should have in mind. It is from this point of view that our space and the space of the nebular physicists are different spaces; the reckoning of inches and pints is different. To avoid possible misunderstanding it is perhaps better to say that we have different *frames of space*—different frames to which we refer the location of objects. Do not, however, think of a frame of space as something consciously artificial; the frame of space comes into our minds with our first perception of space. Consider, for example, the more extreme case when the FitzGerald contraction is one-half. If a man takes a rectangle 2 inches x 1 inch to be a square, it is clear that space must have dawned on his intelligence in a way very different from that in which we have apprehended it.

The frame of space used by an observer depends only on his motion. Observers on different planets with the same velocity (i.e., having zero relative velocity) will agree as to the location of the objects of the universe; but observers on planets with different velocities have different frames of location. You may ask, How can I be so confident as to the way in which these imaginary beings will interpret their observations? If that objection is pressed I shall not defend myself; but those who dislike my imaginary beings must face the alternative of following the argument with mathematical symbols. Our purpose has been to express in a conveniently apprehensible form certain results which follow from terrestrial experiments and calculations as to the effect of motion on electrical, optical and metrical phenomena. So much careful work has been done on this subject that science is in a position to state what will be the consequence of making measurements with instruments traveling at high speed—whether instruments of a technical kind or, for example, a human retina. In only one respect do I treat my nebular observer as more than a piece of registering apparatus; I assume that he is subject to a common failing of human nature, viz. he takes it for granted that it was his planet that God chiefly had in mind when the universe was created. Hence he is (like my reader perhaps?) disinclined to take seriously the views of location of those people who are so misguided as to move at 1000 miles a second relatively to his parish pump.

An exceptionally modest observer might take some other planet than his own as the standard of rest. Then he would have to correct all his measurements for the FitzGerald contraction due to his own motion with respect to the standard, and the corrected measures would give the space-frame belonging to the standard planet as the original measures gave the space-frame of his own planet. For him the dilemma is even more pressing, for there is nothing to guide him as to the planet to be selected for the standard of rest. Once he gives up the naïve assumption that his own frame is the one and only right frame the question arises, Which then of the innumerable other frames is right? There is no answer, and so far as we can see no possibility of an answer. Meanwhile all his experimental measurements are waiting unreduced, because the corrections to be applied to them depend on the answer. I am afraid our modest observer will get rather left behind by his less humble colleagues.

The trouble that arises is not that we have found anything necessarily wrong with the frame of location that has been employed in our system of physics; it has not led to experimental contradictions. The only thing known to be "wrong" with it is that it is not unique. If we had found that our frame was unsatisfactory and another frame was preferable, that would not have caused a great revolution of thought; but to discover that ours is one of many frames, all of which are equally satisfactory, leads to a change of interpretation of the significance of a frame of location.

"Commonsense" Objections

Before going further I must answer the critic who objects in the name of commonsense. Space—*his* space—is so vivid to him. "This object is obviously here; that object is just there. I know it; and I am not going to be shaken by any amount of scientific obscurantism about contraction of measuring rods."

We have certain preconceived ideas about location in space which have come down to us from ape-like ancestors. They are deeply rooted in our mode of thought, so that it is very difficult to criticise them impartially and to realize the very insecure foundation on which they rest. We commonly suppose that each of the objects surrounding us has a definite location in space and that we are *aware* of the right location. The objects in my study are actually in the positions where I am "aware" that they are; and if an observer (on another star) surveying the room with measuring rods, etc., makes out a different arrangement of location, he is merely spinning a scientific paradox which does not shake the real facts of location obvious to any man of commonsense. This attitude rejects with contempt the question, How am I aware of the location? If the location is determined by scientific measurements with elaborate precautions, we are ready enough to suggest all sorts of ways in which the apparatus might have misbehaved; but if the knowledge of location is obtained with no precautions, if it just comes into our heads unsought, then it is obviously true and to doubt it would be flying in the face of commonsense! We have a sort of impression (although we do not like to acknowledge it) that the mind puts out a feeler into space to ascertain directly where each familiar object is. That is nonsense; our commonsense knowledge of location is not obtained that way. Strictly it is *sense* knowledge, not *commonsense* knowledge. It is partly obtained by touch and locomotion; such and such an object is at arm's length or a few steps away. Is there any essential difference (other than its crudity) between this method and scientific measurements with a scale? It is partly obtained by vision—a crude version of scientific measurement with a theodolite. Our common knowledge of where things are is not a miraculous revelation of unquestionable authority; it is inference from observations of the same kind as, but cruder than, those made in a scientific survey. Within its own limits of accuracy the scheme of location of objects that I am instinctively "aware" of is the same as my scientific scheme of location, or frame of space.

When we use a carefully made telescope lens and a sensitized plate instead of the crystalline lens and retina of the eye we increase the accuracy but do not alter the character of our survey of space. It is by this increase of refinement that we have become "aware" of certain characteristics of space which were not known to our ape-like ancestor when he instituted the common ideas that have come down to us. His scheme of location works consistently so long as there is no important change in his motion (a few miles a second makes no appreciable difference); but a large change involves a transition to a different system of location which is likewise self-consistent, although it is inconsistent with the original one. Having any number of these systems of location, or frames of space, we can no longer pretend that each of them indicates "just where things are." Location is not something supernaturally revealed to the mind; it is a kind of conventional summary of those properties or relations of objects which condition certain visual and tactual sensations.

Does not this show that "right" location in space cannot be nearly so important and fundamental as it is made out to be in the Newtonian scheme of things? The different observers are able to play fast and loose with it without ill effects.

Suppose that location is, I will not say entirely a myth, but not quite the definite thing it is made out to be in classical physics; that the Newtonian idea of location contains some truth and some padding, and it is not the truth but the padding that our observers are quarrelling over. That would explain a great deal. It would explain, for instance, why all the forces of Nature seem to have entered into a conspiracy to prevent our discovering the definite location of any object (its position in the "right" frame of space); naturally they cannot reveal it, if it does not exist.

This thought will be followed up in the next chapter. Meanwhile let us glance back over the arguments that have led to the present situation. It arises from the failure of our much-trusted measuring scale, a failure which we can infer from strong experimental evidence or more simply as an inevitable consequence of accepting the electrical theory of matter. This unforeseen behavior is a constant property of all kinds of matter and is even shared by optical and electrical measuring devices. Thus it is not betrayed by any kind of discrepancy in applying the usual methods of measurement. The discrepancy is revealed when we change the standard motion of the measuring appliances, e.g., when we compare lengths and distances as measured by terrestrial observers with those which would be measured by observers on a planet with different velocity. Provisionally we shall call the measured lengths which contain this discrepancy "fictitious lengths."

According to the Newtonian scheme length is definite and unique; and each observer should apply corrections (dependent on his motion) to reduce his fictitious lengths to the unique Newtonian length. But to this there are two objections. The corrections to reduce to Newtonian length are indeterminate; we know the corrections necessary to reduce our own fictitious lengths to those measured by an observer with any other prescribed motion, but there is no criterion for deciding which system is the one intended in the Newtonian scheme. Secondly, the whole of present-day physics has been based on lengths measured by terrestrial observers without this correction, so that whilst its assertions ostensibly refer to Newtonian lengths they have actually been proved for fictitious lengths.

The FitzGerald contraction may seem a little thing to bring the whole structure of classical physics tumbling down. But few indeed are the experiments contributing to our scientific knowledge which would not be invalidated if our methods of measuring lengths were fundamentally unsound. We now find that there is no guarantee that they are not subject to a systematic kind of error. Worse still we do not know if the error occurs or not, and there is every reason to presume that it is impossible to know.

QUESTIONS FOR STUDY, DISCUSSION, AND WRITING

1. What is the FitzGerald contraction?
2. The Michelson-Morley experiment led to the conclusion that statements about motion are neither provable nor disprovable. The fact that we still place a practical trust in measurements would seem to deny the most obvious implication of this conclusion. Why, then, is it important?
3. On page 993 Eddington speaks of mathematical symbols as expository devices alternative to his example of the imaginary observers on various planets. As he states this equivalence of function, he implies that he could roughly translate one kind of exposition into the other. This further implies that they are two languages. What are the key features of these two languages?
4. What would Huxley ("The Method of Scientific Investigation," pp. 950–956) or Peirce ("The Fixation of Belief," pp. 938–949) think of Eddington's essay?

GEORGE GAMOW

Expanding Horizons[1]

The Earth and Its Neighborhood

In the early stages of human civilization, the thing that we call the universe was considered almost ridiculously small. The earth was believed to be a large flat disc floating on the surface of the world ocean which surrounded it. Below was only water as deep as one could imagine, above was the sky, the abode of the gods. The disc was large enough to hold all lands known to the geography of that time, which included the shores of the Mediterranean Sea, with the adjacent parts of Europe, Africa, and a bit of Asia. The northern rim of the Earth disc was limited by a range of high mountains, behind which the Sun hid during the night time when it was resting on the surface of the World Ocean. * * * But in

1. Chapter X of *One Two Three ... Infinity*, 1947.

the third century before Christ there lived a man who disagreed with this simple and generally accepted picture of the world. He was the famous Greek philosopher (so they called scientists at that time) named Aristotle.

In his book *About Heaven* Aristotle expressed the theory that our Earth is actually a sphere, covered partly by land, partly by water, and surrounded by the air. He supported his point of view by many arguments which are familiar and seem trivial to us now. He indicated that the way the ships disappear behind the horizon when the hulk vanishes first and the masts seem to stick out of the water, proves that the surface of the ocean is curved, not flat. He argued that the eclipses of the moon must be due to the shadow of the Earth passing over the face of our satellite, and since this shadow is round, the Earth itself must be round too. But only very few people at that time would believe him. People could not understand how, if what he said was true, those who lived on the opposite side of the globe (the so-called antipodes; Australians to you) could walk upside down without falling off the Earth, or why the water in these parts of the world did not flow toward what they would call the blue sky.

The people at that time, you see, did not realize that the things fall down because they are attracted by the body of the Earth. For them "above" and "below" were absolute directions in space, which should be the same everywhere. The idea that "up" can become "down" and "down" become "up" if you travel halfway around the Earth must have seemed to them just as crazy as many statements of Einstein's theory of relativity seem to many people today. The fall of heavy bodies was explained not by the pull of the Earth, as we explain it now, but by the "natural tendency" of all things to move downward; and so down you go toward the blue sky if you venture to put your foot on the under part of the Earth globe! So strong was the objection and so hard the adjustment to the new ideas that in many a book published as late as the fifteenth century, almost two thousand years after Aristotle, one could find pictures showing inhabitants of the antipodes standing head down on the "underneath" of the Earth, and ridiculing the idea of its spherical shape. Probably the great Columbus himself, setting off for his journey to discover "the-other-way-round road" to India, was not completely sure of the soundness of his plan, and as a matter of fact he did not fulfill it because the American Continent got in the way. And only after the famous around-the-world sailing of Fernando de Magalhães (better known as Magellan) did the last doubt about the spherical shape of the Earth finally disappear.

When it was first realized that the Earth has the shape of a

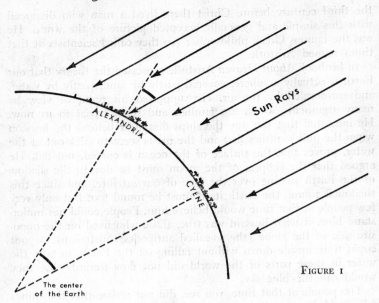

Sun Rays

ALEXANDRIA

CYENE

The center
of the Earth

FIGURE 1

giant sphere, it was natural to ask how large this sphere was in comparison with the parts of the world known at that time. But how would you measure the size of the Earth without undertaking a round-the-world trip, which was of course out of the question for the philosophers of ancient Greece?

Well, there is a way, and it was first seen by the famous scientist of that time named Eratosthenes, who lived in the Greek colony of Alexandria in Egypt during the third century B.C. He had heard from the inhabitants of Cyene, a city on the Upper Nile some 5000 Egyptian stadies south from Alexandria,[2] that during the equinox the noon sun in that city stood directly overhead, so that vertical objects threw no shadow. On the other hand Eratosthenes knew that no such thing ever happened in Alexandria, and that on the same day the sun passes 7 degrees, or one fiftieth of the full cycle, away from the zenith (the point directly overhead). Assuming that the Earth is round, Eratosthenes gave a very simple explanation of that fact, an explanation that you can easily understand by looking at Figure 1. Indeed, since the surface of the earth curves between the two cities, the sun rays falling vertically in Cyene are bound to strike the earth at a certain angle in the more northerly located Alexandria. You can also see from that figure that if two straight lines were drawn from

2. Near present location of the Aswan Dam [Gamow's note].

the center of the earth, one to pass through Alexandria and one through Cyene, the angle that they would make at their convergence would be identical with that made by the convergence of the line passing from the center of the earth to Alexandria (*i.e.*, zenith direction in Alexandria) and the sun's rays at the time that the sun is directly over Cyene.

Since that angle is one fiftieth of the full circle, the total circumference of the Earth should be fifty times the distance between the two cities, or 250,000 stadies. One Egyptian stadie is about 1/10 mile so that Eratosthenes' result is equivalent to 25,000 miles, or 40,000 km; very close indeed to the best modern estimates.

However the main point of the first measurement of the Earth was not in the exactness of the number obtained, but in the realization of the fact that the earth was *so* large. Why, its total surface must be several hundred times larger than the area of all known lands! Could it be true, and if true, what was beyond the known borders?

Speaking about astronomical distances, we must get acquainted first with what is known as *parallactic displacement* or simply as *parallax*. The word may sound a little frightening, but as a matter of fact the parallax is a very simple as well as useful thing.

We may start our acquaintance with parallax by trying to put a thread into a needle's eye. Try to do it with one eye closed, and you will find very quickly that it does not work; you will be bringing the end of the thread either too far behind the needle or stopping short in front of it. With only one eye you are unable to judge the distance to the needle and to the thread. But with two eyes open you can do it very easily, or at least learn easily how to do it. When you look at the object with two eyes, you automatically focus them both on the object. The closer the object the more you have to turn your eyes toward each other, and the muscular feeling arising from such adjustment gives you a pretty good idea about the distance.

Now if instead of looking with both eyes, you close first one and then the other, you will notice that the position of the object (the needle in this case) relative to the distant background (say, the window across the room) has changed. This effect is known as *parallactic displacement* and is certainly familiar to everybody; if you never heard about it, just try it out. * * * The farther away the object, the smaller will be its *parallactic displacement*, so that we can use it for measuring distances. Since *parallactic displacement* can be measured exactly in the degrees of the arc, this method is more precise than a simple judgment of the distance based on the muscular feeling in the eyeballs. But since the two eyes are set in our head only about three inches apart, they are not good for the estimate of distances beyond a few feet; in the case of more distant objects the axes of both eyes become almost parallel and the parallactic displacement becomes immeasurably small. In order to judge greater distances we should need to move our two eyes farther apart, thus increasing the angle of the parallactic displacement. No, no surgical operation is necessary, and the trick can be done with mirrors.

Such an arrangement was used in the Navy (before the invention of radar) to measure the distance to enemy warships during battle. It is a long tube with two mirrors (A, A') in front of each eye, and two other mirrors (B, B') at opposite ends of the tube. Looking through such a range finder you actually see with one eye from the end B and with another from the end B'. The distance between your eyes, or the so-called optical base, becomes effectively much greater, and you can estimate much longer distances. Of course, the Navy men do not rely on just the distance-feeling given by the muscles of their eyeballs. The range finders are equipped with special gadgets and dials measuring parallactic displacement with the utmost precision.

However these naval range finders, working perfectly even when the enemy ship is almost behind the horizon, would fail badly in any attempt to measure the distance even to such a comparatively near-by celestial body as the moon. In fact in order to notice the parallactic displacement of the moon in respect to the background of distant stars the optical base, that is, the distance between the two eyes must be made at least several hundred miles long. Of course it isn't necessary to arrange the optical system that would permit us to look with one eye from, say, Washington, and with another from New York, since all one has to do is to take two simultaneous photographs of the moon among the surrounding stars from these two cities. If you put this double picture in an ordinary stereoscope you will see the moon hanging in space in front of the stellar background. By measuring the photographs of the moon and the surrounding stars taken at the same instant in two different places on the surface of the Earth, astronomers have found that the parallactic displacement of the moon as it would be observed from the two opposite points of the Earth's diameter is 1° 24′ 5″. From this it follows that the distance to the moon equals 30.14 earth-diameters, that is, 384,403 km, or 238,857 miles.

From this distance and the observed angular diameter we find that the diameter of our satellite is about one fourth of the Earth's diameter. Its total surface is only one sixteenth of the Earth's surface, about the size of the African continent.

In a similar way one can measure the distance to the sun,

although, since the sun is much farther away, the measurements are considerably more difficult. Astronomers have found that this distance is 149,450,000 km (92,870,000 miles) or 385 times the distance to the moon. It is only because of this tremendous distance that the sun looks about the same size as the moon; actually it is much larger, its diameter being 109 times that of the Earth's diameter.

If the sun were a large pumpkin, the Earth would be a pea, the moon a poppy seed, and the Empire State Building in New York about as small as the smallest bacteria we can see through the microscope. It is worth while to remember here that at the time of ancient Greece, a progressive philosopher called Anaxagoras was punished with banishment and threatened with death for teaching that the sun was a ball of fire as big perhaps as the entire country of Greece!

In a similar way astronomers are able to estimate the distance of different planets of our system. The most distant of them, discovered only quite recently and called Pluto, is about forty times farther from the sun than the Earth; to be exact, the distance is 3,668,000,000 miles.

The Galaxy of Stars

Our next jump into space will be that from the planets to the stars, and here again the method of parallax can be used. We find, however, that even the nearest stars are so far away that at the most distant available observation points on the Earth (opposite sides of the globe) they do not show any noticeable parallactic shift in respect to the general stellar background. But we still have a way to measure these tremendous distances. If we use the dimensions of the Earth to measure the size of the Earth's orbit around the sun, why don't we use this orbit to get the distances to the stars? In other words is it not possible to notice the relative displacements of at least some of the stars by observing them from the opposite ends of the Earth's orbit? Of course it means that we have to wait half a year between the two observations, but why not?

With this idea in mind, the German astronomer Bessel started in 1838 the comparison of the relative position of stars as observed two different nights half a year apart. First he had no luck; the stars he picked up were evidently too far away to show any noticeable parallactic displacement, even with the diameter of the earth's orbit as the basis. But lo, here was the star, listed in astronomical catalogues as 61 Cygni (61st faint star in the constellation of Swan), which seemed to have been slightly off its position half a year before.

Another half a year passed and the star was again back in its old place. So it was the parallactic effect after all, and Bessel was the first man who with a yardstick stepped into the interstellar space beyond the limits of our old planetary system.

The observed annual displacement of 61 Cygni was very small indeed; only 0.6 angular seconds,[3] that is, the angle under which you would see a man 500 miles away if you could see so far at all! But astronomical instruments are very precise, and even such angles can be measured with a high degree of accuracy. From the observed parallax, and the known diameter of the Earth's orbit, Bessel calculated that his star was 103,000,000,000,000 km away, that is, 690,000 times farther away than the sun! It is rather hard to grasp the significance of that figure. In our old example, in which the sun was a pumpkin and the Earth a pea rotating around it at a distance of 20 ft., the distance of that star would correspond to 30,000 miles!

In astronomy it is customary to speak of very large distances by giving the time they could be covered by light that travels at the tremendous velocity of 300,000 km per sec. It would take light only 1/7 second to run around the Earth, slightly more than 1 second to come here from the moon, and about 8 minutes from the sun. From the star 61 Cygni, which is one of our nearest cosmic neighbors, the light travels to the Earth for about 11 years. If, because of some cosmic catastrophe the light from 61 Cygni were extinguished, or (what often happens to the stars) it were to explode in a sudden flash of fire, we should have to wait for 11 long years until the flash of the explosion, speeding through the interstellar space, and its last expiring ray finally brought to earth the latest cosmic news that a star had ceased to exist.

From the measured distance separating us from 61 Cygni, Bessel calculated that this star, appearing to us as a tiny luminous point quietly twinkling against the dark background of the night sky, is actually a giant luminous body only 30 per cent smaller and slightly less luminous than our own gorgeous sun. This was the first direct proof of the revolutionary idea first expressed by Copernicus that our sun is only one of the myriads of stars scattered at tremendous distances throughout infinite space.

Since the discovery of Bessel a great many stellar parallaxes have been measured. A few of the stars were found to be closer to us than 61 Cygni, the nearest being alpha-Centauri (the brightest star in the constellation of Centaurus), which is only 4.3 light-years away. It is very similar to our sun in its size and luminosity. Most of the stars are much farther away, so far away that even the diameter of the Earth's orbit becomes too small as the base for distance measurements.

Also the stars have been found to vary greatly in their sizes and luminosities, from shining giants such as Betelgeuse (300 light-

3. More exactly 0.600″ ± 0.06 [Gamow's note].

years away), which is about 400 times larger and 3600 times brighter than our sun, to such faint dwarfs as the so-called Van Maanen's star (13 light-years away), which is smaller than our Earth (its diameter being 75 per cent that of Earth) and about 10,000 times fainter than the sun.

We come now to the important problem of counting all existing stars. There is a popular belief, to which you also probably would subscribe, that nobody can count the stars in the sky. However, as is true of so many popular beliefs, this one is also quite wrong, at least as far as the stars visible to the naked eye are concerned. In fact, the total number of stars which may thus be seen in both hemispheres is only between 6000 and 7000, and since only one half of them are above the horizon at any one time, and since the visibility of stars close to the horizon is greatly reduced by atmospheric absorption, the number of stars which are usually visible to the naked eye on a clear moonless night is only about 2000. Thus, counting diligently at the rate of say 1 star per second, you should be able to count them all in about 1/2 hr!

If, however, you used a field binocular, you would be able to see some 50,000 additional stars, and a 2 1/2-inch telescope would reveal about 1,000,000 more. Using the famous 100-inch telescope of the Mt. Wilson Observatory in California you should be able to see about half a billion stars. Counting them at the rate of 1 star per second every day from dusk to dawn, astronomers would have to spend about a century to count them all!

But, of course, nobody has ever tried to count all the stars visible through large telescopes one by one. The total number is calculated by counting the actual stars visible in a number of areas in different parts of the sky and applying the average to the total area.

More than a century ago the famous British astronomer William Herschel, observing the stellar sky through his large self-made telescope, was struck by the fact that most of the stars that are ordinarily invisible to the naked eye appear within the faintly luminous belt cutting across the night sky and known as the Milky Way. And it is to him that the science of astronomy owes the recognition of the fact that the Milky Way is not an ordinary nebulosity or merely a belt of gas clouds spreading across space, but is actually formed from a multitude of stars that are so far away and consequently so faint that our eye cannot recognize them separately.

Using stronger and stronger telescopes we have been able to see the Milky Way as a larger and larger number of separate stars, but the main bulk of them still remains in the hazy background. It would be, however, erroneous to think that in the region of the Milky Way the stars are distributed any more densely than in any other part of the sky. It is, in fact, not the denser distribution of stars but the greater depth of stellar distribution in this direction that makes it possible to see what seems to be a larger number of stars in a given space than anywhere else in the sky. In the direction of the Milky Way the stars extend as far as the eye (strengthened by telescopes) can see, whereas in any other direction the distribution of stars does not extend to the end of visibility, and beyond them we encounter mostly the almost empty space.

Looking in the direction of the Milky Way it is as though we are looking through a deep forest where the branches of numerous trees overlap each other forming a continuous background, whereas in other directions we see patches of the empty space between the stars, as we would see the patches of the blue sky through the foliage overhead.

Thus the stellar universe, to which our sun belongs as one insignificant member, occupies a flattened area in space, extending for large distances in the plane of the Milky Way, and being comparatively thin in the direction perpendicular to it.

A more detailed study by generations of astronomers led to the conclusion that our stellar system includes about 40,000,000,000 individual stars, distributed within a lens-shaped area about 100,000 light-years in diameter and some 5000 to 10,000 light-years thick. And one result of this study comes as a slap in the face of human pride—the knowledge that our sun is not at all at the center of this giant stellar society but rather close to its outer edge.

In more scientific language the system of the Milky Way is known as the *Galaxy* (Latin of course!). The size of the Galaxy is here reduced by a factor of a hundred billion billions, though the number of points that represent separate stars are considerably fewer than forty billions, for, as one puts it, typographical reasons.

One of the most characteristic properties of the giant swarm of stars forming the galactic system is that it is in a state of rapid rotation similar to that which moves our planetary system. Just as Venus, Earth, Jupiter, and other planets move along almost circular orbits around the sun, the billions of stars forming the system of the Milky Way move around what is known as the galactic center. This center of galactic rotation is located in the direction of the constellation of Sagittarius (the Archer), and in fact if you follow the foggy shape of the Milky Way across the sky you will notice that approaching this constellation it becomes much broader, indicating that you are looking toward the central thicker part of the lens-shaped mass. (Our astronomer in Figure 3 is looking in this direction.)

What does the galactic center look like? We do not know that, since unfortunately it is screened from our sight by heavy clouds of dark interstellar material hanging in space. In fact, looking at the broadened part of the Milky Way in the region of Sagittarius[4] you would think first that the mythical celestial road branches here into two "one-way traffic lanes." But it is not an actual branching, and this impression is given simply by a dark cloud of interstellar dust and gases hanging in space right in the middle of the broadening between us and the galactic center. Thus whereas the darkness on both sides of the Milky Way is due to the background of the dark empty space, the blackness in the middle is produced by the dark opaque cloud. A few stars in the dark central patch are actually in the foreground, between us and the cloud.

It is, of course, a pity that we cannot see the mysterious galactic center around which our sun is spinning, along with billions of other stars. But in a way we know how it must look, from the observation of other stellar systems or galaxies scattered through space far beyond the outermost limit of our Milky Way. It is not some supergiant star keeping in subordination all the other members of the stellar system, as the sun reigns over the family of planets. The study of the central parts of other galaxies (which we will discuss a little later) indicates that they also consist of large multitudes of stars with the only difference that here the stars are crowded much more densely than in the outlying parts to which our sun belongs. If we think of the planetary system as an autocratic state where the Sun rules the planets, the Galaxy of stars may be likened to a kind of democracy in which some members occupy influential central places while the others have to be satisfied with more humble positions on the outskirts of their society.

As said above, all the stars including our sun rotate in giant circles around the center of the galactic system. How can this be proved, how large are the radii of these stellar orbits, and how long does it take to make a complete circuit?

All these questions were answered a few decades ago by the Dutch astronomer Oort, who applied to the sysem of stars known as the Milky Way observations very similar to those made by Copernicus in considering the planetary system.

Let us remember first Copernicus' argument. It had been observed by the ancients, the Babylonians, the Egyptians, and others, that the big planets like Saturn or Jupiter seemed to move across the sky in a rather peculiar way. They seemed to proceed along an ellipse in the way the sun does, then suddenly to stop, to back, and after a second reversal of motion, to continue their way in the original direction. In the lower part of Figure 2 we show schematically such

4. Which can be best observed on a clear night in early summer [Gamow's note].

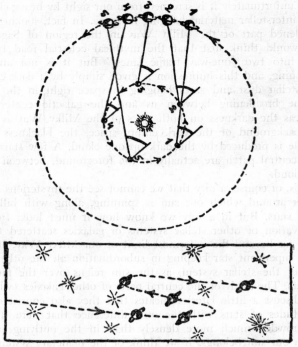

FIGURE 2

a look as described by Saturn over a period of about two years. (The period of Saturn's complete circuit is 29½ years.) Since, on account of religious prejudices that dictated the statement that our Earth is the center of the universe, all planets and the sun itself were believed to move around the Earth, the above described peculiarities of motion had to be explained by the supposition that planetary orbits have very peculiar shapes with a number of loops in them.

But Copernicus knew better, and by a stroke of genius, he explained the mysterious looping phenomenon as due to the fact that the Earth as well as all other planets move along simple circles around the Sun. This explanation of the looping effect can be easily understood after studying the schematic picture at the top of Figure 2.

The sun is in the center, the Earth (small sphere) moves along the smaller circle, and Saturn (with a ring) moves along the larger circle in the same direction as the Earth. Numbers 1, 2, 3, 4, 5 represent different positions of the Earth in the course of a year, and the corresponding positions of Saturn which, as we remember,

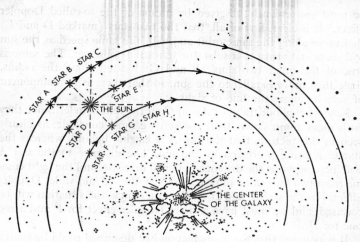

FIGURE 3

moves much more slowly. The parts of vertical lines from the different positions of the Earth represent the direction to some fixed star. By drawing lines from the various Earth positions to the corresponding Saturn positions we see that the angle formed by the two directions (to Saturn and to the fixed star) first increases, then decreases, and then increases again. Thus the seeming phenomenon of looping does not represent any peculiarity of Saturn's motion but arises from the fact that we observe this motion from different angles on the moving Earth.

The Oort argument about the rotation of the Galaxy of stars may be understood after inspection of Figure 3. Here in the lower part of the picture we see the galactic center (with dark clouds and all!) and there are plenty of stars all around it through the entire field of the figure. The three circles represent the orbits of stars at different distances from the center, the middle circle being the oribt of our sun.

Let us consider eight stars (shown with rays to distinguish them from other points), two of which are moving along the same orbit as the sun, but one slightly ahead and one slightly behind it, the others located on somewhat larger and somewhat smaller orbits as shown in the figure. We must remember that owing to the laws of gravity the outer stars have lower and the inner stars higher velocity than the stars on solar orbits (this is indicated in the figure by the arrows of different lengths).

How will the motion of these eight stars look if observed from the sun, or, what is of course the same, from the Earth? We are speaking here about the motion along the line of sight, which can be most conveniently observed by means of the so-called Doppler effect.[5] It is clear, first of all, that the two stars (marked *D* and *E*) that move along the same orbit and with the same speed as the sun will seem stationary to a solar (or terrestrial) observer. The same is true of the other two stars (*B* and *G*) located along the radius, since they move parallel to the sun, so that there is no component of velocity along the line of sight.

Now what about the stars *A* and *C* on the outer circle? Since they both move more slowly than the sun we must conclude, as clearly seen in this picture, that the star *A* is lagging behind, whereas the star *C* is being overtaken by the sun. The distance to the star *A* will increase while the distance to *C* will decrease, and the light coming from two stars must show respectively the red and violet Doppler effect. For the stars *F* and *H* on the inner circle the situation will be reversed, and we must have a violet Doppler effect for *F* and a red one for *H*.

It is assumed that the phenomenon just described could be caused only by a circular motion of the stars, and the existence of that circular motion makes it possible for us not only to prove this assumption but also to estimate the radius of stellar orbits and the velocity of stellar motion. By collecting the observational material on the observed apparent motion of stars all over the sky, Oort was able to prove that the expected phenomenon of red and violet Doppler effect really exists, thus proving beyond any doubt the rotation of the Galaxy.

In a similar way it may be demonstrated that the effect of galactic rotation will influence the apparent velocities of stars perpendicular to the line of vision. Although this component of velocity presents much larger difficulties for exact measurement (since even very great linear velocities of distant stars correspond to extremely small angular displacements on the celestial sphere) the effect was also observed by Oort and others.

The exact measurements of the Oort effect of stellar motion now make it possible to measure the orbits of stars and determine the period of rotation. Using this method of calculation it has been learned that the radius of the solar orbit having its center in Sagittarius is 30,000 light-years, that is, about two thirds the radius of the outermost orbit of the entire galactic system. The time necessary for the sun to move a complete circle around the galactic center is some 200 million years. It is a long time, of course, but

5. The difference between the frequency of sound or light waves when the wave source is in motion and when it is at rest (or in motion at a different rate) relative to the observer. Thus the pitch of a railway crossing bell is first higher, then lower, to a man in a passing train as his distance from the bell first diminishes and then increases. Similarly, light from a star rushing away from our galaxy produces a spectrum that exhibits a "red shift," or displacement toward the red end, in comparison with the spectrum the same star would produce if its distance from the earth were constant.

remembering that our stellar system is about 3 billion years old, we find that during its entire life our sun with its family of planets has made about 20 complete rotations. If, following the terminology of the terrestial year, we call the period of solar rotation "a solar year" we can say that our universe is only 20 years old. Indeed things happen slowly in the world of stars, and a solar year is quite a convenient unit for time measurements in the history of the universe!

Toward the Limits of the Unknown

As we have already mentioned above, our Galaxy is not the only isolated society of stars floating in the vast spaces of the universe. Telescope studies reveal the existence, far away in space, of many other giant groups of stars very similar to that to which our sun belongs. The nearest of them, the famous Andromeda Nebula, can be seen even by the naked eye. It appears to us as a small, faint, rather elongated nebulosity. * * * These nebulae possess a typical spiral structure; hence the name "spiral nebulae." There are many indications that our own stellar structure is similarly a spiral, but it is very difficult to determine the shape of a structure when you are inside it. As a matter of fact, our sun is most probably located at the very end of one of the spiral arms of the "Great Nebula of the Milky Way."

For a long time astronomers did not realize that the spiral nebulae are giant stellar systems similar to our Milky Way, and confused them with ordinary diffuse nebulae like that in the constellation of Orionis, which represent the large clouds of interstellar dust floating between the stars inside our Galaxy. Later, however, it was found that these foggy spiral-shaped objects are not fog at all, but are made of separate stars, which can be seen as tiny individual points when the largest magnifications are used. But they are so far away that no parallactic measurements can indicate their actual distance.

Thus it would seem at first that we had reached the limit of our means for measuring celestial distances. But no! In science, when we come to an insuperable difficulty the delay is usually only temporary; something always happens that permits us to go still farther. In this case a quite new "measuring rod" was found by the Harvard astronomer Harlow Shapley in the so-called pulsating stars or Cepheides.[6]

There are stars and stars. While most of them glow quietly in the sky, there are a few that constantly change their luminosity from bright to dim, and from dim to bright in regularly spaced cycles. The giant bodies of these stars pulsate as regularly as the heart beats,

---

6. So called after the star beta-Cepheus, in which the phenomenon of pulsation was first discovered [Gamow's note].

and along with this pulsation goes a periodic change of their bright-ness.[7] The larger the star, the longer is the period of its pulsation, just as it takes a long pendulum more time to complete its swing than a short one. The really small ones (that is, small as stars go) complete their period in the course of a few hours, whereas the real giants take years and years to go through one pulsation. Now, since the bigger stars are also the brighter, there is an apparent correlation between the period of stellar pulsation, and the average brightness of the star. This relation can be established by observing the Cepheides, which are sufficiently close to us so that their distance and consequently actual brightness may be directly measured.

If now you find a pulsating star that lies beyond the limit of parallactic measurements, all you have to do is to watch the star through the telescope and observe the time consumed by its pulsa-tion period. Knowing the period, you will know its actual bright-ness, and comparing it with its apparent brightness you can tell at once how far away it is. This ingenious method was successfully used by Shapley for measuring particularly large distances within the Milky Way and has been most useful in estimating the general dimensions of our stellar system.

When Shapley applied the same method to measuring the dist-ance to several pulsating stars found imbedded in the giant body of the Andromeda Nebula, he was in for a big surprise. The distance from the Earth to these stars, which, of course, must be the same as the distance to the Andromeda Nebula itself, turned out to be 680,000 light-years—that is, much larger than the estimated diam-eter of the stellar system of Milky Way. And the size of Andromeda Nebula came out only a little smaller than the size of our entire Galaxy. * * *

This discovery dealt the death blow to the earlier assumptions that the spiral nebulae are comparatively "small things" located within our Galaxy, and established them as independent galaxies of stars very similar to our own system, the Milky Way. No astronomer would now doubt that to an observer located on some small planet circling one of the billions of stars that form the Great Andromeda Nebula, our own Milky Way would look much as the Andromeda Nebula looks to us.

The further studies of these distant stellar societies, which we owe mostly to Dr. E. Hubble, the celebrated galaxy-gazer of Mt. Wilson Observatory, reveal a great many facts of great interest and import-ance. It was found first of all that the galaxies, which appear more numerous through a good telescope than the ordinary stars do to the naked eye, do not all have necessarily spiral form, but present

---

7. One must not confuse these pulsat-ing stars with the so-called eclipsing var-iables, which actually represent systems of two stars rotating around each other and periodically eclipsing one another [Gamow's note].

SPHERICAL ELLIPTIC TRANSITIONAL CLOSED SPIRAL OPENED SPIRAL

a great variety of different types. There are *spherical galaxies*, which look like regular discs with diffused boundaries; there are *elliptical galaxies* with different degrees of elongation. The spirals themselves differ from each other by the "tightness with which they are wound up." There are also very peculiar shapes known as "barred spirals."

It is a fact of extreme importance that all the varieties of the observed galactic shapes can be arranged in a regular sequence (Figure 4), which presumably corresponds to different stages of the evolution of these giant stellar societies.

Although we are still far from understanding the details of galactic evolution, it seems very probable that it is due to the process of progressive contraction. It is well known that when a slowly rotating spherical body of gas undergoes a steady contraction, its speed of rotation increases, and its shape becomes that of a flattened ellipsoid. At a certain stage of contraction, when the ratio of the polar radius to the equatorial radius becomes equal to 7/10, the rotating body must assume a lenticular shape with a sharp edge running along its equator. Still further contraction keeps this lenticular shape intact, but the gases forming the rotating body begin to flow away into surrounding space all along the sharp equatorial edge, leading to the formation of a thin gaseous veil in the equatorial plane.

All the above statements have been proved mathematically by the celebrated English physicist and astronomer Sir James Jeans for a rotating gas sphere, but they can also be applied without any alterations to the giant stellar clouds that we call galaxies. In fact, we can consider such a clustering of the billions of stars as a flock of gas in which the role of molecules is now played by individual stars. In comparing the theoretical calculations of Jeans with Hubble's empirical classification of galaxies, we find that these giant stellar societies follow exactly the course of evolution described by the theory. In particular we find that the most elongated shape of elliptic nebulae is that corresponding to the radius-ratio of 7/10 (E7), and that it is the first case in which we notice a sharp equatorial edge. The spirals that develop in the later stages of evolution are apparently formed from the material ejected by the rapid rotation, although up to the present we do not have a completely satisfactory explanation of why and how these spiral forms are formed and what causes the difference between the simple and the barred spirals.

Much is still to be learned from further study of the structure, motion, and stellar content in the different parts of galactic societies of stars. A very interesting result was, for example, obtained a couple of years ago by a Mt. Wilson astronomer, W. Baade, who was able to show that, whereas the central bodies (nuclei) of spiral nebulae are formed by the same type of stars as the spherical and elliptic galaxies, the arms themselves show a rather different type of stellar population. This "spiral-arm" type of stellar population differs from the population of the central region by the presence of very hot and bright stars, the so-called "Blue Giants," which are absent in the central regions as well as in the spherical and elliptical galaxies. Since, as we shall see later, the Blue Giants most probably represent the most recently formed stars, it is reasonable to assume that the spiral arms are so to speak the breeding grounds for new stellar populations. One could imagine that a large part of the material ejected from the equatorial bulge of a contracting elliptic galaxy is formed by primordial gases that come out into the cold intergalactic space and condense into the separate large lumps of matter, which through subsequent contraction become very hot and very bright.

* * * Now we must consider generally the distribution of separate galaxies through the vastness of the universe.

We must state here, first of all that the method of distance measurements based on pulsating stars, though giving excellent results when applied to quite a number of galaxies that lie in the neighborhood of our Milky Way, fails when we proceed into the depth of space, since we soon reach distances at which no separate stars may be distinguished and the galaxies look like tiny elongated nebulosities even through the strongest telescopes. Beyond this point we can rely only on the visible size, since it is fairly well established that, unlike stars, all galaxies of a given type are of about the same size. If you know that all people are of the same height, that there are no giants or dwarfs, you can always say how far a man is from you by observing his apparent size.

Using this method for estimating distances in the far-out-flung realm of galaxies, Dr. Hubble was able to prove that the galaxies are scattered more or less uniformly through space as far as the eye (fortified by the most highly powered telescope) can see. We say "more or less" because there are many cases in which the galaxies cluster in large groups containing sometimes many thousands of members, in the same way as the separate stars cluster in galaxies.

Our own galaxy, Milky Way, is apparently one member of a comparatively small group of galaxies numbering in its membership three spirals (including ours, and the Andromeda Nebula) and six elliptical and four irregular nebulae (two of which are Magellanic clouds).

However, save for such occasional clustering, the galaxies, as seen

through the 100-inch telescope of the Mt. Wilson Observatory, are scattered rather uniformly through space up to a distance of 500,000,-000 light-years. The average distance between two neighboring galaxies is about 2,000,000 light-years, and the visible horizons of the universe contain about 100,000,000 individual stellar worlds!

In our old simile, in which the Empire State building was symbolized by a bacterium, the Earth by a pea, and the sun by a pumpkin, the galaxies might be represented by giant swarms of many billions of pumpkins distributed roughly within the orbit of Jupiter, separate pumpkin clusters being scattered through a spherical volume with a radius only a little smaller than the distance to the nearest star. Yes, it is very difficult to find the proper scale in cosmic distances, so that even when we scale the Earth to a pea, the size of the known universe comes out in astronomical numbers! * * *

We are now prepared to answer the fundamental question concerning the size of our universe. *Shall we consider the universe as extending into infinity and conclude that bigger and better telescopes will always reveal to the inquiring eye of an astronomer new and hitherto unexplored regions of space, or must we believe, on the contrary, that the universe occupies some very big but nevertheless finite volume, and is, at least in principle, explorable down to the last star?*

When we speak of the possibility that our universe is of "finite size," we do not mean, of couse, that somewhere at a distance of several billion light-years the explorer of space will encounter a blank wall on which is posted the notice "No trespassing."

In fact, we have seen that *space can be finite without being necessarily limited by a boundary*. It can simply curve around and "close on itself," so that a hypothetical space explorer, trying to steer his rocket ship as straight as possible will describe a geodesic line in space and come back to the point from which he started.

The situation would be, of course, quite similar to an ancient Greek explorer who travels west from his native city of Athens, and after a long journey, finds himself entering the eastern gates of the city.

And just as the curvature of the Earth's surface can be established without a trip around the world, simply by studying the geometry of only a comparatively small part of it, the question about the curvature of the three-dimensional space of the universe can be answered by similar measurements made within the range of available telescopes. One must distinguish between two kinds of curvatures: the positive one corresponding to the closed space of finite volume, and the negative one corresponding to the saddle-like opened infinite space (*cf.* Figure 5). The difference between these two types of space lies in the fact that, whereas in the *closed space* the number of uniformly scattered objects falling within a given

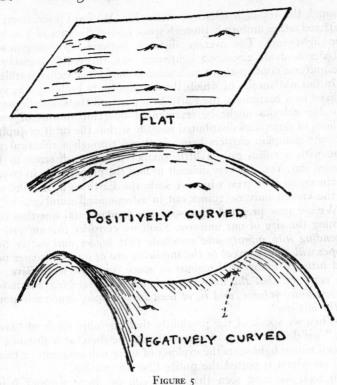

FLAT

POSITIVELY CURVED

NEGATIVELY CURVED

FIGURE 5

distance from the observer increases more slowly than the cube of that distance, the opposite is true in *opened space*.

In our universe the role of the "uniformly scattered objects" is played by the separate galaxies, so that all we have to do in order to solve the problem of the universal curvature is to count the number of individual galaxies located at different distances from us.

Such counting actually has been accomplished by Dr. Hubble, who has discovered that the *number of galaxies seems to increase somewhat more slowly than the cube of the distance, thus indicating the positive curvature and the finiteness of space*. It must be noticed, however, that the effect observed by Hubble is very small, becoming noticeable only near the very limit of the distance that it is possible to observe through the 100-inch Mt. Wilson telescope, and we can hope that the observations with the new 200-inch reflector on Palomar Mountain may throw some more light on this important problem.

Another point contributing to the uncertainty of the final answer concerning the finiteness of the universe lies in the fact that the distances of the faraway galaxies must be judged exclusively on the basis of their apparent luminosities (the law of inverse square). This method, which assumes that all the galaxies possess the same mean luminosity, may, however, lead to the wrong results if the luminosity of individual galaxies changes with time, thus indicating that luminosity depends on age. It must be remembered, in fact, that the most distant galaxies seen through the Mt. Wilson telescope are 500,000,000 light-years away, and are therefore seen by us in the state in which they were 500,000,000 years ago. If the galaxies become gradually fainter as they grow older (owing, perhaps, to a diminishing number of active stellar bodies as individual members die out) the conclusions reached by Hubble must be corrected. In fact, the change of galactic luminosities by only a small percentage in the course of 500,000,000 years (only about one seventh of their total age) would reverse the present conclusion that the universe is finite.

Thus we see that quite a lot of work has yet to be done before we can tell for sure whether our universe is finite or infinite.

GEORGE W. BEADLE
The New Biology and the Nature of Man[1]

In one sense I might say I begin this talk with the humanities, for I start with the consideration of the oldest living language. It is at least three billion years old, and a remarkable language it is. It exists only in written form, that is "written" in submicroscopic molecular code. It is remarkably simple, for it has only four letters. Each of these is one two hundred millionth of an inch across. Each is made of but five kinds of atoms—carbon, hydrogen, oxygen, nitrogen, and phosphorus—and there are only about thirty-two atoms in each letter. All the words in this language appear to be three-letter words, and there are only sixty-four of them possible. This beats Basic English by a very wide margin. Most remarkable of all, this language is the only language known to have a built-in capacity for copying itself. There is no need for secretaries, typewriters, or printing presses.

It is a language in which the specifications for all living organisms, from viruses to man, that have ever existed on earth are written.

The number of letters in the specifications for these organisms varies from five thousand letters for the specifications of the simplest

1. The Dewey F. Fagerburg Memorial Lecture, University of Michigan, 1963. The text is based on a transcript of the lecture, which was delivered informally from notes.

known virus to five billion for the specifications of man. That's over a million-fold difference. What is the name of this language? I call it DNAese, because it is contained in deoxyribose nucleic acid molecules, which we call DNA.

DNA-Deoxyribonucleic Acid

How do we know that DNA carries the specifications of the kind I have said? The answer is very simple. In viruses—some viruses at least—one can strip away all of the components except the DNA, infect a living cell of the proper kind with the DNA and reconstruct another generation of viruses. This means that whatever specifies the unique properties of the virus must be carried in the DNA. The same is true with bacteria. It is possible to take DNA molecules out of a bacterium in the purest possible form, transfer these molecules to another bacterium and alter the genetic specifications that say what the recipient bacterium is going to do. Now, viruses are known to have genes that are transmitted in essentially the same way that our genes are transmitted. Since only DNA is transmitted from generation to generation, the genes must be made of this substance. We don't know this directly in our own case, but we believe it is so in us too.

What do we want to know about the language in which these specifications are written? First of all, we would like to know how we get these specifications and how we transmit them to the next generation; for this is how we receive and transmit our biological inheritances. We want to know how these specifications are written. We want to know how they are copied. We want to know how they are translated—how it is that from these specifications we can build ourselves from a single, almost microscopic, egg cell. We want to know why it is that each of us is unique. No one of us is exactly like any other person on earth—unless we happen to be a set of identical twins or triplets. Although we have common ancestors, we differ in our specifications. How did the specifications come to differ?

Classical Genetics

First, let us talk about how we receive the specifications and how we transmit them. This you recognize immediately as classical genetics. I assume you know all about it, but I shall review it very quickly using a characteristic in man to illustrate the point. In each of us there is an enzyme, a protein, that catalyzes one of the reactions by which melanin pigment is made. Melanin is the pigment that gives color to our hair and our eyes; it is melanin in the skin that responds to light and results in our tanning. Individuals who lack this pigment are called albinos. They are comparable to pink-eyed white rabbits in that they are unable to make melanin.

Individuals unable to make melanin differ from those who make it by a single unit of their set of specifications, a unit called a gene. This particular gene comes in two forms—the form that says make a proper tyrosinase enzyme necessary for melanin synthesis and a defective form that specifies an enzyme unable to catalyze this reaction. Each of us has two representatives of this message, one from the mother, one from the father. Since the message comes in two forms, there are four possible kinds of individuals. From the mother we can get a message that says, "I can now make melanin." From the father we can get one that says the same thing. Then we are pure for the message that says, "I can now make melanin." Or from the mother we can get a positive message and from the father a negative message that says, "I can not make melanin." Because the positive message is dominant and the defective message is recessive, an individual of this kind makes melanin. Another individual may get the defective form from the mother, the active form from the father, that is, have one of each. He will also be able to make melanin. It doesn't make any difference from which parent you get the positive message. But if you get the defective message from both parents, you are pure for the message that says, "I can not make melanin." You will be an albino.

When we pass these messages on to the next generation, one or the other goes into each of the egg or sperm cells—either the one from the mother or the one from the father. If you happen to have the capability of sending both kinds of messages, half of your children will get one form, half will get the other form. And if both parents carry both messages, then it is obvious that those who get the defective form from both parents will be albinos.

I've now given you a short course in classical genetics. Essentially, that's all there is to it, except that there are perhaps a hundred thousand other similar messages that carry their parts of the total set of instructions. If you understand how one works, you understand them all. In general biology courses and courses in genetics, we make it more complicated because we don't want to be responsible for technological unemployment of geneticists. Actually, genetics is a bit more complex if you consider all of the ramifications. For example, genes come in chromosomes; and there are many messages per chromosome. They don't always stay in the same chromosome, but can cross over into the partner or homologous chromosome.

How DNA Carries Information

Now you know how hereditary messages are transmitted. Let's now consider how they are written. As I said, they are written in four "letters," which, of course, are not really letters like those of our alphabet. They are sub-units of molecules—DNA molecules.

We can represent these four different sub-units of a DNA molecule by letters of our alphabet. To illustrate, I shall use the four letters —N, E, A, T—to represent the four molecular sub-units. These units, made of five different atoms, average about thirty-two atoms per unit. Each of these units, or "letters" is about one ten-millionth of an inch across. They differ from one another in the arrangement of the atoms, not in the number of different atoms.

These DNA "letters" are arranged in long chains. One of the characteristics of this language or code is that there appears to be no spacing or punctuation between "words." It's very much simpler than ours. If I add extra letters to the sequence NEAT so that it reads NEATTNETAATNE—I have the beginning of a long message not unlike a DNA message.

In the nucleus of the egg cell from which we started development there are five billion of these "letters." If you were to take all the molecules containing the five billion units and string them end to end, they would form a chain about five feet long. But the molecules are so small in diameter that you would be unable to see the chain with the highest powered light microscope possible. The molecules can just barely be resolved with the most modern electron microscope.

How much information is contained in these five feet of DNA—in five billion units? Since there are only four letters in DNAese, to translate from it into a message of our own language would require some kind of a coding system. One system that we might use would be to have each successive three-letter unit of DNAese stand for a letter of our alphabet. If we transform the language, using the four letters NEAT, into a twenty-six letter language we might say NEA equals A, NAE equals B, and so on, until we have all twenty-six letters of the alphabet. In such a code we could take the five billion DNA "letters" of the nucleus of the egg, translate them into letters of the alphabet and then spell out a message. Since we have five billion units, and it takes three of them to make a letter of the alphabet, we'd end up with about one billion, seven hundred thousand three-letter messages or letters of our alphabet. That many letters of the alphabet will make three hundred thousand words, five letters to a word. If we write our messages in all these letters in words which average five letters, we will get sixty thousand printed pages. If we say there are six hundred pages per average volume, we will have a thousand volumes. In other words, the information in the tiny microscopic nucleus, in this sub-microscopic thread five feet long, will be the equivalent of a thousand ordinary library volumes. That is a set of genetic specifications for making one of us out of an egg cell, given a proper environment, proper raw materials, and so on.

Let's express the size of this five foot thread in another way. If it were wound back and forth, one layer thick, on the head of a pin, it would cover only about one-half of one percent of the head of the pin. That means that you could get a thousand volumes of information on half of one per cent of the head of the pin. If you covered the whole head of the pin, you would have the equivalent of two hundred thousand volumes in a monolayer so thin that you could not detect it by anything less than an electron microscope. That's pretty good miniaturization. Let's go one step further. If we took all the DNA code out of all the eggs that gave rise to all the people on earth today—say three billion people—and wound it back and forth like cordwood, how large a stack would it make? It would make a cube an eighth of an inch on a side! Since each person requires a thousand volumes to specify him genetically, this little cube an eighth of an inch on a side is the equivalent of three trillion volumes of library work. In all history since the invention of the printing press, there have been printed only about 50 million different books. In this small cube we can put the equivalent of three trillion volumes—that's 60,000 times as much as is contained in all the books ever published.

The Molecular Basis of Reproduction

The next question I'd like to ask is, how does this message copy itself? This is an interesting and important question because we know that every living system has somehow to send its specifications on to the next generation. In our case, from the time we get the specifications in the egg cell until the time we send them on to the next generation, we must copy the thousand volumes of information with every cell division. The number of cell divisions from the egg of one generation with which we started to the egg or the sperm which we send on to the next generation will vary with age and sex. It may be ten, twenty, thirty or more successive cell divisions. This means that you must copy your specifications ten, twenty, thirty or more times during your lifetime. Remember that's the equivalent of a thousand volumes with each copying. And, of course, you must not make many mistakes or the next generation won't come out right. This is the equivalent of sitting down with a typewriter and typing a thousand volumes of information and then retyping it ten to thirty times in succession. That's a lot of typing! We now know how this is done because of the work of a large number of people, climaxed by the discovery by James Dewey Watson and Francis H. C. Crick of the structure of the molecules that carry these four kinds of units. They discovered that these molecules are not simple single chains but are double parallel chains that are arranged in such a way that they carry complementary information.

Now what does this mean? Opposite every T there will be an A, and conversely, the letter A will always have opposite it a T. The N will have opposite it an E, and the E will have opposite it an N. This means that if you know the order of the units in a four-letter segment you will know the order of its complementary chain. If I have the message TANE, I will have the double message

T-A-N-E-.
Ä-T̈-Ë-N̈-

This means that this molecule has a very simple way of copying itself. It simply separates into the two single chains. Then each chain serves as a model or a template against which the individual units of new chains line up in the right order. If the molecules come apart, the TANE chain picks up the units that make an ATEN chain, and the ATEN chain picks up the units that make a TANE chain, and you have two pairs. It's as if I started with paired hands, fingers tip-to-tip; took them apart; and imagined that the left hand were to make a right hand, and the right hand were to make a left hand from separate fingers. DNA and closely related molecules are the only ones known to science that can carry out this simple kind of replication.

How do these units know how to tell their complements? How does an A know that it must pick up a T? How does an N know that it must pick up an E? The separate units are floating around in a cell in which DNA molecules are replicating. When the N in the chain comes to an E, they will fit and stick together through specific hydrogen bonding. But if the N tries to pick up any of the other three units, N, A, or T, they will not fit and, therefore, not remain in place. One chain automatically picks up the units to make a new chain. These units are free in your cells right now. And your DNA molecules in some cells are coming apart and making new complements in this simple way.

The Test of DNA Replication

Do they really replicate in this way? It's a beautiful hypothesis, so beautiful that we're almost tempted to believe it without doing any testing. But nature has a way of fooling scientists. It often finds ways of working that scientists don't think of. So obviously it's important to test this hypothesis. One way is to label DNA molecules with stable isotopes. There are eight nitrogen atoms in a typical pair of units. The total molecular weight of the pair is about 700. If we were to substitute nitrogen-15 for the normal nitrogen-14 in one pair, the molecular weight would be increased by eight. Eight in 700 is about one per cent. This would not change the size of the molecule. Therefore, it would be more dense. Now if one could find a way to separate more dense molecules from less dense ones, it would be easy to test the hypothesis. As a matter of fact, three investigators, Mathew Meselson, Frank Stahl and Jerome Vinograd, a few years ago figured out a very simple way to do this. It is very much like the way a farmer separates wheat from chaff by shaking it up in a bucket of water. The chaff floats and the wheat settles and they are, therefore, easily separated. You can do that with DNA molecules. You can separate heavy ones from light ones. It's a little more complicated than that. For one thing, it requires a $25,000 analytical ultracentrifuge instead of a bucket of water, but these days this is no problem because universities like The University of Michigan have them around.

With this method, it was possible for Meselson and Stahl to label the DNA units with nitrogen-15 and make them heavy, then to let them undergo one division in a medium in which only light nitrogen was present. The unit with heavy nitrogen comes apart and picks up light nitrogen. Of the two chains that start heavy, each will take a light partner. The new chains ought to be hybrid and intermediate in density. They are. In the next generation, the hybrid chain, the one with both heavy and light nitrogen, ought to separate into light and heavy chains. Each of these will pick up a light nitrogen partner. There will then be one hybrid chain and one completely light chain. And that, too, is found to be the case. In the next generation it is easy to figure out what happens. It does.

The Synthesis of DNA

An even more dramatic way of testing the hypothesis was used by Arthur Kornberg and his associates, now at Stanford University. They set out to see if they could make DNA molecules copy themselves in a test tube. Everyone said it was impossible—that it was so elaborate a process that no biochemist could hope to make it happen in a test tube. Kornberg set out to do it and he found out, in fact, that it was quite simple. If you take the four DNA units with two extra phosphate groups on each, under the right conditions in a test tube, and drop in molecules of double DNA, the DNA will be replicated. It will make copies of itself. Single DNA chains are even more effective in the system. There are ways of telling that the copies are like the added primer.

Even more remarkable, one can make DNA molecules without having a model. One of these is a DNA that has A-T-A-T-A-T units in one chain and the complement in the other chain, T-A-T-A-T-A. If you use such an artificial DNA as a primer, it will be copied and the copy will be like the primer. Several of Kornberg's associates, using a somewhat different approach, discovered a way of making artificial double DNA molecules in which all the units in one chain are E and all the units in the other chain are N. They were then able to use this as a primer and show that in replication more molecules like the spontaneously formed N-N-N-N are made. E-E-E-E

All of this makes if difficult to believe that the hypothesis is incorrect.

The Translation of DNA

We now come to another interesting part of the story. How do we use a simple language like this—four letters, three-letter words, and only sixty-four words—to build an organism as complex as ourselves? It sounds fantastic. If you think a bit; you see it isn't. Any set of specifications that we can write in our twenty-six letter language can be written in a language with only two symbols, dots and dashes. As a matter of fact, computer language has only two symbols, and everyone knows that with it we can write any kind of information we want. It's true that in a computer you can't normally do it with such nice short words. These nice short three-letter words are what make the language of genetics so simple and elegant.

To know how we use this information to make us, we have to understand how we translate this language. Human beings are enormously complex, being made of many thousands of kinds of molecules. The DNA specifications have somehow to say, "Make all these molecules at the right time and in the right place and put them all together in the right way." To do this, one of the first steps is the translation of the four-letter language with its three-letter words into another kind of language, perhaps the second oldest living language on earth. It may have come into existence somewhat less than three billion years ago, that is, later than DNA. Of course, no one was around to say exactly when. So mine is only a rough guess. This language is called *Proteinese* because it is written in the form of protein molecules. These are long molecules somewhat like DNA molecules in being built of sub-units. But there are twenty sub-units in protein instead of four as in DNA. These sub-units are amino acids. A typical amino acid has four or five kinds of atoms—carbon, hydrogen, oxygen, nitrogen, and, in some, sulphur. Note that they never contain phosphorus. These atoms are arranged in twenty specific ways to make the twenty units out of which we make proteins. We have some ten thousand, twenty thousand, perhaps a hundred thousand kinds of protein. These do many kinds of things. There are structural proteins. Hair is largely protein. So are fingernails. Hemoglobin, the pigment in red blood cells, is protein. All of the enzymes either are protein or contain protein. Enzymes speed up or catalyze almost all of the reactions that go on in a living system.

Let us now look at the characteristics of Proteinese as compared with DNAese. First of all, it differs in that there are twenty letters instead of four. How about the words? The words in protein are not all of the same length. They can range from perhaps hundred-letter words to thousand-letter words. How many kinds of words can you write in protein? Remember, you can write only sixty-four in DNA. But using the information in the sixty-four words of DNA, you can write twenty kinds of words that, when used in a thousand-word message, will specify a protein a thousand units long. The first unit can be any one of twenty, the second unit can be any one of twenty. So it would be twenty times twenty times twenty a thousand times. That is a number so large that for all practical purposes it is inconceivable. It is much, much larger than the total number of elementary atomic particles (electrons, protons, neutrons, and so forth) in the entire known universe. It is literally impossible to exhaust the number of combinations of words that you can make with twenty units, if they can be put together up to a thousand units long and in any proportion and in any sequence. This language, therefore, is essentially unlimited in the number of possible words.

Protein Synthesis

How do we make protein molecules with DNA units? This actually seems to be very simple. To do so we make use of another language, but fortunately it is only a dialect of the first one. How are the four letters of DNA translated into protein? If we write the four letters of DNA—N-E-A-T—we can write the complement of the DNA molecule in the dialect called RNA—ribonucleic acid. The complement of N will be an E which is almost like a DNA E. So we call it E′. E will have the complement, N′; A, the complement T′; T, the complement A′. Now, remember the letters form three-letter words. So, we have a word E′N′T′ that specifies an amino acid, say amino acid number one. We can have another word N′T′A′ that specifies amino acid number two.

How is an amino acid related to a DNA word? It happens in the following way. The DNA code is in the nucleus of the cell. RNA that is complementary to this code is constructed. It moves from the nucleus to the cytoplasm and there enters small microscopic structures called ribosomes. This information-carrying RNA that specifies a protein goes into the ribosome and there serves as a template to collect amino acids in the right sequence. Each of the twenty amino acids is tagged with a small segment of RNA, called transfer RNA, consisting of about eighty units. There are twenty transfer RNA's, corresponding to the twenty amino acids. Each carries a three-letter coding segment complementary to a three-letter coding segment on the template RNA. An enzymatically catalyzed reaction joins the amino acids together to form a protein molecule. This then leaves the ribosome. This is the way we make hemoglobin. You are doing this right now in your red blood cells. Interestingly enough, this process of translating the information from DNA to RNA can be done in a test tube. And the process of transferring the information from RNA to protein can also be carried out in a test tube. It is now possible to make test tube hemoglobin by following these steps. This makes it pretty clear that this is the right interpretation. That all this can be accomplished in a test tube is a remarkable achievement of modern molecular biology.

Enzymes

For what are proteins used? Let's take the protein that catalyzes the reaction by which the amino acid phenylalanine is oxidized. One oxygen atom, added in a particular place, makes the related amino acid tyrosine. We must have both of these amino acids. If we have an enzyme that says we can make tyrosine from phenylalanine, we don't have to have tyrosine in our diets. We can make the tyrosine by this reaction which is catalyzed by an enzyme which was made from a piece of DNA which we call a gene. Some people have a defective form of this enzyme and cannot catalyze the reaction by which tyrosine is made from phenylalanine. If such persons are fed normal amounts of phenylalanine, as in a usual diet, they cannot convert the phenylalanine into tyrosine. They use some of the phenylalanine for protein but the rest of it, the surplus, accumulates and indirectly posions the central nervous system. Such individuals are feeble-minded. This genetic disease is called phenylketonuria, and in English one describes it as feeble-mindedness due to inability to oxidize phenylalanine to tyrosine because of the absence of a protein. The gene that says the same thing in DNAese says so in a "sentence" of perhaps four hundred or a thousand "words."

Genetic Disease

We know of several hundred genetic diseases in man. Phenylketonuria is an interesting one. If diagnosed early, which is simple, and if an artificial diet is provided in which there is only enough phenylalanine to make protein and no excess, and if tyrosine is provided in the right amount, the individual becomes normal. The result is circumvention of a genetic disease by modern medicine. But note that this is accomplished without correcting the fundamental defect in the specifications. Such a "cured" individual will transmit defective specifications to the next generation. This creates a eugenic problem that someday society may have to be concerned about. It isn't quite as bad as it sounds because the build-up of this defect as a result of this achievement of medical science is very slow indeed. It would take many, many generations and many thousands of years before this particular disease would become frequent. On the other hand, there may someday be many genetic diseases similarly circumvented. If so, we will sooner or later have to think about what to do about them. I point out, however, that this isn't a question for science alone. It is a question for society, including scientists. One solution is simple. Persons who are of this type might be persuaded to adopt children instead of having them in a natural way. There would then be no build-up. But as I say, it is not a scientific question, and I am no more competent to advise than is any other informed citizen.

Cytoplasm

I am sure many of you are saying life can't be this simple. Of course it isn't. We have DNA specifications in the nucleus of the cell that are, so to speak, the blueprints or the recipes for making people out of egg cells. But a lot more is essential too. In addition to these specifications the egg also contains cytoplasm. And that too is specific. It must be human cytoplasm. You can't put the nucleus of a human egg into the cytoplasm of a monkey egg and get an organism. It won't work. Of course we don't do this experiment with monkeys and people, but we can do it with two kinds of frogs. We can find that the nucleus has to be in its own species of cytoplasm. Therefore, the cytoplasm is species-specific. We don't know too much about this as yet. We must leave some problems for the Ph.D. candidates of the next generation.

In addition to cytoplasm one must have food—raw materials—to make an organism as complex as one of us from an egg cell, given the proper specifications. This food must be of the right kind, in the right amount, in the right proportions and available at the right time. If these conditions are not all fulfilled, the result is nutritional disease. Each of us has consumed ten, twenty or thirty tons of food up to now, depending on age and appetite. We have used that food to make us, using a set of specifications, tearing it down with enzymes, using the pieces to construct one of us. If the specifications aren't right, or if the raw material isn't right, the individual doesn't come out right.

Mutation

Let us now turn to the last question. How do differences arise? Why am I different from other people? I have different specifications, but how did they come to be different? The answer is pretty simple. Sometimes DNA molecules make a mistake in being copied. An N unit doesn't always pick up an E unit because the hydrogen atoms that must be in the right place to make them stick together by hydrogen bonding have a way of being in alternate positions occasionally. If the hydrogen atoms happen to be in the wrong place exactly when the molecule is going to pick up its partner, the N may pick up an A instead of an E. Let's say that we have a three-letter word, TEN. The complement to that would be ANE. Now let's say that the E picks up a T instead of what it should pick up, an N. Then the complement would be ATE. Now when this ATE replicates in the next round, it is not likely to make a mistake.

The complement of ATE is TAN. By substituting an A for an E, we have now substituted the word TAN for the word TEN. That is what we call a mutation. TAN will not stand for the same amino acid as does TEN. If this change occurs in the message, there will be a wrong amino acid in the protein at a particular place. This type of change is known to happen. For example, there are forms of hemoglobin that differ by one amino acid. Sickle cell hemoglobin, which is an unfavorable kind of hemoglobin to have, differs by one amino acid at a particular place because one symbol in the DNA code was miscopied at some time in the past. This is not the only way a mutation can occur. A letter can be left out, an extra one inserted or letters can be transposed. Or there can be more complex changes like those that occur in typewriting when one gets a hand on the wrong row of keys. Sometimes an entire "chapter" may be present as an "extra." Thus in mongolian idiocy there is present in each cell an entire extra chromosome.

Breaking the Code

How do we know that the DNA words designating amino acids are three-letter words? How do scientists go about discovering this? How do we know what order of the DNA unit stands for what amino acid? That is, what is the coding relation between DNA and protein? This is like trying to decipher any code. What you do is find the equivalent of a Rosetta stone on which you have both messages written. Then, you can find out how one is related to the other. We have, so to speak, found the Rosetta stone of life that relates DNA to protein. This was done in a most interesting way. Professor Severo Ochoa at New York University found that he could make RNA molecules artificially by putting the RNA units together in a test tube under the right conditions. If you put in all A' units, you will get an RNA that has only A' in it. If you put in all T', you will get RNA made only of T'. If you put in T' and A', you will get an RNA that has T' and A'. If the T' and A' are in equal proportions, they will go together at random in equal proportions. If you put in all four DNA units, T'A'N'E', they too will go together at random.

A few years ago Marshall W. Nirenberg and J. Heinrich Matthaei of the National Institutes of Health thought of putting into the test tube system, in which they did the translation of RNA to protein, artificial RNA. When they used an artificial RNA containing only T' units, lo and behold, it did direct synthesis of a very peculiar and previously unknown protein—namely a protein made of only the one amino acid phenylalanine. This is not really a protein but a protein-like polymer called polyphenylalanine. This was a clue to breaking the code. The units had to make sense or they couldn't have made that particular protein. Whatever the coding ratio is, whether it is two-letter words, three-letter words, four-letter words, the amino acid is always the same—phenylalanine. This told Nirenberg and Matthaei that if the words are indeed three-letter words, the coding word for the amino acid phenylalanine must be T'T'T'.[2]

Now you can make a synthetic RNA in which you have T' and A'. If you put in a ratio of five times as many T' as A' and get a random association, it is easy to calculate the relative frequencies of the various possible three-letter words. Words with two T's and one A' will be relatively frequent. So will T'T'T' words. It turns out that two of the amino acids that are incorporated in the protein when this experiment is made are phenylalanine and tyrosine. The coding word for tyrosine is therefore probably two T's and an A'. But there are three possible ways to arrange the word. You put the A' first, second, or last. How do you know which way is the right way? That turns out to be simple too. Professor Ochoa found that if he started out with the one letter A', and then built up an RNA using all T' for the remaining units he got an RNA that had an A' at the end and all the rest T's, that is, . . . T'T'T'T'T'T'T'A'. RNA gets synthesized from right to left; the protein gets built against it from left to right. We know this from radioactive tracers. When Ochoa used this RNA, he got a protein containing, for the most part, phenylalanine, as he should. Remember three T's equal phenylalanine. But, there was a small amount of tyrosine incorporated. It was always at the final end of the chain to be made. Obviously, if tyrosine is two T's and an A', it has to be in the arrangement, T'T'A'. By doing other experiments of this kind, it is possible to work out other code words. This is what workers have done and are doing. As a result, we know code words for nineteen of the amino acids. If you know the order of the amino acids in a protein, such as Frederick Sanger worked out for insulin, you can now come pretty close to reading the DNA message that spelled the amino acid sequence in the protein. I've simplified the story considerably but that is approximately where we are now.

It turns out that there are sixty-four words possible in DNAese, and it only takes twenty to encode the twenty amino acids. What are the other forty-four doing? For one thing, there is pretty clearly some degeneracy in the code. That means there are two or more words that encode the same amino acid. Then too, some of the words are probably used as spacers, to indicate where one protein stops and another begins. Perhaps one tells where to start reading the message. With no spaces, there must be a fixed starting point for reading the message. This kind of code is called a non-overlapping code because the letters must be read three at a time starting at a predetermined

2. The usual symbols for DNA nucleotides are A, T, C, and G. For RNA, A, U, C, and G. I've used the ones I have so as to be able to make 20 three-letter English words [Beadle's note].

point. And it is a degenerate code because one word might stand for the same amino acid as does another word.

Three Letter Words

Now we've answered all the questions except one. How do we know that the words in this language are three-letter words? That turns out to be very simple too. And it's done this way. I have a message ANNNANATETANANTANTATETNTNAEANT, which makes some sense in terms of our own language. It says ANN NAN ATE TAN ANT etc. Crick and some of his associates took a DNA message like this that they knew made sense. Then they made mutations near the left end by adding or substracting units. If they took one letter out, the message no longer made sense. If I take the first letter away from the example given, it now reads NNN ANA TET, etc. Taking one letter out shifted the reading frame by one and scrambled the message. If you take out one letter and then put in another letter, the one you put in will compensate for the one you took out, and the message will make sense at one end, e.g., TNN NAN ATE TAN ANT etc. If you take out two letters, the message won't make sense, e.g., NNA NAT ETA etc. But, if you take out three letters, most of the message will make sense, e.g., NAN ATE TAN ANT etc. Or if you put three in the left end, the right end will retain its sense. But if you take out two or put in two, take out one or put in one, take out four or put in four, the message will not make sense. The only simple way to explain such results is to assume that the language consists of three-letter words.

Evolution

Let us now talk about evolution. These changes—taking out letters, putting them in, and rearranging them—are believed to be the basis of all organic evolution from the beginning of life on earth to the origin of man. We are of course the product of evolution and the result of many, many millions of mutations which had selective advantages. These mutations have given rise to an evolutionary sequence going back from us, if you call man the ultimate form of evolution at the present time, to simpler and simpler forms to something akin to the simplest viruses. Instead of the five billion units in the DNA of humans, the smallest viruses have only a few thousand units of DNA or RNA in their genetic specifications.

Before viruses, it is presumed that there arose spontaneously on earth in the pre-life stages, DNA or RNA molecules that were able to copy themselves. Some presumably collected protein coats that provided protection. This gave them a selective advantage. The units, out of which DNA was made, presumably came from simpler organic molecules by chemical reactions which are inevitable under favorable conditions. They, in turn, came from simpler molecules that were inorganic. These, in turn, came from the elements. We now know that all the elements are capable of coming from hydrogen by nuclear interactions that nuclear physicists know about. Hydrogen fuses to give beryllium-8, beryllium-8 captures helium nuclei and becomes carbon. And so it goes. All of this is known in principle now. If this is correct, it means that from the first postulated primitive universe of hydrogen all of evolution is possible up to man.

That sounds very mechanistic, I know. At this point, I should say it really isn't any more remarkable that there should have been created a universe of hydrogren capable of evolving into man than that there should have been created a universe already containing man. One course is as remarkable as the other. In other words the hypothesis I have advanced does not change the problem of ultimate creation one iota. In that sense, it has nothing to do with religion, which is an entirely separate matter.

Cultural Inheritance

As far as we know, we differ from all other organisms on earth in a quantitative way only. Maybe there is something we do not yet know that makes us qualitatively different from other organisms. If so, we do not know what it is. Quantitatively, however, we have a great deal that other organisms do not have. For one thing, we have a more highly developed nervous system than any other organism on earth. As a result, we have better memories. We are able to reason. Maybe other animals can reason too, but we are much better at it, there is no doubt about that. We have been able to develop a method of communication by speech. Other organisms have primitive ways of communicating by sound, but they do not have speech in the sense in which we have it. We have learned to write down messages that are equivalent to DNA. We have developed through speech and writing very effective methods of communication. These methods of communication and the ability to reason, to store information in our nervous systems, to take it out, to rearrange it, and to communicate it, make possible the evolution of a cultural inheritance, which we alone among all creatures on earth possess. This inheritance includes language, religion, music, literature, art, technology, and science.

No other organism has added this type of cultural inheritance to its biological inheritance. We accumulate our cultural inheritance individually; we transmit it to our fellow man, and we transmit it to the next generation in a cumulative fashion. Our educational institutions are engaged in the process of systematically transmitting such information to the next generation and in adding to it in a cumulative way from one generation to the next. This is in addition to and separate from our biological inheritance in its manner of accumulation, storage and transmission. As a matter of fact, we don't know how the information that we accumulate is stored in our nervous systems. This again is a problem for the next generation, and a very important one. Although we do not know how this is done, we do know that cultural inheritance cannot develop without biological inheritance through DNA—for we know our brains are made according to the specifications in DNA. The two types of inheritance are complementary.

The assumed evolutionary sequence from hydrogen to man has proceeded through a fantastic number of steps, each almost imperceptibly small. Each represents a chemical change such as the fusion of hydrogen to form helium or the modification of a DNA "letter" by a simple chemical reaction. Through science, which is a part of our cultural inheritance, we have identified many of these evolutionary steps. The humanities, too, are a part of our cultural inheritance. In this sense, the two areas are closely related. If we are to understand and appreciate our total cultural inheritance, as we believe liberally educated men and women should, we cannot reasonably disregard any of its major components.

QUESTIONS FOR STUDY, DISCUSSION, AND WRITING

1. *In which paragraph does Beadle set out his organizational plans? What is the plan and what principles seem to have determined it?*
2. *Which of Beadle's questions seemed hardest for him to answer? Why?*
3. *What is Beadle's implicit definition of language? How does it compare with Francis' ("Revolution in Grammar," pp. 104–121)? Why does Beadle usually talk about writing in the passive voice?*
4. *What is the social problem created by genetic disease?*
5. *How does Beadle's conception of the relation between religion and science compare with Huxley's ("Letter to Kingsley," p. 328)? How would you account for the difference?*

EDWARD S. DEEVEY, JR.
Bogs

Matthew Arnold could never have expressed his feeling for Dover Beach with such words as: "The heath is calm tonight,/ The swamp is full, the moon lies fair/ Upon the peat." For the poetic geographer a bog is Gothic when it is not downright menacing, a "ghoul-haunted woodland" or a trysting place for witches. Myths of bogland are very old, and may be based on a well-founded dread of savage woodsmen; Western civilization, originating near the Mediterranean shores, has fought the forest and its denizens at every step, and has successively driven the Goth, the Pict, the Caledonian and the Seminole into dank morasses of oblivion. Today the connection between Picts and pixies, bogs and bogeys is generally forgotten. By odd coincidence, however, the bog itself offers a historical record of changing landscape and climate that leads back into those murky mists of memory. Close study suggests also that the boglands of the Northern Hemisphere may be cast to play an ominous role in changes of the earth's climate that are yet to come.

The true bog must be distinguished from the reedy marsh. Marshes form near salt water and contain mainly grasses; few trees other than mangroves can stand much salt around their roots. Bogs are found in the drier interiors of continents as well as near the ocean, but they require some rainfall—deserts have few bogs. If the rainfall is great enough and the summers are cool enough for trees to grow on the uplands of a region, bogs may be expected in the lowlands. Bogs in rainy areas may be more sodden than a tropical rain forest, but the rain water they soak up contains few salts and other nutrients. Only plants that partake sparingly of nutrients, like the shrubs and perennials of arctic barrens and cold steppes, can survive in a bog.

Upland and lowland are relative terms, and refer to the flow of water through the ground. Whenever a barrier lies athwart the flow, water is interrupted in its steady descent to the sea and may rise above the surface of the ground behind the dam. So lowlands can occur near the tops of hills. A lake of clear water formed in this way will not last long. An entering stream dumps silt into the lake, and plants growing along the water's edge add their debris. More organic material may be deposited by runoff from land above the lake, especially from swampy flats. Eventually the lake is obliterated and the mud becomes firm enough to support shrubs and then trees. Pools left in the center of the lake may be bridged by plants like the sedge or swamp loosestrife. With their aid other plants form a floating mat on which trees can grow while the water below is yet unfilled. Most bogs are probably made in this way.

The raised bog (the German *Hochmoor*) does not have to start in a lake but can form in any wet meadow. It depends on the presence of sphagnum, commonly known as peat moss. When dry, this remarkable substance resembles a sponge in its ability to take up great quantities of water by capillary action. It holds more water than absorbent cotton and so is useful as a plant mulch or even as a surgical dressing. The accumulation of dead sphagnum in a meadow forms a layer of half-decayed material, or peat, which draws ground water upward, thus permitting still more of the moss to grow on top. Where sphagnum grows in large masses, it actually raises the water table. When thoroughly wet, however, peat is as impervious to more water as dry rock. Rainwater then cannot percolate downward and runs off horizontally. The extra water eventually reaches the edge of the dome-shaped mass of sphagnum, where the peat is thinner. Thus watered at its margins, the bog grows upward and outward, and can even grow uphill. Plants other than sphagnum grow on the surface, and their remains are added to the peat. So long as the bog is growing, this debris, being water-soaked, accumulates almost unchanged. Eventually the bog reaches a size at which evaporation from the surface balances the rainfall and upward flow of ground water, and growth on the bog halts. Plant debris on the surface then decays about as fast as it accumulates, and little or no new peat forms. Material below the outer skin of the bog does not decay because oxygen cannot reach it, and plant remains—even corpses of men—do not decompose for centuries. Heather or other shrubs of the same family may grow on the stabilized surface, but few trees are to be seen. A growth of forest on a raised bog probably implies a recent change toward a drier climate.

All bogs are stores of peat with sluggish circulation. The water at the surface is poor in salts and bases, partly because much of it is rain water, and partly also because the peat absorbs dissolved matter like a chemist's Amberlite resin. In most boggy districts there is a third reason: The local rock is usually granite, which contributes almost no minerals to the ground water flowing through it. The result is that bog plants are starved for lime, phosphorus and nitrogen. The deeper the peat, the more this is true. In consequence bogs are enclaves of subarctic life; they abound in plants like black spruce, cotton grass and Labrador tea. The bogs of Cape Cod support cranberries; those of New Jersey, blueberries. Both these plants are heaths of northern lands. Even subarctic animals like the bog lemming and the olivebacked thrush may be found far south of their regular ranges, giving bogs in temperate regions a northern flavor. In a sense they were left behind as the last continental ice sheet retreated northward, taking with it the belts of tundra and taiga (spruce forest) that lay beyond its margin when it covered the present locations of New York and Chicago. Probably no area has been continuously boggy since those days, but any partly closed-in bog in the northern U.S. can be thought of, from a lemming's point of view, as tundra enclosed by taiga.

Amid the plants of the muskeg, however, are others reminiscent of the tropics. Sogginess and nitrogen deficiency are common to rain forests as well as to bogs. So a few of the hardier orchids have ventured northward to meet the Labrador tea. Insectivorous plants, mainly tropical, are also successful in bogs, since their unorthodox behavior solves the problem of nitrogen deficiency; sundews, butterwort and pitcher plants grow in bogs. The pitcher plants, in fact, go north almost to the arctic tree-line, and their rain-filled leaves serve not only as traps for unwary insects but, being enriched in nitrogen and phosphorus, form an aquatic habitat for the larvae of other insects (particularly those of midges, blowflies and mosquitoes) which can withstand the digestive enzymes in the leaves. The pitcher plant mosquito (*Wyeomyia smithii*) has followed its host northward.

Although cool, cloudy summers are essential for the existence of a raised bog, a few hot days will not destroy it, but will merely dry out its surface. A bog can then be crossed dry-shod. In damp or cooler weather it squishes underfoot like the arctic muskeg. A change in temperature or rainfall over a long period of time, however, upsets the stability of a bog. Raised bogs especially are sensitive indicators of climate. If the climate becomes moister or cooler, the bogs renew their growth both upward and outward. In drier or warmer conditions the surface will stabilize, but air will penetrate deeper into the drying peat and the zone of decay will thicken downward. If the drought is long-continued, the peat will be deeply weathered, the decay zone extending even into the older peat, and the bog will dwindle away in the sun like an ice cube.

Sensitive indicators of weather are nowhere hard to find. In tune with the variable march of the seasons, some insects emerge, some birds arrive or depart, some flowers bloom. The term of such an indicator, however, is short. Bogs exist for such long periods and respond to weather so slowly that they integrate weather into climate. Best of all, they also record it. When we cut into a bog for fuel and garden mulch, it resembles a cake of three, four, five or more layers, each marking a change in climate. At each boundary the dark, well-oxidized peat which formed, or rather weathered, when that layer was at the surface is topped by a brighter, fresher (and less combustible) peat representing renewed growth.

The episodes of rejuvenation indicated by the layers in any one bog may not mean anything important. The local water table could rise and fall for many reasons. But when all the bogs for miles around have layers formed at the same time, the implication can only be that the climate has changed repeatedly. Bright-colored layers composed of raw sphagnum peat, rich in the remains of such water plants as cotton grass, record a stage of flooding which lasted for years: the climate was cooler, and rainfall was more effective. Dark-colored, humus-rich peat—poor in recognizable fossils because of oxidation, but sometimes containing the remains of heather, birch, or alder—records a stage of stability or destruction during a run of drier, warmer summers.

This matchless record of past climates needs only a time scale to be read with assurance. The climatic chronology determined by the pollen method—according to ratios of fossilized pollen grains from different plants—is relatively coarse. Pollen is plentiful in the peat, but a pollen period is thousands of years long, covering the span of two or three bog layers. Nevertheless one point of equivalence with the pollen chronology became obvious early in the science of bogs. Before 1916, when the pollen method was founded by the great Swedish geologist Lennart von Post, C. A. Weber had noticed that one of the episodes of bog rejuvenation in northern Germany was especially well-marked and widespread. Von Post soon realized that Weber's *Grenzhorizont*[1] coincided with the beginning of his own last pollen period, the "sub-Atlantic climatic deterioration" when northern countries such as Germany and Sweden became cold and rainy. Refinements such as radiocarbon dating confirm von Post's deduction that Europe's climate took a turn for the worse about 600 B.C. The upland vegetation responded to the new conditions slowly—some plants thriving, others dying out—and the pollen count reflects this. But the bogs record a finer embroidery of moisture changes superimposed on the longer swings of temperature.

Human history has not been unrelated to these events. The decline of Greece and the rise of Rome clearly correlate with climatic change shortly after 600 B.C. The climate was somewhat better when Rome's power was at its height, but Rome's conquest of Britain was given up, in part for climatic reasons, at the time of another change, about A.D. 400. As Gibbon put it, "The masters of the fairest and most wealthy climates on the globe turned with contempt . . . from the cold and lonely heaths over which the deer of the forest were chased by a troop of naked barbarians." Since that time, or at most since 600 B.C., the extraordinary blanket-bog has crept like a glacier down the slopes of the Irish and Scottish mountains, and down the Pennines in England, overwhelming pine forests and cropland alike. Today the British Isles are very different from the sunny, forested land the Neolithic farmers knew in the third millennium B.C. Already in the Middle Bronze Age (about 1200 B.C.) the bogs were getting out of hand. Wooden tracks were laid over the increasingly squishy countryside, in an effort to keep trade routes open. Such tracks, datable by pollen, by artifacts and by radiocarbon, often turn up when British bogs are dug.

Most of Europe's forests were cut down long ago. Peat is not so good a fuel as wood, but it will burn, and the heat can be used for distilling. Fortified with peat-smoke-flavored alcohol, a man can tolerate the sight of a treeless landscape and can even come to prefer a heath to a forest. The raised bogs have been drained and dug extensively in Ireland, Scotland, Denmark, western Scandinavia, northern Germany, and to a smaller extent in Maine and New Brunswick, where wood is more plentiful. As a fuel resource the peat bogs of the world are not to be despised. George Kazakov, a Russian peat expert now living in this country, computes that there

1. Boundary line.

are 223 billion dry tons of peat available on earth, more than half of it in the U.S.S.R.

So large a supply of combustible carbohydrate, delicately poised between growth and destruction, can seriously affect the earth's carbon balance. The carbon-dioxide content of air has increased by 11 per cent since about 1870 and apparently is still increasing. Radiocarbon assays by Hans Suess, now of the Scripps Institution of Oceanography, prove that most of the added carbon dioxide is compounded of modern carbon. It is much too young, judging by its high radiocarbon content, to have all come from the burning of fossil fuels by industry. Fossil fuels can account for only a small portion of the increase. The rest of the new carbon dioxide must be modern, and a finger of suspicion points to bogs as the source.

The warming of the world's climate since the last century may well have set a slow fire to the peat, simply by favoring surface oxidation by soil bacteria. If the world's climate should become so warm and dry that all the peat is oxidized, about 366 billion tons of carbon dioxide would be released. This is a sixth of the amount now present in the atmosphere, and the whole reserve of carbon in land plants and animals is only 15 times as much. The estimate does not include the carbon of humus in ordinary soils which would also be oxidized if the climate changed. So it is not impossible that the carbon dioxide added to the earth's atmosphere may have come mainly from peat and humus.

Though the changes of climate and of the amount of carbon dioxide have run parallel, we cannot yet be sure which is cause and which effect. Carbon dioxide added to air causes it to absorb more heat from the sun, and it may be that the climate has become warmer because of the extra 11 per cent of "dephlogisticated air."[2] If so, we may be in for trouble. A doubling in the carbon dioxide content of the air would almost certainly warm the climate enough to cause the glaciers to melt. The added water would raise the sea level perhaps by 100 feet, drowning the largest cities of the world. It may be that before such a calamity happens, a new balance will be struck; the carbon dioxide should be dissolved in the oceans, and it is a major mystery why the extra 11 per cent has not been dissolved already. But if the added carbon dioxide does not go into the oceans, New York and London will simply have to move, and the pixies too will need new haunts, for the bogs will be thin air.

2. Here, carbon dioxide, although the usual term (drawn from eighteenth-century chemistry) was "phlogisticated air." "Phlogiston" was the hypothetical element believed to be contained in all combustible substances and liberated from them in the process of combustion. The "air" in a closed space was said to be "phlogisticated" when nothing more could be burned in it; hence gases that would not support combustion (including carbon dioxide) were "phlogisticated air." "Dephlogisticated air," on the other hand, was Priestley's term for the "air" that absorbs "phlogiston" readily and hence supports violent combustion—oxygen.

JOHN D. STEWART
Vulture Country

Spain is the stronghold of the vultures. There are four listed species in Europe, two common and two rare; if they are anywhere, they are in Spain. The bearded vulture and the black survive there, the Egyptian flourishes, and the great griffon swarms. The further south you go the more numerous they become, until you reach the hot grazing plains of Andalusia. There, summer and winter through, they hang in hordes in the roofless sky, for Andalusia is the vulture country.

There are three essential qualities for vulture country: a rich supply of unburied corpses, high mountains, a strong sun. Spain has the first of these, for in this sparsely populated and stony land it is not customary, or necessary, to bury dead animals. Where there are vultures in action such burial would be a self-evident waste of labor, with inferior sanitary results. Spain has mountains, too, in no part far to seek; and the summer sun is hot throughout the country. But it is hottest in Andalusia, and that is the decisive factor.

The sun, to the vulture, is not just something which makes life easier and pleasanter, a mere matter of preference. His mode of life is impossible without it. Here in Andalusia the summer sun dries up every pond and lake and almost every river. It drives the desperate frogs deep into the mud cracks and forces the storks to feed on locusts. It kills the food plants and wilts the fig trees over the heads of the panting flocks. Andalusia becomes like that part of ancient Greece, "a land where men fight for the shade of an ass."

All animals, both tame and wild, weaken in these circumstances, and the weakest go to the wall and die. The unpitying sun glares down on the corpses and speeds their putrefaction, rotting the hide and softening the sinews and the meat, to the vulture's advantage. But the sun plays a still greater part in his life. Its main and vital function, for him, is the creation of thermal currents in the atmosphere, for without these he would be helpless.

The vulture must fly high—high enough to command a wide territory, for, except at times of catastrophe, dead animals are never thick on the ground. His task is to soar to ten thousand feet, more or less, two or three times in a day, and to hang there and keep constant survey. A male griffon weighs up to sixteen pounds, so that to hoist himself up to that necessary viewpoint would call for fifty-three thousand calories, the equivalent of fifty pounds of meat. To find and eat three times his own weight in a day is clearly impossible; a short cut must be made. In the dawn of any day, in Andalusia, you may see the vulture discovering that short cut.

The eagles, buzzards, kites, and falcons are already on the wing, quartering the plain fast and low, seeking reptiles and small game. But the vulture sits on a crag and waits. He sees the sun bound up out of the sierra, and still he waits. He waits until the sun-struck rocks and the hard earth heat up and the thermal currents begin to rise. When the upstream is strong enough, he leaps out from the cliff, twists into it and without one laborious wingbeat, spirals and soars.

By the time the vulture reaches his station, a half hour later and maybe more, the sun is blazing down on the plain and betraying every detail to his telescopic eye, and the updraft is strengthening as the day approaches its zenith. His ceiling for this day is fixed by two factors. One is the strength and buoyancy of his chosen thermal, which will vary with the strength of the sun and the behavior of the upper winds. But the more important factor, for it fixes his horizontal bearings as well, is the distribution of neighboring vultures in the sky, his colleagues and competitors.

He cocks his head from side to side and checks their various positions. There they hang, dotted across the clear sky at intervals of a mile or so—at the corners of one-mile squares. Height and lateral distances all adjusted, the vulture settles, circling slowly on his invisible support, and begins his long and lonely vigil.

This griffon vulture, which I select from the four species as being by far the most prevalent and typical, is almost sure to be a male. The female rarely leaves her nest from early March, when she lays her rough white egg, until August, when her huge poult is fledged and flying. The father has to feed and carry for all three.

At first glance, from below, he appears as one great wing, ten feet from tip to tip and two feet broad. His tail is square and very short, which is all it needs to be, for there are no sharp or sudden quirks in his flight that would call for a strong rudder. His movements are premeditated, stressless, and leisurely, for his energy must be conserved at all costs and never wasted on aerobatics.

The vulture's head and neck, too, protrude very little in front of his wing plane, and this distinguishes his flight silhouette from the eagle's. His neck is, in fact, some two feet long, but since it is bare—and must be bare—he folds it back into his collar to keep it warm. His head, apart from its nakedness, is like an eagle's; his yellow claws, which never kill and rarely carry, are shorter and not so strong. His plumage is a uniform sandy color, faded and tattered by work and waiting and, perhaps, by old age. It is relieved only by his coffee-colored ruff and the broad black primary wing feathers fingering the air.

The vulture sails in silence, for no vocal signals could serve him at such a distance from his fellows. He croaks, growls, and whistles only in his family circle, and at his feasts. He circles by almost imperceptible adjustments of his wing planes, aided by slight twists of his tail. But his head is in constant and active movement. He swivels it from one side to the other, bringing each eye in turn to bear on the earth. Then he bends his neck to right or left to check on one of his neighbors to north, south, east or west.

The whole vulture network is interdependent. Each vulture can give and receive two signals or, as the scientists call them, "visual stimuli." Circling means "Nothing doing"; dropping, or its result-ant hole in the sky, calls "Come here!" Like all other vultures, he rests reassured by the first and is rapidly and relentlessly drawn by the second.

It is demonstrable how, with a special density of nerve endings on his retina, the vulture can see a small animal from a great height. Many other birds—gannets, for example—have the same propensity. Their eyesight is surprising only when we compare it with the poor standards of our own. But a mystery remains: how does the bird know that the animal is dead? The sense of smell is to be ruled out straightway. It is impossible that it would operate at such a distance, even allowing for the upward current of air. Birds are not, generally, well endowed in this respect, and in the vulture's case this may be especially fortunate.

No book, no expert, could answer this question for me, and I carried it through the vulture country for years, the one tantalizing imponderable, the broken link. Then, one hot afternoon, I lay down beside an old swineherd in the shade of a cork oak on the foothills overlooking the great plan of La Janda. For fifty years, he told me, he had watched pigs on that plain—the pigs, yes, and the vultures. I put my problem to him.

The swineherd's theory is not to be proved, but it is a wise one and I shall hold it until I find a better. No, he said, it is not the white belly skin that distinguishes the dead animals. White fur may fix the vulture's eye, but it does not offer him evidence of death. All herds and flocks, said the old man, lie down together and at one time. They have their place and their hour of rest. When a vulture sees an animal lying alone and apart, he is bound to notice it. The next time he crosses, the same image strikes his eye and startles him again. Over and over again he marks it and waits and watches; but now, alerted, he watches it more closely.

The next day the animal is still there; his attention is fixed upon it now, so he circles a little lower, his eye riveted, seeking the slight-est movement of limb or lung. He sees none, but he continues to wait, said the old man. It takes him two days, at least, to confirm death. He goes on circling, but lower. He becomes more engrossed, and more sure. The other vultures note his behavior and move over a little in the sky. Every time he falls, they move closer. Now he is very low. He seeks the heaving of the flanks or eye movements; he sees neither. At some point, perhaps, he receives a visual stimulus in some death sign—the protruding tongue or the wide and whitened eye. Then he falls quickly, landing heavily at a little distance from the corpse.

The swineherd and I watched the first vulture land. We watched him sidling and circling the dead goat standing erect to see better, wing tips trailing, naked neck stretched to the full, head swiveling rapidly to bring alternate eyes to bear. He hopped closer and paused, peering intently. If he could smell, even as well as we, his doubts would have been over. But he stood there, irresolute, famished yet fearful, with his bill open and his wings ready for use.

Then a big shadow swept across the brown grass, and the vulture glanced upwards. His involuntary signal had been answered, and a tall column of vultures wheeled overhead. He hopped to close quarters, stretched forward, pecked the corpse, and leapt back. He watched it for a second more; no movement. Then he croaked once, as though to bless himself, and threw himself on the body. He struck his heavy beak into the flank, flapped for balance, and thrust backwards with feet and wings to strip the hide from the ribs and belly.

Almost immediately there were eight more vultures at the corpse, and we saw that all of them sought and fought for the same place. Their aim was to penetrate, their object the viscera. Watching them thrusting their long necks deep into the belly cavity and withdrawing them befouled and bloodstained, I saw why those necks must be bare. Yes, said the swineherd, and that is the one part the vulture cannot reach to clean. His mate may clean it for him later, for pure greed, but if he had feathers there he would have maggots in them.

Now sixteen more vultures swept down, landing heavily in their haste and flap-hopping to the feast—the second square from the sky pattern. The corpse was covered, submerged in a heaving, struggling mass of broad brown wings. A new column wheeled above us, circling lower. There should be twenty-four up there, I reckoned. There were twenty-three.

The latecomers landed on nearby trees, including ours, and their weight bent thick limbs to the ground. From points four miles distant, we could expect thirty-four more, and at the height of the carnival I counted just short of one hundred birds.

A mule lasts two hours, said the old man, and an ox, three. This goat became bones in the sun in half an hour.

As the hundred fed, or hoped and waited, many more vultures circled high above, assessing the situation and the prospects and treasuring their altitude. Toward the end, when the feasters scattered and exposed the small skeleton, the watchers flapped and drifted wearily away to resume their distant stations. But they had fulfilled their function. They had marked the spot and drawn the Egyptian vultures and the kites.

Now the little Egyptian vultures landed daintily and dodged nimbly through the throng of giants. They are bare on the face and throat only, with well-feathered head and neck, and so, perforce, they are cleaner feeders. The dirty work has been done; now the long and delicate beak comes into play. The Egyptian vultures attack the skull, the large joints, and the crevices of the pelvic girdle—all parts inaccessible to the griffon's heavy beak. They extract brains, membranes, and the spinal cord, and clip out tendons and ligaments. They dodge out through the encircling griffons with their spoils, gobble them swiftly, and dance back for more. The griffons, gorged with meat and panting in the sun, pay them scant attention.

Finally, when all but the whistling kites have left the scene, comes the great solitary bearded vulture, the fierce lammergeier. His whole head is feathered, so he despises carrion. He lives aloof from all the rest of the vulture tribe, but they serve his interests, so he keeps them within sight. The old swineherd calls him *Quebrantahuesos*—the bone smasher—and Aeschylus noted him, long ago, for the same behavior. The lammergeier seizes the largest bones, carries them high, in his claws, and drops them on the rocks. Then he swoops down and rakes out the marrow.

Like an eagle, he can kill as well as carry with his claws, and he has not the true vulture's patient, soaring habit. He attacks flocks and herds and carries off the lambs and kids and piglets. After his work has been done nothing will remain except an empty skull and some small bones, which the ants and carrion beetles pick and polish.

Our griffon, first on the scene, will not be the first to leave it. He is sure to have gorged himself with his advantage. Crop, throat, and neck distended, he squats back on his tail, with his wings spread to steady him and his beak hanging open. From time to time he chokes and belches and gags, and it is an hour, maybe, before the meat subsides in him.

When he is ready, the griffon runs and leaps across the plain, thrashing heavily with his big wings, and labors into the air. He finds a thermal, circles in it to his altitude, then slips sideways and sweeps gently across the sierra to his distant nest.

The griffon vultures are gregarious in nesting, with colonies throughout the mountains at fairly regular intervals of thirty miles. They are said to pair for life. Certainly they return every year to the same nest. In January they begin to repair the nest, a broad and battered saucer of strong branches, topped with twigs and grass. They are careless builders, and many nests have bare rock protruding in them. No attempt is made to cover it. The egg is laid in late February and incubated for forty days. The new chick is bare and blue-skinned and looks as though he might become a dragon, but soon he sprouts white down and begins to assert the characteristics of his race. In a month he is voracious, and by the end of April he will demand four pounds of meat every day. Before he is fledged he will need eight pounds. Providentially, his demands coincide with the heyday of death.

When the male vulture arrives at the nest he settles on a nearby ledge, vomits, and sorts out the result with his beak. The female helps with this assessment, feeding herself hungrily on the larger relics. Then she offers her gape and crop to her cowering, whistling infant. The chick gobbles madly. With vultures it can never be "little and often," for animals die irregularly, as they must, so the birds, young and old, must gorge to the neck when opportunity offers. That is their instinct and their nature.

A male vulture with family responsibilities cannot rest for long. Now that his load is delivered and eaten, he is likely to be the hungriest of the family. This, too, is as it should be, for the hunger sends him out and up again, however little daylight may remain, to circle in the sky until the sunset reddens the sierra.

Time was when the summer drought killed thousands of beasts every year and the floods of winter hundreds more. Nowadays there are fewer casualties, but the vultures still have a fairly constant food supply in the charnel gorges, which lie below most mountain villages.

Grazalema, Arcos, Casares, and a hundred more were built, for protection from the raiding Moors, on the edge of the precipice. All dead and dying animals, as well as all the garbage of the town, are simply pushed over the cliff and left to the birds. There is a bird in Andalusia for every class and size of refuse. From the escarpment you can watch all the scavengers of the air, soaring below you or fighting on the feast. The great black vulture may be here, the griffon and Egyptian for sure, and two kinds of kites. The cunning ravens and carrion crows wait on the outskirts, dashing in to snatch their choice. Clouds of choughs and jackdaws wheel and cry above them.

There is a new feeding ground in the unfenced highways of Andalusia. As motor traffic increases, these offer more and more dead dogs, cats, kids, pigs, and rabbits. If you are abroad at dawn, it is a common thing to run down a vulture intent on scraping a dead dog off the asphalt. Even so, with an apparently limitless population of these great birds, each looking for some thirty pounds of meat every day, one wonders how they flourish.

Their wonderful feeding system has, it seems to me, one fatal flaw. They can signal "Food here," but not how much. At the feast which I have described only some succeeded in feeding at all, and only two or three ate their fill. A majority came the distance and lost their height for little or for nothing.

In Africa, also vulture country, there is no such difficulty, for there all the game is big game, and every funeral is worth attending. It may be that some of our Andalusian vultures go there in the winter. Certainly our vulture population increases here, but that is because the vultures from further north crowd in as the heat decreases and the air currents weaken in their homelands. Fortunately, there is a seasonal food supply ready for them all, for it is the time of birth, with all its failures and fatalities. After the winter storms, too, the torrents offer up their toll of corpses. And in winter, each bird has only himself to feed. But you would not doubt, if you knew the constant panic for food which dominates him summer and winter alike, that the vulture leads a competitive and anxious life. He has strong forces for survival. It is held—and we know it to be true of eagles—that the vulture has a very long life. If this longevity is a fact, then the solitary chick each year may add up to a good replacement rate.

The nest is inaccessible, and the hen guards it constantly against the only possible natural enemy—other vultures or raptors. So the survival rate must be high as is proved by the evident increase toward saturation point.

At times, lying on my back on the plain with binoculars trained on the sky, I have seen vultures circling in two or three layers, each one high above the other. What can this mean? A hungry duplication, or triplication, hopelessly covering the same feeding ground and using the only available thermals? Or the opposite—idle and well-fed reserves standing by for surplus?

No one can tell me. But here in the vulture country there are no birds more spectacular, more fascinating to watch and to study. In time we may find out the last of their secrets. I lie on the plains and keep on watching them. And they, I know, keep on watching me.

QUESTIONS FOR STUDY, DISCUSSION, AND WRITING

1. On page 1036 Stewart explains the vulture's aerodynamics. What is the crucial problem and how does the bird's genetic "design" permit him to solve it?
2. The feast which is concluded on page 1040 might reasonably be taken as the climax of the essay, but in fact Stewart goes on to do more. What does his continuation add to the essay?
3. Why do the vultures keep watching Stewart and what are the implications of that last sentence?
4. How would Huxley ("The Method of Scientific Investigation," pp. 950–956) classify the old swineherd's assertion that lying apart from the herd is the sign of death that attracts the vulture?
5. Answer Question 4 on page 831.

WILHELM GOETSCH

Warfare and Hunting[1]

Most ant societies are organized for total warfare. The workers, which make up the mass of the population, become fighters when necessary, and the queen often takes part, at least when it comes to defending the nest. These are joined by the slower soldiers with their oversized weapons. Only the males are left out; since they possess neither poison gland nor stinger and their jaws are underdeveloped, they lack all aptitude for war, which is carried on by the female in these Amazonian societies.

Fighting goes on constantly in nearly all ant colonies, mostly in single combats. Battles are continuously in progress on the borders of the colonies, which include not only the nest but the nearby hunting grounds. Among ants, as among men, a strong state tries to spread out as much as possible and must keep defending its conquests.

Among the seed-gathering *Messor* ants, which we shall later examine more closely, we often find the borders guarded by sentinels. These ants assume a special position: the antennae are laid back, the legs are drawn close, and the whole body is pressed against the earth. This posture, in which the ants remain motionless for hours, has been called the sentinel's position, but we find ants in the same posture in the middle of the nest. At such times the ant is probably resting. Ants are not always hard at work; like bees, they often take long rests. An anthill always seems to be bustling because under natural conditions we cannot observe the animals that are resting. A *Messor* ant that is wandering around with nothing to do will assume the rest position if it comes upon a protected spot, such as a connecting passage in the nest. * * * *Messor* ants also take up this position when they find themselves in an unfamiliar situation. A young ant emerging from the nest, already tired and afraid to venture out into the unknown, may stop to rest in this manner. When one ant sees another in this position, it too may sit down; whole congregations are formed in this way. The arrival of another ant may, however, induce a sitter to move on; if the newcomer happens to be tired he will sit down in his turn. In this way one relays the other.

Ants sometimes rest in the open, usually at the edge of the hunting ground where the unknown begins. In this way the sentries form a ring around the hunting ground, but we need not assume

1. From Chapter VI of *The Ants*, 1953.

that they are "consciously" guarding the area any more than are the ants that block the nest entrances by sitting down to rest in them.

In both instances the habit of the sentinel's position is useful to the community: the resting ants are on guard the moment anything out of the ordinary happens. The passage of a strange ant acts as a violent stimulus. The sentry thrusts her head forward, or may even leap at the enemy. Once the foe is seized, the assailant recoils swiftly without releasing her grip, drawing the enemy into her own territory; here she finishes it off with her jaws, her stinger, or the poison from her abdominal gland. Sometimes her fellows join in, and the fight becomes a mass battle.

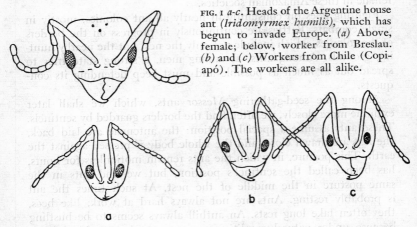

FIG. 1 *a-c*. Heads of the Argentine house ant (*Iridomyrmex humilis*), which has begun to invade Europe. (*a*) Above, female; below, worker from Breslau. (*b*) and (*c*) Workers from Chile (Copiapó). The workers are all alike.

The best way to observe one of these battles is to put members of different colonies into an artificial nest. The two parties spring wildly at one another spraying their poison, thrusting with their stingers, and trying to bite off one another's heads or abdomens. Even the severely wounded sometimes continue the battle. In one such battle two *Messor* ants whose abdomens had been entirely severed kept attacking their weary enemies after the other combatants had subsided in exhaustion and both parties had withdrawn into corners.

I once witnessed a violent battle when I put a few Argentine house ants (*Iridomyrmex humilis*, Fig. 1) into an artificial nest inhabited by a group of the Italian *Pheidole pallidula*. In the ensuing battle the two adversaries used entirely different techniques. The Italians, workers and soldiers at once, attacked furiously, gnashing wildly about like bulldogs, using no caution. The Argentines, on the other hand, never came close to the dangerous mandibles, but danced round their assailants like cautious boxers. Waiting for an unguarded spot, they would attack the enemy from the side or from behind and seize him by the leg. Once this was done, the Argentine pulled back and a second Argentine seized another leg. Now the Italian was done for; with its legs pulled in opposite directions, it was held fast, unable to use its own weapons. In a moment its legs were bitten off. All this happened in less time than you have taken to read the last three sentences. The Argentines with their treacherous effective tactics were always victorious, even against larger opponents such as wood ants.

The Argentine ant is now on a far-flung warpath. It is spreading all over the world, and wherever it shows up the native ants begin to disappear. Authorities now believe that *Iridomyrmex* originally migrated to Argentina from the warmer territories of Brazil and Bolivia. From Argentina it has embarked on its campaigns of conquest, making long journeys over the sea in shipments of fruits and plants. *Iridomyrmex* has no fixed nests, but sets up colonies wherever it can find food. The queens, who are wanderers too, soon join the new colonies, and so the breed spreads. This ant came to New Orleans in 1891, probably in a shipment of coffee, and soon spread as far as Tennessee, North Carolina, and Texas, where it became a familiar household pest. In the West it found a home in California, where its presence was first noted in 1907; I have found the breed in Copiapó, Chile, and other observers have seen it in Concepción.

The Argentine ant first appears in ports. In 1908, during the Boer War, it was brought to Cape Town in shipments of fodder; since that time it has made itself at home in all South Africa. In Teneriffe and other Canary Islands it lives in the open as well as in houses. From 1882 on the same sort of battles that took place in my artificial nest must have raged on a large scale in the Azores and Madeira, for since that date, when the Argentine ant was introduced, the *Pheidole* has disappeared from Madeira. In Lisbon and Oporto the battle is apparently still going on, but the Argentine ant is already in the majority. It has marched victoriously through Spain, southern France, and Bosnia, and in all these regions is found in the open as well as in houses. The same is true of Naples and its environs, where I first noted its presence in 1936. It has recently conquered the islands of Capri, Ischia, and Majorca (1953).

Wherever it cannot live in the open all year, the Argentine ant invades houses; it has been reported in Brussels, in Paris, where a hotel once had to be evacuated on its account, in Berlin, and most recently in Hamburg. In the Breslau Botanical Gardens it has become a serious nuisance.

Why does the Argentine ant attract such attention as a household pest? First of all, it multiplies at a stupendous rate. Between April and September one colony grew from a population of 100 to 10,000. The ants invade a house en masse and get into everything, even into the beds. They attack every conceivable human food-stuff. From the highest attic to the deepest cellar nothing edible is safe from them, and it is useless to set food in water, because the Argentine ants swim right through it. They are particularly fond of sweets; one swarm emptied a jar of jam in a few hours. They also enjoy meat and are quite capable of attacking young birds in the nest and little chickens in the coop. The fact that they do away with all vermin and leave no bugs of any sort alive is but feeble consolation.

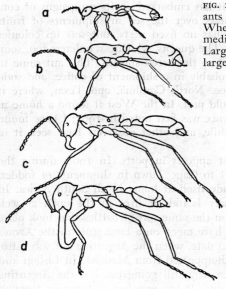

FIG. 2. *a-d*. Legionary or driver ants *(Eciton hamatum).* (After Wheeler.) *(a)* Worker. *(b)* Intermediate form. *(c)* Soldier. *(d)* Large soldier with greatly enlarged jaws.

The wars of the Argentine ant, as of other species turn out to be large-scale hunting expeditions; the victims, even the ants, are always used for food. The corpses of their own adult dead, however, are usually spared; these serve as food only in case of extreme need. The expeditions of the so-called hunting or driver ants are organized somewhat differently. We have numerous descriptions of the campaigns of the South American *Eciton* species, most of which are blind, and of the African *Anomma* species (cf. Fig. 2). Vosseler gives an excellent account of the Ethiopian hunting ant which the Africans call *siafu:*

The nomadic ants are imbued with a restless spirit. Wherever they go, you see nothing but hustling, hunting, battle, and murder. First a few scouts appear, rushing restlessly back and forth, sounding out the terrain. Before one is aware of their purpose, impatient hordes begin to pour out of a little cleft in the earth; the hole soon widens, and as if by magic hundreds turn to thousands and hundreds of thousands. Like a shoreless river they pour in all directions over the ground and the low shrubbery, covering the earth with their dense swarm. A mad scampering begins on all sides. Crickets, cockroaches, spiders, caterpillars, maggots—any creatures large or small, armed or unarmed, that may have felt secure in their cover—take aimless and headlong flight from the ruthless army.

Now begins a silent, bloody drama with scarcely its equal for excitement. A great bear-caterpillar loses its confidence in the protective covering of its long hairs and races with bent back along the edge of the path, followed by the ants as by a pack of bloodthirsty wild dogs. The chase continues up a steep wall, the hunters on the heels of the game. The caterpillar slips down, and for a moment the ants lose the trail. But before the game can get to its feet again, twenty ants have bitten fast into its hair; in an instant it is covered by hundreds of them, cut to pieces, and immediately dragged nestward by the hunters, who are heedless of the difficulties of the terrain. A cricket summons up all the strength of its sinewy legs to spring out of danger—in vain. It is surrounded, held fast by its legs, feelers, and wings, and skillfully dissected by dozens of sharp jaws; the pieces follow those of the caterpillar.

The field is quickly swept clean by the forward swarming ants. Now the reserves march up six to ten abreast, forming columns one or two fingers wide, which relieve or reinforce the troops at the front. Where the murderous swarm has passed roads are taking shape, weaving in and out in a dense network. Along these roads fresh soldiers advance while others haul the booty to the rear. The embattled confusion moves forward. The highways are smoothed out, and their sides are occupied by sentries. These large soldiers stand "shoulder to shoulder" at right angles to the road, their heads in constant movement as they watch for intruders.

At the slightest sign of a foe the sentries rear up, thorax and head erect, and rest their antennae on their wide-open pincers, poised to attack. If no enemy shows up, the sentries are reduced in number; the giants and a few others line the roads at irregular intervals, head upraised, feelers tingling, jaws in readiness. Their flanks secured, the diligent ants stream along for days. Often there is a two-way traffic, one army advancing while another, heavily laden, makes its way back to the nest. But these nomadic ants never inhabit a nest for long; like gypsies, they have no permanent home and soon move on with bag and baggage, hunting and waging war as they go.

I myself have seen similar expeditions in the jungle of the upper Paraná.

The scene is very much the same when these ant armies swarm over a human dwelling. Everybody leaves—insects, animals, and men. Since the ants quickly move on, the house is soon habitable again, and a visit from the ant hordes is not always unwelcome; for all the vermin, including rats, mice, and even snakes, are destroyed or driven away.

JOHN LIVINGSTONE LOWES

Time in the Middle Ages[1]

We live in terms of *time*. And so pervasive is that element of our consciousness that we have to stand, as it were, outside it for a moment to realize how completely it controls our lives. For we think and act perpetually, we mortals who look before and after, in relation to hours and days and weeks and months and years. Yesterday and to-morrow, next week, a month from now, a year ago, in twenty minutes—those are the terms in which, wittingly or automatically, we act and plan and think. And to orient ourselves at any moment in that streaming continuum we carry watches on our wrists, and put clocks about our houses and on our public towers, and somewhere in our eye keep calendars, and scan time-tables when we would go abroad. And all this is so utterly familiar that it has ceased to be a matter of conscious thought or inference at all. And—to come to the heart of the business—unless we are mariners or woodsmen or astronomers or simple folk in lonely places, we never any longer reckon with the *sky*. Except for its bearing on the weather or upon our moods, or for contemplation of its depths of blue or fleets of white, or of the nightly splendor of its stars, we are oblivious of its influence. And therein lies the great gulf fixed between Chaucer's century and ours.

For Chaucer and his contemporaries, being likewise human, also lived in terms of time. But their calendar and time-piece was that sky through which moved immutably along predestined tracks the planets and the constellations. And no change, perhaps, wrought by the five centuries between us is more revealing of material differences than that shift of attitude towards "this brave o'erhanging firmament," the sky. And it is that change, first of all, that I wish, if I can, to make clear.

There could be, I suspect, no sharper contrast than that between the "mysterious universe" of modern science, as interpreters like Eddington and Jeans have made even laymen dimly perceive it, and the nest of closed, concentric spheres in terms of which Chaucer and his coevals thought. The structure of that universe may be stated simply enough. Its intricacies need not concern us here. About the earth, as the fixed center, revolved the spheres of the seven then known planets, of which the sun and the moon were two. Beyond these seven planetary spheres lay the sphere of the fixed stars. Beyond that in turn, and carrying along with it in its "diurnal sway" the eight spheres which lay within it, moved the *primum mobile*,

---

1. From Chapter I, "Backgrounds and Horizons," of *Geoffrey Chaucer*, 1934.

a ninth sphere with which, to account for certain planetary eccentricities, the Middle Ages had supplemented the Ptolemaic system. We must think, in a word, of Chaucer's universe as geocentric—the "litel erthe," encompassed by "thilke speres thryes three."[2] As an interesting fact which we have learned, we know it; to conceive it as reality demands an exercise of the imagination. And only with that mental *volte-face* accomplished can we realize the cosmos as Chaucer thought of it.

Now the order of succession of the planetary spheres had far-reaching implications. Starting from the earth, which was their center, that succession was as follows: Moon, Mercury, Venus, Sun, Mars, Jupiter, Saturn. And implicit in that order were two fundamental consequences—the astrological status of the successive hours of the day, and the sequence of the days of the week. The two phenomena stood in intimate relation, and some apprehension of each is fundamental to an understanding of the framework of conceptions within which Chaucer thought, and in terms of which he often wrote.

There were, then, in the first place—and this is strange to us—two sorts of *hours*, with both of which everybody reckoned. There were the hours from midnight to midnight, which constituted the "day natural"—the hours, that is, with which we are familiar—and these, in Chaucer's phrase, were "hours equal," or "hours of the *clock*." But there were also the hours which were reckoned from sunrise to sunset (which made up "day artificial"), and on from sunset to sunrise again. And these, which will most concern us, were termed "hours inequal," or "hours of the *planets*." And they were the hours of peculiar significance, bound up far more closely with human affairs than the "hours of the clock." It is worth, then, a moment's time to get them clear.

They were termed "inequal" for an obvious reason. For the periods between sunrise and sunset, and sunset and sunrise, respectively, change in length with the annual course of the sun, and the length of their twelfths, or hours, must of necessity change too. Between the equinoxes, then, it is clear that the inequal hours will now be longer by day than by night, now longer by night than by day. And only twice in the year, at the equinoxes, will the equal hours and the inequal hours—the hours of the clock and the hours of the planets—be identical. Moreover, each of the inequal hours (and this is of the first importance) was "ruled" by one of the seven planets, and it was as "hours of the planets" that the "hours inequal" touched most intimately human life. And that brings us at once to the days of the week, and their now almost forgotten implications. Why, to be explicit, is to-day Saturday? And why to-morrow Sun-

2. Those spheres thrice three.

day? To answer those two questions is to arrive at one of the determining concepts of Chaucer's world.

Let me first arrange the seven planets in their order, starting (to simplify what follows) with the outermost. Their succession will then be this: Saturn, Jupiter, Mars, Sun, Venus, Mercury, Moon. Now Saturn will rule the first hour of the day which, for that reason, bears his name, and which we still call *Saturday*. Of that day Jupiter will rule the second hour, Mars the third, the Sun the fourth, Venus the fifth, Mercury the sixth, the Moon the seventh, and Saturn again, in due order, the eighth. Without carrying the computation farther around the clock it is obvious that Saturn will also rule the fifteenth and the twenty-second hours of the twenty-four which belong to his day. The twenty-third hour will then be ruled by Jupiter, the twenty-fourth by Mars, and the twenty-fifth by the Sun. But the twenty-fifth hour of one day is the first hour of the next, and accordingly the day after Saturn's day will be the Sun's day. And so, through starry compulsion, the next day after Saturday *must* be Sunday. In precisely the same fashion—accomplished most quickly by remembering that each planet must rule the twenty-second hour of its own day—the ruling planet of the first hour of each of the succeeding days may readily be found. And their order, so found, including Saturn and the Sun, is this: Saturn, Sun, Moon, Mars, Mercury, Jupiter, Venus—then Saturn again, and so on *ad libitum*. And the days of the week will accordingly be the days of the seven planets in that fixed order.

Now Saturn's day, the Sun's day, and the Moon's day are clearly recognizable in their English names of Saturday, Sunday, and Monday. But what of the remaining four—to wit, the days of Mars, Mercury, Jupiter, and Venus, which we call Tuesday, Wednesday, Thursday, and Friday? French has preserved, as also in Lundi, the planetary designations: Mardi (*Martis dies*), Mercredi (*Mercurii dies*), Jeudi (*Jovis dies*), and Vendredi (*Veneris dies*). The shift of the names in English is due to the ousting, in those four instances, of the Roman pantheon by the Germanic. Tiw, Woden, Thor, and Frig (or Freya) have usurped the seats of Mars, Mercury, Jupiter, and Venus, and given their barbarous names to the days. And in France a fourth, even more significant substitution has taken place. For the sun's day is in French *dimanche*, and *dimanche* is *dominica dies*, the Lord's day. And so between Saturn's planet and Diana's moon is memorialized, along with Mercury and Jupiter and Venus and Mars, the second Person of the Christian Trinity. The ancient world has crumbled, and its detritus has been remoulded into almost unrecognizable shapes. But half the history of Europe and of its early formative ideas is written in the nomenclature of the week. And that nomenclature depends in turn upon the succession of the planetary hours. And it was in terms of those hours that Chaucer and his contemporaries thought.

In the *Knight's Tale*, to be specific, Palamon, Emily, and Arcite go to pray, each for the granting of his own desire, to the temples respectively of Venus, Diana, and Mars. And each goes, as in due observance of ceremonial propriety he must, in the hour of the planet associated with the god to whom he prays. Palamon goes to the temple of Venus, "And *in hir houre* he walketh forth." A few lines earlier that hour has been stated in everyday terms: it was "The Sonday night, er day bigan to springe . . . Although it nere nat day by houres two"—two hours, that is, before sunrise. The day that was springing after Sunday night was Monday, and the hour of Monday's sunrise is the hour of the Moon. And the hour two hours earlier, in which Palamon walked forth, was the hour ruled by Venus, to whose temple he was on the way. And Emily and Arcite, as the tale goes on, performed their pilgrimages at similarly reckoned hours. To Chaucer and his readers all this was familiar matter of the day, as instantly comprehensible as are now to us the hours which we reckon by the clock. For us alas! it has become a theme for cumbrous exposition, because the hours of the planets have vanished, with the gods whose names they bore. All that is left of them is the time-worn and wonted sequence of the seven designations of the days.

Nothing, indeed, is more characteristic of the period in which Chaucer wrote than the strange, twisted mythology, transmogrified and confused, which emerged from the association of the planets and the gods. Not even Ovid had conceived such metamorphoses.[3] For the gods were invested with the attributes of planets, and as such became accountable for the most bizarre occurrences, and kept amazing company. Under the aegis of Mars, to take one instance only, were enrolled the butchers, hangmen, tailors, barbers, cooks, cutlers, carpenters, smiths, physicians, and apothecaries—a band about as "martial" as Falstaff's Thomas Wart and Francis Feeble.[4] And so, in "the temple of mighty Mars the rede" in the *Knight's Tale*, there were depicted, together with the "open werre" which was his by virtue of his godhead, the disastrous chances proceeding from his malign ascendancy as planet—the corpse in the bushes with cut throat, the nail driven, like Jael's, into the temple,[5] the sow eating the child in the cradle, the cook scalded in spite of his long ladle. And from among the members of what Chaucer twice calls Mars' "divisioun" there were present—together with the pickpurse, and "the smyler with the knyf under the cloke"—the barber

---

3. Ovid's *Metamorphoses* includes poetical renderings of myths dealing with the transformation of men and women into birds, flowers, trees, etc.

4. Recruits in Shakespeare's *Henry IV, Part 2*.

5. See Judges iv, 17-22.

and the butcher and the smith. And in the next paragraph Mars becomes again "this god of armes"—god of war and wicked planet inextricably interfused.

Moreover, as the day and week were conceived in terms of planetary sequence, so the year stood in intricate relation to the *stars*. The sun, with the other planets, moved annually along the vast starry track across the sky which then, as now, was called the zodiac —so called, as Chaucer lucidly explains to "litel Lowis" in the *Treatise on the Astrolabe*, because (and his etymology is sound) "*zodia* in langage of Greek sowneth [signifies] 'bestes' . . . and in the zodiak ben the twelve signes that han names of bestes." These twelve signs, as everybody knows, are Aries, Taurus, Gemini, Cancer, Leo, Virgo, Libra, Scorpio, Sagittarius, Capricornus, Aquarius, Pisces—or, to follow Chaucer's praiseworthy example and translate, Ram, Bull, Twins, Crab, Lion, Virgin, Scales, Scorpion, Archer, Goat, Water-carrier, Fishes. There they were, "eyrish bestes," as Chaucer calls them in a delightful passage that will meet us later, and along their celestial highway passed, from one sign to another, and from house to house, the seven eternal wanderers. To us who read this—though not to countless thousands even yet—the twelve constellations of the zodiac are accidental groupings, to the eye, of infinitely distant suns. To Chaucer's century they were strangely living potencies, and the earth, in the words of a greater than Chaucer, was "this huge stage . . . whereon the stars in secret influence comment." Each sign, with its constellation, had its own individual efficacy or quality—Aries, "the colerik hote signe"; Taurus, cold and dry; and so on through the other ten. Each planet likewise had its own pecular nature—Mars, like Aries, hot and dry; Venus hot and moist; and so on through the other five. And as each planet passed from sign to sign, through the agency of the successive constellations its character and influence underwent change. Chaucer in the *Astrolabe* put the matter in its simplest terms: "Whan an hot planete cometh in-to an hot signe, then encresseth his hete; and yif a planete be cold, thanne amenuseth [diminshes] his coldnesse, by -cause of the hote signe." But there was far more to it than that. For these complex planetary changes exercised a determining influence upon human beings and their affairs. Arcite behind prison bars cries out:

> Som wikke aspect or disposicioun
> Of Saturne, *by sum constellacioun*,
> Hath yeven us this.

And "the olde colde Saturnus" names the constellation:

> Myn is the prison in the derke cote...
> *Whyl I dwelle in the signe of the Leoun.*

The tragedy of Constance, as the Man of Law conceived it,

comes about because Mars, at the crucial moment, was in his "derkest hous." Mars gave, on the other hand, the Wife of Bath, as she avers, her "sturdy hardinesse," because Mars, at her birth, was in the constellation Taurus, which was, in astrological terminology, her own "ascendent." And since the constellation Taurus was also the "night house" of Venus, certain other propensities which the wife displayed had been thrust upon her, as she cheerfully averred, by the temporary sojourn of Mars in Venus's house, when she was born.

But the march of the signs along the zodiac touched human life in yet another way. "Everich of thise twelve signes," Chaucer wrote again to his little Lewis, "hath respecte to a certein parcelle of the body of a man and hath it in governance; as Aries hath thyn heved, and Taurus thy nekke and thy throte. Gemini thyn armholes and thyn armes, and so forth." And at once one recalls Sir Toby Belch and Sir Andrew Aguecheek in *Twelfth Night*. "Shall we not set about some revels?" asks Sr. Andrew. "What shall we do else?" replies Sir Toby. "Were we not born under Taurus?" "Taurus!" exclaims Sir Andrews, "that's sides and heart." "No, sir," retorts Sir Toby, "it is legs and thighs." And you may still pick up, in the shops of apothecaries here and there, cheaply printed almanacs, designed to advertise quack remedies, in which the naked human figure is displayed with lines drawn from each of the pictured zodiacal signs—Ram, Bull, Crab, Scorpion—to the limbs or organs, legs, thighs, sides, or heart, which that particular sign (in Chaucerian phrase) "hath in governance." It is not only in worn stone and faded parchments that strange fragments of the elder world survive.

QUESTIONS FOR STUDY, DISCUSSION, AND WRITING

1. Arrange the steps of Lowes' explanation of medieval time in a different order. Is your order superior to Lowes' or inferior? By what criteria?
2. When the advertising man and the engineer from the electronics laboratory become suburban gardeners, why may they have to reckon with the sky and neglect their watches and calendars?
3. In "Cotton" (p. 436–450) Agee describes southern tenant farmers who are certainly aware of the "inequal hours," but their awareness is no more medieval than that of the suburban gardeners. What is missing from the modern awareness?
4. List some ways in which the abstractions of watch and calendar (and time table) "rule" our lives. This list will be a selection from the particulars of daily life. What generalizations about our society will these particulars justify? Does our society, as focused in these generalizations, have a mythology—a set of hypothetical or typical characters going through hypothetical or typical experiences?

LEWIS MUMFORD
The Monastery and the Clock[1]

Where did the machine first take form in modern civilization? There was plainly more than one point of origin. Our mechanical civilization represents the convergence of numerous habits, ideas, and modes of living, as well as technical instruments; and some of these were, in the beginning, directly opposed to the civilization they helped to create. But the first manifestation of the new order took place in the general picture of the world: during the first seven centuries of the machine's existence the categories of time and space underwent an extraordinary change, and no aspect of life was left untouched by this transformation. The application of quantitative methods of thought to the study of nature had its first manifestation in the regular measurement of time; and the new mechanical conception of time arose in part out of the routine of the monastery. Alfred Whitehead has emphasized the importance of the scholastic belief in a universe ordered by God as one of the foundations of modern physics: but behind that belief was the presence of order in the institutions of the Church itself.

The technics of the ancient world were still carried on from Constantinople and Baghdad to Sicily and Cordova: hence the early lead taken by Salerno in the scientific and medical advances of the Middle Age. It was, however, in the monasteries of the West that the desire for order and power, other than that expressed in the military domination of weaker men, first manifested itself after the long uncertainty and bloody confusion that attended the breakdown of the Roman Empire. Within the walls of the monastery was sanctuary: under the rule of the order surprise and doubt and caprice and irregularity were put at bay. Opposed to the erratic fluctuations and pulsations of the worldly life was the iron discipline of the rule. Benedict added a seventh period to the devotions of the day, and in the seventh century, by a bull of Pope Sabinianus, it was decreed that the bells of the monastery be rung seven times in the twenty-four hours. These punctuation marks in the day were known as the canonical hours, and some means of keeping count of them and ensuring their regular repetition became necessary.

According to a now discredited legend, the first modern mechanical clock, worked by falling weights, was invented by the monk named Gerbert who afterwards became Pope Sylvester II near the close of the tenth century. This clock was probably only a water clock, one of those bequests of the ancient world either left over

1. Section two of "Cultural Preparation," Chapter I of *Technics and Civilization*, 1934.

directly from the days of the Romans, like the water-wheel itself, or coming back again into the West through the Arabs. But the legend, as so often happens, is accurate in its implications if not in its facts. The monastery was the seat of a regular life, and an instrument for striking the hours at intervals or for reminding the bell-ringer that it was time to strike the bells, was an almost inevitable product of this life. If the mechanical clock did not appear until the cities of the thirteenth century demanded an orderly routine, the habit of order itself and the earnest regulation of time-sequences had become almost second nature in the monastery. Coulton agrees with Sombart in looking upon the Benedictines, the great working order, as perhaps the original founders of modern capitalism: their rule certainly took the curse off work and their vigorous engineering enterprises may even have robbed warfare of some of its glamor. So one is not straining the facts when one suggests that the monasteries—at one time there were 40,000 under the Benedictine rule—helped to give human enterprise the regular collective beat and rhythm of the machine; for the clock is not merely a means of keeping track of the hours, but of synchronizing the actions of men.

Was it by reason of the collective Christian desire to provide for the welfare of souls in eternity by regular prayers and devotions that time-keeping and the habits of temporal order took hold of men's minds: habits that capitalist civilization presently turned to good account? One must perhaps accept the irony of this paradox. At all events, by the thirteenth century there are definite records of mechanical clocks, and by 1370 a well-designed "modern clock had been built by Heinrich von Wyck at Paris. Meanwhile, bell towers had come into existence, and the new clocks, if they did not have, till the fourteenth century, a dial and a hand that translated the movement of time into movement through space, at all events struck the hours. The clouds that could paralyze the sundial, the freezing that could stop the water clock on a winter night, were no longer obstacles to time-keeping: summer or winter, day or night, one was aware of the measured clank of the clock. The instrument presently spread outside the monastery; and the regular striking of the bells brought a new regularity into the life of the workman and the merchant. The bells of the clock tower almost defined urban existence. Time-keeping passed into time-serving and time-accounting and time-rationing. As this took place, Eternity ceased gradually to serve as the measure and focus of human actions.

The clock, not the steam-engine, is the key-machine of the modern industrial age. For every phase of its development the clock is both the outstanding fact and the typical symbol of the machine: even today no other machine is so ubiquitous. Here, at the very beginning of modern technics, appeared prophetically the accurate automatic machine which only after centuries of further effort, was also to prove the final consummation of this technics in every department of industrial activity. There had been power-machines, such as the water-mill, before the clock; and there had also been various kinds of automata, to awaken the wonder of the populace in the temple, or to please the idle fancy of some Moslem caliph: machines one finds illustrated in Hero and Al-Jazari. But here was a new kind of power-machine, in which the source of power and the transmission were of such a nature as to ensure the even flow of energy throughout the works and to make possible regular production and a standardized product. In its relationship to determinable quantities of energy, to standardization, to automatic action, and finally to its own special product, accurate timing, the clock has been the foremost machine in modern technics: and at each period it has remained in the lead: it marks a perfection toward which other machines aspire. The clock, moreover, served as a model for many other kinds of mechanical works, and the analysis of motion that accompanied the perfection of the clock, with the various types of gearing and transmission that were elaborated, contributed to the success of quite different kinds of machine. Smiths could have hammered thousands of suits of armor or thousands of iron cannon, wheelwrights could have shaped thousands of great water-wheels or crude gears, without inventing any of the special types of movement developed in clockwork, and without any of the accuracy of measurement and finesse of articulation that finally produced the accurate eighteenth century chronometer.

The clock, moreover, is a piece of power-machinery whose "product" is seconds and minutes: by its essential nature it dissociated time from human events and helped create the belief in an independent world of mathematically measurable sequences: the special world of science. There is relatively little foundation for this belief in common human experience: throughout the year the days are of uneven duration, and not merely does the relation between day and night steadily change, but a slight journey from East to West alters astronomical time by a certain number of minutes. In terms of the human organism itself, mechanical time is even more foreign: while human life has regularities of its own, the beat of the pulse, the breathing of the lungs, these change from hour to hour with mood and action, and in the longer span of days, time is measured not by the calendar but by the events that occupy it. The shepherd measures from the time the ewes lambed; the farmer measures back to the day of sowing or forward to the harvest: if growth has its own duration and regularities, behind it are not simply matter and motion but the facts of development: in short, history. And while mechanical time is strung out in a succession of mathematically isolated instants, organic time—what Bergson calls duration—is cumulative in its effects. Though mechanical time can, in a sense, be speeded up or run backward, like the hands of a clock or the images of a moving picture, organic time moves in only one direction—through the cycle of birth, growth, development, decay, and death—and the past that is already dead remains present in the future that has still to be born.

Around 1345, according to Thorndike, the division of hours into sixty minutes and of minutes into sixty seconds became common: it was this abstract framework of divided time that became more and more the point of reference for both action and thought, and in the effort to arrive at accuracy in this department, the astronomical exploration of the sky focused attention further upon the regular, implacable movements of the heavenly bodies through space. Early in the sixteenth century a young Nuremberg mechanic, Peter Henlein, is supposed to have created "many-wheeled watches out of small bits of iron" and by the end of the century the small domestic clock had been introduced in England and Holland. As with the motor car and the airplane, the richer classes first took over the new mechanism and popularized it: partly because they alone could afford it, partly because the new bourgeoisie were the first to discover that, as Franklin later put it, "time is money." To become "as regular as clockwork" was the bourgeois ideal, and to own a watch was for long a definite symbol of success. The increasing tempo of civilization led to a demand for greater power: and in turn power quickened the tempo.

Now, the orderly punctual life that first took shape in the monasteries is not native to mankind, although by now Western peoples are so thoroughly regimented by the clock that it is "second-nature" and they look upon its observance as a fact of nature. Many Eastern civilizations have flourished on a loose basis in time: the Hindus have in fact been so indifferent to time that they lack even an authentic chronology of the years. Only yesterday, in the midst of the industrializations of Soviet Russia, did a society come into existence to further the carrying of watches there and to propagandize the benefits of punctuality. The popularization of time-keeping, which followed the production of the cheap standardized watch, first in Geneva, then in America around the middle of the last century, was essential to a well-articulated system of transportation and production.

To keep time was once a peculiar attribute of music: it gave industrial value to the workshop song or the tattoo or the chantey of the sailors tugging at a rope. But the effect of the mechanical clock is more pervasive and strict: it presides over the day from the hour of rising to the hour of rest. When one thinks of the day as an

abstract span of time, one does not go to bed with the chickens on a
winter's night: one invents wicks, chimneys, lamps, gaslights, electric lamps, so as to use all the hours belonging to the day. When one
thinks of time, not as a sequence of experiences, but as a collection
of hours, minutes, and seconds, the habits of adding time and saving
time come into existence. Time took on the character of an enclosed
space: it could be divided, it could be filled up, it could even be
expanded by the invention of labor-saving instruments.

Abstract time became the new medium of existence. Organic
functions themselves were regulated by it: one ate, not upon feeling hungry, but when prompted by the clock: one slept, not when
one was tired, but when the clock sanctioned it. A generalized time-
consciousness accompanied the wider use of clocks: dissociating time
from organic sequences, it became easier for the men of the Renas-
cence to indulge the fantasy of reviving the classic past or of reliving
the splendors of antique Roman civilization: the cult of history, appearing first in daily ritual, finally abstracted itself as a special discipline. In the seventeenth century journalism and periodic literature
made their appearance: even in dress, following the lead of Venice
as fashion-center, people altered styles every year rather than every
generation.

The gain in mechanical efficiency through co-ordination and
through the closer articulation of the day's events cannot be over-
estimated: while this increase cannot be measured in mere horse-
power, one has only to imagine its absence today to forsee the
speedy disruption and eventual collapse of our entire society. The
modern industrial regime could do without coal and iron and steam
easier than it could do without the clock.

BERTON ROUECHÉ
A Game of Wild Indians

During the second week in August, 1946, an elderly man, a
middle-aged woman, and a boy of ten dragged themselves, singly
and painfully, into the Presbyterian Hospital, in the Washington
Heights section of Manhattan, where their trouble was unhesitatingly identified as typhoid fever. This diagnosis was soon confirmed
by laboratory analysis, and on Thursday morning, August 15th, a
report of the outbreak was dutifully telephoned to the Department
of Health. It was received and recorded there, in accordance with
the routine in all alarms of an epidemiological nature, by a clerk in
the Bureau of Preventable Diseases named Beatrice Gamso. Miss
Gamso is a low-strung woman and she has spent some thirty callous-
ing years in the Health Department, but the news gave her a turn.

She sat for an instant with her eyes on her notes. Then, steadying herself with a practiced hand, she swung around to her typewriter and set briskly about dispatching copies of the report to all adminis-trative officers of the Department. Within an hour, a reliable inves-tigator from the Bureau was on his way to Washington Heights. He was presently followed by one of his colleagues, a Department public-health nurse, several agents from the Bureau of Food and Drugs, and an inspector from the Bureau of Sanitary Engineering.

Typhoid fever was among the last of the massive pestilential fevers to yield to the probings of medical science, but its capitu-lation has been complete. It is wholly transparent now. Its clinical manifestations (a distinctive rash and a tender spleen, a fiery fever and a languid pulse, and nausea, diarrhea, and nosebleed), its cause (a bacillus known as *Eberthella typhosa*), and its means of transmis-sion have all been clearly established. Typhoid is invariably con-veyed by food or drink contaminated with the excreta of its victims. Ordinarily, it is spread by someone who is ignorant, at least momentarily, of his morbid condition. One reason for such unawareness is that for the first several days typhoid fever tends to be disarmingly mild and indistinguishable from the countless fleeting malaises that dog the human race. Another is that nearly five per cent of the cases become typhoid carriers, continuing indefinitely to harbor a lively colony of typhoid bacilli in their systems. The existence of typhoid carriers was discovered by a group of German hygienists in 1907. Typhoid Mary Mallon, a housemaid and cook who was the stubborn cause of a total of fifty-three cases in and around New York City a generation ago, is, of course, the most celebrated of these hapless menaces. About seventy per cent, by some unexplained, physiological fortuity, are women. The names of three hundred and eighty local carriers are currently on active file in the Bureau of Preventable Diseases. They are called on regularly by public-health nurses and are permanently enjoined from any employment that involves the handling of food. More than a third of all the cases that occur here are traced to local carriers but, because of the vigilance of the Health Department, rarely to recorded carriers; new ones keep turning up. Most of the rest of the cases are of unknown or out-of-town origin. A few are attribuable to the products of polluted waters (clams and oysters and various greens).

The surveillance of carriers is one of several innovations that in little more than a generation have forced typhoid fever into an abrupt tractability throughout most of the Western world. The others include certain refinements in diagnostic technique, the institution of public-health measures requiring the chlorination of city-supplied water and proscribing the sale of unpasteurized milk, and the development of an immunizing vaccine. Since late in the ninetenth century, the local incidence of typhoid fever has dropped from five or six thousand cases a year to fewer than fifty, and it is very possible that it may soon be as rare as smallpox. Banishment has not, however, materially impaired the vigor of *Eberthella typhosa*. Typhoid fever is still a cruel and withering affliction. It is always rambunctious, generally prolonged, and often fatal. It is also one of the most explosive of communicable diseases. The month in which it is most volcanic is August.

The investigator who led the sprint to Washington Heights that August morning in 1946 was Dr. Harold T. Fuerst, an epidemiologist, and he and Dr. Ottavio J. Pellitteri, another epidemiologist, handled most of the medical inquiry. One afternoon, when I was down at the Bureau, they told me about the case. Miss Gamso sat at a desk nearby, and I noticed after a moment that she was following the conversation with rapt attention. Her interest, it turned out, was entirely understandable. Typhoid-fever investigations are frequently tedious, but they are seldom protracted. It is not unusual for a team of experienced operatives to descry the source of an outbreak in a couple of days. Some cases have been riddled in an afternoon. The root of the trouble on Washington Heights eluded detection for almost two weeks, and it is probable that but for Miss Gamso it would never have been detected at all.

"I got to Presbyterian around eleven," Dr. Fuerst told me. "I found a staff man I knew, and he led me up to the patients. It was typhoid, all right. Not that I'd doubted it, but it's routine to take a look. And they were in bad shape—too miserable to talk. One—the woman—was barely conscious. I decided to let the questioning go for the time being. At least until I'd seen their histories. A clerk in the office of the medical superintendent dug them out for me. Pretty skimpy—name, age, sex, occupation, and address, and a few clinical notations. About all I got at a glance was that they weren't members of the same family. I'd hoped, naturally, that they would be. That would have nicely limited the scope of the investigation. Then I noticed something interesting. They weren't a family, but they had a little more in common than just typhoid. For one thing, they were by way of being neighbors. One of them lived at 502 West 180th Street, another at 501 West 178th Street, and the third at 285 Audubon Avenue, just around the corner from where it runs through the five-hundred block of West 179th Street. Another thing was their surnames. They were different, but they weren't dissimilar. All three were of Armenian origin. Well, Washington Heights has an Armenian colony—very small and very clannish. I began to feel pretty good. I didn't doubt for a minute that the three of them knew each other. Quite possibly they were friends. If so, it was reasonable to suppose that they might recently have shared a meal. It wasn't very likely, of course, that they had been the only ones to share it. Ten-year-old boys don't usually go out to meals without their parents. Maybe there had been a dozen in on it. It could even have been some sort of national feast. Or a church picnic. Picnic food is an ideal breeding ground for the typhoid organism. It can't stand cooking, but it thrives in raw stuff—ice cream and mayonnaise and so on. And if a carrier had happened to have a hand in the arrangements . . . I decided we'd do well to check and see if there was an Armenian carrier on our list."

"We found one, all right," Dr. Pellitteri said. "A widow named Christos—she died a year or two ago—who lived on West 178th Street."

"To be sure, we had only three cases," Dr. Fuerst went on. "But I didn't let that bother me. I've never known an outbreak of typhoid in which everybody who was exposed got sick. There are always a certain number who escape. They either don't eat whatever it is that's contaminated or they have a natural or an acquired immunity. Moreover, the incubation period in typhoid—the time it takes for the bug to catch hold—varies with the individual. Ten days is about the average, but it can run anywhere from three to thirty. In other words, maybe we had seen only the vanguard. There might be more to come. So in the absence of anything better, the Armenian link looked pretty good. I called the Bureau and told Bill Birnkrant—he was acting director at the time—what I thought, and he seemed to think the same. He said he'd start somebody checking. I went back upstairs for another try at the patients."

"That's when the rest of us began to come into the picture," Dr. Pellitteri said. "My job was the recent social life of the Armenian colony. Ida Matthews, a public-health nurse, took the carrier angle. Neither of us had much luck. The file listed twelve carriers in Washington Heights. As I remember, the only Armenian was Mrs. Christos. At any rate, the nurse picked her first. I remember running into Miss Matthews somewhere on Audubon toward the end of that first afternoon. She told me what progress she had made. None. Mrs. Christos was old and sick, and hadn't been out of her apartment for a month. Miss Matthews said there was no reason to doubt the woman's word, as she had a good reputation at the Department—very coöperative, obeyed all the rules. Miss Matthews was feeling pretty gloomy. She'd had high hopes. Well, I knew how she felt. I'd hit nothing but dead ends myself. Our patients didn't seem to be friends. Apparently, they just knew each other. The priest at the Gregorian church in the neighborhood— Holy Cross Armenian Apostolic, on West 187th Street—knew of no recent feasts or festivals. He hadn't heard of any unusual amount of illness in the parish, either. No mysterious chills and fevers. And the Armenian doctors in the neighborhood said the same. They had seen nothing that resembled typhoid except the cases we already had. Before I gave up for the day, I even got in touch with an Armenian girl who used to work at the Department. The only thing I could think of at the moment was a check of the Armenian restaurants. When I mentioned that, she burst out laughing. It seems Armenians don't frequent Armenian restaurants. They prefer home cooking."

"I got Pellitteri's report the next morning," Dr. Fuerst said. "And Miss Matthews'. I was back at the hospital, and when I called Birnkrant, he gave me the gist of them. I can't say I was greatly surprised. To tell the truth, I was relieved. The Armenian picnic I'd hypothesized the day before would have created a real mess. Because the hospital had reported two new cases. Two women. They lived at 500 West 178th Street and 611 West 180th Street, but they weren't Armenians. One was Italian. The other was plain American. So we were right back where we started. Only, now we had five cases instead of three, and nothing to tie them together but the fact that they all lived in the same neighborhood. And had the same brand of typhoid. There are around a dozen different strains, you know, which sometimes complicates matters. About the only thing Birnkrant and I could be sure of was that the feast theory— any kind of common gathering—was out. I'd had a word with the new patients. They had never even heard of each other. So the link had to be indirect. That gave us a number of possibilities. The source of infection could be water—either drinking water or a swimming pool. Or it could be commercial ice. Or milk. Or food. Drinking water was a job for Sanitary Engineering. The others, at the moment, were up to us—meaning Pellitteri and me. They were all four conceivable. Even ice. You can find a precedent for anything and everything in the literature on typhoid. But just one was probable. That was food. Some food that is sold already prepared —like potato salad or frozen custard—or one that is usually eaten raw. All we had to do was find out what it was, and where they got it, and how it got that way. Birnkrant and I figured out the area involved. It came to roughly four square blocks. I don't know if you know that part of Washington Heights. It's no prairie. Every building is a big apartment house, and the ground floors of most are stores. At least a fourth have something to do with food."

"I was in the office when Fuerst called," Dr. Pellitteri said. "Before he hung up, I got on the phone and we made the necessary arrangements about questioning the patients and their families— who was to see who. Then I took off. I wasn't too pessimistic. The odds were against a quick answer, but you never know. It was just possible that they all bought from the same store. Well, as it happened, they did. In a way. The trouble was it wasn't one store. It was practically all of them. Fuerst had the same experience. We ended up at the office that evening with a list as long as my arm—

half a dozen fruit-vegetable stands, four or five groceries, a market that sold clams, and an assortment of ice-cream parlors and confectioneries and delicatessens. Moreover, we couldn't even be sure the list included the right store. Most people have very strange memories. They forget and they imagine. You've got to assume that most of the information they give you may be either incomplete or inaccurate, or both. But there *was* a right store—we knew that. Sanitary Engineering had eliminated drinking water, and we had been able to rule out swimming and milk and ice. Only one of the group ever went swimming, all but one family had electric refrigerators, and none of them had drunk unpasteurized milk. It had to be contaminated food from a store. That much was certain."

"It was also certain that we had to have some help," Dr. Fuerst said, "Pellitteri and I could have handled a couple of stores. Or even, at a pinch, three or four. But a dozen or more—it would take us weeks. Let me give you an idea what an investigation like that involves. You don't just walk in the store and gaze around. You more or less take it apart. Every item of food that could conceivably cause trouble is examined, the physical setup is inspected for possible violations of the Sanitary Code, and all employees and their families are interviewed and specimens taken for laboratory analysis. So we needed help, and, of course, we got it. Birnkrant had a conference with the Commissioner the next morning and they talked it over, and the result was an engineer and another nurse and a fine big team from Food and Drugs. Very gratifying."

"And Miss Matthews," Dr. Pellitteri said. "We had her back again. She had finally finished with her carriers. They were all like the first. None had violated any of the rules."

"As expected," Dr. Fuerst said. "The average carrier is pretty coöperative. Well, that was Saturday. By Monday, we had made a certain amount of progress. We hadn't found anything yet, but the field was narrowing down. And all of a sudden we got a little nibble. It came from a confectionery called Pop's, on 178th Street, around noon. Pop's had been well up on our list. They sold ice cream made on the premises, and the place was a neighborhood favorite. Which meant it got a very thorough going over. But we were about ready to cross it off—everything was in good shape, including the help—when it developed that the place had just changed hands. Pop had sold out a week before, and he and his wife, who'd helped him run it, were on the way to California. Needless to say, Pop's went back on the list, and at the top. Also, somebody did some quick checking. Pop and his wife were driving, and their plan was to spend a few days with friends in Indianapolis. That gave us a chance. We called Birnkrant and he called Indianapolis—the State Health Department. They were extremely interested. Naturally. They said they'd let us know."

Dr. Fuerst lighted a cigarette. "Then we got a jolt," he said. "Several, in fact. The first was a call from the hospital. Four new cases. That brought the total up to nine. But it didn't stay there long. Tuesday night, it went to ten. I don't mind saying that set us back on our heels. Ten cases of typhoid fever in less than a week in one little corner of the city is almost unheard of in this day and age. The average annual incidence for the whole of Washington Heights is hardly half a case. That wasn't the worst of it, though. The real blow was that tenth case. I'll call him Jones. Jones didn't fit in. The four Monday cases, like the three Armenians and the Italian and the American, all lived in that one four-block area. Jones didn't. He lived on 176th Street, but way over west, almost on Riverside Drive. An entirely different neighborhood. I had a word with Jones the first thing Wednesday morning. I remember he worked for the post office. That's about all I learned. He hardly knew where he was. When I left the hospital, I called on his wife. She wasn't much help, either. She did all the family marketing, she told me, and she did it all within a block or two of home. That was that. She was very definite. On the other hand, there was Mr. Jones. He had typhoid, which doesn't just happen, and it was the same strain as all the rest. So either it was a very strange coincidence or she was too upset to think. My preference, until proved otherwise, was the latter. I found a phone, and called Birnkrant and gave him the latest news. He had some news for me. Indianapolis had called. They had located Pop and his wife and made the usual tests. The results were negative."

"I don't know which was the most discouraging," Dr. Pellitteri said. "Jones, I guess. He meant more work—a whole new string of stores to check. Pop had been ninety per cent hope. He merely aroused suspicion. He ran a popular place, he sold homemade ice cream, and when the epidemic broke, he pulled out. Or so it appeared from where we stood. It hurt to lose him. Unlikely or not, he had been a possibility—the first specific lead of any kind that we had been able to find in a week of mighty hard work. During the next few days, it began to look more and more like the last. Until Friday evening. Friday evening we got a very excited call from the laboratory. It was about a batch of specimens we had submitted that morning for analysis. One of them was positive for *E. typhosa.* The man's name doesn't matter. It didn't even then. What did matter was his occupation. He was the proprietor of a little frozen-custard shop—now extinct—that I'll call the Jupiter. The location was interesting, too. It was a trifle outside our area, but still accessible, and a nice, easy walk from the Joneses'. Food and Drugs put an embargo on the Jupiter that night. The next morning, we began to take it apart."

"I missed that," Dr. Fuerst said. "I spent Saturday at the hospital. It was quite a day. We averaged a case an hour. I'm not exaggerating. When I finally left, the count was nine. Nine brand-new cases. A couple of hours later, one more turned up. That made twenty, all told. Fortunately, that was the end. Twenty was the grand total. But, of course, we didn't know that then. There was no reason to believe they wouldn't just keep coming."

"The rest of us had the same kind of day," Dr. Pellitteri said. "Very disagreeable. There was the owner of the Jupiter—poor devil. You can imagine the state he was in. All of a sudden, he was out of business and a public menace. He didn't even know what a typhoid carrier was. He had to be calmed down and instructed. That was the beginning. It got worse. First of all, the Jupiter was as clean as a whistle. We closed it up—had to, under the circumstances—and embargoed the stock, but we didn't find anything. That was peculiar. I can't explain it even now. He was either just naturally careful or lucky. While that was going on, we went back to the patients and questioned them again. Did they know the Jupiter? Were they customers? Did they ever buy anything there? We got one yes. The rest said no. Emphatically. If there had been a few more yeses—even three or four—we might have wondered. But they couldn't all be mistaken. So the Jupiter lead began to look pretty wobbly. Then the laboratory finished it off. They had a type report on the Jupiter organism. It wasn't the *E. typhosa* we were looking for. It was one of the other strains. That may have been some consolation to Mr. Jupiter. At least, he didn't have an epidemic on his conscience. But it left us uncomfortably close to the end of our rope. We had only a handful of stores still to check. If we didn't find the answer there, we were stumped. We didn't. We crossed off the last possibility on Tuesday morning, August 27th. It was Number Eighty. We'd examined eighty stores and something like a thousand people, and all we had to show for it was a new carrier."

"Well, that was something," Dr. Fuerst said. "Even if it was beside the point. But we also had another consolation. None of the patients had died. None was going to. They were all making excellent progress."

"That's true enough," Dr. Pellitteri said. "But we couldn't claim much credit for that." He paused, and shifted around in his chair. "About all we can take any credit for is Miss Gamso, here," He smiled. "Miss Gamso saved the day. She got inspired."

Miss Gamso gave me a placid look. "I don't know about inspired," she said. "It was more like annoyed. I heard them talking —Dr. Birnkrant, and these two, and all the rest of them—and I read the reports, and the days went by and they didn't seem to be getting anywhere. That's unusual. So it was irritating. It's hard to explain, but I got to thinking about that carrier Mrs. Christos.

There were two things about her. She lived with a son-in-law who was a known food handler. He was a baker by trade. Also, where she lived was right in the middle of everything—519 West 178th Street. That's just off Audubon. And Audubon is the street where practically all our cases did most of their shopping. Well, there was one store in particular—a fruit-and-vegetable market called Tony's—on almost everybody's list. The address was 261 Audubon Avenue. Then I really got a brainstorm. It was right after lunch on Tuesday, August 27th. I picked up the telephone and called the bureau that registers house numbers at the Borough President's office, and I asked them one question. Did 519 West 178th Street and 261 Audubon Avenue happen by any chance to be the same building? They asked me why I wanted to know. I wasn't talking, though. I just said was it, in a nice way, and the man finally said he'd see. When he came back, I was right. They were one and the same. I was so excited I thought I'd burst. Dr. Pellitteri was sitting right where he is now. He was the first person I saw, so I marched straight over and told him. He kind of stared at me. He had the funniest expression." Miss Gamso smiled a gentle smile. "I think he thought I'd gone crazy."

"I wouldn't say that," Dr. Pellitteri said. "I'll admit, however, that I didn't quite see the connection. We'd been all over Tony's—it was almost our first stop—and there was no earthly reason to question Miss Matthews' report on Mrs. Christos. The fact that they occupied the same building was news to me. To all of us, as I recall. But what if they did? Miss Gamso thought it was significant or suspicious or something. The point escaped me. When she mentioned the son-in-law, though, I began to get a little more interested. We knew him, of course—anybody who lives with a carrier is a potential cause of trouble—and checked on him regularly. But it was just possible that since our last checkup he had become infected. That happens. And although we hadn't found him working in any of the stores, he could have come and gone a couple of weeks before we started our investigation. At any rate, it was worth looking into. Almost anything was, by then. I went up that afternoon. I walked past Tony's on the way to 519. There wasn't any doubt about their being in the same building. Tony's is gone now, like Mrs. Christos, but the way it was then, his front door was about three steps from the corner, and around the corner about three more steps was the entrance to the apartments above. The Christos flat was on the fifth floor—Apartment 53. Mrs. Christos and her son-in-law were both at home. They let me in and that's about all. I can't say they were either one delighted to see me. Or very helpful. She couldn't add anything to what she had already told Miss Matthews. The son-in-law hardly opened his mouth. His last regular job, he said, had been in January, in a cafeteria over in Astoria. Since then, he'd done nothing but odd jobs. He wouldn't say what, when, or where. I couldn't completely blame him. He was afraid that if we got to questioning any of his former employers, they'd never take him on again. When I saw how it was, I arranged for a specimen, and, for the moment, let it go at that. There was no point in getting rough until we knew for sure. I told him to sit tight. If he was positive, I'd be back in a hurry. I got the report the next day. He wasn't. He was as harmless as I am. But by then it didn't matter. By that time, it was all over. To tell the truth, I had the answer before I ever left the building."

Dr. Pellitteri shook his head. "I walked right into it," he said. "It was mostly pure luck. What happened was this. On the way out, I ran into the superintendent—an elderly woman. I was feeling two ways about the son-in-law—half sympathetic and half suspicious. It occurred to me that the superintendent might have some idea where he'd been working the past few weeks. So I stopped and asked. She was a sour old girl. She didn't know and didn't care. She had her own troubles. They were the tenants, mainly. She backed me into a corner and proceeded to unload. The children were the worst, she said—especially the boys. Always thinking up some new devilment. For example, she said, just a few weeks ago, toward the end of July, there was a gang of them up on the roof playing wild Indians. Before she could chase them off, they'd stuffed some sticks down one of the plumbing vent pipes. The result was a stoppage. The soil pipe serving one whole tier of apartments blocked and sprang a leak, and the bathroom of the bottom apartment was a nice mess. I hadn't been paying much attention until then. But at that point—Well, to put it mildly, I was fascinated. Also, I began to ask some questions. I wanted to know just what bathroom had flooded. The answer was Apartment 23. What were the other apartments in that tier? They were 33, 43, and 53. What was underneath Apartment 23? A store—Tony's Market, on the corner. Then I asked for a telephone. Birnkrant's reaction was about what you'd expect. Pretty soon, a team from Sanitary Engineering arrived. They supplied the details and the proof. Tony stored his fruits and vegetables in a big wooden walk-in refrigerator at the rear of his store. When Sanitary Engineering pulled off the top, they found the soil pipe straight overhead. The leak had been repaired almost a month before, but the sawdust insulation in the refrigerator roof was still damp from the waste that had soaked through. It wasn't Tony's fault. He hadn't known. It wasn't anybody's fault. It was just one of those things. So that was that."

"Not entirely," Dr. Fuerst said. "There was still Jones to account for. It wasn't necessary. The thing was settled. But I was curious. I had a talk with him the next day. We talked and talked. And in the end, he remembered. He was a night walker. Every evening after dinner, he went out for a walk. He walked all over Washington Heights, and usually, somewhere along the line, he stopped and bought something to eat. It was generally a piece of fruit. As I say, he finally remembered. One night, near the end of July, he was walking down Audubon and he came to a fruit stand and he bought an apple. On the way home, he ate it."

QUESTIONS FOR STUDY, DISCUSSION, AND WRITING

1. "*Typhoid is invariably conveyed . . .*" (p. 1059). *If you change* invariably *to* all, *you have the major premise of a syllogism: All typhoid is conveyed . . . victims. On August 15 the Bureau of Preventable Diseases was given a minor premise: Three people in Washington Heights have typhoid. What is the conclusion of this syllogism and how did it govern the entire investigation?*
2. *What is the relation of the bureau's file of carriers to this syllogism?*
3. *How does Roueché's narrative correspond to the process of investigation? What is the effect of his narrative?*
4. *How far did methodical or systematic investigation get the bureau? What else was necessary to complete the investigation?*
5. *On page 981 Platt ("Style in Science") distinguishes work method from style. How could the typhoid investigation be said to show an interplay between the two?*

Prose Forms: Parables

[When we read a short story or a novel, we are less interested in the working out of ideas than in the working out of characters and their destinies. In Dickens' Great Expectations, for example, Pip the hero undergoes many triumphs and defeats in his pursuit of success, only to learn finally that he has expected the wrong things, or the right things for the wrong reasons; that the great values in life are not always to be found in what the world calls success. In realizing this meaning we entertain, with Dickens, certain concepts or ideas that organize and evaluate the life in the novel, and that ultimately we apply to life generally. Ideas are there not to be exploited discursively, but to be understood as the perspective which shapes the direction of the novel and our view of its relation to life.

When ideas in their own reality are no longer the primary interest in writing, we have obviously moved from expository to other forms of prose. The shift need not be abrupt and complete, however; there is an area where the discursive interest in ideas and the narrative interest in characters and events blend. In allegory, for example, abstract ideas are personified. "Good Will" or "Peace" may be shown as a young woman, strong, confident, and benevolent in her bearing but vulnerable through her sweet reasonableness to the single-minded, fierce woman who is "Dissension." Our immediate interest is in their behavior as characters, but our ultimate interest is in the working out, through them, of the ideas they represent. We do not ask that the characters and events be entirely plausible in relation to actual life, as we do for the novel; we are satisfied if they are consistent with the nature of the ideas that define their vitality.

Ideas themselves have vitality, a mobile and dynamic life with a behavior of its own. The title of the familiar Negro spiritual "Sometimes I Feel Like a Motherless Child," to choose a random instance, has several kinds of "motion" as an idea. The qualitative identity of an adult's feelings and those of a child; the whole burgeoning possibility of all that the phrase "motherless child" can mean; the subtle differences in meaning—the power of context—that occur when it is a Negro who feels this and when it is a white; the speculative possibilities of the title as social commentary or psychological analysis; the peculiar force of the ungrammatical "like"—these suggest something of the "life" going on in and around the idea. Definition,

1069

analogy, assumption, implication, context, illustration are some of the familiar terms we use to describe this kind of life.

There is, of course, another and more obvious kind of vitality which an idea has: its applicability to the affairs of men in everyday life. Both the kind and extent of an idea's relevance are measures of this vitality. When an essayist wishes to exploit both the life in an idea and the life it comprehends, he often turns to narration, because there he sees the advantage of lifelike characters and events, and of showing through them the liveliness of ideas in both the senses we have noted. Ideas about life can be illustrated in life. And, besides, people like stories. The writer's care must be to keep the reader's interest focused on the ideas, rather than on the life itself; otherwise, he has ceased being essentially the essayist and has become the short-story writer or novelist.

The parable and the moral fable are ideal forms for his purpose. In both, the idea is the heart of the composition; in both the ideas usually assume the form of a lesson about life, some moral truth of general consequence to men; and in both there are characters and actions. Jesus often depended on parables in his teaching. Simple, economical, pointed, the parables developed a "story," but more importantly, applied a moral truth to experience. Peter asked Jesus how often he must forgive the brother who sins against him, and Jesus answered with the parable of the king and his servants, one of whom asked and got forgiveness of the king for his debts but who would not in turn forgive a fellow servant his debt. The king, on hearing of this harshness, retracted his own benevolence and punished the unfeeling servant. Jesus concluded to Peter, "So likewise shall my heavenly Father do also unto you, if ye from your hearts forgive not every one his brother their trespasses." But before this direct drawing of the parallel, the lesson was clear in the outline of the narrative.

Parables usually have human characters; fables often achieve a special liveliness with animals. In March's "The Fisherman and the Hen," the old hen is clearly just a chicken, clucking, picking at worms, scratching the ground. But when the fisherman has struck her to steal her worm for bait, and the old hen, responding to his compassion for having wronged her, gets another worm in order to be struck and so to be fondled afterwards, the old hen is almost magically transformed into a peculiar psychological truth about human behavior. The story creates its own interest as a story, but by its end the reader realizes that the story exists for the sake of an idea—and that its relevance is a lesson about himself.

The writer will be verging continually on strict prose narrative when he writes the parable or fable, but if he is skillful and tactful, he will preserve the essayist's essential commitment to the definition and development of ideas in relation to experience.]

ANONYMOUS: The Whale[1]

The whale is the largest of all the fishes in the sea. If you saw one floating on the surface, you would think it was an island rising from the sea sands. When he is hungry, this huge fish opens his mouth and sends forth a breath—the sweetest thing on earth—from his gaping jaws. Other fish, enticed by this sweetness, draw near and hover in his mouth, happy in their ignorance of his deception. The whale then snaps shut his jaws, sucking in all these fish. He thus traps the little fish; the great he cannot ensnare.

This fish lives near the bottom of the sea until the time when equinoctial storms stir up all the waters, as winter struggles to supplant summer, and the sea bottom becomes so turbulent that he cannot stay there. Then he leaves his home and rises to the surface, where he lies motionless. In the midst of the storm, ships are tossed about on the sea. The sailors fearing death and hoping to live, look about them and see this fish. They think he is an island, and, overjoyed, they head their ships for him and drop anchor. They step ashore and, striking sparks from stone and steel into their tinder, they make a fire on this marvel, warm themselves, and eat and drink. The fish soon feels the fire and dives to the bottom, drawing the sailors down with him. He kills them all without leaving a wound.

Application: The devil is determined and powerful, with the craftiness of witches. He makes men hunger and thirst after sinful pleasures and draws them to him with the sweetness of his breath. But whoever follows him finds only shame. His followers are the men of little faith; men of great faith he cannot ensnare, for they are steadfast, body and soul, in true belief. Whoever listens to the devil's teachings will at last regret it bitterly; whoever anchors his hope on the devil will be drawn down by him to the gloomy depths of hell.

1. From *A Bestiary*, an anonymous thirteenth-century English work, translated by Alan B. and Lidie M. Howes.

MARTIN BUBER: The Demon in the Dream

"What do you see?" asked the demon in the dream.

"A very long wall," I said.

"That is," he explained, "the boundary wall between the land of things and the land of thoughts. On this wall we demons live. It seems narrow to you, does it not, and not very roomy? But for us it is broad and comfortable enough. And we feel at home on it as well. Yes, I even allow myself to fancy that our feelings are better than yours, for you think yourself at home in both lands and are really at home in neither.

"You man! You act as if this wall were only a boundary which is otherwise not there, so to speak; as if one could neither squat on the wall, as I am squatting on it now, nor dance on it, as you saw me doing a moment ago. You believe such a foolish thing only because you know nothing of us. And if one knows nothing of us, how shall he know anything of the world or of the subtlest of its kingdoms, this wall?

"You know nothing of us. You only 'suspect' something. Oh, your suspicions! They arouse disgust in all beings—things and thoughts and demons. There, out of the darkness, a slimy grasping arm shoots towards you and then past you. Ugh, man, how unappetizing! I should rather be a crude tree-trunk and experience only what is necessary than be a being full of suspicions.

"You have a suspicion of us, then. But we know you to your very ground and deeper, too. We know you better than anything else, and in another way. But you are also more important to us than anything else. Yes, reluctantly I admit it, we are directly dependent on you. For we live off you. We can receive the strength of the world only through you. We can enjoy all things only through you. Your experience is our food, and we have no other.

"The more forcefully you live, the more avidly do we enjoy ourselves. The content of your living does not much matter to us; your joy and anger, sin and holiness, heroism and despair, are all the same to us. But whether you live fully or faintly, that does concern us. Your moderation is a meager crumb, your temperance a tough morsel that sticks in the throat. But where some fellow is horrified at the world and rushes against it and rages over its appeasements and is shattered on the wall of the great indifference; or where some fellow falls madly in love and again and again draws forth new power from out of his extravagance and converts it into amorousness until he revolves around some envisioned axis like a hundred-spoked fire-wheel, flaring up and crackling in a blissful smoke—there we feast, there we thrive.

"What you call contents is for us only gaily-colored variety, a cupboard of agreeable spices, no more. It does not occur to us to prefer one kind to another. Whether your passion pursues sensuality or politics, business or deeds of mercy, that does not affect our enjoyment; it only plays round it. But on the violence of your passion, on that we do depend.

"You have a No for every Yes, and for every value a disvalue. You effect transitions from one to the other, and you call the Yes good and the No bad, or vice versa, and are very concerned about whether your passion is on the side of the Yes or on the side of the No. But we are not especially interested in all this. The juggling amuses us, yet I assure you that we cannot otherwise express our esteem for your virtue and your moderate high-mindedness than by leaving it alone.

"But you must not think that we amuse ourselves on this wall and coolly await what ascends to us from excited human power. We would have a hard life then! For you are accustomed to 'let things happen' and to allow the possibilities in you to remain merely possibilities. It is fatiguing and disagreeable, you think, to give all of yourself; it is not even seemly. If it were not for us you would sleep through all your opportunities. We descend to you, we become things or thoughts in order not to startle you, we mingle with you, and—we tempt you. We taste the food, and when we find it flat we undertake the temptation: thereupon the bite becomes tasty. We rustle your passion out of its hiding-place. We inflame to feeling your capacity to feel. We actualize you. Naturally we do all this for our own sake; but, incidentally, what would become of you if we did not stir you up!

"There are some among you who imagine that one is tempted only to sin. That attitude fits them well, my dear: for they possess no other art than that which inclines them towards what they call sin. But in reality we are not at all specialized: we desire that out of your *potentia* should come *actus*, nothing more. We do not mix in your sophistries.

"We have, indeed—I may not conceal it from you—our sad chapter. We consume ourselves in the act of tempting. To tempt men is no child's play. We spring head over heels into each new undertaking, and it swallows all we are and all we can be. We could, in fact, say that we risk ourselves. Yes, we do enjoy it; but the enjoyment is exclusive and pitiless. When we are finished with this enjoyment, we collapse into ourselves. This collapsing of ours is not like your sleep; it is a dispersion, a scattering, a being wiped away. It lasts until a desire for fresh enjoyment steals over us and collects us. From this you can well imagine how much continuity there is in our lives. Hardly a vague trace remains in memory from one adventure to another! We seem continually to be starting life over again. Indeed it appears each time as if the escapade were really worth while—but that is, after all, a moot point.

"Though we are constantly starting all over again, we cannot remember a real beginning in our lives. Seriously, it seems to me as if we had nothing that might be called a real beginning. At times there descends on me a dull feeling as if I already always existed. But we do have an end, that is certain. Sometimes a final enjoyment will arrive which will swallow me and not deliver me up again. And until then . . .! Well, it is a melancholy bliss, I cannot deny it.

"And once there was even one among us who . . . I shall tell you about it although I can hardly believe you capable of fully understanding; for it is a story with long roots—but you have a nice way of looking at one, as if you . . . no matter!

"There was one demon who was discontented. He longed for continuity. Moments—he loathed moments if he could not advance upright from one to another, but one lay there and was more insignificant than a drunken man! He refused to take part any longer in this foolish rhythm of power and weakness. But you must not fancy that he conducted himself like your famous human rebels and harangued some god. When he realized he was fed up, he stood up and took a step outside of time. Once outside he sat down again.

"There he sat and was no longer affected by the whole game. There was no enjoyment, but there was no more emptiness—for where time no longer beats there is no emptiness, only the shape of the stillness. Thus he who had been discontented waxed in power and in duration. He took on security as a tree takes on rings. His power became ever stronger until he became aware that it could never again flag. Confident that he was wholly his own, it seemed to him as if the world was wholly his possession. You should have seen him when he stepped back into time!

"He began to tempt men again. But because his power had grown so great, each of his temptations drove his victim to his uttermost. Each ability of this man was intensified to the maximum, every longing was strained to its extreme. The uttermost of man, as you may well know, is a wonderful thing. The uttermost of man creates. That is a dangerous activity. It creates modes of being, essence, immortality. It lures men into madness and destruction, but it transforms the uttermost moment into eternity. And it cannot be exhausted through our enjoyment of it; its deep sweetness remains untasted, an eternally inaccessible remainder.

"He who had come back had been able to enjoy himself despite this remainder before he stepped out of time. Now he could do so no longer. Now, under the influence of the stillness, something greater than enjoyment sprang up in him: he sensed the inexhaustible over against him; he suffered, he burned. He was no longer merely discontented as before; he was wretched and alien. And he grew ever more miserable the higher his temptations reached on the ladder of creativeness. His strength, his capacity for enjoyment, was not impaired; it even grew from time to time without slackening. He went upright from one adventure to the next, yet each time the remainder pained him ever more acutely. Ever more silly the enjoyment appeared that could only satiate itself through intensity; ever more furiously he longed for the vision. To grasp the remainder, to fathom the qualities, to take possession of creativity, to see! But a demon can see as little as he can create.

"And while my brother's great game kindled awesome raptures, triumphs, downgoings on earth, driving the human soul upward to perform its greatest deed; while a gigantic burnt offering ascended to the tempter out of tumult and beauty, tyranny and grace, my brother recognized: 'What I enjoy is not the essence, the essence is beyond my reach; the essence is given to this little man with whom I play. While I play with him I evoke in him the essence, I make the essence in him alive.' And in the tempter there awoke this desire: 'I want to become a man: man, plaything—I want immortality—I want a creating soul!' For immortality, he perceived, is nothing but the creating soul."

The demon in my dream had altered. His grin had turned into an awkward smile, like the first smile on an infant's face, and his initially strident voice now sounded like the voice of the wine-growers I once heard sing the ancient melody of the dead to the words of a harvest song. Then sleep loosened, and the intertwined worlds slipped away from each other's embrace.

HENRY FIELDING: A Trifling Incident[1]

Tom Jones, when very young, had presented Sophia with a little bird, which he had taken from the nest, had nursed up, and taught to sing.

Of this bird, Sophia, then about thirteen years old, was so extremely fond, that her chief business was to feed and tend it, and her chief pleasure to play with it. By these means little Tommy, for so the bird was called, was become so tame, that it would feed out of the hand of its mistress, would perch upon the finger, and lie contented in her bosom, where it seemed almost sensible of its own happiness; though she always kept a small string about its leg, nor would ever trust it with the liberty of flying away.

One day, when Mr. Allworthy and his whole family dined at Mr. Western's, Master Blifil, being in the garden with little Sophia, and observing the extreme fondness that she showed for her little bird, desired her to trust it for a moment in his hands. Sophia presently complied with the young gentleman's request, and after some previous caution, delivered him her bird; of which he was no sooner in possession, than he slipped the string from its leg and tossed it into the air.

The foolish animal no sooner perceived itself at liberty, than forgetting all the favors it had received from Sophia, it flew directly from her, and perched on a bough at some distance.

Sophia, seeing her bird gone, screamed out so loud, that Tom Jones, who was at a little distance, immediately ran to her assistance.

He was no sooner informed of what had happened, than he cursed

1. Chapters 3 and 4 from Book IV of *Tom Jones, The History of a Foundling.*

Blifil for a pitiful malicious rascal; and then immediately stripping off his coat he applied himself to climbing the tree to which the bird escaped.

Tom had almost recovered his little namesake, when the branch on which it was perched, and that hung over a canal, broke, and the poor lad plumped over head and ears into the water.

Sophia's concern now changed its object. And as she apprehended the boy's life was in danger, she screamed ten times louder than before; and indeed Master Blifil himself now seconded her with all the vociferation in his power.

The company, who were sitting in a room next the garden, were instantly alarmed, and came all forth; but just as they reached the canal, Tom (for the water was luckily pretty shallow in that part) arrived safely on shore.

Thwackum fell violently on poor Tom, who stood drooping and shivering before him, when Mr. Allworthy desired him to have patience; and turning to Master Blifil, said, "Pray, child, what is the reason of all this disturbance?"

Master Blifil answered, "Indeed, uncle, I am very sorry for what I have done; I have been unhappily the occasion of it all. I had Miss Sophia's bird in my hand, and thinking the poor creature languished for liberty, I own I could not forbear giving it what it desired; for I always thought there was something very cruel in confining anything. It seemed to be against the law of nature, by which everything has a right to liberty; nay, it is even unchristian, for it is not doing what we would be done by; but if I had imagined Miss Sophia would have been so much concerned at it, I am sure I never would have done it; nay, if I had known what would have happened to the bird itself; for when Master Jones, who climbed up that tree after it, fell into the water, the bird took a second flight, and presently a nasty hawk carried it away."

Poor Sophia, who now first heard of her little Tommy's fate (for her concern for Jones had prevented her perceiving it when it happened), shed a shower of tears. These Mr. Allworthy endeavored to assuage, promising her a much finer bird; but she declared she would never have another. Her father chid her for crying so for a son of his, his backside should be well flead.

foolish bird; but could not help telling young Blifil, if he was a

Sophia now returned to her chamber, the two young gentlemen were sent home, and the rest of the company returned to their bottle; where a conversation ensued on the subject of the bird, so curious, that we think it deserves a chapter by itself.

Square had no sooner lighted his pipe, than, addressing himself to Allworthy, he thus began: "Sir, I cannot help congratulating you on your nephew; who, at an age when few lads have any ideas but of sensible objects, is arrived at a capacity of distinguishing right from wrong. To confine anything, seems to me against the law of nature, by which everything hath a right to liberty. These were his words; and the impression they have made on me is never to be eradicated. Can any man have a higher notion of the rule of right and the eternal fitness of things? I cannot help promising myself, from such a dawn, that the meridian of this youth will be equal to that of either the elder or the younger Brutus."

Here Thwackum hastily interrupted, and spilling some of his wine, and swallowing the rest with great eagerness, answered, "From another expression he made use of, I hope he will resemble much better men. The law of nature is a jargon of words, which means nothing. I know not of any such law, nor of any right which can be derived from it. To do as we would be done by, is indeed a Christian motive, as the boy well expressed himself; and I am glad to find my instructions have borne such good fruit."

"If vanity was a thing fit," says Square, "I might indulge some on the same occasion; for whence only he can have learnt his notions of right or wrong, I think is pretty apparent. If there be no law of nature, there is no right nor wrong."

"How!" says the parson, "do you then banish revelation? Am I talking with a deist or an atheist?"

"Drink about," says Western. "Pox of your laws of nature! I don't know what you mean, either of you, by right and wrong. To take away my girl's bird was wrong, in my opinion; and my neighbor Allworthy may do as he pleases; but to encourage boys in such practices is to breed them up to the gallows."

Allworthy answered, "That he was sorry for what his nephew had done, but could not consent to punish him, as he acted rather from a generous than unworthy motive." He said, "If the boy had stolen the bird, none would have been more ready to vote for a severe chastisement than himself; but it was plain that was not his design;" and indeed, it was as apparent to him, that he could have no other view but what he had himself avowed. (For as to that malicious purpose which Sophia suspected, it never once entered into the head of Mr. Allworthy.) He at length concluded with again blaming the action as inconsiderate, and which, he said, was pardonable only in a child.

Square had delivered his opinion so openly, that if he was now silent, he must submit to have his judgment censured. He said, therefore, with some warmth, "That Mr. Allworthy had too much respect to the dirty consideration of property. That in passing our judgments on great and mighty actions, all private regards should be laid aside; for by adhering to those narrow rules, the younger Brutus had been condemned of ingratitude, and the elder of parricide."

"And if they had been hanged too for those crimes," cried

Thwackum, "they would have had no more than their deserts. A couple of heathenish villains! Heaven be praised we have no Brutuses nowadays! I wish, Mr. Square, you would desist from filling the minds of my pupils with such antichristian stuff; for the consequence must be, while they are under my care, its being well scourged out of them again. There is your disciple Tom almost spoiled already. I overheard him the other day disputing with Master Blifil that there was no merit in faith without works. I know that is one of your tenets, and I suppose he had it from you."

"Don't accuse me of spoiling him," says Square. "Who taught him to laugh at whatever is virtuous and decent, and fit and right in the nature of things? He is your own scholar, and I disclaim him. No, no, Master Blifil is my boy. Young as he is, that lad's notions of moral rectitude I defy you ever to eradicate."

Thwackum put on a contemptuous sneer at this, and replied, "Ay, ay, I will venture him with you. He is too well grounded for all your philosophical cant to hurt. No, no, I have taken care to instil such principles into him——"

"And I have instilled principles into him too," cries Square. "What but the sublime idea of virtue could inspire a human mind with the generous thought of giving liberty? And I repeat to you again, if it was a fit thing to be proud, I might claim the honor of having infused that idea."

"And if pride was not forbidden," said Thwackum, "I might boast of having taught him that duty which he himself assigned as his motive."

"So between you both," says the squire, "The young gentleman hath been taught to rob my daughter of her bird. I find I must take care of my partridge-mew. I shall have some virtuous religious man or other set all my partridges at liberty." Then slapping a gentleman of the law, who was present, on the back, he cried out, "What say you to this, Mr. Counsellor? Is not this against law?"

The lawyer with great gravity delivered himself as follows:

"If the case be put of a partridge, there can be no doubt but an action would lie; for though this be *ferae naturae*, yet being reclaimed, property vests: but being the case of a singing bird, though reclaimed, as it is a thing of base nature, it must be considered as *nullius in bonis*. In this case, therefore, I conceive the plaintiff must be non-suited; and I should disadvise the bringing any such action."

"Well," says the squire, "if it be *nullus bonus*, let us drink about, and talk a little of the state of the nation, or some such discourse that we all understand; for I am sure I don't understand a word of this. It may be learning and sense for aught I know; but you shall never persuade me into it. Pox! you have neither of you mentioned a word of that poor lad who deserves to be commended: to venture breaking his neck to oblige my girl was a generous-spirited action: I have learning enough to see that. D——n me, here's Tom's health! I shall love the boy for it the longest day I have to live."

Thus was the debate interrupted; but it would probably have been soon resumed, had not Mr. Allworthy presently called for his coach and carried off the two combatants.

Such was the conclusion of this adventure of the bird, and of the dialogue occasioned by it; which we could not help recounting to our reader, though it happened some years before that stage or period of time at which our history is now arrived.

FRANZ KAFKA: Parable of the Law[1]

"Before the Law stands a doorkeeper. To this doorkeeper there comes a man from the country who begs for admittance to the Law. But the doorkeeper says that he cannot admit the man at the moment. The man, on reflection, asks if he will be allowed, then, to enter later. 'It is possible,' answers the doorkeeper, 'but not at this moment.' Since the door leading into the Law stands open as usual and the doorkeeper steps to one side, the man bends down to peer through the entrance. When the doorkeeper sees that, he laughs and says: 'If you are so strongly tempted, try to get in without my permission. But note that I am powerful. And I am only the lowest doorkeeper. From hall to hall, keepers stand at every door, one more powerful than the other. And the sight of the third man is already more than even I can stand.' These are difficulties which the man from the country has not expected to meet, the Law, he thinks, should be accessible to every man and at all times, but when he looks more closely at the doorkeeper in his furred robe, with his huge pointed nose and long thin Tartar beard, he decides that he had better wait until he gets permission to enter. The doorkeeper gives him a stool and lets him sit down at the side of the door. There he sits waiting for days and years. He makes many attempts to be allowed in and wearies the doorkeeper with his importunity. The doorkeeper often engages him in brief conversation, asking him about his home and about other matters, but the questions are put quite impersonally, as great men put questions, and always conclude with the statement that the man cannot be allowed to enter yet. The man, who has equipped himself with many things for his journey, parts with all he has, however valuable, in the hope of bribing the doorkeeper. The doorkeeper accepts it all, saying, however, as he takes each gift: 'I take this only to keep you from feeling that you have left something undone.' During all these long years the man watches the doorkeeper almost incessant-

1. From the chapter, "In the Cathedral," of *The Trial* (1925).

ly. He forgets about the other doorkeepers, and this one seems to him the only barrier between himself and the Law. In the first years he curses his evil fate aloud; later, as he grows old, he only mutters to himself. He grows childish, and since in his prolonged study of the doorkeeper he has learned to know even the fleas in his fur collar, he begs the very fleas to help him and to persuade the doorkeeper to change his mind. Finally his eyes grow dim and he does not know whether the world is really darkening around him or whether his eyes are only deceiving him. But in the darkness he can now perceive a radiance that streams inextinguishably from the door of the Law. Now his life is drawing to a close. Before he dies, all that he has experienced during the whole time of his sojourn condenses in his mind into one question, which he has never yet put to the doorkeeper. He beckons the doorkeeper, since he can no longer raise his stiffening body. The doorkeeper has to bend far down to hear him, for the difference in size between them has increased very much to the man's disadvantage. 'What do you want to know now?' asks the doorkeeper, 'you are insatiable.' 'Everyone strives to attain the Law,' answers the man, 'how does it come about, then, that in all these years no one has come seeking admittance but me?' The doorkeeper perceives that the man is nearing his end and his hearing is failing, so he bellows in his ear: 'No one but you could gain admittance through this door, since this door was intended for you. I am now going to shut it.' "

"So the doorkeeper deceived the man," said K. immediately, strongly attracted by the story. "Don't be too hasty," said the priest, "don't take over someone else's opinion without testing it. I have told you the story in the very words of the scriptures. There's no mention of deception in it." "But it's clear enough," said K., "and your first interpretation of it was quite right. The doorkeeper gave the message of salvation to the man only when it could no longer help him." "He was not asked the question any earlier," said the priest, "and you must consider, too, that he was only a doorkeeper, and as such fulfilled his duty." "What makes you think he fulfilled his duty?" asked K. "He didn't fulfill it. His duty might have been to keep all strangers away, but this man, for whom the door was intended, should have been let in." "You have not enough respect for the written word and you are altering the story," said the priest. "The story contains two important statements made by the doorkeeper about admission to the Law, one at the beginning, the other at the end. The first statement is: that he cannot admit the man at the moment, and the other is: that this door was intended only for the man. If there were a contradiction between the two, you would be right and the doorkeeper would have deceived the man. But there is no contradiction. The first statement, on the contrary, even implies the second. One could almost say that in suggesting to the man the possibility of future admittance the doorkeeper is exceeding his duty. At that time his apparent duty is only to refuse admittance and indeed many commentators are surprised that the suggestion should be made at all, since the doorkeeper appears to be a precisian with a stern regard for duty. He does not once leave his post during these many years, and he does not shut the door until the very last minute; he is conscious of the importance of his office, for he says: 'I am powerful'; he is respectful to his superiors, for he says: 'I am only the lowest doorkeeper'; he is not garrulous, for during all these years he puts only what are called 'impersonal questions'; he is not to be bribed, for he says in accepting a gift: 'I take this only to keep you from feeling that you have left something undone'; where his duty is concerned he is to be moved neither by pity nor rage, for we are told that the man 'wearied the doorkeeper with his importunity'; and finally even his external appearance hints at a pedantic character, the large, pointed nose and the long, thin, black, Tartar beard. Could one imagine a more faithful doorkeeper? Yet the doorkeeper has other elements in his character which are likely to advantage anyone seeking admittance and which make it comprehensible enough that he should somewhat exceed his duty in suggesting the possibility of future admittance. For it cannot be denied that he is a little simple-minded and consequently a little conceited. Take the statements he makes about his power and the power of the other doorkeepers and their dreadful aspect which even he cannot bear to see—I hold that these statements may be true enough, but that the way in which he brings them out shows that his perceptions are confused by simpleness of mind and conceit. The commentators note in this connection: 'The right perception of any matter and a misunderstanding of the same matter do not wholly exclude each other.' One must at any rate assume that such simpleness and conceit, however sparingly manifest, are likely to weaken his defense of the door; they are breaches in the character of the doorkeeper. To this must be added the fact that the doorkeeper seems to be a friendly creature by nature, he is by no means always on his official dignity. In the very first moments he allows himself the jest of inviting the man to enter in spite of the strictly maintained veto against entry; then he does not, for instance, send the man away, but gives him, as we are told, a stool and lets him sit down beside the door. The patience with which he endures the man's appeals during so many years, the brief conversations, the acceptance of the gifts, the politeness with which he allows the man to curse loudly in his presence the fate for which he himself is responsible—all this lets us deduce certain feelings of pity. Not every doorkeeper would have acted thus. And finally, in answer to a gesture of the man's he bends down to give him the chance of putting a last question. Nothing but mild impatience—the doorkeeper knows that this is the end of it all—is discernible in the words: 'You are insatiable.' Some push this mode of interpretation even further and hold that these words express a kind of friendly admiration, though not without a hint of condescension. At any rate the figure of the doorkeeper can be said to come out very differently from what you fancied." "You have studied the story more exactly and for a longer time than I have," said K. They were both silent for a little while. Then. K. said: "So you think the man was not deceived?" "Don't misunderstand me," said the priest, "I am only showing you the various opinions concerning that point. You must not pay too much attention to them. The scriptures are unalterable and the comments often enough merely express the commentators' despair. In this case there even exists an interpretation which claims that the deluded person is really the doorkeeper." "That's a farfetched interpretation," said K. "On what is it based?" "It is based," answered the priest, "on the simple-mindedness of the doorkeeper. The argument is that he does not know the Law from inside, he knows only the way that leads to it, where he patrols up and down. His ideas of the interior are assumed to be childish, and it is supposed that he himself is afraid of the other guardians whom he holds up as bogies before the man. Indeed, he fears them more than the man does, since the man is determined to enter after hearing about the dreadful guardians of the interior, while the doorkeeper has no desire to enter, at least not so far as we are told. Others again say that he must have been in the interior already, since he is after all engaged in the service of the Law and can only have been appointed from inside. This is countered by arguing that he may have been appointed by a voice calling from the interior, and that anyhow he cannot have been far inside, since the aspect of the third doorkeeper is more than he can endure. Moreover, no indication is given that during all these years he ever made any remarks showing a knowledge of the interior, except for the one remark about the doorkeepers. He may have been forbidden to do so, but there is no mention of that either. On these grounds the conclusion is reached that he knows nothing about the aspect and significance of the interior, so that he is in a state of delusion. But he is deceived also about his relation to the man from the country, for he is inferior to the man and does not know it. He treats the man instead as his own subordinate, as can be recognized from many details that must be still fresh in your mind. But, according to this view of the story, it is just as clearly indicated that he is really subordinated to the man. In the first place, a bondman is always subject to a free man. Now the man from the country is really free, he can go where he likes, it is only the Law that is closed to him, and access to the Law is forbidden him only by one individual, the doorkeeper.

When he sits down on the stool by the side of the door and stays there for the rest of his life, he does it of his own free will; in the story there is no mention of any compulsion. But the doorkeeper is bound to his post by his very office, he does not dare go out into the country, nor apparently may he go into the interior of the Law, even should he wish to. Besides, although he is in the service of the Law, his service is confined to this one entrance; that is to say, he serves only this man for whom alone the entrance is intended. On that ground too he is inferior to the man. One must assume that for many years, for as long as it takes a man to grow up to the prime of life, his service was in a sense an empty formality, since he had to wait for a man to come, that is to say someone in the prime of life, and so he had to wait a long time before the purpose of his service could be fulfilled, and, moreover, had to wait on the man's pleasure, for the man came of his own free will. But the termination of his service also depends on the man's term of life, so that to the very end he is subject to the man. And it is emphasized throughout that the doorkeeper apparently realizes nothing of all this. That is not in itself remarkable, since according to this interpretation the doorkeeper is deceived in a much more important issue, affecting his very office. At the end, for example, he says regarding the entrance to the Law: 'I am now going to shut it,' but at the beginning of the story we are told that the door leading into the Law always stands open, and if it always stands open, that is to say at all times, without reference to life or death of the man, then the doorkeeper cannot close it. There is some difference of opinion about the motive behind the doorkeeper's statement, whether he said he was going to close the door merely for the sake of giving an answer, or to emphasize his devotion to duty, or to bring the man into a state of grief and regret in his last moments. But there is no lack of agreement that the doorkeeper will not be able to shut the door. Many indeed profess to find that he is subordinate to the man even in knowledge, toward the end, at least, for the man sees the radiance that issues from the door of the Law while the doorkeeper in his official position must stand with his back to the door, nor does he say anything to show that he has perceived the change." "That is well argued," said K., after repeating to himself in a low voice several passages from the priest's exposition. "It is well argued, and I am inclined to agree that the doorkeeper is deceived. But that has not made me abandon my former opinion, since both conclusions are to some extent compatible. Whether the doorkeeper is clear-sighted or deceived does not dispose of the matter. I said the man is deceived. If the doorkeeper is clear-sighted, one might have doubts about that, but if the doorkeeper himself is deceived, then his deception must of necessity be communicated to the man. That makes the doorkeeper not, indeed, a deceiver, but a creature so simple-minded that he ought to be dismissed at once from his office. You mustn't forget that the doorkeeper's deceptions do himself no harm but do infinite harm to the man." "There are objections to that," said the priest. "Many aver that the story confers no right on anyone to pass judgment on the doorkeeper. Whatever he may seem to us, he is yet a servant of the Law; that is, he belongs to the Law and as such is beyond human judgment. In that case one must not believe that the doorkeeper is subordinate to the man. Bound as he is by his service, even only at the door of the Law, he is incomparably greater than anyone at large in the world. The man is only seeking the Law, the doorkeeper is already attached to it. It is the Law that has placed him at his post; to doubt his dignity is to doubt the Law itself." "I don't agree with that point of view," said K., shaking his head, "for if one accepts it, one must accept as true everything the doorkeeper says. But you yourself have sufficiently proved how impossible it is to do that." "No," said the priest, "it is not necessary to accept everything as true, one must only accept it as necessary." "A melancholy conclusion," said K. "It turns lying into a universal principle."

WILLIAM MARCH: Aesop and King Croesus

King Croesus decided to put heavier taxes on his people who were even then sullen and discontented with the burdens they already bore, and he discussed the matter with his trusted messenger, the slave Aesop. Aesop could find no flaw in the king's reasoning, but if Croesus put the matter so bluntly to his subjects, he feared there would be barricades and bloodshed—a situation which could be avoided if Croesus would permit him, Aesop, to break the bad news in a fable.

This was agreed upon, and later Aesop spoke to the assembled people: "The lion decided to take even heavier tribute from his subjects, and as a result there was anger among them, some of them advocating an open rebellion, but the wise fox said, 'What can we gain by desperate measures? If we depose the lion, whose greedy ways we at least understand, we may find ourselves with a tyrant worse then he is; if we lose, we may have taken from us the little we now have. Isn't it wiser, therefore, to endure the evils we are familiar with than to invite strange evils of which we know nothing?'"

When Aesop finished, the people wept and went away, accepting their new burdens as something that could not be avoided, since the fable is, and always has been, the platitude's natural frame.

WILLIAM MARCH: The Panther and the Woodcutter

There was once a panther who, famished by a cold winter, became so bold that he crept up to a woodcutter's cottage and tried to lure the owner outside so that he could eat him. He tapped on the window and stood in the dark while the woodcutter cracked his shutters and asked who had summoned him from his bed. The panther made his voice soft and seductive. He said, "I'm a rich traveler, and I've lost my way in the forest. If you'll come outside and show me the road, I'll reward you with a bagful of gold."

"I'm not interested in gold," said the woodcutter. "What can gold buy that I value?"

The panther said, "Then I promise to take you to my kingdom and give you great power. Everybody will bow down when you pass by."

"That would be tiresome," said the woodcutter. "I can think of nothing sillier than having people bow down when I take a walk." He closed his shutters and got back into bed at once.

Then the defeated panther slunk off to the edge of the forest and lay down, pressing his famished belly against the earth, but his tricks were not all used up, and he began to moan and sob like a man in distress. "Save me! Save me!" he cried. "Save me from the panther who is going to eat me!"

At that the woodcutter ran out of his cottage without calculating the danger, bent only on doing a merciful deed, and a moment later the panther sprang and fixed his teeth in the man's throat, bearing him down to the frozen earth and shaking out the little life that remained in him. When he had finished his meal, the panther rolled his eyes and said, "I've learned an important lesson tonight: some men are betrayed more easily through compassion than through avarice."

WILLIAM MARCH: The Fisherman and the Hen

When he reached the brook where he intended to fish, an angler found he had left his bait at home, but after considering matters, he thought he might be able to catch grasshoppers and use them instead. He got down on his hands and knees, but try as he would, he wasn't successful. He had about abandond the idea of getting bait that way, when he saw an old hen in the grass, seeking her breakfast. As he watched, he realized the old hen, despite her infirmities, was a better grasshopper-catcher than he, for almost at once she pounced on a large, lively one and held it in her bill.

The fisherman crept toward the old hen, hoping to take the grasshopper from her before she could swallow it, but the hen, guessing his intention, flushed her wings and ran through the grass. She might have escaped if the fisherman had not thrown a stick at her. He caught her squarely and she fell in the weeds, her tail feathers twitching from side to side.

He pulled the half-swallowed grasshopper from her throat, put it in his pocket, and turned away; but noticing how pathetic the old hen looked there in the grass, he picked her up and stroked her head. "Poor old thing!" he said. "I'm sorry for what I did just now!" He lifted her higher and rubbed his cheek against her wings. "I was a brute to hit you so hard," he said.

It was the first time the old hen had had any affection in years, and she lay back in the fisherman's arms, making a clucking sound in her throat, until he put her down and went back to his fishing. Shortly thereafter, he dismissed the incident from his mind, being engaged with his own pleasures, so he was somewhat puzzled when he heard a soft, seductive noise behind him. He turned, and there was the old hen with another grasshopper in her beak. When she saw she had his attention, she moved away slowly, glancing back at him over her shoulder, awaiting his blow with resignation, since an old hen will put up with anything if you'll give her a little affection now and then.

WILLIAM MARCH: Aesop's Last Fable

Aesop, the messenger of King Croesus, finished his business with the Delphians and went back to the tavern where he had taken lodgings. Later, he came into the taproom where a group of Delphians were drinking. When they realized who he was, they crowded about him. "Tell us," they began, "is Croesus as rich as people say?"

Aesop, since the habit of speaking in fables was so strongly fixed in him, said, "I can best answer your question with a parable, and it is this: The animals gathered together to crown their richest member king. Each animal in turn stated what he possessed, and it was soon apparent that the lion had the largest hunting preserves, the bee the most honey, the squirrel the largest supply of acorns, and so on; but when the voting began, the difficulty of arriving at a decision was plain to all, for to the bee, the nuts that represented the wealth of the squirrel were of no consequence; to the lion, the hay that the zebra and the buffalo owned was worthless; and the panther and the tiger set no value at all on the river that the crane and crocodile prized so highly."

Then Aesop called for his drink, looking into the faces of the Delphians with good-natured amusement. He said, "The moral of the fable is this: Wealth is an intangible thing, and its meaning is not the same to all alike."

The stolid Delphians looked at one another, and when the silence was becoming noticeable, one of then tried again: "How was the weather in Lydia when you left home?"

"I can best answer that question with another fable," said Aesop, "and it is this: During a rain storm, when the ditches were flooded and the ponds had overflowed their banks, a cat and a duck met on the road, and, wanting to make conversation they spoke at the same instant. 'What a beautiful day this is,' said the delighted duck. 'What terrible weather we're having,' said the disgusted cat."

Again the Delphians looked at one another, and again there was silence. "The moral of that tale," said Aesop, "is this: What pleases a duck distresses a cat." He poured wine into his glass and leaned against the wall, well satisfied with the start he had made in instructing the barbarous Delphians.

The Delphians moved uneasily in their seats, and after a long time, one of them said, "How long are you going to be here?"

"That," said Aesop, "can best be answered in the Fable of the Tortoise, the Pelican, and the Wolf. You see, the pelican went to visit his friend the tortoise and promised to remain as long as the latter was building his new house. Then one day as they were working together, with the tortoise burrowing and the pelican carrying away the dirt in his pouch, the wolf came on them unexpectedly, and—"

But Aesop got no farther, for the Delphians had surrounded him and were, an instant later, carrying him toward the edge of the cliff on which the tavern was built. When they reached it, they swung him outward and turned him loose, and Aesop was hurled to the rocks below, where he died. "The moral of what we have done," they explained later, "is so obvious that it needs no elaboration."

WILLIAM MARCH: The Unique Quality of Truth

When the old scholar heard that Truth was in the country, he decided to find her, as he had devoted his life to studying her in all her forms. He set out immediately, and at last he came upon the cottage in the mountains where Truth lived alone. He knocked on the door, and Truth asked what he wanted. The scholar explained who he was, adding that he had always wanted to know her and had wondered a thousand times what she really was like.

Truth came to the door soon afterwards, and the scholar saw that the pictures he had formed of her in his imagination were wrong. He had thought of Truth as a gigantic woman with flowing hair who sat nobly on a white horse, or, at the very least, as a sculptured heroic figure with a wide white brow and untroubled eyes. In reality, Truth was nothing at all like that; instead, she was merely a small shapeless old woman who seemed made of some quivering substance that resembled india rubber.

"All right," said the old lady in a resigned voice. "What do you want to know?"

"I want to know what you are."

The old lady thought, shook her head, and answered, "That I don't know. I couldn't tell you to save my life."

"Then have you any special quality that makes you an individual?" asked the scholar. "Surely you must have some characteristic that is uniquely yours."

"As a matter of fact, I have," said the old lady; then, seeing the question on the scholar's lips, she added, "I'll show you what I mean. It's easier than trying to explain."

The shapeless old woman began to bounce like a rubber ball, up and down on her doorstep, getting a little higher each time she struck the floor. When she was high enough for her purpose, she seized the woodwork above her door and held on; then she said, "Take hold of my legs and walk back the way you came, and when you know what my unique quality is, shout and let me know."

The old scholar did as he was told, racking his brains in an effort to determine what quality it was that distinguished Truth. When he reached the road, he turned around, and there in the distance was Truth still clinging to the woodwork above her door.

"Don't you see by this time?" she shouted. "Don't you understand now what my particular quality is?"

"Yes," said the old scholar. "Yes, I do."

"Then turn my legs loose and go on home," said Truth in a small petulant voice.

PLATO: The Allegory of the Cave[1]

And now, I said, let me show in a figure how far our nature is enlightened or unenlightened: Behold! human beings living in an underground den, which has a mouth open towards the light and reaching all along the den; here they have been from their childhood, and have their legs and necks chained so that they cannot move, and can only see before them, being prevented by the chains from turning round their heads. Above and behind them a fire is blazing at a distance, and between the fire and the prisoners there is a raised way; and you will see, if you look, a low wall built along the way, like the screen which marionette players have in front of them, over which they show the puppets.

I see.

1. From Book VII of *The Republic*.

And do you see, I said, men passing along the wall carrying all sorts of vessels, and statues and figures of animals made of wood and stone and various materials, which appear over the wall? Some of them are talking, others silent.

You have shown me a strange image, and they are strange prisoners.

Like ourselves, I replied; and they see only their own shadows, or the shadows of one another, which the fire throws on the opposite wall of the cave?

True, he said; how could they see anything but the shadows if they were never allowed to move their heads?

And of the objects which are being carried in like manner they would only see the shadows?

Yes, he said.

And if they were able to converse with one another, would they not suppose that they were naming what was actually before them?

Very true.

And suppose further that the prison had an echo which came from the other side, would they not be sure to fancy when one of the passers-by spoke that the voice which they heard came from the passing shadow?

No question, he replied.

To them, I said, the truth would be literally nothing but the shadows of the images.

That is certain.

And now look again, and see what will naturally follow if the prisoners are released and disabused of their error. At first, when any of them is liberated and compelled suddenly to stand up and turn his neck round and walk and look towards the light, he will suffer sharp pains; the glare will distress him and he will be unable to see the realities of which in his former state he had seen the shadows; and then conceive some one saying to him, that what he saw before was an illusion, but that now, when he is approaching nearer to being and his eye is turned towards more real existence, he has a clearer vision—what will be his reply? And you may further imagine that his instructor is pointing to the objects as they pass and requiring him to name them—will he not be perplexed? Will he not fancy that the shadows which he formerly saw are truer than the objects which are now shown to him?

Far truer.

And if he is compelled to look straight at the light, will he not have a pain in his eyes which will make him turn away to take refuge in the objects of vision which he can see, and which he will conceive to be in reality clearer than the things which are now being shown to him?

True, he said.

And suppose once more, that he is reluctantly dragged up a steep and rugged ascent, and held fast until he is forced into the presence of the sun himself, is he not likely to be pained and irritated? When he approaches the light his eyes will be dazzled and he will not be able to see anything at all of what are now called realities.

Not all in a moment, he said.

He will require to grow accustomed to the sight of the upper world. And first he will see the shadows best, next the reflections of men and other objects in the water, and then the objects themselves; then he will gaze upon the light of the moon and the stars and the spangled heaven; and he will see the sky and the stars by night better than the sun or the light of the sun by day?

Certainly.

Last of all he will be able to see the sun, and not mere reflections of him in the water, but he will see him in his own proper place, and not in another; and he will contemplate him as he is.

Certainly.

He will then proceed to argue that this is he who gives the season and the years, and is the guardian of all that is in the visible world, and in a certain way the cause of all things which he and his fellows have been accustomed to behold?

Clearly, he said, he would first see the sun and then reason about him.

And when he remembered his old habitation, and the wisdom of the den and his fellow-prisoners, do you not suppose that he would felicitate himself on the change, and pity them?

Certainly, he would.

And if they were in the habit of conferring honors among themselves on those who were quickest to observe the passing shadows and to remark which of them went before, and which followed after, and which were together; and who were therefore best able to draw conclusions as to the future, do you think that he would care for such honors and glories, or envy the possessors of them? Would he not say with Homer,

> Better to be the poor servant of a poor master,

and to endure anything, rather than think as they do and live after their manner?

Yes, he said, I think that he would rather suffer anything than entertain these false notions and live in this miserable manner.

Imagine once more, I said, such an one coming suddenly out of the sun to be replaced in his old situation; would he not be certain to have his eyes full of darkness?

To be sure, he said.

And if there were a contest, and he had to compete in measuring the shadows with the prisoners who had never moved out of the den, while his sight was still weak, and before his eyes had become steady (and the time which would be needed to acquire this new habit of sight might be very considerable) would he not be ridiculous? Men would say of him that up he went and down he came without his eyes; and that it was better not even to think of ascending; and if any one tried to loose another and lead him up to the light, let them only catch the offender, and they would put him to death.

No question, he said.

This entire allegory, I said, you may now append, dear Glaucon, to the previous argument; the prison-house is the world of sight, the light of the fire is the sun, and you will not misapprehend me if you interpret the journey upwards to be the ascent of the soul into the intellectual world according to my poor belief, which, at your desire, I have expressed—whether rightly or wrongly God knows. But, whether true or false, my opinion is that in the world of knowledge the idea of good appears last of all, and is seen only with an effort; and, when seen, is also inferred to be the universal author of all things beautiful and right, parent of light and of the lord of light in this visible world, and the immediate source of reason and truth in the intellectual; and that this is the power upon which he who would act rationally either in public or private life must have his eye fixed.

I agree, he said, as far as I am able to understand you.

Moreover, I said, you must not wonder that those who attain to this beatific vision are unwilling to descend to human affairs; for their souls are ever hastening into the upper world where they desire to dwell; which desire of theirs is very natural, if our allegory may be trusted.

Yes, very natural.

And is there anything surprising in one who passes from divine contemplations to the evil state of man, misbehaving himself in a ridiculous manner; if, while his eyes are blinking and before he has become accustomed to the surrounding darkness, he is compelled to fight in courts of law, or in other places, about the images or the shadows of images of justice, and is endeavouring to meet the conceptions of those who have never yet seen absolute justice?

Anything but surprising, he replied.

Any one who has common sense will remember that the bewilderments of the eyes are of two kinds, and arise from two causes, either from coming out of the light or from going into the light, which is true of the mind's eye, quite as much as of the bodily eye; and he who remembers this when he sees any one whose vision is perplexed and weak, will not be too ready to laugh; he will first ask whether that soul of man has come out of the brighter life, and is unable to see because unaccustomed to the dark, or having turned from darkness to the day is dazzled by excess of light. And he will count the one happy in his condition and state of being, and he will pity the other; or, if he have a mind to laugh at the soul which comes from below into the light, there will be more reason in this than in the laugh which greets him who returns from above out of the light into the den.

That, he said, is a very just distinction.

JAMES THURBER: The Glass in the Field

A short time ago some builders, working on a studio in Connecticut, left a huge square of plate glass standing upright in a field one day. A goldfinch flying swiftly across the field struck the glass and was knocked cold. When he came to he hastened to his club, where an attendant bandaged his head and gave him a stiff drink. "What the hell happened?" asked a sea gull. "I was flying across a meadow when all of a sudden the air crystallized on me," said the goldfinch. The sea gull and a hawk and an eagle all laughed heartily. A swallow listened gravely. "For fifteen years, fledgling and bird, I've flown this country," said the eagle, "and I assure you there is no such thing as air crystallizing. Water, yes; air, no." "You were probably struck by a hailstone," the hawk told the goldfinch. "Or he may have had a stroke," said the sea gull. "What do you think, swallow?" "Why, I—I think maybe the air crystallized on him," said the swallow. The large birds laughed so loudly that the goldfinch became annoyed and bet them each a dozen worms that they couldn't follow the course he had flown across the field without encountering the hardened atmosphere. They all took his bet; the swallow went along to watch. The sea gull, the eagle, and the hawk decided to fly together over the route the goldfinch indicated. "You come, too," they said to the swallow. "I—I—well, no," said the swallow. "I don't think I will." So the three large birds took off together and they hit the glass together and they were all knocked cold.

Moral: He who hesitates is sometimes saved.

JAMES THURBER: The Unicorn in the Garden

Once upon a sunny morning a man who sat in a breakfast nook looked up from his scrambled eggs to see a white unicorn with a gold horn quietly cropping the roses in the garden. The man went up to the bedroom where his wife was still asleep and woke her. "There's a unicorn in the garden," he said. "Eating roses." She opened one unfriendly eye and looked at him. "The unicorn is a mythical beast," she said, and turned her back on him. The man walked slowly downstairs and out into the garden. The unicorn was still there; he was now browsing among the tulips. "Here, unicorn," said the man, and he pulled up a lily and gave it to him. The unicorn ate it gravely. With a high heart, because there was a unicorn in his garden, the man went upstairs and roused his wife again. "The unicorn," he said, "ate a lily." His wife sat up in bed and looked at him, coldly. "You are a booby," she said, "and I am going to have you put in the booby-hatch." The man, who had never liked the words "booby" and "booby-hatch," and who liked them even less on a shining morning when there was a unicorn in the garden, thought for a moment. "We'll see about that," he said. He walked over to the door. "He has a golden horn in the middle of his forehead," he told her. Then he went back to the garden to watch the unicorn; but the unicorn had gone away. The man sat down among the roses and went to sleep.

As soon as the husband had gone out of the house, the wife got up and dressed as fast as she could. She was very excited and there was a gloat in her eye. She telephoned the police and she telephoned a psychiatrist; she told them to hurry to her house and bring a strait-jacket. When the police and the psychiatrist arrived they sat down in chairs and looked at her, with great interest. "My husband," she said, "saw a unicorn this morning." The police looked at the psychiatrist and the psychiatrist looked at the police. "He told me it ate a lily," she said. The psychiatrist looked at the police and the police looked at the psychiatrist. "He told me it had a golden horn in the middle of its forehead," she said. At a solemn signal from the psychiatrist, the police leaped from their chairs and seized the wife. They had a hard time subduing her, for she put up a terrific struggle, but they finally subdued her. Just as they got her into the strait-jacket, the husband came back into the house.

"Did you tell your wife you saw a unicorn?" asked the police. "Of course not," said the husband. "The unicorn is a mythical beast." "That's all I wanted to know," said the psychiatrist. "Take her away. I'm sorry, sir, but your wife is as crazy as a jay bird." So they took her away, cursing and screaming, and shut her up in an institution. The husband lived happily ever after.

Moral: Don't count your boobies until they are hatched.

OSCAR WILDE: The Doer of Good

It was night-time, and He was alone.

And He saw afar off the walls of a round city, and went towards the city.

And when He came near He heard within the city the tread of the feet of joy, and the laughter of the mouth of gladness, and the loud noise of many lutes. And He knocked at the gate and certain of the gate-keepers opened to Him.

And He beheld a house that was of marble, and had fair pillars of marble before it. The pillars were hung with garlands, and within and without there were torches of cedar. And He entered the house.

And when He had passed through the hall of chalcedony and the hall of jasper, and reached the long hall of feasting, He saw lying on a couch of sea-purple one whose hair was crowned with red roses and whose lips were red with wine.

And He went behind him and touched him on the shoulder, and said to him:

"Why do you live like this?"

And the young man turned round and recognized Him, and made answer, and said: "But I was a leper once, and you healed me. How else should I live?"

And He passed out of the house and went again into the street.

And after a little while He saw one whose face and raiment were painted and whose feet were shod with pearls. And behind her came slowly, as a hunter, a young man who wore a cloak of two colours. Now the face of the woman was as the fair face of an idol, and the eyes of the young man were bright with lust.

And He followed swiftly and touched the hand of the young man, and said to him: "Why do you look at this woman and in such wise?"

And the young man turned round and recognized Him, and said: "But I was blind once, and you gave me sight. At what else should I look?"

And He ran forward and touched the painted raiment of the woman, and said to her: "Is there no other way in which to walk save the way of sin?"

And the woman turned round and recognized Him, and laughed, and said: "But you forgave me my sins, and the way is a pleasant way."

And He passed out of the city.

And when He had passed out of the city, He saw, seated by the roadside, a young man who was weeping.

And he went towards him and touched the long locks of his hair, and said to him: "Why are you weeping?"

And the young man looked up and recognized Him, and made answer: "But I was dead once, and you raised me from the dead. What else should I do but weep?"

On Religion

JAMES THURBER
The Owl Who Was God

Once upon a starless midnight there was an owl who sat on the branch of an oak tree. Two ground moles tried to slip quietly by, unnoticed. "You!" said the owl. "Who?" they quavered, in fear and astonishment, for they could not believe it was possible for anyone to see them in that thick darkness. "You two!" said the owl. The moles hurried away and told the other creatures of the field and forest that the owl was the greatest and wisest of all animals because he could see in the dark and because he could answer any question. "I'll see about that," said a secretary bird, and he called on the owl one night when it was again very dark. "How many claws am I holding up?" said the secretary bird, "Two," said the owl, and that was right. "Can you give me another expression for 'that is to say' or 'namely'?" asked the secretary bird. "To wit," said the owl. "Why does a lover call on his love?" asked the secretary bird. "To woo," said the owl.

The secretary bird hastened back to the other creatures and reported that the owl was indeed the greatest and wisest animal in the world because he could see in the dark and because he could answer any question. "Can he see in the daytime, too?" asked a red fox. "Yes," echoed a dormouse and a French poodle. "Can he see in the daytime, too?" All the other creatures laughed loudly at this silly question, and they set upon the red fox and his friends and drove them out of the region. Then they sent a messenger to the owl and asked him to be their leader.

When the owl appeared among the animals it was high noon and the sun was shining brightly. He walked very slowly, which gave him an appearance of great dignity, and he peered about him with large, staring eyes, which gave him an air of tremendous importance. "He's God!" screamed a Plymouth Rock hen. And the others took up the cry "He's God!" So they followed him wherever he went and when he began to bump into things they began to bump into things, too. Finally he came to a concrete highway and he started up the middle of it and all the other creatures followed him. Presently a hawk, who was acting as outrider, observed a truck coming toward them at fifty miles an hour, and he reported to the secretary bird and the secretary bird reported to the owl. "There's danger ahead," said the secretary bird. "To wit?" said the owl. The secretary bird told him. "Aren't you afraid?" He asked. "Who?" said the owl calmly, for he could not see the truck. "He's God!" cried all the creatures again, and they were still crying "He's God!" when the truck hit them and ran them down. Some of the animals were merely injured, but most of them, including the owl, were killed.

Moral: You can fool too many of the people too much of the time.

HERODOTUS
Croesus and the Oracle[1]

The messengers who had the charge of conveying these treasures to the shrines, received instructions to ask the oracles whether Croesus should go to war with the Persians, and if so, whether he should strengthen himself by the forces of an ally. Accordingly, when they had reached their destinations and presentd the gifts, they proceeded to consult the oracles in the following terms: "Croesus, king of Lydia and other countries, believing that these are the only real oracles in all the world, has sent you such presents as your discoveries deserved, and now inquires of you whether he shall go to war with the Persians, and if so, whether he shall strengthen himself by the forces of a confederate." Both the oracles agreed in the tenor of their reply, which was in each case a prophecy that if Croesus attacked the Persians, he would destroy a mighty empire, and a recommendation to him to look and see who were the most powerful of the Greeks, and to make alliance with them.

At the receipt of these oracular replies Croesus was overjoyed, and feeling sure now that he would destroy the empire of the Persians, he sent once more to Pytho, and presented to the Delphians, the number of whom he had ascertained, two gold staters apiece. In return for this the Delphians granted to Croesus and the Lydians the privilege of precedency in consulting the oracle, exemption from all charges, the most honorable seat at the festivals, and the perpetual right of becoming at pleasure citizens of their town.

1. From "Clio," Book I of the *Histories*.

After sending these presents to the Delphians, Croesus a third time consulted the oracle, for having once proved its truthfulness, he wished to make constant use of it. The question whereto he now desired an answer was—"Whether his kingdom would be of long duration?" The following was the reply of the Pythoness:

> Wait till the time shall come when a mule is monarch of Media;
> Then, thou delicate Lydian, away to the pebbles of Hermus;
> Haste, oh! haste thee away, nor blush to behave like a coward.

Of all the answers that had reached him, this pleased him far the best, for it seemed incredible that a mule should ever come to be king of the Medes, and so he concluded that the sovereignty would never depart from himself or his seed after him.[2]

* * *

With respect to Croesus himself, this is what befell him at the taking of the town. He had a son, of whom I made mention above, a worthy youth, whose only defect was that he was deaf and dumb. In the days of his prosperity Croesus had done the utmost that he could for him, and among other plans which he had devised, had sent to Delphi to consult the oracle on his behalf. The answer which he had received from the Pythoness ran thus:

> Lydian, wide-ruling monarch, thou wondrous simple Croesus,
> Wish not ever to hear in thy palace the voice thou hast prayed for,
> Utt'ring intelligent sounds. Far better thy son should be silent!
> Ah! woe worth the day when thine ear shall first list to his accents.

When the town was taken, one of the Persians was just going to kill Croesus, not knowing who he was. Croesus saw the man coming, but under the pressure of his affliction, did not care to avoid the blow, not minding whether or no he died beneath the stroke. Then this son of his, who was voiceless, beholding the Persian as he rushed towards Croesus, in the agony of his fear and grief burst into speech, and said, "Man, do not kill Croesus." This was the first time that he had ever spoken a word, but afterwards he retained the power of speech for the remainder of his life.

Thus was Sardis taken by the Persians, and Croesus himself fell into their hands, after having reigned fourteen years, and been besieged in his capital fourteen days; thus too did Croesus fulfill the oracle, which said that he should destroy a mighty empire—by destroying his own.

2. Croesus then took the Spartans as allies and went to war against Cyrus, the Persian king, who turned out to be a "mule," since his parents were of different races and different social classes. Cyrus finally besieged and captured the town to which Croesus had withdrawn with his soldiers.

RONALD A. KNOX
The Nature of Enthusiasm[1]

I have called this book *Enthusiasm*, not meaning thereby to name (for name it has none) the elusive thing that is its subject. I have only used a cant term, pejorative, and commonly misapplied, as a label for a tendency. And, lest I should be accused of setting out to mystify the reader, I must proceed to map out, as best I may, the course of this inquiry. There is, I would say, a recurrent situation in Church history—using the word "church" in the widest sense— where an excess of charity threatens unity. You have a clique, an *élite*, of Christian men and (more importantly) women, who are trying to live a less worldly life than their neighbors; to be more attentive to the guidance (directly felt, they would tell you) of the Holy Spirit. More and more, by a kind of fatality, you see them draw apart from their co-religionists, a hive ready to swarm. There is provocation on both sides; on the one part, cheap jokes at the expense of over-godliness, acts of stupid repression by unsympathetic authorities; on the other, contempt of the half-Christian, ominous references to old wine and new bottles, to the kernel and the husk. Then, while you hold your breath and turn away your eyes in fear, the break comes; condemnation or secession, what difference does it make? A fresh name has been added to the list of Christianities.

The pattern is always repeating itself, not in outline merely but in detail. Almost always the enthusiastic movement is denounced as an innovation, yet claims to be preserving, or to be restoring, the primitive discipline of the Church. Almost always the opposition is twofold; good Christian people who do not relish an eccentric spirituality find themselves in unwelcome alliance with worldlings who do not relish any spirituality at all. Almost always schism begets schism; once the instinct of discipline is lost, the movement breeds rival prophets and rival coteries, at the peril of its internal unity. Always the first fervors evaporate; prophecy dies out, and the charismatic is merged in the institutional. "The high that proved too high, the heroic for earth too hard"—it is a fugal melody that runs through the centuries.

If I could have been certain of the reader's goodwill, I would have called my tendency "ultrasupernaturalism." For that is the real character of the enthusiast; he expects more evident results from the grace of God than we others. He sees what effects religion can have, does sometimes have, in transforming a man's whole life and outlook; these exceptional cases (so we are content to think them) are for him the average standard of religious achievement. He will have no

1. From Chapter I of *Enthusiasm*, 1950.

"almost-Christians," no weaker brethren who plod and stumble, who (if the truth must be told) would like to have a foot in either world, whose ambition is to qualify, not to excel. He has before his eyes a picture of the early Church, visibly penetrated with supernatural influences; and nothing less will serve him for a model. Extenuate, accommodate, interpret, and he will part company with you.

Quoting a hundred texts—we also use them but with more of embarrassment—he insists that the members of his society, saved members of a perishing world, should live a life of angelic purity, of apostolic simplicity; worldly amusements, the artifices of a polite society, are not for them. Poor human nature! Every lapse that follows is marked by pitiless watchers outside the fold, creates a harvest of scandal within. Worse still, if the devout circle has cultivated a legend of its own impeccability; we shall be told, in that case, that actions which bring damnation to the worldling may be inculpable in the children of light. We must be prepared for strange alternations of rigorism and antinomianism as our history unfolds itself.

Meanwhile, it must not be supposed that the new birth which the enthusiast preaches can be limited to a mere reformation of manners. It involves a new approach to religion; hitherto this has been a matter of outward forms and ordinances, now it is an affair of the heart. Sacraments are not necessarily dispensed with; but the emphasis lies on a direct personal access to the Author of our salvation, with little of intellectual background or of liturgical expression. The appeal of art and music, hitherto conceived as a ladder which carried human thought upwards, is frowned upon as a barrier which interferes with the simplicity of true heart-worship. An inward experience of peace and joy is both the assurance which the soul craves for and its characteristic prayer-attitude. The strength of this personal approach is that it dominates the imagination, and presents a future world in all the colours of reality. Its weakness—but we are not concerned here to criticize—is an anthropocentric bias; not God's glory but your own salvation preoccupies the mind, with some risk of scruples, and even of despair.

But the implications of enthusiasm go deeper than this; at the root of it lies a different theology of grace. Our traditional doctrine is that grace perfects nature, elevates it to a higher pitch, so that it can bear its part in the music of eternity, but leaves it nature still. The assumption of the enthusiast is bolder and simpler; for him, grace has destroyed nature, and replaced it. The saved man has come out into a new order of being, with a new set of faculties which are proper to his state; David must not wear the panoply of Saul. Especially, he decries the use of human reason as a guide to any sort of religious truth. A direct indication of the Divine will is communicated to him at every turn, if only he will consent to abandon the "arm of flesh"—Man's miserable intellect, fatally obscured by the Fall. If no oracle from heaven is forthcoming, he will take refuge in sortilege; anything, to make sure that he is leaving the decision in God's hands. That God speaks to us through the intellect is a notion which he may accept on paper, but fears, in practice, to apply.

A new set of faculties, and also a new status; man saved becomes, at last, fully man. It follows that "the seed of grace," God's elect people, although they must perforce live cheek by jowl with the sons of perdition, claim another citizenship and own another allegiance. For the sake of peace and charity, they will submit themselves to every ordinance of man, but always under protest; worldly governments, being of purely human institution, have no real mandate to exercise authority, and sinful folk have no real rights, although, out of courtesy, their fancied rights must be respected. Always the enthusiast hankers after a theocracy, in which the anomalies of the present situation will be done away, and the righteous bear rule openly. Disappointed of this hope, a group of sectaries will sometimes go out into the wilderness, and set up a little theocracy of their own, like Cato's senate at Utica. The American continent has more than once been the scene of such an adventure; in these days, it is the last refuge of the enthusiast.

QUESTIONS FOR STUDY, DISCUSSION, AND WRITING

1. What devices does Knox use in constructing his definition of enthusiasm?
2. What explanation does Knox imply for the fact that "enthusiasm" is regarded as a pejorative term?
3. What does Knox mean by "ominous references to old wine and new bottles, to the kernel and the husk"?
4. What illustrations might Knox give for his last sentence?

SAMUEL H. MILLER
But Find the Point Again[1]

When the climate of a culture changes, people are so preoccupied with their traditional habits and ways of looking at things that they do not see what is happening before their eyes. Revolutions come and go, states and empires fall, miracles rise from the ruins, yet they read their daily papers, eat and drink and sleep, suffer their sorrows, as if everything remained the same. They are supported by the structures of the past, to which they have been accustomed, and the new age coming into being rises unseen all about them.

1. An address delivered at the convocation service of the Harvard Divinity School on September 30, 1959.

They are anachronisms, belonging to another age yet living in this one.

In religion the conserving tendency of faith exaggerates this indifference to the changing world. Thus the church[2] may long deceive itself by its spectacular success in numbers and prestige without knowing how hollow it has become, or how feeble and unintelligible its message sounds to a world which has moved into new dimensions of knowledge and fear. The pulpit may continue to talk of matters long after their cogency has vanished, except in the sacred vocabulary of the preacher.[3] The ministry may be exhausted by the aggressive zeal of its diversified activities without touching the heart of darkness at the center of our troubled time.

Testy old Carlyle, in all his flamboyance, perceived this fact when he declared:

That a man stand there, and speak of spiritual things to me, it is beautiful; even in its great obscurity and decadence it is among the beautifulest, most touching objects one sees on this earth. This speaking man has indeed, in these times, wandered terribly from the point; has, alas, as it were, totally lost sight of the point, yet at bottom whom have we to compare with him? Of all such functionaries boarded and lodged on the industry of modern Europe, is there one worthier of the board he has? ... The speaking function, with all our writing and printing function, has a perennial place, could he but find the point again![4]

Worthy of his bed and board—if he could but find the point again! Age after age he had served well. According to the needs of previous epochs, he had stood in the teeth of the storm and despite unpopularity or even martyrdom, he had not wavered from the point or betrayed the nature of his leadership. Think only of the apostles who had fashioned the profound bases of Christian civilization, sustaining for centuries the life and culture of many peo-

2. "Certainly by every test but that of influence the Church had never been stronger than it was at the opening of the twentieth century, and its strength increased steadily. Everyone was a Christian, and almost everyone joined some church, though few for reasons that would have earned them admission to Jonathan Edwards' Northampton congregation. The typical Protestant of the twentieth century inherited his religion as he did his politics, though rather more casually, and was quite unable to explain the differences between denominations. He found himself a church member by accident and persisted in his affiliation by habit; he greeted each recurring Sunday service with a sense of surprise and was persuaded that he conferred a benefit upon his rector and his community by participating in church services. The church was something to be 'supported' like some aged relative whose claim was vague but inescapable.

"Never before had the church been materially more powerful or spiritually less effective." Henry Steele Commager, *The American Mind*, (New Haven: Yale University Press, 1950) [Miller's note].

3. "The great Biblical key ideas of sovereign divine creation, election, sin, mercy, judgment, conversion, rebirth, reconciliation, justification, sanctification, Kingdom of God, are utterly alien, and consequently irrelevant to people whose minds are molded and dominated by the conquest of the kingdom of man. They are undecipherable hieroglyphs, with which, strangely enough, Church people still seem to play." Hendrik Kraemer, *The Communication of the Christian Faith* (Philadelphia: Westminster Press, 1956), p. 94 [Miller's note].

4. Thomas Carlyle, *Past and Present*, Bk. IV, Chap. 1 ("Collected Works," Vol. VII, London: 1870) [Miller's note].

ples; or of the priests who had labored in many fields, in the arts and in philosophy during the Middle Ages, elaborating a world which reached its climax in cathedral and *summa*;[5] or of the reformers who had endured the ordeal of a radical revolution in the ways of faith and modes of action, transforming the institutions of the state and church in terms of new freedoms. Where did Carlyle's speaking man lose the point? Was he meandering, fiddling at inconsequentials? Was he blind, or stupid, or wicked? A world was in the making, as every epoch makes its world, and this man did not keep to his job. He strayed and in his straying the bonds of faith were loosed and the world fell apart.

Now you and I are standing in that man's shoes. We too have been called to minister to the world. Will we have anything to say, not merely to please the world, but to fit its real needs? Will we be able to find the point again, and thus provide a firm base for society, perspectives sufficient for the arts and culture, and an intellectual integrity profound enough to discipline the destructive forces of our present chaos?

Our fundamental embarrassment as we stand face to face with this world is that we may become relevant to its demands all too easily, conforming to that standard which the world sets for us, and losing the very point of being a minister in the world at all. One of the tragedies of our time is that the minister is both overworked and unemployed; overworked in a multitude of tasks that do not have the slightest connection with religion, and unemployed in the serious concerns and exacting labors of maintaining a disciplined spiritual life among mature men and women. It is a scandal of modern Protestantism that young men called to the high venture of the Christian way, disciplined by seminary training in the arduous dimensions of such faith, are graduated into churches where the magnitude of their vocation is as Joseph Sittler has said, *macerated*, chopped into small pieces, by the pressure of the petty practices of so-called parish progress. One wonders how much of the compulsive frenzy of the parish minister comes from the guilty realization that he has not attended to his prime calling at all, but is merely filling up time with a nervous pandemonium of jerks and jabs in the direction of people in order to make the church popular. Wherever the current ideal of the minister comes from—the big operator, the smart salesman, the successful tycoon—it still remains a puzzle why the minister should fall prey to such false images unless he has completely confused what he is supposed to be doing with what most churches want him to do.

Herman Melville, as flamboyant a rhetorician as Carlyle, yet with profound perceptions of what was involved in the minister's

---

5. A comprehensive treatise by a church philosopher.

task, described the pulpit in the New Bedford Chapel where the one-time harpooner, Father Mapple, preaches.

> The pulpit is ever this earth's foremost part. All the rest comes in its rear; the pulpit leads the world. From thence it is the storm of God's quick wrath is first described, and the bow must bear the earliest brunt. From thence it is that the God of breezes fair or foul is first invoked for favorable winds. Yes, the world's a ship on its passage out, and not a voyage complete; and the pulpit is its prow.[6]

This might easily have been accepted at face value in the early 19th century but for us it would be easier to believe it was written tongue in cheek, a rather fatuous inflation of words and little more. The truth is that the pulpit, at least now, is certainly not the *prow* of this world, either in generating power or in initiating ideas.[7] It is set back now in quieter waters, out of the haste and the traffic where strife is real and decisions must be made.

The world is still a ship on its passage out. There is no doubt of that, nor that the voyage is incomplete. Indeed, we are more uncertain than Melville as to where we are going. Our charts seem obsolete in the light of new facts and forces, so we prove the unknown with a dread as terrifying as that the first man must have felt when he ventured out of sight of land under strange skies. The minister no less than others has been overwhelmed by the catastrophic changes of history.

If the ministry is to regain its magnitude and integrity, it must be validated at a much more serious level of life than that of success and prestige. To succumb either to sentimental popularity or to institutional professionalism is to betray not only our own calling but the world's need as well. The ministry has a point, a tip of light which breaks the darkness like a sharpened spear, a bright moment when the diversity and contradictions of life break into a unity, a unity never complete and never permanent, but always redemptive and profoundly satisfying. We prove ourselves at the point where we enter into history, where the world is being made and unmade, where life turns into hell or opens into heaven, where, like Jacob of old, men and women are caught in the middle of the darkness, alone and in agony, wrestling with the unnamed mysteries of existence, striving to exact a blessing from the exigencies of their human lot. We come to life as a profession when we stand forth beyond the superficial safety and the limits of praise and blame, to speak the clumsy, daring word which only faith may speak of things unseen but powerful with portent to be, of realities

6. Herman Melville, *Moby Dick* (Boston: Houghton Mifflin Co., 1956), p. 50 [Miller's note].

7. Several years ago the *Saturday Review* conducted a survey of sources of ideas in contemporary life. The results were as follows: 49% from radio and TV, 21% from newspapers, 11% from magazines, 11% from movies, and 8% from books [Miller's note].

waiting to be born at the far edge of all things known, of a realm mysterious with blessing for any who can become like little children, able to leap beyond themselves to a greatness dimly surmised.

Yet any man who steps into this kind of pulpit, into this prow where the storms strike first and the dark is thickest, knows right well the terror of his position. The ministry in any age is caught between the offense of God and the offense of the world, between the awful terror of making God plain, of speaking the *verbum dei*, and the terrifying muddle of this world's jumble of circumstances in which human life is crucified. Like a lonely figure, the ministry in our age stands separated from the confident assurance of any infallible or perhaps even divine message easily inherited from the past, and as well from the arrogance of an age which finds all authority in itself. We may stand at the prow, but not with the sustaining authority our forefathers found in their Bibles, their creeds and their churches; and the seething waters that break across our bow are from deeper seas than any man has ever sailed.

This is a world [says J. Robert Oppenheimer] in which each of us, knowing his limitations, knowing the evils of superficiality and the terrors of fatigue, will have to cling to what is close to him, to what he knows, to what he can do, to his friends and his tradition and his love, lest he be dissolved in a universal confusion and know nothing and love nothing....

This balance, this perpetual, precarious, impossible balance between the infinitely open and the intimate, this time—our twentieth century—has been long in coming; but it has come. It is, I think, for us and our children, our only way.... This cannot be an easy life. We shall have a rugged time of it to keep our minds open and to keep them deep....[8]

Only the utmost honesty, perhaps the confession of our poverty, will enable us in this extremity to prove ourselves a skilled profession worthy of its bed and board.

Our Fading Heritage

To say the least, our situation is bewildering. T. S. Eliot described it by saying that much of our heritage is Christian but it is vastly less so than it used to be. The truth is that the whole imaginative structure of Christian truth, elaborated in myth and symbol, has for the most part crumbled under the impact of the last three centuries of revolutionary thought, scientific methods, and historical studies. The vision of reality articulated in this great Biblical formulary has evaporated and no longer serves as the frame of reference for elucidating the mysteries of being human. We have not deliberately renounced our Christian heritage, but it no longer plays a dynamic role either in the motivation of our actions or in the judgments which evaluate our satisfactions. Men are no longer moved by the words which once thrust men to war or turned them

8. J. Robert Oppenheimer, *Man's Right to Knowledge*, 2nd Series (New York: Columbia University Press, 1935), p. 115 [Miller's note].

from the world to God. The charts which men have used for centuries now seem quite inadequate in the face of new conditions. The character of reality for human beings has changed, and the ancient vision is no longer sufficient.

It is precisely at this point that we must ask whether we shall labor to create a new Christian culture with materials coming from the new discoveries, disciplines, and attitudes of our time or succumb to an essentially non-religious one, that is, a sub-pagan culture.[9] It has always been the function of faith to supply a structure of myth and symbol, and to enact in appropriate rites a vision of reality capable of sustaining the larger inferences of meaning in the life of a people, thus providing a margin sufficiently suggestive for the exercise of freedom in human possibilities but not reducible to precise, black and white, static literalisms.[1] It is such a symbolic structure of the imagination which both ties together the disparate realities and forces of human existence, and at the same time becomes a vocabulary, verbal, visual, and active, by which a community can be established and under certain conditions can rise to the level of communion. Wherever this symbolic structure evaporates, loses its power of suggestion, becomes dogmatically rigid and then superficially literal, the people lose their means of coherence. The ancient dictum that where there is no vision of commonly recognized reality the people perish as a people, society falls apart, and civilization and culture are thrown into anarchy and self-destruction is still true. Lewis Mumford, in his Bampton Lectures, declared:

Perhaps the fatal course all civilizations have so far followed has been due, not to natural miscarriages, the disastrous effects of famines and floods and diseases, but to accumulated perversions of the symbolic functions.[2]

Our disorders, I suspect, derive from the fact that the vision of reality conceived in redemptive terms and elaborated by Dante and Aquinas is simply no longer an instrument of suggestiveness for multitudes conditioned by the popular influences of science and industry. The minister, if he is to find the point at all of being useful to the rehabilitation of society and the redemption of the individual, cannot offer the twentieth century the image which the thirteenth century found eminently satisfactory. The new age has a style of its own, a language peculiar to itself, and whatever image

9. "The civilization characteristic of Christendom has not disappeared, yet another civilization has begun to take its place . . . Our whole life and mind is saturated with the slow upward filtration of a new spirit—that of an emancipated atheistic international democracy." George Santayana, *Winds of Doctrine* (New York: Harper & Row, 1957), p. 1 [Miller's note].

1. "The great social ideal for religion is that it should be the common basis for the unity of civilization . . . In that way it justifies its insight beyond the transient clash of brute force." Alfred North Whitehead, *Adventures of Ideas* (New York: The Macmillan Co., 1933), p. 221 [Miller's note].

2. Lewis Mumford, *Art. Technics* (New York: Columbia University Press, 1952), p. 51 [Miller's note].

of reality is to be conjured up must be of the very substance of our time. On the other hand, the minister can scarcely believe that the twentieth century, unlike all others, has transcended the limitations of time and history so that it is sufficient to itself.[3] A vision of reality limited only to our own epoch is incredibly arrogant and stupidly parochial. The golden-tongued Chrysostom put it well, as he put many things: "A priest must be sober and clear-eyed, with a thousand eyes in every direction."

New Images of Reality

New configurations of experience have arisen in the Renaissance, the Industrial Revolution, and in the rise of science, each with its own system of values and perspectives of discrimination by which life is ordered. We have moved out of the Magical Age, as I. A. Richards has put it, into the Scientific. We have reached a new maturity of freedom from superstition and credulity. With this Mundigkeit, or adulthood, as Bonhoeffer describes it, there has occurred an extraordinary activity and excitement in all the creative aspects of man's mind and spirit. New life is erupting in fresh but ambiguous forms needing identification and judgment. To evaluate such a burgeoning mass of new work is not easy, but it is evident that in the midst of it there is much which approximates or reflects the ancient and traditional expressions of religious concerns about the elemental mysteries of human existence.

Into the vacuum left by the slow evaporation of the Biblical image of reality the burgeoning powers of this age have understandably and desperately pushed their way, seeking to formulate a new vision of reality more congenial to the terms of our contemporary sensibilities and knowledge. The arts have gone philosophical. Beckman, Klee, Picasso, Henry Moore deliver their gnomic elucidations about the nature of reality with religious seriousness. The sciences, too, finding themselves on the brink of this same vacuum, have not always been slow to make a leap of faith concerning ultimate things, or if the scientists themselves modestly desisted, their friends have rushed in with cosmic conclusions. Even business, for all its pragmatic traditions and prejudices, has become quite confidently responsible and evangelical, urging upon men and their families the "business way of life."

Thus the minister must confront these twin terrors of the pulpit —at his back what seems to be an obsolete order of things and before him a confusion from which nothing is exempt. He stands for a whole

---

3. "Any modern re-formation of the religion (based upon certain historical occasions scattered irregularly within a period of about 1200 years from the earlier prophets to the stabilization of theology by Augustine) must first concentrate upon the moral and metaphysical intuitions scattered throughout the whole epoch." Whitehead, *op. cit.*, p. 212 [Miller's note].

congeries of notions which have become mere words, the realities seemingly no longer a part of modern existence, and he must deal with a turbulent age doing its best to create a new order of intelligible meaning. Now that the Christian vision no longer reverberates in the life of the contemporary man, how will the minister find the insight or the courage to proclaim "good news"? How will he rehabilitate the heights and depths of sensibility which have atrophied in the recent frenzy of naturalizing the world? How will he demonstrate the reality of life at levels from which man has long since withdrawn to busy himself in other areas? How will he speak to the point when man has nothing in his experience to provide the peg on which to hang such realities as grace and spirit?

Can the minister supply a vision of reality? Can he offer the Bible to a people disabused of its validity? Can he recall heaven and hell to a people who have laughed them out of existence? Can he talk to them of God, when they find God quite unimaginable in such a world, scientifically structured in iron law? Can he explain faith, redemption, grace, while they wonder what such things have to do with the defense mechanisms of the ego or the libidinous expressions of the id? Can he continue to conduct the rites of the church, and speak of "holy" things when life itself has been naturalized and even the church transfers its own significance to statistical categories and popular prestige?

Sharing in this demythologized epoch, he may have no vision of reality to offer. But if there is no vision, there is no preacher, no message, no church. He cannot peddle Dante or Thomas, Luther or Calvin, as if nothing had happened in the world since their time. As Kierkegaard so succinctly put it, one cannot crib the answers to the problems of the age from the back of the book.

The Need for a Learned Ministry

If ever the conditions of the world demanded the highest and most rigorous intellectual preparation for the ministry, they do so now. The founders of this University were profoundly convinced that no well-ordered society could long endure without a "learned ministry." Well into the 18th century this passionate conviction continued to be expressed until the twin forces of pietism and romanticism began to dull the edge of all discipline in American life. Slackness, emotionalism, and a fever of optimism spread through the church and corrupted its ways. There was a general levelling down of all classes in the name of democracy, and a revolt against all theological thoroughness in the name of simplicity and practical concerns. By and large, it was a loose vulgarisation of the Christian faith which by the early 20th century had transformed it into a shadow of the moral enthusiasm and respectability of the secular world. We need again to reassert the fundamental necessity for a learned ministry if the church is to survive as a potent source of that vision by which society unites its life in a meaningful order of truth and goodness. Its present tactics are scarcely more than an effort to keep its body alive by repudiating its soul.

It is only by dint of the severest intellectual discipline that a man may provide a vision of reality for such an age as this. If that vision is in the Christian tradition, he must discover how to unwrap it, reveal its dynamic suggestiveness, make plain its elucidation of the human problem. If it is not in the Christian tradition he must discover where it is and what it is. In all he must be able to make wise and revealing judgments, not confusing truth with novelty, or tradition with truth, but discerning the distinctions between appearance and reality, between the authentic and the popular. To attain the intellectual acumen to be wise about the living past in the present, to be able to confirm the eternal in the temporal, and to discriminate sharply between sophisticated skepticism and skeptical faith is an order of considerable magnitude. It is certainly no job for an ecclesiastical mechanic or a general manager of parish programs. The radical thrust of this work is in the direction of the profoundest perceptiveness, imagination, rational daring, and penetrating insight.

As in other professions, and nowhere more disastrously, American practicality has contrived short cuts in the training of the ministry. Concerned only with shortsighted results, it has reduced theological education to a vulgarized form of a trade school, where facile schemes, glib formulae, and manipulative methods prepare a man for disillusionment and heartsickening bitterness when he discovers all too late that such bright and shining stones are no food for the hunger of honest men and women, touched by this world's tragic pain. If there is to be a vision of reality, if the minister really desires to find the point again and to be worthy of his board, he can do it only by probing the Bible to its deepest ground, exploring the wide reaches of faith in its historical elaboration, and articulating as explicitly as his imagination and reason allow, the theological structure of human relationships and circumstantial mysteries. Certainly no portion of his intellectual ability can be left undeveloped. A great deal of nonsense especially in pietistic circles, supported by a native American anti-intellectualism, has been uttered in this regard. The attainment of the saints has been praised as if it were achieved either without assistance from or in spite of their intelligence. Neither history nor biography corroborate such an illusion. A soft-headed saint is simply no saint. Although the saints may not have been scholars, their intelligence was undeniable. One can scarcely fulfill the love of God in Jesus' prime commandment by avoiding the passionate expression of the "whole mind." Let the minister be sure his mind is sharpened to its utmost, lest he blunder about the world with a rough and stupid carelessness, hoping that he might hit upon the will of God merely because of his good intentions.

The minister has a job cut from monumental dimensions. The specifications for rehabilitating a usable, imaginable, worshipful vision of reality in our time are such as to thrust a man beyond all normal limits of his resources. He must probe the past till he finds the quick of it—and knows beyond the peradventure of a doubt the broad and everlasting realities in it which run like a living stream into our own day. He must probe the present, suffer the full brunt of its tumultuous power and passion, separating with painful threshing the wheat from the chaff in his own mind and heart. He must take the Bible, a very old book fashioned in archaic languages and forms, and unveil the present intimacy of its radical realities. He must handle the mixed and perplexing chaos of mortal circumstance, the old and the new, the great and the inconsequential, the sacred and the profane, and by an alchemy of his own he must make sense of things, or be honest, and humble in knowing he can do no more than to face them wisely and bravely. He must learn to see the primordial truth in small events, the sublime in common unexpected places, the glory of grace in humble persons, the son of God in a "litter of scorn." Everywhere he must have eyes to see what mortal eyes too often miss, and the intelligence both to look for it and to confirm it when it is found.

When André Malraux, the novelist, has one of his characters ask, "How can one make the best of one's life?" the answer is given, "By converting as wide a range of experience into conscious thought as possible." This is in a sense the function of the minister, especially if we keep in mind the tremendous scope of "experience" and the dialectical forces of history producing it. The intelligence of the minister is redemptive, in that he not only turns experience into conscious thought, but he seeks to make sense out of the diversity and incompleteness of experience. It is his task to bring experience to conscious fulfillment, and to articulate that fulfillment in terms of an ultimate whole. The vision of reality is seen in small events and single revelations; it becomes the symbol of the total way of life in which all things work together for good to them that love God. He will sadly know how true it is, as Proust once said, that most lives are like camera film, exposed to passing events but never developed. It is the joy and anguish of the minister to "develop" the experience of men to a vision of reality.

I should like to risk the privilege of using some words of Albert Camus, spoken when he received the Nobel prize, as a thrust of light in this direction. Although he is speaking of art, I should like to substitute our own thoughts of religion.

To me art is not a solitary delight. It is a means of stirring the greatest number of men with a privileged image of our common joys and sorrows. Hence it forces the artist [minister] not to isolate himself; it subjects him to the humblest and most universal truth.

Not one of us is great enough for such a vocation. . . . Whatever our personal frailties may be, the nobility of our calling will always be rooted in two commitments difficult to observe: refusal to lie about what we know and resistance to oppression.

Faced with a world threatened by disintegration, in which our grand inquisitors may set up once and for all the kingdoms of death, this generation knows that, in a sort of mad race against time, it ought to reestablish among nations a peace not based on slavery, to reconcile labor and culture again, and to reconstruct with all men an Ark of the Covenant.[4]

"To reconstruct with all men an Ark of the Covenant"! To bind together in one household the humanity of our time, to recover the ground of truth on which we all must stand and the vision of hope in which freedom may be boldly exercised, to lift up our eyes to that higher dream of which Dante spoke in which the exuberance of our epoch may become, not a haunted nightmare or a burden of despair, but a song of joy and peace for all people. This is a calling beyond our strength, and yet nothing less than such a kingdom could demand or deserve our all. It is Dante again who emblazons the text for such a calling in his unforgettable words, "I crown and mitre thee above myself." Not in our strength, not in our wisdom, but in the power of that which waits to be born, in the new Ark of the Covenant, we stake our faith.

The Scope of Theological Training

To train men for such a profession has never been an easy task. In our day an educated man may pass as such by having a wide smattering of slight contacts, innumerable opinions, and a name-dropping vocabulary. Sometimes theological education has contented itself with informing men with more than they can think, and encouraging a kind of lust for knowledge which accumulates a body of inert ideas in lieu of wisdom. Certainly if we can keep in mind that Ark of the Covenant for which Camus is striving out of motives far removed from the Christian faith, we too will know that there is something greater than our particular art, or our special skill. The fragmentation of the world is mirrored in our divisive authorities. Our vocabularies tend to become departmental or even private. The paths of communication and of possible unity become clogged with protective devices and defensive barriers for our private satisfaction.

---

4. Albert Camus, quoted by Charles Rolo, "Albert Camus: A Good Man," *The Atlantic Monthly*, Vol. 201, No. 5 (May 1958) [Miller's note].

The ramifying walls which separate so much of our learning in seemingly water-tight compartments are not in life. We make them ourselves, sometimes for our convenience, often for our prestige; but we must find a way to breach them if we are to train men to love God with their whole mind.[5]

A learned ministry is not necessarily pedantic. Indeed, a minister is in many respects a disciplined amateur. He is amateur because he works forever at the edge of unprecedented possibilities in the freedom by which the spirit fulfills events and needs. He is amateur because he is concerned with everything human across the entire spectrum of sensibility from feeling to idea to action. He is amateur because he is the lover of this world, intent on fulfilling its deepest and most radical reality through its diversified institutions and cultures. As amateur, he will want to draw together insight and perception from every corner of time and space. He will meditate, day and night, on those primordial myths in which the experience of multitudes was strained, concentrated, and objectified in archaic figures and forms. He will read the long and troubled contours of the past, the profound penetrations of prophet and priest, the dreams and corruption and heroism of the church, the anguish of centuries and the hope of eternity. To know, to know accurately and deeply, to respect the fullness of our inheritance, to study it with earnest discipline and to explore it humbly and expectantly for its peculiar gift to the wisdom of the ages and the opening of the deeper levels of present existence requires intelligence of the most disciplined sort, but not pedantry.

Every profession of our time increasingly demands a skill of theoretical knowledge and practical application; and the ministry no less than any other must be a disciplined profession. By and large, we are not so at present. We have bartered our professional birthright of an honored place in the economy of a community by reducing our office to a mad dervish dance of unenlightened public activities. Our duty is still an intellectual one in the highest sense of that term.

I will not say that you cannot be ordained as a minister without some vision of reality by which human experience can be elucidated, its heights and depths articulated, and its risk of waste redeemed for meaning and joy; I will not say you cannot serve the church in many different ways without such a scheme of measurement and discernment; I will not say that you cannot help people in many of

---

5. "The doctor, the teacher, the administrator, the judge, the clergyman, the architect are each in his own way professionally concerned with man as a whole, and the conditions of human life as a whole. Preparation for these professions is unthinking and inhuman if it fails to relate us to the whole." Karl Jaspers, *The Idea of the University* (Boston: Beacon Press, 1959), p. 47 [Miller's note].

their crises when the spirit despairs and life grows dark; but I will say that if you enter the ministry and hope to stand in the pulpit as the prow of the world, in the foremost part where directions are discerned and determined; if you expect to serve the real needs and not the apparent ones of the time in which you live; if you are going to find the point again where the ministry can be validated as a profession competently intent on doing its own job, then you must find a way to pull life together in a frame of reference or in a vision of reality so that men will know the dignity of belonging to this vast venture under God. Only by stretching ourselves to the utmost, by submitting both to the discipline of training and to the conditions of the time under which we work, will we prepare ourselves to make meaning out of the cataclysms of history or the humble events of human experience. Until we find the point again, and stand by it boldly, intelligently, the pulpit will be no more than an easy refuge from the strife and pain of life. But if we find the point again, if the vision is restored and the word is spoken for which every age waits, then no man will claim our place.

QUESTIONS FOR STUDY, DISCUSSION, AND WRITING

1. Miller's piece was delivered as an address at a convocation service of the Harvard Divinity School. How did occasion and audience influence his presentation?
2. Miller implies certain goals in the education of students for the ministry. What are these goals and how far are they appropriate for other kinds of students? To what extent would he agree with the goals implied by Robert Frost in "Education by Poetry" (pp. 594–603)?
3. On page 1108, Miller mentions distinctions between truth and novelty, tradition and truth, appearance and reality, and the authentic and the popular. How are these distinctions important to his central idea and how are they developed, explicitly and implicitly, elsewhere in his address?
4. How does Miller use the metaphor from Melville's Moby Dick? For what purpose does he refer to it again later in his address?
5. On page 1107 Miller speaks of "the moral enthusiasm and respectability of the secular world." How does his use of the term "enthusiasm" here differ from Knox's (pp. 1098–1100)?
6. On page 1110 Miller distinguishes between "wisdom" and "a kind of lust for knowledge which accumulates a body of inert ideas in lieu of wisdom." Explain how closely this distinction corresponds to Perry's distinction between "bull" and "cow" (p. 208).
7. Compare Miller's view of "belief" with that of Charles Sanders Peirce (pp. 938–949).
8. Compare Miller's suggestions about the true function of religion in society with Thurber's satirical view of religion in society in "The Owl Who Was God" (pp. 1095–1096).

NICHOLAS OF CUSA
The Icon of God[1]

If I strive in human fashion to transport you to things divine, I must needs use a comparison of some kind. Now among men's works I have found no image better suited to our purposes than that of an image which is omnivoyant—its face, by the painter's cunning art, being made to appear as though looking on all around it. There are many excellent pictures of such faces—for example, that of the archeress in the market-place of Nuremberg; that by the eminent painter, Roger, in his priceless picture in the governor's house at Brussels; the Veronica in my chapel at Coblenz, and, in the castle of Brixen, the angel holding the arms of the Church, and many others elsewhere. Yet, lest ye should fail in the exercise, which requireth a figure of this description to be looked upon, I send for your indulgence such a picture as I have been able to procure, setting forth the figure of an omnivoyant, and this I call the icon of God.

This picture, brethren, ye shall set up in some place, let us say, on a north wall, and shall stand round it, a little way off, and look upon it. And each of you shall find that, from whatsoever quarter he regardeth it, it looketh upon him as if it looked on none other. And it shall seem to a brother standing to eastward as if that face looketh toward the east, while one to southward shall think it looketh toward the south, and one to westward, toward the west. First, then, ye will marvel how it can be that the face should look on all and each at the same time. For the imagination of him standing to eastward cannot conceive the gaze of the icon to be turned unto any other quarter, such as west or south. Then let the brother who stood to eastward place himself to westward and he will find its gaze fastened on him in the west just as it was afore in the east. And, as he knoweth the icon to be fixed and unmoved, he will marvel at the motion of its immovable gaze.

If now, while fixing his eye on the icon, he walk from west to east, he will find that its gaze continuously goeth along with him, and if he return from east to west, in like manner it will not leave him. Then will he marvel how, being motionless, it moveth, nor will his imagination be able to conceive that it should also move in like manner with one going in a contrary direction to himself. If he wish to experiment on this, he will cause one of his brethren to cross over from east to west, still looking on the icon, while he himself moveth from west to east; and he will ask the other as they meet if the gaze of the icon turn continuously with him; he will hear that it doth move in a contrary direction, even as with himself,

1. Preface to *The Vision of God*.

and he will believe him. But, had he not believed him, he could not have conceived this to be possible. So by his brother's showing he will come to know that the picture's face keepeth in sight all as they go on their way, though it be in contrary directions; and thus he will prove that that countenance, though motionless, is turned to east in the same way that it is simultaneously to west, and in the same way to north and to south, and alike to one particular place and to all objects at once, whereby it regardeth a single movement even as it regardeth all together. And while he observeth how that gaze never quitteth any, he seeth that it taketh such diligent care of each one who findeth himself observed as though it cared only for him, and for no other, and this to such a degree that one on whom it resteth cannot even conceive that it should take care of any other. He will also see that it taketh the same most diligent care of the least of creatures as of the greatest, and of the whole universe.

MATTHEW
Parables of the Kingdom[1]

The same day went Jesus out of the house, and sat by the sea side.

And great multitudes were gathered together unto him, so that he went into a ship, and sat; and the whole multitude stood on the shore.

And he spake many things unto them in parables, saying, Behold, a sower went forth to sow;

And when he sowed, some seeds fell by the way side, and the fowls came and devoured them up:

Some fell upon stony places, where they had not much earth: and forthwith they sprung up, because they had no deepness of earth:

And when the sun was up, they were scorched; and because they had no root, they withered away.

And some fell among thorns; and the thorns sprung up, and choked them:

But other fell into good ground, and brought forth fruit, some an hundredfold, some sixtyfold, some thirtyfold.

Who hath ears to hear, let him hear.

And the disciples came, and said unto him, Why speakest thou unto them in parables?

He answered and said unto them, Because it is given unto you to know the mysteries of the kingdom of heaven, but to them it is not given.

For whosoever hath, to him shall be given, and he shall have

1. Matthew xiii.

more abundance: but whosoever hath not, from him shall be taken away even that he hath.

Therefore speak I to them in parables: because they seeing see not; and hearing they hear not, neither do they understand.

And in them is fulfilled the prophecy of Esaias, which saith, By hearing ye shall hear, and shall not understand; and seeing ye shall see, and shall not perceive:

For this people's heart is waxed gross, and their ears are dull of hearing, and their eyes they have closed; lest at any time they should see with their eyes, and hear with their ears, and should understand with their heart, and should be converted, and I should heal them.

But blessed are your eyes, for they see: and your ears, for they hear.

For verily I say unto you, That many prophets and righteous men have desired to see those things which ye see, and have not seen them; and to hear those things which ye hear, and have not heard them.

Hear ye therefore the parable of the sower.

When any one heareth the word of the kingdom, and understandeth it not, then cometh the wicked one, and catcheth away that which was sown in his heart. This is he which received seed by the way side.

But he that received the seed into stony places, the same is he that heareth the word, and anon with joy receiveth it;

Yet hath he not root in himself, but dureth for a while: for when tribulation or persecution ariseth because of the word, by and by he is offended.

He also that received seed among the thorns is he that heareth the word; and the care of this world, and the deceitfulness of riches, choke the word, and he becometh unfruitful.

But he that received seed into the good ground is he that heareth the word, and understandeth it; which also beareth fruit, and bringeth forth, some an hundredfold, some sixty, some thirty.

Another parable put he forth unto them, saying, The kingdom of heaven is likened unto a man which sowed good seed in his field:

But while men slept, his enemy came and sowed tares among the wheat, and went his way.

But when the blade was sprung up, and brought forth fruit, then appeared the tares also.

So the servants of the householder came and said unto him, Sir, didst not thou sow good seed in thy field? from whence then hath it tares?

He said unto them, An enemy hath done this. The servants said unto him, Wilt thou then that we go and gather them up?

But he said, Nay; lest while ye gather up the tares, ye root up also the wheat with them.

Let both grow together until the harvest: and in the time of harvest I will say to the reapers, Gather ye together first the tares, and bind them in bundles to burn them: but gather the wheat into my barn.

Another parable put he forth unto them, saying, The kingdom of heaven is like to a grain of mustard seed, which a man took, and sowed in his field:

Which indeed is the least of all seeds: but when it is grown, it is the greatest among herbs, and becometh a tree, so that the birds of the air come and lodge in the branches thereof.

Another parable spake he unto them; The kingdom of heaven is like unto leaven, which a woman took, and hid in three measures of meal, till the whole was leavened.

All these things spake Jesus unto the multitude in parables; and without a parable spake he not unto them:

That it might be fulfilled which was spoken by the prophet, saying, I will open my mouth in parables; I will utter things which have been kept secret from the foundation of the world.

Then Jesus sent the multitude away, and went into the house: and his disciples came unto him, saying, Declare unto us the parable of the tares of the field.

He answered and said unto them, He that soweth the good seed is the Son of man;

The field is the world; the good seed are the children of the kingdom; but the tares are the children of the wicked one;

The enemy that sowed them is the devil; the harvest is the end of the world; and the reapers are the angels.

As therefore the tares are gathered and burned in the fire; so shall it be in the end of this world.

The Son of man shall send forth his angels, and they shall gather out of his kingdom all things that offend, and them which do iniquity;

And shall cast them into a furnace of fire: there shall be wailing and gnashing of teeth.

Then shall the righteous shine forth as the sun in the kingdom of their Father. Who hath ears to hear, let him hear.

Again, the kingdom of heaven is like unto treasure hid in a field; the which when a man hath found, he hideth, and for joy thereof goeth and selleth all that he hath, and buyeth that field.

Again, the kingdom of heaven is like unto a merchant man, seeking goodly pearls:

Who, when he had found one pearl of great price, went and sold all that he had, and bought it.

Again, the kingdom of heaven is like unto a net, that was cast into the sea, and gathered of every kind:

Which, when it was full, they drew to shore, and sat down, and gathered the good into vessels, but cast the bad away.

So shall it be at the end of the world: the angels shall come forth, and sever the wicked from among the just,

And shall cast them into the furnace of fire: there shall be wailing and gnashing of teeth.

Jesus saith unto them, Have ye understood all these things? They say unto him, Yea, Lord.

Then said he unto them, Therefore every scribe which is instructed unto the kingdom of heaven is like unto a man that is an householder, which bringeth forth out of his treasure things new and old.

And it came to pass, that when Jesus had finished these parables, he departed thence.

And when he was come into his own country, he taught them in their synagogue, insomuch that they were astonished, and said, Whence hath this man this wisdom, and these mighty works?

Is not this the carpenter's son? is not his mother called Mary? and his brethren, James, and Joses, and Simon, and Judas?

And his sisters, are they not all with us? Whence then hath this man all these things?

And they were offended in him. But Jesus said unto them, A prophet is not without honour, save in his own country, and in his own house.

And he did not many mighty works there because of their unbelief.

GERARD MANLEY HOPKINS
The Fall of God's First Kingdom

A.M.D.G.[1]

FOR SUNDAY EVENING JAN. 25 1880, SEPTUAGESIMA SUNDAY, AT ST. FRANCIS XAVIER'S, LIVERPOOL—on *the Fall of God's First Kingdom*—"Every kingdom divided against itself shall be made desolate and every city (commonwealth) or house divided against itself shall not stand (Matt. xii 25)."

I am to speak tonight of the fall of God's first kingdom, of the Fall of Man. Those of you who have heard this month's evening sermons will understand how this comes now in due course. God entered in the beginning into a contract with man that they two should make one commonwealth for their common good, which

---

1. Abbreviation for *Ad Maiorem Dei Gloriam,* "for the greater glory of God."

was that God might be glorified in man and man in God; God was the sovereign in this commonwealth and kingdom and man the subject; God by his providence, his laws and appointments and man by his obedience and execution of them undertook to bring this good about; both parties were bound by justice and in justice lived, which in man was called original justice, but lasted / [2] not long. It ended with the Fall, of which I am now to speak.

Before God was king of man he was king of angels and before man fell angels had fallen. Then man was made that he might fill the place of angels. But Satan, who had fallen through pride and selflove, resolved that through pride and selflove man should be brought to fall and that, whereas a breach had been made in God's kingdom in heaven, God's kingdom on earth should be broken utterly to pieces. And as he could not do it by force he would do it by fraud. Now the wise assailant attacks the weakest spot, therefore Satan tempted Eve the woman.

He chose his disguise, he spoke by the serpent's mouth; he watched his time, he found Eve alone. And here some say she should have been warned when she heard a dumb beast speaking reason. But of this we cannot be sure: St. Basil says that all the birds and beasts spoke in Paradise: not of course that they were not dumb and irrational creatures by nature then as now, but if a black spirit could speak by them so could a white and it may be that the angels made use of them as instruments to sing God's praises and to entertain man. Neither would Satan needlessly alarm the woman, rather than that he would invisibly have uttered voices in the air. But when she heard what the serpent said, *then* she should have taken alarm. So then to listen to a serpent speaking might be no blame; but how came Eve to be alone? for God had said of Adam /*It is not good for man to be alone: let us make him a helpmate like himself*/; and Eve was without the helpmate not like only but stronger than herself. She was deceived and Adam, as St. Paul tells us, was not nor would have been. Then why was Eve alone?

Now, I know, my brethren, that the Scripture does not tell us this and we cannot with certainty answer the question, but yet it is useful to ask it because it throws a great light on what God's first kingdom was and how it came to fall. Take notice then that, besides those things which we must do whether we like or no, which we cannot help doing, such as breathe, eat, and sleep, there are three sorts of things that we may lawfully do, that are right in us, that we are within our rights in doing. The first are *our bounden duties*, as to hear mass on Sunday: these God commands. The second are *what God sanctions* but does not command nor in any special way approve, as to amuse ourselves. The third are what God does not

2. This sign is used throughout the sermon as a rhetorical notation for phrasing to be used in its delivery.

command but specially approves when done, as to hear mass on a week-day: these are called works *of supererogation.* All these are good, not only the things God commands and the things he specially approves and accepts but also the things he only sanctions, for he sanctions nothing but what is good, that is to say / nothing but what is in itself harmless and which his sanction then makes positively good, and when a man says / *I do this because I like it and God allows me* / he submits himself to God as truly as if it were a duty and he said / *I do this because God wills it and commands me.* But though all are good they are not equally good; far from that. In the things God sanctions and we do for our own pleasure the whole good, the only good, comes from God's sanction and our submission to his sovereign will; for that he may reward us, but not for anything else: for the rest, we are doing our own pleasure and our own pleasure is our work's reward. But when we do what God commands or what God specially approves, then he is ready to reward us not only for our submission of ourselves to his sovereign will but also for the work done, for the pains taken; for we were doing *his* pleasure, not our own. Now you will easily understand, indeed you know, that it is the mark of a truly good will to do the good God approves of but does not bind us to, to do, in other words, works of supererogation: it shews that good is loved of itself and freely. And it is the mark of a cold heart, of poor will, I will not say a bad one, to do nothing that God especially approves, only what he commands or else sanctions: it shews that there is little love of good for good's sake. And though no one can be lost but for sin, yet those who do the least good they lawfully can are very likely indeed to fall into doing *less than that least* and so to sin. Now if this applies to us now / very strongly does it apply to man unfallen. For Adam and Eve though they were in God's kingdom not sovereign but subject, yet they were king and queen of all this earth, they were like vassal princes to a sovereign prince, God's honor was more in their hands than it is in any one of ours; we are but ourselves, they represented mankind, they represented the commons in God's commonwealth; if I dishonor God today one of you may make up by honoring him, but if they left him unhonored who was to honor him? the beasts and birds and fishes? When Adam obeyed God / mankind was obeying its sovereign; when Adam offered God of his own free will unbidden sacrifice / mankind was all engrossed in a work of supererogation, in giving God fresh glory; when Adam was doing his own pleasure / mankind was in its duty indeed but God's honor was not growing, the commonwealth was idle. Now, brethren, with this thought turn to Eve's temptation and look for what shall appear there.

Eve was alone. It was no sin to be alone, she was in her duty, God had given her freedom and she was wandering free, God had made her independent of her husband and she need not be at his side. Only God had made her for Adam's companion; it was her office, her work, the reason of her being to companion him and she was not doing it. There is no sin, but there is no delicacy of duty, no zeal for the sovereign's honor, no generosity, no supererogation. And Adam, he too was alone. He had been commanded to dress and keep Paradise. What flower, what fruitful tree, what living thing was there in Paradise so lovely as Eve, so fruitful as the mother of all flesh, that needed or could repay his tendance and his keeping as she? There was no sin; yet at the one fatal moment when of all the world care was wanted care was not forthcoming, the thing best worth keeping was unkept. And Eve stood by the forbidden tree, which God had bidden them not to eat of, which *she* said God had bidden them not even touch; she neither sinned nor was tempted to sin by standing near it, yet she would go to the very bounds and utmost border of her duty. To do so was not dangerous of itself, as it would be to us. When some child, one of Eve's poor daughters, stands by a peachtree, eyeing the blush of color on the fruit, fingering the velvet bloom upon it, breathing the rich smell, and in imagination tasting the sweet juice, the nearness, the mere neighborhood is enough to undo her, she looks and is tempted, she touches and is tempted more, she takes and tastes. But in Eve there was nothing of this; she was not mastered by concupiscence, *she* mastered *it*. There she stood, beautiful, innocent, with her original justice *and with nothing else*, nothing to stain it, but nothing to heighten and brighten it: she felt no cravings, for she was mistress of herself and would not let them rise; she felt no generous promptings, no liftings of the heart to give God glory, for she was mistress of herself and gave them no encouragement. Such was Eve before her fall.

Now, brethren, fancy, as you may, that rich tree all laden with its shining fragrant fruit and swaying down from one of its boughs, as the pythons and great snakes of the East do now, waiting for their prey to pass and then to crush it, swaying like a long spray of vine or the bine of a great creeper, not terrible but beauteous, lissome, marked with quaint streaks and eyes or flushed with rainbow colors, the Old Serpent. We must suppose he offered her the fruit, as though it were the homage and the tribute of the brute to man, of the subject to his queen, presented it with his mouth or swept it from the boughs down before her feet; and she declined it. Then came those studied words of double meaning the Scripture tells us of: *What! and has God forbidden you to eat of the fruit of Paradise?* Now mark her answer: you would expect her to reply: No, but of this one fruit only: he has given us free leave for all the trees in Paradise excepting one—but hear her: *Of the fruit of the trees in Paradise we do eat*—no mention of God's bounty here, it is all their freedom, what they do: "we do eat"—*but the fruit*

of the tree in the midst of Paradise—as though she would say /
of the best fruit of all—*God has commanded us not to eat of, nor
so much as touch it, or we shall die*: then she remembers God
when it is question of a stern and threatening law. She gave her
tempter the clue to his temptation—that God her sovereign was
a tyrant, a sullen lawgiver; that God her lord and landlord was
envious and grudging, a rackrent; that God her father, the author of
her being was a shadow of death. The serpent took the hint and
bettered it. Well was he called subtle: he does not put her suggestion into words and make it blacker; she would have been
shocked, she would have recoiled; he gives the thing another turn,
as much as to say: Why yes, God would be all this if you took his
law according to the letter. No no; what does "death" mean? you
will not die: you will die to ignorance, if you will, and wake to
wisdom: *God knows, on the day you eat of it your eyes will be
opened and you will be as gods, knowing good and evil.* And with
these words he dealt three blows at once against God's kingdom—
at God as a lawgiver and judge, at God as an owner or proprietor,
at God as a father; at God as a lawgiver and judge, for the Serpent
said / God has made this the tree of the knowledge of good and
evil, that is / which shall decide for him whether to call you good
or evil, good if you keep from it, evil if you touch it: be your
own lawgivers and judges of good and evil; be as God yourselves, be
divinely independent, why not? make it *good* to try the tree, *evil*
to leave it untasted; at God as a proprietor, for as owner of man
and the earth and all therein and sovereign of the commonwealth
God had given the other trees of Paradise to his subjects but
reserved this one to the crown: the Serpent advised them to trespass boldly on these rights and seize crown-property; and at God
as a father, for God like a fatherly providence found them food and
forbad them poison: the Serpent told them the deadly poison was
life-giving food. It was enough: Eve would judge for herself. She
saw that the tree was good to eat, that it was *not* poison, it was
the food of life—and here was the pride of life; *that it was beautiful to the eyes,* a becoming object to covet and possess—and
here was the desire of the eyes; *and that it was delightful to behold,*
that is / sweet and enjoyable in imagination even and forecast,
how much more in the eating and the reality!—and here was the
desire of the flesh; she freely yielded herself to the three con-
cupiscences; *she took and eat* of this devil's-sacrament; she rebelled,
she sinned, she fell.

She fell, but still God's kingdom was not fallen yet, because it
turned upon the man's obedience, not the woman's. Then came
the meeting between the husband and the wife and she learnt that
she was deceived and undone. Then her husband must share her
lot for better and worse; this selfish and fallen woman would drag

her husband in her fall, as she had had no thought of God's honor in her innocence, so in her sin she had no charity for her husband: she had so little love for him that she said, if he loved her he must share her lot. Most dearly he loved her, and she stood before him now lovely and her beauty heightened by distress, a thing never seen before in Paradise, herself a Tree of Knowledge of Good and Evil and offering him its fruit; herself a Tree of Life, the mother of all flesh to be. For he thought his hope of offspring would go with her. He was wrong: God, who gave back to Abraham for his obedience his all but sacrificed son, would have given back to Adam for his obedience his fallen wife; but he did not pause to make an act of hope. He listened to her voice. He left his heavenly father and clave to his wife and they two were in one fallen flesh; for her he took the stolen goods and harbored the forfeit person of the thief, rebelling against God, the world's great landlord, owner of earth and man, who had bestowed upon him Paradise, who had bestowed upon him the body of his wife; for her he eat the fatal fruit, making a new contract, a new commonwealth with Eve alone, and rebelling against God his lawgiver and judge. With that the contract with God was broken, the commonwealth undone, the kingdom divided and brought to desolation. God was left upon his throne but his subject had deserted to the enemy, God was left with his rights but the tenant had refused him payment, God was left a father but his children were turned to children of wrath. Then followed the disinheriting of the disobedient son; then followed the first and most terrible of evictions, when Cherubim swayed the fiery sword and man was turned from Paradise; then followed the judgment of death and the execution of the sentence which we feel yet. *Wretched men that we are, who shall deliver us from this body of death? The grace of God through Jesus Christ our Lord* (Rom. vii 24, 25.). *For the wages of sin are death, but the grace of God is eternal life in Christ Jesus our Lord* (ib. vi 23.), *a blessing etc.*)

L. D. S.[3]

3. Abbreviation for *Laus Deo Semper,* "glory to God for ever."

QUESTIONS FOR STUDY, DISCUSSION, AND WRITING

1. Compare Hopkins' account of the fall with the account in Genesis iii. How far does Hopkins' account go beyond the brief recital of the facts in Genesis? What justification does Hopkins have in Genesis for his interpretation? Does he add anything to it?
2. Hopkins speaks of God in the first part of his sermon as a "king" or "sovereign" who "entered . . . into a contract with man" and then later has Eve refer to Him as a "tyrant," a "sullen lawgiver," and a "landlord . . . a rackrent." What are the differences in con-

notation and denotation of these various metaphors for God? How does Hopkins use them to develop the central idea of his sermon?

3. What is the importance for the discourse of the threefold classification of "things that we may lawfully do"? What other examples might be given for each category?

4. Does Hopkins give Eve's case a fair hearing? Explain.

5. Hopkins said that when he delivered this sermon he was required (presumably by his superiors in the church) to "leave out or reword all passages speaking of God's kingdom as falling." How would these omissions affect the central idea and the forcefulness of the sermon?

6. In the light of his address "But Find the Point Again," what do you think Miller's comments on Hopkins' goals as a preacher and effectiveness as a speaker might be?

JOHN DONNE

Quis Homo?[1]

We are all conceived in close prison; in our Mothers wombs, we are close prisoners all; when we are born, we are born but to the liberty of the house[2]; prisoners still, though within larger walls; and then all our life is but a going out to the place of execution, to death. Now was there ever any man seen to sleep in the cart, between Newgate, and Tyburn?[3] Between the prison, and the place of execution, does any man sleep? And we sleep all the way; from the womb to the grave we are never thoroughly awake; but pass on with such dreams, and imaginations as these, I may live as well, as another, and why should I die, rather than another? But awake, and tell me, says this text *Quis homo?* Who is that other that thou talkest of? *What man is he that liveth, and shall not see death?*

1. "Who [is] the man?" From a sermon delivered at Easter communion, March 28, 1619, when the king was dangerously ill at Newmarket.
2. Donne distinguishes between a prisoner confined to a cell and one given somewhat more liberty.
3. London prisoners were taken in carts from Newgate prison to nearby Tyburn for execution.

JOHN DONNE

Let Me Wither

Let me wither and wear out mine age in a discomfortable, in an unwholesome, in a penurious prison, and so pay my debts with my bones, and recompense the wastefulness of my youth, with the beggary of mine age; Let me wither in a spittle under sharp, and foul, and infamous diseases, and so recompense the wantonness of my youth, with that loathsomeness in mine age; yet if God withdraw not his spiritual blessings, his grace, his patience, If I can call my suffering his doing, my passion his action, All this that is temporal, is but a caterpiller got into one corner of my garden, but a mildew fallen upon one acre of my corn; The body of all, the substance of all is safe, as long as the soul is safe. But when I shall trust to that, which we call a good spirit, and God shall deject, and impoverish, and evacuate that spirit, when I shall rely upon a moral constancy, and God shall shake, and enfeeble, and enervate, destroy and demolish that constancy; when I shall think to refresh my self in the serenity and sweet air of a good conscience, and God shall call up the damps and vapors of hell itself, and spread a cloud of diffidence, and an impenetrable crust of desperation upon my conscience; when health shall fly from me, and I shall lay hold upon riches to succor me, and comfort me in my sickness, and riches shall fly from me, and I shall snatch after favor, and good opinion, to comfort me in my poverty; when even this good opinion shall leave me, and calumnies and misinformations shall prevail against me; when I shall need peace, because there is none but thou, O Lord, that should stand for me, and then shall find, that all the wounds that I have, come from thy hand, all the arrows that stick in me, from thy quiver; when I shall see, that because I have given my self to my corrupt nature, thou hast changed thine; and because I am all evil toward thee, therefore thou hast given over being good toward me; When it comes to this height, that the fever is not in the humors, but in the spirits,[1] that mine enemy is not an imaginary enemy, fortune, nor a transitory enemy, malice in great persons, but a real, and an irresistible, and an inexorable, and an everlasting enemy, The Lord of Hosts himself, The Almighty God himself, the Almighty God himself only knows the weight of this affliction, and except he put in that *pondus gloriae*, that exceeding weight of an eternal glory, with his own hand, into the other scale, we are weighed down, we are swallowed up, irreparably, irrevocably, irrecoverably, irremediably.

QUESTIONS FOR STUDY, DISCUSSION, AND WRITING

Both Hopkins and Donne are more famous as poets than as preachers, yet all that any author writes will in one way or another bear the stamp of his thought and personality. Read the following poems, one by Donne, one by Hopkins, and compare the poems to sermons. Does the conception of God suggested by each poem resemble that in the sermon by the same author? Do the poems accomplish any of the same purposes as the sermons? Are the sermons "poetic" in any way? What differences arise from the fact that

1. Not in one of the four chief fluids of the body or "humors" (blood, yellow bile, phlegm, and black bile), but in the more subtle fluids.

in the sermons both are speaking to congregations, in the poems both are addressing God?

Thou art indeed just, Lord, if I contend
With thee; but, sir, so what I plead is just.
Why do sinners' ways prosper? and why must
Disappointment all I endeavour end?
    Wert thou my enemy, O thou my friend,
How wouldst thou worse, I wonder, than thou dost
Defeat, thwart me? Oh, the sots and thralls of lust
Do in spare hours more thrive than I that spend,
Sir, life upon thy cause. See, banks and brakes
Now, leavèd how thick! lacèd they are again
With fretty chervil, look, and fresh wind shakes
Them; birds build—but not I build; no, but strain,
Time's eunuch, and not breed one work that wakes.
Mine, O thou lord of life, send my roots rain.

                    —GERARD MANLEY HOPKINS

Batter my heart, three person'd God; for, you
As yet but knocke, breathe, shine, and seeke to mend.
That I may rise, and stand, o'erthrow mee, and bend
Your force, to breake, blowe, burn and make me new.
I, like an usurpt towne, to another due,
Labour to admit you, but Oh, to no end,
Reason your viceroy in mee, mee should defend,
But is captiv'd, and proves weake or untrue.
Yet dearely I love you, and would be loved faine,
But am bethroth'd unto your enemie;
Divorce mee, untie, or breake that knot againe,
Take mee to you, imprison mee, for I
Except you enthrall mee, never shall be free,
Nor ever chast, except you ravish mee.

                          —JOHN DONNE

JONATHAN EDWARDS

Sinners in the Hands of an Angry God[1]

Their foot shall slide in due time.[2]
—DEUT. xxxii. 35

    In this verse is threatened the vengeance of God on the wicked unbelieving Israelites, who were God's visible people, and who lived under the means of grace; but who, notwithstanding all God's

1. Only the first part of the sermon is printed here; the "application" is omitted.

2. The complete verse reads: "To me belongeth vengeance, and recompence; their foot shall slide in due time: for the day of their calamity is at hand, and the things that shall come upon them make haste." It occurs in the middle of a long denunciatory "song" spoken by Moses to the Israelites.

wonderful works towards them, remained (as ver. 28.)[3] void of counsel, having no understanding in them. Under all the cultivations of heaven, they brought forth bitter and poisonous fruit; as in the two verses next preceding the text. The expression I have chosen for my text, *Their foot shall slide in due time*, seems to imply the following things, relating to the punishment and destruction to which these wicked Israelites were exposed.

1. That they were always exposed to *destruction*; as one that stands or walks in slippery places is always exposed to fall. This is implied in the manner of their destruction coming upon them, being represented by their foot sliding. The same is expressed, Psalm lxxiii. 18. "Surely thou didst set them in slippery places; thou castedst them down into destruction."

2. It implies that they were always exposed to sudden unexpected destruction. As he that walks in slippery places is every moment liable to fall, he cannot foresee one moment whether he shall stand or fall the next; and when he does fall, he falls at once without warning: Which is also expressed in Psalm lxxiii. 18, 19. "Surely thou didst set them in slippery places; thou castedst them down into destruction. How are they brought into desolation as in a moment!"

3. Another thing implied is, that they are liable to fall of *themselves*, without being thrown down by the hand of another; as he that stands or walks on slippery ground needs nothing but his own weight to throw him down.

4. That the reason why they are not fallen already, and do not fall now, is only that God's appointed time is not come. For it is said, that when that due time, or appointed time comes, *their foot shall slide*. Then they shall be left to fall, as they are inclined by their own weight. God will not hold them up in these slippery places any longer, but will let them go; and then, at that very instant, they shall fall into destruction; as he that stands on such slippery declining ground, on the edge of a pit, he cannot stand alone, when he is let go he immediately falls and is lost.

The observation from the words that I would now insist upon is this—"There is nothing that keeps wicked men at any one moment out of hell, but the mere pleasure of God"—By the *mere* pleasure of God, I mean his *sovereign* pleasure, his arbitrary will, restrained by no obligation, hindered by no manner of difficulty, any more than if nothing else but God's mere will had in the least degree, or in any respect whatsoever, any hand in the preservation of wicked men one moment. The truth of this observation may appear by the following considerations.

1. There is no want of *power* in God to cast wicked men into hell at any moment. Men's hands cannot be strong when God rises up.

---

3. Verse 28: "For they are a nation void of counsel, neither is there any understanding in them."

The strongest have no power to resist him, nor can any deliver out of his hands. He is not only able to cast wicked men into hell, but he can most easily do it. Sometimes an earthly prince meets with a great deal of difficulty to subdue a rebel, who has found means to fortify himself, and has made himself strong by the numbers of his followers. But it is not so with God. There is no fortress that is any defense from the power of God. Though hand join in hand, and vast multitudes of God's enemies combine and associate themselves, they are easily broken in pieces. They are as great heaps of light chaff before the whirlwind; or large quantities of dry stubble before devouring flames. We find it easy to tread on and crush a worm that we see crawling on the earth; so it is easy for us to cut or singe a slender thread that any thing hangs by: thus easy is it for God, when he pleases, to cast his enemies down to hell. What are we, that we should think to stand before him, at whose rebuke the earth trembles, and before whom the rocks are thrown down?

2. They *deserve* to be cast into hell; so that divine justice never stands in the way, it makes no objection against God's using his power at any moment to destroy them. Yea, on the contrary, justice calls aloud for an infinite punishment of their sins. Divine justice says of the tree that brings forth such grapes of Sodom, "Cut it down, why cumbereth it the ground?" Luke xiii. 7. The sword of divine justice is every moment brandished over their heads, and it is nothing but the hand of arbitrary mercy, and God's mere will, that holds it back.

3. They are already under a sentence of *condemnation* to hell. They do not only justly deserve to be cast down thither, but the sentence of the law of God, that eternal and immutable rule of righteousness that God has fixed between him and mankind, is gone out against them, and stands against them; so that they are bound over already to hell. John iii. 18. "He that believeth not is condemned already." So that every unconverted man properly belongs to hell; that is his place; from thence he is, John viii. 23. "Ye are from beneath:" And thither he is bound; it is the place that justice, and God's word, and the sentence of his unchangeable law assign to him.

4. They are now the objects of that very same *anger* and wrath of God, that is expressed in the torments of hell. And the reason why they do not go down to hell at each moment, is not because God, in whose power they are, is not then very angry with them; as he is with many miserable creatures now tormented in hell, who there feel and bear the fierceness of his wrath. Yea, God is a great deal more angry with great numbers that are now on earth; yea, doubtless, with many that are now in this congregation, who it may be are at ease, than he is with many of those who are now in the flames of hell.

So that it is not because God is unmindful of their wickedness, and does not resent it, that he does not let loose his hand and cut them off. God is not altogether such an one as themselves, though they may imagine him to be so. The wrath of God burns against them, their damnation does not slumber; the pit is prepared, the fire is made ready, the furnace is now hot, ready to receive them; the flames do now rage and glow. The glittering sword is whet, and held over them, and the pit hath opened its mouth under them.

5. The *devil* stands ready to fall upon them, and seize them as his own, at what moment God shall permit him. They belong to him; he has their souls in his possession, and under his dominion. The scripture represents them as his goods, Luke xi. 12. The devils watch them; they are ever by them at their right hand; they stand waiting for them, like greedy hungry lions that see their prey, and expect to have it, but are for the present kept back. If God should withdraw his hand, by which they are restrained, they would in one moment fly upon their poor souls. The old serpent is gaping for them; hell opens its mouth wide to receive them; and if God should permit it, they would be hastily swallowed up and lost.

6. There are in the souls of wicked men those hellish *principles* reigning, that would presently kindle and flame out into hell fire, if it were not for God's restraints. There is laid in the very nature of carnal men, a foundation for the torments of hell. There are those corrupt principles, in reigning power in them, and in full possession of them, that are seeds of hell fire. These principles are active and powerful, exceeding violent in their nature, and if it were not for the restraining hand of God upon them, they would soon break out, they would flame out after the same manner as the same corruptions, the same enmity does in the hearts of damned souls, and would beget the same torments as they do in them. The souls of the wicked are in scripture compared to the troubled sea, Isa. lvii. 20. For the present, God restrains their wickedness by his mighty power, as he does the raging waves of the troubled sea, saying, "Hitherto shalt thou come, but no further;" but if God should withdraw that restraining power, it would soon carry all before it. Sin is the ruin and misery of the soul; it is destructive in its nature; and if God should leave it without restraint, there would need nothing else to make the soul perfectly miserable. The corruption of the heart of man is immoderate and boundless in its fury; and while wicked men live here, it is like fire pent up by God's restraints, whereas if it were let loose, it would set on fire the course of nature; and as the heart is now a sink of sin, so if sin was not restrained, it would immediately turn the soul into a fiery oven, or a furnace of fire and brimstone.

7. It is no security to wicked men for one moment, that there are no visible means of death at hand. It is no security to a natural

man, that he is now in health, and that he does not see which way he should now immediately go out of the world by any accident, and that there is no visible danger in any respect in his circumstances. The manifold and continual experience of the world in all ages, shows this is no evidence, that a man is not on the very brink of eternity, and that the next step will not be into another world. The unseen, unthought-of ways and means of persons going suddenly out of the world are innumerable and inconceivable. Unconverted men walk over the pit of hell on a rotten covering, and there are innumerable places in this covering so weak that they will not bear their weight, and these places are not seen. The arrows of death fly unseen at noon-day; the sharpest sight cannot discern them. God has so many different unsearchable ways of taking wicked men out of the world and sending them to hell, that there is nothing to make it appear, that God had need to be at the expense of a miracle, or go out of the ordinary course of his providence, to destroy any wicked man, at any moment. All the means that there are of sinners going out of the world, are so in God's hands, and so universally and absolutely subject to his power and determination, that it does not depend at all the less on the mere will of God, whether sinners shall at any moment go to hell, than if means were never made use of, or at all concerned in the case.

8. Natural men's prudence and care to preserve their own lives, or the care of others to preserve them, do not secure them a moment. To this, divine providence and universal experience do also bear testimony. There is this clear evidence that men's own wisdom is no security to them from death; that if it were otherwise we should see some difference between the wise and politic men of the world, and others, with regard to their liableness to early and unexpected death: but how is it in fact? Eccles. ii. 16. "How dieth the wise man? even as the fool."

9. All wicked men's pains and *contrivance* which they use to escape hell, while they continue to reject Christ, and so remain wicked men, do not secure them from hell one moment. Almost every natural man that hears of hell, flatters himself that he shall escape it; he depends upon himself for his own security; he flatters himself in what he has done, in what he is now doing, or what he intends to do. Every one lays out matters in his own mind how he shall avoid damnation, and flatters himself that he contrives well for himself, and that his schemes will not fail. They hear indeed that there are but few saved, and that the greater part of men that have died heretofore are gone to hell; but each one imagines that he lays out matters better for his own escape than others have done. He does not intend to come to that place of torment; he says within himself, that he intends to take effectual care, and to order matters so for himself as not to fail.

But the foolish children of men miserably delude themselves in their own schemes, and in confidence in their own strength and wisdom; they trust to nothing but a shadow. The greater part of those who heretofore have lived under the same means of grace, and are now dead, are undoubtedly gone to hell; and it was not because they were not as wise as those who are now alive: it was not because they did not lay out matters as well for themselves to secure their own escape. If we could speak with them, and inquire of them, one by one, whether they expected, when alive, and when they used to hear about hell, ever to be the subjects of that misery: we doubtless, should hear one and another reply, "No, I never intended to come here: I had laid out matters otherwise in my mind; I thought I should contrive well for myself: I thought my scheme good. I intended to take effectual care; but it came upon me unexpected; I did not look for it at that time, and in that manner; it came as a thief: Death outwitted me: God's wrath was too quick for me. Oh, my cursed foolishness! I was flattering myself, and pleasing myself with vain dreams of what I would do hereafter; and when I was saying, Peace and safety, then suddenly destruction came upon me."

10. God has laid himself under *no* obligation, by any promise to keep any natural man out of hell one moment. God certainly has made no promises either of eternal life, or of any deliverance or preservation from eternal death, but what are contained in the covenant of grace, the promises that are given in Christ, in whom all the promises are yea and amen. But surely they have no interest in the promises of the covenant of grace who are not the children of the covenant, who do not believe in any of the promises, and have no interest in the Mediator of the covenant.

So that, whatever some have imagined and pretended about promises made to natural men's earnest seeking and knocking, it is plain and manifest, that whatever pains a natural man takes in religion, whatever prayers he makes, till he believes in Christ, God is under no manner of obligation to keep him a moment from eternal destruction.

So that, thus it is that natural men are held in the hand of God, over the pit of hell; they have deserved the fiery pit, and are already sentenced to it; and God is dreadfully provoked, his anger is as great towards them as to those that are actually suffering the executions of the fierceness of his wrath in hell, and they have done nothing in the least to appease or abate that anger, neither is God in the least bound by any promise to hold them up one moment; the devil is waiting for them, hell is gaping for them, the flames gather and flash about them, and would fain lay hold on them, and swallow them up; the fire pent up in their own hearts is struggling to break out: and they have no interest in any Mediator, there are no means within reach that can be any security to them. In short, they have no refuge, nothing to take hold of; all that preserves them every moment is in the mere arbitrary will, and uncovenanted, unobliged forbearance of an incensed God.

QUESTIONS FOR STUDY, DISCUSSION, AND WRITING

1. Trace the steps by which Edwards gets from his text to his various conclusions about man's state. Are they all logical? What assumptions does he add to those implied by the text in developing his argument? (Before answering these questions you will probably want to check the entire context of the text in Deuteronomy xxxii.)
2. What kinds of evidence does Edwards use in supporting his argument? Are they equally valid?
3. How do the concrete details, the imagery, and the metaphors that Edwards uses contribute to the effectiveness of his argument?
4. Compare Edwards' method with that of the preacher in Joyce, "The Spiritual Torments of Hell" (pp. 1132–1138). Do the two preachers use the same kinds of arguments? Do they develop and support their arguments in the same way? Which is the more effective, and why?
5. One might make the assumption that a society's conception of hell reflects, at least indirectly, some of that society's positive values. What positive values are reflected in Edwards' picture of hell? Explain whether the same positive values are reflected in Joyce's hell.
6. Edwards' sermon was delivered to a congregation, exhorting them to virtue; the sermon in the selection from Joyce (pp. 1132–1138) occurs in a work of fiction and illustrates the effects of a moving experience upon a young boy. Could the two sermons be exchanged and remain equally effective for their purposes? Explain.
7. What can you deduce about the nature of the congregations that Edwards and Hopkins (pp. 1117–1122) are preaching to? About differences between the two men?
8. One of his pupils described Edwards' delivery: "His appearance in the desk was with a good grace, and his delivery easy, natural and very solemn. He had not a strong, loud voice, but appeared with such gravity and solemnity, and spake with such distinctness and precision, his words were so full of ideas, set in such a plain and striking light, that few speakers have been so able to demand the attention of an audience as he. His words often discovered a great degree of inward fervor, without much noise or external emotion, and fell with great weight on the minds of his hearers. He made but little motion of his head or hands in the desk, but spake as to discover the motion of his own heart, which tended in the most natural and effectual manner to move and affect others." Would this manner of delivery be effective for the sermon printed here?

JAMES JOYCE
The Spiritual Torments of Hell[1]

The preacher began to speak in a quiet friendly tone. His face was kind and he joined gently the fingers of each hand, forming a frail cage by the union of their tips.

—This morning we endeavored, in our reflection upon hell, to make what our holy founder calls in his book of spiritual exercises, the composition of place. We endeavored, that is, to imagine with the senses of the mind, in our imagination, the material character of that awful place and of the physical torments which all who are in hell endure. This evening we shall consider for a few moments the nature of the spiritual torments of hell.

—Sin, remember, is a twofold enormity. It is a base consent to the promptings of our corrupt nature to the lower instincts, to that which is gross and beastlike; and it is also a turning away from the counsel of our higher nature, from all that is pure and holy, from the Holy God Himself. For this reason mortal sin is punished in hell by two different forms of punishment, physical and spiritual.

Now of all these spiritual pains by far the greatest is the pain of loss, so great, in fact, that in itself it is a torment greater than all the others. Saint Thomas, the greatest doctor of the Church, the angelic doctor, as he is called, says that the worst damnation consists in this that the understanding of man in totally deprived of divine light and his affection obstinately turned away from the goodness of God. God, remember, is a being infinitely good and therefore the loss of such a being must be a loss infinitely painful. In this life we have not a very clear idea of what such a loss must be but the damned in hell, for their greater torment, have a full understanding of that which they have lost and understand that they have lost it through their own sins and have lost it for ever. At the very instant of death the bonds of the flesh are broken asunder and the soul at once flies towards God as towards the center of her existence. Remember, my dear little boys, our souls long to be with God. We come from God, we live by God, we belong to God: we are His, inalienably His. God loves with a divine love every human soul and every human soul lives in that love. How could it be otherwise? Every breath that we draw, every thought of our brain, every instant of life proceed from God's inexhaustible goodness. And if it be pain for a mother to be parted from her child, for a man to be exiled from hearth and home, for friend to be sundered

---

1. Part of a sermon preached at the retreat which Stephen Dedalus attends in *A Portrait of the Artist as a Young Man*, 1916.

from friend, O think what pain, what anguish, it must be for the poor soul to be spurned from the presence of the supremely good and loving Creator Who has called that soul into existence from nothingness and sustained it in life and loved it with an immeasurable love. This, then, to be separated for ever from its greatest good, from God, and to feel the anguish of that separation, knowing full well that it is unchangeable, this is the greatest torment which the created soul is capable of bearing, *poena damni*, the pain of loss.

The second pain which will afflict the souls of the damned in hell is the pain of conscience. Just as in dead bodies worms are engendered by putrefaction so in the souls of the lost there arises a perpetual remorse from the putrefaction of sin, the sting of conscience, the worm, as Pope Innocent the Third calls it, of the triple sting. The first sting inflicted by this cruel worm will be the memory of past pleasures. O what a dreadful memory will that be! In the lake of alldevouring flame the proud king will remember the pomps of his court, the wise but wicked man his libraries and instruments of research, the lover of artistic pleasures his marbles and pictures and other art treasures, he who delighted in the pleasures of the table his gorgeous feasts, his dishes prepared with such delicacy, his choice of wines, the miser will remember his hoard of gold, the robber his illgotten wealth, the angry and revengeful and merciless murderers their deeds of blood and violence in which they revelled, the impure and adulterous the unspeakable and filthy pleasures in which they delighted. They will remember all this and loathe themselves and their sins. For how miserable will all those pleasures seem to the soul condemned to suffer in hellfire for ages and ages. How they will rage and fume to think that they have lost the bliss of heaven for the dross of earth, for a few pieces of metal, for vain honours, for bodily comforts, for a tingling of the nerves. They will repent indeed: and this is the second sting of the worm of conscience, a late and fruitless sorrow for sins committed. Divine justice insists that the understanding of those miserable wretches be fixed continually on the sins of which they were guilty and moreover, as Saint Augustine points out, God will impart to them His own knowledge of sin so that sin will appear to them in all its hideous malice as it appears to the eyes of God Himself. They will behold their sins in all their foulness and repent but it will be too late and then they will bewail the good occasions which they neglected. This is the last and deepest and most cruel sting of the worm of conscience. The conscience will say: You had time and opportunity to repent and would not. You were brought up religiously by your parents. You had the sacraments and graces and indulgences of the church to aid you. You had the minister of God to preach to you, to call you back when you had strayed, to forgive you your sins, no matter how many, how abominable, if only you had confessed and repented. No. You would not. You flouted the ministers of holy religion, you turned your back on the confessional, you wallowed deeper and deeper in the mire of sin. God appealed to you, threatened you, entreated you to return to Him. O, what shame, what misery! The Ruler of the universe entreated you, a creature of clay, to love Him Who made you and to keep His law. No. You would not. And now, though you were to flood all hell with your tears if you could still weep, all that sea of repentance would not gain for you what a single tear of true repentance shed during your mortal life would have gained for you. You implore now a moment of earthly life wherein to repent: in vain. That time is gone: gone for ever.

—Such is the threefold sting of conscience, the viper which gnaws the very heart's core of the wretches in hell so that filled with hellish fury they curse themselves for their folly and curse the evil companions who have brought them to such ruin and curse the devils who tempted them in life and now mock them in eternity and even revile and curse the Supreme Being Whose goodness and patience they scorned and slighted but Whose justice and power they cannot evade.

—The next spiritual pain to which the damned are subjected is the pain of extension. Man, in this earthly life, though he be capable of many evils, is not capable of them all at once inasmuch as one evil corrects and counteracts another, just as one poison frequently corrects another. In hell, on the contrary, one torment instead of counteracting another, lends it still greater force: and, moreover, as the internal faculties are more perfect than the external senses, so are they more capable of suffering. Just as every sense is afflicted with a fitting torment so is every spiritual faculty; the fancy with horrible images, the sensitive faculty with alternate longing and rage, the mind and understanding with an interior darkness more terrible even than the exterior darkness which reigns in that dreadful prison. The malice, impotent though it be, which possesses these demon souls is an evil of boundless extension, of limitless duration, a rightful state of wickedness which we can scarcely realize unless we bear in mind the enormity of sin and the hatred God bears to it.

—Opposed to this pain of extension and yet co-existent with it we have the pain of intensity. Hell is the center of evils and, as you know, things are more intense at their centers than at their remotest points. There are no contraries or admixtures of any kind to temper or soften in the least the pains of hell. Nay, things which are good in themselves become evil in hell. Company, elsewhere a source of comfort to the afflicted, will be there a continual torment: knowledge, so much longed for as the chief good of the intellect, will there be hated worse than ignorance: light, so much coveted by all creatures from the lord of creation down to the humblest plant in the forest, will be loathed intensely. In this life our sorrows are either not very long or not very great because nature either overcomes them by habits or puts an end to them by sinking under their weight. But in hell the torments cannot be overcome by habit, for while they are of terrible intensity they are at the same time of continual variety, each pain, so to speak, taking fire from another and reendowing that which has enkindled it with a still fiercer flame. Nor can nature escape from these intense and various tortures by succumbing to them for the soul is sustained and maintained in evil so that its suffering may be the greater. Boundless extension of torment, incredible intensity of suffering, unceasing variety of torture—this is what the divine majesty, so outraged by sinners, demands, this is what the holiness of heaven, slighted and set aside for the lustful and low pleasures of the corrupt flesh, requires, this is what the blood of the innocent Lamb of God, shed for the redemption of sinners, trampled upon by the vilest of the vile, insists upon.

—Last and crowning torture of all the tortures of that awful place is the eternity of hell. Eternity! O, dread and dire word. Eternity! What mind of man can understand it? And remember, it is an eternity of pain. Even though the pains of hell were not so terrible as they are yet they would become infinite as they are destined to last for ever. But while they are everlasting they are at the same time, as you know, intolerably intense, unbearably extensive. To bear even the sting of an insect for all eternity would be a dreadful torment. What must it be, then, to bear the manifold tortures of hell for ever? For ever! For all eternity! Not for a year or for an age but for ever. Try to imagine the awful meaning of this. You have often seen the sand on the seashore. How fine are its tiny grains! And how many of those tiny little grains go to make up the small handful which a child grasps in its play. Now imagine a mountain of that sand, a million miles high, reaching from the earth to the farthest heavens, and a million miles broad, extending to remotest space, and a million miles in thickness: and imagine such an enormous mass of countless particles of sand multiplied as often as there are leaves in the forest, drops of water in the mighty ocean, feathers on birds, scales on fish, hairs on animals, atoms in the vast expanse of the air: and imagine that at the end of every million years a little bird came to that mountain and carried away in its beak a tiny grain of that sand. How many millions upon millions of centuries would pass before that bird had carried away even a square foot of that mountain, how many eons upon eons of ages before it had carried away all. Yet at the end of that immense stretch of time not even one instant of eternity could be said to have ended. At the end of all those billions and trillions of years eternity would have scarcely begun. And if that mountain rose again after it had been all carried away and if the bird came again and carried it all away again grain by grain: and if it so rose and sank as many times as there are stars in the sky, atoms in the air, drops of water in the sea, leaves on the trees, feathers upon birds, scales upon fish, hairs upon animals, at the end of all those innumerable risings and sinkings of that immeasurably vast mountain not one single instant of eternity could be said to have ended; even then, at the end of such a period, after that eon of time the mere thought of which makes our very brain reel dizzily, eternity would scarcely have begun.

—A holy saint (one of our own fathers I believe it was) was once vouchsafed a vision of hell. It seemed to him that he stood in the midst of a great hall, dark and silent save for the ticking of a great clock. The ticking went on unceasingly; and it seemed to this saint that the sound of the ticking was the ceaseless repetition of the words: ever, never; ever, never. Ever to be in hell, never to be in heaven; ever to be shut off from the presence of God, never to enjoy the beatific vision; ever to be eaten with flames, gnawed by vermin, goaded with burning spikes, never to be free from those pains; ever to have the conscience upbraid one, the memory enrage, the mind filled with darkness and despair, never to escape; ever to curse and revile the foul demons who gloat fiendishly over the misery of their dupes, never to behold the shining raiment of the blessed spirits; ever to cry out of the abyss of fire to God for an instant, a single instant, of respite from such awful agony, never to receive, even for an instant, God's pardon; ever to suffer, never to enjoy; ever to be damned, never to be saved; ever, never; ever, never. O, what a dreadful punishment! An eternity of endless agony, of endless bodily and spiritual torment, without one ray of hope, without one moment of cessation, of agony limitless in intensity, of torment infinitely varied, of torture that sustains eternally that which it eternally devours, of anguish that everlastingly preys upon the spirit while it racks the flesh, an eternity, every instant of which is itself an eternity of woe. Such is the terrible punishment decreed for those who die in mortal sin by an almighty and a just God.

—Yes, a just God! Men, reasoning always as men, are astonished that God should mete out an everlasting and infinite punishment in the fires of hell for a single grievous sin. They reason thus because, blinded by the gross illusion of the flesh and the darkness of human understanding, they are unable to comprehend the hideous malice of mortal sin. They reason thus because they are unable to comprehend that even venial sin is of such a foul and hideous nature that even if the omnipotent Creator could end all the evil and misery in the world, the wars, the diseases, the robberies, the crimes, the deaths, the murders, on condition that he allowed a single venial sin to pass unpunished, a single venial sin, a lie, an angry look, a moment of willful sloth, He, the great omnipotent God could not do so because sin, be it in thought or deed, is a transgression of His law and God would not be God if He did not punish the transgressor.

—A sin, an instant of rebellious pride of the intellect, made Lucifer and a third part of the cohorts of angels fall from their glory. A sin, an instant of folly and weakness, drove Adam and Eve out of Eden and brought death and suffering into the world. To retrieve the consequences of that sin the Only Begotten Son of God came down to earth, lived and suffered and died a most painful death, hanging for three hours on the cross.

—O, my dear little brethren in Christ Jesus, will we then offend that good Redeemer and provoke His anger? Will we trample again upon that torn and mangled corpse? Will we spit upon that face so full of sorrow and love? Will we too, like the cruel Jews and the brutal soldiers, mock that gentle and compassionate Saviour Who trod alone for our sake the awful winepress of sorrow? Every word of sin is a wound in His tender side. Every sinful act is a thorn piercing His head. Every impure thought, deliberately yielded to, is a keen lance transfixing that sacred and loving heart. No, no. It is impossible for any human being to do that which offends so deeply the divine Majesty, that which is punished by an eternity of agony, that which crucifies again the Son of God and makes a mockery of Him.

—I pray to God that my poor words may have availed today to confirm in holiness those who are in a state of grace, to strengthen the wavering, to lead back to the state of grace the poor soul that has strayed if any such be among you. I pray to God, and do you pray with me, that we may repent of our sins. I will ask you now, all of you, to repeat after me the act of contrition, kneeling here in this humble chapel in the presence of God. He is there in the tabernacle burning with love for mankind, ready to comfort the afflicted. Be not afraid. No matter how many or how foul the sins if only you repent of them they will be forgiven you. Let no worldly shame hold you back. God is still the merciful Lord who wishes not the eternal death of the sinner but rather that he be converted and live.

—He calls you to Him. You are His. He made you out of nothing. He loved you as only a God can love. His arms are open to receive you even though you have sinned against Him. Come to Him, poor sinner, poor vain and erring sinner. Now is the acceptable time. Now is the hour.

The priest rose and turning towards the altar knelt upon the step before the tabernacle in the fallen gloom. He waited till all in the chapel had knelt and every least noise was still. Then, raising his head, he repeated the act of contrition, phrase by phrase, with fervor. The boys answered him phrase by phrase. Stephen, his tongue cleaving to his palate, bowed his head, praying with his heart.

> —*O my God!*—
> —*O my God!*—
> —*I am heartily sorry*—
> —*I am heartily sorry*—
> —*for having offended Thee*—
> —*for having offended Thee*—
> —*and I detest my sins*—
> —*and I detest my sins*—
> —*above every other evil*—
> —*above every other evil*—
> —*because they displease Thee, my God*—
> —*because they displease Thee, my God*—
> —*Who are so deserving*—
> —*Who are so deserving*—
> —*of all my love*—
> —*of all my love*—
> —*and I firmly purpose*—
> —*and I firmly purpose*—
> —*by Thy Holy grace*—
> —*by Thy Holy grace*—
> —*never more to offend Thee*—
> —*never more to offend Thee*—
> —*and to amend my life*—
> —*and to amend my life*—

PAUL TILLICH

The Riddle of Inequality

> For to him who has will more be given; and from him
> who has not, even what he has will be taken away.
>
> —MARK iv. 25

One day a learned colleague called me up and said to me with angry excitement: "There is a saying in the New Testament which I consider to be one of the most immoral and unjust statements ever made!" And then he started quoting our text: "To him who has will more be given," and his anger increased when he continued:

"and from him who has not, even what he has will be taken away."
We all, I think, feel offended with him. And we cannot easily
ignore the offense by suggesting what *he* suggested—that the
words may be due to a misunderstanding of the disciples. It appears
at least four times in the gospels with great emphasis. And even
more, we can clearly see that the writers of the gospels felt exactly
as we do. For them it was a stumbling block, which they tried to
interpret in different ways. Probably none of these explanations satisfied them fully, for with this saying of Jesus, we are confronted
immediately with the greatest and perhaps most painful riddle of
life, that of the inequality of all beings. We certainly cannot hope to
solve it when neither the Bible nor any other of the great religions
and philosophies was able to do so. But we can do two things: We
can show the breadth and the depth of the riddle of inequality and
we can try to find a way to live with it, even if it is unsolved.

I

If we hear the words, "to him who has will more be given," we
ask ourselves: What *do* we have? And then we may find that much is
given to us in terms of external goods, of friends, of intellectual
gifts and even of a comparatively high moral level of action. So we
can expect that more will be given to us, while we must expect
that those who are lacking in all that will lose the little they already
have. Even further, according to Jesus' parable, the one talent they
have will be given to us who have five or ten talents. We shall be
richer because they will be poorer. We may cry out against such
an injustice. But we cannot deny that life confirms it abundantly.
We cannot deny it, but we can ask the question, do we *really*
have what we believe we have so that it cannot be taken from
us? It is a question full of anxiety, confirmed by a version of our
text rendered by Luke. "From him who has not, even what he
thinks that he has will be taken away." Perhaps our having of those
many things is not the kind of having which is increased. Perhaps
the having of few things by the poor ones is the kind of having
which makes them grow. In the parable of the talents, Jesus confirms this. Those talents which are used, even with a risk of losing
them, are those which we really have; those which we try to preserve without using them for growth are those which we do not
really have and which are being taken away from us. They slowly
disappear, and suddenly we feel that we have lost these talents,
perhaps forever.

Let us apply this to our own life, whether it is long or short. In
the memory of all of us many things appear which we had without
having them and which were taken away from us. Some of them
became lost because of the tragic limitations of life; we had to
sacrifice them in order to make other things grow. We all were
given childish innocence; but innocence cannot be used and

increased. The growth of our lives is possible only because we have sacrificed the original gift of innocence. Nevertheless, sometimes there arises in us a melancholy longing for a purity which has been taken from us. We all were given youthful enthusiasm for many things and aims. But this also cannot be used and increased. Most of the objects of our early enthusiasm must be sacrificed for a few, and the few must be approached with soberness. No maturity is possible without this sacrifice. Yet often a melancholy longing for the lost possibilities and enthusiasm takes hold of us. Innocence and youthful enthusiasm: we had them and had them not. Life itself demanded that they were taken from us.

But there are other things which we had and which were taken from us, because we let them go through our own guilt. Some of us had a deep sensitivity for the wonder of life as it is revealed in nature. Slowly under the pressure of work and social life and the lure of cheap pleasures, we lose the wonder of our earlier years when we felt intense joy and the presence of the mystery of life through the freshness of the young day or the glory of the dying day, the majesty of the mountains or the infinity of the sea, a flower breaking through the soil or a young animal in the perfection of its movements. Perhaps we try to produce such feelings again, but we are empty and do not succeed. We had it and had it not, and it has been taken from us.

Others had the same experience with music, poetry, the great novels and plays. One wanted to devour all of them, one lived in them and created for oneself a life above the daily life. We *had* all this and did not have it; we did not let it grow; our love towards it was not strong enough and so it was taken from us.

Many, especially in this group, remember a time in which the desire to learn to solve the riddles of the universe, to find truth has been the driving force in their lives. They came to college and university, not in order to buy their entrance ticket into the upper middle classes or in order to provide for the preconditions of social and economic success, but they came, driven by the desire for knowledge. They had something and more could have been given to them. But in reality they did not have it. They did not make it grow and so it was taken from them and they finished their academic work in terms of expendiency and indifference towards truth. Their love for truth has left them and in some moments they are sick in their hearts because they realize that what they have lost they may never get back.

We all know that any deeper relation to a human being needs watchfulness and growth, otherwise it is taken away from us. And we cannot get it back. This is a form of having and not having which is the root of innumerable human tragedies. We all know about them. And there is another, the most fundamental kind of having and not having—our having and losing God. Perhaps we were rich towards God in our childhood and beyond it. We may remember the moments in which we felt his ultimate presence. We may remember prayers with an overflowing heart, the encounter with the holy in word and music and holy places. We had communication with God; but it was taken from us because we had it and had it not. We did not let it grow, and so it slowly disappeared leaving an empty space. We became unconcerned, cynical, indifferent, not because we doubted about our religious traditions—such doubt belongs to being rich towards God—but because we turned away from that which once concerned us infinitely.

Such thoughts are a first step in approaching the riddle of inequality. Those who have, receive more if they really have it, if they use it and make it grow. And those who have not, lose what they have because they never had it really.

II

But the question of inequality is not yet answered. For one now asks: Why do some receive more than others in the very beginning, before there is even the possibility of using or wasting our talents? Why does the one servant receive five talents and the other two and the third one? Why is the one born in the slums and the other in a well-to-do suburban family? It does not help to answer that of those to whom much is given much is demanded and little of those to whom little is given. For it is just this inequality of original gifts, internal and external, which arouses our question. Why is it given to one human being to gain so much more out of his being human than to another one? Why is so much given to the one that much *can* be asked of him, while to the other one little is given and little *can* be asked? If this question is asked, not only about individual men but also about classes, races and nations, the everlasting question of political inequality arises, and with it the many ways appear in which men have tried to abolish inequality. In every revolution and in every war, the will to solve the riddle of inequality is a driving force. But neither war nor revolution can remove it. Even if we imagine that in an indefinite future most social inequalities are conquered, three things remain: the inequality of talents in body and mind, the inequality created by freedom and destiny, and the fact that all generations before the time of such equality would be excluded from its blessings. This would be the greatest possible inequality! No! In face of one of the deepest and most torturing problems of life, it is unpermittably shallow and foolish to escape into a social dreamland. We have to live now; we have to live this our life, and we must face today the riddle of inequality.

Let us not confuse the riddle of inequality with the fact that each of us is a unique incomparable self. Certainly our being individuals belongs to our dignity as men. It is given to us and must be used and intensified and not drowned in the gray waters of conformity which threaten us today. One should defend every individuality and the uniqueness of every human self. But one should not believe that this is a way of solving the riddle of inequality. Unfortunately, there are social and political reactionaries who use this confusion in order to justify social injustice. They are at least as foolish as the dreamers of a future removal of inequality. Whoever has seen hospitals, prisons, sweatshops, battlefields, houses for the insane, starvation, family tragedies, moral aberrations should be cured from any confusion of the gift of individuality with the riddle of inequality. He should be cured from any feelings of easy consolation.

III

And now we must make the third step in our attempt to penetrate the riddle of inequality and ask: Why do some use and increase what was given to them, while others do not, so that it is taken from them? Why does God say to the prophet in our Old Testament lesson that the ears and eyes of a nation are made insensible for the divine message?

Is it enough to answer: Because some use their freedom responsibly and do what they ought to do while others fail through their own guilt? Is this answer, which seems so obvious, sufficient? Now let me first say that it *is* sufficient if we apply it to ourselves. Each of us must consider the increase or the loss of what is given to him as a matter of his own responsibility. Our conscience tells us that we cannot put the blame for our losses on anybody or anything else than ourselves.

But if we look at others, this answer is not sufficient. On the contrary: If we applied the judgment which we *must* apply to anyone else we would be like the Pharisee in Jesus' parable. You cannot tell somebody who comes to you in distress about himself: Use what has been given to you; for he may come to you just because he is unable to do so! And you cannot tell those who are in despair about what they are: Be something else; for this is just what despair means—the inability of getting rid of oneself. You cannot tell those who did not conquer the destructive influences of their surroundings and were driven into crime and misery that they should have been stronger; for it was just of this strength they had been deprived by heritage or environment. Certainly they all are men, and to all of them freedom is given; but they all are also subject to destiny. It is not up to us to condemn them because they were free, as it is not up to us to excuse them because they were under their destiny. We cannot judge them. And when we judge ourselves, we must be conscious that even this is not the last word, but that we like them are under an ultimate judgment. In it the riddle of inequality is eternally answered. But this answer is not ours. It is our predicament that we must ask. And we ask with an uneasy conscience. Why are they in misery, why not we? Thinking of some who are near to us, we can ask: Are we partly responsible? But even if we are, it does not solve the riddle of inequality. The uneasy conscience asks about the farthest as well as about the nearest: Why they, why not we?

Why has my child, or any of millions and millions of children, died before even having a chance to grow out of infancy? Why is my child, or any child, born feeble-minded or crippled? Why has my friend or relative, or anybody's friend or relative, disintegrated in his mind and lost both his freedom and his destiny? Why has my son or daughter, gifted as I believe with many talents, wasted them and been deprived of them? And why does this happen to any parent at all? Why have this boy's or this girl's creative powers been broken by a tyrannical father or by a possessive mother?

In all these questions it is not the question of our own misery which we ask. It is not the question: Why has this happened to *me*?

It is not the question of Job which God answers by humiliating him and then by elevating him into communion with him. It is not the old and urgent question: Where is the divine justice, where is the divine love towards me? But it is almost the opposite question: Why has this *not* happened to me, why has it happened to the other one, to the innumerable other ones to whom not even the power of Job is given to accept the divine answer? Why—and Jesus has asked the same question—are many called and few elected?

He does not answer; he only states that this is the human predicament. Shall we therefore cease to ask and humbly accept the fact of a divine judgment which condemns most human beings away from the community with him into despair and self-destruction? Can we accept the eternal victory of judgment over love? We cannot; and nobody ever could, even if he preached and threatened in these terms. As long as he could not see himself with complete certainty as eternally rejected, his preaching and threatening would be self-deceiving. And who could see himself eternally rejected?

But if this is not the solution of the riddle of inequality at its deepest level, can we trespass the boundaries of the Christian tradition and listen to those who tell us that this life does not decide about our eternal destiny? There will be occasions in other lives, as our present life is determined by previous ones and what we have achieved or wasted in them. It is a serious doctrine and not completely strange to Christianity. But if we don't know and never will know what each of us has been in the previous or future lives, then it is not really *our* destiny which develops from life to life, but in each life it is the destiny of someone else. This answer also does not solve the riddle of inequality.

There is no answer at all if we ask about the temporal and eternal destiny of the single being separated from the destiny of the whole. Only in the unity of all beings in time and eternity can a humanly possible answer to the riddle of inequality be found. *Humanly* possible does not mean an answer which removes the riddle of inequality, but an answer with which we can live.

There is an ultimate unity of all beings, rooted in the divine life from which they come and to which they go. All beings, non-human as well as human, participate in it. And therefore they all participate in each other. We participate in each other's having and we participate in each other's not-having. If we become aware of this unity of all beings, something happens. The fact that others have-not changes in every moment the character of my having: It undercuts its security, it drives me beyond myself, to understand, to give, to share, to help. The fact that others fall into sin, crime and misery changes the character of the grace which is given to me: It makes me realize my own hidden guilt, it shows to me that those who suffer for their sin and crime, suffer also for me; for I am guilty of their guilt—at least in the desire of my heart—and ought to suffer as they do. The awareness that others who *could* have become fully developed human beings and never *have*, changes my state of full humanity. Their early death, their early or late disintegration, makes my life and my health a continuous risk, a dying which is not yet death, a disintegration which is not yet destruction. In every death which we encounter, something of us dies; in every disease which we encounter, something of us tends to disintegrate.

Can we live with this answer? We can to the degree in which we are liberated from the seclusion within ourselves. But nobody can be liberated from himself unless he is grasped by the power of that which is present in everyone and everything—the eternal from which we come and to which we go, which gives us *to* ourselves and which liberates us *from* ourselves. It is the greatness and the heart of the Christian message that God—as manifest in the Cross of the Christ—participates totally in the dying child, in the condemned criminal, in the disintegrating mind, in the starving one and in him who rejects him. There is no extreme human condition into which the divine presence would not reach. This is what the Cross, the most extreme of all human conditions, tells us. The riddle of inequality cannot be solved on the level of our separation from each other. It is eternally solved in the divine participation in all of us and every being. The certainty of the divine participation gives us the courage to stand the riddle of inequality, though finite minds cannot solve it. Amen.

LUCRETIUS

Death Is Nothing to Us[1]

Death is nothing to us and no concern of ours, since our tenure of the mind is mortal. In days of old, we felt no disquiet when the hosts of Carthage poured in to battle on every side— when the whole earth, dizzied by the convulsive shock of war, reeled sickeningly under the high ethereal vault, and between realm and realm the empire of mankind by land and sea trembled in the balance. So, when we shall be no more—when the union of body and spirit that engenders us has been disrupted—to us, who shall then be nothing, nothing by any hazard will happen any more at all. Nothing will have power to stir our senses, not though earth be fused with sea and sea with sky.

If any feeling remains in mind or spirit after it has been torn from our body, that is nothing to us, who are brought into being by the wedlock of body and spirit, conjoined and coalesced. Or even if the matter that composes us should be reassembled by time after our death and brought back into its present state—if the light of life were given to us anew—even that contingency would still be no concern of ours once the chain of our identity had been snapped. We who are now are not concerned with ourselves in any previous existence: the sufferings of those selves do not touch us. When you look at the immeasurable extent of time gone by and the multiform movements of matter, you will readily credit that these same atoms that compose us now must many a time before have entered into the selfsame combinations as now. But our mind cannot recall this to remembrance. For between then and now is interposed a breach in life, and all the atomic motions have been wandering far astray from sentience.

If the future holds travail and anguish in store, the self must be in existence, when that time comes, in order to experience it. But from this fate we are redeemed by death, which denies existence to the self that might have suffered these tribulations. Rest assured, therefore, that we have nothing to fear in death. One who no longer is cannot suffer, or differ in any way from one who has never been born, when once this mortal life has been usurped by death the immortal.

When you find a man treating it as a grievance that after death he will either molder in the grave or fall a prey to flames or to the jaws of predatory beasts, be sure that his utterance does not ring true. Subconsciously his heart is stabbed by a secret dread, however loudly the man himself may disavow the belief that after

1. From Book III of *On the Nature of Things*.

death he will still experience sensation. I am convinced that he
does not grant the admission he professes, nor the grounds of it; he
does not oust and pluck himself root and branch out of life, but
all unwittingly makes something of himself linger on. When a
living man confronts the thought that after death his body will be
mauled by birds and beasts of prey, he is filled with self-pity. He
does not banish himself from the scene nor distinguish sharply
enough between himself and that abandoned carcass. He visualizes
that object as himself and infects it with his own feelings as an
onlooker. That is why he is aggrieved at having been created
mortal. He does not see that in real death there will be no other
self alive to mourn his own decease—no other self standing by to
flinch at the agony he suffers lying there being mangled, or indeed
being cremated. For if it is really a bad thing after death to be
mauled and crunched by ravening jaws, I cannot see why it should
not be disagreeable to roast in the scorching flames of a funeral
pyre, or to lie embalmed in honey, stifled and stiff with cold, on
the surface of a chilly slab, or to be squashed under a crushing
weight of earth.

"Now it is all over. Now the happy home and the best of wives
will welcome you no more, nor winsome children rush to snatch
the first kiss at your coming and touch your heart with speechless
joy. No chance now to further your fortune or safeguard your
family. Unhappy man," they cry, "unhappily cheated by one
treacherous day out of all the uncounted blessings of life!" But
they do not go on to say: "And now no repining for these lost
joys will oppress you any more." If they perceived this clearly with
their minds and acted according to the words, they would free their
breasts from a great load of grief and dread.

"Ah yes! *You* are at peace now in the sleep of death, and so you
will stay to the end of time. Pain and sorrow will never touch you
again. But to *us*, who stood weeping inconsolably while you were
consumed to ashes on the dreadful pyre—to us no day will come
that will lift the undying sorrow from our hearts." Ask the speaker,
then, what is so heart-rending about this. If something returns to
sleep and peace, what reason is that for pining in inconsolable grief?

Here, again, is the way men often talk from the bottom of their
hearts when they recline at a banquet, goblet in hand and brows
decked with garlands: "How all too short are these good times that
come to us poor creatures! Soon they will be past and gone, and
there will be no recalling them." You would think the crowning
calamity in store for them after death was to be parched and
shriveled by a tormenting thirst or oppressed by some other vain
desire. But even in sleep, when mind and body alike are at rest,
no one misses himself or sighs for life. If such sleep were prolonged to eternity, no longing for ourselves would trouble us. And

yet the vital atoms in our limbs cannot be far removed from their sensory motions at a time when a mere jolt out of sleep enables a man to pull himself together. Death, therefore, must be regarded, so far as we are concerned, as having much less existence than sleep, if anything can have less existence than what we perceive to be nothing. For death is followed by a far greater dispersal of the seething mass of matter: once that icy breach in life has intervened, there is no more waking.

Suppose that Nature herself were suddenly to find a voice and round upon one of us in these terms: "What is your grievance, mortal, that you give yourself up to this whining and repining? Why do you weep and wail over death? If the life you have lived till now has been a pleasant thing—if all its blessings have not leaked away like water poured into a cracked pot and run to waste unrelished—why then, you silly creature, do you not retire as a guest who has had his fill of life and take your care-free rest with a quiet mind? Or, if all your gains have been poured profitless away and life has grown distasteful, why do you seek to swell the total? The new can but turn out as badly as the old and perish as unprofitably. Why not rather make an end of life and labor? Do you expect me to invent some new contrivance for your pleasure? I tell you, there is none. All things are always the same. If your body is not yet withered with age, nor your limbs decrepit and flagging, even so there is nothing new to look forward to—not though you should outlive all living creatures, or even though you should never die at all." What are we to answer, except that Nature's rebuttal is justified and the plea she puts forward is a true one?

But suppose it is some man of riper years who complains—some dismal greybeard who frets unconscionably at his approaching end. Would she not have every right to protest more vehemently and repulse him in stern tones: "Away with your tears, old reprobate! Have done with your grumbling! You are withering now after tasting all the joys of life. But, because you are always pining for what is not and unappreciative of the things at hand, your life has slipped away unfulfilled and unprized. Death has stolen upon you unawares, before you are ready to retire from life's banquet filled and satisfied. Come now, put away all that is unbecoming to your years and compose your mind to make way for others. You have no choice." I cannot question but she would have right on her side; her censure and rebuke would be well merited. The old is always thrust aside to make way for the new, and one thing must be built out of the wreck of another. There is no murky pit of Hell awaiting anyone. There is need of matter, so that later generations may arise; when they have lived out their span, they will all follow you. Bygone generations have taken your road, and those to come will take it no less. So one thing will never cease to spring from another. To none is life given in freehold; to all on lease. Look back at the eternity that passed before we were born, and mark how utterly it counts to us as nothing. This is a mirror that Nature holds up to us, in which we may see the time that shall be after we are dead. Is there anything terrifying in the sight— anything depressing—anything that is not more restful than the soundest sleep?

As for all those torments that are said to take place in the depths of Hell, they are actually present here and now, in our own lives. There is no wretched Tantalus, as the myth relates, transfixed with groundless terror at the huge boulder poised above him in the air. But in this life there really are mortals oppressed by unfounded fear of the gods and trembling at the impending doom that may fall upon any of them at the whim of chance.

There is no Tityos lying in Hell for ever probed by birds of prey. Assuredly they cannot find food by groping under those giant ribs to glut them throughout eternity. No matter to what length that titanic frame may lie outstretched, so that he covers not a paltry nine acres with his spread-eagled limbs but the whole extent of earth, he will not be able to suffer an eternity of pain nor furnish food from his body for evermore. But Tityos is here in our midst—that poor devil prostrated by love, torn indeed by birds of prey, devoured by gnawing jealousy or rent by the fangs of some other passion.

Sisyphus too is alive for all to see, bent on winning the insignia of office, its rods and ruthless axes, by the people's vote and embittered by perpetual defeat. To strive for this profitless and never-granted prize, and in striving toil and moil incessantly, this truly is to push a boulder laboriously up a steep hill, only to see it, once the top is reached, rolling and bounding down again to the flat levels of the plain.

By the same token, to be for ever feeding a malcontent mind, filling it with good things but never satisfying it—the fate we suffer when the circling seasons enrich us with their products and their ever-changing charms but we are never filled with the fruits of life—this surely exemplifies the story of those maidens in the flower of life for ever pouring water into a leaking vessel which can never by any sleight be filled.

As for Cerberus and the Furies and the pitchy darkness and the jaws of Hell belching abominable fumes, these are not and cannot be anywhere at all. But life is darkened by the fear of retribution for our misdeeds, a fear enormous in proportion to their enormity, and by the penalties imposed for crime—imprisonment and ghastly precipitation from Tarpeia's Crag, the lash, the block, the rack, the boiling pitch, the firebrand and the branding iron. Even though these horrors are not physically present, yet the conscience-ridden mind in terrified anticipation torments itself with its own goads and whips. It does not see what term there can be to its suffering nor where its punishment can have an end. It is afraid that death may serve merely to intensify pain. So at length the life of misguided mortals becomes a Hell on earth.

Here is something that you might well say to yourself from time to time: "Even good king Ancus looked his last on the daylight— a better man than you, my presumptuous friend, by a long reckoning. Death has come to many another monarch and potentate, who lorded it over mighty nations. Even that King of Kings who once built a highway across the great deep—who gave his legions a path to tread among the waves and taught them to march on foot over the briny gulfs and with his charges trampled scornfully upon the ocean's roar—even he was robbed of the light and poured out the spirit from a dying frame. Scipio, that thunderbolt of war, the terror of Carthage, gave his bones to the earth as if he had been the meanest of serfs. Add to this company the discoverers of truth and beauty. Add the attendants of the Muses, among them Homer who in solitary glory bore the scepter but has sunk into the same slumber as the rest. Democritus, when ripe age warned him that the mindful motions of his intellect were running down, made his unbowed head a willing sacrifice to death. And the Master himself, when his daylit race was run, Epicurus himself died, whose genius outshone the race of men and dimmed them all, as the stars are dimmed by the rising of the fiery sun. And will *you* kick and protest against your sentence? You, whose life is next-door to death while you are still alive and looking on the light. You, who waste the major part of your time in sleep and, when you are awake, are snoring still and dreaming. You, who bear a mind hag-ridden by baseless fear and cannot find the commonest cause of your distress, hounded as you are, poor creature, by a pack of troubles and drifting in a drunken stupor upon a wavering tide of fantasy."

Men feel plainly enough within their minds, a heavy burden, whose weight depresses them. If only they perceived with equal clearness the causes of this depression, the origin of this lump of evil within their breasts, they would not lead such a life as we now see all too commonly—no one knowing what he really wants and everyone for ever trying to get away from where he is, as though mere locomotion could throw off the load. Often the owner of some stately mansion, bored stiff by staying at home, takes his departure, only to return as speedily when he feels himself no better off out of doors. Off he goes to his country seat, driving his carriage and pair hot-foot, as though in haste to save a house on fire. No sooner has he crossed its doorstep than he starts yawning or retires moodily to sleep and courts oblivion, or else rushes back to revisit the city. In so doing the individual is really running away from himself. Since he remains reluctantly wedded to the self whom he cannot of course escape, he grows to hate him, because he is a sick man ignorant of the cause of his malady. If he did but see this, he would cast other thoughts aside and devote himself first to studying the nature of the universe. It is not the fortune of an hour that is in question, but of all time—the lot in store for mortals throughout the eternity that awaits them after death.

What is this deplorable lust of life that holds us trembling in bondage to such uncertainties and dangers? A fixed term is set to the life of mortals, and there is no way of dodging death. In any case the setting of our lives remains the same throughout, and by going on living we do not mint any new coin of pleasure. So long as the object of our craving is unattained, it seems more precious than anything besides. Once it is ours, we crave for something else. So an unquenchable thirst for life keeps us always on the gasp. There is no telling what fortune the future may bring—what chance may throw in our way, or what upshot lies in waiting. By prolonging life, we cannot subtract or whittle away one jot from the duration of our death. The time after our taking off remains constant. However many generations you may add to your store by living, there waits for you none the less the same eternal death. The time of not-being will be no less for him who made an end of life with yesterday's daylight than for him who perished many a moon and many a year before.

GEORGE SANTAYANA
Classic Liberty

When ancient peoples defended what they called their liberty, the word stood for a plain and urgent interest of theirs: that their cities should not be destroyed, their territory pillaged, and they themselves sold into slavery. For the Greeks in particular liberty meant even more than this. Perhaps the deepest assumption of classic philosophy is that nature and the gods on the one hand and man on the other, both have a fixed character; that there is consequently a necessary piety, a true philosophy, a standard happiness, a normal art. The Greeks believed, not without reason, that they had grasped these permanent principles better than other peoples. They had largely dispelled superstition, experimented in government, and turned life into a rational art. Therefore when they defended their liberty what they defended was not merely freedom to live. It was freedom to live well, to live as other nations did not, in the public experimental study of the world and of human nature.

This liberty to discover and pursue a natural happiness, this liberty to grow wise and to live in friendship with the gods and with one another, was the liberty vindicated at Thermopylae by martyrdom and at Salamis by victory.

As Greek cities stood for liberty in the world, so philosophers stood for liberty in the Greek cities. In both cases it was the same kind of liberty, not freedom to wander at hazard or to let things slip, but on the contrary freedom to legislate more precisely, at least for oneself, and to discover and codify the means to true happiness. Many of these pioneers in wisdom were audacious radicals and recoiled from no paradox. Some condemned what was most Greek: mythology, athletics, even multiplicity and physical motion. In the heart of those thriving, loquacious, festive little ant-hills, they preached impassibility and abstraction, the unanswerable scepticism of silence. Others practised a musical and priestly refinement of life, filled with metaphysical mysteries, and formed secret societies, not without a tendency to political domination. The cynics railed at the conventions, making themselves as comfortable as possible in the role of beggars and mocking parasites. The conservatives themselves were radical, so intelligent were they, and Plato wrote the charter[1] of the most extreme militarism and communism, for the sake of preserving the free state. It was the swan-song of liberty, a prescription to a diseased old man to become young again and try a second life of superhuman virtue. The old man preferred simply to die.

Many laughed then, as we may be tempted to do, at all those absolute physicians of the soul, each with his panacea. Yet beneath their quarrels the wranglers had a common faith. They all believed there was a single solid natural wisdom to be found, that reason could find it, and that mankind, sobered by reason, could put it in practice. Mankind has continued to run wild and like barbarians to place freedom in their very wildness, till we can hardly conceive the classic assumption of Greek philosophers and cities, that true liberty is bound up with an institution, a corporate scientific discipline, necessary to set free the perfect man, or the god, within us.

Upon the dissolution of paganism the Christian church adopted the classic conception of liberty. Of course, the field in which the higher politics had to operate was now conceived differently, and there was a new experience of the sort of happiness appropriate and possible to man; but the assumption remained unchallenged that Providence, as well as the human soul, had a fixed discoverable scope, and that the business of education, law, and religion was to bring them to operate in harmony. The aim of life, salvation, was involved in the nature of the soul itself, and the means of salvation

1. The reference is to Plato's *Republic*.

had been ascertained by a positive science which the church was possessed of, partly revealed and partly experimental. Salvation was simply what, on a broad view, we should see to be health, and religion was nothing but a sort of universal hygiene.

The church, therefore, little as it tolerated heretical liberty, the liberty of moral and intellectual dispersion, felt that it had come into the world to set men free, and constantly demanded liberty for itself, that it might fulfil this mission. It was divinely commissioned to teach, guide, and console all nations and all ages by the self-same means, and to promote at all costs what it conceived to be human perfection. There should be saints and as many saints as possible. The church never admitted, any more than did any sect of ancient philosophers, that its teaching might represent only an eccentric view of the world, or that its guidance and consolations might be suitable only at one stage of human development. To waver in the pursuit of the orthodox ideal could only betray frivolity and want of self-knowledge. The truth of things and the happiness of each man could not lie elsewhere than where the church, summing up all human experience and all divine revelation, had placed it once for all and for everybody. The liberty of the church to fulfil its mission was accordingly hostile to any liberty of dispersion, to any radical consecutive independence, in the life of individuals or of nations.

When it came to full fruition this orthodox freedom was far from gay; it was called sanctity. The freedom of pagan philosophers too had turned out to be rather a stiff and severe pose; but in the Christian dispensation this austerity of true happiness was less to be wondered at, since life on earth was reputed to be abnormal from the beginning, and infected with hereditary disease. The full beauty and joy of restored liberty could hardly become evident in this life. Nevertheless a certain beauty and joy did radiate visibly from the saints; and while we may well think their renunciations and penances misguided or excessive, it is certain that, like the Spartans and the philosophers, they got something for their pains. Their bodies and souls were transfigured, as none now found upon earth. If we admire without imitating them we shall perhaps have done their philosophy exact justice. Classic liberty was a sort of forced and artificial liberty, a poor perfection reserved for an ascetic aristocracy in whom heroism and refinement were touched with perversity and slowly starved themselves to death.

Since those days we have discovered how much larger the universe is, and we have lost our way in it. Any day it may come over us again that our modern liberty to drift in the dark is the most terrible negation of freedom. Nothing happens to us as we would. We want peace and make war. We need science and obey the will to believe, we love art and flounder among whimsicalities, we believe in general comfort and equality and we strain every nerve to become millionaires. After all, antiquity must have been right in thinking that reasonable self-direction must rest on having a determinate character and knowing what it is, and that only the truth about God and happiness, if we somehow found it, could make us free. But the truth is not to be found by guessing at it, as religious prophets and men of genius have done, and then damning every one who does not agree. Human nature, for all its substantial fixity, is a living thing with many varieties and variations. All diversity of opinion is therefore not founded on ignorance; it may express a legitimate change of habit or interest. The classic and Christian synthesis from which we have broken loose was certainly premature, even if the only issue of our liberal experiments should be to lead us back to some such equilibrium. Let us hope at least that the new morality, when it comes, may be more broadly based than the old on knowledge of the world, not so absolute, not so meticulous, and not chanted so much in the monotone of an abstracted sage.

HERBERT J. MULLER

A Credo[1]

"What kind of people do they think we are?" exclaimed Winston Churchill during the last war. A major cause of Hitler's undoing was that the British proved to be a much sturdier people than he thought. Even so he had reason to think poorly of them, judging by the mediocrity of their leaders before Churchill, and by the gloominess of many of their intellectuals. The behavior of the British points to simplicities that thinkers are prone to forget. Before we get solemn about the ultimate issues we might take a hard look at these simplicities.

Thus it is a commonplace that American soldiers in the last war had a dim idea of what they were fighting for. Presumably they have no clearer idea of why they went to Korea, and certainly they have no passion for dying for any cause. Nevertheless they have fought sturdily, sweating it out, grumbling it through to the end. As ordinary men they have a toughness of spirit that carries them through crises while clear-eyed intellectuals indulge in despair. In one aspect this is insensitiveness or simple coarseness. In another it is simple loyalty to the company—the chance unit of buddies. The "cause" comes down to such common sentiments as fellow-feeling, pride in workmanship, and self-respect. Our religions, our

1. From "Conclusion: The Uses of the Future," the final chapter of *The Uses of the Past*, 1952.

philosophies, and our histories too seldom take adequate account of these rudiments of human idealism. A philosophy of history might well begin and end with a report I have heard on the French underground that took care of Allied airmen and escaped prisoners in the last war. The report was that the most effective workers in this underground were priests and prostitutes.

In this unphilosophical, unspiritual view we may better understand why democracy has not degenerated into the anarchy and tyranny predicted by its critics, from Plato down—why, on the contrary, it has been able to mobilize its resources for mighty national efforts, and to emerge from two world wars without loss of its basic civil liberties. The very limitations of ordinary men may be sources of strength. The depressing conventionality of Americans, for example, has contributed to their unusual cohesiveness and stability. Their favorite national myth, the success story, has strengthened their faith in themselves and helped to maintain the habits of enterprise and self-reliance. Their spiritual slackness, or incapacity for flaming idealism, is at least in part a saving realism and modesty. The chances for world order and peace are better because they no longer expect wars to end war, and have little sense of manifest destiny, little zeal for making the world safe for democracy at any cost. In a period of deep confusion they can carry on the democratic tradition because they carry much of it unconsciously, in sentiments of equality and fair play learned in kindergarten, habits of tolerance and compromise engrained by everyday give and take. "A very great deal of the Western way of life," writes Crane Brinton, "is thus embedded somewhere in quite ordinary Americans, not in their cerebral cortexes, probably, but in a much safer place which the physiologist hasn't quite located— we used to say, in the heart."

Yet such realism also forbids us to be complacent about these homely virtues, or about any faith learned by heart. Much paltry sentiment and belief have been learned in the same way.[2] Embedded still deeper are the primitive instincts of fear and rage, which now give desperate overtones to the tribal chant of the nation's might and right. Conventional patriotism, oratory, heroics, the

2. An instance is the almost universal assumption of Americans that the profit motive is the only motive that can stimulate men to exert their best efforts. This implies an essentially cynical view of human nature, or at least American nature, and confirms what the Russians say about us; yet it is also an excuse for high moral indignation. One may recall the outraged protests in Congress and editorial offices during the last war, when President Roosevelt proposed that incomes be limited to $25,000 for the duration. The most sober conservatives argued that any such restriction would destroy the incentive of the businessmen on whom we depended for war production. It should be added, however, that like ordinary soldiers and workers—not to mention scientists, ministers, teachers, and other simple folk— many businessmen apparently did a conscientious job without expecting as much as $25,000; so we may believe that they are not necessarily the swine their champions assume they are. Or so we must hope, else we are certainly doomed [Muller's note].

fervor of hatred and fear—the conditioned reflexes of national life might still carry us through the present emergency; but they could not make a world order. For the long run we need more sober, lucid, responsible convictions about the kind of people we have been, and will have to be. For wherever the democratic faith is embedded in ordinary Americans, it was not born there and did not settle there by chance. It was engendered by conscious thought; it was propagated by conscious effort. In a revolutionary world it cannot survive indefinitely as mere habit. If we begin and end with the priest and the prostitute, in between we still need more conscious thought and effort.

And so with Western civilization as a whole. The familiar refrains about its "breakdown" may obscure the extraordinary unflagging creativeness that has made it the richest, most dramatic spectacle in history. It has maintained a high level of creative activity over a longer period of time than have previous societies, which rested on their oars after bursts of great achievement. In particular, as Whitehead observed, thought has been more creative. Whereas in other societies thought served chiefly to explain and conserve, Western man embarked on an endless "adventure of ideas" and put the ideas to work. He has thrived on the continuous disagreement and disharmony from which he has suffered; his life has always been charged with high tension. Since the dawn of the Middle Ages Europe has known the sense of crisis—the symptoms diagnosed by the specialists in "breakdowns." During its most complacent periods, such as the *ancien régime* and the Victorian age, revolutionary forces were agitating the more sensitive spirits and engendering further crises.

Now it may be that the long era of expansion is drawing to a close, and that even if we escape a universal catastrophe the future will be an era of contraction. All history might be charted in terms of such pendulum swings, which are the natural terms of action and reaction. An obvious sign in our time is the growth of totalitarianism—a "dynamic" reversion to the closed, tribal society. Another sign is the swelling appeal to religion, which might betoken a quest for spiritual freedom but looks more like a yearning for security and rest. At best, such tendencies to contraction represent a healthy desire to order, consolidate, and conserve, to restore community and natural piety, in a healthy recognition of the abuses of freedom and the limitations of reason. Yet we are not likely to enjoy the best, nor are we in a position to make consolidation the order of the day. Immediately we have to deal with another revolutionary development, in the unlocking of atomic energy; to conserve anything at all we shall have to make over our traditional institutions and policies. Given science, we must expect more revolutionary developments, in both our conceptions of the universe and our operations on it. We cannot count on history to repeat itself.

Hence I should stress first of all, in very general terms, our continued need of an adventurous spirit—of still more creative thought, bold, imaginative, experimental, self-reliant, critical of all "infallible" authority. This stress may seem unnecessary in an age notorious for its skepticism and irreverence, and at a moment when revolutionaries are the apparent menace. Nevertheless these revolutionaries are much less bold and independent than they appear, what with their childish faith in guaranteed totalitarian solutions. Our conservatives are even less enterprising than they appear; the frequent violence of their tactics masks a fearful timidity and unimaginativeness in their basic strategy, when not a downright panic. And we all have to be wary of another contradiction in our heritage. While the spirit of adventure has been the genius of Western thought, at its heart has remained the venerable assumption of a static, finished world, in which truth is timeless, standards are absolute and fixed, and human nature is always and everywhere the same. Our religion, our ethics, our poetry, our political and economic theory, our proverbs and maxims for daily life—our idealism and our common sense alike are steeped in this assumption, which is at variance both with our scientific knowledge of human history in an evolving world, and with the conditions of life in a revolutionary world.

All along I have been identifying the adventurous spirit with humanism, liberalism, rationalism, the scientific spirit, the ideals of freedom, individualism, and the "open society." Since these have constituted the distinctive faith of our secular civilization, I appear to be calling for business as usual, at the same old stand —the kind of business that has brought on the present crisis. I should therefore repeat that the adventure in freedom is inevitably precarious. Yet I deny that this faith is the main source of our folly and evil. In the world of affairs the obvious menace is the inveterate self-interest, individual and national, upon which all faiths have foundered. In the world of thought the chief menaces are the various forms of authoritarianism and irrationalism. The worst folly of liberals has been a facile optimism that blinked both the ancients evils and the new complexities.

Today they are apt to echo the common charge that "scientific philosophy" is the root of our evils. Science has indisputably inspired much narrow, harsh philosophy, and much pseudo-science; its disciples have often been inhuman. As inhuman, however, is the fashion of branding all the efforts of intelligence as sinful pride, and all the works of science as mere materialism. It appears that to study meteorology and scientific agriculture is to be materialistic, whereas to pray for rain and good crops is to be spiritual. Actually, both procedures have utilitarian motives; the immediate choice is between more or less intelligent, efficacious means of attaining human ends; and as for "higher" values, pure science is a more disinterested, more genuinely spiritual activity than ordinary prayer or worship. At least science cannot be charged with the nationalism and imperialism that now threaten catastrophe. No war has ever been fought over scientific causes. No nation—least of all Soviet Russia—has proposed its aims or resolved its issues in a scientific spirit. Science has had very little to do, indeed, with the administration of our economic and political life. It remains the author of our major problem, in its gift of tremendous power that has been terribly abused; but for the wise use of this power we need more, not less, of the objective, dispassionate scientific spirit. For our philosophical purposes we need more of its integrity and its basic humility, its respect at once for fact and for mystery.

Many men now take a strange pleasure in emphasizing the limits of scientific knowledge, as if the validity of poetic, metaphysical, or religious claims to higher truth were thereby automatically proved, and ignorance were not merely bliss but wisdom. Many are attacking the claims of reason itself, in the name of faith, intuition, instinct, the heart, the voice of the blood. In the world of affairs such attitudes are translated into the kind of common sense that scorns all "theory," ridicules "brain-trusts," and identifies learning with absent-mindedness. The way is thus cleared for the positive irrationalism of the dictators, the brutal contempt of mind exhibited in their policy when not their creed. We may then realize that a denial of the claims of reason naturally leads to a denial of the claims of the heart too, and that if its powers are as inadequate as many seem pleased to think, there can be no hope of avoiding catastrophe.

If we must make these imprecise, invidious distinctions, we had better try to keep our heads. Scientific knowledge is no less useful because of ultimate uncertainty; it serves the quite sufficient purpose of enabling us to go about our business in a world whose metaphysical "reality" we do not absolutely need to know. Reliable knowledge is not enough by itself but nothing can take its place— no arbitrary assertion of higher truths and goods. Whatever higher faculties man may have—of feeling, intuition, or imagination, in vision, trance, or ecstasy—can be trusted only after they have been interpreted and judged by reason. Otherwise anything goes: the visions of Buddha, Christ, Mohammed, Marx, Whitman, Nietzsche, and Hitler are on the same footing; and what goes best is apt to be blind unreason or brute force. No product of social intercourse is more precious than reasonableness, or more essential to attain-

ing and sharing the goods of life; for love itself is a partial sentiment that often goes wrong, leading to division, jealousy, and
hatred.

In this spirit reason must then add that love and hatred remain
more elemental. Its claims need to be qualified by modest ideas of
its functions and its powers; its ideal product is not pure rationality but reasonableness. Traditional rationalism has taken too supercilious an attitude toward the instinctive, spontaneous life, the
sentiment and passion that alone can give force to its ideals. In this
century many social scientists have displayed an incredibly naive
confidence in the power of intelligence to control the "behavior
patterns" with which they play, talking as if social conflict could be
handled in the same way as infectious disease. Liberals generally
have set their sights too high, overestimating the rationality and
virtue of free men. Yet it is still reason that warns us against such
unreasonable expectations. In its most mournful judgments of its
frail powers it still proves its necessity, its responsibility, and its
power.

To live intelligently, in short, we must recognize that man is not
simply a "rational animal." To live decently we must also recognize
that this definition of him is more adequate than such popular
definitions as a beast of prey, an illusioned robot, or an imprisoned
soul. He shares his basic drives and reflexes with other animals,
and he may or may not have an immortal soul; what most plainly
and positively distinguishes him from other animals is the power
of conscious thought and responsible behavior. If we respect him
at all we must treat him as if he were rational, and enlist his free
consent in joint enterprises. The whole argument for liberty and
democracy ultimately rests on Pascal's dictum that thought makes
the whole dignity of man, and that the endeavor to think well is
the basic morality. "The chief virtue of democracy," concluded
Carl Becker, "and in the long run the sole reason for cherishing
it, is that with all its defects it still provides the most favorable
conditions for the maintenance of that dignity and the practice of
that morality."

This is also the reason for cherishing the individual, as the
essential carrier of that dignity and agent of that morality. In his
newly won freedom to think and act for himself he has indeed
done himself much harm. He has identified his cause with a
gospel of economic individualism that meant slavery to a profit
system, a loss of dignity for the many and a warped, impoverished
humanity even for the successful. He has tended to forget that the
sense of community is indispensable even to full self-realization. His
excesses have therefore called out an extreme revulsion. Social scientists have referred to the individual as a "discredited hypothesis,"
defining him as a mere cell of the social organism, while dictators

have discredited him in fact or put him in cells. Yet there is no doing away with him, or without him. The great creative individual, as John Stuart Mill said, not only personifies but initiates all the wise and noble things that the race has done. In everyday life we are as dependent on free relations with the ordinary decent person. We may best appreciate him in a time of crisis, for he is capable of more wisdom and virtue than collective man ever can be. He is often superior to the best institutions—the greatest States and Churches—which repeatedly fall short of the integrity and the decency we can count on in private life.

The related ideal of equality is more vulnerable. Undeniably it has worked to dignify mediocrity and lower standards of excellence. It has produced the new tyranny of the masses, the chief enemy of true individuality. And always it entails apparent absurdities. "In the eighteenth century," wrote Ortega y Gasset, "certain minority groups discovered that every human being, by the mere fact of birth, and without requiring any special qualification whatsoever, possessed certain fundamental political rights, the so-called rights of the man and the citizen." Bright sophomores delight in pointing out the self-evident truth that men are *not* created free or equal. We shall always be asked to contemplate the ignoramus and the expert marching to the polls, to cast one vote apiece.

But what are the alternatives? In the past almost all political and religious orders were based on the aristocratic principle of the natural inequalities of man. The ideal argument for this principle is rule by the superior. In practice, however, the ruling classes have seldom been disposed to permit any natural test of their claims to superiority—they simply clung to inherited privileges. We have seen that mediocrity thrives in such societies too; even imbecility has sat on thrones and worn haloes. And the logic of the aristocratic principle is no less vulnerable to analysis. There is no universal standard of superiority, no scale for weighing the diverse claims of strength, skill, valor, intelligence, shrewdness, learning, breeding, virtue, piety, and what have you. For men are not unequal in every respect. Any little man may rightly say that he is a better artisan, a better soldier, a better friend, a better husband and father, or a better Christian than the genius; and he may even be a better citizen than some experts.[3] At the same time, all men are in fact equal in respect of their common structure and their common destiny. The egalitarian principle does more justice to both the diversity and the unity of our common humanity. In these terms

3. The common man's limitations as voter may seem less hopeless when he is set beside his betters. His gullibility is hardly more dangerous than the conservatism and self-interest of the wealthy, educated classes, who can usually be counted on to prefer a "safe" candidate —a mediocrity like Calvin Coolidge. It was primarily the common man who elected the greater presidents, such as Jefferson, Jackson, Lincoln, Wilson, and F. D. Roosevelt—all of whom were violently hated by large segments of the well-to-do [Muller's note].

the supreme gift of the West to mankind is that it has promoted the sentiment of equality and realized a measure of actual equality, political, economic, and social. It has thereby laid the only possible basis for a world federation.

All these ideals, once more, necessarily lead to disagreement, disquiet, disharmony, disorder, disunity. Still, such costs are not necessarily prohibitive. They seem more alarming because of the conservative disposition to be alarmed by all change, and to spare the past its troubles. Historically, there is no clear correlation between harmony and health, much less growth—no great society has realized the degree of spiritual unity common in primitive societies. Although freedom in thought and political life has always got societies into trouble, none have died of it; dying societies have been marked rather by rigidity, the traditionalism of which Rome in decline is the conspicuous example. The most encouraging sign in the Western world is that it not only recognizes the evils in its way of life but continues to struggle against them. It has not yet lost the pioneering spirit that has made its whole history a migration. There will always be some hope for it so long as it retains its distinctive hope that life on earth can and must be improved.

To this hope—to the whole humanistic endeavor—Christianity, finally, can lend strong support. Although it did not lead the way, it contributed the germinal ideals of spiritual freedom and equality. Today many of its leaders are outgrowing the traditional exclusiveness that has militated against its ideal of universal brotherhood. Some are willing to believe that religion too is properly an adventure—a progress toward more adequate conceptions of God and the spiritual life, instead of the final truth about them. Meanwhile Christianity remains the most accessible source of saving experience for the West. It can comfort, bind up wounds, and cure as no secular faith can. And simply because it is no longer a flaming, crusading faith it can preach more effectively its gospel of charity and humility, help to keep alive the possibilities of peace. Churchmen of all sects are combating the tendency of political and military leaders to buy slight tactical advantages at great moral cost (as Monte Cassino was blasted, to no gain whatever). The Christian conscience might avert the ultimate horror of a total war to preserve freedom—a war waged in a total disregard of the values that alone make freedom precious, and rehabilitation possible.

Nevertheless I have been arguing that Christianity does not constitute our best hope, at least for our earthly future. An established religion remains by nature a deeply conservative force, not a creative one. The churches have long brought up the intellectual rear of our civilization, and despite their awakened social conscience their claims to spiritual leadership are still weakened by their engrained tendency to resist new knowledge and aspiration. Most are still disposed to a dogmatic supernaturalism that saps the intellectual honesty and courage essential for a responsible idealism.[4] Churchmen persistently narrow our choices by equating "religious" and "spiritual," obscuring all the shriveled, deformed spirituality to be found within the churches and all the healthy idealism to be found outside them. Much of what passes for religious faith today amounts to a side bet, covering a vague belief that "there must be something" or that man needs to believe (especially when in foxholes); often it verges on sentimentality—the indulgence of feeling without commitments in thought and action. Many churchmen are trying to reanimate such faith by exploiting the theology of crisis, the ethos of fear—preaching not merely humility but humiliation. Given the historic record, we cannot be simply heartened by the possibility that the future may belong to the churches again.

Humanism, or the religion of humanity, may not do either. Toynbee attacks it as peculiar, perverse, "even pathological." It is in fact peculiar enough—it has not had the chance of religion. No doubt it makes too heavy demands on human nature in its present state, especially when it asks men to put humanity above the tribe —something they have never succeeded in doing under the fatherhood of God. Yet I still hold that the Western humanistic faith is not perverse, and not so pathological as historic religion has often been. It has proved itself in many good men, by many good works. It has brought finer possibilities of life to masses of men who in the past could invest their hope only in a hypothetical life to come. The utter defeat of this cause would be the worst tragedy in history. Meanwhile the notorious pride of the modern world is dangerous because it is not a clear, proud faith in the dignity of man or in the uses of mind. The enemy today wears the mask of pride, but its true name is fear.

4. Thus the greatest of the Christian churches recently affronted the intellectual conscience of many other Christians by proclaiming the new dogma of the Virgin's bodily ascent into heaven, despite the absence of scriptural or historical evidence of such an event. Protestant leaders lamented that the Catholic Church should elect the most crucial moment in Western history to emphasize dogmatic differences, and thereby raise a further barrier to a united Christendom. Although the Pope has made one concession, observing that "human intelligence sometimes experiences difficulties in forming a judgment about the credibility of the Catholic faith," he has also warned Catholics against any compromise on their dogmas, insisting that reunion is possible only on the impossible terms set by the Church. Spirituality is further confused when an authoritarian church denounces the tyranny of Communism while it supports Franco as it once supported Mussolini, a dictator whom Pius XI hailed as "a man sent by Divine Providence" [Muller's note].

QUESTIONS FOR STUDY, DISCUSSION, AND WRITING

1. Muller says (p. 1157) that "as for 'higher' values, pure science is a more disinterested, more genuinely spiritual activity than ordinary prayer or worship." What does he mean by this? What evidence elsewhere in the essay supports this view?

2. Muller asserts that "much of what passes for religious faith today

amounts to a side bet." What advantages over this kind of faith does he perceive in "humanism, or the religion of humanity"?

3. In the paragraph on page 1158 beginning "To live intelligently . . ." Muller mentions several definitions of man and then goes on to qualify and expand one of them to construct his own definition. Why does he feel the need to qualify and expand? Would Jonathan Edwards have agreed with Muller's definition?

4. Muller asserts (p. 1159) that "all men are in fact equal in respect of their common structure and their common destiny." Explain "structure" and "destiny" in this context.

5. What does Muller mean when he says that "religion too is properly an adventure"? Explain whether Miller (pp. 1109–1112) is in any way making a similar point.

GILBERT HIGHET
The Mystery of Zen

The mind need never stop growing. Indeed, one of the few experiences which never pall is the experience of watching one's own mind, and observing how it produces new interests, responds to new stimuli, and develops new thoughts, apparently without effort and almost independently of one's own conscious control. I have seen this happen to myself a hundred times; and every time it happens again, I am equally fascinated and astonished.

Some years ago a publisher sent me a little book for review. I read it, and decided it was too remote from my main interests and too highly specialized. It was a brief account of how a young German philosopher living in Japan had learned how to shoot with a bow and arrow, and how this training had made it possible for him to understand the esoteric doctrines of the Zen sect of Buddhism. Really, what could be more alien to my own life, and to that of everyone I knew, than Zen Buddhism and Japanese archery? So I thought, and put the book away.

Yet I did not forget it. It was well written, and translated into good English. It was delightfully short, and implied much more than it said. Although its theme was extremely odd, it was at least highly individual; I had never read anything like it before or since. It remained in my mind. Its name was *Zen in the Art of Archery*, its author Eugen Herrigel, its publisher Pantheon of New York. One day I took it off the shelf and read it again; this time it seemed even stranger than before and even more unforgettable. Now it began to cohere with other interests of mine. Something I had read of the Japanese art of flower arrangement seemed to connect with it; and then, when I wrote an essay on the peculiar Japanese poems called *haiku*, other links began to grow. Finally I had to read the book once more with care, and to go through some other works which illuminated the same subject. I am still grappling with the theme; I have not got anywhere near understanding it fully; but I have learned a good deal, and I am grateful to the little book which refused to be forgotten.

The author, a German philosopher, got a job teaching philosophy at the University of Tokyo (apparently between the wars), and he did what Germans in foreign countries do not usually do: he determined to adapt himself and to learn from his hosts. In particular, he had always been interested in mysticism—which, for every earnest philosopher, poses a problem that is all the more inescapable because it is virtually insoluble. Zen Buddhism is not the only mystical doctrine to be found in the East, but it is one of the most highly developed and certainly one of the most difficult to approach. Herrigel knew that there were scarcely any books which did more than skirt the edge of the subject, and that the best of all books on Zen (those by the philosopher D. T. Suzuki) constantly emphasize that Zen can never be learned from books, can never be studied as we can study other disciplines such as logic or mathematics. Therefore he began to look for a Japanese thinker who could teach him directly.

At once he met with embarrassed refusals. His Japanese friends explained that he would gain nothing from trying to discuss Zen as a philosopher, that its theories could not be spread out for analysis by a detached mind, and in fact that the normal relationship of teacher and pupil simply did not exist within the sect, because the Zen masters felt it useless to explain things stage by stage and to argue about the various possible interpretations of their doctrine. Herrigel had read enough to be prepared for this. He replied that he did not want to dissect the teachings of the school, because he knew that would be useless. He wanted to become a Zen mystic himself. (This was highly intelligent of him. No one could really penetrate into Christian mysticism without being a devout Christian; no one could appreciate Hindu mystical doctrine without accepting the Hindu view of the universe.) At this, Herrigel's Japanese friends were more forthcoming. They told him that the best way, indeed the only way, for a European to approach Zen mysticism was to learn one of the arts which exemplified it. He was a fairly good rifle shot, so he determined to learn archery; and his wife co-operated with him by taking lessons in painting and flower arrangement. How any philosopher could investigate a mystical doctrine by learning to shoot with a bow and arrow and watching his wife arrange flowers, Herrigel did not ask. He had good sense.

A Zen master who was a teacher of archery agreed to take him as a pupil. The lessons lasted six years, during which he practiced every single day. There are many difficult courses of instruction in the world: the Jesuits, violin virtuosi, Talmudic scholars, all have long and hard training, which in one sense never comes to an end; but Herrigel's training in archery equaled them all in intensity. If I were trying to learn archery, I should expect to begin by looking at a target and shooting arrows at it. He was not even allowed to aim at a target for the first four years. He had to begin by learning how to hold the bow and arrow, and then how to release the arrow; this took ages. The Japanese bow is not like our sporting bow, and the stance of the archer in Japan is different from ours. We hold the bow at shoulder level, stretch our left arm out ahead, pull the string and the nocked arrow to a point either below the chin or sometimes past the right ear, and then shoot. The Japanese hold the bow above the head, and then pull the hands apart to left and right until the left hand comes down to eye level and the right hand comes to rest above the right shoulder; then there is a pause, during which the bow is held at full stretch, with the tip of the three-foot arrow projecting only a few inches beyond the bow; after that, the arrow is loosed. When Herrigel tried this, even without aiming, he found it was almost impossible. His hands trembled. His legs stiffened and grew cramped. His breathing became labored. And of course he could not possibly aim. Week after week he practiced this, with the Master watching him carefully and correcting his strained attitude; week after week he made no progress whatever. Finally he gave up and told his teacher that he could not learn: it was absolutely impossible for him to draw the bow and loose the arrow.

To his astonishment, the Master agreed. He said, "Certainly you cannot. It is because you are not breathing correctly. You must learn to breathe in a steady rhythm, keeping your lungs full most of the time, and drawing in one rapid inspiration with each stage of the process, as you grasp the bow, fit the arrow, raise the bow, draw, pause, and loose the shot. If you do, you will both grow stronger and be able to relax." To prove this, he himself drew his massive bow and told his pupil to feel the muscles of his arms: they were perfectly relaxed, as though he were doing no work whatever.

Herrigel now started breathing exercises; after some time he combined the new rhythm of breathing with the actions of drawing and shooting; and, much to his astonishment, he found that the whole thing, after this complicated process, had become much easier. Or rather, not easier, but different. At times it became quite unconscious. He says himself that he felt he was not breathing, but being breathed; and in time he felt that the occasional shot was not being dispatched by him, but shooting itself. The bow and arrow were in charge; he had become merely a part of them.

All this time, of course, Herrigel did not even attempt to discuss Zen docrine with his Master. No doubt he knew that he was approaching it, but he concentrated solely on learning how to shoot. Every stage which he surmounted appeared to lead to another stage even more difficult. It took him months to learn how to loosen the bowstring. The problem was this. If he gripped the string and arrowhead tightly, either he froze, so that his hands were slowly pulled together and the shot was wasted, or else he jerked, so that the arrow flew up into the air or down into the ground; and if he was relaxed, then the bowstring and arrow simply *leaked* out of his grasp before he could reach full stretch, and the arrow went nowhere. He explained this problem to the Master. The Master understood perfectly well. He replied, "You must hold the drawn bowstring like a child holding a grownup's finger. You know how firmly a child grips; and yet when it lets go, there is not the slightest jerk—because the child does not think of itself, it is not self-conscious, it does not say, 'I will now let go and do some- thing else,' it merely acts instinctively. That is what you must learn to do. Practice, practice, and practice, and then the string will loose itself at the right moment. The shot will come as effortlessly as snow slipping from a leaf." Day after day, week after week, month after month, Herrigel practiced this; and then, after one shot, the Master suddenly bowed and broke off the lesson. He said "Just then it shot. Not you, but *it*." And gradually thereafter more and more right shots achieved themselves; the young phi- losopher forgot himself, forgot that he was learning archery for some other purpose, forgot even that he was practicing archery, and became part of that unconsciously active complex, the bow, the string, the arrow, and the man.

Next came the target. After four years, Herrigel was allowed to shoot at the target. But he was strictly forbidden to aim at it. The Master explained that even he himself did not aim; and indeed, when he shot, he was so absorbed in the act, so selfless and unanx- ious, that his eyes were almost closed. It was difficult, almost impossible, for Herrigel to believe that such shooting could ever be effective; and he risked insulting the Master by suggesting that he ought to be able to hit the target blindfolded. But the Master accepted the challenge. That night, after a cup of tea and long meditation, he went into the archery hall, put on the lights at one end and left the target perfectly dark, with only a thin taper burning in front of it. Then, with habitual grace and precision, and with that strange, almost sleepwalking, selfless confidence that is the heart of Zen, he shot two arrows into the darkness. Herrigel went out to collect them. He found that the first had gone to the heart of the bull's eye, and that the second had actually hit the first arrow and splintered it. The Master showed no pride. He said,

"Perhaps, with unconscious memory of the position of the target, *I* shot the first arrow; but the second arrow? *It* shot the second arrow, and *it* brought it to the center of the target."

At last Herrigel began to understand. His progress became faster and faster; easier, too. Perfect shots (perfect because perfectly unconscious) occurred at almost every lesson; and finally, after six years of incessant training, in a public display he was awarded the diploma. He needed no further instruction: he had himself become a Master. His wife meanwhile had become expert both in painting and in the arrangement of flowers—two of the finest of Japanese arts. (I wish she could be persuaded to write a companion volume, called *Zen in the Art of Flower Arrangement*; it would have a wider general appeal than her husband's work.) I gather also from a hint or two in his book that she had taken part in the archery lessons. During one of the most difficult periods in Herrigel's training, when his Master had practically refused to continue teaching him—because Herrigel had tried to cheat by *consciously* opening his hand at the moment of loosing the arrow— his wife had advised him against that solution, and sympathized with him when it was rejected. She in her own way had learned more quickly than he, and reached the final point together with him. All their effort had not been in vain: Herrigel and his wife had really acquired a new and valuable kind of wisdom. Only at this point, when he was about to abandon his lessons forever, did his Master treat him almost as an equal and hint at the innermost doctrines of Zen Buddhism. Only hints he gave; and yet, for the young philosopher who had now become a mystic, they were enough. Herrigel understood the doctrine, not with his logical mind, but with his entire being. He at any rate had solved the mystery of Zen.

Without going through a course of training as absorbing and as complete as Herrigel's, we can probably never penetrate the mystery. The doctrine of Zen cannot be analyzed from without: it must be lived.

But although it cannot be analyzed, it can be hinted at. All the hints that the adherents of this creed give us are interesting. Many are fantastic; some are practically incomprehensible, and yet unforgettable. Put together, they take us toward a way of life which is utterly impossible for westerners living in a western world, and nevertheless has a deep fascination and contains some values which we must respect.

The word Zen means "meditation." (It is the Japanese word, corresponding to the Chinese Ch'an and the Hindu Dhyana.) It is the central idea of a special sect of Buddhism which flourished in China during the Sung period (between A.D. 1000 and 1300) and entered Japan in the twelfth century. Without knowing much about it, we might be certain that the Zen sect was a worthy and noble one, because it produced a quantity of highly distinguished art, specifically painting. And if we knew anything about Buddhism itself, we might say that Zen goes closer than other sects to the heart of Buddha's teaching: because Buddha was trying to found, not a religion with temples and rituals, but a way of life based on meditation. However, there is something eccentric about the Zen life which is hard to trace in Buddha's teaching; there is an active energy which he did not admire, there is a rough grasp on reality which he himself eschewed, there is something like a sense of humor, which he rarely displayed. The gravity and serenity of the Indian preacher are transformed, in Zen, to the earthy liveliness of Chinese and Japanese sages. The lotus brooding calmly on the water has turned into a knotted tree covered with spring blossoms.

In this sense, "meditation" does not mean what we usually think of when we say a philosopher meditates: analysis of reality, a long-sustained effort to solve problems of religion and ethics, the logical dissection of the universe. It means something not divisive, but whole; not schematic, but organic; not long-drawn-out, but immediate. It means something more like our words "intuition" and "realization." It means a way of life in which there is no division between thought and action; none of the painful gulf, so well known to all of us, between the unconscious and the conscious mind; and no absolute distinction between the self and the external world, even between the various parts of the external world and the whole.

When the German philosopher took six years of lessons in archery in order to approach the mystical significance of Zen, he was not given direct philosophical instruction. He was merely shown how to breathe, how to hold and loose the bowstring, and finally how to shoot in such a way that the bow and arrow used him as an instrument. There are many such stories about Zen teachers. The strangest I know is one about a fencing master who undertook to train a young man in the art of the sword. The relationship of teacher and pupil is very important, almost sacred, in the Far East; and the pupil hardly ever thinks of leaving a master or objecting to his methods, however extraordinary they may seem. Therefore this young fellow did not at first object when he was made to act as a servant, drawing water, sweeping floors, gathering wood for the fire, and cooking. But after some time he asked for more direct instruction. The master agreed to give it, but produced no swords. The routine went on just as before, except that every now and then the master would strike the young man with a stick. No matter what he was doing, sweeping the floor or weeding in the garden, a blow would descend on him apparently out of nowhere; he had always to be on the alert, and yet he was constantly receiving unexpected cracks on the head or shoulders. After some months of this, he saw his master stooping over a boiling pot full of vegetables; and he thought he would have his revenge. Silently he lifted a stick and brought it down; but without any effort, without even a glance in his direction, his master parried the blow with the lid of the cooking pot. At last, the pupil began to understand the instinctive alertness, the effortless perception and avoidance of danger, in which his master had been training him. As soon as he had achieved it, it was child's play for him to learn the management of the sword: he could parry every cut and turn every slash without anxiety, until his opponent, exhausted, left an opening for his counterattack. (The same principle was used by the elderly samurai for selecting his comrades in the Japanese motion picture *The Magnificent Seven.*)

These stories show that Zen meditation does not mean sitting and thinking. On the contrary, it means acting with as little thought as possible. The fencing master trained his pupil to guard against every attack with the same immediate, instinctive rapidity with which our eyelid closes over our eye when something threatens it. His work was aimed at breaking down the wall between thought and act, at completely fusing body and senses and mind so that they might all work together rapidly and effortlessly. When a Zen artist draws a picture, he does it in a rhythm almost the exact reverse of that which is followed by a Western artist. We begin by blocking out the design and then filling in the details, usually working more and more slowly as we approach the completion of the picture. The Zen artist sits down very calmly; examines his brush carefully; prepares his own ink; smooths out the paper on which he will work; falls into a profound silent ecstasy of contemplation—during which he does not think anxiously of various details, composition, brushwork, shades of tone, but rather attempts to become the vehicle through which the subject can express itself in painting; and then, very quickly and almost unconsciously, with sure effortless strokes, draws a picture containing the fewest and most effective lines. Most of the paper is left blank; only the essential is depicted, and that not completely. One long curving line will be enough to show a mountainside; seven streaks will become a group of bamboos bending in the wind; and yet, though technically incomplete, such pictures are unforgettably clear. They show the heart of reality.

All this we can sympathize with, because we can see the results. The young swordsman learns how to fence. The intuitional painter produces a fine picture. But the hardest thing for us to appreciate is that the Zen masters refuse to teach philosophy or religion directly, and deny logic. In fact, they despise logic as an artificial distortion of reality. Many philosophical teachers are difficult to understand because they analyze profound problems with subtle intricacy: such is Aristotle in his *Metaphysics*. Many mystical writers are difficult to understand because, as they themselves admit, they are attempting to use words to describe experiences which are too abstruse for words, so that they have to fall back on imagery and analogy, which they themselves recognize to be poor media, far coarser than the realities with which they have been in contact. But the Zen teachers seem to deny the power of language and thought altogether. For example, if you ask a Zen master what is the ultimate reality, he will answer, without the slightest hesitation, "The bamboo grove at the foot of the hill" or "A branch of plum blossom." Apparently he means that these things, which we can see instantly without effort, or imagine in the flash of a second, are real with the ultimate reality; that nothing is more real than these; and that we ought to grasp ultimates as we grasp simple immediates. A Chinese master was once asked the central question, "What is the Buddha?" He said nothing whatever, but held out his index finger. What did he mean? It is hard to explain; but apparently he meant "Here. Now. Look and realize with the effortlessness of seeing. Do not try to use words. Do not think. Make no efforts toward withdrawal from the world. Expect no sublime ecstasies. Live. All *that* is the ultimate reality, and it can be understood from the motion of a finger as well as from the execution of any complex ritual, from any subtle argument, or from the circling of the starry universe."

In making that gesture, the master was copying the Buddha himself, who once delivered a sermon which is famous, but was hardly understood by his pupils at the time. Without saying a word, he held up a flower and showed it to the gathering. One man, one alone, knew what he meant. The gesture became renowned as the Flower Sermon.

In the annals of Zen there are many cryptic answers to the final question, "What is the Buddha?"—which in our terms means "What is the meaning of life? What is truly real?" For example, one master, when asked "What is the Buddha?" replied, "Your name is Yecho." Another said, "Even the finest artist cannot paint him." Another said, "No nonsense here." And another answered, "The mouth is the gate of woe." My favorite story is about the monk who said to a Master, "Has a dog Buddha-nature too?" The Master replied, "Wu"—which is what the dog himself would have said.

Now, some critics might attack Zen by saying that this is the creed of a savage or an animal. The adherents of Zen would deny that—or more probably they would ignore the criticism, or make some cryptic remark which meant that it was pointless. Their position—if they could ever be persuaded to put it into words—would be this. An animal is instinctively in touch with reality, and so far is living rightly, but it has never had a mind and so cannot perceive the Whole, only that part with which it is in touch. The philosopher sees both the Whole and the parts, and enjoys them all. As for the savage, he exists only through the group; he feels himself as part of a war party or a ceremonial dance team or a ploughing-and-sowing group or the Snake clan; he is not truly an individual at all, and therefore is less than fully human. Zen has at its heart an inner solitude; its aim is to teach us to live, as in the last resort we do all have to live, alone.

A more dangerous criticism of Zen would be that it is nihilism, that its purpose is to abolish thought altogether. (This criticism is handled, but not fully met, by the great Zen authority Suzuki in his *Introduction to Zen Buddhism*.) It can hardly be completely confuted, for after all the central doctrine of Buddhism is—Nothingness. And many of the sayings of Zen masters are truly nihilistic. The first patriarch of the sect in China was asked by the emperor what was the ultimate and holiest principle of Buddhism. He replied, "Vast emptiness, and nothing holy in it." Another who was asked the searching question "Where is the abiding-place for the mind?" answered, "Not in this dualism of good and evil, being and non-being, thought and matter." In fact, thought is an activity which divides. It analyzes, it makes distinctions, it criticizes, it judges, it breaks reality into groups and classes and individuals. The aim of Zen is to abolish that kind of thinking, and to substitute—not unconsciousness, which would be death, but a consciousness that does not analyze but experiences life directly. Although it has no prescribed prayers, no sacred scriptures, no ceremonial rites, no personal god, and no interest in the soul's future destination, Zen is a religion rather than a philosophy. Jung points out that its aim is to produce a religious conversion, a "transformation": and he adds, "The transformation process is incommensurable with intellect." Thought is always interesting, but often painful; Zen is calm and painless. Thought is incomplete; Zen enlightenment brings a sense of completeness. Thought is a process; Zen illumination is a state. But it is a state which cannot be defined. In the Buddhist scriptures there is a dialogue between a master and a pupil in which the pupil tries to discover the exact meaning of such a state. The master says to him, 'If a fire were blazing in front of you, would you know that it was blazing?'

"Yes, master."

"And would you know the reason for its blazing?"

"Yes, because it had a supply of grass and sticks."

"And would you know if it were to go out?"

"Yes, master."

"And on its going out, would you know where the fire had gone? To the east, to the west, to the north, or to the south?"

"The question does not apply, master. For the fire blazed because it had a supply of grass and sticks. When it had consumed this and had no other fuel, then it went out."

"In the same way," replies the master, "no question will apply to the meaning of Nirvana, and no statement will explain it."

Such, then, neither happy nor unhappy but beyond all divisive description, is the condition which students of Zen strive to attain. Small wonder that they can scarcely explain it to us, the unilluminated.

QUESTIONS FOR STUDY, DISCUSSION, AND WRITING

1. What difficulties does Highet face in discussing Zen? How does he manage to give a definition in spite of his statement that Zen "cannot be analyzed"?
2. Why does Highet describe the training in archery in such detail?
3. On page 1170 Highet says that "Zen is a religion rather than a philosophy." How has he led up to this conclusion? What definitions of "religion" and "philosophy" does he imply?
4. By what means does Highet define "meditation"? Would other means have worked as well? Explain.
5. To what extent is Zen "the creed of a savage or an animal"? How does Highet go about refuting this charge?

O. HOBART MOWRER

Psychiatry and Religion

As we move forward, with ever-accelerating tempo, into what we are pleased to call the Age of Science, we are faced by an awesome paradox. As man, through science, acquires more and more control over the external world, he has come to feel less and less capable of controlling himself, less and less the master of his own soul and destiny. In the same decade in which we produced the atomic submarine and started probing interstellar space, we have also seen, significantly, the emergence of the Beatnik; personality disintegration has become endemic; and society itself is commonly said to be "sick." We remain optimistic about what man can continue to do through science by way of dealing with his environment, but we have become extremely pessimistic about man.

This reciprocal relationship is not accidental: the same presuppositions and intellectual operations that have given us such unprecedented power over nature when extended to ourselves produce a pervasive feeling of helplessness, confusion, resignation, desperation. We seem to be the hapless pawns of a great mechanical, impersonal juggernaut called the cosmos. By the very principles and premises that have led to the conquest of the outer world, we ourselves lose our autonomy, dignity, self-mastery, responsibility, indeed, our very identity. Little wonder, then, that we feel weak, lost, fearful, "beat." Being part of nature, we, too, apparently obey strict cause-and-effect principles; and if this be true, if our own experience and conduct are as rigidly determined and predetermined as is the rest of nature, the whole notion of purpose, responsibility, meaning seems to vanish. At the moment of our greatest technological triumphs, which include the tapping of almost unlimited sources of physical energy and the achievement of fabulous mechanical, chemical, and biological know-how, we become uncertain, lose confidence, and brood about annihilation. At the same time, some highly pertinent developments are quietly and unobtrusively occurring in psychological and sociological thought which hold promise of delivering us from our current predicament, both philosophically and practically.

Pre-Reformation Catholicism held man "doubly responsible," which is to say, capable of both good and evil. When, in this context, one behaved badly, it was to his discredit; and when one behaved well, it was decidedly to his credit. There was thus for each individual a sort of moral balance sheet, as it has been called, and ultimate salvation or damnation depended, quite simply and directly, on the number and magnitude of the entries on the two sides of this fateful ledger.

Obviously there was much in common sense and everyday experience to support such an ethical system, but there were also, unfortunately, broad opportunity and temptation for those responsible for its administration to pervert and abuse it. The problem of justice in *this* life presents difficulties enough, and when one enters into the subtleties of a life to come, the only restraints upon dogmatic assertion and egregious exploitation are the fertility of ecclesiastical imagination and the credulity of the faithful. For at least four hundred years prior to the Reformation, the will to resist such perversity had continued to decline, and by the beginning of the sixteenth century, the great triumphant Church Universal was fairly riddled with connivance, sophistry, sloth, and extortion.

Men of learning and independence of thought were, of course, well aware of this sad state of affairs long before the outbreak of what we think of as the Reformation proper. And pre-eminent among such men was the Dutch scholar and humanist Desiderius Erasmus, who made a two-pronged attack upon the situation. In his immediately successful and popular book *In Praise of Folly* (1511), he focused a delicate but deadly wit upon the Church's hypocrisy and corruption, and behind his Greek edition of the *New Testament* (1516) was the momentous imputation that it was not the Church that was the ultimate authority in religious matters but the Bible itself.

When, in 1517, Martin Luther nailed the ninety-five theses to the door of the Castle Church of Wittenberg, it was therefore not surprising that Erasmus was interested. The essence of Luther's position, particularly as it has filtered down to us through John Calvin and other Protestant expositors, is that man is responsible, so to say, in only one direction: capable of choosing the wrong and fully accountable for having done so, he is, however, supposedly unable to do anything whatever toward his own redemption and must wait, helplessly, upon the unpredictable favor, or "grace," of God. It is, of course, not difficult to see why such a curious and one-sided doctrine was conceived and advocated with such insistence: it cut the whole logic from under the Church's emphasis upon good works, including both penances and indulgences, and thus succeeded where more moderate programs of reform had failed.

Erasmus (in the tradition of the Apostle James, Pelagius, Jerome, and, later, Arminius) had insisted upon human freedom and responsibility in the matter of both evil and good and had asked only for greater honesty in the assignment of the credit for each kind of action. But Luther and Calvin, seizing upon selected segments in the teachings of Saint Paul and Saint Augustine, stridently repudiated this position, and in so doing were able to produce an ideological and institutional change of enormous historical significance.

We are no doubt justified in looking back upon the Reformation as representing, in many ways, a magnificent achievement. But we have been slow to appreciate, it seems, how dearly it has cost us. Protestantism, whatever its virtues and strengths, has also had the tragic consequence of leaving us without clear and effective means of dealing with personal guilt. And it is this fact, I submit, more than any other that is responsible for what Paul Tillich has aptly called "the psychic disintegration of the masses" in modern times.

By the turn of the century, the influence of religion and moral suasion had so far declined that the medical profession was being inundated by a new type of illness. Purely functional in origin but often expressed somatically, the new malady was characterized by a pervasive "loss of nerve," which, as a matter of medical convenience, was dubbed "neurosis." But the condition needed more than a name; it called for specific treatment, which medicine tried, without success, to provide. Hydrotherapy, hypnotism, electrical massage, bromides, and a dozen other nostrums came and went, but neurosis remained, unfathomed and unconquered.

In this era of confusion and crisis, psychoanalysis had its inception and spectacular proliferation. Religion had disqualified itself for dealing honestly and effectively with man's deepest moral and spiritual anguish. Freud's discoveries purported to rescue man from the perplexities of the Protestant ethic and the ravages of unresolved guilt, not by restoring him to full ethical responsibility but by relieving him of all responsibility. In short, the notion was that one should not feel guilty about anything. Freud tacitly agreed with Luther and Calvin that man is helpless to save (cure) himself, but he took the momentous further step of also holding no one accountable for having fallen into "neurosis"—which is just a medical euphemism for what had formerly been known as a state of sin—in the first place. "All behavior is caused" became the sanctimonious rallying cry for the new movement, for at one stroke it gave the appearance of advancing the science of mind and providing a powerful therapeutic procedure. Now, instead of mistreating the criminal, the insane, and the neurotic, we would understand and help them, treat them (for a fee). And this was all to be achieved not by a return to the outmoded principle of double responsibility but by adoption of a new and radical doctrine of double *irresponsibility*.

This innovation was, of course, acclaimed as a great scientific and cultural gain. Not only would we now be able to turn to others for treatment, thus confirming the Protestant thesis that we cannot help ourselves; we could also hold others accountable for our having got into such a predicament in the first place.

But as the clock of history has ticked off the decades of this century, we have gradually discovered that Freud's great postulate, not of total depravity but of total determinism, has liberated us only in the sense of dumping us from the frying pan into the fire. At long last we seem to be waking up to the fact that to be "free" in the sense of embracing the doctrine of double irresponsibility is not to be free at all, humanly speaking, but lost.

Within the past five years there has been a growing realization, at least in the disciplines most intimately concerned with such matters, of the futility, the deadly peril of this general trend. After an extensive study of the therapeutic claims and accomplishments of psychoanalysis, the English psychologist Dr. Hans Eysenck has recently summed up the situation with this laconic statement: "The success of the Freudian revolution seemed complete. Only one thing went wrong: *the patients did not get any better*." And this verdict has been amply borne out by numerous other inquiries of a similar kind.

Naturally, the doctrine of total determinism radiated from the field of psychopathology to criminology, and we were soon being told that not even those individuals convicted of legal crimes were really responsible; instead, they too were sick and in need of treatment rather than correction or conversion. Lawyers, judges, legislators, and psychiatrists are at present deeply embroiled in the question of criminal responsibility versus the doctrine of the irresistible impulse, but there have been several developments which suggest that the status of "expert testimony" may be undergoing serious reappraisal. The psychoanalytically oriented physician or psychiatrist who argues the doctrine of psychic determinism for others must either consistently apply it—and render himself irresponsible, incompetent, sick—or else assume an aura of omnipotence. The position of the psychiatric expert in our courts is currently not an enviable one.

Two years ago, Professor Richard La Piere of the Department of Sociology of Stanford University published a sobering volume with the tongue-in-cheek title *The Freudian Ethic,* in which he holds that in generally abandoning the Protestant ethic, whatever its shortcomings (and they are grievous), and espousing psychoanalysis we have moved, as an entire society, not toward salvation but perdition. With many other social analysts, La Piere agrees that, as a people, we are indeed sick, but argues that the very essence of our sickness is that we so freely resort to this concept instead of holding ourselves and others accountable.

While psychoanalysis was developing as a predominantly medical enterprise, a parallel movement with similar philosophic and practical implications was also taking form and gaining momentum in academic circles. I refer to the radical repudiation, in the first two or three decades of this century, of all that was inward, subjective, and personal, known as behaviorism, with its new and exclusive emphasis upon that form of cause-effect relationship implied by the so-called stimulus-response, or S-R, formula. Here determinism, although couched in somewhat different terms, was no less absolute than in psychoanalysis, and the individual was again relieved—or should we say deprived?—of all semblance of accountability. Behavior or action or conduct was the inevitable consequence of "antecedent stimulus conditions" (causes), and moral accountability became, in this context, a meaningless and, indeed, opprobrious concept. The conditioned and unconditioned reflex, in the language of Pavlov and Watson, was the "functional unit" of all behavior; and Thorndike, in his slightly different theory of habit, likewise spoke of stimulus-response "connections" or "bonds." All of which had at least the incidental effect, if not intent, of obliterating the whole notion of freedom, choice, responsibility by reducing behavior, absolutely and completely, to S-R connections and reflexes.

Some years ago the ambiguity of this situation came home to me in a particularly dramatic way. At that time I was still trying to do a little psychotherapy of the conventional kind, and on more than one occasion graduate students came to me for help who, in the course of our interviews, spontaneously remarked that one of the main inducements for them to go into psychology as a vocation was that they had long suffered from unresolved guilt, which psychology, with its scientific emphasis upon stimulus-response, cause-effect connections, seemed logically to eliminate. But the fact that these students were now in therapy was palpable proof that this stratagem had not worked. The behavioristic doctrine of total determinism manifestly does not deliver us from the one-sided determinism of Luther and Calvin any more effectively than does that brand of complete irresponsibility adduced by Freud. If the doctrines of Luther and Calvin disposed the Western world to "Christian despair," those of Freud and Watson have, it seems, engulfed us in a despair that is infinitely deeper and more absolute.

It is only within the last decade or so that we have begun to see a way out. The existentialists, in their very legitimate protests against the general abrogation of responsibility—first one-sidedly, in Protestant theology, and then more systematically, in psychoanalysis and behaviorism—have recently been attracting some well-deserved attention. But when they go on to reject the scientific approach, totally and inherently, they are on dangerous ground and may shortly find themselves, in this regard, discredited.

Having denounced Protestant predestination and psychological determinism alike, what do the existentialists offer, alternatively? Only a counsel of brave despair, an admonition to have the courage to be, on the assumption that being (existence) is an ironic joke and ultimate tragedy. Just how do we come by this courage? By lifting ourselves by our own bootstraps? In practice, it seems that this philosophy leaves us quite as helpless and hopeless as does the Protestant principle, with its emphasis upon man's inevitable guilt and God's uncertain grace.

If one takes the time to examine contemporary behavior theory, one finds that scientific developments in psychology have moved a long way from the naïve and primitive assumptions of behaviorism. Now it is generally agreed that there is by no means a reflexive or ineluctable connection between stimulation and response. Now we are quite certain that the coupling between our sensory receptors and our muscles is much looser and infinitely more complicated than the earlier theories implied. According to present views, stimulation may suggest a given response or course of action, but whether we "give consent," as Catholic theologians would say, to the suggestion, thought, or image is dependent upon the hopes and fears which we weigh and ponder in deciding whether to act or refrain from acting. In other words, given a stimulus, a particular and predetermined response does not automatically pop out of the organism, as our earlier, push-button psychology seemed to demand. Response—and responsibility—in this new frame of reference is crucially dependent upon the anticipated consequences of our actions. In short, we have rediscovered reason. Instead of being merely stimulated (the Latin term for "goaded"), living organisms become goal-directed, purposive, deliberate, or, if you will, free and responsible.

Beginning with the naïve and oversimplified behaviorism of

Watson, academic psychology in this century has thus achieved a relatively advanced degree of sophistication; whereas psychoanalysis, which started with Freud's highly elaborated and ingenious speculations, has rather steadily involuted, regressed. The original emphasis on unconscious (irresponsible) motivation has, of late years, given way to a new accent on "ego psychology," which involves frequent reference to "ego strength" and "ego weakness" in a manner unmistakably reminiscent of the older notions of character and will power; and with the ink hardly dry on this ego-psychology literature, psychoanalysts are now beginning to show a new respect for and interest in the superego, or conscience.

These developments, I say, are retrogressive as far as Freud's original formulations go, but in terms of common sense they are decidedly in the right direction. However, they are suicidal as far as psychoanalysis itself is concerned, which was conceived and laid its claim to recognition as an independent discipline along very different lines.

All the developments just reviewed thus strike a new note, or at least one that has considerable novelty for contemporary men and women. Once more we are coming to perceive man as pre-eminently a social creature, whose greatest and most devastating anguish is experienced not in physical pain or biological deprivation but when he feels alienated, disgraced, guilty, debased as a person. And the thrust of much current therapeutic effort is in the direction of trying to help such individuals recover their sociality, relatedness, community identity.

Here, surely, is a promising meeting ground for psychology, psychiatry, and sociology and for much that is common to both classical Judaism and authentic Christianity. But, logically and programmatically, it strikes at the heart of the Protestant principle. Yesterday, as a Presbyterian, I attended church and heard the minister quote Reinhold Niebuhr, with approval, to the effect that "Christian faith is more profound than mere moral idealism," thus echoing the contempt which Protestantism has always had for the "merely moral man." And the preceding Sunday I heard another minister preach a fine "Reformation" sermon on the theme that "the fruit of grace is responsibility for action in the world"; that is, the theme that we are good because—and if—we are saved, not the reverse. Scientific and humanistic thought can never, I believe, come to terms with such hyperbole. The fact that Protestant theologians keep reverting in their sermons to the question of just what it means to be "saved by grace," rather than by works, suggests that they are themselves not quite certain.

As a psychologist, I have no competence to judge the effectiveness of religion in saving men's immortal souls, and, I confess, this is not my major interest. But I do maintain that religion has great potential for serving, and saving, men and women in this world which is not now being at all adequately realized. If, in the secular sciences, we have rediscovered something of the logic and conditions of responsible action, perhaps this will be an encouragement to the theologians themselves to take a more courageous and responsible position and quit hiding behind a preposterous piece of medieval sophistry.

C. E. M. JOAD

Mr. Hoyle and the Physical Universe[1]

The immediate occasion of the writing of this book was the delivery in the summer of 1950 of a series of broadcast talks by Mr. Fred Hoyle, subsequently published in a book entitled *The Nature of the Universe.* They set me pondering again over questions to which I had given little thought since the astronomers gave our laymen's minds their last jolt some twenty years ago. Sir James Jeans and Sir Arthur Eddington possessed great gifts of popular exposition and their books helped us to understand something of the revolution which had taken place since the beginning of the century in man's conception of the nature of the physical universe. The universe was, it seemed, not only much larger but much more complicated than we had believed.

Now, twenty years later, the universe revealed by the astronomers is again different; it is again larger and it is not a whit less mysterious. The presentation of this revised picture should not, I suppose, logically affect our outlook. Physics and astronomy are concerned to accumulate facts; philosophy and religion to interpret them. The discovery that the sun is more likely to explode and roast the earth than to grow cold and freeze it, or the injunction to add a nought or so to our estimates of the size of space or the span of time which were already inconceivably large, even the conception of the continuous creation of matter, have not, as far as I can see, any *necessary* bearing upon our views as to the nature of the universe as a whole, more particularly as regards its origin, purpose, destiny and end. Nevertheless, these things do make a difference—they do, at any rate, to me—if only because they reinforce my sense of the mystery of the universe and its awesomeness.

Stages in Man's Attitude to the Cosmos

Man's attitude to the universe seems to have passed roughly through three stages. First, there is the attitude of the savage set in a world that he is unable to understand, living his life at the mercy of natural forces whose genesis escapes detection and whose

1. Chapter II of *The Recovery of Belief,* 1951.

workings evade control. His universe is not only mysterious, but forbidding, and to lessen the mystery, to diminish the menace, he peoples it with semi-human figures of his own imagining, gods and goddesses, spirits good and bad, demons and devils. These, too, for the most part, are fearful, but, unlike the impersonal forces of nature, they are also accessible. They can be propitiated, for example, and bribed.

Secondly, there are the triumphant advance of science and the apparently limitless possibilities of explanation opened up by the scientific method. The first effect of the discoveries of the sciences was to reduce the importance of man by enlarging the scale of the known universe, so that life in general and human life in particular seemed no more than a tiny glow, flickering uncertainly in the vast immensities of geological time and astronomical space. The discoveries of science further exhibited—or were thought some fifty years ago to exhibit—the universe as essentially material and human life as a sort of outside passenger traveling across a fundamentally alien environment. Point and purpose, design and intention were eliminated so effectively that even such a doughty champion of science as H. G. Wells declared in consternation: "Unless there is a more abundant life before mankind, this scheme of space and time is a bad joke beyond our understanding, a flare of vulgarity, an empty laugh braying across the mysteries."

But though they made man small and the universe large, the scientists, during their period of explanatory triumph which reached its climax some seventy years ago, did make it comprehensible; so much so that Professor Tyndall, in his presidential address to the British Association in 1874, could look forward to a day when science would be able to envisage and explain all that has happened and all that will happen in terms of "the ultimately purely natural and inevitable march of evolution from the atoms of the primeval nebula to the proceedings of the British Association for the Advancement of Science." As for life and mind, T. H. Huxley, lecturing to the British Association, did not hesitate to assert that "the thoughts to which I am now giving utterance and your thoughts regarding them are expressions of the molecular changes in the matter of life."

Today that phase has passed and we know too much about the universe to think that we know anything for certain. We have, indeed, entered upon a third phase in which mystery has returned with a vengeance and the physical universe shows itself to be not only queerer than we understand but, it may be, queerer than we can understand. Each fresh advance in human knowledge reveals a greater unknown. Nor, on reflection, is this surprising. If you think of knowledge as a little glowing patch, a circle of light, set in an area of environing darkness, the darkness of the unknown, then the more you enlarge the circle of the known, the more also you enlarge its area of contact with the unknown.

Mr. Hoyle's Picture of the Physical World

Such, at any rate, has been the effect of this book of Hoyle's upon myself, nor have the severe strictures to which it has subsequently been exposed on the ground that he presents personal speculations as agreed conclusions and suggests that the sketch of the universe whose outlines he has drawn is in some sense a final picture instead of being a temporary daub, liable to be superseded as its many predecessors have been superseded, substantially weakened the impression that it has produced. For it seems unlikely that any subsequent modifications of Mr. Hoyle's sketch will have the effect of lessening the magnitude and mystery of the universe. Whether it is because of a change in myself, a change from the confidence of the young to the hesitations of the older man, or whether the universe has, in fact, come to seem more mysterious, as it has come to be better known, I am impressed by its magnitude and wonder as never before. It was, in the circumstances, natural enough that I should be set thinking again of the mind that planned it.

Mr. Hoyle apparently agrees. "It is my view," he writes, "that man's unguided imagination could never have chanced on such a structure as I have put before you in these talks. No literary genius could have invented a story one hundredth part as fantastic as the sober facts that have been unearthed by astronomical science." "I think," he adds, "that Newton would have been quite unprepared for any such revelation, and that it would have had a shattering effect on him."

Particularly striking are the conceptions of the receding galaxies and the continuous creation of matter. As new galaxies condense out of what Mr. Hoyle calls "inter-stellar gas," they begin to recede. While the nearest are moving at the rate of several million miles an hour, the further they recede the faster they move, so that the most distant observable through our biggest telescope are traveling at the rate of over two hundred million miles an hour. This consideration leads to the concept of the limits of the observable universe. At a sufficient distance from us the galaxies will be moving at the speed of light itself. This means that "the further a galaxy is away from us the more its distance will increase during the time required by its light to reach us," so that, if it is far enough away, its light will never reach us at all. The limiting distance is, in fact, about two thousand million light years. The largest of our telescopes, which is on Mount Palomar, can penetrate to about half that distance; that is to say, about half the theoretically observable universe is already under our observation. Double that area, and the limit of what the human eye can or could observe is reached. Beyond that limit lies what?

So far as the word of astronomy goes, the answer can only be "much the same as lies on this side." "Theory," says Mr. Hoyle, "requires the galaxies to go on for ever, even though we cannot see them. That is to say, the galaxies are expanding out into an infinite space." It seems likely enough. It would be an odd and very arbitrary coincidence if the limits of the universe coincided with the limits of our possible observation. The universe, then, is not finite as the theory of relativity was at one time thought to suggest, but infinite. Indeed, it is only to one particular system of space and time that Einstein's special theory of relativity applies. But it is far from clear that astronomy is here entitled to have the last word.

The Philosophers on Space and Time

For at this point the philosophers put a question: can we, they ask, think of space that extends for ever? I doubt if we can. The concept is not, as it seems to me, one that the mind can grasp. Can we, on the other hand, think of it as coming to an end, as in fact bounded? Again we cannot. For if it is bounded it must be bounded by something; it must, so to say, have an edge. And beyond that edge lies what? Either something or nothing. The "something," if it is a physical something—and it is difficult to see what else could be a boundary to space—must itself be in space; and "nothing" is equivalent to empty space. Here, then, is a contradiction.

In this situation philosophers have traditionally made two inferences. Either they have said, space is not wholly real, since it will not in the last resort bear thinking about but leads the mind into contradictions and reality cannot be self-contradictory, or our minds are not capable of fully grasping it.

Similarly with time. Twenty years ago Sir James Jeans presented us with a graphic picture of a universe which was gradually running down in accordance with the second law of thermo-dynamics. Throughout the universe processes of energy diffusion due to the breaking down of the radio-active atoms were everywhere observable. Nowhere was any instance of the contrary process observed. When all the energy originally stored in the radio-active atoms had been equally diffused, there would be no more happenings of any kind in the universe which would come to rest in a universal stagnation. The process of ubiquitous energy diffusion seemed to entail an act or process of energy concentration. If the contents of a parcel are being continuously and uniformly scattered, somebody must have done the parcel up. Hence Jeans was led to postulate an act or series of acts of creation. "Everything," he wrote, "points with overwhelming force to a definite event or series of events of creation at some time or times not infinitely remote."

But this picture, too, has changed. A series of ingenious arguments leads Mr. Hoyle to conclude—and the view is apparently widely shared—that what is apparently empty space is not, in fact, empty but contains inter-stellar gas which simply appears. The inter-stellar gas is extremely thinly spread—"the average rate of appearance amounts to no more than the creation of one atom in the course of about a year in a volume equal to St. Paul's Cathedral." Nevertheless, the total rate of appearance for "the observable universe alone is about a hundred million million million million million tons per second." The inter-stellar gas condenses to form galaxies, the galaxies, stars, and from the explosions of the stars are born planets. Thus it is the creation of inter-stellar gas that drives the universe forward. It also invalidates Sir James Jeans's picture. The inter-stellar gas consists of hydrogen atoms. "Hydrogen is being steadily converted into helium and the other elements throughout the universe and this conversion is a one-way process." Unless new hydrogen were being continuously created, it would all have been used up long ago. Nevertheless, the matter of the universe today still consists almost entirely of hydrogen. If, Mr. Hoyle notes, "matter were infinitely old, this would be quite impossible." (Yet it doesn't seem incompatible with Jeans's notion of the creation of the universe at a time *not* infinitely remote.)

Also if matter were infinitely old, and new matter were *not* constantly being created, all the galaxies would long ago have receded beyond the limits of our possible observation. Hence Mr. Hoyle's conclusion that "material simply appears—it is created." This creation, he thinks, has been going on and will go on endlessly. For this reason, if we were to make a film of the universe from any position in space, and the film were run indefinitely, a spectator, however long he watched, would notice a "general sameness" about it. The universe would also look the same, if the film were run backwards. For "whether we run the film backwards or forwards, the large-scale features of that universe remain unchanged." The conclusion is that time, like space, is endless in both directions. And the philosopher's comment is the same: can you, he asks, conceive of endless time? For my part, I do not think that I can. Can you, then, he asks again, think of time coming to an end? Again my answer is that I cannot. For at or after the end of time there would assuredly be either something or nothing. The something would require to be in time and there is no such thing as nothing. Also the ending would itself presumably have to occur *at* a time so that the end of time is also in time which means, presumably, that it is not, after all, the end. Time, in fact, will bear thinking about even less than space.

The Creation of Matter

Reading Mr. Hoyle, I tried to bring myself to make the imaginative effort required to conceive the nature of matter. The current theory of the ultimate constitution of matter requires us to think of it in terms of atoms. Now the atom is itself a universe in which the planetary electrons in their orbits are relatively as far from the nucleus as the earth is from the sun, while one orbit is—allowing for the difference of scale—as far from another as the orbit of the earth is from that of Pluto. Yet the entire universe of the atom is so small that, in a striking phrase of Ritchie Calder, "if the entire population of the world were to work in eighty-four hour shifts, counting incessantly day and night, it would take them three years to count a thimble full of atoms."

Facts of this kind ought not, I know, to impress me, nor, as I remarked above, ought they to make any difference to one's general concept of the universe. For, what is size that so much should be made of it? It is no more wonderful, it may be said, for God to have made the vastness of the galaxies or the smallness of the atom than to have made the sea, the sky, the earth, the frost or the rain.

Agreed. Yet I *am* impressed, nevertheless, impressed beyond measure by the size and majesty of the universe and by the insignificance of our attempts to comprehend it. What, for example, are we to make of Mr. Hoyle's conception of the continuous creation of inter-stellar gas? The universe, it seems, is being continually furnished with fresh raw material in the shape of hydrogen atoms. Where does this material come from? Apparently from nowhere. It just appears. But if it comes from nowhere it is created and, if created, uncaused. For creation means the appearance of something where there was nothing, or, alternatively, the occurrence of events for which there can be assigned no causes of which the occurrent events can be regarded as the effects. It contradicts, therefore, the assumption upon which physical science, as we have known it, has been built, the assumption, namely, that nature is an orderly scheme in which each event is the determined result of the set of conditions that produced it. If uncaused events can occur, if, indeed, they are occurring all the time, what becomes of the claim of science to enable us to calculate and predict, a claim which, one would suppose, can be sustained only in so far as there are *no* uncaused events, since these must, from the very nature of the case, evade calculation and prediction?

Science and Explanation

What, further, becomes of the claim of science to tell us the whole truth about the world? Scientists, you may say, never made such a claim—or at any rate they don't make it now. Perhaps, perhaps not; but what is not doubtful is that the *plain man believes* that science makes it. He believes, that is to say, that though much, nay, most of the universe is still unknown to science at the present time, much has also been discovered and that what remains is theoretically discoverable by an extension of the same methods as those which have already met with such signal success and will be found amenable to the operation of the same laws as those whose workings have already been mapped. But to revert only to the notions upon which I have briefly touched, to space, to time, and to the continuous creation of matter, so far from being explicable, they are not, so far as I can see, even conceivable in the terms of the concepts which science employs for its thinking.

Moreover, even if science is no longer a stick with which to beat religion, the plain man's indifference to or contempt for religion is largely the effect of science. For he has grown up in an intellectual climate which science has formed for him to accept the criterion of reality with which science has provided him. Not only does he believe the world of matter that science explores to be real, but he believes that whatever else is real must be of the same nature as matter. Now matter is what you can see and touch. Hence to enquire into the nature of the things we see and touch, to analyze them into their elements and atoms, is to deal directly with reality; to apprehend values or to enjoy religious experience—in fact, to enjoy any experience which does not spring from contact with the physical—is to wander in a world of shadows. In sum, to use the eye of the body to view the physical world is to acquaint oneself with what is real; to use that of the soul to see visions is to become the victim of illusion. Such I take to be the instinctive beliefs of contemporary common sense.

Parallel with the belief that the real must be a substance tangible and visible is the belief that it must be subject to the laws which are observed to operate in the physical world—that it must work, in sort, like a machine. As Professor Eddington puts it, nineteenth-century science was disposed, as soon as it scented a piece of mechanism, to exclaim: "Here we are getting to bedrock. This is what things should resolve themselves into. This is ultimate reality." The implication was that whatever did not work like a machine—the sense of value, for example, or the feeling of moral obligation, or belief in God—was not quite real, or, even if the sense, the feeling and the belief were admitted to be real since, after all, they really were experienced, that the objects to which they apparently pointed were not. Common sense again agrees.

But to judge from the works and conversation of *contemporary* physicists, there is no longer any basis even in science for these beliefs. Now, it was the growing conviction that the reasons which science was formerly thought to afford, or which most people thought that it afforded, for dismissing the religious view of the universe, were no longer valid, that set me exploring this time-honored ground once again. For whatever the universe might as a whole, whatever it might at bottom be like, science, I became convinced, could not tell us. Not only were the methods of science far from being exhaustive; when applied to certain kinds of facts with which they were not fitted to deal, they were lamentably unsatisfactory.

A Scientist on the Mind

Reflect, for example, upon the implications of the fact that the correlations which scientists establish are known by a mind. What has science to say about mind? This is a large question and the answer to it cannot be given at the end of a chapter. But that I may bring the chapter to an end by providing one striking illustration of its main contention, let us consider what Mr. Hoyle has to say about the mind.

At the end of his book, Mr. Hoyle, having surveyed first the materialist and then the religious hypothesis, asks the question whether our minds survive bodily death and points out very properly that the answer to the question depends at least in part upon what is meant by a mind. If, he comments, we knew, "we should be well on the way to getting an answer." Unfortunately, we don't, he thinks, know what a mind is. But one thing he holds to be clear, namely, that "the mind, if it exists in the religious sense, must have some physical connections," and must, therefore, be "capable of physical detection."

Why should it be so capable? Not a scrap of evidence is advanced in favor of this assertion. Of course, if the mind is physical, it must have physical connections. But why should it be physical? Why, in short, should it be taken for granted that that in me, whatever it is, that recognizes that A^2-B^2 equals $(A-B)$ $(A+B)$, and can follow the chain of reasoning upon which the equation is based, must be a piece of matter analyzable into charges of positive and negative electricity? Is it credible that it *could* be a piece of matter, or credible that it could be another piece of matter that finds it credible? Could one piece of matter find another piece either credible or incredible? Can a piece of matter, indeed, do anything at all except move, that is, alter its position in space? But if it cannot—and for my part I find it self-evident that it cannot and regard all such phrases as "matter become conscious of itself" as mere beggings of the question—the mind cannot either be, or be of the same nature as, a piece of matter. Why, then, must it have "physical connections" and "be capable of physical detection"? The answer, such as it is, that Mr. Hoyle gives is that "survival after death would be meaningless and unthinkable without some interaction with the physical world." Again, one may ask, *why* should it be meaningless? Because, presumably, our minds, when they animate our bodies, do manifestly often interact with the physical world and Mr. Hoyle takes it for granted that what they often do now they must always do.

But (i) there is absolutely no ground for this assumption. Mind may have pre-existed the body and it may survive it. Shorn of its

bodily connection, it may cease to have any contact with the physical world and yet continue *to be*. We do not know that this is so,
but we certainly do not know that it is not so.

(ii) There is no ground for supposing that a mind which is *not*
at every moment interacting with matter is meaningless and
unthinkable. I can think of many kinds of mental activities which
certainly do not seem *prima facie* to involve any interaction with the
physical world, as, for example, my realization of the truth of the
algebraic equation given above, the train of mental activity upon
which I engage when I do mental arithmetic or my recognition of
such necessary relations as that, if *P* implies *Q* and *Q* implies *R*,
then *P* also implies *R*.

Mr. Hoyle may, of course, mean merely that in order that it may
engage in these *prima facie* purely mental activities my mind must
interact with my brain upon which, apparently, he believes it wholly
to depend; he may even believe its activities to be wholly caused
by *movements* in the brain. And it may be the case that this is
true. But whether it is true or not, this is not the point here at
issue, which is not whether all the minds we know anything of now
are wholly dependent upon brains, which is the materialist contention, but whether it is meaningless to think of minds which do not
have any contact with the physical world. For my part, I am totally
unable to see why it should be meaningless. Even if all those activities of mind with which we are familiar involved bodily dependence, it would certainly not be meaningless to suppose that there
may be other activities that do not involve it. And, in fact, we do
know of such activities. Telepathy, for example, whose occurrence
must, I think, now be regarded as demonstrated, certainly *seems*
to involve *direct* communication between minds, that is to say, communication otherwise than through the medium of brains and
bodies. Precognition, again, certainly appears to occur, but precognition can hardly involve interaction between mind and the precog-
nized events in the physical world, for if these events are really in
the future, they have not yet occurred and do not, presumably, exist.

(iii) The view that a mind must have some physical connections
is exceedingly ambiguous. If it means that it must interact with
matter or that it must be related to or dependent upon a brain,
then the observations just made apply. But it *may* mean that it
must have physical connections, as it were, tacked on to it, links
or hooks, perhaps, attaching it to the brain, or perhaps some tail
or trail of tenuous matter. Now this view *is*, I think, strictly
unthinkable, for if the mind is not material—and to say that it is
brings us back to the materialism which Mr. Hoyle explicitly repudiates—there is nothing for the hypothecated physical hooks and
links to tack on to. There could only be such a point of attachment
if the mind was, in fact, material. What the relation of mind to the
brain may be I shall discuss in other chapters.

Conclusion in Regard to Scientific Method

I mentioned Mr. Hoyle's treatment of mind here in order that I might bring out two points. First, in spite of his explicit repudiation of materialism, his thought is still unconsciously dominated by materialist conceptions. (It is rare to meet a scientist whose thought is *not*.) He still thinks of reality in terms of matter, and takes the physical as the standard, the sole standard, of the real. Moreover, matter is still conceived imaginatively after the model of that which we can see and touch, which of course involves the implied assumption that whatever else is real must be of the same nature as that which we can see and touch, and the implied corollary that to appreciate values, to enjoy religious experience, indeed, to enjoy any experience which does not involve interaction with the physical, is to wander in a world of shadows. In effect, then, though he would, I dare say, repudiate the suggestion, Mr. Hoyle has not moved from the position adopted by T. H. Huxley nearly a hundred years ago, as expressed, for example, in the utterance quoted above, "the thoughts to which I am now giving utterance, and your thoughts regarding them are the expression of molecular changes in the matter of life." Indeed, he might even subscribe to the grandiose claim of Professor Tyndall.[2]

I conclude that directly scientists leave the domain of science and seek to interpret its findings, they are apt to go astray, if only because of their tendency to import the concepts and modes of thinking proper to science into spheres to which they are not relevant, as an alternative to denying the existence of such spheres altogether. Having by this means reached startling results, they are apt to take refuge in such purely dogmatic assertions as "Survival after death would be meaningless and unthinkable without some interaction with the physical world."

Prominent among these spheres is the sphere of religion. The conclusion seems to follow that though science may succeed in increasing our knowledge of the nature of the constitution of the physical world, it can have no contribution to make to the religious interpretation of the universe.

2. See above, p. 1179.

C. S. LEWIS

On "Special Providences"[1]

In this book the reader has heard of two classes of events and two only—miracles and natural events. The former are not interlocked with the history of Nature in the backward direction—i.e., in the time before their occurrence. The latter are. Many pious people,

1. An appendix to *Miracles*, 1947.

however, speak of certain events as being "providential" or "special providences" without meaning that they are miraculous. This generally implies a belief that, quite apart from miracles, some events are providential in a sense in which some others are not. Thus some people thought that the weather which enabled us to bring off so much of our army at Dunkirk was "providential" in some way in which weather as a whole is not providential. The Christian doctrine that some events, though not miracles, are yet answers to prayer, would seem at first to imply this.

I find it very difficult to conceive an intermediate class of events which are neither miraculous nor merely "ordinary." Either the weather at Dunkirk was or was not that which the previous physical history of the universe, by its own character, would inevitably produce. If it was, then how is it "specially" providential? If it was not, then it was a miracle.

It seems to me, therefore, that we must abandon the idea that there is any special class of events (apart from miracles) which can be distinguished as "specially providential." Unless we are to abandon the conception of Providence altogether, and with it the belief in efficacious prayer, it follows that all events are equally providential. If God directs the course of events at all then he directs the movement of every atom at every moment; "not one sparrow falls to the ground"[2] without that direction. The "naturalness" of natural events does not consist in being somehow outside God's providence. It consists in their being interlocked with one another inside a common space-time in accordance with the fixed pattern of the "laws."

In order to get any picture at all of a thing, it is sometimes necessary to begin with a false picture and then correct it. The false picture of Providence (false because it represents God and Nature as being both contained in a common Time) would be as follows. Every event in Nature results from some previous event, not from the laws of Nature. In the long run the first natural event, whatever it was, has dictated every other event. That is, when God at the moment of creation fed the first event into the framework of the "laws"—first set the ball rolling—He determined the whole history of Nature. Foreseeing every part of that history, He intended every part of it. If He had wished for different weather at Dunkirk He would have made the first event slightly different.

The weather we actually had is therefore in the strictest sense providential; it was decreed, and decreed for a purpose, when the world was made—but no more so (though more interestingly to us) than the precise position at this moment of every atom in the ring of Saturn.

2. The allusion is to Matthew x. 29-31: "Are not two sparrows sold for a farthing? and one of them shall not fall on the ground without your Father. / But the very hairs of your head are all numbered. / Fear ye not therefore, ye are of more value than many sparrows."

It follows (still retaining our false picture) that every physical event was determined so as to serve a great number of purposes.

Thus God must be supposed in pre-determining the weather at Dunkirk to have taken fully into account the effect it would have not only on the destiny of two nations but (what is incomparably more important) on all the individuals involved on both sides, on all animals, vegetables and minerals within range, and finally on every atom in the universe. This may sound excessive, but in reality we are attributing to the Omniscient only an infinitely superior degree of the same kind of skill which a mere human novelist exercises daily in constructing his plot.

Suppose I am writing a novel. I have the following problems on my hands: (1) Old Mr. A. has got to be dead before Chapter 15. (2) And he'd better die suddenly because I have to prevent him from altering his will. (3) His daughter (my heroine) has got to be kept out of London for three chapters at least. (4). My hero has somehow got to recover the heroine's good opinion which he lost in Chapter 7. (5) That young prig B., who has to improve before the end of the book, needs a bad moral shock to take the conceit out of him. (6) We haven't decided on B's job yet; but the whole development of his character will involve giving him a job and showing him actually at work. How on earth am I to get in all these six things? . . . I have it. What about a railway accident? Old A. can be killed in it, and that settles him. In fact the accident can occur while he is actually going up to London to see his solicitor with the very purpose of getting his will altered. What more natural than that his daughter should run up with him? We'll have her slightly injured in the accident: that'll prevent her reaching London for as many chapters as we need. And the hero can be on the same train. He can behave with great coolness and heroism during the accident—probably he'll rescue the heroine from a burning carriage. That settles my fourth point. And the young prig B.? We'll make him the signalman whose negligence caused the accident. That gives him his moral shock and also links him up with the main plot. In fact, once we have thought of the railway accident, that single event will solve six apparently separate problems.

No doubt this is in some ways an intolerably misleading image: firstly because (except as regards the prig B.) I have been thinking not of the ultimate good of my characters but of the entertainment of my readers: secondly because we are simply ignoring the effect of the railway accident on all the other passengers in that train: and finally because it is I who make B. give the wrong signal. That is, though I pretend that he has free will, he really hasn't. In spite of these objections, however, the example may perhaps suggest how Divine ingenuity could so contrive the physical "plot" of the universe as to provide a "providential" answer to the needs of innumerable creatures.

But some of these creatures have free will. It is at this point that we must begin to correct the admittedly false picture of Providence which we have hitherto been using. That picture, you will remember, was false because it represented God and Nature as inhabiting a common Time. But it is probable that Nature is not really in Time and almost certain that God is not. Time is probably (like perspective) the mode of our perception. There is therefore in reality no question of God's at one point in time (the moment of creation) adapting the material history of the universe in advance to free acts which you or I are to perform at a later point in Time. To Him all the physical events and all the human acts are present in an eternal Now. The liberation of finite wills and the creation of the whole material history of the universe (related to the acts of those wills in all the necessary complexity) is to Him a single operation. In this sense God did not create the universe long ago but creates it at this minute—at every minute.

Suppose I find a piece of paper on which a black wavy line is already drawn. I can now sit down and draw other lines (say in red) so shaped as to combine with the black line into a pattern. Let us now suppose that the original black line is conscious. But it is not conscious along its whole length at once—only of each point on that length in turn.

Its consciousness in fact is travelling along that line from left to right retaining point A only as a memory when it reaches B and unable until it has left B to become conscious of C. Let us also give this black line free will. It chooses the direction it goes in. The particular wavy shape of it is the shape it wills to have. But whereas it is aware of its own chosen shape only moment by moment and does not know at point D which way it will decide to turn at point F, I can see its shape as a whole and all at once. At every moment it will find my red lines waiting for it and adapted to it. Of course: because I, in composing the total red-and-black design have the whole course of the black line in view and take it into account. It is a matter not of impossibility but merely of designer's skill for me to devise red lines which at every point have a right relation not only to the black line but to one another so as to fill the whole paper with a satisfactory design.

In this model the black line represents a creature with free will, the red lines represent material events, and I represent God. The model would of course be more accurate if I were making the paper as well as the pattern and if there were hundreds of millions of black lines instead of one—but for the sake of simplicity we must keep it as it is.[3]

3. Admittedly all I have done is to turn the tables by making human volitions the constant and physical destiny the variable. This is as false as the opposite view; the point is that it is no falser. A subtler image of creation and freedom (or rather, creation of the free and the unfree in a single timeless act) would be the *almost* simultaneous mutual adaptation in the movements of two expert dancing partners [Lewis' note].

It will be seen that if the black line addressed prayers to me I might (if I chose) grant them. It prays that when it reaches point N it may find the red lines arranged around it in a certain shape. That shape may by the laws of design require to be balanced by other arrangements of red lines on quite different parts of the paper —some at the top or bottom so far away from the black line that it knows nothing about them: some so far to the left that they come before the beginning of the black line, some so far to the right that they come after its end. (The black line would call these parts of the paper, "The time before I was born," and, "The time after I'm dead.") But these other parts of the pattern demanded by that red shape which Black Line wants at N, do not prevent my granting its prayer. For his whole course has been visible to me from the moment I looked at the paper and his requirements at point N are among the things I took into account in deciding the total pattern.

Most of our prayers if fully analyzed, ask either for a miracle or for events whose foundation will have to have been laid before I was born, indeed, laid when the universe began. But then to God (though not to me) I and the prayer I make in 1945 were just as much present at the creation of the world as they are now and will be a million years hence. God's creative act is timeless and timelessly adapted to the "free" elements within it: but this timeless adaptation meets our consciousness as a sequence of prayer and answer.

Two corollaries follow:

1. People often ask whether a given event (not a miracle) was really an answer to prayer or not. I think that if they analyze their thought they will find they are asking, "Did God bring it about for a special purpose or would it have happened anyway as part of the natural course of events?" But this (like the old question, "Have you left off beating your wife?") makes either answer impossible. In the play, *Hamlet*, Ophelia climbs out on a branch overhanging a river: the branch breaks, she falls in and drowns. What would you reply if anyone asked, "Did Ophelia die because Shakespeare for poetic reasons wanted her to die at that moment—or because the branch broke?" I think one would have to say, "For both reasons." Every event in the play happens as a result of other events in the play, but also every event happens because the poet wants it to happen. All events in the play are Shakespearian events; similarly all events in the real world are providential events. All events in the play, however, come about (or ought to come about) by the dramatic logic of events. Similarly all events in the real world (except miracles) come about by natural causes. "Providence" and Natural causation are not alternatives; both determine every event because both are one.

2. When we are praying about the result, say, of a battle or a medical consultation the thought will often cross our minds that (if only we knew it) the event is already decided one way or the

other. I believe this to be no good reason for ceasing our prayers. The event certainly has been decided—in a sense it was decided "before all worlds." But one of the things taken into account in deciding it, and therefore one of the things that really cause it to happen, may be this very prayer that we are now offering. Thus, shocking as it may sound, I conclude that we can at noon become part causes of an event occurring at ten o'clock. (Some scientists would find this easier than popular thought does.) The imagination will, no doubt, try to play all sorts of tricks on us at this point. It will ask, "Then if I stop praying can God go back and alter what has already happened?" No. The event has already happened and one of its causes has been the fact that you are asking such questions instead of praying. It will ask, "Then if I begin to pray can God go back and alter what has already happened?" No. The event has already happened and one of its causes is your present prayer. Thus something does really depend on my choice. My free act contributes to the cosmic shape. That contribution is made in eternity or "before all worlds"; but my consciousness of contributing reaches me at a particular point in the time-series.

The following question may be asked: If we can reasonably pray for an event which must in fact have happened or failed to happen several hours ago, why can we not pray for an event which we know *not* to have happened? *e.g.*, pray for the safety of someone who, as we know, was killed yesterday. What makes the difference is precisely our knowledge. The known event states God's will. It is psychologically impossible to pray for what we know to be unobtainable; and if it were possible the prayer would sin against the duty of submission to God's known will.

One more consequence remains to be drawn. It is never possible to prove empirically that a given, non-miraculous event was or was not an answer to prayer. Since it was non-miraculous the sceptic can always point to its natural causes and say, "Because of these it would have happened anyway," and the believer can always reply, "But because these were only links in a chain of events, hanging on other links, and the whole chain hanging upon God's will, they may have occurred because someone prayed." The efficacy of prayer, therefore, cannot be either asserted or denied without an exercise of the will—the will choosing or rejecting faith in the light of a whole philosophy. Experimental evidence there can be none on either side. In the sequence M.N.O. event N, unless it is a miracle, is always caused by M and causes O; but the real question is whether the total series (say A–Z) does or does not originate in a will that can take human prayers into account.

This impossibility of empirical proof is a spiritual necessity. A man who knew empirically that an event had been caused by his prayer would feel like a magician. His head would turn and his heart would be corrupted. The Christian is not to ask whether this or that event happened because of a prayer. He is rather to believe that all events without exception are *answers* to prayer in the sense that whether they are grantings or refusals the prayers of all concerned and their needs have all been taken into account. All prayers are heard, though not all prayers are granted. We must not picture destiny as a film unrolling for the most part on its own, but in which our prayers are sometimes allowed to insert additional items. On the contrary; what the film displays to us as it unrolls already contains the results of our prayers and of all our other acts. There is no question *whether* an event has happened because of your prayer. When the event you prayed for occurs your prayer has always contributed to it. When the opposite event occurs your prayer has never been ignored; it has been considered and refused, for your ultimate good and the good of the whole universe. (For example, because it is better for you and for everyone else in the long run that other people, including wicked ones, should exercise free will than that you should be protected from cruelty or treachery by turning the human race into automata.) But this is, and must remain, a matter of faith. You will, I think, only deceive yourself by trying to find special evidence for it in some cases more than in others.

QUESTIONS FOR STUDY, DISCUSSION, AND WRITING

1. Why does Lewis find it "necessary to begin with a false picture and then correct it"? Trace the steps by which he makes the "correction."
2. What point does Lewis illustrate with his sketch of the plot of an imaginary novel? Explain whether the illustration is appropriate or not.
3. Compare Lewis' extended analogy of the black wavy line with one of the briefer analogies among the parables in Matthew xiii (pp. 1114–1117). What do they have in common? How do they differ?
4. Why does Lewis add his two corollaries? Explain whether his essay would have been incomplete without them.
5. How might Lewis' piece differ if it had been prepared as a sermon to be preached from a pulpit?

A Compendious Rhetoric
and Rhetorical Index

A Compendious Rhetoric

and Rhetorical Index

Saying Something That Matters

There is no point in the hard labor of writing unless you expect to *do* something to somebody—perhaps add to his store of information, perhaps cause him to change his mind on some issue that you care about. Determining just what that something is is half the battle; hence the importance of knowing your main point, your central purpose in writing, your **thesis.** It may seem that this step—perhaps in the form of a "thesis sentence" or exact statement of the main point—is inevitably prior to everything else in writing, but in actual practice the case is more complicated. Few good writers attain a final grasp of their thesis until they have tried setting down their first halting ideas at some length; to put it another way, you discover more precisely what it is you have to say in the act of trying to say it. Formulating and refining upon a thesis sentence as you work your way through a piece of writing helps you see what needs to be done at each stage; the finished piece, though, instead of announcing its thesis in any one sentence, may simply imply it by the fact of its unity, the determinate way the parts hang together. Nowhere in Edith Hamilton's treatment of Xenophon (p. 677) is the main point summed up in a single sentence, yet that point is solidly there: Xenophon came through when the chips were down because he possessed in a high degree certain qualities of mind and character summed up in the word *Greek*. But whether you state the main point or leave it to be inferred, you need to decide what your piece is about, what you want to say about it, why, and to whom.

Sometimes a thesis will rest on a good many **assumptions,** related ideas that the writer may not mention but depends upon his reader to understand and agree to (if he is an honest writer) or to overlook and hence fail to reject (if his real purpose is to mislead). Herbert Gold (p. 191) assumes that getting medical care for an accident victim takes priority over satisfying a bureaucratic demand for detailed information for the record, and we probably agree without hesitation. The same could be said for the assumption that readers are thoroughly familiar with the conventional value associations of "black" and "white" in Harold R. Isaacs' essay (p. 389). In neither of these cases is it absolutely necessary for us to scrutinize what we are taking for granted; nevertheless the habit of scrutiny guards us against the careless or cunning writer whose unstated assumptions may be highly questionable. The same habit, turned on our own minds when we become writers, can save us from the unthinking use of assumptions that we would be hard pressed to defend.

Assumptions brought to light
Étienne Gilson, "Education and the Higher Learning" (p. 213)
Geoffrey Crowther, "Two Heresies" (p. 235)
C. E. M. Joad, "Mr. Hoyle and the Physical Universe" (p. 1178)
Samuel Johnson, "On Self-love and Indolence" (p. 616)
J. B. Bury, "Darwinism and History" (p. 909)
Niccolò Machiavelli, "The Morals of the Prince" (p. 690)
Abraham Lincoln, "Liberty" (p. 709)
Francis Bacon, "Of Simulation and Dissimulation" (p. 633)
Francis Bacon, "Idols of the Mind" (p. 260)

Some theses lend themselves to verification by laboratory methods or the like; they deal with **questions of fact.** The exact order of composition of Shakespeare's plays could conceivably be settled finally if new evidence turned up. Whether or not the plays are great literature, on the other hand, is a **question of opinion;** agreement (though not hard to reach in this instance) depends on the weighing of arguments rather than on tests or measurements. Not that all theses can be neatly classified as assertions either of fact or of opinion (consider "Shakespeare's influence has been greater than Newton's"); still the attempt to classify his own effort can help a writer understand what he is doing.

Answers to questions of fact
Roberta Wohlstetter, "Surprise" (p. 273)
John Livingstone Lowes, "Time in the Middle Ages" (p. 1048)
John D. Stewart, "Vulture Country" (p. 1036)
A. S. Eddington, "The Downfall of Classical Physics" (p. 984)
Douglas Southall Freeman, "Over the River" (p. 815)

Answers to questions of opinion
Charles Sanders Peirce, "The Fixation of Belief" (p. 938)
Lionel Trilling, "The Morality of Inertia" (p. 621)
Thomas Jefferson, "Slaves and Taxes" (p. 717)
Oliver Wendell Holmes, Jr., "United States *v.* Schwimmer" (p. 769)
Talbot Smith, "Salmon *v.* Bagley Laundry Company" (p. 776)

Sometimes a writer addresses himself more specifically to his readers' **understanding,** sometimes he addresses himself chiefly to their **emotions.** Although the processes of thinking and of feeling are almost always mixed, still it is obvious that a description of a chemical process and a description of a candidate you hope to see elected to office will differ considerably in tone and emphasis. Accordingly you need to give some thought to the kind of result you hope to produce: perhaps simply an addition of information, perhaps a change of attitude, perhaps a commitment of the will to action.

Appeals to understanding
Harold R. Isaacs, "Blackness and Whiteness" (p. 389)
James B. Greenough and George L. Kittredge, "Language Is Poetry" (p. 574)

The Means of Saying It

No worthwhile thesis comes without work, and the work of arriving at a thesis is much like the work of writing itself—developing, elaborating, refining upon an idea that is perhaps at first hazy. For convenience the process may be divided into setting bounds, or defining; marshaling evidence; and drawing conclusions.

DEFINING in a broad sense may be thought of as what you do to answer the question "What do you mean?" It sets bounds by doing two things to an idea: grouping it with others like it and showing how it differs from those others. "An island is a tract of land" (like a lot or prairie or peninsula) "completely surrounded by water and too small to be called a continent" (and therefore different from a lot, etc.). This process of classifying and distinguishing may take many forms, depending on the kind of thing you are dealing with and your reason for doing so. (Artifacts, for example, can hardly be defined without reference to purpose; a lock is a device *for securing* a door; a theodolite is an instrument used *to measure* horizontal or vertical angles.) Some of the standard methods are these: by giving **examples,** pointing to an instance as a short way of indicating class and individual characteristics (*That* is a firebreak"; "A liberal is a man like Jefferson"); by **negating,** explaining what your subject is *not* —i.e., process of elimination ("Love vaunteth not itself, is not puffed up"); by **comparing and contrasting,** noting the resemblances and differences between your subject and something else ("A magazine is sometimes as big as a book but differs in binding and layout"); by **analyzing,** breaking down a whole into its constituent parts ("A play may be seen as exposition, rising action, and denouement"); by seeking a **cause** of the thing in question or an **effect** that it has produced ("Scurvy is the result of a dietary deficiency and often leads to anemia"); or by attributing to a thing an **end** or **means,** seeing it as a way of fulfilling purpose or as the fulfillment of a purpose ("Representation is the end of the electoral system and the means to good government").

When we turn to specimens of writing, we see immediately that the various methods of defining may serve not only for one-sentence "dictionary" definitions but also as methods of organizing paragraphs or even whole essays, where unfolding the subject is in a sense "defining" it, showing where its boundaries lie. "What is democracy?" says E. B. White, in effect: "I will explain it to you by pointing to examples where I see it operating" (p. 767). "The characteristics of Newspeak," says George Orwell (p. 95), "are best described by negation: it was *not* like language as we know it in these important respects. . . ." John Rader Platt begins by saying in effect, "To understand what is meant by 'style' in science, let us compare two characteristic attitudes toward scientific investigation" (p. 973). In response to the implicit question, "Why do men not always think straight?" Francis Bacon (p. 260) offers an analysis: "Error in general may be broken down into the following four kinds or 'idols'...." Herbert Spencer, seeking to understand force in words, traces it to its cause in the principle of economy (p. 90). Finally, Walter Lippmann (p. 761) opens our eyes to realities that are not immediately apparent by showing us that political opposition is indispensable if the party in power is to provide effective leadership. The choice of method in the above examples, it will be noted, is not random; each author selects according to his purpose in writing, and what suits one purpose exactly might be exactly wrong for another.

Defining by example
C. E. M. Joad, "Mr. Hoyle and the Physical Universe" (p. 1178)
Edward Hallett Carr, "The Historian and His Facts" (p. 920)

Defining by negation
E. M. Forster, "Not Listening to Music" (p. 500)
Carl Becker, "Democracy" (p. 759)

Defining by comparison and contrast
Learned Hand, "Sources of Tolerance" (p. 180)
Kenneth Clark, "The Blot and the Diagram" (p. 503)

Defining by analysis
Charles Sanders Peirce, "The Fixation of Belief" (p. 938)
George Santayana, "Classic Liberty" (p. 1150)

Defining by cause or effect
W. J. Cash, "Reconstruction and the Southern Quandary (p. 886)
Edward S. Deevey, Jr., "Bogs" (p. 1030)

Defining by end or means
Walter Lippmann, "The Indispensable Opposition" (p. 761)
Stephen Potter, "The Game Itself" (p. 636)

MARSHALING EVIDENCE. Once you have said what you mean, the next question is likely to be "How do you know?" Marshaling evidence may be thought of as what you do to answer that question. Where the matter at hand involves questions of fact, **factual evidence** will be most directly appropriate. (A diary, a letter—perhaps a cryptogram hidden in the text— might prove even to die-hard Baconians that Shakespeare himself did in fact write the plays which have been credited to him). Writers on scientific subjects—William H. Ittelson and Franklin P. Kilpatrick (p. 267), for example, or George W. Beadle (p. 1015)—inevitably draw chiefly on facts, often intricately arrayed, to support their conclusions. But it should not be assumed that factual evidence turns up mainly in scientific writing. Much of what Edith Hamilton has to say about Xenophon and the Greek character (p. 677) derives ultimately from historical and archaeological facts, and even the preacher John Donne, arguing that the arrow of temptation often overtakes us simply because we cannot bring ourselves to walk resolutely away from it (p. 629), plainly appeals to facts with which most of us are only too familiar.

Factual evidence is generally thought to carry more weight than any other kind, though the force of a fact is greatly diminished if it is not easily verifiable or attested to by reliable witnesses. Where factual evidence is hard to come by (consider the problems of proving that Bacon did not write Shakespeare's plays), the opinion of **authorities** is often invoked, on the assumption that the men most knowledgeable in a field are most likely to judge truly in a particular case. The testimony of authorities is relevant, of course, not only in questions of fact but also in questions of opinion. William G. Perry (p. 203), arguing for the student who "bulled" his way through an examination, implicitly invokes college professors *en masse* as authority for the idea that "bull" is closer than might be supposed to the goal of a liberal education. In general, however, the appeal to authority in matters of opinion has lost the rhetorical effectiveness it once had. Edmund Wilson's treatment of Emily Post (p. 354) is representative of a modern tendency—not necessarily unhealthy—to be highly skeptical of "authoritative" opinions.

As changes in the nature of the question draw in a larger and larger number of "authorities," evidence from authority shades into what might be called "the **common consent** of mankind," those generalizations about human experience that large numbers of readers can be counted upon to accept and that often find expression in proverbs or apothegms: "Risk no more than you can afford to lose" and "The first step toward Hell is halfway there." Such generalizations, whether proverbial or not, are a common ground on which writer and reader meet in agreement. The writer's task is to find and present the ones applicable to his particular thesis and then demonstrate that applicability, as Jefferson does in the Declaration of Independence (p. 744).

Marshaling factual evidence
Douglas Southall Freeman, "Over the River" (p. 815)
Thomas Henry Huxley, "The Method of Scientific Investigation" (p. 950)
A. S. Eddington, "The Downfall of Classical Physics" (p. 984)

Marshaling evidence from authority
Douglas Southall Freeman, "Over the River" (p. 815)
John D. Stewart, "Vulture Country" (p. 1036)
Herbert Spencer, "Force in Words" (p. 90)

Marshaling evidence based on common consent
Francis Bacon, "Of Simulation and Dissimulation" (p. 633)
Samuel Johnson, "On Self-love and Indolence" (p. 616)
Bernard Shaw, "The Gospel of St. Andrew Undershaft" (p. 430)

DRAWING CONCLUSIONS. One of the ways of determining the consequences of thought—that is, drawing conclusions—is the process of applying generalizations (**deduction**): "If we should risk no more than we can afford to lose, then we had better not jeopardize the independence of our universities by seeking federal aid." Another way of arriving at conclusions is the process of **induction,** which consists in forming generalizations from a sufficient number of observed instances: "Since universities *A, B,* and *C* have been accepting federal aid through research grants for years without loss of independence, it is probably safe for any university to do so." Typically deduction and induction work reciprocally, each helping to supply for the other the materials upon which inference operates. We induce from experience that green apples are sour; we deduce from this generalization that a particular green apple is sour. A third kind of inference, sometimes regarded as only a special kind of deduction or induction, is **analogy,** the process of concluding that two things which resemble each other in one way will resemble each other in another way also: "Federal aid has benefited mental hospitals enormously, and will probably benefit universities just as much." An analogy proves nothing, although it may help the reader see the reasonableness of an idea and is often extremely valuable for purposes of illustration, since it makes an unknown clearer by relating it to a known.

Turning to our essays, we can see something of the variety of ways in which these three kinds of inference manifest themselves in serious writing: Jefferson advancing the principle that a people subject to tyranny has the right to free itself and then deducing that the American colonies should sever ties with Britain (p. 744); New York City health inspectors deducing the source of an outbreak of typhoid fever in Roueché's "A Game of Wild

Indians" (p. 1058); Deevey proceeding from examination of a number of bogs to inductive conclusions about the way bogs are formed (p. 1030); Francis showing how the same process of thought has led to a new understanding of the "parts of speech" (p. 104); a New Testament parable adumbrating the kingdom of heaven by drawing an analogy between it and a mustard seed (p. 1114); C. S. Lewis explicating a knotty point in the Christian idea of God by likening God to a novelist (p. 1187).

Such a list of examples suggests that in good writing the conclusions the writer draws, the consequences of his thought, are "consequential" in more than one sense: not only do they follow logically from the evidence he has considered, they are also *significant;* they relate directly or indirectly to aspects of our lives that we care about. To the questions suggested earlier as demands for definition and evidence, then, we must add a third. "What do you mean?" calls for precision yet admits answers vast in scope. "How do you know?" trims the vastness down to what can be substantiated but may settle for triviality as the price of certainty. The appropriate question to raise finally, then, is simply "So what?" and the conclusions we as writers draw need to be significant enough to yield answers to that question. We have come full circle back to the idea of saying something that matters.

Drawing conclusions by deduction
James Madison, "The Merits of a Republic" (p. 753)
Samuel L. Clemens, "Fenimore Cooper's Literary Offenses" (p. 549)

Drawing conclusions by induction
Van Wyck Brooks, "Mark Twain's Humor" (p. 560)
Thomas Henry Huxley, "The Method of Scientific Investigation" (p. 950)

Drawing conclusions by analogy
Thomas De Quincey, "The Palimpsest of the Human Brain" (p. 310)
Henry David Thoreau, "The Battle of the Ants" (p. 829)

And the Style

One theory of style in writing sees form and content as distinct: style is the way a thing is said, the thing itself an unchanging substance that can be decked out in various ways. Mr. Smith not only *died,* he *ceased to be,* he *passed away,* he *croaked,* he *was promoted to glory*—all mean "the same thing." According to a second theory, however, they are ways of saying different things: variations in **diction** imply variations in reference. To say that Smith *ceased to be* records a privative and secular event; to say that he *was promoted to glory* (a Salvation Army expression) rejoices in an event of a different order altogether. Content and form in this view are inseparable; a change in one is a change in the other.

In **metaphor** we can see that the two theories, instead of contradicting each other, are more like the two sides of a coin: when one idea is expressed in terms of another, it is the same and yet not the same. To view the passage from life to death as if it were a promotion from one military rank to a higher one is to see a common center of reference and widening circles of association at the same time. This seeing *as if* opens up a whole range of expression, since many meanings reside in the relationship between the two parts of a comparison rather than in either part by itself. Nicholas of Cusa (p. 1113), for example, offers an insight that could be arrived at in no other way when he attempts to explain the nature of God by presenting him as an omnivoyant figure in a painting.

But style is by no means dependent on diction and metaphor alone. Grammatical relationships yield a host of stylistic devices, most of which can be described in terms of **repetition and variation.** Repetition may exist at every level; as commonly understood, its chief application is to the word (including the pronoun as a word-substitute), but the same principle governs the use of parallelism (repetition of a grammatical structure) within and between sentences, even between paragraphs. Failure to observe that principle—that similarity in idea calls for similarity in form—can be detected wherever a change in form implies that a distinction is being made when actually none is relevant to the context: "Their conversation was interrupted by dinner, but they resumed their discussion afterwards"; "She rolled out the dough, placed it over the pie, and pricked holes in it. She also trimmed off the edge." The corollary of the principle of appropriate repetition is the principle of appropriate variation—that difference in idea calls for difference in form. For every failure to repeat when repetition is called for there is a corresponding failure to vary when variation is called for: "Their discussion was interrupted when class discussion of the day's assignment began"; "It had been raining for many days near the river. It had been rising steadily toward the top of the levee." Failures of this sort, which suggest a similarity in idea or parallelism in thought where none exists, often strike the ear as a lack of euphony or appropriate rhythm: "A boxer must learn to react absolutely instantly"; "The slingshot was made of strips of inner tubes of tires of cars." The principle of appropriate variation applies, too, to sentences as wholes: if a separate sentence is used for each detail, or if every sentence includes many details, the reader may be given a false impression of parallelism or equality of emphasis. Here again variation may be a way to avoid misleading grammatical indications of meaning. In a writer like Samuel Johnson (p. 616), who works deliberately for a high degree of parallelism, correspondence between repetition and sameness of meaning, or variation and difference of meaning, is perhaps most conveniently illustrated.

All stylistic techniques come together to supply an answer to the question "Who is behind these words?" Every writer establishes an impression of himself—his **identity**—through what he says and the way he says it, and the quality of that impression obviously has much to do with his reader's willingness to be convinced. Honesty and straightforwardness come first—though the honesty of an ignoramus and the straightforwardness of a fool are unlikely to win assent. The writer must therefore choose a suitable role for himself and develop some sense of what that role implies: is he an expert or a humble seeker after truth, a wry humorist or a gadfly deliberately exacerbating hidden guilt? Even within the same general circumstances (in this case the academic world), William G. Perry (p. 203) is one sort of a person, Herbert Gold (p. 191) clearly another. A self will be revealed in every phrase the writer sets down—even in details of spelling, grammar, and punctuation, which, if ineptly handled, may suggest to his readers a carelessness that destroys their confidence.

Identities strongly marked by style
Lionel Trilling, "The Morality of Inertia" (p. 621)
Anatole France, "Children's Playthings" (p. 496)
Gertrude Stein, "Poetry and Grammar" (p. 86)
Max Beerbohm, "A Relic" (p. 54)
Allan Seager, "The Joys of Sport at Oxford" (p. 11)
Stanley Milgram, "A Behavioral Study of Obedience" (p. 290)
Herbert Gold, "A Dog in Brooklyn, A Girl in Detroit" (p. 191)
Nathaniel Hawthorne, "Abraham Lincoln" (p. 811)
Margaret Culkin Banning, "Letter to Susan" (p. 320)
James Anthony Froude, "Defeat of the Armada" (p. 832)
Bernard Shaw, "The Gospel of St. Andrew Undershaft" (p. 430)
Thomas Babington Macaulay, "Boswell" (p. 670)
James Agee, "Cotton" (p. 436)
John Ruskin, "Traffic" (p. 644)

(including the pronoun as a word-substitute), but the same principle governs the use of parallelism (repetition of a grammatical structure) within and between sentences, even between paragraphs. Failure to observe that principle—that similarity in idea calls for similarity in form—can be detected wherever a change in form implies that a distinction is being made when actually none is relevant to the context. "Their conversation was interrupted by dinner, but they resumed their discussion afterwards"; "She rolled out the dough, placed it over the pie, and pricked holes in it. She also trimmed off the edge." The corollary of the principle of appropriate repetition is the principle of appropriate variation—that difference in idea calls for difference in form. For every failure to repeat when repetition is called for there is a corresponding failure to vary when variation is called for." Their discussion was interrupted when class discussion of the day's assignment began"; "It had been raining for many days near the river. It had been rising steadily toward the top of the levee." Failures of this sort, which suggest a similarity in idea or parallelism in thought where none exists, often strike the ear as a lack of euphony or appropriate rhythm. A bovet must learn to react absolutely instantly". The slingshot was made of strips of inner tubes of tires or crust. The principle of appropriate variation applies, too, to sentences as wholes: if a separate sentence is used for each detail, or if every sentence includes many details, the reader may be given a false impression of parallelism or equality of emphasis. Here, again variation may be a way to avoid misleading grammatical indications of meaning. In a writer like Samuel Johnson (p. 616), who works deliberately for a high degree of parallelism, correspondence between repetition, and sameness of meaning, or variation and difference of meaning, is perhaps most conveniently illustrated.

All stylistic techniques come together to supply an answer to the question "Who is behind these words?" Every writer establishes an impression of himself—his identity—through what he says and the way he says it, and the quality of that impression obviously has much to do with his reader's willingness to be convinced. Honesty and straightforwardness come first—though the honesty of an ignoramus and the straightforwardness of a fool are unlikely to win assent. The writer must therefore choose a suitable role for himself and develop some sense of what that role implies: is he an expert or a humble seeker after truth, a wry humorist or a godly deliberately exacerbating hidden guilt. Even within the same general circumstances (in this case the academic world), William C. Perry (p. 203) is one sort of a person, Herbert Gold (p. 101) clearly another. A self will be revealed in every phrase the writer sets down—even in details of spelling, grammar, and punctuation, which, if ineptly handled, may suggest to his readers a carelessness that destroys their confidence.

Identities through marked by style

Authors

Authors

[An * indicates the source of a selection in this anthology. Only a few of each author's works are cited.]

Joseph Addison (1672-1719)
English critic and essayist; author, with Richard Steele, of *The Spectator, a series of essays issued in periodical form.

James Agee (1909-1955)
American journalist, novelist, film critic, screenwriter; author of *A Death in the Family* (novel), *Let Us Now Praise Famous Men* (social commentary).

Hannah Arendt (1906-   )
German-born American political analyst; author of *The Origins of Totalitarianism, The Human Condition, *Eichmann in Jerusalem.

Matthew Arnold (1822-1888)
English man of letters, poet, and literary critic; author of *Poems, Essays in Criticism, *Culture and Anarchy, Literature and Dogma.*

Roger Ascham (1515-1568)
English scholar, tutor of Queen Elizabeth I; author of *Toxophilus* and *The Scholemaster.*

W. H. Auden (1907-   )
English-born American poet, playwright, critic; author of *In Time of War, The Sea and the Mirror, Poems, *The Dyer's Hand;* with Christopher Isherwood, of *Ascent of F-6, The Dog Beneath the Skin* (plays); with Louis MacNeice, of *Letters from Iceland.*

Sir Francis Bacon (1561-1626)
English politician, statesman and philosopher; author of *Essays, Advancement of Learning, *New Organon, New Atlantis.*

James Baldwin (1924-   )
American essayist and novelist; Harlem-bred, onetime expatriot in Paris, political activist for civil-rights causes; author of *Go Tell It on the Mountain* and *Another Country* (novels), *Notes of a Native Son, Nobody Knows My Name,* and *The Fire Next Time* (commentary).

Margaret Culkin Banning (1891-   )
American novelist; author of *Too Young to Marry, Out in Society, *Letters to Susan, The Case for Chastity.*

George Wells Beadle (1903-   )
American geneticist, chancellor of the University of Chicago; author, with Alfred H. Sturtevant, of *An Introduction to Genetics.*

Carl Becker (1873-1945)
American historian (Cornell); author of *Progress and Power, The Declaration of Independence, *Modern Democracy.*

Sir Max Beerbohm (1872-1956)
English essayist and caricaturist; author of *Zuleika Dobson* (novel); *A Christmas Garland, *And Even Now.*

Henri Bergson (1859-1941)
French philosopher; author of *The Two Sources of Morality and Religion, Time and Free Will, *On Laughter.*

George Berkeley (1685-1753)
Irish cleric, philosopher; author of *Principles of Human Knowledge, Dialogue between Hylas and Philonous, Theory of Vision.*

Bruno Bettelheim (1903-   )
Austrian-born American psychologist (University of Chicago) and psychoanalyst; author of *Love Is Not Enough, *The Informed Heart.*

Ambrose Bierce (1842-1914?)
American short-story writer and journalist; author of *Tales of Soldiers and Civilians, The Cynic's Word Book* (retitled *The Devil's Dictionary).*

William Blake (1757-1827)
English poet, artist, and engraver; author of *Songs of Innocence, Songs of Experience, *The Marriage of Heaven and Hell, The Book of Thel.*

Wayne C. Booth (1921-   )
American literary critic, professor of English (University of Chicago); author of *The Rhetoric of Fiction.*

Jacob Bronowski (1908-   )
English mathematician and government administrator, part-time essayist, and radio-script writer; author of *The Poet's Defence; William Blake, A Man without a Mask; *Science and Human Values.*

Van Wyck Brooks (1886-1963)
American critic, literary historian; author of *The Ordeal of Mark Twain, The Pilgrimage of Henry James, Makers and Finders: A History of The Writer in America, 1800-1915

(a series of volumes including *The Flowering of New England, The Time of Melville and Whitman*).

Sir Thomas Browne (1650-1682)

English physician; author of *Religio Medici, Vulgar Errors, *Urn Burial.*

Martin Buber (1878-   )

Austrian-born Jewish theologian and biblical scholar, now living in Israel; author of *I and Thou, Between Man and Man.*

J. B. Bury (1861-1927)

English historian and classical scholar (Cambridge); author of *Idea of Progress, History of the Freedom of Thought, History of the Later Roman Empire.*

Thomas Carlyle (1795-1881)

Scots essayist, historian; author of *Sartor Resartus; The French Revolution; On Heroes, Hero-Worship, and the Heroic in History; History of Frederick the Great.*

Edward Hallett Carr (1892-   )

English historian (Cambridge), journalist, and statesman; author of *The Romantic Exiles; The Bolshevik Revolution, 1917–1923; *What Is History?*

W. J. Cash (1901-1941)

American journalist; author of *The Mind of the South.*

Lord Chesterfield (1694-1773)

Philip Dormer Stanhope, fourth earl; English statesman and diplomat, well-known letter-writer (*Letters to His Son*).

Sir Kenneth Clark (1903-   )

English art historian and critic; author of *Landscape into Art, The Nude, Leonardo Da Vinci, Looking at Pictures.*

Samuel Langhorne Clemens (1835-1910)

"Mark Twain"; American humorist, novelist, essayist, journalist; author of *Life on the Mississippi, The Innocents Abroad, *Roughing It, The Adventures of Tom Sawyer, The Adventures of Huckleberry Finn.*

Robert Coles (1926-   )

American child psychiatrist (Harvard).

Joseph Conrad (1847-1924)

Pen name for Teodor Josef Konrad Korzeniowski; Polish-born English sea captain, later a novelist; author of *The Nigger of the Narcissus, Lord Jim, Victory, Under Western Eyes.*

Sir Geoffrey Crowther (1907-   )

English economist and journalist, former editor of *The Economist.*

Edward S. Deevey, Jr. (1914-   )

American biologist (Yale).

Daniel Defoe (1660?-1731)

English journalist and novelist; author of *Robinson Crusoe, Moll Flanders, *A Journal of the Plague Year.*

Thomas De Quincey (1785-1859)

English essayist and literary journalist; author of *Confessions of an English Opium Eater, *Autobiographic Sketches.*

Emily Dickinson (1830-1886)

American poet; a New England recluse whose poetry was published almost entirely posthumously.

John Donne (1573-1631)

English poet and clergyman, Dean of St. Paul's Cathedral, founder and chief exemplar of the Metaphysical School in English poetry; author of *Songs and Sonnets, Devotions upon Emergent Occasions.*

John Dos Passos (1896-   )

American novelist; author of *Three Soldiers, Manhattan Transfer, U. S. A.* (a trilogy containing *The 42nd Parallel, 1919,* and *The Big Money*).

William O. Douglas (1898-   )

American jurist, law professor (Columbia and Yale), since 1939 an Associate Justice of the U. S. Supreme Court, and traveler and mountain climber; author of *Of Men and Mountains, *Strange Lands and Friendly People, We the Judges, A Living Bill of Rights.*

Finley Peter Dunne (1867-1936)

American journalist and humorist, creator of the Irish-American political and social commentator Mr. Dooley; author of *Mr. Dooley in Peace and War.*

John Earle (1601?-1665)

English churchman, Bishop of Salisbury; author of *Microcosmographie, a series of character sketches.

A. S. Eddington (1882-1944)

English astrophysicist (Cambridge); author of technical works on relativity, stellar evolution, and motions of the stars and of *The Nature of the Physical World.*

Jonathan Edwards (1703-1758)

American Puritan preacher and theologian in Massachusetts Bay Colony.

Ralph Waldo Emerson (1803-1882)

American essayist, poet, expositor of the intellectual movement known as Transcendentalism; author of *Nature, Representative Men, English Traits.*

Desiderius Erasmus (1465-1536)

Dutch humanist-scholar, satirist; author of *The Praise of Folly, Colloquies, *The Education of a Christian Prince.*

Thomas F. Farrell (1891-   )

American engineer; as a wartime U. S. Army major general was deputy commander of the Atomic Bomb Project in 1945-1946.

Henry Fielding (1707-1754)

English magistrate, novelist, essayist, and dramatist; author of *Joseph Andrews, *Tom Jones, Amelia.*

Donald Fleming (1923-   )

American historian of science (Harvard); author of *John William Draper, William Henry Welch and the Rise of Modern Medicine.*

E. M. Forster (1879-   )

English novelist and essayist; author of *The Longest Journey, Howard's End, A Passage to India* (novels); *Aspects of the Novel, *Two Cheers for Democracy* (criticism).

Anatole France (1844-1924)

French novelist, essayist, poet; author of *Thaïs, Penguin Island, The Revolt of the Angels.*

W. Nelson Francis (1910-   )

American linguist (Brown); author of *The Structure of American English* and *The English Language: An Introduction.*

Felix Frankfurter (1882-   )

American jurist, former professor of law (Harvard) and Associate Justice of the U. S. Supreme Court (1939-1962); author of *The Public and Its Government, Of Law and Men, Law and Politics.*

Benjamin Franklin (1706-1790)

American statesman, delegate to the Continental Congress and Constitutional Convention, ambassador to France during the American Revolution, inventor, newspaper publisher, and practical philosopher; author of *Poor Richard's Almanack, *Autobiography.*

Douglas Southall Freeman (1886-1953)

American editor (Richmond *News Leader*), professor of journalism (Columbia), historian; biographer of Robert E. Lee (*R. E. Lee, Lee's Lieutenants*).

Robert Frost (1874-1963)

American poet, lecturer, teacher.

James Anthony Froude (1818-1894)

English historian, editor, educator; author of *History of England from the Fall of Wolsey to the Defeat of the Spanish Armada, The English in Ireland in the Eighteenth Century,* biographies of Carlyle.

Thomas Fuller (1608-1661)

English clergyman, historian, gazetteer, biographer; author of *The Holy State and the Profane State, Church History of Britain, The Worthies of England.*

George Gamow (1904-   )

American theoretical physicist and popularizer of science; author of *Mr. Tompkins in Wonderland, *One, Two, Three . . . Infinity, The Creation of the Universe, Gravity.*

Edward Gibbon (1737-1794)

English historian; author of *History of the Decline and Fall of the Roman Empire.*

Walker Gibson (1919-   )

American professor of English (New York University); author of *The Reckless Spenders, Seeing and Writing, *The Limits of Language.*

Étienne Gilson (1884-   )

French Catholic philosopher; author of *The Philosophy of St. Thomas Aquinas,* *The Mystical Philosophy of St. Bernard, Painting and Reality.*

Wilhelm Goetsch (1887-   )

Austrian zoologist; author of *The Ants, Comparative Biology of Insect Colonies.*

Herbert Gold (1924-   )

American novelist, short-story writer, critic; author of *Birth of a Hero, First Person Singular, The Man Who Was Not With It, The Optimist.*

James Bradstreet Greenough (1883-1901)

American philologist (Harvard); author of *Analysis of the Latin Subjunctive, Latin Grammar* (with J. H. Allen), *Words and Their Ways in English Speech* (with G. L. Kittredge).

Donald Hall (1928-   )

American poet and professor of English (University of Michigan); author of *The Dark Houses, Exiles and Marriages, *String Too Short to Be Saved.*

Edith Hamilton (1867-1963)

American classical and biblical scholar, teacher (Bryn Mawr School); author of *The Greek Way, The Roman Way, Echo of Greece, Witness to the Truth.*

Learned Hand (1872-1961)

American jurist, U. S. District Court of and Circuit Court of Appeals Judge; author of *The Spirit of Liberty.*

Nathaniel Hawthorne (1804-1864)

American novelist, short-story writer, essayist; author of *Twice-told Tales, Mosses from an Old Manse, The Scarlet Letter, The House of the Seven Gables.*

William Hazlitt (1778-1830)

English essayist, critic; author of *Characters of Shakespeare's Plays; English Comic Writers; Table Talk, or Original Essays on Men and Manners; *Characteristics.*

Herodotus (c. 484-424? B.C.)

Greek historian, "father of history"; author of *Histories,* the nine books of which are named after the nine Muses (*Clio, Euterpe,* etc.).

Gilbert Highet (1906-   )

Scots-born American classicist and teacher (Columbia); author of *The Art of Teaching, *Talents and Geniuses.*

Paul Hollander (1932-   )

Hungarian-born (fled Budapest during 1956 revolt) American sociologist (Harvard), with special interests in Soviet society, the sociology of literature, and socially deviant behavior.

Oliver Wendell Holmes, Jr. (1841-1935)

American jurist, professor of law (Harvard), chief justice of the Massachusetts Supreme Court, Associate Justice of the U. S. Supreme Court; author of *The Common Law.*

Gerard Manly Hopkins (1844-1889)
English Jesuit, poet, essayist.

David Hume (1711-1776)
Scots philosopher, historian; author of *Essays Moral and Political*, **Enquiry Concerning Human Understanding*, *History of Great Britain*.

Thomas Henry Huxley (1825-1895)
English biologist, popularizer of science; author of *Evolution and Ethics*, *Scientific Memoirs*, **Darwiniana*.

Harold R. Isaacs (1910-   )
American journalist, foreign-affairs analyst, lecturer (Massachusetts Institute of Technology); author of *No Peace for Asia*, *The Tragedy of the Chinese Revolution*, *The New World of Negro Americans*.

William H. Ittelson (1920-   )
American psychologist (Brooklyn College; author of *Visual Space Perception*.

Henry James (1843-1916)
American novelist and essayist, brother of William, longtime resident of London; author of *Portrait of a Lady*, *The Ambassadors*, *The Wings of the Dove*, *The American*.

William James (1842-1910)
American philosopher and pioneer psychologist (Harvard), pragmatist, brother of Henry; author of **Principles of Psychology*, *The Varieties of Religious Experience*, *Pragmatism*.

Thomas Jefferson (1743-1826)
Third President of the United States, first Secretary of State, founder of the University of Virginia, drafter of the **Declaration of Independence* and the statute of Virginia for religious freedom, founder of the Democratic party; also renowned for his talents as an architect and inventor; for his political and social views see **Notes on the State of Virginia*.

C. E. M. Joad (1891-1953)
English philosopher; author of *Common Sense Ethics*, *Good and Evil*, **The Recovery of Belief*.

Samuel Johnson (1709-1784)
English lexicographer, critic, moralist; journalist (*The Idler*, **The Rambler*); author of *A Dictionary of the English Language*, *Lives of the Poets*; subject of Boswell's *Life*.

James Joyce (1882-1941)
Irish short-story writer, novelist; longtime resident in Paris; author of *Dubliners*, **Portrait of the Artist as a Young Man*, *Ulysses*, *Finnegans Wake*.

Franz Kafka (1883-1924)
Czech novelist and short-story writer; author of **The Trial*, *The Castle*, *Amerika*.

Murray Kempton (1918-   )
American journalist, political analyst; author of **Part of Our Time*, a collection of his columns.

X. J. Kennedy (1929-   )
Pseudonym of Joseph C. Kennedy; poet, critic, professor of English (Tufts); author of *Nude Descending a Staircase*.

Franklin P. Kilpatrick (1929-   )
American social psychologist (Brookings Institution); author of *Human Behavior from the Transactional Point of View*.

George Lyman Kittredge (1860-1941)
American philologist and professor of English (Harvard); author of **Words and Their Ways in English Speech* (with J. B. Greenough), *Chaucer and His Poetry*, *Shakespeare*, *Sir Thomas Malory*, and editor of *The Complete Works of Shakespeare*.

Ronald Knox (1888-1957)
English Roman Catholic prelate; author of *The Belief of Catholics*; *The Body in the Silo*; *Let Dons Delight*; **Enthusiasm, a Chapter in the History of Religion*.

Charles Lamb (1775-1834)
English essayist, critic; author of **Essays of Elia* and, with his sister, *Tales from Shakespeare*.

François, duc de la Rochefoucauld (1613-1680)
French moralist; author of *Memoirs*, **Reflections or Sentences and Moral Maxims*.

T. E. Lawrence (1888-1935)
"Lawrence of Arabia"; English archaeologist, army officer, assisted Arabs in their revolt against the Turks during World War I; author of *The Seven Pillars of Wisdom*.

Stephen Leacock (1896-1914)
Canadian humorist, economist (McGill), and historian; author of *The Unsolved Riddle of Social Justice* and, among his lighter works, *Nonsense Novels* and *Moonbeams from the Larger Lunacy*.

C. S. Lewis (1898-1963)
English literary scholar and critic, novelist, theologian; author of *A Preface to Paradise Lost*, *The Screwtape Letters*, *Mere Christianity*, **Miracles*.

A. J. Liebling (1904-1963)
American journalist (*The New Yorker*), who counted wine and boxing among many other interests; author of *Back Where I Came From*, *The Honest Rainmaker*, *The Earl of Louisiana*.

Abraham Lincoln (1809-1865)
Sixteenth President of the United States; lawyer, Congressman, celebrated for his debates with Stephen Douglas on the question of slavery's extension. His voluminous state papers include the Emancipation Proclamation, the Gettysburg Address, the Second Inaugural.

Walter Lippmann (1889-   )
American political philosopher and journalist-statesman; author of *Public Opinion*, *A Preface to Morals*,

The New Imperative, The Public Philosophy, The Communist World and Ours.

Lester D. Longman (1905-   )

American art historian (University of Iowa); author of *Outline of Art History, History and Appreciation of Art.*

John Livingstone Lowes (1867-1945)

American literary critic, scholar, and teacher (Harvard); author of **Geoffrey Chaucer, The Road to Xanadu.*

Lucretius (*c.* 99-55 B.C.)

Titus Lucretius Carus; Roman poet; author of *De Rerum Natura (On the Nature of Things).*

Robert Lynd (1879-1949)

Irish essayist, journalist; author of *The Pleasures of Ignorance, Solomon in All His Glory, Dr. Johnson and Company, *It's a Fine World.*

Thomas Babington Macaulay (1800-1859)

English historian, member of Parliament, and first Baron Macaulay; author of *History of England, Lays of Ancient Rome.*

Niccolò Machiavelli (1469-1527)

Florentine statesman and political philosopher during the reign of the Medici; author of *The Art of War, History of Florence, Discourses on Livy, *The Prince.*

Archibald MacLeish (1892-   )

American poet, former Librarian of Congress, professor of English (Harvard); author of the verse play *J. B.* and *Poetry and Experience.*

James Madison (1751-1836)

Fourth President of the United States and Secretary of State under Jefferson; drafter of the Virginia plan, the basis of the U. S. Constitution, and keeper of notes of the proceedings of the Constitutional Convention; like Jefferson, a Virginian, proponent of religious freedom, and opponent of slavery; author, with Hamilton and Jay, of *The Federalist,* papers arguing for the ratification of the Constitution.

Katherine Mansfield (1888-1923)

Pseudonym of Katherine Middleton Murry; New Zealand-born English short-story writer; author of *Bliss, The Garden Party, The Dove's Nest.*

William March (1893-1954)

Pseudonym of William Edward March Campbell; American businessman, novelist, short-story writer, fabulist; author of *Company K, The Little Wife and Other Stories, Some Like Them Short, *99 Fables.*

Matthew

One of the twelve Apostles of Christ, author of **The Gospel according to St. Matthew.*

W. Somerset Maugham (1874-   )

English novelist, dramatist, short-story writer; author of *Of Human Bondage* (novel), *The Moon and Sixpence* (stories), *The Circle* (play), **The Summing Up* (autobiography).

Margaret Mead (1901-   )

American anthropologist (American Museum of Natural History and Columbia); author of *Coming of Age in Samoa, *Male and Female, New Lives for Old.*

Stanley Milgram (1933-   )

American social psychologist (Yale).

John Stuart Mill (1806-1873)

English political and social philosopher, economist, and social reformer, civil servant in India, a proponent of utilitarianism and political freedom; author of *A System of Logic, On Liberty, Utilitarianism, Autobiography.*

Samuel Miller (1900-   )

American clergyman, dean of the Harvard Divinity School; author of *The Life of the Soul, The Life of the Church, Great Realities, Prayers for Daily Use.*

C. Wright Mills (1916-1962)

American sociologist (Columbia) concerned with society's power structure; author of *White Collar, The Power Elite.*

Charles W. Morton (1899-   )

American journalist, editor (*The Atlantic*); author of *Frankly, George; How to Protect Yourself against Women and Other Vicissitudes, A Slight Sense of Outrage.*

O. Hobart Mowrer (1907-   )

American psychologist of learning theory (University of Illinois); author of *Learning Theory and Behavior, Learning Theory and the Symbolic Processes.*

Herbert Joseph Muller (1905-   )

American professor of English and government (Indiana University); author of *Thomas Wolfe, *The Uses of the Past, The Spirit of Tragedy, The Loom of History.*

Lewis Mumford (1895-   )

American critic of architecture and city planning; author of *Sticks and Stones, The Brown Decades, *Technics and Civilization, The Culture of Cities.*

John Henry Newman (1801-1890)

English Catholic prelate and cardinal; author of *Tracts for the Times, *The Idea of a University, Apologia pro Vita sua.*

Nicholas of Cusa (*c.* 1400-1464)

German Catholic prelate (bishop and cardinal) and philosopher, argued in favor of church councils over the pope and for the principle of consent as the basis of government; author of *De concordantia catholica, De docta ignorantia, *De visione Dei (The Vision of God).*

J. Robert Oppenheimer (1904-   )

American nuclear physicist, one of the key men in harnessing atomic energy, director of the Institute for Advanced

Study at Princeton; author of *Science and the Common Understanding,* *The Open Mind.*

George Orwell (1903-1950)

Pseudonym of Eric Blair; English novelist, essayist, and social commentator, satirist of totalitarianism; author of *Down and Out in London and Paris, Homage to Catalonia,* *Nineteen Eighty-Four, Animal Farm.*

Sir Thomas Overbury (1581-1613)

English courtier, poet, and essayist; author of *Characters.*

Francis Parkman (1823-1893)

American historian of colonial America, including *History of the Conspiracy of Pontiac,* *LaSalle and the Discovery of the Great West, Montcalm and Wolfe.*

Blaise Pascal (1623-1662)

French mathematician, moralist, and essayist; author of *Pensées.*

Walter Pater (1839-1894)

English man of letters, interpreter of Renaissance humanism; author of *Studies in the History of the Renaissance, Marius the Epicurean, Appreciations.*

Charles Sanders Peirce (1839-1914)

American philosopher, scientist, and logician; author of *Chance, Love, and Logic; Essays in the Philosophy of Science, Values in a Universe of Chance.*

William G. Perry (1913-   )

American educator, director of the Bureau of Study Counsel at Harvard.

Plato (427?-347 B.C.)

Greek philosopher, pupil and friend of Socrates, teacher of Aristotle, founder of the Academy, proponent of an oligarchy of intellectuals based on the assumption that virtue is knowledge; author of *The Republic.*

John Rader Platt (1918-   )

American physicist (University of Chicago).

Stephen Potter (1900-   )

English writer-producer (BBC), critic, and humorist; author of *D. H. Lawrence, A First Study; The Muse in Chains; A Study in Education,* and, among his lighter things, *Gamesmanship, Lifemanship, One-Upmanship.*

Berton Roueché (1911-   )

American journalist (*The New Yorker*), chronicler of medical history; author of *Eleven Blue Men, The Incurable Wound, The Neutral Spirit.*

John Ruskin (1819-1900)

English essayist, art critic, social reformer; author of *Modern Painters, The Stones of Venice,* *The Crown of Wild Olive.*

Samuel

The subject of two books of the Old Testament; leader of Israel, anointer of Saul and of David.

George Santayana (1863-1952)

American philosopher (Harvard), author of *The Life of Reason, The Realm of Essence, The Realm of Truth,* and *Soliloquies in England.*

Jean-Paul Sartre (1905-   )

French existential philosopher, dramatist, novelist, short-story writer, editor (*Les Temps Modernes*); author of *The Flies, No Exit,* and *Dirty Hands* (plays), *Nausea* (novel), *Being and Nothingness* (philosophy), *The Words* (autobiography).

Allan Seager (1906-   )

American novelist and short-story writer, professor of English (University of Michigan); author of *Amos Berry, Hilda Manning,* *A Frieze of Girls.*

John Selden (1584-1654)

English politician, jurist, oriental scholar, and member of Parliament; author of many political tracts and works on law and *Table Talk.*

George Bernard Shaw (1856-1950)

Irish playwright and essayist; author of the plays *Saint Joan,* *Man and Superman,* *Major Barbara, Caesar and Cleopatra.*

Talbot Smith (1899-   )

American jurist, U. S. District Court Judge (in Michigan), former professor of law (University of California) and associate justice of the Supreme Court of Michigan.

Herbert Spencer (1820-1903)

English philosopher of science and evolution, trained as an engineer, and editor, journal contributor; author of *First Principles, Principles of Biology, Principles of Psychology, Principles of Sociology, Principles of Ethics.*

Wallace Stegner (1909-   )

American essayist, novelist, professor of English (Stanford); author of *Remembering Laughter, The Women on the Wall, Beyond the Hundredth Meridian, A Shocking Star,* *Wolf Willow.*

Gertrude Stein (1874-1946)

American experimental writer, expatriate in Paris, lecturer; author of *The Making of Americans, Operas and Plays, The Autobiography of Alice B. Toklas, Ida.*

John Steinbeck (1902-   )

American novelist, columnist, Nobel prize-winner; author of *In Dubious Battle, Of Mice and Men, The Grapes of Wrath, East of Eden.*

Laurence Sterne (1713-1768)

English cleric, novelist, and humorist; author of *Tristram Shandy, Sentimental Journey, Sermons.*

John D. Stewart (1930-   )

English essayist, fiction writer, dramatist, civil servant, contributor to English and American magazines.

Jonathan Swift (1667-1745)

Anglo-Irish clergyman, statesman, satirist; author of *Gulliver's Travels, The Tale of a Tub, Drapier Letters.*

Theophrastus (*c.* 371-287 B.C.)
Greek philosopher, naturalist, and successor to Aristotle; author of **Characters, Metaphysics, On Plants.*

Dylan Thomas (1914-1953)
Welsh poet, story writer, radio-script writer and broadcaster; author of *Collected Poems (1934-1952), Under Milk Wood* (poems), *Adventures in the Skin Trade and Other Stories, Portrait of the Artist as a Young Dog* (novel).

Henry David Thoreau (1817-1862)
American philosopher, essayist, naturalist, poet, disciple of Emerson, foremost exponent of self-reliance; author of *Descent into Hell, War in* ence," **Journals.*

James Thurber (1894-1963)
American humorist, cartoonist, social commentator (*The New Yorker*), playwright; author of *My Life and Hard Times; *Fables for Our Time; Men, Women, and Dogs; The Beast in Me and Other Animals.*

Paul Tillich (1886-   )
German-born American theologian (Union Theological Seminary and Harvard); author of *The Interpretation of History, The Shaking of the Foundations, Systematic Theology, The Dynamics of Faith, Christianity and the Encounter of the World Religions.*

Lionel Trilling (1905-   )
American literary critic and social commentator, professor of English (Columbia); author of *Matthew Arnold, The Liberal Imagination, Freud and the Crisis of Our Culture, *A Gathering of Fugitives.*

E. B. White (1899-   )
American essayist, journalist, editor (*The New Yorker*); author of *One Man's Meat, The Wild Flag, The Second Tree from the Corner.*

Walt Whitman (1819-1892)
American poet, Civil War journalist; author of *Leaves of Grass* (poems), *Democratic Vistas* and **Specimen Days* (essays).

Oscar Wilde (1856-1900)
Irish wit, dramatist, poet, story writer, critic; author of *The Picture of Dorian Gray* (novel), *The Importance of Being Earnest* (play).

Charles Williams (1886-1945)
English man of letters (novelist, poet, playwright, theologian, editor); author of **Walden,* "Of Civil Disobedi-*Heaven, All Hallows' Eve* (novels), **Witchcraft, The Descent of the Dove.*

Raymond Williams (1921-   )
English literary critic and journalist, lecturer (Cambridge); author of *The Long Revolution, *Culture and Society.*

Roger Williams (*c.* 1603-1683)
English clergyman, exiled from Massachusetts Bay Colony for advocating separation of church and state, founder of Rhode Island.

Edmund Wilson (1895-   )
American man of letters, critic, and novelist; author of *To the Finland Station* (history), **Classics and Commercials* and *Axel's Castle* (criticism), *Memoirs of Hecate County* (novel).

William Edward Wilson (1906-   )
American professor of English (Indiana University); author of *Big Knife: The Story of George Rogers Clark.*

John Winthrop (1588-1649)
First governor of Massachusetts Bay Colony, keeper of a journal published posthumously as **The History of New England.*

Roberta Wohlstetter
American social scientist (Rand Corporation); author of **Pearl Harbor; Warning and Decision.*

William Butler Yeats (1865-1939)
Irish poet, dramatist, statesman; author of *A Vision, Autobiography.*

Index

Index